The Writer's Craft

ANNOTATED TEACHER'S EDITION

SENIOR AUTHOR
SHERIDAN BLAU
University of California at Santa Barbara

CONSULTING AUTHOR
PETER ELBOW
University of Massachusetts at Amherst

SPECIAL CONTRIBUTING AUTHORS
Don Killgallon
Baltimore County Public Schools

Rebekah Caplan
Oakland Unified School District

SENIOR CONSULTANTS
Arthur Applebee
State University of New York at Albany

Judith Langer
State University of New York at Albany

McDougal, Littell & Company
Evanston, Illinois

Dallas • Phoenix • Columbia, SC

ISBN 0-8123-8663-9

Box 1667, Evanston, Illinois 60204

Printed in the United States of America.

1 2 3 4 5 6 7 8 9 10–VJM–99 98 97 96 95 94

Contents of the Annotated Teacher's Edition

Using *The Writer's Craft*

Teacher's Workshops

Student Text with Annotations

Excellence in Three Parts

The Writer's Craft **presents a perfect blend of literature, writing, and grammar. But the real value of the series lies in its flexible approach to teaching. This flexibility results from a unique three-part arrangement.**

The Writer's Workshops

Real-world writing experiences show students how writing can help them affect and make sense of their world. References to the two Handbooks help them solve any writing problems that arise.

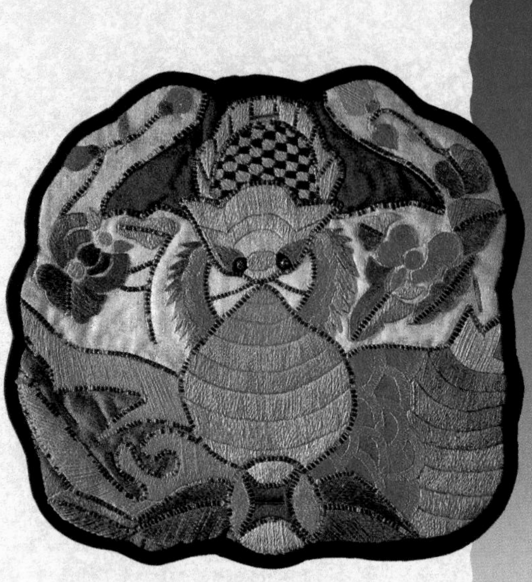

The design of this embroidered pillow contains several symbols often used in Chinese folk art and stories. The bat represents good luck, the peach stands for long life, and the coin symbolizes prosperity.

Writer's Workshops

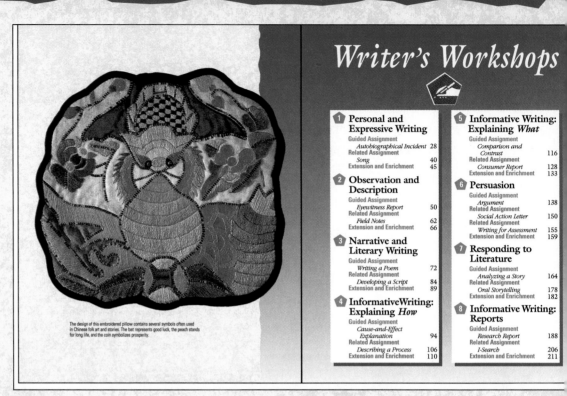

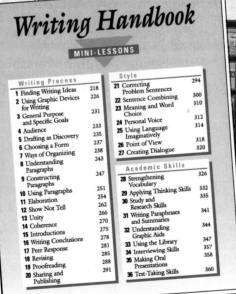

This yarn drawing is an example of the artistry of the Huichol people, who live in a mountainous region of central Mexico. The deer, cow, cactus, and sun symbols commonly appear in Huichol textiles.

Writing Handbook

MINI-LESSONS

Grammar and Usage Handbook

MINI-LESSONS

The Writing Handbook

Mini-lessons on the writing process, style, and academic skills allow both teachers and students to find just the right help at just the right time.

The Grammar and Usage Handbook

Strong grammar instruction is taken out of isolation and presented in the context of drafting, revision, proofreading, and literature. Students apply their skills immediately after learning them.

Writer's Workshops

Each Writer's Workshop explores a writing mode or skill through one Guided Assignment and one Related Assignment.

Guided Assignments Hands-on activities provide in-depth suggestions and strategies for each stage of the writing process.

Related Assignments These streamlined writing experiences build on and extend the skills presented in the Guided Assignments by allowing students to problem solve within motivating, less traditional formats:

- Collage
- Children's Book
- Field Notes
- Graphics
- Commercials
- Oral History
- Song
- Script
- Magazine

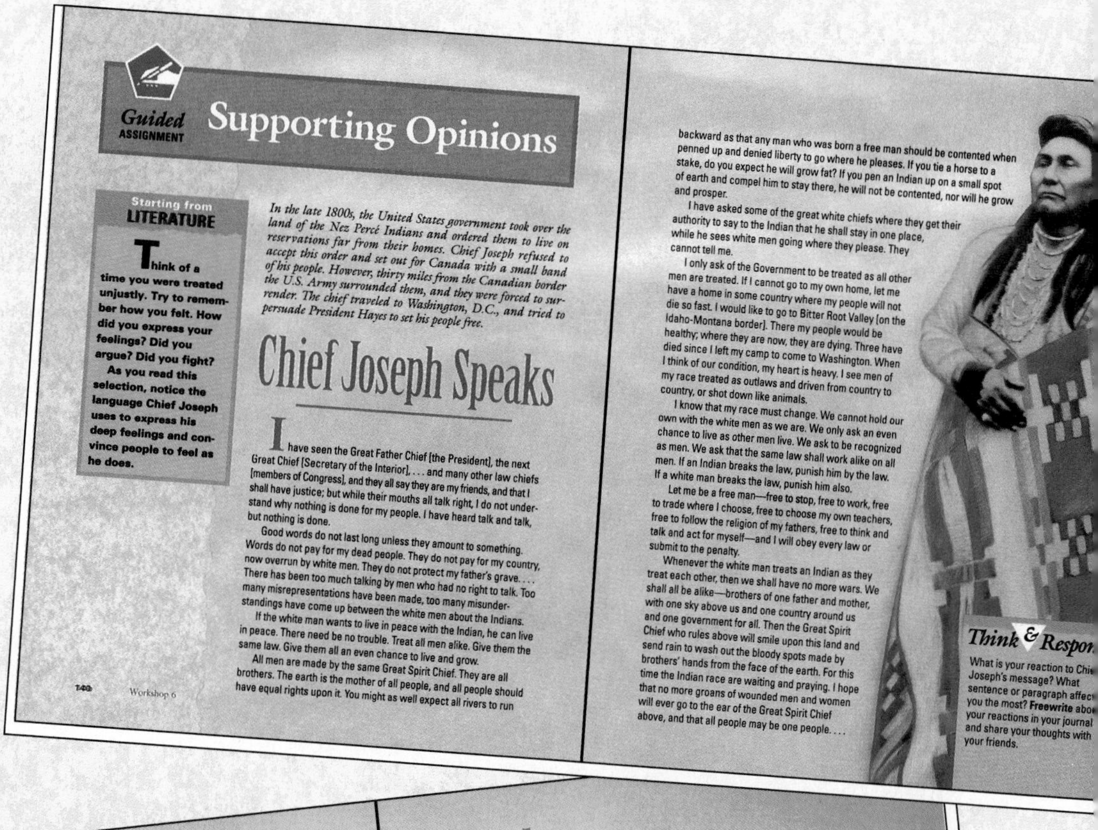

Guided ASSIGNMENT

Supporting Opinions

Starting from LITERATURE

Think of a time you were treated unjustly. Try to remember how you felt. How did you express your feelings? Did you argue? Did you fight? As you read this selection, notice the language Chief Joseph uses to express his deep feelings and convince people to feel as he does.

In the late 1800s, the United States government took over the land of the Nez Percé Indians and ordered them to live on reservations far from their homes. Chief Joseph refused to accept this order and set out for Canada with a small band of his people. However, thirty miles from the Canadian border the U.S. Army surrounded them, and they were forced to surrender. The chief traveled to Washington, D.C., and tried to persuade President Hayes to set his people free.

Chief Joseph Speaks

I have seen the Great Father Chief [the President], the next Great Chief [Secretary of the Interior], . . . and many other law chiefs [members of Congress], and they all say they are my friends, and that I shall have justice; but while their mouths all talk right, I do not understand why nothing is done for my people. I have heard talk and talk, but nothing is done.

Good words do not last long unless they amount to something. Words do not pay for my dead people. They do not pay for my country, now overrun by white men. They do not protect my father's grave. . . . There has been too much talking by men who had no right to talk. Too many misrepresentations have been made, too many misunderstandings have come up between the white men about the Indians.

If the white man wants to live in peace with the Indian, he can live in peace. There need be no trouble. Treat all men alike. Give them the same law. Give them all an even chance to live and grow.

All men are made by the same Great Spirit Chief. They are all brothers. The earth is the mother of all people, and all people should have equal rights upon it. You might as well expect all rivers to run backward as that any man who was born a free man should be contented when penned up and denied liberty to go where he pleases. If you tie a horse to a stake, do you expect he will grow fat? If you pen an Indian up on a small spot of earth and compel him to stay there, he will not be contented, nor will he grow and prosper.

I have asked some of the great white chiefs where they get their authority to say to the Indian that he shall stay in one place, while he sees white men going where they please. They cannot tell me.

I only ask of the Government to be treated as all other men are treated. If I cannot go to my own home, let me have a home in some country where my people will not die so fast. I would like to go to Bitter Root Valley [on the Idaho-Montana border]. There my people would be healthy; where they are now, they are dying. Three have died since I left my camp to come to Washington. When I think of our condition, my heart is heavy. I see men of my race treated as outlaws and driven from country to country, or shot down like animals.

I know that my race must change. We cannot hold our own with the white men as we are. We only ask an even chance to live as other men live. We ask to be recognized as men. We ask that the same law shall work alike on all men. If an Indian breaks the law, punish him by the law. If a white man breaks the law, punish him also.

Let me be a free man—free to stop, free to work, free to trade where I choose, free to choose my own teachers, free to follow the religion of my fathers, free to think and talk and act for myself—and I will obey every law or submit to the penalty.

Whenever the white man treats an Indian as they treat each other, then we shall have no more wars. We shall all be alike—brothers of one father and mother, with one sky above us and one country around us and one government for all. Then the Great Spirit Chief who rules above will smile upon this land and send rain to wash out the bloody spots made by brothers' hands from the face of the earth. For this time the Indian race are waiting and praying. I hope that no more groans of wounded men and women will ever go to the ear of the Great Spirit Chief above, and that all people may be one people. . . .

Think & Respon

What is your reaction to Chie Joseph's message? What sentence or paragraph affec you the most? **Freewrite** abo your reactions in your journal and share your thoughts with your friends.

148 Workshop 6

Related ASSIGNMENT

Advertisement

Starting from ADVERTISING

With so many similar products on the market today, what makes you buy one brand rather than another? Sometimes you buy things because you're used to them or because your friends recommend them. Many times, though, you buy a product simply because you've seen a catchy ad for it. As you read this ad, notice how the writer used persuasive language to deliver the ad's message.

Blade through the day with Roller Bran

Start your day off on the right foot with the newest cereal to hit the streets. This unique blend of supersoluble oat bran and corn gives you all the nutrition and energy you need to glide through the day and perform your best. And the taste leaves other breakfast cereals by the side of the road.

Watch for Roller Bran on your grocer's shelf.

And grab it while you can—this cereal's on the move.

Think & Respond

What audience was the advertiser trying to reach? Do you think you would buy the cereal? Why? What words or pictures in the ad are most persuasive?

152 Workshop 6

Guided Assignment

Guided ASSIGNMENT

Comparison and Contrast

Starting from LITERATURE

Our solar system has nine planets, each with its own unique characteristics. What would life be like on another planet—Mars, for example? Brad Darrach and Steve Petranek wondered too, and decided the simplest way to explain the red planet would be to show how it was similar to and different from the earth. As you read their informative essay, from *Life* magazine, notice how they compare and contrast these two planets in our solar system.

A LAND OF STAGGERING PROPORTIONS

by Brad Darrach and Steve Petranek

Oh, what a fascinating walk you could take near the Martian equator next December, in the middle of a summer day. The weather would be perfect—high 60s and a bright orange Creamsicle-colored sky—but shirtsleeves would be out. You'd be wearing a light space suit to keep your blood from boiling because the "air" on Mars is so thin, about the same density as Earth's at 20 miles above sea level. The space suit would help with two other problems—the deadly ultraviolet light from the Sun, and the unbreathable Martian atmosphere, which is 95 percent carbon dioxide, with traces of nitrogen and argon.

The physical act of walking would seem effortless; you could endlessly hop, skip or jump along because gravity is only about a third of what it is on Earth. A 100-pound woman would feel as if she weighed 38 pounds, and a world-class athlete could run 100 meters in less than five seconds. The vista would remind you of the Arizona and California deserts—fine sand littered with rocks and boulders. But the sand would be pink and reddish-brown, because Martian soil is about 13 percent iron, much of which has turned to rust. Of course, there wouldn't be any cacti or scrub plants like tumbleweed, any darting lizards or rabbits. The terrain would be much drier than any desert on Earth, so dry that an ice cube placed on the ground would quickly disappear, evaporating before it could melt, going straight from solid to vapor.

You could walk just about anywhere you wanted on Mars, because the entire surface is land; there are no lakes, rivers or oceans. All the water is underground or frozen at the north and south poles. There's as much land on Mars as there is on Earth, even though Mars is only half as big as Earth and weighs only a tenth as much. Because of its weaker gravity, Mars is not as dense as Earth; it's puffed up. A thousand feet below the surface of Earth you would probably hit solid rock, but a thousand feet below the crust of Mars you would find porous material, perhaps even a gravelly slurry of rock and ice. . . .

A day's walk on Mars would offer about as much Sun time as on Earth; Mars rotates once every 24 hours, 37 minutes. But the summer would last twice as long because Mars takes 687 days to orbit the Sun.

A trek to any of Earth's natural wonders would pale by comparison to what can be seen on Mars. Mount Everest, at just over 29,000 feet, would seem a foothill compared to the Tharsis bulge, a broad raised equatorial plain the size of the United States. On Tharsis sit extraordinary volcanoes, among them Olympus Mons, at 90,000 feet the highest known elevation in the solar system. The mighty Colorado River's cut through the Grand Canyon would seem a drainage ditch next to Valles Marineris, a gorge that would stretch from Seattle to Miami. . . .

You could spend a lifetime on the surface of Mars and never run out of new formations to see . . . . Just one thing, though. You would want to get back to base before dark. Most nights, even in summer, the temperature drops to about -125° F.

Think & Respond

What aspects of the Martian environment do you find most intriguing? Why? Give some examples from the essay that show how the authors help you to understand the environment of Mars.

116 Workshop 5

Starting from Literature

The authors of *The Writer's Craft* believe that writing is an exciting journey of discovery where students explore ideas, examine options, problem solve, and share what they have done with others. Every assignment in each Writer's Workshop builds upon these ideas.

Literary and Professional Writing

Each Guided and Related Assignment begins with a model that focuses on a specific writing type or strategy. The introduction to the model presents the writing type to be covered, previews the literature, and sets a purpose for reading.

- **Models** cover a wide range of writing types, from traditional and contemporary literature, to newspaper and magazine articles, to consumer reports and TV scripts. Topics often lead to strong cross-curricular ties, and students gain a sense of how writing functions in the real world.
- **Think and Respond** questions allow students to respond to what they have read and prepare them to begin writing a piece of their own.

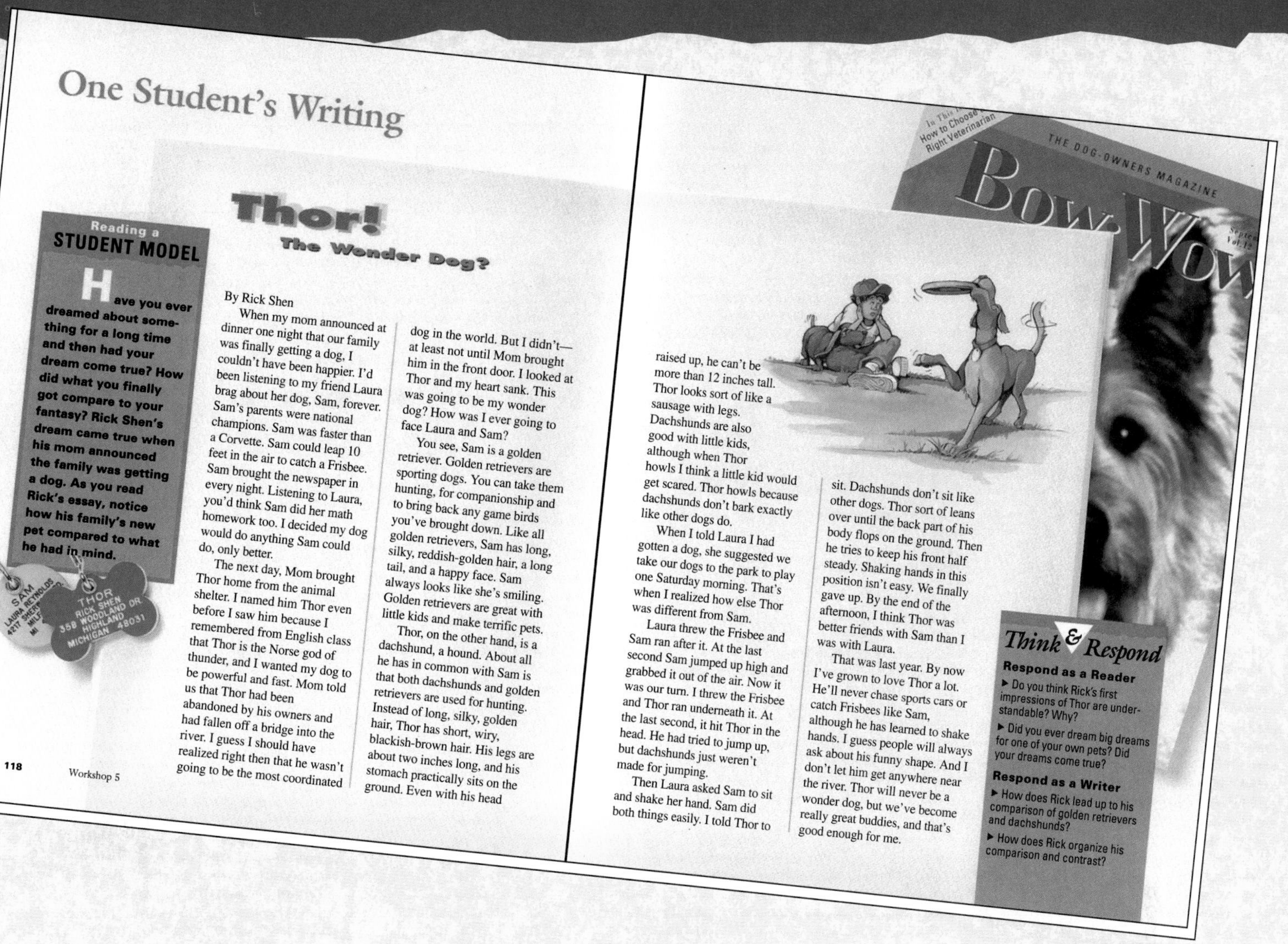

One Student's Writing

Reading a STUDENT MODEL

Have you ever dreamed about something for a long time and then had your dream come true? How did what you finally got compare to your fantasy? Rick Shen's dream came true when his mom announced the family was getting a dog. As you read Rick's essay, notice how his family's new pet compared to what he had in mind.

THOR
RICK SHEN
358 WOODLAND DR.
HIGHLAND
MICHIGAN 48031

Thor! The Wonder Dog?

By Rick Shen

When my mom announced at dinner one night that our family was finally getting a dog, I couldn't have been happier. I'd been listening to my friend Laura brag about her dog, Sam, forever. Sam's parents were national champions. Sam was faster than a Corvette. Sam could leap 10 feet in the air to catch a Frisbee. Sam brought the newspaper in every night. Listening to Laura, you'd think Sam did her math homework too. I decided my dog would do anything Sam could do, only better.

The next day, Mom brought Thor home from the animal shelter. I named him Thor even before I saw him because I remembered from English class that Thor is the Norse god of thunder, and I wanted my dog to be powerful and fast. Mom told us that Thor had been abandoned by his owners and had fallen off a bridge into the river. I guess I should have realized right then that he wasn't going to be the most coordinated dog in the world. But I didn't—at least not until Mom brought him in the front door. I looked at Thor and my heart sank. This was going to be my wonder dog? How was I ever going to face Laura and Sam?

You see, Sam is a golden retriever. Golden retrievers are sporting dogs. You can take them hunting, for companionship and to bring back any game birds you've brought down. Like all golden retrievers, Sam has long, silky, reddish-golden hair, a long tail, and a happy face. Sam always looks like she's smiling. Golden retrievers are great with little kids and make terrific pets.

Thor, on the other hand, is a dachshund, a hound. About all he has in common with Sam is that both dachshunds and golden retrievers are used for hunting. Instead of long, silky, golden hair, Thor has short, wiry, blackish-brown hair. His legs are about two inches long, and his stomach practically sits on the ground. Even with his head raised up, he can't be more than 12 inches tall. Thor looks sort of like a sausage with legs. Dachshunds are also good with little kids, although when Thor howls I think a little kid would get scared. Thor howls because dachshunds don't bark exactly like other dogs do.

When I told Laura I had gotten a dog, she suggested we take our dogs to the park to play one Saturday morning. That's when I realized how else Thor was different from Sam.

Laura threw the Frisbee and Sam ran after it. At the last second Sam jumped up high and grabbed it out of the air. Now it was our turn. I threw the Frisbee and Thor ran underneath it. At the last second, it hit Thor in the head. He had tried to jump up, but dachshunds just weren't made for jumping.

Then Laura asked Sam to sit and shake her hand. Sam did both things easily. I told Thor to sit. Dachshunds don't sit like other dogs. Thor sort of leans over until the back part of his body flops on the ground. Then he tries to keep his front half steady. Shaking hands in this position isn't easy. We finally gave up. By the end of the afternoon, I think Thor was better friends with Sam than I was with Laura.

That was last year. By now I've grown to love Thor a lot. He'll never chase sports cars or catch Frisbees like Sam, although he has learned to shake hands. I guess people will always ask about his funny shape. And I don't let him get anywhere near the river. Thor will never be a wonder dog, but we've become really great buddies, and that's good enough for me.

THE DOG-OWNERS MAGAZINE
Bow Wow

Think & Respond

Respond as a Reader

▸ Do you think Rick's first impressions of Thor are understandable? Why?

▸ Did you ever dream big dreams for one of your own pets? Did your dreams come true?

Respond as a Writer

▸ How does Rick lead up to his comparison of golden retrievers and dachshunds?

▸ How does Rick organize his comparison and contrast?

118 Workshop 5

Reading Student Writing

A student-written paper follows the opening model, demonstrating to students the importance of their own writing and the usefulness of the skills they will be learning.

Student Models

Each student model shows students the importance of becoming invested in their writing. A variety of publishing formats suggests the many ways writing can be shared.

- **Placement** of the complete model at the front of the lesson allows teachers to use the whole-to-part teaching strategy so successful with middle school students.
- **Think and Respond** questions focus on both reader response and on analyzing the writer's technique.

Writing
ON YOUR OWN
Comparison and Contrast

INVITATION TO *Write*

Like Brad Darrach and Steve Petranek, Rick Shen used comparison and contrast techniques as part of an informative essay. In both pieces of writing, the authors explained and described by showing how things are alike and different.

Write an informative essay that uses comparison and contrast to explain or describe something or someone.

PROBLEM SOLVING

"How can I find a topic I care about?"

For additional suggestions for finding a writing topic, see

- Handbook 1, "Discovering Writing Ideas," pages 218–223

PREWRITE AND EXPLORE

1. Look for comparisons and contrasts. When you compare and contrast persons or things, you try to find similarities and differences. What types of comparisons interest you? To find out, try some of the following activities.

Exploring Topics

- **One on one** Which team is better, the Chicago Bulls or the Los Angeles Lakers? What are the differences between laser discs and videocassettes? Which exercise gives you the best workout—cross-country skiing or tennis? Get together with some classmates and **brainstorm** to create a list of people, objects, and ideas you could compare and contrast, one on one. Make a list of the ideas you come up with.
- **Decisions, decisions** Personal decisions often involve comparison and contrast. Which summer camp will you attend? What clubs will you join at school? Which jeans will you buy? Recall decisions you have made in the past, or think about decisions you're facing now. **Freewrite** about one that involved comparing or contrasting two choices.

120 Workshop 5

- **Time machine** If you could travel forward into the future or back to the past, what would be different? What would be the same? Choose a new lifetime and make a **chart** that shows what things are different and what things are the same.
- **Reading literature** Have any of your favorite stories or novels been made into movies? How are the two versions alike? How are they different? **Freewrite** about one such example.

What types of ideas have you gathered? Which one strikes you as the most interesting, unusual, or challenging? Choose one you'd like to explore in a comparison and contrast essay.

2. Investigate similarities and differences. To explore your topic, you need to find a way to sort out similarities and differences. One way is to figure out what features you want to compare and contrast. For example, if you were comparing compact discs and tapes, you might consider such features as sound quality, durability, and cost. Then you could make a chart to show how your two subjects measure up.

Another way is to make a Venn diagram. In the outer part of each circle, list what is different about each subject you are comparing. In the space where the circles overlap, list the similarities.

One Student's Process

Rick Shen used a Venn diagram to help him clearly see how Sam and Thor were alike and different.

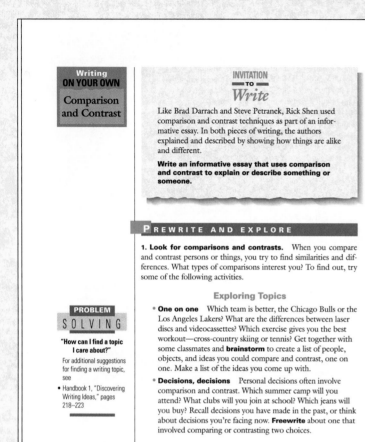

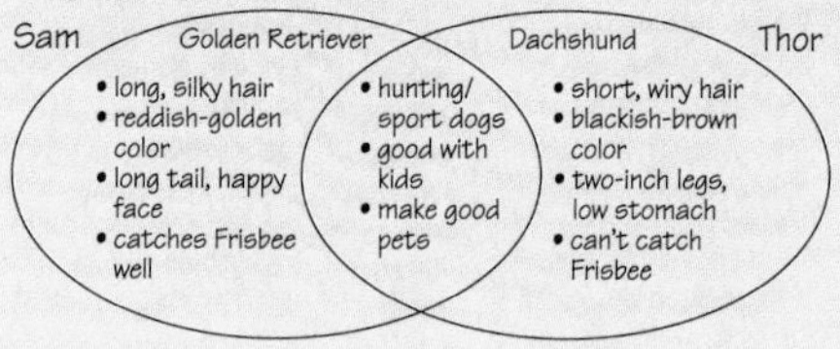

Comparison and Contrast 121

Moving to Writing

After discussing the model, your students are invited to write on their own. The detailed Guided Assignments lead students through each stage of the writing process, where they are presented with different strategies and encouraged to experiment, problem solve, and collaborate with others.

Writing on Your Own

A variety of features helps students make the transition from reading to writing.

- **Invitation to Write** refers to the professional and student models and describes the assignment students are to complete.
- **Exploring Topics** provides creative activities to help students find writing ideas they can care about.
- **Problem Solving** notes appear throughout the lesson and offer cross-references to the Handbooks. This provides you with ideas for mini-lessons and shows your students where they can look for additional help.
- **One Student's Process** follows a student writer through every stage of the assignment.

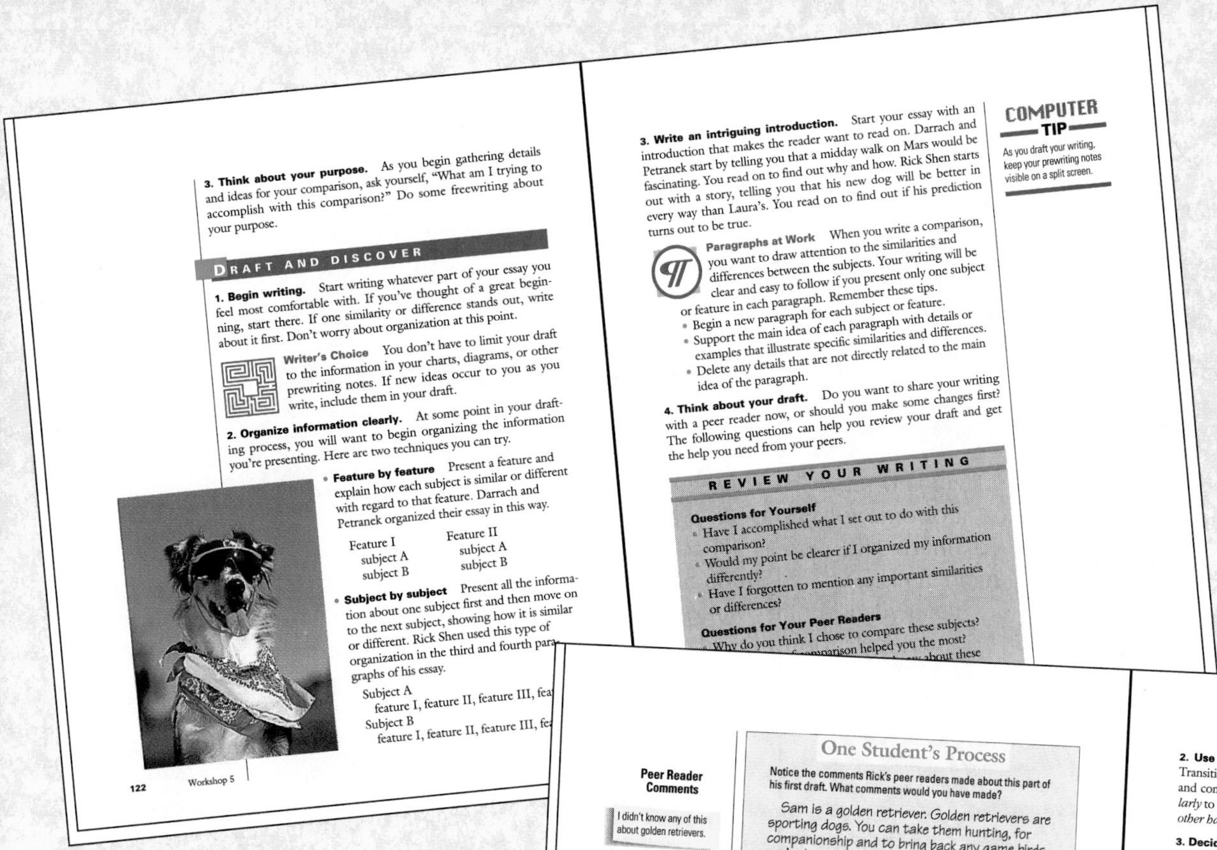
3. **Think about your purpose.** As you begin gathering details and ideas for your comparison, ask yourself, "What am I trying to accomplish with this comparison?" Do some freewriting about your purpose.

DRAFT AND DISCOVER

1. **Begin writing.** Start writing whatever part of your essay you feel most comfortable with. If you've thought of a great beginning, start there. If one similarity or difference stands out, write about it first. Don't worry about organization at this point.

Writer's Choice You don't have to limit your draft to the information in your charts, diagrams, or other prewriting notes. If new ideas occur to you as you write, include them in your draft.

2. **Organize information clearly.** At some point in your drafting process, you will want to begin organizing the information you're presenting. Here are two techniques you can try.

- **Feature by feature** Present a feature and explain how each subject is similar or different with regard to that feature. Darrach and Petranek organized their essay in this way.

Feature I
subject A
subject B

Feature II
subject A
subject B

- **Subject by subject** Present all the information about one subject first and then move on to the next subject, showing how it is similar or different. Rick Shen used this type of organization in the third and fourth para[graphs] of his essay.

Subject A
feature I, feature II, feature III, fea[ture]
Subject B
feature I, feature II, feature III, fe[ature]

122 Workshop 5

3. **Write an intriguing introduction.** Start your essay with an introduction that makes the reader want to read on. Darrach and Petranek start by telling you that a midday walk on Mars would be fascinating. You read on to find out why and how. Rick Shen starts out with a story, telling you that his new dog will be better in every way than Laura's. You read on to find out if his prediction turns out to be true.

Paragraphs at Work When you write a comparison, you want to draw attention to the similarities and differences between the subjects. Your writing will be clear and easy to follow if you present only one subject or feature in each paragraph. Remember these tips.
- Begin a new paragraph for each subject or feature.
- Support the main idea of each paragraph with details or examples that illustrate specific similarities and differences.
- Delete any details that are not directly related to the main idea of the paragraph.

4. **Think about your draft.** Do you want to share your writing with a peer reader now, or should you make some changes first? The following questions can help you review your draft and get the help you need from your peers.

COMPUTER TIP
As you draft your writing, keep your prewriting notes visible on a split screen.

REVIEW YOUR WRITING

Questions for Yourself
- Have I accomplished what I set out to do with this comparison?
- Would my point be clearer if I organized my information differently?
- Have I forgotten to mention any important similarities or differences?

Questions for Your Peer Readers
- Why do you think I chose to compare these subjects?

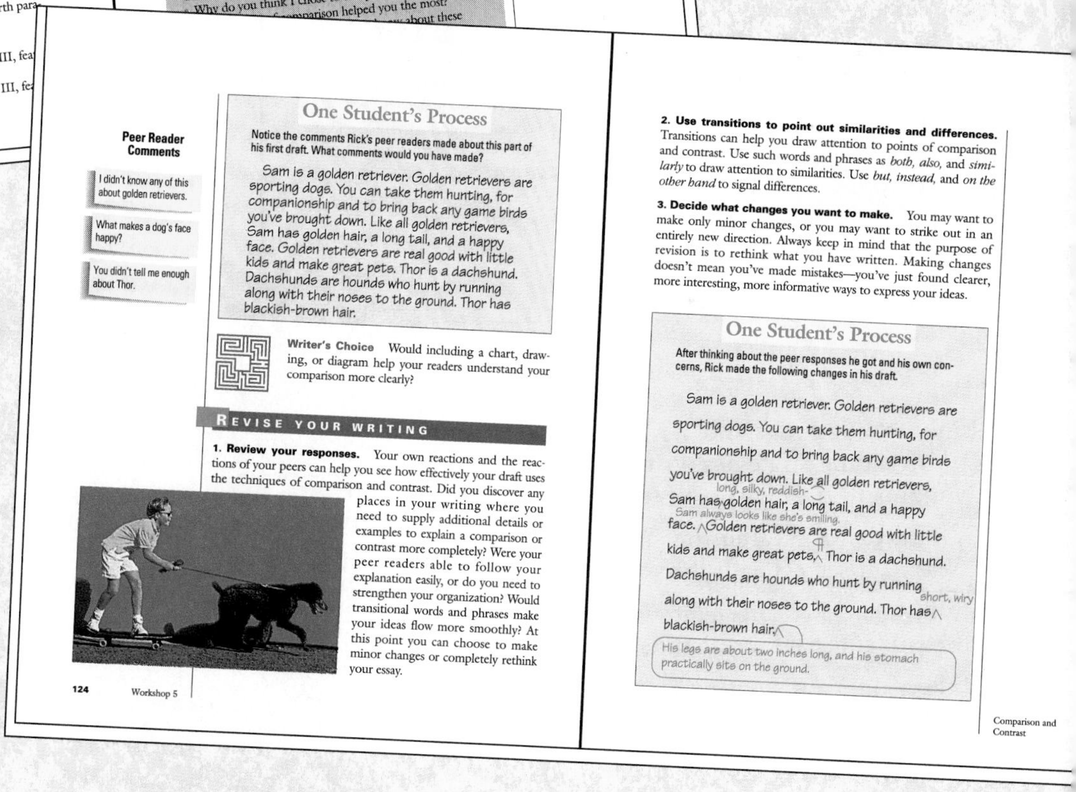
Peer Reader Comments

I didn't know any of this about golden retrievers.

What makes a dog's face happy?

You didn't tell me enough about Thor.

One Student's Process

Notice the comments Rick's peer readers made about this part of his first draft. What comments would you have made?

Sam is a golden retriever. Golden retrievers are sporting dogs. You can take them hunting, for companionship and to bring back any game birds you've brought down. Like all golden retrievers, Sam has golden hair, a long tail, and a happy face. Golden retrievers are real good with little kids and make great pets. Thor is a dachshund. Dachshunds are hounds who hunt by running along with their noses to the ground. Thor has blackish-brown hair.

Writer's Choice Would including a chart, drawing, or diagram help your readers understand your comparison more clearly?

REVISE YOUR WRITING

1. **Review your responses.** Your own reactions and the reactions of your peers can help you see how effectively your draft uses the techniques of comparison and contrast. Did you discover any places in your writing where you need to supply additional details or examples to explain a comparison or contrast more completely? Were your peer readers able to follow your explanation easily, or do you need to strengthen your organization? Would transitional words and phrases make your ideas flow more smoothly? At this point you can choose to make minor changes or completely rethink your essay.

124 Workshop 5

2. **Use transitions to point out similarities and differences.** Transitions can help you draw attention to points of comparison and contrast. Use such words and phrases as *both, also,* and *similarly* to draw attention to similarities. Use *but, instead,* and *on the other hand* to signal differences.

3. **Decide what changes you want to make.** You may want to make only minor changes, or you may want to strike out in an entirely new direction. Always keep in mind that the purpose of revision is to rethink what you have written. Making changes doesn't mean you've made mistakes—you've just found clearer, more interesting, more informative ways to express your ideas.

One Student's Process

After thinking about the peer responses he got and his own concerns, Rick made the following changes in his draft.

Sam is a golden retriever. Golden retrievers are sporting dogs. You can take them hunting, for companionship and to bring back any game birds you've brought down. Like all golden retrievers, Sam has golden hair (long, silky, reddish-), a long tail, and a happy face. (Sam always looks like she's smiling.) Golden retrievers are real good with little kids and make great pets. ¶ Thor is a dachshund. Dachshunds are hounds who hunt by running along with their noses to the ground. Thor has (short, wiry) blackish-brown hair. (His legs are about two inches long, and his stomach practically sits on the ground.)

Comparison and Contrast

- **Drafting Strategies** and **Writer's Choice** options remind students that there are many ways to complete any piece of writing.
- **Writing Tips, Computer Tips,** and **Grammar Tips** provide helpful advice where students need it.
- **Paragraphs at Work** tailors tips on paragraphing to each specific type of writing.
- **Review questions** for both the writer and the peer reader make revision a rich, interactive process.
- **Revision in progress** shows peer response at work.

Standards for Evaluation

INFORMATIVE WRITING

Comparison and contrast writing
- introduces the subjects being compared in an interesting, intriguing manner
- discusses how the subjects being compared are similar and different
- organizes ideas logically, using feature-by-feature or subject-by-subject organization
- includes transitional words and phrases to make similarities and differences clear
- ends with a satisfying conclusion

LINKING GRAMMAR AND WRITING

Comparative and Superlative Forms

Whenever you use comparison and contrast, you will be comparing at least two subjects. Sometimes you may be working with more than two subjects. Depending on how many subjects you're comparing and contrasting, you will need to use different forms of adjectives and adverbs.

Use the **comparative** forms of adjectives and adverbs when you are comparing or contrasting two subjects.

Diamonds are <u>harder</u> than rubies.

Use the **superlative** forms of adjectives and adverbs when you are comparing or contrasting three or more subjects.

Diamonds are the <u>hardest</u> of all precious stones.

Rick Shen used the comparative form to compare Sam with a sports car.

Sam is <u>faster</u> than a Corvette.

Had Rick wanted to compare Sam with more than one other subject, he would have used the superlative form.

Of all the dogs in the park that day, Sam was <u>fastest</u>.

PROOFREAD

1. Proofread your work. Check your informative essay for errors in grammar, spelling, punctuation, and capitalization.

2. Make a clean copy of your paper. Use the Standards for Evaluation in the margin to make one final check of your writing. Then prepare a final copy of your informative essay.

126 Workshop 5

PUBLISH AND PRESENT

- **Add graphics to your essay.** Photographs, drawings, and other visual aids can add interest to your informative essay.
- **Participate in a paper exchange.** Exchange essays with students in another class at your school or even at a different school. Attach a letter to the essay you've been asked to respond to, telling the writer what you liked about his or her work.
- **Make a bulletin board display.** Include a comparison and contrast chart about your subjects.

REFLECT ON YOUR WRITING

FOR YOUR **PORTFOLIO**

1. Add your writing to your portfolio. You have now written your own informative essay based on comparison and contrast. How did your writing experience go? Did you find this type of writing enjoyable? What was the most interesting or frustrating part of your writing experience? Write a brief note to yourself or your teacher that talks about your writing process. These questions may help you focus your thoughts.

- What did I learn about these subjects by comparing and contrasting them? Did anything surprise me?
- Was I surprised by any of the responses I got from my peer readers? Did I make any of the changes my peer readers suggested?
- Did I enjoy exploring comparisons and contrasts? Did this assignment give me any ideas for other comparisons I would like to investigate?
- Other than in an informative essay like Brad Darrach's and Steve Petravek's, in what other types of writing could I use comparison and contrast techniques?

2. Explore additional writing ideas. See the suggestions for writing a consumer report on pages 130–132, and Springboards on page 133.

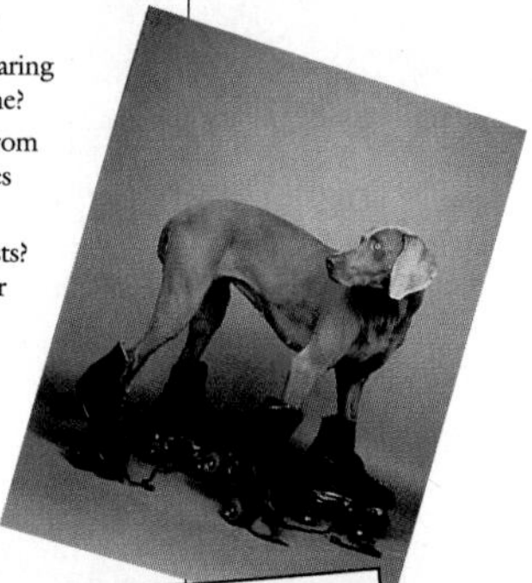

Roller Rover (1987), William Wegman.

127

Related ASSIGNMENT

Consumer Report

Reading a CONSUMER REPORT

How do you decide what basketball shoe or blue jeans to buy? With so many brands to choose from, you have to be a smart consumer to get the most for your money. One way to spend your cash intelligently is to check out similar products in a consumer magazine. As you read this consumer report about frozen yogurt, think about the features of this warm-weather treat that the author focuses on. What other features would you have compared?

from ZILLIONS

WHY IS EVERYBODY EATING FROZEN YOGURT?

Why is frozen yogurt the fastest growing new food of the 1990's?

It's cold and sweet. Smooth and creamy. A lot like ice cream—but with a difference. Frozen yogurt has less fat and fewer calories. In these nutrition-conscious 90's, a healthier choice that tastes terrific is sure to find new fans.

Did we say *tastes terrific*? Whipping air and sugar into icy yogurt may not sound tempting to your taste buds. Isn't yogurt just sour milk? Doesn't it have a certain tang? It can't really compare to ice cream, can it? To find out, we asked 26 *Zillions* readers around the country to visit local frozen yogurt stores and check out some low-fat flavors.

What They Thought

Each member of the Yogurt Team tasted chocolate and one other flavor at three different stores. In all, they visited 80 stores and tried 160 samples. . . . Everyone found a favorite, and (surprise! surprise!) no one complained about this assignment. "Frozen yogurt doesn't taste as sour as I thought it would," said Adam. Cammie agreed: "I was really amazed at the similarity to ice cream."

The kids found the best samples were smooth (not icy), fairly sweet, with a gentle yogurt tang and good flavor.

- **Linking Grammar and Writing** and **Proofreading** strategies provide a springboard to language instruction.
- **Standards for Evaluation** shares assessment secrets with the students.
- **Publish and Present** suggestions make sure students have a real audience.
- **Reflect on Your Writing** encourages students to use a portfolio and to think about what they've learned.

Related Assignment

In this activity, students apply skills learned in the Guided Assignment. Here, the consumer report builds on skills presented in the compare-contrast assignment.

Writing Handbook

When do you want to teach your students about transitional devices? When they write a story? Before they explain a process? Perhaps you want to review the concept with each lesson. With the unique Writing Handbook, *you* decide what your students need to learn and when they need to learn it.

The Writing Handbook is divided into three sections, each with a wealth of mini-lessons:

Writing Process
Style
Academic Skills

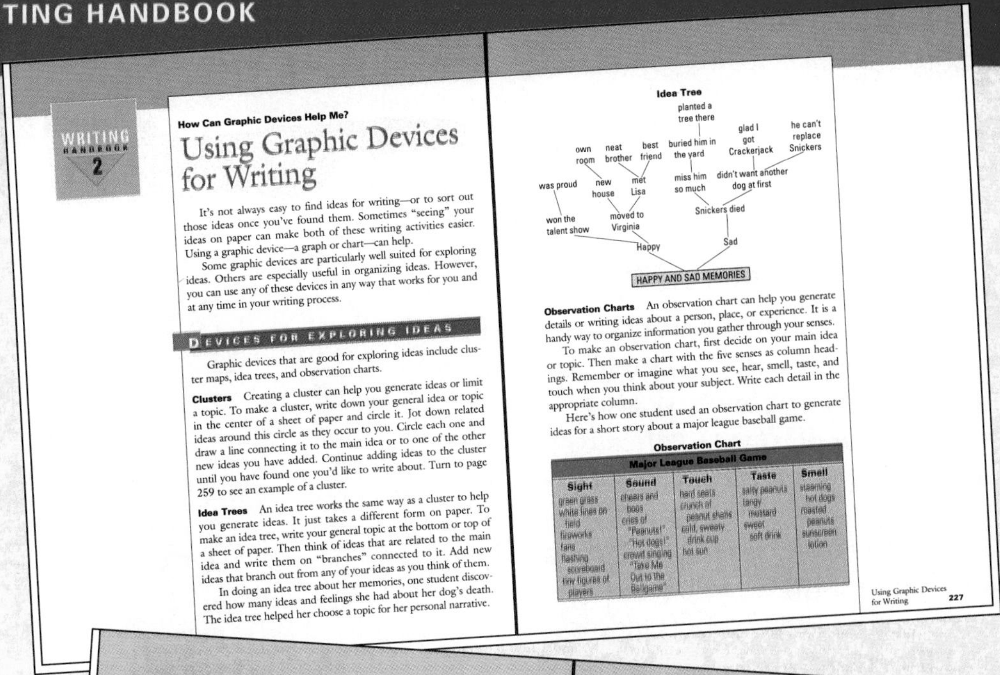

WRITING HANDBOOK 2

How Can Graphic Devices Help Me?

Using Graphic Devices for Writing

It's not always easy to find ideas for writing—or to sort out those ideas once you've found them. Sometimes "seeing" your ideas on paper can make both of these writing activities easier. Using a graphic device—a graph or chart—can help.

Some graphic devices are particularly well suited for exploring ideas. Others are especially useful in organizing ideas. However, you can use any of these devices in any way that works for you and at any time in your writing process.

DEVICES FOR EXPLORING IDEAS

Graphic devices that are good for exploring ideas include cluster maps, idea trees, and observation charts.

Clusters Creating a cluster can help you generate ideas or limit a topic. To make a cluster, write down your general idea or topic in the center of a sheet of paper and circle it. Jot down related ideas around this circle as they occur to you. Circle each one and draw a line connecting it to the main idea or to one of the other new ideas you have added. Continue adding ideas to the cluster until you have found one you'd like to write about. Turn to page 259 to see an example of a cluster.

Idea Trees An idea tree works the same way as a cluster to help you generate ideas. It just takes a different form on paper. To make an idea tree, write your general topic at the bottom or top of a sheet of paper. Then think of ideas that are related to the main idea and write them on "branches" connected to it. Add new ideas that branch out from any of your ideas as you think of them.

In doing an idea tree about her memories, one student discovered how many ideas and feelings she had about her dog's death. The idea tree helped her choose a topic for her personal narrative.

Idea Tree

Observation Charts An observation chart can help you generate details or writing ideas about a person, place, or experience. It is a handy way to organize information you gather through your senses.

To make an observation chart, first decide on your main idea or topic. Then make a chart with the five senses as column headings. Remember or imagine what you see, hear, smell, taste, and touch when you think about your subject. Write each detail in the appropriate column.

Here's how one student used an observation chart to generate ideas for a short story about a major league baseball game.

Observation Chart

Major League Baseball Game				
Sight	**Sound**	**Touch**	**Taste**	**Smell**
green grass white lines on field fireworks fans flashing scoreboard tiny figures of players	cheers and boos cries of "Peanuts!" "Hot dogs!" crowd singing "Take Me Out to the Ballgame"	hard seats crunch of peanut shells cold, sweaty drink cup hot sun	salty peanuts tangy mustard sweet soft drink	steaming hot dogs roasted peanuts sunscreen lotion

Using Graphic Devices for Writing 227

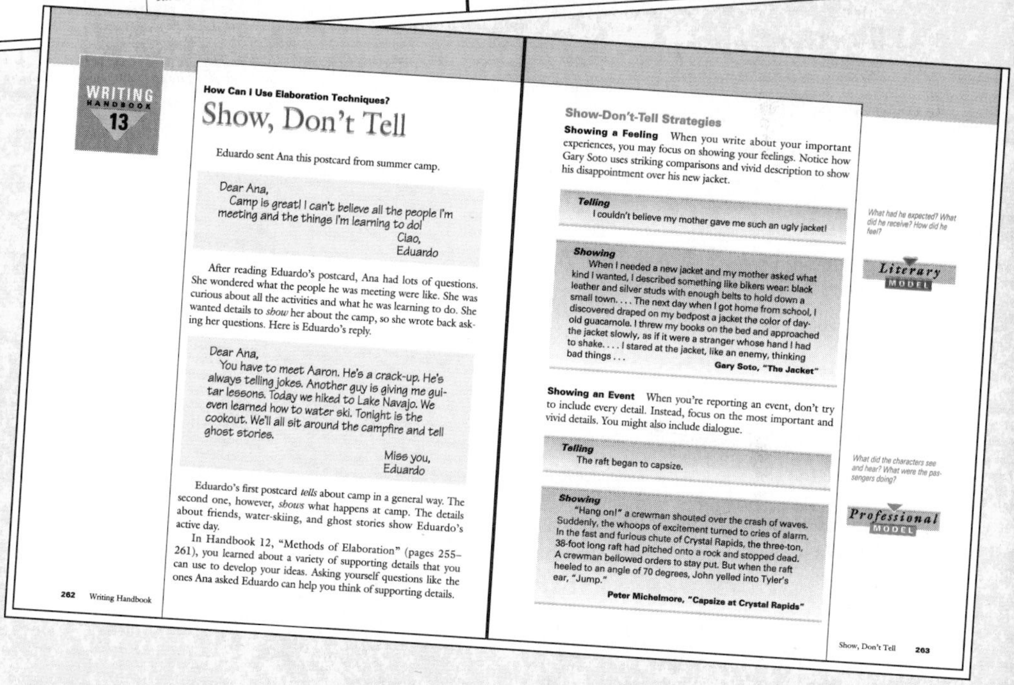

WRITING HANDBOOK 13

How Can I Use Elaboration Techniques?

Show, Don't Tell

Eduardo sent Ana this postcard from summer camp.

> Dear Ana,
> Camp is great! I can't believe all the people I'm meeting and the things I'm learning to do!
> Ciao,
> Eduardo

After reading Eduardo's postcard, Ana had lots of questions. She wondered what the people he was meeting were like. She was curious about all the activities and what he was learning to do. She wanted details to *show* her about the camp, so she wrote back asking her questions. Here is Eduardo's reply.

> Dear Ana,
> You have to meet Aaron. He's a crack-up. He's always telling jokes. Another guy is giving me guitar lessons. Today we hiked to Lake Navajo. We even learned how to water ski. Tonight is the cookout. We'll all sit around the campfire and tell ghost stories.
> Miss you,
> Eduardo

Eduardo's first postcard *tells* about camp in a general way. The second one, however, *shows* what happens at camp. The details about friends, water-skiing, and ghost stories show Eduardo's active day.

In Handbook 12, "Methods of Elaboration" (pages 255–261), you learned about a variety of supporting details that you can use to develop your ideas. Asking yourself questions like the ones Ana asked Eduardo can help you think of supporting details.

262 Writing Handbook

Show-Don't-Tell Strategies

Showing a Feeling When you write about your important experiences, you may focus on showing your feelings. Notice how Gary Soto uses striking comparisons and vivid description to show his disappointment over his new jacket.

Telling
I couldn't believe my mother gave me such an ugly jacket!

What had he expected? What did he receive? How did he feel?

Showing
When I needed a new jacket and my mother asked what kind I wanted, I described something like bikers wear: black leather and silver studs with enough belts to hold down a small town. . . . The next day when I got home from school, I discovered draped on my bedpost a jacket the color of day-old guacamole. I threw my books on the bed and approached the jacket slowly, as if it were a stranger whose hand I had to shake. . . . I stared at the jacket, like an enemy, thinking bad things . . .

Gary Soto, "The Jacket"

Literary MODEL

Showing an Event When you're reporting an event, don't try to include every detail. Instead, focus on the most important and vivid details. You might also include dialogue.

Telling
The raft began to capsize.

What did the characters see and hear? What were the passengers doing?

Showing
"Hang on!" a crewman shouted over the crash of waves. Suddenly, the whoops of excitement turned to cries of alarm. In the fast and furious chute of Crystal Rapids, the three-ton, 38-foot long raft had pitched onto a rock and stopped dead. A crewman bellowed orders to stay put. But when the raft heeled to an angle of 70 degrees, John yelled into Tyler's ear, "Jump."

Peter Michelmore, "Capsize at Crystal Rapids"

Professional MODEL

Show, Don't Tell 263

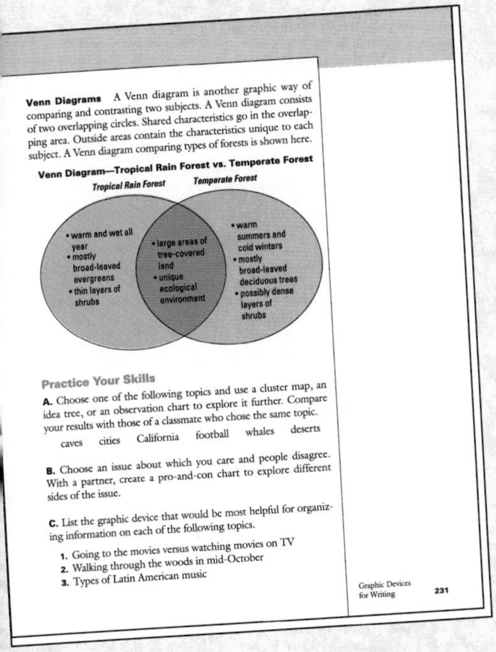

Venn Diagrams A Venn diagram is another graphic way of comparing and contrasting two subjects. A Venn diagram consists of two overlapping circles. Shared characteristics go in the overlapping area. Outside areas contain the characteristics unique to each subject. A Venn diagram comparing types of forests is shown here.

Venn Diagram—Tropical Rain Forest vs. Temperate Forest

Practice Your Skills

A. Choose one of the following topics and use a cluster map, an idea tree, or an observation chart to explore it further. Compare your results with those of a classmate who chose the same topic.

caves cities California football whales deserts

B. Choose an issue about which you care and people disagree. With a partner, create a pro-and-con chart to explore different sides of the issue.

C. List the graphic device that would be most helpful for organizing information on each of the following topics.

1. Going to the movies versus watching movies on TV
2. Walking through the woods in mid-October
3. Types of Latin American music

Graphic Devices for Writing 231

Use the cross-references in the Writer's Workshops to decide when to present lessons, or teach them whenever *you* see the need. You can also encourage your students to use the lessons independently as they problem solve their way through a piece of writing.

- **One key concept or skill** is the focus of each mini-lesson.
- **Charts and graphic devices** clarify difficult strategies and concepts.
- **Literary, professional, and student models** provide examples of different techniques and strategies.
- **Abundant practice** enables students to practice their new skills or hone abilities they already have.

Grammar and Usage Handbook

Research has shown that grammar and usage lessons, taught in isolation, do not improve student writing. *The Writer's Craft* solves this problem with its innovative Grammar and Usage Handbook. Every lesson provides instruction and practice in the context of drafting, revision, proofreading, and literature.

Covering the Basics

Each lesson begins with clear teaching and a quick student check.

- **Thorough introductions to the concept** begin each lesson. Numerous charts and examples clarify the explanation.

- **Thematic exercises and examples** center around a subject that can be used as a springboard to writing.
- **Concept Checks** review the basic idea of the lesson in a simple format.

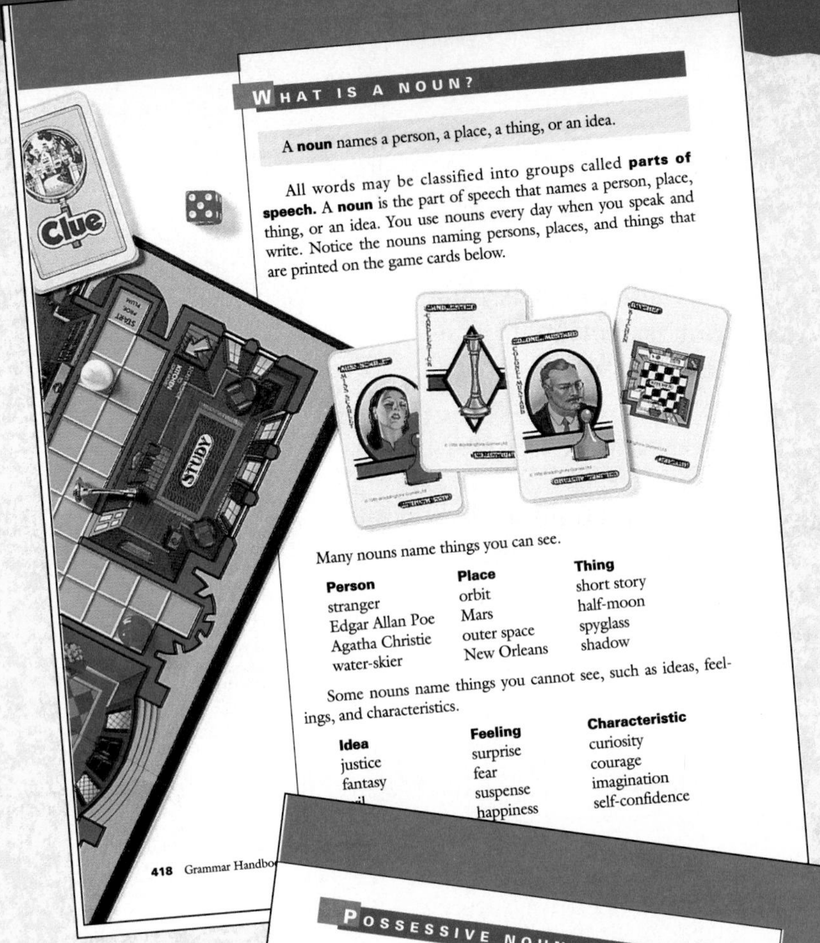

WHAT IS A NOUN?

A **noun** names a person, a place, a thing, or an idea.

All words may be classified into groups called **parts of speech.** A **noun** is the part of speech that names a person, place, thing, or an idea. You use nouns every day when you speak and write. Notice the nouns naming persons, places, and things that are printed on the game cards below.

Many nouns name things you can see.

Person	Place	Thing
stranger	orbit	short story
Edgar Allan Poe	Mars	half-moon
Agatha Christie	outer space	spyglass
water-skier	New Orleans	shadow

Some nouns name things you cannot see, such as ideas, feelings, and characteristics.

Idea	Feeling	Characteristic
justice	surprise	curiosity
fantasy	fear	courage
	suspense	imagination
	happiness	self-confidence

418 Grammar Handbo

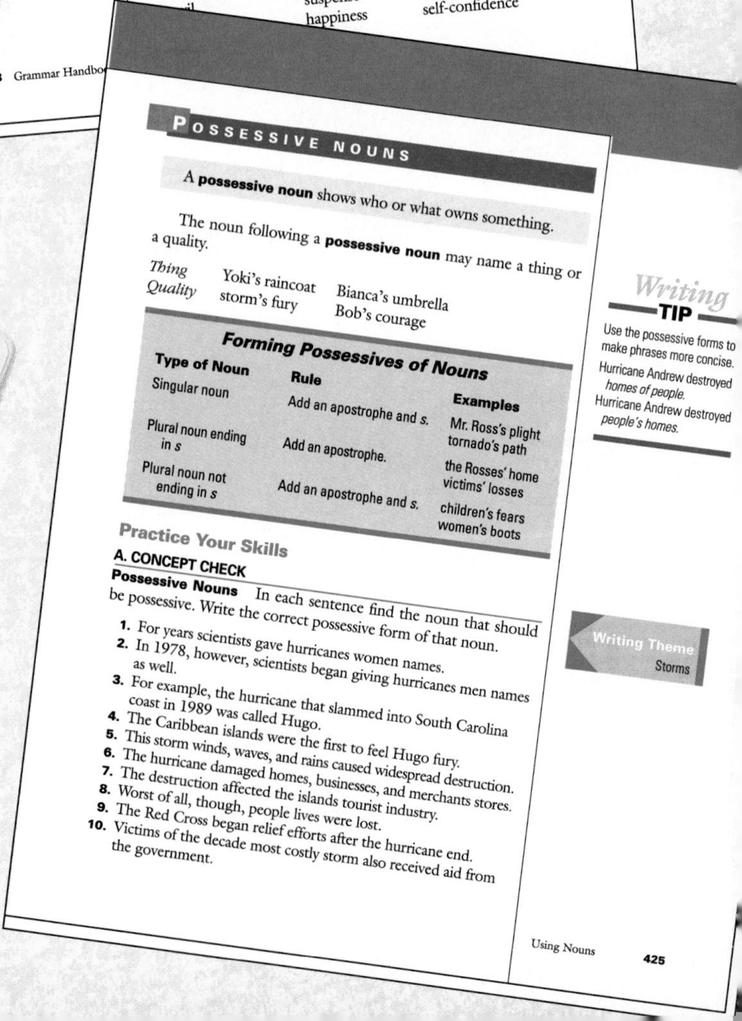

POSSESSIVE NOUNS

A **possessive noun** shows who or what owns something.

The noun following a **possessive noun** may name a thing or a quality.

Thing	Yoki's raincoat	Bianca's umbrella
Quality	storm's fury	Bob's courage

Forming Possessives of Nouns

Type of Noun	Rule	Examples
Singular noun	Add an apostrophe and *s*.	Mr. Ross's plight tornado's path
Plural noun ending in *s*	Add an apostrophe.	the Rosses' home victims' losses
Plural noun not ending in *s*	Add an apostrophe and *s*.	children's fears women's boots

Practice Your Skills

A. CONCEPT CHECK

Possessive Nouns In each sentence find the noun that should be possessive. Write the correct possessive form of that noun.

1. For years scientists gave hurricanes women names.
2. In 1978, however, scientists began giving hurricanes men names as well.
3. For example, the hurricane that slammed into South Carolina coast in 1989 was called Hugo.
4. The Caribbean islands were the first to feel Hugo fury.
5. This storm winds, waves, and rains caused widespread destruction.
6. The hurricane damaged homes, businesses, and merchants stores.
7. The destruction affected the islands tourist industry.
8. Worst of all, though, people lives were lost.
9. The Red Cross began relief efforts after the hurricane end.
10. Victims of the decade most costly storm also received aid from the government.

Writing TIP

Use the possessive forms to make phrases more concise.
Hurricane Andrew destroyed *homes of people.*
Hurricane Andrew destroyed *people's homes.*

Writing Theme
Storms

Using Nouns 425

Applying in Context

A variety of creative exercises provides meaningful application of each concept:

- **Drafting** and **Revision Skills** exercises put the concept to work through such activities as sentence combining and elaboration.
- **Application in Literature** activities show the concept at work in professional writing.
- **Application in Writing** allows students to experiment with different formats while applying new skills.
- **Proofreading activities** provide opportunities to sharpen editing skills.
- **Writing Connections** tie the concept back to the Writer's Workshops.

B. REVISION SKILL

Using Adverbs There are many adverbs available for writers to use. Write the following paragraph, replacing the italicized adverbs with other adverbs that convey a similar meaning.

[11]When you think of mummies, do you think of the *very* old mummies of the ancient Egyptian Pharaohs? [12]It was *once* thought that the Egyptian embalmers used mysterious methods and secret formulas to preserve the bodies *totally*. [13]*Today* scientists know that it was the climate, which is *extremely* dry,

FOR MORE PRACTICE
See page 529.

Writing Theme
Discovering New Planets

Using Modifiers 513

B. APPLICATION IN LITERATURE

Recognizing Adjectives Notice how Ray Bradbury uses adjectives to create vivid, interesting images in the selection below. For each sentence in the paragraph, write the adjectives and the words they modify. Do not include articles. If there are no adjectives in the sentence, write *None*. You should find a total of twelve adjectives.

[13]They set foot upon the porch. [14]Hollow echoes sounded from under the boards as they walked to the screen door. [15]Inside they could see a bead curtain hung across the hall entry, and a crystal chandelier and a Maxfield Parrish painting on one wall over a comfortable Morris chair. . . . [16]You could hear the tinkle of ice in a lemonade pitcher. [17]In a distant kitchen, because of the heat of the day, someone was preparing a cold lunch.

Ray Bradbury,
The Martian Chronicles

C. APPLICATION IN WRITING

A Description Imagine that you are writing a script for a science fiction play. Write a brief description of the scene as the main character walks on stage. What does he or she see, hear, and feel? Use five of the adjectives listed below in your description.

shimmering	weird	immense
purple	American	cold
quiet	slimy	happy
	three	several

FOR MORE PRACTICE
See page 509.

B. PROOFREADING SKILL

Correct Comparative Forms Proofread and write the following paragraph, correcting errors in grammar, capitalization, punctuation, and spelling. Pay special attention to the use of comparative forms. (10 errors)

The United States has one of the most richest cooking traditions in the world. Santa Fe cooking is a cheif example. Its a blend of at least four traditions. The older tradition comes from Native Americans. Their more important contributions are the corn tortilla and chilies. Then the Spanish arrived they brought fruit from their homeland. Later, mexicans settled in the area, bringing New spices and sauces. People from other parts of the United States were the recenter arrivals. Together these cultures have made Santa Fe cooking among the wonderfullest anywhere.

FOR MORE PRACTICE
See page 510.

CHECK POINT
MIXED REVIEW • PAGES 496–503

Write the italicized adjectives in each sentence. Then label each adjective as either *Common* or *Proper*. Label any predicate adjectives *Predicate Adjective*. In addition, if an adjective is used in a comparison, label it as either *Comparative* or *Superlative*.

[1]In March 1925, a *serious* epidemic of diphtheria broke out in Nome, Alaska. [2]The *winter* snows hampered rescue attempts. [3]*Alaskan* dog-sled drivers loaded their sleds with

Writing Theme
Dog-Sled Racing

WRITING CONNECTIONS

Elaboration, Revision, and Proofreading

Revise the following draft of part of a report, using the directions given on this page. Then proofread for errors in grammar, capitalization, punctuation, and spelling. Pay particular attention to the use of adverbs.

[1]Before the worlds largest ocean liner ever sailed, [2]it was advertised as unsinkable. [3]People celebrated as it triumphant pulled away from it's port in Southampton, England on April 10, 1912 it was the first and last voyage of the Titanic. [4]less than three hours after hitting the iceberg, fifteen hundred passengers and crew members found themselves in the icy northern Atlantic ocean. [5]The water in the south Pacific Ocean is usually much warmer. ... On the night of April 14, disaster struck. [7]The Ship hit ...n iceberg and sank more quicker than anyone would have ...elieved. [8]The titanic did have lifeboats, but not near ...ough for everyone. [9]A ship that was nearby did not ...pond to the Titanic's call for help. [10]Following this ...ident, an International convention was held in london, ...land. [11]The convention acted quick to set up new rules ...ea travel. [12]All ships would be required to maintain ...operatons continuously. [13]Each ship would be ...ped with enough lifeboats to hold everyone on board. ...lifeboat drills would be conducted regular. [15]A ... patrol was also organized too warn ships of ...

...nce 2, add an adverb to emphasize how unsinkable the ...

...e sentence that doesn't belong.

...ence 4 to a more logical position

Informative Writing: Reports

Writing a report involves gathering information and presenting it in a clear and organized way. (See Workshop 8.) When you revise a report, make sure you have included all the facts your readers need to know in order to understand your topic. Look for ways you can use adverbs to add precision to your writing.

Special Features

Throughout the pupil's editions, special features provide opportunities for students to enjoy themselves as they learn.

- **Sketchbook** Sometimes funny, sometimes thought-provoking, the Sketchbooks let students experiment with "no-risk writing." A special "Show, Don't Tell" feature provides important practice with elaboration.
- **Sentence Composing** By imitating the sentences of professional writers, students develop their own more sophisticated style.
- **Springboards** Creative suggestions allow students to apply their writing skills across the curriculum.
- **On the Lightside** Your students will learn that language study can be fun.

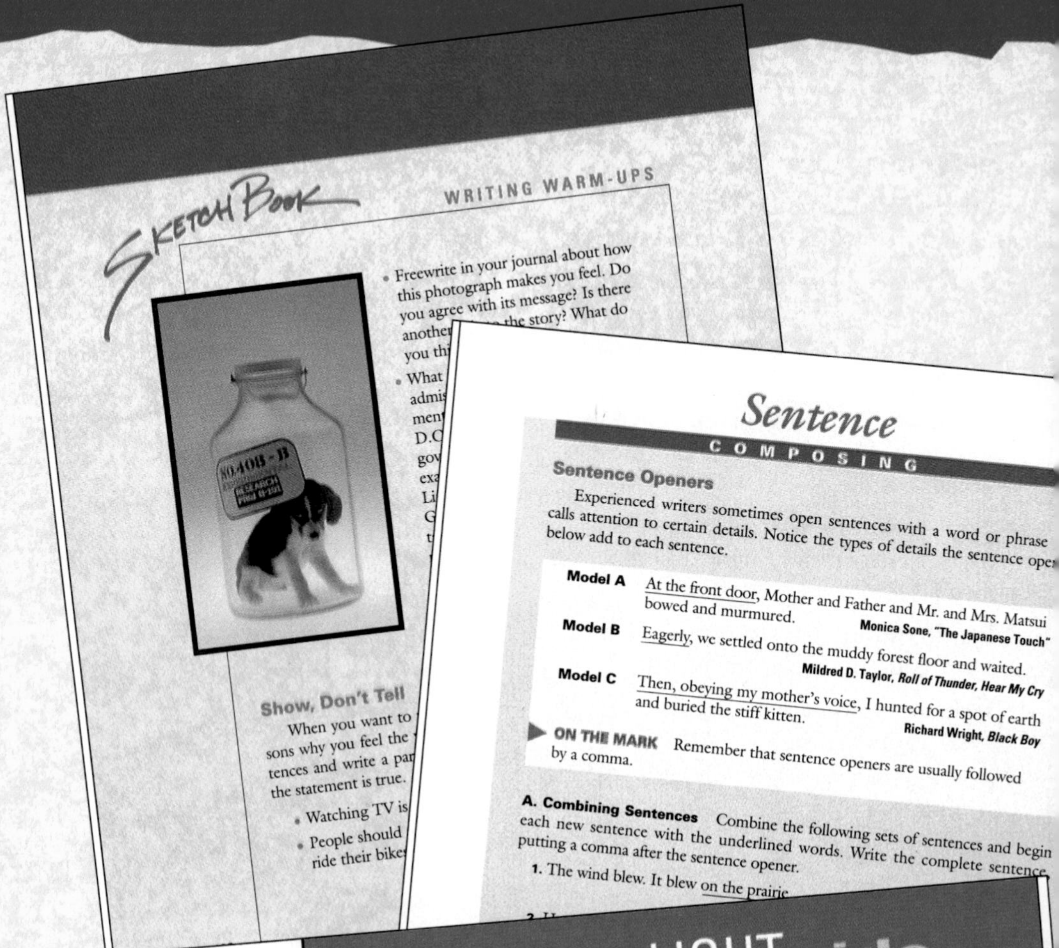

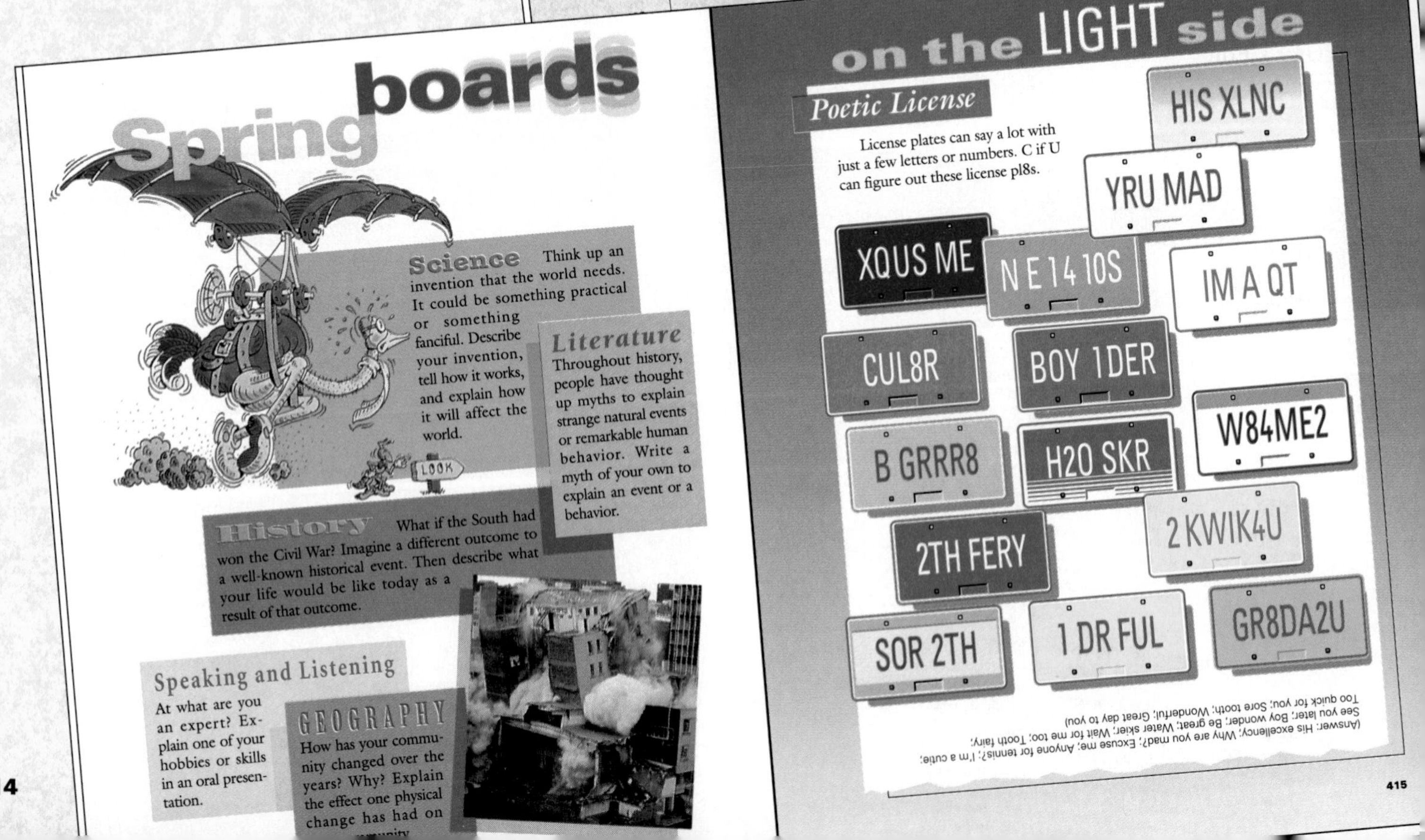

Springboards
Science Think up an invention that the world needs. It could be something practical or something fanciful. Describe your invention, tell how it works, and explain how it will affect the world.
LOOK
Literature Throughout history, people have thought up myths to explain strange natural events or remarkable human behavior. Write a myth of your own to explain an event or a behavior.
History What if the South had won the Civil War? Imagine a different outcome to a well-known historical event. Then describe what your life would be like today as a result of that outcome.
Speaking and Listening
At what are you an expert? Explain one of your hobbies or skills in an oral presentation.
GEOGRAPHY How has your community changed over the years? Why? Explain the effect one physical change has had on
on the LIGHT side
Poetic License
License plates can say a lot with just a few letters or numbers. C if U can figure out these license pl8s.
HIS XLNC
YRU MAD
XQUS ME
N E 14 10S
IM A QT
CUL8R
BOY 1DER
W84ME2
B GRRR8
H2O SKR
2 KWIK4U
2TH FERY
SOR 2TH
1 DR FUL
GR8DA2U
(Answer: His excellency; Why are you mad?; Excuse me; Anyone for tennis?; I'm a cutie; See you later; Boy wonder; Be great; Water skier; Wait for me too; Tooth fairy; Too quick for you; Sore tooth; Wonderful; Great day to you)
415

Review and Assessment

How can you check your students' progress? The Pupil's Edition and Teacher's Resource File for *The Writer's Craft* offer a wide variety of assessment tools.

Writing Assessment

- **Writing Prompts** Based on state assessments across the country, these prompts allow you to check students' writing progress. (Pupil book and Resource File)
- **Guides to Analytic and Holistic Scoring** Guidelines help you check achievement on any writing assignment. Models of student writing provide benchmarks to compare against. (Resource File)
- **Portfolio Assessment Suggestions** Guidelines in this Teacher's Edition and in the Resource File will help you use this effective evaluative technique.

Grammar and Usage Assessment

- **Checkpoints** These activities in the pupil book provide a mixed review after every two or three lessons.
- **Section Reviews** Cumulative activity sets allow you to evaluate student progress after every main Handbook section.
- **Skills Assessments** Structured like many state assessments, these appear throughout the handbooks and allow a mixed review of language concepts.
- **Pretests and Mastery Tests** The standardized format of these tests provides you with a quick way to evaluate student understanding. (Resource File)

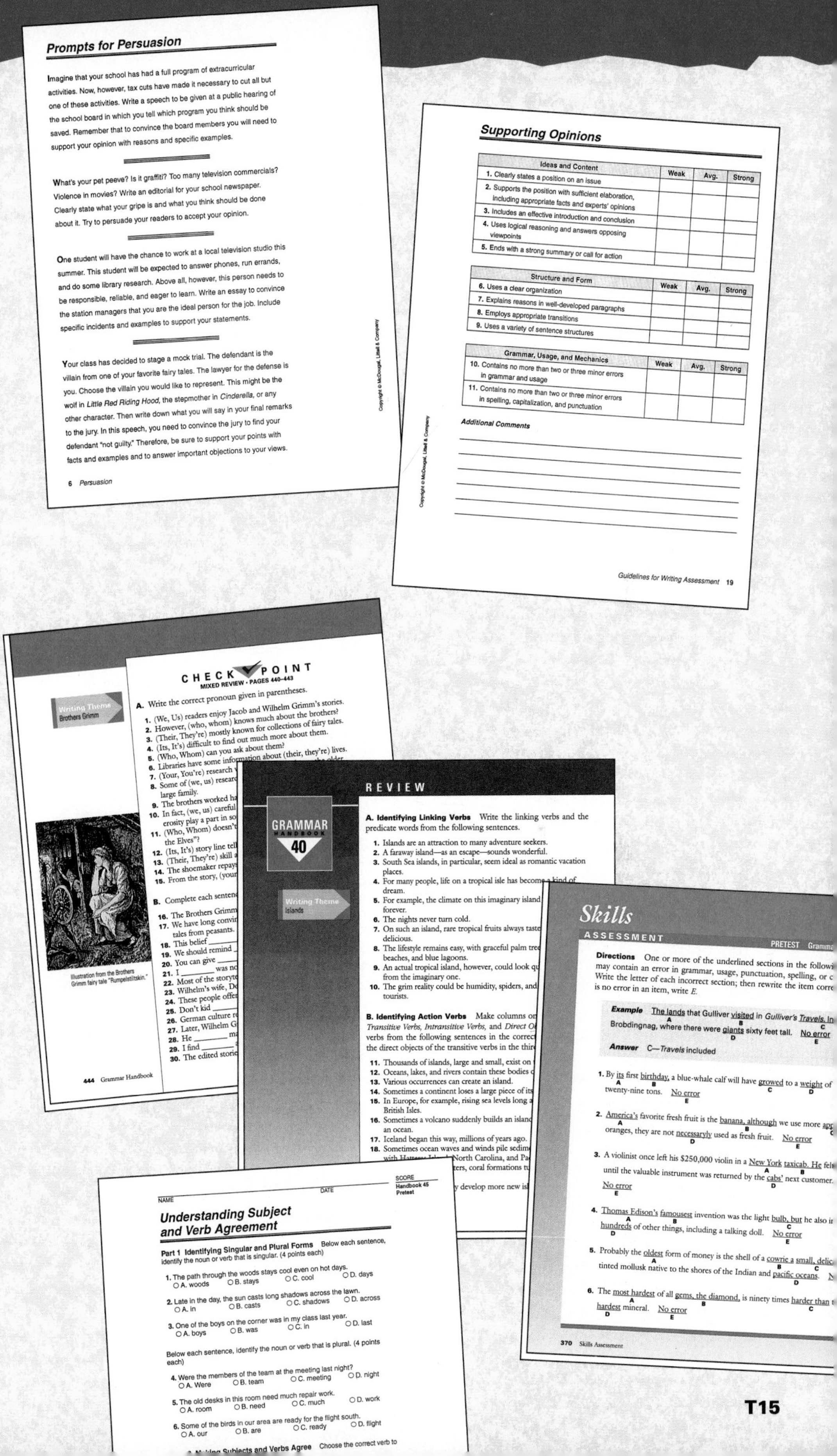

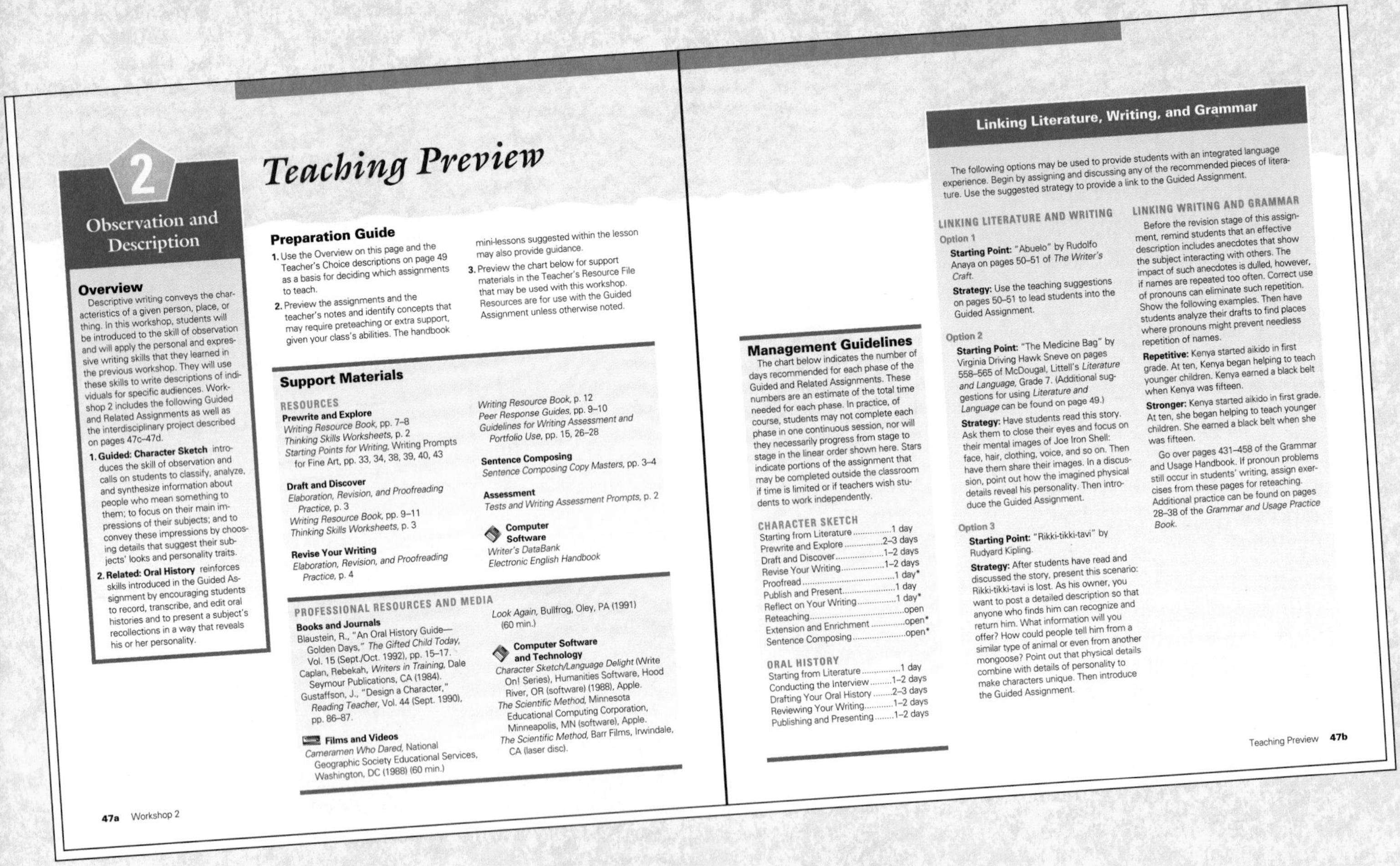

2

Observation and Description

Overview

Descriptive writing conveys the characteristics of a given person, place, or thing. In this workshop, students will be introduced to the skill of observation and will apply the personal and expressive writing skills that they learned in the previous workshop. They will use these skills to write descriptions of individuals for specific audiences. Workshop 2 includes the following Guided and Related Assignments as well as the interdisciplinary project described on pages 47c–47d.

1. **Guided: Character Sketch** introduces the skill of observation and calls on students to classify, analyze, and synthesize information about people who mean something to them; to focus on their main impressions of their subjects; and to convey these impressions by choosing details that suggest their subjects' looks and personality traits.
2. **Related: Oral History** reinforces skills introduced in the Guided Assignment by encouraging students to record, transcribe, and edit oral histories and to present a subject's recollections in a way that reveals his or her personality.

Teaching Preview

Preparation Guide

1. Use the Overview on this page and the Teacher's Choice descriptions on page 49 as a basis for deciding which assignments to teach.
2. Preview the assignments and the teacher's notes and identify concepts that may require preteaching or extra support, given your class's abilities. The handbook mini-lessons suggested within the lesson may also provide guidance.
3. Preview the chart below for support materials in the Teacher's Resource File that may be used with this workshop. Resources are for use with the Guided Assignment unless otherwise noted.

Support Materials

RESOURCES

Prewrite and Explore
Writing Resource Book, pp. 7–8
Thinking Skills Worksheets, p. 2
Starting Points for Writing, Writing Prompts for Fine Art, pp. 33, 34, 38, 39, 40, 43

Draft and Discover
Elaboration, Revision, and Proofreading Practice, p. 3
Writing Resource Book, pp. 9–11
Thinking Skills Worksheets, p. 3

Revise Your Writing
Elaboration, Revision, and Proofreading Practice, p. 4
Writing Resource Book, p. 12
Peer Response Guides, pp. 9–10
Guidelines for Writing Assessment and Portfolio Use, pp. 15, 26–28

Sentence Composing
Sentence Composing Copy Masters, pp. 3–4

Assessment
Tests and Writing Assessment Prompts, p. 2

Computer Software
Writer's DataBank
Electronic English Handbook

PROFESSIONAL RESOURCES AND MEDIA

Books and Journals
Blaustein, R., "An Oral History Guide—Golden Days," *The Gifted Child Today*, Vol. 15 (Sept./Oct. 1992), pp. 15–17.
Caplan, Rebekah, *Writers in Training*, Dale Seymour Publications, CA (1984).
Gustaffson, J., "Design a Character," *Reading Teacher*, Vol. 44 (Sept. 1990), pp. 86–87.

Films and Videos
Cameramen Who Dared, National Geographic Society Educational Services, Washington, DC (1988) (60 min.)
Look Again, Bullfrog, Oley, PA (1991) (60 min.)

Computer Software and Technology
Character Sketch/Language Delight (Write On! Series), Humanities Software, Hood River, OR (software) (1988), Apple.
The Scientific Method, Minnesota Educational Computing Corporation, Minneapolis, MN (software), Apple.
The Scientific Method, Barr Films, Irwindale, CA (laser disc).

47a Workshop 2

Management Guidelines

The chart below indicates the number of days recommended for each phase of the Guided and Related Assignments. These numbers are an estimate of the total time needed for each phase. In practice, of course, students may not complete each phase in one continuous session, nor will they necessarily progress from stage to stage in the linear order shown here. Stars indicate portions of the assignment that may be completed outside the classroom if time is limited or if teachers wish students to work independently.

CHARACTER SKETCH
Starting from Literature ....1 day
Prewrite and Explore ....2–3 days
Draft and Discover ....1–2 days
Revise Your Writing ....1–2 days
Proofread ....1 day*
Publish and Present ....1 day
Reflect on Your Writing ....1 day*
Reteaching ....open
Extension and Enrichment ....open*
Sentence Composing ....open*

ORAL HISTORY
Starting from Literature ....1 day
Conducting the Interview ....1–2 days
Drafting Your Oral History ....2–3 days
Reviewing Your Writing ....1–2 days
Publishing and Presenting ....1–2 days

Linking Literature, Writing, and Grammar

The following options may be used to provide students with an integrated language experience. Begin by assigning and discussing any of the recommended pieces of literature. Use the suggested strategy to provide a link to the Guided Assignment.

LINKING LITERATURE AND WRITING

Option 1

Starting Point: "Abuelo" by Rudolfo Anaya on pages 50–51 of *The Writer's Craft*.

Strategy: Use the teaching suggestions on pages 50–51 to lead students into the Guided Assignment.

Option 2

Starting Point: "The Medicine Bag" by Virginia Driving Hawk Sneve on pages 558–565 of McDougal, Littell's *Literature and Language*, Grade 7. (Additional suggestions for using *Literature and Language* can be found on page 49.)

Strategy: Have students read this story. Ask them to close their eyes and focus on their mental images of Joe Iron Shell: face, hair, clothing, voice, and so on. Then have them share their images. In a discussion, point out how the imagined physical details reveal his personality. Then introduce the Guided Assignment.

Option 3

Starting Point: "Rikki-tikki-tavi" by Rudyard Kipling.

Strategy: After students have read and discussed the story, present this scenario: Rikki-tikki-tavi is lost. As his owner, you want to post a detailed description so that anyone who finds him can recognize and return him. What information will you offer? How could people tell him from a similar type of animal or even from another mongoose? Point out that physical details combine with details of personality to make characters unique. Then introduce the Guided Assignment.

LINKING WRITING AND GRAMMAR

Before the revision stage of this assignment, remind students that an effective description includes anecdotes that show the subject interacting with others. The impact of such anecdotes is dulled, however, if names are repeated too often. Correct use of pronouns can eliminate such repetition. Show the following examples. Then have students analyze their drafts to find places where pronouns might prevent needless repetition of names.

Repetitive: Kenya started aikido in first grade. At ten, Kenya began helping to teach younger children. Kenya earned a black belt when Kenya was fifteen.

Stronger: Kenya started aikido in first grade. At ten, she began helping to teach younger children. She earned a black belt when she was fifteen.

Go over pages 431–458 of the Grammar and Usage Handbook. If pronoun problems still occur in students' writing, assign exercises from these pages for reteaching. Additional practice can be found on pages 28–38 of the *Grammar and Usage Practice Book*.

Teaching Preview 47b

The Teacher's Edition

The Teacher's Edition of *The Writer's Craft* provides you with all the help you will need to prepare comprehensive, exciting lessons.

Teaching Preview

These pages appear before every Writer's Workshop and contain the following information:

- **Workshop Overview** Introduces the focus of the workshop and explains the relationships among the Guided and Related Assignments.
- **Preparation Guide** Guides your planning decisions and provides a chart of available support materials in the Teacher's Resource File, as well as lists of compatible computer software and other technology components.
- **Workshop Management Guidelines** Indicates recommended number of days for each part of the assignment, with suggestions for independent study.
- **Linking Literature, Writing, and Grammar** Presents three options for basing each writing assignment on literature and shows how to link any option with a grammar and usage mini-lesson.

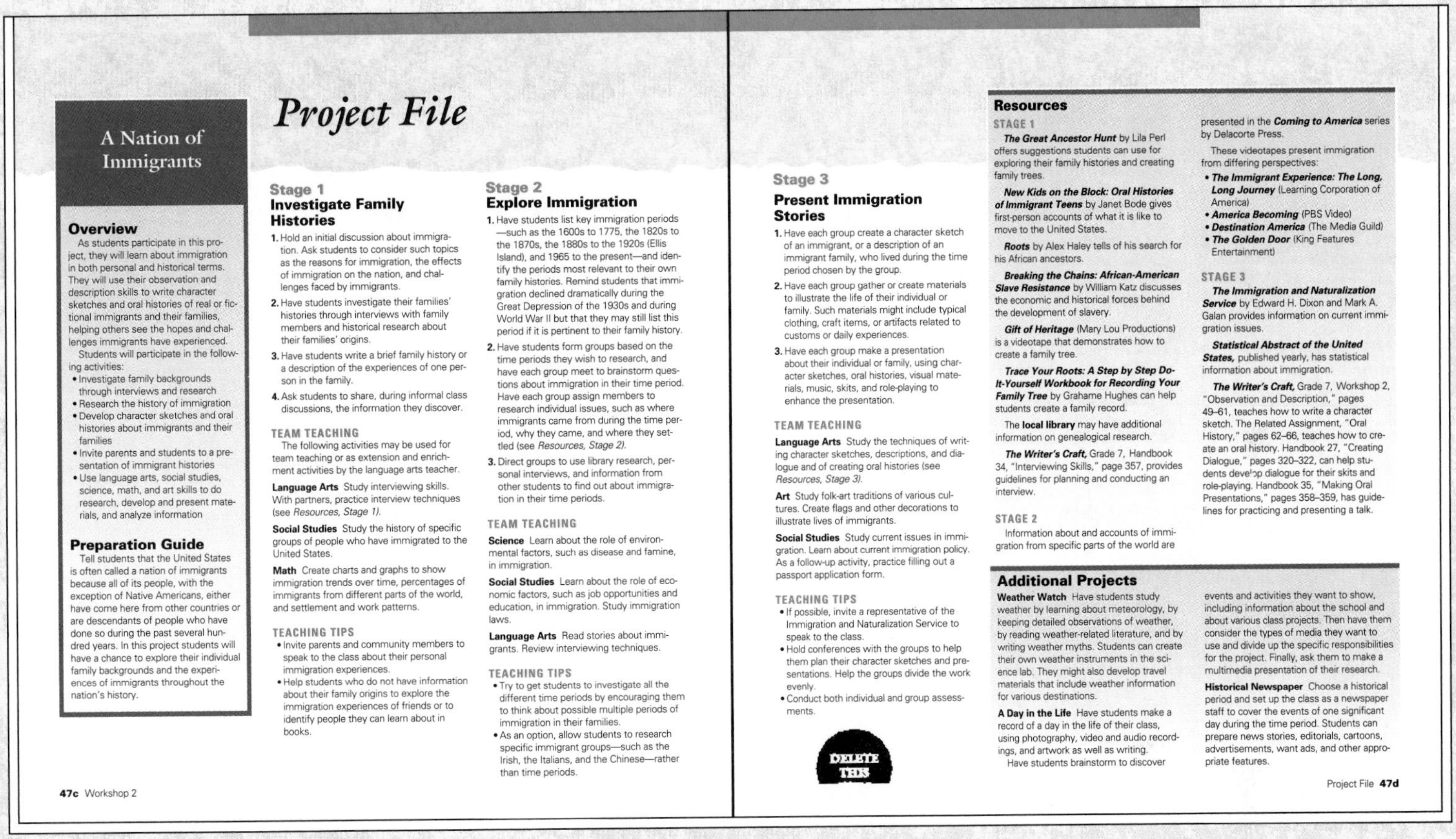

A Nation of Immigrants

Project File

Overview

As students participate in this project, they will learn about immigration in both personal and historical terms. They will use their observation and description skills to write character sketches and oral histories of real or fictional immigrants and their families, helping others see the hopes and challenges immigrants have experienced.

Students will participate in the following activities:

- Investigate family backgrounds through interviews and research
- Research the history of immigration
- Develop character sketches and oral histories about immigrants and their families
- Invite parents and students to a presentation of immigrant histories
- Use language arts, social studies, science, math, and art skills to do research, develop and present materials, and analyze information

Preparation Guide

Tell students that the United States is often called a nation of immigrants because all of its people, with the exception of Native Americans, either have come here from other countries or are descendants of people who have done so during the past several hundred years. In this project students will have a chance to explore their individual family backgrounds and the experiences of immigrants throughout the nation's history.

Stage 1
Investigate Family Histories

1. Hold an initial discussion about immigration. Ask students to consider such topics as the reasons for immigration, the effects of immigration on the nation, and challenges faced by immigrants.
2. Have students investigate their families' histories through interviews with family members and historical research about their families' origins.
3. Have students write a brief family history or a description of the experiences of one person in the family.
4. Ask students to share, during informal class discussions, the information they discover.

TEAM TEACHING

The following activities may be used for team teaching or as extension and enrichment activities by the language arts teacher.

Language Arts Study interviewing skills. With partners, practice interview techniques (see *Resources, Stage 1)*.

Social Studies Study the history of specific groups of people who have immigrated to the United States.

Math Create charts and graphs to show immigration trends over time, percentages of immigrants from different parts of the world, and settlement and work patterns.

TEACHING TIPS

- Invite parents and community members to speak to the class about their personal immigration experiences.
- Help students who do not have information about their family origins to explore the immigration experiences of friends or to identify people they can learn about in books.

Stage 2
Explore Immigration

1. Have students list key immigration periods —such as the 1600s to 1775, the 1820s to the 1870s, the 1880s to the 1920s (Ellis Island), and 1965 to the present—and identify the periods most relevant to their own family histories. Remind students that immigration declined dramatically during the Great Depression of the 1930s and during World War II but that they may still list this period if it is pertinent to their family history.
2. Have students form groups based on the time periods they wish to research, and have each group meet to brainstorm questions about immigration in their time period. Have each group assign members to research individual issues, such as where immigrants came from during the time period, why they came, and where they settled (see *Resources, Stage 2)*.
3. Direct groups to use library research, personal interviews, and information from other students to find out about immigration in their time periods.

TEAM TEACHING

Science Learn about the role of environmental factors, such as disease and famine, in immigration.

Social Studies Learn about the role of economic factors, such as job opportunities and education, in immigration. Study immigration laws.

Language Arts Read stories about immigrants. Review interviewing techniques.

TEACHING TIPS

- Try to get students to investigate all the different time periods by encouraging them to think about possible multiple periods of immigration in their families.
- As an option, allow students to research specific immigrant groups—such as the Irish, the Italians, and the Chinese—rather than time periods.

Stage 3
Present Immigration Stories

1. Have each group create a character sketch of an immigrant, or a description of an immigrant family, who lived during the time period chosen by the group.
2. Have each group gather or create materials to illustrate the life of their individual or family. Such materials might include typical clothing, craft items, or artifacts related to customs or daily experiences.
3. Have each group make a presentation about their individual or family, using character sketches, oral histories, visual materials, music, skits, and role-playing to enhance the presentation.

TEAM TEACHING

Language Arts Study the techniques of writing character sketches, descriptions, and dialogue and of creating oral histories (see *Resources, Stage 3)*.

Art Study folk-art traditions of various cultures. Create flags and other decorations to illustrate lives of immigrants.

Social Studies Study current issues in immigration. Learn about current immigration policy. As a follow-up activity, practice filling out a passport application form.

TEACHING TIPS

- If possible, invite a representative of the Immigration and Naturalization Service to speak to the class.
- Hold conferences with the groups to help them plan their character sketches and presentations. Help the groups divide the work evenly.
- Conduct both individual and group assessments.

DELETE THIS

Resources

STAGE 1

The Great Ancestor Hunt by Lila Perl offers suggestions students can use for exploring their family histories and creating family trees.

New Kids on the Block: Oral Histories of Immigrant Teens by Janet Bode gives first-person accounts of what it is like to move to the United States.

Roots by Alex Haley tells of his search for his African ancestors.

Breaking the Chains: African-American Slave Resistance by William Katz discusses the economic and historical forces behind the development of slavery.

Gift of Heritage (Mary Lou Productions) is a videotape that demonstrates how to create a family tree.

Trace Your Roots: A Step by Step Do-It-Yourself Workbook for Recording Your Family Tree by Grahame Hughes can help students create a family record.

The **local library** may have additional information on genealogical research.

The Writer's Craft, Grade 7, Handbook 34, "Interviewing Skills," page 357, provides guidelines for planning and conducting an interview.

STAGE 2

Information about and accounts of immigration from specific parts of the world are presented in the ***Coming to America*** series by Delacorte Press.

These videotapes present immigration from differing perspectives:

- ***The Immigrant Experience: The Long, Long Journey*** (Learning Corporation of America)
- ***America Becoming*** (PBS Video)
- ***Destination America*** (The Media Guild)
- ***The Golden Door*** (King Features Entertainment)

STAGE 3

The Immigration and Naturalization Service by Edward H. Dixon and Mark A. Galan provides information on current immigration issues.

Statistical Abstract of the United States, published yearly, has statistical information about immigration.

The Writer's Craft, Grade 7, Workshop 2, "Observation and Description," pages 49–61, teaches how to write a character sketch. The Related Assignment, "Oral History," pages 62–66, teaches how to create an oral history. Handbook 27, "Creating Dialogue," pages 320–322, can help students deve!ɔp dialogue for their skits and role-playing. Handbook 35, "Making Oral Presentations," pages 358–359, has guidelines for practicing and presenting a talk.

Additional Projects

Weather Watch Have students study weather by learning about meteorology, by keeping detailed observations of weather, by reading weather-related literature, and by writing weather myths. Students can create their own weather instruments in the science lab. They might also develop travel materials that include weather information for various destinations.

A Day in the Life Have students make a record of a day in the life of their class, using photography, video and audio recordings, and artwork as well as writing.

Have students brainstorm to discover events and activities they want to show, including information about the school and about various class projects. Then have them consider the types of media they want to use and divide up the specific responsibilities for the project. Finally, ask them to make a multimedia presentation of their research.

Historical Newspaper Choose a historical period and set up the class as a newspaper staff to cover the events of one significant day during the time period. Students can prepare news stories, editorials, cartoons, advertisements, want ads, and other appropriate features.

Project File

Detailed suggestions for an exciting cross-curricular project follow each set of Preview pages and contain the following material:

- **Project Overview** Introduces the goals of the project and lists the key activities.
- **Guidelines for Implementation** Provides suggestions and management for implementing each stage of the project.
- **Team Teaching Suggestions** Shows the language arts teacher how to assign tasks among the disciplines or independently make connections to other subject areas.
- **Resources** Offers a wealth of print, video, and technological resources for each stage of the project.
- **Additional Projects** Presents capsulized summaries of other exciting cross-curricular projects.

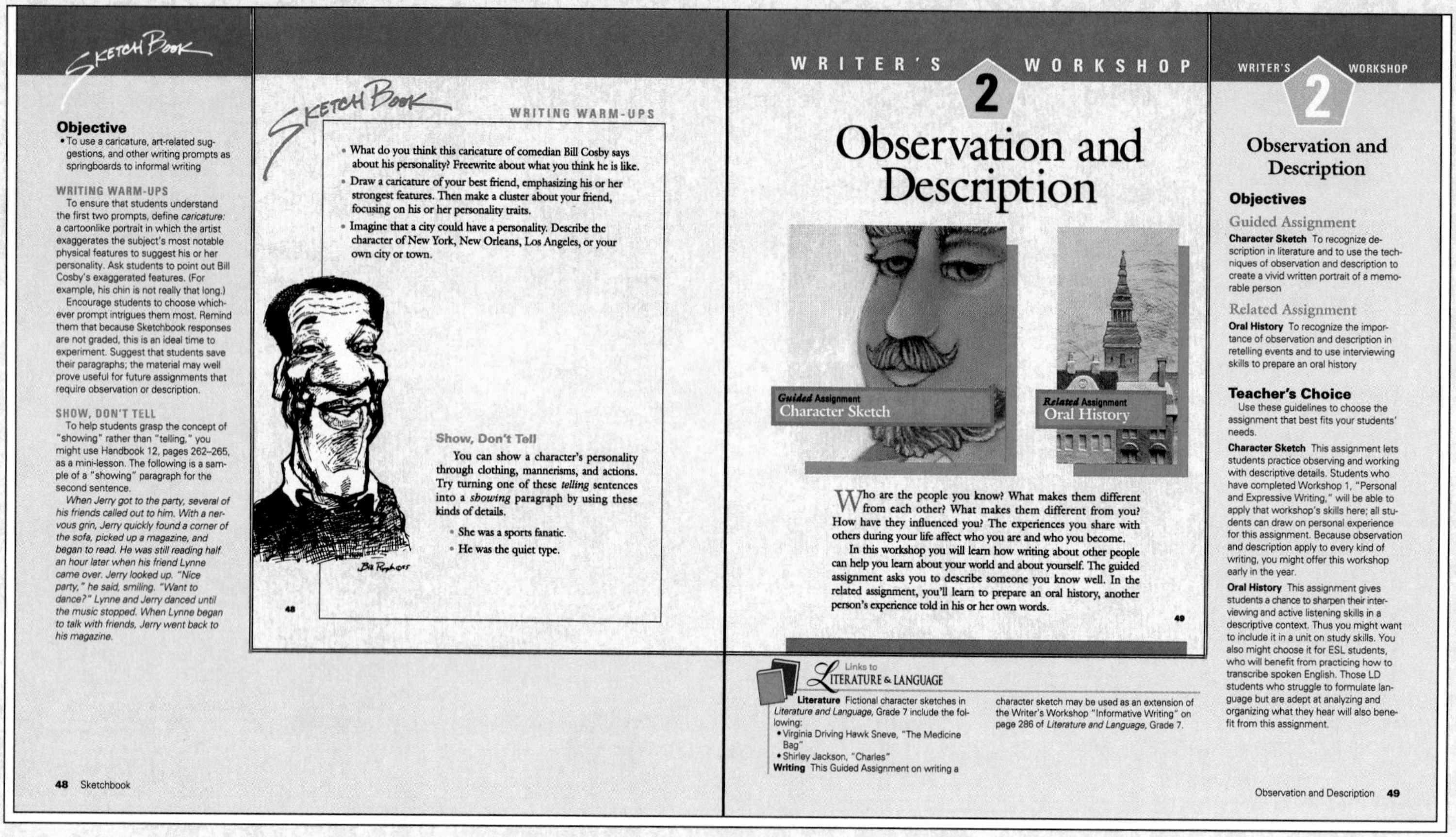

SKETCHBOOK

Objective

- To use a caricature, art-related suggestions, and other writing prompts as springboards to informal writing

WRITING WARM-UPS

To ensure that students understand the first two prompts, define *caricature:* a cartoonlike portrait in which the artist exaggerates the subject's most notable physical features to suggest his or her personality. Ask students to point out Bill Cosby's exaggerated features. (For example, his chin is not really that long.)

Encourage students to choose whichever prompt intrigues them most. Remind them that because Sketchbook responses are not graded, this is an ideal time to experiment. Suggest that students save their paragraphs; the material may well prove useful for future assignments that require observation or description.

SHOW, DON'T TELL

To help students grasp the concept of "showing" rather than "telling," you might use Handbook 12, pages 262–265, as a mini-lesson. The following is a sample of a "showing" paragraph for the second sentence.

When Jerry got to the party, several of his friends called out to him. With a nervous grin, Jerry quickly found a corner of the sofa, picked up a magazine, and began to read. He was still reading half an hour later when his friend Lynne came over. Jerry looked up. "Nice party," he said, smiling. "Want to dance?" Lynne and Jerry danced until the music stopped. When Lynne began to talk with friends, Jerry went back to his magazine.

SKETCHBOOK

WRITING WARM-UPS

- What do you think this caricature of comedian Bill Cosby says about his personality? Freewrite about what you think he is like.
- Draw a caricature of your best friend, emphasizing his or her strongest features. Then make a cluster about your friend, focusing on his or her personality traits.
- Imagine that a city could have a personality. Describe the character of New York, New Orleans, Los Angeles, or your own city or town.

Show, Don't Tell

You can show a character's personality through clothing, mannerisms, and actions. Try turning one of these *telling* sentences into a *showing* paragraph by using these kinds of details.

- She was a sports fanatic.
- He was the quiet type.

48

48 Sketchbook

WRITER'S 2 WORKSHOP

Observation and Description

Guided Assignment
Character Sketch

Related Assignment
Oral History

Who are the people you know? What makes them different from each other? What makes them different from you? How have they influenced you? The experiences you share with others during your life affect who you are and who you become.

In this workshop you will learn how writing about other people can help you learn about your world and about yourself. The guided assignment asks you to describe someone you know well. In the related assignment, you'll learn to prepare an oral history, another person's experience told in his or her own words.

49

Links to LITERATURE & LANGUAGE

Literature Fictional character sketches in *Literature and Language*, Grade 7 include the following:

- Virginia Driving Hawk Sneve, "The Medicine Bag"
- Shirley Jackson, "Charles"

Writing This Guided Assignment on writing a character sketch may be used as an extension of the Writer's Workshop "Informative Writing" on page 286 of *Literature and Language*, Grade 7.

WRITER'S 2 WORKSHOP

Observation and Description

Objectives

Guided Assignment

Character Sketch To recognize description in literature and to use the techniques of observation and description to create a vivid written portrait of a memorable person

Related Assignment

Oral History To recognize the importance of observation and description in retelling events and to use interviewing skills to prepare an oral history

Teacher's Choice

Use these guidelines to choose the assignment that best fits your students' needs.

Character Sketch This assignment lets students practice observing and working with descriptive details. Students who have completed Workshop 1, "Personal and Expressive Writing," will be able to apply that workshop's skills here; all students can draw on personal experience for this assignment. Because observation and description apply to every kind of writing, you might offer this workshop early in the year.

Oral History This assignment gives students a chance to sharpen their interviewing and active listening skills in a descriptive context. Thus you might want to include it in a unit on study skills. You also might choose it for ESL students, who will benefit from practicing how to transcribe spoken English. Those LD students who struggle to formulate language but are adept at analyzing and organizing what they hear will also benefit from this assignment.

Observation and Description 49

Workshop Introduction

In the Pupil's Edition, this page allows both students and teachers to see—at a glance—the focus of the Workshop and the writing types they will be exploring. The Teacher's Edition provides this additional support:

- **Workshop Objectives** Lists general objectives for the Workshop as a whole.
- **Teacher's Choice** Helps the teacher choose assignments by describing each one, suggesting which students might benefit most, and recommending when it might best be taught.
- **Links to *Literature and Language*** Shows the teacher how to tie *The Writer's Craft* to McDougal, Littell's popular integrated language arts program.

Using The Models

Teacher notes accompany both the professional and student models to help introduce the characteristics of the writing that students will be working on.

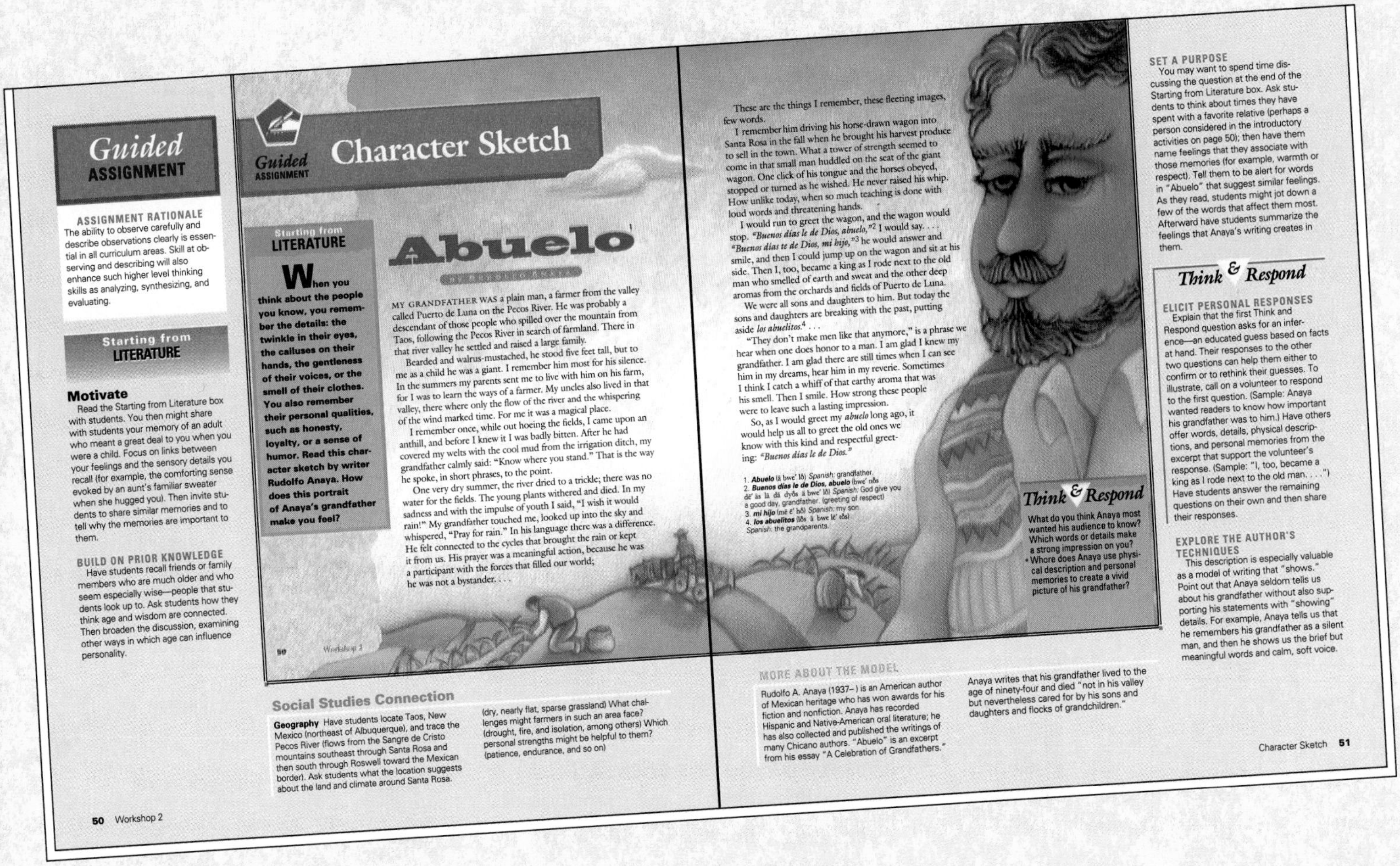

Guided ASSIGNMENT

ASSIGNMENT RATIONALE
The ability to observe carefully and describe observations clearly is essential in all curriculum areas. Skill at observing and describing will also enhance such higher level thinking skills as analyzing, synthesizing, and evaluating.

Starting from LITERATURE

Motivate
Read the Starting from Literature box with students. You then might share with students your memory of an adult who meant a great deal to you when you were a child. Focus on links between your feelings and the sensory details you recall (for example, the comforting sense evoked by an aunt's familiar sweater when she hugged you). Then invite students to share similar memories and to tell why the memories are important to them.

BUILD ON PRIOR KNOWLEDGE
Have students recall friends or family members who are much older and who seem especially wise—people that students look up to. Ask students how they think age and wisdom are connected. Then broaden the discussion, examining other ways in which age can influence personality.

Guided ASSIGNMENT

Character Sketch

Starting from LITERATURE

When you think about the people you know, you remember the details: the twinkle in their eyes, the calluses on their hands, the gentleness of their voices, or the smell of their clothes. You also remember their personal qualities, such as honesty, loyalty, or a sense of humor. Read this character sketch by writer Rudolfo Anaya. How does this portrait of Anaya's grandfather make you feel?

Abuelo[1]

MY GRANDFATHER WAS a plain man, a farmer from the valley called Puerto de Luna on the Pecos River. He was probably a descendant of those people who spilled over the mountain from Taos, following the Pecos River in search of farmland. There in that river valley he settled and raised a large family.

Bearded and walrus-mustached, he stood five feet tall, but to me as a child he was a giant. I remember him most for his silence. In the summers my parents sent me to live with him on his farm, for I was to learn the ways of a farmer. My uncles also lived in that valley, there where only the flow of the river and the whispering of the wind marked time. For me it was a magical place.

I remember once, while out hoeing the fields, I came upon an anthill, and before I knew it I was badly bitten. After he had covered my welts with the cool mud from the irrigation ditch, my grandfather calmly said: "Know where you stand." That is the way he spoke, in short phrases, to the point.

One very dry summer, the river dried to a trickle; there was no water for the fields. The young plants withered and died. In my sadness and with the impulse of youth I said, "I wish it would rain!" My grandfather touched me, looked up into the sky and whispered, "Pray for rain." In his language there was a difference. He felt connected to the cycles that brought the rain or kept it from us. His prayer was a meaningful action, because he was a participant with the forces that filled our world; he was not a bystander. . . .

50 Workshop 2

These are the things I remember, these fleeting images, few words.

I remember him driving his horse-drawn wagon into Santa Rosa in the fall when he brought his harvest produce to sell in the town. What a tower of strength seemed to come in that small man huddled on the seat of the giant wagon. One click of his tongue and the horses obeyed, stopped or turned as he wished. He never raised his whip. How unlike today, when so much teaching is done with loud words and threatening hands.

I would run to greet the wagon, and the wagon would stop. *"Buenos días le de Dios, abuelo,"*[2] I would say. . . . *"Buenos días te de Dios, mi hijo,"*[3] he would answer and smile, and then I could jump up on the wagon and sit at his side. Then I, too, became a king as I rode next to the old man who smelled of earth and sweat and the other deep aromas from the orchards and fields of Puerto de Luna.

We were all sons and daughters to him. But today the sons and daughters are breaking with the past, putting aside *los abuelitos*.[4] . . .

"They don't make men like that anymore," is a phrase we hear when one does honor to a man. I am glad I knew my grandfather. I am glad there are still times when I can see him in my dreams, hear him in my reverie. Sometimes I think I catch a whiff of that earthy aroma that was his smell. Then I smile. How strong these people were to leave such a lasting impression.

So, as I would greet my *abuelo* long ago, it would help us all to greet the old ones we know with this kind and respectful greeting: *"Buenos días le de Dios."*

1. **Abuelo** (ä bwe' lô) *Spanish:* grandfather.
2. **Buenos días le de Dios, abuelo** (bwe' nôs dē' äs lä dä dyôs ä bwe' lô) *Spanish:* God give you a good day, grandfather. (greeting of respect)
3. **mi hijo** (mē ē' hô) *Spanish:* my son.
4. **los abuelitos** (lôs ä bwe lē' tôs) *Spanish:* the grandparents.

Think & Respond

What do you think Anaya most wanted his audience to know? Which words or details make a strong impression on you?
- Where does Anaya use physical description and personal memories to create a vivid picture of his grandfather?

SET A PURPOSE
You may want to spend time discussing the question at the end of the Starting from Literature box. Ask students to think about times they have spent with a favorite relative (perhaps a person considered in the introductory activities on page 50); then have them name feelings that they associate with those memories (for example, warmth or respect). Tell them to be alert for words in "Abuelo" that suggest similar feelings. As they read, students might jot down a few of the words that affect them most. Afterward have students summarize the feelings that Anaya's writing creates in them.

Think & Respond

ELICIT PERSONAL RESPONSES
Explain that the first Think and Respond question asks for an inference—an educated guess based on facts at hand. Their responses to the other two questions can help them either to confirm or to rethink their guesses. To illustrate, call on a volunteer to respond to the first question. (Sample: Anaya wanted readers to know how important his grandfather was to him.) Have others offer words, details, physical descriptions, and personal memories from the excerpt that support the volunteer's response. (Sample: "I, too, became a king as I rode next to the old man. . . .") Have students answer the remaining questions on their own and then share their responses.

EXPLORE THE AUTHOR'S TECHNIQUES
This description is especially valuable as a model of writing that "shows." Point out that Anaya seldom tells us about his grandfather without also supporting his statements with "showing" details. For example, Anaya tells us that he remembers his grandfather as a silent man, and then he shows us the brief but meaningful words and calm, soft voice.

Social Studies Connection

Geography Have students locate Taos, New Mexico (northeast of Albuquerque), and trace the Pecos River (flows from the Sangre de Cristo mountains southeast through Santa Rosa and then south through Roswell toward the Mexican border). Ask students what the location suggests about the land and climate around Santa Rosa. (dry, nearly flat, sparse grassland) What challenges might farmers in such an area face? (drought, fire, and isolation, among others) Which personal strengths might be helpful to them? (patience, endurance, and so on)

MORE ABOUT THE MODEL

Rudolfo A. Anaya (1937–) is an American author of Mexican heritage who has won awards for his fiction and nonfiction. Anaya has recorded Hispanic and Native-American oral literature; he has also collected and published the writings of many Chicano authors. "Abuelo" is an excerpt from his essay "A Celebration of Grandfathers." Anaya writes that his grandfather lived to the age of ninety-four and died "not in his valley but nevertheless cared for by his sons and daughters and flocks of grandchildren."

50 Workshop 2

Character Sketch 51

- **Assignment Rationale** Explains the thinking behind the assignment and the reasons for its inclusion.
- **Motivate** Helps teachers prepare their students for reading the literature through ties to prior knowledge and setting a purpose.
- **Connections** Links to literature, science, social studies, and the fine arts.
- **More About the Model** Provides interesting background material or extended learning opportunities tied to the literature.
- **Think and Respond** Suggestions for eliciting personal responses and exploring the authors' techniques ensure that students will get the most from what they read.
- **Draw Conclusions** A summary after the student model encourages comparison of the two readings and helps students draw conclusions about the writing they will study.

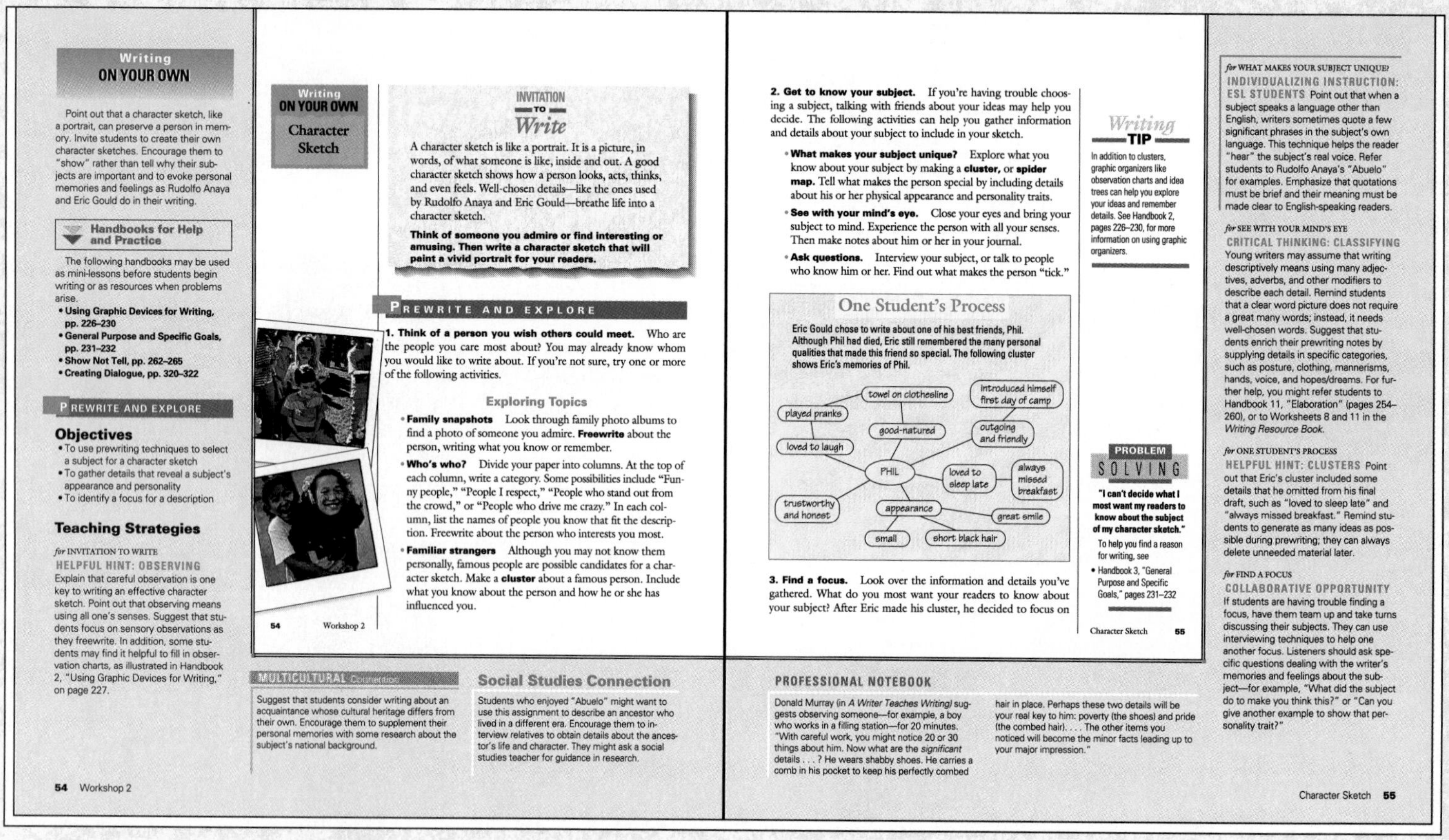

Writing ON YOUR OWN

Point out that a character sketch, like a portrait, can preserve a person in memory. Invite students to create their own character sketches. Encourage them to "show" rather than tell why their subjects are important and to evoke personal memories and feelings as Rudolfo Anaya and Eric Gould do in their writing.

Handbooks for Help and Practice

The following handbooks may be used as mini-lessons before students begin writing or as resources when problems arise.
- Using Graphic Devices for Writing, pp. 226–230
- General Purpose and Specific Goals, pp. 231–232
- Show Not Tell, pp. 262–265
- Creating Dialogue, pp. 320–322

PREWRITE AND EXPLORE

Objectives
- To use prewriting techniques to select a subject for a character sketch
- To gather details that reveal a subject's appearance and personality
- To identify a focus for a description

Teaching Strategies

for INVITATION TO WRITE
HELPFUL HINT: OBSERVING
Explain that careful observation is one key to writing an effective character sketch. Point out that observing means using all one's senses. Suggest that students focus on sensory observations as they freewrite. In addition, some students may find it helpful to fill in observation charts, as illustrated in Handbook 2, "Using Graphic Devices for Writing," on page 227.

Writing ON YOUR OWN — Character Sketch

INVITATION TO Write

A character sketch is like a portrait. It is a picture, in words, of what someone is like, inside and out. A good character sketch shows how a person looks, acts, thinks, and even feels. Well-chosen details—like the ones used by Rudolfo Anaya and Eric Gould—breathe life into a character sketch.

Think of someone you admire or find interesting or amusing. Then write a character sketch that will paint a vivid portrait for your readers.

PREWRITE AND EXPLORE

1. Think of a person you wish others could meet. Who are the people you care most about? You may already know whom you would like to write about. If you're not sure, try one or more of the following activities.

Exploring Topics
- **Family snapshots** Look through family photo albums to find a photo of someone you admire. **Freewrite** about the person, writing what you know or remember.
- **Who's who?** Divide your paper into columns. At the top of each column, write a category. Some possibilities include "Funny people," "People I respect," "People who stand out from the crowd," or "People who drive me crazy." In each column, list the names of people you know that fit the description. Freewrite about the person who interests you most.
- **Familiar strangers** Although you may not know them personally, famous people are possible candidates for a character sketch. Make a **cluster** about a famous person. Include what you know about the person and how he or she has influenced you.

54 Workshop 2

2. Get to know your subject. If you're having trouble choosing a subject, talking with friends about your ideas may help you decide. The following activities can help you gather information and details about your subject to include in your sketch.
- **What makes your subject unique?** Explore what you know about your subject by making a **cluster**, or **spider map**. Tell what makes the person special by including details about his or her physical appearance and personality traits.
- **See with your mind's eye.** Close your eyes and bring your subject to mind. Experience the person with all your senses. Then make notes about him or her in your journal.
- **Ask questions.** Interview your subject, or talk to people who know him or her. Find out what makes the person "tick."

One Student's Process

Eric Gould chose to write about one of his best friends, Phil. Although Phil had died, Eric still remembered the many personal qualities that made this friend so special. The following cluster shows Eric's memories of Phil.

3. Find a focus. Look over the information and details you've gathered. What do you most want your readers to know about your subject? After Eric made his cluster, he decided to focus on

Writing TIP

In addition to clusters, graphic organizers like observation charts and idea trees can help you explore your ideas and remember details. See Handbook 2, pages 226–230, for more information on using graphic organizers.

PROBLEM SOLVING

"I can't decide what I most want my readers to know about the subject of my character sketch."

To help you find a reason for writing, see
- Handbook 3, "General Purpose and Specific Goals," pages 231–232

Character Sketch 55

for WHAT MAKES YOUR SUBJECT UNIQUE?
INDIVIDUALIZING INSTRUCTION: ESL STUDENTS Point out that when a subject speaks a language other than English, writers sometimes quote a few significant phrases in the subject's own language. This technique helps the reader "hear" the subject's real voice. Refer students to Rudolfo Anaya's "Abuelo" for examples. Emphasize that quotations must be brief and their meaning must be made clear to English-speaking readers.

for SEE WITH YOUR MIND'S EYE
CRITICAL THINKING: CLASSIFYING
Young writers may assume that writing descriptively means using many adjectives, adverbs, and other modifiers to describe each detail. Remind students that a clear word picture does not require a great many words; instead, it needs well-chosen words. Suggest that students enrich their prewriting notes by supplying details in specific categories, such as posture, clothing, mannerisms, hands, voice, and hopes/dreams. For further help, you might refer students to Handbook 11, "Elaboration" (pages 254–260), or to Worksheets 8 and 11 in the *Writing Resource Book.*

for ONE STUDENT'S PROCESS
HELPFUL HINT: CLUSTERS Point out that Eric's cluster included some details that he omitted from his final draft, such as "loved to sleep late" and "always missed breakfast." Remind students to generate as many ideas as possible during prewriting; they can always delete unneeded material later.

for FIND A FOCUS
COLLABORATIVE OPPORTUNITY
If students are having trouble finding a focus, have them team up and take turns discussing their subjects. They can use interviewing techniques to help one another focus. Listeners should ask specific questions dealing with the writer's memories and feelings about the subject—for example, "What did the subject do to make you think this?" or "Can you give another example to show that personality trait?"

MULTICULTURAL Connection

Suggest that students consider writing about an acquaintance whose cultural heritage differs from their own. Encourage them to supplement their personal memories with some research about the subject's national background.

Social Studies Connection

Students who enjoyed "Abuelo" might want to use this assignment to describe an ancestor who lived in a different era. Encourage them to interview relatives to obtain details about the ancestor's life and character. They might ask a social studies teacher for guidance in research.

PROFESSIONAL NOTEBOOK

Donald Murray (in *A Writer Teaches Writing*) suggests observing someone—for example, a boy who works in a filling station—for 20 minutes. "With careful work, you might notice 20 or 30 things about him. Now what are the *significant* details . . . ? He wears shabby shoes. He carries a comb in his pocket to keep his perfectly combed hair in place. Perhaps these two details will be your real key to him: poverty (the shoes) and pride (the combed hair). . . . The other items you noticed will become the minor facts leading up to your major impression."

54 Workshop 2

Character Sketch 55

Lesson Notes

The Teacher's Edition continues to help the teacher throughout the Workshop. Each lesson contains the following material:

- **Objectives** Specific goals for each part of the lesson.
- **Handbook Suggestions** Ideas for mini-lessons from the Handbooks.
- **Teaching Strategies** Point-of-use notes that truly make this one book for all students. Included are suggestions for

Modeling Suggestions for making yourself a co-writer in the classroom

Speaking and Listening Opportunities

Critical Thinking

Individualizing Instruction Tips for teaching LEP, LD, and students with different ability levels or learning styles

Collaborative Opportunities

Spot Checks

Peer Response Suggestions

Stumbling Blocks Potential problems and tips to avoid them

Managing the Paper Load Ideas for cutting down on grading and review

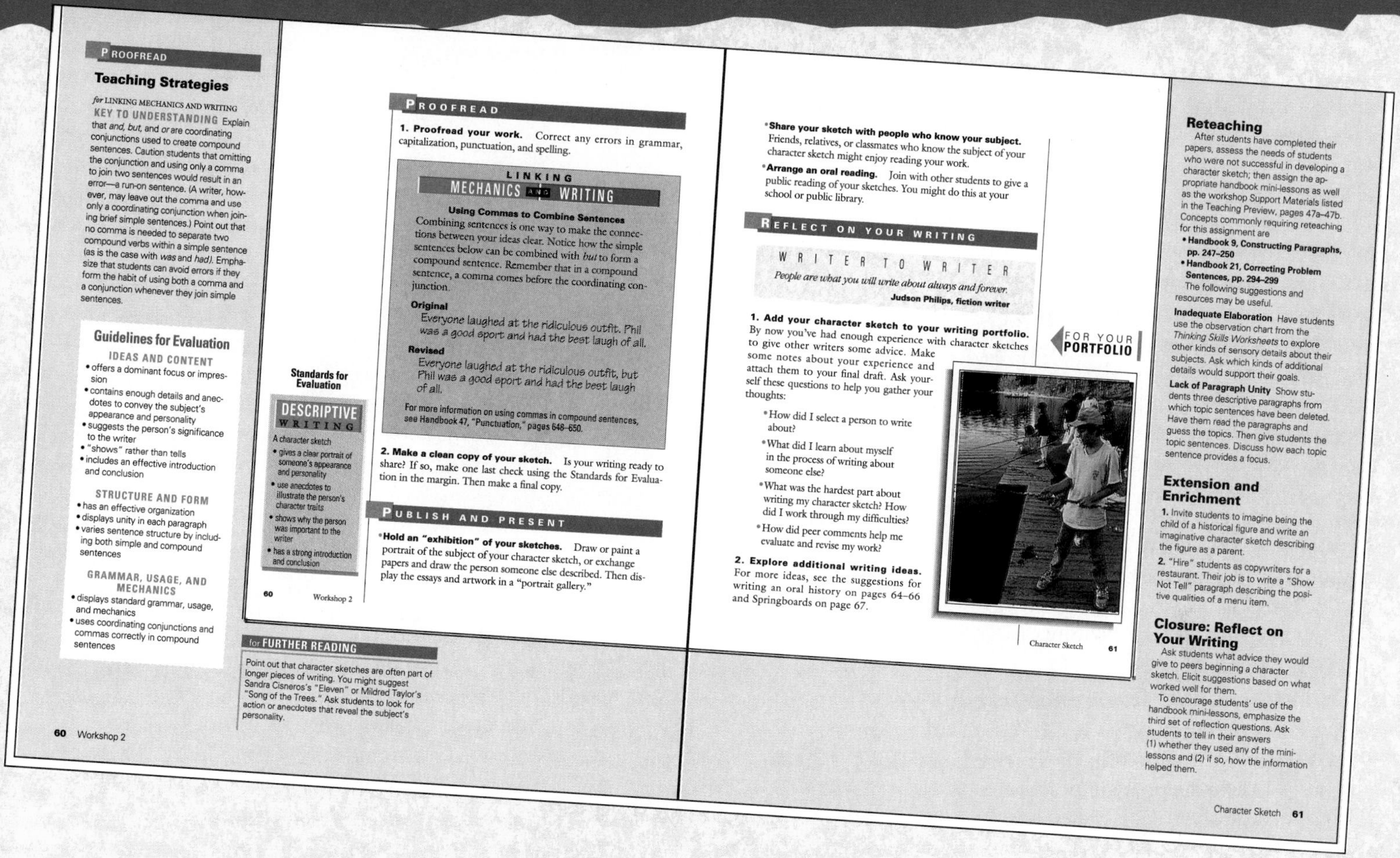

PROOFREAD

Teaching Strategies

for LINKING MECHANICS AND WRITING

KEY TO UNDERSTANDING Explain that *and, but,* and *or* are coordinating conjunctions used to create compound sentences. Caution students that omitting the conjunction and using only a comma to join two sentences would result in an error—a run-on sentence. (A writer, however, may leave out the comma and use only a coordinating conjunction when joining brief simple sentences.) Point out that no comma is needed to separate two compound verbs within a simple sentence (as is the case with *was* and *had*). Emphasize that students can avoid errors if they form the habit of using both a comma and a conjunction whenever they join simple sentences.

Guidelines for Evaluation

IDEAS AND CONTENT
- offers a dominant focus or impression
- contains enough details and anecdotes to convey the subject's appearance and personality
- suggests the person's significance to the writer
- "shows" rather than tells
- includes an effective introduction and conclusion

STRUCTURE AND FORM
- has an effective organization
- displays unity in each paragraph
- varies sentence structure by including both simple and compound sentences

GRAMMAR, USAGE, AND MECHANICS
- displays standard grammar, usage, and mechanics
- uses coordinating conjunctions and commas correctly in compound sentences

Standards for Evaluation

DESCRIPTIVE WRITING

A character sketch
- gives a clear portrait of someone's appearance and personality
- use anecdotes to illustrate the person's character traits
- shows why the person was important to the writer
- has a strong introduction and conclusion

PROOFREAD

1. Proofread your work. Correct any errors in grammar, capitalization, punctuation, and spelling.

LINKING MECHANICS AND WRITING

Using Commas to Combine Sentences

Combining sentences is one way to make the connections between your ideas clear. Notice how the simple sentences below can be combined with *but* to form a compound sentence. Remember that in a compound sentence, a comma comes before the coordinating conjunction.

Original

Everyone laughed at the ridiculous outfit. Phil was a good sport and had the best laugh of all.

Revised

Everyone laughed at the ridiculous outfit, but Phil was a good sport and had the best laugh of all.

For more information on using commas in compound sentences, see Handbook 47, "Punctuation," pages 648–650.

2. Make a clean copy of your sketch. Is your writing ready to share? If so, make one last check using the Standards for Evaluation in the margin. Then make a final copy.

PUBLISH AND PRESENT

- **Hold an "exhibition" of your sketches.** Draw or paint a portrait of the subject of your character sketch, or exchange papers and draw the person someone else described. Then display the essays and artwork in a "portrait gallery."

60 Workshop 2

- **Share your sketch with people who know your subject.** Friends, relatives, or classmates who know the subject of your character sketch might enjoy reading your work.
- **Arrange an oral reading.** Join with other students to give a public reading of your sketches. You might do this at your school or public library.

REFLECT ON YOUR WRITING

WRITER TO WRITER

People are what you will write about always and forever.

Judson Philips, fiction writer

1. Add your character sketch to your writing portfolio. By now you've had enough experience with character sketches to give other writers some advice. Make some notes about your experience and attach them to your final draft. Ask yourself these questions to help you gather your thoughts:

- How did I select a person to write about?
- What did I learn about myself in the process of writing about someone else?
- What was the hardest part about writing my character sketch? How did I work through my difficulties?
- How did peer comments help me evaluate and revise my work?

2. Explore additional writing ideas. For more ideas, see the suggestions for writing an oral history on pages 64–66 and Springboards on page 67.

FOR YOUR PORTFOLIO

Character Sketch 61

Reteaching

After students have completed their papers, assess the needs of students who were not successful in developing a character sketch; then assign the appropriate handbook mini-lessons as well as the workshop Support Materials listed in the Teaching Preview, pages 47a–47b. Concepts commonly requiring reteaching for this assignment are
- **Handbook 9, Constructing Paragraphs, pp. 247–250**
- **Handbook 21, Correcting Problem Sentences, pp. 294–299**

The following suggestions and resources may be useful.

Inadequate Elaboration Have students use the observation chart from the *Thinking Skills Worksheets* to explore other kinds of sensory details about their subjects. Ask which kinds of additional details would support their goals.

Lack of Paragraph Unity Show students three descriptive paragraphs from which topic sentences have been deleted. Have them read the paragraphs and guess the topics. Then give students the topic sentences. Discuss how each topic sentence provides a focus.

Extension and Enrichment

1. Invite students to imagine being the child of a historical figure and write an imaginative character sketch describing the figure as a parent.

2. "Hire" students as copywriters for a restaurant. Their job is to write a "Show Not Tell" paragraph describing the positive qualities of a menu item.

Closure: Reflect on Your Writing

Ask students what advice they would give to peers beginning a character sketch. Elicit suggestions based on what worked well for them.

To encourage students' use of the handbook mini-lessons, emphasize the third set of reflection questions. Ask students to tell in their answers (1) whether they used any of the mini-lessons and (2) if so, how the information helped them.

for **FURTHER READING**

Point out that character sketches are often part of longer pieces of writing. You might suggest Sandra Cisneros's "Eleven" or Mildred Taylor's "Song of the Trees." Ask students to look for action or anecdotes that reveal the subject's personality.

60 Workshop 2

Character Sketch 61

- **Guidelines for Evaluation** Rubrics for evaluating student papers.
- **Reteaching Suggestions** Suggestions for providing additional instruction in areas where students were not successful.
- **Extension and Enrichment** Ideas for moving students beyond the assignment.
- **Reflect on Your Writing** Ideas that help students learn from each assignment and build writing portfolios.
- **For Further Reading** Other readings that are related to the model.

Other Features

Answer Keys Answers or suggested responses to all student activities.

Professional Notebook Quotes and suggestions from experts on teaching and the writing process.

Multicultural Connections Opportunities to broaden learning to include a variety of cultures.

Spice Box Motivating quotes and activities.

Teacher's Lounge Humor from the bulletin boards to you.

Teacher's Resource File

Motivation, reinforcement, creative approaches to writing, and practical teaching support are the hallmarks of the Teacher's Resource File.

Transparency Pack

A wealth of transparencies enhances all of your writing lessons.

- **Fine Art Transparencies** Classic and contemporary art reproductions offer springboards to writing. Worksheets provide writing prompts for a variety of modes.

- **Thinking Skills Transparencies** These graphic organizers can be used to help students find or develop ideas. Worksheets provide practice with each device.

- **Elaboration, Revision, and Proofreading Transparencies** Transparencies and worksheets give students extra experience with three key writing skills.

Guidelines for Writing Assessment and Portfolio Use

This booklet includes evaluation guidelines; models of strong, average, and weak student responses; and materials to aid in portfolio building.

Sentence Composing Copy Masters

These activities provide additional practice in composing sentences based on literary models.

McDougal, Littell
Starting Points for Writing

Another Vanishing Cowboy (1988), Stephen Rosser.

Stephen Rosser (1954–) is an Oklahoma arti[st]... bright colors, bold shapes, and a playful style to... the horror movies and television programs he w... A movie character called the Invisible Man insp... this "invisible" cowboy... realized that he was als... pearing from the West...

McDougal, Littell
Thinking Skills

Problem-Solution Ch...

| Problem: | **What** Choice: track team or community theater |
| | **Why** Not enough time for both and homework |

Possible Solutions	Results—Pros and Cons
1. Choose track	**Pro** Lots of friends on the team
	May get to go to regionals

Informative Writing: Explaining What
Elaboration

(1) When you sleep, something strange happens

beneath your eyelids. (2) While your lids are closed,

dart rapidly back... your e...

sign...

sleep...

plac...
it takes...
90...

Your hear...
slow do...
but you...

Informative Writing: Explaining What
Elaboration

The following paragraph is from the beginning of a definition of *REM* sleep. Use the **Suggestions for Elaboration** to develop the paragraph further by adding information to sentences or by making up new sentences. You may find details and other ideas in the Data Bank. Write your paragraph on a separate sheet of paper.

First Draft

(1) When you sleep, something strange happens beneath your eyelids. (2) While your lids are closed, your eyeballs sometimes move. (3) The movement is a sign that you are in REM, or Rapid Eye Movement, sleep. (4) During REM sleep, other changes also take place in your body. (5) REM sleep occurs about every 90 minutes. (6) It's during REM sleep that you dream.

Data Bank

■ eyelids closed ■ eyeballs dart ■ move back and forth rapidly ■ as if watching fast game of tennis ■ occurs about every 90 minutes ■ takes up 25% of sleep time ■ heart rate and breathing often speed up or slow down ■ slight twitching of muscles ■ body seems paralyzed

Suggestions for Elaboration

- Elaborate on Sentence 2 by adding details and a comparison that shows how the eyeballs of a person in REM sleep move.
- Support Sentence 4 by adding examples of other changes that occur in the body during REM sleep.
- Following Sentence 5, add information telling how much of an average night is taken up with REM sleep.

Elaboration: Informative Writing/Explaining What 9

Writing from Personal Experience
Strong Response

A Perfect Bunt

I've always talked about giving people a chance, but I'd never tested my belief until one hot, dusty Saturday on the ballfield near my house. We were choosing up sides for the weekly softball team, and I was one of the captains. I noticed a new kid, Raul. He was short and skinny. Let Daryl choose him for his team, I thought. I want to win!

I chose Luiza, who was fast as a sprinter, Rob, who had a powerful arm, and five others. Soon it was down to Raul and Loren. I wanted Loren, but I stopped before calling her name. Should I give the new kid a chance?

My palms sweated as I thought. Raul might lose the game for us. I had to decide quickly, though. "Raul!" I shouted, swallowing hard. "You catch."

Raul struck out twice before the ninth inning. Then we...

The introduction establishes the setting and personal nature of this narrative. It encourages the reader to continue.

Specific details help show the writer's feelings.

Subject–Verb Splits: Phrases

Put a phrase between subject and verb to add details about the subject and give variety to your sentences. Here are examples of phrases as S–V splits.

Model A The other six, *two brothers and four sisters,* lived with their parents in a spacious house at 426 Twenty-Ninth Street, in Oakland.
Frank B. Gilbreth, Jr., and Ernestine Gilbreth Carey, *Cheaper by the Dozen*

Model B The boy, *regaining his balance,* dragged Sounder off the porch and to the corner of the cabin.
William H. Armstrong, *Sounder*

Model C Johnny, *trained in a silver shop to do such work,* made a bullet mold.
Esther Forbes, *Johnny Tremain*

A. Combining Sentences At the caret (ˌ) in the first sentence, insert the underlined part of the second sentence as an S–V split. Add commas.

1. Mafuto ˌ heard a scornful laugh. He was *standing tense in the shadows.*
Armstrong Sperry, *Call It Courage*

2. The voice of a different frog ˌ croaked from the nearest bank. This voice was *hoarser and not so deep.*
Natalie Babbitt, *Tuck Everlasting*

3. A long table ˌ took up almost the whole dining room. The table was *loaded with food.*
Norma Fox Mazer, "I, Hungry Hannah Cassandra Glen . . ."

4. Mr. Lema ˌ greeted me and assigned me a desk. He was *the sixth grade teacher.*
Francisco Jiménez, "The Circuit"

Paragraphs a... used effective... to present dialogue and show the nex... scene in the narrative.

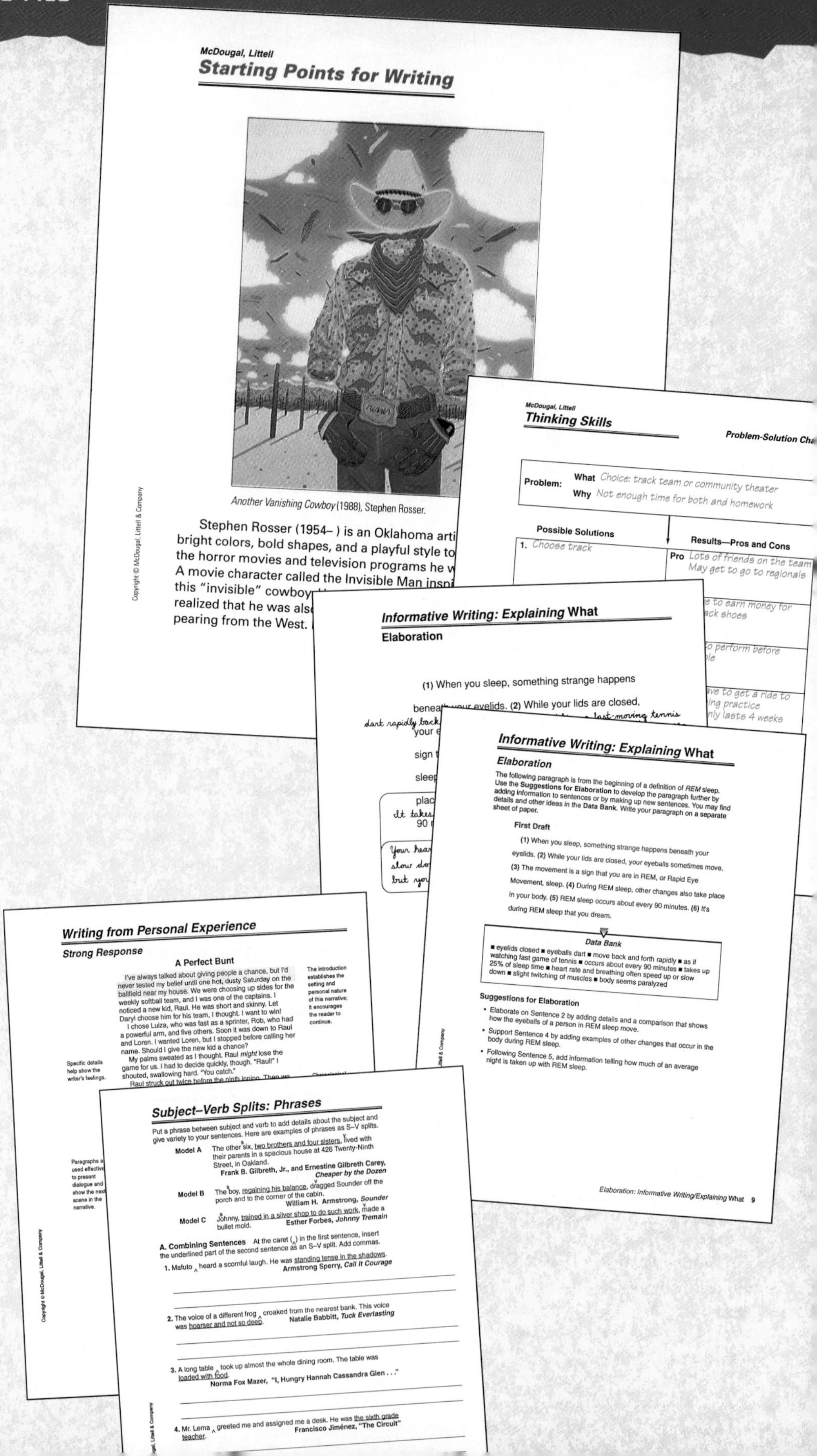

Peer Response Guides

Students are given prompts to guide them through peer response sessions for each Guided Assignment.

Writing Resource Book

Practice and reteaching exercises are provided for each Writer's Workshop and each section of the Writing Handbook.

Grammar and Usage Practice Book

A variety of practice and reteaching exercises reinforce concepts taught in the Grammar Handbook. A special section of Proofreading exercises helps students improve proofreading skills.

Spelling and Vocabulary Booklet

Ten spelling lessons and thirty-six vocabulary lessons improve student vocabulary through activities and word lists based on SAT and ACT examinations.

Tests and Writing Assessment Prompts

This complete testing and assessment package offers Pretests and Mastery Tests for all grammar, usage, and mechanics concepts. Writing Prompts for Assessment are provided for each Guided Assignment in the text to help prepare students for evaluation situations.

Writing from Literature

Writing prompts designed to accompany fourteen frequently taught literary selections provide students opportunities to practice the types of writing covered in the Guided Assignments.

Standardized Test Practice

Provides practice and teaches students strategies for standardized test question formats such as spelling, vocabulary, usage, and reading comprehension.

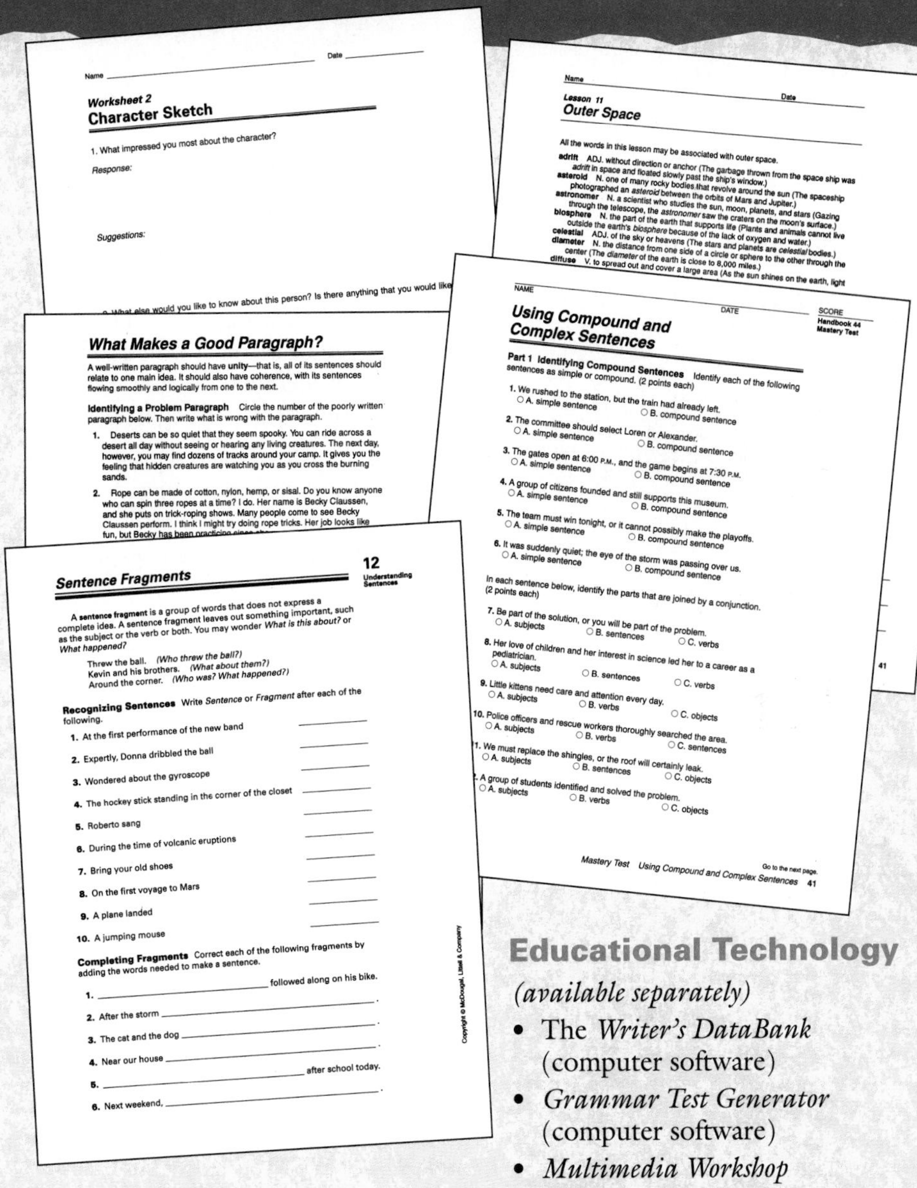

Educational Technology

(available separately)

- The *Writer's DataBank* (computer software)
- *Grammar Test Generator* (computer software)
- *Multimedia Workshop* (computer software)
- *Electronic English Handbook* (computer software)
- *On Assignment!* (interactive videodisc program)

What makes my students different?

Teaching Young Adolescents: The Middle Years

Author:

Susan Hynds, Associate Professor and Director of English Education, Syracuse University, Syracuse, New York

Middle school students are, indeed, *in the middle* of childhood and young adulthood. But rather than living in some nether world between the two, they seem to be straddling them. Sometimes they tip more to the side of childhood, at other times to the side of young adulthood. That very quality is what makes them a delight to teach on one day, and an exercise in hair-pulling exasperation the next.

Physically, socially, intellectually, and emotionally, young adolescents seem more different from each other and seem to change more dramatically in four short years than children of almost any age. For example . . .

Physically . . .

Middle school students have three main characteristics: energy, energy, and energy! Just stand in a middle school hallway at the change of classes and feel the vibrating chaos as hundreds of spirited young bodies stream from classrooms, banging their lockers, flying up stairways, screaming at their peers and streaming past their teachers. But this seemingly endless reservoir of energy is fluctuating and unpredictable. The same students who were just screaming and hitting each other in the hallways can be seen a few minutes later, lounging in their desks in a near-catatonic state the minute classes begin again.

Because they always seem poised on the brink of hyperactivity or boredom, middle school students need to be invited to read about, write about, and explore topics that are personally meaningful and easily related to their own worlds in some way. They also need language activities that allow them to get up out of their desks, to switch intellectual gears, and to interact with other students.

Socially . . .

There is no question that middle school students are very social creatures. Often, it's only through the support of their peers that they discover and develop their own personal identities. Their social identities, like their moods, are in a perpetual and dramatic state of flux.

To move from the safe, self-contained classroom of the elementary school to the middle school with its changes of classes and teachers makes young adolescents needy of little touches that say they are cared about and part of a classroom family. If you are a middle school teacher, you know how often you seem to be dispensing paper clips, pencils, hall passes, hugs, and bandaids.

Young adolescents need to belong in another way as well. The friends of elementary school are often quickly forgotten, but middle school students are beginning to forge the bonds of friendships that can last a lifetime. At the same time, they are beginning to think of themselves as members of a society. They are curious about how issues of race, gender, poverty, and crime touch their own lives or neighborhoods. They are also becoming aware of social and cultural differences. For this reason, they need to be presented with situations that allow them to explore a variety of human relationships and cultural perspectives. Teachers need to invite them to write and talk about these perspectives with others, and to capitalize on their irrepressibly social natures.

Intellectually . . .

For many years, it was assumed that students between the ages of ten and fourteen were beginning to move from what Piaget called "concrete operations" into what he called "formal operations"—basically, that they could think abstractly about themselves and the world. For that reason, many instructional materials for junior high school students were geared to lead students up through the ranks from concrete to more abstract levels of thinking.

Today, we know that most middle school students—indeed, many high school students, and even adults—have not yet moved fully into formal operational thinking in the purest sense of that term. This doesn't mean that middle school learners can't think abstractly. It means that they need teachers who can help them make concrete connections between abstract ideas and their own personal worlds.

A middle school student writing about one of the Greek myths might remark: "He's just a male chauvinist!" or "She's just stupid!" They don't typically gravitate to more abstract comments like: "Greed is a common human characteristic," or "People should follow the spirit and not the letter of the law." Because young adolescents often believe that all eyes are on them, it's hard for them to look past their own viewpoints.

This doesn't mean that middle school learners can't think abstractly about people and events; it means that they need to be invited to think beyond themselves. They need to be challenged with statements like, "Tell me all the reasons that

you believe this solution is a good one," or "Does this historical event remind you of anything in today's world?" or "How could your experience be turned into a story with meaning for everyone?" They need to be led back and forth from the world of concrete, personal experience, into the realm of imagining, speculating, and hypothesizing.

Emotionally . . .

Middle school students are intense! Perhaps because life seems so intense for them, middle school students have a powerful need to be recognized, listened to. They need to have opportunities to perform, to be at center stage, and to express their feelings and concerns. A wide range of writing and speaking activities—journals, songs, scripts, opinion pieces, discussion groups, and storytelling—are all excellent ways for students to sort through and share all of the new emotions they are experiencing.

At the same time, because they are so intense, they have a very strong need for routine. This does not mean a need for boring drill and practice exercises, but for comfortable rituals which invite them to take risks and be creative. They need little routines that say "we are a classroom family, and we do things this way in *our* room." Providing predictable structures for portfolio conferences and writers' and readers' workshops will give students this sense of safety and comfort.

The Nineties: Harsh Realities

Unfortunately, there are many issues that may not have faced us in the days when we went to junior high school. We are beginning to see some of the effects of parental substance abuse, sexual abuse, and domestic violence on the intellectual and emotional capacities of young adolescents. These problems of abuse and neglect know no racial, ethnic, or socioeconomic lines. They are as present in suburbs as they are in cities.

There is also a great deal of media openness which treats virginity as a social disease, which promotes materialism, and makes a life of crime seem like a glamorous occupation. On top of this, young adolescents are reaching puberty earlier than their cohorts did at the turn of the century, and, perhaps regrettably, many of them are experimenting with issues and experiences that once were considered beyond the realm of children their age.

Finally, as productive members of society, middle school students are, quite literally, useless. Years ago, young people worked on farms or in the village when they weren't in school. They were an integral part of the larger social community. Today, although they might be loved, they aren't needed for much of anything. And so, they often become consumers of junk food, video games, or other kinds of mindless diversion.

Teachers need to realize that the teaching of literature and writing can provide a way for students to deal with sensitive or personal issues that may have no other outlet. They need to offer a range of topics for writing and discussion so that students who are uncomfortable with certain subjects can maintain a comfortable distance, while others can be free to explore those topics. Teachers also need to help young adolescents to feel integral and involved in their community and the larger world.

The Writer's Craft invites young adolescents to explore a whole array of personally meaningful topics and issues through a variety of different formats, both written and oral. A host of language activities invites students to work collaboratively or individually, moving beyond their own perspectives and considering the viewpoints of others. Best of all, *The Writer's Craft* invites you to create a sense of classroom community and to give your middle school students the self-confidence to become more involved in the world beyond the walls of school.

Related Reading

George, P. S.; Stevenson, C.; Thomason, J; & Beane, J. (1992). *The middle school and beyond.* Alexandria, VA: Association for Supervision and Curriculum Development.

Hester, J. P. & Hester, P. J (1983). Brain research and the middle school curriculum. *Middle School Journal 15* (1), pp. 4–7.

Johnson, J. H. & Markle, G. C. (1986). *What research says to the middle level practitioner.* Columbus, OH: National Middle School Association.

Lawrence, V. (1988). The teacher in the middle school. *Early Adolescence Magazine, 2* (3), pp. 19–21.

Silvern, S. B. (1990). Connecting classroom practice and research. *Journal of Research in Childhood Education, 5* (1), pp. 85–86.

Wiles, J. & Bondi, J. (1986). *Making middle schools work.* Alexandria, VA: Association for Supervision and Curriculum Development.

Is there a better way to teach writing?

Philosophy and Rationale

Authors:

Peter Elbow, Professor of English, University of Massachusetts at Amherst

Sheridan Blau, Senior Lecturer in English and Education, University of California at Santa Barbara

Teachers are constantly bombarded with confident pronouncements from experts and textbooks about the teaching of writing. But tidy theories don't usually hold up in the complex realities of the middle school classroom. This book, therefore, is based on the classroom experience of many teachers teaching in many different circumstances: experiences of success and of frustration and of puzzlement.

The truth is, writing is not a body of theoretical knowledge or precepts. Writing, rather, is a body of practices and strategies and activities—above all, a *craft.* Therefore if we truly want to teach writing, we must engage students in the activities of craftspersons. We must ask them to be writers and see themselves as writers. The premise of the book, then, is that we can and should treat our students as writers—putting strong faith in them yet also making strong demands on them.

The best way to explain what this book is about is to list some of the important things we know about writers:

Writers are not all alike. Therefore, there is no single "writing process" or lock step set of procedures that works for all writers or is appropriate for all students. Indeed, even the same person needs different processes on different occasions and for different kinds of writing. *The Writer's Craft* is based on the premise that students are no more like each other than other writers are, and that it is counterproductive to try to impose one alleged "writing process" on all students for all writing.

Writers make choices. Since writers are *not* alike, it follows, then, that they encounter different problems as they work and employ different strategies. Therefore this book is not organized in a linear fashion where every student follows the same path. Rather, it assumes that students will blaze their own trails. As each assignment is presented in the book, students are given numerous important but necessary decisions to make. (For example, "Do you want to start out by making an outline before you have done any writing, or wait until you've explored your ideas on paper or written a discovery draft? Good writers proceed in both ways.") Some assignments offer a great deal of guidance to the student and others offer very little. In short, the assignments as a whole follow a coherent path, yet there are many opportunities for choice.

Writers learn to write by writing. This book, therefore, does not require a lot of reading *about* writing. Instead it constantly invites the student to write: to write often, in many different forms and contexts, and for different audiences.

Writers learn by reflecting. Writers think about what they do. They observe themselves, learn from practice, think about the choices they make. They talk to others who are engaged in the same business, sharing problems and successes, and comparing the writing choices each of them made. So this book asks students to look not only at *what* they write but at *how* they write, to reflect for themselves on the complicated vagaries of their own writing processes, and to talk with other students and with teachers about how things went.

Writers learn by reading. Thus the book puts a big emphasis on reading the writing of others: the writing of fellow students in the class, the writing of well-known published writers, and some writing by students in other parts of the country (which is included in the book). The readings by published writers in the wider world are not just literary pieces: they also represent a wide range of other types of writing—from magazine articles to scripts to workaday on-the-job writing. The book reprints these writings as chances for students to see what other writers have done: not as pieces to revere—to put under glass like paintings in a museum—but rather as opportunities for students to come at them as fellow writers and questioners. Always, throughout the book, the question is, "Let's see: what choices was the writer making here?"

There is a community of writers. A few writers may squirrel themselves away from others and write entirely on their own, but, as the last two points above illustrate, most writers have important connections with other writers and with a larger community. The teachers behind this book have consciously emphasized this connected model of the writer. The book asks students to work with the smaller community of other writers in the class: to talk about writing and compare notes and drafts and discuss the writing process and give responses to each other. And it also asks students to work with and see themselves as part of the larger community of writers and readers in the world.

Writers must care about what they write. If they just do exercises, if they just find ideas and transmit them *like telegraph operators*, they will have no personal investment in what they write. This book shows students how to find writing ideas that matter to them. It encourages them to take responsibility for what they write, take ownership, take pride.

Writers have a lot to say. Because students are young and inexperienced—because they sometimes even tell us, "I have nothing to write about"—it is tempting to think of them as empty vessels that must be filled. But the teachers behind this book have found that their best teaching comes when they emphasize not what students *don't* know and can't do, but what they *do* know and can do. When we build on the considerable knowledge and language skills that students already have, they learn new things much faster. Experienced writers trust their own thinking, and students, too, must be given some confidence in themselves to function at their best.

Good writers explore and discover as they write. The book helps students to learn how to start from what they *don't* know as well as from what they do know—and then write their way to understanding. In short, writing is thinking, not just recording what is already worked out in some book or in one's mind. To write is to observe, to analyze, to solve problems, to make decisions. This book gives students continual practice in various forms of thinking.

Writers should experiment. The teachers behind this book made a conscious choice to push for a variety of writing experiences. Students should write in diverse modes. They should push at the edges of their experience and develop skills that come from trying various kinds of writing—from narratives to essays to oral histories to songs to visual collages. And not all writing need be earnest and heavy. Writers and students need low-stakes writing, too, in order to learn to take some of the risks and have some of the fun that is necessary if a writer is to develop. So while the book asks that most major assignments go through multiple drafts and be carefully revised, it also asks students in the "Sketchbook" and journal sections to make quick sketches and learn to play with writing.

Teachers have a unique opportunity with this program. The perspective that writing is a craft, and that students learn most from writing, provides teachers with an exciting role. Instead of feeling compelled to lecture or provide ready-made advice that fits all students and all situations, a teacher can instead be a coach, guide, responder, and nudger—one who will encourage those students who are too timid or fearful, and yes, push those who need a push.

How do I set up my classroom?

Establishing a Writing Workshop Classroom

Author:
Linda Lewis, Writing Specialist,
Ft. Worth Independent School District

How can a teacher organize a classroom for effective writing instruction? Perhaps predictably, there is no one best way. Outstanding writing classrooms take many different forms, each reflecting the preferences and personalities of the teacher and students who form that particular writing community. All effective classrooms, however, provide a caring, supportive environment that encourages even the most reluctant students to grow as writers. This environment is based on certain expectations:

- Everyone writes.
- Everyone shares.
- Everyone responds.

If these expectations are met, a key goal is achieved:

- Everyone succeeds.

Creating a Favorable Atmosphere

An effective writing classroom is actually a social place—an interactive community of writers. In such a classroom, the students are responsible for their own growth as writers; however, they are equally responsible for the learning and development of others.

Establishing expectations The teacher's approach to writing can have a tremendous impact on the classroom. Therefore, the following attitudes should be evident in every day's activities.

- **Writing is a meaningful activity.** To help students realize that writing has purpose, they should be encouraged to read as much as possible and to become aware of the power of the written word. Magazine excerpts, speeches, scripts, and newspaper articles are all excellent vehicles for making this point. To reinforce this understanding, the students' own writing must be done for real purposes and real audiences. *The Writer's Craft* can be used to give students opportunities to apply their skills in activities as diverse as oral histories and children's books.
- **Everyone can write.** The basic assumption that underlies an effective writing classroom is that everyone has both something to say and the basic tools with which to say it. Even reluctant writers should be engaged in producing whole texts, not just sentences or paragraphs. The teacher can reinforce this expectation by emphasizing and evaluating not only the student's final writing product, but also his or her individual process and progress.
- **Writing involves sharing and responding.** The purpose of almost all writing is communication. Therefore, students should be encouraged to share their writing at every stage of the writing process and to solicit the types of responses that they need from their peers. See pages T32–T35 for more information on peer response and collaborative learning.

Setting up the classroom The arrangement and content of the classroom itself can dynamically reinforce and enhance the feeling of a writing community.

- **The furniture** Student desks or tables can be arranged in many different configurations to facilitate various aspects of the writing activity. For example, some teachers prefer to have the class carry out individual and large-group activities with desks in traditional rows, rearranging them in clusters for collaborative work or peer-response sessions and in a large circle for sharing finished work. Others designate specific areas of the room for various writing activities, perhaps providing an editing corner, a conference table, tables for group response activities, and an area with student desks for private writing.
- **Displays of illustrative materials** Writing—by the students, the teacher, and professional writers—should be profusely displayed in the classroom, and changed as the teacher or students discover exciting new models. Several drafts of a given piece of writing, quotations by published authors about their writing process and products, and favorite writing samples can be included in these displays. A special motivational display, for example, could include brief autobiographical blurbs and pictures that students compile for their hypothetical future books.
- **Reference sources** In addition to providing an appropriate arrangement of furniture and motivational displays, an effective writing classroom should include a reference area stocked with various dictionaries, thesauruses, handbooks, and other reference books. Some teachers also provide files of writing done by students in previous classes.

Roles of Teacher and Students

To promote the individual and collaborative goals of effective writing instruction, both the teacher and the students must be aware of the different roles they can play in the classroom.

The teacher's roles There is no one writing process that will work for all students in all writing situations. Therefore, an effective writing teacher is a co-writer, collaborator, coach, and facilitator, rather than a lecturer.

- **The teacher as co-writer and collaborator** Probably one of the best ways for a teacher to advance the expectations of a writing classroom is to become a writer along with the students. In sharing not only finished writing products, but also work in progress, the teacher can instruct students through direct involvement and interaction.
- **The teacher as coach and facilitator** In addition to writing with students, the teacher can facilitate their learning in many ways. For example, during exploratory activities the teacher can help students find topics in which they can become invested; during drafting, support and problem solve with individual students as needed; and during revision, provide guidance and individual or small-group instruction. Providing time for one-on-one conferences is an excellent way of providing this kind of help while encouraging young writers to grow.

The students' roles Like the teacher, the students in an interactive writing classroom play many different roles.

- **The student as writer** It is important that students view themselves as writers with ideas to communicate to others, not as students completing an assignment for the teacher. The kinds of "real world" writing assignments included in *The Writer's Craft* can help create this attitude in the classroom. So can the use of peer response groups and an emphasis on other actual audiences. Probably the most important way to make students feel like writers, however, is to *treat* them as writers, to respect their ability as craftspersons and encourage them to analyze writing problems, explore options, and experiment with techniques.
- **The student as collaborator** In a writing workshop classroom, students are encouraged to share work in progress, help each other problem solve, and contribute ideas to the work of peers, if asked. Students who are not used to such an arrangement may at first have difficulty with this more open approach to writing, and should be allowed to work independently. However, teachers can encourage interaction by having writers work with single partners initially, and then combine to form groups as they become conversant and comfortable with sharing.
- **The student as responder** Student writing improves dramatically when students share their writing with each other. (See Peer Sharing and Peer Response on pages T32–T33.) There are several specific ways that teachers can help students become effective peer responders: (1) have students evaluate "training papers" by students from other classes before addressing the writing of classmates, (2) have them role-play successful and unsuccessful response groups and critique the interactions, and (3) model appropriate comments using transparencies such as those available in the Teacher's Resource File.

Ensuring Success

The success of a writing classroom depends largely on three factors: (1) clarity of goals, (2) commitment to working toward them, and (3) criteria for assessing progress and achievement. The teacher who is able to establish a favorable atmosphere for writing, and clear goals for writers as described above, is well on the way to success. Developing concrete standards of evaluation and making students aware of them is another important factor.

Standards of evaluation Students are more apt to become successful writers if they understand the specific criteria by which their writing will be judged before they undertake an assignment. The Standards for Evaluation in the Guided Assignments, as well as *Guidelines for Writing Assessment and Portfolio Use* in the Teacher's Resource File, can help students become familiar with and learn to identify the qualities of good writing and develop strategies for effecting them as they write.

Using portfolios In addition, students should be encouraged to reflect on their writing process as they complete each piece and to save selected works in a portfolio. They should also examine these writing portfolios from time to time and note their consistent strengths and weaknesses as well as specific aspects of their development as writers.

A writing workshop classroom can be a lively and stimulating place. And when it is successful, the teacher's expectations and those of the students become reality: everyone writes, everyone shares, everyone responds, and everyone succeeds.

How can I combine literature, writing, and grammar?

Integrating the Language Arts

Authors:

Arthur N. Applebee, Professor of Education, State University of New York at Albany

Judith A. Langer, Professor of Education, State University of New York at Albany

The English language arts curriculum has always been compartmentalized into a variety of special topics, including literature, writing, and grammar. Thought of as separate subjects, they have competed for time and attention in the classroom and in instructional materials. In this view, if we give more time to writing, then we must give less time to literature or grammar. This compartmentalization reflects a "building block" approach to student learning, implying that the various aspects of the language arts can be taught separately and yet still be put together by the student into some meaningful whole. This approach lends itself well to neatly organized segments of curriculum planning, presented in elaborate scope-and-sequence charts meant to coordinate the teaching of particular skills within each particular segment of the English curriculum.

Yet this building block approach does not fit very well with the ways in which human beings learn and use language. Rather than learning skills in isolation, we learn them best in the context of experiences. Young children learn to talk because they want to communicate their needs and share their interests with those around them. Older students similarly learn to read and write most effectively when they are reading, writing, and talking about things that interest and matter to them—and when they have a purpose for reading and writing about these things. An integrated approach to the language arts is much more effective in promoting "higher literacy" in students than the building block approach.

The Workshops in *The Writer's Craft* reflect the importance of an integrated approach to student language learning, and offer a variety of ways in which teachers can foster the integration of writing with literature and grammar. Some general suggestions follow.

Integrating Writing with Literature

The primary emphasis in many English classrooms is on the teaching of literature. The following suggestions provide ideas for integrating literature with the kinds of writing activities suggested in *The Writer's Craft:*

1. Let students think through writing. Use the students' responses to the literature—their developing understandings and interpretations—as the prompt for a writing activity. As students discuss and debate their responses, the motivation and opportunity to work out their ideas in writing can develop naturally out of their discussions. This is particularly true with the selections in McDougal, Littell's *Literature and Language* series, which places a similar emphasis on a process-oriented approach to the teaching of English language arts.

2. Use literary selections as springboards. The literature students read may suggest similar situations they want to explore, or concepts they want to analyze, or it may prompt them to create their own contribution to a particular genre. *The Writer's Craft* and *Literature and Language* were carefully planned to allow just this kind of interaction. The Writer's Workshops in the two series were built around the same scope and sequence, and a special "Links" feature in both Teacher's Editions suggests how to structure lessons that tie literature selections to the Writer's Workshops.

3. Use selections as both literature models and as examples of how other writers have gone about the craft of writing. Students can profitably spend some time discussing their responses to the selections, sorting out their differing evaluations and interpretations, before examining the ways in which the selections have been shaped and crafted.

4. Let students explore their understandings of and reactions to other students' writing. Examples of student work can be discussed in the same ways that you discuss published selections. If drafts are available, student work may be particularly useful in highlighting the choices a writer makes and the effects those choices have on readers. The Workshops in *The Writer's Craft* contain a variety of activities to help integrate students' writing with the literature they are reading.

Integrating Grammar Instruction

Students gain effective control of the conventions of written English when they are given many opportunities to use them in the context of their own writing. Isolated exercises in punctuating dialogue, for example, are likely to mean very little to students; learning how to punctuate dialogue because they want to incorporate it into a narrative of their own is much more likely to lead to long-term learning. To integrate grammar with writing and literature:

1. Encourage students to examine unusual features of the literature they read. With them, discuss how those features influence their reactions. For example, students may become aware of the effect of short, simple sentences in reading a folk tale by Virginia Hamilton, or alternatively of the more complex syntax characteristics in a novel by Madeleine L'Engle.

2. Emphasize specific writing conventions that may help while students are drafting or revising particular types of writing. Information about how to punctuate dialogue is likely to be particularly relevant when writing a story or reporting on an interview, for example. Information about formal versus informal usage is likely to be most relevant in writing to unknown or distant audiences.

3. Use opportunities for publication to provide instruction in grammar and usage tailored to individual students. Problems with the conventions of written English are usually highly individualized. In any given class, one student may have trouble with pronoun referents, another with managing verb tense, and still another with semicolons. Instruction to deal with such problems will be most effective as each student is revising a work to share with others. At that point, they will usually have a fairly clear idea of what they want to say, and are likely to be ready for help in saying it as clearly and effectively as they can. The mini-lessons in the Grammar and Usage Handbook are particularly useful in this context.

4. Let students teach one another. Some of the most effective instruction in grammar can come from peer responses to student writing. Because different students have different strengths, they can provide very effective help in "polishing" one another's drafts for publication—and the process of explaining the suggestions they make will strengthen each student's understanding of effective grammar and usage. For example, student pairs can help by reading each other's work and marking a "check" on any portion of the paper that doesn't "sound right" to them. The "check" can highlight questions about spelling, mechanics, grammar, or word choice and can signal useful places the writer can rethink when polishing the piece.

Each of the Workshops in *The Writer's Craft* highlights one or another aspect of grammar and usage in the context of the particular types of writing that students are being asked to do. Rather than isolated skill and drill, this grammar content is designed to highlight the relationship between knowledge of the conventions of language and the craft of writing. Each Workshop encourages students to experiment with language to make their own writing more effective.

The Language Arts Trio: Literature, Writing, and Grammar

Approached in these ways as interrelated segments of larger activities, the language arts "building blocks" can be taught just as systematically as the old scope-and-sequence charts implied—but much more effectively. When teachers integrate literature, writing, and grammar in their instructional program, the language arts will build upon and support each other. Instead of completing isolated lessons that assume the students will later be able to transfer the separate language arts skills to real literacy situations, students will learn language skills in complete and meaning-laden contexts in the first place. Thus, students' reading, writing, and language skills will develop in concert, in ways both students and their teachers recognize as meaningful, purposeful, and useful.

Is there a way to get students more involved?

Peer Sharing and Peer Response

Author:

Peter Elbow, Professor of English, University of Massachusetts at Amherst

Paul Goodman once said, "If we learned to speak the way we learn to write, there'd be lots more people who can't speak." Why? Because in many classrooms the context for writing is inexorable: the student writes, the teacher grades, and the teacher is the only audience. Imagine what speaking would be like if we spoke only to one person, and if every time we ever spoke, we were evaluated. Is this really the best way for students to learn to write? Does this diet of nothing but teacher grades and "corrected" papers really provide students with the nourishment they need to be better writers? And do tall stacks of papers only for teachers' eyes make for sane writing teachers?

There is another alternative: peers as audience and peers as responders. Peers are not a substitute for teachers as audience and responders, but a supplement or addition. Classmates are not asked to evaluate or correct each other's papers but rather to do what they are best at: to function as an audience, and provide an honest account of how they understand the text, how they reacted, and what was going on in their minds as they read. More and more teachers are finding peer responding a crucially helpful strand in their teaching.

Why Use Peer Response?

The use of peer response groups helps teachers to create a powerful change in their classrooms. Why is peer response so effective?

Students need audiences. One of the greatest weaknesses in student writing is a lack of awareness and connection with audience. When students write only for the teacher (which usually means for a grade), they often fall into certain bad habits—treating writing as an empty school exercise, and attempting simply to just "get it right" or "give teachers what they want." Yet surprisingly, students often care less about what they turn in to teachers than they do about what they read to or share with each other. They often hand writing to teachers that they don't really believe in.

When students write for their peers, however, they become very concerned about what they say and how they say it. In fact, the most powerful thing about the regular use of peer sharing and response groups is that students naturally and easily begin to learn that writing is not so much a matter of "figuring out what the teacher wants" but rather of discovering what they themselves have to say and then seeing whether they have gotten it across effectively to readers.

Just as this textbook tries to teach students that not everyone writes in the same way, so too does it teach students that not everyone reads in the same way. Peer response introduces students to the complex but ultimately empowering truth that the same text often produces different responses in different readers. The writer is then left in the position of having to evaluate those different responses and make writerly decisions about how to revise.

Teachers need relief. Another powerful reason teachers are making more and more use of peer response groups is brutally practical: the paper load for teachers.

Students don't learn to write well unless they write a great deal—which means writing more papers than teachers have time to read carefully and comment on. Peer sharing and response groups provide a way to increase the amount of writing that students do while assuring them of a response. For even though students may not be skilled at providing evaluation and advice, they are excellent at providing the one thing that writers need most—*an audience.*

Types of Response

Most students have never written words that they didn't turn in to a teacher for evaluation and criticism. Yet limiting feedback to this kind of response can cripple students' writing. Student writing almost always takes a big turn for the better when this traditional audience-relation is balanced by use of the other relationships described below. Indeed, this variety of types is crucial, for it provides the ideal "balanced audience diet" that students need—a balance among different relations to readers.

Private writing Students need opportunities to write privately—to do some writing that they don't show to anyone. This provides a crucial foundation of safety and comfort in writing and an arena for risk-taking.

Pure sharing Students need opportunities to share their writing with readers —but sometimes just for the sake of sharing with no response at all. This increases the risk ("going public"), and yet still provides a strong degree of safety since there is no feedback. The emphasis is placed on *communicating* rather than *feedback.* Sharing heightens the social dimension of writing, and there is also an enormous amount of extremely efficient learning that goes on, especially when the sharing is oral. Nothing teaches us so much about writing as the feel of our own sentences in our mouths and the sound of them in our ears. The process also gives students experience in working in groups before having to learn feedback techniques.

Limited feedback Students sometimes need opportunities to share writing and get responses—but not get criticism. By holding off the question of "how good is the writing?" students discover what is probably the most useful kind of feedback—learning how readers *understand* their words. Limited feedback, therefore, involves more risk, more feedback, and more learning. But because there is no criticism or advice, students find it a rewarding way to share, and can listen nondefensively to responses from readers.

Full feedback By working in peer groups in the two ways previously described, students heighten their reading and responding skills. Now they are ready to give and receive responses to the more demanding writerly questions like these: "What worked well and not so well? What suggestions do you have?"

This textbook provides a rich range of specific suggestions, prompts, and examples to enable students to learn how to become good peer responders to each other. By taking advantage of these techniques, students will find an audience, their teacher will gain time to teach, and writing will remain the exciting exchange of ideas and opinions it should always be.

Is there a way to get students more involved?

Collaborative and Cooperative Learning

Learning to use one's knowledge in collaboration with others is essential for success in and out of school. Consequently, group learning is becoming central to classrooms across the curriculum.

Collaborative learning is defined as any group activity that asks students to work together on a task. Advocates of collaborative learning assert that it motivates students to learn, improves social skills, and promotes self-esteem in students of all abilities. The students work together, and the teacher focuses on the different groups, carefully listening, watching, suggesting, and being prepared to work through any problems that naturally arise in the context of group work.

In **cooperative learning,** a more structured type of collaborative work, the success of one individual is linked to that of others. Each group member is responsible for helping other members to learn and for contributing a piece to a whole. Cooperative learning might be used, for example, if students were directed to stage a play, create an advertising campaign, complete a complex report, or produce a book of oral histories. Each student is held accountable for his or her own contributions and each student's mastery is assessed.

Getting Started

Divide the class into groups. Group students of differing abilities or talents together; pay particular attention to students with special needs: ESL and LD students, for example. Assure all students that creativity, problem-solving abilities, listening skills, empathy, and writing skills share equal importance in group work. Also, remind students that while they are responsible for their own learning, they are also responsible for helping others in the group to learn. Students should work together in an atmosphere of care, acceptance, trust, and support. Competition has no role in collaborative learning.

The size of groups depends on the purpose of the collaborative effort. Small groups of two or three students each are most appropriate when students are sharing personal writing and will benefit most from the individual attention one or two peers can offer. Larger groups of no more than six members can be effective too, particularly if the assignment is large or complex.

Specify objectives and purpose. Set clear, specific goals and objectives for each collaborative learning session. Also make sure students understand on what criteria they will be assessed.

Provide a structure. Assign specific responsibilities to students working in groups, or have the students do so themselves. For example, students working in a discussion group can take on specific roles, such as facilitator or discussion leader, recorder, reporter, and materials manager. If students are working cooperatively on a larger project, such as a research report, the assignment itself may be divided into parts and assigned; each student is responsible for completing his or her share of the work and for helping to join the pieces into a cohesive whole.

Monitor progress and achievement. The teacher's role during cooperative learning is that of facilitator or consultant. As group members work together, the teacher should circulate among them, mentally noting behavior and participation for future performance assessment. If necessary, the teacher should enter a group to clear up any misunderstandings or to ask questions that will direct students' thinking. If more than one group is having difficulty, the teacher may interrupt to reteach or clarify a point with the entire class.

Address assessment. Certain informal collaborative situations, such as peer response, require no evaluation procedure. Some situations, however, require assessment and grading to keep students

Author:

David Wallace, Researcher with the Center for the Study of Writing at Carnegie-Mellon University accountable for successful group process, for their own learning, and for that of other group members. Options for using grades to reward students for group learning include

- averaging individual scores within each group;
- giving a single score to all group members who have worked cooperatively on a single product;
- giving individual scores plus bonus points for successful group performance and the development of social skills.

Students should share in the assessment process by evaluating their own performance and that of their group. Students may judge that they've been successful if they have met the designated goals of the collaborative learning session. In evaluating group process, they might consider such questions as, "Did I feel supported? challenged? confronted? Were feelings hurt or were ideas shared and feedback given in an encouraging, supportive way? How might we improve the process next time?" Teachers and students should discuss what works and what doesn't work in group process and brainstorm together on ways of improving collaborative learning skills.

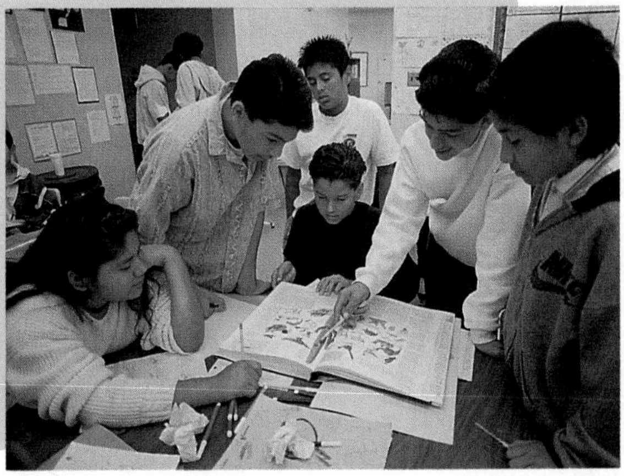

Ideas for Collaborative Learning

The Writer's Craft encourages students to work together in groups to explore concepts and ideas, problem solve, brainstorm, and collaborate during all phases of the writing process. The collaborative learning activities that follow can be effectively adapted for use in the English classroom.

Collaborative planning While students working alone during the planning stage rarely go beyond deciding what information to include in their texts, students planning in pairs or small groups consider the full range of writing variables and keep them in mind throughout the writing process. Developed at the Center for the Study of Writing at Berkeley and Carnegie-Mellon University under co-director Linda Flower, collaborative planning helps students learn to monitor their own learning about writing.

Before students begin to draft a writing assignment, divide the class into pairs or groups of three; have them take turns in the roles of writer and partner, talking through their writing ideas. While the writer talks about his or her ideas for content, audience, purpose, and form, partners help the writer by acting as a sounding board, listening carefully, asking for clarification or elaboration, and suggesting alternatives.

Jigsaw projects Students may choose to work collaboratively on any large or complex project, dividing the assignment into "pieces" and assigning each student to a piece. Students creating a video, for example, could divide the project into such "pieces" as research, scriptwriting, direction, and production. Students would then work together to meld the pieces into a coherent whole.

Learning partners After presenting new information on a topic or giving an assignment to the entire class, have students review the material out loud with a peer, using their notes as necessary to summarize or explain. For example, students could meet in small groups after grammar instruction. They could take turns paraphrasing the new rules out loud, presenting examples of the concept at work, or finding examples in their reading. The whole group can then complete or review the answers to the practice activities together, make necessary corrections, and submit a single set of answers for grading.

Research groups Students may conduct research on a topic and pool information into a written or oral report. Students will need to divide the workload equally, with each person responsible for researching a particular aspect of their outline. Students will join the pieces of information into a cohesive whole; one grade can be assigned to the entire group.

Team teaching Teachers from different subject areas may work together to develop theme-based projects that can lead to student learning and involvement across the curriculum. Because of their scope, such projects are ideal for collaborative learning activities. The Project Files preceding each Workshop in this Teacher's Edition provide detailed guidelines for this type of project. If team teaching is not utilized in a particular school, the projects can still be executed within the language arts classroom.

Are tests the only way to check progress?

Assessment and Response to Student Writing

Traditionally, much of the work in the teaching of writing has occurred in the process of responding to and assessing what students write. Teachers have given students topics to write about, and then have spent a great deal of time marking the papers that result—giving grades, making suggestions for ways the writing could have been improved, and correcting errors.

Such an approach is exhausting for teachers—the paperload quickly becomes overwhelming—and discouraging for students—whose papers "bleed" with the teachers' red penciling. Such an approach also works against what we know about the writing process. When students write about topics that have substance and depth, we can expect their work to be characterized by growth and change over time. They will try out and abandon ideas. They will reorganize sections. This is the "normal" state of affairs among the best of writers, and characterizes the *process* of crafting a text.

Response and Assessment

For students to engage in the kinds of thoughtful exploration described above, evaluation—judgments about how well the work has been done—needs to be separated from response—reactions to the paper and ideas for further development that come from an interested reader. This is because evaluation, although well-intentioned, can become too much a focus of ongoing instruction, and therefore inhibiting to students; it teaches them not to take risks, not to try new forms, not to draft and redraft, but to concentrate on letter-perfect work that says little and goes nowhere.

Response is the critical feature in writing instruction; it helps students know what works, what doesn't, and how to go about improving what they have written. The ideal writing environment invites students to engage in exploratory writing and offers response to work-in-process. Evaluation and grades are postponed until later.

Providing Effective Response

Teachers can use a number of strategies to ensure that students receive sufficient and helpful response to their work. The most powerful is the use of peer readers and peer response groups (see pages T32–T33). The following suggestions should also be kept in mind:

1) Limit the amount of writing to which you, the teacher, respond. Writers need frequent responses from interested readers, but that does not mean that the teacher needs to read everything that is written. Instead students may be asked to share with each other initial brainstorming about a topic, to reflect upon one another's notes and journals, and to respond to early drafts.

These early drafts and explorations have served their purpose once they have been discussed with an interested reader or mined for the nuggets that will become part of later drafts. Therefore, there is no reason for the teacher to read them, too: indeed, the teacher can become a bottleneck and may inadvertently turn students back toward thoughts already abandoned.

2) Respond to work in progress as a collaborator rather than an evaluator. Teachers can, of course, be very helpful while students are working on their drafts. They can show new ways to solve writing problems, suggest other issues to consider, and offer their own responses as readers about what parts are clear, what parts are interesting, and what parts fail to convince. These kinds of responses are instructional in the best sense: the teacher's suggestions about work in progress can become part of the developing writer's repertoire of strategies and models, available for use in other contexts.

Authors:

Arthur N. Applebee, Professor of Education, State University of New York at Albany

Judith A. Langer, Professor of Education, State University of New York at Albany

Exploring Assessment

Reader response is certainly the most productive way to respond to student writing, but evaluation is, of course, necessary. Report cards demand grades, and students want to know how they are doing. But there are a number of ways in which evaluation can be managed so it supports rather than subverts the processes of teaching and learning.

Choose criteria carefully. Since writing should be considered a process for exploring ideas and sharing them with others, it follows that conventions of writing should be treated as part of this process rather than as the focus of instruction. It is easy, however, for both writers and teacher to get bogged down in usage and mechanics.

Therefore, to prevent both writers and evaluators from losing track of the key issues of writing, it is important to have clear, consistent standards about what "writing well" will mean in your class. If "writing well" is to mean exploring ideas and experimenting with ways to share them effectively, then students who try to do this should be rewarded with higher grades—even if their experiments lead them to make mistakes. A new and difficult task, completed with some uncertainty, may reflect much more growth in writing achievement than a simple task completed with little thought and no "error."

Use a variety of evaluation methods. In recent years, teachers have developed a number of different ways to formalize their evaluations of student writing. Most of these have been used in the context of large-group assessment, where the concern is with how well students are doing *relative to* one another or to some external criterion. Using such procedures (for example, general impression [or holistic] scoring, analytic scoring, or primary trait scoring) is generally inappropriate within a classroom when used in a formal sense, but can be extremely helpful when used informally to guide teachers' and students' mutual understandings of the goals of the writing task. These methods, however, should be used sparingly and combined with more flexible techniques such as peer response and portfolio assessment.

For those occasions when holistic or analytic evaluations are desired, the Writer's Workshops in *The Writer's Craft* include specific criteria for evaluation of various types of writing, as does the booklet *Guidelines for Writing Assessment and Portfolio Use* in the Teacher's Resource File. Underlying these criteria are a few broad questions that can be used in assessing how well the writing succeeds:

- Is the writer's purpose clear? Has it caught my interest?
- Is there enough detail for me to accept or reject what the writer has said?
- Does the writing carry me through clearly from beginning to end, or are there places where I get lost or miss the point?
- Do the drafts indicate the student is learning to use the responses of readers effectively, or are successive drafts little more than neater versions of the same text?
- Has the writer taken care in the final draft to avoid distracting, careless errors in presentation?

Using Portfolios

Writers vary in how well they write from topic to topic and day to day. Again, this is normal and natural, but we often forget about it when judging how well a writer writes. To offer a well-grounded evaluation of a student's writing skills, we need to examine a broad sample of that student's work.

Portfolios of student work offer one of the best vehicles for classroom-based assessment for two reasons: 1) They typically contain a variety of different samples of student work, and 2) they make it easy to separate evaluation from the process of instruction. Evaluation can be based on the diverse samples of work in the portfolio rather than on the day-to-day progress of an individual piece of classroom work.

Portfolios take almost as many forms as there are teachers and can be tailored to virtually any classroom situation. The major options involve the form that portfolios take, what is included in them, and how they are evaluated.

continued

Portfolio Options

Form. Portfolios are a cumulative collection of the work students have done. The most popular forms include

- a traditional "writing folder" in which students keep their work
- a bound notebook with separate sections kept for work in progress and final drafts
- a looseleaf notebook in which students keep their drafts and revisions
- a published collection of carefully selected and hand-bound work

Content. Portfolios provide an ideal way to illustrate how a student's work has developed over time, and will give students, parents, administrators, and other teachers a much stronger sense of what students can do. Portfolios may contain

- everything a student writes for a particular class
- a selection of "best work" representing the diverse kinds of writing that a student has done
- selections chosen to represent each of the types of writing a student has done during a grading period
- a diverse collection of a student's performance including drawings and illustrations, tape recordings or videotapes of group work, and readings or dramatic presentations of the student's writing
- drafts and revisions
- a selection of finished work, chosen by the student, the teacher, or the student and teacher working together

Students can also be encouraged to reflect further upon their own progress as writers, providing an introductory essay summarizing their work as they see it in the portfolio. Like the reflective activities included at the end of each workshop in this textbook, such reflection can help students become aware of and take control over their own growth as writers.

Evaluating Content. Just as teachers vary in the form and content of the portfolios they ask their students to build, they also vary in how they use portfolios to determine students' grades.

An approach that many teachers have found to be particularly effective is to base grade a selection of work from the portfolio— chosen to reflect the range of types of writing that students have done during the grading period. Students can be asked to select the pieces to be graded, making the choice themselves or in conjunction with the teacher. With this approach, they should be given guidelines for what to choose: a narrative, an expository piece, and a persuasive essay, perhaps, plus an additional piece of their own choosing. The particular guidelines should reflect the goals and assignments in the writing program during the grading period.

The ability to choose works to be graded —rather than being graded on everything—can be a powerful motivational device as well. Many teachers give their students the opportunity to work further on the selections they want to have graded. Returning to these writings at a later point, students often recognize for themselves ways to make their writing more effective, and may reshape them substantially before offering them for evaluation.

The students' own impressions of their work should not be left out of the evaluation process. Young writers should be encouraged to comment on each piece added to their portfolios and to comment on their progress over time. Forms and guidelines in *Guidelines for Writing Assessment and Portfolio Use* in the Teacher's Resource File can help both students and teachers complete effective evaluations of finished pieces.

Weaning students from excessive evaluation. Many teachers who are new to such a workshop approach—postponing evaluation rather than interjecting it into the writing process—worry that students want quicker grades. If they aren't graded, will they do the work? One transitional device that works well in many classrooms is to give points when students have completed each separate part of the work. Everyone who completes a first draft, for example, might get a point, with another for doing a revision. These points can be totaled across the marking period to become part of the final grade.

If evaluation is separated from instruction, if criteria for evaluation are kept consistent with those stressed during instruction, and if response becomes a responsibility shared with students as well as the teacher, assessment can become an effective complement to the process of learning to write.

How do I meet the needs of different students?

Teaching Writing to Language-Minority Students

Author:

Marguerite Calderone, Associate Professor of Education in Psychology, University of Texas, El Paso

Increases in the immigrant population during the past two decades have dramatically transformed the cultural makeup of many American classrooms. Not since the great wave of immigrations around the turn of the last century have English teachers in American schools been so challenged to meet the special language needs of their students.

Few veteran English teachers are likely to feel professionally prepared to operate successfully in a multicultural, multilingual classroom. What follows here are some strategies for teaching writing to language-minority students—strategies that research has shown are especially effective with non-English speaking students but which are equally applicable to all students.

Developing Prior Knowledge

The more experience a writer has with the concepts and terms associated with a topic for writing, the easier it will be to write about that topic. Similarly, the more knowledge a teacher has of the culture and background of minority students, the easier it will be to adapt teaching strategies and writing assignments to meet their needs.

Hold class discussions. Clarify cultural references and provide general information to the entire class. Encourage language-minority students to comment on similarities to and differences from their own cultures.

Explore teaching alternatives. The use of visual aids and hands-on experiences are effective strategies for building prior knowledge and student confidence.

Encourage students to write about their native customs, holidays, geography, and foods. Such topics will be more comfortable for language-minority students. Additionally, the felt-pride from sharing their native culture will act as strong motivation for writing.

Provide opportunities for reading popular American magazines and newspapers. These activities will familiarize language-minority students with American people, places, and events. Television, movies, theater, and similar cultural activities will have the same impact.

Developing Vocabulary and Genre Knowledge

Mastering English vocabulary and patterns of discourse is essential to building writing proficiency among language-minority students. Students who are asked to write about a school or government election, for example, must be familiar with the terms and concepts of the subject, such as *parties, platform, campaign, run-off, running mate,* and so on. Ideally, preteaching vocabulary would become a regular part of each assignment.

Similarly, students who are asked to write a mock political campaign speech will feel entirely unable to do so unless they know what one looks and sounds like. All students should be given the opportunity to read a number of models of whatever type of writing they are being asked to produce.

Peer Interaction

Through group discussion, students with limited-English proficiency can build a repertoire of concepts, phrases, and rhetorical strategies by trial-and-error, questioning, and modeling. Whenever possible, divide the class into small discussion groups. Each group should include at least one language-minority student. Establish a protocol that requires all students to speak within the group. In this way language-minority students will be exposed to vocabulary and rhetorical strategies they can model and be encouraged to try out their developing English proficiency.

Writing in the Primary Language

There is strong research evidence showing that limited-English proficiency students in American schools can make significant progress toward literacy in English by reading and writing for some time in their primary language, making the transition to writing exclusively in English as they acquire English fluency. Allowing students to write in their primary language during the early stages of English acquisition offers the following advantages:

- It establishes a firm basis for acquiring universal reading and writing skills that are easily transferred from one language to another.
- It promotes success, enhances self-esteem, and builds students' confidence in their abilities as readers and writers.
- It enables students to function at the highest levels of their cognitive abilities, unhampered by their limited-English proficiency.

How can writing in languages other than English become a realistic instructional strategy in classes where teachers don't speak the primary language or languages of their non-English speaking students? Following are some strategies for implementing this instructional strategy:

- Encourage students to write in their primary language whenever they encounter a particularly demanding or complex writing assignment. This will enable them to clarify their thinking about the topic even if no one else can read what they've written.
- Have students write in their primary language only during the prewriting stage. Allowing them to focus their topic, generate ideas, and organize their material in a familiar language will lead to enhanced comprehension and increased motivation.
- Seek out individuals fluent in the student's primary language to act as responders. Such individuals might be teacher aides, parents, or classmates who speak the student's primary language but who are also fluent in English. Of course, if there are several students who share the same primary language, they can act as peer reviewers for one another.
- Invite students to translate their own primary language essays. Such translations should not be treated as final drafts, however, but as rough draft translations produced for the benefit of the teacher. Teachers who receive these translations can respond to the ideas contained in the translated essay rather than on problems in English language usage.

Additional Strategies

Following are some additional strategies for working with language-minority students:

- Preview the assignment to spot potential areas of difficulty—with cultural concepts, language requirements, research needs, and so on. Provide preteaching as necessary.
- Read aloud difficult parts of the assignment or lesson, allowing time for questions and clarification.
- Precede writing activities with similar oral activities to allow students to separate the task of clarifying ideas from that of translating them into written form.
- Provide guided practice, especially with prewriting and revising techniques.

Increased, individualized feedback and monitoring will enhance student comprehension and offer support—both of which lead to more successful writing experiences.

References

Calderone, M.; Tinajero, J.; & Hertz-Lazarowitz, R. (1990). "Effective Transition into English Reading Through CIRC." Baltimore, MD: Center for Research on Effective Education for Disadvantaged Students, Johns Hopkins University.

California State Department of Education (1981). *Schooling and Language Minority Students: A Theoretical Framework.* California State University, Los Angeles, EDAC.

Cummins, J. (1986). *Empowering Minority Students.* Sacramento, CA: California Association for Bi-Lingual Education.

Damon, W. (1984). "Peer Education: The Untapped Potential." *Journal of Applied Development Psychology:* 5, 331–343.

Stevens, R. J.; Madden, N. A.; Slavin, R. E.; & Farnish, A. M. (1987). "Cooperative Integrated Reading and Composition (CIRC)." Baltimore, MD: Center for Research on Elementary and Middle Schools, John Hopkins University.

How do I meet the needs of different students?

Addressing Different Learning Styles

People of all ages perceive and process information in different ways. A familiarity with learning styles can help educators develop teaching strategies to meet the needs of all students in the classroom.

The Types of Learners

Research on left- and right-brain functions has led to a variety of theories about preferred learning styles. The left brain is thought to be the center for analytical, logical, verbal, sequential, and convergent thinking, while the right brain is thought to be the center for emotion and visual, spatial, creative, experiential, and divergent cognitive styles. Left-brain students, who have traditionally been rewarded by the educational system, tend to excel in such school subjects as reading, mathematics, and computer programming. Right-brain dominant students tend to excel in art, dance, music, and geometry.

In addition to left/right-brain classification, students are often categorized according to three learning styles: visual, auditory, and kinesthetic.

Visual learners best comprehend and retain information presented in the form of graphs, charts, diagrams, and other visual images, such as fine art and photographs. Often, they benefit from a multimedia approach to learning.

Auditory learners, like visual learners, often benefit from a multimedia approach to learning. They need not only to read it and see it, but to hear it and discuss it.

Kinesthetic learners process information through tactile sensations, learning from activities that enable them to work with their hands or create meaning through movement and physical expression.

Harvard psychologist Howard Gardner has taken the analysis of learning styles and left- and right-brain dominance to yet another level in his theory of multiple intelligences.

The Seven Types of Intelligence

Linguistic	Verbal excellence, reading and writing skills
Logical-Mathematical	Conceptual, logical, abstract thinking
Spatial	Interest in visual images and pictures; designing, building, and inventing
Musical	Sensitivity to rhythm, singing, moving to and playing music
Bodily-Kinesthetic	Communicating with body language; processing information through bodily sensations
Interpersonal	Organizing, communicating, socializing, understanding others
Intrapersonal	Preferring to work alone and being independent, private, and self-motivated

Everyone has multiple intelligences and different styles of learning. However teachers, who tend to be left-brain oriented and strong in linguistic and logical-mathematical intelligences, often teach primarily in the modes most comfortable for them. They may therefore be unconsciously leaving a number of students out of the learning process. Yet how can any teacher adequately address the bewildering array of learning styles that may be present in any one classroom?

With its integrated approach to the development of writing, *The Writer's Craft* helps solve this problem by providing students with opportunities to work in a variety of learning modes. Teachers need only encourage students to take advantage of various learning strategies to maximize their intellectual and creative potential.

Applications in *The Writer's Craft*

Teacher's notes throughout the text point out the following learning opportunities:

Fine Art and Illustrations The art program throughout *The Writer's Craft* provides visual or spatial learners with an engaging and entertaining way into the material. Invite students to consider how the art enhances and reflects concepts in the text, and use the illustrations as springboards to creative writing.

Workshops and Related Assignments At each grade level, Workshops and Related Assignments include a broad range of activities, not all of which are writing based. Visual and spatial learners, for example, will particularly enjoy creating collages, graphic aids, and picture books. Auditory and musical learners will especially like creating videos, writing lyrics, and making oral presentations.

Exploratory Activities Workshops begin with a wide range of Exploratory Activities, providing students with options for entering writing assignments comfortably and naturally. The teacher can encourage students to experiment with the options until they find those that work best.

Graphic Organizers Graphic devices such as clusters, idea trees, flow charts, and pie graphs can be a tremendous boon to visual and kinesthetic students who learn from the physical act of writing ideas, organizing them spatially, and seeing and making the connections among them. Left-brain dominant students can organize their information with time lines, charts, and analysis frames.

Publishing Options The wide variety of publishing options offered throughout the Workshops allows students to tailor their work to their own learning styles. In different assignments, for example, students may be encouraged to include photographs or drawings, build models, incorporate music, or use videotapes, recordings, slides, or photos in a multimedia presentation.

Collaborative and Independent Learning Auditory and interpersonal learners may enjoy working collaboratively to brainstorm solutions to problems, discuss ideas, and share their writing. (See pages T34–T35.) Peer response sessions are also ideal for these kinds of learners. However, each lesson is so complete that the intrapersonal, or solitary, learner can succeed with little help from others.

Special Help with Learning Disabilities

Learning disabled students typically have average or above-average potential; however, specific areas of deficiency (which vary from student to student) make the processing of information and the acquisition of skills more difficult.

Students with learning disabilities often display some or all of the following characteristics:

- Low reading level
- Low motivation
- Difficulty organizing work or ideas
- Poor memory
- Difficulty sequencing and processing information
- Difficulty following directions and completing assignments
- Difficulty thinking, reasoning, and generalizing
- Hyperactivity and distractibility
- Poor fine-motor coordination and handwriting

It is essential to remember that learning disabilities are often physiologically based and beyond the student's control. What can appear to be inattentiveness or an uncooperative attitude may, in fact, reflect an inability to learn through conventional channels.

Whenever possible, teachers should provide opportunities for LD students to process information in their own preferred learning style. This approach will allow them to maximize their intellectual and creative potential in school. The following general strategies, along with any of the alternative strategies described in the section on learning styles, will help students get the most from classroom experiences:

- Seat students toward the front of the classroom where there are no obstructions to seeing or hearing.
- Present essential directions or material from the text both orally and in writing.
- Supply visual aids whenever possible to reinforce material from the text.
- To help students compensate for poor short- and long-term memory, repeat important ideas frequently and begin each lesson with a summary of material covered the previous day.
- When giving an assignment, model sample problems on the board, breaking the process down into clearly ordered steps.
- Encourage collaborative learning. Carefully monitor sessions to make sure they take place in an atmosphere of care, empathy, and support.
- Occasionally pair students according to ability for special peer-review sessions. For example, pair an LD student who has difficulties with sequencing and ordering events with a student who is particularly strong in those areas.

I've got a computer . . . Now what?

Teaching English in the Electronic Age

Author:
Dawn Rodrigues, Associate Professor of English, Colorado State University

New technology brings exciting changes to the curriculum. In the English classroom, the most visible of these changes has been the arrival of the computer, with all of its attendant software. The sheer volume of available material has proven to be occasionally intimidating, but teachers *can* take control of the technology by selectively integrating computer programs and strategies into their teaching.

Benefits of the Computer

Although research on the use of the computer in English classrooms is still somewhat limited, many studies have revealed some significant benefits of using a word processor:

- Students enjoy composing on a computer, tending to write more and work harder at their writing.
- Students do not resist revision, since changes can be more easily executed.
- Collaboration among students increases.

Computers have also proven to be especially helpful with low-ability students or those with handicaps and learning disabilities. First, the actual *physical* act of writing becomes easier, and the process as a whole becomes less intimidating—when words on a screen can be instantly deleted, writing anxiety diminishes.

Second, the process of using the computer forces special-needs students to focus more directly on their task. Finally, the clean, printed text eliminates some students' embarrassment over poor handwriting—for the first time in their lives, they can be proud of their writing.

New Strategies for Writing Instruction

With the increasing availability of computers, teachers can recommend that students use composing and collaborative strategies that were not possible before. Many of these strategies, such as invisible writing, listmaking, and the development of a writer's file, can be found in *The Writer's Craft* in the feature labeled Computer Tip. Some other strategies follow:

- Students can leave gaps in their paper where they need to add material or where they want to invite response from others. Notes such as the following, to themselves or their peer readers, can provide the cues:

CAN YOU HELP ME THINK OF A BETTER EXAMPLE HERE? or MAYBE THIS WOULD WORK AS THE INTRO—TRY LATER.

- Students can work on portions of the draft that they are most comfortable with, and then electronically paste the pieces together as their ideas take shape.
- Teachers and peer readers can read drafts on screen and leave notes to the writer at the appropriate points.

Making It Work

Making students comfortable with computers does not require that the entire class meet regularly in a lab. At many schools, a teacher can reserve a computer lab on occasion for the entire class. On those days, the teacher can introduce valuable computer-writing techniques, such as the use of an "alternate screen" to store outlines or notes while composing in the other window.

Spell-checkers, on-line thesauruses, and specialized software programs such as McDougal, Littell's *Electronic English Handbook* or *Writer's DataBank* can also be introduced. If a lab is not available, the teacher can occasionally bring a computer into the classroom to demonstrate various techniques.

No matter how the computer is used, however, it is important to remember that not all students adapt to word processing in the same way. Therefore, the teacher must be prepared to provide plenty of individual instruction. For example, freed from the restrictions of pen and paper, some students may overwrite. These individuals must be shown how to evaluate content and delete unnecessary material. Other students may have trouble adapting pen-and-paper planning or revision to the screen. These writers could be encouraged to use printouts in combination with composing on screen until they become more comfortable with the computer.

Conclusion

Computers, when used creatively, can be a powerful addition to a writing class. The computer has the amazing ability to transform itself into whatever the teacher or writer wants it to be—a magic slate for writing, an electronic window to an audience, or an endless resource for ideas and strategies. It allows teachers to create an almost unlimited set of instructional techniques and a chance to re-envision writing instruction.

Assignment Chart

Concept Development in *The Writer's Craft*
Varied, real-life writing assignments grow more sophisticated as your students do and provide opportunities for writing across the curriculum. **Guided Assignments** are listed in bold, followed by Related Assignments in each strand below.

Writing Strands	Grade 6	Grade 7	Grade 8
Personal and Expressive Writing	• **Writing from Your Journal** • Friendly Letter	• **Writing from Personal Experience** • Collage	• **Autobiographical Incident** • Song
Observation and Description	• **Describing People and Places** • Cultures and Customs	• **Character Sketch** • Oral History	• **Eyewitness Report** • Field Notes
Narrative and Literary Writing	• **Personal Narrative** • Writing a Poem	• **Short Story** • Children's Book	• **Writing a Poem** • Developing a Script
Informative Writing: Explaining *How*	• **Directions** • Explaining with Graphics	• **Problems and Solutions** • Group Discussion	• **Cause-and-Effect Explanation** • Describing a Process
Informative Writing: Explaining *What*		• **Informing and Defining** • Comparison and Contrast	• **Comparison and Contrast** • Consumer Report
Persuasion	• **Sharing an Opinion** • Public Opinion Survey • Writing for Assessment	• **Supporting Opinions** • Advertisement • Writing for Assessment	• **Argument** • Social Action Letter • Writing for Assessment
Responding to Literature	• **Personal Response** • Book Review	• **Interpreting Poetry** • Focusing on Media	• **Analyzing a Story** • Oral Storytelling
Informative Writing: Reports	• **Report of Information** • Family History	• **Multimedia Report** • Feature Article	• **Research Report** • I-Search

The Writer's Craft

THE McDOUGAL, LITTELL STUDENT BOARD

Dear Pat,
We pitched our tent a few yards from a stream, and yesterday I saw two deer come down to get water. Birds like the ones in the photo are all around our campsite. They wake me up at 5:00 in the morning!
Chris

The Writer's Craft

SENIOR AUTHOR

SHERIDAN BLAU

University of California at Santa Barbara

CONSULTING AUTHOR

PETER ELBOW

University of Massachusetts at Amherst

SPECIAL CONTRIBUTING AUTHORS

Don Killgallon

Baltimore County Public Schools

Rebekah Caplan

Oakland Unified School District

SENIOR CONSULTANTS

Arthur Applebee

State University of New York at Albany

Judith Langer

State University of New York at Albany

McDougal, Littell & Company
Evanston, Illinois

Dallas • Phoenix • Columbia, SC

SENIOR AUTHOR

Sheridan Blau, Senior Lecturer in English and Education and former Director of Composition, University of California at Santa Barbara; Director, South Coast Writing Project; Director, Literature Institute for Teachers

The Senior Author, in collaboration with the Consulting Author, helped establish the theoretical framework of the program and the pedagogical design of the Workshop prototype. In addition, he guided the development of the spiral of writing assignments, served as author of the literary Workshops, and reviewed completed Writer's Workshops to ensure consistency with current research and the philosophy of the series.

CONSULTING AUTHOR

Peter Elbow, Professor of English, University of Massachusetts at Amherst; Fellow, Bard Center for Writing and Thinking

The Consulting Author, in collaboration with the Senior Author, helped establish the theoretical framework for the series and the pedagogical design of the Writer's Workshops. He also reviewed Writer's Workshops and designated Writing Handbook lessons for consistency with current research and the philosophy of the series.

SPECIAL CONTRIBUTING AUTHORS

Don Killgallon, English Chairman, Educational Consultant, Baltimore County Public Schools. Mr. Killgallon conceptualized, designed, and wrote all of the features on sentence composing.

Rebekah Caplan, Coordinator, English Language Arts K–12, Oakland Unified School District, Oakland, CA; Teacher-Consultant, Bay Area Writing Project, University of California at Berkeley. Ms. Caplan developed the strategy of "Show, Don't Tell," first introduced in the book *Writers in Training,* published by Dale Seymour Publications. She also wrote the Handbook lessons and Sketchbook features for this series that deal with that concept.

SENIOR CONSULTANTS

These consultants reviewed the completed prototype to ensure consistency with current research and continuity within the series.

Arthur N. Applebee, Professor of Education, State University of New York at Albany; Director, Center for the Learning and Teaching of Literature; Senior Fellow, Center for Writing and Literacy

Judith A. Langer, Professor of Education, State University of New York at Albany; Co-director, Center for the Learning and Teaching of Literature; Senior Fellow, Center for Writing and Literacy

MULTICULTURAL ADVISORS

The multicultural advisors reviewed the literary selections for appropriate content and made suggestions for teaching lessons in a multicultural classroom.

Andrea B. Bermúdez, Professor of Multicultural Education; Director, Research Center for Language and Culture, University of Houston —Clear Lake

Alice A. Kawazoe, Director of Curriculum and Staff Development, Oakland Unified School District, Oakland, CA

Sandra Mehojah, Project Coordinator, Office of Indian Education, Omaha Public Schools, Omaha, NE

Alexs D. Pate, Writer, Consultant, Lecturer, Macalester College and the University of Minnesota

STUDENT CONTRIBUTORS

The following students contributed their writing.

Alyce Arnick, Aurora, CO; Gil Atanasoff, Kenosha, WI; Jaime Carr, York, PA; Celeste Coleman, Clovis, CA; Kara DeCarolis, Golden, CO; Jason Edwards, Clovis, CA; Ben Everett, Charleston, IL; Doug Frieburg, Lisle, IL; Jeff Hayden, St. Louis, MO; Latoya Hunter, Mt. Vernon, NY; Alisa Monnier, Arlington Heights, IL; Jonathan Moskaitis, Easton, PA; Vanessa Ramirez, Santa Barbara, CA; Dave Smith, Brookfield, WI; Tim Stanley, Las Vegas, NV; Melissa Starr, Houston, TX; Anna Quiroz, Kenosha, WI

The following students reviewed selections to assess their appeal.

Joseph Blandford, Barrington, IL; Janet Cheung, Chicago, IL; Andrea Dobrowski, Kenilworth, IL; Stephen Malcom, Chicago, IL; Utíca Miller, Evanston, IL; Andrea Ramirez, Kenosha, WI; Joy Rathod, Chicago, IL; Debra Simmet, Zion, IL; Elizabeth Vargas, Chicago, IL

TEACHER CONSULTANTS

The following teachers served as advisors on the development of the Workshop prototype and/or reviewed completed Workshops.

Wanda Bamberg, Aldine Independent School District, Houston, TX

Karen Bollinger, Tower Heights Middle School, Centerville, OH

Barbara Ann Boulden, Issaquah Middle School, Issaquah, WA

Sherryl D. Broyles, Language Arts Specialist, Los Angeles Unified School District, Los Angeles, CA

Christine Bustle, Elmbrook Middle School, Elm Grove, WI

Denise M. Campbell, Eaglecrest School, Cherry Creek School District, Aurora, CO

Cheryl Cherry, Haven Middle School, Evanston, IL

Gracie Garza, L.B.J. Junior High School, Pharr, TX

Patricia Fitzsimmons Hunter, John F. Kennedy Middle School, Springfield, MA

Mary F. La Lane, Driftwood Middle School, Hollywood, FL

Barbara Lang, South Junior High School, Arlington Heights, IL

Harry Laub, Newark Board of Education, Newark, NJ

Sister Loretta Josepha, S.C., Sts. Peter and Paul School, Bronx, NY

Jacqueline McWilliams, Carnegie School, Chicago, IL

Joanna Martin, Thompson Junior High School, St. Charles, IL

Karen Perry, Kennedy Junior High School, Lisle, IL

Patricia A. Richardson, Resident Teacher-Trainer, Harold A. Wilson Professional Development School, Newark, NJ

Pauline Sahakian, Clovis Unified School District, Clovis, CA

Elaine Sherman, Curriculum Director, Clark County, Las Vegas, NV

Richard Wagner, Language Arts Curriculum Coordinator, Paradise Valley School District, Phoenix, AZ

Beth Yeager, McKinley Elementary School, Santa Barbara, CA

ISBN 0-8123-8662-0

Box 1667, Evanston, Illinois 60204

1 2 3 4 5 6 7 8 9 10 – VJM – 99 98 97 96 95 94

Table of Contents

OVERVIEW

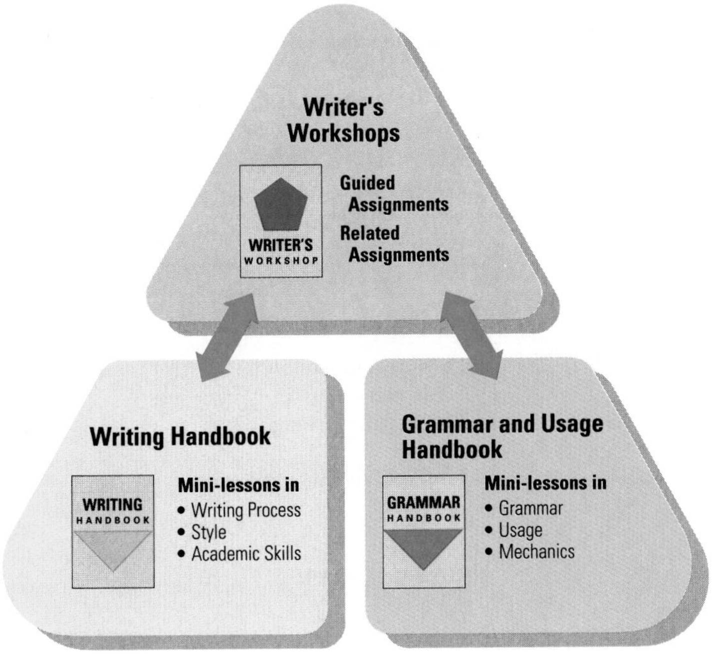

You are special. You think and act in ways that are uniquely your own. This book recognizes the fact that you are an individual. On every page you will be encouraged to discover techniques best suited to your own personal writing style. Just as important, you will learn to think your way through every writing task.

In each of the Writer's Workshops, you will experiment with ideas and approaches as you are guided through a complete piece of writing. Cross-references to the Handbooks will allow you to find additional help when you need it. Then, as you write, you will discover what you think about yourself—and about the world around you.

Getting Ready explains the philosophy of *The Writer's Craft* to students and introduces the idea of a community of writers.

Understanding the Writing Process explains that the stages of the writing process are flexible and recursive.

Using This Book shows the relationship of the parts of this text to the writing process.

The **Discovery Workshop** allows students to try out the writing process.

Starting Points

For more in-depth treatment of each stage of the writing process, see the Writing Handbook Mini-lessons on pages 188–332.

Writer's Workshops

WRITER'S WORKSHOP 1

Personal and Expressive Writing

In each **Writer's Workshop,** students learn to write by writing, not by reading about writing.

Students can explore a particular type of writing in two different assignments in each Writer's Workshop.

Each workshop begins with a **Guided Assignment** that provides information about a type of writing and gives detailed guidance in completing each stage of the writing process.

A **Related Assignment** allows students an opportunity to apply, in a less structured format, what they learned in the Guided Assignment.

Assignments such as "Friendly Letter" take writing outside the classroom and encourage students to do writing related to the real world.

A literary work, or other professional writing, and a Student Model introduce each type of writing and encourage student writers.

The writing of one student is cited throughout the stages of the writing process.

The features **Linking Mechanics and Writing** and **Linking Grammar and Writing** demonstrate the connections between effective writing and standard grammar, usage, and mechanics.

Assignments such as "Culture and Customs" increase multicultural awareness and foster respect for cultural diversity.

The **Springboards** feature appears in each workshop and offers additional suggestions for writing topics.

WRITER'S WORKSHOP 2

Observation and Description

WRITER'S WORKSHOP 3

Narrative and Literary Writing

The no-risk activities in each **Sketchbook** encourage students to experiment with writing.

Each Guided Assignment suggests exploratory activities that can help students find topics that are meaningful to them.

Various writing strategies are presented at appropriate stages of the writing process.

Publish and Present gives students opportunities to share their writing in many formats and with varied audiences.

In **Sentence Composing** students analyze and imitate the style of professional writers' sentences, thereby learning how to add variety to their own.

In the strategies demonstrated in the drafting and revising stages, students find creative answers to their questions about writing.

Questions for both the writer and the peer reader guide students in self-assessment and peer response.

Paragraphs at Work show students how to create effective paragraphs for each writing form.

Different learning styles are highlighted in assignments such as "Explaining with Graphics."

The **On the Lightside** feature offers unusual facts, offbeat reflections, and lighthearted humor about language.

WRITER'S WORKSHOP 4

Informative Writing: Explaining *How*

x

WRITER'S WORKSHOP 5

Persuasion

Important writing modes and purposes are covered in traditional and non-traditional formats.

Multiple drafting and revising strategies help students mold the writing process to each of their own writing tasks.

The checklist format of **Standards for Evaluation** allows students to decide how well their writing meets the general criteria for a specific writing type.

Assignments such as "Public Opinion Survey" send writing into the realm of the real world.

"Writing for Assessment" gives students opportunities to practice responding to assessment prompts and enhances their chances for success across the curriculum.

Students are guided in creating a written response to a work of literature.

In each assignment, students are encouraged to shape the writing process so that it suits their topic and style.

Portfolio activities, as well as other applications to help students grow as writers, are offered in **Reflect on Your Writing.**

Assignments such as "Book Review" promote critical thinking skills.

WRITER'S WORKSHOP 6

Responding to Literature

WRITER'S WORKSHOP 7

Informative Writing: Reports

Students gather, organize, synthesize, and document material in "Report of Information."

The model, a report of information with a list of sources, demonstrates one student's response to a similar assignment.

Practical suggestions guide students to do efficient library research and make responsible use of sources.

Standard MLA style is presented.

"Family History" explores a nontraditional format and emphasizes oral communication skills.

The **Writing Handbook** provides extra support for students. Cross-referenced in the Writer's Workshops, the Handbook enables teachers to present mini-lessons to the class or to individual students at appropriate times.

Students discover graphic devices as tools to effective writing.

Handbooks 1–18 contain detailed information on the writing process and may be used for preteaching or to help students solve writing problems.

The mini-lessons have activities for both practice and reinforcement.

Handbooks 8, 9, and 10 cover paragraph skills in depth.

Writing Handbook

MINI-LESSONS

Sketchbook

WRITING PROCESS

Models from literature and professional and student writers demonstrate writing concepts.

Handbook 11 shows students how to move smoothly from one idea to the next.

Showing, not telling, is the focus of Handbook 12, and specific strategies for developing writing are included.

Practical approaches to giving and receiving peer response are presented in Handbook 16.

Handbooks 19–24 deal with style and help students increase the sophistication of their writing.

Sentence variety is covered in Handbook 24.

Handbooks 25–33 cover academic skills that are needed for classroom success.

Handbook 29 familiarizes students with library organization and important reference works and thus enables them to locate resources for research tasks.

Critical thinking skills are essential to effective writing and are particularly useful with Writer's Workshop 5, "Persuasion."

Oral communication skills are introduced in Handbooks 31 and 32 and are used throughout the workshops.

Grammar and Usage Handbook

MINI-LESSONS

The **Grammar and Usage Handbook** presents grammar mini-lessons with the context of writing.

Instruments to gauge student learning are provided in the **Skills Assessment** pages, which include a pretest, a post-test, and four proficiency tests. A standardized test format, like that often found in state assessment examinations, is used for the Skills Assessments.

Each Handbook includes Concept Checks; Drafting, Revision, and Proofreading activities; Applications in Literature; and Applications in Writing.

Exercises focus on writing themes; these themes can become springboards to writing ideas.

Checkpoints provide a mixed review of concepts and are interspersed after every few mini-lessons.

Additional Practice and **Review** exercises can be used for a variety of purposes: as refreshers, for review, for more practice, or to check student mastery.

Writing Connections enables students to integrate grammar and writing as they elaborate upon, revise, and proofread a draft. Each Writing Connections feature reinforces skills introduced in a specific Writer's Workshop.

Resources that writers commonly use are located in the **Appendix.**

The **Glossary for Writers** contains definitions of key writing terms.

ART NOTE Ask students to look carefully at the wall hanging shown on this page. It is the first of many pieces of folk art from around the world that they will find in this book.

Explain that folk art varies from culture to culture because it usually stems from the crafts and traditions of the particular society in which it is produced. Folk artists often don't even consider themselves artists—or their products works of art since they usually create them as part of performing a function. For example, a craftsperson might create a wall hanging to tell a story, or a bowl to perform a ritual.

This contemporary Peruvian wall hanging by an anonymous artist depicts a scene from daily life in a village near Lima, Peru. Ask someone to locate Peru on a map.

You might ask students to imagine that they are anthropologists, social scientists who study the way people live. Then ask students what they can tell about life in this particular Peruvian society, from the wall hanging. Tell students to base their guesses only on what they see in the illustration. (They may conclude that the people live in a fertile valley or plain near mountains; that they are agricultural people who grow apples, carrots, and potatoes [purple strings]; that the climate is dry [prickly pear cactus]; that they use llamas for transportation; that they live in brick or stone houses with thatched roofs.)

Ask students to think like folk artists themselves: What objects or scenes would they choose for a wall hanging depicting the daily life of their community?

This Peruvian wall hanging illustrates the daily life of people in the mountains near Lima, Peru. The apple, carrot, potato, and prickly pear (fruit-bearing cactus) images represent some of the staples in the people's diet. They use the llamas to transport goods through mountains to the markets in Lima.

Starting Points

Do you write only when you have to? If so, you may be surprised to learn that writing isn't just a way of showing teachers what you know or telling your parents where you'll be after school. Writing is also an amazing tool that can help you in all kinds of everyday situations.

The Writer's Craft will help you discover all the possibilities of writing. It will show you how to use your pen or word processor to sort through your thoughts and feelings, to explore the answers to problems, and even to invent new worlds with words. All *you* have to do is read on—and start writing.

Starting Points

This introductory chapter is designed to help teachers create a classroom atmosphere in which students will want to write and will have an opportunity for initial success in writing. The Starting Points chapter includes the four sections described below.

- **Getting Ready** motivates students and emphasizes writing as discovery and as a source of personal satisfaction. It also acquaints students with journal writing, freewriting, and writing with peers.
- **Understanding the Writing Process** provides an overview of the stages of the writing process. This section presents explanations and examples of the kinds of activities that characterize each stage and stresses the nonlinear and recursive nature of the process.
- **Using This Book** offers students an overview of the textbook. It describes the content of the Writer's Workshops and the Handbooks and also explains how the sections are related.
- The **Discovery Workshop** invites students to experience the joy and personal satisfaction of writing, as they work on an open-ended assignment. In this workshop, students choose their own goals and learn that the content of writing can shape its form, as they experiment with the stages of the writing process.

Getting Ready

As the class reads and discusses the material in this motivational section, remind them that they probably do their best writing when they are writing about something that interests them. Point out the reference to journals in paragraph 3. Students may have used journals in the past, and this is a good time to suggest that they keep one during this school year. Explain that a journal is a place in which they can explore their feelings, their ideas, their hopes, their frustrations, or anything else that they see or hear that interests them—even cartoons or original sketches or quotations from literature. Tell them that what they have written in their journals can sometimes give them ideas for topics for papers.

Getting Ready

WHY SHOULD I WRITE?

Writing can help you with just about anything—from remembering the important details of a conversation to making sense of the changes going on inside you and around you. What's more, in the process of writing you can make all sorts of discoveries about yourself and the world—about what you know and what you might like to learn more about. Think for a minute about all the special purposes you can use writing for.

To Discover

Writing can help you discover what you think and feel. If you have a question or a problem, writing about it can lead you to an answer. If you have a feeling you can't quite pin down, putting that feeling into words can help you identify it. If you've had a confusing experience, writing about it may help you to make sense of it.

To Remember

Are there people, places, and experiences you never want to forget? memories you treasure? Writing in a journal about what you've seen, heard, tasted, touched, smelled, thought, and felt can capture these experiences on paper. Even when you've forgotten the events you've recorded, your writing will bring everything back to you. In this way, a journal can be your own personal time capsule. Years from now, it can give you gifts from the past.

To Explore and Invent

When you write, you can create your own world. You can go anywhere you want and do anything you want—anything you can imagine. You can explore ancient pyramids in Mexico or figure out what an eleven-year-old might do if he could pick up cellular-phone conversations on his braces. You can predict the future, change the past, invent a special gadget—even dance on the moon.

To Plan and Prepare

Putting your ideas on paper can help you plan what you'll do next Saturday afternoon or how you'll spend that money you've been earning by recycling cans. Jotting down a few key phrases or ideas can help you prepare for that all-important phone conversation with someone special. You can even use pen and paper to plan a party by making lists of the friends you want to invite and the foods you will serve. Writing is an ideal way to organize your thoughts.

To Learn

When you're reading or studying, do questions pop into your mind? Writing down those questions can remind you to look for the answers later. When you're reading a book or watching television, do you find yourself talking back to the characters? Why not write down your comments instead? Writing your reactions can help you tune in to what you're thinking and feeling.

Taking notes on what you're reading or hearing can also help you fix the information in your mind. If the information is confusing, writing it down can even help you make better sense of it. So whether you're covering a student council meeting for the school newspaper or listening to your grandfather talk about what life was like during the Great Depression, keep a pen and some paper handy.

Getting Ready 5

FREEWRITING

Point out the reference to freewriting in paragraph 3 and give students an opportunity to try it out. Assure them that their efforts at freewriting are for their eyes only. Then invite students to write for three minutes about whatever comes into their minds, no matter how trivial it seems. Tell them not to erase or stop to make corrections. If they can't think of anything more to say, they can repeat the last word until they think of another idea.

When the time limit is up, suggest that students reread what they have written and underline the parts that they particularly like. Tell them to save their freewriting because they might want to use some of the ideas in future writing assignments.

WAYS OF WRITING

Everyone has different moods. For example, sometimes you want to be alone, and at other times you want to be around people. In the same way, sometimes you'll want to write on your own, and at other times you'll prefer to write with others. This book gives you opportunities to do both.

Writing on Your Own

Whether you want to explore very personal thoughts and feelings or you just want to experiment with some new ideas and ways of expressing yourself, try writing on your own. In private writing you can take risks and say whatever is on your mind, because no one else ever has to read what you've written.

There are many ways to get started writing on your own. For instance, you might begin by writing in your journal or by freewriting. **Freewriting** is a way of exploring ideas or feelings by writing freely for a specific length of time. The activities in Handbooks 1 and 2 on pages 192–202 can also help you get started.

Writing with Others

You *may* choose to write alone and keep your writing to yourself. However, writing with others as well as sharing your writing can be very enjoyable, encouraging, and helpful. You and your classmates can help one another by

- brainstorming together to find topics
- listening to one another's ideas
- sharing ways you've solved writing problems
- responding, if you wish, to one another's work

Understanding the Writing Process

Every time you write, the experience is different. On one occasion, all your ideas might come out in a rush. Another time, you might need more help getting started. You might need to read, sketch, freewrite, or discuss your ideas with others. Most times you write, however, you will find yourself doing some or all of these activities: prewriting, drafting, revising, proofreading, publishing, presenting, and reflecting.

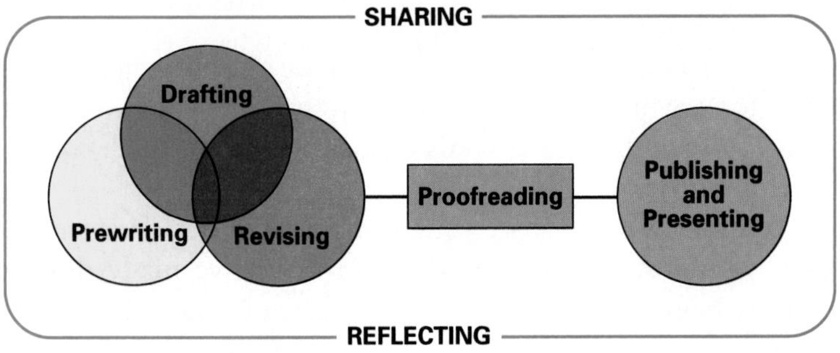

PREWRITE AND EXPLORE

Prewriting is what you do to find your topic and material for writing. You might draw pictures, talk with friends, freewrite, read, or daydream. You might even take a walk or rummage through a cluttered closet. Prewriting is whatever you do to figure out what you care about, what you think, what you know, and what you need to find out.

There may be times when you need to do very little prewriting before you draft. However, when you do want to explore your ideas to discover a topic or gather details, you may find the prewriting techniques in Handbooks 1–5 on pages 192–214 very helpful.

UNDERSTANDING THE WRITING PROCESS

As you read this page with students, focus on the diagram. Point out that the prewriting, drafting, and revising stages are shown as overlapping circles because they can be done at any time during the process and are not three steps that follow one after the other in a neat pattern.

Explain that in the next few pages, they will become better acquainted with the stages of the writing process. Then students will have an opportunity to try out what they have learned, in the Discovery Workshop on pages 13–23.

PREWRITE AND EXPLORE

Invite students to share favorite strategies for finding ideas for writing. Remind them that a wide range of activities, including just sitting and thinking, can be sources of things to write about.

DRAFT AND DISCOVER

Remind students that *draft* is another word for *write.* Tell students that when they are drafting, they are beginning to form their ideas into sentences and paragraphs.

Direct students' attention to the Writer to Writer quotation. Explain that they will see similar quotations throughout the book; these quotations are ideas and suggestions from other student writers, as well as from professional writers.

REVISE YOUR WRITING

Assure students that writers—even professional ones—often draft and revise a number of times as they work on a piece of writing. It is not unusual for writers to draft and revise, then draft and revise again, as their ideas become clearer.

DRAFT AND DISCOVER

WRITER TO WRITER

Just try to write continuously—flow.

Tonia Lowe, student
Hummlestown, Pennsylvania

The process of **drafting** involves putting your ideas down on paper. It's a time for experimenting—for trying out ideas and seeing where they lead you. As you write, you may find that a new idea takes you in a surprising direction. That's all right. Just get everything down on paper. Later, you can go back and smooth out any rough spots.

After you finish a draft, it's a good idea to put your writing away for a while. Just a little time away from your work can help you see if there are words or ideas you want to change or develop further.

You may want to share your writing with your classmates—**peer readers.** Sharing the discoveries you've made during drafting helps you enjoy your writing and understand it better. Sometimes you will want to get responses to your writing. At other times you may just want to hear how your words sound. In any case, sharing your writing helps you see your work the way your readers do. You can then tell what's working and what needs changing.

REVISE YOUR WRITING

After drafting, you're ready to **revise,** or improve, what you've written. Usually the first step is taking a fresh look at your writing to see how it's working. Peer comments can help you with this. What you do next, though, depends on the kinds of improvements you decide to make. For example, to clear up a paragraph a reader found confusing, you might add information or rearrange your sentences. To make a description clearer, you might add transitions or replace some words with more vivid or specific ones. As you revise, you might also take new directions and make additional changes you hadn't thought of before.

PROOFREAD

Proofreading means carefully checking your writing and correcting any errors in grammar, usage, spelling, and punctuation. The symbols in Handbook 18, "Proofreading," on page 262 can help. After you've corrected any errors, you can make a final copy of your work.

PUBLISH, PRESENT, AND REFLECT

Although you've probably shown your writing to others as you've worked, **publishing and presenting** involves *formally* sharing your finished piece of writing with an audience. In this book you'll find many suggestions for publishing and presenting.

After you've finished your writing, it's helpful to think about what you've written and what you've learned about your topic and yourself as a writer. This kind of thinking, or **reflecting,** may involve asking yourself the following questions. How have my feelings about the subject changed since I started working on this piece? Did I write differently from the way I usually write? How? Why? What helped me to do a good job, and what got in my way?

Using This Book

Tell students that pages 10–12 provide a guide to what is included in this textbook. Have students note the diagram of the three main sections of the textbook. Tell them to note how these sections differ and how they work together.

Using This Book

Think of this book as your own personal writing coach, ready to offer you the advice, support, and direction you need to become a better writer. Like a good coach, *The Writer's Craft* tries to understand your needs, offers you helpful suggestions, and provides you with a variety of enjoyable and interesting opportunities for writing.

As you go through *The Writer's Craft,* you'll find that it is divided into three sections: **Writer's Workshops,** a **Writing Handbook,** and a **Grammar and Usage Handbook.**

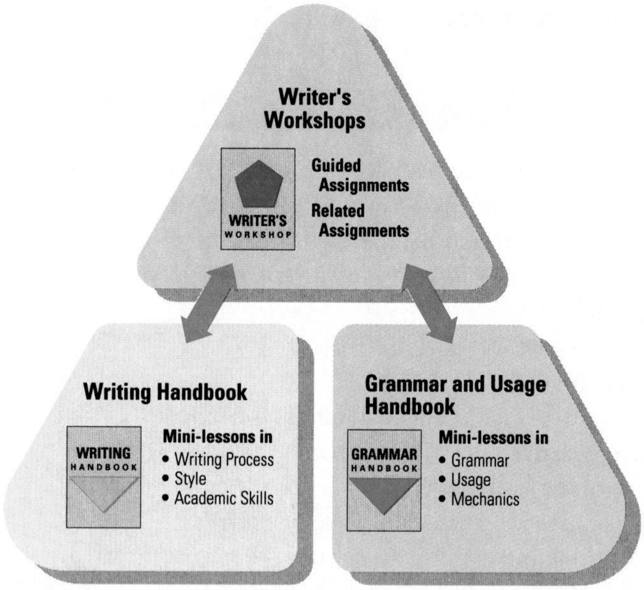

WRITER'S WORKSHOPS

The Writer's Workshops invite you to try many different kinds of writing—descriptions, stories, poems, jokes, family histories. Each Writer's Workshop consists of one Guided

Assignment and one Related Assignment. Special features that appear just before and after each Writer's Workshop—and in other places throughout *The Writer's Craft*—offer additional opportunities for writing.

Guided Assignments

Each Guided Assignment introduces you to a certain kind of writing—personal writing, writing to explain, writing about literature—and then guides you through the process of creating that kind of writing. Along the way, you get to see how a professional writer and another student have approached the same kind of writing assignment. As you work, **Problem Solving** notes in the margins point you to other parts of the book that can help you solve writing problems you may face.

Related Assignments

A Related Assignment follows each Guided Assignment. It gives you a chance to apply the skills you've just learned by experimenting with a related type of writing—a poem, perhaps, or a public-opinion survey. In the Related Assignments, you have the freedom to develop your writing in your own special way.

Additional Writing Opportunities

In addition to the workshops, throughout this book there are many other opportunities to write. For example, if you just want to play with your writing skills, you can turn to one of the Sketchbooks that appear before the workshops. These **Sketchbooks** offer "no-risk" writing warm-ups. To apply your writing skills to other school subjects or to find additional ideas to write about, you can flip to the **Springboards** at the end of each workshop. Springboards suggest interesting ways to use the writing skills you've learned.

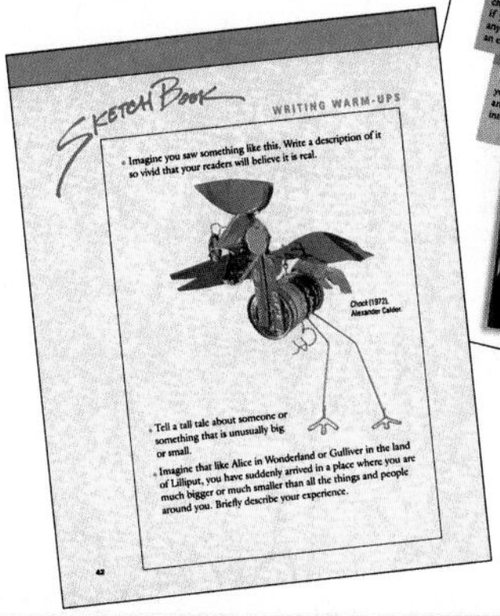
SKETCH BOOK
WRITING WARM-UPS
- Imagine you saw something like this. Write a description of it so vivid that your readers will believe it is real.

Chock (1972), Alexander Calder

- Tell a tall tale about someone or something that is unusually big or small.
- Imagine that like Alice in Wonderland or Gulliver in the land of Lilliput, you have suddenly arrived in a place where you are much bigger or much smaller than all the things and people around you. Briefly describe your experience.

42

Springboards

History What historical event do you wish you could have experienced? The first walk on the moon? The eruption of Mount Vesuvius? Write a journal entry describing your imaginary experience.

Literature Pretend that you are a character in one of your favorite stories. What if you could get up off the page and do anything you wanted? Write a narrative about an experience you would have.

Music Make up a rap in which you retell a personal experience. Use the rhythm and sound of your words to make your rap interesting and lively.

AMERICA

Social Studies How would you explain to someone in another country what a day in your life is like? Write your thoughts in a letter to a pen pal.

23

Using This Book 11

Finally, if you like experimenting with words and phrases, you may like the **Sentence Composing** activities. In these activities you learn new ways to vary your sentences by imitating sentences written by professional writers. In the process you may discover your own personal style.

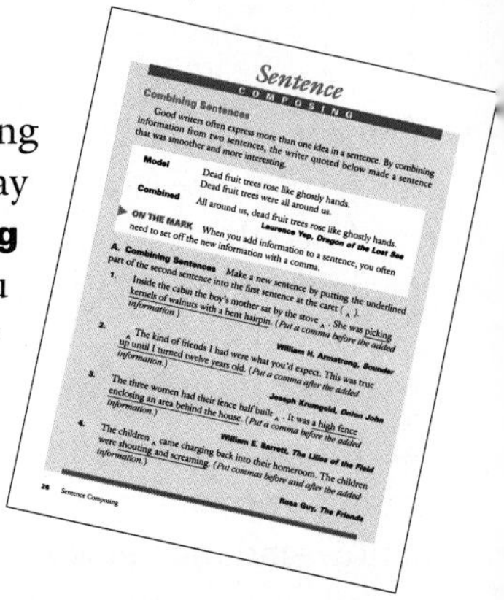

Sentence
COMPOSING

Combining Sentences

Good writers often express more than one idea in a sentence. By combining information from two sentences, the writer quoted below made a sentence that was smoother and more interesting.

Model Dead fruit trees rose like ghostly hands.
Dead fruit trees were all around us.

Combined All around us, dead fruit trees rose like ghostly hands.

Laurence Yep, *Dragon of the Lost Sea*

ON THE MARK When you add information to a sentence, you often need to set off the new information with a comma.

A. Combining Sentences Make a new sentence by putting the underlined part of the second sentence into the first sentence at the caret (^).

1. Inside the cabin the boy's mother sat by the stove ^ . She was picking kernels of walnuts with a bent hairpin. (*Put a comma before the added information.*)

William H. Armstrong, *Sounder*

2. ^ The kind of friends I had were what you'd expect. This was true up until I turned twelve years old. (*Put a comma after the added information.*)

Joseph Krumgold, *Onion John*

3. The three women had their fence half built ^ . It was a high fence enclosing an area behind the house. (*Put a comma before the added information.*)

William E. Barrett, *The Lilies of the Field*

4. The children ^ came charging back into their homeroom. The children were shouting and screaming. (*Put commas before and after the added information.*)

Rosa Guy, *The Friends*

26 Sentence Composing

THE HANDBOOKS

The Writing Handbook and the Grammar and Usage Handbook offer the special help and practice you need to carry out the assignments in the workshops. Although Problem Solving notes in the workshops point out when certain handbook sections may be useful, you may also want to explore the handbooks on your own.

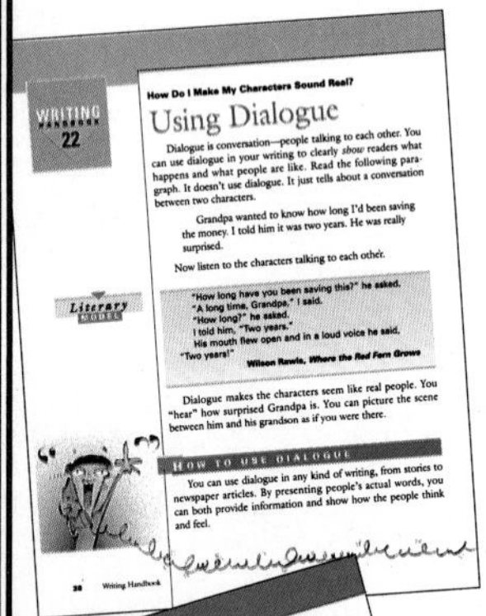

WRITING HANDBOOK 22

How Do I Make My Characters Sound Real?

Using Dialogue

Dialogue is conversation—people talking to each other. You can use dialogue in your writing to clearly *show* readers what happens and what people are like. Read the following paragraph. It doesn't use dialogue. It just tells about a conversation between two characters.

Grandpa wanted to know how long I'd been saving the money. I told him it was two years. He was really surprised.

Now listen to the characters talking to each other.

Literary MODEL

"How long have you been saving this?" he asked.
"A long time, Grandpa," I said.
"How long?" he asked.
I told him, "Two years."
His mouth flew open and in a loud voice he said,
"Two years!"
Wilson Rawls, *Where the Red Fern Grows*

Dialogue makes the characters seem like real people. You "hear" how surprised Grandpa is. You can picture the scene between him and his grandson as if you were there.

HOW TO USE DIALOGUE

You can use dialogue in any kind of writing, from stories to newspaper articles. By presenting people's actual words, you can both provide information and show how the people think and feel.

38 Writing Handbook

The Writing Handbook

This handbook is made up of mini-lessons that offer help and practice in everything from finding ideas and making your writing sound like you to using the library. Literary, professional, and student models show you how other writers use the skills and strategies you are learning. For example, the model on this page shows you how one author uses dialogue in his writing.

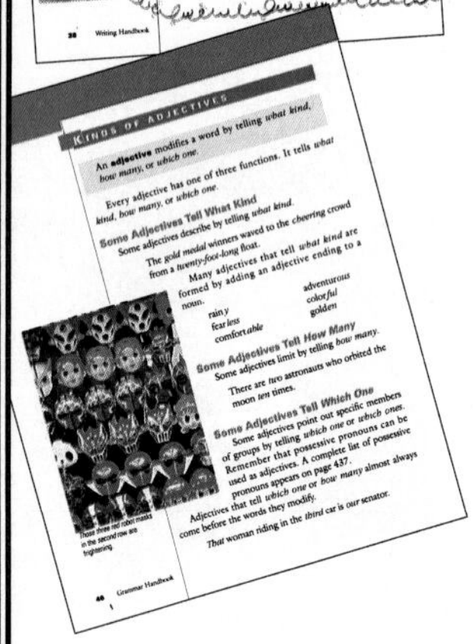

KINDS OF ADJECTIVES

An **adjective** modifies a word by telling *what kind, how many,* or *which one.*

Every adjective has one of three functions. It tells *what kind, how many,* or *which one.*

Some Adjectives Tell What Kind
Some adjectives describe by telling *what kind.*

The *gold medal* winners waved to the *cheering* crowd from a *twenty-foot-long* float.

Many adjectives that tell *what kind* are formed by adding an adjective ending to a noun.

rain*y* adventur*ous*
fear*less* color*ful*
comfort*able* gold*en*

Some Adjectives Tell How Many
Some adjectives limit by telling *how many.*

There are *two* astronauts who orbited the moon *ten* times.

Some Adjectives Tell Which One
Some adjectives point out specific members of groups by telling *which one* or *which ones.* Remember that possessive pronouns can be used as adjectives. A complete list of possessive pronouns appears on page 437.

Adjectives that tell *which one* or *how many* almost always come before the words they modify.

That woman riding in the *third* car is *our* senator.

Those three red robot masks in the second row are frightening.

46 Grammar Handbook

The Grammar and Usage Handbook

When you want a better understanding of how the English language works, the mini-lessons that make up this handbook can help. These lessons explain everything from the parts of speech to capitalization and punctuation. The page shown here, for example, teaches about adjectives.

12 Starting Points

Discovery Workshop

Whenever you want to learn to do something new—whether it's planting a garden or painting a picture of one—you probably ask someone to show you how to do it. The Writer's Workshops in this book give you that kind of guidance. Each one tells you what form of writing you will work on and offers you suggestions on how to create that particular form.

One of the most wonderful things about writing, though, is that there isn't just one way to do it. In fact, when you let yourself write freely, writing can be a series of fascinating surprises.

In this Discovery Workshop, you'll have a chance to experience writing as an adventure. In addition, from the blue notes in the margins you'll learn how to use the sections and features of the Writer's Workshops that follow.

STARTING POINTS

Discovery Workshop

The Discovery Workshop is different from the other workshops in this text, and this difference makes it uniquely valuable. All the workshops allow students to choose their own topics, but only the Discovery Workshop guides students in selecting their own form.

Author Peter Elbow explains: "The Discovery Workshop comes at the beginning for a reason. It provides a writing framework in which a student can start with anything that's on his or her mind, explore the issue, and watch it evolve, so that content ultimately leads to form. Learning to let content determine form gives students an important skill that they'll use in many other writing situations—in this book, in other classes, at work, in life."

As students develop their piece of writing, they also discover the many variables in the writing process. More importantly, they learn that writing can have personal meaning, as they begin to identify and respond to their own goals. Thus the Discovery Workshop provides students with a strong foundation that enables them to approach writing tasks with confidence and flexibility. This foundation can extend beyond the classroom and help make students lifelong writers.

The Discovery Workshop begins with a Student Model. Because this workshop centers on the process of writing, rather than on one form, the Student Model is actually several "discovery" drafts on the same topic. Teaching suggestions offer ways to use the model as a springboard to students' own writing.

The Discovery Workshop can also offer students a chance to see something they don't often experience—you, their teacher, as a writer. If possible, write along with students during this workshop. Share your experiences and responses with them and encourage them to share theirs.

Guided ASSIGNMENT

Starting from LITERATURE

Motivate

Share with students the story of a time when you did something because you felt pressured by others to do it. What was the situation? How did you feel about it? How did it end? What were your feelings then? Invite students to share similar stories. (If some of the situations that students describe seem dangerous, you might want to remind them that blindly following the crowd can have negative consequences.)

BUILD ON PRIOR KNOWLEDGE

Ask students what forms of writing are shown on these pages. (journal entry, poem, postcard, story) Ask students when someone might use each form. Encourage them to identify which of the four forms they prefer to use and to offer reasons for the choice.

SET A PURPOSE

Tell students that all writing pieces on these pages were created by the same student, Maggie Skeffington. Then read Starting from Literature with them. Point out the purpose-setting suggestion ("look for similarities and differences") and question at the end of the box. Remind students to think about these issues as they read Maggie's journal entry, poem, postcard, and story.

Guided ASSIGNMENT

Writing to Discover

Starting from LITERATURE

Where do you get your writing ideas? A journal entry gave Maggie Skeffington the idea to write about her first jump from a high board. As you read the different forms Maggie's writing took, look for similarities and differences between them. Why would she have written about the same experience in so many different ways?

The ***Starting from Literature*** and ***Reading a Student Model*** boxes give you important information about the professional and student models.

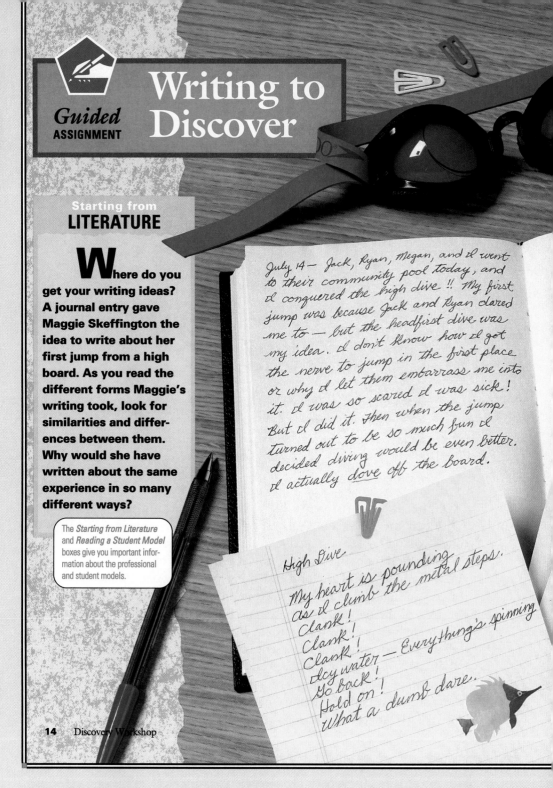

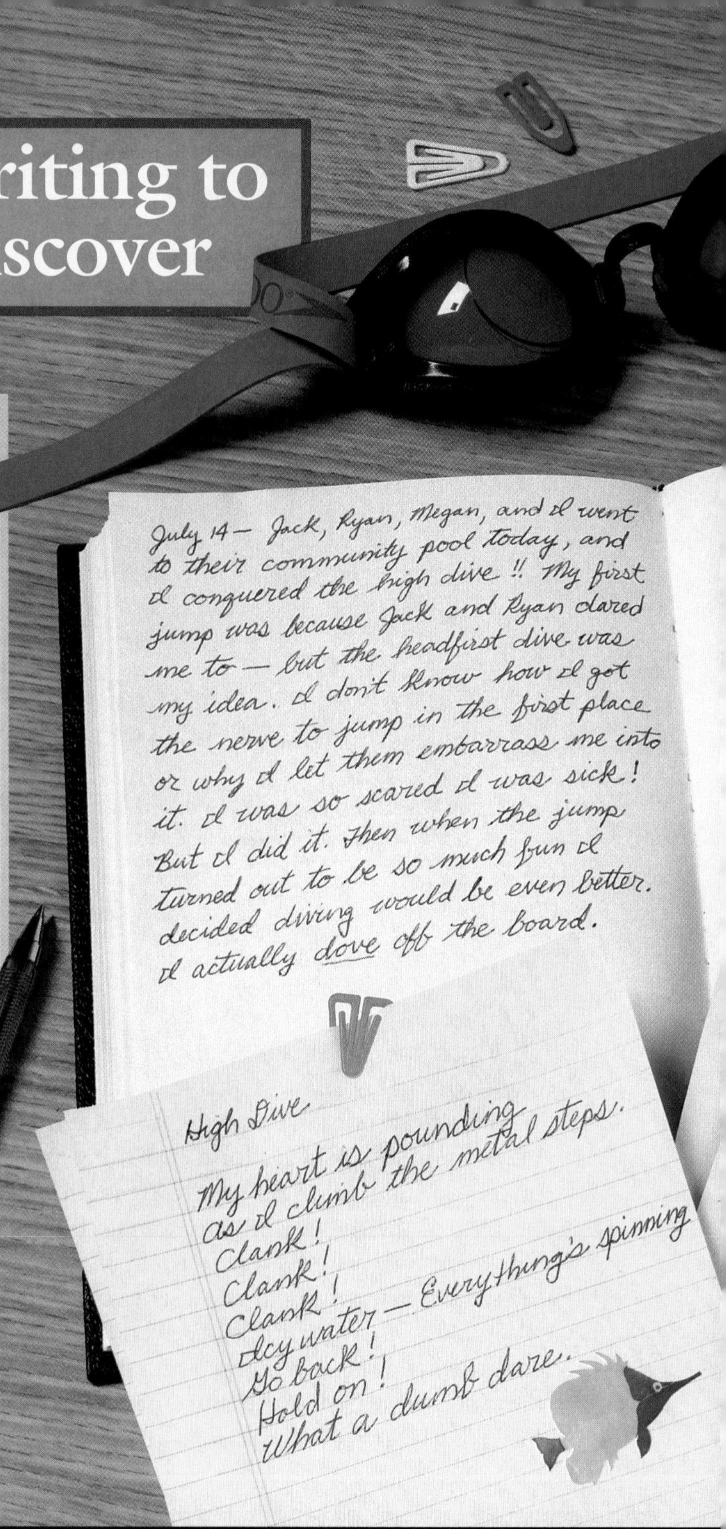
July 14— Jack, Ryan, Megan, and I went to their community pool today, and I conquered the high dive!! My first jump was because Jack and Ryan dared me to—but the headfirst dive was my idea. I don't know how I got the nerve to jump in the first place or why I let them embarrass me into it. I was so scared I was sick! But I did it. Then when the jump turned out to be so much fun I decided diving would be even better. I actually dove off the board.
High Dive
My heart is pounding
as I climb the metal steps.
Clank!
Clank!
Clank!
Icy water—Everything's spinning
Go back!
Hold on!
What a dumb dare...

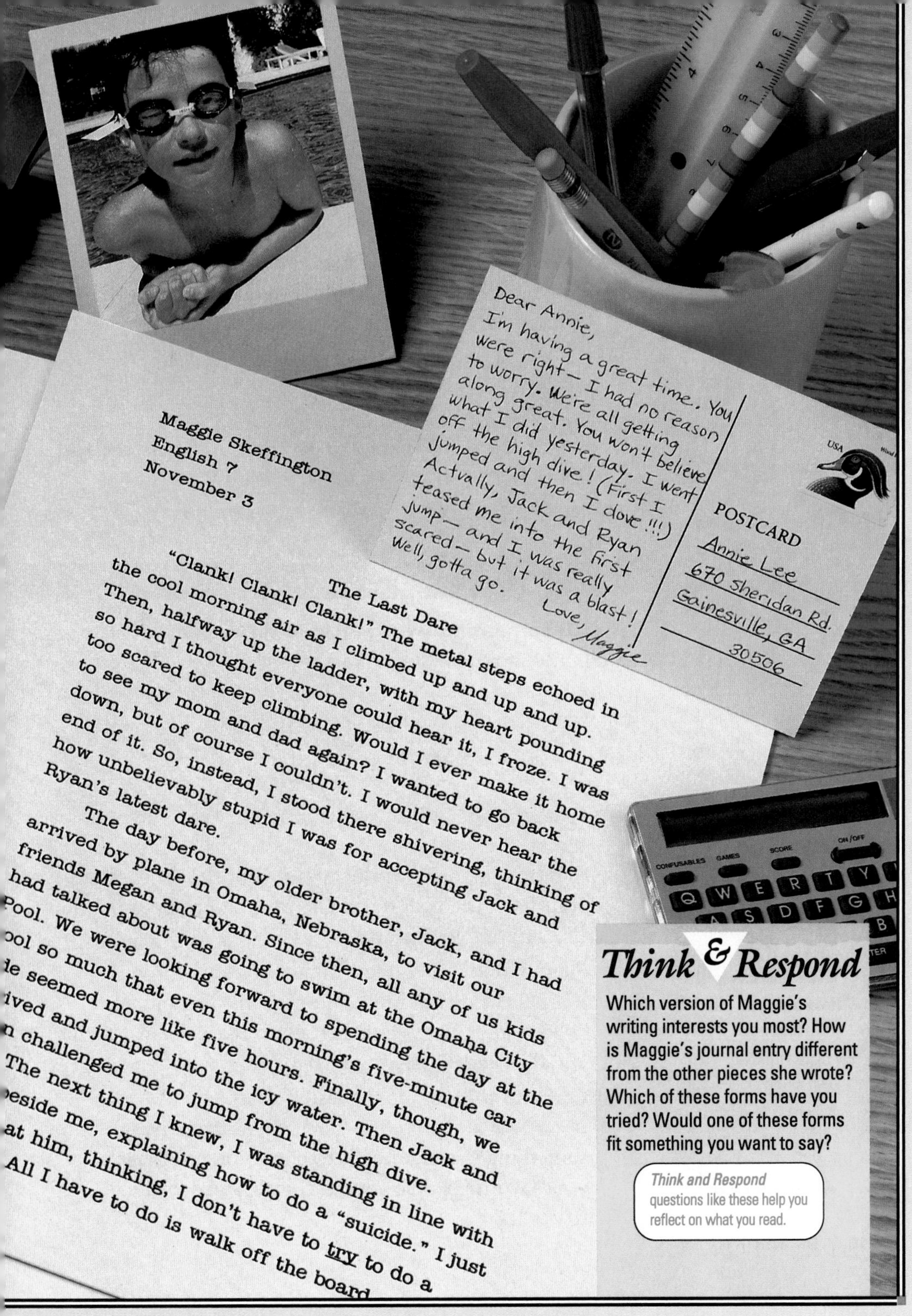

Dear Annie,
I'm having a great time. You were right — I had no reason to worry. We're all getting along great. You won't believe what I did yesterday. I went off the high dive! (First I jumped and then I dove!!!) Actually, Jack and Ryan teased me into the first jump — and I was really scared — but it was a blast! Well, gotta go.
Love,
Maggie
USA
POSTCARD
Annie Lee
670 Sheridan Rd.
Gainesville, GA
30506
Maggie Skeffington
English 7
November 3
The Last Dare
"Clank! Clank! Clank!" The metal steps echoed in the cool morning air as I climbed up and up and up. Then, halfway up the ladder, with my heart pounding so hard I thought everyone could hear it, I froze. I was too scared to keep climbing. Would I ever make it home to see my mom and dad again? I wanted to go back down, but of course I couldn't. I would never hear the end of it. So, instead, I stood there shivering, thinking of how unbelievably stupid I was for accepting Jack and Ryan's latest dare.
The day before, my older brother, Jack, and I had arrived by plane in Omaha, Nebraska, to visit our friends Megan and Ryan. Since then, all any of us kids had talked about was going to swim at the Omaha City Pool. We were looking forward to spending the day at the ool so much that even this morning's five-minute car le seemed more like five hours. Finally, though, we ived and jumped into the icy water. Then Jack and n challenged me to jump from the high dive.
The next thing I knew, I was standing in line with eside me, explaining how to do a "suicide." I just at him, thinking, I don't have to try to do a
All I have to do is walk off the board
CONFUSABLES GAMES SCORE ON/OFF
Q W E R T Y
A S D F G H
B

Think & Respond

Which version of Maggie's writing interests you most? How is Maggie's journal entry different from the other pieces she wrote? Which of these forms have you tried? Would one of these forms fit something you want to say?

Think and Respond questions like these help you reflect on what you read.

Think & Respond

ELICIT PERSONAL RESPONSES

Before students respond to the questions, ask them to answer the purpose-setting question on page 14: "Why would she have written about the same experience in so many different ways?" (Sample: It was an experience that was very important to her.)

As students respond to the first question, have them explain why a particular version of Maggie's writing interested them.

For the second question, ask students to list as many differences as possible. Write their responses on the board. (Samples: The audience is Maggie; it doesn't have the specific details of the story.)

Have students respond in writing to the final two questions. Tell them that these responses are for themselves. If after beginning their writing assignment they decide that the form doesn't work, they do not have to stick with it.

Writing ON YOUR OWN

The Invitation to Write creates a bridge between the model and the writing assignment. In this instance, you might remind students that Maggie chose an event in her life that was very important to her. By writing about it in several forms, Maggie discovered more about what her topic meant to her. Then point out that, like Maggie, students are invited to choose topics that they care about and to try several forms of writing as they follow their own processes of exploration and discovery.

PREWRITE AND EXPLORE

Objectives

- To use prewriting techniques to discover and explore a topic
- To identify several possible writing forms

Teaching Strategies

GENERAL NOTE

KEY TO UNDERSTANDING Remind students that the more Maggie wrote about the dive, the more its importance became clear to her. Tell students that the more they write, and the more forms of writing they try, the more clearly their thoughts will come into focus. For these reasons, encourage students to try following all the suggestions in this workshop.

Writing ON YOUR OWN

Writing to Discover

This is an invitation especially for you! It asks you to explore a topic that interests you.

INVITATION TO *Write*

Each time Maggie Skeffington wrote about her high-diving experience she made new discoveries. Some were about the experience. Others were about herself. Now you have the chance to make your own discoveries through writing.

Write to explore something you care about—an experience, a feeling, or an idea that matters to you. Then see where your thoughts lead you.

PREWRITE AND EXPLORE

Discover and explore exciting writing ideas by trying the activities in this section.

1. Find something worth spending time with. The topics you'll most enjoy writing about are the ones that matter to you, so look for experiences and ideas you really care about. The following activities can help you find a topic.

Problem Solving features help you find answers to your writing questions. When you feel stuck, these features will point you to helpful mini-lessons.

PROBLEM SOLVING

"How else can I find ideas?"

For more information on finding writing ideas, see

- Handbook 2, "Finding a Starting Point," pages 197–202

Exploring Topics

- **Freewriting** What's on your mind? What have you been thinking about lately? What are you feeling right now? To find out, just start writing about your thoughts. Then, as your first idea leads to others, write more about the things that interest you most.
- **Flash back** Take a few minutes to look through your journal entries or family photographs. Dig out any toys, collections, or souvenirs that you've saved. What memories and feelings do they bring to mind?
- **Favorite things** Is there someplace you love to go? The beach? An amusement park? Is there someone or something that never fails to cheer you up? Make a list of your favorite people, places, things, and activities.

2. Explore your ideas. Jot down the most interesting ones you've found. Then talk about them with others, or freewrite about one or two possibilities for a while.

One Student's Process

When Maggie was looking for writing ideas, a short poem she'd written reminded her of the time she conquered the high dive. She then did some freewriting to recall more about the experience.

I remember that climb. My heart really was pounding hard. Worse, though, was that halfway up I just froze on the ladder. I was too scared to keep climbing, but I knew I couldn't go back. If I had, Ryan and Jack would never have let me hear the end of it. So I just stood there feeling terrified, wishing I hadn't taken their stupid dare.

Talk about your dumb dares. That one was certainly at the top of the list. I'm never ever going to let myself be pushed into doing anything I'm that scared of doing again. I'm just glad everything worked out OK.

In One Student's Process, you'll see the prewriting, drafting, and revising done by a student writer like yourself. Your own writing process may be similar—or it may be very different.

3. Take stock. Think about all the ideas you've just explored. Have you discovered one that you'd like to spend some time with? If not, look at some other journal entries or at some of the items you've paused over, or try more talking or freewriting.

4. Gather details. Once you've found a topic you like, begin gathering details you can use to flesh out a draft. If you've done some freewriting, you may already have a lot of material. Otherwise, you can simply spend some time thinking about your topic or create lists or graphic organizers. For example, you might list the facts or background information you know about your topic. You might also list sensory details—how things looked, sounded, smelled, tasted, and felt.

PROBLEM SOLVING

"How do I find details?"

For information on finding details, see

- Handbook 4, "Developing a Topic," pages 205–210

GENERAL NOTE

HELPFUL HINT Maggie used a journal entry as the basis for her story. Not all students keep journals, however. If you have students who do not have journals, suggest they do an exercise in guided imagery: a mental tour of an event, a game, or an experience, noting details, as if the tour were real. After they have finished their mental tours, they can write about them.

for ONE STUDENT'S PROCESS

KEY TO UNDERSTANDING The One Student's Process feature provides a sample of a student's work at various stages of the writing process. When you discuss this feature, be sure students understand that they do not have to use the technique that is illustrated, but are free to choose other strategies.

The accompanying teaching notes for this feature suggest ways to link the sample to students' own work. For example, you might point out that in her freewriting, Maggie starts by trying to remember the details of what happened. She ends up by writing about accepting dumb dares. Assure students that jumping from one subject to another as Maggie did is fine in freewriting. Among the many ideas, writers can generally find several that capture their interest..

DRAFT AND DISCOVER

Objectives

- To write successive drafts, focusing on the same subject but using different writing forms
- To identify personal writing goals

Teaching Strategies

GENERAL NOTE

HELPFUL HINT Stress the word *discover* in "Draft and Discover." Remind students that drafting, or writing, is a discovery process as they seek to find out what a subject means to them. Unlike the prewriting in other workshops, the prewriting students have just completed was more of a warm-up than a plan for how to proceed. Therefore, suggest that students look over their prewriting, put it aside, and begin drafting, expecting surprises along the way. Encourage them to try more than one form as Maggie did.

for READ WHAT YOU'VE WRITTEN

KEY TO UNDERSTANDING Remind students that in this workshop, they are learning how to choose a form, organize their material, develop a topic, and decide on a goal. Explain that the questions in this section can help them accomplish these tasks.

for DEVELOPMENT

KEY TO UNDERSTANDING As developing writers, students do not always realize when they have gotten to the heart of what they want to say. Tell them that a sense of satisfaction can guide them. They might not feel completely satisfied, but they should feel they are on the right track.

The Writer's Choice features remind you of some of your options and allow you to select what's right for you.

Writer's Choice You can choose a form before drafting, or you can just begin writing and see what happens. However, even if you select a form before drafting, you can change your mind later.

DRAFT AND DISCOVER

In this section you'll find plenty of suggestions for getting your ideas down on paper.

1. Begin writing. At this point all you need to do is get something down on paper. You don't need to know where your ideas will take you. Just begin writing and see what takes shape on the page. Let your ideas flow from your pen right onto the page without stopping to judge them.

2. Read what you've written. Take a moment to look at your draft. Do you like what you see? Do you know what form you would like your writing to take? Have you given any thought to your personal goals for writing? Jotting down your answers to some of the following questions may help you figure out what you want to do next.

Questions to Ask Yourself

Form and Organization	• What's a good way to present my ideas? Has my draft led me to a particular form of writing—such as a story, a poem, or a report? • What order should my ideas follow? What should my readers see first? next? last?
Development	• Have I included all of the most important details? • Have I gotten across the heart of what I want to say?
Personal Goals	• What do I want this writing to do? • Do I want to share this writing with an audience, or do I want to keep it private?

PROFESSIONAL NOTEBOOK

Advice from the Authors Share this suggestion from Peter Elbow to help students experiment with a variety of forms: "Try it [your idea] as a dialogue, a poem, or a TV show. Try it as a letter from someone on Mars or as a six-year-old kid might write. Trying out different forms and different voices strengthens your own writing voice."

3. Consider sharing your writing. You don't *have* to share your writing. However, it can feel good to find out that someone else understands and likes what you've written. Furthermore, peer reactions can show you what is working in your draft and what you might need to add or change. If you do decide to share your draft, try asking your readers questions like these:

- What do you think my writing is about?
- What parts of my draft do you like best?
- What, if anything, do you want to know more about?

Peer reader comments in the margin show you the responses and suggestions that one student gave to another. When you feel ready, you can ask your own peer readers to give you feedback on your writing too.

One Student's Process

Maggie found herself writing the story of what happened on the high dive. Here is part of her first draft of that story, along with the peer comments she got on it.

The sound of my feet pounding on the metal steps echoed in the morning air as I climbed. Then, halfway up, with my heart pounding, I froze. What I wanted was I wanted to go back down, but of course I couldn't. So, instead, I stood there feeling cold and thinking of how unbelievably stupid I was for accepting Jack and Ryan's latest dare.

Peer Reader Comments

I really like the part where you're frozen on the ladder.

Why did you want to go back down?

I've let myself be embarrassed into doing some pretty scary things too.

REVISE YOUR WRITING

In this section you'll learn strategies for reworking your writing to make it as good as it can be.

1. Take a fresh look at your writing. Use your own ideas and your peer readers' comments to discover what's working in your draft and what you might want to change. Then decide on the improvements you want to make.

2. Check your content and organization. Have you said everything you wanted to say? Is your material organized in a way that makes sense?

for CONSIDER SHARING YOUR WRITING

KEY TO UNDERSTANDING Peer response is a valuable tool for finding out how others respond to a draft. Students do not have to ask for a response from peers; when they do, however, they retain authority over their drafts by having peer readers respond to specific questions. Most Guided Assignments offer students two sets of questions: one for the peer reader and one for the writer. (See page 57 for an example.)

for ONE STUDENT'S PROCESS

HELPFUL HINT: PEER RESPONSE Point out the kinds of comments the peer reader made. If peer response is new to your students, go over Handbook 16, pages 253–256, and the pages on peer response in the Appendix. Then you might have students suggest additional comments about Maggie's draft.

REVISE YOUR WRITING

Objective

- To evaluate and revise a draft

Teaching Strategies

HELPFUL HINT If students are unsure about which form they should be using, encourage them to think about content. For example, a writer focusing on feelings about another person might use the form of a friendly letter. A writer focusing on an interesting process might create a how-to article.

for ONE STUDENT'S PROCESS

HELPFUL HINT Explain that Maggie added the "Clank! Clank! Clank!" from her poem to her story to make the beginning more vivid. If students have experimented with more than one form, suggest that they see if they can include something interesting from one of their other pieces of writing.

PROOFREAD

Teaching Strategies

GENERAL NOTE

KEY TO UNDERSTANDING This section introduces students to proofreading. Be sure that they understand that proofreading is done only after the paper has been completely written and the writer is satisfied with its content, development, and organization.

In other Guided Assignments, a feature titled Linking Grammar and Writing (or Linking Mechanics and Writing) appears in this section. These features focus on grammar and mechanics that are appropriate for each writing assignment, and they include cross-references to the *Grammar and Usage Handbook.* See pages 38 and 82 for examples.

for PROOFREADING SYMBOLS

HELPFUL HINT Students should note the location of this proofreading chart so that they can refer to it when they proofread future assignments. This information also appears in Handbook 18, pages 260–262.

Writing TIP

Reading your revised draft aloud to yourself can help you make sure that your revision flows smoothly.

Marginal notes like these offer writing and grammar tips as well as suggestions for using a computer when you write.

One Student's Process

Here are some changes Maggie made to her draft. She would make even more changes later.

Clank! Clank! Clank!

^The sound of my feet pounding on the metal steps echoed in the morning air as I climbed. Then, halfway up, with my heart pounding, I froze. ~~What I wanted was~~ I wanted to go back down, but of course I couldn't.^ I would never hear the end of it. So, instead, I stood there feeling cold and thinking of how unbelievably stupid I was for accepting Jack and Ryan's latest dare.

^ I was too scared to keep climbing. Would I ever make it home to see my mom and dad again?

PROOFREAD

This section reminds you of all the little details you need to attend to before making a final copy of your draft.

Carefully check your writing and correct any errors in grammar, usage, spelling, and punctuation. The symbols on this chart can help you mark the changes you want to make.

Proofreading Symbols

Symbol	Meaning	Symbol	Meaning
∧	Add letters or words.	/	Make a capital letter lowercase.
⊙	Add a period.	¶	Begin a new paragraph.
≡	Capitalize a letter.	∾	Switch the positions of letters or words.
⁀‿	Close up space.	— or ℓ	Take out letters or words.
∧,	Add a comma.		

PUBLISH AND PRESENT

To share your work with others—your classmates, your teacher, or an even wider audience—try one or more of the following ideas.

Each workshop suggests a variety of ways for you to share your writing with a wide audience.

- **Plan a writing magazine.** As a class, begin plans to publish writing you want to share with students in other classes. Such writing might include letters, movie reviews, journal entries, fiction, and even freewriting.
- **Go beyond the classroom.** Take your work home to share it with family members and friends.
- **Market your manuscript.** Submit your writing to a magazine that features student writing or to a school or community newspaper.

REFLECT ON YOUR WRITING

Reflecting on any experience can help you discover what you liked about it, what you learned from it, and what you want to do differently next time. So take some time now to think about the writing you've just completed, jotting down your answers to the following questions. Then, if you are using a portfolio, add your reflections to your portfolio as a note along with your finished piece.

After you complete each piece of writing, you'll have an opportunity to reflect on what you've learned about writing and about yourself.

- How did I discover what I wanted to say?
- How did I figure out what form I wanted to use?
- How do I feel about the piece I've written? What part of this piece am I most proud of?
- Which parts of the writing process were the most difficult for me?
- If I had this writing assignment to do over again, how might I do it differently?

GENERAL NOTE

ASSESSMENT Since this workshop is of a personal and exploratory nature, consider marking papers on a credit/no credit basis. All of the other Guided Assignments contain evaluation standards, which appear in the margin of the Proofreading sections or the Publish and Present sections in the student book. More detailed evaluation standards appear in the teacher's edition. (For an example, see page 60.)

Closure: Reflect on Your Writing

This section directs students to write briefly about their experiences with the assignment. If your class is using portfolios, they can add their reflections to them. The purpose of this section is to increase each student's awareness of his or her own writing process and to focus students' attention on their growth as writers. Suggest that they choose one or two questions and write a thoughtful response.

One Student's WRITING

Maggie Skeffington's final draft appears on these two pages. After students have read it, have them compare it with Maggie's journal entry, poem, and postcard that appear on pages 14–15. What is the major difference between those earlier writings and her final draft? (The earlier writings do not have the kind of detail that Maggie has in her final piece.) Which parts did students find particularly effective?

As students discuss their responses, remind them that writing is a process that takes time and that Maggie had to make time to create her final draft. She did not sit down, write a page, correct it, and turn it in. It took considerable time for her to discover what she should say. The results of her efforts were a well-developed piece of personal writing and a place in a sixth-grade textbook!

One Student's Writing

Maggie Skeffington
English 7
November 3

The Last Dare

"Clank! Clank! Clank!" The metal steps echoed in the cool morning air as I climbed up and up and up. Then, halfway up the ladder, with my heart pounding so hard I thought everyone could hear it, I froze. I was too scared to keep climbing. Would I ever make it home to see my mom and dad again? I wanted to go back down, but of course I couldn't. I would never hear the end of it. So, instead, I stood there shivering, thinking of how unbelievably stupid I was for accepting Jack and Ryan's latest dare.

The day before, my older brother, Jack, and I had arrived by plane in Omaha, Nebraska, to visit our friends Megan and Ryan. Since then, all any of us kids had talked about was going to swim at the Omaha City Pool. We were looking forward to spending the day at the pool so much that even this morning's five-minute car ride seemed more like five hours. Finally, though, we arrived and jumped into the icy water. Then Jack and Ryan challenged me to jump from the high dive.

The next thing I knew, I was standing in line with Jack beside me, explaining how to do a "suicide." I just looked at him, thinking, I don't have to try to do a suicide. All I have to do is walk off the board and I'll be dead! The ground was too far away—and spinning. Then it was my turn.

"Come on! Hurry up!" My brother stood below me, screaming. I looked down, wanting to say something smart, but immediately realized that was a mistake. So I continued up, up THE STEPS TO DEATH.

"Clank! Clank! Clank!" All too soon I reached the tiny platform. With my heart pounding faster than ever, I stepped forward, and suddenly there was nothing under me.

For a moment I felt like one of those cartoon characters who has just stepped off a cliff and is still managing to hang in the air by pedaling his feet fast. Then, with my stomach churning, I began to fall.

Just when I was getting used to falling, "Boom!" I hit the water. Was this it? Was I dying? Sort of. I could hardly believe what was happening, but I was dying to do it again!

Of course, I was also still a little mad at myself for having gone through with something so terrifying just so that I wouldn't seem like a chicken. No more stupid dares, I promised myself. Then I got back in the high-dive line—this time to dive headfirst—but for me, because I wanted to dive, and not to prove anything to anyone else.

Writing to Discover 23

ART NOTE Although drypainting is found in other cultures (in India, Tibet, Australia, Latin America, Japan), the Navajo are the people most famous for using drypainting as a sacred art. The Navajo believe that humans must live in harmony or balance *(hózhó)* with the universe and that lack of harmony causes illness and misfortune. They have developed many traditional healing ceremonies designed to restore this delicate balance and to control dangerous forces in the universe.

After a long apprenticeship, a singer or medicine man can perform one or more of these special rituals, or chants. They may last from one to nine nights and involve songs, prayers, plant medicines, sand painting, and sacred objects. Sand paintings created for these religious rituals are deliberately destroyed at the end of the ceremony.

To create a sand painting, singers first clear a smooth place on the ground of a *hogan,* a Navajo home. They use only their right hands as they carefully apply colored sands in a precise circular design of stylized figures and symbols. The Navajo believe that sand paintings are holy altars that attract gods who come to see their portraits and to identify the person in need of healing. During their visit, the gods take away the evil that is troubling the person and replace it with their own goodness and power.

The sand painting shown here is for a chant to cure or prevent sickness, the Hand-tremblingway. Ask students what symbols they can recognize. Can they find the branching big star? (in the center) the Rainbow guardian? (the outermost figure that rings the painting) What other symbols can they identify?

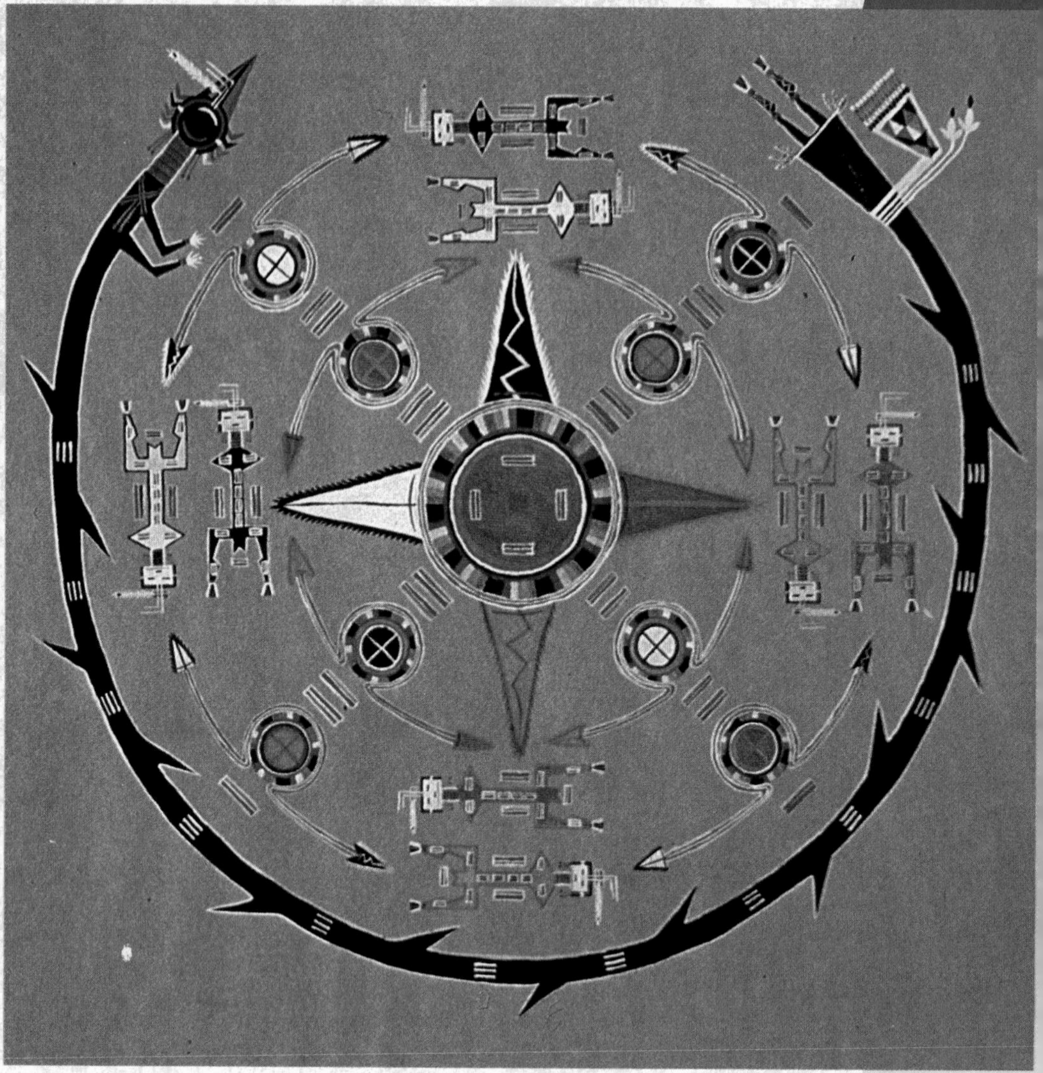

Big Star with Big Flies and Mountains Guarded by Arrows (1973), artist unknown. Navajo artisans create sand paintings for religious ceremonies by sprinkling dry pigments and other colored substances onto a flat surface. The outermost image in this sand painting is a Rainbow Guardian in black flint armor. The Big Flies, portrayed here with white faces, are important symbols in Navajo mythology. The small circles represent the mountains that border Navajo homelands.

Writer's Workshops

Writer's Workshops

1

Personal and Expressive Writing

Overview

Personal and expressive writing draws on personal feelings, experiences, and observations. In this workshop, students will keep private journals and then use journal entries as the basis for a piece of writing that can be shared. Workshop 1 includes the following Guided Assignment and Related Assignment, as well as the interdisciplinary project described on pages 25c–25d.

1. **Guided: Writing from Your Journal** calls on students to record their feelings and observations in a private journal, to analyze and evaluate their journal entries, to explore ideas they would like to share, and to choose an appropriate form in which to share their ideas.
2. **Related: Friendly Letter** guides students through the process of relating their personal experiences in a letter, one of the forms suggested in the Guided Assignment. It encourages students to write conversationally for a familiar audience.

Teaching Preview

Preparation Guide

1. Use the Overview on this page and the Teacher's Choice descriptions on page 27 as a basis for deciding which assignments to teach.
2. Preview the assignments and the teacher's notes and identify concepts that may require preteaching or extra support, given your class's abilities. The handbook mini-lessons suggested within the lesson may also provide guidance.
3. Preview the chart below for support materials in the Teacher's Resource File that may be used with this Workshop. Resources are for use with the Guided Assignment unless otherwise noted.

Support Materials

WRITER'S CRAFT RESOURCES

Prewrite and Explore
Thinking Skills Worksheets, pp. 5, 7
Thinking Skills Transparencies, pp. 5–5a, 7–7a
Writing Resource Book, p. 1

Draft and Discover
Elaboration, Revision, and Proofreading Practice, p. 1
Elaboration, Revision, and Proofreading Transparencies, pp. 1–2
Writing Resource Book, p. 2

Revise Your Writing
Elaboration, Revision, and Proofreading Practice, p. 2
Elaboration, Revision, and Proofreading Transparencies, pp. 3–4
Guidelines for Writing Assessment and Portfolio Use, pp. 14, 22–24
Peer Response Guides, pp. 7–8

Assessment
Tests and Writing Assessment Prompts, p. 1

Extension Activities
Sentence Composing Copymasters, pp. 1–2
Starting Points for Writing, pp. 32–34, 36, 38–39
Writing from Literature, pp. 3–4, 11–12, 21–24
Standardized Test Practice

Educational Technology (available separately)
Writer's DataBank
Electronic English Handbook
Multimedia Workshop
On Assignment! (videodisc)

OTHER RESOURCES

Books and Journals
Bernabei, G. S. "What Sixth Graders Learn from the Journal of Bobby G." *English Journal.* 81 (Sept. 1992): 78–80.
Hesse, Karen. *Letters from Rifka.* New York: Holt, 1992.

Films and Videos
Homesick: My Own Story, SRA, 1993.

Educational Technology
The Diary of Anne Frank. Image Entertainment. (videodisc)
Diaries and Journals. Electronic Bookshelf. Apple Series, IBM, MS-DOS, Macintosh.

Linking Literature, Writing, and Grammar

The following options may be used to provide students with an integrated language experience. Begin by assigning and discussing any of the recommended pieces of literature. Use the suggested strategy to provide a link to the Guided Assignment.

LINKING LITERATURE AND WRITING

Option 1

Starting Point: An excerpt from *Homesick: My Own Story,* by Jean Fritz on pages 28–29 of *The Writer's Craft.*

Strategy: Use the teaching suggestions on pages 28–29 to lead students into the Guided Assignment.

Option 2

Starting Point: An excerpt from *Woodsong* by Gary Paulsen on pages 50–54 of McDougal, Littell's *Literature and Language,* Grade 6. (Additional suggestions for using *Literature and Language* can be found on page 27.)

Strategy: Have students read the autobiographical excerpt. Ask students how Paulsen was able to remember this incident so vividly. Suggest that he may have recorded some of the details in a diary or journal immediately after the incident. Use the discussion to introduce the Guided Assignment.

Option 3

Starting Point: "The Jacket" by Gary Soto.

Strategy: Have students read the short story and discuss the feelings of wanting to fit in and wear the same kind of clothing that peers do. Suggest that these are the kinds of feelings that might be included in a journal and later used in a story. Use the discussion to lead students into the Guided Assignment.

LINKING WRITING AND GRAMMAR

Before the drafting or revision stages of this assignment, keep a journal of your own for a few days. Tell students that there are some differences between the way we write privately for ourselves and the way we write for an audience. To illustrate the point, read aloud examples of sentence fragments from your journal; then write the fragments on the board. Point out that the meaning of the words was clear to you, but that to help your audience understand your ideas, you want to express them in complete sentences. Have students help you add the missing subjects or verbs to the fragments. Suggest that they look for fragments in their own work.

Go over pages 344–346 of the Grammar and Usage Handbook covering sentence fragments. If problems persist, assign the exercises on those pages for reteaching. Additional practice can be found in the *Grammar and Usage Practice Book* on pages 3–4.

Management Guidelines

The chart below indicates the number of days recommended for each phase of the Guided and Related Assignments. These numbers are an estimate of the total time needed for each phase. In practice, of course, students may not complete each phase in one continuous session, nor will they necessarily progress from stage to stage in the linear order shown here. Stars indicate portions of the assignment that may be completed outside the classroom if time is limited or if teachers wish students to work independently.

WRITING FROM PERSONAL EXPERIENCE

Starting from Literature	1 day
Keeping a Journal	1–2 weeks*
Prewrite and Explore	1 day
Draft and Discover	2–3 days*
Revise Your Writing	1–2 days*
Proofread	1 day*
Publish and Present	1–2 days*
Reflect on Your Writing	1 day
Extension and Enrichment	open*

FRIENDLY LETTER

Starting from Literature	1 day
Keeping in Touch	1 day*
Taking a Final Look	1 day*
Sentence Composing	open*

Project File

All About Me: A Self-portrait

Overview

During this project students will think deeply about themselves and will investigate ways to create a self-portrait that they can share with others. The project will culminate in multimedia presentations and the development of a class album.

Students will participate in the following activities:

- Examine autobiographies and artists' self-portraits
- Decide what elements self-portraits might include
- Use reflection, interviewing, and other techniques to gather information about themselves and their backgrounds
- Plan and present their own multimedia self-portraits
- Use language arts, science, math, social studies, and art skills to complete their research and to develop and present their writing

Preparation Guide

Point out to students that they are the world's foremost experts on at least one thing—themselves. Lead them in a class discussion of what self-portraits are and what developing a self-portrait might entail. Students should understand that self-portraits can take many forms and can involve several media.

Tell students that in this project they will use the skills of personal writing, as well as other skills, to create self-portraits that they can share with classmates.

Stage 1
Explore Self-portraits

1. Invite students to read autobiographies and to view artists' self-portraits (see *Resources, Stage 1*).
2. Discuss differences in what written and visual self-portraits reveal and omit about their creators.
3. Tell students to brainstorm a list of possible elements of multimedia self-portraits. Possibilities include collages, family trees, videos, photographs, displays of mementos, music, poetry, art, monologues, skits, and talent shows.
4. Have students write in their journals about what they consider to be the most important aspects of who they are.

TEAM TEACHING

The following activities may be used for team teaching or as enrichment and extension activities by the language arts teacher.

Language Arts Read autobiographies and journals (see *Resources, Stage 1*).

Art Compare the self-portraits of several artists, for example Norman Rockwell and Vincent van Gogh. How do the portraits reveal their personalities?

Social Studies Learn how social scientists define personality. Study the value placed on individuals versus groups in various cultures and time periods.

Science Study infant and childhood development. Learn how personality is formed.

TEACHING TIPS

- Have students create a bulletin-board display with unidentified photos of themselves as babies; let them try to guess the identities of the babies.
- Show video portraits of writers, artists, artisans, or others. Discuss elements in the videos that would also be effective in self-portraits.

Stage 2
Focus on Yourself

1. Have students explore who they are in terms of family background and cultural heritage. Encourage them to interview family members—in person or by letter or telephone—and to create family trees (see *Resources, Stage 2*).
2. Have students explore who they are in terms of where they live. Ask them to create brief descriptions of their communities.
3. Have students explore who they are personally. Suggest they develop lists of their likes and dislikes (for example, movies, music, books, and clothing styles), their special interests, and their talents.
4. Tell students to plan their self-portraits and presentations. Remind them of the many possibilities involving various media.

TEAM TEACHING

Science Investigate the role of heredity in determining personal traits (see *Resources, Stage 2*).

Social Studies Explore family histories and cultural heritages. Map ancestors' travels (see *Resources, Stage 2*). Identify characteristics and influences of communities.

Math Fill out and tabulate interest inventories. Calculate the durations and distances of ancestors' travels. Graph family or personal data.

Music Explore music related to family histories or cultural heritages.

Language Arts Study interviewing and letter-writing skills (see *Resources, Stage 2*).

TEACHING TIPS

- Have students map their communities, marking places of importance to them.
- Encourage students to investigate the histories of their first and last names (see *Resources, Stage 2*).
- Make audiovisual equipment available to interested students.

Stage 3
Create and Present a Self-portrait

1. Direct students to create self-portraits, using writing and at least one other medium. Written materials might include family trees, poems, captions for photos or drawings, personal memoirs, and family histories.
2. Schedule one or two "That's Me!" days during which students will present their self-portraits to their classmates.
3. Direct students to compile their written materials into a class album, adding introductions or explanations as needed.

TEAM TEACHING

Language Arts Review techniques of personal writing (see *Resources, Stage 3*).

Art Create visuals for the presentations.

Music Choose or compose music to accompany the presentations.

Science Explain principles of heredity and personality or other science material related to the presentations.

Social Studies Explain relevant historical or geographic information.

TEACHING TIPS

- Arrange facilities and equipment for students' presentations.
- Encourage students to invite family members to attend the presentations.
- If possible, duplicate the class album at the end of the school year so that each student can keep a copy.

Resources

STAGE 1

Autobiographies for students to explore include the ***Self-Portrait*** books by the children's-book illustrators Erik Blegvad, Trina Schart Hyman, and Margot Zemach); ***The Lost Garden*** by Laurence Yep; ***The Adventures of Davy Crockett*** by Crockett himself; ***The Endless Steppe*** by Esther Hautzig; ***Patrick Des Jarlait: The Story of an American Indian Artist; The Land I Lost*** by Huynh Quang Nhuong; ***Waheenee: An Indian Girl's Story Told by Herself,*** compiled by Gilbert L. Wilson; and ***Rosa Parks: My Story.***

STAGE 2

Where Did You Get Those Eyes? by Kay Cooper and ***Ancestor Hunting*** by Lorraine Henriod cover making family trees, interviewing family members, and researching family history. Henriod also discusses genealogists in various cultures, such as griots and other tribal historians.

The Great Ancestor Hunt by Lila Perl and ***Who Do You Think You Are?*** by Suzanne Hilton are engaging, thorough guides for more advanced students tracing their families' roots.

Last Names First by Mary P. Lee and Richard S. Lee tells how to investigate the origins of last and first names and discusses laws and customs related to names.

Heredity by Robert E. Dunbar and ***Me and My Family Tree*** by Paul Showers explain how traits are inherited and survey the science of genetics from Mendel through the discovery of the structure of DNA.

The Writer's Craft, Grade 6, Workshop 1, "Personal and Expressive Writing," pages 40–43, teaches the writing of friendly letters. Handbook 31, "Interviewing Skills," page 323, offers useful tips for questioning and listening.

STAGE 3

The Writer's Craft, Grade 6, Workshop 1, "Personal and Expressive Writing," pages 26–44, teaches techniques of personal writing.

Kidpix (Broderbund) and **PosterWorks** (S. H. Pierce & Co.) are software that lets students use computers to generate illustrations and posters.

Additional Projects

Letters from Space For this project, encourage students to research conditions on other planets in the solar system, to choose a planet, and then to imagine themselves as part of a team sent to explore it. They should write a series of personal letters to family members and friends back on earth, describing their findings and experiences. They can present their letters with "photos," sketches, models of their spacecraft, and "specimens" of plant and animal life they have encountered.

Message to the Future Have students create time capsules for their future grandchildren, including personal writings describing their daily lives, their thoughts, their frustrations, and their hopes. Students should also choose photos, drawings, and other items to include. After presenting their materials to classmates, they can decide how and where to store the time capsules.

Media Blitz Suggest that students decide which TV commercials they find most effective and which they find most offensive, using journal writing and discussion to explore their responses to the commercials. Then have them write personal essays detailing their feelings and create commercials that meet their standards for excellence. They may submit their writings to a local newspaper, or they may send them to the performers on whose shows the commercials air or to the presidents of the companies whose products are advertised.

Sketch Book

Objective

- To use objects and suggested writing prompts as springboards to informal writing

WRITING WARM-UPS

Encourage students to respond freely and informally to at least one of the Sketchbook prompts. Before freewriting about their memories, students may enjoy discussing their childhood collections with the rest of the class. Assure them that their written responses will not be graded and may provide useful material for future assignments.

For example, freewriting about collections could lead to a friendly letter or to a piece of writing to share in Writer's Workshop 1. Writing about an important event might be the basis of a personal narrative in Writer's Workshop 3.

SHOW, DON'T TELL

The following is a sample of a showing paragraph for the first prompt:

I don't know what I would do without my friends. Whom would I share secrets with, if Katie didn't call me at exactly eight o'clock every night? Whom would I scream with at horror movies, if Akiko weren't brave enough to go with me? How would I have gotten up the nerve to try out for the lead in the class play, if Doug hadn't told me I was good enough?

Sketch Book

WRITING WARM-UPS

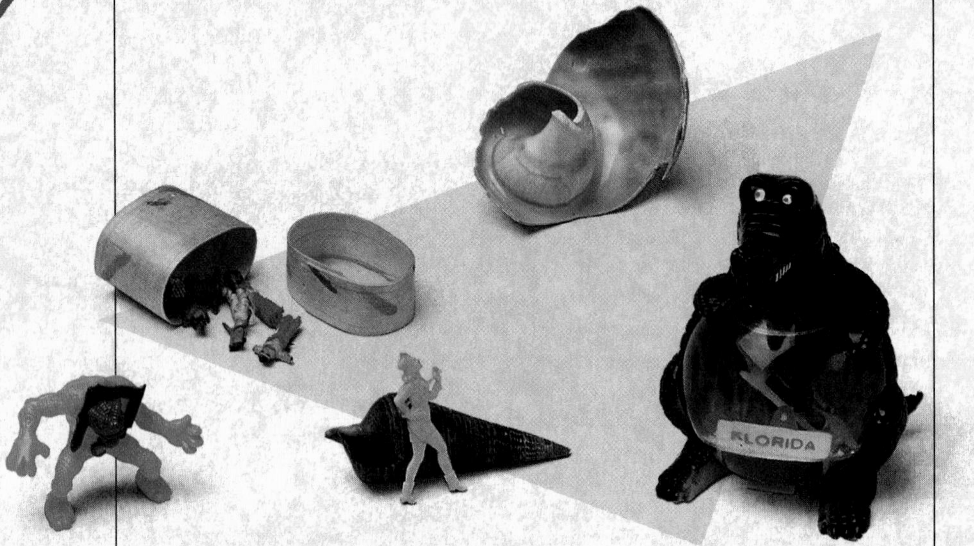

- Do any of these objects remind you of your childhood? Make a list of things you collected when you were younger, and freewrite about the memories they spark.

- What was the most important event in your life last year? What made it so important?

Show, Don't Tell

A writer keeps a journal to capture important thoughts, ideas, and feelings. Some writers expand journal entries into longer pieces of writing that *show* rather than *tell* their experiences. Try turning one of the *telling* sentences below into a *showing* paragraph.

- I don't know what I would do without my friends.
- I felt grown up.

26

Personal and Expressive Writing

Guided Assignment
Writing from Your Journal

Related Assignment
Friendly Letter

Do you ever wish you could keep track of what you do every day—the places you go, things you see, conversations you have? Do you ever feel shy about telling someone how you feel? Keeping a journal may be the answer. You can discover what you think and how you feel by writing in this safe and private place.

In this workshop you'll keep a private journal. Then you'll learn how you can take an idea from your journal and turn it into a piece of writing to share with others. In a related assignment, you'll have a chance to write a letter to a friend or relative.

Personal and Expressive Writing

Objectives

Guided Assignment

Writing from Your Journal To respond to samples of personal writing, to keep a journal, and to use journal entries as the basis of a piece of personal writing to share with an audience.

Related Assignment

Friendly Letter To respond to a friendly letter by a well-known author and to write a letter to a friend or relative.

Teacher's Choice

Use the following guidelines to choose the assignment that best suits students' needs.

Writing from Your Journal This assignment will benefit all students by providing an outlet for expressing personal feelings and observations, as well as an opportunity to learn how a piece of public writing can be developed from personal writing. Have students begin writing in their journals as soon as the school year starts. You may want to have students write in their journals for several weeks before they begin the drafting phase of this assignment.

Friendly Letter This assignment will motivate most students by providing a specific, familiar audience for their personal writing. You may want to suggest this assignment as an alternative when students choose a form for writing in the Guided Assignment.

Links to LITERATURE & LANGUAGE

Literature For examples of personal and expressive writing in different writing forms, see *Literature and Language,* Grade 6:

- Gary Paulsen, From *Woodsong*
- Gish Jen, "The White Umbrella"
- Eleanor Farjeon, "The Quarrel"
- Maya Angelou, "Life Doesn't Frighten Me"

Writing This guided assignment may be used as an extension of the Writer's Workshop, "Personal Writing: A Letter About Me," on page 58 of *Literature and Language,* Grade 6.

Guided ASSIGNMENT

ASSIGNMENT RATIONALE

Journal writing is one of the most useful forms of personal writing; it helps students develop the habit of expressing and reflecting on their feelings, observations, and ideas. Drawing on material from their journals for writing assignments that can be shared with others increases students' sense of personal investment in schoolwork and reinforces the fact that their personal point of view is of value.

Starting from LITERATURE

Motivate

Ask students whether they think most adults remember what it is like to be a child or a teenager. Then ask whether they have read any fiction or nonfiction in which an adult author captures the feelings of a twelve-year-old. Have them discuss authors they admire for this reason.

BUILD ON PRIOR KNOWLEDGE

Ask students if they have ever experienced a conflict between the way they feel and the way adults expect them to act. Invite them to discuss their experiences. Then read aloud the excerpt from Anne Frank's *The Diary of a Young Girl* in the Literature Connection at the bottom of this page. Have students discuss whether people have more than one side to their personalities. Lead students to see that Anne Frank was able to express in her diary the different sides of her personality. Point out that Jean Fritz recaptured her childhood conflicts in her autobiography (see More About the Model on page 29).

Guided ASSIGNMENT Writing from Your Journal

Starting from LITERATURE

Jean Fritz was born in Hankow, China. She lived there until she was twelve years old, when her family decided to move back to the United States. In *Homesick: My Own Story*, she writes about her last two years in China.

As you read this excerpt from Jean Fritz's autobiography, notice the way she shows how she felt about herself and her name. Have you ever had any of the thoughts or feelings Jean Fritz describes? How would you write about such feelings in a diary or journal?

from

Homesick: My Own Story

by Jean Fritz

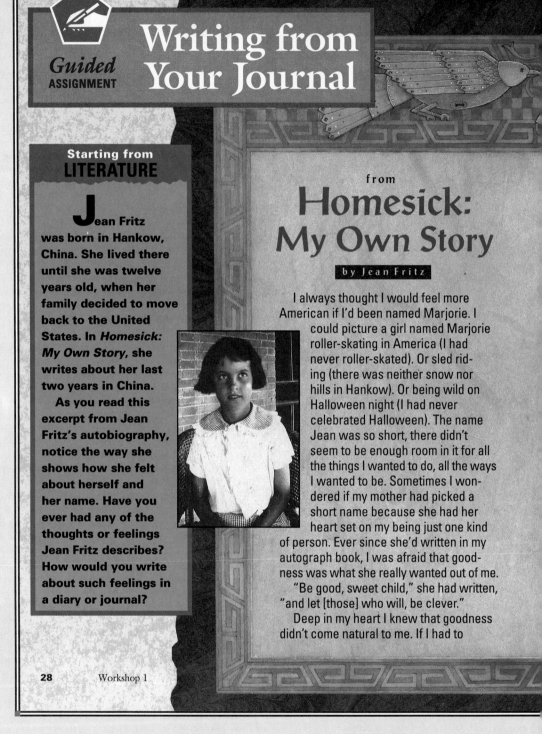

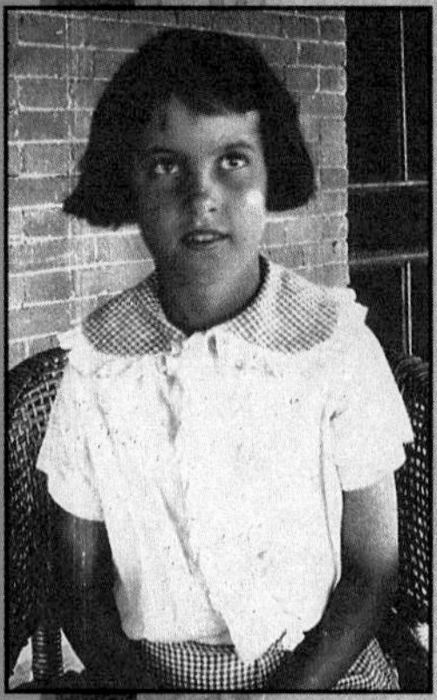

I always thought I would feel more American if I'd been named Marjorie. I could picture a girl named Marjorie roller-skating in America (I had never roller-skated). Or sled riding (there was neither snow nor hills in Hankow). Or being wild on Halloween night (I had never celebrated Halloween). The name Jean was so short, there didn't seem to be enough room in it for all the things I wanted to do, all the ways I wanted to be. Sometimes I wondered if my mother had picked a short name because she had her heart set on my being just one kind of person. Ever since she'd written in my autograph book, I was afraid that goodness was what she really wanted out of me.

"Be good, sweet child," she had written, "and let [those] who will, be clever."

Deep in my heart I knew that goodness didn't come natural to me. If I had to

Literature Connection

Students can compare Jean Fritz's feelings as a young girl to those Anne Frank expressed in *The Diary of a Young Girl:* ". . . I have, as it were, a dual personality. . . . I'm awfully scared that everyone who knows me as I always am will discover that I have another side. . . . I'm afraid they'll laugh at me, think I'm ridiculous. . . . If I'm quiet and serious, everyone thinks it's a new comedy and then I have to get out of it by turning it into a joke. . . . I start by getting snappy, then unhappy, and finally I twist my heart round again, so that the bad is on the outside and the good is on the inside. . . ."

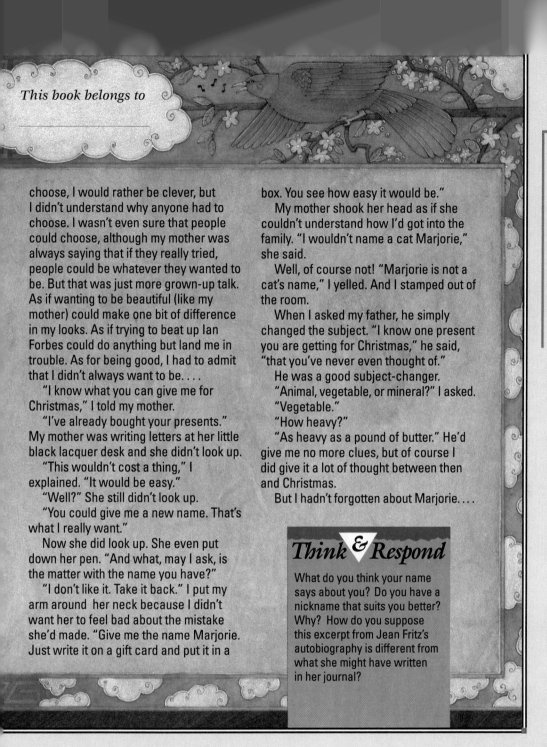

choose, I would rather be clever, but I didn't understand why anyone had to choose. I wasn't even sure that people could choose, although my mother was always saying that if they really tried, people could be whatever they wanted to be. But that was just more grown-up talk. As if wanting to be beautiful (like my mother) could make one bit of difference in my looks. As if trying to beat up Ian Forbes could do anything but land me in trouble. As for being good, I had to admit that I didn't always want to be. . . .

"I know what you can give me for Christmas," I told my mother.

"I've already bought your presents." My mother was writing letters at her little black lacquer desk and she didn't look up.

"This wouldn't cost a thing," I explained. "It would be easy."

"Well?" She still didn't look up.

"You could give me a new name. That's what I really want."

Now she did look up. She even put down her pen. "And what, may I ask, is the matter with the name you have?"

"I don't like it. Take it back." I put my arm around her neck because I didn't want her to feel bad about the mistake she'd made. "Give me the name Marjorie. Just write it on a gift card and put it in a box. You see how easy it would be."

My mother shook her head as if she couldn't understand how I'd got into the family. "I wouldn't name a cat Marjorie," she said.

Well, of course not! "Marjorie is not a cat's name," I yelled. And I stamped out of the room.

When I asked my father, he simply changed the subject. "I know one present you are getting for Christmas," he said, "that you've never even thought of."

He was a good subject-changer.

"Animal, vegetable, or mineral?" I asked.

"Vegetable."

"How heavy?"

"As heavy as a pound of butter." He'd give me no more clues, but of course I did give it a lot of thought between then and Christmas.

But I hadn't forgotten about Marjorie. . . .

Think & Respond

What do you think your name says about you? Do you have a nickname that suits you better? Why? How do you suppose this excerpt from Jean Fritz's autobiography is different from what she might have written in her journal?

from Literature box, have them read the excerpt from Jean Fritz's autobiography *Homesick: My Own Story.* Encourage students to compare Jean Fritz's feelings with their own.

Think & Respond

ELICIT PERSONAL RESPONSES

Have students consider the questions in the Think & Respond box. You might ask them to do some freewriting, expressing their feelings about their own names or names they wish they had.

Students may enjoy imagining what Jean Fritz might have written in her diary on the day she asked her mother for a new name. You might ask students to write an imaginary diary entry from Jean Fritz's point of view.

EXPLORE THE AUTHOR'S TECHNIQUES

The excerpt from Jean Fritz's autobiography is full of specific details remembered from her childhood. The details show readers ways in which her childhood was different from that of children in the United States ("I had never celebrated Halloween") and ways in which it was typical (wanting to change her name, feeling that her parents did not understand her, worrying about the contradictory parts of her personality and her mother's feelings, and wondering what her Christmas present would be). Point out to students how Fritz uses dialogue and creates a scene with conflict and suspense, shaping her memories into a good story that will hold readers' attention and move them emotionally.

MORE ABOUT THE MODEL

Author Note The daughter of missionaries, Jean Fritz (1915–) spent the first twelve years of her life in China. As a child, she loved her parents' stories about life in the United States and even felt homesick for a country she had not known. Needing an outlet, Fritz began a journal at an early age. At first, she recorded quotations from books she liked, but soon she began to record her private thoughts and feelings. This journal provided material for her later books, including her autobiography, *Homesick: My Own Story.*

Reading a STUDENT MODEL

This student model includes excerpts from the diary of a contemporary twelve-year-old who captured her feelings and experiences so well that her diary was eventually published. In the workshop pages that follow, students will see how these private journal entries could have formed the basis of a short story.

Motivate

Ask students if they have ever kept a diary and if they let anyone read what they wrote in it. Then ask whether they can imagine using any entries from their diaries as the basis of a short story, a personal narrative, or any other piece of writing that they might share with friends.

BUILD ON PRIOR KNOWLEDGE

Have students describe diaries they have seen. They might describe leather-bound books with locks, having designated spaces for writing about each day of the year. You might mention that a journal can be simply a blank book or notebook in which a person jots down ideas, feelings, or observations. Journals may also include drawings, photos, and clippings from other people's writing. Diaries, on the other hand, are usually more like daily records of whatever is important to the writer.

SET A PURPOSE

If your students have entered junior high school this year, have them meet in small groups to complete charts with the following heads: *What I Expected* and *What It's Really Like.* Then have the class discuss their charts. Later, as they read Latoya Hunter's diary entries, they can compare their expectations and experiences with hers.

If your students will not change schools until next year, have them discuss just their expectations, comparing them with Latoya's.

One Student's Writing

Reading a STUDENT MODEL

Writers sometimes keep their journals and diaries private. At other times, though, writers want to share the experiences they've written about. Twelve-year-old Latoya Hunter revised and published the diary she kept during her first year in junior high school. As you read these excerpts from *The Diary of Latoya Hunter: My First Year in Junior High School*, ask yourself whether you have ever had the kinds of experiences Latoya writes about.

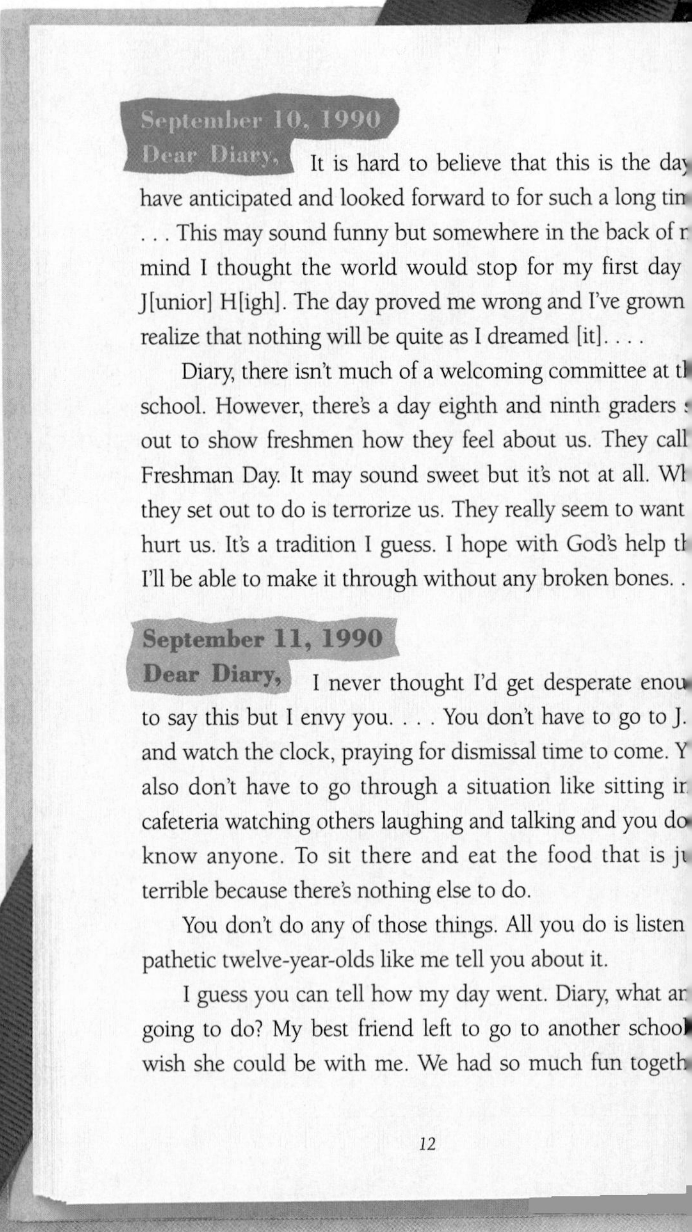

September 10, 1990
Dear Diary, It is hard to believe that this is the day I have anticipated and looked forward to for such a long tim . . . This may sound funny but somewhere in the back of r mind I thought the world would stop for my first day J[unior] H[igh]. The day proved me wrong and I've grown realize that nothing will be quite as I dreamed [it]. . . .

Diary, there isn't much of a welcoming committee at t school. However, there's a day eighth and ninth graders out to show freshmen how they feel about us. They call Freshman Day. It may sound sweet but it's not at all. Wh they set out to do is terrorize us. They really seem to want hurt us. It's a tradition I guess. I hope with God's help t I'll be able to make it through without any broken bones. .

September 11, 1990
Dear Diary, I never thought I'd get desperate enou to say this but I envy you. . . . You don't have to go to J. and watch the clock, praying for dismissal time to come. Y also don't have to go through a situation like sitting in cafeteria watching others laughing and talking and you do know anyone. To sit there and eat the food that is ju terrible because there's nothing else to do.

You don't do any of those things. All you do is listen pathetic twelve-year-olds like me tell you about it.

I guess you can tell how my day went. Diary, what ar going to do? My best friend left to go to another school wish she could be with me. We had so much fun togeth

12

30 Workshop 1

MORE ABOUT THE MODEL

When Latoya Hunter's class at P.S. 94 in the Bronx graduated from the sixth grade, the event was described in an article in *The New York Times.* An editor at a publishing company read the article and was struck by Latoya's teacher's praise of the girl's "incredible writing talent." The editor got in touch with the teacher to ask if Latoya would be interested in keeping a diary of her first year at junior high school. Latoya was willing, and her diary was published in 1992.

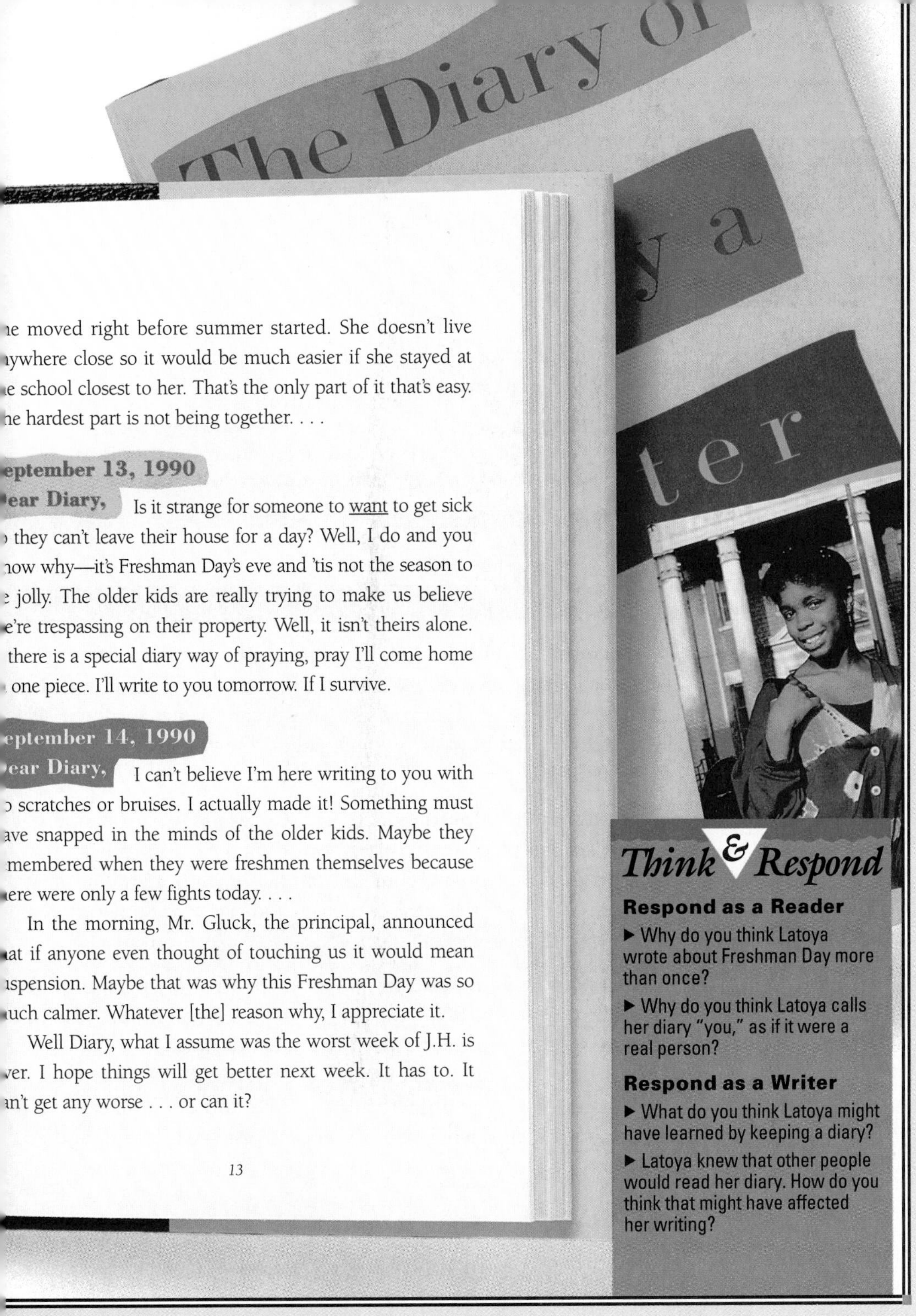

ıe moved right before summer started. She doesn't live ıywhere close so it would be much easier if she stayed at ıe school closest to her. That's the only part of it that's easy. ıe hardest part is not being together. . . .

eptember 13, 1990

ear Diary, Is it strange for someone to want to get sick ı they can't leave their house for a day? Well, I do and you ıow why—it's Freshman Day's eve and 'tis not the season to ː jolly. The older kids are really trying to make us believe e're trespassing on their property. Well, it isn't theirs alone. there is a special diary way of praying, pray I'll come home one piece. I'll write to you tomorrow. If I survive.

eptember 14, 1990

ear Diary, I can't believe I'm here writing to you with ɔ scratches or bruises. I actually made it! Something must ave snapped in the minds of the older kids. Maybe they membered when they were freshmen themselves because ıere were only a few fights today. . . .

In the morning, Mr. Gluck, the principal, announced ıat if anyone even thought of touching us it would mean ıspension. Maybe that was why this Freshman Day was so ıuch calmer. Whatever [the] reason why, I appreciate it.

Well Diary, what I assume was the worst week of J.H. is ver. I hope things will get better next week. It has to. It ın't get any worse . . . or can it?

13

Think & Respond

Respond as a Reader

▸ Why do you think Latoya wrote about Freshman Day more than once?

▸ Why do you think Latoya calls her diary "you," as if it were a real person?

Respond as a Writer

▸ What do you think Latoya might have learned by keeping a diary?

▸ Latoya knew that other people would read her diary. How do you think that might have affected her writing?

Think & Respond

RESPOND AS A READER

▶ Freshman Day was on Latoya's mind for several days. Have students point out details that show how worried she was.

▶ Students who have kept diaries may be able to explain that writing in a diary is like talking to a close friend. Tell students that some diary writers even give their diaries a person's name; Anne Frank called her diary "Kitty."

RESPOND AS A WRITER

▶ Students might say that Latoya learned to describe and to reflect on her feelings. To help them consider other benefits of diary writing, students should try to imagine how Latoya might react if, later in the school year, she reread her entries for this week. (Sample: She might be surprised at how worried and unhappy she had been at the time.) Ask what people can learn by looking back at their personal writing later on. (Samples: how to keep things in perspective, how experience and time affect how you feel)

▶ Students may say that Latoya might have left out incidents that were too personal or embarrassing, that she might not have expressed all her negative feelings about people, or that she might have been more careful about her language and grammar.

Writing
ON YOUR OWN

Remind students of the kinds of feelings and experiences Latoya Hunter recorded in her diary and the kinds of feelings and experiences Jean Fritz recalled and shared in her autobiography. Tell them that they will begin this assignment by writing privately for themselves in their journals. Later, they will identify some thoughts and feelings they would like to share with an audience.

Handbooks for Help and Practice

The following handbooks may be used as mini-lessons before students begin writing or as resources when problems arise.

- **Show, Don't Tell, pp. 239–242**
- **Peer Response, pp. 253–256**
- **Revising, pp. 257–259**
- **Personal Voice, pp. 276–277**

KEEP A JOURNAL

Objectives

- To choose tools with which to keep a journal
- To decide what kinds of material to include in a journal
- To freewrite daily in a journal and reread journal entries at a later date

Teaching Strategies

for COMPUTER TIP

HELPFUL HINT: PRIVACY Students may want to create a different file for each journal entry, and put the dates on the disk label. If students keep their files on a disk that is available to other people, they may want to protect their privacy by creating a private password that restricts access to their files.

Writing ON YOUR OWN
Writing from Your Journal

INVITATION TO *Write*

A journal is a place where you can freely write for yourself about the things that matter to you most. Jean Fritz and Latoya Hunter are two writers who found a way to share such personal writing with a wider audience.

Keep a journal and write in it regularly. Then turn one or more entries from your journal into a piece of writing you can share with others.

KEEP A JOURNAL

1. Use the writing tools that are right for you. Writing in your journal should feel comfortable and inviting, so use your favorite writing materials. Do you prefer a spiral or loose-leaf notebook or a book with blank pages? Do you like to use pencil or pen?

2. Remember, journals are private property. Your journal is a special place for writing about what's important to you. What's more, you are your only audience. Although you might later choose to share parts of your journal with someone else, no one should read the parts you want to keep private.

3. Write in your journal. Try to spend at least ten minutes each day freewriting in your journal. Remember, journal writing doesn't need to be planned, and it doesn't need to look polished. Therefore, you can start anywhere and write freely about whatever subjects are on your mind. On days when you're not sure what to write about, just start writing and see what happens.

COMPUTER TIP

Would you like to use a computer for your journal? If so, store your journal files on a separate disk to make sure your writing stays private. Remember to put a label with your name on it on your disk.

PROFESSIONAL NOTEBOOK

If, as a writing teacher, you think it is important to have access to students' journals, the following advice from Arlene Silberman in *Growing Up Writing* may help: "Journals of this sort may be worthwhile, but parents and teachers still wonder about the need for privacy. . . . The Boston Writing Project *Newsletter* proposed a solution: students may clip together any pages they do not want read. If students don't abuse the practice . . . their individual privacy can be respected, yet teachers will still be able to seek evidence of improved writing and expanded interests."

Journal Writing Ideas

Topics	Questions	Idea Starters
Memories	• What happened in the past? • What do I remember about special places or events?	• a stuffed animal, a tape or CD, an autograph, a ticket stub
People	• Who's most important to me and why? • Whom do I most admire?	• photo albums, family, friends
Issues and Ideas	• What problems in the world or at home worry me? • How would I solve them?	• newspapers, magazines, TV, relationships at home
Daily Events	• What happened today? • What are my future plans and dreams?	• classes, conversations, after-school activities

Writer's Choice Do you want to fill your journal with only your personal writing? Do you want to use your journal as a kind of scrapbook and include drawings, snapshots, or clippings?

4. Be a reader of your own writing. A journal is more than a place to write. Your journal is a wonderful book to read as well. It is the ever-changing story of *you.* Reread your writing each week and you'll discover what you've been thinking about most and how your thinking changes over time. You'll also see if you are expressing yourself clearly.

PREWRITE AND EXPLORE

1. Find a journal entry to turn into a finished piece. Your journal will have many entries about your experiences, thoughts, and feelings. Which entry or entries could be used as the basis for another piece of writing? Look for one or more of the following types of entries to find the best starting point for writing from your journal.

Writing **TIP**

Some writers find it helpful to reflect on what they've written in their journals. Write an entry every couple of weeks about what you've been writing in your journal. This kind of reflective journal writing may help you learn more about yourself and your writing.

GENERAL NOTE

HELPFUL HINT Tell students that the Sketchbook activities on pages 26 and 70 may help them find writing ideas.

for JOURNAL WRITING IDEAS

KEY TO UNDERSTANDING Point out to students that in their journals, they can write not only about real events and people but also about their daydreams and fantasies. These entries may provide useful material for future imaginative writing projects.

for WRITER'S CHOICE

INDIVIDUALIZING INSTRUCTION: LEP STUDENTS If writing, even for themselves, is difficult for these students, encourage them to focus on the scrapbook aspects of their journals. Then periodically ask whether you can look at some of the material they have chosen to include in their journals. By asking thoughtful yet probing questions about these materials, you can help these students put their feelings into words.

for BE A READER . . .

CRITICAL THINKING: DRAWING CONCLUSIONS After the first week of journal writing, set aside time for students to reflect on their writing. First, give students time to read silently all their entries for the week. Then lead a class discussion in which students share their feelings about journal writing and their conclusions about how journal writing will help them personally and as writers.

PREWRITE AND EXPLORE

Objectives

- To use prewriting techniques to find journal entries on which to base a piece of writing to be shared with an audience
- To explore a topic through freewriting

Social Studies Connection

To encourage journal writing about social issues, you may want to team-teach this assignment with your students' social studies teacher. The two of you can make sure that appropriate newspapers and magazines are available in the classroom and that time for journal writing can be set aside in both classes. Also, you or the social studies teacher may want to teach a mini-unit on reading a newspaper. (Many local newspapers provide educational materials for teaching such a unit.) Encourage students to develop their journal writing into public writing forms, such as a letter to the editor or a persuasive essay.

Teaching Strategies

for EXPLORING TOPICS

MODELING Students may feel more comfortable about moving from journal writing to public writing if they see you participating in the process. Consider sharing some of your journal entries and modeling the evaluating process you use in deciding which entries to use as the basis for a piece of public writing.

for EXPLORING TOPICS

PEER RESPONSE Encourage students to discuss their ideas in peer conferences. Peers should listen to each other's ideas and ask questions about whatever interests them. Caution them, however, not to tell the writer which topic to pursue, since this is the writer's decision alone.

for ONE STUDENT'S PROCESS

HELPFUL HINT To connect the freewriting in One Student's Process with the Writing Tip beside it, tell students that before she started freewriting Latoya might have asked herself the following questions: "*What* was I thinking about most during my first week of junior high school? *Why* was that topic so important to me? *How* do I feel about it now?" Encourage students to ask themselves similar questions as they explore their topics.

Exploring Topics

- **Feelings** Look through your journal for an entry in which you expressed the way you really felt about something. Did you write about a time when you were especially angry, sad, confused, or joyful?
- **Exclamation points** Did you write about something exciting that happened to you—a field trip, a day at the circus, your first concert? Find an entry about an event you'll want to remember years from now.
- **Common problems** Check your journal for an entry about a problem you faced and that other people might also face. Did you write about possible solutions? Would your solutions help others as well?

2. Do some freewriting about your entry or entries. First, ask yourself which parts of your journal writing are most worth sharing with others. Then, explore your ideas in writing. Don't recopy your journal; let your freewriting take you places you haven't yet explored.

Writing TIP

Try using the questions *who, what, when, where, why,* and *how* to examine your topic. You could even show your answers on a chart in your journal.

One Student's Process

Many of Latoya Hunter's September diary entries focused on her fears about Freshman Day. If Latoya chose this subject idea to write about, she could start by exploring it through freewriting.

Freshman Day—still remember it like it was yesterday. I was nervous for days. I took the rumors the older kids spread about what they would do to us so seriously. It's funny to think about now tho. I thought it would be so much worse than it was! My imagination really went wild—it took over everything I did. In my mind, school felt like a scary place for a few days. Maybe I can do something with that idea.

PROFESSIONAL NOTEBOOK

In *Growing Up Writing,* Arlene Silberman tells about a football coach who had his athletes keep journals: "Every Monday morning in season he has the members of the team write about the joy or dismay they felt after the previous Saturday's game and analyze why certain tactics either worked well or went awry. . . . One player wrote, 'This loss burns inside of me,'. . . and [another] concluded, 'Our desire was there, fate wasn't.' Clearly, students who are recognized for physical prowess can express themselves powerfully—provided they are writing about something that matters to them."

DRAFT AND DISCOVER

1. Start drafting. Use your journal and any freewriting you may have done to help you get started. Then write some more. You might begin by looking for bits of information you need to say more about. Also look for telling sentences you can turn into showing paragraphs.

2. Choose a form for your writing. What direction is your writing starting to take? Have you been drafting a letter? a personal narrative? a poem? This chart shows you some forms your writing might take.

If my journal entry is about...	A possible form might be...
• a specific event	• story, skit, letter to a friend
• an intense feeling, memory, or experience	• poem, personal narrative, series of revised journal entries
• a social issue or world problem	• letter to the editor or to a politician

Notice that Jean Fritz focused on a specific memory and wrote a personal narrative.

3. Let yourself shine through. The best writing comes straight from the heart, so be yourself. If you pretend to be someone you're not, your writing will sound phony and your readers may not believe what you say.

4. Think about your draft. Once you've completed a draft, take a break. When you come back to your writing, you'll be able to review it with a fresh eye. Reread your piece and decide if you're ready to share it with one or more peer readers. Would you rather make some changes first, before you show your draft to someone else? The questions at the top of the next page will help you and your readers review your draft.

PROBLEM SOLVING

"How can I turn my notes into an interesting piece of writing?"

To help you present your ideas, see

• Handbook 12, "Show, Don't Tell," pages 239–242

PROBLEM SOLVING

"How can I make my writing sound like me?"

To help you develop your writing voice, see

• Handbook 21, "Personal Voice," pages 276–277

DRAFT AND DISCOVER

Objectives

- To draft a piece of writing based on journal entries
- To respond to one's own draft and to that of a peer

Teaching Strategies

for CHOOSE A FORM . . .

KEY TO UNDERSTANDING: FORM Make sure that students understand that a *form* of writing is a particular shape or structure that the writing takes. Point out that a writer's purpose often determines the form he or she uses to express feelings or ideas. Mention that there are many forms of writing other than those in the chart. Brainstorm with students to come up with additional forms, such as an interview, a personal essay, or an editorial.

for CHOOSE A FORM . . .

INDIVIDUALIZING INSTRUCTION: LEP STUDENTS If these students are uncomfortable about sharing their feelings in writing, they may enjoy collaborating to create a skit. Have them meet in a group to identify a conversation, school event, or after-school activity that they all mentioned in their journals. Then have them act out the event, dramatizing what was done and said, as well as suggesting what was going on in the minds of the persons involved.

for LET YOURSELF SHINE THROUGH

KEY TO UNDERSTANDING: PERSONAL VOICE Tell students that occasionally, for other assignments, they may want to either imitate another writer's style or write from another person's point of view. In this assignment, however, each student should express his or her feelings or ideas in his or her own voice.

MULTICULTURAL Connection

Memories of ethnic celebrations and religious rituals can evoke strong feelings and lasting memories. If students have recorded such memories in their journals, encourage them to share them in forms unique to their cultural background, such as a form of poetry or song that they have heard at home.

for QUESTIONS FOR YOURSELF

INDIVIDUALIZING INSTRUCTION: BASIC STUDENTS If these students become frustrated with the requirements of the short story or poem form, suggest they switch to a more familiar form, such as the friendly letter presented in the Related Assignment. Telling their experiences to a close friend or relative may help them loosen up and write in a more natural personal voice.

for QUESTIONS FOR YOUR PEER READERS

PEER RESPONSE If a peer reader identifies sections of the draft that do not sound natural, have the writer tell the reader about the event, idea, or feeling he or she wrote about in those sections. The peer reader can write down some of the writer's spoken words; the writer may then use these notes to make the written text sound more natural.

for ONE STUDENT'S PROCESS

KEY TO UNDERSTANDING: POINT OF VIEW Tell students that stories can be told from the first-person point of view or the third-person point of view. In first-person narration, the story is told by using the pronouns *I*, *me*, and *my*, just as in journal writing. Point out that in third-person narration, the story is told by using the pronoun *he* or *she* when referring to the main character. Have students read Latoya's draft aloud, replacing the pronouns *she* and *her* with the pronouns *I* and *me.* Ask whether the story sounds more personal that way.

for ONE STUDENT'S PROCESS

CRITICAL THINKING: EVALUATING Have students evaluate Latoya's decision to begin her short story with the scene on the steps of her new school. What details does she use to show her fear and the cause of it? Do these details catch students' attention? What details could she have added? Can students think of a better way she might have begun her short story?

PROBLEM SOLVING

"How can others help me write?"

For help in working with your peers, see

- Handbook 16, "Peer Response," pages 253–256

REVIEW YOUR WRITING

Questions for Yourself

- Why did I pick this idea to write about? What parts of my draft feel most important to me?
- What form is my writing taking? What other form might be worth trying?
- Have I included enough details for my readers to understand my ideas?

Questions for Your Peer Readers

- How does my writing make you feel? What parts of my writing were most interesting to you?
- What questions do you have about my subject?
- Does my writing sound like me? What doesn't sound natural?

One Student's Process

Latoya's diary entries about Freshman Day and her first awkward days in a new school make a terrific starting point for a short story. Here's part of a draft for that story. (A friend's responses are shown in the margin. What would you have said?)

She stood outside of her new school feeling small and afraid. The steps rose high in front of her. She took the flyer out of her pocket and read it again. It said Freshman Day is Tuesday. Freshmen beware. When the first bell sounded from inside, the kids in the upper grades rushed past her. Up the steps and through the double doors. She was afraid because she had heard about what was in store for the new kids. The warning was right there on the flyer. The final bell rang and jolted her out of her daydream.

Peer Reader Comments

I was scared before Freshman Day too. Can you add some details that would show how she felt?

I wonder what it would be like if you wrote the story from your own point of view. Do you think it might sound more like you?

REVISE YOUR WRITING

1. Judge your responses. Think about your own answers to the questions on page 36. Which of your peer readers' comments seem most helpful? What ideas do you now have about how to make your writing stronger?

2. Decide what changes to make. First, see if you want to try a new form. If not, look for more specific changes you can make. Do you need to reorder ideas, add details, or clarify any information?

Paragraphs at Work When you're drafting about a personal feeling or experience, you may end up with one or two long paragraphs. As you revise, break your writing into paragraphs. Begin a new paragraph at these times:

- whenever there's a change in the action or setting
- whenever a new character begins to speak

LINKING GRAMMAR AND WRITING

Making Changes at the Best Time

When you work from your journal, translate notes to yourself into writing that others can understand. Turn abbreviations into words and brief fragments into sentences. Here are two revised lines from Latoya's journal.

Original

Cant believe Im here writing 2 U w/no scratches or anything I made it!

Revised

I can't believe I'm here writing to you with no scratches or bruises. I made it!

PROBLEM SOLVING

"How can I make my writing better?"

For information about revising your work, see

- Handbook 17, "Revising," pages 257–259

REVISE YOUR WRITING

Objectives

- To evaluate responses to a draft of personal writing and to revise a draft with those responses in mind
- To evaluate the form and details of a draft
- To analyze the structure of a draft, paragraph by paragraph

Teaching Strategies

GENERAL NOTE

MANAGING THE PAPER LOAD
Spot-check students' papers to see how well sensory details have been used to develop ideas. Point out areas where writers might provide more details.

for PARAGRAPHS AT WORK

STUMBLING BLOCK If this is students' first major writing assignment of the year, they may need some help with paragraphing and might benefit from Handbook 10, "Improving Paragraphs," pages 230–233. Students using dialogue in their stories or personal narratives should consult Handbook 22, "Using Dialogue," pages 278–280, and Handbook 43, "Punctuation," pages 586–589.

for LINKING GRAMMAR AND WRITING

KEY TO UNDERSTANDING: SENTENCE FRAGMENTS AND RUN-ON SENTENCES Tell students that their journal entries, like the original note in Latoya's journal, may contain sentence fragments and run-on sentences. In most cases, students would need to correct these sentence errors when drafting or revising a piece of writing intended for an audience. As an example, point out how Latoya added the subject *I* to the beginning of her sentence fragment. She then put a period after *bruises,* so that "I made it" is set off as a complete sentence on its own. If students need help with correcting sentence fragments and run-on sentences, refer them to pages 344–346. For additional practice, use *Grammar and Usage Practice Book,* pages 3–4.

TEACHER'S LOUNGE

"You'll find 'Classroom Discipline in 3 Easy Lessons' in fiction."

for ONE STUDENT'S PROCESS

SPEAKING AND LISTENING Have students listen as you read the revised draft. Point out that Latoya did decide to tell her story from the first-person point of view, as her peer reader suggested. Ask how the details that Latoya added improve the draft. For example, why is "hugging my books and looking back over my shoulder" better than "feeling small and afraid"? (The details of her physical movements *show* how Latoya is feeling, enabling readers to picture her clearly and vividly and sense how she feels.) Why is "like a dangerous mountain peak" better than simply "high"? (The simile provides the reader with a mental picture of how afraid Latoya feels.) Have students point out other details in the draft that show, rather than tell about, Latoya's fear.

for ONE STUDENT'S PROCESS

KEY TO UNDERSTANDING: PARAGRAPHING Ask why Latoya decided to start a new paragraph with the sentence "When the warning bell. . . ." (to signal a change in the action) Urge students to review their own drafts to see whether their paragraphing could be improved.

PROOFREAD

Teaching Strategies

for PROOFREAD YOUR WORK

COLLABORATIVE OPPORTUNITY After students have proofread their work, suggest they choose a partner with whom they can exchange papers. Then have them proofread each other's work. Tell students that sometimes a fresh eye can spot errors that the writer of a draft might overlook.

GENERAL NOTE

ASSESSMENT Because this assignment is so personal and may be students' first writing assignment of the year, you may want to give an informal response to students' work. You might also want to write comments that encourage students to continue keeping a journal and exploring their thoughts, feelings, and ideas in writing.

One Student's Process

Here's how Latoya might have revised her draft based on her reader's responses.

I ~~She~~ stood outside of my ~~her~~ new school hugging my books and looking back over my shoulder. ~~feeling small and afraid.~~ The steps rose ~~high~~ in front of me like a dangerous mountain peak. ~~her.~~ I ~~She~~ took the flyer out of my ~~her~~ pocket and read it again. ~~It said~~ "Freshman Day is Tuesday. Freshmen beware!"

¶ When the warning bell sounded from inside the school, the kids in the upper grades rushed past me ~~her~~. Up the steps and through the double doors. What surprises were ~~She was afraid because she had heard about what was~~ in store for us ~~the~~ new kids?

Terror. Pain. The older kids seemed to want to hurt us. Our arms would be branded with an "F" for "freshman" in permanent ink so we'd always know our place.

PROOFREAD

1. Proofread your work. Correct mistakes you have made in grammar, spelling, punctuation, capitalization, and paragraphing.

2. Make a clean copy. Make any last-minute changes you want. Then make a clean copy or printout of your work.

PUBLISH AND PRESENT

- **Form a reader's circle.** Get together with several classmates and take turns reading your work aloud. After each piece has been read, discuss how it made you feel.

- **Make a journal sampler.** Collect everyone's writing in a loose-leaf notebook. As a class, decide on a title for your sampler and write a one-page introduction. You might even paste a photograph of your class on the cover.
- **Design a bulletin board.** Find photographs or make drawings that suit the subject or mood of your writing. Then post your work on a classroom bulletin board.

REFLECT ON YOUR WRITING

WRITER TO WRITER

I've recently done a lot of experiments with scrapbooks. I'll read in the newspaper something that reminds me of or has relation to something I've written. I'll cut out the picture or article and paste it in a scrapbook beside the words from my book.

William Burroughs, writer

FOR YOUR **PORTFOLIO**

1. Add your writing to your portfolio. How did it feel to share your writing with others? Think about the following questions. Then write a note to yourself in which you reflect on your writing. Clip it to your final draft.

- What am I learning about myself by keeping a journal?
- How did I change my original journal entry to get it ready to share with others?
- What was easiest about doing this kind of writing? What was hardest?
- How might keeping a journal help me with future writing assignments?

2. Explore additional writing ideas. See the suggestions for writing a friendly letter on pages 42–43 and Springboards on page 44.

Reteaching

After students have completed their papers, assess the needs of students who were not successful in developing an effective piece of personal writing; then assign the appropriate handbook mini-lessons, as well as the appropriate Workshop Support Materials listed in the Teaching Preview on pages 25a–25b.

Concepts commonly requiring reteaching for this assignment are:

- **Handbook 10, Improving Paragraphs, pp. 230–233**
- **Handbook 12, Show, Don't Tell, pp. 239–242**

The following suggestions and resources may also be useful.

Lack of "Showing" Details Bring in photos of people expressing emotions. Have students list physical details that show the persons' feelings.

Absence of Personal Voice Have students record their journal entries for a week, then transcribe them.

Extension and Enrichment

1. Students may enjoy designing their own personalized journals with special covers, bindings, and page layouts.
2. Have students choose a form other than that used in the Guided Assignment to create other personal writing based on the same journal entry.

Closure: Reflect on Your Writing

Explain to students that thinking about how they might answer the questions will help them become aware of their development as writers. Invite them to choose one or two of the questions and write responses in their journals.

SPICE BOX

Students may enjoy starting a class scrapbook in which they can place concert programs, photos of school events, and other mementos. Invite them to include entries from their journals that comment on any of these events.

Related ASSIGNMENT

Starting from LITERATURE

Objectives

- To respond to a friendly letter
- To write a friendly letter telling about oneself and expressing an interest in the other person by asking questions
- To proofread a friendly letter and address an envelope correctly

Motivate

Ask if students visit friends or relatives who live some distance away and how else they stay in touch. (Samples: by audio or videotape, telephone, or computer) Have students list three persons they wish to see more often, and write one thing they would like to ask or tell each.

BUILD ON PRIOR KNOWLEDGE

Ask students if they and the people they know send and receive many personal letters. Why or why not? Ask students what they like best about getting a letter or card from a friend. (Samples: knowing that someone is thinking of them, getting a surprise in the mail, finding out what the friend is doing and thinking, being able to read the letter again)

SET A PURPOSE

Before students read the letter by C. S. Lewis, remind them that he is British, that the letter was written in 1945, and that some of the language is not the kind of language they use in informal writing today. As students read, encourage them to look for characteristics that give the letter a casual, friendly tone.

Related ASSIGNMENT

Friendly Letter

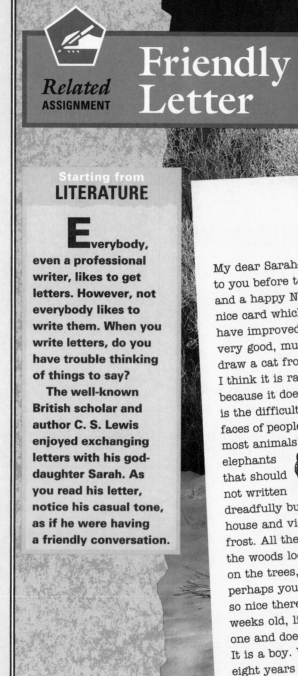

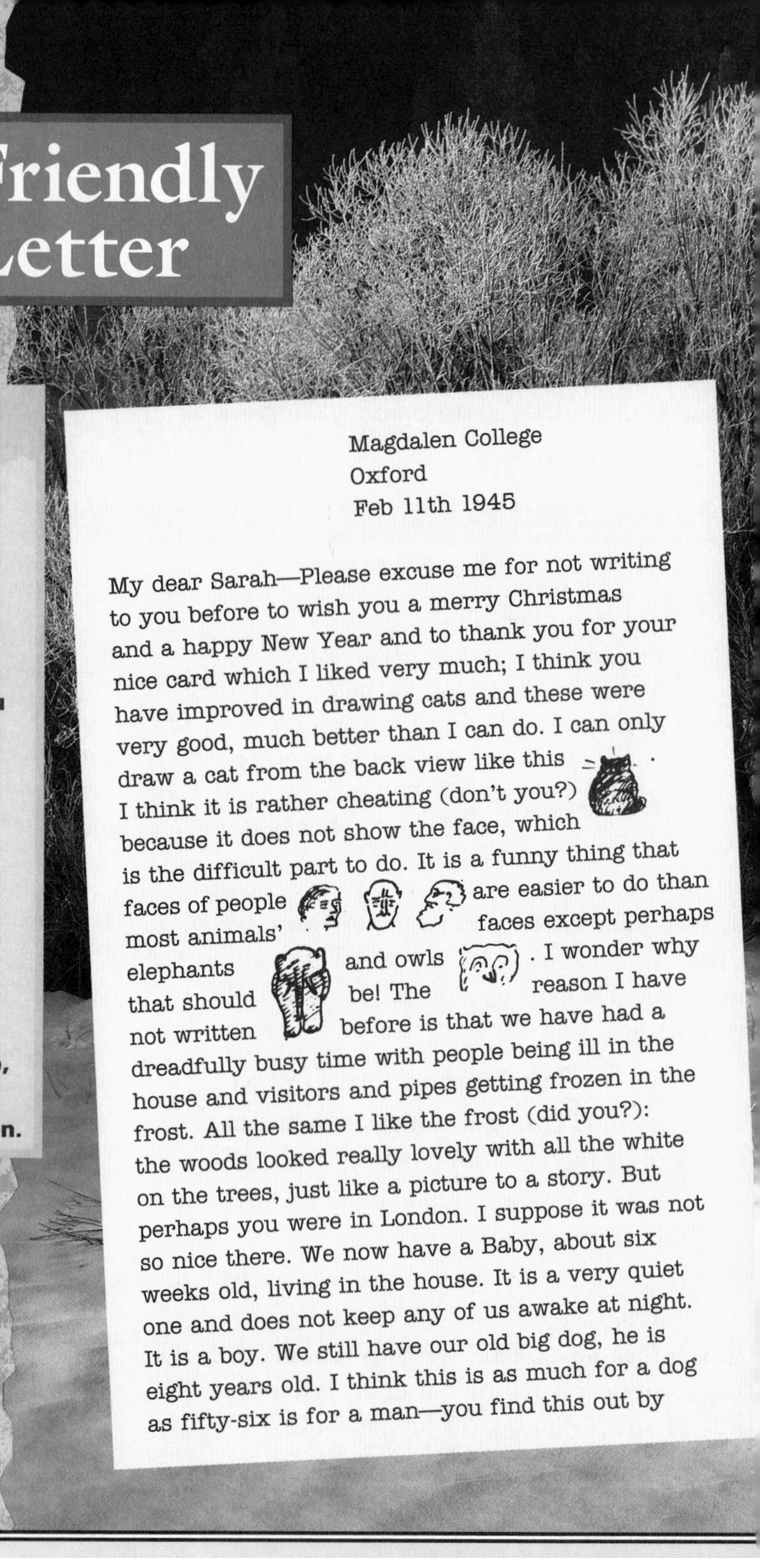

Starting from LITERATURE

Everybody, even a professional writer, likes to get letters. However, not everybody likes to write them. When you write letters, do you have trouble thinking of things to say?

The well-known British scholar and author C. S. Lewis enjoyed exchanging letters with his goddaughter Sarah. As you read his letter, notice his casual tone, as if he were having a friendly conversation.

Magdalen College
Oxford
Feb 11th 1945

My dear Sarah—Please excuse me for not writing to you before to wish you a merry Christmas and a happy New Year and to thank you for your nice card which I liked very much; I think you have improved in drawing cats and these were very good, much better than I can do. I can only draw a cat from the back view like this . I think it is rather cheating (don't you?) because it does not show the face, which is the difficult part to do. It is a funny thing that faces of people are easier to do than most animals' faces except perhaps elephants and owls . I wonder why that should be! The reason I have not written before is that we have had a dreadfully busy time with people being ill in the house and visitors and pipes getting frozen in the frost. All the same I like the frost (did you?): the woods looked really lovely with all the white on the trees, just like a picture to a story. But perhaps you were in London. I suppose it was not so nice there. We now have a Baby, about six weeks old, living in the house. It is a very quiet one and does not keep any of us awake at night. It is a boy. We still have our old big dog, he is eight years old. I think this is as much for a dog as fifty-six is for a man—you find this out by

40 Workshop 1

Links to LITERATURE & LANGUAGE

Writing This related assignment may be used as an extension of the Writer's Workshop, "Personal Writing: A Letter About Me," on page 58 of *Literature and Language,* Grade 6.

from

Letters to Children

by C. S. Lewis

finding what is seven times the dog's age. So he is getting rather gray and very slow and stately. He is great friends with the two cats, but if he sees a strange cat in the garden he goes for it at once. He seems to know at once whether it is a stranger or one of our own cats even if it is a long way off and looks just like one of them. His name is Bruce. The two cats are called Kitty-Koo and Pushkin. Kitty-Koo is old and black and very timid and gentle but Pushkin is gray and young and rather fierce. She does not know how to velvet her paws. She is not very nice to the old cat. I wonder how you are all getting on? Are you at school now and how do you like it? It must be about half way through term by now, I should think. Do you keep a "calendar" and cross off the days till the end of term? I am not going to post this till tomorrow because I want to put in a "book-token." You take it to a book-shop and they give you a book instead of it. This is for a kind of Christmas present, only it is very late. Now I have written you a letter you must write me one—that is, if you like writing letters but not otherwise. I used to like it once but I don't much now because I have so many to write, but my Brother does some of them for me on his type-writer which is a great help. Have you seen any snow-drops yet this year? I saw some two days ago. Give my love to the others—and to yourself

Your affectionate godfather
C. S. Lewis

Think & Respond

If you were Sarah, what things in the letter do you think you would have particularly enjoyed? Why? What details show that C. S. Lewis had Sarah's interests in mind?

Think & Respond

ELICIT PERSONAL RESPONSES

Before students answer the questions in the Think & Respond box, ask how old they think Sarah was when C. S. Lewis wrote to her and what details in the letter make them think so.

For the first question, accept any reasonable responses. Students may mention the drawings, the descriptions of the dog and cats, the mention of the "book token," or the questions.

In response to the second question, students may mention similar details: Lewis included the drawings because Sarah had included her own drawings in her card to him. He included a long description of his cats because he knew she liked cats.

EXPLORE THE AUTHOR'S TECHNIQUES

Point out that Lewis begins his letter by thanking Sarah for the card she sent him and by complimenting her on her drawings. In exchange, he includes his own drawings to entertain her. Tell students that people with an ongoing correspondence often exchange gifts, thank-you's, compliments, jokes, stories, advice, and questions.

Point out the unusual lack of paragraphing in the letter and say that this is an extreme example (not necessarily to be imitated) of modeling a letter on a conversation, in which unrelated ideas often flow together. Also point out the conversational asides in parentheses "(don't you?)" and "(did you?)." These enhance the feeling that the writer is talking directly to the reader in a friendly conversation.

The rest of the letter is filled with day-to-day news that might interest the reader, as well as questions for the reader to answer in her next letter.

for FURTHER READING

Letters to Read You might want to read aloud other selections from the book *Letters to Children* by C. S. Lewis. Students can compare and contrast the tone and subject matter Lewis used with different children, depending on his relationship to them and what he knew about their interests. In addition, students might enjoy reading the letters of some other well-known authors, such as Emily Dickinson, E. B. White, and Mark Twain.

Writing ON YOUR OWN

Remind students that in his letter, C. S. Lewis used a writing style that resembled his way of talking with a friend. Encourage students to imagine they are talking, as they write.

Handbooks for Help and Practice

The following handbooks may be used as mini-lessons before students begin writing or as resources when problems arise:

- **Personal Voice, pp. 276–277**
- **Letter Form, p. 609**

Teaching Strategies

for TELL ABOUT YOURSELF

HELPFUL HINT If students have been keeping journals, suggest that they review their recent journal entries to bring to mind what has been happening in their lives lately and what they have been thinking and feeling about their experiences. Then urge them to consider which events, feelings, and ideas they would most like to share with their correspondent.

for TELL ABOUT YOURSELF

COOPERATIVE LEARNING If students know a classmate who is sick or has moved away, they may want to work together to produce a scrapbook of letters, photos, and souvenirs to send to him or her. They might even produce a video letter to cheer up the classmate and keep him or her up-to-date on class activities.

for ASK SOME QUESTIONS

CRITICAL THINKING: MAKING INFERENCES Tell students that they can infer what kinds of information and questions a reader will respond to by briefly reviewing what they know about the person: his or her hobbies, age, pets, important friends and relatives, recent achievements, major or minor problems, and so on.

Writing ON YOUR OWN

Friendly Letter

INVITATION TO *Write*

Letter writing is a wonderful way to share your feelings with someone you care about. In today's world when everyone uses a telephone to stay in touch, a friendly letter is a special way to communicate.

Write a letter that shares with a reader something about yourself and your life.

KEEP IN TOUCH

1. Tell about yourself. You might write to someone you know and share news and information that is important to you and that will interest your reader. Notice that many of the subjects C. S. Lewis writes about—the cat drawings, his old dog, the frost, the book-token—are things that will have meaning to Sarah.

2. Ask some questions. Don't just write about yourself and your news. Also show an interest in your reader. What is happening in his or her life? Take your time and concentrate on writing interesting questions that call for more than just a yes or no answer. Remember that your questions give your reader a reason to write back.

3. What comes first? Do you want to share your news first, or do you want to begin with questions you have? For example, you might write to an uncle who has always been interested in your sports activities to tell him about your last soccer match. A letter to a friend who recently moved might begin with questions about his or her new home.

42 Workshop 1

PROFESSIONAL NOTEBOOK

Some teachers use the friendly-letter format to dialogue with students. In her book *In the Middle,* Nancie Atwell addresses her students in the following note:

"Your notebook is a place for you, me, and your friends to talk this year about books, reading, authors, and writing. You'll be chatting about literature in letters to me and friends; we'll write letters back to you. . . . In your letters talk with us about what you've read. . . . Tell what you thought and felt and why. . . . Tell what these books said and meant to you. . . . And write back about our ideas, feelings, experiences, and questions."

4. Be yourself. A friendly letter is like one side of a conversation. Choose words that are comfortable and natural to you. Use your own writing voice. Be funny or serious, depending on your mood.

TAKE A FINAL LOOK

Even though a friendly letter is casual and informal, what you write should be clear and understandable. Keep these suggestions in mind as you look over your letter.

1. Read your letter to yourself. Have you included everything you planned to say? Does your writing sound like you?

2. Details matter. Look for errors in grammar, punctuation and spelling that may confuse a reader. Since friendly letters are often handwritten, you might want to be sure that your writing is neat and readable.

3. Letters follow a form. A friendly letter usually includes a date, a salutation or greeting, a body, a friendly closing, and sometimes a return address. For more information about letter forms see page 609.

Address your envelope carefully so that your letter gets to the right place. Include your own address as the return address.

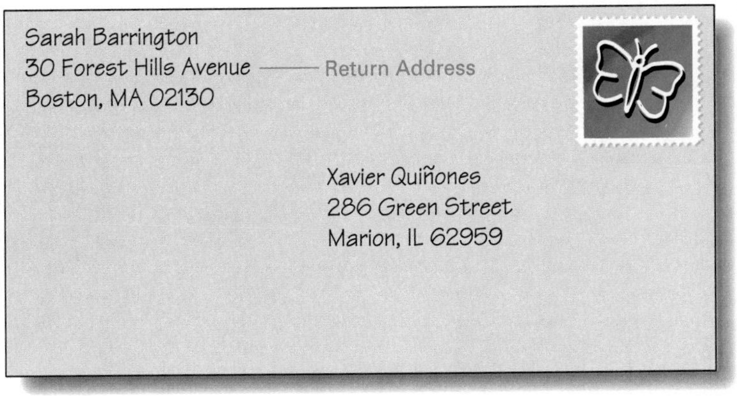
Sarah Barrington
30 Forest Hills Avenue
Boston, MA 02130
Return Address
Xavier Quiñones
286 Green Street
Marion, IL 62959

PROBLEM SOLVING

"What is my own writing voice?"

To write in a way that sounds like you, see

- Handbook 21, "Personal Voice," pages 276–277

for BE YOURSELF

INDIVIDUALIZING INSTRUCTION: ESL STUDENTS Recent immigrants with friends and relatives in their country of origin may write letters using their native language. If they wish, these students can work with English-proficient peers to translate their letters and share them with the class.

for READ YOUR LETTER . . .

PEER RESPONSE Although many students may not need or want peer response to their informal letters, some may want a second opinion as whether the tone or subject matter of their letter is appropriate for its intended reader. For example, the writer might ask, "If you were sick in the hospital, would this letter make you laugh?" or "Do you think I described our school's last football game in an interesting way?"

for DETAILS MATTER

INDIVIDUALIZING INSTRUCTION: LD STUDENTS If possible, allow students with poor fine-motor skills to tape record their letters. They then can ask a peer to transcribe the letters onto notepaper. Point out that even C. S. Lewis was forced during busy times to ask his brother to type letters for him.

Guidelines for Evaluation

AN EFFECTIVE FRIENDLY LETTER

- includes a date, a salutation or greeting, a body, a friendly closing, and sometimes a return address
- shows an interest in the reader
- is phrased in a way that sounds comfortable and natural to the writer
- is neat and readable

Social Studies Connection

Ask students if they would enjoy contacting sixth-grade students who live in another part of the country where the geography and life style are somewhat different from their own. Before students write, have them research the other town or area and then come up with questions they might ask the students in that part of the country.

Many teachers' magazines provide lists of classes that would like to correspond with classes at another school. Students may even decide to communicate by computer bulletin board or by exchanging videos, if the necessary equipment is available.

Teaching Strategies

for HISTORY

HELPFUL HINT The following books may be available in your library: *American Women: Their Lives in Their Words* by Doreen Rappaport (ALA Best Book), *To Be a Slave* by Julius Lester (Newbery Honor), *The Way We Lived* by Martin W. Sandler, and *Voices from the Civil War* by Milton Meltzer. Mr. Meltzer is also the author of the award-winning *A History in Their Own Words* series, which includes volumes on the Chinese, Latino, and African-American people.

for SOCIAL STUDIES

HELPFUL HINT To identify international pen pals for your students, query the following organization: International Pen Friends, P.O. Box 65, Brooklyn, NY 11229.

Encourage students who receive letters from abroad to post their letters on a classroom wall so as to share what they learn about the interests of their peers in other countries.

for ART

SPEAKING, LISTENING, AND VIEWING Display posters of several paintings for a week or have a showing of the art works in the *Fine Art Transparency Pack*. Then have students respond to one or more pictures in their journals. Once they have completed their entries, have students discuss their varying responses to the art. Emphasize that differences of opinion are to be expected.

Springboards

History What do you think life was like for women living on the Western frontier during the 1800s? Take a new look at a period in history by reading a historical journal or a diary. Your librarian can help you locate a journal. Use the journal entries to create a story based on a person's life.

SOCIAL STUDIES
With your teacher's help, find and write to an international pen pal. Tell about a hobby, sport, or topic of interest to you. Ask your pen pal similar questions to learn about his or her interests.

Art
Look through art books to find a painting that especially interests you. Use your journal to jot down your feelings about the painting.

Literature
Have you ever wanted to talk to a character in a story? Try writing a letter instead. You might offer advice, share a secret, or ask a question.

Three Musicans (1921), Pablo Picasso.

ART NOTE

Art critics have described Picasso's *Three Musicians* as a jigsaw puzzle of bright interlocking shapes. Done in the cubist style, the painting features rearrangements of the components of three-dimensional objects into flat, overlapping geometric planes. The painting also has aspects of a *collage,* an art form in which an image is formed from pasted scraps of different materials. The three musicians are a clown, a monk, and a harlequin. Have students discuss the mood of the picture. (Sample: Some may see it as cheerful or funny, while others may find it spooky or dreamlike.)

on the LIGHT side

Word Puzzles

If you have ever eaten a sausage, onion, mushroom, green pepper, olive, and pepperoni pizza, you probably know what this is:

everything
pizza

Since *everything* is sitting on top of *pizza,* this word puzzle says "pizza with everything on it."

Now see if you can figure out what popular phrase or expression each of these word puzzles says. Try inventing some of your own and sharing them with friends.

league

every right thing

R
G rosie I
N

T M
A U
H S
W T

F R I E N D S **standing miss** **F R I E N D S**

new leaf

wear
long

Answers: Little League; right in the middle of everything; ring around the rosie; what goes up must come down; misunderstanding between friends; turn over a new leaf; long underwear

Students might enjoy collaborating on a book of these and other word puzzles. Encourage them to submit their puzzles for publication in a school or local newspaper or to include them in their letters to friends.

Imitating Sentences

Objectives

- To analyze sentences by dividing them into meaningful "chunks"
- To recognize sentences with similar patterns
- To implement the techniques of professional writers through sentence imitation

Teaching Strategies

for CHUNKING SENTENCE PARTS

SPEAKING AND LISTENING To help students identify the correctly chunked sentences, ask volunteers to read each pair of choices aloud, pausing slightly at the slash marks. Have listeners decide which version is easier to understand. Afterward, lead students to see that a sentence part set off by commas usually makes up a single chunk.

Additional Resource

Sentence Composing Copy Masters, pp. 1–2

Answer Key

A. Chunking Sentence Parts

1. b
2. b
3. a
4. b

Sentence

COMPOSING

Imitating Sentences

Life would be boring if you did the same things every day. Likewise, writing can be boring if you write every sentence the same way. You can learn new ways to vary your sentences by imitating sentences written by professional writers. Notice how each sentence in the description below is different.

Model A The sword Dyrnwyn, blazing white with flame, leaped from Taran's hand and fell beyond his reach.

Model B The Horned King stood over Taran.

Model C With a cry, Eilonwy sprang at the antlered man.

Model D Snarling, the giant Horned King tossed her aside.

Lloyd Alexander, *The Book of Three*

ON THE MARK Use commas to set off information that breaks up the flow of a sentence.

A. Chunking Sentence Parts People read and write sentences in meaningful "chunks." That is, they break down sentences into groups of words that work together. Choose the sentence in each pair below that is divided into chunks of words that work together.

1. a. The sword / Dyrnwyn, blazing white with / flame, leaped from Taran's / hand and fell beyond his reach.
b. The sword Dyrnwyn, / blazing white with flame, / leaped from Taran's hand / and fell beyond his reach.

2. a. The Horned / King stood over / Taran.
b. The Horned King / stood / over Taran.

3. a. With a cry, / Eilonwy sprang / at the antlered man.
b. With a / cry, Eilonwy sprang at the antlered / man.

4. a. Snarling, the / giant Horned / King tossed her aside.
b. Snarling, / the giant Horned King / tossed her aside.

B. Identifying Imitations Divide the sentences below into chunks. Then decide which sentences have chunks that match the models on page 46.

1. Choose the sentence that imitates Model A.
   - **a.** Crashing over the rocks, the raft bounced and swirled as it sped through the rapids.
   - **b.** My brother Bob, smiling broadly with pride, crossed over the finish line and waved to the crowd.
2. Choose the sentence that imitates Model B.
   - **a.** The third baseman walked toward home plate.
   - **b.** The dog and cat, usually enemies, became friends.
3. Choose the sentence that imitates Model C.
   - **a.** In a flash, the horses bolted from the starting gate.
   - **b.** The toddler peered up with a cute grin, charming everyone.
4. Choose the sentence that imitates Model D.
   - **a.** As the game ended, the fans ran out onto the court.
   - **b.** Diving, the shortstop snared the line drive.

C. Writing Imitations Break each of the following model sentences from *The Book of Three* by Lloyd Alexander into meaningful chunks. Then write your own sentences made up of chunks that imitate the structure of the chunks in each model.

1. She unstrung the bow and picked up the arrows she had dropped.
2. To save his energy, he lay down on the straw and tried to relax.
3. He clambered easily to the top and perched there like an enormous crow, scanning the land in the direction they had traveled.

Grammar Refresher To learn more about sentence parts and how they work together, see Handbook 34, "Understanding Sentences," pages 338–373.

B. Identifying Imitations

Chunks may vary slightly but should represent logical sentence divisions. The asterisked items are the ones that match the models.

1a. Crashing over the rocks, / the raft bounced and swirled / as it sped through the rapids.
***1b.** My brother Bob, / smiling broadly with pride, / crossed over the finish line / and waved to the crowd.
***2a.** The third baseman / walked / toward home plate.
2b. The dog and cat, / usually enemies, / became friends.
***3a.** In a flash, / the horses bolted / from the starting gate.
3b. The toddler peered up / with a cute grin, / charming everyone.
4a. As the game ended, / the fans ran out / onto the court.
***4b.** Diving, / the shortstop / snared the line drive.

C. Writing Imitations

Chunks may vary slightly but should represent logical sentence divisions. Imitative sentences will vary as well but should follow the basic pattern.

1. She unstrung the bow / and picked up the arrows / she had dropped.
2. To save his energy, / he lay down on the straw / and tried to relax.
3. He clambered easily to the top / and perched there like an enormous crow, / scanning the land / in the direction they had traveled.

2 Observation and Description

Teaching Preview

Overview

Observation and description skills provide a solid foundation for informative, narrative, and persuasive writing. In this workshop students sharpen their powers of observation and learn to choose details that show, rather than tell, what they have observed. Workshop 2 includes the following Guided Assignment and Related Assignment, as well as the interdisciplinary project described on pages 47c–47d.

1. **Guided: Describing People and Places** calls on students to closely observe a person or place and then choose precise sensory details, examples, and comparisons to bring the subject to life for readers. This assignment encourages students to make judgments about their main impression of a subject, to select details that support their impression, and to classify and organize those details in an effective way.
2. **Related: Culture and Customs** invites students to observe and share details of an ethnic or religious tradition and to explain the custom's significance.

Preparation Guide

1. Use the Overview on this page and the Teacher's Choice descriptions on page 49 as a basis for deciding which assignments to teach.
2. Preview the assignments and the teacher's notes and identify concepts that may require preteaching or extra support, given your class's abilities. The handbook mini-lessons suggested within the lesson may also provide guidance.
3. Preview the chart below for support materials in the Teacher's Resource File that may be used with this Workshop. Resources are for use with the Guided Assignment unless otherwise noted.

Support Materials

WRITER'S CRAFT RESOURCES

Prewrite and Explore
Thinking Skills Worksheets, pp. 1, 9
Thinking Skills Transparencies, pp. 1–1a, 9–9a
Writing Resource Book, pp. 3–4

Draft and Discover
Elaboration, Revision, and Proofreading Practice, pp. 3, 17–19
Elaboration, Revision, and Proofreading Transparencies, pp. 5–6, 31–34
Writing Resource Book, pp. 5–7

Revise Your Writing
Elaboration, Revision, and Proofreading Practice, pp. 4, 17–19
Elaboration, Revision, and Proofreading Transparencies, pp. 7–8, 31–34
Guidelines for Writing Assessment and Portfolio Use, pp. 15, 25–27
Peer Response Guides, pp. 9–10
Writing Resource Book, p. 8

Assessment
Tests and Writing Assessment Prompts, p. 2

Extension Activities
Sentence Composing Copymasters, pp. 3–4
Starting Points for Writing, pp. 27–30, 37, 39
Writing from Literature, pp. 1–2, 9–10, 13–14, 17–20, 25–26
Standardized Test Practice

Educational Technology
(available separately)
Writer's DataBank
Electronic English Handbook
Multimedia Workshop
On Assignment! (videodisc)

OTHER RESOURCES

Books and Journals
Cisneros, Sandra. *The House on Mango Street.* Arte Publico, 1985.
Gustaffson, J. "Design a Character." *Reading Teacher.* 44 (Sept. 1990): 86–87.

Films and Videos
Pool Party. Fast Forward/Gary Soto, 1992.

Educational Technology
"Character Sketch/Language Delight." *Write On! Series.* Humanities Software, Apple.
Rain Forest. Image Entertainment. (videodisc)
Where in the World Is Carmen Sandiego? Broderbund. PC, PC/CD-ROM.

Linking Literature, Writing, and Grammar

The following options may be used to provide students with an integrated language experience. Begin by assigning and discussing any of the recommended pieces of literature. Use the suggested strategy to provide a link to the Guided Assignment.

LINKING LITERATURE AND WRITING

Option 1

Starting Point: "The Monkey Garden" by Sandra Cisneros on pages 50–51 of *The Writer's Craft.*

Strategy: Use the teaching suggestions on pages 50–51 to lead students into the Guided Assignment.

Option 2

Starting Point: "Ibrahima" by Walter Dean Myers on pages 234–243 of McDougal, Littell's *Literature and Language,* Grade 6. (Additional suggestions for using *Literature and Language* can be found on page 49.)

Strategy: Have students read the biographical selection. Then ask them to describe their main impressions of Ibrahima and his African homeland. Have them find descriptive details that support their impressions. Use the discussion to introduce the Guided Assignment.

Option 3

Starting Point: "A Backwoods Boy" by Russell Freedman.

Strategy: Have students read the biographical selection. Ask what impression of Lincoln the biography gave them and what details Freedman used to create that impression. Use the discussion to introduce the Guided Assignment.

LINKING WRITING AND GRAMMAR

Before the drafting or revision stages of this assignment, tell students that when they describe people and places, they may want to combine several descriptive details in one sentence. Write the following sentences on the board and ask how students might combine them in one sentence.

My Uncle Jeff is muscular. He is very tanned. He is also as tall as a mountain.

Show how the sentences could be combined, using a series of adjectives. Point out the commas that are needed to separate items in a series.

My Uncle Jeff is muscular, very tanned, and as tall as a mountain.

Suggest that students occasionally use a series of adjectives, verbs, or nouns in their descriptions.

Go over pages 574–580 of the Grammar and Usage Handbook. If problems in using commas persist, assign the exercises on those pages for reteaching. Additional practice can be found in the *Grammar and Usage Practice Book* on page 96.

Management Guidelines

The chart below indicates the number of days recommended for each phase of the Guided and Related Assignments. These numbers are an estimate of the total time needed for each phase. In practice, of course, students may not complete each phase in one continuous session, nor will they necessarily progress from stage to stage in the linear order shown here. Stars indicate portions of the assignment that may be completed outside the classroom if time is limited or if teachers wish students to work independently.

WRITING FROM PERSONAL EXPERIENCE

Starting from Literature	1 day
Prewrite and Explore	1–2 days
Draft and Discover	2 days*
Revise Your Writing	1 day*
Proofread	1 day*
Publish and Present	1 day
Reflect on Your Writing	1 day
Extension and Enrichment	open*

CULTURE AND CUSTOMS

Exploring Customs	1–2 days*
Describing a Custom	2 days*
Reviewing Your Writing	1 day*
Publishing and Presenting	2–3 days
Sentence Composing	open*

Project File

Celebrating Diversity: An International Fair

Overview

In this project, students will choose cultures to study in depth. They will then organize an international fair to present aspects of the cultures they have investigated. During the course of the project, students will learn about and come to appreciate many different cultures.

Students will participate in the following activities:

- Choose a culture and study it in depth
- Write a description of a specific aspect of a culture
- Create an exhibit presenting an important aspect of a culture they have studied
- Plan and put on an international fair
- Use language arts, science, social studies, math, and art skills to complete their research and develop materials

Preparation Guide

Tell students that appreciating and understanding cultural variety can make the difference between peace and conflict both in world politics and in interactions with neighbors. Students should understand that the term *culture* refers to all the elements—including traditions, customs, arts, crafts, and ways of life—that characterize a group of people.

Tell students that by presenting an international fair, they will learn more about their own cultures and those of others.

Stage 1
Explore Ideas

1. Invite students to discuss ethnic fairs they have attended or heard about. Encourage them to recall the kinds of exhibits and activities featured.
2. Propose that students organize an international fair. Ask students to brainstorm lists of the aspects of cultures that interest them most. They might list such items as the following:
   - toys and handicrafts
   - foods and customs related to food
   - songs, dances, and music
   - games, stories, plays, and books
   - clothing
   - holiday traditions
   - fine arts
   - interpretations of natural phenomena
   - famous people
3. Have students share customs and traditions from their own backgrounds with the class.

TEAM TEACHING

The following activities may be used for team teaching or as enrichment and extension activities by the language arts teacher.

Social Studies Have students investigate how historians and other scholars study cultures. Have them read books about cultures and study how museum exhibits are put together (see *Resources, Stage 1*).

Math Estimate how many people will attend the fair and calculate the approximate area needed. Study math tools, like the abacus, that are used by specific cultures.

Language Arts Read stories about cultural traditions and customs.

TEACHING TIPS

- Plan for the class to attend a local ethnic fair or an "international" picnic or field day held by a student-exchange organization such as the American Field Service (see *Resources, Stage 1*).
- Invite exchange students to speak to the class about their countries and cultures.
- Encourage students both to explore their own cultural heritages and to investigate cultures they know little about.

Stage 2
Research and Describe Cultures

1. Tell students to form groups and to choose the cultures they will present at the fair.
2. Direct the groups to research their chosen cultures in preparation for the fair, focusing specifically on the subjects of the exhibits they wish to develop, such as foods, crafts, costumes, and music (see *Resources, Stage 2*).
3. Have students write detailed descriptions of the exhibits they are planning.

TEAM TEACHING

Science Learn how traditions such as harvest and food-storage customs relate to the ecology of a specific area. Explore the nutritional values of traditional foods. Study holidays and traditions linked to solstices and equinoxes.

Social Studies Investigate the history, geography, and climate of a country or cultural area. Learn about daily life, religion, and customs.

Art Examine the fine arts of a particular culture. Learn about traditional costumes and find or create costumes for the exhibits.

Music Learn traditional songs and dances and prepare to perform them at the fair (see *Resources, Stage 2*).

Language Arts Learn descriptive-writing skills (see *Resources, Stage 2*).

TEACHING TIPS

- This project could involve a number of classes or perhaps the whole school.

- Explain to students that their written descriptions will provide a focus as they plan and create their exhibits.
- Remind students to consider practical issues related to the fair, such as the availability of the gym or playground and of facilities for preparing and serving food.

Stage 3
Plan and Hold a Fair

1. Encourage students to use art, photos, displays, costumes, food samples, music, demonstrations, and performances to present cultures in their exhibits (see *Resources, Stage 3*).
2. Direct students to publicize the fair at school or in the community by creating posters and signs, contacting local newspapers and radio stations, and creating a short presentation they can give to other classes or other schools. Tell them to invite parents and friends to attend the international fair.
3. Have students put on their international fair.
4. After the fair, hold a discussion, helping students to reflect on the project experience.

TEAM TEACHING

Science Make exhibits focusing on aspects of climate, such as seasonal variations in temperature and precipitation, that impact on specific cultures.

Social Studies Learn about specific cultural groups in your community. Learn about the importance of specific food products in various cultures.

Math Draw up schedules for the fair. Figure food quantities needed and adapt recipes. Lay out activity and display areas.

TEACHING TIPS

- Arrange student access to audiovisual equipment.
- Help students to divide up the setup and cleanup tasks fairly.
- Invite local media coverage.

Resources

STAGE 1

To find out about intercultural fairs and exchange students in your area, check with the **American Field Service** chapter at your local high school, or contact the organization's main office in New York.

Students can get overviews of cultures from the **Enchantment of the World** series (Childrens Press), which includes over 80 photo-rich books, each focusing on one country, describing people, foods, cultures, history, and more.

The Writer's Craft, Grade 6, Handbook 26, "Reading Skills," pages 298–301, teaches effective reading.

STAGE 2

Games and Sports the World Around by Sarah E. Hunt examines favorite play activities of many cultures.

Holidays Around the World by Joseph Gaer, with one section for each of five major world religions, gives details and backgrounds of holiday celebrations.

Folksongs and Footnotes, compiled by Theodore Bikel, contains songs from cultures around the world, arranged by theme.

A Treasury of the World's Finest Folk Song compiled by Leonhard Deutsch includes European songs, arranged by country.

The Writer's Craft, Grade 6, Workshop 2, "Observation and Description," pages 48–67, teaches descriptive writing. Handbook 12, "Show, Don't Tell," pages 239–242, offers in-depth instruction in this effective technique.

STAGE 3

Folk Crafts for World Friendship by Florence Temko gives instructions for handicrafts of many cultures and discusses their uses during festivals and holidays.

The Good Housekeeping International Cookbook, edited by Dorothy B. Marsh, offers international recipes categorized by country.

Public libraries shelve cookbooks of many cultures under the Dewey decimal number 641.5.

The Writer's Craft, Grade 6, Handbook 32, "Oral Reports," pages 324–325, can help students prepare oral presentations for their exhibits.

Additional Projects

School as Art Have students combine skills of observation and description with art skills to create a photo essay or a video showing the events, large and small, of a typical school day. Suggest that they photograph or videotape daily events over several weeks. As they edit their shots, they will learn about art elements and will practice critical viewing skills. Students should also write an introduction, a descriptive narration or set of captions, and an afterword to accompany their images. They can show their project at school or submit it to a local newspaper or TV station.

The Science of Toys In this project observation and description are used to link science, language arts, and several other content areas. Have students research child development and then visit preschools, observe individual children, and write descriptions of the children's behavior, based on what they have learned about developmental stages. Suggest that students, individually or in groups, design, make, and deliver toys appropriate to the needs, development, and interests of the children they have observed.

Sketch Book

Objective

- To use a cartoon and writing prompts as springboards to informal writing

WRITING WARM-UPS

Tell students that their responses to this activity will not be graded, so they should respond freely and informally to at least one of the Sketchbook prompts. They might begin by discussing their ideas and experiences in small groups and then freewriting in their journals. Students' responses may provide useful material for other writing assignments.

Writing about a dream, for example, could lead to a personal narrative or a poem in Writer's Workshop 3. All the prompts encourage generous use of details, a technique useful in Writer's Workshop 2 as students describe persons and places.

SHOW, DON'T TELL

The following is a sample of a showing paragraph for the first prompt:

The park on the first warm day of spring was a sea of moving faces and bodies for as far as I could see. There were old women dressed in hats and white gloves, and kids in cutoffs who seemed to have come straight from school or the playground. People were bicycling, roller-blading, jogging, strolling, tossing Frisbees, and walking dogs of every breed, from Chihuahuas to Saint Bernards. One man ambled by with a bright blue parrot on his shoulder. The most amazing thing, though, was that almost everybody was smiling.

Sketch Book

"Now now, Billy . . . How could you have seen a monster if you can't even describe him?"

- Write a description of a truly horrible monster.
- Tell about a dream you remember. Include as many details as you can recall.
- What is it like to be awake late at night? Describe what you feel, hear, see, smell, and taste, and also what you think about.

Show, Don't Tell

When you write about the world, instead of telling what you see, use details that show what you see—details that will bring a scene to life. Choose one of the telling sentences below and write a paragraph that shows the subject, using specific details.

- The crowd was interesting.
- Main Street is the center of activity in our town.

Observation and Description

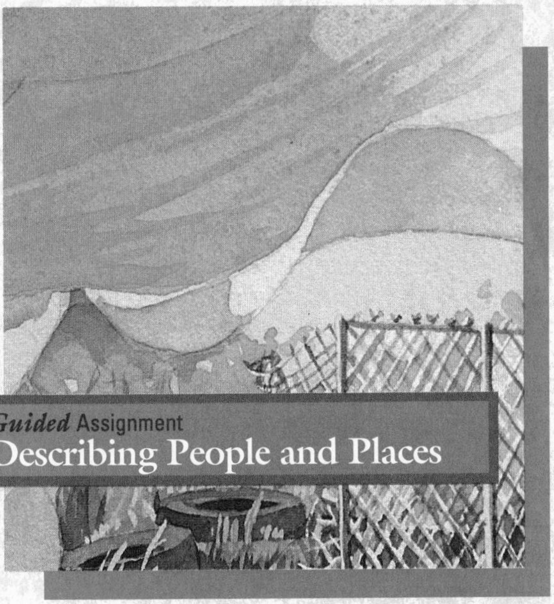

Guided Assignment
Describing People and Places

Related Assignment
Culture and Customs

Imagine a camera that captures not only how objects look but also how they sound, smell, taste, and feel. Impossible, right?

Wrong. You are that camera. What's more, the "pictures" you take don't have to remain trapped in your head. You can share everything you observe, feel, and think about a person, a place, or an object simply by writing a description of it.

In this workshop you will learn to observe and describe a person or place. In a related assignment, you'll see how the same skills can help you present the customs of a culture.

WRITER'S WORKSHOP 2

Observation and Description

Objectives

Guided Assignment

Describing People and Places To recognize techniques of observation and description in literature and to create a piece of descriptive writing that uses sensory details

Related Assignment

Culture and Customs To analyze the techniques used to describe the customs of a culture and to create a description of a custom, using those techniques

Teacher's Choice

Use the following guidelines to choose the assignment that best suits students' needs.

Describing People and Places This assignment will benefit most students by giving them a chance to develop the techniques of observation and description. The ability to observe details and use them descriptively is important in elaboration and in developing a personal writing style. Because descriptive writing is often used with other modes of writing, you will probably want to introduce students to the skills of observation and description early in the year.

Culture and Customs This assignment will help students see how descriptive details can be used in writing to explain.

Links to LITERATURE & LANGUAGE

Literature For literature that includes vivid descriptions of people and places, see *Literature and Language,* Grade 6:

- Walter Dean Myers, "Ibrahima"
- Toshi Maruki, *Hiroshima No Pika*
- Sue Alexander, *Nadia the Willful*
- Russell Freedman, "Frontier Schools"

Writing This guided assignment on observation and description may be used as an extension of the Writer's Workshop, "Descriptive Writing: 'You Are There' Biography," on page 148 in *Literature and Language,* Grade 6.

Guided ASSIGNMENT

ASSIGNMENT RATIONALE

Descriptive writing helps students to focus and sharpen their powers of observation and to choose precise and vivid language with which to express their observations. Studying description early in the year provides students with a solid foundation for narrative, informative, and persuasive writing, all of which call on descriptive skills for elaboration and for showing meaning.

Starting from LITERATURE

Motivate

Display to the class two objects that closely resemble each other but are not exactly alike. Then describe one of the objects. Begin with general statements that could apply to both objects. Let your description get more and more specific until the class can guess which of the two objects you are describing. Point out that specific details are what distinguish one person, place, or thing from another.

BUILD ON PRIOR KNOWLEDGE

Ask students to close their eyes and imagine that they are in a garden on a hot summer day. Then draw a cluster diagram on the board for the word *garden.* Have students contribute details. Help them categorize their contributions. (Samples: plants, animals, smells, colors, feelings) Point out that although everybody's idea of a garden is different, all have much in common.

Guided ASSIGNMENT

Describing People and Places

Starting from LITERATURE

Imagine reading this in a letter from a friend: "We just moved into a new apartment. I hate the wallpaper, but I guess I like the view out my bedroom window." Would you be able to picture the apartment or what your friend sees out the window? Would you need more details?

As you read Sandra Cisneros's description of a garden, see if you can picture the garden. Notice, too, the many details that appeal to your senses.

FROM The Monkey Garden

BY SANDRA CISNEROS

The monkey doesn't live there anymore. The monkey moved—to Kentucky—and took his people with him. And I was glad because I couldn't listen anymore to his wild screaming at night, the twangy yakkety-yak of the people who owned him. The green metal cage, the porcelain table top, the family that spoke like guitars. Monkey, family, table. All gone.

And it was then we took over the garden we had been afraid to go into when the monkey screamed and showed its yellow teeth.

There were sunflowers big as flowers on Mars and thick cockscombs bleeding the deep red fringe of theater curtains. There were dizzy bees and bow-tied fruit flies turning somersaults and humming in the air. Sweet sweet peach trees. Thorn roses and thistle and pears. Weeds like so many squinty-eyed stars and brush that made your ankles itch and itch until you washed with soap and water. There were big green apples hard as knees. And everywhere the sleepy smell of rotting wood, damp earth and dusty hollyhocks thick and perfumy like the blue-blond hair of the dead.

Yellow spiders ran when we turned rocks over and pale worms blind and afraid of light rolled over in their sleep. Poke a stick in the sandy soil and a few blue-skinned beetles would appear, an avenue of ants, so many crusty ladybugs. This was a garden, a wonderful thing to look at in the spring. But bit by bit, after the monkey left, the garden began to take over itself. Flowers stopped obeying the little bricks that kept them from growing beyond their paths. Weeds mixed in. Dead cars appeared over-night like mushrooms. First one and then another and then a pale blue pickup with the front windshield missing. Before you knew it, the monkey garden became filled with sleepy cars.

Things had a way of disappearing in the garden, as if the garden itself ate them or as if with its old-man memory it put them away and forgot them. Nenny found a dollar and a dead mouse between two rocks in the stone wall where the morning-glories climbed, and once when we were playing hide-and-seek, Eddie Vargas laid his head beneath a hibiscus tree and fell asleep there like a Rip Van Winkle until somebody remembered he was in the game and went back to look for him.

This, I suppose, was the reason why we went there. Far away from where our mothers could find us. We and a few old dogs who lived inside the empty cars.

Think & Respond

Discuss the "pictures" or details you liked best in Cisneros's description. What words and phrases did Cisneros use to make these details stand out for you? To which of your senses do these words and phrases appeal? Do you have a similar place—a park, a backyard, a vacant lot—where you play? Describe your place to your classmates in a way that they will remember.

Links to Literature & Language

Literature For another example of writing by Sandra Cisneros, see the short story "Eleven" on page 68 of *Literature and Language,* Grade 6.

SET A PURPOSE

To help students focus on the purpose-setting statement at the end of Starting from Literature, ask them to think about how they gathered details about the garden. Did they use their senses? Which ones? As they read Sandra Cisneros's description, have them try to imagine her garden. What words help them visualize it? Suggest that they note the senses to which those words appeal.

Think & Respond

ELICIT PERSONAL RESPONSES

After students have had a chance to discuss the details they like in Cisneros's description, ask them whether the description of the monkey garden reminds them of any special places of their own. Invite volunteers to describe places they particularly like. You might also describe a special childhood place of your own or a favorite place where you and your friends gather.

EXPLORE THE AUTHOR'S TECHNIQUES

To help students use the excerpt as a model for writing, draw a chart on the board with columns labeled *Sight, Sound, Smell, Taste,* and *Touch.* Invite students to list words and phrases from the model that appeal to each sense. (Samples: *Sight*—"The deep red fringe of theater curtains," "an avenue of ants;" *Sound*—"wild screaming," "twangy yakkety-yak," "guitars humming;" *Smell*—"rotting wood, damp earth, and dusty hollyhocks;" *Taste*—"sweet sweet peach trees, big green apples;" *Touch*—"thorn roses and thistle," "itch and itch," "hard as knees," "crusty") Challenge students to look for color words and for comparisons that use the words *like* or *as.* (Samples: "big as flowers on Mars," "Dead cars . . . like mushrooms") Tell students they may want to use sensory details like these in their own descriptive writing.

Reading a STUDENT MODEL

Like Sandra Cisneros, student Alisa Monnier chose to write about a special place. Her description is the final draft of the piece that students will see in process on the workshop pages that follow.

Motivate

Ask students whether they ever travel to interesting places. Do they like to send or collect postcards so their friends can see where they have been? Have they ever wanted to go to a far-off place someone else told them about? Invite student responses. Tell students that in the description they will read, Alisa Monnier shares such a far-off place with them.

BUILD ON PRIOR KNOWLEDGE

Ask students to share what they know about Japan. If possible, ask someone to locate it on a map or globe. What do students notice about it? (It is a group of islands, set in the ocean. It is very mountainous.) Students may be interested to know that Japan is a little smaller geographically than the state of California but has more than four times as many people. Ask students what we import from Japan. (Samples: cars, electronic equipment) What do they think Japan is like? (Samples: crowded, modern)

SET A PURPOSE

Remind students to look for details that appeal to the senses, as they read. How do such details help them form a picture in their minds? (Sample: They tell what colors, shapes, and sizes things are and how they taste, smell, sound, and feel.) Encourage students to note the details that Alisa uses to help them picture Japan.

One Student's Writing

Reading a STUDENT MODEL

Sandra Cisneros described in vivid detail a place that was very special to her as a young girl. Like Cisneros, each of us has someplace or someone that is special to us.

The special place of sixth grader Alisa Monnier is Japan. As you read her description of Japan, notice the details that help you to experience the city streets and mountain views as if you were there.

Japan
Alisa Monnier

Japan is a group of wonderful islands off the coast of Asia. I look forward to going there every year. When I go to Japan with my mother and sister, we stay with relatives: my aunt Tomoko, my uncle Hideyuki and his wife, my cousin Hidenori, and my grandma Hideko. I enjoy exploring the cities of Kitakyushu and Beppu. I also love the large green mountains right behind the house where my relatives live.

Kitakyushu, my mother's hometown, is a big city. It has a population of over 1 million. It is filled with modern skyscrapers and department stores. Each summer Kitakyushu has a large day-long festival called Gion Matsuri [gē′ôn mät so͞o′dē]. This festival is an exciting combination of sights and sounds. People wear Japanese kimonos and other brightly colored outfits, and special entertainers dance down the street to the rhythm of music and the beat of a drum. Many vendors set up little tents along the streets where they sell cotton candy, barbecued meat, toys, and even pet turtles and goldfish. The party continues all day and lasts late into the night, filling the air with the delicious smell of barbecue and the wonderful sounds of music and laughter. I cherish living in such an exciting city as Kitakyushu during the summer.

MULTICULTURAL Connection

Encourage students who have lived in or visited their families' countries of origin to describe those countries to the class. Urge them to bring photos, costumes, and other items to display. Suggest that these places may make good writing topics for this assignment.

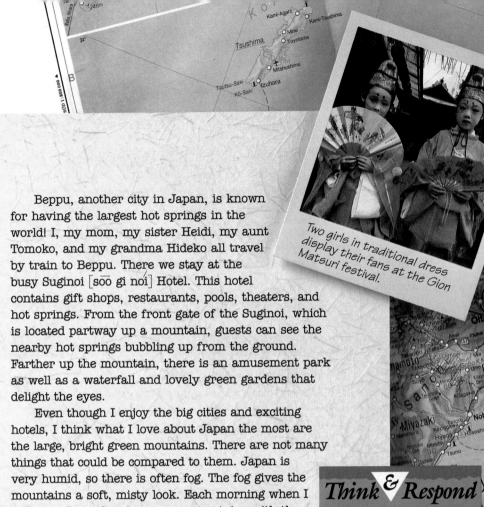

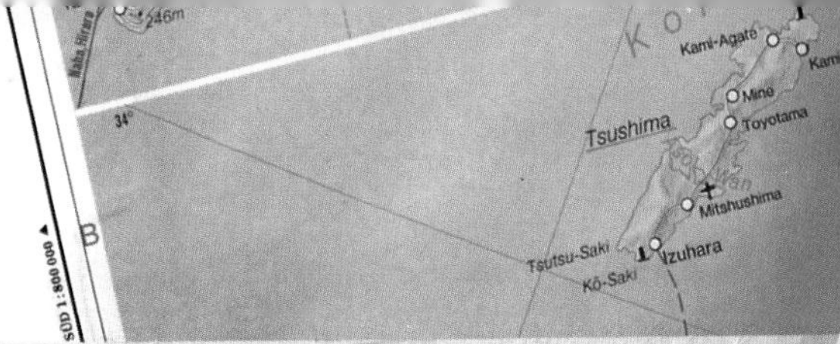

Two girls in traditional dress display their fans at the Gion Matsuri festival.

Beppu, another city in Japan, is known for having the largest hot springs in the world! I, my mom, my sister Heidi, my aunt Tomoko, and my grandma Hideko all travel by train to Beppu. There we stay at the busy Suginoi [sōō gi noi´] Hotel. This hotel contains gift shops, restaurants, pools, theaters, and hot springs. From the front gate of the Suginoi, which is located partway up a mountain, guests can see the nearby hot springs bubbling up from the ground. Farther up the mountain, there is an amusement park as well as a waterfall and lovely green gardens that delight the eyes.

Even though I enjoy the big cities and exciting hotels, I think what I love about Japan the most are the large, bright green mountains. There are not many things that could be compared to them. Japan is very humid, so there is often fog. The fog gives the mountains a soft, misty look. Each morning when I wake up, I see these gorgeous mountains with the sun rising behind them. I always look forward to seeing the mountains when I go to Japan. They are another beautiful part of our world.

Japan is a great place to visit. I love the summer festival in Kitakyushu, the hotel and hot springs in Beppu, and the beauty of the mountains. Japan is exciting, relaxing, and beautiful.

Think & Respond

Respond as a Reader

▶ What part of Alisa's description do you picture most clearly and vividly?

▶ What did you learn from her first paragraph?

Respond as a Writer

▶ What are some of the details that help bring Kitakyushu, Beppu, and the mountains to life?

▶ How does Alisa's use of paragraphs help her make clear the details she provides about Kitakyushu, Beppu, and the mountains?

Think & Respond

RESPOND AS A READER

▶ As students choose the parts of the description that they can picture most vividly, ask them to point out details that helped them form their mental pictures.

▶ Students may say that Japan is a group of islands with cities and large green mountains; some of the writer's relatives live in Japan.

RESPOND AS A WRITER

▶ Students may choose such details as "many vendors set up little tents" at the festival in Kitakyushu (paragraph 2); "gift shops, restaurants, pools, theaters, and hot springs" at Beppu (paragraph 3); and the "soft, misty look" of the mountains (paragraph 4).

▶ Students should note that Alisa begins with a paragraph that introduces her subject by telling three things she likes about Japan. Then she devotes one paragraph to each of these three things. In the last paragraph, she concludes by summing up why she likes Japan.

Draw Conclusions

To make sure that students understand this introduction to descriptive writing, ask them to list the characteristics they have noted thus far. Responses may include:

- a main impression
- sensory details
- vivid language

Social Studies Connection

Students who have moved from one part of the country to another or who frequently visit relatives in other places might like to write about another region or state. Encourage them to think of details that show how their subject is special and different from where they now live.

Writing ON YOUR OWN

Remind students of everyday occasions on which they describe something to friends, parents, or teachers. Say that in this Guided Assignment, they will have a chance to sharpen their powers of observation and description. Remind them of how Sandra Cisneros and Alisa Monnier used words and details that appeal to the senses. Ask students to look for similar details to include in their descriptions.

Handbooks for Help and Practice

The following handbooks may be used as mini-lessons before students begin writing or as resources when problems arise.

- **Thinking with Pictures, pp. 192–196**
- **Finding a Starting Point, pp. 197–202**
- **Organizing Details, pp. 217–221**
- **Show, Don't Tell, pp. 239–242**
- **Appealing to the Senses, pp. 266–273**

PREWRITE AND EXPLORE

Objectives

- To use prewriting techniques to select a subject for descriptive writing
- To gather sensory details for descriptive writing

Teaching Strategies

for EXPLORING TOPICS

HELPFUL HINT: IDENTIFYING TOPICS You might point out that Sandra Cisneros chose a fairly limited topic, a garden, whereas Alisa Monnier chose a larger one, Japan. Have students review Alisa's description for other ideas that she might have developed into compositions. (Samples: the Gion Matsuri festival, the Suginoi Hotel grounds, and the mountains) Ask how Alisa might have developed each of these topics. (Sample: by gathering more details and describing it more fully)

Writing ON YOUR OWN

Describing People and Places

INVITATION TO *Write*

Sandra Cisneros and Alisa Monnier both described places that were special to them. Through their descriptions, you explored an overgrown garden and visited Japan.

Choose a person or place that matters to you or interests you. Then write a vivid description that brings your subject to life.

This float is one of many in a *Gion Matsuri* parade. This Japanese festival dates back to the year 869 and commemorates the end of a terrible epidemic that had struck Kyoto.

PREWRITE AND EXPLORE

1. Find an interesting subject. Have you been someplace you wish your friends could have seen? Do you know someone you'd like your parents to meet? If so, you may already have a subject you'd like to describe. If not, try one or more of the following activities.

Exploring Topics

- **Be on the lookout.** Your subject might be someone or someplace you see every day. For example, Sandra Cisneros wrote about an abandoned garden that she used to play in.
- **Take a photo safari.** Hunt through old snapshots to find people and places you might want to capture in a description. **List** the possible subjects you find.
- **Dig up the past.** Reread old letters, postcards, or journal entries to recall some of the people and places that have been part of your life. Note the subjects you find especially interesting or still care about. Then explore them further by **freewriting.**

2. Choose a subject. Pick the subject that interests you most. If you can't make up your mind, freewriting about some of your favorites may help.

3. Gather details. To paint word pictures, you need details. These activities can help you gather details:

- **Go right to the source.** Look at photographs, postcards, souvenirs, and other items that might trigger memories of your subject. If your subject is a person, ask questions of him or her. If your subject is a place you can revisit, do so to gather details.
- **Close your eyes and open your mind.** Imagine your subject. Ask yourself what you see, hear, smell, taste, and feel. Then draw a **sketch** or complete an **observation chart** or an **idea tree.**
- **Listen to yourself.** Describe your subject to a friend, letting your friend ask you questions. Then jot down the incidents, examples, sensory details, and comparisons you used as you answered your friend's questions.

One Student's Process

Here's an idea tree that Alisa Monnier created to gather details about Kitakyushu, Japan.

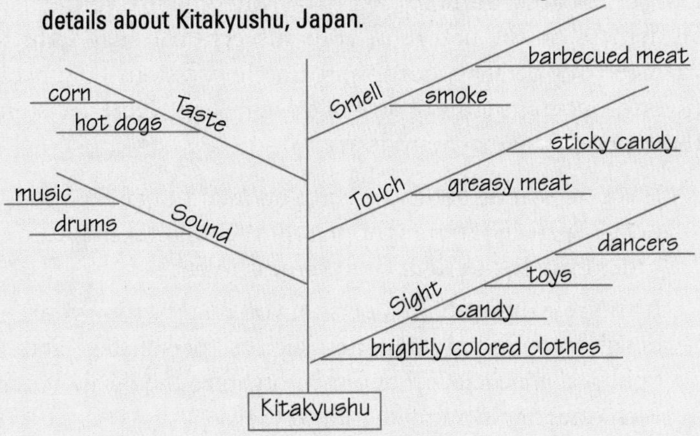

Writing TIP

You will have more fun writing if you choose a subject that you care about.

PROBLEM SOLVING

"Where can I find out more about graphic devices?"

For more information on graphic devices, see

- Handbook 1, "Thinking with Pictures," pages 192–196

GENERAL NOTE

HELPFUL HINT Tell students that the Sketchbook activities on pages 48 and 70 may help them find writing ideas.

for GATHER DETAILS

STUMBLING BLOCK Students who choose to describe a place may fall into the trap of trying to cover too large an area. Suggest that they imagine that they are taking a picture and limit their description to what will fit into just one or two photographs. They can decide whether to take a distance shot or a close-up, but point out that if they take in too wide an area, much of the detail will be lost.

for GATHER DETAILS

KEY TO UNDERSTANDING: SENSORY DETAILS To get students thinking about sensory details, lead the class in brainstorming lists of words and details that appeal to each sense. Point out that some details can appeal to more than one sense; for example, *mud puddle* might appeal to both sight and touch; *lilacs* appeal to both sight and smell.

for GATHER DETAILS

INDIVIDUALIZING INSTRUCTION: ESL STUDENTS Students with limited English vocabularies may find it helpful to gather details in their first language. Then pair them with fluent English speakers who can help them use a bilingual dictionary to find exact translations and vivid English words for sensory details.

for ONE STUDENT'S PROCESS

HELPFUL HINT: GRAPHIC DEVICES Point out that Alisa's idea tree contains a branch for each kind of sensory experience: sight, sound, taste, touch, and smell. Whatever sort of graphic they create, students should try to include all five categories.

DRAFT AND DISCOVER

Objectives

- To draft a descriptive piece of writing
- To respond to one's own draft and to that of a peer

Teaching Strategies

for START WRITING

HELPFUL HINT: DRAFTING Remind students that they can draft their ideas in any order and move the paragraphs around later. Suggest that they may find it easier to write introductions after they have created their detail paragraphs.

for ORGANIZE YOUR DETAILS

INDIVIDUALIZING INSTRUCTION: VISUAL LEARNERS Some students may find it easier to understand spatial organization if they work from a picture. Show these students a photograph and ask them to list the details in a particular order––top to bottom, right to left, near to far, or from the edges to the center. Then encourage them to use the same technique in organizing details in their written descriptions.

Writing TIP

If you find as you draft that you don't have much to say about your subject, do more prewriting and exploring to gather additional details or to find a new subject.

PROBLEM SOLVING

"How can I show what I think and feel?"

For tips on showing instead of telling, see

- Handbook 12, "Show, Don't Tell," pages 239–242

DRAFT AND DISCOVER

1. Start writing. Now begin drafting your description. You might start by describing the feature you like best or the one that is clearest in your mind. Then move on to descriptions of other details of your subject.

2. Create a main impression. As you write, decide what is most important to you about your subject. Then choose details that help show this feature or quality of your subject. For example, Cisneros focuses on the wildness of the garden, including many details that show what a free and untamed place the garden was.

3. Show, don't tell. For instance, you might describe specific incidents that show what a person or place is like. Cisneros provides two incidents to show that "things had a way of disappearing in the garden, as if the garden itself ate them or as if with its old-man memory it put them away and forgot them." She writes, "Nenny found a dollar and a dead mouse between two rocks in the stone wall . . . and once . . . Eddie Vargas laid his head beneath a hibiscus tree and fell asleep there like a Rip Van Winkle. . . ."

4. Organize your details. The way you organize your details will depend on the nature of your subject. You may want to organize your details according to the impressions they made on you—putting the most striking details first. Here are some other options you may want to try:

- If you're writing about a place, you might organize your details spatially. You might present them, for example, in order from left to right or from near to far.
- If you're writing about a person, you might group your details into general categories, such as "personality" and "physical appearance," and then organize the details within each category in a way that makes sense.

PROFESSIONAL NOTEBOOK

Advice from the Authors Rebekah Caplan recommends daily writing practice in which students write showing responses to telling sentences. Caplan believes that regular practice is as necessary for writers as for football players, ballet dancers, or pianists. She says, "The practice of showing, not telling, through daily sentence expansions provides a framework in which students can experiment and discover ways of showing ideas. It is a time for self-exploration in the attempt to attach meaning to experience; it is also a time for increasing fluency and creating a style and voice."

5. Think about your draft. How is your draft shaping up? Are you ready to share your writing with a peer reader? Here are some questions to ask yourself and your peer readers about your writing.

REVIEW YOUR WRITING

Questions for Yourself

- What is the main impression I want to create? Have I supported this impression with details?
- What matters to me most about my subject? Have I gotten this across?
- Do I want to show my thoughts and feelings or just hint at them?
- Where do I need to add more information or details?

Questions for Your Peer Readers

- What do you remember best about my description?
- What does my description make you think and feel?
- What details came across most clearly? least clearly?
- What else would you like to know about my subject?

One Student's Process

Here is part of Alisa Monnier's first draft, along with the comments her peer readers made. What comments would you make about Alisa's draft?

Kitakyushu is my mother's hometown. It is a big city. Each summer Kitakyushu has a large festival called Gion Matsuri. People wear Japanese clothes and special entertainers dance down the street to the music. Many vendors sell food and toys. The party lasts late into the night. Kitakyushu is an exciting place to be in the summer.

Peer Reader Comments

Just how big is Kitakyushu? I want to know more about it!

What kinds of food and toys can you get?

Your description makes me wish that I could go there.

for REVIEW YOUR WRITING

INDIVIDUALIZING INSTRUCTION: AUDITORY LEARNERS Auditory learners will benefit from hearing their descriptions read aloud. Suggest that as peers read their descriptions aloud, they listen for places where they might add details to support their main impression.

for ONE STUDENT'S PROCESS

PEER RESPONSE Brainstorm with students other questions they might ask if they were Alisa's peer readers. Suggest that they first ask themselves *What else would I like to know about this festival?* Sample questions might include *What does the festival celebrate? What do the clothes look like? Who plays the music? What kind? What makes the entertainers "special"? How late does the party last?*

REVISE YOUR WRITING

Objectives

- To review and evaluate responses to a draft of descriptive writing and to revise a draft with those responses in mind
- To use details, metaphors, and similes to make descriptions vivid
- To evaluate the structure of a draft, paragraph by paragraph
- To use transitions to connect details logically

Teaching Strategies

for USE SENSORY DETAILS . . .

INDIVIDUALIZING INSTRUCTION: BASIC STUDENTS You might help students prepare a checklist that includes an example of each kind of sensory detail as well as a brief definition and example of both a simile and a metaphor. Have students compare their drafts to the checklist, and encourage them to add details and figures of speech to make their drafts more specific and vivid.

for USE SENSORY DETAILS . . .

CRITICAL THINKING: ANALYZING Have students analyze Sandra Cisneros's description to find additional examples of sensory details, similes, and metaphors. Then ask them to analyze their own drafts and to elaborate on ideas that need more support.

for CHECK YOUR BEGINNING AND ENDING

STUMBLING BLOCK Have students who cannot think of an attention-getting opener look at Alisa Monnier's piece. Point out that she simply began by naming three things she especially liked, and ended by mentioning them again. Students should note that the introduction tells readers what to expect, and the conclusion draws the information together again so that readers will know they have reached the end.

REVISE YOUR WRITING

1. Review your responses. Look over your peer readers' comments as well as your own notes. Then make any changes you think will improve your description.

2. Use sensory details, similes, and metaphors. Vivid sensory details, similes, and metaphors can help readers feel as if they are experiencing your subject firsthand. In the following passages, such details and devices bring readers ankle-deep into the monkey garden.

> "There were sunflowers big as flowers on Mars and thick cockscombs bleeding the deep red fringe of theater curtains."

> ". . . brush that made your ankles itch and itch until you washed with soap and water."

> "There were big green apples hard as knees. And everywhere the sleepy smell of rotting wood, damp earth and dusty hollyhocks thick and perfumy. . . ."

Writer's Choice Descriptions can create different feelings, or moods. A description might create a feeling of suspense, mystery, or peace. Choose the mood you want to get across. Then select words, metaphors, and similes that will help create this feeling—for example, "The wind moaned like a sad old ghost."

3. Review your organization. Is the word picture you have painted clear? If not, you might be able to improve your draft by organizing your details differently. Also, check to make sure that you start a new paragraph each time you begin a new part of your description.

4. Check your beginning and ending. Think about how you want to begin and end your description. What details might you use at the beginning to get your readers' attention?

PROBLEM SOLVING

"How do I create similes and metaphors?"

To learn more about similes and metaphors, see

- Handbook 19, "Appealing to the Senses," pages 266–273

PROBLEM SOLVING

"What are some other ways to organize my details?"

To learn more about organizing details, see

- Handbook 7, "Organizing Details," pages 217–221

What might you say at the end of your description to give your readers a sense of closure—a sense that they've reached the end? Do you want to leave your readers with a powerful word picture or with some final thoughts about your subject?

Paragraphs at Work Alisa Monnier describes each of her favorite places in Japan in a separate paragraph. The way you paragraph your description will depend on your subject and your organization.

- Start a new paragraph whenever you begin describing a new area within a place, such as a city within a country or a room within a building.
- Begin a new paragraph whenever you introduce a new aspect of a person, such as appearance or personality.
- Develop the main idea of each paragraph with vivid details that are organized in a way that makes sense.

One Student's Process

These are the changes Alisa made to her draft after she and her friends reviewed it. She would make even more changes as she revised her work.

tall buildings and department stores.
Kitakyushu ~~is~~, my mother's hometown, ~~It~~ is a
It has a population of over one million. It is filled with
big city. Each summer Kitakyushu has a large
festival called Gion Matsuri. People wear
kimonos
Japanese ~~clothes~~ and special entertainers
dance down the street to the music. Many ven-
cotton candy, barbecued meat,
dors sell ~~food and~~ toys, The party lasts late into
filling the air with great smells and sounds.
the night, Kitakyushu is an exciting place to be in
the summer. and pet turtles and goldfish.

Writing TIP

If your organization is sensible but your details are hard to follow, you may just need to connect your details with transitions. For more information on using transitions, see Handbook 11, "Transitions," pages 234–238.

for PARAGRAPHS AT WORK

KEY TO UNDERSTANDING: ORGANIZATION You may want to point out that there is no one right way to organize a paragraph but that related ideas belong together. Have students look at paragraphs 3, 4, and 5 of "The Monkey Garden" (pages 50–51) and explain how the ideas in each paragraph are related to one another. (Sample: paragraph 3, what the garden was like when the children took it over; paragraph 4, how the garden changed over time; paragraph 5, how things disappeared)

for ONE STUDENT'S PROCESS

CRITICAL THINKING: ANALYZING Have students read Alisa's changes aloud and decide how she improved the original. (Sample: Alisa added information and specific details.) Encourage students to analyze their own descriptions and to add details and change general words to specific ones.

PROOFREAD

Teaching Strategies

for LINKING MECHANICS AND WRITING

KEY TO UNDERSTANDING: COMMAS IN A SERIES Ask students to locate other examples of commas in a series in Alisa Monnier's description. Samples include her list of relatives in paragraph 1; the street vendors' wares in paragraph 2; and the adjectives in the final sentence of paragraph 5. When students are listing three or more items in their writing, they need to separate them with commas.

Guidelines for Evaluation

IDEAS AND CONTENT

- creates a main impression of a person or a place
- uses sensory details, and possibly similes and metaphors, to create a clear and vivid word picture
- reveals the writer's feelings and thoughts about the subject
- includes an effective beginning and ending

STRUCTURE AND FORM

- uses well-developed paragraphs
- reveals a clear organization
- uses appropriate transitions

GRAMMAR, USAGE, AND MECHANICS

- displays standard grammar, usage, and mechanics
- uses commas correctly to separate items in a series

GENERAL NOTE

MANAGING THE PAPER LOAD In grading students' descriptions, you might want to concentrate on how well students created a single main impression and supported it with sensory details and comparisons.

PROOFREAD

1. Proofread your work. Check your spelling, grammar, usage, and punctuation.

LINKING MECHANICS AND WRITING

Using Commas in a Series

When you write descriptions, you will often use series of details. Remember to use commas to separate the items in a series—including a comma just before the conjunction *and* or *or.*

Original

I love the summer festival in Kitakyushu the hotel and hot springs in Beppu and the beauty of the mountains.

Revised

I love the summer festival in Kitakyushu, the hotel and hot springs in Beppu, and the beauty of the mountains.

For more information on using commas properly, see Handbook 43, "Punctuation," pages 566–599.

2. Make a clean copy of your description. Review your writing one last time, using the Standards for Evaluation in the margin. Then make a final copy.

Standards for Evaluation

DESCRIPTIVE WRITING

A description

- creates a main impression and supports that impression with details
- paints a clear and vivid picture of the subject
- shows readers what matters most about the subject to the writer
- reveals the writer's thoughts and feelings about the subject
- is well-organized
- possesses an attention-getting beginning and a satisfying ending

PUBLISH AND PRESENT

- **Share your writing with someone who likes to draw.** Ask an interested classmate to create a drawing or painting based on your description.

- **Illustrate your description.** Re-create your subject in a sketch, painting, or sculpture. Then, on a bulletin board or in a special area of your classroom, display your artwork beside your written description.
- **Submit your description to a local newspaper.** Neighborhood newspapers often publish articles about special local people and places. So if you have described a person or a place in your community, consider submitting your description to the local paper.

Mt. Fuji, with an elevation of 12,388 feet, is the highest mountain in Japan.

REFLECT ON YOUR WRITING

WRITER TO WRITER

If you can first get away from worrying about spelling and following grammar rules, you'll find that your imagination is free to write.

Paul Zindel, novelist

1. Add your writing to your portfolio. In a note to yourself, jot down what you've learned in writing your description. Then attach your note to the final copy of your description. Thinking about the following questions may help you focus your thoughts:

- What did I notice or realize about my subject that I had never noticed or realized before?
- Did my attitude toward my subject change? If so, how?
- What would I have liked to get across more vividly?
- What helped me the most in doing this assignment? What got in my way?

FOR YOUR **PORTFOLIO**

2. Explore additional ideas. See the suggestions for writing a description of a cultural custom on pages 64–66 and Springboards on page 67.

Reteaching

After students have completed their papers, assess the needs of students who were not successful in developing an effective description; then assign the appropriate handbook mini-lessons as well as the Workshop Support Materials listed in the Teaching Preview, pages 47a–47b. Concepts commonly requiring reteaching for this assignment are:

- **Handbook 11, Show, Don't Tell, pp. 239–242**
- **Handbook 19, Appealing to the Senses, pp. 266–273**

The following suggestions and resources also may be useful.

Weak Beginnings Locate in books or stories several introductory paragraphs that begin with vivid descriptions. Read each of these introductions aloud and have students explain what main impression they get and what details help them see the scene or the person.

Lack of Specific Details Have students use the Observation Chart from the *Thinking Skills Worksheets* to list details about their topics. Students working in pairs should ask each other questions and make suggestions that will flesh out their topics.

Extension and Enrichment

1. Ask students to imagine that they are entering a magazine contest. To win, they must describe their dream rooms in two hundred words or less.

2. Challenge students to describe a familiar object so that it can be identified without being named. Have students read their descriptions aloud to find out whether their classmates can guess the object.

Closure: Reflect on Your Writing

Have students meet in small groups to discuss their answers to the questions before writing them down. Encourage students to also discuss how working with peer readers helped them revise their drafts.

Related ASSIGNMENT

Starting from LITERATURE

Objectives

- To respond to and analyze a piece of writing that describes a culture and its customs
- To create a piece of descriptive writing about a culture and its customs

Motivate

Before directing students to read Starting from Literature, ask them to name their favorite holiday and tell why they like it. Encourage students to describe favorite holidays from their family's cultural traditions. Tell students that in this assignment, they will have a chance to describe one of their favorite holidays or customs and to show what makes it special.

BUILD ON PRIOR KNOWLEDGE

Have students describe some of the ways in which people celebrate holidays; for example with certain foods, costumes or fancy clothes, colors, decorations, the exchange of presents, songs, games, and the lighting of candles. Tell students that they are going to read about a holiday in the country of Nepal, near India. Ask them to speculate about what a holiday in Nepal might be like.

SET A PURPOSE

Explain to students that they will be reading a description of a holiday with which they probably are not familiar. Remind them to look for details that describe the holiday, the people who observe it, and the place where it is observed. Urge students to look for sensory details and comparisons that help them picture the event.

Related ASSIGNMENT

Culture and Customs

Starting from LITERATURE

What are some of the customs of your family or group? When you lose a tooth, do you sleep with it under your pillow? Do you take part in special religious ceremonies? Is there a day each year when you dress up in special clothing?

In this excerpt, Elizabeth Murphy-Melas describes a festival in Nepal (nə pôl′) known as Yomarhi Purnima (yō mä′ dē po͞o nē′ mä). As you read her description, think about what the details reveal about the people of Nepal and the way they live.

YOMARHI PURNIMA

by Elizabeth Murphy-Melas

Tiny Nepal is an enchanting land of deep, picturesque valleys surrounded by the rugged, snowcapped Himalayas. In the heart of the country lies the beautiful Katmandu Valley. There, the Nepalese till the rich soil as they have for generations. . . . And each December, the people of the Katmandu Valley celebrate a special festival called Yomarhi Purnima in thanksgiving for their bountiful harvest. . . .

Yomarhi Purnima begins on the day of the full moon in December. Yomarhi is a Nepali word formed from yo ("fig") and marhi ("cake"); purnima is a Sanskrit word meaning "full moon." The Yomarhi cake is a sweet cake the Nepalese eat during the harvest celebration, just as Americans eat fruitcake at Thanksgiving and Christmas.

for FURTHER READING

Books to Read Students curious about different thanksgiving celebrations around the world might read *The Thanksgiving Book* by Lucille Recht Penner. It describes the history and customs of Thanksgiving in the United States and of similar holidays in other countries. Students also might enjoy *The Book of Holidays Around the World*, a 365-day calendar of festivals with a brief description of each, by Alice van Straalen.

On the eve of the full moon, also called the harvest moon, the women and girls of the household spend all day baking Yomarhi cakes in brick ovens. The small cakes, about the size of a child's fist, are molded by hand into the shapes of animals, people, and Hindu gods and goddesses. In the evening, the family says prayers and visits local temples and shrines, making offerings of the cakes. The scent of incense from the shrines fills the streets.

The family then returns home for an evening of feasting and merrymaking. Children dress in their best festival clothes—the boys wearing trousers, high-necked tunics, and soft cotton topis; the girls, bright, colorful saris with bracelets and earrings. Because it's a special occasion, chicken or eggs are cooked. The Nepalese also eat rice mixed with dal, a thick sauce made from peas or lentils. It's fun to sit upon woolen rugs on the floor, sip tea, and savor the meal!

That night, two special Yomarhi cakes—one shaped like Ganesh, the elephant-headed Hindu god of good luck, and one shaped like Laxmi, the goddess of wealth—are locked away in a cupboard. There they will remain for the four days of the harvest celebration. According to tradition, a miracle will occur, increasing the size of the cakes and bringing blessings to the family. At the end of Yomarhi Purnima, a family member unlocks the cupboard, and the cakes are enjoyed by all at a final feast.

Yomarhi Purnima is also a time of thanksgiving for merchants in the villages. They place Yomarhi cakes in their safe-deposit boxes, shops, and offices, hoping Laxmi will be pleased with their generosity and bring prosperity in the coming year. Students often wedge a few cakes in between their textbooks to bring them good luck in passing their school examinations!

Think & Respond

Which Yomarhi Purnima customs do you like best? How are the customs described here similar to or different from your own holiday traditions? Point out some of the ways Elizabeth Murphy-Melas brings the Yomarhi Purnima festival to life by showing it rather than just telling about it.

Think & Respond

ELICIT PERSONAL RESPONSES

Have volunteers tell which Yomarhi Purnima customs appeal to them most and why. How do these Nepalese customs compare to others they know about? (Sample: The Nepalese have a thanksgiving feast that celebrates the harvest, just as Americans do, but the traditional foods are different. People sit on the floor, not around a table.)

EXPLORE THE AUTHOR'S TECHNIQUES

Examples of showing details that students might mention include the brick ovens; the Yomarhi cakes, which are "molded by hand" into many shapes; the scent of incense that fills the streets; the costumes; the foods; sitting on "woolen rugs on the floor"; what people do with the special cakes; and how students carry the cakes in between their textbooks for luck. They might also mention the comparisons that the author makes between the Yomarhi cakes and fruitcake and between the cakes and the size of a child's fist.

You also might ask students to point out details that the author includes to explain things that her readers might not otherwise know. (Samples: what the words *Yomarhi* and *purnima* mean, what *dal* is, who Ganesh and Laxmi are, and why merchants put cakes in their safe-deposit boxes) Students should note that the description would be much less clear without these details. As students prepare to write, encourage them to think about what information their audience needs to know.

MULTICULTURAL Connection

Many cultures have similar holidays, including a new year festival, a festival of lights in midwinter, a celebration of renewal and rebirth in the spring, and a harvest festival or thanksgiving in the fall. Most countries also celebrate an independence day, as well as holidays associated with heroes or national leaders. Invite students to compare the celebration of some of these kinds of holidays with similar ones in the United States.

Writing ON YOUR OWN

Remind students of the way Elizabeth Murphy-Melas used details about Yomarhi Purnima to help her readers picture the festival in far-off Nepal. Then note that this assignment will help them observe and record details and then use them to show their readers a holiday or custom, as Murphy-Melas did.

Handbooks for Help and Practice

The following handbooks may be used as mini-lessons before students begin writing or as resources when problems arise.

- **Show, Don't Tell, pp. 239–242**
- **Introductions, pp. 247–249**
- **Conclusions, pp. 250–252**

Teaching Strategies

for FIND A CUSTOM

HELPFUL HINT Tell students that all cultures have what are called rites of passage. Generally, these relate to birth, the taking on of adult responsibilities, marriage, and death. Invite students to consider, as topics for writing, their experiences with these customs.

for INTERVIEW

SPEAKING AND LISTENING Discuss questions interviewers might ask, such as "What holidays and special occasions do you celebrate?" or "Do you eat special foods then?" and so on. You might mention the *who, what, when, where, why,* and *how* questions, explaining how these questions can help them collect useful information in interviews. Pair students and have them use their questions to interview each other briefly about customs. Then bring students together as a class to discuss the ideas they got from these mini-interviews. You might direct students who would like to know more about interviewing skills to page 107, "Guidelines for Interviewing," in the *Writing Resource Book.*

Writing ON YOUR OWN
Culture and Customs

INVITATION TO *Write*

In the process of describing Yomarhi Purnima, Elizabeth Murphy-Melas brings her readers into the homes and hearts of the people of Nepal.

Now write a description of an ethnic or religious custom that's familiar to you or one that you would like to learn more about.

The *Mani Rimdu* festival takes place each May in the Khumbu region of eastern Nepal. Monks dressed in colorful masks enact ancient legends that are based on the theme of good triumphing over evil.

EXPLORING CUSTOMS

1. Find a custom. Can you think of a cultural or religious tradition you'd like to understand better or help someone else to understand? This tradition might come from your own culture or from any culture that interests you. Freewrite to come up with ideas, or try doing some of the following activities:

- **Holiday hop.** Make a list of holidays that have special meaning to you and your family—one, for example, might be Rosh Hashana, Cinco de Mayo, Tet, or Easter. Create a **cluster** that explores the traditions associated with each holiday.
- **Interview.** Talk with someone who has visited or lived in a culture different from yours. Ask questions and take notes on the customs of that culture.
- **Consider do's and taboos.** What have you been taught about the traditions and customs of your culture? Do you always wear a head covering? Do you bow when you meet someone? Do you wear traditional clothing? Create a list of your customary practices and ways of behaving.

Music Connection

Many holidays have special music that is commonly sung during the festivities. Encourage students to investigate music associated with their topic. If possible, they might bring in tapes and records and play them for the class. Suitable songs might be taught to the class for a songfest.

After exploring for a while, choose a custom that you would like to describe. Freewriting can help you discover which custom you want to describe and even what you want to say.

Writer's Choice You may write about a custom of your own culture or one from another culture. Similarly, you may choose to describe a religious tradition that you know well or one you're interested in learning about.

2. Observe the custom and record details. If possible, become familiar with the traditional practice first hand by watching it or by doing it yourself. If that isn't possible, "observe from memory" by recalling the practice as vividly as possible. Then record the details of the custom in a **list** or a **cluster** or by creating an **observation chart** or a **sketch.** Be sure to include plenty of sensory details.

DESCRIBING A CUSTOM

1. Start your draft. Using your prewriting notes and your mind's eye, describe the sights, sounds, smells, tastes, and feelings you associate with the custom you've chosen. As much as possible, show rather than tell. Also, try to get yourself to write at top speed, without worrying about your word choices, grammar, or punctuation.

2. Consider your audience. Think about what your readers will need to know to understand the custom you are describing. Then make sure to include this information. For example, Murphy-Melas explains, "The Yomarhi cake is a sweet cake the Nepalese eat during the harvest celebration, just as Americans eat fruitcake at Thanksgiving and Christmas."

3. Think about your draft. Look for ways to improve your description. If you're comfortable sharing your draft, ask peer readers to comment on your description too.

PROBLEM SOLVING

"How can I show rather than tell?"

For help in turning telling into showing, see

- Handbook 12, "Show, Don't Tell," pages 239–242

Writing TIP

Comparisons of unfamiliar practices with familiar ones can help your readers better understand the unfamiliar practices. Similes (comparisons with *like* or *as*) can also help.

for OBSERVE THE CUSTOM . . .

MODELING To help students get started gathering details, model creating a cluster diagram or filling in an observation chart with observations from your own memories of a holiday celebration or custom.

for START YOUR DRAFT

CRITICAL THINKING: ANALYZING Suggest that before they start to write, students look over their notes to see whether they have collected enough material. They might compare the number of specific details they have gathered with those Elizabeth Murphy-Melas included in her description. Ask them which of the senses their details involve. If students decide that they need more material, they might try brainstorming or freewriting.

for THINK ABOUT YOUR DRAFT

PEER RESPONSE Suggest that students ask a peer to read their descriptions aloud to them while they listen to see whether their main impression comes through clearly and whether their showing details are vivid and sharp. If students are not sure, urge them to question their peers about specific sentences, paragraphs, or ideas.

PROFESSIONAL NOTEBOOK

James Beane comments on the ideal middle school curriculum: "Early adolescents have the same concerns as people in general, regardless of their developmental stage. Moreover, their questions about themselves are often personal versions of larger-world questions. . . . The emerging vision of a middle school curriculum, then, is one that is organized around these rich and provocative themes. . . . Imagine, for example, a unit . . . in which students examine how self-perceptions are formed, how culture influences their self-concepts, how various cultures express their identities, and how increasing cultural diversity promises to reshape politics and the economy."

for CHECK YOUR BEGINNING AND ENDING

CRITICAL THINKING: ANALYZING

Have students look again at Elizabeth Murphy-Melas's first paragraph and identify the questions that the author answers. (Samples: Where is Nepal? What is it like? What do people do there? What holiday do they celebrate? Why? When?) Ask students why these would be good questions to consider. (Sample: They give readers the basic information they need in order to understand the description.) Encourage students to consider answering such questions in their introductions.

Guidelines for Evaluation

AN EFFECTIVE DESCRIPTION OF A CUSTOM

- conveys a vivid impression of the culture described
- uses sensory images and details
- shows, rather than tells
- considers its audience's knowledge of the topic
- has an effective introduction and conclusion

GENERAL NOTE

MANAGING THE PAPER LOAD

You might share the Guidelines for Evaluation (above) with students before they turn in their papers. Then limit your comments to those items on the list.

REVIEWING YOUR WRITING

1. Rework your description. Look at your own notes and your peers' comments. What needs improvement? Remember that adding sensory details, showing instead of telling, and replacing general words with more specific ones can all help bring a description to life.

2. Check your beginning and ending. In your introduction you should interest your readers in your subject and tell them what they will be reading about. To do this, you might begin by vividly describing an important feature of the custom. Another good way to begin is by pointing out a mistaken idea people have about the custom. You could also start by briefly telling about your first encounter with the tradition.

Your conclusion should leave your readers with a clear understanding of the custom you have described. Therefore, you may want to end by summarizing the important details you presented. You may also want to share what the custom means to you or what it taught you.

PROBLEM SOLVING

"How do I write an effective introduction and conclusion?"

For information on introductions and conclusions, see

- Handbook 14, "Introductions," pages 247–249
- Handbook 15, "Conclusions," pages 250–252

PUBLISHING AND PRESENTING

- **Compile an anthology of cultural customs.** Include illustrations or photos. A brief biography of each writer also would be a nice touch.
- **Create a multicultural calendar.** Meet with classmates who wrote about holiday traditions. Then, for each month of the year, create an illustrated description of how one or more cultures celebrate holidays in that month. For some months, you may need to create a collage of illustrations.
- **Reenact customs.** Create short skits about the customs you and your classmates have described. Perform your skits in class or at a school assembly.

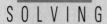

Springboards

CONSUMER ECONOMICS

Script a radio advertisement for a product of your own invention. Use words that will help listeners picture your product and understand its purpose. Then, if possible, tape-record your advertisement, using music and sound effects.

Social Studies

Choose an object from another time or place—a spinning wheel, a piñata, or a guillotine, for example. Then write about it in a way that describes its purpose or significance.

History

What historical events that are usually forgotten do you think people should celebrate or remember? Invent a holiday based on a historical event, and describe at least one custom you would observe on that day.

SCIENCE

Imagine you are an astronaut approaching a planet from space. This planet may be one you've heard of before or one that exists only in your imagination. What do you see from the cockpit of your spacecraft? What are your thoughts and feelings? Write a description of what you're seeing, thinking, and feeling.

Teaching Strategies

GENERAL NOTE

HELPFUL HINT Remind students that for these descriptive writing prompts, they will need to gather sensory details and specific showing details, as they did in the Guided Assignment.

for CONSUMER ECONOMICS

INDIVIDUALIZING INSTRUCTION: VISUAL LEARNERS Students who learn best by seeing things might be encouraged to focus on the storyboard for a TV advertisement, illustrating each main scene in their advertisements and then writing a script for each scene.

for SCIENCE

CRITICAL THINKING: COMPARING AND CONTRASTING Remind students that people can understand something unfamiliar by comparing and contrasting it to something familiar. As students list the characteristics of the distant planet, urge them to think of something familiar on Earth that is the same and then to make that comparison in their description.

Unscrambling Sentences

Objectives

- To identify phrases and clauses as sentence parts
- To unscramble sentence parts and to imitate the sentence structure of professional models

Teaching Strategies

for UNSCRAMBLING SENTENCES

MODELING Model the way to unscramble sentence parts, thinking aloud as you go through the process; for example: "First, I read the model. I see that it begins with a subject and a form of *be.* Which chunk in the scrambled sentence does that? ('the baby was. . . .') Continue modeling the procedure so that students understand it and know how to look for clues to sentence structure. Invite a volunteer to talk through the structure of the student imitation, explaining how it imitates the original model.

Additional Resource

Sentence Composing Copy Masters, pp. 3–4

Answer Key

A. Unscrambling and Imitating Sentences

Unscrambled sentences are given. Imitative sentences will vary but should follow the same pattern.

1. After the rain stopped, there was a rainbow in the sky.
2. Thrilled by the comeback of their team, the fans rushed onto the field, yelling and screaming with delight.

Sentence

COMPOSING

Unscrambling Sentences

Effective sentences often contain sentence parts, or chunks, that can be arranged in different ways. You can add variety to your writing by trying out different positions for your sentence chunks. Notice how you can unscramble sentence chunks and imitate sentences by professional writers.

Model	I was plain and tall, too tall for fourteen years, and without any shape. **Rosa Guy, *The Friends***
Scrambled Chunks	and lacking any hair / very quiet for a newborn / the baby was small and quiet
Unscrambled Chunks	The baby was small and quiet, very quiet for a newborn, and lacking any hair.
Student Imitation	The diner is crowded and noisy, so noisy you can't always hear the waitress, and near the train station.

ON THE MARK You generally place commas where you want readers to pause when they read your sentences.

A. Unscrambling and Imitating Sentences Unscramble each set of sentence chunks below to create a sentence that has the same order of chunks and punctuation as the model. Then write a sentence of your own that imitates the model.

1. Model When I awoke, there were snowflakes on my eyes.
Charles Portis, *True Grit*

in the sky / there was a rainbow / after the rain stopped

2. Model Drawn by the scent of fish, the wild dogs sat on the hill, barking and growling at each other.
Scott O'Dell, *Island of the Blue Dolphins*

yelling and screaming with delight / thrilled by the comeback of their team / the fans rushed onto the field

3. Model Leaping out of the thickets like stags, the men of Soror were upon us before we could lift our weapons to our shoulders.

Pierre Boulle, *Planet of the Apes*

while the old dog watched / the young dog brought the Frisbee to the girl / with mild interest / running across the park like lightning

4. Model She started quickly down the walk, waving to the boy who was making his way slowly up the street on a green motor scooter.

Betsy Byars, *The Summer of the Swans*

glancing toward the secretary / Wilbur walked nervously into the principal's office / with her finger on the trigger / who was holding the water gun securely

B. Unscrambling Sentences Sometimes you can arrange sentence chunks in more than one acceptable order. Write two different sentences from each set of chunks below, adding punctuation as necessary. Then select the one you like best. Be prepared to explain why you prefer it.

1. staring out the window / I spent the entire day sulking / waiting for the rain to stop **Rosa Guy, *The Friends***

2. like sensible folk / and then / they waved until the boys were around the first bend in the road / they all went home to breakfast

Alexei Panshin, *Rite of Passage*

3. to meet him / each year / the faithful Sounder would come hobbling on three legs far down the road / after he had been gone for a whole winter and returned **William H. Armstrong, *Sounder***

4. in the very dead of night / then suddenly / clear, resonant, and unmistakable / there came a sound to my ears

Sir Arthur Conan Doyle, *The Hound of the Baskervilles*

Grammar Refresher You can use commas between sentence parts to avoid confusion. For more information about using commas, see Handbook 43, "Punctuation," pages 566–599.

3. Running across the park like lightning, the young dog brought the Frisbee to the girl while the old dog watched with mild interest.

4. Wilbur walked nervously into the principal's office, glancing toward the secretary who was holding the water gun securely with her finger on the trigger.

B. Unscrambling Sentences

The following are the authors' original sentences. Accept any sentences that clearly express a complete thought.

1. I spent the entire day sulking, staring out the window, waiting for the rain to stop.

2. They waved until the boys were around the first bend in the road, and then, like sensible folk, they all went home to breakfast.

3. Each year, after he had been gone for a whole winter and returned, the faithful Sounder would come hobbling on three legs far down the road to meet him.

4. Then suddenly, in the very dead of night, there came a sound to my ears, clear, resonant, and unmistakable.

for GRAMMAR REFRESHER

HELPFUL HINT In these sentences, commas are used to set off introductory elements, interrupters, appositives, and participial phrases. However, students may benefit most from listening to the sentences as they are read aloud and noting that most commas come at natural pauses. Encourage them to follow the models for punctuation as well as for sentence structure.

3

Narrative and Literary Writng

Overview

Narrative and literary writing can include various forms to interpret personal experience. In this workshop, students express themselves in two forms—the personal narrative and the poem. Workshop 3 includes the following Guided and Related Assignments, as well as the interdisciplinary project described on pages 69c–69d.

1. **Guided: Personal Narrative** calls on students to interpret an incident from their own experience, using skills of narration and description to select significant details and arrange them in a logical order.
2. **Related: Writing a Poem** allows students to express their feelings in imaginative ways as they explore the creative use of language.

Teaching Preview

Preparation Guide

1. Use the Overview on this page and the Teacher's Choice descriptions on page 49 as a basis for deciding which assignments to teach.
2. Preview the assignments and the teacher's notes and identify concepts that may require preteaching or extra support, given your class's abilities. The handbook mini-lessons suggested within the lesson may also provide guidance.
3. Preview the chart below for support materials in the Teacher's Resource File that may be used with this Workshop. Resources are for use with the Guided Assignment unless otherwise noted.

Support Materials

WRITER'S CRAFT RESOURCES

Prewrite and Explore
Thinking Skills Worksheets, pp. 1, 5
Thinking Skills Transparencies, pp. 1–1a, 5–5a
Writing Resource Book, pp. 9–10

Draft and Discover
Elaboration, Revision, and Proofreading Practice, pp. 5, 20–22
Elaboration, Revision, and Proofreading Transparencies, pp. 9–10, 35–38
Writing Resource Book, pp. 11–13

Revise Your Writing
Elaboration, Revision, and Proofreading Practice, pp. 6, 20–22
Elaboration, Revision, and Proofreading Transparencies, pp. 11–12, 35–38
Guidelines for Writing Assessment and Portfolio Use, pp. 16, 28–30
Peer Response Guides, pp. 11–12, 27–28
Writing Resource Book, pp. 14–15

Assessment
Tests and Writing Assessment Prompts, p. 3

Extension Activities
Sentence Composing Copymasters, pp. 5–6
Starting Points for Writing, pp. 27–29, 31, 34–36
Writing from Literature, pp. 3–4, 11–12 19–20, 23–28
Standardized Test Practice

Educational Technology
(available separately)
Writer's DataBank
Electronic English Handbook
Multimedia Workshop
On Assignment! (videodisc)

OTHER RESOURCES

Books and Journals
Elbow, Peter. "Poetry as No Big Deal." *Writing with Power.* New York: Oxford UP, 1981.
Koch, Kenneth. *Wishes, Lies, and Dreams: Teaching Children to Write Poetry.* New York: Harper/Collins, 1980.

Films and Videos
First Choice: Poems and Poets. Pied Piper.

Educational Technology
Creation. Toucan/Queue. Apple II, PC.
Poetry Palette. Mindplay. Apple II.
Poets Journal. Hartley Courseware. Apple.

Linking Literature, Writing, and Grammar

The following options may be used to provide students with an integrated language experience. Begin by assigning and discussing any of the recommended pieces of literature. Use the suggested strategy to provide a link to the Guided Assignment.

LINKING LITERATURE AND WRITING

Option 1

Starting Point: An excerpt from *A Child of the Movement* by Sheyann Webb on pages 72–73 of *The Writer's Craft.*

Strategy: Use the teaching suggestions on pages 72–73 to lead students into the Guided Assignment.

Option 2

Starting Point: An excerpt from *Sweet Summer* by Bebe Moore Campbell on pages 365–372 of McDougal, Littell's *Literature and Language,* Grade 6. (Additional suggestions for using *Literature and Language* can be found on page 71.)

Strategy: Have students read the excerpt from Campbell's autobiography. Then ask them to explain why Campbell's sixth-grade year—and especially her choice of a book—was so important to her. Have students consider important moments in their own lives. Use the discussion to introduce the Guided Assignment.

Option 3

Starting Point: "Snapshot of a Dog" by James Thurber.

Strategy: Read aloud the last paragraph of Thurber's essay, in which he tells the story of how a beloved family dog died. Ask students why this personal experience was important to Thurber. Have them discuss their own memories of important incidents involving pets. Use the discussion to introduce the Guided Assignment.

LINKING WRITING AND GRAMMAR

Before the drafting or revision stages of this assignment, tell students that good dialogue can help bring a personal narrative to life, but poorly paragraphed dialogue can confuse readers. It can even make them stop reading, if they cannot tell when one person finishes speaking and another person starts. By starting a new paragraph each time the speaker changes, writers can help readers follow the dialogue, without having to repeat the speakers' names over and over. Write the following example on the board and have students check the paragraphing in their own dialogues.

Incorrect: "Where are you going?" Darren asked. "I have to find my little sister," Jim answered. "What time did she leave here?" "I have no idea."

Correct: "Where are you going?" Darren asked.

"I have to find my little sister," Jim answered. "What time did she leave here?"

"I have no idea."

Suggest that students review page 280 of Writing Handbook 22, "Using Dialogue." If problems with paragraphing dialogue persist, assign the exercises on that page for reteaching.

Management Guidelines

The chart below indicates the number of days recommended for each phase of the Guided and Related Assignments. These numbers are an estimate of the total time needed for each phase. In practice, of course, students may not complete each phase in one continuous session, nor will they necessarily progress from stage to stage in the linear order shown here. Stars indicate portions of the assignment that may be completed outside the classroom if time is limited or if teachers wish students to work independently.

PERSONAL NARRATIVE

Starting from Literature	1 day
Prewrite and Explore	2 days
Draft and Discover	2–3 days*
Revise Your Writing	1–2 days*
Proofread	1 day*
Publish and Present	1–2 days
Reflect on Your Writing	1 day
Extension and Enrichment	open*

WRITING A POEM

Starting from Literature	1 day
Exploring Your World	1–2 days*
Drafting Your Poem	1–2 days*
Reviewing Your Poem	1 day*
Publishing and Presenting	1–2 days
Sentence Composing	open*

Project File

Go Fly a Kite!

Overview

This project uses the study of kites and a kite-flying competition to demonstrate how several areas of the curriculum can come together to teach teamwork and collaboration, to show the interdisciplinary nature of much learning, and to provide engaging activities. The project culminates in a kite-flying day, when students fly kites they have made and participate in events and competitions.

Students will participate in the following activities:

- Express thoughts and feelings about kites by writing poems or personal narratives
- Research and report orally on the history, the cultural uses, the types, and the construction of kites
- Working with partners, design and make kites
- Plan and participate in a kite-flying event
- Use language arts, science, math, music, physical education, social studies, and art skills to complete the project

Preparation Guide

Ask students to describe their favorite kinds of kites and to tell about flying their own kites. Point out that kites are more than high-flying fun—they have been around for centuries and have been used in situations ranging from wars to religious ceremonies.

Tell students that in this project they will use research skills and the skills of narrative and literary writing as they explore the history of kites, the meaning of flight, and varieties of kite design.

Stage 1
Exploring Kites, Flight, and You

1. Invite students to discuss their experiences with kites. Lead students to explore the meaning of flight and its traditional link to concepts of freedom.
2. Direct students to draw on their experiences with kites, along with ideas from the class discussion, as they create personal narratives or poems for Writer's Workshop 3.
3. Have students brainstorm to develop a list of topics related to kites that they would like to investigate. They may list topics such as the following:
   - history of kites
   - uses of kites
   - kites of specific cultures
   - aerodynamics of kite flying
   - kite design
   - kite-flying competitions
4. Form groups and have each group choose a topic to research. Direct students to share their findings with the class (see *Resources, Stage 1*).

TEAM TEACHING

The following activities may be used for team teaching or as enrichment and extension activities by the language arts teacher.

Language Arts Write personal narratives and poems.

Art Study kites as an art form.

Social Studies Study the history of kite flying, the ceremonial and social functions of kites in Asian cultures, and the many uses of kites through the ages.

Science Study the aerodynamics of kite flying. Compare kite flying and hang gliding. Trace the role of experimentation with kites in the development of the airplane.

TEACHING TIPS

- As students work through Writer's Workshop 3, discuss imaginative language and poetic form (see *Resources, Stage 1*).
- Teach or review research techniques and oral presentation skills (see *Resources, Stage 1*).
- Offer students the option of sharing their poems or narratives either orally or in a class album.

Stage 2
Creating a Kite

1. Instruct each group to work together to design and make a kite. Tell them to use their earlier research findings to make a kite that reflects a specific culture or a special design (see *Resources, Stage 2*).
2. Invite students to include other forms of self-expression in their kite-making activities. For example, they might create drawings, paintings, or videos of their work on the kites, or they might turn their kite poems into songs.

TEAM TEACHING

Science Study and experiment with various kite-making materials and various shapes, sizes, and tail lengths.

Art Try out various colors and designs for decorating kites. Create drawings or take photos of the kites.

Math Specify measurements of the kites and create scale drawings or scale models of them.

Music Turn a kite poem into a song.

TEACHING TIPS

- Set up work surfaces and provide, or ask students to bring in, materials for making kites.
- Have tape recorders, video cameras, and art supplies available for students.

Stage 3
Planning and Participating in a Kite-Flying Day

1. Direct students to plan a kite-flying event. Depending on the types of kites they have made, this could include any of the following activities:
   - a stunt-kite demonstration
   - a tournament of Chinese dragon kites
   - a battle of Indian fighting kites
   - a cooperative effort to use kites in innovative ways (aerial photography is one possibility)
   - a design competition
   - a competition for greatest height or time aloft
   - an exhibit and demonstration of kites from various cultures
2. Tell students to choose an appropriate place for the kite-flying day and to make necessary arrangements. Suggest that they divide the day into segments for different events (see *Resources, Stage 3*).
3. Encourage students to write poems and stories about the event. Help interested students make videotapes of the event.

TEAM TEACHING

Physical Education Organize teams and events.

Science While flying kites, observe and record effects of wind velocity, increased or decreased string tension, and other factors (see *Resources, Stage 3*).

Social Studies Follow traditional kite-flying customs of specific cultures.

Math Estimate a kite's altitude, using the angle of elevation and the length of its string.

TEACHING TIPS

- Invite parents to be spectators at students' kite-flying event.
- Arrange local media coverage, or encourage students to take photographs or make videos of the event.

Resources

STAGE 1

High Fliers: Colorful Kites from Japan by Tadao Saito uses vivid illustrations to trace the history of Japanese kites, to tell of their uses, and to show how to make them.

Come Fight a Kite by Dinesh Bahadur displays Indian fighting kites, outlines their history, and tells how to make and fly them.

In ***From Kite to Kitty Hawk,*** a book about the history of flight, Richard W. Bishop includes a chapter on kites.

The World on a String by Jane Yolen is challenging for sixth graders but is packed with interesting details about the history, aerodynamics, and types of kites and about their uses in cultures around the world. It includes kite-making instructions and a bibliography.

The Writer's Craft, Grade 6, Workshop 3, "Narrative and Literary Writing," pages 70–89, teaches the writing of narratives and poems. Handbook 19, "Appealing to the Senses," pages 266–273, discusses language that appeals to the senses. Handbook 32, "Oral Reports," pages 324–325, explains how to prepare and deliver effective oral reports.

STAGE 2

Getting Started in Kitemaking by Leslie L. Hunt covers the making and flying of many types and designs.

Kites for Kids by Burton and Rita Marks includes a directory of sources for kite-making equipment and supplies.

Fun with Kites by John and Kate Dyson contains huge color photos and simple instructions for making kites in eighteen bright, unusual designs.

Video Power: A Complete Guide to Writing, Planning, and Shooting Videos by Tom Shachtman and Harriet Shelare gives clear instructions and tips.

STAGE 3

The **American Kiteflyers Association,** 1559 Rockville Pike, Rockville, MD 20852, publishes the journal ***Kiting*** and a brief manual, ***How to Fly a Kite,*** discussing suitable areas, safety rules, tips for success, and interesting facts about kites.

Better Kite Flying for Boys and Girls by Ross R. Olney and Chan Bush is a book of tips from two pros, with sections on flying special types, such as Chinese dragon kites and Indian fighting kites.

Additional Projects

Making Books This project gives students an opportunity to integrate science, math, and art skills with the skills of narrative and literary writing. Have them use Writer's Workshop 3 to write several personal narratives and poems. Then encourage them to research how to create handmade papers, how to assemble and sew book pages, and how to make and attach book covers. Have each student choose one or more of his or her writings and create a handmade book.

Talk to the Animals Take students to visit an animal shelter, or arrange for a presentation by a humane society's education department. Have students conduct interviews and do research to learn about the dangers faced by neglected and unwanted pets. Then suggest that they write poems to or about the animals they have seen or personal narratives based on their experiences with the animals. They can compile their writings into a booklet; add art, an introduction, and notes alerting readers to the problem of neglected and unwanted pets; and present their booklet to the humane society.

Sketch Book

Objective

- To use fine art, a quotation, and writing prompts as springboards to informal writing

WRITING WARM-UPS

Encourage students to respond freely and informally to at least one of the Sketchbook prompts. Students may begin by discussing their reactions in small groups and then freewriting in their journals. Remind them that their responses will not be graded and may provide them with useful material for other narrative and literary writing.

Encourage students to respond to the story of Icarus. Such responses may generate material that could be the basis for writing a personal response to literature in Writer's Workshop 6. Telling the story of a memorable journey or an imaginary flight may lead to a personal narrative that can be developed in Writer's Workshop 3.

SHOW, DON'T TELL

For the first prompt, suggest that students use all their senses to describe a frightening storm. Encourage them to use vivid verbs and modifiers to describe what happened.

For the second prompt, suggest that students imagine that they went to the Monkey House with a group of their friends. Encourage them to tell a story about the visit, using dialogue and description to show the action.

Sketch Book

WRITING WARM-UPS

Detail of color engraving *The Fall of Icarus* (1731), Bernard Picart.

Icarus, beating his wings in joy, felt the thrill of the cool wind on his face and the clear air above and below him. He flew higher and higher into the blue sky until he reached the clouds. His father called out in alarm. He tried to follow, but he was heavier and his wings would not carry him. Up and up Icarus soared, through the soft moist clouds and out again toward the glorious sun. He was bewitched by a sense of freedom; he beat his wings frantically so that they would carry him higher and higher to heaven itself.

"The Flight of Icarus,"
traditional Greek myth,
RETOLD BY SALLY BENSON

- Imagine that you could spread your wings and fly away. Tell the story of your flight.
- Tell a story about a memorable journey you have taken.

Show Don't Tell

Turn one of these *telling* sentences into a *showing* paragraph that has dialogue, action, description, or a combination of these techniques.

- Jason said the storm was frightening.
- We walked through the Monkey House at the zoo.

70

Narrative and Literary Writing

Guided Assignment
Personal Narrative

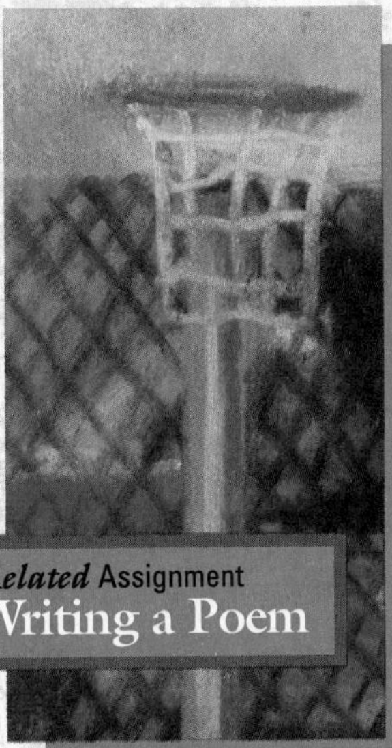

Related Assignment
Writing a Poem

You have special stories to share, and only you can tell them. No one else thinks what you think, knows the people you know, or has done what you have done. How can you help other people understand what it's like to be you? One way is to write about your personal experiences.

In this workshop, you will have the chance to explore your experiences in two ways. The guided assignment will help you write a personal narrative, or story. In the related assignment, you will write a poem to share your thoughts and feelings.

WRITER'S WORKSHOP 3

Narrative and Literary Writing

Objectives

Guided Assignment

Personal Narrative To re-create a personal experience in writing and express the importance of that experience

Related Assignment

Writing a Poem To use language creatively to express personal feelings and ideas

Teacher's Choice

Use the following guidelines to choose the assignment that best suits students' needs.

Personal Narrative This assignment will interest most students because it allows them to write about the subject with which they are most familiar—themselves. It gives them the opportunity to explore a personal experience, share it with others, and reflect on its importance. You may wish to present this assignment early in the year to help students appreciate the importance of their own ideas and experiences.

Writing a Poem This lesson allows students to explore the expressive possibilities of language. It encourages them to play with words and ideas and to stretch their imaginations.

Links to LITERATURE & LANGUAGE

Literature For examples of personal narratives, see Grade 6 *Literature and Language:*

- Bebe Moore Campbell, from *Sweet Summer*
- Gary Paulsen, from *Woodsong*
- Virginia Hamilton, "Carrying the Running-Aways"

Writing This guided assignment may be used as an extension of the Writer's Workshop, "Personal Writing: A Letter About Me," on page 58 of *Literature and Language,* Grade 6.

Guided ASSIGNMENT

ASSIGNMENT RATIONALE

Writing a personal narrative requires students to combine the elements of description, narration, analysis, and synthesis. It also helps students recognize the value of their own experiences. After students master the personal narrative, they can move on to more sophisticated forms of narrative and literary writing.

Starting from LITERATURE

Motivate

Before students read Starting from Literature, ask them to think of historical events they have studied. Which ones do they wish they could have witnessed or taken part in? Why? Then explain that the personal narrative they are about to read reveals one child's personal experience of an important historical event.

BUILD ON PRIOR KNOWLEDGE

Ask students what they know about Martin Luther King, Jr., and the civil rights movement he led in the 1950s and 1960s. Ask knowledgeable students to explain how Dr. King drew attention to the injustices facing African-Americans at the time. Use the discussion to point out that protest marches and other nonviolent tactics were important parts of the civil rights movement. You might bring in library books, pictures, or videotapes about the movement to give students a feeling for the times. Then tell students that the literary excerpt they will now read was written by a woman who marched with Dr. King when she was a child.

Guided ASSIGNMENT

Personal Narrative

Starting from LITERATURE

Sheyann Webb was eight years old in 1965 when she began participating in marches and rallies to help gain civil rights for African Americans. She was one of about seven hundred followers of Dr. Martin Luther King, Jr., who began a protest march from Selma to Montgomery, Alabama, that reached a violent climax on the Edmund Pettus bridge. As you read Sheyann's personal narrative, think about why she was able to conquer her fears that day.

from

A Child of the Movement

by Sheyann Webb

I remember being afraid on the first attempt of the Selma-to-Montgomery march (March 7, 1965). That was the first time that I was really afraid. The night before the march I slipped to the mass meeting. They began to talk about the strategies, like not fighting back. That right there told me that there was a possibility that there could be some fights. They were saying if you're

72 Workshop 3

hit, or if something is said to you, just bow down. Out of all the times my parents had talked to me about what could happen, this is when it really came to me. But somehow I was still determined to go.

I got up the next morning, frightened to march. The people began to congregate and line up. I was looking for Mrs. Moore (a teacher who had befriended me) and I found her. I remember not wanting to get close to the front of the line because I was afraid. I remember Mrs. Moore telling me that I should go back home, and I was saying I was going to march. I got in the midway of the march. As usual, we knelt down to pray, and after we had prayed, we began to sing. A little of that fear began to leave me as we sang, because people were still joyful.

As we marched down the street to the downtown area, I began to see more spectators, blacks as well as whites, and this was different to me. Normally you didn't see a whole lot of spectators. And I began to see more police officers riding around on motorcycles. It was a little bit more exciting. We still clapped, and we sang all the way down. The closer we got to the bridge, the more I began to get frightened. At this time I could see hundreds of policemen. The helmets, state troopers, dogs and horses, police cars. I got even more frightened then. I began to hold Mrs. Moore's hand tighter, and the person's hand on the other side of me. My heart was beginning to beat real, real fast. I looked up at Mrs. Moore, and I wanted to say, "I want to go home," but I didn't. She was looking straight ahead. Then the people began to kneel down and pray again.

We were still on the Edmund Pettus bridge. Going up, you can't see what's on the other side. But I had gotten up to the top, which is midway on the bridge, and you could see down. The big picture that I saw frightened me more. When we were asked to kneel down and pray, I knelt down with everybody. Shortly after we got up, a burst of tear gas began. I could see the troopers and policemen swinging their billy clubs. People began to run, and dogs and horses began to trample them. You could hear people screaming and hollering. And I began to run. I don't know what happened with Mrs. Moore. All I wanted to do was make my way back home. As I got almost down to the bottom of the bridge, Hosea Williams picked me up. I told him to put me down 'cause he wasn't running fast enough. I just continued to run.

Think & Respond

Discuss with your classmates how you would have felt if you had been marching alongside Sheyann Webb. What words and phrases signal the order of events in Sheyann's narrative?

SET A PURPOSE

Ask students to think about times when they were afraid. How did they cope with their fears? As they read Sheyann Webb's narrative, ask them to notice how she dealt with her fears.

Think & Respond

ELICIT PERSONAL RESPONSES

Have students discuss their feelings about the model in small groups. Students might brainstorm a list of words and phrases to describe what they might have felt, such as fear, excitement, or a pounding heart. Some students may also wish to freewrite their responses in their journals.

EXPLORE THE AUTHOR'S TECHNIQUES

Tell students that Webb's narrative, like most personal narratives, is told in chronological order. Point out that Webb helps her reader follow the events of her narrative by using transition words and phrases that show time order. Have students identify these transitions. (Samples: "The night before the march"—first paragraph; "the next morning"—second paragraph; "As we marched," "At this time," and "Then"—third paragraph; and "When we were asked to kneel down and pray," "Shortly after," and "As I got almost down"—fourth paragraph)

for FURTHER READING

For students interested in learning more about the civil rights movement, suggest the following books: *Martin Luther King, Jr., and the Freedom Movement* by Lillie Patterson (Facts on File, 1989); *Martin Luther King, Jr.* by Robert Jakoubek (Chelsea House, 1989).

Reading a STUDENT MODEL

Not everyone has the opportunity to participate in a historic event, as Sheyann Webb did. Yet everyone has experiences that make lasting impressions on him or her. This student model deals with a very personal event of great significance to the writer. It is the final draft of the piece that students will see in process on the workshop pages that follow.

Motivate

Ask students, "What are your most memorable experiences?" On the board, write headings such as these: *Embarrassing, Unusual, Frightening, Amusing, Painful, Satisfying.* Use the discussion to help students realize that many memorable things have happened to them, each worth thinking and writing about.

BUILD ON PRIOR KNOWLEDGE

Point out that sometimes people are deeply affected by things that happen to others who are close to them. Ask students whether they can think of examples from their own lives, such as the time when a best friend moved away or a pet died. Encourage students to discuss how these experiences made them feel and what they learned from living through them.

SET A PURPOSE

Point out that in the narrative they are about to read, Tim, the writer, tells what happened when his grandfather died. Equally important, Tim explores what the death meant to him. Ask students to be aware of their responses to Tim's experience as they read.

One Student's Writing

Reading a STUDENT MODEL

What have you felt, seen, thought, or done that you will always remember? For one middle school student, Tim Stanley, the death of his grandfather was an experience he would never forget. He wrote this personal narrative about what happened and why it was important to him. As you read his narrative, think about how it makes you feel.

Grandpa

"Wake up, Tim," said Mom.

"What time is it?" I asked.

"About eleven-thirty," she answered.

"Eleven-thirty?" That's when I sensed that something was definitely wrong. I suddenly felt very scared, not for myself or my life, just scared that something bad was going to happen.

"Why did you wake me up?"

"Grandma just called."

"Which one?"

"Grandma Coberly."

My heart went into my throat. My Grandma and Grandpa Coberly were the older grandparents I had. They were also the more frail.

"What did she say?" I asked.

"Grandpa's in the hospital. He had a heart attack."

"Is he OK?" I asked.

"It doesn't look good," she replied.

I can remember thinking not about Grandpa but why everyone always says, "It doesn't look good," instead of saying what they mean.

My grandpa died of kidney failure that night

74 Workshop 3

Our first catch!

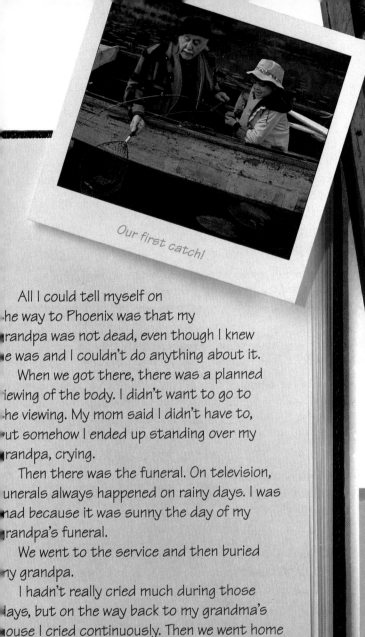

All I could tell myself on
-he way to Phoenix was that my randpa was not dead, even though I knew e was and I couldn't do anything about it.

When we got there, there was a planned iewing of the body. I didn't want to go to -he viewing. My mom said I didn't have to, ut somehow I ended up standing over my randpa, crying.

Then there was the funeral. On television, unerals always happened on rainy days. I was nad because it was sunny the day of my randpa's funeral.

We went to the service and then buried ny grandpa.

I hadn't really cried much during those lays, but on the way back to my grandma's ouse I cried continuously. Then we went home and went on with our lives, but there's still a hole where my grandpa was. It's the first ime I faced death.

Think & Respond

Respond as a Reader

▶ How do you think writing about this experience helped Tim understand it better?

▶ What experiences of your own does Tim's experience remind you of?

Respond as a Writer

▶ How does the dialogue draw you into Tim's story?

▶ In what part of his story does Tim tell why it was so important to him? Why do you think he told about it there?

Think & Respond

RESPOND AS A READER

▶ You might start by asking how writing about an experience can help writers understand it better. Help students see that the act of writing forces writers to look closely at a subject, enabling them to make connections and draw conclusions. Then ask students to respond specifically to the first question.

▶ Students may not have experienced a loss as profound as the death of a family member. However, students may have experienced other kinds of loss that will enable them to relate to the writer's experience and to his feelings.

RESPOND AS A WRITER

▶ Students may say that the dialogue reveals character, action, and setting in a compelling way. Tim Stanley may have started his narrative with dialogue because he remembers that important conversation so vividly.

▶ Tim concludes his narrative by saying why this experience is so important to him. Perhaps he felt it made a powerful conclusion. The passage of time has given Tim some perspective on the experience, and he shares his new understanding in the final two lines of his narrative. You might ask students where else Tim could have put his final statement.

Draw Conclusions

To make sure students understand this introduction to personal narrative writing, challenge them to list the characteristics they have noted thus far. Responses may include the following:

- tells a story that is important to the writer
- presents events in the order in which they happened
- makes clear why the experience is meaningful to the writer

Links to LITERATURE & LANGUAGE

Literature Tim's essay explores how a child feels when a family member dies. Another example of a narrative about change and loss within the family is the excerpt from *"How It Feels When Parents Divorce"* by Jill Krementz in *Literature and Language*, Grade 6.

Writing ON YOUR OWN

Point out to students that whenever they tell others about events that have happened to them, they are constructing a narrative. In this Guided Assignment, they will be asked to create a narrative about a personal experience. As they write, they should keep in mind the way Sheyann Webb and Tim Stanley organized their narratives. They should also show why their own personal experiences were important to them.

Handbooks for Help and Practice

The following handbooks may be used as mini-lessons before students begin writing or as resources when problems arise:

- **Finding a Starting Point, pp. 197–202**
- **Show, Don't Tell, pp. 239–242**
- **Appealing to the Senses, pp. 266–273**
- **Personal Voice, pp. 276–277**
- **Using Dialogue, pp. 278–280**

PREWRITE AND EXPLORE

Objectives

- To use prewriting techniques to choose a topic for a personal narrative
- To gather details for the narrative

Teaching Strategies

for UNFORGETTABLE FIRSTS

INDIVIDUALIZING INSTRUCTION: ESL STUDENTS Encourage students who have come from other countries to consider writing a personal narrative about an unforgettable "first." For example, they might write about their first day in a new school or making their first friend in the United States. Suggest that they focus their narratives on an aspect of experiencing a new culture for the first time.

Writing ON YOUR OWN
Personal Narrative

INVITATION TO *Write*

Sheyann Webb and Tim Stanley each wrote about an experience that made a difference in their lives. Personal narratives aren't always about major events like these, however. Sometimes writing about a small moment in your life can help you understand the moment's special meaning.

Write a narrative about a personal experience and tell why it was important to you.

PREWRITE AND EXPLORE

1. Search for ideas. Which incidents in your life do you remember best? Try some of the activities below to find personal experiences you might want to write about.

Exploring Topics

- **Unforgettable firsts** How did you meet your first friend? What was your first trip away from home like? List all the firsts you can think of. Then make some notes about ones that meant a lot to you.
- **Lifeline** What are the most memorable experiences in your life? **Graph** these experiences by marking off the years of your life on a horizontal line. Write each good experience above the year in which it occurred. Write each bad experience below the year in which it occurred.
- **Favorite things** Look through your scrapbooks or photo albums, or listen to some music. What memories do these images and songs spark? Freewrite about memories that have a special meaning to you.

2. Choose an idea for your narrative. Which of your ideas do you care most about? You might want to exchange story ideas with some of your classmates. Do other people's experiences give you any new ideas?

3. Think with your pencil. Freewrite about one or two of your favorite experiences. Just keep your pencil moving and see where your writing takes you.

Writer's Choice Do you want to write about something that happened to you, or do you want to write about something that happened to someone else? The important thing is to choose a story that means a lot to you.

4. Explore your story. Begin gathering facts and feelings for your narrative. Try to relive the experience. Go there in your mind and write what you see, hear, smell, taste, and feel. You might want to freewrite for a few minutes about why this experience stands out in your memory. You could also explore your ideas in a cluster or make a time line listing the events of your story in the order in which they occurred.

One Student's Process

Tim Stanley wanted to write about his grandfather's death because his grandfather had meant so much to him. He made a cluster to help him explore his feelings.

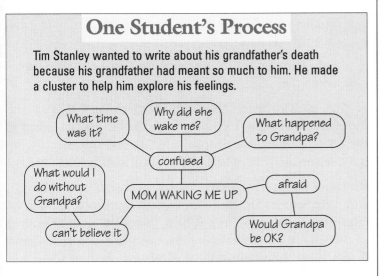

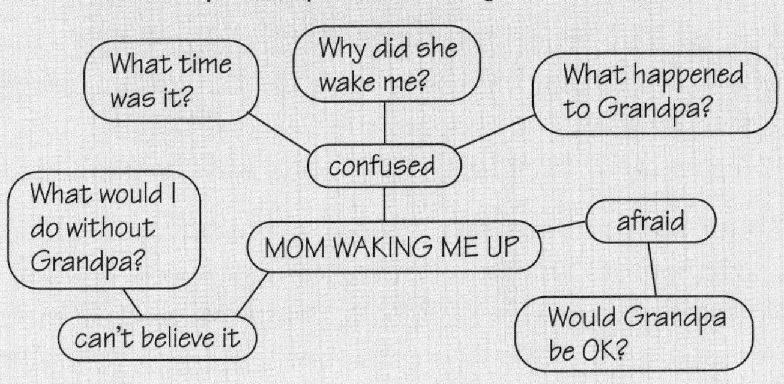

PROBLEM SOLVING

"How can I find an idea I care about?"

For help discovering the story you want to tell, see

- Sketchbook, page 70
- Springboards, page 89
- Handbook 2, "Finding a Starting Point," pages 197–202

Teaching Strategies

GENERAL NOTE

HELPFUL HINT Tell students that the Sketchbook activities on pages 70 and 140 may help them find writing ideas.

for CHOOSE AN IDEA . . .

STUMBLING BLOCK Some students may be worried because they think other students have had more "interesting" or more dramatic experiences than they. Stress that any experience has value as long as it has personal meaning to the writer.

for THINK WITH YOUR PENCIL

CRITICAL THINKING: ANALYZING

After students explore an experience in freewriting, have them reread what they have written. Then suggest that they write some more and explore *why* the experience is important to them. Have them consider such questions as these: Why do I remember this experience? What did I learn from it?

for EXPLORE YOUR STORY

HELPFUL HINT: GRAPHIC DEVICES

Point out that another way to gather details for a narrative is to make a chart that answers these questions: *Who? What? When? Where? Why?* and *How?* Students can put each question at the top of a column and then list details in the appropriate columns. Direct students to the *Thinking Skills Transparency Pack* in the Teacher's Resource File for other graphic devices that can help them explore the events of their narratives.

DRAFT AND DISCOVER

Objectives

- To draft a personal narrative
- To organize a draft into a beginning, middle, and end
- To respond to one's own draft and to that of a peer

Teaching Strategies

for START WRITING

INDIVIDUALIZING INSTRUCTION: LD STUDENTS Consider having students tape-record their first draft. Then have them work with a peer to transcribe the tape.

for THINK ABOUT USING DIALOGUE

INDIVIDUALIZING INSTRUCTION: LEP AND ESL STUDENTS Students may wish to include dialect or foreign words in the dialogue to enliven their narratives.

for ORGANIZE YOUR DRAFT

KEY TO UNDERSTANDING Help students to see that although it is important to make the sequence of events clear in a narrative, a good narrative is more than a string of events presented in chronological order. The importance and impact of the events must be made clear. As an example, remind students of how Sheyann Webb included in her narrative what she was thinking and feeling as she marched from Selma to the Edmund Pettus bridge.

DRAFT AND DISCOVER

1. Start writing. A good way to begin is just to tell what happened. Feel free to explore new ideas as you put your thoughts down on paper. You also might begin thinking about what you want your readers to understand or to feel after they read your narrative.

2. Think about using dialogue. Sometimes letting people speak for themselves can help readers experience events along with you. For example, notice how Tim Stanley records the conversation he had with his mother, telling most of the first part of his story in dialogue. In her narrative, Sheyann Webb uses a quotation to show how vulnerable she felt during the march. "I looked up at Mrs. Moore, and I wanted to say, 'I want to go home,' but I didn't."

3. Organize your draft. Once you have put your ideas down on paper, you can start arranging them. Your narrative should have the following parts:

- **beginning**—sets the scene, or possibly tells why the experience was important to you
- **middle**—usually tells the story in chronological order (the order in which things happened)
- **end**—sums up the story or explains why it was important to you

Notice how Tim begins his narrative with dialogue that sets the scene: it's late at night, and he's in bed. He then tells the events in the order in which they happened. Tim ends his narrative by summing up the story and explaining why it was important to him.

4. Think about your draft. Look over your draft. How do you feel about it? Do you want to continue working on it, or are you ready to get some feedback from your classmates now? The questions on the following page can help you review your draft and get the information you need to make it better.

PROBLEM SOLVING

"How can I make my narrative interesting to readers?"

For help finding lively details, see

- Handbook 12, "Show, Don't Tell," pages 239–242
- Handbook 19, "Appealing to the Senses," pages 266–273

PROFESSIONAL NOTEBOOK

Advice from the Authors Encourage students to be adventurous during drafting. "We want to try to train them to take risks in drafting," says Peter Elbow in *Writing with Power.* Remind students that when they are drafting, they are writing for themselves. "There needs to be this element of safety . . . [of] not thinking about quality and readers' needs all the time."

REVIEW YOUR WRITING

Questions for Yourself

- How can I help readers share my experience?
- What part of my story do I like best? What makes it so interesting?
- Have I forgotten to mention any important details? How can I work them into my narrative?

Questions for Your Peer Readers

- What part of my narrative was most interesting to you? Tell me why.
- How did reading my story make you feel?
- Did you have any trouble following the events in my story? If so, where did you get lost?
- What would you like to know more about?

One Student's Process

Tim decided to ask some classmates to read and comment on the beginning of his draft. Read their comments. What would you say about Tim's draft?

"Wake up, Tim. What time is it?
About eleven-thirty."
"Eleven-thirty?" That's when I sensed something was definitly wrong.
"Why'd you wake me up?"
"Grandma just called."
"Which one?"
"Grandma Coberly."
She said that Grandpa was in the hospital.
"Is he OK."
"It doesn't look good." I remember thinking why does everyone always say it doesn't look good. Why don't they just say that someone's dying?

Peer Reader Comments

Your beginning makes me want to know what happens, but I'm not sure who's talking.

Can you say more about why you felt something was wrong?

Yeah, I agree! People should just say what they mean.

for QUESTIONS FOR YOURSELF

HELPFUL HINT Point out that students don't need to answer all the questions at once. They may want to focus on a different question each time they read their drafts.

for QUESTIONS FOR YOUR PEER READERS

PEER RESPONSE You may wish to have students use the *Peer Response Guide* for personal narrative on pages 11–12 in the Teacher's Resource File.

for ONE STUDENT'S PROCESS

KEY TO UNDERSTANDING Draw students' attention to the peer comments. Reinforce the point that it is important for readers to share with their peers how the writing affects them—what it makes them think and how it makes them feel as they are reading.

PROFESSIONAL NOTEBOOK

Advice from the Authors Peter Elbow writes, "It's crucial to think of peers not as fixers but as *audience*. There has to be an emphasis on peer questions that will help the relationship between writer and reader, build trust, promote discussion, find out what happens inside readers' minds."

REVISE YOUR WRITING

Objectives

- To evaluate responses to a draft of a personal narrative and to revise with those responses in mind
- To evaluate the personal dimension of the narrative
- To analyze the structure of a draft, paragraph by paragraph

Teaching Strategies

for GET PERSONAL

HELPFUL HINT Point out that one way for students to achieve a personal tone is to imagine they are talking to a close friend about their experiences.

for PARAGRAPHS AT WORK

HELPFUL HINT Draw students' attention to the first sentence in each paragraph of Sheyann Webb's narrative. Point out that each sentence signals a change in the action. Her transitions make the order of events clear.

for DECIDE WHAT CHANGES . . .

INDIVIDUALIZING INSTRUCTION: ADVANCED STUDENTS As students revise, encourage them to experiment with techniques that break up the chronological progression of the narrative, such as flashback or flash-forward.

REVISE YOUR WRITING

1. Think about the responses to your narrative. What good things did you or your peer readers notice about your narrative? Did your readers help you to see your draft in new ways? If you want to add more information or make parts of your draft more clear, check your prewriting notes. You may have jotted down details you can use as you revise.

2. Get personal. Since this is a personal narrative, help your readers get to know you. Does the writing sound like the way you speak now or spoke when the event took place? Have you showed how you felt about the experience?

For example, Sheyann Webb shows how she felt as an eight-year-old child during the march. "I began to hold Mrs. Moore's hand tighter, and the person's hand on the other side of me. My heart was beginning to beat real, real fast."

Paragraphs at Work In a personal narrative, paragraph breaks will help your readers follow your story. Divide your narrative into separate paragraphs to make the flow of events clear. As you revise, remember these tips:

- Begin a new paragraph whenever the scene or action changes.
- Begin a new paragraph when a different person begins speaking.
- Use transitional words and phrases such as *first, next, later, at the same time,* and *finally* to make the order of events clear.

3. Decide what changes you want to make in your draft. You may want to make only minor changes. Don't be afraid, however, to make major revisions or even to start over again. Do whatever is needed to turn your writing into something you care about and want to share with readers.

PROBLEM SOLVING

"How can I make my writing sound like me?"

For help with finding your personal style, see

- Handbook 21, "Personal Voice," pages 276–277

COMPUTER TIP

Try different ways of expressing an idea by moving your cursor down a line and typing in different wording. Keep the version you like best.

Grammar Connection

Remind students to use verb tense consistently. Ask students to identify the tense Sheyann Webb used in her narrative. (past tense) Then demonstrate how shifts in tense can be confusing by reading a portion of Webb's narrative, changing verb tense from past to present.

One Student's Process

After reviewing his draft and his peer readers' comments, Tim decided to make the following changes in his draft. He would change it even more before he was satisfied with his story.

"Wake up, Tim[," said Mom. ¶"] What time is it?[" I asked.]

["]"About eleven-thirty[,]" [she answered.]

"Eleven-thirty?" That's when I sensed something was definitly [e] wrong.

"Why'd you wake me up?"

"Grandma just called."

"Which one?"

"Grandma Coberly."

She said that Grandpa was in the hospital. [He had a heart attack.]

"Is he OK[?]"

"It doesn't look good." I remember thinking why does everyone always say it doesn't look good. Why don't they just say [what they mean?] ~~that someone's dying?~~

[¶ My heart went into my throat. My Grandma and Grandpa Coberly were the older grandparents I had. They were also the more frail.]

PROOFREAD

1. Proofread your work. When you proofread a personal narrative, make sure that you have spelled the names of people and places correctly. If you used dialogue, make sure you punctuated it properly. Then check for other errors in grammar, spelling, punctuation, and capitalization.

for ONE STUDENT'S PROCESS

COLLABORATIVE OPPORTUNITY
Point out how the changes Tim made in this draft respond specifically to the peer comments on page 79. Then ask groups of students to discuss further changes that Tim might consider as he continues to revise his narrative.

PROOFREAD

Teaching Strategies

for PROOFREAD YOUR WORK

HELPFUL HINT Point out that one technique students can use to discover misspelled words is to read their narrative backwards, one word at a time. Such a reading will force them to slow down and look at each word separately.

for LINKING MECHANICS AND WRITING

HELPFUL HINT Draw students' attention to the revised dialogue to make sure they understand that commas and periods almost always belong inside the quotation marks. Have them look for examples of dialogue in newspaper and magazine articles and observe how the dialogue is punctuated.

Guidelines for Evaluation

IDEAS AND CONTENT

- tells an engaging story
- expresses why the story is meaningful to the writer
- uses descriptive details and dialogue to show the writer's experience

STRUCTURE AND FORM

- draws readers in with an interesting introduction
- uses chronological order effectively
- uses transitions to make the order of events clear
- has a satisfying conclusion

GRAMMAR, USAGE, AND MECHANICS

- uses verb tenses consistently
- punctuates dialogue correctly
- spells proper names correctly

Standards for Evaluation

PERSONAL WRITING

A personal narrative

- tells a story that is important to the writer
- has an introduction that draws readers in
- presents events in an order that makes sense
- makes it clear why the story is meaningful
- has a satisfying conclusion

LINKING MECHANICS AND WRITING

Writing Dialogue

When you write dialogue, be sure to indicate clearly who is speaking. Enclose the exact words of the speaker in quotation marks. Place commas, periods, and question marks inside the quotation marks as needed. Also, remember to begin a new paragraph each time the speaker changes.

Notice how Tim corrected his use of quotation marks when he revised his writing.

Original

"Wake up, Tim. What time is it?
About eleven-thirty."

Revised

"Wake up, Tim," said Mom.

"What time is it?" I asked.

"About eleven-thirty," she answered.

For more information about using quotation marks, see Handbook 43, "Punctuation," pages 586–588.

2. Make a clean copy of your narrative. Take a last look at your narrative, using the Standards for Evaluation shown in the margin as a guide. Then make a final copy of your work.

PUBLISH AND PRESENT

- **Make a class booklet.** Collect stories in a booklet that can be displayed in class or in the school library.
- **Read your narrative aloud.** If possible, add music, photographs, or other props.

- **Submit your narrative to the school magazine.** If the school does not have a magazine, your class could start one.
- **Turn your story into a dramatic skit.** Act out your story with the help of your classmates.

REFLECT ON YOUR WRITING

WRITER TO WRITER

The story's about you.

Horace, Roman poet

FOR YOUR **PORTFOLIO**

1. Add your writing to your portfolio. You have now read two personal narratives and written one of your own. Think about what you have learned from this experience. Then write your thoughts in a paragraph and attach it to your narrative.

Think about questions like these:

- How did writing about my experience help me to understand the event? What new thoughts or memories came to me while writing?
- What was easiest about writing my narrative? What was hardest?
- How did sharing my writing with my peers help me? How could I have gotten more help?
- What would I do differently if I wrote about the same experience again?

2. Explore additional writing ideas. See the suggestions for writing a poem on pages 86–88 and Springboards on page 89.

Reteaching

After students have completed their papers, assess the needs of students who were not successful in developing an effective personal narrative; then assign the appropriate handbook minilessons as well as the Workshop Support Materials listed in the Teaching Preview, pages 69a–69b. Concepts commonly requiring reteaching for this assignment are:

- **Handbook 7, Organizing Details, pp. 217–221**
- **Handbook 13, Creating Longer Pieces of Writing, pp. 243–246**

The following suggestions and resources also may be useful:

Weak Sentences In retelling events, students may produce run-on or stringy sentences. Handbook 23, "Correcting Sentence Errors," pages 281–284, can help students revise their writing.

Show, Don't Tell Remind students that they want their readers to be able to imagine themselves experiencing the events of the narrative. Direct students to "Showing an Experience" on page 13 of the *Writing Resource Book* for more practice using sensory details in personal narratives.

Extension and Enrichment

1. Suggest that students write stand-up comedy routines in which they retell humorous personal experiences.
2. Challenge students to write a fictional narrative. They might start with a real experience and then use their imaginations to change and develop the sequence of events and the outcome.

Closure: Reflect on Your Writing

As students consider the questions, encourage them to think about the unexpected twists and turns their writing took as they drafted.

Related ASSIGNMENT

Starting from LITERATURE

Objectives

- To respond to three poems
- To experiment with expressing feelings and ideas creatively
- To draft, review, and present a poem

Motivate

Ask students to discuss characteristics of poetry. Use the discussion to correct any misconceptions students may have about poetry (e.g. all poems must rhyme). Explain that poetry is a form that gives writers great freedom: it offers many options and has few rules. Tell students that this assignment will give them a chance to play with language and experiment with ways to express their thoughts and feelings.

BUILD ON PRIOR KNOWLEDGE

Ask students to name their favorite singing groups. Then ask them to explain what they like about those performers' songs. Prompt students to recognize that one important aspect of any song is the lyrics—the words that have been set to music. Point out that lyrics are a form of poetry. Song lyrics, like the poems students are about to read, use language creatively to express feelings and ideas.

SET A PURPOSE

Point out that writing poetry is another way in which writers share their personal reactions to the world around them. As students read the poems on these pages, suggest that they notice any particularly vivid words and phrases.

Related ASSIGNMENT Writing a Poem

Starting from LITERATURE

A poem can capture a thought, a feeling, a scene, or any other experience. Writing poetry gives you a chance to play with language. You can think about how words sound and look, as well as about what they mean. You can be silly or serious, simple or sophisticated. As you read these poems, notice the different ways the poets use language.

Rain

Rain hits over and over
on hot tin,
on trucks,
on wires and roses.
Rain hits apples, birds, people,
coming in strokes of white,
gray, sometimes purple.
Rain cracks against my eyelids,
runs blue on my fingers,
and my shadow floats on the sidewalk
through trees and houses.

Adrien Stoutenburg

MORE ABOUT THE MODEL

Author Notes Adrien Stoutenburg and Eloise Greenfield have written many books of poetry for young people. Stoutenburg has worked as a writer, librarian, political reporter, and editor. She once said, "I always . . . desired to be a poet and write reams of poetry in my spare time." Greenfield worked as a clerk-typist for the U.S. Patent Office before becoming a writer. She said that having her first writing projects rejected taught her that writing was "not the result of talent alone, but of talent combined with skills that had to be developed."

Scrapyard

Old, old cars, rusting away,
Some cars whole—in these we play.
Now I am swerving round a corner,
Streaking round a bend,
Zooming past the finishing line
To the checkered flag—
Finishing a perfect first,
Ready for the autograph hunters.

Michael Benson

Reggie

It's summertime
And Reggie doesn't live here anymore
He lives across the street
Spends his time with the round ball
Jump, turn, shoot
Through the hoop
Spends his time with arguments
    and sweaty friends
And not with us
He's moved away
Comes here just to eat and sleep
    and sometimes pat my head
Then goes back home
To run and dribble and jump and stretch
And stretch
And shoot
Thinks he's Kareem
And not my brother

Eloise Greenfield

Think & Respond

What feeling do you get from reading each of these poems? Which poem do you like best? Why? What words strike you the most? What ideas do these poems give you for your own writing?

Think & Respond

ELICIT PERSONAL RESPONSES

Before students answer the questions in Think & Respond, ask these questions about the poems: Why does Stoutenburg say that rain "hits"? (to show that rain can strike forcefully) What is Michael Benson pretending to be in the scrapyard? (a race-car driver) What emotion does Eloise Greenfield describe? (Sample: sadness or loneliness)

EXPLORE THE AUTHORS' TECHNIQUES

You may wish to begin by pointing out some of the ways in which poetry differs from other types of writing:

- Poetry is written in lines, not in sentences. The length of each line is part of the effect of the poem. For example, Eloise Greenfield draws attention to some words by placing them in very short lines.
- Poets play with the sound and rhythm of words. Notice how Adrien Stoutenburg uses the phrases "Rain hits . . ." and "Rain cracks . . ." to give her poem a distinct visual and sound pattern. Michael Benson repeats words ending in *-ing* to give his poem a lively rhythm, contrasting motion with rest.
- Poems are condensed; poets make every word count.

PROFESSIONAL NOTEBOOK

Poet Georgia Heard shares this advice with students: "Poems have to be about something that is *so* important to me, I have a physical feeling of that topic inside me. You know how when you are scared, really scared, you can feel it in your body, or when you are so, so happy, and your body sings? . . . Feelings are the source of a poem, but you can't just write the feelings onto paper. Instead of trying to tell the reader my feelings, I go back in my mind's eye and locate the feeling in specific concrete things that we see and hear. I get a picture in my mind and then re-create that picture so the reader can feel what I felt."

Writing ON YOUR OWN

Remind students that each of the poems on the previous two pages is a personal look at something that was important to the poets. Tell students that they can write a poem about anything that is interesting to them. The subject can be large or small, important or trivial, funny or sad.

Handbooks for Help and Practice

The following handbooks may be used as mini-lessons before students begin writing or as resources when problems arise:

- **Appealing to the Senses, pp. 266–273**
- **Personal Voice, pp. 276–277**

Teaching Strategies

for LOOK INSIDE YOUR HEAD

HELPFUL HINT Another useful way to begin gathering ideas for a poem is to make a cluster diagram. In the center of a piece of paper, students should write a subject, circle it, and then see how many related ideas, words, and phrases they can generate from it.

for EXPLORE IDEAS

HELPFUL HINT The images in the *Fine Art Transparency Pack* in the Teacher's Resource File can be good starting points for poetry ideas. Students can use the suggested prompts or simply free-write their personal reactions to the images.

Writing ON YOUR OWN
Writing a Poem

INVITATION TO *Write*

A poem can be about a subject as common as rain or as personal as your brother. The only limit to what you say—and how you say it—is your own imagination.

Write a poem about something you've seen, felt, thought, or dreamed.

EXPLORING YOUR WORLD

1. Look inside your head. Close your eyes and try to focus your thoughts inward. What images or ideas come to mind? Also check your journal for subjects you've been thinking about lately.

2. Explore ideas. You might try freewriting about your observations and feelings. Write down or sketch words and images that occur to you, no matter how odd they seem. Look for these kinds of details:

- **Sensory images** What do you see, hear, smell, taste, and feel when you think about your subject?
- **Words and phrases** What words, phrases, or sounds remind you of your subject?
- **Comparisons** Is your subject like anything else? Look for unexpected or unusual comparisons.

For example, notice the strong sensory images Stoutenburg uses to help readers see and feel the rain—"hot tin," "strokes of white, /gray, sometimes purple," "cracks against my eyelids," and "my shadow floats on the sidewalk."

PROBLEM SOLVING

"How can I turn my ideas into a poem?"

To help bring your ideas to life, see

- Handbook 19, "Appealing to the Senses," pages 266–273

TEACHER'S LOUNGE

DRAFTING YOUR POEM

1. Write and rewrite. You actually started writing your poem when you began exploring your world. Now begin experimenting with images, ideas, words, and meanings. Keep the ones you like best and try out new ones. Many poets write their poems over and over before they really discover what they want to say.

2. Play with language. As you write, read your drafts aloud. Listen to the sound of the words. Try using words that use sound in an interesting way.

Words and Sounds

Words can

- begin with the same sound (slippery snow)
- end in the same sound (dark ink)
- have the same vowel sound (gray lake)
- sound like what they mean (buzz, crackle)

Writer's Choice Some poems rhyme and some don't. Experiment with your poem to see if rhyming the last words of lines makes your poem seem more rhythmic, more musical.

3. Think about the rhythm and shape of your poem. Notice the rise and fall of your voice as you read your poem. Also notice the way the poem looks on paper. Experiment with different words and ways of arranging them. Try short lines and long lines and different stanzas, or groupings of lines.

Notice how both Stoutenburg and Greenfield repeat certain words to give their poems rhythm. Stoutenburg repeats the word *on:* "on hot tin, / on trucks, / on wires and roses." Greenfield repeats the word *and:* "To run and dribble and jump and stretch / And stretch / And shoot."

for WRITE AND REWRITE

PERSONAL TOUCH You may wish to write a poem along with the class. By doing so, you can impress on students the value of experimenting and reworking drafts in order to hone ideas and language. Unless you model the process, students may stop working once they have completed a draft.

for PLAY WITH LANGUAGE

INDIVIDUALIZING INSTRUCTION: ESL STUDENTS The sensory images that make poetry so expressive can be difficult for ESL students to compose on their own. Urge these students to sketch their ideas in words and images. Then work with them to find precise words and phrases to convey the ideas and images they have drawn.

for THINK ABOUT THE RHYTHM AND SHAPE . . .

SPEAKING AND LISTENING You may wish to break the class into small groups and have students read their drafts aloud to one another. Encourage students to respond to the way the poems sound (the rhythm of the words) as well as to what the poems say.

Music Connection

You might want to give students the option of writing a song setting their poetry to music. For example, they could write new lyrics to a melody they already know.

for PLAY IT BY EAR

SPEAKING AND LISTENING
Encourage students to review "Words and Sounds" on page 87 before they read their own poems aloud. Then they should ask themselves, "Did I use sounds as effectively as I could have? Would repeating a sound in a particular line help the sound and rhythm of my poem?"

for CUT IT DOWN

MODELING As you write your own poem along with the class, show how you eliminate unnecessary words and phrases as you go over your draft again and again. Verbalize your thinking process, so that students can hear the considerations that lead you to drop a word or phrase. Point out that poetry doesn't have to state everything directly. Providing a few good clues to the meaning is often a more effective way of interesting the reader.

for CUT IT DOWN

HELPFUL HINT Remind students that they can accent certain words by placing them alone in lines. Stress that the look of the poem on the page—the length of the various lines—also affects the reader.

Guidelines for Evaluation

AN EFFECTIVE POEM

- focuses on a single experience or feeling
- uses vivid language and images
- takes advantage of the sound and rhythm of words

REVIEWING YOUR POEM

1. Play it by ear. Put your poem aside for a few hours or a day. Then read it again, aloud. Listen for places where you stumble or don't like the way it sounds. Can you think of better words to use? Do you need to find more vivid images?

2. Share your poem with your peers. Read your poem aloud to your classmates. Then have them read it silently or aloud. Ask your classmates why they think you wrote this poem. What words and phrases do they especially like or dislike? What images create the most vivid pictures?

3. Cut it down. Poetry is a way of saying a lot with a few well-chosen words. Look for ways you can trim unnecessary words or thoughts. You might want to focus on only one part of an experience, a scene, or a feeling.

For example, in his poem, Benson tells readers that pretending to be a race-car driver in an old, junky car makes the speaker feel important and powerful. One line of the poem—"Ready for the autograph hunters"—says it all.

4. Make sure that your poem expresses who you are. As you rework your poem, consider the comments of your peers. Remember, though, that the poem represents your vision, and you get to decide what you say and how you say it.

Grammar TIP

In poetry, the first word of every line is sometimes capitalized. However, you can use capitalization and punctuation in any way that helps you express your ideas clearly and strongly.

PUBLISHING AND PRESENTING

- **Have a poetry reading.** Read poems aloud with your classmates. Invite another class to listen.
- **Make a poetry collection.** Gather your class's poems into a booklet.
- **Create a bulletin-board display.** Post your poems in the classroom. Add artwork to illustrate the poems.

Grammar Connection

You may wish to explain the concept of "poetic license." Poets often take liberties with the rules of capitalization and punctuation that students are expected to follow in other kinds of writing. For example, both "Scrapyard" and "Reggie" do not use traditional punctuation. Point out that students' main concern should be to make their meaning clear and not confuse their readers.

Springboards

History What historical event do you wish you could have experienced? The first walk on the moon? The eruption of Mount Vesuvius? Write a journal entry describing your imaginary experience.

Music Make up a rap in which you retell a personal experience. Use the rhythm and sound of your words to express your true feelings.

Literature Pretend that you are a character in one of your favorite stories. What if you could get up off the page and do anything you wanted? Write a narrative about an experience you would have.

Social Studies How would you explain to someone in another country what a day in your life is like? Write your thoughts in a letter to a pen pal.

Springboards

Teaching Strategies

for HISTORY

SPEAKING AND LISTENING
Another way to experience history is by interviewing persons who have participated in historic events. Encourage students to interview parents, grandparents, or other adults about important events they have experienced. Then have students write a narrative retelling the event from the point of view of the person interviewed.

for LITERATURE

COLLABORATIVE LEARNING As an alternative, small groups of students can work together to write and perform a skit about the experiences of a character from a story the class has studied.

for SOCIAL STUDIES

INDIVIDUALIZING INSTRUCTION: ESL STUDENTS Students from other countries might write letters to their classmates, describing what life is like in their native countries.

Combining Sentences

Objectives

- To make sentences smoother and more interesting by combining information from two sentences
- To imitate the sentence patterns of professional writers

Teaching Strategies

for COMBINING SENTENCES

MODELING You may wish to model the sentence-combining process on the board, using these sample sentences from *The Forgotten Door* by Alexander Kay:

After a minute, two of the creatures moved hesitantly down the slope and stood looking at him curiously.

The creatures were *a doe and her fawn.* (Put commas before and after the added information.)

Answer: After a minute, two of the creatures, a doe and her fawn, moved hesitantly down the slope and stood looking at him curiously.

Sentence COMPOSING

Combining Sentences

Good writers often express more than one idea in a sentence. By combining information from two sentences, the writer quoted below made a sentence that was smoother and more interesting.

Model Dead fruit trees rose like ghostly hands.
Dead fruit trees were all around us.

Combined All around us, dead fruit trees rose like ghostly hands.

Laurence Yep, *Dragon of the Lost Sea*

ON THE MARK When you add information to a sentence, you often need to set off the new information with a comma.

A. Combining Sentences Make a new sentence by putting the underlined part of the second sentence into the first sentence at the caret (^).

1. Inside the cabin the boy's mother sat by the stove ^ . She was picking kernels of walnuts with a bent hairpin. (*Put a comma before the added information.*)

   William H. Armstrong, *Sounder*

2. ^ The kind of friends I had were what you'd expect. This was true up until I turned twelve years old. (*Put a comma after the added information.*)

   Joseph Krumgold, *Onion John*

3. The three women had their fence half built ^ . It was a high fence enclosing an area behind the house. (*Put a comma before the added information.*)

   William E. Barrett, *The Lilies of the Field*

4. The children ^ came charging back into their homeroom. The children were shouting and screaming. (*Put commas before and after the added information.*)

   Rosa Guy, *The Friends*

B. Combining and Imitating Sentences Combine each group of sentences below by adding the underlined chunks to the first sentence. Make a sentence that has the same order of chunks as the model. Then write a sentence of your own that imitates the model.

1. *Model:* A shaft of sunlight, warm and thin like a light patchwork quilt, lay across his body.

   Marjorie Kinnan Rawlings, *The Yearling*

   A creature from outer space stepped from the flying saucer. The creature was <u>tall and glowing like a giant firefly.</u>

2. *Model:* Closer and closer they came, bumping and jolting each other, clawing and snorting in their own eager fury.

   Norton Juster, *The Phantom Tollbooth*

   Faster and faster they ran. They were <u>pumping and stretching their legs.</u> They were <u>straining and sweating toward the finish line.</u>

3. *Model:* Behind it stretched a graveyard, with groves of trees planted among the tombstones.

   Cynthia Voigt, *Homecoming*

   Before us stood the teacher. He stood <u>with a stack of report cards.</u> The report cards were <u>held in his hand.</u>

4. *Model:* From every window blows an incense, the all-pervasive blue and secret smell of summer storms and lightning.

   Ray Bradbury, *Dandelion Wine*

   After every touchdown comes a celebration. It is <u>a loud and joyous moment.</u> The moment is one <u>of spirited cheers and laughter.</u>

   Peter S. Beagle, *The Last Unicorn*

Grammar Refresher When you combine sentences, the information you add is often a fragment. It does not express a complete thought by itself. To learn more about sentences and fragments, see Handbook 34, "Understanding Sentences," pages 338–373.

Additional Resource

Sentence Composing Copy Masters, pp. 5–6

Answer Key

A. 1. Inside the cabin the boy's mother sat by the stove, picking kernels of walnuts with a bent hairpin.
2. Up until I turned twelve years old, the kind of friends I had were what you'd expect.
3. The three women had their fence half built, a high fence enclosing an area behind the house.
4. The children, shouting and screaming, came charging back into their homeroom.

B. Combined sentences are given. Students' imitations will vary but should follow the same pattern as the model.
1. A creature from outer space, tall and glowing like a giant firefly, stepped from the flying saucer.
2. Faster and faster they ran, pumping and stretching their legs, straining and sweating toward the finish line.
3. Before us stood the teacher, with a stack of report cards held in his hand.
4. After every touchdown comes a celebration, a loud and joyous moment of spirited cheers and laughter.

4

Informative Writing: Explaining *How*

Overview

Informative writing that explains *how* focuses on causes and effects or on the steps of a process. In this workshop, students apply skills of analyzing, sequencing, and describing to create written and visual explanations of processes. Workshop 4 includes the following Guided and Related Assignments, as well as the interdisciplinary project described on pages 91c–91d.

1. **Guided: Directions** invites students to analyze and sequence the steps of a process in order to write directions for an activity they have mastered. It gives students practice in writing descriptive details, arranging details in chronological and spatial order, and considering the needs of an audience.
2. **Related: Explaining with Graphics** calls on students to explain a process, using visual devices along with captions. Using a different medium, it allows students to exercise the same skills of analysis and sequencing required for the Guided Assignment.

Teaching Preview

Preparation Guide

1. Use the Overview on this page and the Teacher's Choice descriptions on page 93 as a basis for deciding which assignments to teach.
2. Preview the assignments and the teacher's notes and identify concepts that may require preteaching or extra support, given your class's abilities. The handbook mini-lessons suggested within the lesson may also provide guidance.
3. Preview the chart below for support materials in the Teacher's Resource File that may be used with this Workshop. Resources are for use with the Guided Assignment unless otherwise noted.

Support Materials

WRITER'S CRAFT RESOURCES

Prewrite and Explore
Thinking Skills Worksheets, pp. 2, 6
Thinking Skills Transparencies, pp. 2–2a, 6–6a
Writing Resource Book, pp. 16–17

Draft and Discover
Elaboration, Revision, and Proofreading Practice, p. 7
Elaboration, Revision, and Proofreading Transparencies, pp. 13–14
Writing Resource Book, pp. 18–20

Revise Your Writing
Elaboration, Revision, and Proofreading Practice, p. 8
Elaboration, Revision, and Proofreading Transparencies, pp. 15–16
Guidelines for Writing Assessment and Portfolio Use, pp. 17, 31–33
Peer Response Guides, pp. 13–14
Writing Resource Book, p. 21

Assessment
Tests and Writing Assessment Prompts, p. 4

Extension Activities
Sentence Composing Copymasters, pp. 7–8
Starting Points for Writing, pp. 27, 30, 35, 37, 40
Writing from Literature, pp. 9–12
Standardized Test Practice

Educational Technology (available separately)
Writer's DataBank
Electronic English Handbook
Multimedia Workshop
On Assignment! (videodisc)

OTHER RESOURCES

Books and Journals
Freeman, E. B. "Informational Books: Models for Student Report Writing." *Language Arts.* 68 (Oct. 1991): 470–473.
Stine, Bob. *How to Be Funny.* New York: Scholastic, 1991.

Films and Videos
Tell Me a Story: How a Picture Book Is Made. SRA, 1993. (20 min.)
The Animated Encyclopedia. SVE, 1991.

Educational Technology
Following Directions: Behind the Wheel. Mindscape Educ./SVE. Apple II.
How We Classify Animals. Aims Media. (videodisc)

Linking Literature, Writing, and Grammar

The following options may be used to provide students with an integrated language experience. Begin by assigning and discussing any of the recommended pieces of literature. Use the suggested strategy to provide a link to the Guided Assignment.

LINKING LITERATURE AND WRITING

Option 1

Starting Point: "Take Tracks Home" by Ed Ricciuti on pages 94–95 of *The Writer's Craft.*

Strategy: Use the teaching suggestions on pages 94–95 to lead students into the Guided Assignment.

Option 2

Starting Point: "The All-American Slurp" by Lensey Namioka on pages 293–300 of McDougal, Littell's *Literature and Language,* Grade 6. (Additional suggestions for using *Literature and Language* can be found on page 93.)

Strategy: Have students read the story and share experiences of learning table manners or learning how to eat certain foods. Challenge them to create step-by-step directions for someone who has never eaten spaghetti, fried chicken, or corn on the cob. Use the activity to introduce the Guided Assignment.

Option 3

Starting Point: "How to Read Faster" by Bill Cosby.

Strategy: Have students read the essay and tell whether the directions are easy to follow. What techniques did Cosby use to help readers follow the directions? Use the discussion to introduce the Guided Assignment.

LINKING WRITING AND GRAMMAR

Before the drafting or revision stages of this assignment, tell students that prepositional phrases that tell *where* and *when* can be very important in directions, but the phrases must be properly placed in the sentence in order to make sense. Tell students that one of the following sentences might belong in a set of directions on how to fish. Ask which sentence makes sense and why.

At the bottom of the lake, you hope a big fish will see the bait and swim to the surface to nibble it.

You hope that a big fish *at the bottom of the lake* will see the bait and swim to the surface to nibble it. (CORRECT)

You hope that a big fish will see the bait *at the bottom of the lake* and swim to the surface to nibble it.

Go over pages 504–515 of the Grammar and Usage Handbook. If problems in the use of prepositional phrases persist, assign the exercises on those pages for reteaching. Additional practice can be found in the *Grammar and Usage Practice Book* on pages 69–72.

Management Guidelines

The chart below indicates the number of days recommended for each phase of the Guided and Related Assignments. These numbers are an estimate of the total time needed for each phase. In practice, of course, students may not complete each phase in one continuous session, nor will they necessarily progress from stage to stage in the linear order shown here. Stars indicate portions of the assignment that may be completed outside the classroom if time is limited or if teachers wish students to work independently.

DIRECTIONS

Starting from Literature	1 day
Prewrite and Explore	2 days
Draft and Discover	2 days*
Revise Your Writing	1–2 days*
Proofread	1 day*
Publish and Present	1–2 days
Reflect on Your Writing	1 day
Extension and Enrichment	open*

EXPLAINING WITH GRAPHICS

Planning Your Graphic Device	1 day
Creating Your Graphic Device	2 days*
Reviewing Your Graphic Device	1 day
Publishing and Presenting	1–2 days
Sentence Composing	open*

It's Your Move: Creating a Board Game

Overview

Students participating in this project will study the characteristics of successful board games, and they will design and create their own games. They will learn and apply the skills of writing directions as they create the directions for their own games. They will practice critical thinking and will draw on many content areas as they work out the various aspects of their games.

Students will participate in the following activities:

- Examine favorite board games and analyze their appeal
- Design and create board games
- Plan and hold a games day
- Solicit feedback about their games and make needed adjustments
- Use language arts, science, social studies, math, and art skills to complete their research and develop materials

Preparation Guide

Tell students that board games have been part of human civilization throughout recorded history. In Egyptian tombs, for example, archaeologists have found game boards over 4,000 years old. Through class discussion, lead students to see that the games people play can reflect their history, their interests, and their dreams.

Tell students that during this project they will create their own board games. They will write directions for their games and get feedback about the games from their classmates.

Project File

Stage 1
Focus on Board Games

1. Invite students to bring their favorite board games to class and to explain how the games are played. On the chalkboard, list the aspects of each game that students find most appealing.
2. Discuss "classic" board games, such as Monopoly, Scrabble, Sorry, Chutes and Ladders, chess, and checkers. Have students consider why these games remain popular.
3. Have students brainstorm to develop a list of the qualities of a successful game. They may mention qualities like the following:
   - appearance
   - interaction among players
   - topic
   - tie to everyday life
   - challenge
4. Form groups and have each group choose a specific game to analyze. Have the groups present their findings to the class, and hold a discussion about similarities among the various games.
5. Have students brainstorm about characteristics of games they might invent themselves.

TEAM TEACHING

The following activities may be used for team teaching or as enrichment and extension activities by the language arts teacher.

Science Interested students might survey computer games and examine the principles behind them. They may want to learn about the technology that makes computer games possible.

Social Studies Study the history of board games. Learn about board games in many cultures. Consider how games can reflect cultural interests and values—for example, Monopoly reflects an interest in business and money and Scrabble and other word games show that our culture values education (see *Resources, Stage 1*).

TEACHING TIPS

- Invite the owner or manager of a toy store to speak to the class about the most popular games today and the reasons for their popularity. Ask him or her to discuss the classic games. What characteristics make them appealing?
- If possible, invite a game designer to share his or her experiences with the class.
- Offer students the option of designing variations on games they already play.

Stage 2
Create a Game

1. Divide students into groups and have the members of each group work together to devise a plan for a board game. Each group should decide the age range of their intended audience, the goal of the game, the number of players, the general plan of the board, and the materials the game will require (see *Resources, Stage 2*).
2. Have the groups create their games and try them out.
3. Instruct the groups to write directions for playing the game they created (see *Resources, Stage 2*).

TEAM TEACHING

Math Discuss the concept of probability and the chances that certain numbers will appear when dice are rolled or a spinner is spun. Examine the scoring systems of various board games.

Art Design an appealing game board. Create a flowchart to show how the game will work (see *Resources, Stage 2*).

Science As an option, create a computer game or a game based on ecology or another scientific topic.

Language Arts Learn about writing directions (see *Resources, Stage 2*). If appropriate, write background information about the game, describing characters, setting the scene, and so forth.

TEACHING TIPS

- Make computers available for students designing game boards as well as for those who choose to create computer games.
- Tell students to test their game as they are developing it. Trying out the game will help them create game strategies that are challenging but also clear and logical.
- As preparation for writing their own game directions, suggest that students notice the way directions for their favorite games are written. Have them think about ways to improve those directions.

Stage 3
Play and Reflect

1. Have students plan a games day during which they will try out one another's games. Tell each group to create peer-response forms for players to fill out after trying the group's game.
2. Hold the games day.
3. After the games day, ask the groups to reconvene to go over their peers' responses and to discuss the effectiveness of their games and their directions.
4. Instruct students to revise their games and directions as needed.

TEAM TEACHING

Math Calculate game scores. Tally responses from peer response sheets.

Art Make needed changes in game boards.

Language Arts Review revision techniques and techniques for working with peer responses (see *Resources, Stage 3*).

TEACHING TIPS

- Encourage students to decorate the classroom for the games day.
- On the games day, have one member of each group stay with the group's game to act as host and help new players. Group members should take turns hosting.
- Suggest that interested students submit descriptions and sketches of their games to companies that manufacture board games.

Resources

STAGE 1

Public libraries shelve materials about games of many cultures, ancient and modern, under Dewey decimal numbers 790.9 through 796.

Back issues of ***Calliope,*** a world history magazine for young people, include information about games throughout history.

The Chess Book by Jane Sarnoff and Reynold Ruffins uses a pictorial format to trace the history, as well as the rules and strategies, of chess.

STAGE 2

Games and Puzzles You Can Make Yourself by Harvey Weiss offers instructions for making playing boards and playing pieces. It also offers an overview of the principles behind various types of board games.

How to Create Computer Games by Christopher Lampton provides instructions that let students write programs for computer game prototypes.

Moving Graphics: Alien Invaders by Marcus Milton shows students how to create a basic computer game that they can adapt in various ways.

Math Puzzles by Peggy Adler and Irving Adler and ***Calculator Fun*** by David Adler include examples of number games and schematic puzzles that may give students ideas for board games.

The Writer's Craft, Grade 6, Workshop 4, "Informative Writing: Explaining *How,*" pages 92–110 teaches how to write directions and how to make flowcharts.

STAGE 3

The New Games Book by the New Games Foundation offers guidelines for creating win/win games and for planning an outdoor games day; students may be able to adapt some suggestions for planning their games day.

The Writer's Craft, Grade 6, Handbook 16, "Peer Response," pages 253–256, and Handbook 17, "Revising," pages 257–259, will help students evaluate the responses to their games and directions and make desired changes.

Additional Projects

Fix-It Manual Have students use informative-writing skills to compile a booklet of directions for repairing items they use regularly, drawing both on their own expertise and on interviews with experts. As they plan and create the booklet, they can design illustrations and study the scientific principles involved in the workings of technological devices as simple as zippers or as complex as computers.

Sixth Grade Then and Now Suggest that students use informative-writing skills to explain how schools have—and have not—changed since their parents or grandparents were in sixth grade. Have them conduct interviews and do research to gather information. To share their findings with classmates, they can create multimedia presentations that take audiences step by step through the events of a typical school day in an earlier era.

Where Music Comes From Encourage students to investigate music-related topics, such as how to play musical instruments, how musical instruments have evolved throughout history, how orchestras are organized, how popular songs are created and recorded, and how CD players and other audio devices work. Have them use informative writing, charts and other visuals, and demonstrations to present their findings.

Sketchbook

Objective

- To use the picture and suggested writing prompts as a springboard to informal writing

WRITING WARM-UPS

Encourage students to respond freely and informally to at least one of the Sketchbook prompts. Students may begin by discussing their reactions in small groups and then freewriting in their journals. Remind students that their responses will not be graded and may provide them with useful material for other assignments.

By explaining how an object might be used or how a game is played, students are practicing skills they will develop further when they give directions or explain with graphics in Writer's Workshop 4. They are also gaining experience useful for the related assignment "Describing Customs and Cultures" in Writer's Workshop 2.

SHOW, DON'T TELL

The following is a sample of a showing paragraph for the second prompt:

I have trouble being a good sport. Why? Because I love to win and hate to lose, but I also hate poor losers. I want to be a good sport when I've just missed a foul shot or just come in second in the swimming heat or just blown a Trivial Pursuit question. So here's what I do. I try to WIN at being a good sport. I grin wider than anyone else when I miss that foul shot. I congratulate my opponent more cheerfully than anybody when she wins the swim heat. And when I lose at Trivial Pursuit, I'm the first to suggest another game. You know something? It does take effort. But it also makes games more enjoyable and creates better team spirit.

Sketchbook

WRITING WARM-UPS

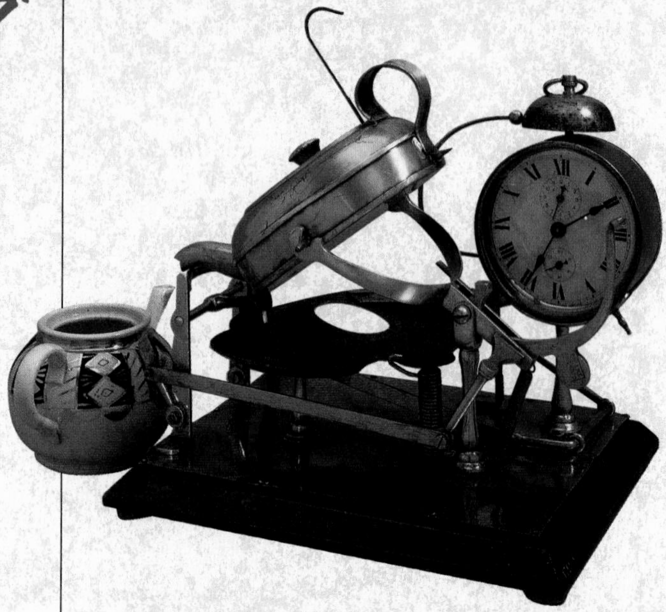

- Guess the purpose of the item in the picture. Explain how someone might use it.
- Imagine you're from another planet. Observe an Earth game such as baseball or soccer. Beam instructions for playing the game to your home planet.

Show, Don't Tell

When you give directions for making or doing something, you strive to *show* the steps of a process, using descriptive details to help readers follow your thinking. Try turning one of the *telling* sentences below into a *showing* paragraph using specific directions.

- A successful party takes planning.
- Becoming a good sport takes effort.

92

Informative Writing: Explaining *How*

Guided Assignment
Directions

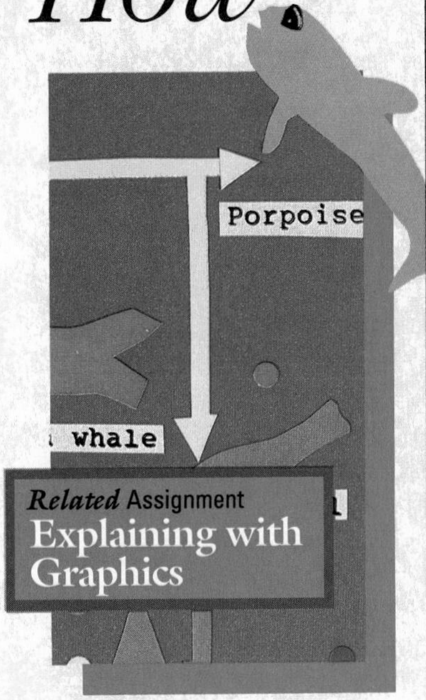

Related Assignment
Explaining with Graphics

Wave one French fry in air for emphasis while you talk. Pretend to conduct an orchestra. Then place four fries in your mouth at once and chew. Turn to your sister, open your mouth, and stick out your tongue. . . . Close mouth and swallow. Smile.

Delia Ephron, *How to Eat Like a Child*

Directions can tell people how to perform all sorts of activities—even how to eat French fries. In this workshop you'll learn how to write clear directions. Then, in a related assignment, you'll learn visual ways of explaining how something works.

93

WRITER'S WORKSHOP 4

Informative Writing: Explaining *How*

Objectives

Guided Assignment

Directions To respond to written directions and to write directions that specify needed materials and explain a process

Related Assignment

Explaining with Graphics To respond to a visual depiction of a process and to create a captioned graphic that explains a process

Teacher's Choice

Use the following guidelines to choose the assignment that best suits students' needs.

Directions This assignment will benefit most students as they respond to sets of written directions and then write directions of their own. The assignment introduces expository writing, while drawing on skills of descriptive and narrative writing; therefore, you might offer this workshop after students have had experience writing with descriptive details and using chronological and spatial order.

Explaining with Graphics Students completing this assignment will create graphics with labels and notes to explain the steps in a process. This assignment will be especially engaging for those LD students who work well with visuals but who struggle with language. Because the assignment focuses on the natural sciences, you might include it in a unit whose theme relates to plant or animal life, or you might collaborate with a science teacher in its presentation.

Links to LITERATURE & LANGUAGE

Literature For literature that includes directions on how to do something, see *Literature and Language,* Grade 6:

- Lensey Namioka, "The All-American Slurp"
- Betty Miles, from "Save the Earth"
- John D. MacDonald, "Fire"

For literature that takes an imaginative approach to explaining *how,* see the folk tales in Unit 6 of *Literature and Language.*

Writing This guided assignment may be used as an extension of the Writer's Workshop, "Informative Writing: How-to Speech," on page 319 of *Literature and Language,* Grade 6.

Guided ASSIGNMENT

ASSIGNMENT RATIONALE

Writing clear directions requires students to identify and explain the steps in a process, a skill useful in all curriculum areas. As students learn to write clear directions, they also will improve their ability to understand and follow instructions. This ability will help students in almost every aspect of their daily lives. In addition, students engaged in writing directions will practice the critical thinking skills of sequencing, speculating, analyzing, and synthesizing.

Starting from LITERATURE

Motivate

Before students read Starting from Literature, you might ask the class to list the kinds of oral and written directions they have followed or asked others to follow in the past week. These may include directions for making a sandwich, using an appliance, opening a locker, and taking a written test. Students should see that they already have a lot of experience with directions.

BUILD ON PRIOR KNOWLEDGE

Ask students what kinds of wild birds and animals they have recently seen in their neighborhoods or on trips. Invite them to share what they know—and wonder—about the habits of these animals. Are the animals more active at night or during the day? In what kinds of places do they live? What do they eat? How might students learn more about them?

Guided ASSIGNMENT Directions

Starting from LITERATURE

Think about a time when you gave someone directions on how to get someplace or do something. Did you add any special tips or suggestions?

In this article from *Field and Stream* magazine, Ed Ricciuti explains how to make plaster casts of animal tracks, or footprints. As you read his directions, notice that he includes suggestions and descriptions so that you will understand exactly what materials to use and what to do.

One of the ways that many animals survive is by staying out of sight. They keep under cover and often move only at night. So even if they are around, you seldom see them, though you can tell they're in the area by what they leave behind—tracks.

Collecting tracks is a great way to keep a record of wildlife that lives in your area—or places you visit. You can even use tracks to make a natural history museum in your home.

How do you collect tracks? If you have artistic talent, you can sketch them. If you have a camera and know how to use it, you can photograph them. Another way is to make plaster casts of tracks.

All you need is plaster of Paris, water, stiff paper, and a paper clip or piece of tape. The thin cardboard of a cereal box will work for the paper, and so will the covers of some

MORE ABOUT THE MODEL

Author Note Ed Ricciuti (1938–) has studied wildlife throughout the world: whales in Hudson Bay, sharks off the coasts of North America, animals of the Everglades and the Okefenokee, and rain forest animals in Puerto Rico. Among his books for young readers are *An Animal for Alan* and *Killers of the Sea*.

note pads, or manila folders. You'll want to identify the tracks you find. You can get field guides to track identification at a library or bookstore. Bring a book with you when you're out looking for tracks. . . .

Carry the plaster in a tightly sealed container.

A canteen will do for toting water. You can mix the water and plaster in an empty tin can, but make sure it's clean.

When you find a track, make a one- to two-inch-high circular collar around it with the paper. Secure it with a piece of tape or a paper clip. Then combine the plaster and the water in the can and stir. This is the tricky part: the mix cannot be too thick or too thin. It should be slightly more fluid than pancake batter. You can follow the directions that come with the plaster, or figure on two parts plaster to one part water.

Mix quickly because plaster thickens and sets fast.

When the mixture is ready, carefully pour it into the track. Make sure it fills the track entirely, and even overflows a little. Next, wait for the plaster to completely harden. It takes at least a half hour, so be patient. While you're waiting, you may want to make some notes. Describe the surroundings of the track—the vegetation, and whether the print was in mud, sand, or some other kind of soil. If there is a trail of tracks, make notes about its path.

When the cast is hard, dig around it with a pocket knife or garden trowel. Be careful not to cut into the plaster. Then remove the cast from the ground. You can clean it later with water and a toothbrush. . . .

If you spend enough time scouting around for tracks,

you can build a nice collection, and at the same time, you'll learn about the habits of wildlife.

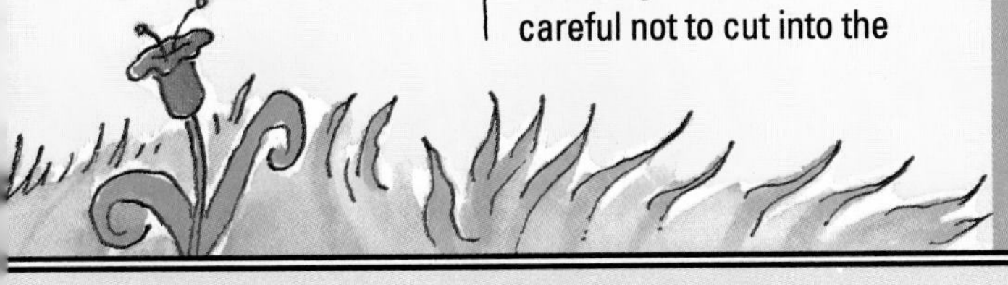

Think & Respond

Did Ricciuti's directions tempt you to try collecting tracks? Do you think you could follow Ricciuti's directions successfully? Why or why not? Can you think of activities you know how to do well enough to explain them to someone else?

SET A PURPOSE

Read Starting from Literature with students; call their attention to the purpose-setting statement. Ask, "How would you make plaster casts of animal tracks? What materials would you need?" Have them check their guesses as they read.

Think & Respond

ELICIT PERSONAL RESPONSES

If students respond to the first question in the Think & Respond box with a flat "Yes" or "No," invite them to discuss why. Ask how making plaster casts of animal tracks does or does not fit in with their interests. Students considering the second question may say that the writer should have provided more information about plaster of Paris and where it can be purchased. (It's the material used to make casts for broken bones; it's sold in hardware stores and art supply stores.) For the third question, students may wish to freewrite or brainstorm in small groups to generate a list of possibilities.

EXPLORE THE AUTHOR'S TECHNIQUES

To help students identify some of Ed Ricciuti's techniques for making a complicated process easy to follow, explain that his article is organized like a recipe. Ask students to find the place near the beginning where he lists "ingredients" and equipment. (paragraph 4) Point out that Ricciuti breaks his process into steps, just as recipe writers do. Ask students to identify the steps. (making a collar, mixing the plaster, pouring it, letting it set, taking notes, removing the cast, cleaning the cast)

Then point out how Ricciuti's article differs from a recipe: He gives interesting background information; he explains how readers can benefit from his ideas; he offers warnings and advice about tricky parts. Encourage students to keep these techniques in mind as they write directions of their own.

for FURTHER READING

Books to Read Students interested in natural history might enjoy the following books:

- Sterling North, *Rascal*
- Bill Peet, *Cappyboppy*
- Molly Burkett, *The Year of the Badger*
- Joy Adamson, *Elsa*
- Gavin Maxwell, *Ring of Bright Water*

Reading a STUDENT MODEL

Ed Ricciuti introduces readers to an interesting hobby. Student Doug Frieburg offers more "practical" advice. Both writers, however, give specific how-to information in a step-by-step format. Doug's "How to Clean Your Room in Ten Easy Minutes" is the final draft of the work in progress that appears on the pages of this workshop.

Motivate

Tell students that everyone has trouble following directions at one time or another, whether it's a matter of following a recipe, assembling a bicycle, or using a friend's map to find a park. You might recount one of your worst frustrations in following directions. Then ask students to share some of their experiences. Encourage students to speculate about why the directions were hard to follow.

BUILD ON PRIOR KNOWLEDGE

Ask what students' least favorite household chores are. Encourage them to elaborate on what makes the chores unpleasant. Then ask them to share any methods they have for getting these chores out of the way quickly.

SET A PURPOSE

To help students identify similarities between Doug's directions and Ed Ricciuti's, tell them to look for similarities in the structures of the essays. For example, both Ricciuti and Doug use the beginnings of their essays to get readers interested. Have students look for other similarities in the beginning, middle, and end sections of the two essays. Ask students also to look for similarities in the use of words such as *next, then,* and *while* to signal steps in a process.

One Student's Writing

Reading a STUDENT MODEL

Ed Ricciuti's purpose was to explain how to make plaster casts of animal tracks. Here, sixth-grader Doug Frieburg writes to explain how to clean your room. As you read Doug's piece, look for the similarities between his directions and those written by Ricciuti.

How to Clean Your Room in Ten Easy Minutes

by Doug Frieburg

Hey, Kids! Have you ever wondered how to clean your room without taking up your whole afternoon? I have that special answer for you in Doug's patented room-cleaning method.

BEGIN by dusting. Whirl away dresser dust with a blow-dryer set on high. Then terminate those nasty cobwebs by draping a not-so-well-liked T-shirt over the end of a baseball bat and running the bat around the ceiling infield.

NEXT, make your dirty clothes disappear in seconds by putting them in any of four major places. Stuff them into a laundry bag at the back of your closet. Mix your dirty clothes with the clean clothes in your dresser drawers. Simply shove them under your bed, or just pile them behind your door.

THEN have a little fun hanging up your clean clothes by turning this task into a game. Just tape a free-throw line on the floor a short distance from your closet. Then, one at a time, drape the items on hangers and toss them toward your

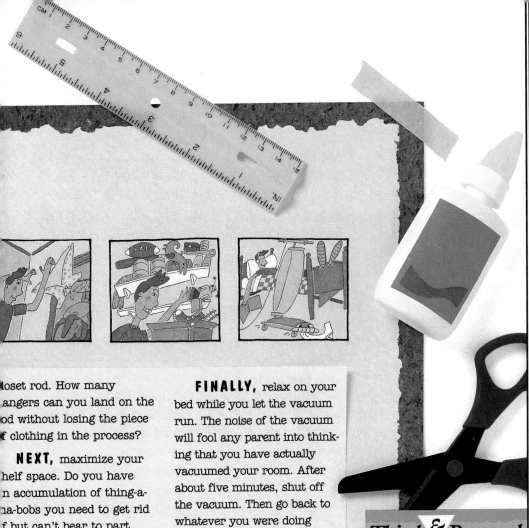

loset rod. How many angers can you land on the od without losing the piece f clothing in the process?

NEXT, maximize your helf space. Do you have n accumulation of thing-a-na-bobs you need to get rid f but can't bear to part vith? Well, you can keep verything and still make our room look neat and rganized just by putting hese items into containers. Raid your mom's stash of ld plastic containers and nargarine tubs. Old coffee ans work well too.

FINALLY, relax on your bed while you let the vacuum run. The noise of the vacuum will fool any parent into thinking that you have actually vacuumed your room. After about five minutes, shut off the vacuum. Then go back to whatever you were doing before you started cleaning.

Many kids think cleaning their room is boring and a waste of time. However, if you follow my patented room-cleaning method, not only will you have fun cleaning your room, but you'll also be done in record time.

Think & Respond

Respond as a Reader

- ▶ Did you enjoy reading Doug's directions? Why or why not?
- ▶ What parts did you like best?

Respond as a Writer

- ▶ How does Doug get your attention in his opening paragraph?
- ▶ How are Doug's directions similar to Ricciuti's? How are they different?

Think & Respond

RESPOND AS A READER

▶ Ask students how they liked Doug's first sentence and first paragraph. Point out that students' initial responses can color their reactions to the rest of the piece.

▶ Students should identify the parts they found particularly funny or clever. (For example, some students may enjoy the tips that turn tasks into games.)

RESPOND AS A WRITER

▶ Students may say that the catchy "Hey, Kids!" opener shows that the writer is speaking directly to them. Students may also say that Doug's tempting offer of a shortcut to a tiresome chore and the humorous line "Doug's patented room-cleaning method" also captured their attention.

▶ Students may note that both sets of directions use steps, get readers interested in the topic in the first paragraph, and address the reader directly as "you." Two differences are that Doug doesn't list needed equipment at the beginning, whereas Ricciuti does; and that Doug devotes a paragraph to each step, whereas Ricciuti combines steps in some paragraphs. In addition, Doug uses humor to engage his readers.

Draw Conclusions

To check students' understanding of this introduction to informative writing that explains *how,* ask them to list the characteristics they have noted thus far. Responses may include the following:

- explains how to do something
- catches readers' interest
- tells what materials are needed
- breaks the process into logical steps and illustrates each step with details

Writing ON YOUR OWN

Point out that in making an activity clear to their readers, students can learn more about it themselves. Invite them to choose an activity that promises to be fun to write about. Remind them that Ed Ricciuti and Doug Frieburg captured their audiences' attention in the first paragraph, then presented the steps in the process in a clear and logical order.

Handbooks for Help and Practice

The following handbooks may be used as mini-lessons before students begin writing or as resources when problems arise:

- **Organizing Details, pp. 217–221**
- **Transitions, pp. 234–238**

PREWRITE AND EXPLORE

Objectives

- To use prewriting techniques to identify a topic for a set of directions
- To generate a list of steps, tools, and materials for an activity

Teaching Strategies

for LOOK FOR TOPICS

KEY TO UNDERSTANDING Remind students that Doug chose an activity he disliked, but his imagination and sense of humor made it fun. Urge students to consider writing ideas that arise from their less favorite as well as their preferred activities.

for TAKING STOCK

HELPFUL HINT After students generate a list of activities, hobbies, and skills, suggest that they organize these items into other categories, such as "most fun," "requires most equipment," "hardest," and "most familiar." Doing so can help students begin the evaluation process that will eventually lead to picking a topic.

Writing ON YOUR OWN

Directions

INVITATION TO *Write*

Although Ed Ricciuti and Doug Frieburg explain how to do very different activities, both make their directions clear.

Now it's your turn. Write directions that explain an activity you know how to do well.

PREWRITE AND EXPLORE

1. Look for topics. What are your favorite games or hobbies? What tasks do you do so often that you could probably do them in your sleep? To find a topic, freewrite about some of the things you do in a typical day or try doing some of the following activities.

Exploring Topics

- **Taking stock** Are you the high scorer on a tricky video game? Do you bake cakes for special occasions? Are you a caretaker of fish, gerbils, or other pets? Take a moment to list your favorite activities, hobbies, and special skills.
- **Making a game of your search** Get together with a few classmates and pick a subject. Then spend a few minutes alone, listing everything about that subject you know how to do. For example, if you picked bicycles, you might list "riding with no hands," "patching inner tubes," and "changing flats." Then compare your list with those of your classmates. Who has the longest list? Did others think of any entries that you might add to your list?

98 Workshop 4

MULTICULTURAL Connection

Encourage students to consider topics related to their cultural heritage. For example, they might write directions for doing a craft, performing a dance, playing a musical instrument, or preparing a food that is linked to a tradition or holiday in a particular culture. Remind them to define terms and include background information that will help readers understand the activity.

- **Completing sentences** Brainstorm alone or with friends or classmates to complete one or more of the following sentences. If you prefer, you can try completing a sentence of your own.

  "I know how to win at . . ."

  "You too can succeed at . . ."

  "Making a __________ requires some planning."

  "Being a good __________ takes know-how."

2. Pick a topic. The activity you pick may be the one you know how to do best, one you think others should learn how to do, or one you think you'll have fun explaining. For help in making a selection, freewrite about your favorites to see which one interests you most.

3. Think about your activity. If possible, carry out your chosen task or project. Then jot down the steps you follow. If performing your activity is not possible, simply imagine yourself doing the task. Also, note any materials and tools you need to perform your activity.

One Student's Process

Doug Frieburg thought about how he could add some fun to an unpleasant task as he imagined himself going through the motions of cleaning his room. Then he jotted down the following notes.

Steps	Tools and Materials
pick up dirty clothes	vacuum cleaner
put away clean clothes	blow-dryer
play closet "free throw"	laundry bag
dust	baseball bat
get rid of cobwebs	old T-shirt
vacuum	

COMPUTER TIP

Listing your steps on a computer can make it easier to rearrange them or insert missed steps.

GENERAL NOTE

HELPFUL HINT Tell students that the Sketchbook activities on pages 48 and 92 may help them find writing ideas.

for COMPLETING SENTENCES

MODELING Show students how you would complete some of the sentences in the text. Demonstrate that the sentences can be changed slightly to fit students' needs. To complete the first sentence, for example, you could say "I know how to win at Monopoly," "I know how to avoid having a dead car battery on a cold morning," "I've been taught how to give the cat its medicine," and so on.

for PICK A TOPIC

CRITICAL THINKING: MAKING COMPARISONS If students are having trouble deciding on a topic, suggest that they freewrite briefly about each contender and then compare the freewritings. Doing so can help students see which topic they enjoy the most or know the most about.

for THINK ABOUT YOUR ACTIVITY

INDIVIDUALIZING INSTRUCTION: LD STUDENTS Sequencing the steps in a process can be especially difficult for some students. Encourage students to number the steps in the process as they visualize following them. Some students might also benefit from drawing each step in the process.

for ONE STUDENT'S PROCESS

KEY TO UNDERSTANDING Point out that the steps in Doug's prewriting notes aren't in the same order as those in his final draft on pages 96–97. Explain that before he began his draft, he probably numbered the steps to show which comes first, second, and so on. Tell students that they can use the same technique in their own prewriting.

Science Connection

Students interested in ecology might consider "How *not* to" topics, such as "How *Not* to Destroy the Ozone Layer," "How *Not* to Pollute Groundwater," and so on. Alternatively, students can try a tongue-in-cheek approach, writing directions on topics such as "How to Destroy the Ozone Layer" and "How to Wipe Out the Rain Forests in Just a Few Short Years." Encourage students to work with science teachers if possible.

DRAFT AND DISCOVER

Objectives

- To draft an informative piece of writing that gives directions
- To respond to one's own draft and that of a peer

Teaching Strategies

for BEGIN WRITING

HELPFUL HINT Tell students that they needn't start writing with the introduction. They can start with the first step in the activity and add the introduction later, after they have set down their main ideas.

GENERAL NOTE

MANAGEMENT TIP To avoid time-consuming problems, ask students to place numbers in the margins of their papers to show where each new step in their directions occurs. Then confer briefly with students, reviewing the sequence to make sure that the steps are in logical order and that none are missing.

Writer's Choice Do you want to treat your subject in a straightforward way, as Ed Ricciuti did? Would you rather take a humorous approach, as Doug Frieburg did?

Grammar **TIP**

Imperative statements such as "Begin by dusting" can help you state your directions simply and clearly.

DRAFT AND DISCOVER

1. Begin writing. If you took any notes or listed steps during prewriting, you might start by expanding on what you wrote. Otherwise, go through the activity in your mind and write about the steps as you picture them.

2. Think about your organization. As you write, make sure that you are presenting your information in a sensible order. For example, you would probably list any necessary tools and materials early on. Then present the steps in the order in which they should be followed—that is, in chronological order.

3. Keep your audience in mind. For example, what might you need to do to make your directions easy for a younger audience to follow? Make sure you explain what readers unfamiliar with your activity need to know. Sometimes making a comparison to something your readers are sure to be familiar with can help. Notice that Ed Ricciuti explains that the mixture of plaster and water "should be slightly more fluid than pancake batter."

4. Draw pictures. Sometimes it's easier to understand directions if you have a map or picture to follow. Would including a diagram, map, or picture help your readers?

5. Evaluate your directions. Could someone unfamiliar with your activity follow your directions? To find out, you might have a peer reader try following your directions—if that's possible. The questions below can also help you evaluate your draft.

REVIEW YOUR WRITING

Questions for Yourself

- Have I missed any steps?
- What might I add or change to make the steps easier to follow?
- Where do I mention the tools and materials my readers will need? Is that the best place for them?
- Which terms might be unfamiliar to my readers?

Questions for Your Peer Readers

- Which steps come across most clearly? least clearly?
- Are my directions organized so that they're easy to follow? If not, where did you get lost or confused?
- What additional information, if any, would you need in order to follow these directions? Am I missing anything?

One Student's Process

Here is part of Doug's first draft. Read it and then review the peer comments.

Begin by dusting. Blow away dresser dust with a blow-dryer set on high. Then terminate those nasty cobwebs with a not-so-well-liked T-shirt and a baseball bat. Make your dirty clothes disappear in seconds by stuffing them into a laundry bag at the back of your closet, shoving them under your bed, or piling them behind your door.

Peer Reader Comments

I like your blow-dryer idea.

What do I do with the T-shirt and bat?

I stick my dirty clothes in with my clean ones.

for REVIEW YOUR WRITING

PEER RESPONSE You might suggest that writers begin by asking peer readers the following questions:

- Which part of my draft do you like best?
- Which part sounds most like me?

Responses to these questions can show students where their writing is strongest, even if the steps in their directions are not yet completely clear.

for ONE STUDENT'S PROCESS

CRITICAL THINKING: ANALYZING Point out that this paragraph in Doug's first draft became two paragraphs in his final draft on pages 96–97. Ask how breaking the paragraph in two makes Doug's final draft easier to follow. (Sample: Two major steps—dusting and picking up clothes—are involved; devoting a paragraph to each step improves clarity.)

for ONE STUDENT'S PROCESS

SPEAKING AND LISTENING If students need practice with peer-response skills, you might use the student model in a role-playing exercise. If necessary assign Handbook 16, "Peer Response," pages 253–256, as a mini-lesson. Then group students; ask one student in each group to take the role of Doug. Ask the others to be peer readers. Tell peer readers to read Doug's draft in the text and to offer their own questions and comments. Encourage "Doug" to listen reflectively, making sure he or she understands their responses and asking questions if he or she does not.

REVISE YOUR WRITING

Objectives

- To evaluate responses to a draft of informative writing and to revise a draft with those responses in mind
- To analyze and revise paragraphs in an informative draft to improve their structure and development

Teaching Strategies

for BE SPECIFIC

STUMBLING BLOCK Help students to understand why precise nouns and verbs are so important in written directions. For example, if you say, "glue the pieces of the model," your readers will know what to do. If you say, "assemble the pieces," they will wonder what materials to use.

for USE TRANSITIONS AS NEEDED

HELPFUL HINT Point out that many of the transitions needed for writing directions are words telling *when.* Students probably have used these transitions before—for example, in narrative writing. For practice with these transitions, assign Handbook 11, "Transitions," pages 234–238.

for USE TRANSITIONS AS NEEDED

INDIVIDUALIZING INSTRUCTION: BASIC STUDENTS Point out to students that directions consisting only of a series of steps connected by transition words such as *then* and *next* may be informative but dull. Remind students of Ed Ricciuti's relaxed, friendly writing voice and of Doug Frieburg's humorous one. Emphasize that good "how to" writing can be made both interesting and fun for the reader by adding descriptive details and vivid verbs.

for THINK ABOUT YOUR BEGINNING

KEY TO UNDERSTANDING Explain that the introduction to a set of directions needn't be long or complicated. A snappy opening line (such as Doug's "Hey, Kids!") or a single intriguing fact (such as Ed Ricciuti's observation that many animals survive by staying out of sight) can capture the reader's interest.

REVISE YOUR WRITING

1. Think about your responses. Read your peer responses as well as your own notes. Decide which parts of your directions are coming across clearly and which parts may need to be improved. Also, if a peer reader tried following your directions, pay attention to the outcome. Was he or she successful? Why or why not? Do you need to add information or make your wording more precise?

2. Add examples. Examples and suggestions can help your readers understand exactly what you mean. For instance, after telling his readers that they will need stiff paper, Ed Ricciuti adds, "The thin cardboard of a cereal box will work for the paper, and so will the covers of some note pads, or manila folders."

3. Be specific. Wherever possible, replace vague nouns and verbs with more precise ones. For example, don't say, "Write about the place" when saying "Describe the surroundings of the track" would be more precise.

4. Use transitions as needed. Transitions, or signal words, can make the order of your steps clear and guide your readers smoothly from one step to the next. Therefore, to introduce the steps in your directions, you may want to use transitions such as *first, second, third, then, next, before, after, meanwhile,* and *finally.*

5. Think about your beginning. Directions, like other forms of writing, have a beginning, a middle, and an end. Make sure that in your beginning you introduce your readers to the activity you're going to explain and get them interested in this activity. You may also want to give your readers a good reason for reading your directions. Ed Ricciuti, for example, promises his readers that they can learn about wildlife. Doug Frieburg promises to teach his readers how to clean their rooms quickly and easily.

Grammar TIP

Adverbs can help make your directions more precise. In addition to telling how, when, or where to do something, as in "mix *quickly,*" adverbs can tell readers to what extent, as in "mix *very* quickly."

PROBLEM SOLVING

"Where can I learn more about using transitions?"

For more information about transitions, see

- Handbook 11, "Transitions," pages 234–238

TEACHER'S LOUNGE

"I don't understand how mechanical objects work. . . . Nor do I understand written instructions. Am I the only American car driver, for instance, who can't figure out how to heat or cool the car? The lever that operates this mechanism is in a slot that offers these choices: COOL, NORM, MAX, AVG, HI-LO, VENT, and HEAT. How can one selection give me both HI and LO? How does HI differ from HEAT, or from MAX? . . . Who is NORM? I have almost never found the right amount of heat for my car except by chance. The temperature somehow rises to MAX and I open all the windows to compensate. Surely this is not what Detroit had in mind."
—William Zinsser, in *Writing with a Word Processor*

6. Review your ending. You can simply end with your last step. You can also end by describing the result of following your directions. For example, Ricciuti ends his article by reminding readers of what they can gain by following his directions:

> If you spend enough time scouting around for tracks, you can build a nice collection, and at the same time, you'll learn about the habits of wildlife.

Paragraphs at Work You can use paragraphs to make your directions easier to follow.

- Make sure to start a new paragraph whenever you introduce a new step or direction.
- Make sure that each paragraph contains two or more sentences that include all the details a reader will need.

One Student's Process

Read part of Doug's revised draft to see the kinds of changes he decided to make.

Begin by dusting. ~~Blow~~ Whirl away dresser dust with a blow-dryer set on high. Then terminate those nasty cobwebs ~~with~~ by draping a not-so-well-liked T-shirt ~~and~~ over the end of a baseball bat and running the bat around the ceiling infield. ¶ Next, Make your dirty clothes disappear in seconds by ~~stuffing them into a laundry bag at the back of your closet,~~ putting them in any of four major places. Stuffing them into a laundry bag at the back of your closet. Shoving them under your bed, or just piling them behind your door. Mix them in with the clean clothes in your dresser drawer.

GENERAL NOTE

COLLABORATIVE OPPORTUNITY

You might encourage students to revise in small groups, consulting one another and exchanging ideas. If possible, group students who have not yet worked together.

for PARAGRAPHS AT WORK

HELPFUL HINT Emphasize that one sentence is not enough to make a paragraph, even though students may have seen one-sentence "paragraphs" in some cookbooks and instruction manuals. For information about the kinds of details that can be used to develop paragraphs, refer students to Handbook 4, "Developing a Topic," pages 205–210.

for ONE STUDENT'S PROCESS

KEY TO UNDERSTANDING Point out that Doug improved his draft in two main ways: He added information and replaced vague verbs and nouns with precise ones. Ask students to locate examples. (Added information: putting the T-shirt over the bat; running the bat around the ceiling; mixing dirty clothes in with clean ones. More precise words: *whirl, draping, the end* [of a baseball bat].) Also note that Doug broke this part of his draft into two separate paragraphs, one for each step in the process.

PROOFREAD

Teaching Strategies

for LINKING GRAMMAR AND WRITING

HELPFUL HINT Ask students to improve the placement of the italicized prepositional phrases in the following sentences.

- Just tape a free-throw line a short distance from your closet *on the floor.*
- Then, one at a time, drape the items and toss them toward your closet rod *on hangers.*

(Corrected sentences are found in paragraph 4 of the Student Model on pages 96–97.)

Guidelines for Evaluation

IDEAS AND CONTENT

- explains each step involved in performing a single activity
- lists needed supplies and equipment
- includes details, examples, and suggestions to make the steps clear
- has an effective beginning and ending
- uses precise nouns and verbs

STRUCTURE AND FORM

- presents steps in a sensible order
- devotes one paragraph to each step
- uses transitions to guide the reader

GRAMMAR, USAGE, AND MECHANICS

- employs standard grammar, usage, spelling, and mechanics
- places prepositional phrases correctly to avoid confusion

PROOFREAD

1. Proofread your work. Correct any errors in grammar, usage, spelling, and mechanics.

2. Make a clean copy of your paper. Use the Standards for Evaluation in the margin to check your directions one last time. Then make a final copy.

LINKING GRAMMAR AND WRITING

Using Prepositional Phrases

A prepositional phrase is a group of words that begins with a preposition and ends with its object—for example, "Just tape a free-throw line *on the floor.*" Because prepositional phrases often answer the questions *how, when,* and *where,* they are very useful in directions. When you use prepositional phrases, however, be sure to position them correctly. Improper positioning can result in confusing or even silly sentences.

Improperly Positioned

Finally, relax while you let the vacuum run on your bed.

Properly Positioned

Finally, relax on your bed while you let the vacuum run.

For more information on prepositional phrases, see Handbook 40, "Understanding Prepositions and Conjunctions," pages 502–525.

Standards for Evaluation

INFORMATIVE WRITING

Directions

- focus on a single activity
- tell readers which tools and materials they need
- contain specific words, suggestions, and examples that explain each step clearly and completely
- present the steps in an order that makes sense
- define terms that may be unfamiliar to readers
- use paragraphs and transitions to signal the start of each new step

PUBLISH AND PRESENT

- **Give a demonstration.** Read your directions aloud for classmates, and demonstrate each step as you read.

PROFESSIONAL NOTEBOOK

Amuse and instruct students with this comment from Robert C. Pinckert's *Pinckert's Practical Grammar:* "Since most [prepositional] phrases are adverbs, and since adverbs can easily be misplaced, you will, from time to time, misplace a phrase, as was done in the unsettling song lyric, *Throw mama from the train a kiss.* Here are other misplacements: *With his strength, the coach made Csonka the fullback. She stuck her tongue out at him through the window. These cats have short tails with blue eyes.*"

- **Make a "how-to" booklet.** Form a class booklet of directions. Consider grouping directions under general headings, such as "Building Things," "Making Repairs," and "Cooking."
- **Mail your directions to a magazine.** Magazines for younger readers often publish articles about making craft items, conducting science experiments, caring for pets, and similar subjects. Your teacher or librarian may be able to help you contact one of these magazines.

REFLECT ON YOUR WRITING

WRITER TO WRITER

I put down words fairly easily. It's being satisfied with what you write that's a problem.

Ralph Ellison, novelist

FOR YOUR **PORTFOLIO**

1. Add your directions to your portfolio. Now that you have written a set of directions and read two others, think about what you have learned. In a note, write down your thoughts and feelings. Attach this note to your final draft. The following questions may help you focus your thoughts:

- Is giving directions in writing harder or easier than giving directions orally?
- What advice would I give someone who was just starting this assignment?
- How was writing directions similar to other kinds of writing? How was it different?
- Were my peers' responses helpful? Why or why not?

2. Explore additional writing ideas. Try the suggestions for making a graphic on pages 108–109. You might also try the Springboards on page 110.

Reteaching

After students have completed their papers, assess the needs of students who were not successful in developing an effective set of directions; then assign the appropriate handbook mini-lessons along with Informative Writing: Explaining *How* Worksheets, pages 16–21 in the *Writing Resource Book*. Concepts commonly requiring reteaching for this assignment are:

- **Handbook 5, Goals and Audience, pp. 211–213**
- **Handbook 9, Creating Paragraphs, pp. 226–229**

The following suggestions and resources may also be useful:

Lack of Transitions Using their written directions, students should fill out the sequence chart on page 2 of the *Thinking Skills Worksheets*. Then go over the transitions on page 104 of the text, helping them find the best ones to link boxes in the sequence chart.

Incomplete Sentences Bring in examples of directions—some that use numbered sentence fragments and some that use complete sentences and paragraphs. Let students examine both kind of directions and discuss the differences. Then have students work in groups to turn the fragments into complete sentences.

Extension and Enrichment

1. Ask students to bring sets of directions to class. Have them work in small groups to determine why the directions work well or how they could be improved.
2. Invite students to write a Do-It-Yourself column for a class newspaper. Using experience or imagination, they can explain how to make improvements at home or at school.

Closure: Reflect on Your Writing

Students who wish to focus on the second question can write their advice as a set of directions. Answering this question reinforces the idea that different audiences require different information.

Related ASSIGNMENT

Starting from LITERATURE

Objectives

- To respond to and interpret an illustrated chart that explains a process
- To create, review, and present a graphic that explains a process

Motivate

Before reading Starting from Literature with students, you might draw a circle on the board. Then draw a slightly smaller circle in the middle of it. Ask, "What's this a picture of?" Elicit a variety of guesses (target, doughnut, porthole, and so on) before writing the caption: "Person in wide-brimmed hat, seen from above." Point out that using words and pictures together can create a clearer message than words or pictures alone.

BUILD ON PRIOR KNOWLEDGE

Ask, "What's the largest creature in the sea?" (Some students may name the great blue whale; most will say whales.) Then ask, "What's the smallest creature in the sea?" (Accept reasonable answers; students may not know about zooplankton and single-celled organisms.)

SET A PURPOSE

Read Starting from Literature with students; then direct their attention to the purpose-setting statement. To further focus students' examination of the chart, you might suggest that they look for sea animals and plants that are new to them.

Related ASSIGNMENT Explaining with Graphics

Starting from A GRAPHIC

Ana Ortiz decided to create this chart of an ocean food chain to show who eats whom among the creatures in the sea. As you look at Ana's graphic, notice what other things you can learn about these creatures as well.

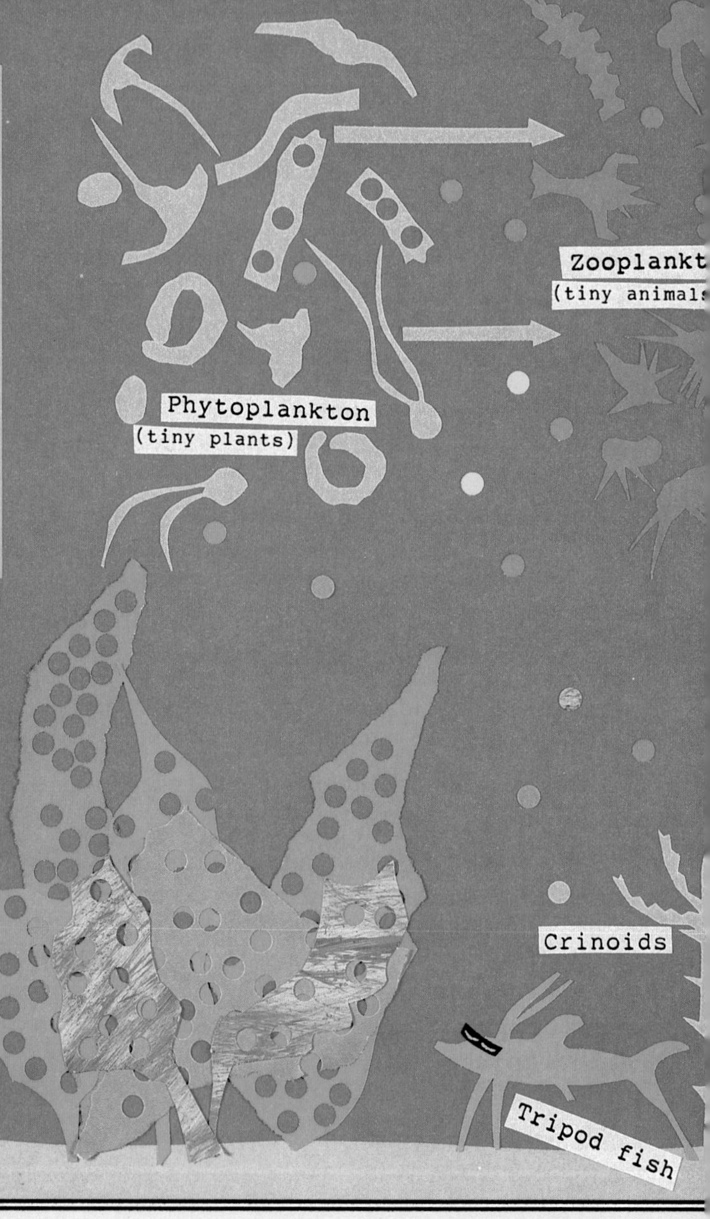

106 Workshop 4

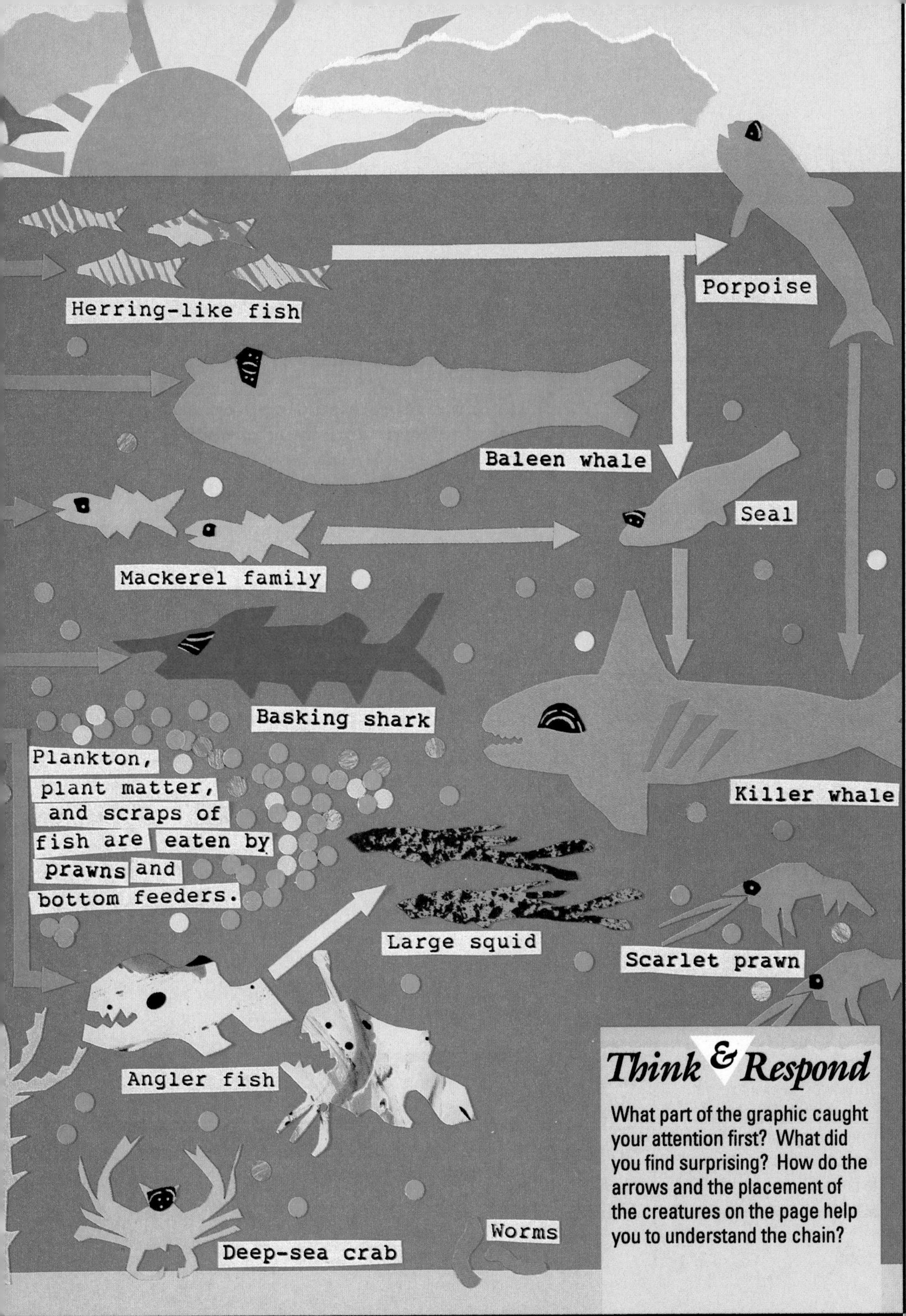

Think & Respond

What part of the graphic caught your attention first? What did you find surprising? How do the arrows and the placement of the creatures on the page help you to understand the chain?

Think & Respond

ELICIT PERSONAL RESPONSES

For the first question, you might ask students which they looked at first: words or pictures. Ask which pictures first caught their attention. Then ask which words they read first.

For the second question, elicit a variety of responses. Tell students that the variety of their responses shows that a graphic can convey many kinds of information.

For the third question, you might ask for a specific fact, such as "What do baleen whales eat?" (zooplankton) Then ask, "How does the chart tell us that?" (with an arrow that links the zooplankton to the baleen whale) Have the class discuss what the arrows and the placement of illustrations show. Stress that a graphic can explain a great deal in a small space. (If the information on this two-page chart were conveyed in words alone, it would take many paragraphs.)

EXPLORE THE AUTHOR'S TECHNIQUES

Point out that Ana Ortiz uses pictures, symbols, labels, and definitions to convey the information in her chart. Write those four terms on the board as headings; then have students name examples to list under each heading. (Samples: *Pictures*—killer whale, porpoise, seal; *Symbols*—arrows, dots for uneaten plant matter and scraps of fish; *Labels*—"phytoplankton," "herring-like fish," "mackerel family"; *Definitions*—parenthetical notes under "zooplankton" and "phytoplankton.") Encourage students to keep these devices in mind as they plan their own graphics.

for FURTHER READING

Books to Read Students can find fascinating information, as well as examples of more ways of using graphics to explain, in Aliki's *Mummies Made in Egypt,* Franklyn M. Branley's *Superstar: The Supernova of 1987,* and Patricia Lauber's *Earthquakes.*

Writing ON YOUR OWN

Explain to students that in this related assignment, they'll create a graphic to explain a process they find interesting. Along the way, they will have a chance to experiment with words and pictures until they find the combination that works best.

Handbooks for Help and Practice

The following handbooks may be used as mini-lessons before students begin writing or as resources when problems arise:

- **Thinking with Pictures, pp. 192–196**
- **Reading Skills, pp. 298–301**

Teaching Strategies

GENERAL NOTE

COOPERATIVE LEARNING Since professional visuals, charts, and other graphics are often team efforts, consider allowing students to work in groups as they complete this assignment. They can work together to find topics, generate content, and plan the graphic. They can then divide up the tasks of creating the verbal and visual components of the graphic.

for PLANNING YOUR GRAPHIC DEVICE

INDIVIDUALIZING INSTRUCTION: ADVANCED STUDENTS You may wish to allow these students to add another dimension to their graphics by creating collages or models. For example, students might use papier-mâché to create a mobile of the solar system or a cutaway sphere showing the layers within the earth. They might create ball-and-toothpick models of molecules or plaster of Paris landscapes to illustrate topography.

Writing ON YOUR OWN

Explaining with Graphics

INVITATION TO *Write*

Ana Ortiz's chart helped you to understand feeding relationships among some of the creatures of the sea. Graphic devices such as this one often provide a simple way to explain difficult ideas.

Now explain a relationship or process by using a graphic device of your own choosing.

PLANNING YOUR GRAPHIC DEVICE

1. Find a subject. Are you writing a report for which you could use a graphic? If so, you may already have a subject. If not, brainstorm with classmates to come up with processes, cycles, or relationships you've learned about in science, social studies, or other classes. For example, you might consider showing how a tadpole becomes a frog.

2. Pick a subject. Choose something that you think you could explain more quickly and clearly in a graphic device than you could explain in words alone.

3. Jot down what you know. Try freewriting, sketching, or creating a cluster to gather details about your subject.

Writing TIP

You don't have to be an artist to make your graphic attractive. For example, you can use photographs and magazine clippings to help illustrate the ideas you want to present.

CREATING YOUR GRAPHIC DEVICE

1. Choose a visual way to present your material. The graphic devices shown at the top of the next page are just two of the many forms your graphic can take. For other ideas, see Handbook 26, "Reading Skills," on pages 298–301.

MULTICULTURAL Connection

Encourage students to think about their own cultural heritage when looking for ideas for graphics. For example, a map might illustrate the migration of a particular cultural group. A chart might show a culture's clothing or musical styles. Urge students to freewrite or cluster to discover subjects related to their backgrounds.

Social Studies Connection

Students might create a "visual cluster"—a cluster of pictures, rather than words—to illustrate the life and achievements of a favorite historical figure. Encourage students to label each image, to explain briefly the importance of events and achievements, and to include dates and place names where appropriate.

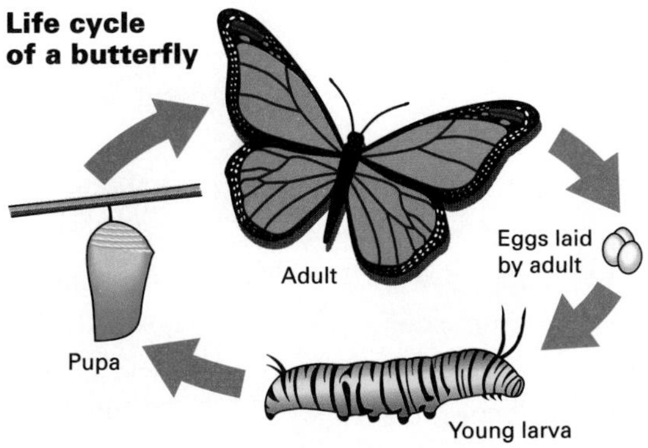

2. Use symbols. Make key relationships easy to spot by using symbols that your readers are sure to recognize. For example, you might use arrows, plus signs, or question marks in your visual.

3. Name and label your graphic. Title your graphic and label any important items or steps. The labels on the model, for example, identify the ocean creatures.

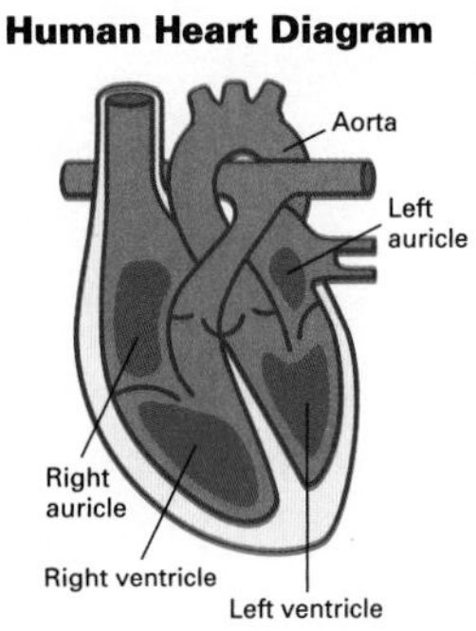

REVIEWING YOUR GRAPHIC DEVICE

1. Get feedback on your visual. Show your graphic to a friend or classmate. Your friend's questions and comments can give you ideas for improving your visual.

2. Revise your graphic. Adjust your graphic until you're sure that your relationship or process comes across clearly.

PUBLISHING AND PRESENTING

- **Be the teacher.** Use your graphic organizer to teach classmates about the relationship or process you've chosen.
- **Display your graphic.** Would your visual make a great poster? Join with other students to create a display for your classroom or library. Add titles if necessary.

for LIFE CYCLE OF A BUTTERFLY

CRITICAL THINKING: INTERPRETING Ask students what information would be left out if the butterfly life cycle were shown in a straight line from an egg to an adult butterfly. (the fact that the adult butterfly lays eggs) Point out that the form of a graphic can help provide information.

for USE SYMBOLS

INDIVIDUALIZING INSTRUCTION: VISUAL LEARNERS Point out to students that colors, like symbols, can convey ideas quickly to readers. For example, a diagram of a molecule of sugar might use black for carbon atoms, white for oxygen atoms, and blue for hydrogen atoms. Color-coding labels is another way to add information. Students will need to create a key that assigns a specific meaning to each color.

for NAME AND LABEL YOUR GRAPHIC

MODELING You might want to demonstrate how to make a key to the symbols and colors used in a graphic. Remind students that the key is usually placed in a corner of the graphic.

Guidelines for Evaluation

AN EFFECTIVE GRAPHIC DEVICE

- shows a relationship or the steps in a process
- uses pictures, words, and symbols to explain each element or step
- has a form appropriate to content

for REVIEWING YOUR GRAPHIC DEVICE

MANAGING THE PAPER LOAD Have students present their graphics to the class. You can base your evaluation on the following criteria: (1) clarity of process or relationship, (2) amount of detail, and (3) originality and creativity.

Springboards

Teaching Strategies

GENERAL NOTE

KEY TO UNDERSTANDING Ask students what all the springboards have in common. Make sure students understand that all the springboards ask them to give directions. Lead students to see that giving directions is an important skill in many subject areas.

Springboards

HOME ECONOMICS What household tasks can you do expertly? Make breakfast? Babysit? Dishes? Write a set of directions that explain to a friend how to do the job. Your directions can be humorous or serious.

HEALTH Create a poster for a younger audience. Show how to perform a simple task important to good health. You might show how to floss your teeth or how to stretch before exercising.

Science Have you ever done a science experiment? If so, write directions explaining what to do. Be sure to explain especially well any parts of the experiment you found tricky or confusing.

Art Explain how to produce a particular kind of painting, sculpture, or craft.

Geography Write out a set of directions for getting from one city or town to another. If you wish, you might include a map that shows the exact route.

For Your Eyes Only!

If you want to send a private message to a friend, write it in a secret code. Try these codes, then make up one of your own.

Tick-Tack-Toe Code

Did you know  spells *theater?* The tick-tack-toe board below is your guide to this alphabet of symbols.

To write the letter **T**, for example, draw the outline of the part of the tick-tack-toe board that holds the letter: . Then place a dot in the middle part of the outline where the letter **T** is shown: .

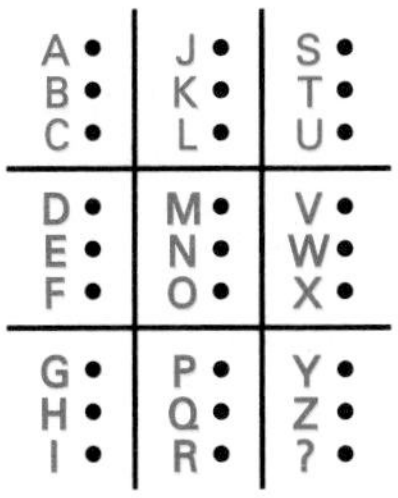

Can you read this message?

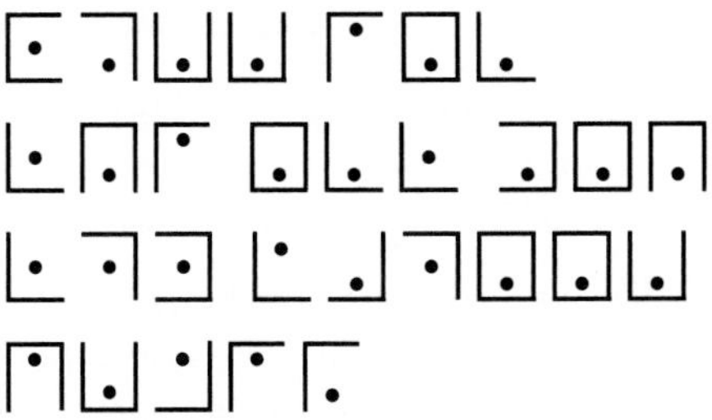

Letter Scramble

If you want to send the message *Meet me after the show,* scramble the letters by rewriting the sentence as two words. Put the first letter, **M**, at the beginning of the first word and the second letter, **e**, at the beginning of the second word. Build each of the two words from every other letter of the message.

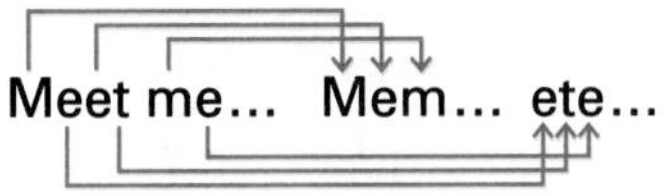

You end up with

Ematrhso etefetehw

If you wish, divide your two-word letter scramble into more words: **Mem atrh so ete fetehw.** To decode the message, divide the total number of letters in half. Write the second half directly below the first, and then read the letters from top to bottom.

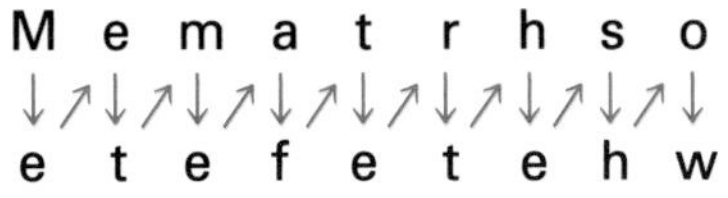

What does this message say?

Ia et gfih hvsa ergt

Answers: I have stage fright. Will you try out for the school play?

on the LIGHT side

Ask students if they have ever used codes to send secret messages to friends. Have students describe some of their codes. What else do they know about codes? You might point out that probably thousands of codes have been used throughout history. Leonardo da Vinci, for example, protected his ideas by writing his notes backward. Military communications are often sent in code during wartime, and other codes, such as the Morse code and semaphore, were invented to send messages over long distances.

After students read the feature, have them form small groups. Ask each group to write a brief message using one of the two codes shown. Then have each group write its coded message on the board. Challenge the other groups to see who can decode each message first.

Sentence Openers

Objectives

- To identify sentence openers
- To compose and correctly punctuate sentences that begin with sentence openers

HELPFUL HINT: COMMAS To help students understand how and why commas are used with sentence openers, ask volunteers to read each of the model sentences aloud. Point out that students pause naturally after the openers. The pause often signals the need for a comma. If students need additional practice, refer them to "Commas That Set Off Special Elements" in Handbook 43, "Punctuation," pages 576–577.

Additional Resource

Sentence Composing Copy Masters, pp. 7–8

Answer Key

A. Combining Sentences

1. Without the slightest hesitation, he went to the door on the right and opened it.
2. After Uncle Daniels had finished with his lamb-chop dinner, I set the cream puffs on the coffee table and stood back looking at them.
3. Still angry, still outraged by his attempt to betray me, I looked at him with scorn and hatred, unable to imagine what I had ever seen in him.
4. When she got to her door, she dragged the boy inside, down a hall, and into a large kitchenette-furnished room at the rear of the house.

Sentence

COMPOSING

Sentence Openers

You can use single words or groups of words as sentence openers to add emphasis and to vary the rhythm of your writing.

Model A Outside, he murmured to himself.
William H. Armstrong, *Sounder*

Model B Hobbling on one foot, Wanda opened the closet door and turned on the light.
Betsy Byars, *The Summer of the Swans*

Model C Ever since I can remember, I had wanted to know about the Land of the Golden Mountain, but my mother had never wanted to talk about it.
Laurence Yep, *Dragonwings*

ON THE MARK Put a comma after a sentence opener to separate it from the rest of the sentence.

A. Combining Sentences Make a new sentence by adding the underlined part of the second sentence to the first sentence as a sentence opener. Write the complete sentence, putting a comma after the sentence opener.

1. He went to the door on the right and opened it. He opened it without the slightest hesitation. **Frank R. Stockton, "The Lady, or the Tiger?"**
2. I set the cream puffs on the coffee table and stood back looking at them. This was after Uncle Daniels had finished with his lamb-chop dinner. **Rosa Guy, *Edith Jackson***
3. I looked at him with scorn and hatred, unable to imagine what I had ever seen in him. I was still angry, still outraged by his attempt to betray me. **James Gould Cozzens, "The Animals' Fair"**
4. She dragged the boy inside, down a hall, and into a large kitchenette-furnished room at the rear of the house. She did this when she got to her door. **Langston Hughes, "Thank You, M'am"**

B. Unscrambling and Imitating Sentences Unscramble each set of sentence chunks below. Create a sentence that has a sentence opener, the same order of chunks, and the same punctuation as the model. Then write a sentence of your own that imitates each model.

1. Model With his remaining strength, he dragged himself from the swirling waters. **Richard Connell, "The Most Dangerous Game"**

onto their shoulders / the girls lifted their coach / after their stunning victory

2. Model Barely touching my waist and my fingers, he began to dance with me. **Alice Munro, "Red Dress—1946"**

to cross above us / the tightrope walker started / carefully keeping her balance and her concentration

3. Model When we arrived home, we took a cold shower underneath a water hose. **Francisco Jimenez, "The Circuit"**

the scouts told stories / as the stars twinkled above / around the campfire

C. Expanding Sentences Use your imagination to add a sentence opener, followed by a comma, where the caret (‸) appears in each sentence below.

1. ‸ We could hear axes ringing in the woods, voices, and sometimes the fall of a tree. **Alexei Panshin, *Rite of Passage***

2. ‸ Ralph laid the small end of the shell against his mouth and blew. **William Golding, *Lord of the Flies***

3. ‸ Mama Bellini picked him up by his antennae, tossed him into the cricket cage and locked the gate behind him. **George Selden, *The Cricket in Times Square***

Grammar Refresher Some sentence openers are prepositional phrases. To learn more about prepositional phrases, see Handbook 40, "Understanding Prepositions and Conjunctions," pages 502–525.

B. Unscrambling and Imitating Sentences

Student imitations may vary. Unscrambled sentences are shown below.

1. After their stunning victory, the girls lifted their coach onto their shoulders.
2. Carefully keeping her balance and her concentration, the tightrope walker started to cross above us.
3. As the stars twinkled above, the scouts told stories around the campfire.

C. Expanding Sentences

Student sentences will vary. Professional models are shown below.

1. As we worked, we could hear axes ringing in the woods, voices, and sometimes the fall of a tree.
2. Doubtfully, Ralph laid the small end of the shell against his mouth and blew.
3. Muttering with rage, Mama Bellini picked him up by his antennae, tossed him into the cricket cage and locked the gate behind him.

for GRAMMAR REFRESHER

KEY TO UNDERSTANDING A prepositional phrase consists of a preposition, a noun or pronoun serving as the object of the preposition, and words modifying the object. (An example from the first model in Exercise B is *With his remaining strength.*) Prepositional phrases can act as modifiers. When they describe nouns or pronouns, they are called adjective phrases. When they describe verbs, adjectives, or other adverbs, they are called adverb phrases.

5

Persuasion

Overview

Persuasive writing is used to convince readers that they should accept the writer's opinion on an issue. In this workshop, students apply observation, analysis, problem-solving, and research skills to write about issues that concern them. Workshop 5 includes the following Guided and Related Assignments, as well as the interdisciplinary project on pages 113c–113d.

1. **Guided: Sharing an Opinion** invites students to identify an issue they care about, formulate an opinion about it, and support the opinion with convincing facts, examples, and statistics in a persuasive paper aimed at a particular audience.
2. **Related: Public Opinion Survey** guides students through the steps of designing, administering, and reporting the results of a survey of opinion.
3. **Related: Writing for Assessment** helps students apply their persuasive writing skills in responding to a writing prompt like those that appear in writing tests.

Teaching Preview

Preparation Guide

1. Use the Overview on this page and the Teacher's Choice descriptions on page 115 as a basis for deciding which assignments to teach.
2. Preview the assignments and the teacher's notes and identify concepts that may require preteaching or extra support, given your class's abilities. The handbook mini-lessons suggested within the lesson may also provide guidance.
3. Preview the chart below for support materials in the Teacher's Resource File that may be used with this Workshop. Resources are for use with the Guided Assignment unless otherwise noted.

Support Materials

WRITER'S CRAFT RESOURCES

Prewrite and Explore
Thinking Skills Worksheets, p. 5
Thinking Skills Transparencies, pp. 5–5a
Writing Resource Book, pp. 22–23

Draft and Discover
Elaboration, Revision, and Proofreading Practice, p. 9
Elaboration, Revision, and Proofreading Transparencies, pp. 17–18
Writing Resource Book, pp. 24–26

Revise Your Writing
Elaboration, Revision, and Proofreading Practice, p. 10
Elaboration, Revision, and Proofreading Transparencies, pp. 19–20
Guidelines for Writing Assessment and Portfolio Use, pp. 18, 34–36
Peer Response Guides, pp. 15–16
Writing Resource Book, p. 27

Assessment
Tests and Writing Assessment Prompts, p. 5

Extension Activities
Sentence Composing Copymasters, pp. 9–10
Starting Points for Writing, pp. 31–32, 37–40
Writing from Literature, pp. 1–2, 5–12, 15–22
Standardized Test Practice

Educational Technology (available separately)
Writer's DataBank
Electronic English Handbook
Multimedia Workshop
On Assignment! (videodisc)

OTHER RESOURCES

Books and Journals
Caplan, Rebekah. "The Argumentative Essay." *Writers in Training.* Palo Alto: Dale Seymour, 1984"
Rybczynski, M. "Audience Adaptation and Persuasive Strategies." *Journal of Research and Development in Education.* 26 (Fall 1992): 15–23.

Films and Videos
Join the Resistance. Carousel, 1992.

Educational Technology
Ace Inquirer. Mindplay. Apple Series.
Fact or Opinion: Smart Shopper. Mindscape/SVE. Apple II.

Management Guidelines

The chart below estimates the number of days needed for each phase of the Guided and Related Assignments. Students may not complete each phase in one continuous session, nor necessarily progress from stage to stage in the linear order shown here. Stars indicate portions of the assignment that may be completed outside the classroom if time is limited or if teachers wish students to work independently.

SHARING AN OPINION

Starting from Literature ....1 day
Prewrite and Explore ....3 days
Draft and Discover........................3 days*
Revise Your Writing......................2 days*
Proofread ....1 day*
Publish and Present..................1–2 days
Reflect on Your Writing................1 day
Extension and Enrichment ....open*

PUBLIC OPINION SURVEY

Finding a Focus ....1 day
Creating Your Survey................2–3 days*
Completing the Survey.............4–5 days*
Sharing Your Results....................1 day

WRITING FOR ASSESSMENT

Reading the Question ....1 day*
Getting Ready to Answer
and Writing Your Answer........1 day
Reviewing Your Answer..............1 day
Sentence Composing......................open*

Linking Literature, Writing, and Grammar

The following options may be used to provide students with an integrated language experience. Begin by assigning and discussing any of the recommended pieces of literature. Use the suggested strategy to provide a link to the Guided Assignment.

LINKING LITERATURE AND WRITING

Option 1

Starting Point: "Video 'Web' Weaves an Inadequate Tale" by Barbara Brotman on pages 116–117 of *The Writer's Craft.*

Strategy: Use the teaching suggestions on pages 116–117 to lead students into the Guided Assignment.

Option 2

Starting Point: "Save the Earth" by Betty Miles on pages 333–338 of McDougal, Littell's *Literature and Language,* Grade 6. (Additional suggestions for using *Literature and Language* can be found on page 115.)

Strategy: Have students read the selection. Then ask their opinions of the activities of the Toxic Avengers. Have students give reasons for their opinions. Use the discussion to introduce the Guided Assignment.

Option 3

Starting Point: "If I Were in Charge of the World" by Judith Viorst.

Strategy: Ask a student to read the poem aloud. Then ask which of Viorst's ideas students agree with and why. What things about the world would they change if they could? Use their ideas to introduce the Guided Assignment.

LINKING WRITING AND GRAMMAR

Before the drafting or revision stages of this assignment, tell students that mistakes in grammar and usage can distract readers from the ideas a writer is trying to present and can even make a piece of writing less persuasive. One common usage problem is subject-verb agreement. Tell students to ignore the nouns in prepositional phrases when they are deciding whether to use a singular or plural verb. Put the following examples on the board and have students select the correct verb. If they have difficulty, cross out the prepositional phrases.

The causes of this problem (is, *are*) hard to figure out.

The cause of these problems (*is,* are) a lack of money.

Go over pages 526–541 of the Grammar and Usage Handbook. If problems with subject-verb agreement still appear in students' papers, assign the exercises on those pages for reteaching. Additional practice can be found in the *Grammar and Usage Practice Book* on pages 78–83.

Project File

Right On! A Students' Bill of Rights

Overview

During this project, students will investigate the rights, responsibilities, and restrictions placed on students by society. They will study the Bill of Rights in the U.S. Constitution, and they will write a Students' Bill of Rights to address what they believe should be the rights of students. The project will culminate with students' publication of their document and with feedback from the school community.

Students will participate in the following activities:

- Examine the Bill of Rights
- Research minors' legal rights
- Draft and revise a Students' Bill of Rights
- Solicit feedback on the draft from other students
- Write essays explaining their opinions about one item covered by their Students' Bill of Rights
- Use language arts, math, social studies, and art skills to complete their research and to develop their materials

Preparation Guide

Ask students what they think some of their legal rights are. Ask them to share what they remember about court cases involving students. For example, students have been involved in protesting school dress codes and administration censorship of school newspapers. Lead students to see that an understanding of their rights can empower them to make changes.

Explain that for this project students will learn about the legal status of people their age and will use persuasive writing skills in creating a Students' Bill of Rights.

Stage 1
Focus on Students' Rights

1. Have students read the Bill of Rights, the first ten amendments to the U.S. Constitution.
2. Ask students if they think that the Bill of Rights applies to them. Encourage them to discuss situations in which they do, and do not, seem to have the freedoms supported by the Bill of Rights. They may bring up any of the following issues:
   - curfews
   - censorship of music or books
   - movie ratings
   - restrictions on skateboarding or in-line skating
   - dress codes
   - parental restrictions on television viewing
   - equal access to protection under the law
3. Propose that students brainstorm a list of rights that they would like to include in a Students' Bill of Rights.
4. Instruct students to design and administer a survey to find out which rights are important to the other students in the school (see *Resources, Stage 1*). Have students add items to, or cut items from, their list, as indicated by survey results.

TEAM TEACHING

The following activities may be used for team teaching or as enrichment and extension activities by the language arts teacher.

Social Studies Learn about the history of the Bill of Rights. Learn the legal definition of *child* and study laws regulating the behavior of children.

Language Arts Learn techniques for devising and conducting surveys (see *Resources, Stage 1*).

Math Compile and tabulate survey results.

TEACHING TIPS

- Suggest that when students read the Bill of Rights, they paraphrase it to enhance comprehension.
- Invite an attorney to speak to the class about children's civil rights and civil liberties.
- Have students use interviews or other research to learn whether they have the same rights as adults.

Stage 2
Draft a Bill of Rights

1. Direct students to create broad categories of rights that concern them. For example, they might make categories such as "rights at home," "rights at school," and "rights in the community." Then have them create subcategories such as freedom of dress (under rights at school) or freedom to choose their own friends (under freedom at home). Suggest that each subcategory be addressed in a section of the Students' Bill of Rights.
2. Ask students to work in groups to research their existing legal rights in each category and to develop proposals for the wording of the corresponding section of the Students' Bill of Rights.
3. Have students present their proposals for the class to discuss.

TEAM TEACHING

Social Studies Research how the Supreme Court has viewed the rights of children; study how the Supreme Court's views affect the law (see *Resources, Stage 2*).

Language Arts Learn research skills. Practice oral presentation techniques (see *Resources, Stage 2*).

TEACHING TIPS

- Schedule a library tour focusing on information about the judicial and legal systems.
- Challenge students developing proposals to avoid "We want" statements, such as "We want to be allowed to wear earrings to school." Have them use statements involving subcategories instead, such as "Students should be free to dress as they wish."

Stage 3
Publish and Evaluate

1. Direct students to revise their proposals based on the class discussion, to make a final draft of their Bill of Rights, and to publish it by posting it in a central area or delivering a copy of it to each homeroom.
2. Have students hold hearings or a vote to get the reactions of students and teachers throughout the school.
3. Instruct students to use the information they have collected to write essays in which they express their opinion of one item in the Students' Bill of Rights (see *Resources, Stage 3*).

TEAM TEACHING

Art Create a design for the finished document.

Math Tabulate votes or chart reactions to the Students' Bill of Rights.

Language Arts Learn techniques of writing to share opinions.

TEACHING TIPS

- During hearings, encourage students to explain and defend their views. Be sure all viewpoints have a chance to be heard.
- Have students vote on the Student Bill of Rights as if it were a constitutional amendment. (At least three-fourths of all students must vote yes for the Bill to be approved.)

Resources

STAGE 1

The Bill of Rights: How We Got It and What It Means by Milton Meltzer paraphrases the Bill of Rights and examines its history and implications.

Your Legal Rights by Linda Atkinson and ***You Have a Right*** by Leland S. Englebardt outline children's civil rights.

In ***The Writer's Craft,*** Grade 6, Workshop 5, "Persuasion," pages 128–132, teaches students how to create and conduct a public opinion survey.

STAGE 2

Blue Jeans and Black Robes: Teenagers and the Supreme Court by Peter P. Sgroi reviews Supreme Court rulings relating to the rights of teenagers.

Your Rights, Past and Present by James Haskins examines changing views of the rights of minors.

Up Against the Law: Your Legal Rights as a Minor by Ross Olney and Patricia Olney discusses the rights of minors under the law and gives many examples of actual and hypothetical cases.

In Defense of Children: Understanding the Rights, Needs, and Interests of the Child: A Resource for Parents and Professionals by Thomas Nazario reviews the rights of children.

The Writer's Craft, Grade 6, Handbook 25, "Study and Research Skills," pages 294–297 teaches research techniques. Handbook 32, "Oral Reports," pages 324–325 provides guidelines for effective oral reports.

STAGE 3

The Writer's Craft, Grade 6, Workshop 5, "Persuasion," pages 114–127, teaches students how to write about their opinions.

I Am Not a Short Adult! Getting Good at Being a Kid by Marilyn Burns deals with various aspects of childhood, including legal rights.

Additional Projects

Presenting Popcorn Have students participate in an ongoing class popcorn sale, with the proceeds to be used for a field trip or celebration at the end of the year. They should use persuasive techniques as they create an advertising campaign to publicize their product. Tell students to create ads, make posters, write product descriptions, and find other ways to persuade buyers. Ask students to track the effects of their advertisements by using sales records and customer surveys to discover which advertisements are most effective. Students should change their ads regularly in response to their findings.

Community Safety Ask students to identify community safety issues that they are concerned about. For example, they might focus on a dangerous intersection in need of a stoplight or on a neighborhood lacking a safe place for children to play. Encourage students to use interviews, surveys, and other research to learn more about the issues and about other people who share their concerns. Have students create multimedia presentations including posters and videos to increase awareness of the issues. Also have them write persuasive letters that explain their concerns and urge action on the issues. Students could mail their letters to community leaders and local newspapers.

Sketch Book

Objective

- To use a visual prompt and writing prompts as springboards to informal writing

WRITING WARM-UPS

Encourage students to respond freely and informally to at least one of the Sketchbook prompts. Students may begin by freewriting in their journals about the painting. Remind them that their responses will not be graded and may provide them with useful material for other writing assignments.

Sharing and explaining an opinion about a work of art often involves the persuasive techniques presented in Writer's Workshop 5. Working through the last prompt provides an opportunity for students to examine their own responses to a work of art. This experience sets the stage for responding to a piece of literature in Writer's Workshop 6.

SHOW, DON'T TELL

The following is a sample of a showing paragraph for the first prompt:

When Tom Sawyer persuades other boys to whitewash his aunt's fence, he's doing the same thing I try to do with my little sister. When she doesn't want to pick up toys and books that are scattered around the house, I make up a game or start a contest to see who can work faster. That way we get the job done without thinking of it as work.

Sketch Book

"For today's youth, no issue ranks as high as the environment in shaping the world in which they are growing up," says the [Peter D. Hart Research Associates] report.

Connie Koenenn
LOS ANGELES TIMES

- What's your opinion about the environment? Jot down some of your thoughts.
- What issues do you care about? List some of them.

Show, Don't Tell

You can show your opinion on a subject by offering reasons and examples to support your point of view. Write a *showing* paragraph for one of the following *telling* sentences.

- I knew I was right.
- Television commercials are (are not) interesting.

Persuasion

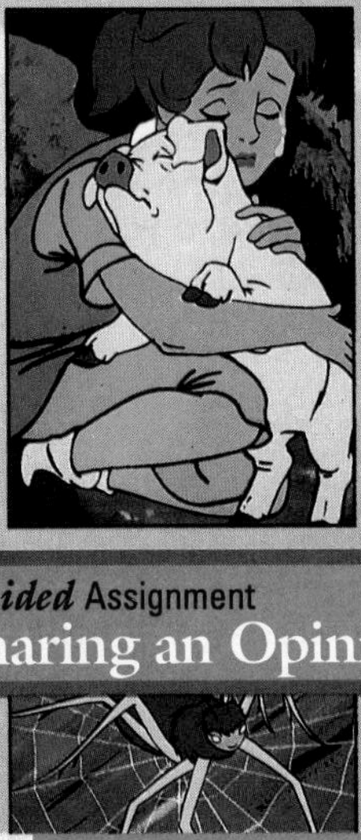

Guided Assignment
Sharing an Opinion

Related Assignment
Public Opinion Survey

Related Assignment
Writing for Assessment

You express opinions every day. You're disappointed in a movie. You think a certain team is better than people realize. You think the rain forests should be protected. If some of your opinions seem stronger and more reasonable than others, it's probably because you have better reasons for them.

In this workshop you will learn to express your opinions effectively in writing. In the related assignments you'll conduct a public opinion survey and describe the opinions of others. You'll also practice writing a persuasive piece for assessment.

Persuasion

Objectives

Guided Assignment

Sharing an Opinion To recognize persuasion in literature and to create a piece of writing that states an opinion and uses facts to support it

Related Assignments

Public Opinion Survey To analyze a survey and accompanying report, then to design and administer a survey and to report on the results

Writing for Assessment To analyze sample essay-test questions and to prepare an editorial in response to a writing prompt

Teacher's Choice

Use the following guidelines to choose the assignment that best suits students' needs.

Sharing an Opinion This assignment will benefit most students because it introduces persuasive writing as a way to share opinions. Students will have a chance to explore their feelings about an issue and gather support for their views.

Public Opinion Survey This assignment should appeal to social learners because the process of eliciting opinions will give them an opportunity to work with others. Since students may benefit from presenting their survey results as percentages or on graphs, you might wish to coordinate this survey with a math lesson.

Writing for Assessment This assignment will help students respond to a type of question found on state and national tests.

Links to LITERATURE & LANGUAGE

Literature For literature that may inspire persuasive writing, see *Literature and Language,* Grade 6:

- Betty Miles, "Save the Earth"
- Maya Angelou, "Life Doesn't Frighten Me"
- Myra Cohn Livingston, "74th Street"
- Les Crutchfield, "A Shipment of Mute Fate"

Writing This Guided Assignment may be used as an extension of the Writer's Workshop, "Persuasive Writing: Community-Issues Brochure," on page 376 of *Literature and Language,* Grade 6, or the Writer's Workshop, "Persuasive Writing: Letter to the Editor," on page 421.

Guided ASSIGNMENT

ASSIGNMENT RATIONALE

As students mature, they will share their opinions in social and classroom settings with increasing frequency; they also will be expected to provide support for those opinions. The ability to express and support one's opinions effectively is thus an important social and academic skill. It draws on such high-level thinking skills as drawing conclusions and evaluating.

Starting from LITERATURE

Motivate

Share an experience in which you saw a movie that was based on a book you had read. Which did you like better, the movie or the book? Why? Invite volunteers to share similar experiences.

BUILD ON PRIOR KNOWLEDGE

Ask students if they have read *Charlotte's Web* by E. B. White. Have volunteers share information about the characters of Fern, Wilbur, and Charlotte. What did they like about each character? What do they think makes this novel, first published in 1952, still so popular?

SET A PURPOSE

Tell students that they are going to read one person's opinion about the video *Charlotte's Web.* Then have students read Starting from Literature. To help students focus on the purpose-setting statement, you might use the analysis frame on page 7 of the *Thinking Skills Worksheets.* After students have read the article, they can write the opinion in the top box and the supporting evidence in the other boxes.

Guided ASSIGNMENT

Sharing an Opinion

Starting from LITERATURE

What do you do when you get steamed up about something—when you find yourself holding a really strong opinion? Do you complain? Do you try to persuade others?

Journalist Barbara Brotman had a strong opinion about a video she saw. As you read her column, notice how she shows the reader why she feels the way she does. Also think about whether you agree with her.

Video "Web" Weaves an Inadequate Tale • by Barbara Brotman

There is a certain video you should know about. You should know about it because, despite what anyone else might say, you should not watch it.

The tape is an outrage. It is video refuse. It is a symbol of the decline of American civilization.

It is *Charlotte's Web.*

You may think little permanent damage could be done by watching a cute video featuring talking barnyard animals.

But you are wrong.

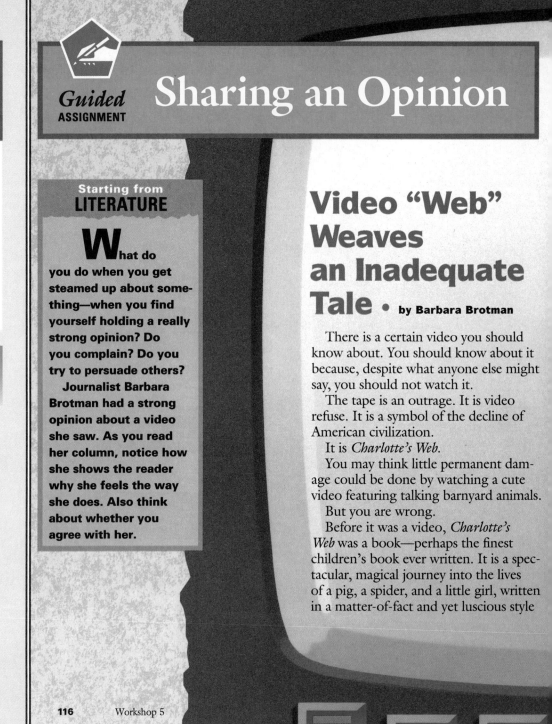

Before it was a video, *Charlotte's Web* was a book—perhaps the finest children's book ever written. It is a spectacular, magical journey into the lives of a pig, a spider, and a little girl, written in a matter-of-fact and yet luscious style by E. B. White, a master of the English language.

It is a first taste of the miracle that is reading. Imagine: You can sit alone in a room, and hear Charlotte the spider cheerily say, "Salutations!" as clearly as you can hear yourself being called for dinner, and maybe more so.

You can smell the rotten goose egg that breaks and renders the barn "untenable," as Charlotte puts it (and if any children's book deserves to not be made into a video, it is one that uses the word *untenable*).

And if at the end of the book your heart does not break, you do not have one.

Charlotte's Web is a sweet video. But as I watch it, it seems terribly wrong.

In the book, Fern, who rescues Wilbur the pig from an untimely death, is a dreamy, mildly unkempt tomboy. In the video she is a generic animated girl. She could be Ariel in *The Little Mermaid*, or Belle in *Beauty and the Beast;* it doesn't seem to matter.

The book's Charlotte is a somewhat cerebral spider with a dry sense of humor and an aversion to sentimentality. She would never sing, "Up with your chinny-chin-chin!" in the voice of Debbie Reynolds. The video Charlotte would, and does.

Reading a book is a partnership. The author creates characters and action; you perceive them, through the wonders of imagination.

A video serves up the entire stew predigested. Imagination is neither required nor encouraged. You, the reader, deserve so much more.

This I wish for all of you:

That you may live in the big-sky prairie with Laura Ingalls Wilder; that you may watch the dancing light in Anna Karenina's eyes go tragically dark; that you may laugh and weep, sitting in rooms that are silent except for the eloquence of the written word; and that it may all start with a girl and a pig and a spider in Homer Zuckerman's barn.

Think & Respond

What parts of Brotman's column did you find most effective? What parts were not convincing? Can you think of times when watching a video of a book might be a good thing to do?

Think & Respond

ELICIT PERSONAL RESPONSES

Have students consider the questions in the Think & Respond box and freewrite a response. After discussing students' responses, ask those students who have both read the book *Charlotte's Web* and seen the video, whether they agree with Brotman or not, and why.

EXPLORE THE AUTHOR'S TECHNIQUES

Focus students' attention on the organization of the model. Point out that after her introduction and presentation of an opposing view, Brotman discusses what is great about the book. She then describes what is wrong with the video and concludes by examining the difference between reading a book and watching a video. Ask students to identify the specific examples that Brotman provided to support her opinions. (Samples: Charlotte's vocabulary; the contrast between the written description of Fern and the Fern in the video version. The video version of Fern is like Disney's generic female characters, such as Ariel and Belle.)

MORE ABOUT THE MODEL

In her final paragraph, Barbara Brotman refers to Laura Ingalls Wilder and to Anna Karenina. Explain that Laura Ingalls Wilder wrote a series of books, based on her own experiences, about pioneer days. The best known is *Little House on the Prairie,* which was later made into a television series.

Anna Karenina is a character in a novel of the same name. Leo Tolstoy, the famous Russian author, narrates Anna's series of choices that made "the dancing light in [her] eyes go tragically dark."

Reading a STUDENT MODEL

The perceived failings of a video version of a book constitute only one issue that people can feel strongly about. A student writer, Dave Smith, addresses another. This model is the final draft of the piece that students will see in process on the workshop pages that follow.

Motivate

Write the following statement on the board: *I believe that everyone should be paid the same amount of money, regardless of type of work, experience, or education.* Invite student reaction to this statement.

BUILD ON PRIOR KNOWLEDGE

Ask students to name some people who are paid a great deal of money. (Students will probably name professional athletes, entertainers, and heads of large corporations.) Ask students what they think are the reasons why such people command large salaries. (Samples: Some are paid for their expertise or talent; some are paid well because audiences will pay well to see them.)

SET A PURPOSE

Direct students to the purpose-setting statement in the Reading a Student Model box. You might also suggest that students watch for the words *first, second,* and *finally,* and that they examine the information in the bar graph.

One Student's Writing

Reading a STUDENT MODEL

Barbara Brotman felt that the *Charlotte's Web* video was an outrage, and she said so. Her feelings became the basis of a strong opinion essay.

Dave Smith, a sixth-grade student, has strong feelings about money and how much of it some people are paid. As you read his newspaper opinion piece, notice how he supports his opinions with strong, persuasive facts.

Kidviews

Those Sky-high Salaries

by DAVE SMITH

Many people in the United States today make somewhere between $5 and $10 an hour. That's not bad. But while they are making $5 to $10 an hour, there are some people making $12,000 an hour!

Who are these people? Who else? The professional athletes! The outrageous salaries of professional at letes just don't make sense.

First, no one is worth much money as these at letes make. These peop make millions of dollars year, and they're not eve doing that much work. The qualifications are throwing fastball ninety-plus mil an hour, hitting a twenty-foot jump shot sixty percent

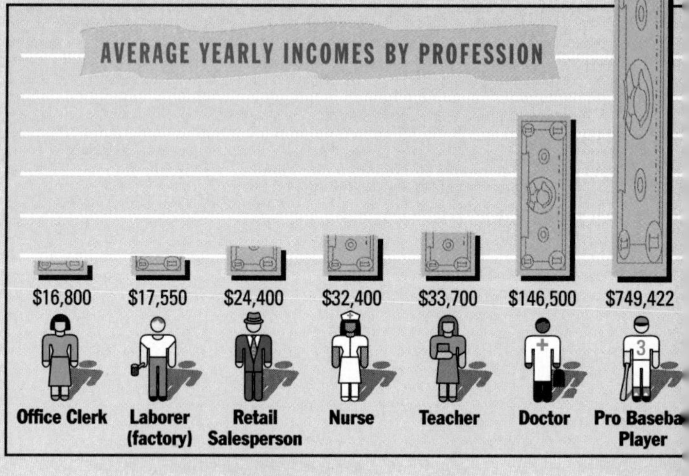

Mathematics Connection

A bar graph is one way to present evidence that involves numbers. Other kinds of graphs and tables can also be appropriate means of presenting figures. If students choose a topic that involves mathematical evidence, suggest that a math teacher help them determine the most effective presentation.

Section 1F	
Inside:	
HOT SUMMER'S COOL LOOKS	2F
MOVIE-VIEWS: RAVES & REJECTS	5F

the time, or completing ty-yard passes.

Bobby Bonilla and the ew York Mets, for example, greed to a five-year, $29 mil- on contract. That averages $5.8 million a year. Crazy, n't it? I know this contract ounds outrageous, but it's ecoming commonplace in ofessional sports today.

Second, there is no need r such a large salary. Aver- ge working Americans can e decently, yet they won't en come close to making in lifetime what some pro ath- tes make in a year.

Let's use a factory worker illustrate this point. We'll y this factory worker has orked for ten years and akes $30,000 a year. This ard-working factory worker ould have to work two undred years just to make much as Bobby Bonilla ill make in one year.

Finally, it doesn't make nse that people are making so much money when so many Americans are homeless, when the world needs money to fund research on deadly diseases such as AIDS and cancer, and when our country has such a large national debt.

Why can't we put salary caps on the earnings of professional athletes and have some of the money go toward good causes like the ones just listed? I wish more athletes were like NFL quarterback Warren Moon, who donates a large portion of his salary to good causes.

If you only remember one thing from this essay, I hope it's this: No one is worth the kind of money pro athletes make today. But if anyone is going to receive that much money, it should be the men and women who get up early every morning, go to work, and work their hardest to support their families.

Think & Respond

Respond as a Reader

▶ What do you think of Dave's suggestion to limit salaries?

▶ How would professional athletes respond to Dave's opinion?

Respond as a Writer

▶ How does Dave use examples to make his point?

▶ How does he show when he is moving from one reason to the next?

Think & Respond

RESPOND AS A READER

▶ In thinking about the first question, students should consider the pros and cons of limiting salaries. Possible advantages are that ticket prices might go down, and worthy causes would benefit if the extra money were given to them. Possible disadvantages are that players might be less motivated to excel, and team owners might keep more of the profits for themselves.

▶ Students will probably agree that many athletes would not like Dave's idea. These athletes might cite the high risk of injury that they face and the short duration of their careers. Many football players, for example, suffer injuries that plague them for the rest of their lives. Athletes also might object to being singled out and might point to the high earnings of movie stars and popular entertainers.

RESPOND AS A WRITER

▶ Students should note that rather than just stating his reasons, Dave uses specific examples—those of Bobby Bonilla, the factory worker, and Warren Moon—to support his opinion.

▶ Students may point to the transition words *first, second,* and *finally,* which help readers find the reasons. Point out that these words begin paragraphs.

Draw Conclusions

Have students list characteristics of an opinion essay—those that they have noted thus far. Responses may include the following:

- a statement of opinion
- the use of reasons, examples, and facts to support the opinion
- a strong introduction and conclusion

Social Studies Connection

Letters to the editors of newspapers and magazines provide "real world" examples of shared opinions. Invite students to create a classroom display of such letters. Along with each letter, students should include a note-card caption that identifies the intended audience and the writer's opinion.

Writing ON YOUR OWN

Have students identify issues that matter to them; then invite them to write their own opinion essays. Encourage them to support their opinions with examples and facts, as Barbara Brotman and Dave Smith did.

Handbooks for Help and Practice

The following handbooks may be used as mini-lessons before students begin writing or as resources when problems arise:

- **Developing a Topic, pp. 205–210**
- **Goals and Audience, pp. 211–213**
- **Levels of Language, pp. 274–275**
- **Thinking Skills, pp. 320–322**

PREWRITE AND EXPLORE

Objectives

- To use prewriting techniques to find and select a topic for an opinion essay
- To gather facts and examples to support an opinion

Teaching Strategies

for EXPLORING TOPICS

HELPFUL HINT As students explore ideas for topics, they might want to choose one for which they have both an opinion and a solution. For example, Dave Smith believes that athletes' salaries are too high, so he proposes putting a limit on the amount of money an athlete can make. Barbara Brotman believes that *Charlotte's Web* is an inferior video, so she encourages the audience to read the book instead.

Writing ON YOUR OWN

Sharing an Opinion

INVITATION TO *Write*

Both Barbara Brotman and Dave Smith had strong opinions and expressed them in writing. Feeling strongly about an issue makes it easier to write about it. Writing about an issue also helps you sort out your thinking.

Write an essay stating your opinion on an issue that you feel strongly about.

PREWRITE AND EXPLORE

1. Search for opinions. Do you believe in limiting violence in television programs? Should grading systems be changed? Should some kinds of music have warning labels? To discover issues you care about, try some of the following activities.

Exploring Topics

- **What bugs me is . . .** Alone or with classmates, **brainstorm** about what makes you mad or about problems you feel should be corrected. Make a list of things that bother you. For example, do you disagree with Barbara Brotman about the video of *Charlotte's Web?*
- **Journal search** Look through your journal for issues or problems that you have written about over and over again or with great emotion.
- **What's news?** Listen to the local or national news on the radio or watch it on TV. You might also browse through newspapers or newsmagazines to see what's going on in the world. What controversial issues do you have an opinion about? Try making a **cluster** to explore your writing options.

SPICE BOX

Debates and discussions are natural ways for students to develop ideas for persuasive writing. Suggest that a group of four interested students choose a proposition to debate before the class. The proposition should state a position on a controversial subject; for example: No limits should be placed on the salaries of professional athletes. Explain that in the debate two students will need to argue in favor of the proposition and two will need to argue against it.

One Student's Process

Dave Smith thought about the opinions he had on various subjects like recycling, rock song lyrics, and the homeless. Then he decided to try a cluster diagram based on one of his major interests. He started with "sports" and branched out in different directions. He realized he had a strong opinion about salaries in professional sports.

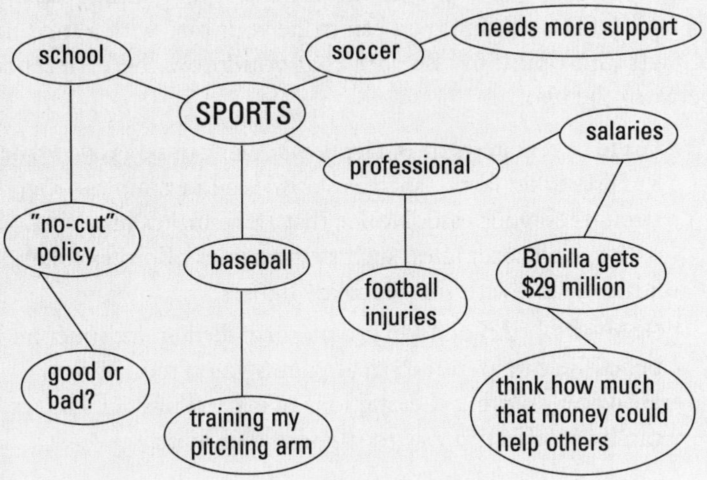

2. Pick an issue. Which issues do you care the most about? Try **freewriting** about some of them. Then choose the one you're most interested in writing about.

3. Explore ideas. In small groups, find out what your classmates think about your issue. You might get some new ideas. Then freewrite some more about the topic. Ask yourself, what is my opinion? Why do I feel this way?

4. Gather information. Do some research on your topic to find details you can use to support your opinion. Ask your librarian about books, newspapers, magazines, and other resources that might be helpful.

PROBLEM SOLVING

"What do I want my essay to do?"

For help in pinpointing your purpose and personal goals, see

- Handbook 5, "Goals and Audience," pages 211–214

GENERAL NOTE

HELPFUL HINT Tell students that the Sketchbook activities on pages 114 and 140 may help them find writing ideas.

for ONE STUDENT'S PROCESS

CRITICAL THINKING: ANALYZING

To show students how a cluster can help them discover an issue to focus on, have them analyze Dave Smith's cluster. Use questions such as the following: What was Dave's general subject? (sports) In how many directions did he take that topic? (four—school, baseball, professional, soccer) How did he arrive at his topic? (He started from professional sports and had two ideas—football injuries and salaries; he had more specific information about salaries.)

for EXPLORE IDEAS

INDIVIDUALIZING INSTRUCTION: LD STUDENTS As an alternative to freewriting, these students may appreciate using a tape recorder to generate and explore possible topics.

for GATHER INFORMATION

STUMBLING BLOCK The word *research* often scares students. Explain that research does not always involve long hours in the library. Research can also mean talking to someone who has knowledge about a subject or expanding on what one already knows. For example, since Dave Smith already knew about the high salaries of some players, he might have simply asked a librarian for help in finding the exact figures.

Social Studies Connection

You might suggest that students consider some of the issues they have examined in social studies classes, as they search for topics. You might ask a social studies teacher to suggest some topics and then offer students the option of coordinating this assignment with their social studies class.

DRAFT AND DISCOVER

Objectives

- To draft an opinion essay
- To review one's own draft and that of a peer

Teaching Strategies

for SUPPORT YOUR OPINION

INDIVIDUALIZING INSTRUCTION: BASIC STUDENTS Some students may have difficulty in recognizing the difference between a fact and an opinion. Therefore, you might teach a mini-lesson on this subject, using "Supporting an Opinion I," on page 24 in the *Writing Resource Book.* In addition, you might work through page 9 of *Elaboration, Revision, and Proofreading Practice* with students so that they can see how another writer supports opinions.

for WRITER'S CHOICE

SPEAKING AND LISTENING Interviewing others can be a valuable way to find support for an opinion. Be sure that students understand that the person should be someone who can speak with authority about a topic. Remind them to write down their questions before they conduct the interview and to take notes during the interview. For a list of guidelines, refer students to Handbook 31, "Interviewing Skills," on page 323.

for THINK ABOUT YOUR READERS

HELPFUL HINT Suggest that students name their intended audience at the top of their paper. Urge them to refer to that notation often, to guide their writing.

DRAFT AND DISCOVER

1. Start writing. If you're not really sure what you want to say, just begin putting down some ideas. You can change, organize, and add to them later. Try stating your opinion in one or two sentences. Then explain why you feel that way.

2. Support your opinion. Writing an opinion paper means not just stating your opinion but backing it up—giving reasons for it. Like Dave Smith, you can make your case with a mixture of facts and opinions. Be sure that you know the difference between the two.

- **Facts** A statement of fact is one that can be proved true or false. Solid facts—such as statistics and examples—can strengthen your case. Notice that Dave makes his point with specific examples, such as the names of professional athletes, and with specific salary figures.
- **Opinions** An opinion is a personal feeling, attitude, or belief. Be careful not to treat your own opinion as fact. However, quoting the opinions of experts in your subject can be an effective way to support your ideas.

Writer's Choice Do you want to interview several people to get some quotes you can use for supporting evidence? Perhaps you can find an expert on your subject to interview.

3. Think about your readers. Aim your writing at your particular audience. Do they need more background information? If you think your readers disagree with you, how can you deal with their arguments against your ideas?

4. Organize your writing. Try to catch the reader's attention, as Barbara Brotman did, and state your opinion. Then give the background and present your reasons. It's often wise to save your best reason for last. For a conclusion, you might restate or summarize your opinion, as Dave Smith did.

PROBLEM SOLVING

"How can I back up my opinion?"

For help in finding material to support your opinion, see

- Handbook 4, "Developing a Topic," pages 205–214

122 Workshop 5

5. Think about your draft. Are you ready to share your writing now, or do you want to make some changes first? The following questions can help you review your draft and get good suggestions from your peer readers.

REVIEW YOUR WRITING

Questions for Yourself

- Have I shown the importance of the issue I am writing about?
- Have I gathered enough evidence?
- Have I left out any reasons that support my opinion?
- Have I taken into account arguments on the other side?

Questions for Your Peer Readers

- Is my opinion on this issue clear? Tell it to me in a sentence or two.
- What part of this paper was most convincing to you?
- Did I support my opinion with enough facts and examples?
- What is your opinion on this issue?

One Student's Process

Here is the first draft of the beginning of Dave's paper. He asked some classmates for their responses. Would you add anything else?

The outrageous salaries of professional athletes just doesn't make sense. Ordinary working people don't make that kind of money. Many people in the United States today only make a few dollars an hour. But while they're making a few dollars an hour, there are some people making huge fortunes. It's insane. Who are these people? Who else? Professional athletes!

Peer Reader Comments

I like your point. I agree that the salaries are too high.

Some more facts would help me. What are the different salaries?

for THINK ABOUT YOUR DRAFT

MANAGEMENT TIP To help students create a better piece of writing, encourage them to wait at least overnight before they review their writing. When they approach their drafts again, they will have a more objective view of their work.

for REVIEW YOUR WRITING

STUMBLING BLOCK If students express concern about how to take into account arguments for the other side, point out how Barbara Brotman brings up an opposing argument in the fourth paragraph of her essay. If you are writing an opinion essay along with students, tell how you are considering opposing arguments.

for REVIEW YOUR WRITING

PEER RESPONSE Rather than ask the reader to restate the writer's opinion orally, encourage the reader to write the opinion; this may enable the writer of the draft to grasp the true response and avoid the temptation to hear only what he or she wants to hear.

for ONE STUDENT'S PROCESS

CRITICAL THINKING: MAKING INFERENCES Dave Smith has not said who his audience is. Who do students think the intended audience is, and why? (Sample: peers; the tone and style are casual.) How would Dave's writing be different if he were writing to the baseball commissioner? (It would be more formal.)

Grammar Connection

Dave's paragraph ends with two sentence fragments. The use of fragments in an essay may bother students who have been told to avoid using fragments. Ask students what reason they think Dave had for using fragments. (He wanted his piece to sound as if he were holding a conversation, and fragments are often used in speaking.)

Explain that fragments can be acceptable when the writer has used them on purpose to achieve a certain effect; however, the writer should be sure that fragments are acceptable to the intended audience.

REVISE YOUR WRITING

Objectives

- To evaluate the responses to a draft of an opinion essay and to revise the draft with those responses in mind
- To evaluate the support for an opinion
- To analyze the organization of a draft
- To evaluate a draft for precise word choice

Teaching Strategies

for GIVE THE FACTS

HELPFUL HINT Suggest that students put a check mark by each fact or example they have given to support their reasons. If students do not have more than two check marks, they may need to add more facts or examples.

for PARAGRAPHS AT WORK

HELPFUL HINT Have students refer to Dave's finished essay on pages 118–119. Ask students to explain the organization of paragraphs 3–6. (Paragraphs 3 and 5 state reasons; paragraphs 4 and 6 support those reasons with specific examples.)

for WATCH YOUR LANGUAGE

INDIVIDUALIZING INSTRUCTION: ESL STUDENTS These students often do not understand the connotations of the words they choose. You might pair these students with strong native English speakers for a special peer review of word choices.

REVISE YOUR WRITING

1. Think about your responses. If your readers thought your opinion was unclear, try stating it in just one sentence. Then build from there.

2. Check your reasons. You've probably heard young children support their opinions by simply saying "Because." Their friends say, "Because why?" Make sure you have supplied the "why."

3. Give the facts. Have you used facts or examples to support all of your reasons? Could you prove them if asked to do so? Dave Smith used real people and salary figures to back up his opinion.

PROBLEM SOLVING

"How can I check my reasoning?"

To make sure your ideas make sense and you have used language effectively, see

- Handbook 30, "Thinking Skills," pages 320–322
- Handbook 20, "Levels of Language," pages 274–275

Paragraphs at Work When you state an opinion, you need to back it up with reasons. It's usually a good idea to put each of your reasons into a separate paragraph, along with the supporting facts, examples, and other details. Remember these tips.

- State your opinion in a separate paragraph at the beginning of your essay.
- Begin a new paragraph for each main reason you give to support your opinion.
- Make sure that all details in a paragraph are related.

4. Watch your language. Precise words make for clearer opinions. Some words cause emotional reactions. If you use words like *good* and *bad* or *right* and *wrong,* you should show readers what you mean. Barbara Brotman and Dave Smith used words like *outrageous,* but they based their opinions on reason as well as emotion.

5. Check your introduction and conclusion. Have you written an interesting introduction that makes your readers want to continue reading? Is your conclusion a strong one that your readers will remember?

One Student's Process

After reviewing his draft with classmates, Dave Smith decided to change the beginning, add some facts, and change the organization. Here are the changes he made.

The outrageous salaries of professional athletes just ~~doesn't~~ don't make sense. ~~Ordinary working people don't make that kind of money.~~ ¶ Many people in America today ~~only~~ make ~~a few dollars~~ somewhere between $5 and $10 an hour. That's not bad. But while they're making ~~a few dollars~~ $5 to $10 an hour, there are some people making ~~huge fortunes. It's insane.~~ $12,000 an hour! ¶ Who are these people? Who else? Professional athletes!

PROOFREAD

1. Proofread your work. Look over your revised paper for errors in grammar, spelling, punctuation, and capitalization. Double-check numbers and statistics. In explaining your reasons for your opinion, you may have used transition words and phrases such as *for example, in addition, next,* and *finally.* Check with your teacher about the use of commas with these transition words.

for ONE STUDENT'S PROCESS

CRITICAL THINKING: ANALYZING
Have students compare this section of the draft with Dave Smith's final introduction on page 118. Ask them why Dave moved the first sentence. (He originally had ended the paragraph by saying that professional athletes are the ones who make so much money. However, in the first sentence he already had stated that the salaries of professional athletes are outrageous; therefore, the sequence wasn't logical.) Discuss how moving that sentence affects the introduction. (It makes the introduction stronger because it enables Dave to build up to the fact that professional athletes are the focus of his remarks.)

for ONE STUDENT'S PROCESS

HELPFUL HINT: SPECIFIC DETAILS Point out that Dave replaced general information ("a few dollars" and "huge fortunes") with specific—in fact, statistical—details ("$5 to $10 an hour" and "$12,000 an hour"). Encourage students to use specific details wherever they can in their writing.

PROOFREAD

Teaching Strategies

for PROOFREAD YOUR WORK

COLLABORATIVE OPPORTUNITY
You might suggest that students work with partners and proofread each other's writing for errors in grammar, spelling, punctuation, and capitalization.

for LINKING GRAMMAR AND WRITING

HELPFUL HINT Other words that sometimes cause similar subject-verb agreement problems are *each* and *neither.* See pages 533–537 of Handbook 41, "Subject-Verb Agreement."

Guidelines for Evaluation

IDEAS AND CONTENT

- clearly states an opinion
- uses reasons, facts, and examples to support the opinion
- takes into account arguments on the other side
- has a strong introduction and conclusion

STRUCTURE AND FORM

- states an opinion in a separate paragraph at the beginning
- uses a separate paragraph for each supporting reason

GRAMMAR, USAGE, AND MECHANICS

- displays standard grammar, usage, spelling, and mechanics
- uses verbs that agree with their subjects

LINKING GRAMMAR AND WRITING

Subject–Verb Agreement

Remember, a verb must always agree in number with its subject. The noun or pronoun closest to the verb is not always the subject of that verb. For example, if you refer to *one* of the factors in a problem or *one* of the reasons for your opinion, you should check for subject-verb agreement.

Dave corrected a problem in subject–verb agreement when he proofread and revised his writing. The plural word *reasons* is next to the verb in the following sentence, but the subject of the sentence is *one.* The singular verb *is* agrees with the subject.

Original

One of the reasons <u>are</u> that no one is worth that much money.

Revised

One of the reasons <u>is</u> that no one is worth that much money.

Standards for Evaluation

PERSUASIVE WRITING

An opinion paper

- has a strong introduction
- clearly states the writer's opinion
- provides support for ideas
- has a strong conclusion

2. Make a clean copy of your paper. Once you are satisfied with your paper, review it one last time, using the Standards for Evaluation listed in the margin. Then make your final copy.

PUBLISH AND PRESENT

- **Write a letter.** Turn your opinion piece into a letter to the editor of a school or community newspaper. Perhaps you can pair it with another piece, expressing a different opinion on the same topic.

PROFESSIONAL NOTEBOOK

Advice from the Authors You might consider this advice from Peter Elbow on evaluating student writing. Elbow states that "if we evaluate *everything* students write, they tend to remain tangled up in the assumption that their whole job in school is to give teachers 'what they want.' Constant evaluation makes students worry more about psyching out the teacher than about what they are really learning. . . . Most of all, constant evaluation by someone in authority makes students reluctant to take the risks that are needed for good learning—to try out hunches and trust their own judgment."

- **Turn your opinion into a poster.** Create headlines and illustrations to present your opinion.
- **Hold a class discussion.** Get together with your classmates and present your papers orally. Then share your reactions to each other's work.
- **Present your case.** Deliver your opinion personally to someone in a position of authority who might be able to help.

REFLECT ON YOUR WRITING

WRITER TO WRITER

One role of the writer today is to sound the alarm.

E. B. White, American writer

1. Add your writing to your portfolio. Include a note, to be attached to your paper, in which you reflect on your experience in writing your opinion paper. In this note you may want to write about the following questions:

FOR YOUR **PORTFOLIO**

- How did I find a topic to write about?
- How did my opinion change as I thought and wrote about my topic?
- What happened when my classmates read my paper? How did their responses help me or get in my way?
- How would I change my essay now, if I were to revise it again?

2. Explore additional writing ideas. See the suggestions for writing a review on pages 130–132, and Springboards on page 137.

Reteaching

After students have completed their papers, assess the needs of students who were not successful in developing an effective opinion essay and assign the appropriate handbook mini-lessons as well as the Workshop Support Materials listed in the Teaching Preview, pages 113a-113b.

Concepts commonly requiring reteaching for this assignment are

- **Handbook 7, Organizing Details, pp. 217–221**
- **Handbook 30, Thinking Skills, pp. 320–322**

The following suggestions and resources also may be useful:

Lack of Supporting Reasons, Facts, and Examples Use page 7, "Analyzing," of the *Thinking Skills Worksheets* to help students generate reasons for an opinion. Then suggest working with partners to list facts and examples that support these reasons.

Ignoring Opposing Views Have students compare and contrast the Strong Response and the Weak Response on pages 34 and 36 of *Guidelines for Writing Assessment and Portfolio Use* in the Teacher's Resource File. Point out passages in which the writer responds to or ignores opposing views.

Extension and Enrichment

1. If students could make any change at school, what would it be? Ask them to write a persuasive letter that outlines the change and deals with at least one possible objection.

2. Supply this scenario: You are in charge of publicity for a rock group. Design a poster to advertise a concert. The poster must persuade middle school students to attend but also appeal to parents.

Closure: Reflect on Your Writing

As students reflect on what to include in their note, encourage them to give special consideration to the final question. Explain that even professional writers think about ways in which they can improve a finished piece of writing.

Related ASSIGNMENT

Reading a PUBLIC OPINION SURVEY

Objectives

- To analyze and respond to a public opinion survey
- To identify a purpose and audience for a survey
- To create and complete a survey and write a report on the results

Motivate

Informally administer the survey on page 128 to your students, reading the directions and the questions and writing the qualities on the board. Tally the results; then list the qualities in the order in which your class ranked them. Tell students that they will compare their answers with those of another group of students.

BUILD ON PRIOR KNOWLEDGE

Ask students to share any experiences they have had with taking or reading the results of public opinion surveys. Then share your experiences, perhaps with market research surveys, political surveys, or opinion surveys given by schools, government groups, or organizations. Discuss the type and purpose of the survey, and the likely use of the results.

SET A PURPOSE

After students have read Reading a Public Opinion Survey, explain that they now will find out how their results compare with Tina's. Remind students to think about a question on which they would like to know others' opinions.

Related ASSIGNMENT

Public Opinion Survey

Reading a PUBLIC OPINION SURVEY

Tina Smith, a sixth-grade student, was curious about the ideas and opinions of her classmates. So she satisfied her curiosity by taking an opinion survey. Then she wrote a report of her findings. Look at her survey form, shown here, and then read her report on the opposite page. Can you think of other questions you'd like to ask?

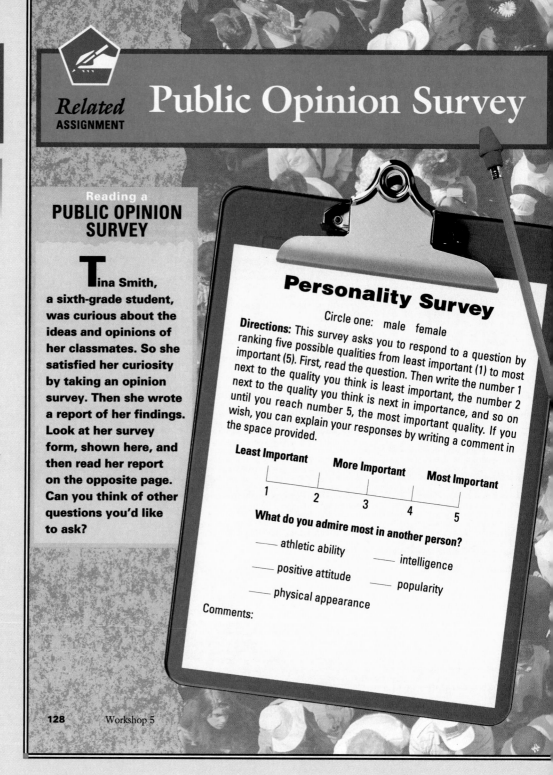

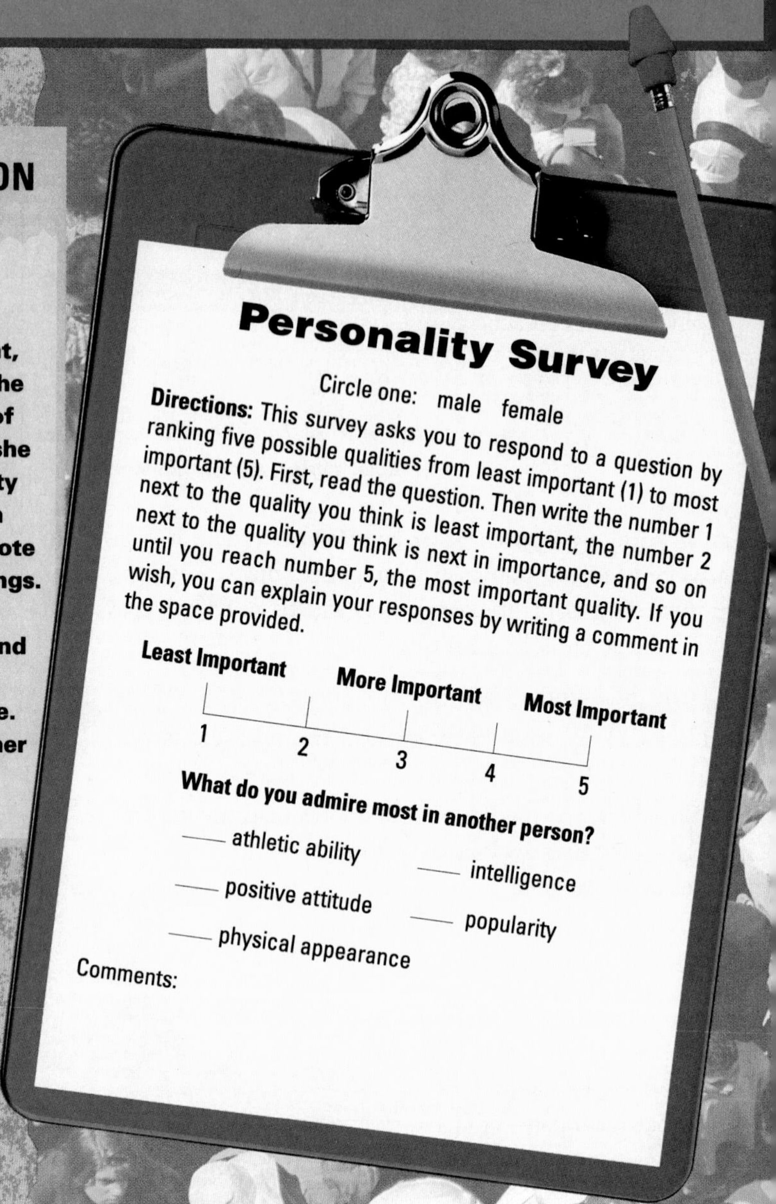

Personality Survey

Circle one: male female

Directions: This survey asks you to respond to a question by ranking five possible qualities from least important (1) to most important (5). First, read the question. Then write the number 1 next to the quality you think is least important, the number 2 next to the quality you think is next in importance, and so on until you reach number 5, the most important quality. If you wish, you can explain your responses by writing a comment in the space provided.

Least Important **More Important** **Most Important**

1 2 3 4 5

What do you admire most in another person?

___ athletic ability ___ intelligence

___ positive attitude ___ popularity

___ physical appearance

Comments:

Mathematics Connection

If possible, you might invite a math teacher who is familiar with statistics to talk informally about designing and analyzing surveys. The teacher can explain the importance of the size of the sample in analyzing the results. For example, with a large sample, very small differences in numbers are not statistically significant. With a small sample, however, such differences can result in a markedly different interpretation.

Personality Survey

Question

I've often wondered why my friends like some people more than others. I started asking them what they admired most in a person. Some said intelligence was most important. Others mentioned good looks or personality. Sometimes, though, I wasn't sure they were being honest. So I decided to take an opinion survey. I wrote down five qualities that people mentioned the most. Then I made up a questionnaire.

Method

I conducted this survey at my school in March. I gave the survey form to 100 sixth-grade students, 50 girls and 50 boys. When I got the forms back, I added up all the numbers. If someone ranked a quality as number five, I gave that answer five points. The second choice got four points, and so on. Here are the choices the students made and the total points each quality got.

SURVEY RESULTS

Quality	Girls	Boys	Total
Positive Attitude	236	222	458
Intelligence	193	189	382
Athletic ability	117	132	249
Physical appearance	122	118	240
Popularity	81	89	170

Results

The most important quality of the five turned out to be a positive attitude. Out of the 100 students, 39 girls and 32 boys put it at the top of the list. The next most important trait was intelligence. It was rated number 2 by 35 girls and 26 boys. Almost one-fourth of the boys even gave it the highest rating. Third place was pretty close to a tie, but athletic ability came out a little ahead of physical appearance. Popularity came in last.

Conclusion

This survey tells me that boys and girls admire similar things. Both think a positive attitude and intelligence are most important. Girls seem to value physical appearance a little more than athletic ability, and with boys it's the other way around. Everyone put popularity last. I learned that most kids value more lasting things.

Think & Respond

What do you find to be the most interesting result of Tina's survey? Can you think of any reason why girls and boys disagreed about what to rank third? How do Tina's findings compare with your own experience?

Think & Respond

ELICIT PERSONAL RESPONSES

Have students freewrite responses to the questions in the Think & Respond box. Then discuss students' responses. If there are major differences between Tina's findings and their statistics, ask students why the results differ.

EXPLORE THE AUTHOR'S TECHNIQUES

Point out that Tina's survey has two main parts—the survey itself (page 128) and the report of her findings (page 129). Ask students what makes the survey easy to complete. (Samples: clear directions, a scale showing how to respond, and a fill-in-the-blank format for responding) Also, point out that Tina wanted to look at the differences between the responses of girls and those of boys; therefore, she asked respondents to indicate their gender. Then focus attention on the organization of the report, emphasizing the four sections and the presentation of the statistical information. You might mention that the format of the report is similar to the format of laboratory reports in science.

Grammar Connection

Students may not know how to deal with numbers in their reports—that is, whether to use numerals or spell out the numbers as words. In actuality, style for treating numbers varies. Refer students to the "Method" and "Results" sections of Tina's report. Note that numbers under 10 and fractions are spelled out. Numbers with more than one digit are written as numerals. Point out that in a chart or other graphic aid, numbers are always written as numerals.

Writing ON YOUR OWN

Remind students of the features that made Tina's survey easy to complete and to tabulate (clear directions and format, the use of a numerical scale for responses). Suggest that students consider Tina's approach as they plan their own public opinion surveys.

Handbooks for Help and Practice

The following handbooks may be used as mini-lessons before students begin writing or as resources when problems arise:

- **Finding a Focus, pp. 203–204**
- **Organizing Details, pp. 217–221**
- **Interviewing Skills, p. 323**

Teaching Strategies

for CONSIDER YOUR AUDIENCE

HELPFUL HINT Remind students that, like Tina, they may want to compare the responses of different segments of their audience, such as girls and boys or different age groups. Explain that in order to do this, students must include at the beginning of their survey questions that elicit the respondents' age, gender, and so on.

for CHOOSE THE SIZE . . .

HELPFUL HINT You might suggest an audience size that you think is reasonable for students to survey; for example, students should not feel pressured to survey 100 people just because the model uses this number; however, caution students against inadvertently skewing their results by limiting their audience to their friends or to people they know well. Also, advise students to survey an equal number of people in each group they wish to compare, such as boys and girls, unless they want only the opinion of one group.

Writing ON YOUR OWN

Public Opinion Survey

INVITATION TO *Write*

Tina Smith used a survey to find out what her classmates admired most in other people. Then she reported on her findings. You, too, can gather information about people's opinions by taking a survey.

Design a public opinion survey on a subject that interests you. Give the survey to a group of people, and then write a report about the results.

FINDING A FOCUS

1. Find a reason to take a survey. You can conduct a survey to get support for an idea—for example, that television violence is harmful to kids. You might use a survey to help you make a decision, such as which product to sell to raise money for your club. Perhaps you are simply curious about how other people think about an issue you care about, such as cafeteria menus or the length of the school day.

2. Consider your audience. Who will take your survey? That depends on what you want to learn. You may want to target certain groups, such as sports fans or skateboarders. On the other hand, you may simply want to survey students in general.

3. Choose the size of your survey. If, for example, you want to know how students feel about cafeteria menus, you would need to survey as many students as possible in order to get the most reliable information. If you want to know how the members of your club feel about meeting times, your survey would be limited to the club members.

Literature Connection

Students might enjoy taking a survey about the kind of reading classmates do for pleasure. They could use broad categories, such as books, magazines, and comic books—or more specific ones, such as realistic fiction, science fiction, historical fiction, or nonfiction.

Music Connection

Interested students might take a survey to find out what musical instruments their classmates would like offered in the music curriculum. Students also could ask a librarian for help in finding music representative of several generations, then create a survey about attitudes toward the music.

CREATING YOUR SURVEY

1. Consider the form. What form works best for the type of survey you are doing? Tina asked people to rank qualities from least to most important. The resulting data gave her numbers that she could compare. Multiple-choice questions are another useful form. They can be used for issues such as which radio stations are more popular or what kinds of books students like to read.

2. Write the questions. Think about what you want to know. Brainstorm with some friends to come up with possible questions. Then try out different ways of wording the questions to make them as clear as possible.

3. Write directions. Tell people what you want them to do. Your directions need to be very clear or else you may get answers that you do not understand or cannot count. Sometimes a sample question and answer helps clarify directions for the people who take your survey.

4. Test your form. Try out your survey on a few of your classmates. Can they follow your directions? Do they understand your questions? If necessary, change the wording of questions or directions before giving your survey to a larger number of people.

COMPLETING THE SURVEY

1. Have people take the survey. Find a convenient time and place for people to read and complete your survey. Collect the completed forms and keep them together until you are ready to count the answers.

2. Keep track of the responses. Set up a chart or a list with which you can count responses and figure out the results of your survey.

for CREATING YOUR SURVEY

INDIVIDUALIZING INSTRUCTION: INDEPENDENT LEARNERS These students should enjoy making up their own survey. Because independent learners usually prefer to trust their own judgment, however, they may need support in seeking the opinions of others. Therefore, you might want to pair such students with social learners who can help distribute or administer the survey.

for CONSIDER THE FORM

KEY TO UNDERSTANDING Tell students that their survey must be in a form that can be tabulated easily. For example, open-ended questions that require people to write their own answers cannot be tabulated easily. Therefore, whatever form the surveys take should provide answer choices. Their form might be like Tina's, or they might take the form of multiple-choice, yes-or-no, or true-or-false questions.

Students should also think about the length of their surveys. People often do not want to spend much time answering a lot of questions, and a survey of more than one page will be expensive to duplicate.

for WRITE THE QUESTIONS

HELPFUL HINT Caution students to phrase their questions as impartially as possible. Loaded language or false either/or reasoning can skew their results. To emphasize this point, ask students to critique this sample survey question:

> Schools load excessive homework on overworked students. T F

for TEST YOUR FORM

INDIVIDUALIZING INSTRUCTION: LEP STUDENTS Work individually with students who have difficulty in writing clear directions, or pair them with strong English speakers.

for WRITE A REPORT

PEER RESPONSE After students have finished writing, you might have them exchange reports and seek feedback. Suggest that peer readers summarize the methods, findings, and conclusions for the writer, to make sure the report is clear. Then have students revise their reports as necessary.

for PRESENT THE RESULTS

INDIVIDUALIZING INSTRUCTION: LD STUDENTS Working with numerical data may be difficult for students who tend to transpose numbers. You might check that these students have tallied their results correctly before they create their graphic presentations.

Guidelines for Evaluation

AN EFFECTIVE SURVEY REPORT

- includes a logically structured survey form with clear directions and questions
- states the purpose of the survey, to whom it was administered, and how it was administered
- effectively presents and summarizes the results

3. Write a report. Think of an effective way of presenting the results of the survey. Your report will probably have the following sections:

- **Discuss the issue.** You can start your report by describing the purpose of your survey. Be sure to explain why you are interested in this information.
- **Describe the methods you used.** Explain who filled out the survey form. Describe how these people were chosen and when and where the survey was conducted.
- **Present the results.** Write a conclusion summing up the results. This might be a good place for a graphic presentation, perhaps a graph or a chart like the one Tina used. Then comment on the results of your survey. Tell why your results are interesting or important.

SHARING YOUR RESULTS

- **Display the findings.** Post the survey form and your report of the results on a school bulletin board. You might also give an oral report about the results of your survey.
- **Write an article.** Write an article for your school or community paper. Describe your survey and explain what you learned.
- **Share your report.** Give a copy of your survey report to those who might be particularly interested, such as student organizations or school administrators.

Related ASSIGNMENT

Writing for Assessment

More and more, writing is becoming an important part of the tests you take in school. You'll do better on a test if you know what to expect. One kind of test asks you to write a brief essay to show what you've learned about a school subject. In another type of test, a writing assessment, you write to show how well you can express your own thoughts and feelings.

Two of the questions on this page are essay-test questions and two are prompts for writing assessments. What does each question ask you to do?

- **SOCIAL STUDIES** The ancient Egyptians believed in an afterlife. Define afterlife and tell the steps Egyptians took to prepare for the afterlife.
- **SCIENCE** Dinosaurs lived on the earth millions of years ago. Discuss the theories about why they became extinct.
- **WRITING TEST** You have received a letter from a sixth grader living in China who wants to know what life is like in the United States. Write a letter to this student. Describe what a typical school day is like for you.
- **WRITING TEST** Imagine that your town is considering a law that would forbid people from skating on downtown sidewalks. Write a letter to the editor of your community newspaper. State your opinion on whether or not skating should be banned. Give reasons to back up your opinion.

Related ASSIGNMENT

Objectives

- To analyze essay-test questions and writing prompts
- To plan, write, revise, and proofread an answer to a writing prompt

Motivate

Ask students how many of them feel confident when they are about to take a test. What makes them feel more confident or less so? Do students prefer taking tests in which they are given a choice of answers, or tests in which they are asked to write an essay? In this workshop, students will study how to write a strong essay response.

BUILD ON PRIOR KNOWLEDGE

Invite students to share their feelings about essay tests. What makes the tests easy or hard? What difficulties do students have with the tests? Then have students tell their strategies for answering essay tests. Do they highlight key words in the question? Do they plan their answers, or do they begin writing immediately? Do they budget their time? Do they revise and proofread their answers?

SET A PURPOSE

After students have read the boxed text, ask them to identify the purpose of an essay test and of a writing assessment test. (The first tests knowledge of a specific subject; the second tests writing skill.) Tell students to keep this difference in mind as they read the questions to identify what each one asks.

Writing ON YOUR OWN

Tell students that the two writing-test prompts on the preceding page are the type of questions they might see on standardized tests. In this assignment, they will use what they learned in the Guided Assignment to write an effective response to the last prompt.

Handbooks for Help and Practice

The following handbooks may be used as mini-lessons before students begin writing or as resources when problems arise:

- **Goals and Audience, pp. 211–213**
- **Conclusions, pp. 250–252**
- **Taking Tests, pp. 326–333**

Teaching Strategies

for FIND OUT WHAT . . . TO DO

INDIVIDUALIZING INSTRUCTION: BASIC STUDENTS Emphasize the importance of finding the key words in essay directions. Point out that the key words indicate the kind of information to give in the answer. Have students find the key words in the questions on page 133.

for KNOW YOUR AUDIENCE

CRITICAL THINKING: ANALYZING Have students examine the first, second, third, and fourth prompts on page 133 and identify the audience for each. Ask what kind of language they would use for each audience: (First and second prompts: the audience is the teacher—use formal language; third prompt: the audience is a Chinese student—use informal language; fourth prompt: the audience is a newspaper editor and newspaper readers, including elected town leaders—use formal language.)

Writing ON YOUR OWN
Writing for Assessment

INVITATION TO Write

Questions like those on page 133 test your knowledge, your thinking skills, and your writing ability. You can learn to examine test questions and find the clues that will help you write effective answers.

Follow the directions for the last question on page 133. Write a letter to the editor that tells your opinion and supports it.

PROBLEM SOLVING

"What's the best way to study for a test?"

For more information on preparing for tests, see

- Handbook 33, "Taking Tests," pages 326–333

READING THE QUESTION

1. Find out what you need to do. Key words in the directions can tell you what writing strategy to use. If you see words like *explain* or *compare* or *persuade,* for example, you know how your answer should be presented. Here are some key words to look for.

describe	discuss	persuade
explain	compare	contrast
define	tell how	give reasons

2. Know your audience. Some questions tell you to write for a specific person or group. Knowing the audience will tell you what kind of language to use or how much to explain. For example, the audience for the third question on page 133 is a sixth grader in China. You might use friendly, informal language for that reader.

3. Determine your format. Check to see what form your writing should take. You could be asked to write a letter, an editorial, or an essay, for example.

Writing TIP

If a question doesn't specify the audience, it is often best to assume that your teacher is your audience.

GETTING READY TO ANSWER

1. Plan your time. Before you start writing, take a few moments to decide how to use your time. For example, if you have thirty minutes to write an answer, you might budget ten minutes to plan your answer, fifteen minutes to write it, and five minutes to revise and proofread it.

2. Do some prewriting. You might want to make a list or a cluster or do some freewriting to find the ideas to include in your answer. Jot down ideas as they come to you. If possible, sketch out a quick outline of your answer.

One Student's Process

Leroy Collins jotted down a rough outline for an answer to the first test question.

Beliefs	Burial practices
— afterlife like real life	— ~~mummies 5000 years old~~
~~— worshipped sun god~~	— food & weapons too
— dead needed bodies	— pets and servants
— dead should be comfortable	
— mummies preserved	

WRITING YOUR ANSWER

1. Start with your main idea. Since time is limited, get right to the point. Try to state your main idea in a sentence or two. Then look at your prewriting notes to find details, facts, or reasons you can use to back up your main idea.

2. End with a strong conclusion. You might want to sum up the point you have made or restate your main idea.

Writing TIP

One good way to start prewriting is to list the topic, audience, format, and writing strategy you plan to use.

Egyptian male mummy mask, painted wood, about 1400 B.C.

for WRITING TIP

INDIVIDUALIZING INSTRUCTION: BASIC STUDENTS Draw attention to the Writing Tip, which is especially helpful for these students. Explain that identifying the "writing strategy" means finding in the question the key word, such as *compare* or *persuade,* that tells what kind of information to give. Note that by making this list, students can be sure that they have identified what the question calls for.

for DO SOME PREWRITING

STUMBLING BLOCK Students often cringe when they hear the word *outline* because they think of a formal outline with all its letters and numbers. Assure students that the outline for planning a test answer can be as simple as the one shown in One Student's Process.

for ONE STUDENT'S PROCESS

CRITICAL THINKING: ANALYZING Have students note the changes that Leroy Collins made in his outline and explain the reason for each change. (He deleted "worshipped sun god" and "mummies 5000 years old" because they are unrelated to the question on the Egyptian afterlife. He moved "mummies preserved" because it was a burial practice, not a belief.)

ART NOTE

In ancient Egypt, the dead bodies of royalty—along with some of their servants, members of the court, and sacred animals—were preserved as mummies. This elaborately painted portrait mask fit over a mummy's head and shoulders.

for ONE STUDENT'S PROCESS

CRITICAL THINKING: ANALYZING
Ask students to explain the reason for each change that Leroy made in his answer. Note that the changes were relatively minor. In a testing situation, there is rarely time for major revisions.

Guidelines for Evaluation

AN EFFECTIVE WRITING-TEST ANSWER

- addresses the topic and audience and follows the writing strategy and format that the prompt calls for
- clearly states the main idea
- provides supporting details, facts, or reasons
- uses language appropriate for the audience
- has a logical organization

GENERAL NOTE

HELPFUL HINT You might want to give students more practice in writing from prompts by occasionally assigning a prompt from *Starting Points for Writing* or *Tests and Writing Assessment Prompts* in the Teacher's Resource File. Students can then compare the effectiveness of their responses over a period of time.

REVIEWING YOUR ANSWER

1. Reread the question. Make sure that you have fully answered the question. In the margins or between the lines, make any changes you want in your answer.

2. Proofread your work. Look for mistakes in grammar, spelling, capitalization, and punctuation.

One Student's Process

Here is how Leroy Collins's paper looked when he had finished it.

The Egyptians beleived that life continued after death. They called this idea the Afterlife. The Egyptians believed the afterlife would be much ~~the same~~ like real life. Therefore, They wanted the dead to have everthing they would need to enjoy the afterlife.

Once an Egyptian died, ~~his~~ the body was perserved as a mummy. This was so the soul would ~~be able to come back to it~~ have a place when it returned. Then the body was placed in a tomb along with food and some of the person's favorite things. Sometimes the bodies of servants or cats and dogs were also included. The insides of the tomb were often painted with beautiful scenes from the person's life.

Defines afterlife

Explains why they had to prepare the dead

Tells the steps Egyptians followed to prepare the dead for the afterlife

Includes specific details

136 Workshop 5

PROFESSIONAL NOTEBOOK

Advice from the Authors Often, students see little point in working hard at essay questions because they do not believe such writing has any value beyond the test situation. Sheridan Blau offers this advice:

"Among the most effective strategies teachers can use to help students discover the value of their own ideas (and hence the value of clarifying and communicating them) is that of taking those ideas seriously—examining them not with the eye of a corrector but with the respect of one who would learn from them."

Springboards

CONSUMER EDUCATION Write a consumer review of a product you have used. Tell your readers whether you recommend they use the product. Be sure to give specific reasons for your recommendation.

Keds (1961), Roy Lichtenstein

MEDIA Imagine that you work for an advertising agency. Choose a product and write an advertisement that will make people want to buy it. Illustrate your ad with your own drawings or with pictures you cut out of magazines.

MUSIC Who is your choice for best musical group, or best individual artist, performing today? Write a paper that presents—and supports—your opinion.

Science How would you support the opinion that the earth is flat? How would you oppose it? Choose a scientific concept that we take for granted today. Then write a paper that either supports the concept or opposes it.

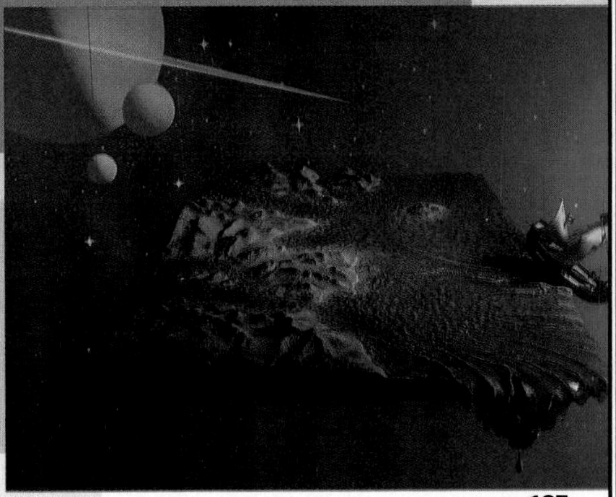

Speaking & Listening Write a campaign speech for any candidate—living or dead—of your choice. Convince your listeners that they should vote for your candidate.

137

Teaching Strategies

for MEDIA

INDIVIDUALIZING INSTRUCTION: VISUAL LEARNERS You might pair a visual learner with a strong persuasive writer to work as an advertising team for this assignment. Remind students that the use of emotional appeals and other persuasive techniques are accepted practice in advertising.

for MUSIC

HELPFUL HINT Remind students that opinions should be supported with reasons, facts, or examples. As support, students might cite music awards or sales; still, since "best" is a subjective judgment, they might simply describe their reasons for liking the music.

for SPEAKING AND LISTENING

HELPFUL HINT If students have access to video equipment, suggest that they videotape their speeches and review the tape to evaluate both the speech and their delivery. Then they can revise their speeches and practice their delivery before they make their presentation to the class.

ART NOTE

Painter Roy Lichtenstein is a leading figure of the pop art movement that gained popularity in the late 1950s and early 1960s. He often enlarges a single product or a single comic-strip frame to draw attention to the ordinary and to satirize serious subjects. *Blam,* another work by Lichtenstein, can be found in the *Fine Art Transparency Pack*.

Subject-Verb Splits

Objectives

- To combine sentences, using subject-verb splits
- To unscramble sentence chunks and create sentences that imitate models with subject-verb splits
- To write original sentences that imitate models with subject-verb splits
- To expand sentences by adding subject-verb splits

CRITICAL THINKING: ANALYZING Have students examine the models. In Model A, ask them to identify the word the subject-verb split modifies *(mother)*. Have them continue with Models B *(meat)* and C *(Little Jon)*. Point out that the words between the subject and the verb should modify the subject; otherwise, the sentence will not make sense.

SPEAKING AND LISTENING Have volunteers read the sentences aloud. Tell students to listen for the natural pauses. Advise students that noting the pauses can help them remember to place commas around subject-verb splits.

Additional Resource

Sentence Composing Copy Masters, pp. 9–10

Answer Key

A. Combining Sentences

1. Boysie, who slept in the kitchen, heard the door shut and came to the living room.
2. The physical education teacher, dancing past energetically in the arms of a Grade Ten boy, gave me an inquisitive look.
3. The truck drivers, when they heard that Maxie Hammerman had been released, were furious.
4. The clerk, a snappy-looking fellow, wearing a red bow tie, with a pink baby face but not a wisp of hair on his head, tried to talk me into buying one big bottle.

Sentence

COMPOSING

Subject-Verb Splits

The underlined parts of the sentences below separate the subject (S) from the verb (V). Notice how these subject-verb splits add information about the subject of each sentence.

Model A Agatha's (S) mother, frantic now, beat (V) the door of the vault with her hands. **O. Henry, "A Retrieved Reformation"**

Model B The meat (S), preserved for the feeding of the dogs, hung (V) in the smokehouse. **Marjorie Kinnan Rawlings, *The Yearling***

Model C Little Jon (S), whose eyes were quicker than most, should (V) have seen the hole, but all his attention was on the stars. **Alexander Key, *The Forgotten Door***

ON THE MARK Put commas before and after a subject-verb split to separate it from the rest of the sentence.

A. Combining Sentences Put the underlined part of the second sentence into the first sentence at the caret (‸) as a subject-verb split. Write the complete sentence, putting commas before and after the subject-verb split.

1. Boysie ‸ heard the door shut and came to the living room. Boysie was the one who slept in the kitchen. **Betsy Byars, *The Summer of the Swans***
2. The physical education teacher ‸ gave me an inquisitive look. The teacher was dancing past energetically in the arms of a Grade Ten boy. **Alice Munro, "Red Dress—1946"**
3. The truck drivers ‸ were furious. This happened when they heard that Maxie Hammerman had been released. **Jean Merrill, *The Pushcart War***
4. The clerk ‸ tried to talk me into buying one big bottle. He was a snappy-looking fellow, wearing a red bow tie, with a pink baby face but not a wisp of hair on his head. **Robert Cormier, *Take Me Where the Good Times Are***

B. Unscrambling and Imitating Sentences Unscramble each set of sentence chunks below. Create a sentence that has a subject-verb split and the same order of chunks and punctuation as the model. Then write a sentence of your own that imitates each model.

1. Model Mr. McAlester, who kept the store, was a good Arkansas man.

Charles Portis, *True Grit*

who coaches our team / Andre's father / is a former professional football player

2. Model His little legs, bent sharply at the knees, had never before seemed so fragile, so thin. **James Hurst, "The Scarlet Ibis"**

surrounded completely by birch trees / had always seemed so comfortable, so cozy / their summer cottage

3. Model My stomach, a large distressing lump, quaked and thrilled, making it hard for me to breathe the thin and tasteless air.

James Gould Cozzens, "The Animals' Fair"

a beautiful blue macaw / making it difficult for me / the parrot / to take a nap in peace / squawked and talked

C. Expanding Sentences Use your imagination to add a phrase as a S-V split where the caret appears in each of the following sentences. Set off each phrase with commas.

1. The lion ^ stared at the animals as hard as if he was going to burn them up with his mere stare. **C. S. Lewis, *The Magician's Nephew***

2. My aunt ^ pulled a chair up next to me, careful not to rake the legs across her shag carpet. **Gary Soto, *A Summer Life***

3. Mr. Miyagi ^ simply beamed. **B. B. Hiller, *The Karate Kid***

Grammar Refresher Adding words between the subject and the verb does not change subject-verb agreement. For more information, see Handbook 41, "Mastering Subject-Verb Agreement," pages 526–545.

B. Unscrambling and Imitating Sentences

Unscrambled sentences are given. Imitation sentences will vary but should follow the same pattern.

1. Andre's father, who coaches our team, is a former professional football player.
2. Their summer cottage, surrounded completely by birch trees, had always seemed so comfortable, so cozy.
3. The parrot, a beautiful blue macaw, squawked and talked, making it difficult for me to take a nap in peace.

C. Expanding Sentences

Answers will vary. Professional models are shown below.

1. The lion, whose eyes never blinked, stared at the animals as hard as if he was going to burn them up with his mere stare.
2. My aunt, chicken-print dish towel in hand, pulled a chair up next to me, careful not to rake the legs across her shag carpet.
3. Mr. Miyagi, never one to show much emotion, simply beamed.

for GRAMMAR REFRESHER

HELPFUL HINT Remind students that the words between the commas can never contain the subject of the sentence. When students are checking subject-verb agreement, tell them to pretend that the subject-verb split does not exist.

The dancer, wobbling on her toes, (twist, twists) her ankle.

The dancer (twist, twists) her ankle.

Twists agrees with the subject *dancer.*

6

Responding to Literature

Overview

Responding to literature means a sharing one's personal reactions to short stories, poems, and books of fiction and nonfiction. In this workshop, students apply skills such as analyzing, inferring, making comparisons, drawing conclusions, evaluating, and making critical judgments, as they express their opinions of works of literature. Workshop 6 includes the following Guided and Related Assignments, as well as the interdisciplinary project described on pages 139c–139d.

1. **Guided: Personal Response** invites students to share their personal reactions to a short story or poem of their choice, as they relate the work to their own personal experience. It builds on Workshop 5 by offering further practice in supporting an opinion.
2. **Related: Book Review** challenges students to extend their evaluation skills to a fiction or nonfiction book.

Teaching Preview

Preparation Guide

1. Use the Overview on this page and the Teacher's Choice descriptions on page 141 as a basis for deciding which assignments to teach.
2. Preview the assignments and the teacher's notes and identify concepts that may require preteaching or extra support, given your class's abilities. The handbook mini-lessons suggested within the lesson may also provide guidance.
3. Preview the chart below for support materials in the Teacher's Resource File that may be used with this Workshop. Resources are for use with the Guided Assignment unless otherwise noted.

Support Materials

WRITER'S CRAFT RESOURCES

Prewrite and Explore
Thinking Skills Worksheets, p. 4
Thinking Skills Transparencies, pp. 4–4a
Writing Resource Book, pp. 29–30

Draft and Discover
Elaboration, Revision, and Proofreading Practice, p. 11
Elaboration, Revision, and Proofreading Transparencies, pp. 21–22
Writing Resource Book, p. 31

Revise Your Writing
Elaboration, Revision, and Proofreading Practice, p. 12
Elaboration, Revision, and Proofreading Transparencies, pp. 23–24
Guidelines for Writing Assessment and Portfolio Use, pp. 19, 37–39
Peer Response Guides, pp. 17–18
Writing Resource Book, pp. 32–33

Extension Activities
Sentence Composing Copymasters, pp. 11–12
Starting Points for Writing, pp. 28, 31–33, 35–36
Writing from Literature, pp. 1–2, 9–12, 15–20, 23–26
Standardized Test Practice

Educational Technology
(available separately)
Writer's DataBank
Electronic English Handbook
Multimedia Workshop
On Assignment! (videodisc)

OTHER RESOURCES

Books and Journals
James, Elizabeth, and Carol Barkin. *How to Write Your Best Book Report.* New York: Morrow, 1986.
White, B. "Preparing Middle School Students to Respond to Literature." *Middle School Journal.* 24 (Sept. 1992): 21–23.

Films and Videos
"Book Review," and "Readers Theatre." *Literature to Enjoy and Write About.* Series 2. Pied Piper, 1990. (22 min. each)
How to Read a Book and Live to Tell About It. SRA, 1990. (25 min.)

Educational Technology
Essay Ease. Mindplay. Apple II.

Linking Literature, Writing, and Grammar

The following options may be used to provide students with an integrated language experience. Begin by assigning and discussing any of the recommended pieces of literature. Use the suggested strategy to provide a link to the Guided Assignment.

LINKING LITERATURE AND WRITING

Option 1

Starting Point: "The Circuit" by Francisco Jiménez on pages 142–145 of *The Writer's Craft.*

Strategy: Use the teaching suggestions on pages 142–145 to lead students into the Guided Assignment.

Option 2

Starting Point: "Eleven" by Sandra Cisneros on pages 68–71 of McDougal, Littell's *Literature and Language,* Grade 6. (Additional suggestions for using *Literature and Language* can be found on page 141.)

Strategy: Read the story aloud to students. Then have them consider whether they ever have moments when they feel younger than they really are. Ask them to freewrite their feelings about the whole story or any part of it. Use the responses to introduce the Guided Assignment.

Option 3

Starting Point: "Sarah Cynthia Sylvia Stout Would Not Take the Garbage Out" by Shel Silverstein.

Strategy: Have volunteers take turns reading stanzas of the poem aloud. Students will probably burst out laughing at some points. Have them discuss their favorite lines and explain why they found them funny. Use their responses to introduce the Guided Assignment.

LINKING WRITING AND GRAMMAR

Before the drafting or revision stages of this assignment, tell students that they will probably want to quote passages from the work to which they are responding. Model this process, using the following examples that might appear in a response to "The Circuit."

I wanted to cry at the end of the story, when Panchito was saying, "Everything we owned was neatly packed in cardboard boxes."

The author shows how hard farm work is when he has Panchito say, "The buzzing insects, the wet sweat, and the hot dry dust made the afternoon seem to last forever."

Have students proofread their own papers carefully, checking to make sure that they quoted accurately from the work of literature and that they used quotation marks and other punctuation correctly.

Go over pages 586–589 of the Grammar and Usage Handbook. If problems with quotations still appear in students' papers, assign the exercises on those pages for reteaching. Additional practice can be found in the *Grammar and Usage Practice Book* on page 95.

Management Guidelines

The chart below indicates the number of days recommended for each phase of the Guided and Related Assignments. These numbers are an estimate of the total time needed for each phase. In practice, of course, students may not complete each phase in one continuous session, nor will they necessarily progress from stage to stage in the linear order shown here. Stars indicate portions of the assignment that may be completed outside the classroom if time is limited or if teachers wish students to work independently.

PERSONAL RESPONSE

Starting from Literature	1 day
Prewrite and Explore	2 days
Draft and Discover	2–3 days*
Revise Your Writing	1 day*
Proofread	1 day*
Publish and Present	1 day
Reflect on Your Writing	1 day
Extension and Enrichment	open*

BOOK REVIEW

Choosing a Book	1 week*
Writing Your Book Review	2 days*
Reviewing Your Writing	1 day
Publishing and Presenting	1 day
Sentence Composing	open*

Project File

Media Myths: Responding to the Media

Overview

For this project, students will examine the way people, communities, and events are portrayed by the mass media. The project will culminate in presentations in which students use videotapes, audiotapes, and excerpts from print media to demonstrate their findings; offer research to verify any inaccuracies found in the images; and share their personal responses to the images.

Students will participate in the following activities:

- Analyze the various elements of a television program
- Examine images presented in films, television shows, radio programs, commercials, and print media
- Use research and personal experience to evaluate the accuracy of media images
- Write responses to media images
- Use language arts, math, social studies, science, and art skills to complete their research and to present their work

Preparation Guide

Tell students that media images influence our views of events and even of other people; ask students for examples. Lead students to see that developing an ability to evaluate the accuracy of media images will help them learn to rely on and trust their own responses to what they see, hear, and read. Be sure students know that the term *media* refers to movies, TV, radio, and print materials.

Explain that for this project students will apply literary response skills as they evaluate the media.

Stage 1
Explore Media and Images

1. Invite students to list the television shows and commercials they have seen often. Discuss elements such as people, setting, and events in several shows and commercials. Ask if students think these elements are realistic.
2. Select one "classic" TV series about a family (possibilities include *The Brady Bunch* or *The Cosby Show*), and have students work in groups to analyze its image of the family, of children and teenagers, of work, and of community. Instruct them to examine the roles and relationships of the family members and events in the family's life.
3. Tell student groups to read or recall current articles about families. Have them identify and discuss similarities and differences in the television images they have analyzed, the images presented by print media, and the images they have formed from their own experience (see *Resources, Stage 1*).

TEAM TEACHING

The following activities may be used for team teaching or as enrichment and extension activities by the language arts teacher.

Language Arts Practice discussion skills and group problem-solving skills.

Social Studies Learn about the features and varieties of family groups, the role of teenagers in society, and any laws regulating the media.

TEACHING TIPS

- As students examine a classic family series, ask them to consider the income level, the style of dress, the language used, the type of work, and the living arrangements of the characters. Do they believe that the television family represents most families?
- Provide magazines that contain articles about families or about aspects of family life.
- Make it clear that the purpose of this project is not to lessen enjoyment of the media but to encourage thoughtful responses.

Stage 2
Research and Respond to Media Images

1. Tell students to brainstorm a list of media images they would like to explore further. Images might include the following:
   - teenagers
   - families
   - men
   - women
   - children
   - work
   - communities
   - wars and disasters
2. Have students work in groups to select images from the list and search for examples in television, movies, radio, magazines, and newspapers.
3. Instruct groups to analyze their examples and to decide which messages, stereotypes, or assumptions are being conveyed. Then have the groups use research to confirm or refute these.
4. Tell students to examine movies, TV shows, and radio programs from five years ago, ten years ago, and so on to see how the image they are researching has been changing.
5. Direct students to write their personal responses to the images they have examined (see *Resources, Stage 2*).

TEAM TEACHING

Social Studies Study the history of television and movies (see *Resources, Stage 2*).

Art Investigate costumes and set design. Learn how the choice of clothing styles and possessions can project specific images.

Language Arts Learn how to write personal responses to reading and other materials.

TEACHING TIPS

- Schedule a library tour focusing on media reference sources.
- Suggest that students examine images in advertisements as well as in articles in current print media.
- Have videotape and audiotape players available for students' use.

Stage 3
Present Responses and Examine Implications

1. Direct groups to plan presentations of their examples and their research findings. The presentations should include group members' personal responses.
2. Have students present video clips, photographs, print and video advertisements, newspaper and magazine clippings, and audiotapes. Have them comment on specific images they find repeated in various media. For example, did they find repeated images of teenagers as rebellious and irresponsible or of fathers as incompetent and foolish?
3. Afterward, invite students to discuss the effects that media images have on viewers' attitudes and expectations. Do media standards of beauty affect how they see themselves? Which images of families do they find to be realistic? Which seem false? Which images are offensive?

TEAM TEACHING

Language Arts Review oral presentation skills.

Social Studies Learn about the ways the media influence events. Use as examples presidential debates and war coverage.

Art Create posters and illustrations for presentations.

Math Gather statistics about the media. Study the TV rating system and learn how the numbers are computed (see *Resources, Stage 3*).

TEACHING TIPS

- Arrange for students to show video clips or to play audiotapes during their presentations.
- Invite social studies classes to attend the presentations.

Resources

STAGE 1

Television and the American Family by Jennings Bryant discusses the impact of television on families.

Dancing in the Dark: Youth, Popular Culture, and the Electronic Media by Quentin J. Schultze investigates how television and radio affect young people and popular culture.

Prime Time Kids: An Analysis of Children and Families on Television by Sally Steenland helps evaluate television images of children and families.

STAGE 2

Film by Richard Platt and ***The TV Book*** by Judy Fireman are large-format, heavily illustrated books tracing the history of the movies and of television. Both include many still photos that may give students ideas about which old movies and TV shows they might explore.

For reviews and other articles on media, check the ***New York Times,*** which dates back to 1851, and the ***Chicago Tribune,*** which dates to 1847.

The Writer's Craft, Grade 6, Writer's Workshop 6, "Responding to Literature," pages 140–160, teaches the writing of responses to written or visual materials.

STAGE 3

The Writer's Craft, Grade 6, Handbook 32, "Oral Reports," pages 324–325, can help students with their oral presentations.

Can You Believe TV Ratings? by Paula Apsell and Mike Tomlinson (Films for the Humanities and WGBH Television) is a TV program originally broadcast on *Nova.* It examines the methods used to measure audiences for TV shows.

Big World, Small Screen: The Role of Television in American Society by Aletha C. Huston discusses the impact of television on society.

Guerrilla Media: A Citizen's Guide to Using Electronic Media for Social Change (Films for the Humanities) by David Hoffman, Tony Schwartz, and Will Duggan gives examples of radio and TV spots and focuses on how the average person can use the media to promote social change.

How to Make a Speech, a McGraw-Hill video narrated by Steve Allen, offers a humorous introduction to creating and delivering effective oral presentations.

Statistical Abstract of the United States, published annually, includes statistics about families and about TV ownership.

Additional Projects

Young Tourists' Guide Ask students to use research, personal response writing, and other skills to create a guidebook to their community and the surrounding area. The guidebook should be intended for peers. Students should compile maps, photos, illustrations, descriptions, and reviews of their favorite and least favorite restaurants, amusement parks, outdoor recreation areas, local events, and so on. Students can donate a copy of the finished guidebook to the local department of tourism or chamber of commerce.

Reading Outreach Ask students to adopt a primary-school class and to visit regularly to read to the children and help them with reading skills. Between visits, students should survey young children's books in libraries and bookstores. Have students prepare reviews, with the primary students as an audience, of the books they think the children will like best. During visits, students should take turns presenting their reviews orally. Afterward, students may read the books to interested children.

The Best Pets Have students research information about specific breeds and types of animals commonly kept as pets. They should present their findings and add the findings to a class data center. Then ask students to choose favorite pet types or breeds; visit owners, breeders, and/or pet stores; and present "pet reviews" combining facts with their personal responses to this kind of pet.

Sketch Book

Objective

- To use a visual prompt and writing prompts as springboards to informal writing

WRITING WARM-UPS

Encourage students to respond freely and informally to at least one of the Sketchbook prompts. Students may begin by brainstorming ideas or questions with the whole class and then exploring their ideas or questions by freewriting in their journals. Remind them that their responses will not be graded and may provide them with useful material for later assignments.

One way to respond to an object is to ask questions about that object. Students will also find this questioning technique helpful as they respond to a piece of literature in Writer's Workshop 6. Questioning can provide an inventory of what more they want to know or what they find puzzling. Asking questions and inventing histories can also suggest some engaging report topics for Writer's Workshop 7.

SHOW, DON'T TELL

The following is a sample for the first prompt that shows rather then tells about personal responses:

Everyone I know has his or her own special way of responding to music. My friend Jesse loves to dance to a rap beat, while my sister dreams away in her bedroom as she listens to tapes of classical piano. As for me, I can't wait to buy the latest country hit and try to play along on my guitar.

Sketch Book

I and the Village (1911), Marc Chagall.

- What do you think about this painting? Jot down your reactions.
- Tell a story about what you see in this painting.
- Is there a book, a poem, a painting, a song, or another work of art that has a special meaning for you? Explain why.

Show, Don't Tell

When you respond to a story or a poem, you try to connect your own experiences to something in the literature. Using examples from your life, you can explain how a piece of literature makes you feel. Select one of the *telling* sentences below and turn it into a *showing* paragraph by using examples from your own experience.

- The character did something that I would do.
- The story made me sad.

Responding to Literature

Guided Assignment
Personal Response

Related Assignment
Book Review

You've just been watching a TV show with friends. You're complaining about the ending, but someone else liked the actors. Still another remembers the funny lines. You're all responding to the show. Sharing your reactions is not only natural and fun, it also helps you understand your own thoughts and feelings about a work.

In this workshop you'll get a chance to write what you think and feel about a short work of literature. In a related assignment, you'll share your responses to a book you've read.

Responding to Literature

Objectives

Guided Assignment

Personal Response To analyze a personal response to a short work of literature and to write a personal response essay on a short literary work of one's choice

Related Assignment

Book Review To evaluate a book review and to write a review of a book of one's choice

Teacher's Choice

Use the following guidelines to choose the assignment that best suits students' needs.

Personal Response This assignment will benefit all students by helping them express and explain their responses to a work of literature. Students are encouraged to explore their own feelings about the work as well as to explore the author's techniques. You may want to tie this assignment to writing activities in your literature program.

Book Review This assignment will be particularly challenging to students of limited English proficiency since they must read and evaluate an entire book; you may want to give these students the option of responding to a shorter work instead. For most students, this assignment may be used as an extension of the Guided Assignment in Workshop 5, "Sharing an Opinion."

Links to Literature & Language

Literature For more examples of short stories about growing up with various cultural and ethnic backgrounds, see *Literature and Language*, Grade 6:

- Sandra Cisneros, "Eleven"
- Lensey Namioka, "The All-American Slurp"
- Gish Jen, "The White Umbrella"

Writing This guided assignment on personal response to literature may be used as an extension of the Writer's Workshop "Personal Writing: Reflections on Reading," on page 103 of *Literature and Language*, Grade 6.

Guided ASSIGNMENT

ASSIGNMENT RATIONALE

The ability to articulate a personal response to literature is not only a key to success in school, but also a skill that can increase students' enjoyment of literature and their awareness of the interactive relationship between the reader and the literary work. This assignment guides students in the process of evaluating a work of literature by relating it to their own experiences. It also offers practice in higher-level thinking skills, such as analyzing, inferring, making comparisons, and drawing conclusions.

Starting from LITERATURE

Motivate

Ask students if they have ever had to change schools because of a family move. Have them describe or speculate on the difficulties that such a move can present. Then ask how they would feel if they had to change homes and schools every year. Tell them that the story they will read is about a boy whose family moves several times a year.

Guided ASSIGNMENT

Personal Response

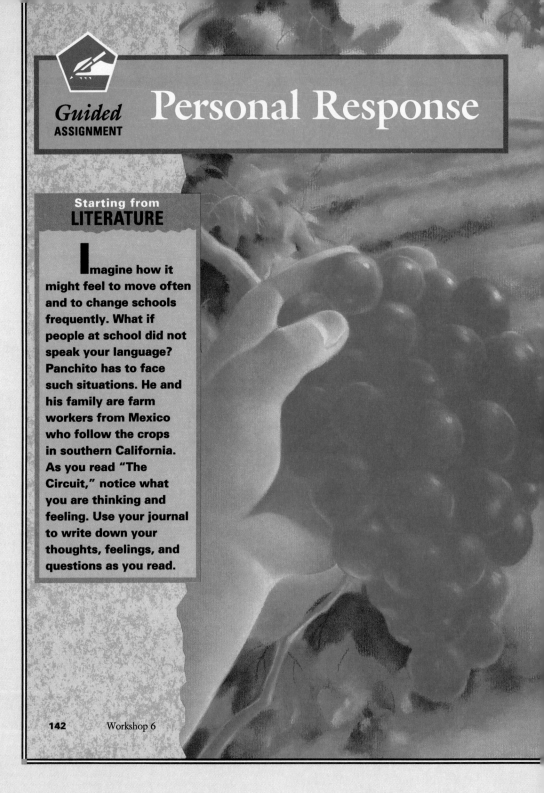

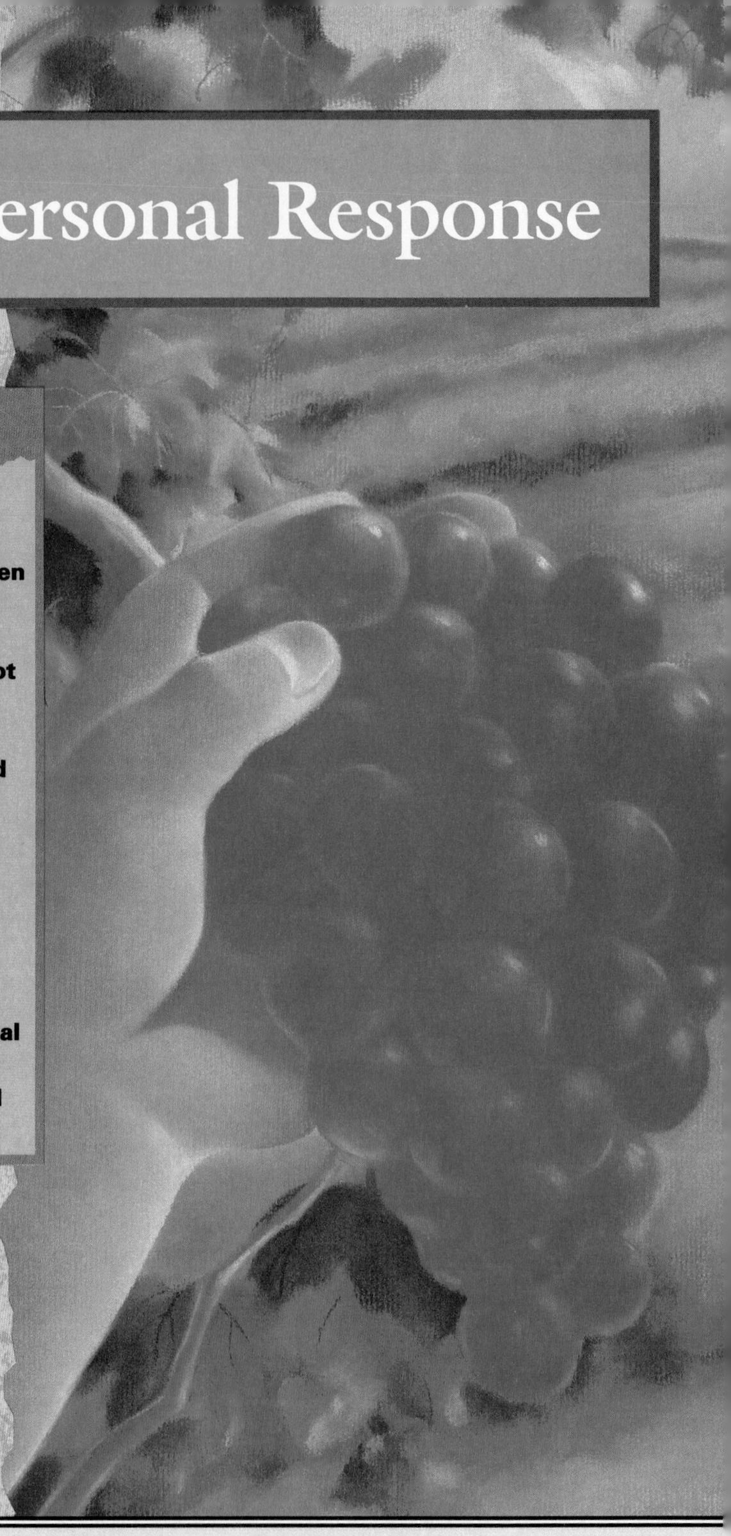

Starting from LITERATURE

Imagine how it might feel to move often and to change schools frequently. What if people at school did not speak your language? Panchito has to face such situations. He and his family are farm workers from Mexico who follow the crops in southern California. As you read "The Circuit," notice what you are thinking and feeling. Use your journal to write down your thoughts, feelings, and questions as you read.

from

The Circuit

by Francisco Jiménez

IT WAS THAT TIME OF YEAR AGAIN. Ito, the strawberry sharecropper, did not smile. It was natural. The peak of the strawberry season was over, and the last few days the workers, most of them *braceros,*[1] were not picking as many boxes as they had during the months of June and July. . . .

Yes, it was that time of year. When I opened the front door to the shack, I stopped. Everything we owned was neatly packed in cardboard boxes. Suddenly I felt even more the weight of hours, days, weeks, and months of work. I sat down on a box. The thought of having to move to Fresno and knowing what was in store for me there brought tears to my eyes.

That night I could not sleep. I lay in bed thinking about how much I hated this move. . . .

As we drove away, I felt a lump in my throat. I turned around and looked at our little shack for the last time.

At sunset we drove into a labor camp near Fresno. Since Papa did not speak English, Mama asked the camp foreman if he needed any more workers. "We don't need no more," said the foreman, scratching his head. "Check with Sullivan down the road. Can't miss him. He lives in a big white house with a fence around it."

When we got there, Mama walked up to the house. She went through a white gate, past a row of rose bushes, up the stairs to the front door. She rang the doorbell. The porch light went on and a tall, husky man came out. They exchanged a few words. After the man went in, Mama clasped her hands and hurried back to the car. "We have work! Mr. Sullivan said we can stay there the whole season," she said, gasping and pointing to an old garage near the stables. . . .

Early next morning Mr. Sullivan showed us where his crop was, and after breakfast, Papa, Roberto, and I headed for the vineyard to pick. . . .

After lunch we went back to work. The sun kept beating down. The buzzing

BUILD ON PRIOR KNOWLEDGE

Ask students if they know who harvests many of America's crops. (Sample: farmers) Then explain that most farms and orchards are huge, and that it often takes dozens of workers to harvest the produce of just one farm. Point out that after the harvest is over, these workers are no longer needed and lose their source of income. Now ask, "If you were a worker who harvested strawberries in the summer, what could you do to keep earning money the rest of the year?" (Sample: find another kind of work or move to another farm to harvest a fruit or vegetable that ripens later in the year)

Tell students that most of the fruits and vegetables grown on large farms or orchards are picked by migrant workers, entire families who travel around the country from season to season as different crops become ready for harvesting. Ask students what problems or difficulties such families might face. (Samples: low wages, no job security or health insurance, no permanent home, children having to miss school or keep changing schools) How would they like being a teenager in such a family? What would bother them most?

SET A PURPOSE

To help students focus on the purpose-setting activity at the end of Starting from Literature, read aloud the first page of the story, and model your own response process by telling students the thoughts, feelings, and questions you might write in your journal in response to the text. For example, your responses might include "Poor kid, I wonder how often he has to move. . . . I've had nights like that when I couldn't sleep because I was dreading something. . . . How relieved they must be to have work for a whole season . . . How would Panchito feel about staying in one place?"

MORE ABOUT THE MODEL

Francisco Jiménez was born in Mexico. When he was four years old, his family moved to the United States to work as migrant farm laborers. He has written many autobiographical stories about his childhood. Jiménez writes in both English and Spanish. He explains, "Because I am bilingual and bicultural, I can move in and out of both American and Mexican cultures with ease; therefore, I have been able to write stories in both languages. I consider that a privilege."

insects, the wet sweat, and the hot dry dust made the afternoon seem to last forever. Finally the mountains around the valley reached out and swallowed the sun. Within an hour it was too dark to continue picking. The vines blanketed the grapes, making it difficult to see the bunches. *"Vamonos,"*[2] said Papa, signaling to us that it was time to quit work. Papa then took out a pencil and began to figure out how much we had earned our first day. He wrote down numbers, crossed some out, wrote down some more. *"Quince,"*[3] he murmured. . . .

The next morning I could hardly move. My body ached all over. I felt little control over my arms and legs. This feeling went on every morning for days until my muscles finally got used to the work.

It was Monday, the first week of November. The grape season was over, and I could now go to school. I woke up early that morning and lay in bed, looking at the stars and savoring the thought of not going to work and of starting sixth grade for the first time that year. Since I could not sleep, I decided to get up and join Papa and Roberto at breakfast. I sat at the table across from Roberto, but I kept my head down. I did not want to look up and face him. I knew he was sad. He was not going to school today. He was not going tomorrow, or next week, or next month. He would not go until the cotton season was over, and that was sometime in February. I rubbed my hands together and watched the dry, acid-stained skin fall to the floor in little rolls.

When Papa and Roberto left for work, I felt relief. I walked to the top of a small grade next to the shack and watched the "Carcanchita"[4] disappear in the distance in a cloud of dust.

Two hours later, around eight o'clock, I stood by the side of the road waiting for school bus number twenty. When it arrived, I climbed in. No one noticed me. Everyone was busy either talking or yelling. I sat in an empty seat in the back.

When the bus stopped in front of the school, I felt very nervous. I looked out the bus window and saw boys and girls carrying books under their arms. I felt empty. I put my hands in my pants pockets and walked to the principal's office. When I entered, I heard a woman's voice say, "May I help you?" I was startled. I had not heard English for months. For a few seconds I remained speechless. I looked at the lady who waited for an answer. My first instinct was to answer her in Spanish, but I held back. Finally, after struggling for English words, I managed to tell her that I wanted to enroll in the sixth grade. After answering many questions, I was led to the classroom.

Mr. Lema, the sixth-grade teacher, greeted me and assigned me a desk. He then introduced me to the class. I was so nervous and scared at that moment when everyone's eyes were on me that I wished I were with Papa and Roberto picking

MULTICULTURAL Connection

Have a student whose first language is Spanish pronounce the footnoted words on page 145 for the class. Ask if the student is familiar with *braceros* and *corridos,* and, if so, have the student give the class a fuller explanation of these workers and songs.

cotton. After taking roll, Mr. Lema gave the class the assignment for the first hour. "The first thing we have to do this morning is finish reading the story we began yesterday," he said enthusiastically. He walked up to me, handed me an English book, and asked me to read. "We are on page 125," he said politely. When I heard this, I felt my blood rush to my head. I felt dizzy. "Would you like to read?" he asked hesitantly. I opened the book to page 125. My mouth was dry. My eyes began to water. I could not begin. "You can read later," Mr. Lema said understandingly.

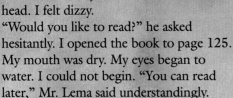

For the rest of the reading period I kept getting angrier and angrier with myself. I should have read, I thought to myself.

During recess I went into the restroom and opened my English book to page 125. I began to read in a low voice, pretending I was in class. There were many words I did not know. I closed the book and headed back to the classroom.

Mr. Lema was sitting at his desk correcting papers. When I entered he looked up at me and smiled. I felt better. I walked up to him and asked if he could help me with the new words. "Gladly," he said.

The rest of the month I spent my lunch hours working on English with Mr. Lema, my best friend at school.

One Friday during lunch hour, Mr. Lema asked me to take a walk with him to the music room. "Do you like music?" he asked me as we entered the building. "Yes, I like Mexican *corridos*,"[5] I answered. He then picked up a trumpet, blew on it, and handed it to me. The sound gave me goose bumps. I knew that sound. I had heard it in many Mexican *corridos*. "How would you like to learn how to play it?" he asked. He must have read my face because before I could answer, he added: "I'll teach you how to play it during our lunch hours."

That day I could hardly wait to get home to tell Papa and Mama the great news. As I got off the bus, my little brothers and sisters ran up to meet me. They were yelling and screaming. I thought they were happy to see me, but when I opened the door to our shack, I saw that everything we owned was neatly packed in cardboard boxes.

---

1. ***braceros*** (brä sä′ rōs): *Spanish:* hired hands; day laborers.
2. ***Vamonos*** (vä′ mô nôs): *Spanish:* Let's go.
3. ***quince*** (kēn′ sä): *Spanish:* fifteen.
4. **"Carcanchita"**: Papa's nickname for the old family car.
5. ***corridos*** (kô rē′ dôs): *Spanish:* ballads.

Think & Respond

How do you think Panchito feels about what happens at the end of the story? What are your thoughts and feelings about the story? **Freewrite** about your response to the whole story or to any part of it. Share your freewriting with your classmates.

145

Think & Respond

ELICIT PERSONAL RESPONSES

As a class or in small groups, have students discuss the questions in the Think & Respond box. Then have them write about their thoughts and feelings in their journals.

Students may say that Panchito felt sad, helpless, angry, or discouraged when he saw that he had to move once again.

EXPLORE THE AUTHOR'S TECHNIQUES

Point out to students that one reason "The Circuit" is such a powerful story is that Francisco Jiménez *shows,* rather than *tells,* what the life of migrant workers is like. Have students find examples from the story. (Samples: In paragraph 2 on page 143, instead of saying, "I found out we had to move again," the author describes what Panchito *saw:* "Everything we owned was neatly packed in cardboard boxes." In paragraph 3, instead of saying that Panchito was sorry to leave, the author describes the boy's physical sensation: "As we drove away, I felt a lump in my throat." On page 145, instead of saying Panchito was nervous about having to read aloud in class, the author again describes the boy's physical sensations: "My mouth was dry. My eyes began to water."

Music Connection

With the help of a music teacher, invite a volunteer to sing some popular Mexican corridos, or ballads. If that is not possible, find recordings of Mexican music and play them for your students. The popular singer Linda Ronstadt is of Mexican heritage and has recorded several albums of songs she heard when she was growing up, including *Mas Canciones* and *Frenesi.* You might also play folk songs about the lives of migrant farm workers. The folk singer Woody Guthrie recorded many of these, including the song "Deportee," which has also been recorded by Judy Collins, Arlo Guthrie, Pete Seeger, and the a cappella group Sweet Honey in the Rock.

Reading a STUDENT MODEL

The models that open this guided assignment differ from those in other workshop assignments; the Student Model is a personal response to the Professional Model. The Student Model is the final draft of the piece that students will see in process on the workshop pages that follow.

Motivate

Tell students about a reading experience you've had, when you said to yourself, "That's amazing! This author knows exactly how I feel; it's as if the writer has read my mind." Ask students if they have ever had this kind of experience, and encourage them to name authors or works that made them feel this way. Point out that writing a personal response essay is one way of expressing their feelings about stories and poems that make a deep impression on them.

BUILD ON PRIOR KNOWLEDGE

Ask students if there are any parts of the story "The Circuit" that they find especially sad or touching. What about those scenes really moves them? Tell students that those parts of a literary work that really touch them often echo their own experiences and are usually the ones that they themselves could write about most powerfully.

SET A PURPOSE

As students read the Student Model, have them notice which part of the story Vanessa focuses on, what details and dialogue she chooses from the story, and the reason why she focuses on those details.

One Student's Writing

Reading a STUDENT MODEL

When Vanessa Ramirez, a sixth-grade student, read "The Circuit," she reacted strongly to one part of the story. That part seemed to touch her own life and experience. She decided to focus on her reaction in her paper. How does she show the reasons for her special response?

Responding to "The Circuit"
by Vanessa Ramirez

When I read and reread "The Circuit" by Francisco Jiménez, I didn't understand why it made me feel sad, but then I realized at the end that it reminded me of when I was small, when I first started school.

In the story a boy named Panchito can't go to school because he has to work in the fields to help his family. When he finally goes to school in November, he forgets how to speak in English.

Panchito says that when he entered the school office, he heard a voice say, "May I help you?" Then he says, "I had not heard English for months. For a few seconds I remained speechless." I put myself in Panchito's place when I read this, because I

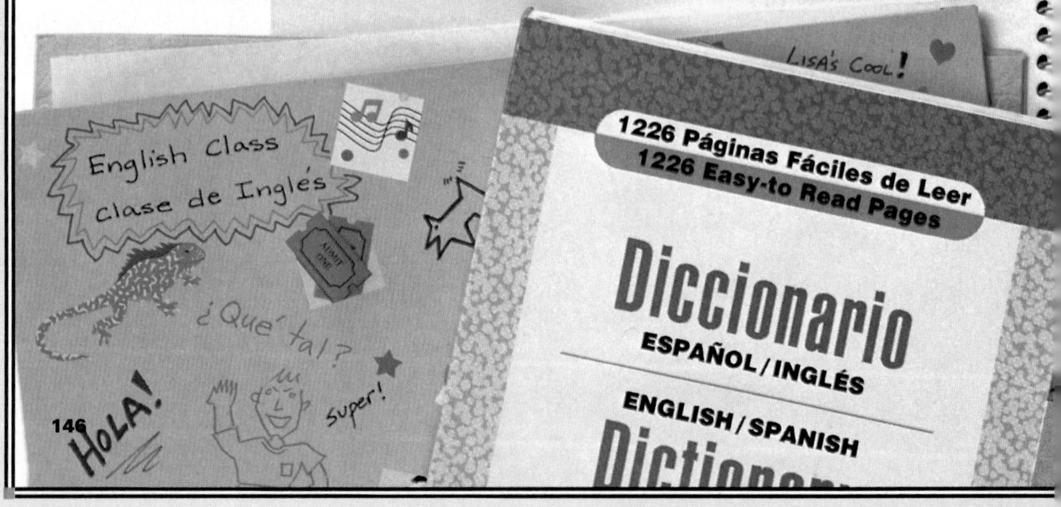

146

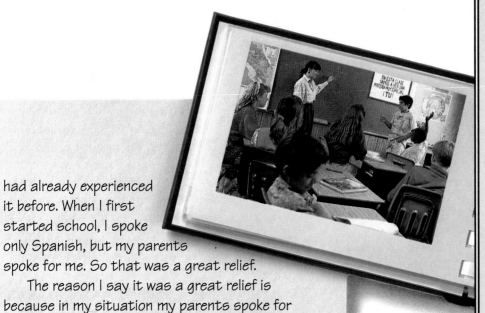

had already experienced it before. When I first started school, I spoke only Spanish, but my parents spoke for me. So that was a great relief.

The reason I say it was a great relief is because in my situation my parents spoke for me in order to enroll me and in his situation Panchito had to speak for himself to enroll in school. This part of the story hit my heart.

When people are used to talking in one language, it is very hard when they realize they're being told something in another language. It must be sad because they don't understand, or maybe they do, but they are embarrassed because they don't know how to speak the other language well. That's how Panchito felt when he went to enroll in school and when the teacher asked him to read in class.

I liked writing about this story because as I was writing, I was imagining that I was there in the story and because it kind of has to do with what happened to me.

Think & Respond

Respond as a Reader

▶ How was Vanessa able to tie the story to her own experience?

▶ In what way was Vanessa's reaction to the story the same as or different from yours?

Respond as a Writer

▶ What parts of Vanessa's essay made the strongest impression on you? Can you say why?

▶ How does the end of Vanessa's paper tie in with the beginning?

Think & Respond

RESPOND AS A READER

▶ Have students identify the part of the first sentence in which Vanessa states how the story relates to her own life. Then have students find examples in the body of her paper that explain or support her opening statement.

▶ Some ESL students may react as Vanessa did to the passages about first entering a school in which classes are conducted in English. Other students may identify more with the experience of moving to a new school or, more generally, with Panchito's experiences of dread, hope, excitement, and disappointment.

RESPOND AS A WRITER

▶ If students have difficulty explaining why a certain passage of Vanessa's essay impressed them, have them read the passage aloud. Then ask them questions to draw out their reasons for responding strongly to that passage.

▶ In both the introduction and the conclusion of her essay, Vanessa points out that Panchito's experiences reminded her of her own.

Draw Conclusions

To make sure students understand this introduction to writing a personal response to literature, challenge them to list the characteristics they have noted thus far. Responses may include the following:

- a clear statement of personal response to a specific work
- reasons from personal experience, and examples and quotations from the literary work
- a general conclusion

Social Studies Connection

Students who are interested in the culture and achievements of Mexican-Americans, as well as the social problems they face, might enjoy reading and reporting on the following books:

Cesar Chavez, by Ruth Franchere

Chicanos: The Story of Mexican-Americans, by Patricia De Garza

Famous Mexican-Americans, by Clarke Newlon

Henry Cisneros: Mexican-American Mayor, by Naurice Roberts

Soy Chicano: I Am Mexican-American, by Robert and Lynne Fitch

Writing ON YOUR OWN

Emphasize to students that in writing a personal response to a work of literature, there are no right or wrong responses. However, point out that supporting their responses with reasons and with examples from the story and from their own experience—as Vanessa did—will help readers understand the writer's unique reactions.

Handbooks for Help and Practice

The following handbooks may be used as mini-lessons before students begin writing or as resources when problems arise.

- **Thinking with Pictures, pp. 192–196**
- **Improving Paragraphs, pp. 230–233**
- **Transitions, pp. 234–238**
- **Show, Don't Tell, pp. 239–242**
- **Revising, pp. 257–259**

PREWRITE AND EXPLORE

Objectives

- To use prewriting techniques to identify a work of literature and to explore responses to that work
- To decide whether to respond to the work as a whole or to a section of the work

Teaching Strategies

for FIND A STORY . . .

INDIVIDUALIZING INSTRUCTION: BASIC STUDENTS Help these students to select works that are at a comfortable reading level. Professionally recorded tapes of the works, if available, will also benefit some of these students.

for SKETCHING A RESPONSE

HELPFUL HINT If students choose to sketch a response, remind them that they need not illustrate the story. Sketching or doodling, like freewriting, is just another way to discover and explore their thoughts and feelings.

Writing ON YOUR OWN
Personal Response

INVITATION TO *Write*

Readers of "The Circuit" will respond to the story in many different ways. Vanessa Ramirez was touched by Panchito's struggle to speak English in school. Remembering her own experiences made it easier for Vanessa to connect to the story and to write about it.

Write a brief response essay, telling your own thoughts and feelings about a short work of literature.

PREWRITE AND EXPLORE

1. Find a story or a poem. Choose a short literary work that you liked or disliked or were puzzled by. You will probably want to select a work that made a strong impression on you.

You could consider "The Circuit" by Francisco Jiménez or a short piece of writing suggested by your teacher. After making your choice, try some of the following activities.

Exploring Topics

- **Writing about it** Notice your thoughts, feelings, and questions as you read. Try **freewriting** about your responses to the whole story or poem.
- **Sketching a response** Try responding to the work with rough sketches or doodles, showing how you think or feel. Then freewrite briefly, explaining your drawing.
- **Talking about it** Share your freewriting or your sketches with a small group of readers. Did others respond to the same work differently? Discuss the different responses. Feel free to change your mind as you listen to other ideas.

Writing **TIP**

If you're having trouble deciding what to write about, find any short passage that you don't understand and write about why it is a problem for you.

Links to LITERATURE & LANGUAGE

Literature For stories that may be appropriate for this assignment, see the *Links to Literature and Language* box at the bottom of page 141. The following poems in *Literature and Language*, Grade 6, may also draw strong responses from students:

- Eleanor Farjeon, "The Quarrel"
- Norma Landa Flores, "Street Corner Flight"
- Abiodun Oyewole, "Another Mountain"
- Denise Levertov, "The Secret"
- Dudley Randall, "Ancestors"
- Maya Angelou, "Life Doesn't Frighten Me"
- Evelyn Tooley Hunt, "Mama Is a Sunrise"
- Langston Hughes, "Words Like Freedom"

2. Reread the piece. Read the story or poem again. This may give you some new ideas. Try some of these activities:

- **"Jump-in" reading** Try this with others who have read the same work. A volunteer begins reading it aloud, then pauses. Someone else jumps in and continues reading. If two jump in at once, they can read together. Afterwards, freewrite a new response.
- **Saying the lines** Readers call out lines they think are important, interesting, or difficult. It's fun and interesting to see what lines others find important.
- **Responding to a single line or sentence** Pick out a line that interests or amuses you or makes you think. Freewrite about why you chose it.

3. Think about your response. Review your notes, drawings, and freewriting to find a response you want to write about.

Writer's Choice Do you want to write about the work as a whole or focus on one part as Vanessa did? Follow your instincts. Write about what is most interesting to you.

One Student's Process

Vanessa wasn't sure how to write about her reactions to the story. So she did some freewriting, jotting down notes to help her sort out her feelings.

This story make me feel sad—I don't know why. When the boy goes to the office somebody says, "May I help you?" and he is embarrassed. That made me feel bad. Also Mr. Lema the sixth grade teacher asks him to read and says "We are on page 125." I know how he might have felt.
I'd like to write about the whole story, but the part about his trouble with English really hit my heart.

GENERAL NOTE

HELPFUL HINT Tell students that the Sketchbook activities on pages 140 and 164 may help them find writing ideas.

for REREAD THE PIECE

MANAGEMENT TIP The first two bulleted activities will work best if students have chosen the same work to write about. You might distribute a list of works from which students can choose, then post sign-up sheets so that students reading the same work can form small groups to explore their responses. Students who prefer to work independently can do the third bulleted activity. You might introduce students to the double-entry journal as a tool for responding to specific lines or passages from literature. See *Writing Resource Book,* page 30, for practice using this kind of journal.

for THINK ABOUT YOUR RESPONSE

CRITICAL THINKING: MAKING COMPARISONS To help students make connections between their own experiences and those of a character in a story, have them ask themselves the following questions: How would I feel if I were this character? What would I do in this situation? When was the last time I felt the way this character feels? How was my response to the situation similar to or different from the character's response?

for WRITER'S CHOICE

INDIVIDUALIZING INSTRUCTION: ESL STUDENTS If these students choose to respond to "The Circuit," invite them to meet in groups to compare their experiences in an English-speaking school with those of Panchito. If all the students in a group speak the same first language, allow them to discuss and freewrite in that language.

SPICE BOX

Pairs of students responding to the same story might enjoy role-playing interviews with the characters in the story. Have one student think of questions to ask one of the characters. Have the other student role-play the character and try to answer the questions. Then have the pairs switch roles. The questioning will help students focus on what impressed them most about the characters and on the reasons for their own reactions.

DRAFT AND DISCOVER

Objectives

- To draft a response to a work of literature
- To respond to one's own draft and to that of a peer

Teaching Strategies

for WRITING TIP

COOPERATIVE LEARNING For practice writing brief plot summaries, have students work together in small groups to compose short summaries of "The Circuit." Then have the groups share their summaries and evaluate them for brevity and accuracy.

for THINK ABOUT THE PARTS . . .

INDIVIDUALIZING INSTRUCTION: BASIC STUDENTS Students who need help organizing their essays can make a chart with these headings: *My Main Feeling About The Story; Details And Quotations From The Story;* and *My Personal Experiences.* Suggest that they state their main feeling in the introduction, use supporting details and experiences in the body, and in the conclusion, share a final thought about the piece or their response to it.

for THINK ABOUT THE PARTS . . .

CRITICAL THINKING: ANALYZING As students read about introductions, bodies, and conclusions, have them turn to pages 146–147 and find these parts in the Student Model. Have volunteers read each part aloud and explain how it functions as an introduction, body, or conclusion.

for THINK ABOUT YOUR READERS

KEY TO UNDERSTANDING: AUDIENCE Have students reread Vanessa's second paragraph, in the model on page 146. Ask what additional details about "The Circuit" she might have included if she had been writing for an audience that had never read the story. (Sample: that Panchito is Mexican-American, a member of a family of migrant farm workers, and a sixth grader)

Writing TIP

Avoid long, detailed plot descriptions. Give the most attention to your own ideas about the work. Summarize only enough to make your point.

DRAFT AND DISCOVER

1. Start writing. Trying to use any freewriting you've already done, write out a rough first draft. Connect your responses to specific things in the story or poem that triggered them. Use quotations from the work to show what you are responding to.

2. Think about the parts of your essay. Some writers prefer not to start with a structure in mind. Still, it may help to think of these three parts of a response:

- **Introduction** Mention the title and the author of the work, then tell what the work is about and why you're interested in it. Notice how Vanessa, in her first paragraph, identified the story, told how she felt about it, and briefly explained why.
- **Body** Here you can give details of how you reacted to the work. If your response is based on your own personal experience, you can explain that. You can even tell a brief story. Vanessa described a key incident in the story and related it to something that had happened to her.
- **Conclusion** You may not need a formal conclusion, but it's good to end with some final thought. You might explain what your response taught you about yourself or about the work. Vanessa ended her response by describing how she felt when writing it.

3. Think about your readers. Who will be reading your response? What do they know about this story or poem? Note that Vanessa told just enough in her second paragraph to set up the incident she wanted to write about.

4. Think about your draft. After you've finished your draft, let it sit awhile. Then read it again and make any changes you need to. Show it to classmates for their response. Here are some questions you might ask.

PROBLEM SOLVING

"How can I think of things to say?"

For help in getting ideas and finding the right details, see

- Handbook 1, "Thinking with Pictures," pages 192–196
- Handbook 12, "Show, Don't Tell," pages 239–242

REVIEW YOUR WRITING

Questions for Yourself

- How honest is my response? Did I say what I really think or feel about this work?
- Have I told my readers enough about the work for them to know what I'm talking about?
- Have I explained why I responded to the work the way I did? Have I told how my own experiences may have caused me to respond this way?

Questions for Your Peer Readers

- What parts of my essay are most interesting to you?
- Did I tell you all you need to know about the work itself to understand my essay?
- Have I explained my thoughts and feelings clearly? Why do you think I reacted to the story the way I did?

One Student's Process

After looking over her prewriting notes, Vanessa wrote a first draft and asked some of her classmates to read it. Notice their comments. What would you have told her?

When I read "The Circuit" by Francisco Jiménez, it made me feel sad. In the story a boy named Panchito doesn't go to school until November, he works in the fields to help his family. He forgets how to speak in English.

Panchito says he heard a voice say "May I help you?" and he was startled. He had not heard English for months and he was embarassed and couldn't say anything right away. For a few seconds he remained speechless. I had already experienced this before. When I first started school, I only spoke Spanish, my parents spoke for me. So that was a great relief.

Peer Reader Comments

I wonder why it makes you feel sad.

That sounds interesting. Where did he hear this voice? In the fields?

for QUESTIONS FOR YOUR PEER READERS

PEER RESPONSE If possible, suggest that students choose peer readers who are not writing a response to the same story or poem. Such readers are more likely to be objective and to be open to the writer's responses. They will also be better able to judge how clearly the writer has explained the story or poem.

for QUESTIONS FOR YOUR PEER READERS

INDIVIDUALIZING INSTRUCTION: SOCIAL LEARNERS These students will benefit more from a face-to-face discussion with their peer readers than from comments written on the draft.

for ONE STUDENT'S PROCESS

PEER RESPONSE Ask students what they notice about the comments made by Vanessa's peer reader. (He or she asked her questions and did not tell her how to change her draft.) Suggest that peer readers try asking *who, what, where, why, when,* and *how* questions about parts of the draft that confuse them. These questions help a writer see where his or her draft is unclear.

PROFESSIONAL NOTEBOOK

When monitoring peer response, keep in mind teacher Nancie Atwell's advice in her book *In the Middle:* "Peer conferences won't work unless writers can trust that their peers won't shoot them down, so I show my kids how to confer, talking to them just as I'd like them to talk with each other. . . . When a response is brutal, or a best friend's empty flattery, I confer on the conferring: "How will that response help the writer?"

REVISE YOUR WRITING

Objectives

- To review and evaluate responses to a draft of a personal response essay and to revise a draft with those responses in mind
- To evaluate the structure of the draft, paragraph by paragraph

Teaching Strategies

for PARAGRAPHS AT WORK

ASSESSMENT: SPOT CHECK As students revise, go around the room and skim a few papers to see how well students are developing their paragraphs and what kinds of paragraphing problems seem to be common.

for PARAGRAPHS AT WORK

STUMBLING BLOCK If students are having difficulty improving their paragraphs, the "Guidelines for Revising a Paragraph" on page 230 of Handbook 10 may help. Encourage students to identify problem paragraphs and to use the guidelines to revise them.

for READ YOUR ESSAY . . .

INDIVIDUALIZING INSTRUCTION: LEP STUDENTS Some students may not read aloud with enough fluency to evaluate how their writing sounds. Offer to read students' essays aloud. Students should listen for parts that need clarification. Share your appreciation of any parts that work particularly well.

PROBLEM SOLVING

"How can I learn to write better paragraphs?"

For help in improving paragraphs, see

- Handbook 10, "Improving Paragraphs," pages 230–233
- Handbook 11, "Transitions," pages 234–238
- Handbook 17, "Revising," pages 257–259

REVISE YOUR WRITING

1. Review your responses. Think about how your readers responded to your essay. Do you want to follow up on any of their ideas or questions?

Paragraphs at Work A good way to handle paragraphs in a response essay is to start a new paragraph whenever you move from one part of your response to the next part. The following guidelines may help you.

- Use at least one paragraph for your introduction.
- Start a new paragraph when you introduce and explain a new idea.
- Support each idea with specific details from the work itself.

2. Read your essay out loud. Listen to your writing in your own voice. Can you hear sentences that don't quite work—words that don't quite say what you mean? Let your ear direct you to the parts that need to be rewritten. You might also try listening carefully as another student reads your essay to you.

3. Decide what changes you want to make. You may think you're satisfied with your draft, but don't be afraid to go on revising it until it *effectively* says what you want it to.

One Student's Process

Vanessa's peer readers were confused about where certain scenes in the story took place and why Vanessa felt sad. So Vanessa made some changes in her draft to make her thoughts clearer.

but then I realized at the end that it reminded me of when I was small, when I first started school.

When he finally goes to school in November,

and reread — I didn't understand why

When I read "The Circuit" by Francisco Jiménez, it made me feel sad. ¶ In the story a boy named Panchito ~~doesn't~~ can't go to school ~~until November,~~ because he has to ~~works~~ work in the fields to help his family. He forgets how to speak in English.

that when he entered the school office,

Panchito says he heard a voice say, "May I help you?" ~~and he was startled. He~~ Then he says, "I had not heard English for months ~~and he was embarassed and couldn't say anything right away~~. For a few seconds ~~he~~ I remained speechless." I had already experienced ~~this~~ it before. When I first started school, I only spoke Spanish, but my parents spoke for me. So that was a great relief.

I put myself in Panchito's place when I read this, because

for ONE STUDENT'S PROCESS

KEY TO UNDERSTANDING: INTRODUCTIONS Point out that by adding information about why she felt sad, Vanessa greatly improved her introduction. In the revised version, Vanessa makes clear from the beginning why she had such a strong personal reaction to the story. This introduction better prepares her reader for what she will say in the rest of the essay. Have students evaluate their introductions to see if they succeed in preparing the reader for what will follow.

for ONE STUDENT'S PROCESS

CRITICAL THINKING: DRAWING CONCLUSIONS Ask students why Vanessa changed the word *doesn't* in paragraph 1 to *can't*. (*Can't* more accurately describes Panchito's situation; *doesn't* suggests a free choice.) Ask why she added the word *because* in the same sentence. (to show more clearly the cause-and-effect relationship between Panchito's working and his not going to school)

for ONE STUDENT'S PROCESS

KEY TO UNDERSTANDING: QUOTING DIALOGUE Point out that before Vanessa made the revisions in paragraph 2, she was paraphrasing Panchito's thoughts instead of sharing his own words. Using the character's exact words helps bring the character to life. Point out, however, that students should not overuse direct quotations; their own ideas should be the focus of a personal response essay. For advice on the mechanics of using quotations from literary works, see page 154.

PROOFREAD

Teaching Strategies

for LINKING MECHANICS AND WRITING

HELPFUL HINT To demonstrate how to use ellipsis marks, use the sample revised quotation in the box but omit the words *For a few seconds.* The revision would read: *Then he says, "I had not heard English for months. . . .I remained speechless."*

GENERAL NOTE

MANAGING THE PAPER LOAD If students discuss their essays in a round-table format as recommended on page 155, you might evaluate them on their participation and their oral presentation of their ideas, rather than on their written essays. If you choose to evaluate written essays, you might concentrate on these criteria: a clear summary, a statement expressing a specific response, and details that support that response.

Guidelines for Evaluation

IDEAS AND CONTENT

- identifies the work by title and author
- gives a brief summary of the work
- relates the work to the writer's personal experience
- uses details and quotations from the work, as well as the writer's personal experience, to support the writer's response

STRUCTURE AND FORM

- includes an introductory paragraph, one or more body paragraphs, and a concluding sentence or paragraph

GRAMMAR, USAGE, AND MECHANICS

- displays standard grammar, usage, and mechanics
- uses quotation marks and, if necessary, ellipsis points correctly
- uses present-tense verbs to summarize plot

PROOFREAD

1. Proofread your writing. Look for mistakes in grammar and spelling. Be careful when you include quotations from the story or poem. Make sure they appear exactly as they do in the original. Use quotation marks correctly, and spell proper nouns correctly.

LINKING MECHANICS AND WRITING

Quoting from Literary Works

- When you quote from someone else's work, always enclose the quotation in quotation marks. Keep capitalization, punctuation, and spelling the way they are in the original.
- If you leave out part of a quotation, show the place where material is omitted by using ellipsis points (. . .).

Notice that when Vanessa quoted directly from the story, she put a comma after the explanatory words *he says* and before the quotation.

Original

Then he says he remained speechless.

Revised

Then he says, "I had not heard English for months. For a few seconds I remained speechless."

For more information about using quotation marks, see Handbook 43, "Punctuation," pages 566–598.

2. Make a clean copy of your response. Read your paper over again, thinking about the Standards for Evaluation shown in the margin. Then make a final copy.

Standards for Evaluation

RESPONDING TO LITERATURE

A personal response

- gives the author and the title of the work
- tells enough about the work for readers unfamiliar with it to understand the response
- clearly expresses a response
- gives the reasons for the response
- draws an overall conclusion

154 Workshop 6

Grammar Connection

On the board, write the following sentences from Vanessa's summary of "The Circuit": "In the story a boy named Panchito can't go to school because he has to work in the fields to help his family. When he finally goes to school in November, he forgets how to speak in English." Underline the verbs can't, has, goes, and forgets. Ask: What tense are the verbs in? (present) Tell students to check their drafts to make sure they consistently use present-tense verbs to summarize the plots of the stories or poems they are writing about.

PUBLISH AND PRESENT

- **Have a round-table discussion.** Discuss responses with classmates who have read the same work.
- **Start a "Literature Response" file for the class.** Group together the responses to a particular work in a file, or bind them as a booklet. Other students can use this as a guide to reading.
- **Start a "Short Takes" review sheet.** For each work reviewed, list title, author, and source, along with a two- or three-line comment. Collect these reviews in a little magazine that can be shown to parents.

REFLECT ON YOUR WRITING

WRITER TO WRITER

'Tis the good reader that makes the good book.

Ralph Waldo Emerson, American poet and essayist

FOR YOUR **PORTFOLIO**

1. Add your writing to your portfolio. Write a brief introductory note for your paper, telling about how you wrote it and what you think of it now. As you write, think about questions like the following:

- How did writing about the work help me learn about it?
- What did I learn about myself?
- How would readers with backgrounds different from mine respond to the work?
- What was hard about writing this essay? What was easy about it?

2. Explore additional writing ideas. See the suggestions for writing a book review on pages 158–159 and Springboards on page 160.

Reteaching

After students have completed their papers, assess the needs of students who were not successful in developing an effective response to a piece of literature; then assign the appropriate handbook mini-lessons, as well as pages 29–33 of the *Writing Resource Book.* Concepts commonly requiring reteaching for this assignment are:

- Handbook 7, Organizing Details; pp. 217–221
- Handbook 10, Improving Paragraphs; pp. 230–233

The following suggestions and resources may also be useful.

Dull Introductions If too many students used a standard "I liked this story because. . ." introduction, have them study the model introductions in Handbook 14. You might also assign *Writing Resource Book* "Ways to Begin Writing," page 66.

Lack of Support for Responses If some students made unsupported statements such as "The characters are unrealistic," work with them to identify the statements and ask questions that will help them articulate the reasons for their responses.

Extension and Enrichment

1. Have students write personality profiles of characters who impressed them in the stories and poems they read.
2. Have students write sequels to the stories they wrote about. Have them attach a brief explanation telling why they added the scenes they did.

Closure: Reflect on Your Writing

To answer how their writing helped them learn about the work of literature, have students compare their prewriting notes with their final draft. What prewriting questions were they able to answer? How did their thinking about the work change as they drafted and revised their essays?

Related ASSIGNMENT

Reading a STUDENT MODEL

Objectives

- To respond to and analyze a book review
- To choose a book, read it, and respond to it by drafting, revising, and presenting a book review

Motivate

Before directing students to the Reading a Student Model box, try this activity. Bring in copies of library books that you know students in your class have read. Line up the books on the chalk tray. Then pass out two easily removable stickers to each student, one saying *Read this book!* and the other, *Stay away!* Invite volunteers to put their stickers on books they would or would not recommend to their classmates.

BUILD ON PRIOR KNOWLEDGE

Ask students how they find good books. Do they get recommendations from friends? Do they read reviews? Point out that book reviews help readers share opinions about books.

SET A PURPOSE

Have students look at the photograph of the book cover on page 158. Ask whether the book is fiction or nonfiction. (nonfiction) Does the subject interest students or arouse their curiosity? Have students read the book review by Jeff Hayden to see if it increases their interest in the book or its subject.

Related ASSIGNMENT

Book Review

Reading a STUDENT MODEL

Sometimes after you've read a good book, do you almost want to force your friends to read it too? Do you sometimes want to warn them to leave it alone? Writing a book review is a good way to share your reactions to what you read. Jeff Hayden, a student at Wilson School in St. Louis, Missouri, wrote a book review that was later published in the magazine *Creative Kids.* As you read, notice how he shows his enthusiasm for the book.

Links to LITERATURE & LANGUAGE

Students who like nonfiction books can read in *Literature and Language,* Grade 6, excerpts from one or all of these books:

- Russell Freedman, *Children of the Wild West*
- Jill Krementz, *How It Feels When Parents Divorce*
- Gary Paulsen, *Woodsong*

Writing This related assignment on a book review may be used as an extension of the Writer's Workshop, "Writing About Literature: Thumbs Up! Thumbs Down!" on page 476 of *Literature and Language,* Grade 6.

Jeff Hayden

A Review of What Would We Do Without You?

How can you help? Just read this book to find out how kids can help kids, how kids can help the environment, and how kids can help adults. In fact, this book shows different ways in which people of all ages can help. What Would We Do Without You? by Kathy Henderson is great for individuals from elementary school to college age. It suggests many different activities to meet the needs of people of all ages.

The chapter "Just Do It: Volunteering on Your Own" tells of activities you can do without special permission. There are guidelines for recycling, cleaning a park or neighborhood, or even about how to become a tutor.

The chapter "Protecting the Environment" gives suggestions as to how kids can save plant life and wildlife. For example, you could cut up soda-can holders before you throw them out. Or you could clean up a beach or a piece of land.

But the chapter "Kids Helping Kids: Peer Support Groups" is my favorite. It tells how kids can invent ways to help their peers who have problems. This chapter involves inventing solutions to everyday dilemmas or writing a story or rap to help kids with health or emotional problems. It tells kids how to organize a fund drive to get money to help save a life.

A really neat part of this book comes at the end of each chapter. It is called For More Information. If you find one chapter to be really interesting and want additional information, addresses are here to write to for more guidance and help.

I hope you read this book. You may find it interesting. And so will the people and animals you help!

Think & Respond

What kinds of information does Jeff Hayden give you about the book? On the basis of his review, would you want to read this book? Why or why not? What ideas does his review give you for books you might review?

Think & Respond

ELICIT PERSONAL RESPONSES

To focus attention on the first question in the Think & Respond box, ask students which chapters of the book Jeff mentions and what the chapters are about. To provide a focus for students' answers to the second question, ask them which parts of the book they would find most or least interesting. In response to the third question, students may describe other kinds of nonfiction books they might want to review. You may want to recommend the titles listed in Links to Literature and Language below.

EXPLORE THE AUTHOR'S TECHNIQUES

Point out that in the first paragraph, Jeff begins his review with an interesting question, identifies the audience for which the book is intended, and then summarizes the book's contents.

In his body paragraphs, he mentions specific types of volunteer activities covered in different chapters of the book, alerting students interested in those activities to the fact that this book has information they can use. He also mentions parts of the book that he finds particularly interesting or noteworthy. He concludes his review with a general recommendation of the book.

for FURTHER READING

Students may enjoy reading and reviewing the following young adult novels, many of which are award winners:

- William Armstrong, *Sounder*
- Betsy Byars, *The Summer of the Swans*
- Madeleine L'Engle, *A Wrinkle in Time*
- Jean Craighead George, *Julie of the Wolves*
- Norton Juster, *The Phantom Tollbooth*
- C.S. Lewis, *The Lion, the Witch, and the Wardrobe*
- L.M. Montgomery, *Anne of Green Gables*
- Katherine Paterson, *Bridge to Terabithia*
- William Rawls, *Where the Red Fern Grows*

Writing ON YOUR OWN

Remind students that Jeff gave his overall impression of the book, as well as many specific details to support and elaborate on that impression. Encourage them to do likewise in their own book reviews.

Handbooks for Help and Practice

The following handbooks may be used as mini-lessons before students begin writing or as resources when problems arise.

- **Finding a Starting Point, pp. 197–202**
- **Drafting, pp. 215–216**

Writing ON YOUR OWN
Book Review

INVITATION TO *Write*

Jeff Hayden gave readers a clear picture of what one book was about and how he felt about the book. A good book review gives readers enough information to decide if they want to read the book themselves.

Write a review of a book that interests you. Give your readers a feeling for what the book is like and how you responded to it.

CHOOSING A BOOK

1. Find a book to read. Do you like mysteries? science fiction? comedy? history? Do you have a favorite author? Is there a subject you'd like to learn more about? Think about your interests. Look for a book that appeals to one of them.

2. Read and respond. Make notes of your reactions as you read. Copy passages you might want to refer to in your review. After reading, freewrite about what pleased or bothered you. Pretend that you are writing a letter to a friend. What would you want to tell him or her about your book? What might you want to ask the author, if you had a chance?

COMPUTER TIP

If you have strong reactions as you read, enter these into your computer. Afterwards, create a split screen if your computer has one, and freewrite about why you had those strong reactions.

WRITING YOUR BOOK REVIEW

1. Begin writing. Check your prewriting notes for ideas. Remember, in a book review you need to tell what the book is about, describe your reactions to it, and say whether you think readers might enjoy it. Start anywhere; get some thoughts down on paper. Later you can decide how to arrange them.

Science Connection

Students interested in science and technology might enjoy reviewing these nonfiction books:

- Isaac Asimov, *How Did We Find Out About Volcanoes?*
- Eve Bunting, *The Great White Shark*
- Heather Couper, *Comets and Meteors*
- Robin McKie, *Lasers*

2. Organize your draft. Here's one good approach:

- **Introduce the book.** Give the title, the author, and perhaps something about the author's background. You may also want to state the main point you intend to make.
- **Summarize the book.** Give readers a general idea about the content of the book, as Jeff does in his review. If the book is fiction, you might discuss plot, setting, and characters. Normally, you shouldn't give away the ending.
- **Evaluate the book.** Tell why you admire or dislike the book. You may want to discuss the author's purpose. Did the book make you laugh or perhaps get you to accept a new idea? Support your reactions with specific examples from the book.
- **Conclude the review.** You can restate your view or perhaps give a recommendation, as Jeff Hayden did.

PROBLEM SOLVING

"How can I get a good start on my draft?"

For help in getting started, see

- Handbook 2, "Finding a Starting Point," pages 197–202
- Handbook 6, "Drafting," pages 215–216

REVIEWING YOUR WRITING

1. Think about your audience. Have you given your readers enough information for them to decide whether they might like the book? Did you explain unfamiliar terms?

2. Apply the final touches. Does your introduction draw the reader in? Is your conclusion convincing? Did you support your reactions? Did you check your grammar and punctuation?

Grammar TIP

Check to be sure you have capitalized and spelled all proper names correctly.

PUBLISHING AND PRESENTING

- **Publish your review**. Submit it to a magazine, as Jeff did, or to a class or school publication.
- **Make an advertisement.** Use words and artwork—as in a movie poster—to show your reactions to the book you reviewed.
- **Hold a book-review round table.** Get together with classmates to discuss, compare, and recommend various books.

Teaching Strategies

for EVALUATE THE BOOK

CRITICAL THINKING: EVALUATING
With the entire class, brainstorm a list of adjectives students might use to describe books they like and books they dislike. Add your own adjectives to the list to expand students' vocabularies. For example: LIKE: *funny, sad, fascinating, surprising, touching, exciting;* DISLIKE: *boring, predictable, outdated, confusing.* Encourage students to use applicable words in their reviews.

for THINK ABOUT YOUR AUDIENCE

PEER RESPONSE After students have had a chance to read each others' drafts, writers might ask readers to tell whether they would like to read the book themselves. If peer readers are not sure, writers can ask what additional information might help them form a definite opinion about the book. Writers may then want to make revisions in their drafts based on their peers' answers.

Guidelines for Evaluation

AN EFFECTIVE BOOK REVIEW

- identifies the book by title and author
- contains a brief summary of the book
- contains an evaluation of the book
- contains specific examples and quotations from the book that support the evaluation
- includes an attention-getting introduction and a convincing conclusion

Teaching Strategies

for SPEAKING AND LISTENING

MANAGEMENT TIP Have students who have read the same literary work meet in small groups. Each member of the group can recommend and read aloud a passage suitable for dramatization or oral interpretation. Tell groups to reach an agreement on which passage to present. Set aside class time for rehearsals and performances.

for MEDIA

COLLABORATIVE OPPORTUNITY Ask students if they have seen programs featuring pairs of movie reviewers who debate the merits of various films. Encourage pairs of students familiar with the format to collaborate in presenting and defending opposing views of the same work or works.

for FINE ARTS

HELPFUL HINT You may want to involve an art teacher in introducing students to various art techniques and in planning an exhibit of finished works.

Springboards

Speaking and Listening

In a book, story, or play, find a scene that you think is particularly moving. Then, with the help of some of your classmates, act it out or present an oral interpretation.

MEDIA Imagine that you are the entertainment critic for your local TV station. Prepare a brief on-air presentation. It should give your personal response to a movie, play, television show, or literary work.

Music Think about current events and personalities in the news. Make up a rap or a folk song that tells your personal response to some person or event.

Reading Write a "lit letter" to a friend. Describe a book you are reading. Tell your friend why you loved or hated the book.

fine Arts Make a drawing, a collage, a painting, a sculpture, a mobile, or another piece of art that expresses your reaction to an event in your life or to a piece of literature. Write a paragraph to go with the art, telling what it means.

Reading Back and Forth

What do the words *eye, pop, dad, mom, noon,* and *civic* have in common?

They are all *palindromes*—words, phrases, or sentences that read the same way backward and forward. Try this one: *No lemon, no melon.*

An old joke says that Adam introduced himself to Eve with a palindrome: "Madam in Eden, I'm Adam."

Perhaps you've heard this famous one: "A man, a plan, a canal, Panama!"

Try reading these palindromes forward and backward.

- Rise to vote, sir.
- Never odd or even.
- Was it a rat I saw?
- Doc, note, I dissent. A fast never prevents a fatness. I diet on cod.
- Now, sir, a war is won.

What happens when you read the word *palindromes* backward? You get a *semordnilap,* a word that is another word in reverse. For example, *on* backward is *no, pots* backward is *stop,* and *star* backward is *rats.* Read *No evil repaid* backward, and you get *Diaper live on.*

Make your own list of palindromes or semordnilaps to share with friends. A dictionary can sometimes help. When you read back and forth, you never know what you might find.

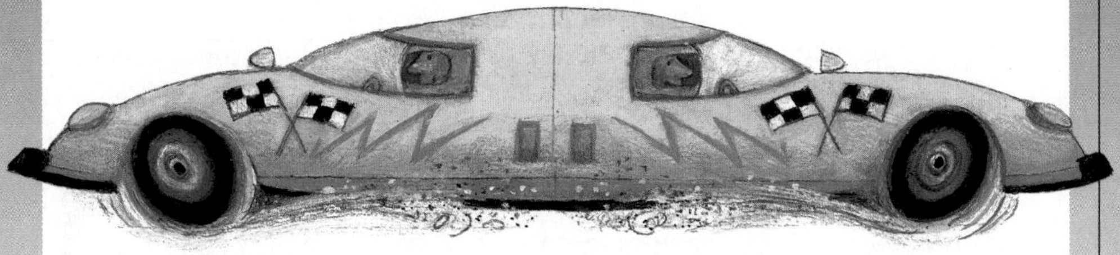

What does *race car* spell backwards?

on the LIGHT side

When discussing this feature, point out to students that the name Eve is itself a palindrome. Ask if students can think of any other names that are palindromes. *(Bob, Nan, Anna, Otto, Ada, Asa)* Then ask if students can think of any proper names that are semordnilaps. *(Pam, Pat, Meg)*

Sentence Closers

Objectives

- To identify sentence closers
- To compose sentences with closers and punctuate the sentences correctly

Teaching Strategies

KEY TO UNDERSTANDING To help students identify closers, have a volunteer read each model sentence aloud without the closer. Point out that even without the closer, each model is a complete sentence. The closer simply adds descriptive details or other information to present a more complete picture.

Sentence COMPOSING

Sentence Closers

At times, the last part of something is the best part—the finale of a fireworks display, dessert at the end of dinner, even the last part of a sentence. Like sentence openers, sentence closers are single words or groups of words that add important details to sentences.

Model A The man was about fifty, overweight but solid-looking.

Frank Bonham, *Chief*

Model B They were in the schoolroom again, the five boys and Lina and the teacher.

Meindert DeJong, *The Wheel on the School*

Model C One of the pups came slowly toward me, a round ball of fur that I could have held in my hand.

Scott O'Dell, *Island of the Blue Dolphins*

ON THE MARK Put a comma before a sentence closer to separate it from the rest of the sentence.

A. Combining Sentences Make a new sentence by adding the underlined part of the second sentence to the first sentence as a sentence closer. Write the complete sentence, putting a comma before the sentence closer.

1. My sister and I were working by our dock. We were scraping and painting the little dinghy. **Shirley Ann Grau, "The Land and the Water"**
2. I jumped to my feet. I was completely thunderstruck. **Antoine de Saint-Exupery, *The Little Prince***
3. She stayed behind because she thought it would be worthwhile trying the door of the wardrobe. She thought this even though she felt almost sure that it would be locked. **C. S. Lewis, *The Lion, the Witch, and the Wardrobe***

4. The pounding came up the stairs. It was crashing on each step.
Shirley Jackson, *The Haunting of Hill House*

5. They were the same kind of thunderheads as on the day of the ball game. The thunderheads were white and piled up over the hills like a sky full of fresh dried laundry. **Joseph Krumgold, *Onion John***

B. Unscrambling and Imitating Sentences Unscramble each set of sentence chunks below. Create a sentence that has a sentence closer and the same order of chunks and punctuation as the model. Then write a sentence of your own that imitates each model.

1. Model Mr. Underhill came out from under his hill, smiling and breathing hard. **Ursula K. Le Guin, "The Rule of Names"**

stood behind the cash register / the sales clerk / chatting and making change

2. Model They were eating borsch, the rich, red soup with sour cream so dear to Russian palates.
Richard Connell, "The Most Dangerous Game"

too difficult for many figure skaters / a dangerous, demanding move / she was practicing a triple jump

3. Model It was a good thing I had no homework that night, for I could not possibly have concentrated.
Jean Stafford, "Bad Characters"

because the storm would definitely have interfered / we took our hike this morning / it was a lucky break

Grammar Refresher Some sentence closers are appositives. To learn more about punctuating appositives, see Handbook 43, "Punctuation," pages 566–599.

Additional Resource

Sentence Composing Copy Masters, pp. 11–12

Answer Key

A. Combining Sentences

1. My sister and I were working by our dock, scraping and painting the little dinghy.
2. I jumped to my feet, completely thunderstruck.
3. She stayed behind because she thought it would be worthwhile trying the door of the wardrobe, even though she felt almost sure that it would be locked.
4. The pounding came up the stairs, crashing on each step.
5. They were the same kind of thunderheads as on the day of the ball game, white and piled up over the hills like a sky full of fresh dried laundry.

B. Unscrambling and Imitating Sentences

Unscrambled sentences are given. Students' imitations will vary but should follow the pattern of the model.

1. The sales clerk stood behind the cash register, chatting and making change.
2. She was practicing a triple jump, a dangerous, demanding move too difficult for many figure skaters.
3. It was a lucky break we took our hike this morning, because the storm would definitely have interfered.

for GRAMMAR REFRESHER

KEY TO UNDERSTANDING: APPOSITIVES An appositive is a noun or a noun phrase that identifies or gives more information about another word in the sentence, usually the word preceding it. Point out that the underlined words in Model 2 of Exercise B form an appositive phrase that defines *borsch.* Appositives are set off with commas when they provide nonessential information, but not when they provide essential information.

7

Informative Writing: Reports

Overview

Reports are longer pieces of informative writing that require research, analysis, and synthesis of information. Workshop 7 includes the following Guided and Related Assignments, as well as the interdisciplinary project described on page 163c–163d.

1. **Guided: Report of Information** calls on students to formulate questions, to research the answers, to analyze, synthesize, and paraphrase information as they take notes, and to draw conclusions to present in an interesting, informative, and logically organized report.
2. **Related: Family History** invites students to conduct interviews with family members, research documents and other primary sources from family history, and arrange details in a chronological narrative to share with the class and with family members.

Teaching Preview

Preparation Guide

1. Use the Overview on this page and the Teacher's Choice descriptions on page 165 as a basis for deciding which assignments to teach.
2. Preview the assignments and the teacher's notes and identify concepts that may require preteaching or extra support, given your class's abilities. The handbook mini-lessons suggested within the lesson may also provide guidance.
3. Preview the chart below for support materials in the Teacher's Resource File that may be used with this Workshop. Resources are for use with the Guided Assignment unless otherwise noted.

Support Materials

WRITER'S CRAFT RESOURCES

Prewrite and Explore
Thinking Skills Worksheets, p. 4, 10
Thinking Skills Transparencies, pp. 4–4a, 10–10a
Writing Resource Book, pp. 34–39

Draft and Discover
Elaboration, Revision, and Proofreading Practice, pp. 13–15
Elaboration, Revision, and Proofreading Transparencies, pp. 25–28
Writing Resource Book, pp. 40–41

Revise Your Writing
Elaboration, Revision, and Proofreading Practice, p. 16
Elaboration, Revision, and Proofreading Transparencies, pp. 29–30
Guidelines for Writing Assessment and Portfolio Use, pp. 20, 40–42
Peer Response Guides, pp. 19–20
Writing Resource Book, p. 42

Extension Activities
Sentence Composing Copymasters, pp. 13–14
Starting Points for Writing, pp. 29–30, 33–34, 38, 40
Writing from Literature, pp. 5–6, 15–18, 25–26
Standardized Test Practice

Educational Technology
(available separately)
Writer's DataBank
Electronic English Handbook
Multimedia Workshop
On Assignment! (videodisc)

OTHER RESOURCES

Books and Journals
Elbow, Peter. "Breathing Experience into Expository Writing." *Writing with Power.* New York: Oxford U Press, 1981.
Hurst, C. O. "Writers, Research, and Report Writing." *Teaching PreK-8.* 23 (Aug./Sept. 1992): 150–152.

Films and Videos
Peru. Altschul Group, 1992. (20 min.).
The Pueblo Dwellers. SRA, 1993. (21 min.)

Educational Technology
Intermediate Library Media Skills. Combase, 1986. Apple II Series.
The Multicultural Chronicles. MicroMedia Publishing, 1993. Hypercard.

Linking Literature, Writing, and Grammar

The following options may be used to provide students with an integrated language experience. Begin by assigning and discussing any of the recommended pieces of literature. Use the suggested strategy to provide a link to the Guided Assignment.

LINKING LITERATURE AND WRITING

Option 1

Starting Point: "A Baseball Pioneer" by Jonathan Moskaitis (student model) on pages 166–169 of *The Writer's Craft.*

Strategy: Use the teaching suggestions on pages 166–169 to lead students into the Guided Assignment.

Option 2

Starting Point: "The Real McCoy" by Jim Haskins on pages 140–143 of McDougal, Littell's *Literature and Language,* Grade 6. (Additional suggestions for using *Literature and Language* can be found on page 165.)

Strategy: Ask if students have ever heard the expression "the real McCoy" and if they know what it means. Then ask if they know the origin of the phrase. Have them read the selection. Explain that curiosity about the origins of things can result in great reports. Then introduce the Guided Assignment.

Option 3

Starting Point: "Volcano" by Patricia Lauber or "The Truth About Dragons" by Rhoda Blumberg.

Strategy: Have students read one of these articles about the natural world. Then ask if there are any mysteries of nature that they have wondered about. Use the discussion to introduce the Guided Assignment.

LINKING WRITING AND GRAMMAR

Before the drafting or revision stages of this assignment, introduce the idea of transitions by having students discuss the importance of watching highway signs during a car trip. Such signs help travelers find their way to a destination by giving helpful clues to what is coming next. In a research report, transition words can help readers follow the trail of a writer's ideas from paragraph to paragraph, from beginning to end. Transitions such as *similarly* and *also* show that the writer is staying on the same path. Transitions such as *however* and *instead* indicate a change in direction. Use the following examples and ask students to look for places in their own reports where transitions could help readers follow the direction of their ideas.

These fuels are convenient and *also* affordable.

These fuels are convenient. *However,* they are polluting our environment.

Go over on pages 234–238 of Writing Handbook 11, "Transitions." If problems with transitions persist, use the exercises on those pages for reteaching.

Management Guidelines

The chart below indicates the number of days recommended for each phase of the Guided and Related Assignments. These numbers are an estimate of the total time needed for each phase. In practice, of course, students may not complete each phase in one continuous session, nor will they necessarily progress from stage to stage in the linear order shown here. Stars indicate portions of the assignment that may be completed outside the classroom if time is limited or if teachers wish students to work independently.

REPORT OF INFORMATION

Starting from Literature	1 day
Prewrite and Explore	2–3 days
Researching	1 week*
Draft and Discover	1 week*
Revise Your Writing	3–4 days*
Proofread	2 days*
Publish and Present	1–2 days
Reflect on Your Writing	1 day
Extension and Enrichment	open*

FAMILY HISTORY

Planning	2 days
Researching	1–2 weeks*
Writing	2 days*
Reviewing	1 day
Publishing and Presenting	1 day
Sentence Composing	open*

Project File

Business Tycoon: Creating Your Own Business

Overview

For this project, students will work to create their own business. They will learn how to find a location, take out a bank loan, hire staff, purchase inventory, set prices, advertise, and keep records. Throughout the project they will use research skills to investigate real-life questions and to gather information about their community. The project culminates when students present their plans or actually open a business at school.

Students will participate in the following activities:

- Write research reports on requirements for starting a successful business
- Develop a list of types of businesses they would like to run
- Present a plan to start up and operate a business or start up a business within their class or school
- Evaluate the success of their business
- Use language arts, math, social studies, and art skills to complete their research and to develop and operate their business

Preparation Guide

Tell students that many young people dream of running their own businesses when they grow up. Ask what they think it would be like to be president of their own company. After they have shared their ideas, tell them that they are about to find out what this is like.

Explain that for this project students will learn research and report-writing skills and will use them to plan a business and, if possible, to start and run a class business—for profit.

Stage 1
Explore and Research Possibilities

1. Invite students to generate a list of factors that they think people would need to consider when starting a business.
2. Assign a topic such as "How to Open a Small Business," and have students complete the Guided Assignment, "Report of Information," in Writer's Workshop 7.
3. After students have completed their reports, ask them to choose several small businesses in their community and to arrange interviews with the owners. Have them compare their research findings with the actual experiences of small business owners.
4. Ask students to brainstorm a list of types of businesses they might want to open themselves.

TEAM TEACHING

The following activities may be used for team teaching or as enrichment and extension activities by the language arts teacher.

Language Arts Learn techniques for doing research and writing reports (see *Resources, Stage 1*).

Social Studies Study the requirements for opening a small business. Learn about community needs and businesses that serve them.

Math Survey local businesses and compile statistics.

TEACHING TIPS

- Schedule a library tour that focuses on business-related materials.
- Arrange for the class to work together to develop questions for small-business owners. Have students practice the techniques of effective interviewing.
- Have students develop case studies describing small businesses they know or have read about.

Stage 2
Focus on a Business

1. Direct students to work in small groups to survey the interests and needs of students in their school or of people in the community. Have students investigate local businesses and identify the type of new business they think might be successful.
2. Tell students to assume that they have $50,000 to start the business of their choice. Have them decide on a business.
3. Have students identify issues that they, as new business owners, must deal with. Issues might include the following:
   - a location for their business
   - budgeting
   - decorating
   - taxes and licenses
   - start-up costs
   - hiring workers
   - purchasing inventory
   - laws regulating businesses
   - loans
4. Direct student groups to choose issues, to research them, and to suggest strategies for dealing with them. Encourage students to interview small-business owners as well as to use library resources.
5. Have groups present their findings and plans orally at a class meeting.
6. Tell the class to agree on a plan of action and to begin developing specific plans or taking steps to open the business.

TEAM TEACHING

Social Studies Study laws regulating businesses. Learn about applying for a bank loan.

Math Devise budgets. Figure taxes and interest. Create payrolls and learn about deductions. Introduce spreadsheets.

Language Arts Practice interviewing techniques (see *Resources, Stage 2*).

TEACHING TIPS

- Encourage students to read about people their age who have opened businesses (see *Resources, Stage 2*).
- Help students create a survey to find out the needs of their potential customers. Help them write survey questions and devise a survey form.
- Suggest that students consider a business they can operate at school. Options might include a juice stand or a music exchange.
- To simplify students' budget planning, specify reasonable, hypothetical amounts for rent and other costs.

Stage 3
Open for Business

1. Have students plan how to introduce their business to potential customers at school and in the community.
2. Direct students to present their plans or to actually open their business.
3. Have students decide how to assess the success of their new venture (see *Resources, Stage 3*).

TEAM TEACHING

Language Arts Write press releases and advertisements for the business. Devise criteria for evaluating the success of the venture.

Art Create layouts and illustrations for print advertisements. Plan interior decoration for the business (see *Resources, Stage 3*).

Math Set up forms for keeping track of income and expenses. Estimate taxes.

TEACHING TIPS

- Ask a small business owner to speak to the class.
- Schedule tours of successful small businesses.
- Encourage students to investigate ways of using the media to publicize their business. They might issue press releases or run classified ads.

Resources

STAGE 1

The Writer's Craft, Grade 6, Workshop 7, "Informative Writing: Reports," pages 164–185, teaches students how to compile and present research material. Handbook 29, "Library Skills," pages 312–319, offers guidance in research techniques. Handbook 31, "Interviewing," page 323, offers help with conducting an interview.

How Business Works by Edwin Hoag gives young people a basic overview of business principles and practices.

The Kids' Money-Making Book by Jim and Jean Young and ***Good Cents: Every Kid's Guide to Making Money*** by the Amazing Life Games Company explain how kids can set up a variety of businesses.

STAGE 2

The Young Tycoons: Ten Success Stories by Gloria Miklowitz and Madeleine Yates profiles nine young teens and one group whose businesses are thriving.

Anatomy of a Start-up: Why Some New Businesses Succeed and Others Fail edited by Elizabeth Longsworth gives twenty-seven real-life case studies.

How to Grow a Hundred Dollars by Elizabeth James, Carol Barkin, and Joel Schick explains how kids can get loans, reinvest, sell shares, advertise, and deal with other essentials of starting and maintaining a business.

The Writer's Craft, Grade 6, Handbook 32, "Oral Reports," pages 324–325, can help students with their oral presentations. Handbook 31, "Interviewing," page 323, gives guidelines for interviews.

STAGE 3

A **Junior Achievement** organization in your area can provide speakers, guidance, and troubleshooting tips for students running their own businesses.

The Writer's Craft, Grade 6, Handbook 30, "Thinking Skills," pages 320–322, explains appeals to emotion and appeals to reason and can help students create effective publicity.

Using Charts and Graphs: One Thousand Ideas for Visual Persuasion by Jan White offers techniques for graphing the progress of a business.

Articles in ***Zillions,*** the magazine of consumer information for young people, provide models for evaluating the success of the business.

Additional Projects

Community Health: Inside View During this project, students volunteer at a local convalescent home or rehabilitation center. They should arrange to interview administrators, staff, and clients. Instruct students to write reports outlining the services offered, sharing success stories and explaining the needs of the facility (such as a need for volunteers or materials) that community members could help with. Students might compile their reports into a pamphlet and distribute it in the community, or they might structure their material as a series of special reports for a local newspaper.

Life Science: Keep It Green Students participating in this project use research to identify local "green" areas and to learn how these areas can best be maintained. Have students launch an ongoing program to preserve or maintain a green area. For example, they might begin a reforestation program in a nearby national forest, volunteer at a wildlife sanctuary, or revitalize an urban park. Students write reports explaining and tracking the program so that next year's students can carry it on.

SketchBook

Objective

- To use writing prompts as springboards to informal writing

WRITING WARM-UPS

Encourage students to respond freely to at least one of the Sketchbook prompts. Students may begin by discussing their opinions in small groups and then freewriting in their journals. Remind students that their responses will not be graded and may provide them with useful material for other informative writing assignments.

For example, students may choose environmental issues as the topics of their reports in Writer's Workshop 7. Students writing to share an opinion (Writer's Workshop 5) may choose some aspect of the environment as the issue they care most about.

SHOW, DON'T TELL

The following is a sample of a showing paragraph for the second prompt:

I made a survey of fifty television commercials over a three-day period recently. I found that while many of the ads were silly and boring, some of them are very clever and creative. I like the use of the latest techniques of computer animation and special effects. I've even read that advertising agencies use some of the best musicians and composers in the business to create the music for commercials.

SketchBook

WRITING WARM-UPS

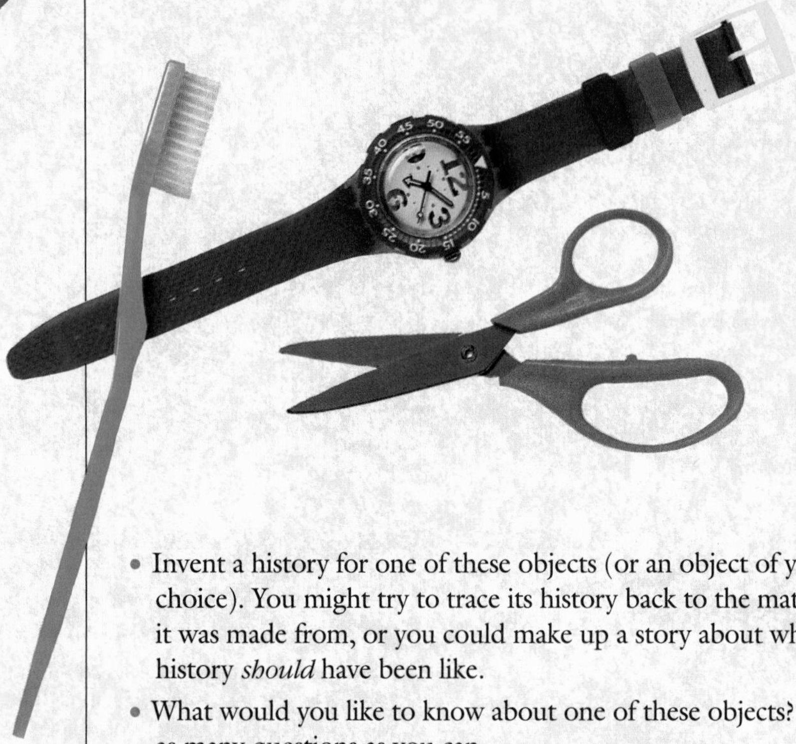

- Invent a history for one of these objects (or an object of your choice). You might try to trace its history back to the materials it was made from, or you could make up a story about what its history *should* have been like.
- What would you like to know about one of these objects? Write as many questions as you can.

Show, Don't Tell

You can make a report interesting by giving facts and examples to *show* what you've learned about a topic. Expand one of the sentences below, adding information that *shows* instead of *tells*.

- Young people like many different kinds of music.
- Leisure activities have changed a great deal in the past fifteen years.

Informative Writing: Reports

Guided Assignment
Report of Information

Related Assignment
Family History

Have you ever learned a little bit about a fascinating subject—and then wished you knew more? In this workshop you'll have the chance to find answers to some of your questions about a topic you care about. Then, you can write a report of information about what you learn, sharing your knowledge with others. You'll also be able to put your report-writing skills to work in a related assignment, as you write your very own family history.

Links to Literature & Language

Literature For more examples of informative writing, see *Literature and Language,* Grade 6.
- Jim Haskins, "The Real McCoy"
- Russell Freedman, "Frontier Schools"
- John Cross Giblin, "Forks in Tokyo, Chopsticks in Chicago"

Writing This Guided Assignment may be used as an extension of the Writer's Workshop, "Informative Writing: Research Report," on page 523 of *Literature and Language,* Grade 6.

Informative Writing: Reports

Objectives

Guided Assignment

Report of Information To recognize the characteristics of report writing, to research a topic, and to create an informational report

Related Assignment

Family History To analyze a family history and to use research and reporting skills to create a family history

Teacher's Choice

Use the following guidelines to choose the assignment that best suits students' needs.

Report of Information This assignment will benefit all students by giving them a chance to learn about the process of doing research and writing a report. The skills involved in report writing draw on students' knowledge of both expository and descriptive writing, so you may wish to offer this assignment after students have had some experience with those two modes of writing.

Family History In this assignment, students will analyze informative writing when applied to a family history. They will then use techniques for researching and writing to prepare a family history of their own. You may wish to give this related assignment to students who are familiar with basic skills of informative writing and who will benefit from applying these skills to a more personal form of writing.

Guided ASSIGNMENT

ASSIGNMENT RATIONALE

The ability to research and report on information is essential to academic success; it is an important skill for business and professional careers and for community activities in later life. Report writing also provides practice in a number of essential thinking skills, including analysis, drawing conclusions, and synthesis.

Reading a STUDENT MODEL

This model is the final draft of the piece that students will see in process on the workshop pages that follow.

Motivate

After students have read Reading a Student Model, ask students what reports they have written recently. Urge volunteers to talk about the challenges they faced in writing their papers. Ask, "What would you do differently if you were going to write the report again?" Tell students that this Student Model and the following assignment will give them ideas for making the next report more successful and easier to write.

BUILD ON PRIOR KNOWLEDGE

Ask students whether they know who Jackie Robinson was. Some students may know that he was the first African-American player in major league baseball. Ask what problems they think someone who is "first" encounters. (Sample: Everyone watches; some people try to make life difficult.) Ask students how they think Robinson's hiring might have changed baseball. (Robinson opened the door for others; many players today are African-American, as are some managers and officials.)

Guided ASSIGNMENT Report of Information

Reading a STUDENT MODEL

Jonathan Moskaitis, a sixth-grade student, needed to write a report for his social studies class. The final report would be displayed on a school bulletin board honoring Black History Month. As you read Jonathan's report, think about how he was able to put his love of baseball to good use in completing this assignment.

Brooklyn Signs Negro Player, First in Organized Baseball

MONTREAL, OCT. 23 (AP)– The first Negro player ever to be admitted to organized baseball was signed tonight by the Brooklyn Dodgers for their International League farm, the Montreal Royals. The Royals wanted

Jackie Robinson, one-time U halfback ace and recent shor the Kansas City Negro Mo put his signature on a contr ing not only for a regular salary but also for a guarante

Dad's pin

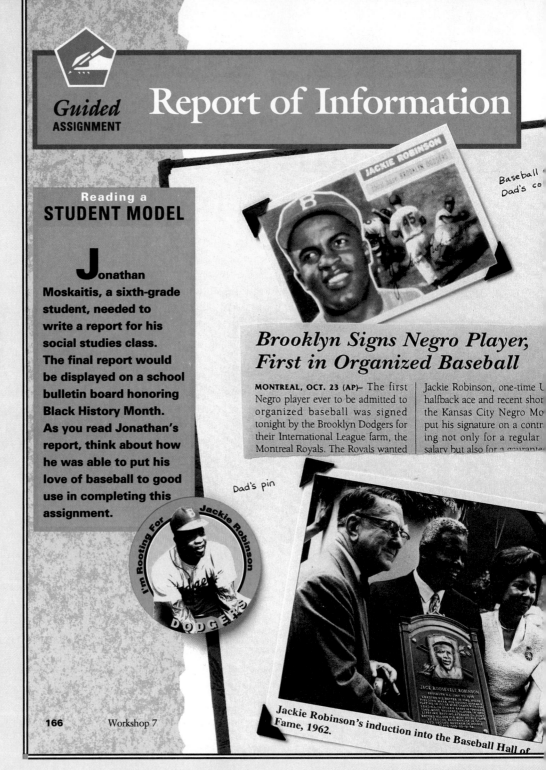

Jackie Robinson's induction into the Baseball Hall of Fame, 1962.

Social Studies Connection

Throughout the year, designated periods such as Black History Month (February) and Women's History Month (March), as well as special holidays such as Cinco de Mayo, may provide topics for writing. Brainstorm with students to develop a list of such topics.

Moskaitis 1

Jonathan Moskaitis

Mrs. Flynn

Social Studies 6B

1 February 1993

A Baseball Pioneer

Jackie Robinson was the first black baseball player in the Major Leagues, but getting there wasn't easy. Because of the color of his skin, he was taunted, hated, and turned away. Jackie was a great athlete, though, and he never gave up.

Jackie Robinson was born in Georgia on January 31, 1919, but his family moved to California when he was a baby. The family was very poor and didn't always have enough to eat. As he was growing up, Jackie hung out with a gang of kids in the neighborhood, and he used to get in trouble with the police all the time. A neighborhood mechanic who really liked Jackie tried to get him to leave the gang and stay out of trouble. With the help of the pastor in the family's church, it worked. They convinced him that it was better to be different and not to follow the crowd. Jackie spent time playing sports instead.

Throughout high school and junior college, Jackie was a star in every sport. He was so good that universities were offering him sports scholarships for his last two years of college. Jackie finally picked UCLA to attend. Jackie was super in all the sports he played, and now professional scouts were observing him!

However, Jackie never made a deal with these sports scouts. Instead, he took a job at a children's camp. He wanted to send some of the money he earned to his mother.

In 1942, Jackie Robinson was drafted into the army. He faced a lot

4/10/47
The Montre
Royals

SET A PURPOSE

Remind students that the purpose of Jonathan's report was to provide information tied to Black History Month. To help students think about how Jonathan applied his love of baseball to this writing assignment, they might ask themselves, "What makes this a good topic?" (Samples: It tells about an important step in African-American history; the writer is interested in it; the writer already knew something about the subject.)

Moskaitis 2

of discrimination there. He played on the military's football team, but he found out other teams wouldn't play against a team that included a black man.

At that time, major-league teams were all white. Minorities had to play in separate leagues. After Jackie left the army in 1944, he joined the Kansas City Monarchs, a baseball team in the Negro leagues. Life in the Negro leagues was tough. The Negro leagues' food, pay, schedules, and hotels weren't nearly as good as those the white leagues got. Players sometimes had to sleep and eat on the bus. Then came the event that changed Jackie's life and the history of baseball forever.

Branch Rickey, the general manager of the Brooklyn Dodgers, asked Jackie to join his team. Rickey knew many players and fans would be against Jackie because he was black. Rickey told Jackie he was looking for a player who would have the guts not to fight when others were cruel to him. Jackie said yes and swore that he'd prove himself by playing great baseball instead of by fighting. Jackie also felt that if he did well, other teams would draft black players too.

Before he could play in Brooklyn, Jackie had to play for the Dodgers' farm team, the Montreal Royals. At first Jackie was rejected by the Royals' fans and his teammates, but as time went on they accepted and liked him. Jackie became a hero in Montreal for his great playing. When he played in other cities, though, the crowd and other teams made fun of Jackie or wouldn't play when he played.

In 1947 Jackie signed a contract with the Dodgers. Again the fans booed him, the team didn't like him, and other teams refused to play with him. But Jackie did what his manager wanted. He ignored the bad things other people said and did to him and tried his hardest to play well. Jackie

168 Workshop 7

MORE ABOUT THE MODEL

Determined to break the color barrier in the major leagues, the Brooklyn Dodgers' Branch Rickey searched for two years before finding someone he thought could stand up to the pressure of such a move. "The first Black in organized baseball," said Rickey, "had to be a great player, certainly. But he also had to be a man of great character. . . . [Robinson] was the ideal choice." Robinson never stopped fighting for racial equality. In 1972, shortly before his death, he told a World Series audience, "I won't be satisfied until I look over at the third-base coaching box and see a Black man there as manager."

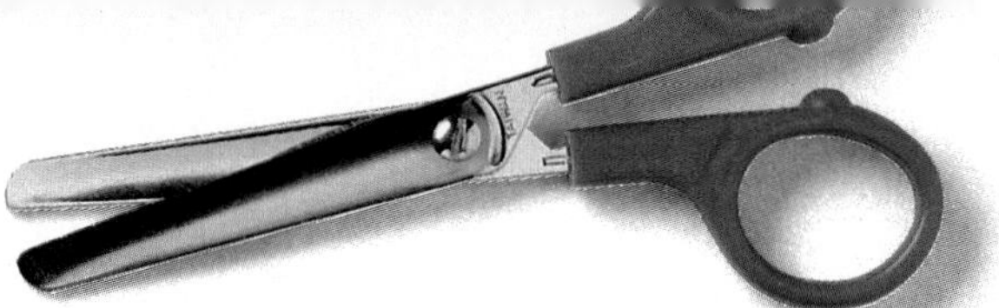

Moskaitis 3

began hitting and stealing more bases. The fans loved it. He was good at defense and hitting in pressure situations, so the team liked him too. At the end of his first year, Jackie's team won the pennant, and Jackie won the National League Rookie of the Year.

During his baseball career with the Dodgers, Jackie led his team to win five pennants. In 1955, the Dodgers even won the World Series! Jackie retired from baseball in 1957. He was inducted into baseball's Hall of Fame in 1962, and the Dodgers retired his number. By then Jackie's real job was done. He had opened the door for blacks, and now more black players were coming into the league.

On October 24, 1972, Jackie Robinson died. We will always remember his contributions to baseball. Of course, we will remember the pennants and World Series he helped win, but probably his most important contribution was his successful fight for blacks' rights on the field and off.

Moskaitis 4

List of Sources

David, Lester. "Jackie Robinson: He Changed Baseball." Boys' Life Feb. 1991: 16.

Epstein, Sam, and Beryl Epstein. Jackie Robinson: Baseball's Gallant Fighter. Champaign: Garrard, 1974.

"Robinson, Jackie." Encyclopaedia Britannica. 1985 ed.

Rudeen, Kenneth. Jackie Robinson. New York: Crowell, 1971.

Scott, Richard. Jackie Robinson. New York: Chelsea House, 1987.

Think & Respond

Respond as a Reader

▶ What new things did you learn about Jackie Robinson?

▶ How does Jonathan get you interested in his topic?

Respond as a Writer

▶ What details does Jonathan include that show how Jackie Robinson struggled to make it in major-league baseball?

▶ What does Jonathan's conclusion say about why he chose to write about Jackie Robinson?

Think & Respond

RESPOND AS A READER

▶ You might want to make a time line on the board and review the main points of Robinson's life and career. Invite students to discuss what they learned about him.

▶ Possible responses to the second question include the attention-getting comments in the opening paragraph ("getting there wasn't easy"; "he was taunted, hated, and turned away"; "he never gave up"). These statements suggest that Robinson's story will have action and conflict—two elements of an exciting piece of writing.

RESPOND AS A WRITER

▶ Students should note such details as "rejected by the Royals' fans and his teammates"; "other teams made fun of Jackie and wouldn't play when he played"; "fans booed him"; "team didn't like him"; and "other teams refused to play with him." Ask students to think about how these details show, rather than tell, Robinson's struggle.

▶ Students should see that Jonathan's conclusion shows that Robinson deserves a place in African-American history not simply because he was a great athlete, but because of what he did to advance the rights of all African-Americans.

Draw Conclusions

To make sure students understand this introduction to report writing, ask them what this model suggests about the characteristics of good reports. Responses may include the following:

- a single, clear topic that is of interest to the writer
- specific information from a variety of named sources
- a strong introduction and conclusion

MULTICULTURAL Connection

Most students will be aware of the struggle by African-Americans for their civil rights. Students from other cultures, however, may not know specific details. Invite students to share some of their knowledge about the struggle to end racial discrimination in the United States.

Writing
ON YOUR OWN

Tell students that in this guided assignment they will have the chance to investigate a subject that interests them and to share their findings. Remind students that Jonathan Moskaitis began with an introduction that quickly grabbed his readers' attention; gave facts and examples to show, rather than merely tell about, his subject; and ended by explaining why his subject was important. Urge students to consider using these techniques in their writing.

Handbooks for Help and Practice

The following handbooks may be used as mini-lessons before students begin writing or as resources when problems arise:

- **Thinking with Pictures, pp. 192–196**
- **Finding a Starting Point, pp. 197–202**
- **Finding a Focus, pp. 203–204**
- **Library Skills, pp. 312–319**

PREWRITE AND EXPLORE

Objectives

- To use prewriting techniques to select a topic for a short report
- To identify the purpose and audience for a report
- To focus a topic for research

Teaching Strategies

for FIND A GREAT TOPIC

HELPFUL HINT Suggest that along with thinking about their interests, students consider doing research on practical ideas that could help them in their daily lives. They might report on preventing accidents in the home, safety for bicycle riders, fire prevention, doing volunteer work in the community, or any other subject that is important to them.

Writing
ON YOUR OWN

Report of Information

INVITATION TO *Write*

For Jonathan Moskaitis, completing a school assignment was a chance to learn more about a subject that had always interested him. When you write a report, you investigate a topic you care about, assemble your information, and share your knowledge with others.

Find a topic you're interested in and learn more about it. Then write a short report that shows what you have learned.

PREWRITE AND EXPLORE

1. Find a great topic. First, think of subjects you already know something about—a special collection or hobby, for example. Then think of subjects you're curious about. Try some of the following activities to find the best report topic.

Jackie Robinson is caught off first base by the Boston Braves' Frank McCormack in 1948.

Exploring Topics

- **Looking inside** Take some time to think about who you are and what you most like to do. Do you have a special talent or skill? Perhaps you're a whiz at computer games or you play a musical instrument well. Maybe you most enjoy reading animal stories or building model airplanes. Make a list of your special interests and **freewrite** about them in your journal.
- **Looking around** What's happening in your world? Look through a newspaper or a magazine aimed at students your age to see what subjects are covered there. You may find stories on everything from space stations to archaeological digs. What catches your eye? Get together with classmates to share ideas and find the best angle on a topic.

Science Connection

Students interested in science might be encouraged to think about topics studied in their science class. They might also scan their local newspapers, or magazines such as *National Geographic World,* for science topics that interest them. You also might advise students to confer with their science teacher for topic ideas and guidance in developing topics.

- **Suiting yourself** Has your teacher assigned a general topic for your report? If so, try to find an angle you care about, a subtopic that will hold your interest. For example, if your teacher assigned a report on nutrition, you might focus on the benefits of a vegetarian diet.

One Student's Process

Jonathan Moskaitis needed to write a report honoring Black History Month. He explored his own interests and discovered ways to connect them to his assignment for school. Notice how Jonathan got stuck in the music and movies categories, but saw real possibilities in the sports category.

Music
Rap or Soul
↓
Write about a musician?
Find out how the music got started?

Sports
Baseball
↓
today vs. yesterday
↓
Negro league — what was that like?
Who was the first black in Major Leagues? Jackie Robinson? Double check w/ Dad.
What was Jackie's life like?

Movies
Comedies
↓
Write about a comedian?

2. Choose the topic that interests you most. Which of your possible topics do you know the most about? Which one do you want to explore further? Choose a topic now and spend some time freewriting about it to make sure it will hold your interest.

Writer's Choice Do you want to investigate a topic that is totally new to you? Would you rather explore something you know quite a bit about already? Which would be more fun for you? The choice is yours.

PROBLEM SOLVING

"How can I find the right topic for my report?"

For help finding the topic that's right for you, see

- Handbook 1, "Thinking with Pictures," pages 192–196
- Handbook 2, "Finding a Starting Point," pages 197–202
- Handbook 3, "Finding a Focus," pages 203–204
- Springboards, page 185

GENERAL NOTE

HELPFUL HINT Tell students that the Sketchbook activities on pages 114 and 164 may help them find writing ideas.

for EXPLORING TOPICS

INDIVIDUALIZING INSTRUCTION: VISUAL LEARNERS You may wish to encourage visual learners to use cluster diagrams to explore their topics. You might model the process, using a topic of your own. You also might have students complete "Reports: Finding a Topic," page 34 of the *Writing Resource Book.*

for ONE STUDENT'S PROCESS

PEER RESPONSE After students have discussed the model notes, point out that they, too, may find that one possible topic is much more fruitful than the others. At that point, encourage students to form into small groups to discuss their ideas. After explaining their topics, they can discuss one another's ideas and give suggestions on aspects of the topics that are most interesting to others. Their comments may open even more possibilities.

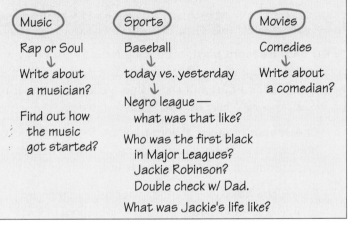

for FOCUS YOUR TOPIC

MODELING Students often have trouble with focusing topics. Suggest that they ask themselves "What about . . . ?" questions; then briefly demonstrate. For example, if the topic is archaeology, you might ask: What about archaeology? (Egyptian archaeology) What about Egyptian archaeology? (The tombs of the Pharaohs) What about the tombs of the Pharaohs? (finding King Tut's tomb) When students reach the point at which they can list specific details, their topic is probably focused narrowly enough.

RESEARCH YOUR TOPIC

Objectives

- To identify sources of information about a topic
- To take notes from research sources

Teaching Strategies

for RESEARCH YOUR TOPIC

INDIVIDUALIZING INSTRUCTION: ESL AND LEP STUDENTS Students who lack proficiency in English may feel overwhelmed by a project that requires them to synthesize information from many sources into a report. You may wish to have these students work with no more than two sources.

BASIC STUDENTS Once these students have focused their topics, review their research plans. Help them select key headings to look for in library catalogs, encyclopedias, and other materials. If necessary, make time to take them to the school library and walk them through the basic steps of library research.

3. Focus your topic. If your topic is too broad, you may have trouble exploring it in a short report. For example, the broad topic *horses* can be narrowed by focusing in on one kind of horse (Clydesdales, for example). Doing some reading or talking with others about your topic can help you narrow it and find a more specific subject.

4. See what you know and what you want to find out. Review any freewriting you may have done on your topic to see what you already know, and put a star by those ideas you want to know more about. Then make a list of questions about your topic that you can find answers to later.

RESEARCH YOUR TOPIC

PROBLEM SOLVING

"How can I find the information I need?"

For help finding what you want to know, see

- Handbook 29, "Library Skills," pages 312–319

1. Go on a treasure hunt. Looking for information on your topic is like going on a treasure hunt. You have an idea about what you'd like to find, but there's no telling what you'll turn up in the process. Where do you begin to look?

- **Check your home.** If your topic is a favorite subject or hobby, you probably already have some useful materials. Look around to see what you can find.
- **Check the library.** Look up your topic in the card catalog or computerized index of your school or local library. Also check the *Readers' Guide to Periodical Literature* for magazine articles on your topic.
- **Talk to people who can help.** A reference librarian can steer you toward useful sources. But don't stop there. Interview experts or your friends, parents, or teachers who know something about your topic. Take careful notes!

2. Review your sources and prepare source cards. Check your sources to make sure that they tell you what you most want to know about your topic. Write down the publication

SPICE BOX

After students have chosen and narrowed their topics, have them write their names and their topic at the top of a sheet of notebook paper. Collect the sheets and pass them to other students. Have those students read the topic and write, on the bottom of the sheet, a question they would like to have answered about it. Then have each student fold the sheet up from the bottom, accordion style, to cover his or her question, and pass the sheet to someone else. When the sheets are full, return them to their owners. Students will have a variety of questions about their topics to consider as they research.

information for each source on a separate index card. Assign a number to each source card for later reference when you take notes. You will also use this information when you create a List of Sources to attach to the end of your report. Always record the author's name (if given) and the title of the book or article. Also write down the following information:

- **Book**—city of publication, publisher's name, copyright date
- **Magazine article**—name of the magazine, issue date, page numbers
- **Encyclopedia**—article title, copyright date

3. Take notes from your sources. You may want to take notes on index cards, using one card for each piece of information. When you're ready to plan your organization or write a draft, you can put the cards in any order you like.

4. Use your own words. It's very important that you take notes using your own words instead of copying out of your sources. Rewriting information helps you understand what you read. Also, using someone else's words in your writing without saying where you got them is called *plagiarism,* and plagiarism is dishonest.

Jonathan took notes from one of his sources on this note card. He recorded details about Jackie Robinson's childhood.

Topic — Source card number — ③

Early life

—very poor, hungry a lot, hung out with a gang of kids

—neighborhood mechanic and the pastor helped Jackie leave gang and learn to think and act for himself

—was encouraged to do well in sports p. 21–23

Note written in Jonathan's own words — Page number from source

Writing TIP

As you take notes from a source, number each note card with the number of the source. That way you'll know where to look in case you have to go back and read some more.

for REVIEW YOUR SOURCES . . .

HELPFUL HINT Suggest that students include on their source cards information that will help them find the book again. They might note the call number along with where the book came from: for example, the school library, public library, home library, or on loan from a friend.

for TAKE NOTES FROM YOUR SOURCES

KEY TO UNDERSTANDING Direct students' attention to the number *3* in the upper right-hand corner of the model note card. Explain that the *3* refers to Jonathan's third source card, which lists the author, the title, and publication information about the source. Ask students, "On which other note cards would Jonathan write a *3* in that corner?" (on any card containing notes from that same source)

for TAKE NOTES FROM YOUR SOURCES

ASSESSMENT: SPOT CHECK When students begin to do research, have them bring at least one source to class. Provide class time for note taking. As students work, circulate around the room, checking to see that they are keeping accurate source cards, taking notes in their own words, and enclosing any direct quotes in quotation marks.

PROFESSIONAL NOTEBOOK

Sixth-grade teacher and researcher Patricia J. Collins recommends a series of mini-lessons centered on immediate needs as students work on reports: "When students were struggling with organizing their information, I did a minilesson on making an outline. As students began writing rough drafts, I presented a mini-lesson on the importance of a good lead. I made overheads of the leads of some of their favorite books and talked about the variety of ways in which they could begin their pieces. I also did procedural mini-lessons on how to set up a bibliography and table of contents.'"

from *Coming to Know,* edited by Nancie Atwell

for CREATE A GRAPHIC . . .

HELPFUL HINT You might point out that although Jonathan used a cluster diagram, he might have used a chart showing chronological order because his subject dealt with a sequence of events in Robinson's life. Ask students to think about the purpose of their reports. Are they solving a problem? Analyzing something? Tracing an event? You might wish to have them choose a graphic from the variety of forms in the *Thinking Skills Transparency Pack.*

for ONE STUDENT'S PROCESS

CRITICAL THINKING: ANALYZING Have students compare Jonathan's cluster diagram with his completed report. Ask them how he incorporated the information in the cluster into his report. (Jonathan included all of the information. Most of the items on the cluster became the topics of paragraphs.)

5. Think about your information. Now that you've done some research, what do you think are the main ideas you want readers to know about your subject? Try sorting your note cards into groups, with each group representing a main idea. Set aside any cards containing information that seems less important to you now.

6. Create a graphic to show the parts of your report. A cluster, a list, or an informal outline can help you see the parts of your report and how they fit together. A graphic can also help you find out where you need to do more research. Use your main ideas as headings, and chart the details beneath the headings.

One Student's Process

Jonathan sorted his note cards into groups for each of his main ideas. Then he made this cluster based on those groups.

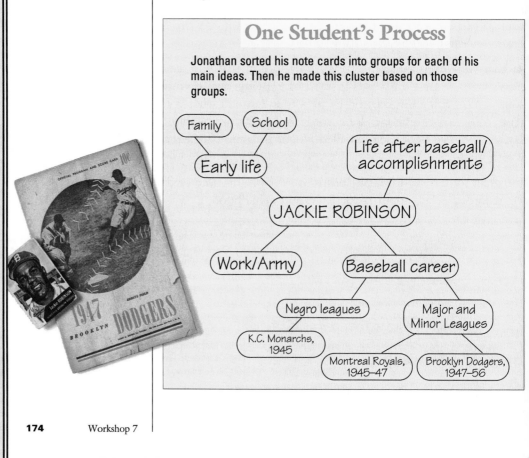

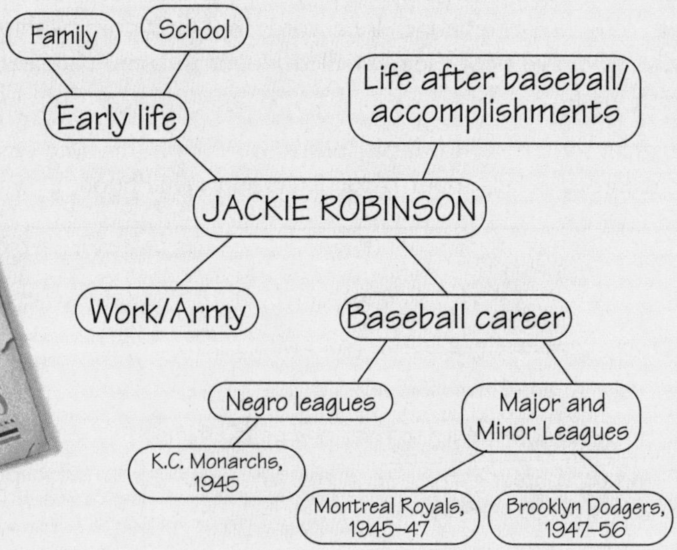

DRAFT AND DISCOVER

1. Start writing any section you wish. You may want to begin drafting the part of your report you've learned the most about. However, if you have a clever idea for an introduction, then start at the very beginning and go from there.

2. Write one or more paragraphs for each main idea. Use your prewriting notes—your graphic and your note cards—as a guide to your writing.

3. Stay open to new ideas. As you write, you may find yourself heading off in unexpected directions. Go back to your sources for more information as you discover what you really want to say.

4. Assemble your draft. Put the pieces of your draft in an order that makes sense. Look again at Jonathan's final report on pages 167–169. You can see that he put his clusters of information in chronological, or time, order. Chronological order works well when you're describing events in history or when you're writing about someone's life. Other organizational patterns—such as order of importance or order of familiarity—may also work for the information you want to present.

5. Write an introduction and a conclusion. Your introduction should include a **thesis statement** that tells the main idea or purpose of your report. Your opening paragraph should also draw your readers into your writing and make them want to read on.

Your conclusion might summarize your main points, ask a question, or make a prediction. Notice how Jonathan's conclusion summarizes the importance of Jackie Robinson's contribution to baseball and to the fight for equality for all people.

6. Think about your draft. Do you want to share your draft with classmates now or work on it some more first? The following questions will help you and your readers review your report.

PROBLEM SOLVING

"What's the best way to organize my ideas? Would a more formal outline help?"

For help outlining your main ideas and ordering your details, see

- Appendix, page 608
- Handbook 7, "Organizing Details," pages 217–221

DRAFT AND DISCOVER

Objectives

- To draft a report of information
- To respond to one's own draft and that of a peer

Teaching Strategies

for WRITE ONE OR MORE PARAGRAPHS . . .

KEY TO UNDERSTANDING You might use Jonathan's cluster diagram on page 174 to point out that he used his plan flexibly. For example, he made "Work/Army," which is one item on his cluster, into two paragraphs; he put "Negro leagues" and "K.C. Monarchs," two items on the cluster, into one paragraph. Urge students to consider what information is most important and to expand those ideas, while combining or even eliminating less important details or items about which they have too little information.

for ASSEMBLE YOUR DRAFT

INDIVIDUALIZING INSTRUCTION: VISUAL AND KINESTHETIC LEARNERS You might suggest that these students try organizing with scissors and tape, cutting their paragraphs apart and trying them in different arrangements until they find an order that makes sense to them. Remind them that they may need to write new transitions when they reorder their reports.

TEACHER'S LOUNGE

"My class size is becoming a problem. By the time I've called roll, class is over."

for REVIEW YOUR WRITING

HELPFUL HINT You might point out to students that the questions they ask their peer readers have different purposes. Some questions simply will check what the writer already believes to be clearly stated or fully developed ideas. Other questions will help writers learn what they did not know. For example, the answers might show writers what is interesting or confusing about their reports. Encourage students to read their work critically and to steer their readers to any points about which they need feedback with questions such as, "Did I tell enough about . . . ?" or "Is this paragraph clear to you?"

for ONE STUDENT'S PROCESS

PEER RESPONSE Point out that Jonathan's peer reader is asking for clarification of ideas and for new information so that he or she can understand the topic. Emphasize that the reader and writer are a team, working together to improve the writing.

REVISE YOUR WRITING

Objectives

- To evaluate the responses to a draft of a report and to revise a draft with those responses in mind
- To evaluate the structure of paragraphs in a report
- To list sources used in writing a report

REVIEW YOUR WRITING

Questions for Yourself

- What is the focus of my report?
- Did I find answers to the questions I had about my topic? What do I still need to research?
- Does my report read smoothly from beginning to end? Is anything missing? What parts should I rearrange?

Questions for Your Peer Readers

- What do you think is the main point of my report?
- Which parts interest you the most?
- Which parts need more explanation?

One Student's Process

Jonathan shared his draft with a friend whose comments appear in the margin.

Before he could play in Brooklyn, Jackie had to play for the Montreal Royals. At first he was rejected by the Royals' fans and his teammates, but as time went on they accepted and liked him. Jackie became a hero in Montreal. Soon Jackie signed up with the Dodgers. Again the fans booed him, the team didn't like him, and other teams refused to play with him. But he began hitting and stealing more bases. The fans loved it! He was good at defence and hitting in pressure situations too, so the team liked him too!

Peer Reader Comments

I've never heard of the Royals. Were they in the Major Leagues back then?

It must have been awfully hard for him! What did Jackie do when he was treated so badly?

REVISE YOUR WRITING

1. Review your responses. Think about how you and your readers responded to your draft. What changes do you want to make? Will you add information and details? Will you take out information that's not related to your main focus?

One Student's Process

Jonathan thought about his friend's comments and added specific details and examples to support his ideas.

for his great playing. When he played in other cities, though, the crowd and other teams made fun of Jackie or wouldn't play when he played.

Before he could play in Brooklyn, Jackie had to play for the Dodgers' farm team, the Montreal Royals. At first Jackie ~~he~~ was rejected by the Royals' fans and his teammates, but as time went on they accepted and liked him. Jackie became a hero in Montreal. ~~Soon~~ ¶ In 1947 Jackie signed ~~up~~ a contract with the Dodgers. Again the fans booed him, the team didn't like him, and other teams refused to play with him. But ~~he~~ Jackie did what his manager wanted. He ignored the bad things other people said and did to him and tried his hardest to play well. Jackie began hitting and stealing more bases. The fans loved it! He was good at defense and hitting in pressure situations ~~too~~, so the team liked him too.

Paragraphs at Work Your outline, list, or cluster headings can help you see where your paragraph breaks should go. Remember these tips.

- Focus on one idea in each paragraph.
- Use a topic sentence to state the main idea.
- Include in each paragraph only those details and examples that support the main idea.

Teaching Strategies

for ONE STUDENT'S PROCESS

PEER RESPONSE Have students compare this portion of Jonathan's draft with the finished model paragraphs 4 and 5 on pages 168–169. Ask them how Jonathan's changes show that he understood and valued his peer reader's opinion. (He added details that responded directly to the questions the reader raised. For instance, he identified the Royals as "the Dodgers' farm team.") Remind students that Jonathan was free to disregard his reader's comments. Ask, "Did he make a good choice? Why?" (Sample: The additional details clarify passages that the reader would probably not have understood and add depth to Robinson's character.)

for LINKING GRAMMAR AND WRITING

CRITICAL THINKING: SEQUENCING Another kind of transition that Jonathan frequently uses helps readers by showing how events are related in time. Have students point out words and phrases that tell when events happened. (Samples: "As he was growing up," "Throughout high school," "In 1942," "Before," and "During his baseball career") Ask students how these transitions help the reader. (They make the order of events clear.)

for MAKE AN ALPHABETICAL LIST . . .

KEY TO UNDERSTANDING Discuss Jonathan's List of Sources (page 169) with students. Ask students to state the rule for writing the author's name (last name, comma, first name, period) and the order of information and its punctuation (Author. Title. Place: Publisher, Date.) Finally, have students explain the preferred form for a magazine article, a source with two authors, and an encyclopedia article.

PROOFREAD

Guidelines for Evaluation

IDEAS AND CONTENT

- focuses on a single topic
- supports main ideas with facts and details
- uses information from more than one source
- includes an effective introduction and conclusion

STRUCTURE AND FORM

- presents information in well-developed paragraphs
- employs appropriate transitions
- includes a List of Sources

GRAMMAR, USAGE, AND MECHANICS

- displays standard grammar, usage, and mechanics
- sets off transitions with commas when necessary

LINKING GRAMMAR AND WRITING

Using Transitions

You can show how your ideas are connected by using **transitions** between sentences and paragraphs. Words such as *however, also, therefore,* and *instead* are transitions that connect ideas. You can also repeat key words to link ideas. Transitions used at the beginning of a sentence are often followed by a comma. The transitions Jonathan uses to connect two paragraphs are underlined below.

Jackie was super in all the sports he played, and now professional scouts were observing him!

However, Jackie never made a deal with these sports scouts. Instead, he took a job at a children's camp.

For more information about using transitions to connect ideas, see Handbook 11, "Using Transitions," pages 234–238.

2. Make an alphabetical List of Sources. Only list those books or articles you actually took notes from and used in writing your report. Also list any people you interviewed. Notice on page 169 how Jonathan prepared his List of Sources.

Standards for Evaluation

INFORMATIVE WRITING

A report

- has an interesting introduction that clearly states the subject
- focuses on a single topic
- includes facts and details to support main ideas
- uses information from more than one source and includes a List of Sources
- ends with a strong conclusion

PROOFREAD

1. Proofread your report. Slowly and carefully reread your report. Correct any mistakes you might have made in grammar, spelling, capitalization, and punctuation.

2. Make a final copy. Read the Standards for Evaluation in the margin and decide if you were successful in completing the assignment. Make any additional changes you feel are necessary. Then write or print out a clean, final copy.

PUBLISH AND PRESENT

- **Present your report to another class.** Add visuals, such as models or graphs, to make your presentation more interesting.
- **Have a panel discussion.** If any classmates researched related topics, present these reports orally. You and the other presenters can then answer questions from the rest of the class.
- **Illustrate your report with drawings or photographs.** Then display your work on a class or school bulletin board.

Jackie Robinson smashed a three-run home run against the Jersey City Giants during his minor league baseball debut, April 18, 1946. Here a teammate congratulates Robinson.

REFLECT ON YOUR WRITING

WRITER TO WRITER

I do a lot of research in books, and I read a lot of old diaries. There's an enormous amount of material available if one will take the time to get it.

Louis L'Amour, writer

FOR YOUR PORTFOLIO

1. Add your report to your portfolio. First, take some time to reflect on your writing process. Attach your answers to these questions to your final draft.

- How did I find my topic?
- What part of this project was most fun for me?
- What are the special strengths of my final draft?
- How have other types of writing I've done helped me to write this report?

2. Explore additional writing ideas. See the suggestions for researching and writing a family history on pages 182–184 and Springboards on page 185.

Reteaching

After students have completed their papers, assess the needs of students who were not successful in developing an effective report of information and assign the appropriate handbook mini-lessons, as well as the Workshop Support Materials listed in the Teaching Preview, pages 163a–163b. Concepts commonly requiring reteaching for this assignment are the following:

- Handbook 7, Organizing Details, pp. 217–221
- Handbook 10, Improving Paragraphs, pp. 230–233

The following suggestions and resources may also be useful:

Lack of Supporting Details Magazines such as *Faces* and *Cobblestone* contain articles that are essentially research reports. With students, read and informally analyze details that make an article interesting.

Weak Conclusions Use Handbook 15, "Conclusions," pages 250–252, to review writing conclusions. Have students examine the successful conclusion in the Strong Response for this workshop on page 40 in the *Guidelines for Writing Assessment and Portfolio Use* booklet in the Teacher's Resource File.

Extension and Enrichment

1. Have students work in pairs to research a topic, perhaps one that has emerged during the class's writing process.
2. Challenge students to collaborate on a class newsletter, working individually or in pairs to research and write reports about issues that relate to school life.

Closure: Reflect on Your Writing

If you had students share their reports, you may want to encourage further reflection by asking them to respond to these questions: "Now that you have heard (read) other people's reports, what would you change in your report *if you had time*? What might you do differently the next time?" Have students record their responses and attach them to their reports as reminders for future report writing.

Related ASSIGNMENT

Starting from LITERATURE

Objectives

- To respond to and analyze a family history
- To plan and research a family history
- To draft, revise, and present a family history

Motivate

Ask volunteers to tell stories about events in their families' histories. Explain that in this assignment, students will write their own family histories.

BUILD ON PRIOR KNOWLEDGE

Ask students how immigrants traveled to the United States one hundred years ago. (primarily via steamship) Ask what they think the journey might have been like. (Samples: long, slow, crowded, difficult) Ask students what problems they think the immigrants faced when they arrived. (Samples: language barriers, finding work, finding a place to live) Why might people have been willing to face such difficulties? (Sample: They thought they would have better opportunities.)

SET A PURPOSE

After students read Starting from Literature, ask them what kinds of experiences their family members talk about. Who tells these stories, and on what occasions? Why are these stories important in their families? As students read Merrill Wilk's family history, urge them to think about how she heard about this story for the first time and why it became important to her.

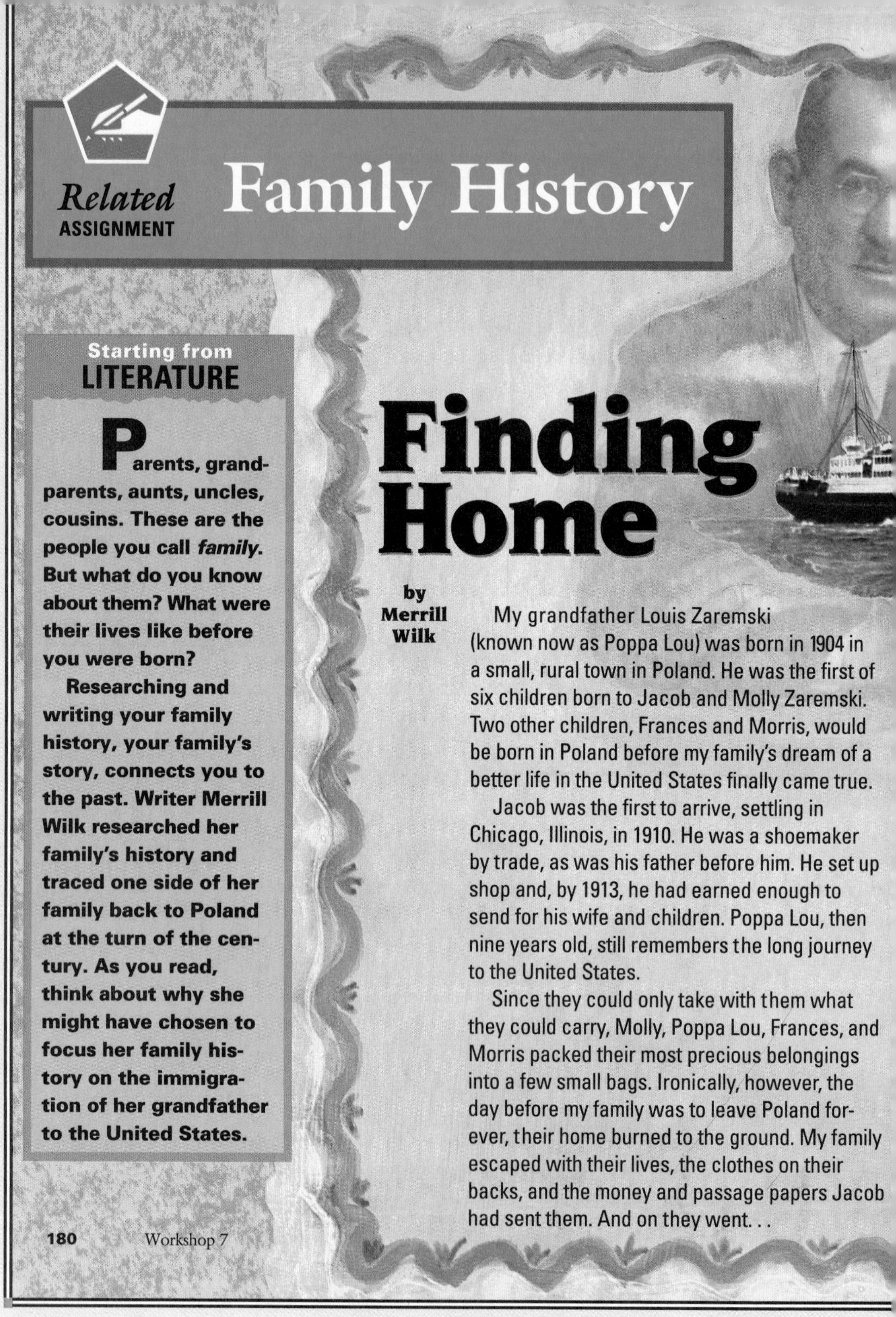

Related ASSIGNMENT

Family History

Starting from LITERATURE

Parents, grandparents, aunts, uncles, cousins. These are the people you call *family*. But what do you know about them? What were their lives like before you were born?

Researching and writing your family history, your family's story, connects you to the past. Writer Merrill Wilk researched her family's history and traced one side of her family back to Poland at the turn of the century. As you read, think about why she might have chosen to focus her family history on the immigration of her grandfather to the United States.

Finding Home

by Merrill Wilk

My grandfather Louis Zaremski (known now as Poppa Lou) was born in 1904 in a small, rural town in Poland. He was the first of six children born to Jacob and Molly Zaremski. Two other children, Frances and Morris, would be born in Poland before my family's dream of a better life in the United States finally came true.

Jacob was the first to arrive, settling in Chicago, Illinois, in 1910. He was a shoemaker by trade, as was his father before him. He set up shop and, by 1913, he had earned enough to send for his wife and children. Poppa Lou, then nine years old, still remembers the long journey to the United States.

Since they could only take with them what they could carry, Molly, Poppa Lou, Frances, and Morris packed their most precious belongings into a few small bags. Ironically, however, the day before my family was to leave Poland forever, their home burned to the ground. My family escaped with their lives, the clothes on their backs, and the money and passage papers Jacob had sent them. And on they went. . .

180 Workshop 7

Social Studies Connection

Ellis Island Between 1892 and 1938, a majority of immigrants from Europe entered the United States through an immigration center on Ellis Island in New York Harbor. Students may wish to find out if any forebears entered the United States at this historic place, now part of Statue of Liberty National Monument.

for FURTHER READING

Books to Read Many young adult books, both fiction and nonfiction, deal with the experience of immigration. One novel students might enjoy is the Newbery Award-winning *Dragonwings*, by Laurence Yep. It tells of the experiences of a Chinese boy who enters the United States in the early 1900s.

Over two thousand immigrants spent more than two weeks in steerage, below the decks of the steamship New Amsterdam. Canvas hammocks for sleeping lined the walls. Benches and long tables filled the room. Each night, heaping platters of boiled herring were served family style, two or three to a table. One night a very large woman sat across from Poppa Lou, quickly eating as much as she could. When she thought no one was looking, she took a whole plate of herring and put it between her feet, hiding it under the skirts of her floor-length dress! My clever grandfather had watched her from the corner of his eye. When he thought she wasn't looking, he slid beneath the table, found the plate of herring, and put it back on the table for everyone to share.

After my family reached New York, they took a train into Chicago's La Salle Street Station. They arrived a day early, however, so Jacob wasn't there to meet them. A traveler's aide who spoke Yiddish and English helped Molly give directions to a driver who then took my family to Jacob's address. Unfortunately, Jacob wasn't home. The driver didn't know what to do, so he asked a police officer for help.

Unwilling to leave them on the street, the officer took my family to jail. Molly, Poppa Lou, Frances, and Morris spent their first night in Chicago on two cots in a jail cell on the second floor of the 48th Street Station. But when the officer brought my family breakfast the next morning before taking them to Jacob's shop, they knew a better life had already begun.

Think & Respond

What details does Merrill Wilk include to bring the characters—and the situations—to life for her readers? What sources might she have used to find this information about her family?

Think & Respond

ELICIT PERSONAL RESPONSES

Give students three or four minutes to review Merrill Wilk's family history and to jot down details that bring the characters and situation to life. Then, in class discussion, have students share specific examples. Some particularly vivid details include those describing steerage, the rich details in the anecdote about Poppa Lou and the plate of herring, and those describing the family's first night in Chicago in a jail cell.

EXPLORE THE AUTHOR'S TECHNIQUES

As students consider where Merrill Wilk may have gotten her information, ask them to think about where they would get information about an event in their grandparents' early lives. Students should note that Merrill Wilk had a number of sources on which to draw. Her grandfather was probably her primary source for this account, but her great-aunt and great-uncle, Frances and Morris, also shared the experience and may have told her about it. In addition, her mother probably heard the story many times and could retell it, as could other aunts and uncles. Merrill's grandfather may also have written about his experiences in a journal, and he may have shared photographs, letters, and his family's passports and naturalization papers.

MULTICULTURAL Connection

Invite students who are immigrants themselves to share their own experiences and provide insight on how it feels to start over in a new country with a different language and unfamiliar customs.

Writing ON YOUR OWN

Ask students what kinds of information Merrill Wilk used to get and hold her readers' attention. (specific details, humorous anecdotes, unusual events) Suggest that as students research and write their own family histories, they try to uncover and include vivid details about their families' adventures.

Handbooks for Help and Practice

The following handbooks may be used as mini-lessons before students begin writing or as resources when problems arise.

- **Show, Don't Tell, pp. 239–242**
- **Interviewing Skills, p. 323**

Teaching Strategies

for PLANNING YOUR FAMILY HISTORY

STUMBLING BLOCK You may wish to confer with adopted or foster children privately and to assure them that the point of the assignment is to do research into the past, using people they know as a resource. They can write about their adopted or foster parents' families, or they might talk to other people they know. For example, an older neighbor might have a fascinating story to share.

Writing ON YOUR OWN

Family History

INVITATION TO *Write*

Writing a family history, like the one Merrill Wilk wrote, makes connections between today and yesterday, between who you are and who your ancestors were. When you write a family history, you research your family's past and write about it in a report.

Gather information about one aspect of your family's past. Then write a family history based on your research.

PLANNING YOUR FAMILY HISTORY

1. Discover what you know. What interesting or funny stories about family members have you heard? What do you know about the lives of your grandparents or great grandparents? Your immediate family members may have much of the information you need. Ask them to go through family photograph albums or scrapbooks with you and to share stories about people and events.

2. Choose a focus. It would be nearly impossible to tell all there is to know about your family in one short report. You could probably fill several books with stories about their past! Instead, think about what part of your family's history you'd most like to write about.

Writer's Choice Would you like to focus on one person's story, as Merrill Wilk did? Would you rather write about the way your relatives' lives were changed by an event in history, such as a natural disaster? Perhaps you'd prefer to trace one side of your family back in time. The choice is yours!

Researching Your History

1. Begin your research. First, make a list of research questions. You may want to know, for example, when and where your ancestors lived and died, when they came to this country, and what kinds of work they did.

2. Talk to members of your extended family. Ask your parents for the names and phone numbers or addresses of other people you might contact. You could even send a questionnaire to family members who live far away. Be sure to include a letter explaining your purpose.

3. Gather documents written by your family members. Journals, diaries, and letters are wonderful sources of information about your family's past. As you review them, take notes on what's most interesting to you and what suits your focus.

Writing TIP

You may wish to tape-record your interviews with family members. That way, you can replay the conversation later and write down the information you want to include in your report.

Writing Your Family History

1. Tell your family's story. You don't want to only list the facts—the "who married whom and when" kind of information. These facts may be part of your report, but be sure to include some of the personal stories your family members shared. Don't just *tell about* what happened to someone; include the kinds of details that *show* what people actually experienced.

2. Share your draft with others. Before you write your next draft, you may wish to share your work with a friend or a family member. A friend might help you find ways to check your organization or make your writing more interesting. A family member might help you fix any mistakes you might have made or fill in any gaps in your story.

Ships such as the one shown in this poster ad carried hundreds of thousands of immigrants from Europe to the United States in the early 1900s.

for BEGIN YOUR RESEARCH

HELPFUL HINT You might suggest that students ask "5W+H" questions *(Who? What? When? Where? Why?* and *How?)*, to help them get started.

for GATHER DOCUMENTS...

HELPFUL HINT Encourage students to use material from journals, diaries, and letters to enliven their family histories. Remind them, however, to ask permission before disclosing private correspondence.

for WRITING TIP

INDIVIDUALIZING INSTRUCTION: LD STUDENTS If students have difficulty transcribing their interviews and assembling information into written form, you might encourage them to draft their family histories on tape recorders and to present their finished work orally.

for TELL YOUR FAMILY'S STORY

HELPFUL HINT: QUOTATIONS
Explain to students that direct quotations can help make family histories more vivid. Allowing relatives to speak in their own words can give readers a better understanding of personalities. Quotations also can be an effective means of showing, rather than telling. If students need help with using quotation marks, you might refer them to pages 586–588 of Handbook 43, "Punctuation."

for REVIEWING YOUR HISTORY

SPEAKING AND LISTENING

Suggest that students ask someone else to read their papers aloud to them. They should listen for places where their reader stumbles, then revise to make the writing flow smoothly.

for PUBLISHING AND PRESENTING

MANAGING THE PAPER LOAD

You may wish to invite volunteers to present their family histories orally to the class and assess those presentations holistically. You might also consider holding a "Family History Day" in which different groups role-play important events in family members' lives.

Guidelines for Evaluation

AN EFFECTIVE FAMILY HISTORY

- focuses on a limited number of people and events
- includes personal details and anecdotes
- is supported by research
- uses transitions to show chronological order

REVIEWING YOUR HISTORY

1. Think about your limits. Check to see if you've tried to do too much in a short report. Are there too many names and dates? Does your history sound like a boring list of facts rather than an interesting story about interesting people? If so, think about how you can narrow your focus in your next draft. For example, you might zoom in on a smaller span of time, describing in detail what happened to two or three family members.

2. Does your story flow smoothly from beginning to end? Family histories are most often told in chronological order. Making a time line of the facts and events you've included can help you check your organization. Rereading your draft aloud is another way to see if the order of events is clear. Is any information out of place? Include any transitions, details, or stories that would make your history easier to follow.

Writing TIP

Drawing a family tree can help you keep the relationships between your family members clear. For your readers' reference, attach a copy of your family tree to your report.

PUBLISHING AND PRESENTING

- **Make copies of your family history.** Share your final piece with any family members who helped you with your research. You may also wish to send copies of your history to family members living far away.
- **Display your family history on a class bulletin board.** Include a drawing of your family tree and photographs of the people you've written about. Be sure to write a caption for each photo so your readers will be able to connect people's names with their faces.

European immigrants at Ellis Island, New York

Springboards

Current Events Pick a topic from the news that interests you, and gather more information on it from several sources. Then stage a radio or television news program—recording it on videotape or audiotape—and present it to other classes.

Social Studies Working in small groups, choose a country that you'd like to learn more about. Each person should select one aspect of that country to research—geography, culture and customs, industry, natural resources, or government, for example. Assemble the reports to make a class encyclopedia.

Village Scene in the Punjab
bout 1820), Gulam Ali Khan.

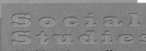

Art Visit an art museum or look through art books at the library to find an artist whose work you especially like. Then find out what you can about the artist or about the artist's style (expressionism or pop art, for example).

LITERATURE Do some research on a place or time period described in a favorite story or novel. Then write up your findings in a report or make an oral presentation to your class. You may wish to read aloud passages from the work that bring the time and place to life.

Springboards

Teaching Strategies

GENERAL NOTE

KEY TO UNDERSTANDING Be sure students understand that all of these prompts involve research. Students will need to identify research questions, locate sources, collect information from several sources, and document the information.

for CURRENT EVENTS

INDIVIDUALIZING INSTRUCTION: AUDITORY LEARNERS Students who learn best from listening might find the current events project especially appealing. Suggest that they do some research by observing television news broadcasts and listening to radio reports. Students should have note cards and pencils handy. They might also want to use a tape or video recorder. A source card should include the time, date, station, name of the newscast, and the reporter's name.

for SOCIAL STUDIES

INDIVIDUALIZING INSTRUCTION: KINESTHETIC AND VISUAL LEARNERS Encourage students who like to draw and paint to make maps and illustrations for the class encyclopedia. Remind them that the details in their drawings must be supported by research.

ART NOTE

The Punjab (from Sanskrit for "five rivers") is an agricultural region on a high, dry plain. In 1947 the Punjab province was divided between India and Pakistan. Ask students what they can guess about daily life in this village.

Reviewing Sentence Composing Skills

Objectives

- To identify and imitate sentence openers, subject-verb splits, and sentence closers
- To unscramble sentence parts and imitate the sentence structure of professional models

Teaching Strategies

for REVIEWING SENTENCE COMPOSING SKILLS

HELPFUL HINT: PUNCTUATING SENTENCE PARTS To reinforce the use of commas with sentence openers, subject-verb splits, and closers, you might ask volunteers to read the model sentences aloud. Call attention to the natural pauses that occur. If students need more practice, direct them to pages 574–580 of Handbook 43, "Punctuation."

Additional Resource

Sentence Composing Copy Masters, pp. 13–14

Answer Key

A. Identifying and Imitating Sentences

Sentence parts are identified. Student imitations will vary but should follow the same pattern.

1. subject-verb split
2. sentence closer
3. subject-verb split
4. sentence opener
5. sentence opener

Sentence

COMPOSING

Reviewing Sentence Composing Skills

In the preceding sentence-composing exercises, you saw different ways professional writers add variety and interest to their sentences.

Sentence Opener	Outside, he murmured to himself. **William H. Armstrong, *Sounder***
Subject-Verb Split	Agatha's mother, frantic now, beat the door of the vault with her hands. **O. Henry, "A Retrieved Reformation"**
Sentence Closer	The man was about fifty, overweight but solid-looking. **Frank Bonham, *Chief***

A. Identifying and Imitating Sentences The sentences below illustrate the sentence-composing skills you have studied. For each sentence, write whether the underlined part is a sentence opener, subject-verb split, or sentence closer. Then write a sentence of your own that imitates each sentence.

1. Templeton, asleep in the straw, heard the commotion and awoke.
E. B. White, *Charlotte's Web*

2. John dusted off his best chair, a rocker with its runners off.
Joseph Krumgold, *Onion John*

3. Mr. Simpson, director of the Order, looked up from the work on his desk and was surprised to see Maggie.
Olive W. Burt, "Banker Maggie Walker"

4. Tall, beautiful, fair, the youth's appearance was greeted with a low hum of admiration and anxiety. **Frank R. Stockton, "The Lady, or the Tiger?"**

5. Then, wildly, like animals escaped from their caves, the children ran and ran in shouting circles. **Ray Bradbury, "All Summer in a Day"**

B. Unscrambling and Imitating Sentences Unscramble each set of sentence chunks below. Create a sentence that has the same order of chunks as the model. Then write a sentence of your own that imitates each model.

1. Model One of them, a tan Jersey named Blind Tillie, was Cold Sassy's champion milk producer.

Olive Ann Burns, *Cold Sassy Tree*

a Vulcan called Spock / an officer on the *Enterprise* / was George's favorite *Star Trek* character

2. Model Instead of answering, the minister let out a startled yelp and sprang to his feet.

Farley Mowat, "Owls in the Family"

the runner reached out his hand / and grabbed for the water bottle / rather than stopping

3. Model I saw Lottie for the first time one afternoon in our own kitchen, stealing chocolate cake.

Jean Stafford, "Bad Characters"

setting the home run record / in the memorable game that year in Atlanta / my grandfather saw Henry Aaron

4. Model When flour was scarce, the boy's mother would wrap the leftover biscuits in a clean flour sack and put them away for the next meal.

William H. Armstrong, *Sounder*

and wash them down with soft drinks / after the game was over / at their favorite stand / would buy hot dogs / the little league team

5. Model The hawk, ruffled in misery, brooding in ferocity, came forth in hunger and hate.

D'Arcy Niland, "The Parachutist"

received their medals with honor and pride / exhausted from competition, glowing from victory / the Olympic team

B. Unscrambling and Imitating Sentences

Unscrambled sentences are given. Student imitations will vary but should follow the same pattern.

1. An officer on the *Enterprise,* a Vulcan called Spock, was George's favorite *Star Trek* character.
2. Rather than stopping, the runner reached out his hand and grabbed for the water bottle.
3. My grandfather saw Henry Aaron in the memorable game that year in Atlanta, setting the home run record.
4. After the game was over, the little league team would buy hot dogs at their favorite stand and wash them down with soft drinks.
5. The Olympic team, exhausted from competition, glowing from victory, received their medals with honor and pride.

ART NOTE The Huichol live in a remote, mountainous region in the Sierra Madre in north-central Mexico. They worship gods associated with nature. They believe these gods control every aspect of their daily lives. Huichol men and women place gourd bowls like these in sacred places as offerings to their gods. The Huichol hope that when the gods come to drink from the bowls, they will drink in the people's prayers and grant their wishes. Therefore, Huichol women artists place an arrow in such bowls and a bit of their embroidery as a prayer for success in their craft.

Upper left. Around the bowl's edge are two human figures, three temples, and two deer—whom the Huichol regard as sacred and call Elder Brother. An offering of coins is pressed into the wax in the bowl's center.

Upper right. Pilgrims journey to collect peyote, a cactus whose small buttons they chew in religious ceremonies.

Lower right. Temples and human figures surround three serpents. The snake is a recurrent theme in Huichol sacred art. Wind, lightning, rivers, rain, corn, arrows, ribbons, and human hair are all depicted as serpents.

Lower left. In a Huichol myth, a man and his dog escape a great flood that devastates the earth. After the flood, the dog turns into a woman and bears the man many children.

Note with students how carefully these bowls are constructed. Bead by bead, the artist creates a design that tells a story and expresses his or her wishes. You might compare the beads to the words students will use in this next section (the Writing Handbook) to tell their stories and express their wishes.

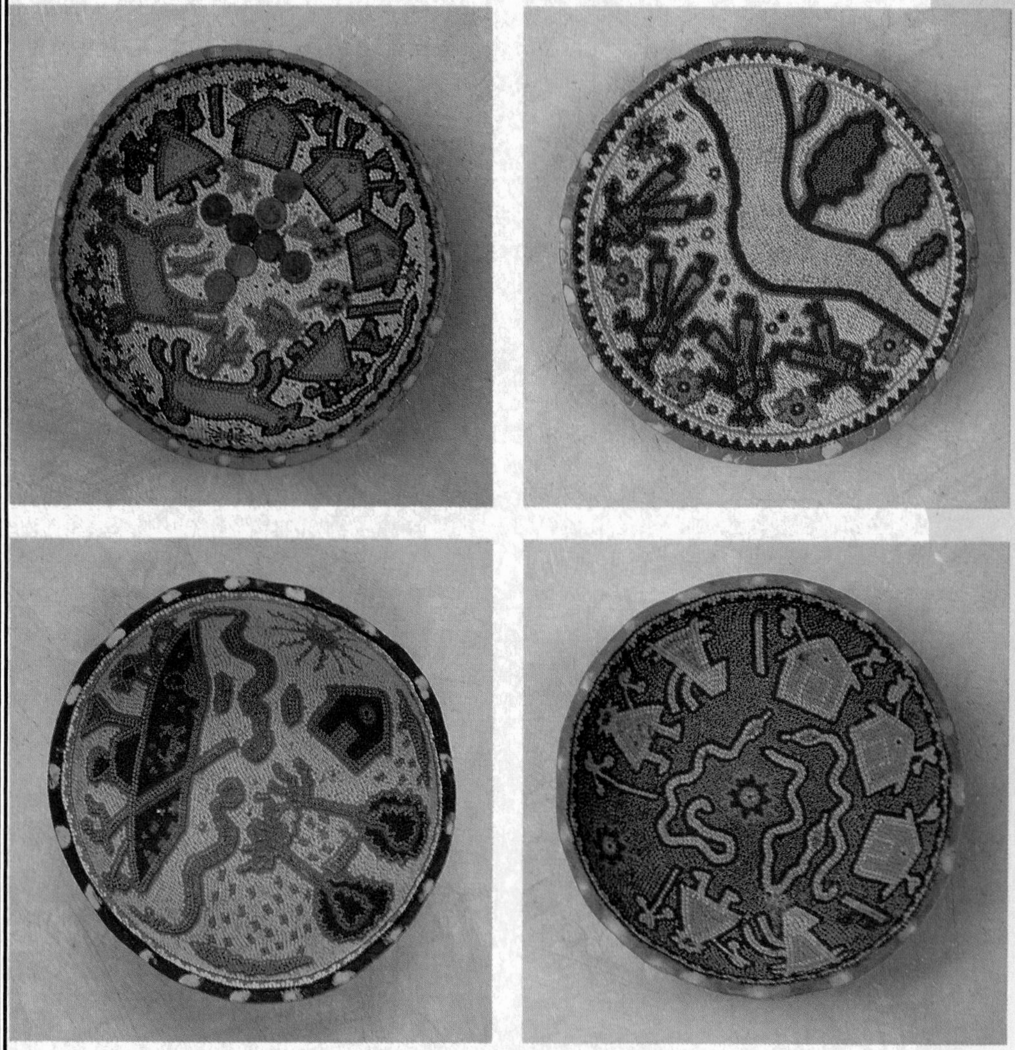

These ceremonial bowls are made by the Huichol people of central Mexico. Each bowl is made from half of a gourd. An artist coats the gourd with wax and then, using a needle, carefully presses glass beads and other objects into the wax. The illustrations on the bowls tell stories from Huichol mythology.

Writing Handbook

MINI-LESSONS

Writing Process

Style

Academic Skills

MINI-LESSONS

Writing Handbook

The mini-lessons in this Handbook may be used for a variety of purposes.

Preteaching—to introduce specific concepts and skills before beginning a Guided or Related Assignment

Reference—to provide extra help and practice as students problem-solve their way through a piece of writing

Reteaching—to remedy specific problems in student writing

To match mini-lessons to an assignment, see "Handbooks for Help and Practice" in the teaching notes for the Writer's Workshops, and handbook cross-references on the pupil page.

SketchBook

Objective

- To use the illustration and suggested writing prompts as springboards to informal writing

WRITING WARM-UPS

Use these ungraded, risk-free activities as warm-ups for the Writing Process Handbooks. After students have responded to at least one prompt, suggest that they retain their responses in their folders for possible use later in the year.

Students who use the first prompt may also wish to respond to the second, which follows logically from it. The third prompt is more general and need not refer to the subject of design.

SketchBook

WRITING WARM-UPS

- What would you like to design? Try drawing some of your ideas.
- Where did you get your ideas for your design? Jot down some of your thoughts.
- What is important to you? Write about some of the things you care about.

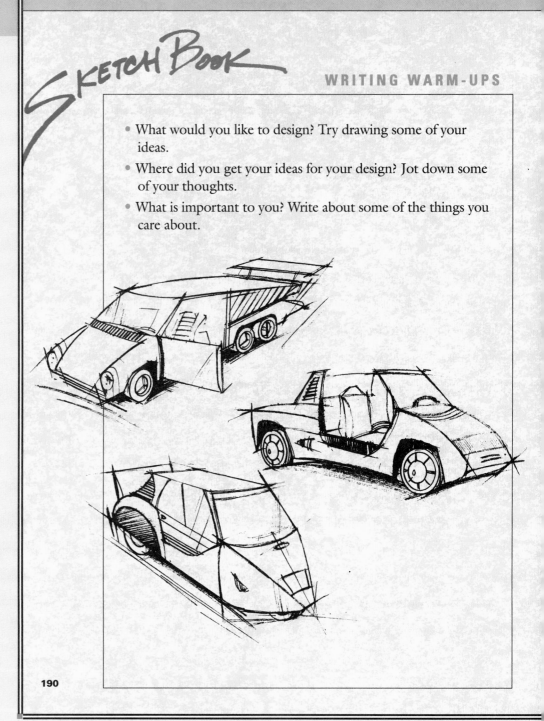

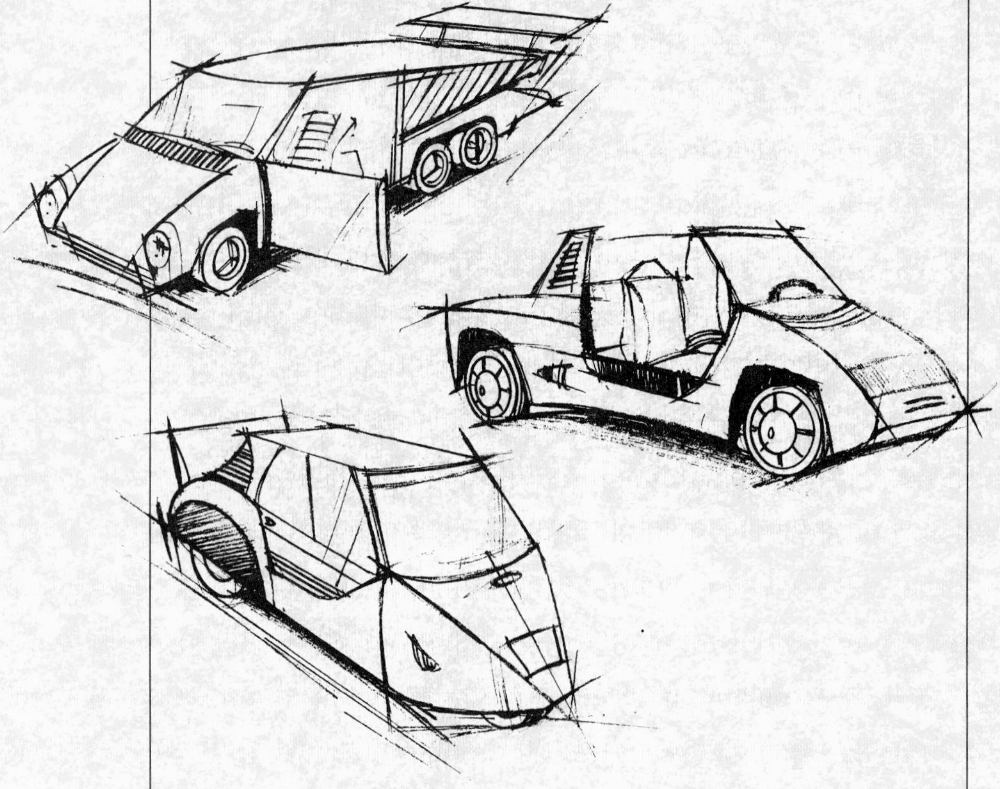

Writing Process

WRITING HANDBOOKS

A lot can happen between the time a designer starts scribbling and the time a project is finished. There may be nany false starts and many trips back to the drawing board. Then, at last, the final design takes shape.

The process of writing can be like that too. As you start xploring your thoughts, you may come up with new ideas, or even change your mind about what you want to say. Finally, hough, your ideas take shape. The handbooks that follow can help you make the most of your own writing process.

WRITING HANDBOOKS

Writing Process

INTRODUCING THE HANDBOOKS

Ask students to discuss how designs such as one of those on page 190 becomes a finished automobile like the one on this page. Whether or not students know a great deal about the manufacturing of automobiles, they will grasp that the process begins in the imagination and ends on the showroom floor.

Encourage students to discuss how writing a paper or a story is, likewise, a process that begins with an individual's idea and ends with a tangible product. Let students know that in the Writing Process Handbooks, they will learn a number of techniques and tips that will help them turn their own writing ideas into realities.

WRITING
HANDBOOK
1

Thinking with Pictures

Objectives

- To understand how various graphic devices are useful for finding and organizing ideas
- To choose appropriate graphic devices and use them to find and organize ideas about given topics

Related Mini-Lessons

For information on topics related to thinking with pictures, see the following mini-lessons:

- **Finding a Starting Point, pp. 197–202**
- **Thinking Skills, pp. 320–322**

Teaching Strategies

GENERAL NOTE

HELPFUL HINT As students work through this handbook, point out how the graphic devices relate to specific thinking tasks. For examples, pictures and diagrams help us think about the way objects are arranged in space. Clusters help us make connections between ideas. Observation charts focus our attention on sensory details, and compare-and-contrast charts prompt us to analyze likenesses and differences.

for GRAPHICS YOU CAN USE

KEY TO UNDERSTANDING Be sure students understand that a *graphic* is any visual device: drawing, chart, map, graph, and so on.

for PICTURES

HELPFUL HINT Tell students that when they write descriptions; drawings will help them observe details that should be noticed and qualities that should be emphasized.

WRITING
HANDBOOK
1

How Do I Get Started?

Thinking with Pictures

"I need an idea!" How many times have you said this? You might need an idea for a Halloween costume or for a theme party. Maybe you're trying to think of that perfect gift for a friend. Perhaps you want to think up a story for a skit at school. You might just need an idea for something to do in your spare time or for a way to solve a misunderstanding with a friend.

GRAPHICS YOU CAN USE

Thinking doesn't always have to involve words. Sometimes sketching a picture or making a chart can help you find an idea you didn't know you had. These graphics can also help you organize ideas you've already collected.

In the following sections, you will learn about graphic devices you can use to help you work out your ideas. Pictures and clusters help you discover new ideas. Observation charts, compare-and-contrast charts, and story maps help you organize and expand ideas you presently have. These devices are useful in everyday situations and also in writing.

Pictures

Drawing a diagram, a picture, or a map can help you try out your ideas. For example, maybe you want to rearrange the furniture in your room. Before you start moving the furniture, you might draw a diagram of the new arrangement to see if you like it. Your diagram might even lead you to discover arrangements you like better.

In the following example, Jody drew a diagram of how she wanted to rearrange the furniture in her room. Notice how the first diagram led to new ideas and a better arrangement of the furniture in the second diagram.

MULTICULTURAL Connection

Some students might want to investigate graphic symbols or designs linked to a cultural heritage. Flags, crests, or seals are obvious starting points for ideas. Students also might investigate graphic designs commonly used in clothing, rugs, jewelry, or furniture. Encourage students to explore any personal meanings these graphic designs or symbols might have for them.

Clusters

A good way to find new ideas and details is to make a **cluster,** a graphic that connects ideas. For example, imagine you are trying to think of a costume to wear for Halloween. To make a cluster, write down your starting point in the middle of a sheet of paper and circle it. Write related ideas around this circle as you think of them. Circle each one and draw a line connecting it to the main idea or to one of the other ideas you added. Continue adding ideas to the cluster until you find one you'd like to use.

Look at the cluster one sixth grader made to find an idea for a costume. Notice that once he decided on a costume, he made a second cluster, listing items needed for the costume.

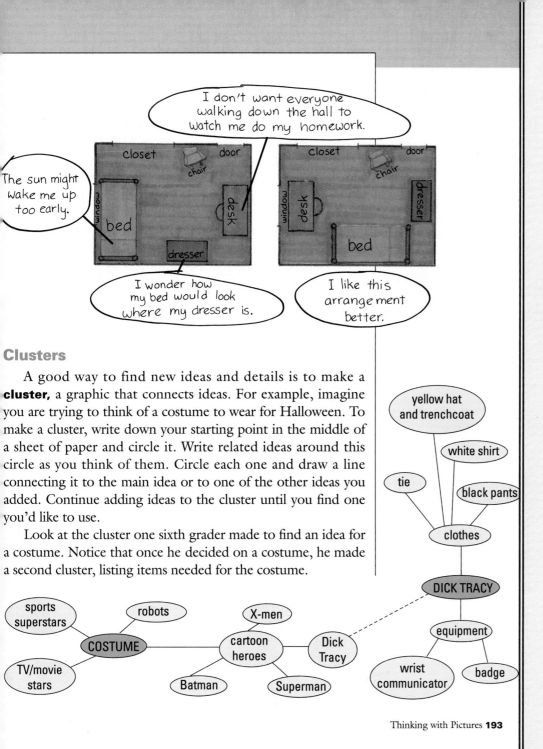

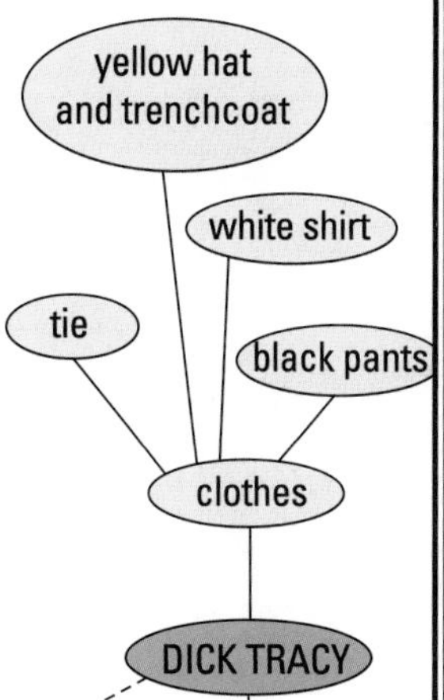

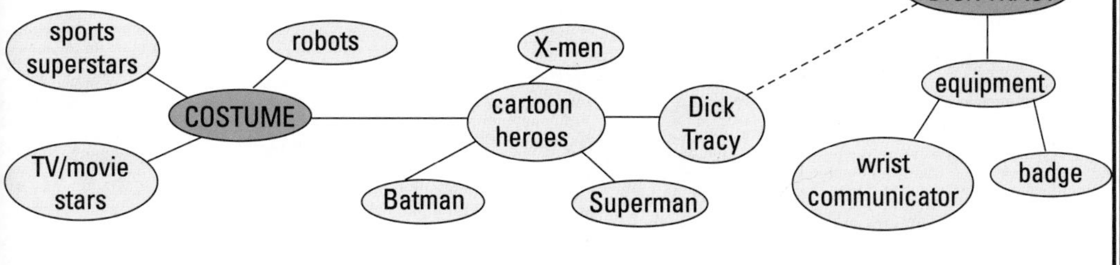

for CLUSTERS

USING THE MODEL Stress the effectiveness of making two or more clusters to explore a topic, using each cluster to narrow the focus further. Point out that in the student model, the second cluster focuses on an idea from the first cluster. You might work with students to create a third, even more focused, cluster. For example, students might put EQUIPMENT at the center, then cluster ideas for improvising various kinds of equipment for a Dick Tracy costume.

for CLUSTERS

CRITICAL THINKING: CLASSIFYING Ask students to decide which items in the Dick Tracy costume cluster represent general categories and which name specific details. ("Clothes" and "equipment" are general; the others are specific, although students might suggest ways of making some of them [such as "tie"] even more specific.)

PROFESSIONAL NOTEBOOK

Gabrielle Rico, who developed the technique of clustering, offers the following insights in her book *Writing the Natural Way:* "[When] I first developed the clustering process, I followed an impulse to circle the words as they spilled out onto the paper, for each word and phrase seemed to be a complex, self-contained mini-whole in my mind, like an image. . . . By its very nature the circle centers, focuses. . . . As the cluster expanded before my eyes, each encircled mini-whole gradually became part of a larger whole, a pattern of meaning that took shape as I began to write."

for OBSERVATION CHARTS

HELPFUL HINT You might suggest that students consider adding a sixth category, *Emotions,* to observation charts. Point out that recording emotions and reactions can be an important part of observing.

for OBSERVATION CHARTS

INDIVIDUALIZING INSTRUCTION: ESL STUDENTS A structured format like an observation chart can help ESL students not only to find ideas but also to build their English vocabularies. Urge students to list at least five entries under each category when they use an observation chart. ESL students also might make personal vocabulary lists with headings for words related to sight, sound, and so on. They can add to these lists throughout the year.

for OBSERVATION CHARTS

COLLABORATIVE OPPORTUNITY Point out that filling in an observation chart could help students in social studies classes to report on a current event, to imagine a moment in history, or to bring into focus what they know about another part of the world. Group students and ask them to brainstorm as to opportunities for using observation charts in other classes.

Observation Charts

Sometimes you need to think of details about a person, a place, a thing, or an experience. Your friends in the neighborhood might be having a homemade-cookie contest with you as a judge. You might be doing a science experiment to find out how the color of food affects taste. You might be making a collage about a day at the beach. An **observation chart** can help you.

To make an observation chart, first choose a subject. Then make five columns, one for each of the senses. Think about details related to the subject—things you see, hear, feel, taste, and smell. Write them in the proper columns.

The observation chart below shows the details one sixth grader thought of for a collage of pictures about a day at the beach.

Observation Chart

A Day at the Beach				
Sight	**Sound**	**Touch**	**Taste**	**Smell**
sand waves sunbathers lifeguards sand castles boats seashells flies	crashing of waves kids laughing lifeguard's whistle blowing music from radio bells on ice cream cart	hot sand cool water greasy sunscreen lotion	salty ocean water soft drinks snacks	salt air seaweed sunscreen lotion

Art Connection

Tell students that making a collage is another way to express thoughts and generate details. You might invite students to bring in collages they have made and to talk about the ideas that the collages express.

Compare-and-Contrast Charts

A **compare-and-contrast chart** can help you chart similarities and differences between items. Perhaps you are doing a science experiment, for example. You want to prove that green plants cannot grow without sunlight. Making a compare-and-contrast chart can help you find the details you need to report your results.

Compare-and-Contrast Chart

Characteristics	Subjects Compared—Changes After Two Weeks	
	Green plant in dark closet	**Green plant in sunlight**
Height	No change	Grew 2.5 cm
Thickness of stem	No change	Increased by 2 mm
Number of leaves	No change	2 new leaves
Appearance	Clear yellow color, wilted, almost dead 	Green color, strong and still growing 

Story Maps

A **story map** helps you to sort out the plot of a story and to see areas that need more work. For instance, imagine that you and your friends want to put on a skit at a neighborhood party. You could use a story map to plan and organize your skit. Start by listing the characters. Then describe the setting, or where the story takes place. Finally, outline the plot, or the events that make up the action of your story. Be sure to organize the events in the order they will take place.

The story map on the next page shows a skit planned by a group of friends for younger children in their neighborhood. The story map also shows a hole in the plot.

for COMPARE-AND-CONTRAST CHARTS

CRITICAL THINKING: INTERPRETING Ask students to interpret the information in the chart. How was the experiment set up? (one green plant placed in a closet, another in sunlight) What happened to the plant that got sunlight? (It grew, sprouted new leaves, and remained green and healthy.) What happened to the one without sunlight? (It didn't grow; it became yellow, wilted, and almost died.) In what ways or characteristics did the two plants differ? (height, thickness of stem, number of leaves, appearance)

for STORY MAPS

KEY TO UNDERSTANDING: PLOT OUTLINES Explain to students that to create a plot outline they would organize events in chronological order—the order in which events occur in time. If students need help with chronological order, you might assign pages 218–219 of Handbook 7, "Organizing Details."

for STORY MAPS

COLLABORATIVE OPPORTUNITY
You might group students and have each group put on the skit outlined in the story map on page 196. Instruct groups to decide how to fill in the hole in the plot. Let each group perform its version of the skit for the rest of the class. Afterward, discuss the various interpretations of the story map.

Thinking with Pictures **195**

GENERAL NOTE

INDIVIDUALIZING INSTRUCTION: ESL STUDENTS Emphasize that pictures, charts, clusters, and story maps that use only key words are excellent ways for writers to get started. These devices enable writers with limited mastery of English to record ideas as quickly as they can think in their native languages.

for PRACTICE YOUR SKILLS

MANAGING THE PAPER LOAD As students work, walk around the room, checking students' progress in developing graphic devices. By making sure now that students are including all appropriate elements, you can reduce your time in assessing final products.

Additional Resources

Writing Resource Book, pp. 43–45
Thinking Skills Transparency Pack

Answers to Practice Your Skills

A. Answers will vary. All drawings, diagrams, or maps, however, should have labels to identify the parts of the picture.

B. Answers will vary. All clusters should show the main idea circled in the center of the page. Related ideas and details should be written around the main idea and circled; they should also be connected by lines to one another or to the main idea.

C. Answers will vary. An observation chart should contain details relating to all five senses. On a compare-and-contrast chart, students should identify the characteristics being compared—that is, the points of comparison and contrast. On a story map, students should identify characters and briefly describe the setting. The plot should consist of background information and story events in order of their occurrence.

Writing **TIP**

Another way to map out a story is to make a series of drawings, like a cartoon strip.

Story Map—A Fairy Tale

Characters	Goldilocks, Papa Bear, Momma Bear, Baby Bear
Setting	The Bears' apartment
Plot	
Background	Momma Bear makes three pizzas. The bears hop on their dirt bikes and go out to buy pop.
Event 1	Goldilocks is on her way to Peggy's apartment for dinner. She gets confused and goes into the Bears' apartment by mistake.
Event 2	She samples each pizza. One is too spicy. One tastes fishy. She eats the whole cheese pizza.
Event 3	She's tired. One bed has a broken spring. She's allergic to the feathers in the second bed. She falls asleep on the water bed.
Event 4	The Bear family returns from the store.
Event 5	(WHAT TWIST SHOULD WE USE NEXT?)
Ending	Goldilocks makes friends with the Bears. They phone Peggy and invite her over for pizza.

Practice Your Skills

A. Choose one of the topics listed below and make a drawing, a diagram, or a map to develop ideas for the invention.

a homework robot   a land-sea-air bike

B. Choose one of the topics listed below and make a cluster to develop ideas for a club for people interested in the subject.

food   computers   travel   fan club

C. Choose one of these topics and make an observation chart, a compare-and-contrast chart, or a story map about it.

a camping trip   meeting friends at the mall   a parade

What Do I Write About?

Finding a Starting Point

WRITING HANDBOOK 2

Ideas for writing can come to you in many ways. Sometimes you can see an idea in a photo, for example. What writing ideas can you get from this photo? Probably the best source of ideas, however, is *you.* Both your personal world and the larger world around you can provide an endless supply of ideas. All you need to do is learn how to tap into them.

WRITER TO WRITER

The first place I go to find ideas is in my head.

Jaime Carr, student
York, Pennsylvania

FINDING IDEAS

"I can't think of anything to write about." If you've said this to yourself, the problem may be that you don't know where to look for writing ideas. Here are some places you can begin your search.

for **FURTHER READING**

Books to Read Point out that viewing fine art can often spark writing ideas. Interested students might enjoy the following books:

- Robert Cumming, *Just Look: A Book About Paintings*
- Beryl Barr, *Wonders, Warriors, and Beasts Abounding*

In addition, allow interested students to peruse the Fine Art Transparency Pack in the Teacher's Resource File, which contains fourteen full-color transparencies of thought-provoking works, such as *The Flying Carriage* by Marc Chagall.

WRITING HANDBOOK 2

Finding a Starting Point

Objectives

- To identify various techniques for finding writing ideas
- To choose an appropriate technique and use it to find writing ideas for a given topic

Related Mini-Lessons

For information on topics related to finding a starting point, see the following mini-lessons:

- **Thinking with Pictures, pp. 192–196**
- **Finding a Focus, pp. 203–204**

Teaching Strategies

GENERAL NOTE

HELPFUL HINT Explain to students that this handbook offers a variety of ways to find and explore writing ideas. Encourage students to experiment with each technique. Tell them that some of the techniques may not seem to fit their personal writing process at this point, but that they will find others that will work well for them.

for WRITER TO WRITER

PERSONAL TOUCH After reading aloud Jaime Carr's comment, share some of your own idea-finding strategies. Then invite students to share some of their favorite ways of finding writing ideas. For example, do any students have a favorite "thinking place"? Does it help to listen to a certain kind of music when they're searching for ideas? How many have found ideas in books, in stories, or from photographs of fine art? How many keep a writing journal or a page in their notebooks for recording writing ideas?

for YOUR PERSONAL WORLD

HELPFUL HINT Emphasize to students that good writing ideas need not always be about things or people they like. Some of the best ideas may be about subjects they dislike or that anger or confuse them. Encourage them to keep track of both likes and dislikes.

for YOUR PERSONAL WORLD

COLLABORATIVE OPPORTUNITY

To help students explore their personal worlds, have them work together to develop questions they can use to probe their personal interests. For example: What character in a movie fascinates me the most? Who is my favorite relative? What was my scariest experience ever? my funniest? What am I good at doing? Have each student write five to ten favorite questions on separate slips of paper and drop them into a hat you have brought in for this purpose. Later you can have each student retrieve from the "thinking cap" a question that he or she can use as a starting point for freewriting.

for THE LARGER WORLD

COLLABORATIVE OPPORTUNITY

Invite students to begin a class clip file. They can bring in clippings (from magazines and other sources) that they find interesting or that they think will intrigue other students. Provide an easily accessible envelope, box, or set of hanging folders to store the clippings. You might review clippings periodically. Encourage students to continue to add to the file throughout the year and to browse through it often.

Your Personal World

The first place to look for writing ideas is in your personal world. Your daily life and all your memories, hobbies, and interests can be sources for writing ideas.

Your Daily Life Your everyday experiences with family, friends, people you meet, things you read, and events you observe may be sources of writing ideas. Your experiences may make you surprised, excited, angry, or disappointed. Behind each of these experiences, there's a story waiting to be told.

Memories How can you jar loose memories of experiences in your life? You might begin by reading your journal or by looking at photos. Talk with family members and friends about memories you share with them. What experiences and feelings come to mind?

Hobbies and Interests You may not realize it, but you are an expert in something. Think about your skills, hobbies, and interests. What might your readers want to know more about?

> *Writing* **TIP**
>
> You might create a stockpile of writing ideas by making your own Top Ten lists of favorite persons, places, or things.

The Larger World

What are people talking about? What's going on in your town and around the world? Look for things around you, in the news, or on TV that interest you, puzzle you, or concern you. The special section of the newspaper shown here has articles about the Olympics, Columbus, and kids in Russia. Are there writing ideas here for you?

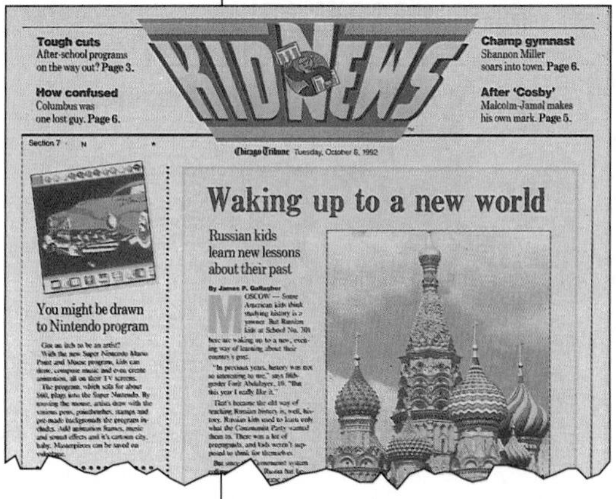
Tough cuts
After-school programs on the way out? Page 3.
How confused
Columbus was one lost guy. Page 6.
KIDNEWS
Champ gymnast
Shannon Miller soars into town. Page 6.
After 'Cosby'
Malcolm-Jamal makes his own mark. Page 5.
Section 7 N
Chicago Tribune Tuesday, October 6, 1992
You might be drawn to Nintendo program
Waking up to a new world
Russian kids learn new lessons about their past
By James P. Gallagher

When you see interesting newspaper articles, ads, and photos, clip them out or copy them. Then save the clippings in a notebook, a folder, or a section of your journal. A clip file can be a gold mine of writing ideas.

WAYS TO TAP IDEAS

Now that you know where to look for writing ideas, you need to know how to dig into these idea sources. Here are some ways you can start getting ideas down on paper.

Freewriting

Just as the name says, **freewriting** means writing freely. You write down anything that comes to mind. Don't worry about spelling, grammar, punctuation, or even making sense. The goal is to discover what you are thinking about. A good way to start is to choose one idea and write for a set period of time—say three minutes. Try to keep your pencil moving, even if you can't think of anything. If you keep at it, something will come to mind.

Look at the example below. This student came up with a wide range of ideas. Notice how he kept finding ideas even after he thought he had run out.

Student MODEL

OK. I like science fiction. Books, movies—Terminator II, Star Trek, Android, Aliens—even comics—Flash Gordon, ray guns. Its funny to see the old movies with their bogus special effects. I saw one where the spaceship looked like a tin can on a string. Now what? My mind is blank. Empty, empty, empty. Outer space is empty. How big is outer space? Are people living on other planets? I can't think of anything else. Nothing. I could list my favorite space movies. I could rate all the movies I've seen. Time's up!

How special effects have changed over the years could be a good topic.

I might want to do some more freewriting on this idea.

I could write a review of some space movies.

for FREEWRITING

HELPFUL HINT Tell students not to read over their freewriting until after they have finished—stopping to read it interrupts the flow of thoughts. Reassure them that it's fine if most of their freewriting does not produce useful material. If students get even one good idea from a full page of freewriting, they will have done well.

for FREEWRITING

USING THE MODEL Point out the place in the model where the student writes "Empty, empty, empty." Tell students that if they run out of things to say when freewriting, they can get going again by repeating a single word or phrase. In this student's case, the repetition prompted another idea. Students might repeat the last word they wrote, or they might repeat a word such as *empty, nothing,* or *blank.* The important thing is to keep their pencils moving.

for FREEWRITING

HELPFUL HINT Invite students to try out freewriting. They might focus on any of the sources listed on page 198, such as memories. They might focus on an object that means something special to them—for example, a favorite old shirt, a childhood toy, or a "lucky" baseball mitt. Alternatively, students might prefer to try answering a question they've picked out of the "thinking cap." (See page 198.) Tell them to begin with their subject or question and see where their ideas lead them.

SPICE BOX

The following activity requires preparation, but it can help students use freewriting to explore their imaginations. You will need an overhead projector, a glass pie pan, a glass of water, food coloring, and a seltzer tablet. Set the pie pan on the glass surface of the projector. Pour about an inch of water into the pie pan and turn on the projector. Slowly add drops of food coloring to the water. Invite students to freewrite about whatever the swirling colors bring to mind. To give the "show" extra pizzazz, add a seltzer tablet.

for TALKING WITH OTHERS

SPEAKING AND LISTENING

Encourage students to be considerate of others' feelings during discussions of ideas. Help them understand that careful listening is sometimes just as helpful as offering their own points of view. Point out that summarizing what they hear (for example, "So what you're saying is . . .") and asking for clarification (for example, "Do you mean . . .?") are two useful listening strategies.

for LISTING

CRITICAL THINKING: CLASSIFYING

Ask students to suggest one or two examples or details that could go under each of the items on Lisa's list of collections. (Sample: Under *Comic Books,* students might suggest superhero comic books, Wonder Woman comics, early Disney comics, and so on.)

Writing TIP

You can use freewriting anytime during the writing process to find ideas or to focus your thinking.

When you have finished freewriting, look over your paper and circle the ideas that catch your interest. Then freewrite on one of those ideas. This second freewriting is a good way to discover details about a subject. It also lets you decide whether you really like the topic enough to continue writing about it.

Talking with Others

A good way to examine a writing idea, and possibly to find a better idea, is to talk with other people. Try bouncing ideas off your classmates, friends, and family members. Give everyone a chance to talk. Build on one another's suggestions. If you listen carefully and ask questions, you may find new ways to look at your topic.

Listing

Another way to tap into writing ideas is to create a list. When you make a list, you start with a broad subject or idea. You then write examples or details related to the broad topic. Here is Lisa's list of things she and her friends collect.

COLLECTIONS
stamps
shells
comic books
bugs
rocks
baseball cards
compact discs
board games

After looking over her list, Lisa decided to explore one of the ideas. She made another list. Then she realized that she had enough ideas to begin drafting.

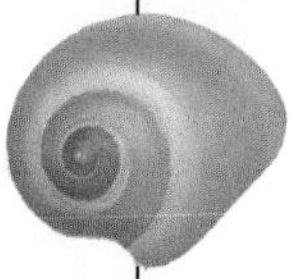

SHELLS

colors	jewelry
labels	conch shells
displays	cowrie shells
shapes	decorations

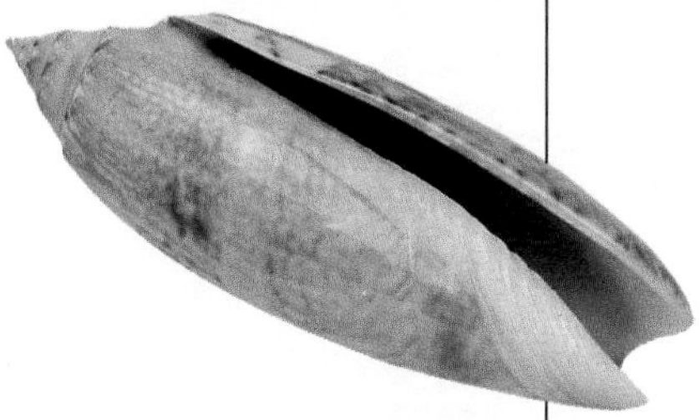

Drawing

You can also draw pictures, diagrams, and charts about people, places, and events that you might want to write about. Your drawings can help you "see" a subject and think about what you want to say. See Handbook 1, "Thinking with Pictures," pages 192–196, for more ideas on using graphic devices to explore ideas.

MAKING AN IDEA YOUR OWN

Writing becomes better when you care—when you have a reason for writing. Look for a personal connection to a topic. Don't just pick "my dog." Find an angle you care about. Was your dog your best friend at a time when you especially needed a friend?

For example, Luis was assigned to write a report on the history of a sport. He knew he wanted to write about baseball, but he wasn't sure where to go from there. To find an idea he truly wanted to write about, he thought about these questions.

- What is my personal experience with this topic?
- What special knowledge do I already have about this topic?
- What do I wish I knew more about?

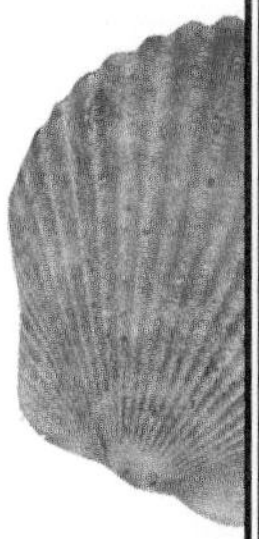

for DRAWING

INDIVIDUALIZING INSTRUCTION: LD STUDENTS Some students who struggle with language may benefit especially from using drawings to generate ideas. To help them make the transition from drawing to writing, encourage them to label the parts of their drawings and to create captions.

for MAKING AN IDEA YOUR OWN

HELPFUL HINT Other questions that might help students find their own angles include the following:

- What's most important to me about this topic?
- How did I get interested in this topic?
- What does this topic have to do with my life?

For more information, refer students to Handbook 5, "Goals and Audience," on page 211.

for MAKING AN IDEA YOUR OWN

HELPFUL HINT Tell students that finding an angle they care about can help them enjoy writing and write better. Reassure students that if they ask in advance, most teachers will let them adapt an assigned topic to fit their interests.

for PRACTICE YOUR SKILLS

ASSESSMENT Because these Practice Your Skills exercises are exploratory, you might check off students' responses rather than evaluate them. Suggest that students keep their responses in their writing journals for later use as idea sources.

Additional Resources

Writing Resource Book, pp. 46–48
Fine Art Transparency Pack
Thinking Skills Transparency Pack

Answers to Practice Your Skills

A. Answers will vary.

B. Answers will vary.

C. Answers will vary.

D. Answers will vary.

Here is the way Luis answered the questions.

Questions	Answers
What is my experience with baseball?	I play in Little League. My family and I went to a professional baseball game last summer.
What special knowledge do I have?	I know the rules of baseball, and I know about junior high leagues.
What do I wish I knew more about?	I wish I knew more about Little League. When did it get started? Who started it?

For additional suggestions about how to make a topic your own, see Handbook 3, "Finding a Focus," pages 203–204.

Practice Your Skills

A. Look through a room in your house to trigger a memory of a person, a place, a conversation, or an experience. Then write about that memory.

B. Use listing, freewriting, or drawing to find writing ideas about a person, a place, an object, an event, or a conversation.

C. Use listing, freewriting, or drawing to find a list of writing ideas related to one of the following subjects.

heroes   school   summer   TV   clothes

D. Choose one of the following subjects. Use one or more of the methods you learned in this lesson to make the subject meaningful to you personally.

jobs   achievement   hobbies   travel   school

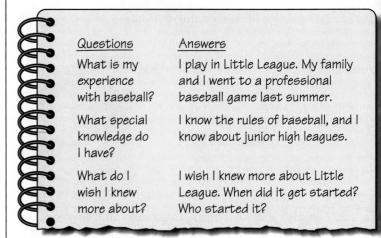

WRITING HANDBOOK 3

What's the Right Size for My Topic?

Finding a Focus

The shoes you wear, the soft drink you buy, and the TV you watch all come in sizes. You buy the size you need or want. In writing too, the size of your topic must fit your needs. To find the right size, think about what your purpose for writing is and what details you want to cover.

NARROWING THE TOPIC

Asking questions and making graphic devices will help you divide a subject into parts. You may decide that you especially want to write about just one of the parts. On the other hand, you may see how several parts fit together to create a topic that you can manage.

Writing TIP

You can use the subheads in an encyclopedia article or the table of contents in a book to find the parts of a topic.

Asking Questions

One student narrowed her topic on pets after asking these *who, what, when, where, why,* and *how* questions.

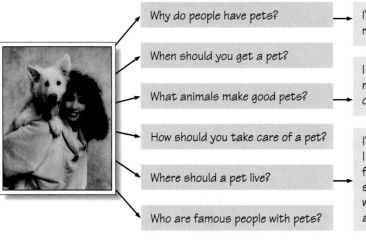

- Why do people have pets? → I'd have fun interviewing my friends.
- When should you get a pet?
- What animals make good pets? → I wonder what animals make good pets in other countries.
- How should you take care of a pet?
- Where should a pet live? → I'll write about this one. I could tell how Digger's first dog house was so small that he got stuck when he tried to turn around in it.
- Who are famous people with pets?

WRITING HANDBOOK 3

Finding a Focus

Objectives

- To understand and use techniques for narrowing writing topics
- To narrow a writing topic appropriately for a given purpose

Related Mini-Lessons

For information on topics related to finding a focus, see the following mini-lessons:

- **Thinking with Pictures, pp. 192–196**
- **Finding a Starting Point, pp. 197–202**

Teaching Strategies

GENERAL NOTE

KEY TO UNDERSTANDING Explain to students that their topic has to fit the length of their writing assignment. For example, a topic with four or five major parts would be too broad for a paragraph.

for ASKING QUESTIONS

INDIVIDUALIZING INSTRUCTION: ESL STUDENTS To use questioning to narrow a topic, these students need a clear understanding of the key words *who, what, when, where, why,* and *how.* Help by using each in sample sentences and translating, if possible.

for ASKING QUESTIONS

USING THE MODEL Call students' attention to the comments that the writer made in the margin. Her comments explore how she might work with the parts of her topic—how she might get information, which questions she has, and how she might use a memory.

Links to LITERATURE & LANGUAGE

You might invite students to notice the author's focus in each of the following poems from *Literature and Language,* Grade 6:

- May Swenson, "Southbound on the Freeway"
- Carl Sandburg, "Fog"
- Issa, Three Haiku

Social Studies Connection

Tell students that *who, what, where, when, why,* and *how*—the 5*W* + *H* questions—can help them check their understanding of important historical or current events. Model the way they might tailor the questions to fit their needs: *Where* did the event occur? *Who* was involved? *When* did it occur? *Why* did it happen? *How* did it happen? *What* were its effects?

for WRITER TO WRITER

KEY TO UNDERSTANDING Explain that *web* is another term for *cluster.*

for USING GRAPHIC DEVICES

HELPFUL HINT Use class discussion to help students see that "one [hurricane] near Grandma's house in Florida" would be a good topic for a two-page paper. Ask students why this topic would be better for a two-page paper than for a paragraph. (The topic has several possible parts.) Then ask why the topics "hurricane," "blizzard," and "tornado" would not be appropriate for two-page papers. (They are too broad; each could be a subject of a whole book.)

Additional Resources

Writing Resource Book, p. 48
Thinking Skills Transparency Pack

Answers to Practice Your Skills

A. Answers may vary. Questions that begin with *who, what, when, where, why,* and *how,* however, should be asked to help focus the topic.

B. Answers will vary. Students should divide the topic into parts by means of a cluster, an observation chart, a list, or another graphic device.

WRITER TO WRITER

I get started by making a web.

Kara DeCarolis, student
Golden, Colorado

Using Graphic Devices

You can also use graphic devices, such as clusters, diagrams, observation charts, lists, and drawings, to see the parts of a topic. Another student started the following cluster about storms. What would you add to the cluster? What do you think would be a good topic about storms for a two-page paper?

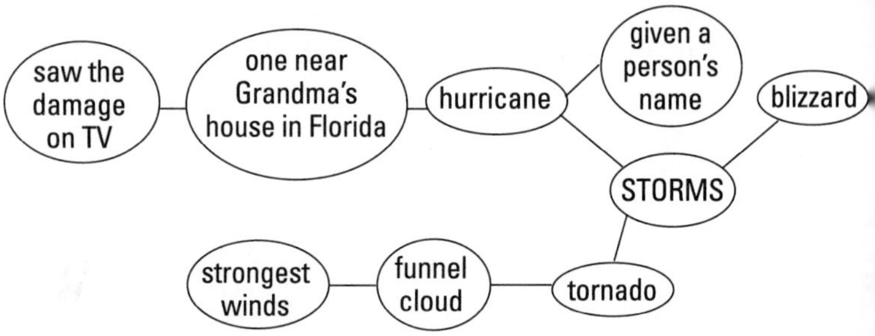

For more information on using graphic devices, see Handbook 1, "Thinking with Pictures," pages 192–196.

Practice Your Skills

A. Choose one of the topics below or one of your own. Then ask questions to focus the topic.

rock music cars art holidays comedy

B. Choose one of the topics below or one of your own. Then use a cluster, an observation chart, a list, or another graphic device to divide the topic into parts.

animals snow cities sports friends

How Do I Explore and Support My Ideas?

Developing a Topic

WRITING HANDBOOK 4

The Wonderful Wizard of Oz: A tornado carries a girl and her dog from their home to another land.

Would you want to read *The Wonderful Wizard of Oz* on the basis of the summary above? If the summary included vivid details, however, you might want to read the book. Details about the tornado, the girl, her dog, their home, and the characters she meets would make the writing come alive. You too can learn ways to make your writing lively. Simply add details that explain, show, or illustrate your message.

KINDS OF SUPPORTING DETAILS

How would you describe the taste of a pizza? What is the nutritional value of pizza? Who invented pizza? To answer each of these questions, you would need to use different kinds of details. The details you choose will vary, depending upon what you want to accomplish. Here are some types of details that can help you in different writing situations.

Sensory Details

You can make descriptions easy to remember by using your senses. Think of ways to tell your readers how things look, sound, feel, smell, and taste. Look at the description of a picnic on the next page. The author could simply state that a delicious selection of food was gathered. But she does much more. (Be careful; her description could make you hungry.)

Writing TIP

You can explore your senses by making an observation chart. See Handbook 1, "Thinking with Pictures," pages 192–196.

PROFESSIONAL NOTEBOOK

Share the following advice from writer Anne Bernays: "Nice writing isn't enough. It isn't enough to have smooth and pretty language. You have to surprise the reader frequently, you can't just be nice all the time. Provoke the reader. Astonish the reader. Writing that has no surprises is as bland as oatmeal. Surprise the reader with the unexpected verb or adjective. Use one startling adjective per page."

WRITING HANDBOOK 4

Developing a Topic

Objectives

- To identify techniques for developing writing topics
- To choose an appropriate technique and develop a writing topic

Related Mini-Lessons

For information related to developing a topic, see the following mini-lessons:

- **Thinking with Pictures, pp. 192–196**
- **Finding a Focus, pp. 203–204**
- **Organizing Details, pp. 217–221**
- **Show, Don't Tell, pp. 239–242**
- **Appealing to the Senses, pp. 266–273**

Teaching Strategies

GENERAL NOTE

KEY TO UNDERSTANDING Explain that effective details are specific ones. For example, "The boy held the money" is fairly general. "The five-year-old clutched the quarter" paints a vivid picture. As students work through the handbook, point out specific details in the models—colors and flavors in the piece by Maya Angelou; dates, addresses, and names in the model about Thomas Edison, and so on.

for SENSORY DETAILS

LINKING GRAMMAR AND WRITING Explain to students that they can bring sensory details to life by avoiding overuse of *is, was,* and other forms of *be.* Urge them to choose verbs that appeal to the senses. For example, on page 206, Maya Angelou writes that meat *sputtered* on the barbecue pit, not that it *was* on the barbecue pit. She writes, "Pound cakes *sagged* with their buttery weight," not that they *were* buttery and heavy.

for SENSORY DETAILS

USING THE MODEL Ask students which images from Angelou's description stand out most for them. Then have students name a favorite food. Ask volunteers to use sensory details to describe the food; urge them to be specific, as Angelou has been.

for FACTS

CRITICAL THINKING: DISTINGUISHING FACTS FROM OPINIONS Remind students that a fact can be proved. Ask them which of the following statements is a fact and which is an opinion. Then ask how each fact could be proved. (Most facts can be verified by checking an encyclopedia or other general reference work.)

- Thomas Edison was the world's greatest inventor. (O)
- The cotton gin was invented by Eli Whitney. (F)
- Navy Admiral Grace Hopper developed the computer language called COBOL. (F)
- Modern clothes would look very different if the zipper had never been invented. (O)

for REASONS

LINKING GRAMMAR AND WRITING Tell students that words such as *because, since, as a result,* and *therefore* are helpful in working reasons smoothly into sentences. To illustrate, share the following examples:

Our school should have an open campus policy at lunch time *because* many students need to go home for lunch.

Since Maria has the most experience with student government, I think she would make a good class president.

Literary MODEL

Sense of sound
Sense of sight
Sense of taste
Sense of touch

On the barbecue pit, chickens and spareribs sputtered in their own fat. . . . Orange sponge cakes and dark brown mounds dripping chocolate stood layer to layer with ice-white coconuts and light brown caramels. Pound cakes sagged with their buttery weight, and small children could no more resist licking the icings than their mothers could avoid slapping the sticky fingers.

Maya Angelou, *I Know Why the Caged Bird Sings*

Facts

You can support your main idea with facts from experts or from reference books, such as encyclopedias and almanacs. A **fact** is any piece of information that can be proved true. The location of Edison's laboratories in New Jersey is a fact. What other facts does the paragraph below tell you about early movies?

Professional MODEL

On February 1, 1893, Edison opened the world's first motion picture studio at his laboratories in West Orange, New Jersey. After producing numerous filmstrips to be viewed through the Kinetoscope [a box-like device for one viewer at a time], Edison opened the first movie theater on April 14, 1894, at 1155 Broadway, New York City. For a nickel, a customer could watch a brief filmstrip of the great bodybuilder Eugene Sandow lifting weights and performing gymnastics, or of Buffalo Bill mounting a horse and shooting his pistols. The new "theater" was a great success.

Charles Panati, *The Browser's Book of Beginnings*

Reasons

Don't leave your readers asking why. Give them reasons to support an opinion or tell why something happened. **Reasons** are explanations or logical arguments. The paragraph on the next page tells why scientists want to know when Merapi, a volcano in Indonesia, will erupt.

Links to LITERATURE & LANGUAGE

Poem to Read Maya Angelou (1928–) is an African-American author who has written poems, songs, and a multivolume autobiography. The first volume, *I Know Why the Caged Bird Sings* (1970), covers her first sixteen years. You might read the poem "Life Doesn't Frighten Me" on page 359 of *Literature and Language,* Grade 6. Like the book *I Know Why the Caged Bird Sings,* this poem draws on Angelou's personal struggle to succeed in an often hostile world. Ask students to identify the details that make this poem vivid and meaningful.

Professional MODEL

Why is it important to know when Merapi might blow? If many of the people living around the volcano's base don't leave in time, they could be killed. Hurricanes of 1,400-degree-Fahrenheit volcanic ash would burn the villagers and farmers. Or flows of mud caused by heavy rain mixed with the ash would bury them alive.

Brianna Politzer, "Magma P.I."

Main reason

Supporting reasons

Examples

Sometimes the best way to help your readers understand a point is to give them an **example,** or instance of something. You can introduce an example with words such as *for instance,* or *to illustrate.* Look for examples in the paragraph below. Which ones support the main idea that the famous airplane pilot Amelia Earhart and her sister were athletic?

The celebrated aviator Amelia Earhart sits in the cockpit of her aircraft after setting a new altitude record, April 1931.

Professional MODEL

From an early age, Amelia and her sister were athletic. They turned a lawn swing into a jungle gym and hung by their knees on the top bar. They played baseball and football with equipment their father bought them. In the barn, they climbed on an old carriage where they took imaginary journeys behind teams of galloping horses while fighting off nonexistent attackers.

Ginger Wadsworth, "The Adventure Begins"

Stories or Events

Another way to add details is to tell a story or describe an event that will help your readers understand your idea. A **story** or **event** can come from your experiences or from talking to others. It can also come from reading or from your imagination.

for EXAMPLES

HELPFUL HINT Explain that examples can be especially useful for helping readers understand a general statement. A strong paragraph might begin with a general topic sentence, then follow up with several examples to show exactly what the topic sentence means. Sometimes a paragraph begins with several specific examples and ends by summing them up in a general topic sentence.

for SECOND PROFESSIONAL MODEL

USING THE MODEL Lead students to see that the second and third sentences in the excerpt from "The Adventure Begins" support the idea that Amelia Earhart and her sister were athletic. To point out the wealth of specific details in these two sentences, ask how the excerpt would be different if Ginger Wadsworth had written instead, "They exercised on lawn furniture and played sports." What would we miss? (vivid examples that help the audience identify with the Earharts)

for EXAMPLES

CRITICAL THINKING: INTERPRETING Ask students to decide what the last sentence in Wadsworth's paragraph suggests about Amelia Earhart and her sister. (Samples: They had good imaginations; they liked to dream of adventure.)

for **FURTHER READING**

Books to Read Students interested in Amelia Earhart might enjoy reading about other adventurous women in the following books:

- Julie Fromer, *Jane Goodall: Living with the Chimps*
- Carole S. Briggs, *Women in Space: Reaching the Last Frontier*
- Charlene W. Billings, *Christa McAuliffe, Pioneer Space Teacher*
- Doreen Rappaport, *Living Dangerously: American Women Who Risked Their Lives for Adventure*

for PROFESSIONAL MODEL

USING THE MODEL Point out that words referring to time help the reader follow the story: *many years ago, one sunny day, Suddenly, before I ever saw it.* Encourage students to use words that signal time when they write stories or describe events.

for WAYS TO EXPLORE A TOPIC FURTHER

KEY TO UNDERSTANDING Explain that students won't always have to gather all their details before they start to draft. They may begin to develop an idea by drafting and later, get more information. They can use strategies in the text to gather more details at any point during the writing process.

for WAYS TO EXPLORE A TOPIC FURTHER

HELPFUL HINT Point out that the first question asks about the writer's purpose. Offer examples of purposes that students might have. Some examples might be to share a memory, to communicate a personal thought or feeling, to tell readers more about a topic, to convince readers of something, or to entertain.

To check students' understanding, ask them how the details needed to share a memory of a day in the mountains would be different from the details needed to convince readers that they should stop logging the forests in the mountains. (Sample: The first topic would need descriptive details; the second would need factual details to support the argument.)

The following paragraph tells a story about a real event that happened to Valerie Taylor, an Australian diver and underwater photographer. The details support the main idea that divers sometimes meet sharks unexpectedly.

***Professional* MODEL**

Valerie remembers one such occasion many years ago. She was diving with two friends along the Great Barrier Reef near her home in Australia one sunny day. "Suddenly I sensed something swimming very close to me," she recalls. "Thinking it was one of the other divers, I looked around—straight into a large black eye. It belonged to a huge tiger shark, nearly fifteen feet long. I knew instinctively it was not going to hurt me. If it had wanted to bite, it would have done so before I ever saw it."

Judith E. Rinard, "Sharks Are Our Business"

WAYS TO EXPLORE A TOPIC FURTHER

During prewriting you explore your ideas and collect some details. To find out if you have enough details to support your ideas, ask yourself these questions:

- Can I accomplish my purpose with the details I have?
- Will the details I have get my ideas across clearly?
- Will my readers need more information to understand my ideas?

WRITER TO WRITER

The thing I like most about writing is the way it allows me to express myself.

Ben Everett, student
Charleston, Illinois

Perhaps you need more details for a paper on the knights of the Round Table. Try these strategies.

Common Ways to Find More Details

Recalling	Remember a movie you've seen about King Arthur and his knights. Have you read a book about Merlin the magician or about King Arthur's magic sword?
Observing	Study an illustrated book to learn about life during the time of King Arthur. Pay close attention to the way the people dressed and the places they lived.
Imagining	Ask yourself questions such as "What if I were a knight of the Round Table?" or "What if I were Guinevere's best friend?"
Interviewing	Plan to talk to your reading teacher or a librarian who knows about your subject. Write out the questions you want to ask. Then interview the person. Listen carefully and ask more questions if you don't understand.
Researching	Visit the library. Look for details in encyclopedias, in books such as *King Arthur and the Knights of the Round Table, The Tale of Sir Gawain,* and *The Legend of King Arthur.* Enjoy movies such as *Knights of the Round Table, Camelot,* and *The Sword in the Stone.*

Try to use several or all of these strategies. The more information you gather, the more familiar you will become with your topic. Then it will be easier for you to include interesting facts, stories, and specific details.

What can you do if you are writing a story about an imaginary character? You will probably rely on imagining. You might, however, blend in details from your memories, observations, and everyday experiences.

PROBLEM SOLVING

"How do I know which facts, stories, and details to include?"

For more information on narrowing your topic and organizing details, see

- Handbook 1, "Thinking with Pictures," pages 192–196
- Handbook 3, "Finding a Focus," pages 203–204
- Handbook 7, "Organizing Details," pages 217–221

for COMMON WAYS TO FIND MORE DETAILS

SPEAKING AND LISTENING To learn more about interviewing, students can turn to Handbook 31, "Interviewing Skills," on page 323.

for COMMON WAYS TO FIND MORE DETAILS

KEY TO UNDERSTANDING Point out that even if students are writing fiction stories, they may still need to research facts, observe specific sensory details, and so on, to bring their narratives to life. For example, to write a story about the knights of the Round Table, students might need to research the obligations of a knight.

for PRACTICE YOUR SKILLS

ASSESSMENT You might use primary trait scoring for student paragraphs. Because this handbook focuses on elaboration rather than on structure, you might make content the primary trait, assigning high scores for adequate development of details.

Additional Resources

Writing Resource Book, pp. 49–50
Elaboration, Revision, and Proofreading Practice

Answers to Practice Your Skills

A. Answers will vary. The following paragraph shows a possible response to the second prompt.

Captain Elsa Zorak announced on Friday, December 10, 2094, that she and her crew had discovered living creatures on Mars. They found three creatures in a burrow twenty feet deep. The wormlike creatures were each two inches long and were bright orange. They had feathery shapes at one end and a corkscrew shape at the other. Captain Zorak said she believes they ate sand.

B. Added details may vary. The main kinds of details, however, should be those shown below. Students may also include other kinds of details in support.

1. examples
2. sensory details
3. facts
4. reasons
5. stories or events

C. Answers will vary.

Practice Your Skills

A. Choose one of the following main ideas. Write a paragraph about it, using the suggestion in parentheses. For this assignment you don't need to do any outside research. You can just make up the kinds of details you need.

1. In the summer heat, the ice cream cone began to melt. (Use sensory details to show what happened.)
2. Living creatures were discovered on Mars in 2094. (Make up the facts about this discovery.)
3. Girls should (or should not) play on the same Little League teams as boys. (Give reasons to support your position.)
4. I like listening to several types of music. (Give examples of the music you like.)
5. You can learn a lot from your mistakes. (Tell a story about what you learned from a mistake you made.)

B. Imagine that you need to add details to support each of the following main ideas. For each idea, name one or more types of details that would make the piece of writing lively and informative. Choose from these types: sensory details, facts, reasons, examples, and stories or events.

1. the ways computers influence our lives today
2. watching a fireworks display
3. the origins of modern basketball
4. why video games are worthwhile
5. your scariest experience

C. Choose one of the topics below or a topic of your own. Write your topic on a piece of paper. Then list two or three concrete details you might use to develop the topic. Use one of the strategies for finding details covered in this handbook.

mummies roller coasters fire alarms sunken ships

210 Writing Handbook

Why Am I Writing and Who Am I Writing for?

Goals and Audience

A gymnast leaps onto the balance beam and begins her routine. All her energy, talent, and training are focused on one audience—the gymnastics judges—and one goal—a medal-winning performance.

You may not expect to win a medal for your writing. Like the gymnast, however, you do need to think about your goals and your audience. Your writing will be more effective if you first consider why you're writing. At the same time keep thinking about your audience.

GOALS

When you write, you usually have some **goal,** or reason for writing, in mind. Think about what makes the subject important to you. Why is it worth writing about? For example, you may want to tell a friend about an exciting baseball game you attended. You may want to express your opinion about a movie you've seen.

You may have more than one goal in mind for a particular piece of writing. For example, you may want to write about a baseball game both to tell what happened that day and to help your friend understand why the game was so special to you. You may want to express your opinion about a movie both to convince your classmates to see it and to share your impression of the star.

Identifying your goals can help you focus your writing. You might begin by asking yourself the following questions:

- Why am I writing?
- What do I want my writing to do?
- How do I want my readers to react?

WRITING HANDBOOK 5

WRITING HANDBOOK 5

Goals and Audience

Objectives

- To recognize writing goals
- To understand how to analyze the needs of an audience
- To apply goals and knowledge of an audience to a writing topic

Related Mini-Lessons

For information on topics related to goals and audience, see the following mini-lessons:

- **Revising, pp. 257–259**
- **Levels of Language, pp. 274–275**

Teaching Strategies

for GOALS

MODELING Using an assignment that you are writing with the class, model the way you would answer the three questions for identifying goals. You also might discuss the ways your goals have changed since you started the piece. Then invite students to apply the questions to a piece of their writing that is still in process. Reassure them that it will be all right if their goals don't become completely clear until the revision stage.

for AUDIENCE

HELPFUL HINT Explain that it is important to think about an audience's general outlook and background. This consideration can help students decide which terms they need to define and which kinds of details their audience will be interested in. For example, in a note to a grandparent, students might define a slang term: "My new skates are rad (that means 'great')." In a letter to a foreign pen pal, students might explain more about their school than they would in a letter to a friend in this country.

for AUDIENCE

HELPFUL HINT Suggest that students try dialoguing to figure out more about their audiences. Explain that dialoguing involves writing an imaginary conversation between the writer and the reader. Writers might ask questions such as "What's most important to you?" and "How can I get you to care about my topic?" They might be surprised at the answers their "readers" give them. This strategy can help students discover how much they already know about their audiences.

Sometimes you will have clear goals in mind before you begin writing. At other times you will discover your goals as you write. You may even change your goals as you draft and revise. Thinking about your goals can help you identify your personal connection to your topic. Clear goals will also help you write clearly and strongly.

AUDIENCE

Just as important as why you are writing is whom you are writing for—your **audience.** These are the people with whom you will share your writing.

Often in your school assignments, your audience will be chosen for you. For example, if your social studies teacher assigns a report on ancient Egypt, your audience will be your teacher and possibly your classmates. In other cases, you will choose your audience. For instance, you might decide to write a letter to a friend or a grandparent, or you might jot down your thoughts and feelings in your journal—for you alone to read.

Thinking about your audience can help you figure out what you want to say. You might ask yourself questions like the following:

- Who is my audience?
- What do they already know about my subject?
- What do I want them to know?
- What details might they find most interesting?

As you consider your audience, also think about the kind of language you will use to present your ideas. For example, if you were writing for younger readers, you would use simpler language and shorter sentences than you would use if you were writing for adults.

Use a graphic organizer like the one shown on the next page to help you think about your goals and audience.

Writing TIP

To help you figure out what kind of language to use in a piece of writing, imagine you are having a conversation with your audience.

Grammar Connection

Point out that in writing for themselves, for friends, for family members, and for younger people, writers often use contractions. Contractions make writing sound friendly and personal. In writing for a more general or formal audience, though, it's generally a good idea *not* to use them. For a review of contractions, refer students to pages 581–582.

Topic: Dolphin language

Goals	**Audience**
Why am I writing? to explain what scientists have learned about how dolphins communicate with one another	**Who is my audience?** my classmates **What do they already know about my subject?** They may have seen a program about dolphins on TV; our class has already learned that dolphins are mammals.
What do I want my writing to do? to make my readers better informed about dolphin communication	**What do I want them to know?** how dolphins make noises, what kinds of noises they make, what the noises might mean, and how scientists study dolphin language
How do I want my readers to react? with interest and amazement	**What details might they find most interesting?** specific examples of how dolphins communicate

Practice Your Skills

A. For each of these topics, suggest one or more possible goals for writing.

1. a funny incident
2. a book you enjoyed reading
3. performing onstage
4. one dark, dreary night
5. tidal waves
6. medieval armor

B. Select two of the topics listed below. For each topic, choose a possible audience and tell the reasons for your choice.

1. why cities need to plant more trees
2. how to get along with a younger brother or sister
3. earthquakes
4. safety tips for in-line skaters
5. the best music videos
6. the best sneakers to buy

for GOALS AND AUDIENCE CHART

USING THE MODEL You might ask students how the different responses in the "Audience" section of the chart might be if the audience were first-graders. (Sample: First-graders would know less; they might be more interested in storylike details.) Then ask how different the responses might be if the audience were the judges of a science fair. (Sample: They would know a lot more; they would want a lot of details showing thorough, up-to-date research.)

for PRACTICE YOUR SKILLS

HELPFUL HINT To let students see the variety of possible goals and of ways to consider audiences, you might go over responses to Practice Your Skills as a class.

Additional Resource

Writing Resource Book, p. 51

Answers to Practice Your Skills

A. Answers will vary. Students should consider why they might be writing and how they would want their readers to react. A possible answer for the first item is shown below.

1. You might want to write about a funny incident in order to share the event and to make a sick friend laugh.

B. Answers will vary. Students should explain why the topic might interest the audience. A possible answer for the first item is shown below.

1. An audience for a piece on why cities should plant more trees might be committees devoted to making cities more attractive places to live. These people would appreciate the natural beauty of trees and also would be aware of environmental issues.

Point out that some of these cowboy sayings include the adjective they explain ("So tall he couldn't tell when his feet were cold"), whereas others expect the listener to infer the adjective ("Like tryin' to scratch yore ear with yore elbow"). Tell students that the alternative expressions they come up with can follow either format.

Explain also that students' sayings don't necessarily have to sound like cowboy talk. In fact, you could challenge students to think of expressions that another specific group of people might use. (Sample: basketball players, farmers, politicians, movie stars, rap singers, even teenagers.) You might ask, for example, "How do you think a basketball player would describe someone extremely tall?"

After students have come up with their own descriptive expressions, try playing this game: One student reads his or her saying aloud, and then the rest of the class guesses what adjective it describes. You might extend the game to include other adjectives, such as *cold, happy, slow, clumsy, mean, easy, absent-minded, generous,* and *noisy.*

on the LIGHT side

Way Out West

Over a period of seventy years, "Frosty" Potter collected a list of sayings he heard cowboys use. Can you come up with other expressions for the adjectives listed here?

Afraid He bolted like a jack rabbit in tall grass.

Brave He'll fight a rattler an' give him first bite.

Crazy He was plumb weak north of his ears.

Hard to do Like tryin' to scratch yore ear with yore elbow.

Hot We had to feed the chickens cracked ice to keep 'em from layin' hard-boiled eggs.

Lazy He was always settin' on the south side of his pants.

Mad Mad 'nough to kick his own dog.

Quiet So quiet yuh could hear daylight coming.

Short Would have to borrow a ladder to kick a grasshopper on the ankle.

Smart As full of information as a mail-order catalog.

Tall So tall he couldn't tell when his feet were cold.

Thin Had to stand twice in the same place to cast a shadow.

Unhappy As unhappy as a woodpecker in a petrified forest.

Worthless His family tree wasn't no more better than a shrub.

Cold Shakin' like a Chihuahua pup with a chill.

214

How Do I Create a First Draft?

Drafting to Explore

Imagine that you have an idea for a painting. How would you begin? You might first draw a sketch of your idea and then follow the sketch as you paint. Perhaps you would rather paint your idea right on the canvas and then make changes or start over as new ideas come to mind.

You can draft your writing ideas using similar methods. **Drafting** is the process of trying out ideas on paper. As you draft, your writing begins to take shape.

HOW DO I START?

As with any creative process, there is no "right" way to draft. Some writers follow a plan they have constructed. Others try out their ideas as they work. Try both techniques.

Follow a Plan

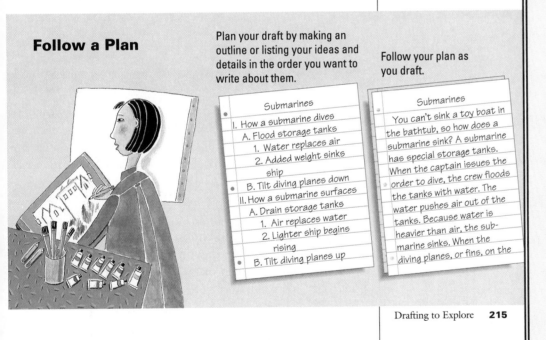

Plan your draft by making an outline or listing your ideas and details in the order you want to write about them.

Submarines

I. How a submarine dives
  A. Flood storage tanks
    1. Water replaces air
    2. Added weight sinks ship
  B. Tilt diving planes down
II. How a submarine surfaces
  A. Drain storage tanks
    1. Air replaces water
    2. Lighter ship begins rising
  B. Tilt diving planes up

Follow your plan as you draft.

Submarines

You can't sink a toy boat in the bathtub, so how does a submarine sink? A submarine has special storage tanks. When the captain issues the order to dive, the crew floods the tanks with water. The water pushes air out of the tanks. Because water is heavier than air, the submarine sinks. When the diving planes, or fins, on the

WRITING
HANDBOOK
6

Drafting to Explore

Objectives

- To identify various approaches to drafting
- To choose an approach to drafting and use it to begin a draft

Related Mini-Lessons

For information on topics related to drafting to explore, see the following mini-lessons:

- **Finding a Starting Point, pp. 197–202**
- **Finding a Focus, pp. 203–204**
- **Creating Longer Pieces of Writing, pp. 243–246**

Teaching Strategies

GENERAL NOTE

KEY TO UNDERSTANDING Tell students that this handbook shows two broad ways to start drafting. However, there are as many specific ways as there are students. If students have written anything as part of their prewriting activities, they may already have the beginning of a draft. The key to drafting is just to get going.

for FOLLOW A PLAN

HELPFUL HINT Point out that following a plan can be especially helpful for longer pieces of writing and for reports. However, emphasize that outlines and lists from a prewriting stage can be changed. If students start drafting and then want to explore a topic not covered in their outlines, they are free to do so. During revising, they can make things fit together smoothly.

for FOLLOW THE FLOW OF YOUR IDEAS

INDIVIDUALIZING INSTRUCTION: KINESTHETIC LEARNERS For students who prefer a hands-on approach, you might suggest Peter Elbow's technique of drafting by doing repeated freewritings. After each freewriting, the writer stops, marks key parts, and then writes a summary of the focus and goals that the freewriting suggests. The summary is the starting point for the next freewriting. After three or four of these freewriting drafts, the piece has enough shape that the writer can put the work away for an interval and then begin revising.

for HOW DO I KNOW WHEN I'M DONE?

HELPFUL HINT Tell students that if they quickly run out of things to say, they should review their prewriting notes. If that fails to generate ideas, they might explore new ideas by brainstorming, freewriting, discussing ideas with a peer, or using other prewriting techniques.

Additional Resource

Writing Resource Book, p. 52

Answers to Practice Your Skills

Answers will vary.

Follow the Flow of Your Ideas

Write down the ideas that are clear in your mind.

Being Left-handed

I think our school should have a club for left-handed people. We lefties could use the support because being left-handed isn't easy. Many school supplies like scissors are made only for right-handers. Even some school desks are made only for ~~righties~~ people who write with their right hands. Once during arts and crafts class, my teacher tried to teach me to knit. It was hopeless! It's harder for a lefty to learn how to do some things from a right-handed teacher.

Arrange the ideas in the order you want them. Delete unrelated ideas.

Add new ideas as they come to mind.

Start over again if you're not happy with the results.

How Do I Know When I'm Done?

You may think you're done after you complete your first draft. That's not the case. After you finish a draft, read your work and decide what you like and what you want to improve. Then start a draft with those changes. Like most writers, you may write several drafts until you are satisfied with your writing.

Practice Your Skills

Look in your journal and choose an entry you would like to turn into a finished piece of writing. Decide whether you want to start by making a plan or by letting your ideas flow as you write. Then write a draft of your piece.

Writing TIP

Once you have completed a draft, it's a good idea to set it aside for an hour or two—or even a day. You may be surprised by the new ideas that occur to you when you look at your draft again.

PROFESSIONAL NOTEBOOK

Students who prefer to start drafting without a detailed plan might appreciate this comment by Aldous Huxley: "I know very dimly when I start what's going to happen. I just have a very general idea, and then the thing develops as I write." That's a professional's definition of exploratory drafting. Inform students that Huxley (1894–1963) was a British novelist and essayist best known for his futuristic novel *Brave New World,* which they are likely to read in higher grades.

What Is the Best Order for My Writing?

Organizing Details

You have chosen a topic, and you have developed that topic with sensory details, facts, reasons, examples, and stories or events. Now you must organize all of these ideas and related details in paragraphs. Where do you begin?

There are different methods of organization you can use, depending on the type of writing you are doing. In some types of writing, such as a story that includes description, you may even use more than one method.

On the following pages you will learn ways in which you can organize details in paragraph form. The chart below is a summary of these methods.

Methods for Organizing Details

Method	Type of Writing	How to Organize Details
main idea with supporting details	reports, opinion	Write the main idea, perhaps as a topic sentence. Support it with facts, reasons, anecdotes, events, or examples.
chronological order	stories, process, directions	Write events or steps as they occur.
spatial order	descriptions	Describe details in a scene by moving up, down, to the left or right, or from near to far or far to near.
order of importance	persuasive, informative	Organize details from most important to least important or from least important to most important.

WRITING HANDBOOK 7

WRITING HANDBOOK 7

Organizing Details

Objectives

- To understand various techniques for organizing details
- To choose an appropriate technique and organize a piece of writing

Related Mini-Lessons

For information on topics related to organizing details, see the following mini-lessons:

- **Thinking with Pictures, pp. 192–196**
- **Examining Paragraphs, pp. 222–225**
- **Creating Paragraphs, pp. 226–229**
- **Improving Paragraphs, pp. 230–233**

Motivate

Draw an analogy between organizing objects and organizing a piece of writing. Ask students to suggest different ways of organizing the objects within an area of the classroom, then decide which arrangement is best. Point out that writers do similar arranging, rearranging, and evaluating of the ideas in their work.

Teaching Strategies

for METHODS FOR ORGANIZING DETAILS

HELPFUL HINT You might tell students that the chart shows four of the most common ways to organize paragraphs. As students probably will notice, however, more than one method of organization may be used, especially in a longer work. For example, a story may follow chronological order, but it may include a descriptive paragraph arranged according to spatial order. It also may include dialogue in which one character uses order of importance to present a persuasive idea.

for PROFESSIONAL MODEL

CRITICAL THINKING: CLASSIFYING Suggest that the support for the main idea falls into two broad categories—"Family" and "Communication." Have students find the details that relate to each category. (for "Family"—close ties to the young; long-term care; the passing along of maternal skills; for "Communication"—sounds, gestures, holding hands, kissing, patting, hugging)

for CHRONOLOGICAL ORDER

HELPFUL HINT If students have trouble keeping track of chronological order when drafting a story or a nonfiction work, such as a history report, suggest that they create timelines to use as guides while drafting.

MAIN IDEA WITH SUPPORTING DETAILS

English zoologist Jane Goodall with friend Flint, at Gombe National Park in northwestern Tanzania, 1965.

Some of the details you have gathered may be reasons, facts, examples, brief stories, or events. You can organize these details by starting with a sentence that expresses the main idea of the paragraph. Then write the reasons, facts, examples, stories, or events that develop and support the main idea.

Notice the development in the paragraph below, about the work of zoologist Dr. Jane Goodall. The first sentence tells the main idea—Goodall found that chimpanzees act like humans in many ways. All of the other sentences provide details that explain how chimpanzees act like humans.

***Professional* MODEL**

Details that support the main idea

Dr. Goodall noticed many ways in which chimpanzee behavior resembles that of humans. Chimpanzee mothers form close ties with their young and care for them for many years. The young learn from their mothers how to raise their own young. Chimpanzees communicate by sounds and gestures. They hold hands and kiss. They pat each other on the back. After being separated for a while, two chimps may hug.

Sharon L. Barry, "Asking Questions, Finding Answers"

PROBLEM SOLVING

"How can I organize the events in my story?"

For information about using story maps, see

• Handbook 1, "Thinking with Pictures," pages 192–196

CHRONOLOGICAL ORDER

The details you have gathered may be events that happened in a certain order in time. Other details may be the steps in which something happens. You can organize these details in **chronological order,** or the order in which events or steps occur, as in the paragraph on the next page.

The alarm sounds at the fire department headquarters in Phoenix, Arizona. A member of the staff rushes over to the computer terminal and punches some figures on its keyboard. Within a few seconds, symbols and words appear on the video screen. . . . Next, the information on the fire is relayed to the computer terminals in all the fire stations in Phoenix.

James A. Baggett, "The Science of Fighting Fires"

Professional MODEL

Transitional words show time relationships.

SPATIAL ORDER

Spatial order is the order in which details are arranged in space. This order helps your readers picture scenes, people, or objects.

To organize details in spatial order, start at a specific place and then move on. For example, you might describe a skyscraper by starting at the bottom and moving up to the top story. You might describe a person from head to toe. You could describe a beach scene from left to right or near to far.

Notice how in the model below, Virginia Hamilton helps her readers picture the inside of a barn. She starts at the entrance and then directs her readers' attention first to the crossbeam above and then to the walls at the sides.

Writing TIP

Transition words and phrases such as *in front, behind, to the left,* and *on the right* can help guide readers through your description.

They entered through identical barn doors, one of which was open to air and light. Inside, the barn was a massive, two-story shell. Walls and roof and one great oak crossbeam spanning the height. Hanging from the beam was an abundance of drying things, thick as fur. Not vegetables, but thousands of herb weeds and dried mushrooms. On the walls from top to bottom hung gourds, their range of colors so bright, they looked painted. There were vertical rows of field corn on lengths of heavy twine hanging down the walls.

Virginia Hamilton, *M. C. Higgins, the Great*

Literary MODEL

for PROFESSIONAL MODEL

HELPFUL HINT Point out to students that they can use transitions (sometimes called signal words) to let readers know the order of events in time. For example, James A. Baggett uses the phrase *Within a few seconds* and the word *Next* to tell readers when events happen.

for SPATIAL ORDER

INDIVIDUALIZING INSTRUCTION: LD STUDENTS Writing about spatial order may challenge students who have difficulty in visualizing information or organizing ideas. Encourage these students to make diagrams, maps, or drawings to use as guides when they write with spatial order. If they use specific labels in their visuals, such as "chair to left of door," they can minimize confusion when they begin writing.

for FURTHER READING

Virginia Hamilton (1936–) is an award-winning author who has written many books and stories for young-adult readers. You might invite students to read *Zeely,* a novel about African-American life in the last century.

for STUDENT MODEL

USING THE MODEL Ask students whether the writer of the student model has convinced them that Florida's coral reefs need protection. (Some students might say that she has at least made a good start.) Then ask what their responses might have been if the order had been switched, with the first sentence reading "Fishing and diving near coral reefs should be limited." (Some students might say that they would have responded with: "Oh, yeah? Why limit people's fun?") Point out that putting the most important detail first can be especially helpful when a main idea is controversial.

for PROFESSIONAL MODEL

USING THE MODEL Call students' attention to the key transition in the professional model. The words *most famous* let readers know that the most important detail is coming up.

for ORDER OF IMPORTANCE

CRITICAL THINKING: PREDICTING After students have read the paragraph by Robert C. Gray, ask them what they think the next paragraph in Gray's piece might be about (the Chincoteague ponies). Explain that putting the most important detail last can build a bridge to the main idea of the next paragraph.

ORDER OF IMPORTANCE

Another way to arrange details is to rank them in **order of importance.** Your most important detail may be the one that impressed you the most or the one that you think your readers might not know. Your least important detail may be the one that impressed you the least or the one your readers know already. Arranging details in order of importance is useful when you present arguments and opinions or write reports.

Look at this student's paragraph presenting an opinion on the destruction of Florida's coral reefs. Notice how she catches her readers' attention at the beginning with a detail that made a great impression on her.

Student MODEL

Most important detail
Less important details

Whenever a careless diver or boater stands on or even bumps into our coral reef, their actions damage a living structure that took nature about six thousand years to create. Also, water pollution and litter from boats contribute to the destruction and death of coral. For these reasons, fishing and diving near the coral reefs should be limited.

You can also put the less important details first, leaving your readers with the most important idea at the end. In the passage below, Robert C. Gray begins with some interesting details about two East Coast islands. Notice how he tells about Assateague's most famous animals at the end of the paragraph.

Professional MODEL

General details about the islands
Wildlife listed in order from common to endangered
Most famous island wildlife mentioned last

A few miles off the eastern shore of Virginia and Maryland lie two small islands: Assateague and its smaller companion, Chincoteague. Assateague is home to great blue herons, sika deer, and even the endangered peregrine falcon. But the island's most famous inhabitants are the wild ponies, called Chincoteague ponies even though they live on Assateague.

Robert C. Gray, "The Wild Ponies of Chincoteague"

SPICE BOX

To give students practice in choosing appropriate organization, ask them which method of organization would be best for the following letters:

- one sent from Bigfoot to a shoe company, describing the kind of shoe he needs
- one left by the former captain of a starship for the new captain, explaining a little quirk in the ship's steering mechanism
- one written to persuade Columbus to let you sail west with him to "India"

Encourage students to invent additional letters and to discuss how to organize them.

Practice Your Skills

A. Imagine you are viewing the scene shown in this painting by Thomas Hart Benton. Write a description of everything that is happening around you. Use spatial organization to present your descriptive details so that your readers can picture the scene just as you see it.

Fire in the Barnyard (1944), Thomas Hart Benton.

B. Reorder each set of details below, using one of the organizational strategies shown in this handbook. Use the strategy that presents the details in the most logical order.

1. Soon the boy surfaced on the other side of the pool.
Pedro stood poised on the high diving board and studied the water beneath him.
He spouted water from his mouth as he let the air out of his lungs.
The hometown crowd exploded into applause and wild cheers.
He bounced once, lifted off the board, shot downward, and sliced through the water.

2. For one thing, skateboarding is fun, and just about anyone can do it.
I think our town should reserve space in the park for a special skateboarding area.
The most important reason, however, is that there are very few public places where kids are allowed to ride their skateboards.
Also, it is very popular among junior-high students.
Instead, dedicated skateboarders must skate in unsupervised, possibly dangerous places.

for PRACTICE YOUR SKILLS

ASSESSMENT Because this handbook focuses on organization, you might use primary trait scoring for the Practice Your Skills exercises, with structure as the primary trait. Content (elaboration) might be appropriate as a secondary trait.

Additional Resources

Writing Resource Book, pp. 53–56
Thinking Skills Transparency Pack

Answers to Practice Your Skills

A. Answers will vary. Descriptions should be spatially ordered, beginning at the teacher's right or left and moving around the room.

B.

1. (chronological order)
Pedro stood poised on the high diving board and studied the water beneath him. He bounced once, lifted off the board, shot downward, and sliced through the water. Soon the boy surfaced on the other side of the pool. He spouted water from his mouth as he let the air out of his lungs. The hometown crowd exploded into applause and wild cheers.

2. (order of importance)
I think our town should reserve space in the park for a special skateboarding area. For one thing, skateboarding is fun, and just about anyone can do it. Also, it is very popular among junior-high students. The most important reason, however, is that there are very few public places where kids are allowed to ride their skateboards. Instead, dedicated skateboarders must skate in unsupervised, possibly dangerous places.

Science Connection

Tell students that chronological and spatial order can be especially helpful in writing about topics in science. Chronological order is effective for writing about scientific processes, such as the life cycle of an insect or the way the heart pumps blood. Spatial order can be useful for scientific descriptions, such as a description of a plant or an animal, the solar system, or an ecosystem.

WRITING
HANDBOOK
8

Examining Paragraphs

Objectives

- To recognize the characteristics of a well-written paragraph
- To judge whether sentences in a paragraph develop its main idea
- To arrange details in a paragraph in a sensible order and to use transitional words

Related Mini-Lessons

For information on topics related to examining paragraphs, see the following mini-lessons:

- **Organizing Details, pp. 217–221**
- **Creating Paragraphs, pp. 226–229**
- **Improving Paragraphs, pp. 230–233**
- **Transitions, pp. 234–238**

Motivate

Retype one of the Starting from Literature models in the Writer's Workshop section of this book, eliminating all paragraph breaks. Duplicate the material and pass out copies to students. After they have read it, ask whether they found it easy to follow, or difficult. Then lead a discussion on the purpose and importance of paragraphing.

Teaching Strategies

for LITERARY MODEL

CRITICAL THINKING: INTERPRETING

Have students describe Sounder's bark in their own words and give details from the paragraph to support their answers. (Samples: loud, clear, musical, rich, full-bodied, echoing)

WRITING
HANDBOOK
8

What Is a Paragraph?

Examining Paragraphs

A paragraph is as easy to spot as a zebra with purple polka dots. All you have to do is look for a group of sentences with the first line indented. However, a well-developed paragraph is more than just a series of sentences.

GOOD PARAGRAPHS

A **paragraph** is a group of sentences that all work together to express and develop the same main idea. In a well-written paragraph, the sentences are also arranged in an order that makes sense. Notice how all the sentences in the following model work together to describe a dog's bark.

Literary MODEL

There was no price that could be put on Sounder's voice. It came out of the great chest cavity and broad jaws as though it had bounced off the walls of a cave. It mellowed into half-echo before it touched the air. It was louder and clearer than any purebred's voice. Each bark bounced from slope to slope in the foothills like a rubber ball. It was not an ordinary bark. It filled up the night and made music.

William Armstrong, *Sounder*

Literature Connection

Tell students to listen for the main idea as you read aloud the passage below from *Julie of the Wolves* by Jean Craighead George.

"Her house was not well built for she had never made one before, but it was cozy inside. She had windproofed it by sealing the sod bricks with mud from the pond at her door, and she had made it beautiful by spreading her caribou ground cloth on the floor. On this she had placed her sleeping skin, a moosehide bag lined with soft white rabbit skins. . . ."

Invite students to identify the main idea of the paragraph. (Sample: The character made herself a warm, cozy house.)

Developing a Main Idea

When you first draft a paragraph, just try to get down everything that comes to mind. Then, to improve your draft, you can do the following:

- Think about your main idea or purpose. What important idea do you want to get across?
- Take out any details that are not related directly to the main idea.
- Add details that help to develop the main idea further and make your paragraph more interesting.

Identify the main idea of the following paragraph. Then check to see whether or not all the details develop this idea.

> During the winter of 1838-39, U.S. troops forced fifteen thousand Cherokee men, women, and children to march from Georgia to Oklahoma through snow and bitter cold. Most were barefoot. All were hungry. Over a fourth of them died on the journey, which became known as the Trail of Tears. Many of the survivors started farms in Oklahoma. Farming was difficult, though, because cattle ranchers often drove their herds of cattle right across the Cherokees' fields.

The details about farming are interesting, but they have nothing to do with the Cherokees' forced march, which is the topic of the paragraph. When the sentences about farming are removed, the main idea comes across much more clearly as in this revised student model.

Student MODEL

> During the winter of 1838-39, U.S. troops forced fifteen thousand Cherokee men, women, and children to march from Georgia to Oklahoma through snow and bitter cold. Most were barefoot. All were hungry. Over a fourth of them died on the journey, which became known as the Trail of Tears.

for DEVELOPING A MAIN IDEA

SPEAKING AND LISTENING After students read the instructional material up to the first sample paragraph, have them close their books and listen as you read the paragraph aloud. Ask them to raise their hands as soon as they hear any details that are not related directly to the main idea of the paragraph. Afterward, discuss with students why the last two sentences in the paragraph do not belong in it, and what the writer might do with them instead (delete them or use them in a new paragraph).

for DEVELOPING A MAIN IDEA

INDIVIDUALIZING INSTRUCTION: BASIC STUDENTS If these students have difficulty in identifying the sentences that do not belong in the paragraph, make two columns with the following headings on the board: *The March from Georgia* and *The New Life in Oklahoma.* Ask a volunteer to read the paragraph aloud. Then have students identify the heading under which each sentence belongs. Write each sentence in the appropriate column. Then tell students that the column with the most sentences represents the main idea of the paragraph and that the two sentences in the other column belong in another paragraph.

for STUDENT MODEL

HELPFUL HINT Have students read the revised Student Model. Then ask what kinds of details the writer might add to this paragraph to develop the main idea even further and make the paragraph more interesting. (Samples: the approximate temperatures, what the Cherokee men, women, and children ate, and how long the trip took) *for* STUDENT MODEL

CRITICAL THINKING: CLASSIFYING After students read the revised Student Model, direct their attention to the single words and the phrase in boldface type. Tell them that these are transitions that help the reader understand the order of the steps and the position of the ingredients in relation to one another. Point out that most of the boldfaced transitions in the revised Student Model indicate time order, but that one of the transitions signals spatial order. Have students identify this transition *(On this layer of sauce).*

for SECOND STUDENT MODEL

HELPFUL HINT To help students practice using transitional words that signal spatial order, have them write a brief description of what a finished snack-sized pizza would look like, from top to bottom. Have them use transitional words and phrases to help their readers visualize the pizza.

Arranging Sentences Sensibly

Once you have settled on the details you want to include in a paragraph, you need to arrange them in a way that makes sense. If you don't do this, you're likely to confuse your readers. For example, read the following paragraph.

> Snack-sized pizzas are easy to make. You just broil them for three to five minutes or until the cheese is melted. First, you have to toast and butter both halves of an English muffin. Then you can add extras such as cooked hamburger, onions, olives, and mushrooms. Don't forget to spread a thin layer of spaghetti sauce or pizza sauce on each half. Put mozzarella cheese on top.

Could you follow these directions? Do you know whether to put the sauce on before or after you add the extras? When do you put on the cheese? When do you broil the pizzas? Now see how much easier it is to follow the directions when the steps are presented in a sensible order.

Student MODEL

The steps are arranged in chronological order.

Transitions help make the order of the steps clearer.

> Snack-sized pizzas are easy to make. **First,** toast and butter both halves of an English muffin. **Next,** spread a thin layer of spaghetti sauce or pizza sauce on each half. **On this layer of sauce,** add extras such as cooked hamburger, onions, olives, and mushrooms. **Then** put mozzarella cheese on top. **Finally,** broil them for three to five minutes or until the cheese is melted.

You can help your readers understand the arrangement of your sentences by using transitional words and phrases. Some of these words and phrases signal time: *soon, after a while.* Others signal place: *to the left, on top.* To learn more about transitions, see Handbook 11, "Transitions," on pages 234–238.

For help in finding the best ways to organize different types of details, you might want to review Handbook 7, "Organizing Details," on pages 217–221.

SPICE BOX

To give students practice in arranging ideas in chronological order, have them bring in comic strips from newspapers or magazines and cut apart the panels. Then have students trade panels with a partner and arrange them in correct order. Finally, have each student write a one-paragraph narrative summary of his or her strip, using transitional words that signal time order. Call on volunteers to read their summaries to the class.

Practice Your Skills

A. Decide which of these two examples is a weak paragraph. Then improve the weak paragraph by getting rid of the sentences that stray from its main idea.

1. People all over the world love baseball. Canadians love it enough to have two teams competing in the Major Leagues. People in many Latin American countries and in Japan love the game enough to have formed their own baseball leagues. What's more, in Japan a single baseball game often attracts more than fifty thousand fans.

2. Wolves communicate by using different types of howls. One kind of howl signals that a wolf wants to "talk." Another type of howl warns that danger is near. Many people think that wolves are vicious beasts, but they aren't. Wolves rarely attack people. In addition, they show mercy to one another. When wolves gather to hunt, they howl to greet one another. Then, to begin the hunt, they let out a wilder sort of howl. If you want to read a good book about wolves, read *Julie of the Wolves.*

B. Use what you've learned about good paragraphs to improve the following paragraph.

Some hot-air balloons hold only two passengers, but others hold more. Just how does a balloonist fly a hot-air balloon? Here are the basics. To take off, the balloonist lights a propane burner under the balloon. To land, the balloonist turns down the burner or opens the vent at the top of the balloon. To make the balloon go higher, the balloonist turns up the propane burner. A group of colorful balloons is quite a sight.

A propane burner heats the air inside a hot-air balloon, causing the air to expand. The balloon rises when the escape of some of the air decreases the overall weight of the balloon.

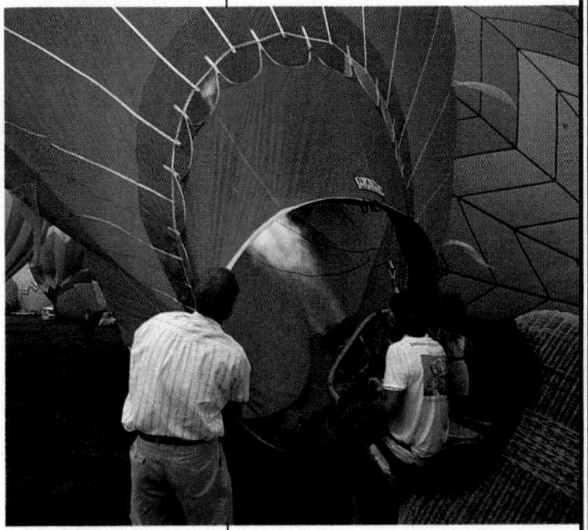

for PRACTICE YOUR SKILLS

INDIVIDUALIZING INSTRUCTION: BASIC STUDENTS To help these students with Exercise A, point out that the first sentence in each of the paragraphs states the main idea. Have students read aloud each of the remaining sentences and tell whether it relates directly to the main idea stated in the first sentence.

Additional Resource

Writing Resource Book, pp. 60–61

Answers to Practice Your Skills

A.

1. No revision is needed.

2. Answers may vary. A sample revision is provided.

Wolves communicate by using different types of howls. One kind of howl signals that a wolf wants to "talk." Another type of howl warns that danger is near. When wolves gather to hunt, they howl to greet one another. Then, to begin the hunt, they let out a wilder sort of howl.

B. Answers will vary. The first and last sentences, however, should be deleted as irrelevant and the remaining sentences rearranged in a sensible order. A sample revision is provided.

Just how does a balloonist fly a hot-air balloon? Here are the basics. To take off, the balloonist lights a propane burner under the balloon. To make the balloon go higher, the balloonist turns up the propane burner. Finally, to land, the balloonist turns down the burner or opens the vent at the top of the balloon.

WRITING HANDBOOK 9

Creating Paragraphs

Objectives

- To write effective topic sentences
- To use supporting details—such as facts, statistics, reasons, and examples—to develop a paragraph

Related Mini-Lessons

For information on topics related to creating paragraphs, see the following mini-lessons:

- **Developing a Topic, pp. 205–210**
- **Examining Paragraphs, pp. 222–225**
- **Improving Paragraphs, pp. 230–233**
- **Show, Don't Tell, pp. 239–242**

Motivate

To motivate students to write attention-getting topic sentences, read aloud the example topic sentences at the top of page 227 before you begin teaching the lesson. Ask students to imagine that these were the first sentences of magazine articles. Ask which sentences would make them want to read on, and why. Remind them that writing good topic sentences is an effective way to get their readers' attention.

Teaching Strategies

for DRAFTING TOPIC SENTENCES

INDIVIDUALIZING INSTRUCTION: ESL STUDENTS It may be helpful for some ESL writers to write a topic sentence and place it at the beginning of each paragraph they plan to develop. Although more sophisticated writers can often vary the placement of the topic sentence or even eliminate it entirely, beginning ESL writers often need the security and focus that a predictable pattern can give them.

WRITING HANDBOOK 9

How Do I Write a Paragraph?

Creating Paragraphs

Look over some of the paragraphs you've written. Which ones seem to work best? What makes them successful?

As you draft other paragraphs, keep in mind what has worked for you in the past. Also, consider using topic sentences and supporting details to express and develop your main ideas.

DRAFTING TOPIC SENTENCES

A **topic sentence** states the main idea or purpose of a paragraph. Here, for example, is the topic sentence from a paragraph about a computer game:

> If you've ever wanted to explore the universe with a crew of creatures from different planets, StarVoyager is the ideal game for you.

You don't have to put a topic sentence in every paragraph you write. However, including a topic sentence is a simple and direct way to make the main idea of a paragraph clear to readers. Furthermore, writing a topic sentence can help you stay focused on your main idea as you draft.

A good topic sentence can also get readers interested in your subject. To create attention-getting topic sentences, use the tips on the following page.

Writing **TIP**

If you put a topic sentence at the beginning of a paragraph, your readers will know right away what your paragraph is about.

PROFESSIONAL NOTEBOOK

In her book *Errors and Expectations,* writing teacher Mina P. Shaughnessy recommends teaching students to write topic sentences by having them form generalizations about a group of pictures on a related subject: "Once aware that the term *topic sentence* implies a *relationship* among sentences, . . . the student should be ready to try developing his own governing statements by making inferences from small pools of data, preferably non-print data at first. . . ." She suggests using pictures of couples or of children at play. Students can use details from the pictures to create their topic sentences.

Writing Effective Topic Sentences

Bring your subject to life with vivid details. Legend says that werewolves are people who develop fangs, fur, claws, and a thirst for blood when the moon is full.

Ask a question. What is life like on the ocean floor?

Talk to your readers. Imagine what it would be like to have an identical twin.

Include an interesting fact or statistic. Every second of every day, enough water splashes over Niagara Falls to fill four thousand bathtubs.

Set the scene. Horns blared and car doors slammed when the garbage truck blocked the intersection.

DEVELOPING PARAGRAPHS

A paragraph is more than just a topic sentence. As you learned in Handbook 8, "Examining Paragraphs," a paragraph is a group of sentences that develops one main idea. In a well-developed paragraph, these sentences contain the details needed to explain the main idea fully. They also support the main idea effectively.

As you develop your paragraphs, remember to do the following:

- Supply your readers with all the important information they need.
- Stay focused on your main idea.
- Explain and support your main idea with details such as facts, statistics, sensory details, incidents, examples, reasons, and quotations.

For more help in developing your ideas with supporting details, review Handbook 4, "Developing a Topic," pages 205–210, and Handbook 12, "Show, Don't Tell," pages 239–242.

Writing TIP

Avoid using wordy phrases such as "This paragraph is about . . . ," "I am going to write about . . . ," or "My topic is. . . ." Instead, just start with what you want to say.

for WRITING . . . TOPIC SENTENCES

COOPERATIVE LEARNING Break the class into groups and give each group a general reference book, such as an almanac, a one-volume encyclopedia, or the *Guinness Book of Records*. Assign each group a topic that can be quickly researched in its reference book. For example, you might assign such topics as planets, popular music, disasters, inventions, and Olympic champions. Invite each group to research its topic and write the most intriguing topic sentence it can for a paragraph that relates to its topic. Suggest that students use one of the types of topic sentences listed at the top of page 227 in their books.

for WRITING . . . TOPIC SENTENCES

CRITICAL THINKING: CLASSIFYING Have a spokesperson from each group share the topic sentence his or her group composed for the Cooperative Learning activity. Ask listeners to classify the type of topic sentence each group wrote, using the categories listed in the chart on page 227 of the pupil book.

for DEVELOPING PARAGRAPHS

KEY TO UNDERSTANDING Point out to students that the kinds of details they use to develop a paragraph will depend on the purpose of the paragraph. Give them the following examples of topic sentences and ask what kinds of details they might use to support them: "It was the most exciting basketball game I've ever seen." (Samples: sensory details, incidents, quotations) "If you go bike riding without a helmet, you're asking for trouble." (Samples: facts, statistics, reasons, incidents, quotations) "What kinds of fashions will you be wearing next fall?" (Samples: sensory details, examples, quotations)

Literature Connection

Read to students this passage from Patricia Lauber's "Gnats, Mammoths, and Saber-toothed Tigers" from *Dinosaurs Walked Here.*

"One day, forty million years ago, a gnat was crawling over the bark of a pine tree. It became trapped in a sticky flow of sap, or resin. Once the gnat was covered with resin, no other animal could eat it. The soft parts of the body did not decay, because bacteria could not feed on them. The gnat was quickly preserved. Much later, the resin hardened into the kind of fossil called amber. . . ."

Point out how the first sentence sets the scene for the process described.

for FIRST STUDENT MODEL

CRITICAL THINKING: ANALYZING
Ask students to tell what sensory details the writer used in the revised paragraph and which senses the details appeal to. ("as golden yellow as maple leaves in autumn"—sight; "easy for my fingers to press down"—touch; "sounds gorgeous"—hearing)

for SECOND STUDENT MODEL

INDIVIDUALIZING INSTRUCTION: BASIC STUDENTS These students may need more practice in writing and evaluating main ideas and supporting details. After they have analyzed the changes made in the second model, ask how the details might change if the "you" addressed in the paragraph referred to parents with young children or to senior citizens, rather than to children between the ages of nine and sixteen.

Now read the following paragraph. Is it well developed?

> My new guitar is great. It looks really neat. I like it a lot.

Why is the new guitar great? What are some of its neat looking features? Why do you like it so much? Since the paragraph fails to support its main idea with details, it is not well developed. A version that's more fully developed with reasons and sensory details gets across the main idea much more effectively.

Student MODEL

> My new guitar is great. Its wood is as golden yellow as maple leaves in autumn. There's a really fancy design around the sound hole. Its nylon strings are easy for my fingers to press down. Best of all, it sounds gorgeous.

Writing TIP

If your paragraph raises more questions than it answers, it is probably missing important information.

Now decide whether or not the following paragraph is well developed.

> Watch out! The advertisers are after you! They're trying to get you to buy all sorts of things.

The second sentence states the paragraph's main idea—but not very precisely. Who, exactly, is "you"? What, specifically, are these advertisers trying to get you to purchase? Notice how much stronger and more complete the paragraph is once it answers these questions.

Student MODEL

> Watch out! If you're between the ages of nine and sixteen, the advertisers are after you! They're trying to get you to buy expensive athletic shoes, computers, and other costly items. Many advertisers are even trying to sell you family products because they know that you can influence how your parents spend their money.

Practice Your Skills

A. Write a topic sentence for the paragraph below. Remember, this sentence should both tell what the paragraph is about and interest readers.

_______________. Tacos and tortilla chips appear on many American restaurant menus and most grocery store shelves. We use Spanish phrases such as "Hasta la vista." Also, the fashion industry has made Mexican symbols, color combinations, and patterns quite popular.

Intricate cross-stitch needlework decorates a Chatino Indian blouse from Oaxaca, Mexico.

B. Read the topic sentences below. If a topic sentence is weak, revise it to make it clearer and more interesting. If the sentence is fine as is, write *No revision needed.*

1. Frightened and injured, the only survivor made his way through the thick jungle.
2. I am going to tell you why you should recycle paper.
3. The Olympic Games are exciting to watch.
4. Have you ever wondered what your doodles mean?
5. This is a story about a bad day I had.

C. Create a well-developed paragraph about either a topic of your choice or one from the following list. The choice of whether or not to include a topic sentence in this paragraph is up to you.

- why your classmates should vote for you (or someone else) for class president
- how to do something you enjoy doing
- an exciting event

for PRACTICE YOUR SKILLS

MANAGING THE PAPER LOAD To cut down on your reading load, you might have students present the paragraphs in Exercise C orally. Students who choose the first prompt can deliver a speech; those who choose the second can give a demonstration; those who choose the third can give oral eyewitness reports.

Additional Resource

Writing Resource Book, pp. 60–61

Answers to Practice Your Skills

A. Answers will vary. Accept any topic sentence that states the main idea of the paragraph in a lively and interesting way. A sample topic sentence is provided.

Have you noticed how the foods, fashions, and language of Mexico are sweeping the United States?

B. Sentences needing revision are 2, 3, and 5. Revisions will vary. Possible answers are shown below.

2. Every time you throw away a newspaper or junk mail, you make America's garbage crisis worse.
3. Dreams fulfilled, dreams shattered, fierce competition, athletic performances of a lifetime—you can see all this and more during the Olympic Games.
5. After pouring sour milk on the last of my favorite cereal, I thought my day couldn't get any worse, but I was wrong.

C. Answers will vary. Be sure that students' paragraphs include a clearly stated or clearly implied main idea. The other sentences in the paragraph should contain details that explain the main idea.

WRITING
HANDBOOK
10

Improving Paragraphs

Objectives

- To evaluate paragraphs and make suggestions for revision
- To revise paragraphs by improving topic sentences, adding needed details, dropping unrelated details, rearranging sentences, and adding transitions

Related Mini-Lessons

For information on topics related to improving paragraphs, see the following mini-lessons:

- **Examining Paragraphs, pp. 222-225**
- **Creating Paragraphs, pp. 226–229**
- **Transitions, pp. 234–238**

Motivate

To illustrate the point made in the opening paragraph on this page, try to find art books in your school or local library that show artists' sketches along with the finished works of art. Have students compare the earlier and later versions and discuss the revision process involved in all creative work, including the writing of a successful paragraph.

Teaching Strategies

for REVISING PARAGRAPHS

HELPFUL HINT If you assign the handbook to individual students, you may want to point out one or two specific guidelines that they especially need to focus on in their writing.

WRITING
HANDBOOK
10

How Do I Create Better Paragraphs?

Improving Paragraphs

When you compare an artist's sketch with a finished painting, you notice many differences. The sketch is usually pretty simple—just pencil lines on paper. The finished painting, however, is much richer. It has color, details, and feelings that aren't present in the sketch.

Think of your drafts as simple sketches. As you revise your writing, try to add color, details, and feelings to your work.

Sailor at Lunch (1914), Diego Rivera. *Sailor's Head,* second version (1914), Diego Rivera. The artist did this pencil sketch as a study for the painting *Sailor at Lunch.*

REVISING PARAGRAPHS

Once you've completed a draft, you can improve your writing by referring to the following guidelines. You may also find it helpful to refer to these guidelines when you're acting as a peer reader.

Guidelines for Revising a Paragraph

- **Make your first sentence a real attention getter.** You may want to start with a question, a startling fact, or vivid details or by addressing the readers.
- **Identify the main idea.** Does your main idea come across clearly? If not, adding a topic sentence can help.
- **Make sure all of your details develop the main idea.** Take out any unrelated details.
- **Check that you've included enough details.** If your paragraph raises more questions than it answers, you probably need to add more information.
- **Be sure the order of your sentences makes sense.** Rearrange sentences and add transitions as necessary.

Literature Connection

Read to students the following passage from *Where the Red Fern Grows* by Wilson Rawls.

"If Santa Claus himself had come down out of the mountains, . . . I would not have been more pleased. I jumped up and down, and cried a whole bucketful of tears. I hugged him and told him what a wonderful papa he was."

Ask students to identify the main idea of the passage (how pleased he was). Then make sure that they observe how the first sentence captures the reader's attention and expresses the author's feelings. Help them describe how the other two sentences support the main idea.

Now look at one student's first draft of a paragraph about his father's weekend hobby. Imagine that you are the writer's peer reader. Can you see ways to improve this paragraph? You may want to refer to the guidelines for help.

> My father goes to his office every Saturday. It's about five miles from our house. Sometimes I come with him. He goes there to play computer games. He's one of the millions of adults who is hooked on computer games. I can see why. On the computer he flies airplanes, drives tanks, and even battles with aliens.

The student writer found a couple of ways to improve his paragraph. He revised his first sentence to make it more of an attention getter. He decided to take out some details that, on second thought, didn't really seem to relate to his main idea. He also added a sentence. Look for these changes as you read his revision.

Student MODEL

> On the weekends, my father flies airplanes, drives tanks, and even battles with aliens. No, he's not a comic-book superhero. He's just one of the millions of adults who is hooked on computer games.

Here is the first draft of another student's paper. This paragraph expresses an opinion about censorship and school newspapers. Think about the ways you might improve this student's paragraph.

> I don't think school officials should tell us what to publish in our student newspaper. Every time the principal tells us to take out an article he doesn't like I get angry. What right does he have to tell us what to print? It's not fair!

for FIRST STUDENT MODEL

CRITICAL THINKING: EVALUATING

Help students ask questions based on the guidelines on page 230 to evaluate the paragraph: "Does the first sentence grab your attention? Can you tell what the main idea is? Do all the sentences relate to the main idea? Are there enough details to support the main idea? Which sentences could be dropped? Does the order of the sentences make sense?"

for SECOND STUDENT MODEL

HELPFUL HINT Have students notice how the student writer moved the details in the last sentence of his first draft to the beginning of his revised paragraph. Tell students that often an idea for a great opening sentence is buried somewhere in the middle of their drafts. If students are now revising a draft, have them search their papers for ideas or details that could be incorporated into an attention-getting opening.

for THIRD STUDENT MODEL

STUMBLING BLOCK Students may have difficulty in evaluating this paragraph unless you remind them that expressions of opinion need to be supported with reasons. Ask, "What is the writer's opinion? Does she give any reasons that support it?" (no)

for THIRD STUDENT MODEL

COLLABORATIVE OPPORTUNITY

Before students read the revised paragraph on page 232, have them work together in pairs to develop a list of reasons supporting the opinion expressed in the topic sentence. Afterward, they can compare their reasons with those given in the revised model on page 232.

for FIRST STUDENT MODEL

KEY TO UNDERSTANDING Have a student read the revised paragraph aloud. Then have the class discuss and evaluate the reasons the writer gave for her opinion. Point out that the writer arranged her reasons in order of importance, with the more important reason last. Have students also note that she used transitional phrases ("first of all"; "second and more importantly") to "signal" each new reason.

for SECOND STUDENT MODEL

INDIVIDUALIZING INSTRUCTION: BASIC STUDENTS These students may need guidance in connecting the changes that were made and the notes in the margin. Help them by asking questions such as "Why did the writer change his first sentence? Do you think he improved it? Why did he move the sentence about the blastoff to the end of the paragraph? Why did he take out the sentence he did?"

ESL STUDENTS Encourage these students to write marginal notes in their native languages on their drafts. The notes can serve to remind them of problems they have identified or changes they want to make.

ADVANCED STUDENTS Ask these students whether they can create an even better attention-grabbing topic sentence than the one in the Student Model. Allow time for volunteers to share their sentences with the class.

Now read the revised paragraph. Can you see what the writer did to improve her paragraph?

Student MODEL

I don't think school officials should tell us what to publish in our student newspaper. First of all, the newspaper is written for students. So why should the articles in it have to please the principal? Second and more importantly, don't sixth-graders have the right to free speech just like every other citizen in this country?

Writing notes to yourself can help you remember what you want to do to improve your draft. When you review your work, you may want to note in the margin the changes you'd like to make. Notice how one writer used his notes to improve his writing.

Student MODEL

I need to rewrite my topic sentence so that it grabs people's attention.

It would make more sense to begin at the beginning of the process, putting the blastoff at the end.

This sentence doesn't really belong.

~~Here is~~ [Have you ever wondered] how a rocket [actually] blasts off[?]~~.~~ Basically, a rocket ~~launches~~ [moves] in one direction by pushing in the opposite direction. As [the] gases force their way out the back of ~~a~~ [the] rocket, they send ~~a~~ [the] rocket skyward. ~~A rocket launch must be an amazing sight~~. The whole process starts with the burning of fuel inside ~~a~~ [the] rocket. The burning fuel produces hot gases. These gases build up inside the rocket until they fill all the space in the compartment where they're being created. At that point, they start escaping through an opening in the back of the rocket.

Practice Your Skills

Read each of the following drafts of student paragraphs. Then read the student comments that accompany each paragraph. Use the student comments in the margin to revise each paragraph. If you have your own ideas about how to make each paragraph better, add those to your revision also.

1. Whales' behavior suggests that a great deal of what they sing about must have to do with relationships. For example, the relationship between a female whale and her child is an extremely strong one. Female whales will risk their lives to protect their young. Whale offspring, called calves, can double in size during their first year of life. Adult whales may grow to weigh as much as 150 tons. What's more, even a fully grown adult may return to its mother during times of trouble. I can understand that. No matter how old I get, when I'm sick or hurt I always want my mom to take care of me. Adult whales will also come to the aid of a sick or injured companion. Furthermore, if a very sick whale decides to beach itself rather than die by drowning, the rest of the whales in its herd may beach themselves too rather than abandon their companion. Clearly, the attachments whales form in life are very strong and important to them.

Peer Reader Comments

Get rid of details that don't develop the main idea.

2. During summer, my brother likes going to the neighborhood pool. I like spending my time at the Hill of Three Oaks. There are lots of great reasons to hang out at the hill. First, the hill is a perfect launching place for my glider. Since no one else is ever there, it's a great place to practice the harmonica. When I try to practice at home, either my mom asks me to stop or my brother makes fun of me. Best of all, though, the hill is a good place to read and think. The book I've been reading lately is *Rumble Fish* by S. E. Hinton.

Write an attention-getting topic sentence.

Get rid of the details that don't develop the main idea.

Add a transition to link the second reason to the others.

for PRACTICE YOUR SKILLS

COOPERATIVE LEARNING Have students work in pairs to revise the paragraphs. They should discuss their reasons for dropping particular details in each paragraph. For paragraph 2, they should discuss their ideas for an improved topic sentence.

Additional Resource

Writing Resource Book, p. 61

Answers to Practice Your Skills

Answers will vary. Sample revisions are provided.

1. Whales' behavior suggests that a great deal of what they sing about must have to do with relationships. For example, the relationship between a female whale and her child is an extremely strong one. Female whales will risk their lives to protect their young. What's more, even a fully grown adult may return to its mother during times of trouble. Adult whales will also come to the aid of a sick or injured companion. Furthermore, if a very sick whale decides to beach itself rather than die by drowning, the rest of the whales in its herd may beach themselves too rather than abandon their companion. Clearly, the attachments whales form in life are very strong and important to them.
2. Do you have a special place in your neighborhood that's perfect for summer afternoons? I like spending my time at the Hill of Three Oaks. There are lots of great reasons to hang out at the hill. First, the hill is a perfect launching place for my glider. Second, since no one else is ever there, it's a great place to practice the harmonica. Best of all, though, the hill is a good place to read and think.

WRITING HANDBOOK 11

Transitions

Objectives

- To analyze the relationships between ideas or details, as signaled by different transitions
- To use transitions to make relationships between ideas and details clear

Related Mini-Lessons

For information on topics related to using transitions, see the following mini-lessons:

- **Organizing Details, pp. 217–221**
- **Improving Paragraphs, pp. 230–233**

Motivate

Have students give directions orally on how to get from your school to another place in the community. Write on the board what each student says and underline transitions, such as *then, when, after, next to, at the third light* and *as soon as.* Point out that people often use such words or phrases when talking, so that others will understand the speaker's ideas are connected. Emphasize that such words and phrases serve the same purpose in writing.

Teaching Strategies

for KINDS OF TRANSITIONS

HELPFUL HINT Tell students that time order transitions are important in narrative writing particularly, because they help readers follow the order of events. Have small groups, or the class as a whole, work together to give a brief summary of the events in a recent sports competition or in a TV drama, using transitions to make the order of events clear.

WRITING HANDBOOK 11

How Can I Connect My Ideas?

Transitions

Not all relationships are as easy to identify as the one between these twins—especially when the relationships are

between ideas or details in a piece of writing. To make such relationships clear, writers sometimes use transitions. **Transitions** are words and phrases that tell readers how details are related to one another. For example, "We have similar tastes in many things. *However,* I like chocolate frozen yogurt, and my sister prefers vanilla."

KINDS OF TRANSITIONS

Writing **TIP**

Transitions can link paragraphs, sentences, and details within sentences.

You can use transitions to tell how details are related in time, space, or importance. You can also use transitions to signal whether details are similar or different.

Time Order When you want to show how details are related in time, you can use the words *first, second,* and *third.* Other words that signal a link to the past, present, or future are shown on the following chart.

Time Order Transitions

Past	Present	Future
before yesterday earlier	now today next during meanwhile	later finally tomorrow afterwards then

Social Studies Connection

To reinforce the importance of transitional words and phrases, have students bring their social studies textbooks to class and turn to a chapter dealing with historical events. Have them identify time order transitions and examples of their use. Point out that these words can help them remember the order in which events occurred. Then have students turn to a chapter on geographic regions. Have them identify spatial order transitions and examples of their use. Point out that these words can help them remember where places are in relationship to one another.

Now notice how J.R.R. Tolkien uses transitions in the following passage to help readers follow Bilbo and his friends on a journey.

Literary MODEL

> **At first** they had passed through hobbit-lands, a wild respectable country inhabited by decent folk, with good roads, an inn or two, and now and then a dwarf or a farmer ambling by on business. **Then** they came to lands where people spoke strangely, and sang songs Bilbo had never heard before. **Now** they had gone on far into the Lone-lands, where there were no people left, no inns, and the roads grew steadily worse.
>
> **J.R.R. Tolkien, *The Hobbit***

Spatial Order To show the position or location of something, try using the following transitions.

Writing TIP

You can create clear word pictures and give precise directions with spatial order transitions.

Spatial Order Transitions

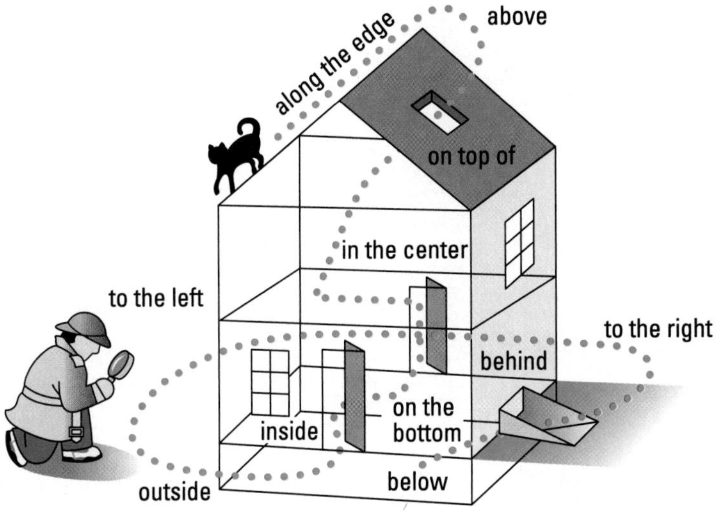

Look for the transitions in the model on the next page. Could you picture the scene as clearly without these transitions?

for LITERARY MODEL

ASSESSMENT: SPOT CHECK To check students' understanding of time order transitions, invite them to replace each boldfaced transition in the model with another transition, having a similar meaning, from the chart on page 234. Make sure students' substitutions do not alter the progression of events in the original paragraph.

for SPATIAL ORDER

INDIVIDUALIZING INSTRUCTION: ESL STUDENTS Ask these students if there are any words in the transition charts whose meanings are unclear to them. If possible, have them work with someone proficient in both English and their first language who will clarify the meanings and give the ESL students additional examples of how the words and phrases are used.

for SPATIAL ORDER

HELPFUL HINT Point out to students that there is always more than one way to describe the position of an object. Pick an object in the room and have students describe its position in as many ways as possible, using a different transition word in each description. For example, the position of a classroom poster might be described by using a variety of transitions, in expressions, such as: "*At the front* of the room is a poster"; "*Behind* the teacher's desk is a poster"; "*To the left* of the board is a poster."

for LITERARY MODEL

SPEAKING, LISTENING, AND VIEWING To demonstrate the importance of spatial order transitions, have students close their eyes and picture the scene in their minds as you read the description aloud. Then read the description again, this time changing the transitions to create a different picture. Afterward, have students use the spatial order transitions to tell how the second description changed the picture in their minds. You might ask an artistically talented student to sketch the two descriptions and share the sketches with the class.

for ORDER OF IMPORTANCE

MODELING Give students examples in which you use *first, second,* and *last* to signal time order; then give examples in which you use those words to signal order of importance. For example, for order of importance you might give three reasons why you think a certain animal makes the best pet. For the last reason, use the transition *Third, and most important.*

Literary MODEL

The hills had flattened and given way to low fields of sedge [grasslike plants]. A scent of brine and brackish water reached Taran's nostrils. **Ahead,** the river widened, flowing into a bay, and **beyond that** to an even greater expanse of water. **To his right, on the far side** of towering rocks, Taran heard the rush of surf.

Lloyd Alexander, *The Castle of Llyr*

Order of Importance When you want to draw attention to how important each detail is, organize your details from least to most important or from most to least important. Then, introduce your details with transitions that show the details' order of importance.

Transitions That Show Order of Importance

First
Second
Third

Good
Better
Best

Least important
More important
Most important

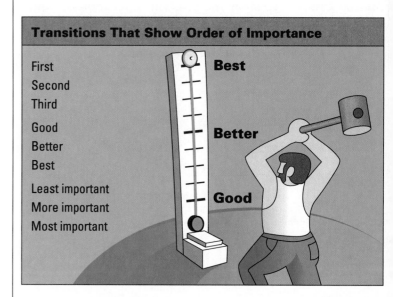

Some transitions can be used to show more than one relationship. For example, *first, second,* and *last* can signal both time order and order of importance. Look at the model on the next page. Notice how transitions show the order of importance of these tips for beginning runners.

Student MODEL

If you're interested in running, it's **important** to start by getting some information on the subject. Do some reading or talk to a coach. Even **more important,** invest in a good pair of shoes. Your feet need support. **Most important,** take it easy at first. Gradually, you will be able to increase your speed and distance.

Comparison and Contrast The following transitions can help you make clear which details are similar to one another and which are different. Remember, comparisons show similarities, while contrasts show differences.

Comparison Transitions

Comparison	
as	both
similarly	like
than	also
likewise	by comparison
Contrast	
yet	instead
but	by contrast
however	on the contrary
unlike	on the other hand

Now read the following model to see how transitions help the narrator point out the similarities and differences between two girls she hasn't seen all summer and a third girl who is new to her.

Literary MODEL

Grace and Carol are browner, less pasty; their features are farther apart, their hair lighter. The third girl is the tallest. **Unlike** Grace and Carol, who are in summer skirts, she wears corduroys and a pullover. **Both** Carol and Grace are stubby-shaped, **but** this girl is thin without being fragile.

Margaret Atwood, *Cat's Eye*

for COMPARISON AND CONTRAST

HELPFUL HINT Tell students that these transitions might come in handy in a piece of descriptive writing that compares two people, places, objects, or activities. Point out that comparison transitions also are useful in explanatory or persuasive writing, when students are comparing one opinion or reason with another.

for COMPARISON AND CONTRAST

MODELING Students probably already use *as, than, also,* and *like* when they are making comparisons in their writing, without actually planning to include them. Also, they probably already use *but* and *instead* when they are making a contrast. Students may need some help, however, in knowing when to use the other transitions in their writing. Model some examples of how to use transitions such as *likewise, similarly, on the contrary,* and *on the other hand.* Use these transitions in oral and written comparisons and contrasts of people, places, objects, or activities with which students are familiar, so that they can see the relationships between the ideas clearly.

Additional Resource

Writing Resource Book, p. 62

Answers to Practice Your Skills

A. Answers may vary. Possible answers are shown below.

1. First
2. Second
3. Then
4. Next
5. Finally

B. Answers may vary. Possible answers are shown below.

2. Then she stole home.
3. By contrast, Mae has a terrible sweet tooth.
4. At the bottom, a bright yellow raft floated along a muddy river.
5. Likewise, his sister has an ear for music.
6. More important, I've only played first base, never catcher.
7. On the other hand, toads have dry, warty skin.
8. Outside, the wind howled and the snow continued to pile up.

Practice Your Skills

A. Choose a time order transition to fill in each blank.

You can make a model volcano erupt in your own kitchen. (1) __________ , you'll need to get some newspapers, a six-ounce paper cup, some modeling clay, four tablespoons of baking soda, and one-fourth cup of vinegar. (2) __________ , cover the table with four layers of newspaper. Put the empty cup, right side up, on the table. (3) __________ , press and shape the clay around the sides of the cup so it looks like a mountain. (4) __________ , put the baking soda into the cup.(5) __________ , add the vinegar and watch your volcano erupt.

B. Each of the following groups of sentences is related. The relationship is stated in parentheses. Rewrite the italicized sentence in each group so that it begins with a transition showing how it is related to the others. The first item has already been done for you.

1. Second, it tastes good. *It's good for you.* (importance) *Most important, it's good for you.*
2. First, Jamie slid into third base. *She stole home.* Now she's up to bat again. (time order)
3. Both Deloris and Marcia prefer salty snacks. They love munching on peanuts and pretzels. *Mae has a terrible sweet tooth.* (contrast)
4. Rico peered into the canyon. *A bright yellow raft floated along a muddy river.* (spatial order)
5. Raji can play any tune after hearing it only once. *His sister has an ear for music.* (comparison)
6. First, I don't know anyone on the team. *I've only played first base, never catcher.* (importance)
7. Frogs have moist, smooth skin. *Toads have dry, warty skin.* (contrast)
8. We warmed ourselves in front of the fireplace. *The wind howled and the snow continued to pile up.* (spatial order)

What's the Best Way to Present My Information?

Show, Don't Tell

WRITING HANDBOOK 12

Two friends are discussing a race one of them ran:

JAMIE: The other runner was gaining on me. She was getting closer and closer. I was afraid she would win.

MARIA: How could you tell she was getting closer? What did you do?

JAMIE: As I rounded the last bend, the crunching of footsteps on the cinder track got louder and louder. Then I felt the brush of her sleeve against mine as she tried to pass me. I pumped my arms and pushed my legs harder, thinking, You've got to do it! You've got to win!

Jamie's first description *tells* what happened in a general way, providing no details. Her second description *shows* what actually happened while she was running. By sharing the thoughts and feelings she experienced during the race, Jamie makes it possible for Maria to experience what happened too.

In writing, as in conversation, the details are what people care about. Whether you're writing a letter or a report for school, you can develop and expand your ideas by including interesting, lively details that capture and hold your readers' attention.

How to *Show* Rather Than *Tell*

Showing an Experience When you write about a personal experience, show what happened by using specific sensory details to bring the people and places to life. Look at the passage from "Baseball in April" on the next page. Notice how Gary Soto uses vivid description to show what he remembers about a visit to Disneyland.

WRITING HANDBOOK 12

Show, Don't Tell

Objectives

- To recognize how sensory details, facts, examples, and reasons can improve various types of writing
- To write paragraphs that show, rather than tell, about a topic

Related Mini-Lessons

For information on topics related to using show-don't-tell strategies, see the following mini-lessons:

- **Organizing Details, pp. 217–221**
- **Appealing to the Senses, pp. 266–273**

Motivate

On the board, write the sentences "I really liked the concert. It was great." Ask students what questions they might ask a friend who had made these statements, if they themselves wanted to find out more about the concert. Write their questions—and add some of your own—on the board. Point out that by providing vivid details in answering these questions, the friend could *show,* rather than *tell,* what the concert had been like.

Teaching Strategies

for SHOWING AN EXPERIENCE

HELPFUL HINT Some students may need to review what sensory details are. Have them list the five senses—sight, hearing, smell, taste, touch. Explain that sensory details appeal to these senses so that readers can imagine what an experience was like.

Literature Connection

Read aloud the following passage from *The Summer of the Swans* by Betsy Byars. Have students identify sensory details that show how scared a mentally handicapped boy feels when lost in the woods:

"The sound of the dogs seemed to him to be everywhere, all around him, so that he ran first in one direction, then in another, like a wild animal caught in a maze. He ran into a bush and the briers stung his face and arms, and he thought this was somehow connected with the dogs and thrashed his arms out wildly, not even feeling the cuts in his skin."

for LITERARY MODEL

CRITICAL THINKING: ANALYZING
Have students identify sensory details in the passage and tell which senses they appeal to. (Samples: "bright flags"—sight, "wild dips and curves"—touch, "screamed"—hearing, "candy that made their teeth blue"—sight)

for LITERARY MODEL

SPEAKING AND LISTENING Have students who have visited Disneyland or other theme parks discuss their experiences. Encourage them to use sensory details to show what they saw, heard, tasted, smelled, and touched. Encourage other students to ask questions to obtain more sensory details about the various experiences.

for SHOWING A PROCESS

HELPFUL HINT Before students read the showing paragraph on the process of training a dog, ask if any students have trained a dog to sit. Ask what details they would add to the telling paragraph. Then have students read the Professional Model and compare their suggestions with the details in Wescott's paragraph.

for PROFESSIONAL MODEL

KEY TO UNDERSTANDING Point out how the writer used time-order transitions to show the sequence of steps. The transition *as* in the second sentence signals three steps that need to be done at the same time. The transition *then* in the middle of sentence 4 signals a step that should be done after another step. Sentence 5 again uses the transition *as* to indicate two actions that should be taken at the same time. If necessary, review Handbook 11 on transitions.

What does Disneyland look like? What's special about it? What fun things did you do?

Literary MODEL

Telling

Disneyland's a great place. Our trip there was fun.

Showing

Disneyland stood tall with castles and bright flags. The Matterhorn had wild dips and curves that took your breath away if you closed your eyes and screamed. The Pirates of the Caribbean didn't scare anyone but was fun anyway, and so were the teacups and It's a Small World. . . . Maria's younger sister, Irma, bought a Pinocchio coloring book and a candy bracelet. Her brothers, Rudy and John, spent their money on candy that made their teeth blue.

Gary Soto, "Baseball in April"

Showing a Process When you explain the steps in a process or give a set of directions, you need to be especially clear and complete. Notice how the telling sentence below leaves many questions unanswered. The showing paragraph includes all the important details.

How do you get him to sit the first time? What do you repeat?

Professional MODEL

Telling

To train your dog to sit, make him sit down, then repeat the command over and over.

Showing

Stand him on your left side, holding the leash fairly short, and command him to sit. As you give the verbal command, pull up slightly with the leash and push his hindquarters down. Do not let him lie down or stand up. Keep him in a sitting position for a moment, then release the pressure on the leash and praise him. Constantly repeat the command as you hold him in a sitting position, thus fitting the word to the action in his mind.

William D. Wescott, *How to Raise and Train a Keeshond*

PROFESSIONAL NOTEBOOK

Advice from the Authors Share with students Peter Elbow's explanation of "show, don't tell" in *Writing with Power:* "That is, if you want readers to feel something, it's no good telling them how to feel ('it was simply *terrifying*'). You have to show them things that will terrify them. . . . Direct all your efforts into experiencing—or re-experiencing—what you are writing about. . . . Be there. See it. *Participate* in whatever you are writing about. . . ."

WRITER TO WRITER

Let us understand your character by what happens to him. . . . Don't tell us that John Smith was angry. Show him kicking over a wastebasket.

Judson Phillips, writer

Showing an Opinion Your opinions and beliefs are based on your experiences and on what you have learned from others. To show rather than tell your opinions, support them with facts, examples, or reasons. This student writer revised her telling sentence. She showed why she believes that solar energy is part of a solution to the world's environmental problems.

Telling

We should rely more on solar energy because it's better for the environment.

Why is solar energy better for the environment? Better than what? How does it compare with other forms of energy?

Showing

To save the environment, we need to rely more on solar energy. Solar energy—energy from the sun—is a cleaner form of energy than the energy that comes from burning fossil fuels, such as coal and oil. That means there will be less pollution and the air will be cleaner. The rate of global warming will slow down, and less wildlife will be displaced or killed by people searching the wilderness for new oil supplies.

Student MODEL

A woman uses a solar box cooker to prepare food.

Showing Information Showing information in a report or essay means supporting each of your main points with plenty of facts, examples, and details.

Telling

Animals play when they're young. That's how they learn survival skills.

Which animals? What survival skills do they learn?

for WRITER TO WRITER

ASSESSMENT: SPOT CHECK To see how well students understand the concept of "show, don't tell," ask what actions they might describe to show that a character was happy, sad, jealous, nervous, or afraid.

for SHOWING AN OPINION

HELPFUL HINT Discuss with students how TV news demonstrates the power of showing, rather than telling, about problems and solutions. For example, telling statements such as "We need to recycle more" or "We should send food aid to starving nations" can go ignored by the audience. But pictures of overflowing landfills or starving children are far more likely to make an impression. Stress that the writer's job is to create such pictures with words.

for STUDENT MODEL

INDIVIDUALIZING INSTRUCTION: BASIC STUDENTS These students may need some help in interpreting the reasons given to support the writer's point of view. If necessary, explain, or have an informed student explain, the terms *fossil fuels* and *global warming* and how they relate to the writer's main idea.

SPICE BOX

Invite students to guess what familiar phrases these word puzzles "show."

MAN / BOARD	*(man overboard)*
ECNALG	*(a backward glance)*
ANOTHER ONE THING	*(one thing after another)*

Then ask students to show "mind over matter," "a broken heart," or phrases of their own choosing.

for PROFESSIONAL MODEL

LINKING GRAMMAR TO WRITING

Tell students that using vivid verbs is one way to show readers what is happening. Point out the verbs *crouch, stalk,* and *pounce* in the passage. Ask readers who own cats if these actions are familiar to them. Have them describe the visual image each verb shows.

for PRACTICE YOUR SKILLS

MANAGING THE PAPER LOAD

Assign the item that relates to the type of writing students are currently doing. If, for instance, students are writing descriptions, you might suggest they work on items 4 or 5.

Additional Resources

Writing Resource Book, pp. 63–64
Thinking Skills Worksheets
Thinking Skills Transparency Pack
Elaboration, Revision, and Proofreading Practice
Elaboration, Revision, and Proofreading Transparency Pack

Answers to Practice Your Skills

A. Answers will vary. A sample revision is provided for paragraph 1.

The movie was disappointing. My favorite actor spoke a total of three lines and wore a clown mask the whole time. The two funny scenes that were in the coming-attractions trailer turned out to be the only laughs in the whole movie. The plot was so confusing that people in the audience kept turning to their friends and whispering questions about what was going on.

B. Answers will vary. A sample revision is provided for paragraph 3.

Our lunch period should be fifteen minutes longer. As soon as the bell rings, I race down to the cafeteria and wait in line for ten minutes. Then I spend another five minutes searching for a table and getting a drink. By the time I start eating, I only have fifteen minutes to gulp down my food and mumble hello to my friends. It is not a relaxing experience, and I usually end up with a stomachache by sixth period.

Professional MODEL

Showing

Do animals really "play"? The next time you're at a zoo, watch how the lion cubs frolic. One will crouch low against the ground, stalk slowly toward its littermate, and then pounce on the surprised "victim." Such roughhouse sessions occur frequently among most carnivores such as wolves, tigers, cheetahs, raccoons, and coyotes. As they play, these young develop the abilities they need to become efficient predators.

Eugene J. Walter, Jr., "Why Do They Do What They Do?"

Practice Your Skills

A. Rewrite the following telling sentences, turning them into showing paragraphs. Use the writing strategies suggested in parentheses.

1. The movie was disappointing. (Show your opinion by supporting it with reasons and other evidence.)
2. There's a greeting card for every occasion. (Show why this is true by giving several examples.)
3. You need to know how to make a good first impression. (Show the steps in this process.)
4. The party was great. (Show the experience by using vivid sensory details to describe what happened.)
5. She stood out from the crowd. (Show this character by describing physical details and actions.)

B. Write a showing paragraph based on each of the following sentences.

1. It was a moment no one would forget.
2. I love making my favorite food. You can do it too.
3. Our lunch period should be fifteen minutes longer.
4. Junk food is being replaced by more healthful food choices for both snacks and meals.
5. I felt out of place.

How Do I Put Everything Together?

WRITING HANDBOOK 13

Creating Longer Pieces of Writing

Exploring an idea can be like tugging on a magician's scarf: you start with one idea and it leads you to another, which leads to another, and so on. What then? If you want to write about all these ideas, you really can't do so in just one paragraph. After all, a good paragraph develops only one main idea. To explore a number of ideas, you write a composition.

WHAT IS A COMPOSITION?

A **composition** is a group of paragraphs that work together to develop a single topic. If this definition reminds you of the definition of a paragraph, that's because the two forms are very much alike. Just look at some of the similarities between a paragraph and a composition.

Paragraph		Composition
Topic Sentence	• states the main idea • gets the reader's attention	Introductory Paragraph
Supporting Sentence		Body Paragraph
Supporting Sentence	• develops the main idea	Body Paragraph
Supporting Sentence		Body Paragraph
Clincher	• reinforces the main idea • paragraph clincher is optional	Concluding Paragraph

Social Studies Connection

One place in which students are likely to find many examples of introduction-body-conclusion structure is in their social studies textbooks. Challenge students to find such a passage in their textbooks, one that is about five or six paragraphs long. Examine one or two examples as a class.

WRITING HANDBOOK 13

Creating Longer Pieces of Writing

Objectives

- To recognize how paragraphs work together in a composition
- To use strategies to create longer pieces of writing
- To use revising guidelines to improve a composition

Related Mini-Lessons

For information on topics related to creating longer pieces of writing, see the following mini-lessons:

- **Improving Paragraphs, pp. 230–233**
- **Introductions, pp. 247–249**
- **Conclusions, pp. 250–252**

Motivate

Show students one frame from a popular comic strip. Ask students to point out the "parts" of the frame (characters, speech balloons, background). Then state that the single frame has all the "parts" of the complete strip and ask students if they would feel satisfied seeing only this one frame. (No; a single frame from a strip does not tell the whole story.) Then point out that a single paragraph from a composition no more tells the whole story than a single frame from a comic strip.

Teaching Strategies

for WHAT IS A COMPOSITION?

HELPFUL HINT You may want to point out that just as not all paragraphs rigidly follow one pattern, neither do all compositions. However, a successful composition will do what is described in the middle column of the chart.

for DRAFTING A COMPOSITION

HELPFUL HINT You may wish to point out that writers choose different ways to begin their compositions. The "best" way to begin differs according to the writer's personal choice and the writing topic. List a variety of choices on the board: 1. prepare detailed outlines; 2. work from rough notes; 3. work slowly and revise while writing; 4. write quickly and revise later; 5. write interesting parts first; 6. write from beginning to end; and so forth. Ask students for their own suggestions and add these to the list. (For more about drafting and editing, see Professional Notebook below.)

for REVISING A COMPOSITION

INDIVIDUALIZING INSTRUCTION: BASIC STUDENTS You may want to review the concepts of *main idea* and *topic* for these students. Students may be better able to distinguish between the concepts if they consider a specific example, such as the following:

Topic: video games

Main idea: Playing video games is a worthwhile hobby.

HOW DO I CREATE A COMPOSITION?

The strategies you use to write good paragraphs will also help you create strong compositions. So keep those techniques and guidelines in mind as you draft.

Drafting a Composition

When you start drafting, you may want just to explore and develop your ideas without giving any thought to how many paragraphs there will be. You can group and organize ideas later. On the other hand, you may know what your main ideas are, and you may want to develop each one as a paragraph. Refer to the guidelines for drafting paragraphs that appear in Handbook 10, "Improving Paragraphs," on pages 230–233.

Writing TIP

You might want to make a rough outline of your composition. Then use each main point in your outline as the main idea of a paragraph.

Revising a Composition

Once you've gotten your ideas down on paper, you can improve your composition by following these guidelines.

Guidelines for Revising a Composition

- **Check to see that your first paragraph identifies your topic and gets your reader's attention.**
- **Make sure that each supporting paragraph develops only one main idea.** Break paragraphs overloaded with ideas into smaller paragraphs, each focusing on one main idea.
- **Check to see that the order of your paragraphs makes sense.** Rearrange paragraphs and add transitions as necessary.
- **Make sure that your last paragraph ties your ideas together effectively and does not introduce new thoughts that need to be developed or explained.**

PROBLEM SOLVING

"I need to know more about developing the different kinds of paragraphs in a composition."

For more information about developing paragraphs in a composition, see

- Handbook 4, "Developing a Topic," pages 205–210
- Handbook 14, "Introductions," pages 247–249
- Handbook 15, "Conclusions," pages 250–252

PROFESSIONAL NOTEBOOK

Advice from the Authors Ask students if they agree with the following comment by Peter Elbow about editing during the drafting stage:

"Editing is usually necessary if we want to end up with something satisfactory. The problem is that editing goes on *at the same time* as producing. The editor is, as it were,constantly looking over the shoulder of the producer and constantly fiddling with what he's doing while he's in the middle of trying to do it. No wonder the producer gets nervous. . . . It's an unnecessary burden to try to think of words and also worry at the same time whether they're the right words."

Now look at how one student used these revision guidelines to improve his composition.

Student MODEL

Are video games worthwhile or not? There are strong arguments to support both answers to this question. ¶ Some people argue that video games are just a waste of time and money. For instance, My dad says, "You should have more to show for the time and money you spend than what you get from those games." He thinks that playing video games just takes time away from doing homework and chores and gives ~~you~~ players nothing in return.

However, other people point out that ~~Video~~ games provide entertainment and help build important skills. Kids get a lot of fun out of playing video games. At the same time, ~~B~~because many games involve quickly pushing buttons or moving a joystick, players also develop faster reflexes and better coordination. ~~When you get one of the top scores you get to put your name on the screen. I've done that in one game already. Your name stays there until someone else gets a better score.~~ Also, with practice, the games make ~~you~~ players able to concentrate better and solve puzzles faster. ¶ Clearly, video games give ~~you~~ players quite a lot in return for ~~your~~ their time and money. Therefore, ~~I~~in my opinion video-game playing is a worthwhile hobby.

Keep opener—question should get my readers' attention.

Begin a new paragraph when a new idea is introduced.

Add a transition to help readers see that this is my next main idea.

Getting off the point here???

Oops—players, not readers

Separate out conclusion and connect the last sentence with a transition word.

for STUDENT MODEL

USING THE MODEL Ask students to compare the writer's changes and comments with the Guidelines for Revising a Composition on page 244. Students should note that the writer checks to see whether he has an attention-getting opening; he decides that he has. Then he checks to see that each paragraph develops only one main idea; he decides to make changes. Discuss these changes with students. Then ask volunteers what kinds of individual word changes the writer has made (the addition of transitions and the use of an accurate, specific noun in place of the vague pronoun *you*). Point out that these relatively small changes greatly improve the composition.

for PRACTICE YOUR SKILLS

MANAGING THE PAPER LOAD

After students have revised the composition on their own, you might display the unrevised version on an overhead projector. Have students work through the revision guidelines, contributing their changes orally.

Additional Resources

Writing Resource Book, p. 65
Elaboration, Revision, and Proofreading Practice, pp. 13–15
Elaboration, Revision, and Proofreading Transparency Pack

Answers to Practice Your Skills

Answers will vary. However, all revisions should have an introductory paragraph, two body paragraphs, and a concluding paragraph. They should not contain the unrelated sentences that mention George and Barbara Bush and Bob Kersee. A sample revision is shown below.

When Gail Devers flashed across the finish line at the 1992 Summer Olympics, her run was an amazing achievement. Not only did she win a gold medal in the 100-meter dash, but she accomplished this feat even though she suffered from a serious illness.

In 1988, Devers came down with Graves' disease, which is a gland problem that often causes weight loss and extreme tiredness. Fortunately, her doctors were able to treat this illness. Unfortunately, however, the treatments they gave Devers ruined her health. After a while, she couldn't even walk.

Then, in 1991, doctors finally figured out how to get rid of the side effects. They changed her treatment. Within a month she was able to walk around a track. Two months later she won a race. One year later she won an Olympic gold medal.

To win an Olympic gold medal at all is a triumph. To win one as Devers did, however, is a truly amazing accomplishment. *Sports Illustrated* called her achievement "the greatest comeback in modern track history."

Practice Your Skills

Revise the draft below by making the following changes:

- Break the writing into four paragraphs, each focusing on one main idea.
- Delete the two sentences that don't support any of the main ideas.
- Add any transitions that are needed to make the connections between details clear.
- Fix the run-on sentence.

When Gail Devers flashed across the finish line at the 1992 Summer Olympics, her run was an amazing achievement. Not only did she win a gold medal in the 100-meter dash, she did so even though she suffered from a serious illness. In 1988, Devers came down with Graves' disease, a gland problem that often causes weight loss and extreme tiredness. George and Barbara Bush also have this disease. Doctors found it difficult to treat her illness. The treatments they gave Devers ruined her health. After a while, she couldn't even walk. In 1991, doctors finally figured out how to get rid of the side effects. They changed her treatment within a month she was able to walk around a track. Two months later she won a race. One year later she won an Olympic gold medal. Her coach at the Olympics was Bob Kersee. To win an Olympic gold medal at all is a triumph. To win one as Devers did is a truly amazing accomplishment. *Sports Illustrated* called her achievement "the greatest comeback in modern track history."

246 Writing Handbook

How Do I Begin My Writing?

Introductions

Worms, flies, a bit of a cheese sandwich—to catch a fish, you've got to use the right bait. To catch a reader's attention, a writer also relies on bait. However, a writer's "bait" is a well-written introduction—not a day-old sandwich.

WRITING HANDBOOK 14

WAYS TO BEGIN

A good introduction both interests readers and lets them know what they will be reading about. Here are some good ways to get started.

Ask a Question

If you start with a question, curiosity will probably cause your readers to read on to find the answer. Would you continue reading to discover the answer to the question that begins the following introduction?

Professional MODEL

> Is the Leaning Tower in Pisa, Italy, falling down? Some Italians think so—even though the 817-year-old monument has survived earthquakes, World War II and nearly one million visitors a year.
>
> **"Pisa in Pieces," *3-2-1 Contact***

WRITING HANDBOOK 14

Introductions

Objectives

- To learn strategies for writing attention-getting introductions
- To write interesting introductions

Related Mini-Lessons

For information on topics related to writing introductions, see the following mini-lessons:

- **Finding a Starting Point, pp. 197–202**
- **Creating Paragraphs, pp. 226–229**

Motivate

Ask students to recall favorite movies or a recent episode of a favorite TV program. Have volunteers describe just the first scenes of these films and programs. Then ask what they think the directors wanted to accomplish with these opening scenes. For example, did the scene reveal something about a character? the plot? If someone had missed the opening, how long would it take him or her to figure out the story? Elicit that the directors were attempting to seize their audiences' attention and give them some idea of the characters, plot, or subject.

Teaching Strategies

GENERAL NOTE

STUMBLING BLOCK Students often settle upon one type of opening and use it for most compositions. Urge students to experiment with all of the strategies.

for PROFESSIONAL MODELS

KEY TO UNDERSTANDING Have students read the Arneke and Heligman introductions aloud. Point out that Arneke's facts help readers grasp the scope of the problem he is introducing. Next, ask students what (besides being questions) the first two sentences in Heligman's introduction have in common. (Both are idiomatic expressions—that is, phrases whose meanings people are not expected to take literally.) Then point out that because readers don't intend to take these questions literally, their curiosity is aroused by the material that follows, which suggests that color and emotions may actually be linked.

for TALK TO YOUR READER

HELPFUL HINT: AUDIENCE Point out to students that it is sometimes easier to write an attention-getting introduction *after* they have explored their subject and determined their audience. When students have a clear picture of their audience in mind, figuring out how to address that audience directly comes more naturally.

for WRITING TIP

STUMBLING BLOCK Remind students that an effective introduction or conclusion can address the reader directly by using the pronoun *you.* However, the pronoun must refer only to the audience. Turn back to page 245 and ask students to examine the unrevised introduction and conclusion in the Student Model. What inconsistency do they see involving the word *you?* (In the introduction, *you* refers to the writer. In the concluding paragraph, *you* refers to video game players.)

Facts First

Jump right in with a surprising fact or statistic that will catch your reader's attention. Here, for example, a writer begins with several startling bits of information.

Professional MODEL

> United States manufacturers sold some 388 million pairs of athletic shoes last year. The beauty of that dizzying number varies greatly from beholder to beholder. Runners see lots of miles run. Retailers see $12.1 billion. And environmentalists see 776 million shoes heading straight for landfills (and those are just last year's shoes).
>
> **David Arneke, "Sole Searching"**

Talk to Your Reader

Have you ever noticed that it's hard to ignore someone who speaks straight at you? Readers tend to find it equally difficult to ignore writing that talks directly to them. Notice, for instance, how you respond to the following introduction.

Professional MODEL

> Are you feeling sad and "blue"? Or are you happy and "in the pink"? Believe it or not, whether you are sad or happy may have a lot to do with color: the color you're wearing, or, more likely, the color you're looking at.
>
> **Deborah Heligman, "There's a Lot More to Color Than Meets the Eye"**

Writing **TIP**

Remember not to use the pronoun *you* unless you really mean "the reader."

Tell a Story

Interest your readers by telling an unusual or a funny story. After all, who can resist a good story? Remember, however, that it's just the introduction to your main subject. So keep the tale short. For example, read the brief tale told in the introduction on the next page.

Literature Connection

Ask students what techniques this introduction by Joan Hunt uses to build interest in her subject, Teddy Roosevelt, a future president.

"Who's the dude?" asked New York assemblyman John Walsh as the 1882 session of the state legislature convened. Young Theodore Roosevelt, wearing a silk hat and pince-nez and carrying a gold-headed cane, flashed a smile. It was the smile of a bulldog who growled at every issue and attacked corrupt politics and politicians." (Sample: uses dialogue/quotation)

It was a chilly October night. A family was driving along a lonely mountain road in northern Oregon. Suddenly, they saw a nine-foot-tall, hairy figure moving swiftly along the roadside. It was caught in the headlights of their car as they passed. But they were too scared to turn around and investigate.

Russell Ginns and Michael Rozek, "Tracking Bigfoot"

Professional MODEL

This story makes readers want to find out what happened next. What did the family see?

WRITER TO WRITER

When I can't think of how to begin a story, I start with dialogue.

Alyce Arnick, student
Aurora, Colorado

Practice Your Skills

A. Look through the models in the Writer's Workshops. Find three introductions that made you want to read more. Tell why each introduction is effective.

B. The following are four weak introductions. Choose two of them. Use what you learned in this handbook to rewrite the two introductions, making them more interesting.

1. Computers can do amazing things. Things that seem fantastic now may be common in the future.
2. Mercury is an interesting planet. It travels around the sun at about 106,000 miles per hour. It is faster than the other planets in the solar system.
3. Bicycle helmets are a great way to protect yourself when you're riding. Everybody should wear one.
4. The weather affects many people's moods. On cold, gray winter days, the lack of sunshine makes some people feel like hibernating.

for PRACTICE YOUR SKILLS

MANAGING THE PAPER LOAD

After students have completed the exercises independently, have them discuss their answers in small groups. Circulate from group to group. Encourage any groups with particularly effective introductions for Exercise B to share them with the class.

Additional Resource

Writing Resource Book, p. 66

Answers to Practice Your Skills

A. Answers will vary.

B. Answers will vary. Sample revisions are shown below.

1. For years people have told computers what to do. Now there are computers that can talk back. Engineers have designed computers that understand and respond to the human voice. They are just one example of the kinds of computers that may be commonplace in the not-too-distant future.
2. What's round and speeds along at about 106,000 miles per hour? It's Mercury, the fastest planet in the solar system.
3. I pedaled my bike furiously. Just three more blocks and I would be home. Suddenly, a car pulled out of a driveway. I squeezed hard on the brakes but couldn't stop. As I tumbled across the pavement, one thought went through my mind: "Boy, am I glad I've got a helmet on."
4. Do you wake up on a gray winter day and feel like burrowing under the covers? You're not alone. Many people find that the weather affects their moods. The lack of sunshine in the winter makes some people feel like hibernating.

SPICE BOX

Ask students to bring in books, stories, or articles with attention-getting introductions. Have them share the introductions in small groups; have the groups analyze the introductions to see what strategies the writers used. Encourage the groups to design and prepare a bulletin board display.

WRITING
HANDBOOK
15

Conclusions

Objectives

- To learn strategies for writing strong conclusions
- To write strong conclusions

Related Mini-Lessons

For information on topics related to writing conclusions, see the following mini-lessons:

- **Creating Paragraphs, pp. 226–229**
- **Revising, pp. 257–259**

Teaching Strategies

for PROFESSIONAL MODEL

CRITICAL THINKING: SPECULATING

Emphasize that a successful conclusion sometimes gives the reader a review of the main points in the composition. Ask students to look closely at the model conclusion and tell what information the article probably included. (Samples: the history of trading baseball cards, when the cards first appeared and with what products, how the hobby has grown, why it is still popular)

WRITING
HANDBOOK
15

How Do I End My Writing?

Conclusions

W R I T E R T O W R I T E R

I don't like it when they just tell you the story and don't have an ending.

Celeste Coleman, student
Clovis, California

Ending a piece of writing without a conclusion is like hanging up in the middle of a phone conversation. You leave your reader wondering, "Is this really the end?"

WAYS TO END WRITING

A good conclusion tells readers, "This is the end," and also leaves them with something to think about. Here, for example, are some good ways to conclude your writing.

Writing **TIP**

Be careful not to introduce any new supporting details or unrelated ideas in your conclusion.

Say It Again

When you want your readers to remember the main points that you've made, restate them in a new way in your conclusion. For example, this writer reminds his readers that collecting baseball cards is and will continue to be a popular hobby.

Professional MODEL

Summarizes the details that support the main idea.

Baseball cards have been sold with everything from the first bubble gum, in the 1930s, to dog food. And baseball fans will keep on buying them, trading them, and treasuring them for as long as players continue to play ball.

"Hot Hobby: Collecting Baseball Cards,"
National Geographic World

Tell Readers What to Think or Do

Sometimes your purpose for writing is to get your readers to change their mind or take an action. Then you may want to end by telling your readers exactly what you feel they should think or do. What actions does this writer suggest?

Professional **MODEL**

> The Bronx Zoo isn't the only place where you'll find bits of wilderness created for zoo animals. Other zoos have been building similar exhibits. Take the time to get to know some of the animals who live there. Remember, they're ambassadors from a disappearing world. And once you've made some new friends, find out how to keep their wilderness homes from disappearing.
>
> **Richard Chevat, "Monkey Business: A Zoo Exhibit Makes Baboons Feel at Home"**

Suggests an action

Suggests something to consider

Suggests an action

End with a Picture

If you want to leave your readers with a powerful word picture, sensory details can help. Here, one writer ends a story about a trip to Mount Rainier with a portrait of the mountain.

Professional **MODEL**

> I step outside the lodge door and into the **softly glowing** night. The earth is **silent,** the land **pure white,** here at the top of the world. Blinking away snowflakes on my eyelashes, I stare at the white slopes, trying to imagine them as meadows in bloom, the way they will look in a few short weeks. It seems impossible. But this is, after all, the magic mountain.
>
> **K. M. Kostyal, "Mount Rainier National Park"**

These sensory details help to make the mountain seem like a magical place.

Words such as *blinking, stare, impossible,* and *magic* help to communicate a feeling of wonder.

Save the Last Event for Last

If you're writing a story, you may just want to end it by telling the last thing that happened. For example, notice the model on the next page that shows how one writer ended a story about a clerk who loses his job in a flower shop.

for FIRST PROFESSIONAL MODEL

INDIVIDUALIZING INSTRUCTION: ESL STUDENTS Some students from cultures whose educational systems are authoritarian in nature may have little experience with making recommendations. Ask them to state orally, in a few words, what they think the problem is and what they think should be done about it; then have them write their recommendations as statements.

GENERAL NOTE

CRITICAL THINKING: CLASSIFYING Encourage students to suggest kinds of writing for which each type of conclusion might be especially useful. Emphasize, however, that it is possible to use any conclusion with any kind of writing.

- Say It Again (writing that explains)
- Tell Readers What to Think or Do (persuasion)
- End with a Picture (descriptions and stories)
- Save the Last Event for Last (telling a story or recounting an autobiographical incident)

Literature Connection

Ask students to notice how biographer Pam Gingold ends her sketch on Mother Jones.

"Mother Jones kept up the fight for workers' rights well into her nineties. She finally passed on, at age one hundred, in 1930, only a few years before labor's greatest victories. But her memory lives on, especially among coal miners. During the Pittston Coal strike of 1989, the wives and daughters of striking miners proudly called themselves 'The Daughters of Mother Jones.'"

(Sample: begins conclusion with last event; makes interesting point—"her memory lives on"; supports point with example)

for PRACTICE YOUR SKILLS

MANAGING THE PAPER LOAD

After students complete the two exercises, ask them to read over their conclusions and to star at least one but not more than two, that they think are especially strong. Comment only on those conclusions that the students feel are their best work.

Additional Resource

Writing Resource Book, p. 67

Answers to Practice Your Skills

A. Revisions will vary. Sample revisions are shown below.

1. I could see the finish line up ahead, but I didn't think I would have the strength to reach it. I was already gasping for air. Meanwhile, the other runners were gaining on me. Then I heard my teammates cheering me on, and somehow I found the energy to keep going. I made it across the finish line with my knees buckling but a big grin on my face. I had won the race.
2. World hunger is a big problem, but that doesn't mean you can't do anything about it. Find out about the organizations in your community that are working to end hunger, and volunteer to help. Kids can make a difference.
3. I'll never forget what our house looked like after the tornado. The roof had caved in, crushing the whole second floor. The refrigerator lay on its side in the kitchen, with broken dishes, bottles, and food all around it. Because of the water spraying out of broken pipes, the mess on the floor was running together and flooding out into the hall. The living room, however, was untouched. Even the pillows on the couch were right where Mom had left them.
4. Science fiction stories can be as gripping as any mystery, novel, or adventure story. So the next time you're looking for something great to read, why not try a book from the sci-fi section—it is sure to be really fantastic.
5. For a while, we didn't know if all the work that went into Lorenzo's party was worth it. When he walked in the door, however, we were glad we'd done it. His jaw dropped about a foot, and he just stood there, totally surprised. Then, very slowly, a huge smile spread across his face.

Literary **MODEL**

The final sentence leaves no doubt that these are the last things that happen.

Teruo took the bills and rang up the cash register. "All right, I'll go now. I feel fine. I'm happy. Thanks to you." He waved his hand to Mr. Sasaki. "No hard feelings." . . .

He walked out of the shop with his shoulders straight, head high, and whistling. He did not come back to see us again.

Toshio Mori, "Say It with Flowers"

Practice Your Skills

A. Below are five weak conclusions. Select three of them. Then rewrite each one to make it stronger.

1. It was the end of the race. I didn't think I would have the strength to reach the finish line. Then I heard my teammates cheering me on, and I won the race.
2. World hunger is a big problem, and people should do something about it. I really wish we could end hunger throughout the world.
3. I'll never forget what our house looked like after the tornado. Everything was completely wrecked—except for the living room.
4. Science fiction stories make really great reading. So the next time you're looking for a really great book, why not try the sci-fi section?
5. It was worth all of the planning and the work to see Lorenzo's reaction. He was completely surprised by the party.

B. The following two ideas are the main points expressed in a composition. Now, write a conclusion to the composition in which you restate these two ideas in a new way.

- Dogs that roam the streets can get hurt in any number of ways.
- People who care about their dogs keep them close to home.

B. Revisions will vary. A sample revision is shown below.

Dogs that run freely around the neighborhood can get hurt by everything from speeding cars to spoiled food. That's why people who care about their dogs shouldn't let them run wild.

WRITING HANDBOOK 16

What Help Can Others Give Me?

Peer Response

WRITER TO WRITER

What helps [when I get stuck] is to read it to a friend and ask for ideas. Maybe read it to two friends.

Melissa Starr, student
Houston, Texas

Have you ever asked a friend to give you advice or to help you solve a problem? If so, you may have gotten a welcome pat on the back along with the advice. Maybe your friend even saw some new ways to solve the problem.

Friends can help you with your writing in the same way. The classmates who read and comment on your work are called **peer readers.** The comments and suggestions they give are **peer responses.** Asking peers to respond to your work may be one of the most important things you can do as a writer.

GETTING PEER RESPONSES

You can get help from peer readers at any time during the writing process. During prewriting, you can bounce your ideas off friends and see how they react. During drafting and revising, you can find out if you've gotten your ideas across clearly. Peer response is helpful at whatever point you choose to use it.

Helping Your Reader

At first your peer readers may not know what kinds of comments you want. They may also be afraid of hurting your feelings. You can help your peer readers by using the guidelines and questions on the next page.

WRITING HANDBOOK 16

Peer Response

Objectives

- To learn strategies for guiding peer readers and to solicit peer comments
- To use response strategies as a peer reader

Related Mini-Lesson

For information on topics related to peer response, see the following mini-lesson:

- **Revising, pp. 257–259**

Motivate

Invite students to tell how they learned to ride a bicycle. Did anyone help them? Was it a friend? Was it a family member? Did they learn faster or better because of the help they received? Then ask if they have ever helped anyone else learn to do something. How did they feel when that person learned or improved? Tell students that in this handbook, they will learn how to help one another become better writers.

Teaching Strategies

for GETTING PEER RESPONSES

HELPFUL HINT Encourage students to ask for peer responses from readers they do not know well, in addition to their friends. Point out that someone who does not know them may offer more fair and impartial comments.

for GUIDELINES FOR PEER RESPONSE

MODELING To help students get the knack of asking for peer responses, you might share a piece of your writing. Then think aloud as you develop questions for peer readers. Continue talking through the piece until you have four or five questions that relate to specific parts of your writing. Ask volunteers to respond to the questions as you model effective listening.

for GIVING PEER RESPONSES

INDIVIDUALIZING INSTRUCTION: ESL STUDENTS Students who are not fluent in English will find it challenging to act as peer readers. To make the task easier for these students, you may wish to pair them with native English speakers who are writing about topics the ESL students are familiar with. Alternatively, you might pair these ESL students with native English speakers who are learning the language with which these ESL students are more comfortable. Such pairings may enable both students in each pair to build their language skills in the course of discussing each other's writing.

Guidelines for Peer Response

Help for Peer Readers

Here are some ways you can guide your peer reader.

- Ask specific questions about your writing (see the questions for peer readers below).
- Ask your readers to respond honestly.
- Tell your peer readers whether your writing is a rough draft or a more finished piece.
- Don't argue with your readers about their responses. Just listen. Whether or not you follow their advice is up to you.

Questions for Peer Readers

You can ask questions like these to find out what your peer readers are thinking.

- What part of my writing was most interesting to you?
- Is there anything you'd like to know more about?
- Was anything confusing?
- Can you point to words or phrases that you like?
- What comes across as my main point?
- What are your ideas on this topic?

GIVING PEER RESPONSES

When you are the peer reader, try putting yourself in the writer's shoes. You are a writer yourself, so all you need to do is to remember how you feel when someone reads your writing. Think about the kinds of comments *you* would like to receive. Then give the writer your honest advice and support. The chart on the next page gives some tips that peer readers should keep in mind.

Responding as a Peer Reader

- **Read carefully.** You may want to read the draft twice so that you are sure you understand it.
- **Be considerate.** Think about the writer's feelings. Remember that you are reading a work in progress.
- **Give useful feedback.** If you are asked specific questions, answer them helpfully and honestly.
- **Be supportive.** A writer needs to know what is good about a piece of writing, too.
- **Be specific.** Don't just say "This was good." Tell what was good and why.
- **Use "I" statements.** You are giving your opinion, not telling a writer what is "right" or "wrong." Don't tell a writer "This sentence isn't clear." Instead, say "I don't understand this."

Ways of Responding

You may find that three kinds of responses—*pointing, summarizing,* and *identifying problems*—are especially helpful when you are a reader. The paragraph below is from a student's first draft. The questions and the responses that follow it show how these kinds of responses work.

Student MODEL

My sister and I learned an important lesson when we went hiking. A sign at the beginning of the trail read "TAKE A FLASHLIGHT." We didn't have one, and it was a sunny day, so we ignored the sign.

After a while we came to a tunnel and walked into total darkness. Walking slowly and cautiously, we crept along. Suddenly, a twig snapped behind us. Then, we heard breathing. Nervously, we stumbled forward. Suddenly the end of the tunnel and daylight were ahead. We squinted in the bright sun and breathed a sigh of relief.

for RESPONDING AS A PEER READER

STUMBLING BLOCK Students may believe that being a peer reader means finding and pointing out mistakes. You might explain that we do not learn as much from our mistakes as we do from our successes. People don't always know how to fix their mistakes, but when told what they did right, they can do it again. Therefore the most helpful comments may be those that point out what is good or what works.

for STUDENT MODEL

PEER RESPONSE Before students turn to the peer responses on page 256, you might have them jot down three or four responses of their own for comparison.

for POINTING, SUMMARIZING . . .

CRITICAL THINKING: CATEGORIZING After students have examined the questions on the pupil page, ask them to look at the questions they wrote. (See the Responding as a Peer Reader note on page 255.) Help students to categorize their responses as Pointing, Summarizing, and Identifying Problems.

Additional Resources

Writing Resource Book, pp. 68–69
Peer Response Guides

Answers to Practice Your Skills

A. Answers will vary. Sample responses are shown below.

1. Pennies are useless. They should be taken out of circulation.
2. "*Making* pennies . . . *make* sense"; "minted"; "two cents worth"; "pitch the penny" (effective alliteration)
3. Does it cost a lot of money to make nine billion pennies? If pennies are so worthless, why are they still made? Could you say a little more about why you think pennies are worthless?
4. I don't understand what Abraham Lincoln has to do with this.
5. Merchants also use pennies to trick people into thinking things cost less than they do—$3.99 sounds like a lot less than $4.00. Without pennies, though, would all sales taxes have to be five or ten percent? Wouldn't that be more expensive in the long run?

B. Answers will vary.

Pointing "What words or phrases do you especially like?"

"I like how you quoted the words on the sign. I like the words *crept* and *stumbled.*"

Summarizing "What do you think is my main idea?"

"Ignoring instructions can lead to trouble. Is that your main idea?"

Identifying Problems "Was there anything you did not understand or that you wanted to know more about?"

"Why did you go into the tunnel? Were you scared? Also, did you find out who or what was behind you?"

Practice Your Skills

A. Read the first draft below. Then respond to the writer's questions that follow.

Making pennies doesn't make sense. In the first place, pennies are practically worthless. Abraham Lincoln's image is on pennies. Pennies are also a nuisance. Each year nine billion pennies are minted, and each year six billion disappear from circulation. Why? No one wants a pocket or purse full of pennies, so the coins get tossed into a drawer or a jar. If you want my two cents worth, we should pitch the penny.

1. What comes across as my main point?
2. Which words or phrases do you especially like?
3. Was there anything you wanted to know more about?
4. Was anything confusing?
5. What are your ideas on this topic?

B. Choose something you have written recently. Read it again and write questions about it to ask a peer reader. Then ask a classmate to respond to your writing by answering the questions you have written.

PROFESSIONAL NOTEBOOK

Advice from the Authors Peter Elbow, in *Writing with Power*, gives students this advice on peer conferences: "Whenever you get feedback, always ask readers to point out the bits that actually made them see something or hear something or experience something. Insist on the real thing: . . . passages that actually caused movies in their heads. It is rare. . . . But when feedback shows you even a few short passages that actually do it, you will be able to think yourself back into what it felt like as you wrote them. This will give you a seat-of-the-pants feeling for what you must do to get power into your words. . . ."

WRITING HANDBOOK 17

How Can I Make My Writing Better?

Revising

You too can improve your writing by revising. Revising can be much more than taking out one unnecessary word, however. It is your chance to look back at your work and see what you like about it and what you want to change. You might want to reword a description or add to an explanation. You may even decide to start over again.

Keep in mind that writing is a very personal activity. Some writers like to revise as they go along. Others wait until they have completed a draft. Use whatever method is right for you.

STRATEGIES FOR REVISING

When you have completed a draft put it aside for a while. When you look at it again, you will be able to see it with fresh eyes. You may be surprised at the things you notice.

One good approach is to read your draft aloud. Hearing the sound of the words can help you decide how well you like your writing. Also, you may find places where you stumble as you read. Think about revising those passages.

Your peers can give you valuable advice for revising your writing. See Handbook 16, "Peer Response," on pages 253–256 for ways to get the best advice from others.

In addition, questions and suggestions like the ones shown on the next page might help you as you revise.

WRITING HANDBOOK 17

Revising

Objectives

- To learn strategies for revising
- To use revision guidelines to improve paragraphs and compositions

Related Mini-Lessons

For information on topics related to revising, see the following mini-lessons:

- **Improving Paragraphs, pp. 230–233**
- **Transitions, pp. 234–238**
- **Peer Response, pp. 253–256**

Teaching Strategies

for STRATEGIES FOR REVISING

KEY TO UNDERSTANDING You may wish to emphasize that revising is seldom an orderly process. Writers may go over a piece of writing numerous times, making a few changes with each pass. Eventually, the piece may even become a mess of arrows, additions, and crossouts.

PROFESSIONAL NOTEBOOK

In her book *Errors and Expectations,* Mina Shaughnessy notes that beginning writers often do not understand the ways in which writing is different from speaking—particularly the necessity for the revision process. "Writers who are not aware of this," says Shaughnessy, "tend to think that the point in writing is to get everything right the first time and that the need to change things is the mark of the amateur." She urges teachers to encourage messiness, for "The messiness is indeed writing—the record of a remarkable interplay between the writer as creator and the writer as reader."

for GUIDELINES FOR REVISING

CRITICAL THINKING: EVALUATING
Have students write at least one more question that relates to each question in the first column. (Samples: What is my main idea? What are my supporting details? How does each sentence relate to the main idea? What transitions can I add? Which words or phrases can I make more vivid?)

for STUDENT MODEL

USING THE MODEL To help students understand how the revisions relate to specific writing techniques, lead a discussion of the reasons why the student made these particular changes. For example, in the opening sentence, a question is more inviting because it draws the reader into the writing; the sentence beginning "At the center . . ." was moved because it was out of sequence.

COMPUTER TIP

A cut-and-paste function can be very helpful for moving or deleting sentences as you revise.

Guidelines for Revising

Ask Yourself	Try This
• Is my main idea obvious?	• Rewrite your introduction or opening sentences.
• Have I included enough information to support my points?	• Add supporting details as needed to make your points clear.
• Should anything be taken out?	• Leave out details that don't develop your main idea.
• Is my writing easy to follow?	• Check the order in which you present information. Start a new paragraph for each main idea. Add transitions where needed.
• Is my writing interesting?	• Spice up your writing with vivid nouns, verbs, and modifiers.

One student made these revisions to a draft.

Student MODEL

Made introduction more interesting
Unimportant details deleted
New paragraph for a new main idea
Details added
Sentence moved
Transition added

Have you ever ~~I've always~~ wondered what was inside a baseball~~.~~? Yesterday I took one apart ~~an old baseball I found in a vacant lot~~ to find out. ¶ The first layer I took off was pieces of leather. They were stitched ~~held~~ together with thick red thread. Then I unwrapped yards and yards ~~layers~~ of wool yarn wound very tightly. At the center I discovered a small ball of cork. Under the yarn I found ~~That was covered by~~ two layers of rubber. Now you won't have to destroy your own baseball to see what's inside.

Practice Your Skills

A. The passages below need to be revised. Use the Guidelines for Revising on page 258 and make any changes you think are needed.

1. Frank Drake, the President of the SETI Institute, said he thinks their new project will succeed. SETI stands for Search for Extraterrestrial Intelligence. SETI and NASA scientists are looking for intelligent life on other planets. They have started a 10-year, $100 million search for radio signals from space.

2. What makes popcorn pop? The Native Americans were the first people to make popcorn. One way they made popcorn was to put an ear of corn on a stick and roast it over a fire. They gathered up the kernels that popped off the ear. The corn kernels that are used for popcorn contain a lot of water. When they are heated, the water expands and turns into steam. This causes the kernel to explode into a mass. The Native Americans scraped kernels from the cob and threw them directly into a fire. They ate the pieces that came out of the fire. One method was more complicated. They heated coarse sand in a shallow clay pan. When the sand was hot, they put corn kernels into it. The cooked kernels popped to the surface of the sand. There is nothing more tasty than fresh-popped popcorn. Eating popcorn became very popular with the explorers and settlers who came to America. Today people in the United States eat almost two pounds of popcorn per person a year.

B. Choose a piece of writing you completed recently, or something from your writer's portfolio. Revise it, using the ideas presented in this handbook. Then write a note to attach to the revised paper. Discuss the changes you made and the reasons you made them.

Additional Resources

Writing Resource Book, p. 70
Elaboration, Revision, and Proofreading Practice
Elaboration, Revision, and Proofreading Transparency Pack

Answers to Practice Your Skills

A. Answers will vary slightly. Sample revisions are shown below.

1. "Our new project is bound to succeed," said Frank Drake, the President of the SETI Institute. SETI stands for Search for Extraterrestrial Intelligence. SETI and NASA scientists have started a 10-year, $100 million search for radio signals from space. They are looking for intelligent life on other planets.

2. What makes popcorn pop? The corn kernels that are used for popcorn contain a lot of water. When they are heated, the water expands and turns into steam. This causes the kernel to explode into a puffy white mass.

The Native Americans were the first people to make popcorn. They developed three ways to make it. One way was to put an ear of corn on a stick and roast it over a fire. Then they gathered up the kernels that popped off the ear. They also scraped kernels from the cob and threw them directly into a fire. They ate the pieces that popped out of the fire. The third method was more complicated. They heated coarse sand in a shallow clay pan. When the sand was hot, they stirred corn kernels into it. The cooked kernels popped to the surface of the sand.

Eating popcorn became very popular with the explorers and settlers who came to America. Today people in the United States eat almost two pounds of popcorn per person a year.

B. Answers will vary.

WRITING HANDBOOK 18

Proofreading

Objectives

- To learn proofreading techniques and symbols
- To use a proofreading checklist and symbols to find and correct mistakes in grammar, capitalization, punctuation, and spelling

Related Mini-Lessons

For information on topics related to proofreading, see the following mini-lessons:

- **Correcting Sentence Errors, pp. 281–284**
- **Capitalization, pp. 547–565**
- **Punctuation, pp. 567–598**

Teaching Strategies

GENERAL NOTE

KEY TO UNDERSTANDING
Emphasize to students the difference between proofreading and revising. Point out that revising involves changes in organization and content, whereas proofreading focuses on changes in grammar, punctuation, capitalization, and spelling.

for PROOFREADING STRATEGIES

HELPFUL HINT You might tell students that newspaper, magazine, and book publishers employ proofreaders, and that some people make proofreading a career. You might want to explain that the techniques outlined on the pupil page are the same ones that professional proofreaders use.

WRITING HANDBOOK 18

How Do I Know My Writing Is Correct?

Proofreading

What would you think if you saw this sign? If you're like most people, you would think that whoever created the sign needs a spelling lesson!

When you write, little errors like the one on the sign can take a reader's attention away from your message. By proofreading your work, you can find and correct errors in spelling, punctuation, capitalization, and grammar. You can help your readers concentrate on your writing, not on accidental mistakes.

PROOFREADING STRATEGIES

To catch the little mistakes in your writing that might slip by, you need to look carefully at your work. Here are some strategies you can try.

Proofread more than once. It's a good idea to read over your work several times. You can look for different kinds of mistakes each time. Put your paper aside between proofreadings. With fresh eyes, you may see errors you missed the first time.

TEACHER'S LOUNGE

A computer spell checker indeed hides hazards aplenty that lie in wait for the unwary. Share this little ditty with your students:

Spellbound

I have a spelling checker,
It came with my PC;
It plainly marks four my revue
Mistakes I cannot sea.
I've run this poem threw it,
I'm sure your please too no,
Its letter perfect in it's weigh,
My checker tolled me sew.

Read aloud for end punctuation. As you read your work aloud, pause where you think each sentence ends. Find the subject and verb. Be sure that you have used the correct end punctuation—a period, a question mark, or an exclamation point—for that type of sentence.

Read aloud for commas within sentences. Notice where you pause naturally. Such a pause may mean that a comma is needed. If you stumble over the words, you may be able to delete a comma that is not needed.

Proofread for initial capitals. Find the end punctuation mark of each sentence. Check to see that the next word begins with a capital letter.

Read your work backwards. Read backwards one word at a time to check your spelling. Circle any spellings you are unsure of. After you finish reading, check the spellings of the circled words in a dictionary.

Proofreading Checklist

Step 1: Look at your sentences.
Do all sentences express complete thoughts?
Are there any run-on sentences?
Do subjects and verbs agree?

Step 2: Look at your words.
Are words spelled correctly?
Have you used the correct forms of verbs to show tense?
Have you used the correct forms of pronouns?
Have you used adjectives and adverbs correctly?

Step 3: Look at your capitalization and punctuation.
Have you capitalized the first words of sentences?
Have you capitalized proper nouns and adjectives?
Have you used commas correctly?
Have you used end marks correctly?
Have you used other punctuation marks correctly?

for PROOFREADING STRATEGIES

PERSONAL TOUCH If you have a preferred proofreading technique, such as laying your work aside for a time between readings, reading from the bottom up, or asking someone else to proofread your work, share it with the class.

for PROOFREADING CHECKLIST

HELPFUL HINT Explain to students that when they proofread, they may need to look for each kind of mistake separately; that is, by making a separate and complete pass through their composition to answer each question under each step on the checklist. Assure students that professional proofreaders always work with a dictionary and a grammar handbook nearby and look up rules frequently to check their knowledge.

SPICE BOX

To stress the importance of a single comma, write these pairs of sentences on the board and have students answer the questions.

- In which case is Jean likely to be in trouble?
  Jean, our babysitter is two hours late!
  Jean, our babysitter, is two hours late!
- Which is more of a compliment?
  Kay's little girl is a pretty, bright child.
  Kay's little girl is a pretty bright child.
- Which shows the speaker knows the man well?
  He is the man I believe.
  He is the man, I believe.

for PRACTICE YOUR SKILLS

INDIVIDUALIZING INSTRUCTION: LD STUDENTS Most students will be able to identify errors in the paragraph and correct them in one clean copy. However, students who are easily distracted or have difficulty processing information may need to have the activity broken down into separate steps. For these students, make an enlarged photocopy of the paragraph. Have the students make their proofreading corrections directly on the page. You might then have them make a clean copy.

Additional Resources

Writing Resource Book, p. 71

Elaboration, Revision, and Proofreading Practice

Elaboration, Revision, and Proofreading Transparency Pack

Answers to Practice Your Skills

In the age of hand-held computer games, it's strange to think that the first computer game was played on a machine that took up a whole room. In January of 1962, students began experimenting with a giant computer at Harvard University. They found a way to make a dot skip across the computer screen. Soon they changed the dot to a spaceship. By February, they had two spaceships flying across the screen. Each spaceship was controlled by a box with a lever and a button on top. Pushing the button made the spaceship shoot at its opponent. Their new game, called Spacewar, set the stage for a new use of computers.

Writing TIP

Keep an eye out for words that have different meanings for different spellings, such as *their, there,* and *they're; to, too,* and *two;* and *your* and *you're.*

Proofreading Symbols

∧ Add letters or words.	/ Make a capital letter lowercase.
⊙ Add a period.	¶ Begin a new paragraph.
≡ Capitalize a letter.	∼ Switch the positions of letters or words.
⁀ Close up a space.	— or ℓ Take out letters or words.
∧, Add a comma.	

Notice how the symbols were used in this passage.

Roller Skates ~~was~~ were invented by Joseph Merlin in ~~1759~~ the 1760s. he biult the skate s so that he could make a stunning entrance at a costume party. Unfortunately he didn't know how to stop he crashed through a miror.

Practice Your Skills

Proofread the paragraph below for mistakes in grammar, capitalization, punctuation, and spelling. Rewrite the paragraph correctly.

In the age of hand-held Computer Games, its strange to think that the first computer game was played on a machine that took up a whole room. In january of 1962 students began expeirmenting with a giant computer at Harvard University. They find a way to make a dot skip across the computer screen, and soon they changed the dot to a spaceship, and by febuary, they had two space-ships flying across the screen. Each spaceship was controlled by a box with a lever and a button on top. Pushing the button made the spaceship shoot at it's opponent. There new game, called Spacewar, set the stage for a new use of computers.

In the News

Under the pressure of a deadline, you work fast, even furiously, to get things done. You probably make mistakes in the process. Even professional journalists goof sometimes, as you can see here.

An eighth of everyone in this country lives in California.

Montreal Gazette

A story in *The Gazette* yesterday incorrectly identified a Cree as James Boffish. In fact, his name is James Babbish. In addition, he was described as an elder. In fact, he is too young, but was an acting elder for this occasion. *The Gazette* regrets the errors.

All river buses are now monitored by an electronic advanced Datatrak system that which enables means that at any time the airport to can be informed of the progress of the boats on their way down-river service.

Pennysaver

Three Ambulances Take Blast Victim to Hospital

KETCHUP CORRECTION
Top-quality ketchup would take at least 75 years to flow across Canada. An incorrect figure was given yesterday, owing to an error in the thinking process.

Ability to Swim May Save Children from Drowning

Storm Delayed by Bad Weather

Helicopter Powered by Human Flies

TODAY IN HISTORY
1775 Paul Revere began his famous ride from Charlestown, S.C., to Lexington, Mass., warning the American colonists that the British were coming.

San Francisco Chronicle

on the LIGHT side

Make sure everyone in the class understands the mistakes in these newspaper headlines and excerpts. You might ask for volunteers to rewrite some of these bloopers so that they are less confusing or jarring. For example: "One eighth of the U.S. population lives in California" or "Human-Powered Helicopter Flies."

As an ongoing class project, have students look for examples of errors in newspapers, magazines, books, and advertisements. Point out the page in your local newspaper where correction notices appear. Also, tell students to check Letters to the Editor pages, where readers often point out mistakes (and where reporters and editors sometimes defend themselves). Keep a bulletin-board collection of the bloopers students find and have each finder act as an editor, adding a corrected version of the erroneous item.

Sketchbook

Objective

- To use the poem and the picture as springboards to informal writing

WRITING WARM-UPS

These fun, ungraded, writing activities can be used to inspire students to think about the meaning of the word *style.* Encourage students to respond to one or more of the prompts and to save their responses in their writing folders for possible use with future assignments.

To begin, have a volunteer read the poem aloud. Students might wish to describe their skateboarding or dancing styles, or to describe themselves as objects, in a free-verse, first-person poem similar to "The Sidewalk Racer." If students choose the prompt that asks them to design their own skateboards, encourage them to draw the design, using appropriate labels and captions.

Sketchbook

WRITING WARM-UPS

Skimming
an asphalt sea
I swerve, I curve, I
sway; I speed to whirring
sound an inch above the
ground; I'm the sailor
and the sail, I'm the
driver and the wheel
I'm the one and only
single engine
human auto
mobile.

Lillian Morrison,
"THE SIDEWALK RACER"

Untitled painting (1986), Keith Haring.

- Describe your special skateboarding style or dancing style, or . . .
- Imagine you are an object. Tell what you are like.
- If you could design your own skateboard, what would it look like?

ART NOTE

Keith Haring was an American artist who drew cartoon-style figures that show no race, sex, or age. Ask students what the figure is doing (skateboarding), how Haring shows motion, and what else they see in the drawing.

Style

WRITING HANDBOOKS

The way you ride a skateboard, dance, or pitch a ball is special. Your personal style shows in the individual way you move. Even the activity you choose is a reflection of who you are.

The way you write has just as much personal style as the way you move. The handbooks that follow will show you how to make your special style come through in your writing.

WRITING HANDBOOKS

Style

INTRODUCING THE HANDBOOKS

Ask students to suggest definitions of the word *style*. Then have them look the word up in the dictionary; ask a volunteer to read the definitions aloud. Discuss questions such as the following: What is Lillian Morrison's style in "The Sidewalk Racer"? What is the style of the skate-boarder on page 265? Point out that the Style Handbooks that follow will help each student achieve a personal writing style.

WRITING HANDBOOK 19

Appealing to the Senses

Objectives

- To recognize details that appeal to the five senses
- To identify and create similes and metaphors
- To use sensory details in a piece of writing

Related Mini-Lessons

For information on topics related to the use of sensory details in writing, see the following mini-lessons:

- **Thinking with Pictures, pp. 192–196**
- **Developing a Topic, pp. 205–210**
- **Show, Don't Tell, pp. 239–242**

Motivate

To help students understand why sensory details are important, write a sentence such as the following on the board: *The pie was good.* Ask students what they know about the pie from this sentence (not much). Invite suggestions about the details they would want to know. (Samples: the kind of pie; how juicy or creamy it was; the texture of the crust)

Teaching Strategies

for LITERARY MODEL

INDIVIDUALIZING INSTRUCTION: VISUAL LEARNERS To help students appreciate Hamilton's use of details that appeal to sight, have them sketch a picture of the girl on the horse. When they have finished, compare sketches and discuss how easy or difficult it was to picture the scene from Hamilton's description.

WRITING HANDBOOK 19

How Can I Bring My Writing to Life?

Appealing to the Senses

Good writers are good observers. They write about the look and feel, the smell and taste, and the sounds of things.

WRITER TO WRITER

What worries me is that each day something out of the ordinary will happen and I won't take notice.

Anna Quiroz, student
Kenosha, Wisconsin

SIGHT

All writers notice details and then search for precise words to describe them. Practice making notes on the sizes, shapes, colors, and conditions of the things around you. In the following description, the writer uses precise words to help readers "see" the scene: *blackest, biggest horse; white, frilly nightcap; arms folded.*

Literary MODEL

Out of the trees on the right side of the house came walking the blackest, biggest horse Thomas could remember seeing. . . . Riding on it was a tiny girl, sitting straight and tall. She had a white, frilly nightcap on her head and she wore red flannel pajamas with lace at the neck and sleeves. She had no shoes on her feet and she sat well forward, her toes clasped in the horse's mane. With her arms folded across her chest, she stared into the distance. She was serene and happy and seemed not to notice Thomas.

Virginia Hamilton, *The House of Dies Drear*

SPICE BOX

You might try this activity to help students become aware of the accuracy of their powers of observation. Place five or six objects on a table and have students observe them for one minute. Cover the objects; then ask students to describe them. Encourage answers that describe each item in accurate detail—for example, not only as a notebook, but as a three-hole-punched red spiral notebook, approximately six inches by nine inches, with the brand name written in black on the cover.

SOUND

Do you ever tune out sounds? To be a good observer, you need to listen carefully. Think of words that describe sounds: *buzz, whir, squeak.* Each word conveys a precise sound. Notice how the writer of the following passage uses precise words to describe sounds. Also note that when you say some of the words aloud, you almost make the sounds yourself.

Writing TIP

Many factual articles begin with descriptions. Use sensory details to catch your readers' interest.

Literary MODEL

Every whale everywhere moves in a sea of total sound. From the moment of its birth until its final hour, day and night, it hears the endless orchestra of life around its massive frame. Silence is an unknown thing. The snapping and crackling of tiny shrimps and crablike organisms, the grunting and grating, puffing and booming, of a hundred fishes, the eerie whining and squealing of dolphins, the sad voices of sea birds overhead, the chatter of its own companions, the undertone of moving water and the drone of wind, all these notes and many more come flooding through its senses all the time. It *feels* the music, too, for water presses firmly on its frame—a smooth continuous sounding board.

Victor B. Scheffer,
The Year of the Whale

for LITERARY MODEL

SPEAKING AND LISTENING To help students appreciate how the model appeals to the sense of hearing, have one student read it aloud as the rest of the class listens. Have students comment on such sound words as *snapping, grunting, booming, chatter,* and *drone.*

for LITERARY MODEL

USING THE MODEL Point out that Scheffer begins his paragraph by stating, "Every whale everywhere moves in a sea of total sound." Ask students how he supports this statement (by giving examples of the various kinds of sounds). Have students identify the nouns formed from verbs that describe the sounds *(snapping, crackling, grunting, grating, puffing, booming, whining, squealing).*

for LITERARY MODEL

CRITICAL THINKING: ANALYZING Scheffer wants his audience to focus on sounds. Ask students, "To what does he compare the sounds of the sea?" (an orchestra) "How does Scheffer remind the audience of this comparison?" (He uses words associated with music, such as *voices, undertone, notes,* and *music.)*

for TOUCH, TASTE, AND SMELL

HELPFUL HINT When students use description, they often focus only on how an object looks. To help students broaden their scope, ask them when they might want to emphasize touch (Samples: to describe a surface, a fabric, the pelt of an animal, clothing); taste (Samples: to describe an unusual food, beverage, water accidentally swallowed in a pool or at the beach); smell (Samples: to describe food, a chemistry experiment, a household cleaner).

for FIRST LITERARY MODEL

USING THE MODEL Write the touch words from the model on the board. Suggest that students think about a donkey or another animal they have petted. Have them add appropriate touch words to the list.

for FIRST LITERARY MODEL

CRITICAL THINKING: ANALYZING Ask students to identify the comparisons Jiménez makes that involve the sense of touch. (He compares the donkey's coat to cotton and its eyes to jet mirrors and to beetles of dark crystal.) Note how Jiménez contrasts the softness of the animal's coat with the hardness of its eyes.

TOUCH, TASTE, AND SMELL

Good writers combine senses to make their descriptions vivid. We often take the senses of touch, taste, and smell for granted. However, they are important tools for all writers.

Touch Read the following description, and notice how the writer uses precise touch words such as *downy, smooth, soft,* and *cotton* to describe a small donkey. He helps you imagine what it might feel like to run your hand over Platero's coat.

Literary MODEL

> Platero is small, downy, smooth—so soft to the touch that one would think he were all cotton, that he had no bones. Only the jet mirrors of his eyes are hard as two beetles of dark crystal.
>
> **Juan Ramón Jiménez, *Platero and I***

Taste and Smell Notice how taste and smell are part of one woman's memories of food she loved in China. The writer uses taste words such as *crunchy, sweet, creamy-soft.* She also describes smells: *good, stinky smell for waking up your nose.*

Literary MODEL

> The lettuce heart, for example, it was thick like a turnip, crunchy but sweet, easy to cook. And the bean curd, we could buy that from a man who rolled his cart by our house every morning, calling, *"Cho tofu! Cho tofu!"* It was fried on the outside, and when you broke it open, inside you'd find a creamy-soft middle with such a good, stinky smell for waking up your nose.
>
> **Amy Tan, *The Kitchen God's Wife***

USING SIMILES AND METAPHORS

Sometimes the best way to describe something you sense is to compare it to something else. Writers often use comparisons to make their descriptions vivid. One kind of comparison, called

for **FURTHER READING**

Poems to Read Poems contain similes, metaphors, and language that appeal to the senses. As examples, some poems you might want to share with students are "Simile: Willow and Ginkgo" by Eve Merriam, "Beach Stones" by Lillian Moore, and "Mama Is a Sunrise" by Evelyn Tooley Hunt.

a **simile,** uses the word *like* or *as.* Read these comparisons:

The icicles were **like** frozen waterfalls.

The sunlight feels **as** sharp **as** a thousand needles.

When you use similes to describe something, be sure to make vivid, interesting comparisons. Finish the following phrases, once with the first words that come to mind, and then with vivid words:

as cold as . . .

as hard as . . .

as slippery as . . .

The first words you thought of may have been *ice, a rock,* and *an eel* because you have heard those comparisons many times before. Words and phrases that have lost their power to interest people are called **clichés.** Good writers avoid clichés by making refreshing new comparisons.

Another kind of comparison is called a **metaphor.** A metaphor compares two things without the word *like* or *as.* The following are examples of metaphors:

The treetops were a soft sea of green.

The seaweed was a slippery golden snake.

In the first metaphor, treetops are compared to the sea. In the second metaphor, seaweed is compared to a snake.

Whether you write similes or metaphors, always search for new comparisons to make your writing lively and appealing.

for SIMILES

MODELING You might want to demonstrate how you would go about finishing one of the comparisons listed. For example, you might say: "Suppose I want to finish the phrase *as hard as.* The first thing that pops into my mind is *rock.* That's too common. The second thing that pops into my mind is *nails.* That's not much better. To come up with an original comparison, I try to think of something that can be hard but is not usually hard—like a cookie. I think about all the reasons that a cookie can be hard. Then I say as hard as a stale cookie or an overbaked cookie or a month-old cookie."

for METAPHORS

KEY TO UNDERSTANDING Students usually have little difficulty in recognizing similes because of the words *like* or *as.* Sometimes, however, students fail to recognize metaphors because the comparison is not stated directly. Tell students that often they can restate a sentence, using the words *like* or *as* to determine whether a group of words is a metaphor. Have them try this approach with the two model sentences at the bottom of the pupil page.

for SENSORY WORD LISTS

HELPFUL HINT Advise students to skim these lists and to refer to them again when they are drafting or revising a piece of writing and want to strengthen the sensory details.

for SENSORY WORD LISTS

STUMBLING BLOCK: SHADES OF MEANING When confronted with these lists, some students may think that they can use these words interchangeably. Caution students that this is not the case. For example, if they are looking for a word to describe fast movement, the words *dash* and *swoop* cannot be used interchangeably because the shades of meaning are different. *Dash* is used to describe an action on the ground, whereas *swoop* describes an action in the air. Encourage discussion of other similar pairs—such as *lean* and *skinny,* or *shiny* and *glowing.*

for SENSORY WORD LISTS

INDIVIDUALIZING INSTRUCTION: LEP AND BASIC STUDENTS When students with a limited vocabulary are using the lists to add sensory words to a piece of writing, encourage them to check with you or with a peer to be sure that they have chosen the word with the correct shade of meaning.

Sight Words

Fast Movements
hurry
scamper
dart
spring
streak
trot

gallop
dash
rush
zoom
zip
hurl
flick
whisk
rip
swerve
dive
swoop
plunge
fly
twirl

Slow Movements
creep
crawl
plod
slouch
tiptoe
amble
saunter
loiter
slink
stalk
edge
sneak
waddle
drag
drift

Shapes
flat
round
domed
curved
wavy
lean
ruffled
flared
oval
skinny
square
chubby
portly
swollen
lumpy
padded
tufted
jutting
angular
tapering
thin
spindly
wiry

Appearance
freckled
spotted
blotched
wrinkled
mottled
striped
bright
shiny
glowing
glossy
shimmering
flowery
flashy
glazed
sheer
transparent
turquoise
green

muddy
grimy
drab
dingy
dull
dark
dismal
worn
untidy
gold
maroon
shabby
ramshackle
arid
awkward
crooked
loose
rigid
cluttered
crowded
jammed
bruised
erect
supple
lively
muscular
pale
small
miniature
massive
dazzling
fiery
sturdy
hardy
healthy

Sound Words

Loud Sounds

crash
thud
explode
roar
screech
whistle
whine
squawk
blare
rumble
grate
slam
stomp
jangle
rasp
clash
racket
thunderous
hubbub
deafening
raucous
piercing
bang

Soft Sounds

sigh
murmur
whisper
whir
rustle
twitter
patter
hum
hiss
bleat
peep
buzz
gurgle
swish
chime
tinkle
clink
mute

Speech Sounds

stutter
stammer
giggle
guffaw

for SENSORY WORD LISTS

HELPFUL HINT Suggest that students list in their journals sensory words they come across in their reading. They can then refer to their list to strengthen their writing.

for SOUND WORDS

LINKING GRAMMAR AND WRITING Often students believe that if they are told to add description to their writing, they should add adjectives or adverbs. Sometimes this is true, but at other times nouns and verbs also can be used to appeal to the senses. For example, have students refer to the list under *Loud Sounds* and note that most of the words are nouns or verbs, or both nouns and verbs.

for TOUCH, TASTE, AND SMELL WORDS

INDIVIDUALIZING INSTRUCTION: ESL STUDENTS All the words on the lists for touch, taste, and smell are adjectives and therefore must be used with a noun. To help students understand the meaning of each word, work with them in a small group to identify a noun that each adjective could describe.

laugh
sing
yell

scream
snort
bellow
growl
chatter
coo
whimper

Touch Words

cool
slimy
icy
lukewarm
dusty
hot
steamy
sticky
damp
slippery
spongy
mushy
oily
waxy
rubbery
leathery
silky
satiny
velvety
smooth
soft
woolly
rough
sharp
furry
feathery
fuzzy
prickly
gritty
sandy

Taste and Smell Words

buttery
salty
bitter
smoky
sweet
sugary
sour
vinegary
fruity
tangy

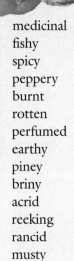

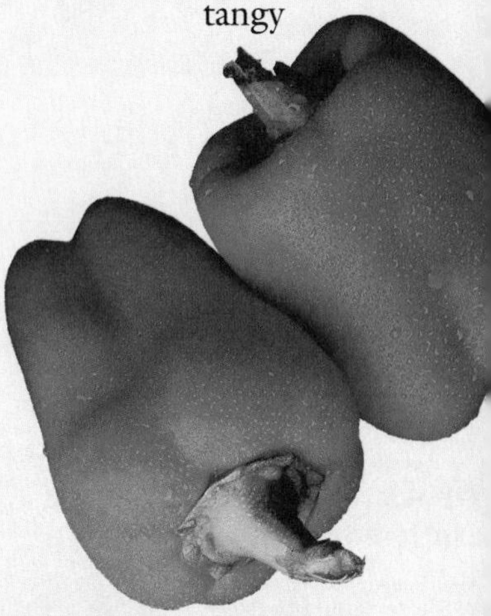

medicinal
fishy
spicy
peppery
burnt
rotten
perfumed
earthy
piney
briny
acrid
reeking
rancid
musty
nutty

PROFESSIONAL NOTEBOOK

To wrap up the lesson, you might share this writing suggestion from Elizabeth George Speare, author of *The Witch of Blackbird Pond, The Bronze Bow*, and *The Sign of the Beaver:* "Take some little incident that you read about in a history book. Try to imagine that you are actually there while the incident is taking place. What would conversations around you be about? What would the place look like? What would it smell like?" Encourage students to ask themselves similar questions as they go on to the Practice Your Skills exercises.

Practice Your Skills

A. Recall the start of a race, a game, a concert, or some other event that you have participated in or observed. Try to relive the moment in your mind. Write down vivid sensory details that describe what you experienced. List the details under the four categories (1) sight, (2) sound, (3) touch, and (4) taste and smell. Use the details to write a description of your experience.

B. Practice describing different things. Choose three of the items below and describe each one in terms of two or three senses. For one item, try your hand at writing a simile or a metaphor to describe it.

1. a campfire
2. a police siren
3. a caterpillar
4. a pickle
5. a fish
6. a skyscraper
7. a rose
8. a bus
9. a baseball glove

C. Sensory details make any writing better—whether it is fiction or nonfiction. Write a story about a true or imaginary incident. Use details to make your writing lively and interesting. The following examples may give you some ideas.

1. A bee tries to land on your sandwich.
2. You are walking home in a rainstorm.
3. A tiny puppy tries to understand your commands.
4. You wait for the school bus on a cold day.
5. Your stomach lets you know it's lunch time.

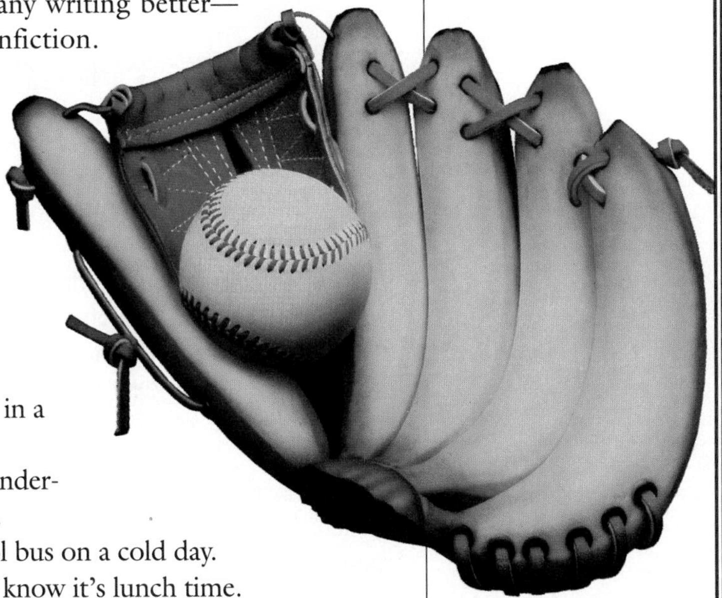

for PRACTICE YOUR SKILLS

HELPFUL HINT For Exercises A and C, suggest that students visualize the scenes before they begin to write. Those students who enjoy drawing might capture more details by sketching the scenes first.

for PRACTICE YOUR SKILLS

ASSESSMENT Each exercise involves writing a description that appeals to the senses. You might want to focus your grading on how well students appeal to more than one sense in their descriptions.

Additional Resources

Writing Resource Book, pp. 72–74
Spelling and Vocabulary Booklet

Answers to Practice Your Skills

A. Answers will vary.
B. Answers will vary.
C. Answers will vary.

WRITING HANDBOOK 20

Levels of Language

Objectives

- To identify standard English, nonstandard English, and slang
- To recognize the differences between formal and informal language
- To use language appropriate for one's audience and type of writing

Related Mini-Lessons

For information on topics related to levels of language, see the following mini-lessons:

- **Goals and Audience, pp. 211–213**
- **Personal Voice, pp. 276–277**
- **Using the Dictionary and the Thesaurus, pp. 308–311**
- **Oral Reports, pp. 324–325**

Motivate

Ask students how they expect to see people dressed in the following situations: at a wedding and at the beach. Explain that just as one's clothing should fit the social situation, so should one's language fit the writing situation.

Teaching Strategies

for CHOOSING THE RIGHT WORDS

INDIVIDUALIZING INSTRUCTION: LEP AND ESL STUDENTS You may have some students who have acquired English by hearing it spoken (by people in the neighborhood, for example, or on TV)—and who thus have never distinguished standard from nonstandard English. Be sensitive to the challenge these students face at this point; be prepared to work with them individually in a nonthreatening atmosphere, to help them determine appropriate language choices.

WRITING HANDBOOK 20

How Do I Make My Language Fit My Audience?

Levels of Language

> Propel, propel, propel your craft
> Smoothly down the liquid solution . . .
> **From *A Prairie Home Companion Folk Song Book***

Perhaps you would prefer to row, row, row your boat gently down the stream. In fact, the version of a well-known song quoted above would be much easier to understand if you replaced its formal vocabulary with more familiar words.

As you write and speak, you make choices about what words you will use. By thinking about your audience (a best friend, classmates, PTA members) and the kind of writing or situation (friendly letter or speech), you can learn to adjust your language to match any occasion.

CHOOSING THE RIGHT WORDS

Careful writers and speakers use **standard English,** language that follows the rules of grammar and usage. **Nonstandard English** is language that does not conform to rules of grammar and usage. Most of the time, you will be using standard English. When you use standard English, however, you will still need to make some decisions. Standard English can vary greatly in style, from formal to informal. **Slang,** for example, is a very informal kind of English used by a particular group. Choose language that is appropriate for your audience and type of writing.

Look at the chart on the next page. It shows some of the characteristics that distinguish formal language from informal language.

Levels of Language

	Formal	**Informal**
Characteristics	Advanced vocabulary, long sentences, no contractions	Simple vocabulary, shorter sentences, contractions
Type of writing	Report, business letter, speech, job application, letter to the editor	Friendly letter, journal entry, note to your best friend
Tone	Serious, reserved	Conversational, casual

Here are some examples of the differences between formal and informal language.

Formal Students who wish to attend the concert should assemble in front of the gymnasium in the morning.

Informal Students who want to go to the concert should meet in front of the gym in the morning.

Formal If you cannot attend, please advise your teacher by 3:00 P.M. today.

Informal If you can't make it, please tell your teacher by 3:00 P.M. today.

Practice Your Skills

Rewrite the passage below in a form appropriate for sending to the mayor of your town.

The kids on our block need your help. The streets are pretty busy here. There isn't a safe place to hang out. The old lot on Elm St. would be a great place for a playground. Right now, it's got heaps of trash. Suppose we kids clean up the lot. Could you OK the change for a playground and give us some equipment?

for LEVELS OF LANGUAGE

CRITICAL THINKING: COMPARING AND CONTRASTING

To make the difference between formal and informal language clear—and fun—ask students to come up with a situation in which informal language would be inappropriate—such as a summer-job interview. Then brainstorm a situation in which formal language would be inappropriate—such as a telephone call with their best friend. Then ask groups of students to generate sentences and alter them to fit each situation. For instance, "I like to watch soap operas" could become "I'm really into the soaps" or "I enjoy watching daytime drama."

Additional Resource

Writing Resource Book, p. 75

Answers to Practice Your Skills

Answers will vary. A possible revision is shown.

The young people in our neighborhood need your help. The streets are very busy, and there is no safe place for us to play. A vacant lot on Elm Street would make an excellent playground, but it is covered with trash. If my friends and I cleaned up the lot, could the city approve the use of the lot as a playground and provide some equipment?

Social Studies Connection

Choose a current news event, and ask two or three volunteers to role-play a discussion of it. Then ask them to role-play being broadcast journalists; tell them to write and then read aloud a one-paragraph story on the same event. Discuss the differences in language level between the two presentations.

WRITING HANDBOOK 21

Personal Voice

Objectives

- To recognize that a writer has a personal voice
- To use journal writing, freewriting, and other strategies to develop a personal voice

Related Mini-Lessons

For information on topics related to developing a personal voice, see the following mini-lessons:

- **Peer Response, pp. 253–256**
- **Levels of Language, pp. 274–275**

Motivate

To help students recognize that writers have individual voices, read aloud two poems that are very different. For example, you might choose "Fog" by Carl Sandburg and a stanza or two from "The Walrus and the Carpenter" by Lewis Carroll. Ask students whether they think both poems are likely to have been written by the same author. Encourage them to focus on some of the stylistic differences as they explain their answers.

Teaching Strategies

for YOUR OWN VOICE

USING THE MODEL Use questions such as these to help students understand why Lindsay's journal entry for September 15 has an unnatural voice:

What form of writing is this? (journal writing)

Who is the usual audience for journal writing? (oneself)

If you did not know that this is a journal entry, who would you think the audience is? (Samples: a teacher; the principal)

WRITING HANDBOOK 21

How Can I Make My Writing Sound Like Me?

Personal Voice

When you call your friends on the phone, do you have to tell them who's calling? Of course not—they recognize your voice. How? Well, there is something unique about the way you sound and the way you put words together.

The same is true of your writing. You have a special way of choosing words and putting them together that is yours and yours alone. It's called your **writing voice.**

YOUR OWN VOICE

Have you ever tried to impress someone by using vocabulary or a formal way of talking that just isn't you? If you did, you most likely sounded unnatural—maybe even completely phony. The same thing can happen with your writing.

Young writers sometimes think they need to use big, important-sounding words and long, complicated sentences to make their writing sound grown-up and sophisticated. Often, though, their writing ends up sounding strained and unnatural. Here, for example, is how Lindsay wrote when she began keeping a journal for her writing class.

September 15

Today we have been assigned the task of keeping a writing journal. Through the coming months, we are to record our personal impressions and thoughts and use them as ideas for future writing projects. I shall attempt to observe the people and nature surrounding me and write about them in meaningful new ways.

At first, Lindsay's journal entries sounded unnatural, as if she were writing to impress some unknown reader. After several weeks, though, she began to find her own voice.

Compare this later journal entry with the first one. Which one sounds more natural to you?

Student MODEL

November 9

It seems like we spent all weekend raking leaves and cleaning up the yard for winter. Will and I piled up a HUGE mound of leaves, then we decided to jump in it like we did when we were little. The leaves went flying. They looked like a flock of red and yellow birds settling on the grass.

LEARN BY DOING

An effective way to discover and develop your writing voice is to write as often as you can. Try these strategies.

- **Write in your journal regularly.** When Lindsay finally relaxed and wrote just for herself in her journal, she discovered her own writing voice.
- **Freewrite at the start of every writing assignment.** You'll be expressing your ideas in your own words.
- **Read your writing aloud.** When you hear your writing spoken, you can more easily tell what sounds natural.
- **Write letters to friends.** Write in the same words you would use if you were speaking to your friends.
- **Use peer readers.** Have friends read your writing. After they finish, ask them, "Is it me? Do you know this writer?"

Practice Your Skills

Read this paragraph. How would *you* express the ideas in this paragraph? Rewrite the paragraph using your own voice.

> I urge all my fellow students to take part in the process of electing officials to govern our class. When one exercises the right to vote, one is taking part in one of our nation's most cherished traditions.

for LEARN BY DOING

INDIVIDUALIZING INSTRUCTION: LEP STUDENTS Encourage these students to find a writing voice by focusing on writing in their journals and on freewriting. Both of these types of writing activities allow students a chance to relax and explore their ideas without worrying about a reader's reactions.

BASIC STUDENTS If students' writing is stilted and wooden, you might suggest that they imagine a sympathetic reader who is interested only in what they want to say—not how they sound when they say it. If students can keep this reader in mind as they write, they will soon allow their natural voices to ring out.

Additional Resource

Writing Resource Book, p. 76

Answers to Practice Your Skills

Answers will vary.

TEACHER'S LOUNGE

"How come when you say we have a problem, I'm always the one who has the problem?"

WRITING
HANDBOOK
22

Using Dialogue

Objectives

- To recognize that dialogue can provide information and show characters' personalities
- To write realistic dialogue that follows conventions of format and mechanics

Related Mini-Lessons

For information on topics related to writing dialogue, see the following mini-lessons:

- **Show, Don't Tell, pp. 239–242**
- **Levels of Language, pp. 274–275**
- **Punctuation, pp. 586–588**

Teaching Strategies

for HOW TO USE DIALOGUE

STUMBLING BLOCK Some students may think that any passage with quotation marks around someone's words is dialogue. Emphasize that dialogue is a conversation that involves at least two people. An expert's opinion quoted in a research report is not dialogue.

WRITING
HANDBOOK
22

How Do I Make My Characters Sound Real?

Using Dialogue

Dialogue is conversation—people talking to each other. You can use dialogue in your writing to clearly *show* readers what happens and what people are like. Read the following paragraph. It doesn't use dialogue. It just tells about a conversation between two characters.

> Grandpa wanted to know how long I'd been saving the money. I told him it was two years. He was really surprised.

Now listen to the characters talking to each other.

Literary MODEL

> "How long have you been saving this?" he asked.
> "A long time, Grandpa," I said.
> "How long?" he asked.
> I told him, "Two years."
> His mouth flew open and in a loud voice he said, "Two years!"
>
> **Wilson Rawls, *Where the Red Fern Grows***

Dialogue makes the characters seem like real people. You "hear" how surprised Grandpa is. You can picture the scene between him and his grandson as if you were there.

HOW TO USE DIALOGUE

You can use dialogue in any kind of writing, from stories to newspaper articles. By presenting people's actual words, you can both provide information and show how the people think and feel.

Providing Information Dialogue can provide information about action, characters, and setting. What can you learn about these parts of a story from the following dialogue?

Literary MODEL

> "Here I am trying to get home to cook me a bite to eat, and you snatch my pocketbook! Maybe you ain't been to your supper either, late as it be. Have you?"
>
> "There's nobody home at my house," said the boy.
>
> "Then we'll eat," said the woman. "I believe you're hungry—or been hungry—to try to snatch my pocketbook!"
>
> "I want a pair of blue suede shoes," said the boy.
>
> "Well, you didn't have to snatch my pocketbook to get some suede shoes," said Mrs. Luella Bates Washington Jones. "You could of asked me."
>
> **Langston Hughes, "Thank You, M'am"**

Showing Personalities Dialogue can also bring out the personalities of the characters and set the tone of your writing. For example, the tone could be humorous, angry, or sad. In the following example, the way the character speaks shows that he is used to ordering people around and that he is a little ridiculous. The dialogue gives the story its humorous tone.

Literary MODEL

> "I want you to get the moon," said the King. "The Princess Lenore wants the moon. If she can have the moon, she will get well again."
>
> "The moon?" exclaimed the Lord High Chamberlain, his eyes widening. This made him look four times as wise as he really was.
>
> "Yes, the moon," said the King. "M-o-o-n, moon. Get it tonight, tomorrow at the latest."
>
> **James Thurber, "Many Moons"**

for FIRST LITERARY MODEL

CRITICAL THINKING: INFERRING

After students read the model dialogue, ask them to infer what has just happened in the story. (A woman confronts a boy who has tried but failed to steal her pocketbook.) Then have students describe what they can tell about each of the two characters. (Samples: Mrs. Jones, a working woman, is firm but compassionate; the young thief may have a poor home life and wants a pair of blue suede shoes.) Write key information on the board. Note how much students were able to learn from a very brief passage of dialogue.

MULTICULTURAL Connection

Dialect Sometimes writers use dialect in dialogue to make characters realistic and to give readers information about both characters and setting. Point out how Langston Hughes uses dialect in this passage from "Thank You, M'am."

for GUIDELINES FOR WRITING DIALOGUE

HELPFUL HINT To help students develop an "ear" for writing dialogue, you might suggest that they listen attentively to conversations of friends and families and even (with the participants' permission) tape-record some to listen to again.

Additional Resource

Writing Resource Book, pp. 77–79

Answers to Practice Your Skills

Answers will vary. A sample answer is shown below.

"So then," said Mr. Lugonez, "why did the Spaniards want to find a new trade route to the Far East? Anybody?"

"Ri-dip," came the reply. It was an unexpected sound. In fact, it was an animal sound. It was the croak of a frog—Carla's frog.

"Carla? I didn't see your hand," said Mr. Lugonez.

"Well, I—"

"Ri-dip. Ri-dip," croaked the frog again.

"Carla—" began Mr. Lugonez, more sternly this time, but Carla gave him no chance to finish.

"Yes, well, you see, um, the Spaniards were absolutely desperate to find a route to the Middle, um, Far East because, um, they needed spices for their food. Food was really boring back then, so people paid a lot for anything to make it taste better. So, um, anyway. . . ." As Carla rattled on, I began to admire the crazy way she was trying to hide her frog.

I guess Mr. Lugonez did too, because when she finally stopped talking, all he said was, "What's the matter, Carla? Did you get a frog in your throat?"

Guidelines for Writing Dialogue

- Dialogue should sound like real people talking. It can include slang and sentence fragments, for example.

"Ken, did you hear me? Don't swim too far out," his mother warned.

"Yeah, yeah," he muttered. "Parents!"

- Use speaker's tags—such as "I said" and "she asked quietly" — to show who is speaking and how the words sound.

"Everybody out of the water," the lifeguard shouted.

"What's going on?" Ken asked anxiously.

- Begin a new paragraph each time the speaker changes.

"Ken," I yelled, "get out of the water! They've seen a shark."

"Wow! Let's get movin'."

- Notice that the first words of quotations are capitalized. The first words of new sentences within a quotation are also capitalized as in the first example above.
- End marks are usually placed inside quotation marks.

PROBLEM SOLVING

"I'm not sure how to use periods and commas with quotation marks."

For information on punctuating dialogue, see

• Handbook 43, "Punctuation," pages 566–599

Practice Your Skills

Rewrite the story described below, using dialogue.

Carla brings her new pet frog to school. Its croaking disrupts Mr. Lugonez's social studies class. Carla tries to cover up the croaking by giving a long and complicated answer to Mr. Lugonez's social studies question, but she eventually runs out of things to say. Mr. Lugonez then asks her if she stopped talking because of a frog in her throat.

How Can I Write Better Sentences?

WRITING HANDBOOK 23

Correcting Sentence Errors

Sometimes you start a sentence and you keep thinking of things to add and your sentence goes on and on and you don't know when to stop. Other times a different problem. Not enough information.

Sentences like these are confusing and hard to follow. To communicate clearly, you need to revise sentences that go on and on, as well as groups of words that do not express complete thoughts. Here are some strategies you can use to write better sentences.

REVISING FRAGMENTS

A sentence expresses a complete thought. A group of words that doesn't express a complete thought is a **fragment.** A subject, a verb, or both are missing from a fragment. The groups of words below are fragments.

Missing a subject	Anxiously waited for the results
Missing a verb	The star of the show
Missing a subject and a verb	From the roof of the building

You can correct fragments by adding the missing parts.

The contestants anxiously waited for the results.
The star of the show *signed autographs for her fans.*
The stuntman jumped from the roof of the building.

Yves Klein's *Saut dans le vide,* 1960, as photographed by Harry Shunk. In English, the French phrase could be translated "leap into the void."

WRITING HANDBOOK 23

Correcting Sentence Errors

Objective

- To identify and correct sentence fragments, run-on sentences, and stringy sentences

Related Mini-Lessons

For information on topics related to correcting sentence errors, see the following mini-lessons:

- **Transitions, pp. 234–238**
- **Revising, pp. 257–259**
- **Sentence Combining, pp. 286–291**

Teaching Strategies

for REVISING FRAGMENTS

STUMBLING BLOCK: IDENTIFYING FRAGMENTS Some students do not recognize sentence fragments because they still have difficulty identifying subjects and verbs. Divide students into pairs and have one member of each pair generate a list of three sentence fragments. Have the other member of each pair revise the fragments into complete sentences. Have the pairs check their work by underlining the subject and double-underlining the verb in each sentence.

Grammar Connection

In most writing, fragments are errors. However, in dialogue—the written form of conversation—fragments are acceptable if they represent the speech of the characters realistically. You might give students an example:

"Going to the game?" Helen asked.
"No," Susan said. "Too much homework."

Ask students to turn the fragments into complete sentences, such as, "Are you going to the game?" and "No, I have too much homework."

for REVISING RUN-ON SENTENCES

INDIVIDUALIZING INSTRUCTION: BASIC STUDENTS You may want to clarify the use of *and, but,* and *or* for these students, using the following examples.

I worked hard in the garden, *and* the plants grew well. (additional information)

I worked hard in the garden, *but* the plants did not grow well. (contrasting idea)

The plants did not get enough water, *or* the soil was poor. (alternatives)

KINESTHETIC LEARNERS Make up index cards with a period, a comma, and the conjunctions *and, but,* and *or.* Then write the example run-on sentences on strips of paper. Have students cut the strips between the complete thoughts and put them back together with appropriate punctuation and conjunctions. If a capital letter is needed, have them write it on a blank card and place it over the lowercase letter.

Sometimes you can correct a fragment by adding it to a complete sentence.

Sentence The ship was thrown off course.

Fragment By the violent storm and strong ocean currents

Revised The ship was thrown off course by the violent storm and strong ocean currents.

For more help with writing sentences that express complete thoughts, see Handbook 34, "Understanding Sentences," pages 338–345. For more suggestions on ways to combine sentences and sentence parts, see Handbook 24, "Sentence Combining," pages 286–291.

REVISING RUN-ON SENTENCES

A **run-on sentence** expresses more than one complete thought. Sometimes there is no end mark at the end of the first thought. At other times a comma incorrectly joins two thoughts. You can correct run-ons by breaking them into separate sentences.

Run-on Julianne plays the flute, her little sister plays the clarinet.

Revised Julianne plays the flute. Her little sister plays the clarinet.

If the thoughts are closely related, you can use a comma and a conjunction to link them.

Run-on The quarterback threw the football the receiver caught it.

Revised The quarterback threw the football, and the receiver caught it.

Run-on The music critic disliked the concert the fans loved it.

Revised The music critic disliked the concert, but the fans loved it.

Writing TIP

You can use the conjunctions *and, but,* and *or* to join sentences. Each word draws attention to a different type of relationship between thoughts.

282 Writing Handbook

W R I T E R   T O   W R I T E R

When I write, I begin by formulating ideas in my head and then listing them. Next, I write them into logical and correct sentences.

Gil Atanasoff, student
Kenosha, Wisconsin

REVISING STRINGY SENTENCES

In a **stringy sentence,** many thoughts are strung together with the word *and.* This type of sentence is dull to read and is often hard to follow. You can break up stringy sentences into separate sentences.

Stringy Blue smoke curled from the stone chimney and light glowed from the windows and we caught the delicious smells of supper cooking.

Separate Ideas Blue smoke curled from the stone chimney. Light glowed from the windows. We caught the delicious smells of supper cooking.

Sometimes writers want to string thoughts together because the ideas are related. However, it is generally better to separate the thoughts by writing them as separate sentences. Then you can use transition words and phrases to show how the thoughts are related.

Stringy We read about the planets and we watched a movie about Venus and Mars and we went to the planetarium.

Separate Thoughts We read about the planets.
We watched a movie about Venus and Mars.
We went to the planetarium.

Revised We read about the planets. *The next day* we watched a movie about Venus and Mars. *Then* we went to the planetarium.

OH, NO..
POOF
ANOTHER VICTIM OF THE CURSE OF THE SKYWRITER:
WHUMP
THE RUN-ON SENTENCE.
MACNELLY

for WRITER TO WRITER

CRITICAL THINKING: EVALUATING Have students read Gil Atanasoff's comment about how he approaches writing. Would they be comfortable using this approach? Have them explain their opinions. Be sure students recognize that there is no one correct way to approach a writing assignment.

for REVISING STRINGY SENTENCES

STUMBLING BLOCK: CHOPPY SENTENCES Sometimes, in an effort to avoid stringy sentences, students wind up writing choppy sentences instead. To help students avoid this error, emphasize the use of conjunctions and transition words to show how ideas are related. Point out that the three separate thoughts in the example about the planets are choppy sentences. Read these sentences aloud so that students can hear how they sound. Then read aloud the revised sentence, stressing the two transitions.

PROFESSIONAL NOTEBOOK

In *Errors and Expectations,* Mina Shaughnessy offers this perspective on students' stringing together ideas with *and:* "The difficulty with this all-purpose *and* is that it is easy on the writer but hard on the reader; it frees the writer from the work of getting his sentences to reflect the different levels of generalization . . . in his thought, but instead imposes upon the reader the work of trying to divine what these relationships are."

for PRACTICE YOUR SKILLS

MANAGING THE PAPER LOAD

Some students may be working on this handbook because of a particular kind of sentence error in their writing. Have students complete only the exercises that relate to their specific type of error. This approach will benefit the student and reduce the amount of grading.

Additional Resources

Writing Resource Book, pp. 80–81
Sentence Composing Copy Masters

Answers to Practice Your Skills

A. Answers will vary.

B. Answers may vary. Sample answers are shown below.

1. We climbed all the way to the top of the hill. We weren't even tired.
2. Arlyn's head ached. She had the flu.
3. Jake thought the animal was an alpaca, but it was a llama.
4. The theater was packed, and there was a line around the block.
5. The doorbell rang. The mail carrier was at the door.

C. Answers may vary. Sample answers are shown below.

1. Brent started to walk to Kathy's house. He stopped to talk to Charlie. Then he stayed to play video games.
2. The wind howled outside, and an owl hooted in the distance. The boards in the old house creaked.
3. I had a dream about *Alice in Wonderland*. I thought I was Alice. I chased the White Rabbit.
4. First we raked the leaves. Then we discovered an old baseball, and we quit raking.
5. Emma knows how to use a computer. She has a program for drawing pictures, and she can print the pictures in color.

For more help with using transitions to link thoughts, see Handbook 11, "Transitions," on pages 234–238.

Practice Your Skills

A. Revise each sentence fragment below. Add a subject, a verb, or a subject and a verb to make a complete sentence.

1. The day before the big game
2. The lead singer of the band
3. Leaped over the fence
4. Through the secret passageway
5. Reminded me of my first piano concert

B. Correct each of the following run-on sentences.

1. We climbed all the way to the top of the hill we weren't even tired.
2. Arlyn's head ached she had the flu.
3. Jake thought the animal was an alpaca, it was a llama.
4. The theater was packed there was a line around the block.
5. The doorbell rang, the mail carrier was at the door.

C. Rewrite these stringy sentences to make the relationships between thoughts clear.

1. Brent started to walk to Kathy's house and he stopped to talk to Charlie and he stayed to play video games.
2. The wind howled outside and an owl hooted in the distance and the boards in the old house creaked.
3. I had a dream about *Alice in Wonderland* and I thought I was Alice and I chased the White Rabbit.
4. First we raked the leaves and we discovered an old baseball and we quit raking.
5. Emma knows how to use a computer and she has a program for drawing pictures and she can print the pictures in color.

284 Writing Handbook

Tongue Twisters

You probably know that Peter Piper picked a peck of pickled peppers. But did you know that Bonnie Bliss blows big beautiful blue bubbles? Or that old, oily Ollie oils oily autos?

Tongue twisters like these have been around for centuries. Test your tongue on these troublesome twisters [from *A Twister of Twists, a Tangler of Tongues,* a torturous collection by Alvin Schwartz].

Betty Botter
bought some butter,
But, she said,
the butter's bitter.
If I put it
in my batter,
It will make
my batter bitter.
But a bit
of better butter—
That would make
my batter better.

A noisy noise annoys an oyster.

Sheep shouldn't sleep in a shack.
Sheep should sleep in a shed.

Which is the witch that
wished the wicked wish?

Which wristwatches are Swiss
wristwatches?

A tooter who tooted a flute
Tried to tutor two tutors to
toot.
Said the two to the tutor,
"Is it harder to toot or
To tutor two tutors to toot?"

Does this shop stock short socks with spots?

For each tongue twister, challenge volunteers to say the twister as quickly as possible without making any mistakes. Declare a class tongue-twister champion by acclamation or by vote. If time permits, you might ask students to recite other tongue twisters they know.

WRITING HANDBOOK 24

Sentence Combining

Objectives

- To recognize sentences that should be combined
- To combine sentences and sentence parts using conjunctions
- To combine sentences by adding single words or groups of words

Related Mini-Lessons

For information on topics related to sentence combining, see the following mini-lessons:

- **Revising, pp. 257–259**
- **Correcting Sentence Errors, pp. 281–284**

Motivate

Read aloud the following paragraph.

The police officer bent down. She bent down until she was eye to eye with the boy. The boy was very young. She could see his face. His face was streaked with tears. He took heavy breaths. He quivered.

Ask students how they feel about the short sentences in the paragraph. (Students may note that the topic is interesting but that the short sentences seem dull.) Explain that many of the short, choppy sentences could be combined to make sentences that are smoother and more interesting.

WRITING HANDBOOK 24

How Do I Fix Choppy Sentences?

Sentence Combining

A pair of jeans, a T-shirt, a vest—by themselves, these clothes might seem fairly dull. Put them together in an interesting way, though, and you've got style.

You can add style to your writing in a similar way. By combining sentences with related ideas and details, you can make your writing livelier and more interesting.

Combining Sentences and Sentence Parts

As you review your writing, look for short, choppy sentences that give information about the same topic. Often, you can combine these sentences into one sentence that includes all the information. You can join related sentences or sentence parts with conjunctions such as *and, but,* and *or.*

Combining Complete Sentences

Sometimes two sentences contain ideas that are alike. You can join the sentences with a comma and the word *and.*

Separate	The baseball stadium is filled with fans. The game is about to begin.
Combined	The baseball stadium is filled with fans**, and** the game is about to begin.

You can use a comma and the word *but* to join two sentences that state contrasting ideas on the same topic.

Separate	The two teams are ready to play. The umpire is nowhere to be found.
Combined	The two teams are ready to play**, but** the umpire is nowhere to be found.

If two sentences offer a choice between ideas, use a comma and the word *or* to join the sentences.

Separate Is the umpire on his way? Did he forget about the game?

Combined Is the umpire on his way**, or** did he forget about the game?

Combining Sentence Parts

Sometimes two sentences are so closely related that some of the same words or ideas appear in both sentences. You can join those sentences by using *and, but,* or *or* and leaving out the repeated words or ideas.

Separate Seals are speedy swimmers. *They are* skillful divers.

Combined Seals are speedy swimmers **and** skillful divers.

Separate Seals need to breathe air. *They* can stay underwater for more than thirty minutes at a time.

Combined Seals need to breathe air **but** can stay underwater for more than thirty minutes at a time.

Separate Are seals fish? *Are they* mammals?

Combined Are seals fish **or** mammals?

Practice Your Skills

A. Combine each pair of sentences, using a comma and the conjunction shown in parentheses.

1. Yellowstone National Park was crowded. Most of the campgrounds were full. (*and*)
2. Did you see Old Faithful? Were you too late? (*or*)
3. A family of bears approached our car. The mother bear led her cubs away. (*but*)
4. We took our new video camera with us. My sister taped some of our adventures in the park. (*and*)

Grammar **TIP**

Use a comma before a conjunction that joins two complete sentences. Don't use a comma before a conjunction that joins two sentence parts.

Teaching Strategies

for COMBINING COMPLETE SENTENCES

INDIVIDUALIZING INSTRUCTION: AUDITORY LEARNERS Students who learn best by listening might find it easier to recognize short, choppy sentences if they hear them spoken. Read the short sample sentences aloud; then read the combined sentences to illustrate the more graceful sound of the longer sentences.

for COMBINING SENTENCE PARTS

STUMBLING BLOCK Students may have trouble recognizing the pronoun in the second sentence of each sample as a repeated idea. Point out that each pronoun refers to the subject of the first sentence. In the first sample, for example, "they" refers to "seals," and so "they" does not need to appear in the combined sentence.

Answers to Practice Your Skills

A.

1. Yellowstone National Park was crowded, and most of the campgrounds were full.
2. Did you see Old Faithful, or were you too late?
3. A family of bears approached our car, but the mother bear led her cubs away.
4. We took our new video camera with us, and my sister taped some of our adventures in the park.

B.

1. I walked along the sandy beach and looked for shells.
2. Pelicans dove into the water to catch fish but often came up with their beaks empty.
3. I saw a dark shape speeding through the water and leaping over the waves.
4. Was that a dolphin or a killer whale?

for ADDING SINGLE WORDS

LINKING GRAMMAR AND WRITING Point out that the examples show how sentences can be combined by adding adjectives or adverbs to the first sentence. Remind students that adjectives are words that modify nouns or pronouns, whereas adverbs are words that modify verbs, adjectives, or other adverbs. Have students identify the added words in the example sentences as either adjectives or adverbs. (*Gleaming, huge, busy, cool,* and *dark* are adjectives; *swiftly* and *silently* are adverbs.)

for ADDING SINGLE WORDS

HELPFUL HINT Students will benefit from seeing these sentence-combining techniques applied to their own writing. Therefore, you might ask students to find passages in their own writing in which they would like to vary their sentences. Then show them how to apply these techniques.

B. Combine the ideas in each pair of sentences. Leave out the words shown in italics.

1. I walked along the sandy beach. *I* looked for shells *in the sand.*
2. Pelicans dove into the water to catch fish. *The birds* often came up with their beaks empty.
3. I saw a dark shape speeding through the water. *I watched it* leaping over the waves.
4. Was that a dolphin? *Could it have been* a killer whale?

ADDING WORDS TO SENTENCES

Using *and, but,* or *or* to connect related ideas is just one way to make your writing livelier. You can also take important words from two or more related sentences and put them together to make a new sentence.

Adding Single Words

You can join sentences by taking an important word from one sentence and adding it to another. Leave out the rest of the words.

Separate The jet rolled quickly down the runway.
The jet was gleaming.
Combined The **gleaming** jet rolled quickly down the runway.

Separate The jet waited to leave the airport.
The plane was huge. *The airport was* busy.
Combined The **huge** jet waited to leave the **busy** airport.

When you add more than one word to the main sentence, you may need to use a comma or the word *and.*

Separate Bats poured out of the cave.
The cave was cool. *It also was* dark.
Combined Bats poured out of the **cool, dark** cave.

288 Writing Handbook

Separate A flock of bats flew over the sleeping city. *The bats flew* swiftly. *They moved* silently.

Combined A flock of bats flew **swiftly and silently** over the sleeping city.

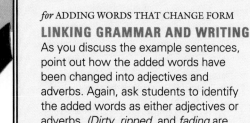

Sometimes the group of words can be put in more than one place in the new sentence.

Combined **Swiftly and silently,** a flock of bats flew over the sleeping city.

Adding Words That Change Form

In some cases you must change the form of a word before you add it to another sentence. For example, you may have to add *-y* to the end of the word.

Separate I threw my jeans into the washer. *They were covered with* dirt.

Combined I threw my **dirty** jeans into the washer.

You may need to use the *-ed* or *-ing* form of the word.

Separate Then I mended the hem. *It had begun to* rip.

Combined Then I mended the **ripped** hem.

Separate I love these jeans. *They are starting to* fade.

Combined I love these **fading** jeans.

You might have to add *-ly* to the word before you use it in the new sentence.

Separate I changed into my jeans. *I was* quick.

Combined I **quickly** changed into my jeans.

Sometimes a word ending in *-ly* fits in more than one place in the new sentence. Pick the place that best suits your meaning.

Combined **Quickly,** I changed into my jeans.
I changed into my jeans **quickly.**

for ADDING WORDS THAT CHANGE FORM

LINKING GRAMMAR AND WRITING
As you discuss the example sentences, point out how the added words have been changed into adjectives and adverbs. Again, ask students to identify the added words as either adjectives or adverbs. *(Dirty, ripped,* and *fading* are adjectives; *quickly* is an adverb.)

for ADDING WORDS THAT CHANGE FORM

HELPFUL HINT In the last example on the page, point out how the different positions of the added word in the sentence change the emphasis. When *quickly* is placed at the beginning of the sentence, the narrator's speed is emphasized. When *quickly* is placed at the end of the sentence, the emphasis falls instead on the narrator's action. You also might add that sometimes the placement depends on the surrounding sentences. A writer might change the position of an added word to vary sentence beginnings in a paragraph.

Answers to Practice Your Skills

A.

1. My friend Ali competed in a bicycle race yesterday. *or* Yesterday my friend Ali competed in a bicycle race.
2. The hot and humid weather was hard on the racers.
3. The race followed a steep trail up a huge mountain.
4. Ali rode his new mountain bike along the rough trail in the race.
5. He carefully steered around the big rocks in the road. *or* He steered carefully around the big rocks in the road.
6. On our map we traced Ali's winding route up the mountain.
7. We met the exhausted cyclists at the end of the difficult race.
8. After the race everyone drank cool, refreshing lemonade.

B.

1. Thousands of noisy people streamed into the stadium for the skating competition.
2. When the stadium lights dimmed, a hush fell over the excited audience.
3. In the spotlight we saw a skater in a ruffled, sparkling green costume.
4. As the music began, she skated across the ice slowly and gracefully. *or* As the music began, she skated slowly and gracefully across the ice.
5. The skater completed many complicated jumps perfectly. *or* The skater perfectly completed many complicated jumps.
6. The delighted crowd cheered when this skater won a silver medal.

Practice Your Skills

A. Combine each group of sentences, following any instructions in parentheses. Omit the words in italics.

1. My friend Ali competed in a race. *It was a* bicycle *race. The race was* yesterday.
2. The weather was hard on the racers. *The day was* hot. *The air felt* humid. (Use *and*.)
3. The race followed a trail up a mountain. *The mountain looked* huge. *The trail was* steep.
4. Ali rode his new mountain bike along the trail in the race. *The path was* rough.
5. He steered around the big rocks in the road. *He tried to be* careful. (Use *-ly*.)
6. On our map we traced Ali's route up the mountain. *The road seemed to* wind *back and forth.* (Use *-ing*.)
7. We met the cyclists at the end of the race. *They were all* exhausted. *The race had been* difficult.
8. After the race everyone drank lemonade. *The lemonade tasted* cool. *It made a* refreshing *drink.* (Use a comma.)

B. Combine the sentences in each of the following groups, leaving out any unnecessary words. You may need to change the forms of some words.

1. Thousands of people streamed into the stadium for the skating competition. The crowd made a lot of noise.
2. When the stadium lights dimmed, a hush fell over the audience. The audience was excited.
3. In the spotlight we saw a skater in a green costume. Her costume sparkled. It was a dress with many ruffles.
4. As the music began, she skated across the ice. Her movements were slow. She skated gracefully.
5. The skater completed many jumps. The jumps were complicated. She performed them perfectly.
6. The crowd cheered when this skater won a medal. She won a silver medal. Everyone was delighted.

ADDING GROUPS OF WORDS TO SENTENCES

Sometimes a group of words in one sentence can add important information to another sentence. You can move the word group from one sentence to the other. If the words you move tell something about a person, a thing, or an action in the other sentence, put them near the name of the person, thing, or action.

Separate Mom asked me to wash the dog. *She asked me* twice today.

Combined Mom asked me **twice today** to wash the dog.

However, the group of words might make sense in more than one place in the new sentence.

Twice today, Mom asked me to wash the dog.

Practice Your Skills

A. Combine each pair of sentences by moving a word group from one sentence to the other. Omit the words in italics.

1. The woman is my grandmother. *She is* wearing a ring.
2. Grandma moved here in 1940. *She came here* from Norway.
3. The most important thing she brought with her was a ring. *It is a* beautiful ruby *ring.*
4. Grandma lost her ring. *She lost it* the year I was born.

B. Combine each pair of sentences by adding important words from one sentence to the other sentence.

1. The postcard is from Grandfather. It is on the table.
2. He is visiting Mexico. He is there for the winter.
3. The card shows the ruins of an ancient city. The city is called Chichén Itzá.
4. Chichén Itzá was built by the Maya. They built the city hundreds of years ago.

Writing **TIP**

After you join two sentences, read the new sentence carefully. Words added in the wrong place can make a sentence confusing, wrong, or even funny—for example, "Mom asked me to wash the dog *twice today.*"

for ADDING GROUPS OF WORDS . . .

INDIVIDUALIZING INSTRUCTION: ESL STUDENTS Some ESL students may have difficulty with the idea that words or groups of words can be placed in various locations in a sentence. In some languages, such as German, grammar rules indicate clearly where such words or phrases should be placed. As a general guideline, tell students to place these words as close as possible to *me* words that are repeated in both sentences. As they gain fluency, students will learn to distinguish between adjectival and adverbial word groups.

Additional Resources

Writing Resource Book, p. 82
Sentence Composing Copy Masters, pp. 5–6

Answers to Practice Your Skills

A.

1. The woman wearing a ring is my grandmother.
2. Grandma moved here from Norway in 1940.
3. The most important thing she brought with her was a beautiful ruby ring.
4. Grandma lost her ring the year I was born.

B.

1. The postcard on the table is from Grandfather.
2. He is visiting Mexico for the winter.
3. The card shows the ruins of an ancient city called Chichén Itzá.
4. Chichén Itzá was built hundreds of years ago by the Maya. *or* Chichén Itzá was built by the Maya hundreds of years ago. *or* Hundreds of years ago, Chichén Itzá was built by the Maya.

Sketch Book

Objective

- To use the book jackets and suggested writing prompts as springboards to informal writing

WRITING WARM-UPS

Use these writing prompts as risk-free ungraded activities that students can enjoy. Unless students wish (and have the time) to do more, suggest that each student respond to only one prompt. Before students begin, point out that all three prompts have a similar focus: students are asked to tell about something that keenly interests them. You might also point out that the authors of the three books in the illustration all chose to write about subjects that interested them individually.

Sketch Book

WRITING WARM-UPS

- What kind of book would you like to write? Jot down some thoughts about what your book would be like.
- What fascinates you? Make a list of things you would like to find out more about.
- What is the most interesting thing you have learned in school this year? Tell why it is important to you.

Academic Skills

WRITING HANDBOOKS

Whether you write them or read them, books can take you to new worlds. To get the most out of these worlds, you need to be able to read, study, think, and research effectively.

The handbooks that follow can teach you skills that will help you explore new worlds, in school and on your own.

WRITING HANDBOOKS

Academic Skills

INTRODUCING THE HANDBOOKS

Here's a thought exercise you might use to introduce the Academic Skills Handbooks. Tell students to imagine that the pupil-edition page is in a foreign language they can't identify. Ask how they would go about learning what the page says.

First, of course, they would think about the problem and develop a strategy for solving it. They might consult a person with expertise in languages. They might also ask a librarian to help them find out what the language is. Perhaps the librarian could help them find a dictionary of that language. While translating the page, students would learn some words of the foreign language, and possibly some English words new to them, as well.

During the whole process just described, students would have used thinking skills, study and research skills, interviewing skills, library skills, dictionary skills, reading skills, and vocabulary skills. If, after succeeding in translating the page, they were to answer questions about their findings, orally and in writing, they would use skills from every mini-lesson in the Academic Skills section. Point out that these are general skills that can help people find information on any subject, from foreign languages to home cooking. They are also, of course, vital to succeeding in school!

WRITING HANDBOOK 25

Study and Research Skills

Objectives

- To use the KWL approach as a way to focus thinking when reading or researching
- To use a learning log to understand a subject better
- To recognize and apply effective techniques for studying and memorizing

Related Mini-Lessons

For information on topics related to study and research skills, see the following mini-lessons:

- **Reading Skills, pp. 298–301**
- **Library Skills, pp. 312–319**
- **Thinking Skills, pp. 320–322**

Motivate

Ask volunteers to describe the biggest study problem they have—for example, scheduling study time. Is the study area noisy and distracting? Do they find memorizing hard? Do they spend a lot of time studying and still receive poor grades because their study methods are ineffective? Make a list of problems on the board and suggest that students look for solutions in this handbook.

Teaching Strategies

for THE KWL APPROACH

MODELING To help students understand the use of the KWL approach, model the first two steps, using a subject you yourself would like to study. On the board, make a "K" list of things you already know, then a "W" list of things you would like to know.

WRITING HANDBOOK 25

How Can I Become a Better Student?

Study and Research Skills

Do you ever wish that it were possible just to open up your head and pour in knowledge? Unfortunately, learning doesn't work that way. To get the most out of your studies, you need to actively participate in the learning process. There are skills you can learn that will make your study time more efficient and enjoyable.

THE KWL APPROACH

Whether you are reading a textbook, doing a research report, or working on a project, using the KWL approach is a good way to focus your thinking. The letters stand for three questions you should ask yourself about your subject:

K **"What do I already know about my subject?"** Before you start studying, make a list of everything you already know about the subject. The list will get you thinking about the subject and about what you don't yet know.

W **"What do I want to know?"** Make a list of the things you would like to know about the subject. As you study, see if you find the answers to your questions.

L **"What did I learn?"** After you have studied the subject, look back and list the things you have learned. Are there still things you want to know? Have your thoughts about the subject changed?

LEARNING LOGS

Writing about a subject helps you understand it better and often prompts you to think about things you hadn't noticed before. One of the best ways to take charge of your learning is to keep a learning log. A **learning log** is a journal you keep for one subject. Like your writing journal, your learning log is a place to record ideas, thoughts, and questions. You might want to keep separate learning logs for each of your subjects.

All sorts of things can go into a learning log. It is a perfect place to record your answers to the KWL questions and to note key facts about the subject. You can write about your reactions to the things you are learning and ask yourself questions about things you don't understand. You can also draw pictures or graphic aids to help you understand the subject.

Science Journal

4/13 Alligators and Crocodiles

K: reptiles, look like floating logs, dangerous huge teeth, short legs, alligators live in swamps in Florida

W: How are alligators and crocodiles different? How can you tell them apart? Do they both attack people?

4/14 Field trip to the zoo

L: I touched an alligator! Alligators aren't as ferocious as crocodiles. The zookeeper could hold the alligator's snout shut with one hand because the muscles to open the jaws are pretty weak. Alligators usually avoid people, but crocodiles will attack. One way to tell them apart is by the shape of the snout.

alligator snout: 

crocodile snout: 

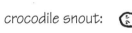

It would be fun to actually see alligators in the wild! Where besides Florida could I find them?

Writing TIP

Writing in your learning log is like thinking with a pencil. Remember, write for yourself—record what will be most useful to you.

Student MODEL

Things you already know

Things you want to know

What you have learned

Key facts

Drawings

Your feelings

Questions you still have

for LEARNING LOGS

HELPFUL HINT Students might like to color-code the KWL information in their learning logs. They might write in one color what they know; in a second color, what they want to know; and in a third color, what they have learned. Color-coding can help them locate different kinds of information in their logs quickly.

for LEARNING LOGS

INDIVIDUALIZING INSTRUCTION: LD STUDENTS To students who have difficulty with phrasing their ideas in writing, suggest using a tape recorder to keep a learning log.

ESL STUDENTS Because of the personal nature of learning logs, ESL students will probably prefer to use their first languages when recording ideas, thoughts, and questions. Tell these students that it is acceptable to use whatever language is more comfortable.

for STUDENT MODEL

USING THE MODEL Ask students what they might add to the list of "K" information and "W" questions. Emphasize the value of the drawings in the "L" part of the model, and note that some information can be conveyed more effectively through graphic aids.

PROFESSIONAL NOTEBOOK

In *The Young Learner's Handbook,* teacher and writer Stephen Tchudi offers this variation on keeping a learning log:

. . . Using a ruler as a guide, draw a line down the center of your notebook pages. Then write the facts in the left-hand column, leaving the right column free for your comments and questions to yourself.

for WRITING TIP

COLLABORATIVE OPPORTUNITY

Encourage students to share the abbreviations and symbols that they use in their notes. Point out that common abbreviations such as *s/b* (should be) and symbols like ≠ (does not equal) are useful in all curriculum areas.

for MEMORIZING

COLLABORATIVE OPPORTUNITY

Some students may find it easier to memorize information by studying with a partner. A partner can prompt oral recitation and identify errors.

Writing **TIP**

Your notes are for your eyes only. Don't worry about grammar, punctuation, and spelling. Feel free to use abbreviations and to make up symbols.

STAY ON TOP OF YOUR STUDIES

Try these ideas to make the most of your study time.

- **Keep track of assignments.** Use a special assignment notebook to record exactly what is expected, what materials you will need, and when the assignment is due.
- **Plan ahead.** Schedule your activities on a weekly calendar to make sure you have time for everything.
- **Keep a separate notebook or folder for each subject.**
- **Take notes as you study.** Include only the main ideas.
- **Review your notes as soon as you can.** Revise or add to them as needed, and highlight important points.

Memorizing

Do you think some people are born with good and bad memories, just as some people are tall and others short? Actually, there are skills anyone can learn to improve memory.

- **Write it, recite it.** The action of writing and the sound of your voice will help you remember information.
- **Find connections between items.** For example, remember items in the order they happened or recall items alphabetically.
- **Create a crazy picture.** Arrange the facts you want to remember in a vivid picture in your mind. Then, when you want to recall those facts, visualize the same picture.
- **Make up catchy sayings.** Develop a sentence or phrase using the initials of the words you want to memorize. For example, HOMES could help you remember the names of the Great Lakes: *H*uron, *O*ntario, *M*ichigan, *E*rie, and *S*uperior.

A crazy picture can help you remember that *core* is the innermost part of the earth.

PROFESSIONAL NOTEBOOK

In *How to Sharpen Your Study Skills,* teacher and writer Sigmund Kalina offers these examples of "memory hooks":

- *word hooks.* In music, the spaces of the treble staff reading upward are f, a, c, e, which spell the word "face."
- *sentence hooks.* Make phrases or sentences that will help fix information in your memory. To remember which way to turn the clock at the start and end of Daylight Saving Time, remember that you "spring" *forward* and "fall" *backward.*

Practice Your Skills

A. Use the KWL approach to write a learning log entry about one of the topics below. First make a list that tells what you already know about the subject. Then list what you want to know about the subject.

pyramids	Olympic Games	sharks
lasers	earthquakes	Australia

B. Obtain a list of the nine planets of the solar system. Use a memorizing strategy to learn the planets. Explain your strategy.

C. Memorize the basic four food groups important for good nutrition: dairy products, meat, fruits and vegetables, and grains. Make up a saying in which each word begins with the first letter of one of the groups.

D. Read the selection below, taking notes as you read. Then share your notes with a small group of classmates. Discuss the main idea of the selection and develop a list of things the group would like to know about the subject.

> It's like being inside a video game. You are in an artificial world where you can interact with the computer-generated objects around you. You might see a ticking clock and decide to pick it up. You watch as your hand reaches down and grabs the clock. You bring it closer and the ticking gets louder. It is not reality. But it isn't just computer graphics either. It's virtual reality.
>
> Virtual reality is a very advanced form of computer simulation. Already, it is being used for everything from letting architects walk through houses before they are built to helping scientists study the surface of Mars. And one day it may be as much a part of your schoolwork as a notebook and pen.
>
> **Nancy Day, "Get Real!" *Odyssey,* June 1992**

Additional Resource

Writing Resource Book, p. 85

Answers to Practice Your Skills

A. Answers will vary, but students' lists should show that they put some thought into answering the "K" and "W" questions.

B. Answers will vary.

C. Answers will vary. Students' sayings need not use the words in the order shown in the exercise. Sample answer: Many friendly dogs growl.

D. Students' notes and lists will vary. The main idea of the selection is that virtual reality is a new computer technology that creates realistic scenes with which people can interact.

WRITING
HANDBOOK
26

Reading Skills

Objectives

- To recognize the uses and techniques of skimming, scanning, and in-depth reading
- To use different reading strategies and parts of a book to find information
- To apply strategies for reading graphic aids

Related Mini-Lessons

For information on topics related to reading skills, see the following mini-lessons:

- **Library Skills, pp. 312–319**
- **Taking Tests, pp. 326–333**

Teaching Strategies

for SKIMMING AND SCANNING

MODELING Model for students the methods of skimming and scanning, using this handbook. To skim the text, read the title, headings, boldfaced words, charts, and graphs. To scan, glance over the pages until you find the tip for reading maps (page 300, in the chart).

WRITING
HANDBOOK
26

How Can I Become a Better Reader?

Reading Skills

Sprinters dash toward the finish line as fast as possible. In contrast, marathon runners carefully pace themselves so that they have enough energy to finish the race. No single method or plan will work for every runner or every race. Similarly, good readers learn to vary the way they read depending on their purpose for reading.

TYPES OF READING

You read for a variety of purposes—to learn about a subject, to find enjoyment, or to locate some specific fact or piece of information. Depending on the kind of material you are reading and your purpose, you may read very quickly or quite slowly and carefully.

Skimming and Scanning

Skimming is a kind of fast reading that helps you get a general idea of what a book or passage is about. To skim, read the most important parts and skip everything else. Look for titles, headings, italicized words, and any pictures, charts, or graphs.

This method of reading is also a useful technique for study and review. Skim headings and topic sentences and then recall specific details.

Scanning is a speedy way to find a specific piece of information. Think of searching for an object with a flashlight. The beam of light focuses on a very small area. Similarly, when you scan, you glance quickly over the page until you spot key words or phrases that show you are near the information you need. Use this skill for tasks such as locating a name and number in the phone book or a certain date in an encyclopedia article.

In-depth Reading

The goal of **in-depth reading** is to get everything you can from a piece of writing. Here are some techniques for in-depth reading.

1. Preview Read the first paragraph of a selection to get a general idea of the topic. Also read titles and headings and look over any charts and graphs. Skim the first sentence of paragraphs within the body of a selection and then read the last paragraph. Writers often summarize or draw conclusions in this last paragraph.

2. Read After you preview, go back and read carefully. Look at topic sentences for key terms and main ideas. Focus on details. Notice how ideas fit together and reread passages until the meaning really sinks in.

3. React and record Respond to the author's ideas. Do you agree or disagree? Take notes as you read and list any questions you may have.

Writing **TIP**

As you read, use your journal, reading log, or notebook to record your questions, reactions, and opinions. Also jot down key information.

USING THE PARTS OF A BOOK

Knowing how to use three parts of nonfiction books can help you locate information efficiently.

Three Parts of a Nonfiction Book

	Table of Contents	Glossary	Index
Where:	Front of the book	Usually back of book	Back of the book
What:	Chapter titles and chapter page numbers	Defines special words used in the book	Lists important topics with page numbers
Use:	Gives an overview of the book. Tells you if the book meets your needs and interests	Quick and easy source for definitions	Helps you find specific details quickly and easily

for IN-DEPTH READING

INDIVIDUALIZING INSTRUCTION: SOCIAL LEARNERS Suggest that these students might benefit from in-depth reading in small groups. Point out that one student can preview the selection aloud; then other students can take turns reading the entire selection. All members of the group can discuss their reactions and questions.

for USING THE PARTS OF A BOOK

ASSESSMENT: SPOT CHECK To make sure students understand *which* parts of a book to use to find information, ask them the following questions:

- In a book on ballet, where would you look to find out what the word *arabesque* means? (glossary)
- In an American history book, where would you look to find out if there is a chapter on the Civil War? (table of contents)
- In a book on classical music, where would you look to find the page numbers for information on Beethoven? (index)

Then, to check students' understanding of *how* to use these three parts of a book, have them turn to the table of contents, the glossary, and the index in the pupil book or another textbook. Ask them specific questions that they can answer by using these parts of the book.

for READING GRAPHIC AIDS

INDIVIDUALIZING INSTRUCTION: VISUAL LEARNERS Bring to class an example of each type of graphic aid listed on the chart. Ask your visual learners to model the Reading Tips and to summarize the information that each graphic aid presents.

for UNDERSTANDING GRAPHS

HELPFUL HINT To provide additional examples of circle graphs and bar graphs, look in newsmagazines such as *Time* or in the newspaper *USA Today.* Encourage students to look for examples in magazines such as *Scholastic UPDATE* or *Zillions.*

READING GRAPHIC AIDS

Graphic aids arrange information in a visual way. For example, one type of graphic aid is a table. What does the table below tell you about different types of graphic aids?

Types of Graphic Aids

	Purpose	Reading Tips
Photograph	Puts ideas into picture form	Read the title or caption.
Diagram	Identifies parts of an object	Read all the labels.
Map	Shows land areas and bodies of water	Read the title and study the symbols in the map key.
Tables and Charts	Presents groups of facts—often in column form	Read the title and column headings.
Graph	Shows how facts or sets of numbers are related	Read the title, symbol key, and all printed text.

UNDERSTANDING GRAPHS

Two common types of graphs are the bar graph and the circle graph. The **circle graph,** or pie chart, is drawn like a pie. Each wedge or slice shows how parts relate to the whole. Compare the size of each slice in the pie chart on the next page. Which "slice" is the largest? What does this tell you?

A **bar graph** uses the lengths of bars to show relationships. Often numbers run along the bottom of the graph, and words run along the left side. What is the subject of the bar graph on the next page?

SPICE BOX

Have students work in small groups to prepare graphic aids that illustrate information about the class. For example, one group could photograph the class, another draw a diagram of the layout of the classroom, another draw a map of the school, and so on. The groups might collect their work in a booklet.

Most Popular Restaurant Desserts

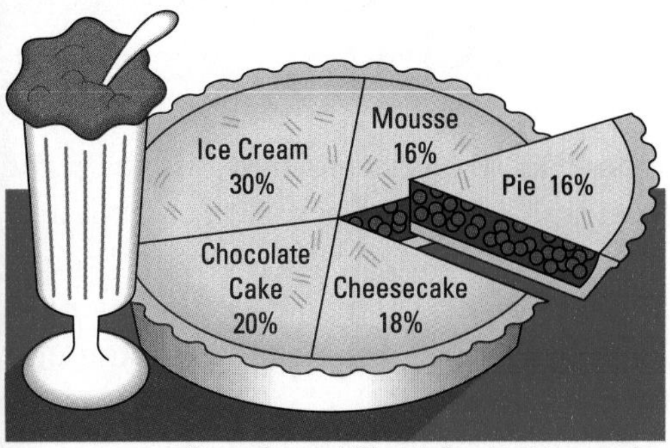

Source: Survey of 400 adults for advertising campaign.

What People Fear Most

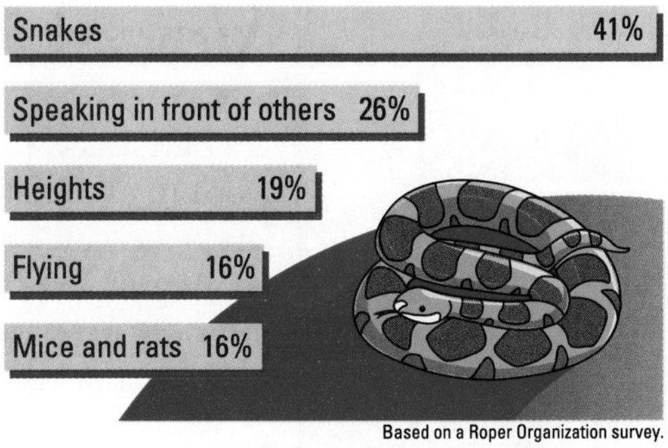

Based on a Roper Organization survey.

Practice Your Skills

A. Answer the questions below about "Take Tracks Home" on pages 94–95 by using the reading strategies shown in parentheses.

1. (Skim) What is the main idea of the passage?
2. (Scan) How long does it take for the plaster cast to harden?
3. (Read in depth) How can you make your own set of plaster casts of tracks?

B. Tell whether you would use the table of contents, glossary, or index in this book to answer the following questions. Then answer the questions.

1. Which pages tell you how to use question marks in quotations?
2. What is the definition of "brainstorming"?
3. What topics are found in Handbook 30, "Thinking Skills"?

C. Answer these questions by referring to the graphs in this lesson.

1. What two categories of things are people least afraid of? How do the numbers in these two categories compare?
2. Which is ordered more often, pie or cheesecake?

for PRACTICE YOUR SKILLS

INDIVIDUALIZING INSTRUCTION: BASIC STUDENTS Students who have difficulty using the glossary or index might benefit from a review of rules for alphabetizing. Review alphabetizing to the first, second, and third letter with these students.

Additional Resource

Writing Resource Book, pp. 86–89

Answers to Practice Your Skills

A. Answers may vary. Sample answers are shown below.

1. Start a collection of animal tracks by making plaster casts.
2. At least one-half hour.
3. Find a track you like. With a strip of stiff paper, make a one- to two-inch high circular collar around the track. Mix about two parts plaster of Paris with one part water and pour the mixture into the track. Be sure to completely fill the track with plaster. After at least half an hour, the plaster will be hard, and you can dig the cast out of the ground with a pocket knife or a garden trowel.

B.

1. index; pages 586-587
2. glossary; a way of generating ideas that involves listing them without stopping to judge them
3. table of contents, common errors in reasoning, appeals to emotion

C.

1. Flying; mice and rats. Both categories have the same numbers (16 percent).
2. Cheesecake (18 percent) is ordered more often than pie (16 percent).

WRITING HANDBOOK 27

Vocabulary Skills

Objectives

- To identify and use strategies for building vocabulary
- To use context clues, base words, prefixes, and suffixes to determine the meaning of unfamiliar words
- To write sentences that use context clues to show the meaning of words

Related Mini-Lessons

For information on topics related to vocabulary skills, see the following mini-lessons:

- **Levels of Language, pp. 274–275**
- **Using the Dictionary and the Thesaurus, pp. 308–311**

Motivate

You might compare a speaker or writer who has a broad vocabulary to an artist who has a wide range of colors to use in painting.

Teaching Strategies

for STRATEGIES FOR BUILDING VOCABULARY

SPEAKING AND LISTENING Many people understand words in print that they do not know how to pronounce. Write the following words on the board and ask volunteers to try pronouncing each one. If students have trouble, advise them to look up the pronunciation in a dictionary.

maneuver (mə-no͞o′-vər): a procedure that includes movement

scheme (skēm): a plan or idea

cerebral (sər′-ə-brəl): relating to the intellect

fugue (fyo͞og): a musical composition

WRITING HANDBOOK 27

How Can I Increase My Vocabulary?

Vocabulary Skills

Like Lucy, have you ever struggled to find just the right word to say what you mean? When you have a strong vocabulary, you won't need to invent strange new words to express your ideas. Instead, you'll be able to communicate clearly right from the start. Here are some simple techniques you can use to increase your vocabulary.

Strategies for Building Vocabulary

Read	One of the easiest ways to build your vocabulary is to do a lot of reading. As you read about many subjects, you will learn a variety of new words.
Ask about meanings of unfamiliar words	When you come across a word you don't understand, ask what the word means. Such questioning is a good way to help you learn about new words.
Keep vocabulary lists	Keep your own list of new words. Write down the new words you read or hear each day in your journal or another notebook. Use a dictionary to look up the words you've listed. Next to each word write its definition.
Write sentences	Create sentences using the new words you have listed and defined. Whenever you use a new word in your writing, you are more likely to remember it.

There are other skills you can develop to help you figure out the meanings of words. Like a detective, you can look for clues. So get out your magnifying glass and become a word sleuth as you learn new ways to unlock word meanings.

SPICE BOX

New slang words are constantly coming into and going out of use. Point out to students that these words often do not appear in a dictionary. Encourage a group of interested students to create a dictionary of the slang words and phrases that they currently use. Have them alphabetize the terms and work together to develop a definition of each one.

USING CONTEXT CLUES

You may find important clues to a word's meaning in its **context,** or the words and pictures around it. These context clues often take the form of definitions, restatements, or examples.

Definitions and Restatements

Sometimes a writer tells you what an unfamiliar word means. The writer may define the word directly or restate its meaning in other words. Here's one example:

> The researcher checked the readings on a *seismograph,* which is a device used to measure earthquakes.

In this sentence, the writer provides a definition of the word *seismograph.* The sentence tells you that *seismograph* means "a device used to measure earthquakes."

Now look at these examples:

> He was a *vagabond,* a wanderer, who traveled the world on his bicycle.

> In 1774, the British placed an *embargo* on Boston Harbor. In other words, they prevented ships from entering or leaving the harbor.

In these sentences, the writer restates the meaning of the words *vagabond* and *embargo.* Whenever you read, look for the following key-word clues. They often signal a definition or restatement.

Key Words That Signal a Definition or Restatement

that is	or	this means
in other words	which is	also called

for DEFINITIONS AND RESTATEMENTS

ASSESSMENT: SPOT CHECK Ask students to identify the definition of *context* in the first paragraph on page 303. Then read the following sentences and ask students to identify the meaning of each italicized word from the context clues.

1. Mr. Keynes is known for being *judicious;* that is, he shows sound judgment.
2. The house suddenly *imploded.* In other words, it fell in upon itself.
3. The play received *plaudits,* or praise, from the critics.

for EXAMPLES

HELPFUL HINT Stress that sometimes readers can get from examples an idea of a word's meaning, but not necessarily an exact definition of the word. Have volunteers look up the definitions of *amphibian* and *barometer* in a dictionary and read them aloud.

for EXAMPLES

ASSESSMENT: SPOT CHECK Ask students to explain the meanings of the italicized words in the following sentences.

1. I wanted to play a *woodwind,* maybe a clarinet or a flute.
2. The magazine was full of photographs of *aristocrats* like the King and Queen of Spain and their relatives.
3. I really liked the store's *merchandise,* especially the jeans and sneakers.

Examples

Sometimes a writer will give you an example that helps you understand the meaning of an unfamiliar word.

> Most *amphibians,* such as frogs and toads, feed on insects.

The sentence above tells you that frogs and toads are two examples of amphibians. These examples give you an idea about the meaning of the word *amphibians.*

Sometimes the example itself is an unfamiliar word. In such a case, you may be able to use the general term to help you understand the meaning of the new word.

> Weather instruments, such as the thermometer and the *barometer,* can help meteorologists forecast the weather days or even weeks in advance.

Although you may be unfamiliar with the term *barometer,* the context clues tell you that a barometer is a type of weather instrument.

In the sample sentences above, the writers use the words *such as* to introduce the examples. Here are other words that writers often use to introduce examples.

Key Words That Signal an Example		
and other	for example	like
especially	for instance	these

USING WORD PARTS

An unfamiliar word is like a secret code. Sometimes you can crack the code by breaking the word into its parts. Each word part has its own meaning. Once you know what each part means, you can put the parts together to figure out the meaning of the whole word.

Literature Connection

Share with students the following passage from *Now Is Your Time* by Walter Dean Myers, an excerpt from which appears on page 234 in Unit 3 of *Literature and Language,* Grade 6. Ask students to point out any context clues to the meaning of *bauxite.*

"Abd al-Rahman Ibrahima was born in 1762 in Fouta Djallon, a district of the present country of Guinea. It is a beautiful land of green mountains rising majestically from grassy plains, a land rich with minerals, especially bauxite."

Base Words

The main word to which other word parts are added is called the **base word.** When you add a word part to a base word, you form a new word. For example, you can add the word part *mis-* to the base word *direct* to form *misdirect,* a word that means "to direct wrongly." In the same way, you can add the word part *-or* to the base word *direct* to form *director* a word that means "a person who directs."

direct mis**direct** **direct**or

Prefixes

A **prefix** is a word part that is added to the beginning of a base word. A prefix changes a base word to a new word with a new meaning. When you know the meanings of common prefixes, you can often figure out the meanings of unfamiliar words that contain those prefixes.

For example, look at the word *illegible.* The prefix *il-* means "not." The base word *legible* means "able to be read." So *illegible* means "not able to be read."

Here are some common prefixes and their meanings.

Prefixes	Meanings	Examples
il-, im-, in-, ir-	not	illegal, impossible, insane, irregular
mis-	wrong	mislead, misplace
non-	not, without	nonfat, nonsense
pre-	before	preheat, prehistory, preschool
re-	again	reappear, rebuild, recharge, reconsider
un-	not	unexpected, uncommon

for PREFIXES

STUMBLING BLOCK Point out to students that sometimes, what looks like a familiar prefix is simply part of a word. For example, the word *reality* has nothing to do with the prefix *re-,* and the word *mister* does not contain the prefix *mis-*. To distinguish such words from ones that do contain prefixes, students need to look for an identifiable base word.

for PREFIXES

HELPFUL HINT Ask students to define each of the example words in the chart by using the given meaning of the prefix. Have students generate and define other example words that include each prefix.

GENERAL NOTE

INDIVIDUALIZING INSTRUCTION: ESL STUDENTS Some students for whom English is a second language might be unfamiliar with Latin or Greek-based prefixes and suffixes. Allow these students time to experiment with affixes in English, but expect errors as they learn to manipulate these word parts. Point out to them that memorizing the meanings of common prefixes and suffixes will expand their vocabulary considerably: they will be able to determine the definitions of many words that include them.

for SUFFIXES

HELPFUL HINT Have students define each of the example words in the chart by using the given meaning of the suffix. Ask them to generate and define additional example words for each suffix.

for PRACTICE YOUR SKILLS

MANAGING THE PAPER LOAD After students have completed the exercises, you might discuss the answers in class. Call on a volunteer to give the answer to each question; allow students to correct their own work.

Additional Resources

Writing Resource Book, pp. 92–96
Spelling and Vocabulary Booklet

Answers to Practice Your Skills

A.

1. polyglot—a person who speaks several languages
2. kiln—an oven used to bake pottery
3. condiments—seasonings or relishes for food

Writing **TIP**

Sometimes the spelling of the base word changes when you add a suffix to it. If you're not sure about the spelling, check a dictionary.

Keep in mind that not all word parts that look like prefixes are prefixes. For example, the *mis-* in *missile* is not a prefix because *-sile* is not a base word. When you analyze word parts, watch out for prefix look-alikes.

Suffixes

A **suffix** is a word part that is added to the end of a base word. Like a prefix, a suffix changes a base word to a new word with a new meaning. For example, the suffix *-ous* means "full of" or "having." When *-ous* is added to the base word *danger,* the new word *dangerous* means "full of danger." When *-ous* is added to *courage,* the new word *courageous* means "having courage."

Here are some common suffixes and their meanings.

Suffixes	Meanings	Examples
-able, -ible	capable of being	washable, collapsible
-en	to make	lengthen, frighten
-er, -or	a person who does	teacher, governor
-ily	in what manner	speedily, happily
-ful, -ous	full of	successful, joyous
-hood, -ness	state of	falsehood, statehood, kindness, goodness
-less	without	heartless, restless
-like	relating to	childlike, lifelike

Practice Your Skills

A. Use the context clues in each sentence to write a definition of the word in italics. Check your definition in a dictionary.

1. Our new neighbor is a *polyglot*—that is, she can speak several languages.
2. They put the pottery in a *kiln,* or oven.
3. Some *condiments,* especially mustard, can really make food appealing.

Grammar Connection

Point out that when a suffix is added to a word, it often changes the word's part of speech. For example, *-er* and *-or* may change verbs to nouns, and *-ible* and *-able* may change verbs to adjectives.

4. The cages held *quetzals* and other tropical birds.
5. Sue is *ambidextrous*—that is, she can use both hands with equal ease.
6. Some *predators,* such as wolves and hyenas, hunt in packs.
7. The concert tickets were *complimentary;* in other words, she got them for free.
8. Some mythological creatures, like the *griffin,* combine the features of several different animals.
9. We heard a *quintet,* a group of five musicians, play folk songs.
10. *Carcinogens,* like cigarette smoke, are the focus of studies on the causes of cancer.

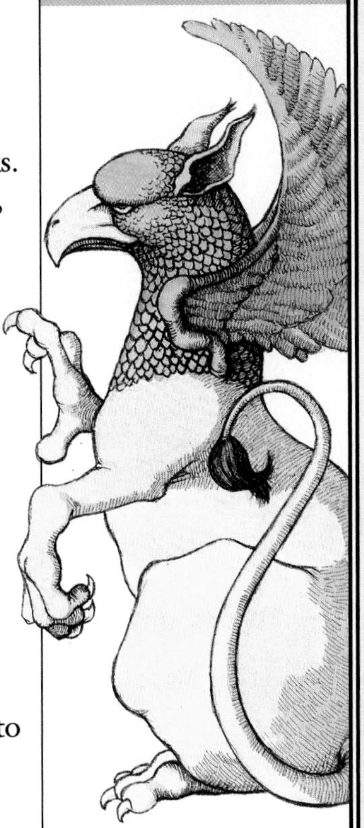

B. Look up the following words in a dictionary. Then use each word in a sentence that contains context clues to the meaning of the word.

1. veranda **2.** opulence **3.** marsupial **4.** artifact

C. Use what you learned about word parts in this handbook to answer the following questions.

1. If *zeal* means "strong feelings" or "intense support for a cause," what does *zealous* mean?
2. If *daunt* means "to discourage," what is a *dauntless* person?
3. If *belligerent* means "ready to fight," what does *nonbelligerent* mean?
4. If *classify* means "to place in a class or category," what does *reclassify* mean?
5. If *attain* means "to gain through effort," what does *attainable* mean?
6. If *natal* means "dating from birth," what does *prenatal* mean?
7. If *toxic* means "poisonous," what does *nontoxic* mean?
8. If *spite* means "feeling of anger or annoyance toward someone," what does *spiteful* mean?

4. quetzal—a kind of tropical bird
5. ambidextrous—able to use both hands equally well
6. predator—an animal that hunts
7. complimentary—free
8. griffin—a mythological creature that possesses the features of several different animals
9. quintet—a group of five musicians
10. carcinogens—substances that cause cancer

B. Sentences will vary. Context clues should, however, take the form of definitions, restatements, or examples.

C.
1. full of strong feelings
2. a person who cannot be discouraged
3. not ready to fight
4. to place in a category again
5. able to be gained through effort
6. dating from before birth
7. not poisonous; harmless
8. full of feelings of anger and annoyance

SPICE BOX

Form students into groups and write a base word, such as *place,* on the board. Set a timer for two minutes and have each group make a list of as many forms of the word as they can using prefixes, or suffixes or both. (Examples include *replace, displace, irreplaceable,* and *placement.)* The group that forms the greatest number of actual words that are correctly spelled wins the round. Continue with other base words, such as *light* and *prove.*

WRITING
HANDBOOK
28

Using the Dictionary and the Thesaurus

Objectives

- To recognize how a dictionary and a thesaurus are organized
- To find information in a dictionary
- To use a thesaurus to find synonyms

Related Mini-Lessons

For information on topics related to using the dictionary and the thesaurus, see the following mini-lessons:

- **Study and Research Skills, pp. 294–297**
- **Vocabulary Skills, pp. 302–307**

Motivate

Call out an unfamiliar word—*whin, yeanling,* or *pilgarlic*—and have students find its meaning in classroom dictionaries. Ask the student who first locates a meaning to read it aloud and describe how he or she found it. Ask students whether they are aware that midgrade school dictionaries contain between 40,000 and 60,000 entries; high school dictionaries, between 75,000 and 100,000. The total number of English words now exceeds four million.

Teaching Strategies

for ALPHABETICAL ORDER

ASSESSMENT: SPOT CHECK To assess students' mastery of alphabetizing, have them number these words in alphabetical order: *cute* (3), *custom* (1), *cuticle* (4), *cutback* (2), *cutlass* (5).

WRITING
HANDBOOK
28

Where Can I Find Information About Words?

Using the Dictionary and the Thesaurus

Mark Twain wrote, "The difference between the *almost right* word and the *right* word is . . . the difference between the lightning bug and the lightning." How can you capture lightning in your writing? A dictionary and a thesaurus can help you find just the right words.

USING A DICTIONARY

You know that a dictionary contains the spellings and definitions of words. There is, however, much more information packed into this helpful book. To use a dictionary effectively you first must know how it is organized.

Alphabetical Order

The words that appear in a dictionary are called **entry words.** Like the names in a phone book, the entry words in a dictionary are listed in alphabetical order—the order of the letters in the alphabet.

Words that begin with the same first letter, such as *elephant* and *envelope,* are alphabetized by the second letter. Words that have the same first and second letters, such as *festival* and *fertile,* are alphabetized by the third letter, and so on.

Guide Words

The two words in boldface type at the top of each page of a dictionary are called **guide words.** Guide words can help you find words in a dictionary quickly and easily.

The guide word on the left tells you the first entry word on that page. The guide word on the right tells you the last entry

Social Studies Connection

Suggest that students locate the glossary in their social studies textbook. Ask them to compare a typical glossary entry with a typical dictionary entry and to note the similarities and differences between the two.

word on that page. As you flip through a dictionary searching for a word, the guide words can help you quickly find the right page. When the word you're looking for falls alphabetically between two guide words, you're on the right page.

drill / drone **417**

thread⟧ a coarse linen or cotton cloth with a diagonal weave, used for work clothes, uniforms, etc.
drill[4](dril) ***n.*** ⟦< ? native term⟧ a short-tailed, bright-cheeked monkey *(Mandrillus leucophaeus)* native to W Africa, resembling the mandrill but smaller

Dictionary Entries

The information a dictionary gives about an entry word is called a **dictionary entry.** Each entry has several parts, as you can see in the example at the top of the next page.

Entry Word The first part of a dictionary entry is the entry word. In most dictionaries, spaces or centered dots divide the entry word into syllables. Knowing how a word is divided into syllables enables you to hyphenate words correctly.

Pronunciation The next part of a dictionary entry is the **pronunciation guide,** often shown in parentheses. The pronunciation guide is a respelling of the word using symbols that stand for sounds. These symbols are explained in a **pronunciation key,** which often is found at the bottom of a dictionary's right-hand pages or at the front of the dictionary.

In the pronunciation guide, words of more than one syllable are shown with accent marks (ʹ). These marks tell you which syllables to emphasize when you pronounce the word.

Part of Speech Most dictionaries tell you the part of speech of each entry word. Some words can be used as more than one part of speech. In those cases, the dictionary defines each part of speech separately. Notice in the dictionary entry on page 310 that *surprise* is defined first as a verb **(vt.).**

Word Origin Next the dictionary entry shows the origin of the word—how the word developed from words in other languages. In the entry for *surprise,* **ME** stands for Middle English, and **OFr** stands for Old French. The abbreviations used are explained in the front of the dictionary.

for DICTIONARY ENTRIES

INDIVIDUALIZING INSTRUCTION: ESL STUDENTS Explain to your ESL students that English dictionaries do not generally list idioms as entry words. However, students may find idioms in their native language listed in a bilingual dictionary. Also explain that some English-language student dictionaries list idioms after the entry word for the main word in each idiom. For example, students can look within the entry for *cat* to find the meaning of "Don't let the *cat* out of the bag."

for DICTIONARY ENTRIES: PRONUNCIATION

SPEAKING AND LISTENING To familiarize students with the pronunciation key, write the phonetic spellings of several words on the board. Ask students to use the key in their class dictionary to sound out the pronunciation.

for DICTIONARY ENTRIES: PART OF SPEECH

KEY TO UNDERSTANDING To help students understand the part of speech entries in their dictionaries, make a list of common abbreviations on the board: noun *(n.)*, verb *(v.)*, pronoun *(pron.)*, adjective *(adj.)*, adverb *(adv.)*, preposition *(prep.)*, conjunction *(conj.)*, and interjection *(interj.)*. Then briefly review the meaning of each part of speech and elicit examples.

for DICTIONARY ENTRIES

STUMBLING BLOCK Ask students to share their own methods for finding an entry for a word whose spelling they are unsure of. (Samples: Try two or three different possible spellings; figure out the first few letters; ask someone else how to spell the word)

for DICTIONARY ENTRIES

ASSESSMENT: SPOT CHECK Have students use the dictionary to answer the following questions:

1. What does *e.g.* mean? (for example)
2. What kind of animal is a *fisher?* (a mammal of the weasel family)
3. What and where is *Ibiza?* (an island off Spain)
4. What is the etymology, or origin, of the word *galaxy?* (from the Greek *galaktos,* meaning "milk")

Ask volunteers to provide the answers and explain how they used the dictionary to find them.

for USING A THESAURUS

KEY TO UNDERSTANDING Make sure students are able to pronounce the word *thesaurus.* You might point out that this word comes from the same Greek root as the word *treasure.* Suggest that students think of a thesaurus as a "treasury of words."

for USING A THESAURUS

COLLABORATIVE OPPORTUNITY Ask students whether they have ever noticed that sportscasters seem to have an endless supply of synonyms for the verb *defeat* when they announce sporting events results. Write on the board these examples: *beat, blitz, conquer, topple.* Emphasize that synonyms have different shades of meaning and that choosing the exact synonym is an important writing skill. For example, of the words listed, which would they use in a headline to suggest that one team defeated another that had long been in first place? *(topple)* Which would they use to suggest that the winning team attacked quickly and never let up? *(blitz)* Which word suggests that even though one team won, the final score was close? *(beat)* Which word implies that the losing team will take a while to recover? *(conquer)*

Pronunciation guide — *Part of speech* — *Word origin*

Entry word — *Definition*

sur·prise (sər prīz′, sə prīz′) ***vt.*** **-prised′**, **-pris′ing** ⟦ME *surprysen* < OFr *surpris,* pp. of *sorprendre,* to surprise, take napping < *sur-* (see SUR-[1]) + *prendre,* to take (see PRIZE[2])⟧ **1** to come upon suddenly or unexpectedly; take unawares **2** to attack or capture suddenly and without warning **3** *a)* to cause to feel wonder or astonishment by

Synonyms

SYN.—**surprise**, in this connection, implies an affecting with wonder because of being unexpected, unusual, etc. *[*I'm *surprised* at your concern*]*; **astonish** implies a surprising with something that seems unbelievable *[*to *astonish* with sleight of hand*]*; **amaze** suggests an astonishing that causes bewilderment or confusion *[amazed* at the

Definition The definition tells you what the entry word means. Many words have more than one definition, and the different definitions are numbered. Usually the oldest definition is given first and the newest definition is given last.

Synonyms Following the definition, a dictionary may provide **synonyms,** or words with similar meanings.

USING A THESAURUS

A thesaurus contains synonyms and antonyms for commonly used words. Synonyms are words that have similar meanings. **Antonyms** are words that have opposite meanings. A thesaurus can help you find the word that best expresses the meaning you have in mind.

Some thesauruses are organized alphabetically. Others have an index at the end. The index tells you where to find the synonyms for a specific word.

Suppose you have used the word *ran. Ran* is a general verb that means "to move quickly." Perhaps a more specific verb would make what you have written more interesting or exciting. Look at the thesaurus entry for *run* at the top of the next page.

TEACHER'S LOUNGE

That teachers must teach connotation and shades of meaning was brought home by the ninth-grader who had, as a vocabulary word, the word *tawdry.*

Looking it up in the dictionary, the youth found it defined as "cheap and tasteless."

The teacher found the word used in this sentence: "The cafeteria serves tawdry sandwiches."—from *Educator's Lifetime Library,* by P. Susan Mamchak and Steven R. Mamchak.

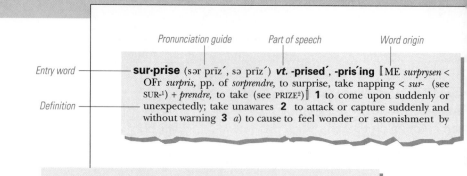

run, *v.* [To go swiftly by physical effort] —*Syn.* rush, hurry, spring, bound, scurry, skitter, scramble, scoot, travel, run off *or* away, dash ahead *or* at *or* on, put on a burst of speed, go on the double, have effect, go on the double-quick, hasten (off), light out, have a free play, make tracks, dart (ahead), gallop, canter, lope, spring, trot, single-foot, amble, pace, flee, speed, spurt, swoop, bolt, race, shoot, tear, whisk, scamper, scuttle.

Words like *bound, scramble, dart,* and *scamper* are all more specific than the word *run. Bound,* for example, means "to move by leaping" and might be a better verb to describe the way a dog runs after a squirrel.

Practice Your Skills

A. Use a dictionary to to find the answer to each of the following questions.

1. From what language did the word *plumage* come? What did it mean originally?
2. What parts of speech can *record* be?
3. How would you pronounce *echidna?* What syllable would you emphasize?
4. What does *gregarious* mean?
5. What is a synonym for *ridiculous?*

B. For each of the following sentences, look up each word in italics in a thesaurus. Then rewrite each sentence using a more precise word.

1. The car *went* slowly up the mountain road.
2. The hungry children *ate* the pizza.
3. The detective *looked* at the footprints in the snow.
4. The exhausted marathon runner *walked* across the finish line.
5. She *carried* the overloaded suitcase through the airport.

for THESAURUS ENTRY

ASSESSMENT: SPOT CHECK To make sure students understand the importance of using specific words, ask them to suggest original sentences that use the synonyms of *run* appropriately. In addition to *scramble, dart,* and *scamper,* students might suggest sentences for *bolt, race,* and *sprint.*

for PRACTICE YOUR SKILLS

MANAGING THE PAPER LOAD
You might have students present their responses to the exercises orally. For Exercise B, you might list the replacement words on the board and have students vote on the most precise one.

Additional Resources

Writing Resource Book, pp. 95–98
Spelling and Vocabulary Booklet

Answers to Practice Your Skills

A.
1. Latin; a feather
2. verb, noun, adjective
3. e-kid′-nə; second
4. sociable
5. absurd, preposterous, laughable

B. Answers will vary. Sample replacement words:
1. crawled, crept
2. gobbled up, wolfed down
3. examined, inspected
4. stumbled, hobbled, staggered
5. lugged, dragged

MULTICULTURAL Connection

Students whose native language is not English might bring to class any bilingual dictionaries that they use to find the meanings of English words and idioms. Ask them to explain how the dictionaries are organized and to describe how they typically use them. Encourage English-speaking students to use the dictionaries to find words and expressions from another language that they would like to learn. Have them check their pronunciations of these words and expressions with their bilingual classmates.

WRITING HANDBOOK 29

Library Skills

Objectives
- To learn how books are arranged in the library
- To interpret the information on a catalog card or in a computerized catalog entry
- To identify the main uses of library reference materials

Related Mini-Lesson

For information on topics related to using the library, see the following mini-lesson.
- **Study and Research Skills, pp. 294–297**

Motivate
Ask students to imagine that they have taken a time-machine trip to a community in the year 2200. One of the places they visit is a technologically advanced library. Ask students to imagine and describe the library of the future, noting how it is different from the typical library today. For instance, would people actually have to go to the library, or could they access most information from their homes?

Teaching Strategies

for THE SECTIONS OF THE LIBRARY

COOPERATIVE LEARNING Have students look at the layout of their school or local library, noting the location of the sections they use most frequently. Then suggest that they work together to draw a rough floor plan of the library, showing the relative locations of the sections they use or expect to use.

WRITING HANDBOOK 29

How Can I Find the Information I Need?

Library Skills

Imagine that there was one place where you could do all of these things: listen to a compact disc, use a computer, find a movie, see an art display, read a book. There is such a place—the library. You can find these resources and more in most libraries today. A world of information, ideas, and activities is available to you at the library.

THE SECTIONS OF THE LIBRARY

You may be surprised at what you can find in the library, if you just know where to look. Most libraries are arranged into the following sections.

Library Floor Plan

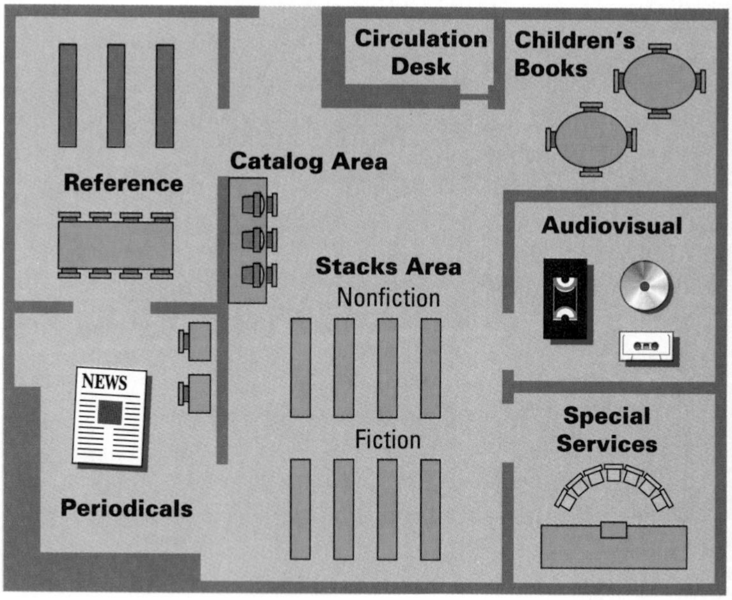

The Way Books Are Arranged

Librarians divide books into two main types, fiction and nonfiction.

Fiction Made-up stories, such as novels and short stories, are fiction. Fiction books are grouped together in one part of the stacks and arranged alphabetically according to the author's last name. For example, a book by Lewis Carroll will be shelved under *C.* If the library has more than one book by the same author, the books by that author will be arranged alphabetically by the first word of the title. Words like *a, an,* and *the* are skipped when alphabetizing. Some libraries keep collections of short stories in a special section of the stacks.

Nonfiction Books that provide factual information about people, events, and other subjects are nonfiction. They are arranged according to their subject. Libraries use special numbering systems to group nonfiction books into broad subject categories. Most school libraries use the Dewey Decimal System to classify books.

Dewey Decimal System

000-099	General Works	Encyclopedias, directories
100-199	Philosophy	Self-help, psychology
200-299	Religion	The Bible, mythology, theology
300-399	Social Science	Politics, education, folklore
400-499	Language	Languages, dictionaries
500-599	Science	Mathematics, astronomy, geology
600-699	Useful Arts	Computers, cooking, business, cars
700-799	Fine Arts	Music, painting, acting, sports
800-899	Literature	Poetry, plays, essays
900-999	History	Biography, travel, geography

for THE WAY BOOKS ARE ARRANGED

CRITICAL THINKING: CLASSIFYING Ask students to list some books they have read or used for research in recent weeks and to note whether they are fiction or nonfiction. For nonfiction titles, ask students to identify the broad subject category for each book, according to the Dewey Decimal System.

for FICTION

PERSONAL TOUCH This might be a good time to discuss how to go about choosing books for pleasure or to satisfy a personal interest or curiosity. Begin by describing how you ycurself select books to read—asking friends for recommendations, looking for new books by favorite authors, browsing through books with interesting titles or covers, reading reviews, scanning summer reading lists, talking with school or community librarians about award winners, and so on. Then have students describe how they choose books and where those books may be found at the library.

for DEWEY DECIMAL SYSTEM

KEY TO UNDERSTANDING Explain that the Dewey Decimal System, developed by Melvil Dewey in 1876, is used in most school and community libraries. Point out that most college, university, and specialized libraries use the Library of Congress system, which uses letters to classify books.

for USING CALL NUMBERS

KEY TO UNDERSTANDING Arrange to have a number of library books in the classroom. Point out their call numbers, explaining the purpose of each set of letters or numbers. Explain that the term *call number* originated in large libraries where the bookshelves, or stacks, were not open to the public. Therefore, users would "call" for a book by writing its classification number on a slip of paper and giving it to a library employee, who would find the book for them.

for USING CALL NUMBERS

HELPFUL HINT After students have read the section letters and what they stand for, suggest that they put these letters at the appropriate locations on the library floor plan they created in the cooperative activity suggested on page 312.

Many libraries have a special area in the nonfiction stacks for biographies and autobiographies. These books are shelved alphabetically according to the last name of the person the book is about. Reference books are also nonfiction books, but they usually are kept in a separate section of the library.

Using Call Numbers

Every nonfiction book in a library has a **call number.** The call number is like a street address. It tells you the location of the book in the stacks. In libraries that use the Dewey Decimal System, the call number is based on the book's Dewey number. Libraries that use other classification systems have different call-number codes.

A call number may show other information, such as the author's initials or **section letters.** Section letters tell you in which section of the library you can find the book. Here are some commonly used section letters:

R, REF = Reference	B, BIO = Biography
C, CHILD = Children's	X, J, JUV = Juvenile
X, Y, YA = Young Adult	F, FIC = Fiction
A V = Audiovisual	P, PER = Periodicals
SF = Science Fiction	MYS = Mystery

Call numbers are usually printed on the book's spine. Look at one library's call number for the book *The Mysterious World of Caves* by Ernst Bauer.

Dewey Decimal number — **551**
B32m — Author's assigned number
Section letter — **JUV**

This book would be found in the children's section of the library. It would be shelved between books that have the Dewey Decimal numbers 550 and 552.

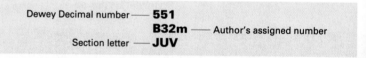

Library Catalogs

When you want to know if the library has a book you are looking for, you don't have to go hunting through the stacks. Instead, you can use a library catalog, which lists every book the library has. Entries in the library catalog give you a great deal of information about a book, including what the book is about and where you can find it.

Some libraries use card catalogs. These are file cabinets filled with cards that list information for every item you can check out. Other libraries have computer catalogs. You type in a key word, such as the subject, the author's name, or the title of the book you want. Then information appears on a computer screen.

Catalog Entries

There are three ways to look for a book in a library catalog. You can look up the subject, the author, or the title of the book. Each of these three types of entries shows the same basic information about a book, but the specific details may appear in a different order for each type.

Subject Entries Do you want to learn more about caves for a class report? A good way to start would be to look under *Caves* in the subject entries of the library catalog. You would probably find several books listed. This subject entry for *The Mysterious World of Caves* is an example from a card catalog. Notice all the information it provides.

Subject Card

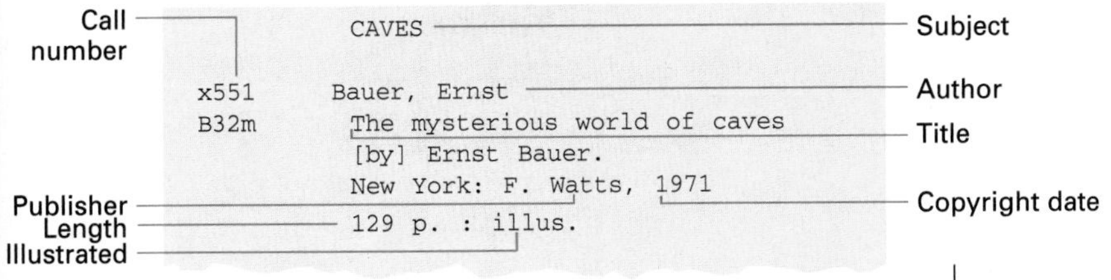

for LIBRARY CATALOGS

HELPFUL HINT Remind students that on the outside of each drawer of a card catalog is a *guide label,* showing the beginning letters of the first and last cards in the drawer. For example, a drawer labeled *Gr–Ha* would contain cards for books on Greenland and Haiti, among other topics. Also point out that within each drawer are *guide cards* with tabs that stick up above the rest of the cards, to help users locate cards quickly.

for LIBRARY CATALOGS

HELPFUL HINT Point out that most catalogs also contain *cross-references.* Explain that a cross-reference will direct users to another subject heading of related interest. For example, if they look up *caves,* they may find a cross-reference that says, "See *spelunking.*" Emphasize that when students are doing research, these cross-references are helpful because they point to possible new sources.

for CATALOG ENTRIES

INDIVIDUALIZING INSTRUCTION: BASIC STUDENTS You might suggest that these students create a subject entry card for a nonfiction book that they would like to write some day. Tell them to refer to the sample entry card at the bottom of the page.

ADVANCED STUDENTS Suggest that students use the library catalog to create a bibliography on a subject of special interest to them.

for SUBJECT ENTRIES

CRITICAL THINKING: MAKING INFERENCES Ask students to suggest why the publication, or copyright, date on each catalog entry may be useful to the reader or researcher when selecting books. (For many subjects, up-to-date information is important. A book with an old copyright date may contain outdated information.)

Science Connection

Point out that one of the most serious threats to a library's collection is the fragility of the paper the books are printed on. Due to the high acid content in most paper, book pages and covers become brittle and deteriorate rather quickly. (One quarter of the Library of Congress's twenty million books, for example, cannot be read without causing damage.) Ask interested students to speculate about the ways in which technology may be providing answers to this problem. (CD roms and other high-tech advances may serve as replacements for books.)

for AUTHOR ENTRIES

ASSESSMENT: SPOT CHECK Ask students to tell how they might find other novels by Wilson Rawls without using the library catalog. (by going directly to the fiction section, which is arranged alphabetically, and looking under *Rawls)* Ask: "Why isn't this possible when you are looking for a nonfiction book?" (Nonfiction books are not arranged alphabetically by author name; they are arranged according to subject.)

for TITLE ENTRIES

STUMBLING BLOCK Share these rules used in alphabetizing entries in your school or local library:

- Abbreviations and numbers are alphabetized as if they were spelled out; *Dr.* is treated as *Doctor* and *100* as *one hundred.*
- All names beginning with *Mc* or *Mac* are alphabetized under *Mac.*

GENERAL NOTE

SPEAKING AND LISTENING: INTERVIEWING Propose that a group of interested students interview a school or local librarian. Suggest they ask questions like the following:

- What are some of the special services now offered by libraries?
- What are some interesting questions that you have been asked by library users?
- How do you think this library will change over the next twenty years?

Author Entries Suppose you especially enjoyed reading *Where the Red Fern Grows* by Wilson Rawls, and you would like to find another of his books. This time you would start by looking up the author's last name in the author entries section of the library catalog. You will find entries for all the library's books by Wilson Rawls. Here is a sample of a single computer catalog entry you might find after doing a search of all the listings for Wilson Rawls. Notice that this computer entry gives the same kinds of information that the card-catalog entry does.

Computer Catalog Author Entry

```
     AUTHOR:   Rawls, Wilson
      TITLE:   Summer of the Monkeys
  PUBLISHER:   Doubleday [1976]
DESCRIPTION:   239 p.

## ----Call number ------Material              Location
1      Y                  Young Adult Book      Jr. Hi Room
```

Title Entries Suppose you needed a book called *The Wright Brothers* for a report about airplanes. How would you find out if this book was in your library? You could look up the title in the library catalog. In a card catalog, title entries are listed alphabetically by the first word in the title. Remember, though, that *A, An,* and *The* do not count as first words for alphabetizing. For example, *The Wright Brothers* is listed under *W,* not *T.* Notice that in a title entry, the first line shows the title of the book, not the author's name as in an author entry.

Title Card

```
             WRIGHT BROTHERS, THE
Y             (by) Freedman, Russell
629.13       The Wright Brothers
             New York: Holiday House, 1991
             129 p.: illus.
```

REFERENCE WORKS

What's the capital of India? How does photosynthesis happen? Who won the Super Bowl in 1992? You can find the answers to these questions and just about any others you might have by looking in the reference section of the library. Your librarian can help you find the works that have the information you are looking for. Here are some of the most common types of reference works.

Library Reference Materials

Reference Source	**Contents**	**Examples**
Encyclopedias	articles on a wide range of topics	*The World Book Encyclopedia*
Almanacs and Yearbooks	up-to-date facts, statistics, and unusual information	*Guinness Book of World Records, Information Please Almanac*
Atlases	maps and geographical information	*Hammond World Atlas*
Periodicals	newspaper and magazine articles	*USA Today, National Geographical World*

Calvin and Hobbes by Bill Watterson

COMPUTER TIP

Many libraries have computer indexes for finding periodical articles.

for LIBRARY REFERENCE MATERIALS

KEY TO UNDERSTANDING Arrange to have an almanac in class for students to examine. Point out that encyclopedias and almanacs both cover a wide range of information. Unlike encyclopedias, however, almanacs give little background material on their subjects. On the other hand, an almanac's charts, lists, and tables provide up-to-date facts and statistics in an easy-to-use format. Also point out that since almanacs are *not* organized alphabetically, it is necessary to use the index to find out where the information you need is located.

for LIBRARY MATERIALS: ATLASES

HELPFUL HINT Point out to students that political and topographical atlases are extremely useful for finding up-to-date names in a rapidly changing world. To illustrate this, give students the following examples and encourage them to add others to the list:

NEW NAME	OLD NAME
Burkina Faso	Upper Volta
Zimbabwe	Rhodesia
C.I.S.	USSR

Many students may not realize that in addition to political and topographical maps, atlases often include economic maps showing information about a region's industries and resources. Also mention special historical atlases that show the progress of military campaigns or the territorial changes in a country or region over time.

for LIBRARY MATERIALS: PERIODICALS

HELPFUL HINT Call on volunteers to describe how to find newspaper or magazine articles on a given topic in their local library. You may want to mention (if students do not) that the *Readers' Guide to Periodical Literature* indexes magazine articles according to subject and author and that newspaper articles are usually available on microfilm.

for USING THE ENCYCLOPEDIA

MODELING If possible, show students the index volume of a set of encyclopedias. Point out that they can use the cross-references in the index to locate articles on subjects related to the topic they are researching. Model this process,using a specific topic.

for USING THE ENCYCLOPEDIA

COOPERATIVE LEARNING Suggest that students list the various encyclopedias available in the school or local library. Then ask them to form small groups, each choosing a set of encyclopedia volumes and examining that encyclopedia's characteristics. Then have the groups use their findings to create a chart that lists advantages and disadvantages of using each encyclopedia. The completed chart can be posted for classroom use.

for USING THE ENCYCLOPEDIA

HELPFUL HINT Point out that encyclopedias must be up-to-date to be useful. Explain that most encyclopedias publish yearbooks containing information about the events of the preceding year and about the latest developments in many fields. Urge students to use these yearbooks, especially when researching current scientific or political topics.

Using the Encyclopedia

The reference work you will probably turn to most often for your school work is the encyclopedia. You can use an encyclopedia to find information on a wide variety of subjects. This information will be helpful to you when you write research papers or other pieces of informative writing. You can also browse through the volumes to get ideas for topics you could write about or just to learn some interesting facts.

You will find encyclopedia articles arranged alphabetically by subject, or you can look up your topic in the index. This sample page from *The World Book Encyclopedia* shows many features that can help you learn about a subject.

Boomerang 487

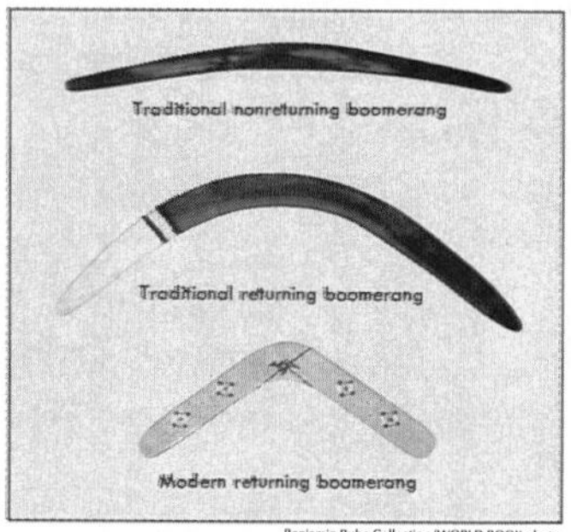

Benjamin Ruhe Collection (WORLD BOOK photo by Vince Finnigan & Assoc.)

Many boomerangs are made of wood, such as the Australian ones shown above. Nonreturning boomerangs are used as tools and weapons. Returning types are thrown mainly for sport.

Boomerang is a curved, flat implement that is thrown as a weapon or for sport. Most boomerangs are made of wood or plastic. Boomerangs measure from 1 to $6\frac{1}{2}$ feet (0.3 to 2 meters) long and $\frac{1}{2}$ to 5 inches (1.3 to 13 centimeters) wide. They weigh from 1 to 80 ounces (30 to 2,300 grams). Boomerangs spin when thrown correctly, and some boomerangs are shaped so they return to the thrower.

Boomerangs are commonly associated with the Aborigines, the original people of Australia, who use them for hunting and many other specialized tasks. However, scientists believe boomerangs were developed independently by a number of prehistoric hunting peoples. Ancient boomerangs have been found in many parts of the world, including Africa, Asia, Europe, and North America.

Kinds of boomerangs. There are two kinds of boomerangs, *returning* and *nonreturning.* Returning

Some Aborigines decorate boomerangs with carved or painted designs that are related to their legends and traditions. They treat these decorated boomerangs with respect and use them in religious ceremonies. The Aborigines also clap boomerangs together to provide rhythm for songs and chants.

How a boomerang flies. A boomerang's flight depends on its shape and size and how it is thrown. Winds also influence its flight. Most boomerangs have a bend near the middle that forms two wings shaped like airplane wings. Each wing is flat on the bottom and curved on top. One edge is thicker than the other. As a boomerang spins wing over wing in flight, its shape causes lower air pressure above each wing than below it. This difference in pressure helps keep the boomerang airborne. Some boomerangs have a shallow, hollowed-out area on the underside of one wing to provide added lift. See **Aerodynamics** (Principles of aerodynamics).

Forces acting on the boomerang, combined with its spin, make it follow a curved path in the air. A skillful thrower can make a returning boomerang travel about 150 feet (45 meters) before it begins its return. Nonreturning boomerangs can be thrown about 300 feet (90 meters). Hanns Peter

Parts of a returning boomerang

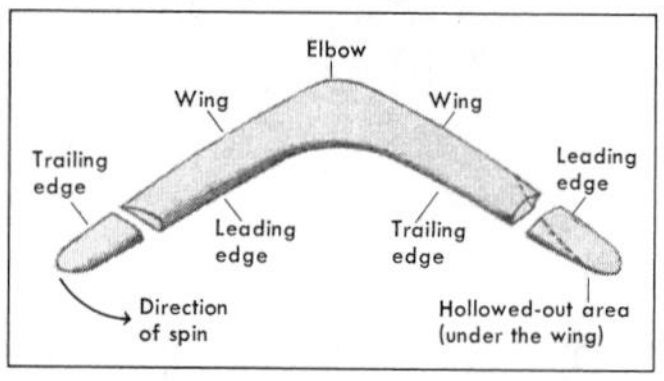

Each wing has a flat bottom and a curved top. When thrown, the boomerang spins forward so the leading edges cut through the air. The hollowed-out area helps the boomerang gain height.

Practice Your Skills

A. Arrange these fiction books in the order in which you would find them in the fiction stacks.

Blume, Judy. *Deenie*
Peck, Richard. *Ghosts I Have Been*
Bonham, Frank. *Chief*
Blume, Judy. *It's Not the End of the World*
Rodgers, Mary. *Freaky Friday*

B. Refer to the Dewey Decimal System chart on page 313. Write the number category for books on each of these topics:

1. the history of Greece
2. ice hockey
3. automobile repair
4. Japanese poetry
5. adding and subtracting fractions

C. Which type of catalog entry—subject entry, author entry, or title entry—would you use for each situation below?

1. You want to read a book by Ursula LeGuin.
2. You want to find the book *Dragondrums.*
3. You want to find a book on beekeeping.

D. Look up one of the topics below in an encyclopedia. On your paper, write down the name of the encyclopedia, the volume number, the title of the article, the guide word at the top of the page where the article begins, any special features the article includes (such as maps, charts, or pictures), and any cross-references.

cliff dwellers	laser
Mohandas Gandhi	volcano

Gandhi beside his spinning wheel, 1946, as photographed by Margaret Bourke-White.

for PRACTICE YOUR SKILLS

MANAGING THE PAPER LOAD

You might call on individuals or pairs of students to complete Exercises A, B, and C orally for the class, explaining their answers fully. If you have a set of encyclopedia volumes in the classroom, assign each topic in Exercise D to a separate student.

Additional Resource

Writing Resource Book, pp. 101–106

Answers to Practice Your Skills

A.
Blume, Judy. *Deenie*
Blume, Judy. *It's Not the End of the World*
Bonham, Frank. *Chief*
Peck, Richard. *Ghosts I Have Been*
Rodgers, Mary. *Freaky Friday*

B.
1. 900–999
2. 700–799
3. 600–699
4. 800–899
5. 500–599

C.
1. author entry
2. title entry
3. subject entry

D. Answers will vary.

ART NOTE

Margaret Bourke-White (1904–1971) photographed Mohandas K. Gandhi in 1946 when he was living among untouchables. For Gandhi, the spinning wheel was a symbol of India's struggle for independence from Britain.

WRITING
HANDBOOK
30

Thinking Skills

Objectives

- To recognize and correct statements that display errors in reasoning
- To recognize and correct statements that display appeals to emotion

Teaching Strategies

for OVERGENERALIZATION

ASSESSMENT: SPOT CHECK To check that students recognize instances of overgeneralization, write on the board the four statements below. Have students identify the examples of overgeneralization (1, 2, and 4) and correct them.

1. Nobody wants to stay indoors on a beautiful spring day. (Sample: Few people want. . . .)
2. All tall people are good basketball players. (Sample: Some tall people. . . .)
3. A low-fat diet is a good idea for most adults.
4. Everyone loves Walt Disney movies. (Sample: Many people love . . . .)

WRITING
HANDBOOK
30

How Can I Present My Ideas Convincingly?

Thinking Skills

"Mom, I want to go to Cheryl's party because it's really important to me. Everyone will be there, and either I show up or I'll be labeled for life!"

Have you ever made a plea like this one? If you have, you probably weren't too successful. To present your ideas clearly and convincingly, you need to think critically. You must be able to judge whether an argument is logical, truthful, and based on facts rather than just on feelings. Then you can judge both your own ideas and those presented to you by others.

COMMON ERRORS IN REASONING

How can you decide whether the ideas in your writing make sense? Study the following common errors in reasoning. Watch for errors like these in your own writing.

Overgeneralization An overgeneralization is a statement that is too broad or general to be true in every case.

> Everyone wants to be rich and famous someday.

This may seem to be true, but think about it. Although everyone may wish to be successful, success may not mean wealth and fame to everyone. Be careful about using such words as *everyone, no one, always,* and *never* in your writing. Would words such as *most, few, usually,* and *seldom* be more accurate?

Circular Reasoning This error occurs when someone tries to support a statement by simply restating it in different words.

> Michele is the most qualified candidate for class president because she is the best person for the job.

What have you learned about Michele's qualifications? Nothing, really. The last part of this statement just repeats what the first part already said.

Always support statements with logical, truthful details: "Michele is the most qualified candidate for class president because she was vice-president last year, she has helped with a number of school projects, and she works well with people."

Either/Or Argument An either/or argument suggests that there are only two sides to an issue.

> Either we raise the price of tickets to this year's class dance, or we will lose money.

Are there really only two ways to deal with the situation? Would cutting costs or having fund-raising activities help?

APPEALS TO EMOTION

When people try to convince others of something, they sometimes appeal to emotion rather than to reason. Watch out for these common appeals to emotion.

Bandwagon Appeal This appeal tries to convince you to do something just because everyone else is.

> You have to learn this new dance! Everyone else has.

Has *everyone* really learned the dance? It's not likely, but does that matter? Just because other people are doing something doesn't mean it's right for you. Always look for sensible reasons *why* you should do something.

Loaded Language Language that stirs up either positive or negative feelings in people is called loaded language. Notice the difference in the two statements on the next page.

for EITHER/OR ARGUMENT

CRITICAL THINKING: ANALYZING

To help students recognize how rare an issue with only two sides is, write the following sentences on the board:

Students should either be willing to stay after school for band practice or not be in the band at all.

Students can either buy cafeteria food or go hungry.

Have students discuss whether these either/or options are really the only ways to solve each matter. For instance, some band members might have other obligations after school. Could there be some band practices during school hours to accommodate them? Encourage students to suggest other alternatives to each pair of options. Remind them that if they keep an open mind when they consider issues about which they feel strongly, they are more likely to find workable solutions to problems that might have seemed impossible to solve.

for BANDWAGON APPEAL

CRITICAL THINKING: EVALUATING

Show students a magazine or newspaper ad that uses bandwagon appeal, or discuss a television ad that does so. Discuss with the class how an advertiser uses this tactic to try to persuade viewers to "jump on the bandwagon" and buy the product. Have students evaluate the effectiveness of the technique in the given advertisement. Then ask them to find additional ads that use bandwagon appeal to discuss in class.

for NAME CALLING

HELPFUL HINT Point out to students that there are times when a criticism of someone's behavior is justified and accurate. For example, if a person responsible for handling public money has shown that he or she is irresponsible, it is probably a good idea to raise this issue for discussion. However, stress to students the importance of supporting any personal criticism with fact-based reasons. In addition, the personal criticisms should be relevant to the issue under discussion. For instance, if a person is running for the office of treasurer of an organization, it is beside the point to criticize his or her taste in music.

for PRACTICE YOUR SKILLS

MANAGING THE PAPER LOAD You might wish to discuss answers to the exercises in class and allow students to correct their own work. Encourage students to recognize the error or errors in each given statement. Also have them judge the facts in each other's corrected statements as relevant or irrelevant to the argument.

Additional Resources

Writing Resource Book, pp. 105–106
Thinking Skills Worksheets
Thinking Skills Transparency Pack

Answers to Practice Your Skills

Rewritten statements will vary. Sample answers are shown below.

1. Name-calling
   Lisa shouldn't choose the music for the party because her taste in music differs from the tastes of most of the other kids.
2. Circular reasoning
   Luciano Pavarotti is famous because he is very talented, and many critics consider him one of the best singers in the world.
3. Bandwagon appeal
   You should buy Rockin Roller in-line skates because they are well designed and reasonably priced.
4. Overgeneralization
   In this age of computers, few people use typewriters anymore.
5. Either/or argument
   Either I sign up for lessons now, or I miss a great opportunity.

> John comes up with unusual and creative ideas.
> John comes up with weird and far-fetched ideas.

Both statements suggest the same thing—that John's ideas are new and different. Yet the second statement gives a very negative impression of John's suggestions. When you write, avoid using such loaded language to persuade your readers.

Name-calling Making statements that attack or criticize a person so that the person's ideas will not be taken seriously is known as name-calling.

> Why would anyone want a loser like Ian on this committee? He's so unpopular.

***Writing* TIP**

You can use facts, statistics, and quotations from experts to back up the statements you make.

Ian may not be the best-known kid in school, but that doesn't mean he's not intelligent or capable of offering useful ideas. When you hear statements like the one above, ask yourself what the *real* issue is. The real issue here is whether Ian can handle certain responsibilities, not whether he can win a popularity contest.

Practice Your Skills

Identify the error in reasoning or the appeal to emotion in each statement below. Then rewrite the statement to correct the error. You can make up any facts you need to correct the statements.

1. Lisa shouldn't choose the music for the party because she's a real featherbrain and she can't even carry a tune.
2. Luciano Pavarotti is famous because he is an internationally known opera star.
3. You should buy Rockin Roller in-line skates because everyone is buying them.
4. In this age of computers, no one uses typewriters anymore.
5. Either I sign up for lessons now, or I'll never learn to play the guitar.

SPICE BOX

Point out that a word that stirs up negative feelings often has a synonym that stirs up positive ones. Put these pairs on the board.

stingy	thrifty
ridiculous	funny
pushy	masterful
immature	youthful

Ask students what they associate with each word. Then invite them to add other pairs of synonyms to the list. You might begin by having them think of positive synonyms for *nosy* and *reckless*, and negative synonyms for *comical* and *peaceful*.

How Can I Become a Better Listener?

Interviewing Skills

An interview can help you get firsthand information to use in your writing. Unlike Calvin, as you ask follow-up questions and listen carefully, you will gather useful information that will make your writing lively and detailed. This handbook will help you prepare and conduct an effective interview.

WRITING HANDBOOK 31

GUIDELINES FOR INTERVIEWING

Planning an Interview

1. **Contact the person.** Set a time and place to meet.
2. **Explore your subject.** Read about the subject and try to learn more about the expert and his or her field.
3. **Prepare questions.** Write a list of questions that require more than a yes or no answer. For example, instead of asking, "Do you enjoy your work?" you could ask a musician you are interviewing, "What kind of music do you most enjoy playing?"
4. **Organize your supplies.** Gather paper, pencils, and perhaps a cassette recorder.

Conducting an Interview

1. **Listen closely.** Take notes as you listen. If you need more time to write, ask the person to repeat his or her answer.
2. **Ask questions.** Use follow-up questions to clear up anything you don't understand.
3. **Review your notes.** Immediately after the interview, go over your notes.

Calvin and Hobbes
by Bill Watterson

WRITING HANDBOOK 31

Interviewing Skills

Objective

- To recognize how to plan and conduct an interview

Teaching Strategies

for PLANNING AN INTERVIEW

COOPERATIVE LEARNING Divide the class into small groups and have each group prepare a set of interview questions. Each group should pick a celebrity to interview; then each student in the group should write a question that conforms to the guidelines in item 3 under *Planning an Interview.* Encourage students to write questions that will help them learn something new about their subject. Groups can share their questions with the rest of the class.

for CONDUCTING AN INTERVIEW

INDIVIDUALIZING INSTRUCTION: LD STUDENTS Advise students who have difficulty in taking notes to use a tape recorder during their interviews.

Additional Resource

Writing Resource Book, p. 107

WRITING
HANDBOOK
32

Oral Reports

Objective

- To prepare, practice, and present an oral report

Related Mini-Lessons

For information on topics related to oral reports, see the following mini-lessons:

- **Developing a Topic, pp. 205–210**
- **Goals and Audience, pp. 211–213**
- **Organizing Details, pp. 217–221**

Motivate

Ask students if they think they would enjoy being TV reporters. Would the job be exciting? Why? From watching TV news, what do they think a TV reporter does, both on and off camera? Point out that one of a reporter's tasks is to prepare and give oral reports, which students will learn how to do in this handbook.

Teaching Strategies

for PREPARING AN ORAL REPORT

CRITICAL THINKING: MAKING COMPARISONS Have students read the steps for preparing an oral report and compare them to preparations for a written one. Note that the written aspect of an oral report usually ends with note cards. Also point out to students that in an oral report, more emphasis is placed on visual aids as a way to keep and focus an audience's interest.

WRITING
HANDBOOK
32

How Can I Make Better Oral Presentations?

Oral Reports

WRITER TO WRITER

Write as if [you] were speaking to an audience.

Jason Edwards, student
Clovis, California

Writing is not the only way to communicate with an audience. Sometimes, speaking directly to a group is the best way to share your ideas. Yet, like many people, you may not know how to make an effective oral presentation. With preparation and practice, you will feel more confident when addressing a group.

PREPARING AN ORAL REPORT

Use what you already know about the writing process as you prepare your oral report. Follow these steps:

- Pick a topic and consider your audience and goals.
- Gather information and explore your ideas through freewriting or drafting.
- Organize and write down the main ideas and key supporting points on note cards.
- Use visual aids such as charts, maps, or pictures to support your ideas. Make sure your visual aids are large enough to be seen by everyone in your audience.

Writing TIP

Highlight key words on your note cards to jog your memory as you present your talk. This will help you unglue your eyes from your notes and look directly at your audience.

PRACTICING AND PRESENTING

The more you practice your talk, the more confident you'll feel when you present it. Here are some guidelines to help you.

Guidelines for Oral Reports

Practicing

1. **Review your notes.** Read through your notes several times.
2. **Rehearse.** Tape-record your report and listen to see if you are speaking clearly and neither too quickly nor too slowly.
3. **Present your report before family members or friends.** Ask for honest feedback and helpful suggestions.

Presenting

1. **Stand up straight and look natural.** Take a deep breath before you begin. This will help you relax.
2. **Establish eye contact with your audience.** Look directly at your audience as much as possible.
3. **Use natural gestures and facial expressions.** Don't smile if you are talking about a sad subject. Keep any gestures simple and natural.
4. **Use your voice effectively.** Speak clearly and loudly enough to be understood by all your listeners. Pause briefly after you make an important point.

Practice Your Skills

Prepare an oral report on a subject listed below or on one of your own choosing. Write down key ideas on your note cards before you rehearse your talk. Finally, present your report in front of your classmates.

how to care for a pet	a movie you have seen recently
robots	hurricanes

GENERAL NOTE

SPEAKING AND LISTENING Interested students might enjoy listening to a recording of a gifted public speaker, such as Winston Churchill, John F. Kennedy, or Martin Luther King, Jr. These students can find recordings of the speaker of their choice, listen, and take notes on how the speaker used his or her voice effectively. Then allow students to share their recordings and analyses with the class.

for PRACTICE YOUR SKILLS

PEER RESPONSE Encourage students to practice their oral reports with a partner before presenting them to the class. Have the peer reviewers critique their partners' performances on the basis of the guidelines for presenting.

for PRACTICE YOUR SKILLS

SPEAKING, LISTENING, AND VIEWING If possible, videotape volunteers as they give their reports to the class. When students are finished, play back the videotape, so that they can observe their own work. Point out any movements or speech patterns that either detract from or add to students' deliveries.

Answers to Practice Your Skills

Students' reports will vary but should follow the guidelines for preparing an oral report.

WRITING HANDBOOK 33

Taking Tests

Objectives

- To recognize strategies for preparing for and taking classroom and standardized tests
- To recognize and apply strategies for answering different types of test questions

Related Mini-Lessons

For information on topics related to taking tests, see the following mini-lessons:

- **Study and Research Skills, pp. 294–297**
- **Reading Skills, pp. 298–301**

Teaching Strategies

for PREPARING FOR A TEST

PERSONAL TOUCH Describe for students a time when you felt especially well prepared for a test. Explain what you did to prepare. Then describe a time when you took a test for which you did not feel prepared. Invite volunteers to share their own test-taking experiences. You might also share with students your approach to composing and giving tests, including your reasons for using certain types of test.

for PREPARING FOR A TEST

HELPFUL HINT Point out to students that when their test preparation involves a lot of memorizing, they might find it useful to study with a partner. Partners can quiz each other on facts and can make sure that each of them knows the required material.

WRITING HANDBOOK 33

How Can I Score Better on Tests?

Taking Tests

No matter what Peppermint Patty says, taking tests doesn't have to be hard. You can improve your test scores by learning how to prepare for a test and how to answer different types of test questions.

PREPARING FOR A TEST

The secret to successful test-taking is careful preparation. The following strategies will help you take charge of any testing situation.

- **Know what to study.** Ask your teacher exactly what the test will cover. That way you can use your study time to focus on the most important information.
- **Make a study plan.** It helps to study a little bit every day. The night before the test, review what you have learned.
- **Review your materials.** Look over the notes you took in class, skim chapters you have read, and review any other materials you may have studied. Think of questions that you would ask if you were making up the test, and try to answer them.
- **Memorize important facts.** Look for and memorize important names, dates, events, vocabulary words, and other important information. For suggestions about how to memorize information, see Handbook 25, "Study and Research Skills," pages 294–297.
- **Rest and relax.** You will perform best when you are alert and well rested. Get a good night's sleep before test day. Then be confident as the test begins. If you studied well, you should do just fine.

TEACHER'S LOUNGE

TYPES OF TEST QUESTIONS

Studying the information that will be covered on a test is important. Just as important is knowing how to answer different types of test questions.

Some test questions ask you to choose one answer from among three or four. Other questions ask you to write a phrase or a sentence. Still others require an entire essay. You might be asked to decide whether a statement is true or false. The following guidelines will help you to recognize and answer different types of test questions. In the process, you will become a better test taker.

True-False Questions

To answer this type of test question, you must read a statement and decide whether it is true or false. The following strategies can help you decide.

- If *any* part of the statement is false, the answer is "false."
- Statements that include such words as *all, never, always,* and *none* are often, though not always, false.
- Statements that include such words as *generally, some, most, many,* and *usually* are often, though not always, true.

1. T (F) All reptiles are coldblooded and walk on four legs.

Although all reptiles are coldblooded, reptiles such as snakes do not have legs. Because the second part of the statement is false, the answer is "false."

Matching Questions

Matching questions ask you to match items in one column with related items in a second column.

for TYPES OF TEST QUESTIONS

CRITICAL THINKING: EXPRESSING OPINIONS Have students discuss which type of test question they prefer and why. Elicit opinions on which questions are most difficult and which are easiest. Explain to the class that knowing how to approach each type of question can make test-taking much less stressful.

for TRUE-FALSE QUESTIONS

ASSESSMENT: SPOT CHECK To be sure students understand the suggestions for answering true-false questions, write the following statements on the board and call on volunteers to label them *true* or *false.* Ask each volunteer to explain which strategy (if any) helped in answering the question.

Some sets of twins are identical.
(T) F

All animals that live in water are fish.
T (F)

Christopher Columbus sailed across the Atlantic Ocean in the 1400s and landed in what is now Massachusetts.
T (F)

Some people are allergic to bee stings.
(T) F

for MATCHING QUESTIONS

INDIVIDUALIZING INSTRUCTION: BASIC STUDENTS A matching test, with its long lists of items, can be overwhelming to some students. Stress to these students that if they are unable to match an item, they should come back to it after they have matched all items they are sure of. They may be able to find the correct answer by a process of elimination.

for MULTIPLE-CHOICE QUESTIONS

HELPFUL HINT Tell students that some multiple-choice questions have two possible answers that are quite similar. Often, one of these two answers is the correct one, as is the case with statements A and B in the example in the pupil book. It is important that they read the two answers carefully to determine how they differ and whether one is correct.

- First read all the items in both columns. Then match the ones you know for sure.
- Cross out the items as you match them. This way you won't be distracted by items you've already matched.

1. Write the letter of the definition next to its term.

B **1.** index		**A.** a list of chapter titles and subheadings
C **2.** glossary		**B.** an alphabetical list of topics
A **3.** table of contents		**C.** an alphabetical list of terms and their definitions

Be sure to choose the most *exact* match for each item. For example, both an index and a glossary are alphabetical lists, but only a glossary includes definitions of terms.

Multiple-Choice Questions

A multiple-choice question asks you to choose the best answer from three or more possible answers.

- Read each choice carefully.
- Cross out any answers that are clearly wrong.
- Choose the answer that is most complete or correct.

1. Which of the following best describes a river?
A. a large stream of saltwater
B. a large stream of water that empties into an ocean, a lake, or another body of water
C. a large body of water separating two continents
D. a body of water completely surrounded by land

Answers *C* and *D* are clearly incorrect. Answer *A* is only partly correct. Therefore, *B* is the correct answer.

Fill-in-the-Blank Questions

Fill-in-the-blank questions ask you to complete a sentence by adding an appropriate word or phrase.

- First fill in the answers that you know for sure.
- Then go back and try to answer the questions you left blank. An "educated guess" is better than no answer at all.
- Check each fill-in for correct capitalization and spelling. Also, be sure your answer fits grammatically with the rest of the sentence.

1. The first writing system was developed by the Sumerians.

This question requires an answer that tells *who* developed the first writing system. Telling *where, when,* or *how* writing was invented would be incorrect.

Sumerian clay tablet, about 1980 B.C.

Short-Answer Questions

Short-answer questions ask you to write a brief answer, usually just a sentence or two.

- First read the directions to find out if each answer must be a complete sentence.
- If you must write a complete sentence, begin by restating the question. Then give the answer.
- Reread the answer to be sure you used correct grammar, spelling, punctuation, and capitalization.

1. Name the three social classes in ancient Rome.
The three social classes in ancient Rome were the elite, the "more humble," and the slaves.

Notice how this answer first restates the question and then provides the answer.

for FILL-IN-THE-BLANK QUESTIONS

HELPFUL HINT To demonstrate how a fill-in-the-blank answer should fit grammatically with the rest of the sentence, discuss what is wrong with the following answer and tell how to correct it.

Segregate is the separation of people by race.

Point out that because it is a verb, the word *segregate* is grammatically incorrect for this sentence. The answer must be a noun or pronoun because it is in the subject position in the sentence. *Segregation,* a noun, is the correct fill-in answer.

for SHORT-ANSWER QUESTIONS

INDIVIDUALIZING INSTRUCTION: ADVANCED STUDENTS Some students may know more about a topic than is required for a short-answer question. Remind them that they should write only the answer to the question. Giving more than the required information will take time away from answering other questions and will not improve their grades.

Grammar Connection

When students take tests with short-answer questions, they must be able to recognize the difference between a sentence fragment and a complete sentence. Remind them to read test instructions carefully to determine whether they can answer in sentence fragments or they must write complete sentences. Refer students who need help in forming complete sentences to Handbook 34, "Understanding Sentences," pages 339–373.

for ESSAY QUESTIONS

INDIVIDUALIZING INSTRUCTION: BASIC STUDENTS Emphasize how key words tell students what kind of information to give in their answers to essay questions. Explain the following key words:

- *compare*—to describe similarities and differences
- *explain*—to tell why or how
- *describe*—to create a word picture of people, places, things, or events
- *identify*—to recognize items as distinct from one another
- *discuss*—to talk about a topic in order to reach a conclusion

for STANDARDIZED TESTS

STUMBLING BLOCK Many test-takers, when confronted by the pages of a standardized test, freeze or become very nervous. Urge students to relax when taking tests. Encourage nervous students to breathe deeply for a moment before beginning a test.

Essay Questions

When you answer an essay question, you must write your answer as one or more paragraphs.

- First identify the topic you are to write about.
- Look for key words that tell how to answer the question, such as *compare, explain, describe, identify,* and *discuss.*
- Note the form you are supposed to use, such as a letter, an explanatory paragraph, or an essay.
- Note also whether your audience is your teacher, other students, or adults.
- Before you start writing, jot down some notes about the key points you want to make.
- Proofread your writing.

Writing TIP

If you want to add additional information after you've finished writing, place it in the margin. Draw an arrow to indicate where the information should go in the paragraph.

STANDARDIZED TESTS

In addition to the tests prepared by your teacher, you will also take standardized tests. These tests, sometimes called achievement tests, are used to measure your understanding of many subjects, including mathematics, reading comprehension, vocabulary, science, and social studies.

Standardized tests often include some of the same types of questions you have already studied. In addition, there are two other types of questions you may come across.

Reading Comprehension Questions

These questions test how well you understand something you have just read. You are given a passage to read, followed by one or more questions about the passage. For example, you might be asked to state the main idea of the passage, recall a detail, or draw a conclusion.

- Read the questions first, if you're allowed to. Then you will know what information to look for as you read.

PROFESSIONAL NOTEBOOK

In their book *How to Be School Smart,* Elizabeth James and Carol Barkin have a useful suggestion for essay test-takers:

"If you're in the middle of an essay question when time runs out, it's a good idea to also jot down an outline for the rest of your answer. This will take only a moment since you already have notes written down. Copy them quickly at the end of your paper so the teacher will know what you planned to say to complete your essay."

Caution your students to keep track of the time as they complete a test, so they can carry out this strategy *before* the time is up.

- Read the passage carefully but quickly.
- Read each question carefully. Then select or write the best, most complete answer.
- If allowed, look back over the test to check answers you're unsure of.

Read the following passage carefully. Then answer the question that follows it.

> Jack London was an American adventurer and writer. Before he was twenty, he sailed the world. He achieved fame and fortune in his lifetime. His travels to Alaska spawned his most well-known adventure tales, *The Call of the Wild* and *White Fang.* London was a self-educated man who wrote about his concerns for the poor and the powerless. His novels and stories emphasize the cruel side of nature.
>
> **1.** In his writing, what was Jack London concerned about?
>
> **A.** fame and fortune **C.** education
>
> **(B.)** the poor and the powerless **D.** sailing

Although all of the answers are mentioned in the passage, only *B* answers the question.

Vocabulary Questions These questions test how well you know the meanings of words. **Synonym questions,** for example, ask you to find words that have the same, or almost the same, meanings as other words.

> Choose the phrase that is closest in meaning to the underlined phrase.
>
> **1.** <u>a costly</u> computer
>
> **A.** a cheap **C.** a thrifty
>
> **(B.)** an expensive **D.** an efficient

for READING COMPREHENSION QUESTIONS

USING THE MODEL Have students carefully examine the passage about Jack London and the question that follows it. Ask volunteers to find the places in the passage where the incorrect answers are mentioned. Point out that in questions that ask for the main idea of a given passage, details from the passage are included in the answer choices; therefore students should read each question carefully to be sure they understand exactly what is being asked.

for VOCABULARY QUESTIONS

INDIVIDUALIZING INSTRUCTION: BASIC STUDENTS Remind these students to use context clues and word parts to decipher unfamiliar words. Show them the base word *cost* in the example. Explain that they can determine the meaning of *costly* if they recognize the meaning of *cost* and the meaning of the suffix *-ly.* Refer students who need additional help to Handbook 27, "Vocabulary Skills," pages 302–307.

Literature Connection

Read students the passage below from *Hatchet* by Gary Paulsen. Then have each student write a reading comprehension question for the passage. Students can exchange papers and try to answer each other's questions.

"Brian Robeson stared out the window of the small plane at the endless green northern wilderness below. It was a small plane, a Cessna 406—a bush plane—and the engine was so loud, so roaring and consuming and loud, that it ruined any chance for conversation."

for ANTONYM QUESTIONS

STUMBLING BLOCK Point out to students that most antonym questions include in the answer choices at least one word that is a synonym of the underlined word. Likewise, most synonym questions include one or more antonyms. Stress that reading the directions carefully will help students see which the required answers must be: antonyms or synonyms. In addition, point out that if students eliminate the synonyms or antonyms not asked for, they will better their chances of selecting the correct answer.

for TAKING A TEST

HELPFUL HINT Tell students that when they are taking a test, they might receive some instructions orally and should listen carefully. For example, a teacher might state that one part of the test will take fifteen minutes and one part will take thirty minutes. Being aware of this information can help students budget their time effectively.

Answer *A* is a word that means the opposite of *costly*. Answers *C* and *D* have different meanings than *costly*. Answer *B* is the word that is closest in meaning.

Antonym questions ask you to find words that have opposite meanings.

Choose the word that is opposite in meaning to the underlined word.

1. a fascinating story

A. interesting	**(C.)** boring
B. challenging	**D.** attractive

Answers *A* and *D* both have meanings that are similar to *fascinating*. Answer *B* has a different meaning, but not an opposite meaning. Only *C* means the opposite of *fascinating*.

TAKING A TEST

When it's time to sit down and take a test, these tips can help you do well.

- **Look over the whole test.** See how long it is and what types of questions it includes.
- **Budget your time.** Read all the directions first. This will let you know whether you will need more time for one type of question, such as an essay.
- **Read the directions carefully.** Ask questions if you don't understand the directions. Follow the directions exactly.
- **Answer easy questions first.** Mark the questions you can't answer right away. Then go back to these questions later.
- **Mark answer sheets carefully.** If the test you're taking includes a computer-scored answer sheet, mark each answer in the correct space, filling in the answer circles or boxes neatly.

PROFESSIONAL NOTEBOOK

Writer and teacher Bertha Davis offers the following advice to standardized test-takers in her book, *How to Take a Test.*

"During timed tests:

Keep Going
KEEP GOING
K E E P G O I N G

"'Keep going' does not mean rush. 'Keep going' means work calmly . . . in the recommended ways, at a steady pace. It is a two-word magic formula . . . . Adopt it as your own."

Remind students to skip any questions they cannot answer immediately, work through the entire test, and then try to answer them.

- **Review your answers.** Check that you have not left out any answers and that your answers make sense. Make any necessary changes.

Practice Your Skills

A. Answer the following questions.

1. T (F) Standardized tests always include reading-comprehension questions.

2. (T) F Before you begin a test you should look over the entire test, if this is allowed.

3. Questions that ask you to choose the best answer from three or more choices are multiple-choice questions.

4. A word that means the opposite of a given word is an antonym .

B. Read the following passage. Then answer the questions.

A desert is a hot, barren region that receives little rainfall. However, scientists do not agree on a specific definition. Some scientists define deserts by the amount of rainfall and evaporation. Some define them by the type of soil or plant life present. Others use a combination of all of these factors. The largest desert in the world is the Sahara in Africa. The Sahara covers an area about the same size as the United States.

1. What factors do some scientists use to define deserts?
A. rainfall and evaporation **C.** plant life
B. type of soil (**D.**) all of the above

2. Which word is closest in meaning to the word *barren?*
(**A.**) empty **C.** tame
B. fertile **D.** rich

for REVIEW YOUR ANSWERS

HELPFUL HINT Sometimes, when students review their work, they are tempted to change several answers. Urge them to be sure of the correct answers before making changes. If they are uncertain of the correct answer to a question, they should stay with their original answer.

Additional Resources

Writing Resource Book, pp. 108–109
Tests and Writing Assessment Prompts

Answers to Practice Your Skills

A. Answers are shown on page.
B. Answers are shown on page.

MULTICULTURAL Connection

In some cultures, test-taking has far more importance than it does in the United States. For example, in Belgium, college students are often graded for the whole year on the basis of a single oral examination. Have interested students research the role of tests in the culture of their choice. They can report back to the class and lead a discussion on the differences and similarities they discovered.

ART NOTE In America, quilting has been a popular art form since the days of the earliest pioneers. Cloth was scarce in Colonial America. Therefore, women recycled clothing until it finally wore out; then they sewed usable scraps into colorful patterned quilts. Quilting remains a popular art form and hobby today, although most quilters do the work with the aid of machines, not strictly by hand.

An anonymous African-American woman worked long hours to produce this beautiful quilt. She was accomplished with a needle—probably a dressmaker who made hand-sewed clothes. She made the quilt from scraps of fine silk, using three techniques: piecing (sewing together scraps to form a large piece of cloth); appliqué (sewing pieces of cloth on top of other cloth); and embroidery (using colored threads to decorate cloth).

It isn't clear whether the quilter is showing the actual daily life of African-Americans of the time or depicting the way she imagines African-Americans will live after the end of slavery. The quilt alternates traditional diamond-shaped designs with "portraits" of log cabins and scenes of fashionably dressed African-Americans chopping wood, visiting, and courting.

You might point out that this quilter "built" her large quilt from scraps of fabric. Similarly, when students write, they create a large work from smaller units called sentences. Tell students that in this section of the text, they will study the basic parts of English sentences, which they'll piece together to build longer pieces of writing.

Detail of a pieced, appliquéd, and embroidered quilt, about 1870. The artist depicts over one hundred colorful log cabins, as well as scenes of community members engaged in a variety of daily tasks. Perhaps the quilt was made to show what life was like for African Americans after the abolition of slavery.

334

Social Studies Connection

Note that this quilt was made five years after the Civil War (1861–1865) ended and seven years after President Lincoln's Emancipation Proclamation (January 1, 1863). You might ask someone to report briefly on the Emancipation Proclamation, which freed only those slaves residing in the states that were rebelling against the Union. Have another student report on how and when slavery ended throughout the United States.

Grammar and Usage Handbook

MINI-LESSONS

MINI-LESSONS

Grammar and Usage Handbook

Pretest

These tests enable you to assess your students' knowledge of grammar, usage, punctuation, spelling, and capitalization. The format of these tests is similar to that of some standardized tests. Use this assessment as a formal diagnostic tool or as an informal means of deciding which concepts in the Grammar and Usage Handbook you will emphasize.

Answer Key

Corrections for run-ons may vary.

1. A—grandpa
2. A—butterfly's
   B—folklore. There
3. B—are
4. C—safely
5. B—Ian and me
   C—cat's *or* cats'
6. A—these *or* those
   B—larger
7. B—his or her
   C—judge
8. C—fuel from
9. A—his or her
   B—Sitting
10. D
11. B—rode
12. B—Arlington, Virginia,
13. B—he
    C—had written
14. B—height
    C—Now,
15. B—ceiling. They

List of Skills Tested

1. A—capitalization—common/proper noun
   B—sentence fragment/run-on
   C—pronoun case
2. A—noun possessive
   B—sentence fragment/run-on
   C—noun plural
3. A—comparative adjective form
   B—subject-verb agreement
   C—noun plural
4. A—spelling
   B—spelling
   C—adjective/adverb confusion
5. A—punctuation—comma
   B—pronoun case
   C—punctuation—possessive

Skills

ASSESSMENT

PRETEST Grammar Handbooks

Directions One or more of the underlined sections in the following sentences may contain an error in grammar, punctuation, spelling, or capitalization. Write the letter of each incorrect section. Then rewrite the section correctly. If there is no error in an item, write *D.*

> ***Example*** The first navigator to sail completely [A] around the world was Juan Sebastián del Cano in 1522. Magellan [B] did not live. To complete [C] the expedition. No error [D]
>
> ***Answer*** C—live to

1. We will visit my Grandpa [A] in Mexico for the *posada* celebration before Christmas. He [B] will make piñatas for all of us [C]. No error [D]

2. The butterflys [A] name may have come from folklore there [B] are stories about witches [C] taking the form of a butterfly to steal butter and milk. No error [D]

3. A drop of water is smaller [A] than you might think. There is [B] 120 drops [C] in a teaspoon. No error [D]

4. The parachute was invented [A] to help people [B] jump out of burning buildings safe [C]. No error [D]

5. First, the [A] veterinarian showed Ian and I [B] how to clip the cats [C] claws. No error [D]

6. Look at them [A] two crystals. The largest [B] one grew more slowly [C] than the other. No error [D]

7. Either of the witnesses [A] will tell their [B] story to the Judge [C]. No error [D]

8. The people of North Africa [A] make food, medicine, cooking oil, bowls, baskets, sandals, rope, and [B] fuel. From [C] parts of the date palm tree. No error [D]

9. Everyone should be careful about their [A] diet. Setting [B] down regularly to meals high in sugar and fat can lead to certain diseases [C]. No error [D]

10. Only fourteen out of every one hundred wives [A] in the United States are [B] older than their [C] husbands. No error [D]

11. In ancient England, the fierce [A] Celtic warrior Boadicea rided [B] into London with her soldiers and burned [C] the city to the ground. No error [D]

12. At the Pentagon [A] building in Arlington Virginia [B] there are almost seventy thousand miles of telephone lines! [C] No error [D]

13. On Christmas Eve, the organ in Joseph Mohr's church broke [A] down. Within three hours, him [B] and the church organist had wrote [C] "Silent Night" so the church members would have music. No error [D]

14. Thousands searched [A] for gold in the Klondike at the hieght [B] of the gold rush. now [C], almost one hundred years later, people are still digging there. No error [D]

15. Balloons [A] were stuck to the ceiling they [B] fell [C] down later. No error [D]

6. A—demonstrative adjective/pronoun confusion
B—comparative adjective form
C—comparative adverb form
7. A—noun plural
B—agreement of possessive pronoun and indefinite pronoun
C—capitalization—common/proper noun
8. A—capitalization—common/proper noun
B—punctuation—comma
C—sentence fragment/run-on
9. A—agreement of possessive pronoun and indefinite pronoun
B—confusing pairs of verbs
C—spelling
10. A—noun plural
B—subject-verb agreement
C—spelling
11. A—spelling
B—verb form
C—verb form
12. A—capitalization—common/proper noun
B—punctuation—comma
C—punctuation—exclamation point
13. A—verb form
B—pronoun case
C—verb form
14. A—verb form
B—spelling
C—capitalization
15. A—spelling
B—sentence fragment'/run-on
C—verb form

Skills Assessment 337

Sketchbook

Objective

- To use writing prompts as springboards to informal writing

WRITING WARM-UPS

Start by reassuring students that they will not be graded for this assignment. The prompts are designed to get students thinking imaginatively about the contents of this Handbook. Although most students will probably respond to just one prompt, encourage volunteers to explore both, if they wish.

Have students work in pairs to brainstorm a list of three famous people whom they would like to interview. Student partners can share their lists and narrow the choices to one person. Partner A can role-play the interviewer, writing the questions. Partner B can create and write the interviewee's responses.

Encourage students who select the second prompt to freewrite for five minutes about their greatest achievement.

Sketchbook

WRITING WARM-UPS

- Imagine you could interview any famous person—living or dead. Write down some questions you would ask and the answers you think the person would give.
- You are telling a reporter about your greatest achievement. Write what you would say.

338

Understanding Sentences

GRAMMAR HANDBOOK 34

After a press conference, reporters must make sense of the information they received. When they tell their readers what was said, they may restate the questions and even quote some of the answers. Reporters will use various kinds of sentences in their articles. The headline may even be a question or an exclamation.

This handbook explains the parts of sentences and shows you the types of sentences you can use in your writing. It can help you write sentences that express your ideas clearly and confidently.

GRAMMAR HANDBOOK 34

Understanding Sentences

Objectives

- To recognize complete sentences
- To identify the two parts of a sentence: subject and predicate
- To identify complete sentences, sentence fragments, and run-on sentences
- To identify the simple predicate, or verb
- To identify the simple subject and recognize it in unusual positions
- To identify the four types of sentences and punctuate them correctly
- To identify the subjects of interrogative, exclamatory, and imperative sentences
- To identify and form compound subjects and predicates

Writing

- To use complete sentences in writing
- To correct fragments and run-ons in writing
- To use vivid verbs in sentences and paragraphs
- To eliminate repetition by forming sentences with compound subjects and compound verbs

INTRODUCING THE HANDBOOK

Students should talk about the different kinds of print journalists: news reporters, sportswriters, and columnists, for example. Then invite students to give examples of different kinds of sentences that reporters might use in an interview, a news story, and a feature article.

Remind students that sentences are basic units of communication in written English. Knowing how to use them helps a writer convey ideas and feelings.

WHAT IS A SENTENCE?

Objectives

- To recognize complete sentences

Writing

- To use complete sentences in a piece of writing

Teaching Strategies

KEY TO UNDERSTANDING: SENTENCES Point out to students that they cannot identify a group of words as a sentence merely by length. Some sentences are very short (for example, *Sam left*.), whereas other long groups of words may not be complete sentences. (*While swimming underwater with my new snorkel and yellow flippers*)

INDIVIDUALIZING INSTRUCTION: LD STUDENTS You may wish to do the first seven items of Exercise A orally with these students. Model the process you use to decide whether a group of words is a complete sentence. Encourage students to add words to complete the thoughts in items 2, 3, 4, and 7. Then allow them to do the last eight items in the exercise independently.

Additional Resources

Tests and Writing Assessment Prompts, Pretest, pp. 7–8
Grammar and Usage Practice Book, p. 1
Grammar Test Generator

Writing Theme: Yellowstone National Park

Suggest that students use these exercises as a springboard to writing. Other related areas that they might explore include the following:

- geysers and Old Faithful
- grizzly bears in Yellowstone National Park
- the effects of forest fires
- wilderness conservation versus recreation

WHAT IS A SENTENCE?

A **sentence** is a group of words that expresses a complete thought.

Look at this group of words:

Visitors to Yellowstone National Park

This group of words is about visitors to Yellowstone National Park. The words do not, however, say what happens to the visitors or what the visitors do. They do not express a complete idea.

Now consider this group of words:

Hike through rugged wilderness

This group of words tells you *what happens*. However, it does not tell *who* or *what* hikes through the wilderness. These words also present only part of an idea.

A **sentence** expresses a complete thought. Every sentence must tell whom or what the sentence is about. It must also tell what happens. Read the following group of words. Since it expresses a complete thought, it is a sentence.

Visitors to Yellowstone National Park hike through rugged wilderness.

Writing TIP

Do not leave your readers with only part of an idea. Make sure every sentence you write tells a complete thought.

Practice Your Skills

A. CONCEPT CHECK

Sentences and Incomplete Sentences Label each group of words *Sentence* or *Not a Sentence.*

Writing Theme Yellowstone National Park

1. The Yellowstone area was part of the Louisiana Purchase. S
2. Belonged to the United States government after 1803. N
3. Home of Native Americans. N
4. Hunted in the Yellowstone region for thousands of years. N

5. President Jefferson sent Lewis and Clark on an expedition. S
6. The two explorers never saw the Yellowstone region. S
7. Heard stories about it from Native Americans. N
8. Around 1807, the trapper John Colter. N
9. Discovered geysers and hot springs. N
10. Other trappers explored the region in the 1830s and 1840s. S
11. Spread stories about the Yellowstone area's natural wonders. N
12. Few people believed these incredible tales. S
13. Finally, in 1870, a United States government expedition. N
14. By 1872, Yellowstone National Park. N
15. The oldest national park in the world. N

B. REVISION SKILL

Correcting Incomplete Sentences Label each group of words *Sentence* or *Not a Sentence.* Add words to change the incomplete sentences to complete sentences.

16. Tourists marvel at the scenery in Yellowstone National Park.
17. More than two hundred geysers and thousands of hot springs.
18. Old Faithful is the most famous geyser.
19. Shoots water and steam 160 feet into the air.
20. During the summer, meadows with beautiful wildflowers.
21. Gazes at their bright colors.
22. Forests of pine trees cover most of the park.
23. Roam freely in the dense forest.
24. Builds a nest in a tree.
25. Large animals, such as grizzly bears.

C. APPLICATION IN WRITING

Paragraph These notes from a journal tell about a vacation in Yellowstone National Park. Use the list and make up details to write a brief paragraph about the trip. Add words to make each note a complete sentence.

long trip in the car	pitched our tent
the warm glow of the fire	hiked through the forest
a huge, brown grizzly bear!	paddled a canoe

FOR MORE PRACTICE
See page 366.

Answers to Practice Your Skills

A. Concept Check
Sentences and Incomplete Sentences

Answers are shown on page.

B. Revision Skill
Correcting Incomplete Sentences

Answers will vary for corrected sentences. Sample answers are given.

16. Sentence
17. Not a Sentence; Yellowstone National Park has more than two hundred geysers and thousands of hot springs.
18. Sentence
19. Not a Sentence: This powerful geyser shoots water and steam 160 feet into the air.
20. Not a Sentence: During the summer, meadows with beautiful wildflowers are a spectacular sight.
21. Not a Sentence; A tourist gazes at their bright colors.
22. Sentence
23. Not a Sentence; Moose roam freely in the dense forest.
24. Not a Sentence; An eagle builds a nest in a tree.
25. Not a Sentence; Large animals, such as grizzly bears, feel at home in Yellowstone National Park.

C. Application in Writing
Paragraph

Answers will vary. Check to see that students have correctly changed each group of words into a complete sentence.

Objectives

- To identify the two parts of a sentence: the subject and the predicate

Writing

- To recognize subjects and predicates in a piece of writing

Teaching Strategies

KEY TO UNDERSTANDING: WORD ORDER Point out to students that normally, the subject comes at or near the beginning of a sentence, whereas the predicate usually occurs in the middle or toward the end. Emphasize to the class that there are exceptions to this general rule and that it is important that students double-check, as they identify the subject and the predicate, by thinking about the meaning of the sentence. Advise students to double-check the subject by asking *whom* or *what* the sentence is about and double-check the predicate by asking *what exists or is occurring.*

Additional Resource

Grammar and Usage Practice Book, p. 2

Writing Theme: Baseball

Suggest that students use these exercises as a springboard to writing. Other related areas that they might explore include the following:

- how a baseball diamond is laid out
- umpiring in the major leagues
- Hank Aaron, home run king
- the career of Babe Ruth

Answers to Practice Your Skills

A. Concept Check

Subjects and Predicates

Answers are shown on page.

SUBJECTS AND PREDICATES

The **subject** of a sentence tells *whom* or *what* the sentence is about. The **predicate** tells what the subject *does* or *is*.

Every sentence has two parts. The **subject** tells whom or what the sentence is about. The **predicate** tells what the subject does or did or what the subject is or was.

Look at the subjects and predicates in these sentences.

Subject (whom or what)	Predicate (what the subject does, did, is, or was)
Babe Ruth	was a superstar in professional baseball.
His great skills	drew huge crowds in the 1920s.
Baseball	is still a popular sport today.
Fans everywhere	flock to ballparks during the summer.

Notice that every sentence can be divided into two parts. All the words in a sentence are part of either the subject or the predicate.

Sentence Diagraming For information on diagraming subjects and predicates, see page 617.

Writing Theme
Baseball

Practice Your Skills

A. CONCEPT CHECK

Subjects and Predicates Write each of the following sentences. Draw one line under the subject and two lines under the predicate.

EXAMPLE The history of baseball dates back hundreds of years.

1. People in England played rounders in the 1600s.
2. This English game was similar to baseball.

342 Grammar Handbook

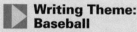

3. Players hit a ball with a bat.
4. American colonists in the 1700s enjoyed rounders too.
5. Americans changed the game into baseball.
6. Alexander Cartwright was probably the father of baseball.
7. He organized the first baseball club in 1845.
8. The name of his team was "Knickerbocker Base Ball Club."
9. The Knickerbocker Club lost its first game.
10. Cartwright developed many of the rules of baseball.
11. He decided the size of the baseball diamond, for example.
12. Today's rules are similar to Cartwright's rules.

B. APPLICATION IN LITERATURE

Subjects and Predicates Label each italicized word or word group *Subject* or *Predicate.*

> 13 *Our team* started to argue with one another. 14 *Our play* was sloppy, nothing like the cool routines back at Hobo Park. 15 Flyballs that lifted to the outfield *dropped at the feet of open-mouthed players.* 16 Grounders *rolled slowly between awkward feet.* 17 The pitching *was sad. . . .*
>
> 18 *My teammates* were grumbling because they thought I was going to strike out, pop-up, roll it back to the pitcher, anything but hit the ball. . . .
>
> 19 *I* came up scared of the fast ball and even more scared of failing. 20 Mary *looked on from the bleachers with a sandwich in her hand.* 21 The coach *clung to the screen . . .*

Gary Soto, "Baseball in April"

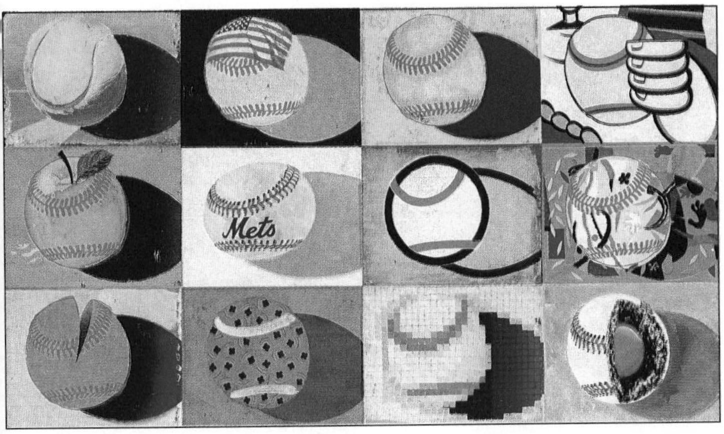

Detail of *Baseball* (1990), Paul Giovanopoulos.

FOR MORE PRACTICE
See page 366.

B. Application in Literature
Subjects and Predicates
13. Subject
14. Subject
15. Predicate
16. Predicate
17. Predicate
18. Subject
19. Subject
20. Predicate
21. Predicate

SENTENCE FRAGMENTS AND RUN-ON SENTENCES

Objectives

- To identify complete sentences, sentence fragments, and run-on sentences

Writing

- To correct fragments and run-ons

Teaching Strategies

KEY TO UNDERSTANDING: FRAGMENTS Point out that sentence fragments are not necessarily short. Illustrate this point by writing the following lengthy fragments on the board:

The bright green parrot sitting on the lowest branch of that tree to the left

Cheered wildly for the home team in the final seconds of the game

Have students read the fragments aloud and discuss why they do not express a complete thought.

INDIVIDUALIZING INSTRUCTION: ESL STUDENTS In some languages, such as Vietnamese, Korean, and Spanish, it is grammatically correct for the subject of a sentence to be omitted, as it can be inferred from the inflected verb. Explain to ESL students that in written English, except for imperative sentences (where the subject is then understood *you*), the subject must be present to make a sentence complete. Point out that *oral* English often contains sentence fragments—people do not always speak in complete sentences. Ask students to write down a conversation overheard in the lunchroom. Have them identify sentence fragments and rewrite them as complete sentences.

ADVANCED STUDENTS Point out that students can use two other methods to correct run-on sentences. If the two ideas are closely related, they can join the ideas by using the word *and* followed by a comma. They may also join the ideas with a semicolon. The semicolon takes the place of a comma and the conjunction.

SENTENCE FRAGMENTS AND RUN-ON SENTENCES

A **sentence fragment** is a group of words that does not express a complete thought. A **run-on sentence** is two or more sentences written as one sentence.

Readers find both sentence fragments and run-on sentences difficult to understand. A sentence fragment is confusing because something is left out. A run-on sentence incorrectly joins ideas that should be separated.

Sentence Fragments

A group of words that is not a sentence is called a **sentence fragment.** Some fragments do not tell what happened. Other fragments do not tell whom or what the sentence is about. You can correct a fragment by adding a missing subject or a missing predicate. Look at these examples:

Fragment	Some kinds of insects. *(What happens?)*
Sentence	Some kinds of insects fool their enemies.
Fragment	Looks like a brown twig. *(What is this about?)*
Sentence	The stick caterpillar looks like a brown twig.

Run-on Sentences

A **run-on sentence** is two or more sentences written as if they were one sentence. Sometimes there is no end mark at the end of the first complete thought. Sometimes a comma is used incorrectly to separate two complete thoughts. To correct a run-on, add the proper end mark at the end of the first sentence. Then capitalize the first letter of the next sentence.

Incorrect	This fox changes color it is white in the winter.
Incorrect	This fox changes color, it is white in the winter.
Correct	This fox changes color. It is white in the winter.

Practice Your Skills

A. CONCEPT CHECK

Fragments and Run-ons Label each group of words *Sentence, Sentence Fragment,* or *Run-on Sentence.*

1. A nest of baby rabbits with gray and brown fur. F
2. Matches the leaves and grass of their surroundings. F
3. A fox approaches, the baby rabbits lie very still. RO
4. Finally, the danger passes. S
5. The baby rabbits are safe they blend in with the background. RO
6. Fawns also fool their enemies. S
7. Sometimes they stand as stiff as trees. S
8. Their color protects them, their fur has specks of white. RO
9. Almost disappear in the sunlight and trees. F
10. Clever tricksters in the animal world. F

Writing Theme
Animal Camouflage

When nestled in foliage, the flap-neck chameleon of Africa is nearly invisible to predators.

B. REVISION SKILL

Correcting Fragments and Run-ons Add words to make the fragments complete sentences. Rewrite the run-on sentences as separate sentences.

11. Insects have very short lives they have many enemies.
12. Their chances of survival.
13. Some insects copy the faces of dangerous animals, the appearance of these insects scares their enemies.
14. Some swallowtail caterpillars have fake eyes on their backs they look like a snake's eyes.
15. Probably frighten away hungry birds.
16. Many other kinds of disguises.
17. The lantern fly lives in Brazil the shape of its head is unusual.
18. Looks like a big hollow peanut.
19. The lantern fly's head has weird markings they are not just for decoration.
20. Markings like the teeth of an alligator, for example.

FOR MORE PRACTICE
See page 367.

SPEAKING AND LISTENING Read aloud some exercise items on page 345 that are run-ons; for example, items 3, 5, and 8 from Exercise A and items 11, 13, and 14 from Exercise B. Run the sentences together with no pause when you read them. Then read each item again, this time inserting a pause between sentences. Encourage students to "hear" where punctuation is needed to correct each run-on.

Additional Resource

Grammar and Usage Practice Book, pp. 3–4

Writing Theme: Animal Camouflage

Other related areas students might wish to explore as writing topics include the following:

- the monarch butterfly's migration
- big cats in the wild
- animals of the Arctic
- why the zebra has stripes
- insect or reptile camouflage

Answers to Practice Your Skills

A. Concept Check
Fragments and Run-ons

Answers are shown on page.

B. Revision Skill
Correcting Fragments and Run-ons

Some answers will vary. Sample answers are given.

11. Insects have very short lives. They have many enemies.
12. Their chances of survival are slim.
13. Some insects copy the faces of dangerous animals. The appearance of these insects scares their enemies.
14. Some swallowtail caterpillars have fake eyes on their backs. They look like a snake's eyes.
15. These phony eyes probably frighten away hungry birds.
16. Many other kinds of disguises protect insects from their enemies.
17. The lantern fly lives in Brazil. The shape of its head is unusual.
18. It looks like a big hollow peanut.
19. The lantern fly's head has weird markings. They are not just for decoration.
20. Markings like the teeth of an alligator, for example, look really scary to other animals.

CHECK POINT

Writing Theme: Washington, D.C.

Other related areas students might wish to explore as writing topics include the following:

- the early history of the White House
- the National Zoo
- the street plan of Washington, D.C.

MIXED REVIEW • PAGES 340–345

You may wish to use this activity to check students' mastery of the following concepts:

- What is a sentence?
- subjects and predicates
- sentence fragments and run-on sentences

Some answers will vary. Possible answers are shown below. Student answers should be listed and should also appear in the rewritten letter.

1. Run-on Sentence; Our trip to Washington, D.C., is really fun. We left on Monday morning.
2. Sentence
3. Fragment; Many visitors from across the United States come here on vacation.
4. Fragment; Huge government buildings are everywhere.
5. Sentence
6. Fragment; A tour guide showed us some of the famous rooms.
7. Run-on Sentence; I liked the Red Room the best. It has beautiful furniture and paintings.
8. Sentence
9. Fragment; This museum contains all sorts of old airplanes and rockets.
10. Fragment; Famous spacecraft of U.S. astronauts are on display there.
11. Fragment; Rocks from the first trip to the moon are also on exhibit.
12. Sentence
13. Fragment; It looks just like a castle in a fairy tale.
14. Run-on Sentence; Then we walked to the Lincoln Memorial. This white marble building reminds me of a great temple.
15. Fragment; The monument honors Abraham Lincoln.
16. Fragment; A gigantic statue of the president stands in the center of the building.
17. Sentence
18. Fragment; The tallest building in Washington, D.C., reaches high into the sky.
19. Sentence
20. Fragment; All the tourists had a great view of the city.

Writing Theme
Washington, D. C.

CHECK POINT
MIXED REVIEW • PAGES 340–345

Read the following letter about a trip to Washington, D.C. Label each numbered group of words *Sentence, Fragment,* or *Run-on Sentence.* Then rewrite the letter. Change each fragment into a complete sentence by adding a subject or a predicate. Correct the run-on sentences.

Dear Adam,

[1]Our trip to Washington, D.C., is really fun, we left on Monday morning. [2]This city is a terrific place. [3]Many visitors from across the United States. [4]Huge government buildings. [5]The White House was our first stop. [6]Showed us some of the famous rooms. [7]I liked the Red Room the best, it has beautiful furniture and paintings. [8]Next, we visited the National Air and Space Museum. [9]Contains all sorts of old airplanes and rockets. [10]Famous spacecraft of U.S. astronauts. [11]Rocks from the first trip to the moon. [12]The Smithsonian Institution building is nearby. [13]Looks just like a castle in a fairy tale.

[14]Then we walked to the Lincoln Memorial this white marble building reminds me of a great temple. [15]Honors Abraham Lincoln. [16]A gigantic statue of the president. [17]We also went to the Washington Monument. [18]The tallest building in Washington, D.C. [19]An elevator inside the monument carried us to the top. [20]Had a great view of the city.

Your friend,
Daryl

A view of Washington, D.C., with the Potomac River in the foreground and the Lincoln Memorial, the Washington Monument, and the Capitol in the distance.

THE SIMPLE PREDICATE, OR VERB

A **verb** is a word that tells about action or that tells what someone or something is. A verb is the most important word in a complete predicate.

You know that a sentence can be divided into two main parts. We call the subject part the **complete subject.** The complete subject includes all of the words that tell whom or what the sentence is about.

The predicate part of the sentence is called the **complete predicate.** The complete predicate includes all of the words that tell what the subject is, what the subject does or did, or what happened to the subject.

Read the following examples of complete subjects and complete predicates.

Complete Subject	Complete Predicate
A large silvery spacecraft	landed.
A large silvery spacecraft	landed in a field.
A large silvery spacecraft	landed in a field near school.
Hairy green aliens	invaded.
Hairy green aliens	invaded the planet..
Hairy green aliens	invaded the planet at midnight.

Look at each complete predicate above. What is the key word in each one? The most important word in the first three complete predicates is *landed.* The most important word in the last three complete predicates is *invaded.*

The most important part of every complete predicate is the **verb.** It is sometimes called the **simple predicate.** In this book, however, we will call the simple predicate the **verb.**

THE SIMPLE PREDICATE, OR VERB

Objectives

- To identify the simple predicate and the complete predicate

Writing

- To use vivid verbs in sentences and paragraphs

Teaching Strategies

KEY TO UNDERSTANDING: PREDICATES Stress that the terms *simple predicate* and *verb* are both names for the same key word or words in the complete predicate of a sentence. Explain that a simple predicate or verb, however, may consist of more than one word. Give students examples of multiword linking verbs such as *will be, has been, have been,* and *had been*—and of multiword action verbs: *will kick, had been eating, might have been told.* Tell students that they will learn more about multiword verbs in Handbook 36, "Understanding Verbs." In the exercises in this lesson, however, most verbs are only one word.

INDIVIDUALIZING INSTRUCTION: SOCIAL LEARNERS Form these students into groups of four. Each group should then form two teams. Have each team create five original sentences and write them on an index card. Then have teams exchange cards and identify the complete subject, the complete predicate, and the verb (simple predicate) in each sentence.

Additional Resource

Grammar and Usage Practice Book, p. 5

Writing Theme: Strange Creatures in Science Fiction

Other related areas students might wish to explore as writing topics include the following:

- strange creatures in *Star Wars*
- Arthur C. Clarke, science fiction writer
- the stories of Ray Bradbury

Answers to Practice Your Skills

A. Concept Check

Verbs

Answers are shown on page.

Writing TIP

Use specific action verbs to make your writing vivid. For example, say a spacecraft *zoomed,* instead of saying it *moved.*

Types of Verbs

There are two types of verbs. Some verbs tell about an action. These are **action verbs.**

Mario *gazed* at the strange creature outside his window.
The alien *leaped* toward the house.
It *banged* on the door with its steel fist.

Other types of verbs may tell that something is, or they may link the subject with words that describe it. These are called **state-of-being verbs.** They are also called **linking verbs.**

The space creature *is* small and chubby.
Sara *seemed* surprised at the alien's sudden appearance.

Common Linking Verbs

am	was	has been	seem	become
are	were	have been	look	feel
is	will be	had been	appear	taste

You will learn more about verbs in Grammar Handbook 36, "Using Verbs," pages 394–430.

Practice Your Skills

Writing Theme
Strange Creatures in Science Fiction

A. CONCEPT CHECK

Verbs Write each sentence on your paper. Underline the complete predicate once. Draw a double line under the verb.

1. *The War of the Worlds* is a story about space monsters.
2. In the story creatures from Mars invade the earth.
3. These invaders are huge and ugly.
4. Their skin looks like wet leather.
5. The Martians carry powerful weapons.
6. They terrify people on the East Coast.
7. The monsters catch a common earth disease.
8. Deadly germs destroy the cruel Martians.
9. Not all aliens in science fiction are mean.

Literature Connection

Slowly read aloud the following passage from "The Circuit" by Francisco Jiménez. Have students identify the predicates, or verbs (underlined below).

"I still felt a little dizzy when we took a break to eat lunch. It was past two o'clock and we sat underneath a large walnut tree that was on the side of the road. While we ate, Papa jotted down the number of boxes we had picked. Roberto drew designs on the ground with a stick."

10. The alien in the movie *E.T.* is lovable and cute.
11. Children learn about friendship from this creature.
12. Many friendly, helpful aliens appeared on *Star Trek*.
13. For example, Mr. Spock worked closely with earth people.
14. He gave Captain Kirk good advice.
15. Like humans, aliens have been both good and evil.

B. REVISION SKILL

Using Vivid Verbs Write the following sentences. Replace each italicized word or phrase with a vivid verb from the list.

EXAMPLE Weird monsters in science fiction *scare* people.
Weird monsters in science fiction *terrify* people.

craved	grew	starred	grabbed	caused
trudged	gobbled	oozed	invaded	stormed

16. Giant creatures without brains *moved* through the jungles on the planet Venus.
17. They *took* everything along the way.
18. In a story by Robert A. Heinlein, a speedy, eight-legged monster *went* across the earth.
19. This hungry alien *ate* metal.
20. It really *wanted* old cars for dinner.
21. The Blob *was* in a popular movie.
22. This famous monster *went into* a small town.
23. It *made* all kinds of trouble.
24. The slimy alien *came* slowly through the town.
25. With each human meal, the Blob *got* bigger and bigger.

C. APPLICATION IN WRITING

Science Fiction Story Write a story about a space creature that lands in your neighborhood. Be sure to describe the creature and its actions. In your story, use five of the vivid verbs in the following list.

rescue	struggle	search	invade
stare	scream	quarrel	command
topple	chuckle	explode	flee

FOR MORE PRACTICE
See page 367.

B. Revision Skill
Using Vivid Verbs

16. trudged, oozed or stormed
17. grabbed
18. stormed
19. gobbled
20. craved
21. starred
22. invaded
23. caused
24. oozed or trudged
25. grew

C. Application in Writing
Science Fiction Story

Answers will vary. Check that students have effectively used at least five vivid verbs to write lively stories.

The Simple Subject

Objective

- To identify the simple subject

Teaching Strategies

KEY TO UNDERSTANDING: SIMPLE SUBJECTS Point out that sometimes a phrase containing one or more nouns can come between the simple subject and the verb in a sentence, as in the sample on the pupil page: *The red dragon **in the cave** thundered mightily.* Ask students to write on the board some sentences with this pattern of a phrase intervening between subject and verb. Have volunteers identify the simple subject in the sentence by finding the verb and then asking *who* or *what?* before the verb.

MANAGING THE PAPER LOAD To limit the number of written exercises to correct, you may wish to have your students complete Exercise A orally. If any students have difficulty in identifying simple subjects in this exercise, remind them to ask *who* or *what* before the verb.

Additional Resource

Grammar and Usage Practice Book, p. 6

The Simple Subject

The **simple subject** is the most important part of the complete subject.

In a complete sentence, every verb has a subject.

Complete Subject	Verb
The princess	danced.
The lovely princess	danced.
The lovely princess in the red gown	danced.
The prince	bowed.
The handsome prince	bowed.
The handsome prince from England	bowed.

Look at each complete subject above. What is the key word in each one? In the first group, the most important word is *princess;* in the second group, it is *prince.*

The most important word in a complete subject is called the **simple subject** of the sentence. Another name for the simple subject is the **subject of the verb.**

To find the subject of a verb, first find the verb. Then ask *who* or *what* before the verb. The answer indicates the simple subject of the sentence. Look at these examples:

The red dragon in the cave thundered mightily.
Verb: *thundered*
Who or what thundered? dragon
Dragon is the subject of *thundered.*

The young girl spun gold from straw.
Verb: *spun*
Who or what spun? girl
Girl is the subject of *spun.*

Elves are magical beings in fairy tales.
Verb: *are*
Who or what are? elves
Elves is the subject of *are.*

Practice Your Skills

A. CONCEPT CHECK

Simple Subjects Write the verb and the simple subject of each of the following sentences.

Writing Theme
Fairy Tales

1. Very few children's books existed before 1700.
2. Children learned lessons about good behavior from these first books.
3. Later stories entertained young readers.
4. Many early books were collections of fairy tales.
5. These tales are among the oldest kinds of literature.
6. People handed fairy tales down from generation to generation.
7. Two brothers collected German fairy tales during the early 1800s.
8. Their names were Jakob and Wilhelm Grimm.
9. German farmers told tales to the brothers.
10. The Grimms wrote down the farmers' exact words.
11. Then they published these ancient tales.
12. Their collection of fairy tales became very popular.
13. Authors in other countries published fairy tales too.
14. In Denmark, Hans Christian Andersen wrote 168 fairy tales.
15. Young readers around the world enjoy Andersen's magical tales.

Arthur Szyk illustrates Hans Christian Andersen's tale "The Nightingale" by showing the little bird singing to cheer an unhappy emperor.

Writing Theme: Fairy Tales

Other related areas students might wish to explore as writing topics include the following:

- African folk tales
- Pecos Bill or another tall tale hero
- Native American tales for children

Answers to Practice Your Skills

A. Concept Check
Simple Subjects
Answers are shown on page.

B. Drafting Skill
Using Subjects and Verbs Creatively

Simple subjects and verbs are underlined on page. Student revisions will vary. Sample revisions are shown below.

16. The Pied Piper played his electric guitar for the homecoming celebration.
17. His inspiring rock-and-roll music charmed all the students at Coolville High School.
18. Unfortunately, the Rats, the Creepyville High School football team, overran their opponents.
19. The number of victories grew higher and higher.
20. The people of Coolville promised strong support for their team this year.
21. The street echoed with cheers of excitement.
22. The sound of the Pied Piper's rock-and-roll music drew people from every part of town.
23. The homecoming parade wound through the town.
24. Bunches of balloons floated through the air.
25. The people threw flowers at the Coolville football players.
26. The famous musician promised the team a victory.
27. During the game, the Pied Piper raced from song to song.
28. The music played faster and louder.
29. The Pied Piper led the team to victory with this music.
30. The townspeople of Creepyville cried over the defeat of their Rats.

C. Application in Writing
Fairy Tale

Answers will vary. Check to see that students have correctly used at least five of the nouns as simple subjects in their fairy tales.

B. DRAFTING SKILL

Using Subjects and Verbs Creatively Find the simple subject and the verb in each sentence. Then rewrite the sentence. Keep the same simple subject and verb, but replace the other words to create a new fairy tale.

EXAMPLE The Pied Piper was a magical musician.
The Pied Piper was a rock-and-roll star.

16. The Pied Piper played a magical fife.
17. His music charmed people and animals.
18. One day, rats overran the town of Hamelin, Germany.
19. The number of rats grew quickly.
20. The people of Hamelin promised the Pied Piper a rich reward for his help.
21. Soon every street echoed with the Pied Piper's magical fife music.
22. The sound of the music drew rats from every house in Hamelin.
23. A great parade of rats wound its way to the river.
24. Bunches of rats floated down the river.
25. Then the selfish people threw the piper out of town without a cent.
26. Angrily, the musician promised revenge.
27. The Pied Piper raced from the city.
28. Years later, the magical fife music again played in the town.
29. This time the Pied Piper led all the children away.
30. The townspeople cried over the loss of their children.

C. APPLICATION IN WRITING

Fairy Tale Write a short fairy tale. Use at least five of the simple subjects below.

king	dragon	frog
forest	knight	princess
sword	horse	giant
apple	castle	cave
cottage	townspeople	countryside
crown	moon	raven

FOR MORE PRACTICE
See pages 367–368.

352 Grammar Handbook

CHECK POINT
MIXED REVIEW • PAGES 347–352

A. Create a chart with two columns. Label one column *Simple Subject* and the other *Verb*. Write the simple subject and the verb of each sentence in the correct columns.

1. In July 1940, the Tacoma Narrows Bridge opened in the state of Washington.
2. This bridge was 2,800 feet long.
3. On a windy day, the deck of the bridge bounced up and down.
4. Newspapers named the wild bridge Galloping Gertie.
5. On Sunday afternoons, traffic was very heavy.
6. Many people drove across the bridge just for fun.
7. The trip was like a ride on a roller coaster.
8. However, the fun stopped in November 1940.
9. The wind blew at forty-two miles an hour.
10. Suddenly, the bridge crashed into the water below.

B. Write each of the following sentences. Draw one line under the simple subject and two lines under the verb.

11. Over eight hundred years ago, architects in Pisa, Italy, designed a beautiful marble tower.
12. However, builders soon discovered a big mistake.
13. The foundation under the tower was only ten feet thick.
14. It was not strong enough for the huge tower.
15. As a result, the foundation sank into the ground.
16. The whole tower tilted to one side.
17. Over the centuries, the base of the tower settled even more.
18. Today this unusual building still tips sideways.
19. Tourists flock to the Leaning Tower of Pisa.
20. Many people consider it one of the wonders of the world.

Writing Theme
Famous Mistakes in Architecture

The Leaning Tower of Pisa, a bell tower, was begun in 1173 and completed between 1360 and 1370 in Pisa, Italy. Built on unstable soil, it tilts an additional twentieth of an inch each year.

CHECK POINT

Writing Theme: Famous Mistakes in Architecture

Other related areas students might wish to explore as writing topics include the following:

- the longest suspension bridge in the world
- the Taj Mahal in India
- the Eiffel Tower in Paris
- designing a dream house

MIXED REVIEW • PAGES 347–352

You may wish to use this activity to check students' mastery of the following concepts:

- the simple predicate, or verb
- the simple subject

A. Answers are shown on page. Student answers should be in columns.

B. Answers are shown on page.

THE SUBJECT IN DIFFERENT POSITIONS

Objectives

- To recognize subjects in unusual positions

Writing

- To vary the position of subjects in sentences

Teaching Strategies

INDIVIDUALIZING INSTRUCTION: KINESTHETIC LEARNERS Write the subject of each of the following sentences on blue index cards. Then write the rest of each sentence on a white card. Ask students to practice rearranging the cards to place the subject in different positions.

After the race, flowers bloomed.

Through the woods raced the deer.

Here are the award-winning books.

Among the crowd appeared the winners.

LINKING GRAMMAR AND WRITING To determine whether the students' writing needs more sentence variety, suggest that they read their drafts aloud to themselves or to a partner. If the word order in a string of sentences sounds monotonous, they may be able to move a prepositional phrase or an adverb to precede the subject.

HELPFUL HINT Explain to students that *here* and *there* are never the subjects of sentences, even though these words often begin complete thoughts.

Additional Resource

Grammar and Usage Practice Book, p. 7

THE SUBJECT IN DIFFERENT POSITIONS

The subject does not always come at the beginning of a sentence.

The subject is usually near the beginning of a sentence and before the verb. Writers, however, can change the order of sentences to add variety to their writing.

Animal paintings appear on the cave walls.
On the cave walls, animal paintings appear.
(The subject is near the end of the sentence but before the verb.)

On the cave walls appear animal paintings.
(The order of the subject and the verb is reversed.)

To find the subject of a sentence in which the order is unusual, first find the verb. Then ask *who* or *what* before the verb.

Who or what *appear? Paintings* appear.
Paintings is the subject of the sentence.

Writing TIP

Give your sentences more variety by putting the subjects of some sentences in different positions.

Sentences Beginning with *Here* and *There*

In a sentence beginning with the word *here* or *there,* the subject usually follows the verb.

There is the paintbrush.
Verb: *is*
Who or what is? paintbrush
Paintbrush is the subject of *is.*

Here are the drawings.
Verb: *are*
Who or what are? drawings
Drawings is the subject of *are.*

Practice Your Skills

A. CONCEPT CHECK

Subjects in Different Positions Write each of the following sentences. Draw one line under the subject of the verb and two lines under the verb.

1. There is a wonderful cave in southern France.
2. Here are the world's oldest paintings.
3. Scientists from all over the world study the paintings in the Grotte de Lascaux.
4. On the walls and ceilings are pictures of animals.
5. Everywhere are creations from the distant past.
6. Inside the dark cave, a scientist imagines a scene from twenty thousand years ago.
7. In the middle of the cave sits an ancient artist.
8. Beside the artist are hollow bones.
9. These bones are the artist's paintbrushes.
10. Near him is a torch.
11. By firelight the artist begins his work.
12. Patiently, the artist draws a buffalo.
13. For early people, rock paintings had a magic purpose.
14. For example, they meant good luck to hunters.
15. Even today, there is mysterious power in these pictures.

B. REVISION SKILL

Varying the Positions of Subjects Rewrite each sentence so that the subject comes after the verb.

16. Many examples of rock art are in southern Africa.
17. Many drawings are there from thousands of years ago.
18. Examples of rock art appear on the walls of cliffs in Rhodesia.
19. An animal scene is over here.
20. A deer comes from the forest.
21. A band of hunters gathers around the deer.
22. Bows and arrows are on the hunters' backs.
23. A huge rhinoceros is nearby.
24. Clouds of smoke are in the distance.
25. Other scenes of events in daily life are next to this drawing.

Writing Theme
Early Art

FOR MORE PRACTICE
See page 368.

Writing Theme: Early Art

Other related areas students might wish to explore as writing topics include the following:

- Egyptian tomb paintings
- Australian aboriginal art
- sculpture and painting in ancient Crete
- early cave painting at Altamira, Spain

Answers to Practice Your Skills

A. Concept Check
Subjects in Different Positions

Answers are shown on page.

B. Revision Skill
Varying the Positions of Subjects

Answers may vary slightly. Possible answers are given.

16. In southern Africa are many examples of rock art.
17. There are many drawings from thousands of years ago.
18. On the walls of cliffs in Rhodesia appear examples of rock art.
19. Over here is an animal scene.
20. From the forest comes a deer.
21. Around the deer gathers a band of hunters.
22. On the hunters' backs are bows and arrows.
23. Nearby is a huge rhinoceros.
24. In the distance are clouds of smoke.
25. Next to this drawing are other scenes of events in daily life.

FOUR KINDS OF SENTENCES

Objectives

- To identify the four kinds of sentences
- To use correct end punctuation for each kind of sentence

Writing

- To vary the kinds of sentences in a piece of writing

Teaching Strategies

KEY TO UNDERSTANDING: PUNCTUATION Remind students that both declarative and imperative sentences can end with periods, but interrogative sentences always end with a question mark and exclamatory sentences with an exclamation point. Some sentences such as *Watch out* can be either imperative or exclamatory. It is up to the writer to decide whether to use a period or an exclamation point, depending on what feeling is to be emphasized.

SPEAKING AND LISTENING Ask for volunteers to read aloud the dialogue in Exercise A. Encourage students to notice how the pitch and inflection of the voice change with different kinds of sentences.

Additional Resource

Grammar and Usage Practice Book, p. 8

Writing Theme: Towns in the Old West

Other related areas students might wish to explore as writing topics include the following:

- Dodge City, Kansas
- Wild Bill Hickok, frontier marshal
- Tombstone, Arizona
- mining for gold today

A. Concept Check
Identifying Kinds of Sentences

1. What is the name of this ghost town? Interrogative
2. Its name is Hamilton. Declarative
3. What a fantastic place this is! Exclamatory

FOUR KINDS OF SENTENCES

Writing **TIP**

Use different types of sentences to make your writing more interesting.

There are four types of sentences: **declarative, interrogative, imperative,** and **exclamatory.**

People use four types of sentences to express different kinds of thoughts and emotions. Sentences can state facts, ask questions, make requests, and show strong feelings.

Type of Sentence	Definition	Punctuation	Example
Declarative	tells or states something	.	The ghost town looks like a western movie set.
Interrogative	asks a question	?	Did you see those crumbling buildings?
Imperative	makes a request or gives an order	.	Imagine life in a ghost town.
Exclamatory	expresses strong feeling	!	This ghost town is amazing!

Practice Your Skills

Writing Theme
Towns in the Old West

A. CONCEPT CHECK

Identifying Kinds of Sentences Write each of the sentences in the following dialogue, adding the correct punctuation. Then label each sentence *Declarative, Interrogative, Imperative,* or *Exclamatory.*

1. JORGE: What is the name of this ghost town
2. LIN: Its name is Hamilton
3. What a fantastic place this is
4. JORGE: How long has the town been deserted
5. LIN: Hamilton has been empty since about 1870
6. JORGE: Why did everyone leave
7. LIN: The silver in the mines ran out

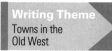

8. JORGE: Where were the mines located
9. LIN: Two of the biggest mines were in that mountain
10. JORGE: That certainly is a steep climb in this desert heat
11. Just imagine the hard life of the miners
12. LIN: Watch your step
13. The board on the sidewalk is loose
14. JORGE: Let's leave now
15. This place is just too spooky

B. PROOFREADING SKILL

Correcting Errors in Sentences Write the following paragraph, correcting errors in grammar, capitalization, punctuation, and spelling. Pay special attention to the punctuation of different kinds of sentences. (10 errors)

Read this newspaper headline from the 1870s! "Miners find gold!" Discoverys of gold and silver in the western states. Created new towns overnight. Why did many of these new towns later turn into ghost towns. After a while, the mines became empty? Than the settlers moved too other towns. However, Last Chance Gulch still exists today, this town is now Helena, montana. Find this city on a map of the united states.

C. APPLICATION IN WRITING

A Travel Brochure Pretend you live in a town next to a gold mine. Write a travel brochure describing your town. Use all four types of sentences in your brochure. Punctuate correctly.

FOR MORE PRACTICE
See pages 368-369.

A ghost town of the Old West

4. How long has the town been deserted? Interrogative
5. Hamilton has been empty since about 1870. Declarative
6. Why did everyone leave? Interrogative
7. The silver in the mines ran out. Declarative
8. Where were the mines located? Interrogative
9. Two of the biggest mines were in that mountain. Declarative
10. That certainly is a steep climb in this desert heat! Exclamatory
11. Just imagine the hard life of the miners. Imperative *or* Exclamatory(!)
12. Watch your step. Imperative *or* Exclamatory(!)
13. The board on the sidewalk is loose. Declarative
14. Let's leave now. Imperative
15. This place is just too spooky! Exclamatory *or* Declarative(.)

B. Proofreading Skill

Errors in proofreading exercises are counted as follows: (a) Each word is counted as one error. For example, a misspelled word is one error; two initials and a last name not capitalized are counted as three errors. (b) Run-on sentences and sentence fragments are each counted as one error, even though the correction involves both punctuation and capitalization.

Correcting Errors in Sentences

Errors are shown on page.

Read this newspaper headline from the 1870s. "Miners find gold!" Discoveries of gold and silver in the western states created new towns overnight. Why did many of these new towns later turn into ghost towns? After a while, the mines became empty. Then the settlers moved to other towns. However, Last Chance Gulch still exists today. This town is now Helena, Montana. Find this city on a map of the United States.

C. Application in Writing

A Travel Brochure

Answers will vary. Check to see that students have used and correctly punctuated all four types of sentences.

FINDING SUBJECTS IN DIFFERENT TYPES OF SENTENCES

Objectives

- To recognize subjects in interrogative, exclamatory, and imperative sentences

Writing

- To punctuate various kinds of sentences correctly

Teaching Strategies

HELPFUL HINT: EXCLAMATORY SENTENCES Point out that exclamatory sentences can have either normal or inverted word order. Give examples such as these:

That roller coaster is awesome!

Wow, was that ride fantastic!

Point out that the first sentence could be a declarative sentence. It is exclamatory because the writer wants to convey excitement or emotion.

HELPFUL HINT Finding the subject in interrogative sentences can be a bit tricky when the subject comes between parts of the verb: for example, *Did Bill go on that ride?* To identify the subject, students should rearrange the word order, turning a question into a declarative sentence.

INDIVIDUALIZING INSTRUCTION: AUDITORY LEARNERS Have these students read aloud the sentences in Exercise A. Encourage them to note the relationship between the emphasis and pitch of their voices and the different kinds of sentences, especially the rising pitch toward the end of interrogative sentences. Volunteers can extend this activity by reading aloud the items in Exercise B, reading first the original sentence, then the changed one, noting any differences in emphasis or pitch.

FINDING SUBJECTS IN DIFFERENT TYPES OF SENTENCES

The subject of an interrogative or exclamatory sentence may be difficult to find. First, rearrange the word order. Then follow the usual steps. In imperative sentences the subject *you* is usually understood.

Interrogative, exclamatory, and imperative sentences often have unusual word order. To find the subject of an interrogative sentence, change it to a declarative sentence. Then find the verb and ask *who* or *what* before it.

Interrogative Sentence	Is Bill afraid of roller coasters?
Declarative Sentence	Bill is afraid of roller coasters.
	Who is? Bill
	Bill is the subject of the verb *is.*

Find the subject of an exclamatory sentence in the same way. First, change it to a declarative sentence. Then find the verb and ask *who* or *what* before it.

Exclamatory Sentence	Was that ride fantastic!
Declarative Sentence	That ride was fantastic.
	What was? ride
	Ride is the subject of the verb *was.*

Most imperative sentences appear to have no subject.

Buy your ticket. Have fun.

In these sentences, *you* is understood to be the subject.

(you) Buy your ticket. (you) Have fun.

Sentence Diagraming For information about diagraming interrogative, exclamatory, and imperative sentences, see page 617.

358 Grammar Handbook

Practice Your Skills

A. CONCEPT CHECK

Subjects in Different Positions Write each of the following sentences. Draw a line under the subject of the verb. If the subject you is understood, write (*you*).

1. Listen to my news about this wild roller coaster. (you)
2. Have you ever heard of Greezed Lightnin'?
3. This exciting ride is at Astroworld in Houston, Texas.
4. It zooms at sixty miles an hour!
5. Are you ready for the thrill of your life?
6. Take an imaginary ride on Greezed Lightnin'. (you)
7. Here comes an eighty-foot loop!
8. Next, climb 138 feet in the air. (you)
9. Your face is as white as a ghost's!
10. Can you stop the screams?

B. REVISION SKILL

Varying the Types of Sentences Change each sentence to the kind described in parentheses. You will need to add or drop words in some of the sentences. Punctuate correctly.

11. Is "The Beast" the name of a roller coaster? (declarative)
12. It is in Kings Island, Ohio. (interrogative)
13. The Beast is terrifying. (exclamatory)
14. Passengers think about the eight scary turns. (imperative)
15. Imagine dropping 135 feet into a tunnel! (interrogative)

C. PROOFREADING SKILL

Correcting Errors in Punctuation Write the following paragraph from a letter, correcting all errors in grammar, capitalization, punctuation, and spelling. Pay special attention to the punctuation of different kinds of sentences. (8 errors)

What a great day we had? Do you remember my freind annie. She and me rode our bikes to the amusement park. The best ride was the roller coaster, it was really scary! The roller coaster was over five storys high. Was it ever fast.

Writing Theme
Roller Coasters

FOR MORE PRACTICE
See pages 368–369.

Additional Resource

Grammar and Usage Practice Book, p. 9

Writing Theme: Roller Coasters

Other related areas students might wish to explore as writing topics include the following:

- When is it fun to be scared?
- a ride that has not yet been invented
- George Washington Gale Ferris and his wheel
- state fairs

Answers to Practice Your Skills

A. Concept Check
Subjects in Different Positions

Answers are shown on page.

B. Revision Skill
Varying the Types of Sentences

Answers will vary. Sample answers are given.

11. "The Beast" is the name of a roller coaster.
12. Is it in Kings Island, Ohio?
13. How terrifying The Beast is!
14. Think about the eight scary turns.
15. Can you imagine dropping 135 feet into a tunnel?

C. Proofreading Skill
Correcting Errors in Punctuation

Errors are shown on page.

What a great day we had! Do you remember my friend Annie? She and I rode our bikes to the amusement park. The best ride was the roller coaster. It was really scary! The roller coaster was over five stories high. Was it ever fast!

CHECK POINT

Writing Theme: Twins

Other related areas students might wish to explore as writing topics include the following:

- nonidentical, or fraternal, twins
- twins in scientific research
- twins in the movies or literature
- family members (or growing up) as twins

MIXED REVIEW • PAGES 354–359

You may wish to use this activity to check students' mastery of the following concepts:

- the subject in different positions
- four kinds of sentences
- finding subjects in different types of sentences

A. Subjects are shown on page.
1. Interrogative
2. Interrogative
3. Imperative
4. Imperative
5. Interrogative
6. Declarative
7. Interrogative
8. Declarative
9. Exclamatory
10. Imperative
11. Interrogative
12. Declarative
13. Declarative
14. Declarative
15. Imperative

B. Answers are shown on page.

Writing Theme
Twins

CHECK POINT

MIXED REVIEW • PAGES 354–359

A. Write each sentence and label it *Declarative, Interrogative, Imperative,* or *Exclamatory.* Underline the subject of each sentence. If the subject *you* is understood write (*you*).

1. Are you interested in twins?
2. Do you like festivals?
3. Find out about a really fun event. (you)
4. First, look at a map of Ohio. (you)
5. Can you find the town of Twinsburg?
6. This little town is near Cleveland, Ohio.
7. Why is this town so special?
8. Since 1976, identical twins have come to Twinsburg each summer for a festival.
9. In 1989, a total of 2,356 sets of twins came here!
10. Picture that many twins in one place. (you)
11. How unusual is this festival?
12. The twins take part in parades and magic acts.
13. There are also more than a hundred contests for twins at the festival.
14. One of the contests is for twins with the widest smiles.
15. Imagine the happy winners. (you)

B. Write the subject and the verb of each of the following sentences.

16. Here is the story of the "Jim twins."
17. Different parents raised them.
18. After thirty-nine years, they finally met each other.
19. Besides their appearance, these twins had many other things in common.
20. Here are some examples.
21. In each of their driveways was the same kind of blue car.
22. Among the favorite hobbies of each twin was woodworking.
23. In the late afternoon, both men got headaches.
24. There were also other similarities.
25. They both named their dog Toy.

360 Grammar Handbook

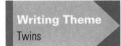

COMPOUND SUBJECTS

A **compound subject** has two or more parts.

Notice that the subject of each sentence below has two parts.

Subject	Predicate
Nick and *Elena*	learned about animals.
Birds and *snakes*	are their favorites.

When a subject has two or more parts, it is called a **compound subject.** *Compound* means "having more than one part."

The word *and* is often used to join the parts of a compound subject, but the word *or* can also be used. The words *and* and *or* are conjunctions. A **conjunction** is a word used to join sentence parts.

Sometimes a subject has three or more parts. Then use commas to separate the parts. Place a conjunction before the last part. Look at this example:

Owls, raccoons, and *squirrels* sometimes live in hollow logs.

Compound subjects can make your writing and speaking flow smoothly. Use them to combine sentences that repeat similar ideas.

Awkward	Moose use their antlers as weapons. Deer use their antlers as weapons.
Better	Deer and moose use their antlers as weapons.
Awkward	Clams and oysters have hard shells. Mussels also have hard shells.
Better	Clams, oysters, and mussels have hard shells.

Grammar TIP

When a compound subject has three or more parts, use a comma before the conjunction. See page 574 in Handbook 43, "Punctuation," for more about punctuating compound subjects.

COMPOUND SUBJECTS

Objectives

- To identify and form compound subjects

Writing

- To combine sentences and form compound subjects and thus eliminate repetition

Teaching Strategies

KEY TO UNDERSTANDING: CONJUNCTIONS Tell students that although the conjunction *and* or the conjunction *or* can be used to link the two parts of a compound subject, these conjunctions cannot be used interchangeably. To illustrate this point, put the following sentences on the board and have students compare their meanings.

Elena *and* Josie will greet the guests.

Elena *or* Josie will greet the guests.

MODELING On the board, write the two sentences in items 12 and 13 of Exercise B on page 362. Then lead students through the process of identifying the compound subject in each item: *bees and butterflies* in item 12; *spiders and ants* in item 13. Show students that combining the subjects in item 13 requires that they choose one of the two predicates: *grow to a giant size* or *grow huge.* Point out that since the meaning of the two predicates is essentially the same, they will not lose any meaningful information by combining the sentences.

COLLABORATIVE OPPORTUNITY Form students into pairs. Have one partner write a sentence with a two-part compound subject on an index card. Then have the other partner expand the first sentence into a three-part subject and write the new sentence underneath the first one. Ask the first student to check the punctuation in the second sentence, and then have the other partner continue the process by writing another sentence with a two-part subject.

Additional Resource

Grammar and Usage Practice Book, p. 10

Writing Theme: The Animal World

Other related areas students might wish to explore as writing topics include the following:

- birds' nests
- beaver dams
- termite mounds
- division of labor in ant colonies

Answers to Practice Your Skills

A. Concept Check
Compound Subjects

Answers are shown on page.

B. Drafting Skill
Sentence Combining

Combined sentences may vary. Sample answers are given.

11. Compound subject: Insects, birds; verb: thrive
12. Bees and beautiful butterflies are everywhere.
13. Spiders and ants grow to a giant size.
14. Hummingbirds and sunbirds sip nectar from flowers.
15. Compound subject: birds, snakes; verb: prey
16. Compound subject: Snakes, lizards, frogs; verb: live
17. Anteaters and opossums hang by their tails.
18. Monkeys and squirrels leap from tree to tree.
19. Compound subject: Deer, antelope; verb: roam
20. Leopards and tigers prowl through the jungle at night.

Writing Theme
The Animal World

Practice Your Skills

A. CONCEPT CHECK

Compound Subjects Write each of the following sentences. Draw two lines under each verb and one line under each part of the compound subject.

1. Carpenters and architects exist in the animal world.
2. Many birds and other animals are excellent builders.
3. Grass, twigs, and leaves are the materials for birds' nests.
4. Birds' beaks and feet make handy tools.
5. Rats and mice build nests in different places.
6. Cracks and corners often become their homes.
7. Feathers, leaves, and bits of fur line their nests.
8. Their jaws, teeth, and claws are their tools.
9. Chipmunks and prairie dogs build underground tunnels.
10. Their paws and noses act like shovels.

B. DRAFTING SKILL

Sentence Combining Find the sentences with compound subjects, and write the parts of the subject and the verb of each. Combine the sentences in items 12, 13, 14, 17, 18, and 20 to form single sentences with compound subjects. You may need to change or drop some words as you combine the sentences.

11. Insects and birds thrive in the rain forest.
12. Bees are everywhere. Beautiful butterflies are everywhere.
13. Spiders grow to a giant size. Ants also grow huge.
14. Hummingbirds sip nectar from flowers. Sunbirds also get their nectar this way.
15. Large birds and snakes prey on smaller animals.
16. Snakes, lizards, and frogs live among the branches.
17. Anteaters hang by their tails. Opossums also hang by their tails.
18. Monkeys leap from tree to tree. Squirrels also leap among the tree branches.
19. Deer and antelope roam the forest floor.
20. Leopards prowl through the jungle at night. Tigers prowl through the jungle at night.

362 Grammar Handbook

COMPOUND PREDICATES

A **compound predicate** has two or more parts.

Notice that the predicate of the sentence below has two parts.

Subject	**Predicate**
King Arthur	*grabbed the sword* and *pulled it from the stone.*

When a predicate has two or more parts, it is called a **compound predicate.** When a predicate has three or more parts, use commas to separate the parts. Place the conjunction before the last part, as in this sentence:

King Arthur *stood before the Round Table, looked at his knights,* and *talked about his plans.*

Compound predicates help make your writing and speaking flow smoothly. Use them to combine sentences with similar ideas.

Awkward	King Arthur rode toward Sir Lancelot. King Arthur welcomed him home.
Better	King Arthur rode toward Sir Lancelot and welcomed him home.

Sentence Diagraming For information about diagraming compound subjects and compound predicates, see page 618.

Practice Your Skills

A. CONCEPT CHECK

Compound Predicates Write the following sentences. Draw one line under the subject, or subjects of each sentence. Then draw two lines under each verb of the compound predicate.

1. King Uther lived in a castle and ruled all of Britain.
2. He and his wife had a baby son and named him Arthur.

Writing Theme
The Legend of King Arthur

COMPOUND PREDICATES

Objectives

- To identify and form compound predicates

Writing

- To combine sentences and form compound predicates and thus eliminate repetition

Teaching Strategies

KEY TO UNDERSTANDING: COMPOUND SENTENCE PARTS
Point out to students that the process of forming two-part and three-part compound predicates closely resembles that of forming compound subjects. Encourage them to experiment with creating sentences with both compound subjects and compound predicates, such as the following:

King Arthur and Sir Lancelot entered the hall and sat at the Round Table.

INDIVIDUALIZING INSTRUCTIONS: ADVANCED STUDENTS Have these students create original sentences that use the conjunctions *or* or *but* to join a two-part predicate. Start the students off with some model sentences like the following:

John pitched *or* played third base.

Bears eat berries *but* prefer honey.

Writing Theme: The Legend of King Arthur
Other related areas students might wish to explore as writing topics include the following:

- the training of a knight
- magicians, wizards, and witches
- another hero with a mysterious origin
- warriors in other countries, such as the samurai of Japan

Answers to Practice Your Skills

A. Concept Check
Compound Predicates
Answers are shown on page.

Additional Resource
Grammar and Usage Practice Book, p. 11

B. Drafting Skill
Sentence Combining

Answers may vary. Sample answers are shown below.

13. King Lot gathered an army and attacked Arthur.
14. During the battle Merlin appeared before Arthur, told him about the powers of the magic sword, and then vanished.
15. Arthur drew his magic sword and leaped toward his enemies.
16. Light flashed from the sword and blinded King Lot and his troops.
17. King Lot and his army fled from the battlefield.
18. Arthur and his loyal followers celebrated the victory.

3. King Uther worried about Arthur and asked Merlin the Magician for advice.
4. Merlin thought for a moment and then advised his king.
5. "You send Arthur away and tell no one about him."
6. Merlin took the baby and placed him in Sir Ector's home.
7. Sir Ector cared for Arthur and taught him about knighthood.
8. After King Uther's death, Sir Ector and Arthur left their home and went to a tournament of knights.
9. At the tournament Arthur saw a sword in a stone and pulled it out.
10. Before Arthur, many brave knights also wanted the sword and pulled at it with all their might.
11. Sir Ector saw the sword in Arthur's hand and told him about King Uther.
12. Arthur finally learned the secret of his birth and became the new king.

B. DRAFTING SKILL

Sentence Combining Combine each of the following sentence pairs into one sentence. Use a conjunction to form a compound subject or a compound predicate.

EXAMPLE King Lot wanted Arthur's lands. Lot's sons also wanted Arthur's lands.
King Lot and his sons wanted Arthur's lands.

13. King Lot gathered an army. King Lot attacked Arthur.
14. During the battle Merlin appeared before Arthur. Merlin told him about the powers of the magic sword and then vanished.
15. Arthur drew his magic sword. Arthur leaped toward his enemies.
16. Light flashed from the sword. The light blinded King Lot and his troops.
17. King Lot fled from the battlefield. His army fled from the battlefield.
18. Arthur celebrated the victory. His loyal followers celebrated the victory.

FOR MORE PRACTICE
See page 369.

CHECK POINT
MIXED REVIEW • PAGES 361–364

Make two columns on your paper. Label them *Subjects* and *Verbs.* Write the subjects of the following sentences in the first column. Write the verbs in the second column.

1. Sequoyah's mother, his uncles, and other people in his village taught him the Cherokee way of life.
2. Traditions and laws were important to the Cherokees.
3. As a young man, Sequoyah fought in battles and was a brave warrior.
4. Friends and relatives admired his courage.
5. Sequoyah also painted pictures and made silver objects.
6. He trapped and hunted animals too.
7. One day Sequoyah and his friends were in the forest.
8. They met and talked with white hunters.
9. One white hunter had a book and read from it.
10. The book and its strange symbols amazed Sequoyah and made him curious.
11. The Cherokees and other Native Americans had no written language.
12. Sequoyah studied the language and created a new alphabet, with a symbol for each syllable in the Cherokee language.
13. English, Greek, and Hebrew were the sources of his symbols.
14. Sequoyah worked on the alphabet for twelve years and finished it in 1821.
15. Both children and older people learned the new Cherokee alphabet easily.
16. Cherokee leaders translated treaties and read them to the people.
17. In 1828, the Cherokees started their own newspaper and called it the *Cherokee Phoenix.*
18. Sequoyah's hard work and creativity earned him respect.
19. The Cherokees honored Sequoyah and named him their president.
20. During the rest of his life, Sequoyah traveled to different countries and studied different languages.

Writing Theme
The Cherokee Language

CHECK POINT

Writing Theme: The Cherokee Language

Other related areas students might wish to explore as writing topics include the following:

- the "Trail of Tears" (1838)
- the Cherokee Bible
- other Native American languages

MIXED REVIEW • PAGES 361–364

You may wish to use this activity to check students' mastery of the following concepts:

- compound subjects
- compound predicates

Answers are shown on page. Student answers should be in columns.

GRAMMAR HANDBOOK 34

ADDITIONAL PRACTICE

Each of these exercises correlates to a section of Handbook 34, "Understanding Sentences." The exercises may be used for more practice, for reteaching, or for review of the concepts presented.

Additional Resource

Grammar and Usage Practice Book, pp. 13–14

Writing Theme: The Western Frontier

Other related areas students might wish to explore as writing topics include the following:

- Rocky Mountain passes
- Willa Cather, Nebraska novelist
- famous sheriffs of the Old West
- Hollywood westerns
- the Homestead Act (1862)

A. Recognizing Complete Sentences

Some answers will vary. Sample answers are given.

1. Sentence
2. Not a Sentence; Unlike today's circuses, frontier circuses traveled in wagons from town to town.
3. Sentence
4. Not a Sentence; A parade of circus animals and colorful wagons marched down the main street.
5. Not a Sentence; People on the sides of the street watched the brass bands and the elephants.
6. Not a Sentence; Wild animals in their cages growled at the spectators.
7. Not a Sentence; Many children followed the parade to the edge of town.
8. Sentence
9. Sentence

GRAMMAR HANDBOOK 34

Writing Theme
The Western Frontier

A. Recognizing Complete Sentences Label each group of words *Sentence* or *Not a Sentence.* Add words to make the incomplete sentences complete.

1. In the 1870s, circuses were very popular on the Western frontier.
2. Unlike today's circuses, traveled in wagons from town to town.
3. Pioneer families loved the circus.
4. A parade of circus animals and colorful wagons.
5. Watched the brass bands and the elephants.
6. Wild animals in their cages.
7. Followed the parade to the edge of town.
8. Then workers put up the big tent for the circus acts.
9. Some children earned free tickets to the circus.
10. Did chores for the circus performers.
11. Watered the elephants, for example.
12. The townspeople applauded the performers.
13. A tightrope walker in a beautiful costume.
14. Silly clowns in enormous shoes.
15. A lion tamer with a whip.

B. Finding Complete Subjects and Predicates Write each of the following sentences. Draw one line under the complete subject and two lines under the complete predicate.

16. A wagon train headed west of the Mississippi River on May 19, 1841.
17. Seventy brave pioneers went on a dangerous journey to California.
18. They traveled along the Oregon Trail.
19. Herds of cattle followed closely behind the wagons.
20. The captain of the wagon train gave a signal at sunset.
21. The wagons left the trail one by one.
22. They formed a large circle.
23. Families started campfires for the evening meal inside the circle.
24. Some boys played tag after dinner.
25. Other children read books by the glow of the campfires.

10. Not a Sentence; They did chores for the circus performers.
11. Not a Sentence; Young boys watered the elephants, for example.
12. Sentences
13. Not a Sentence; A tightrope walker in a beautiful costume performed dangerous tricks.
14. Not a Sentence; Silly clowns in enormous shoes sprayed one another with water.
15. Not a Sentence; A lion tamer with a whip made lions jump through fiery hoops.

B. Finding Complete Subjects and Predicates

Answers are shown on page.

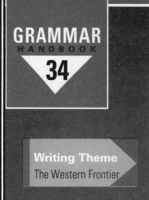

C. Correcting Fragments and Run-ons Add words to each fragment to make a complete sentence. Rewrite each run-on as separate sentences. Write *Correct* if the sentence is correct.

26. Some advertisements twisted the truth about the West.
27. Newspaper editors also spread fabulous stories they made the West seem like a place in a dream.
28. Promised people in the East a better life.
29. The valleys were greener the skies were bluer.
30. Beets grew three feet thick, turnips measured five feet around.
31. Golden wheat with stems as thick as canes.
32. Mines with gold and silver.
33. Headed west in search of riches and adventure.
34. They believed the advertisements and newspaper stories.
35. However, few people became wealthy, many settlers on the Western frontier were poor.

D. Finding the Verb Write the verb in each sentence.

36. Many African Americans were pioneers during the 1800s.
37. For example, Biddy Mason blazed new trails for others.
38. She found adventure and freedom on the Western frontier.
39. Because of her courage, she escaped slavery in the South.
40. Her journey began in Mississippi during the early 1850s.
41. She walked all the way to California behind a wagon train.
42. Slavery was against the law in California.
43. In this free state, Biddy Mason finally won her freedom.
44. Later, she became a rich and powerful woman.
45. She owned businesses and land in Los Angeles.

E. Finding the Verb and Its Subject Write each of the following sentences. Draw two lines under the verb and one line under the subject of the verb.

46. Pioneers in a Kansas town celebrated on July 4, 1871.
47. Harriet wrote about the day's events in her diary.
48. At sunrise a soldier fired a cannon in the center of town.
49. Families in the area decorated their wagons and buggies.
50. Even horses wore tiny American flags.

C. Correcting Fragments and Run-ons

Some answers will vary. Sample answers are given.

26. Correct
27. Newspaper editors also spread fabulous stories. They made the West seem like a place in a dream.
28. These tales about the West promised people in the East a better life.
29. The valleys were greener. The skies were bluer.
30. Beets grew three feet thick. Turnips measured five feet around.
31. Golden wheat with stems as thick as canes covered the fields.
32. Mines with gold and silver offered the chance for wealth.
33. Many pioneers headed west in search of riches and adventure.
34. Correct
35. However, few people became wealthy. Many settlers on the Western frontier were poor.

D. Finding the Verb

Answers are shown on page.

E. Finding the Verb and Its Subject

Answers are shown on page.

F. Finding Subjects in Different Positions
Answers are shown on page.

G. Identifying Kinds of Sentences
73. Interrogative, question mark
74. Interrogative, question mark
75. Imperative, period
76. Imperative, period
77. Declarative, period

51. The settlers rode into town for a day of fun.
52. By the courthouse the sheriff gave a patriotic speech.
53. Then the choir sang "The Star-Spangled Banner."
54. Many people brought food for a big picnic.
55. After lunch the boys played games.
56. Some men competed in wagon races and horse races.
57. At night, fireworks burst in the sky.

F. Finding Subjects in Different Positions Write the subject of each of the following sentences. Then tell whether it comes *before* or *after* the verb.

58. Here are some facts about education on the frontier. A
59. At first there were no schools in the wilderness. A
60. A pioneer woman usually taught boys and girls at home in her cabin. B
61. Around her gathered a circle of children. A
62. With a stick she scratched out numbers on the dirt floor. B
63. Her students learned arithmetic and other subjects. B
64. Later, pioneers built one-room schoolhouses. B
65. There were many one-room schoolhouses in the Wild West.
66. Outside the schoolhouse door hung an iron bell. A
67. Each morning the teacher rang the bell loudly. B
68. Then the students rushed to their seats. B
69. Along one side were rows of hard wooden benches. A
70. In the front of the room was a blackboard. A
71. Near the center of the room was a big potbellied stove. A
72. There were students of all ages in the same classroom. A

G. Identifying Kinds of Sentences Label each of the following sentences *Declarative, Imperative, Interrogative,* or *Exclamatory.* Then write the correct punctuation mark for the end of each sentence.

73. What was life like in Granite, Oklahoma
74. Are you ready for an adventure in history
75. Then take an imaginary journey in a time machine
76. Pretend you are a visitor to this frontier town
77. Pioneer families stop at the shops along Main Street

78. How busy the general store is
79. Horses gallop through the middle of town
80. So much action happens here

H. Finding Subjects and Verbs in Sentences Write each of the following sentences. Draw two lines under the verb and one line under the subject of the verb. If the subject *you* is understood, write it in parentheses.

81. Imagine a square dance in the 1800s. (you)
82. Where is your partner?
83. Find one in a hurry! (you)
84. What a fun time awaits you!
85. Listen to the caller. (you)
86. "Are you all ready?"
87. "Swing your partner round and round." (you)
88. "Form a star and then a chain." (you)
89. "Now stampede!" (you)
90. How loudly the dancers stamp their feet!

I. Finding Compound Subjects and Verbs Write each of the following sentences. Draw two lines under the verb(s) and one line under the subject(s).

91. Pioneer boys and girls had many chores.
92. On an ordinary day, most parents and their children woke up at four o'clock in the morning.
93. Younger children fed the chickens, gathered twigs, and picked berries.
94. Older children plowed the fields, planted the crops, and carried buckets of water.
95. Usually boys and their fathers worked in the fields.
96. In contrast, girls helped their mothers and worked at home.
97. They baked bread, washed clothes, and stitched embroidery.
98. Margaret Mitchell and her family were pioneers in Kansas during the 1870s.
99. As a young girl, she and her sisters trapped wild turkeys and hunted wolves.
100. Margaret, her parents, and her sisters built a log cabin.

78. Exclamatory, exclamation point
79. Declarative, period
80. Exclamatory, exclamation point; *or* Declarative, period

H. Finding Subjects and Verbs in Sentences
Answers are shown on page.

I. Finding Compound Subjects and Verbs
Answers are shown on page.

GRAMMAR HANDBOOK 34

REVIEW

These exercises may be used as a mixed review or as an informal evaluation of the skills presented in Handbook 34, "Understanding Sentences."

Additional Resources

Grammar and Usage Practice Book, p. 15
Tests and Writing Assessment Prompts, Mastery Test, pp. 9–12
Elaboration, Revision, and Proofreading Practice, p. 23

Writing Theme: Exploring Places

Other related areas students might wish to explore as writing topics include the following:

- Francisco Coronado (1510–1544), Spanish explorer
- Prince Henry the Navigator of Portugal (1394–1460)
- Jacques Cartier (1491–1557), French explorer in Canada

A. Subjects and Predicates
Answers are shown on page.

B. Fragments and Run-ons
Some answers may vary. Sample answers are given.

GRAMMAR HANDBOOK 34

Writing Theme
Exploring Places

A. Subjects and Predicates Write the italicized words in the following sentences. Label these words *Subject* or *Predicate.*

1. Your plane *circles above a snowy field.* P
2. You *see a land of lakes and streams from your window.* P
3. *Not a single road* is visible anywhere. S
4. *This huge, lonely, and wild land* is the tundra. S
5. The tundra *stretches north to the ice fields of the Arctic.* P
6. Your plane *lands near an icy patch of land.* P
7. With several other people, *you* explore this unusual place. S
8. Very few trees *grow here because of the cold weather.* P
9. However, *wild animals* roam everywhere. S
10. *Some animals, such as arctic hares and polar bears,* blend in with the snowy background. S
11. Reindeer *graze on the short grasses.* P
12. *A gray wolf* howls in the distance. S
13. Gulls *build their nests on the arctic cliffs.* P
14. Along the coast, *walruses* float on blocks of ice. S
15. *They* use their long white tusks as giant hooks. S

B. Fragments and Run-ons Label each numbered group of words *Sentence, Fragment,* or *Run-on.* Then correct the fragments and run-ons.

[16]Two deep-sea divers explored a cave off the eastern coast of Mexico. [17]One diver was a photographer, the other diver was a scientist. [18]Suddenly, a shark. [19]Held a movie camera in front of the shark. [20]The shark almost bumped the photographer's face mask. [21]The camera surprised the shark it remained very still. [22]Stared peacefully at the divers. [23]The shark's two dozen sharp teeth in the front of its lower jaw. [24]Sharks sometimes attack people. [25]However, the sharks in these caves are gentle their behavior here is very odd.

[26]Carlos Garcia discovered these caves and their unusually calm visitors, at first, the sharks seemed dead. [27]Looked like a graveyard for sharks. [28]Actually, these caves are shark "hotels" under the sea. [29]Sharks visit these caves then they become sleepy. [30]Provide a restful place for sharks.

16. Sentence
17. Run-on; One diver was a photographer. The other diver was a scientist.
18. Fragment; Suddenly, a shark floated near the divers.
19. Fragment; The photographer held a movie camera in front of the shark.
20. Sentence
21. Run-on; The camera surprised the shark. It remained very still.
22. Fragment; The shark stared peacefully at the divers.
23. Fragment; The shark's two dozen sharp teeth in the front of its lower jaw were scary.
24. Sentence
25. Run-on; However, the sharks in these caves are gentle. Their behavior here is very odd.
26. Run-on; Carlos Garcia discovered these caves and their unusually calm visitors. At first, the sharks seemed dead.
27. Fragment; The caves looked like a graveyard for sharks.
28. Sentence
29. Run-on; Sharks visit these caves. Then they become sleepy.
30. Fragment; The caves provide a restful place for sharks.

C. Simple Subjects and Verbs Write the simple subject and verb of each sentence.

31. You follow a sandy path to the top of a hill.
32. At the top, great waves of sand seem endless.
33. These hills of sand are dunes on the Oregon coast.
34. The ocean piles the sand into huge dunes along the coast.
35. Their form changes often.
36. Violent winter winds reshape the dunes almost overnight.
37. Many dunes even "sing."
38. Sometimes the sand shifts in the wind.
39. Then the grains of sand brush across one another.
40. The movement sounds squeaky.

D. Types of Sentences Label each complete sentence *Declarative, Interrogative, Imperative,* or *Exclamatory.* Correct the sentence fragments.

41. Explore the seas with Jacques-Yves Cousteau.
42. Discovered families of octopuses in a bay south of France.
43. Cousteau named this area Octopus City.
44. Dive beneath the ocean's surface.
45. What a strange world this is!
46. Where are the octopuses' homes?
47. Holes under those piles of rocks.
48. Is the octopus a terrible monster?
49. Frightens many people because of its scary appearance.
50. However, the octopus is really a very shy creature.

E. Subjects in Different Positions Write each of the following sentences. Draw one line under the simple subject and two lines under the verb. Write understood subjects of imperative sentences in parentheses.

51. How adventurous are you?
52. Are you ready for a trip to the Southwest?
53. Explore the desert in Arizona. (you)
54. Here is some important advice.
55. Bring canteens of water. (you)

C. Simple Subjects and Verbs
Answers are shown on page.

D. Types of Sentences
Corrected fragments may vary. Sample answers are shown below.
41. Imperative
42. He discovered families of octopuses in a bay south of France
43. Declarative
44. Imperative
45. Exclamatory
46. Interrogative
47. Holes under those piles of rocks are their secret hiding places.
48. Interrogative
49. The octopus frightens many people because of its scary appearance.
50. Declarative

E. Subjects in Different Positions
Answers are shown on page.

56. Wear long pants, high boots, and a hat with a brim. (you)
57. Before your eyes stretches a beautiful desert.
58. How weird it looks!
59. The desert reminds me of a strange planet.
60. There are almost no trees.
61. Only ten inches of rain fall here every year.
62. How strong the sun is!
63. Are you too hot?
64. Under those rocks is a shady place.
65. Be careful! (you)
66. Nearby is a rattlesnake.
67. The sharp fangs on that snake are really scary!
68. Where are the other animals in the desert?
69. See all the different holes in the ground. (you)
70. Creatures in the desert stay cool underground.

F. Compound Subjects and Compound Predicates
Combine each group of sentences into one sentence by making a compound subject or a compound predicate.

71. You walk out on this glacier. You inspect it.
72. The beauty is unmistakable. The power is unmistakable.
73. The blue and green colors are lovely. The shapes are lovely.
74. Great cracks develop in the ice. Towers develop in the ice.
75. Glaciers covered much of North America during the Ice Age. Glaciers shaped the land.
76. Glaciers cut valleys. Glaciers dug lakes. Glaciers carved mountains.
77. Alaska still has glaciers. Canada still has glaciers. Some Rocky Mountain states still have glaciers.
78. Mountains are the homes of today's glaciers. Polar regions are the homes of today's glaciers.
79. Glaciers begin as mounds of snow. Glaciers grow slowly.
80. Snow falls. It builds up each year.
81. The snow gets thicker. It packs into ice.
82. The ice slides downhill. The ice forms a glacier.
83. You go to the glacier's edge. You see a mound of gravel.
84. The glacier scraped up rock. The glacier crushed it.
85. Only heat stops glaciers. Only the sea stops glaciers.

F. Compound Subjects and Compound Predicates

71. You walk out on this glacier and inspect it.
72. The beauty and power are unmistakable.
73. The blue and green colors and the shapes are lovely.
74. Great cracks and towers develop in the ice.
75. Glaciers covered much of North America during the Ice Age and shaped the land.
76. Glaciers cut valleys, dug lakes, and carved mountains.
77. Alaska, Canada, and some Rocky Mountain states still have glaciers.
78. Mountains and polar regions are the homes of today's glaciers.
79. Glaciers begin as mounds of snow and grow slowly.
80. Snow falls and builds up each year.
81. The snow gets thicker and packs into ice.
82. The ice slides downhill and forms a glacier.
83. You go to the glacier's edge and see a mound of gravel.
84. The glacier scraped up rock and crushed it.
85. Only heat and the sea stop glaciers.

WRITING CONNECTIONS

Elaboration, Revision, and Proofreading

Revise the following draft about a personal experience by using the directions at the bottom of the page. Then proofread your revision for errors in grammar, capitalization, punctuation, and spelling. Pay special attention to sentence fragments and run-ons.

[1]Lewis and I were always alike. [2]We were the same age. [3]Had the same interests. [4]We were even the same size. [5]We loved to play basketball against each other for hours at a time the games were always close. [6]My favorite player is Michael Jordan. [7]However, last year Lewis began to grow. [8]He was beating me all the time. [9]At first it made me mad. [10]I accused him of cheating on the score. [11]I said he was fouling me, even when he wasn't. [12]I couldn't beleive that he played basketball better than I did. [13]My attitude changed last labor day, when our familys got together for a picnic. [14]I looked at Lewis's parents and brothers, I noticed something for the first time. [15]Everyone in his family is about a head taller than everyone in mine. [16]The problem isn't that Lewis is better than I am. [17]He's bigger. [18]His height and wieght are things I cant change.

1. Combine sentences 2 and 3 to correct the sentence fragment.
2. Add the transition word "Soon" to the beginning of sentence 8 to make the order of events clearer.
3. Add the phrase "than I am by six inches and twenty-five pounds" to sentence 17.
4. Delete the sentence that doesn't belong.
5. Divide the passage into two paragraphs.

Personal and Expressive Writing

Writing in your journal gives you a chance to explore your thoughts and to record your experiences. (See Workshop 1.) When you revise journal entries for others to read, you need to polish your rough ideas. Make sure that every sentence expresses a complete thought. Correct sentence fragments and run-ons, which may confuse your readers.

WRITING CONNECTIONS

Elaboration, Revision, and Proofreading

This activity will allow students to see some of the concepts presented in this handbook at work in a piece of personal and expressive writing. By revising and proofreading this passage, students will have the chance to correct sentence fragments and run-on sentences and to combine sentences.

You might have students work in small groups to revise the passage. Then discuss the completed revision with the entire class. Revisions may vary slightly. Typical revisions are shown below. Elements involving change are shown in boldface.

Lewis and I were always alike. **We were the same age and had the same interests.** We were even the same size. We loved to play basketball against each other for hours at a time. The games were always close. ~~**My favorite player is Michael Jordan.**~~ However, last year Lewis began to grow. **Soon** he was beating me all the time. At fist it made me mad. I accused him of cheating on the score. I said he was fouling me, even when he wasn't. I couldn't believe that he played basketball better than I did.

My attitude changed last Labor Day, when our families got together for a picnic. I looked at Lewis's parents and brothers. I noticed something for the first time. Everyone in his family is about a head taller than everyone in mine. The problem isn't that Lewis is better than I am. **He's bigger than I am by six inches and twenty-five pounds.** His height and weight are things I can't change.

SKETCH BOOK

Objective

- To use visual prompts and writing prompts as springboards to informal writing

WRITING WARM-UPS

These ungraded, spontaneous journal activities can be used imaginatively to introduce the concepts in this handbook. Suggest that students choose one prompt to respond to and that they save their responses in their writing folders.

You might begin by discussing the funny names and double meanings of the signs in the illustration. This leads naturally to the first prompt, in which students invent a fictional name for a town. Students using the other two prompts might also wish to include funny names as part of their writings.

SKETCH BOOK

- Invent your own town. Give it a name and then explain the meaning of the name.
- Make up the setting for a science fiction story. Write about the weird and wonderful objects in your setting.
- Imagine you have discovered the royal tomb of an Inca ruler. Tell about the fascinating artifacts you have found within it.

Understanding Nouns

GRAMMAR HANDBOOK 35

- What Are Nouns?
- Common and Proper Nouns
- Singular and Plural Nouns
- Nouns That Show Possession

A town can have an unusual name (Muleshoe, Texas) or a plain name (The Plains, Ohio). The names of persons and things can be just as simple or fancy. Dinosaur, Colorado, is a place. A dinosaur is (or was) a thing. Both names are nouns. You need nouns to name the people, places, things, and ideas you write about.

In this handbook you will study the different types of nouns. You will learn how you can use them to make your writing precise and interesting.

GRAMMAR HANDBOOK 35

Understanding Nouns

Objectives

- To identify nouns
- To distinguish between common and proper nouns
- To distinguish between singular and plural nouns
- To form plural nouns correctly
- To identify nouns that show possession
- To form possessive nouns correctly

Writing

- To use nouns that make writing more specific and precise
- To use proper nouns and possessive nouns correctly in writing

INTRODUCING THE HANDBOOK

Invite students to imagine what the world would be like if things didn't have names. They would have to point at everything. Warnings of danger—for example, "Car coming!"—would be almost impossible. People would scarcely be able to share information or to teach and learn skills.

Then introduce the term *noun.* Inform students that a *noun* is the name of one kind of word—a word that is the name of a thing, person, place, or idea. As students move into the handbook, encourage them to look for and to use specific, vivid nouns.

WHAT ARE NOUNS?

Objectives

- To identify nouns as words that name persons, places, things, or ideas

Writing

- To use precise nouns in writing

Teaching Strategies

LINKING GRAMMAR AND WRITING
Write on the board sentences such as the following and ask students to suggest precise nouns that create a clearer picture:

A <u>person</u> is walking a <u>dog.</u>

In front of the <u>building</u> is a <u>car</u>.

COLLABORATIVE OPPORTUNITY
You might divide the class into small groups and have each group suggest categories of things (for example, things that are made of metal). For each category, see which group can write the longest list in a limited time, perhaps two minutes. Make sure every item on the list is a noun. You might continue with categories of persons and places.

INDIVIDUALIZING INSTRUCTION: ESL STUDENTS Extend students' vocabulary of English nouns by pairing them with native speakers to name objects pictured in magazines. Ask each student to take turns naming things that appear in the illustrations. To extend the vocabulary of ESL students, native speakers should supply nouns ESL students do not know.

Additional Resources

Tests and Writing Assessment Prompts, Pretest, pp. 13–14
Grammar and Usage Practice Book, p. 16
Grammar Test Generator

WHAT ARE NOUNS?

A **noun** names a person, a place, a thing, or an idea.

Writing **TIP**

Notice how specific nouns in "Finding Home" on pages 180–181 record the persons, places, things, and ideas that were important to Merrill Wilk's family.

Many names tell who you are. You may be an artist, a student, and a leader. These different names for you are nouns. Nouns are used to name persons, places, things, or ideas.

Many nouns name things that can be seen. Some examples are *spaceship, airport,* and *mountain.* Some nouns name things that can be neither seen nor touched. These include nouns such as *justice, courage, fear,* and *happiness.*

Here are some other examples of nouns.

Persons	**Places**	**Things**	**Ideas**
captain	desert	robot	loyalty
engineer	solar system	meteor	curiosity
Kirk	Asia	Eiffel Tower	knowledge
Uhura	Lima	*Enterprise*	love

Data and Captain Picard from the television series *Star Trek: The Next Generation,* with Captain Kirk and Mr. Spock from the original *Star Trek.*

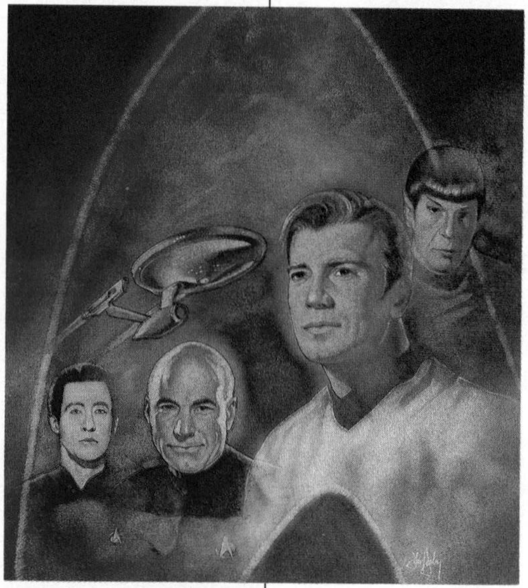

A noun can name something in general, or it can be a precise name. Compare these sentences:

The travelers explored the area.
The astronauts explored the crater.

Did you notice how much more the second sentence tells in the same number of words? The word *astronauts* is more specific than *travelers,* helping a reader guess where these travelers might be. *Crater* gives a picture of the place, while the general term *area* does not. In your writing, always try to use specific nouns. They will make your ideas and descriptions clearer.

Practice Your Skills

A. APPLICATION IN LITERATURE

Nouns Write each of the italicized nouns and tell whether each refers to a *Person,* a *Place,* a *Thing,* or an *Idea.*

> [1]In a far corner of the *universe,* on one of the forest *moons* of the planet *Endor,* there lived a *tribe* of small furry *folk* called *Ewoks.* [2]In a *village* perched high in the *branches* of the ancient *trees* they lived happy *lives,* with *love* and *goodwill* for their fellow Ewoks. . . .
>
> [3]One of these young Ewoks was named *Teebo.* . . . [4]He could daydream and watch the *rivers* of color that flowed across the *sky.* [5]The sky *colors* seemed to sing a bright *song.* . . . [6]In these *songs* Teebo could hear different *voices.* [7]He could sense the *happiness* when the voices rejoiced at the planting of a new *birth-tree,* and the *sorrow* when the voices mourned the *end* of a tree's *lifetime.*
>
> **Joe Johnston, *The Adventures of Teebo***

B. DRAFTING SKILL

Using Precise Nouns Finish the following sentences. Using your imagination, complete each sentence with precise nouns.

8. Keisha rode her ____________ to the ____________.
9. When she reached the ____________, she spoke to the ____________.
10. Keisha didn't know that the ____________ was from another ____________ in the universe.
11. The ____________ from his head made the ____________ blink on and off.
12. Suddenly, a feeling of ____________ came over Keisha as she ran to call the ____________.

C. APPLICATION IN WRITING

Fantasy Imagine you are writing about a strange event that occurs in another universe. Before you begin writing, make a list of nouns you might use in your story. Go over your list to make each noun as specific as possible.

Writing Theme
Fantastic Fiction

Writing TIP

Choose the noun that names exactly what you mean. Do not say *tool* if you mean *hammer.* Do not write *boat* if you mean *canoe.*

FOR MORE PRACTICE
See page 388.

Writing Theme: Fantastic Fiction

Suggest that students use these exercises as a springboard to writing. Other related areas that they might explore include the following:

- *The Hobbit* and other novels by J.R.R. Tolkien
- fantasy novels by Anne McCaffrey, Madeleine L'Engle, or Lloyd Alexander
- *Star Trek* and other TV space adventures
- *E.T.: The Extra-Terrestrial, Star Wars,* and other fantasy movies

Answers to Practice Your Skills

A. Application in Literature
Nouns

Students' answers may vary slightly. Alternate answers are included below.

1. universe, Place; moons, Thing or Place; Endor, Place; tribe, Person; folk, Person; Ewoks, Person
2. village, Place; branches, Thing; trees, Thing; lives, Thing or Idea; love, Idea; goodwill, Idea
3. Teebo, Person
4. rivers, Thing; sky, Thing or Place
5. colors, Thing; song, Thing
6. songs, Thing; voices, Thing
7. happiness, Idea; birth-tree, Thing; sorrow, Idea; end, Thing or Idea; lifetime, Thing or Idea

B. Drafting Skill
Using Precise Nouns

Answers will vary. Sample answers are shown below.

8. bicycle, mall
9. video store, manager
10. clerk, planet
11. rays, lights
12. terror, police

C. Application in Writing
Fantasy

Lists of nouns will vary.

Common and Proper Nouns

Objectives
- To distinguish between common and proper nouns

Writing
- To use proper nouns correctly in writing

Teaching Strategies

KEY TO UNDERSTANDING Tell students that a common noun usually can be preceded by the word *a* or *an*—for example, *a* student (one of a group) or *an* icicle (one of a number of icicles). A proper noun, because it refers to *one* person, place, or thing, is not preceded by an *a* or *an*. Instead it is capitalized to show it is specific.

STUMBLING BLOCK Some students may be confused by the fact that many of the proper nouns listed on the pupil page consist of more than one word. Point out that in each case, the words work together to name specific persons, places, or things.

HELPFUL HINT Call on individuals to continue the lists by suggesting a common noun and an example of a corresponding proper noun. Remind students that they can check whether a word is a noun by asking, "Does the word name a person, place, thing, or idea?"

Additional Resource

Grammar and Usage Practice Book, p. 17

Common and Proper Nouns

A **common noun** is a general name for a person, a place, a thing, or an idea. A **proper noun** names a particular person, place, thing, or idea.

When you call yourself a student, you are giving yourself a name that you share with all the other boys and girls in your school. This name is common to a whole group of people. Many other nouns are also common to whole groups of people, places, or things. Some examples are *photographer, picture, camera,* and *event.* These are called **common nouns.**

Some nouns name particular persons, places, or things. Names like *Ansel Adams, Washington, D.C.,* and *Lincoln Memorial* are called **proper nouns.** Proper nouns are always capitalized. Look at these examples of common nouns and proper nouns.

Common Nouns	Proper Nouns
children	Sara Curtis, Bob Curtis
photographer	Margaret Bourke-White
town	Columbus
magazine	*National Geographic*
river	Hudson River
building	United Nations
continent	Asia
park	Glacier National Park
road	Jefferson Road
lake	Lake Superior
monument	Gateway Arch
boy	Alex Bautista
girl	Sarah Lenz
school	Washington Junior High
store	Oak Street Photo
clerk	Emilia Flores

Writing TIP

Use proper nouns to make your writing more precise. Do not say *teacher* when you mean *Mr. Engel.*

Practice Your Skills

A. CONCEPT CHECK

Common and Proper Nouns Write the nouns from the following sentences. Identify each as a Common or Proper noun.

1. Dorothea Lange was a great photographer.
2. Her reputation was established during the Great Depression.
3. Lange roamed the states in the Dust Bowl.
4. There she took her most famous picture, *Migrant Mother*.
5. She later recalled, "I saw and approached the hungry and desperate mother, as if drawn by a magnet."
6. When Lange returned to her home, she sent the photo to a newspaper in San Francisco.
7. Soon afterward, the government of the United States rushed food to hungry workers.
8. Lange's photos captured the lives and feelings of poor people.
9. John Steinbeck said her work inspired his greatest novel.
10. His book, *The Grapes of Wrath*, won a Pulitzer Prize.

B. DRAFTING SKILL

Using Proper Nouns Effectively Complete each of the following sentences by adding proper nouns.

EXAMPLE Many reporters cover news in ___________.
Many reporters cover news in Washington, D.C.

11. Many photographers work for our newspaper, the ________.
12. These photographers cover local news in our town of _____ .
13. They also travel to the state capital, ____________.
14. They often take pictures of ____________, our governor.
15. At times, even national leaders like ____________ may visit.
16. Sports photographers cover games at the high schools, including ____________.
17. They travel all over the state of __________ to shoot events.
18. Photographers take photos of entertainment stars like_____ .
19. I wish that ___________, ___________, and other celebrities would visit our town.
20. If I were a photographer, I would take pictures of _______ .

Writing Theme
Photographers

Migrant Mother (1936), Dorothea Lange.

FOR MORE PRACTICE
See page 388.

Writing Theme: Photographers

Suggest that students use these exercises as a springboard to writing. Other related areas that they might explore include the following:

- Henri Cartier-Bresson, Edward Steichen, or other famous photographers
- the history of photography
- how a camera works
- holograms (three-dimensional photographs)

Answers to Practice Your Skills

A. Concept Check
Common and Proper Nouns

Answers are shown on page.

B. Drafting Skill
Using Proper Nouns Effectively

Answers will vary. Sample answers are shown below.

11. *St. Louis Post-Dispatch*
12. St. Louis
13. Jefferson City
14. Mel Carnahan
15. Jesse Jackson
16. Hazelwood High School
17. Missouri
18. Meryl Streep
19. Tom Hanks, Bruce Springsteen
20. Union Station

ART NOTE

Dorothea Lange (1895–1965) was hired by the Farm Security Administration to bring to public attention conditions among the poor during the Depression. Her photographs of California's migrant workers, especially *Migrant Mother, Nipomo, California,* were so effective that the government immediately established camps for the migrants. In *Migrant Mother,* a widow with three ragged children stares grimly and stoically at her bleak future. Ask students how this photograph makes them feel.

CHECK POINT

Writing Theme: Favorite Moments on Trips

Other related areas students might wish to explore as writing topics include the following:

- funniest or most exciting moment of a family trip
- a trip students would like to take
- famous travelers, either real (such as Marco Polo) or imaginary (such as Lemuel Gulliver)

MIXED REVIEW • PAGES 376–379

You may wish to use this activity to check students' mastery of the following concepts:

- What are nouns?
- common and proper nouns

A. Application in Literature

Answers may vary slightly. Alternative answers are included below.

1. morning, Common Noun, Thing or Idea; San Francisco, Proper Noun, Place; passengers, Common Noun, Person; deck, Common Noun, Thing or Place
2. breakfast, Common Noun, Thing; front, Common Noun, Place; ship, Common Noun, Thing; railing, Common Noun, Thing
3. *President Taft,* Proper Noun, Thing; speck, Common Noun, Thing
4. ceremony, Common Noun, Thing or Idea; greeting, Common Noun, Idea; Golden Gate, Proper Noun, Place or Thing
5. stretch, Common Noun, Thing; Pacific Ocean, Proper Noun, Place or Thing; San Francisco Bay, Proper Noun, Place or Thing
6. years, Common Noun, Thing or Idea; entrance, Common Noun, Thing or Idea
7. skirt, Common Noun, Thing; Columbus, Proper Noun, Person; Balboa, Proper Noun, Person; America, Proper Noun, Place; distance, Common Noun, Thing or Idea

B. Answers are shown on page. Every underlined word should begin with a capital letter.

Writing Theme
Favorite Moments on Trips

CHECK POINT

MIXED REVIEW • PAGES 376–379

A. APPLICATION IN LITERATURE

Write each underlined noun. Identify it as a *Common* or *Proper Noun.* Tell if it names a *Person,* a *Place,* a *Thing,* or an *Idea.*

EXAMPLE After years in China, the family came home.
years, Common Noun, Thing
China, Proper Noun, Place
family, Common Noun, Person

[1]The morning we were due to arrive in San Francisco, all the passengers came on deck early, but I was the first. [2]I skipped breakfast and went to the very front of the ship where the railing comes to a point. [3]That morning I would be the "eyes" of the *President Taft,* searching the horizon for the first speck of land. [4]My private ceremony of greeting, however, would not come until we were closer, until we were sailing through the Golden Gate. [5]For years I had heard about the Golden Gate, a narrow stretch of water connecting the Pacific Ocean to San Francisco Bay. [6]And for years I had planned my entrance.

[7]Dressed in my navy skirt, white blouse, and silk stockings, I felt every bit as neat as Columbus or Balboa and every bit as heroic when I finally spotted America in the distance.

Jean Fritz, *Homesick: My Own Story*

B. Copy these sentences, capitalizing every proper noun.

8. Last year my family went to washington, d.c.
9. My brother peter kept a list of all the monuments we saw.
10. My favorite moment came when we visited the white house.
11. The president of the united states walked past us!
12. We saw congress in session at the capitol building.
13. My youngest sister, mandy, was only three years old.
14. Her favorite site was the lincoln memorial.
15. She liked the red velvet rope around the statue of lincoln.
16. Driving to the jefferson memorial, dad took a wrong turn.
17. We wound up across the potomac river in virginia.

SINGULAR AND PLURAL NOUNS

A **singular noun** names one person, place, thing, or idea. A **plural noun** names more than one person, place, thing, or idea.

Some nouns name just one person, place, thing, or idea. *Girl,* for example, names one person. It a **singular noun.** Other nouns name more than one person. They are **plural nouns.** *Girls* is a plural noun.

Here are seven rules for forming the plurals of nouns.

1 To form the plurals of most nouns, just add *-s*.

streets islands languages teachers

2 When the singular noun ends in *s, sh, ch, x,* or *z,* add *-es.*

buses bushes coaches boxes waltzes

3 When the singular noun ends in *y* with a consonant before it, change the *y* to *i* and add *-es.*

city—cities country—countries

4 For most nouns ending in *f* or *fe,* add *-s.* For some nouns ending in *f* or *fe,* however, change the *f* to *v* and add *-es* or *-s.*

chief—chiefs	self—selves	loaf—loaves
roof—roofs	life—lives	knife—knives
belief—beliefs	leaf—leaves	wolf—wolves
reef—reefs	half—halves	shelf—shelves
cuff—cuffs	wife—wives	calf—calves

SINGULAR AND PLURAL NOUNS

Objectives

- To form and spell plural nouns correctly

Writing

- To use proofreading skills to correct errors in the spelling of plural nouns
- To use plural nouns correctly in writing

Teaching Strategies

COLLABORATIVE OPPORTUNITY
Have students work in small groups to create a list of ten to twenty singular nouns. The list should include some examples that follow each of the seven rules for forming plurals. Groups should then exchange lists and challenge the recipients to write the plural forms. After the lists have been returned and checked, you might want to teach the most frequently missed plurals to the class as a whole.

INDIVIDUALIZING INSTRUCTION: ESL STUDENTS It may be necessary to review the definition of consonants before presenting rule 3. Note also that ESL students may be discouraged by the complexity of forming English plurals, especially if their native languages have fewer rules for formation of plurals. Assure students that rule 1 applies to most English nouns.

MODELING Demonstrate how to use a dictionary to look up plural forms of nouns. Show students where they should look (right after the pronunciation). Explain that the abbreviations *n., pl.* mean *noun, plural* (form) and that sometimes only the last few syllables of this form are shown.

concerto (kən•cher′ tō) *n., pl.*–**tos**

Emphasize that if a plural form is not listed, it is formed by adding *-s* to the singular form (rule 1, page 381).

Additional Resource

Grammar and Usage Practice Book, pp. 18–19

Writing Theme: Other Ways of Life

Other related areas students might wish to explore as writing topics include the following:

- Masai herders of Tanzania
- Bedouins, nomads of the desert
- life on a Navajo reservation
- the Maya of Guatemala

Answers to Practice Your Skills

A. Concept Check

Singular and Plural Nouns

1. Eskimos or Eskimo
2. lives
3. oxen, deer
4. nets
5. roots, berries
6. families, tents
7. houses
8. knives, snowhouses
9. towns, cities
10. beliefs, ways

5 When the singular noun ends in *o*, add *-s*.

radios halos pianos rodeos

Exceptions: For the following nouns ending in *o*, add *-es*.

echoes heroes potatoes tomatoes

6 In some cases, the plural noun is exactly the same as the singular noun.

salmon bass deer news

7 Some nouns form their plurals in special ways.

child—children goose—geese mouse—mice

Always check a dictionary when you are unsure about how to form the plural of a word. If the plural form is not listed in the dictionary, just add *-s* to the singular form.

Practice Your Skills

A. CONCEPT CHECK

Writing Theme
Other Ways of Life

Singular and Plural Nouns Change each of the nouns in parentheses to its plural form. Write the plural form.

1. The Inuit of Canada and the Inupiat and Yupik of Alaska were once called (Eskimo).
2. In the past, their (life) depended solely on nature.
3. They hunted bears, musk (ox), and (deer) called caribou.
4. They spread (net) to catch fish from the sea.
5. During the summer, they also ate (root), stems, and (berry).
6. In those months, (family) lived in (tent) made of skins.
7. During winter, most Inuit lived in (house) made of sod.
8. Using (knife), some cut blocks of snow to build (snowhouse).
9. Today, however, many Inuit live in modern (town) and (city).
10. Their (belief) and (way) of life have changed.

Literature Connection

Read aloud this passage from *Hatchet* by Gary Paulsen. Have students identify all nouns and tell whether each is singular (underlined) or plural (underlined twice).

"His eyes opened and there was light in the cave, a gray dim light of morning. He wiped his mouth and tried to move his leg, which had stiffened like wood. There was thirst, and hunger, and he ate some raspberries from the jacket. They had spoiled a bit, seemed softer and mushier, but still had a rich sweetness. He crushed the berries against the roof of his mouth with his tongue and drank the sweet juice as it ran down his throat. . . ."

B. PROOFREADING SKILL

Correcting Plural Nouns Proofread the following paragraphs for errors in grammar, punctuation, and spelling. Rewrite the paragraphs correctly. Watch especially for errors in the plural forms of nouns. (15 errors)

Kyoko and her sisters have lived in Hong Kong all their lifes. They go to school only in the morning schools are crowded, so students go in shiftes. They compete strongely among themselfs to get into the best schools. In they're free time, many childrens work in the family business.

This Sundae morning, Kyoko's whole family is going out to breakfast they are celebrating a job promotion for Kyoko's father. Him works in one of the many Hong Kong factorys that produce radioes, televisions, and other electronic devices. The restaurant serves dim sum, which are dumplings. Kyoko isn't sure what kind she will order, because there are more than sixty varietys of dim sum.

At home, Kyoko's mother often prepares wonderfull seafood dishs. There are more than 150 kinds of fish in the nearby waters, plus mussels, oysters, and other shellfish.

FOR MORE PRACTICE
See page 389.

C. APPLICATION IN WRITING

A Description Imagine that you have a pen pal who lives in a distant part of the world and whose life is very different from yours. Write a description of some part of your everyday life that will help your pen pal better understand your world. Use the plural form of at least ten of the following nouns.

potato	food	deer
hobby	wish	people
man	woman	city
bus	student	trout
belief	class	street
radio	life	country

B. Proofreading Skill
Correcting Plural Nouns

Errors in proofreading exercises are counted as follows: (a) Each word is counted as one error. For example, a misspelled word is one error; two initials and a last name not capitalized are counted as three errors. (b) Run-on sentences and sentence fragments are each counted as one error, even though the correction involves both punctuation and capitalization.

Errors are shown on page. The correctly rewritten paragraphs appear below.

Kyoko and her sisters have lived in Hong Kong all their lives. They go to school only in the morning. Schools are crowded, so students go in shifts. They compete strongly among themselves to get into the best schools. In their free time, many children work in the family business.

This Sunday morning, Kyoko's whole family is going out to breakfast. They are celebrating a job promotion for Kyoko's father. He works in one of the many Hong Kong factories that produce radios, televisions, and other electronic devices. The restaurant serves dim sum, which are dumplings. Kyoko isn't sure what kind she will order, because there are more than sixty varieties of dim sum.

At home, Kyoko's mother often prepares wonderful seafood dishes. There are more than 150 kinds of fish in the nearby waters, plus mussels, oysters, and other shellfish.

C. Application in Writing
A Description

Student answers will vary.

NOUNS THAT SHOW POSSESSION

Objectives
- To form possessive nouns correctly

Writing
- To proofread a paragraph, correcting errors in the use of possessive forms of nouns
- To use possessive nouns correctly in writing

KEY TO UNDERSTANDING Write the following sentences on the board:

The shoes *of John* are brand new.

John's shoes are brand new.

Point out that each of the two sentences shows possession, but that the style with the possessive noun is used more often in everyday speech. To know where to place the apostrophe in *Johns shoes,* rephrase the sentence to "the shoes of John." The apostrophe is placed after the name of the owner, *John.* Give students an additional example based on a plural possessive:
- the *girls* (Anne and Mary) father
- the father of the *girls* (Anne and Mary)
- the *girls'* father

STUMBLING BLOCK Students may feel that adding an apostrophe and an *-s* to a word that already ends in an *-s* (such as *Confucius)* results in a word *(Confucius's)* that "looks funny" and "sounds funny." Assure students that this is the correct form and that it will not seem strange when students have become used to it.

ASSESSMENT: SPOT CHECK Ask each student to write four examples of the possessive forms of each of the following kinds of nouns: (a) singular nouns; (b) plural nouns that end in an *-s;* (c) plural nouns that do not end in an *-s*. Have students exchange papers to check each others' examples.

NOUNS THAT SHOW POSSESSION

A **possessive noun** shows who or what owns something.

Everyone owns things, from clothes to toys to pets. When you wish to say that someone owns something, you use the **possessive form** of the noun.

China's civilization is very ancient.
(The possessive form of *China* is *China's.*)
Local rulers constantly challenged the *emperor's* power.
(The possessive form of *emperor* is *emperor's.*)

Making Singular Nouns Show Possession

To form the possessive of a singular noun, add an apostrophe and an *-s.*

Singular Noun	Possessive Form
ruler	ruler's
Confucius	Confucius's

Making Plural Nouns Show Possession

There are two rules to remember for forming the possessive of a plural noun.

1 If the plural noun ends in *s,* simply add an apostrophe to the end of the word.

Plural Noun	Possessive Form
horses	horses'
invaders	invaders'
families	families'
riders	riders'
rulers	rulers'

SPICE BOX

You might ask each student to work with a partner to make up several tongue twisters containing at least one possessive noun. Have students write their tongue twisters on the board. Ask the rest of the class to check for the correct spelling of possessives. For example:

Leonard loves Uncle Lee's lasagna.

Hillary's huge home run won the Hurricanes' home game.

2 If the plural noun does not end in *s*, add an apostrophe and an *-s*.	
Plural Noun	**Possessive Form**
people	people's
women	women's
children	children's

When you form possessives, be careful to place the apostrophe in the correct position. Notice how changing the position of the apostrophe can change the meaning of a phrase. *The peasant's land* means the land belongs to one peasant. *The peasants' land* means the land belongs to two or more peasants. For more information about how to use apostrophes correctly, turn to Handbook 43, "Punctuation," pages 581–598.

Practice Your Skills

A. CONCEPT CHECK

Possessive Nouns Rewrite the following sentences. Use the possessive form for each noun in italics.

1. A youth who lived seven hundred years ago was one of *history* greatest travelers.
2. It was Marco Polo who described *Kublai Khan* empire, China.
3. *Marco Polo* diary told of all the wondrous sights he saw.
4. Polo reported seeing coconuts the size of a *man* head.
5. He noted that the *coconuts* insides were white and delicious.
6. The *explorer* description of a crocodile was amazing.
7. He told of a serpent ten paces long and said that this *reptile* jaws were wide enough to swallow a man.
8. In addition, some of the *cities* features amazed Polo.
9. Underground drainage systems showed the Chinese *people* engineering skills.
10. Beautiful gold-covered carvings demonstrated the native *artists* abilities.

Writing Theme Ancient China

Additional Resource

Grammar and Usage Practice Book, p. 20

Writing Theme: Ancient China

Other related areas students might wish to explore as writing topics include the following:

- Chinese myths
- Chinese pottery
- the sayings of Confucius
- the Great Wall of China

Answers to Practice Your Skills

A. Concept Check

Possessive Nouns

1. history's
2. Kublai Khan's
3. Marco Polo's
4. man's
5. coconuts'
6. explorer's
7. reptile's
8. cities'
9. people's
10. artists'

B. Proofreading Skill
Correcting Possessive Forms of Nouns

No one knows whether China's scientists were the first to invent gunpowder, but they seem to have been the first to use it in fireworks. In fact, the Chinese used gunpowder in fireworks, bombs, and rockets, but their applications never included guns. The inventors' skills became legendary. From the sixth century on, firecrackers were the people's delight in every Chinese religious parade and festival. By the time of Marco Polo's visit in the thirteenth century, Chinese fireworks displays were quite marvelous. In the sixteenth century, another European, Matteo Ricci, saw a fireworks display at a New Year's festival in Nanjing. Ricci's diary reports that the Chinese were experts in "reproducing battles and in making rotating spheres of fire, fiery trees, fruit, and the like." On the occasion of the New Year's festival, Ricci wrote, "I calculated that they consumed enough powder to carry on a sizable war for a number of years."

C. Application in Writing
An Explanation

Answers will vary.

B. PROOFREADING SKILL

Correcting Possessive Forms of Nouns Proofread the following paragraph for errors. Then rewrite it correctly. Pay special attention to errors in the use of possessive forms of nouns. (18 errors)

To celebrate the Chinese New Year, dancers perform the Lion Dance traditionally thought to bring good luck.

No one knows whether Chinas scientists was the first to invent gunpowder, but they seem to have been the first to use it in fireworks. In fact, the chinese used gunpowder in fireworks, bombs, and rockets, but they're applications never included guns. The inventors skills became legendary. From the sixth century on, firecrackers were the peoples' delight in every Chinese religious parade and festival. By the time of Marco Polos visit in the thirteenth century, Chinese fireworks display's were quiet marvelous, in the Sixteenth Century, another european, Matteo Ricci, saw a fireworks display at a New Years festival in Nanjing. Riccis' diary reports that the Chinese were experts in "reproducing battles and in making rotating spheres of fire, fiery trees, fruit, and the like." On the occasion of the New Years' festival, Ricci wrote, "i calculated that they consumed enough powder to carry on a sizable war for a number of years.

C. APPLICATION IN WRITING

An Explanation Choose one of these products, which were invented in China. Write one or more paragraphs to explain how the product is made, how it is used, or both. In your explanation, use at least five possessive nouns.

paper rockets compass movable type

FOR MORE PRACTICE
See page 389.

386 Grammar Handbook

CHECK POINT
MIXED REVIEW • PAGES 381–386

Write the following sentences. Correct all errors in the plural and possessive forms of nouns. If a sentence does not contain any errors, write *Correct.*

1. The peak of Tibets Mount Everest is 29,108 foot above sea level.
2. Until a Japanese woman successfully climbed Everest in 1975, all the mountaineers' who reached the peak were man.
3. However, until September 1988, no female climbers from the United States reached Everests' peak.
4. That month, two U.S. groups with women members began their ascents of the mountain. C
5. Members of one expedition hauled boxs and crates of equipment to a base camp high on the mountain's south side.
6. They carried more supplys to camps higher up that would be used by the climbers during their attempts to reach the top.
7. Small groupes of climbers then set off for the summit.
8. Stacy Allison's team included herself and two men. C
9. At 28,000 feet, the three climber's oxygen supply ran short.
10. Without extra oxygen, the bloods' oxygen level drops.
11. If all three adventureres had continued, their energy and judgment could have suffered.
12. The team members held a lottery to decide who would go on. C
13. The two mens' dreams of reaching the summit ended.
14. Allison took the remaining oxygen and climbed for three more houres before standing at the earth's highest point.
15. She stayed there for forty-five minutes, taking photoes of herself with the flag of the United States and with logos of companys that had sponsored the expedition.
16. Two daies later, another one of the expeditions' female mountaineers, Peggy Luce, reached the summit.
17. Luces' climb was nearly disastrous.
18. Because her goggle's had fogged up, Luce took them off; she was almost snow-blind when she reached the top alone.
19. Then, on her way down, her oxygen tanks supply ran out.
20. She survived, however, as one of the conquerors of Everest. C

Writing Theme
Women Mountaineers

CHECK POINT

Writing Theme: Women Mountaineers

Other related areas students might wish to explore as writing topics include the following:

- mountain climbing equipment and training
- James Ramsey Ullman's *The Age of Mountaineering*
- the world's tallest mountains
- clubs and training for indoor climbing

MIXED REVIEW • PAGES 381–386

You may wish to use this activity to check students' mastery of the following concepts:

- plural forms of nouns
- possessive forms of nouns

Errors are underlined on page.
Corrections are shown below.

1. Tibet's, feet
2. mountaineers, men
3. Everest's
4. Correct
5. boxes
6. supplies
7. groups
8. Correct
9. climbers'
10. blood's
11. adventurers
12. Correct
13. men's
14. hours
15. photos, companies
16. days, expedition's
17. Luce's
18. goggles
19. tank's
20. Correct

GRAMMAR HANDBOOK 35

ADDITIONAL PRACTICE

Each of these exercises correlates to a section of Handbook 35, "Using Nouns." The exercises may be used for more practice, for reteaching, or for review of the concepts presented.

Additional Resource

Grammar and Usage Practice Book, p. 22

Writing Theme: Animal Communications

Other related areas students might wish to explore as writing topics include the following:
- the songs of birds
- the dances of honeybees
- how animals make their territory known
- courtship behavior

A. Finding Nouns
Answers are shown on page.

B. Using Common and Proper Nouns
Answers are shown on page. Every underlined word should begin with a capital letter.

GRAMMAR HANDBOOK 35

Writing Theme
Animal Communications

A. Finding Nouns Write the nouns in each sentence.

1. Many chimpanzees live in the jungles of Africa.
2. These apes are like humans in many ways.
3. People wondered if these animals could learn to speak a language such as English.
4. Fifty years ago, Keith and Catherine Hayes tried to find out.
5. The couple brought a chimpanzee to live in their home.
6. The chimp, named Viki, soon settled into its new world.
7. Viki learned to say only four words.
8. Her voice was a hoarse whisper.
9. Since that time, scientists have learned that the vocal cords of chimps differ from the vocal cords of humans.
10. Once, the Hayeses asked Viki to sort some photographs.
11. Viki separated pictures of people from photos of animals.
12. The chimpanzee made only one mistake.
13. Viki put her own picture in the pile with photos of humans.
14. In a more recent experiment, a gorilla named Koko learned several hundred signs in sign language for words.
15. Koko even asked for a cat to be her pet.

B. Using Common and Proper Nouns Write these sentences, capitalizing each proper noun.

16. Some scientists in the united states study how marine animals can learn languages.
17. One important study took place at a laboratory in hawaii.
18. Dr. louis herman, an animal researcher at the university of hawaii, worked with two dolphins.
19. Phoenix and akeakamai were captured in the gulf of mexico.
20. Their species of dolphin is common in the atlantic ocean.
21. Dr. herman worked in a laboratory near honolulu.
22. One dolphin, phoenix, learned to use whistles for words.
23. The other dolphin, akeakamai, learned sign language.
24. They learned about forty words, roughly what an eighteen-month-old baby learning to speak english would know.
25. Dolphins, which roam the oceans from norway to new zealand and south africa, seem to use their own language of whistles, squeaks, and other noises.

C. Using Plural Nouns Write the following sentences. Correct all errors in the use of the plural forms of nouns.

26. There are many formes of animal communications.
27. Cuckooes, salmon, wolves, and other animals send messages.
28. You probably know that gooses honk, coyotes howl, and sheeps bleat, and that crickets sing by rubbing their two front wings together.
29. Did you know that male deers bellow to scare off rivals?
30. You've probably seen fireflys flashing to attract mates.
31. Different kinds of these insects flash different patternes.
32. One day zookeeperes were watching an elephant named Siri.
33. Siri was making scratchs on the floor with a rock.
34. The zoo employees got Siri paper, paints, and brushs.
35. Siri created hundredes of pages of drawings.
36. Some observers said that her work looked as though it came from art studioes.
37. Vervet monkies use various signals to communicate.
38. They have three main enemys: eagles, snakes, and leopards.
39. To escape leopards, the monkeys go far out on tree branchs, but to escape eagles, they stay close to the tree trunks.
40. Vervets use three different calls to tell one another which enemy is near so they will know how to save their lifes.

D. Writing Possessive Forms Write the correct possessive form of each word in parentheses.

41. Humpback whales make (nature) most complex sounds.
42. The (humpbacks) sounds range from shrieks to groans.
43. Males sing songs during the (whales) mating season.
44. All humpbacks in each of the (ocean) regions sing one song.
45. The (group) song changes during the mating season.
46. Just as (people) taste in music changes, whales seem to get tired of singing the same song over and over.
47. Each (season) singing begins with last year's final song.
48. The songs seem to be a contest among a (region) males.
49. The (singers) breathing stops while they sing because whales cannot breathe and sing at the same time.
50. Most of the (performers) songs last ten to fifteen minutes.

C. Using Plural Nouns
Errors are underlined on page. Corrections are shown below.
26. forms
27. Cuckoos
28. geese, sheep
29. deer
30. fireflies
31. patterns
32. zookeepers
33. scratches
34. brushes
35. hundreds
36. studios
37. monkeys
38. enemies
39. branches
40. lives

D. Writing Possessive Forms
41. nature's
42. humpbacks'
43. whales'
44. ocean's
45. group's
46. people's
47. season's
48. region's
49. singers'
50. performers'

GRAMMAR HANDBOOK 35

REVIEW

These exercises may be used as a mixed review or as an informal evaluation of the skills presented in Handbook 35, "Using Nouns."

Additional Resources

Grammar and Usage Practice Book, p. 23
Tests and Writing Assessment Prompts, Mastery Test, pp. 15–16
Elaboration, Revision, and Proofreading Practice, p. 24

Writing Theme: Tall Tales

Other related areas students might wish to explore as writing topics include the following:

- Pecos Bill and Slue-foot Sue
- John Henry
- Mike Fink
- an original tall tale, set in the present

A. Finding Common and Proper Nouns
Answers are shown on page. Student answers should be in columns.

B. Writing Singular and Plural Nouns
Errors are underlined on page. Corrections are shown below.

11. heroes
12. stories
13. achievements
14. impossibilities
15. children
16. mountains
17. wolves
18. bushes
19. raccoons
20. grizzlies

GRAMMAR HANDBOOK 35

Writing Theme
Tall Tales

A. Finding Common and Proper Nouns Label two columns *Common Nouns* and *Proper Nouns.* Write each noun from this paragraph in the correct column. Capitalize proper nouns. If a noun is used more than once, you need to list it only once.

[1]The story of paul bunyan is a famous tale that began in the united states. [2]People all over america have told the stories of a giant lumberjack who could perform great deeds. [3]The strength and abilities of this man were amazing! [4]He could cut down ten trees at a time with a single swipe of his ax. [5]Paul could drive the stumps into the ground with his bare fist. [6]Our hero could even squeeze water out of boulders. [7]paul dug the mississippi river and cleared the states of iowa and kansas for the farmers. [8]With a blue ox named babe, paul cleared western pastures so cattle could graze. [9]To give babe drinking water, the fantastic lumberjack scooped out the great lakes. [10]The adventures of paul bunyan are still enjoyed by americans.

B. Writing Singular and Plural Nouns Write the following sentences. Correct all errors in the plural forms of nouns.

11. Davy Crockett was one of many tall-tale heros.
12. He was real, but storys about him were bigger than life.
13. His strong opinions and the outrageous achievementes he claimed for himself made news everywhere.
14. Davy loved to exaggerate his adventures outrageously, and other people added more impossibilitys to his accounts.
15. The tales say he wasn't born like normal childs.
16. Davy was born on a meteor that crashed in the mountaines.
17. Many of the tales tell of fights Davy had, often with wild animals like mountain lions, wolfs, bears, and alligators.
18. Once he fought a huge mountain lion all night in the bushs, and by morning they had become lifelong friends.
19. All the raccoon knew that he was a great shot, so when they saw him they laid themselves down and gave up.
20. "When I was a baby," he claimed, "I could lick two grizzlys at once."

Literature Connection

Tall Tales to Read Students might enjoy hearing you read aloud Virginia Hamilton's story "Papa John's Tall Tale," from her collection of African-American folk tales *The People Could Fly.* Hamilton notes that in different regions of America, tall tales are called "toasties, gallyfloppers, windies, whoppers, and long bows." You might ask students what word, if any, they have been using to refer to these tales of exaggeration.

C. Writing Possessive Forms Write the possessive form of each noun given in parentheses.

21. Back in the days of sailing ships, (sailors) lives were filled with hard work.
22. They often sang songs, or chanteys, while hoisting a (ship) sails, weighing anchor, or doing their other duties.
23. One of the (seafarers) favorite songs was "Old Stormalong."
24. The (chantey) hero was named Alfred Bulltop Stormalong.
25. Tales of (Stormy) adventures became popular.
26. This (hero) parents were unknown.
27. A tidal wave washed him onto (Cape Cod) coast, in New England, while he was still a baby.
28. Even then, Stormy was eighteen feet tall and drank milk by the barrel—to the (townsfolk) amazement.
29. When he grew up, many (ships) captains wanted him as a sailor.
30. He had numerous adventures on the seas and saved his fellow (crewmen) lives many times.

D. Proofreading Write the following paragraph on your paper. Correct all errors in the use of proper nouns, plural forms, and possessive forms. (17 errors)

Of all this countries tall-tale heros, Mose was the first to come from a big city. He hailed from new york. People first heard about Mose in a broadway stage show called *A Glance at New York,* by B. A. Baker. From that time on, Mose' legend just grew and grew. Storys of his heroic deeds were told in newspapers and magazines.

Mose was a firefighter back when firefighters's dutys included pulling their wagones themselves. He was eight foot tall and was stronger than ten men. Once a horse-drawn trolley was caught in its track, blocking his fire trucks way. Mose unhooked the horses and picked up the trolley, with the trolleys' passengeres inside. He carried it across the street so that his team and their truck could get to the fire. Hearing a mothers crys, mose entered the burning building and soon carried out a baby—in his hat!

C. Writing Possessive Forms
21. sailors'
22. ship's
23. seafarers'
24. chantey's
25. Stormy's
26. hero's
27. Cape Cod's
28. townsfolk's
29. ships'
30. crewmen's

D. Proofreading

Errors are underlined on page.

Of all this country's tall-tale heroes, Mose was the first to come from a big city. He hailed from New York. People first heard about Mose in a Broadway stage show called *A Glance at New York* by B. A. Baker. From that time on, Mose's legend just grew and grew. Stories of his heroic deeds were told in newspapers and magazines.

Mose was a firefighter back when firefighters' duties included pulling their wagons themselves. He was eight feet tall and was stronger than ten men. Once a horse-drawn trolley was caught in its tracks, blocking his fire truck's way. Mose unhooked the horses and picked up the trolley, with the trolley's passengers inside. He carried it across the street so that his team and their truck could get to the fire. Hearing a mother's cries, Mose entered the burning building and soon carried out a baby—in his hat!

WRITING CONNECTIONS

Elaboration, Revision, and Proofreading

This activity will allow your students to see some of the concepts presented in this handbook at work in a piece of descriptive writing. By revising and proofreading this passage, students will have the chance to use specific nouns and plural and possessive forms of nouns.

You might have students work in small groups to complete the revision; then discuss possible answers with the entire class.

Revisions will vary. A typical revision is shown below. Elements involving change are shown in boldface

A tradition at many celebrations in Mexico and other countries of Latin America is the breaking of a piñata. A piñata is a clay jug or a papier-mâché container covered with layers of brightly colored paper. Many piñatas are made in the shapes of animals, such as burros or birds. The piñata is dangled above the heads of guests. Each **guest** is blindfolded **and** gets three tries to break the piñata with a long stick. When someone succeeds, the piñata's contents **tumble** out. **Sweets, toys, and other small presents fall to the ground.** Everyone scurries to gather up the loot.

The tradition of breaking piñatas started in Spain. Today, it is carried on at celebrations for Christmas, Easter, and other occasions throughout the year. A piñata may also be an attraction at any party for children.

WRITING CONNECTIONS

Elaboration, Revision, and Proofreading

Observation and Description

A good way to learn about other cultures and customs is to describe them. (See Workshop 2.) When you revise this type of descriptive writing, look for ways to add vivid details. Using precise common and proper nouns will help you present information clearly.

Revise the following draft of a description by using the directio at the bottom of the page. Then proofread your work, looking especially for errors in the use of nouns. Also look for other errors in grammar, capitalization, punctuation, and spelling.

[1]A tradition at many celebrations in mexico and other Countries of latin america is the breaking of a piñata. [2]A piñata is a clay jug or a papier-mâché container covered with layer's of brightly colored paper. [3]Many piñatas are made in the shapes of animals, such as burroes or birds. [4]The piñata is dangled above the head's of guests. [5]Each one is blindfolded. [6]Each one gets three tries to break the piñata with a long stick. [7]When someone succeeds, the piñatas contents come out. [8]Everyone scurries to gather up the loot. [9]The tradition of breaking piñatas started in spain. [10]Today, it is carried on at celebrations for christmas, easter, and other ocasions throughout the year. [11]A piñata may also be an attraction at any party for childs.

1. In sentence 5, replace the vague pronoun "one" with the more precise noun "guest."
2. Combine sentences 5 and 6 to make a sentence with a compoun verb.
3. In sentence 7, replace the vague verb "come" with the more expressive "tumble."
4. Add this missing information after sentence 7: "Sweets, toys, and other small presents fall to the ground."
5. Divide the passage into two paragraphs.

392 Grammar Handbook

Sniglets

Have you ever searched for just the right word to describe something—and found that the word you wanted was one you had to make up yourself? If so, then you've invented a **sniglet,** a word that doesn't appear in the dictionary but probably should. What sniglets can you add to this list?

cinemuck *(si' ne muk)* n. The combination of popcorn, soda, and melted chocolate that covers the floors of movie theaters.

glackett *(glak' it)* n. The noisy ball inside a spray-paint can.

oatgap *(oht' gap)* n. The empty space in a cereal box created by "settling during shipment."

pigslice *(pig' slys)* n. The last unclaimed piece of pizza that everyone is secretly dying for.

profanitype *(pro fan' i tipe)* n. The special symbols used by cartoonists to replace swear words (points, asterisks, stars, and so on).

snacktivity *(snak tiv' ih tee)* n. Any amusing table pastime (i.e., putting olives on the ends of one's fingers, "biting faces" into a slice of bread, etc.)

spork *(spork)* n. The combination spoon/fork you find in fast-food restaurants.

wondracide *(wun' druh side)* n. The act of murdering a piece of bread with a knife and cold butter.

Rich Hall and Friends

Have students work in pairs or small groups to come up with additional sniglets. (Maybe someone can even come up with another invented word for *sniglet.)* Suggest that students follow the dictionary-style format used in the text: the sniglet, then the parenthetical pronunciation guide, then the abbreviated part of speech, then the definition.

Students might be interested to know that in his humorous poem "The Owl and the Pussycat," the nineteenth-century English poet Edward Lear coined the sniglet *runcible spoon,* which is essentially the same thing as *spork:* "They dined on mince, and slices of quince, / Which they ate with a runcible spoon. . . . "

SKETCH BOOK

Objective

- To use a poem and writing prompts as springboards to informal writing

WRITING WARM-UPS

Start by reassuring students that they will not be graded for this assignment, which is designed to get them thinking imaginatively about some of the concepts in this Handbook. Most students will probably wish to respond to only one prompt, although some students may wish to write about them both.

For the first prompt, have small groups of students brainstorm what an elephant or another zoo animal might do after the zoo closes and the keepers go home for the night.

Suggest that students who select the second prompt begin by making a cluster diagram of ways in which they relax when there is no one to bother them. Finally, tell students that these prompts will require them to use vivid action words, which they will learn more about in this Handbook.

SKETCH BOOK

WRITING WARM-UPS

I wonder if the elephant
Is lonely in his stall
When all the boys and girls are gone
And there's no shout at all,
And there's no one to stamp before,
No one to note his might.
Does he hunch up, as I do,
Against the dark of night?

Gwendolyn Brooks
"PETE AT THE ZOO"

- Write a humorous description of what you think animals do when no one is around.
- Write about what you like to do when no one else is around.

Understanding Verbs

GRAMMAR HANDBOOK 36

The people on this safari hope to shoot photos that will show all the activity of African wildlife: *running, grazing, stalking, playing, stampeding*—even *lounging* like these cheetahs. The photos will bring the African landscape to life for all who see them.

You can use verbs to make your writing come to life. Verbs are the engines that drive your sentences. They describe the action, tell that something exists, or link ideas.

In this handbook, you will learn ways to use verbs to capture the true spirit of the ideas you want to communicate.

GRAMMAR HANDBOOK 36

Understanding Verbs

Objectives

- To identify action verbs and linking verbs
- To distinguish between main verbs and helping verbs
- To recognize direct objects of verbs
- To identify linking verbs and predicate words
- To recognize and form the present, past, and future tenses of verbs
- To identify the three principal parts of regular and irregular verbs
- To choose correct forms of these pairs of often-confused verbs: *can, may; let, leave; lie, lay; teach, learn; rise, raise; sit, set*

Writing

- To use vivid verbs in sentences and paragraphs
- To correct errors in verb tenses in sentences and paragraphs
- To use irregular verb forms and often-confused verbs correctly

INTRODUCING THE HANDBOOK

Call on volunteers to share their ideas about the art on this page. What actions does the photograph suggest? Call students' attention to the verbs they use to describe the scene. Then tell them that verbs are the core of written and spoken language, because they express actions or state the condition of people, objects, or ideas. Vivid, specific verbs are among a writer's most powerful tools.

KINDS OF VERBS

Objectives

- To identify action verbs and linking verbs

Writing

- To use specific action verbs in a piece of writing

Teaching Strategies

KEY TO UNDERSTANDING: ACTION VERBS Students may have difficulty with the concept that some action verbs describe unseen actions. On the board, write some additional examples of verbs that express actions not perceived with the senses: for example, *remember, forget, guess,* and *sympathize.* Point out that many of these words relate to activities of the mind or of the emotions. Call on volunteers to compose sentences using these verbs.

HELPFUL HINT: LINKING VERBS To reinforce the concept that certain verbs work to connect the subject and predicate, use the following activity. Tell students that all the verbs at the bottom of page 396 are forms of the verb *to be.* Have students make up a sentence using each verb form. Then ask them to explain which words in each sentence are linked to the subject by the verb.

ASSESSMENT: SPOT CHECK To be sure students are able to recognize verbs in sentences, hand out clippings from a school or local newspaper. Ask students to identify the verb or verbs in each sentence. Write these verbs on the board. Then invite other students to classify each verb as an action verb or as a linking verb.

KINDS OF VERBS

Verbs are words that tell about action or state that something *is.*

You use two kinds of verbs when you speak or write. These are **action verbs** and **state-of-being** or **linking verbs.**

Action Verbs

Some verbs tell about action you can see.

The young boy *saddled* his pony.
The two *galloped* across the field.

Other verbs tell about action you cannot see. That is, there is no physical movement.

The boy *wished* for a long ride.
He *enjoyed* the time with his pony.

State-of-Being or Linking Verbs

Some verbs do not show action. They tell what something is, or they link the subject with a word or words in the predicate. Such verbs are called **state-of-being verbs** or **linking verbs.** Since state-of-being verbs and linking verbs are very similar, we will refer to both of them as linking verbs from this point on. These are the most common linking verbs.

am	are	were	being
is	was	be	been

FRANK & ERNEST® by Bob Thaves

Look at the linking verbs in the following sentences.

The pony *is* a reddish color.
He *was* a year old last month.
His movements *are* graceful.

These are some other familiar linking verbs.

look	appear	become	taste	seem
feel	sound	remain	smell	

The clip-clop of the pony's hooves *sounds* hollow.
The pony *seems* relaxed now.
The pony *becomes* nervous around strangers.

Practice Your Skills

A. CONCEPT CHECK

Verbs Write the verb from each of the following sentences.

Writing Theme
John Steinbeck

1. Salinas, California, was John Steinbeck's home.
2. John wandered freely through the valley as a boy.
3. His family seemed warm and happy.
4. At age four, he received a Shetland pony.
5. Young John felt proud of this new responsibility.
6. Family friends traveled to the Pacific Ocean in summer.
7. John's family often made the trip by train.
8. The salty spray smelled wonderful to him.
9. Long hikes were a daily activity at the beach.
10. Starfish beckoned from tide pools.
11. Magnificent shells glittered in the sun.
12. The young children went for swims as often as possible.
13. John remained at the beach only part of the summer.
14. His uncle invited him to his ranch near King City.
15. The ranch appeared very different from the ocean.
16. The sun beat harshly on the hills and fields.
17. John searched for special places in the hills.
18. These places inspired special thoughts and feelings.
19. John used the ranch as the setting for his story "The Red Pony."
20. In the story, Jody seems much like young John.

MANAGING THE PAPER LOAD To limit the number of written exercises you have to correct, you may wish to do Exercise A orally with your class. Call on different students to read the individual sentences aloud and identify the verbs. You may also want to ask students whether each verb they identify is an action verb or a linking verb.

Additional Resources

Tests and Writing Assessment Prompts, Pretest, pp. 17–18
Grammar and Usage Practice Book, p. 24
Grammar Test Generator

Writing Theme: John Steinbeck

Suggest that students use these exercises as a springboard to writing. Other related areas that they might explore include the following:

- the setting of "The Red Pony"
- the childhood of a favorite writer
- books and stories about special animals

Answers to Practice Your Skills

A. Concept Check
Verbs

Answers are shown on page.

B. Application in Literature
Identifying Verbs

21. was, Linking
22. took, Action; stepped, Action
23. glittered, Action
24. touched, Action; rubbed, Action
25. relaxed, Action
26. brushed, Action
27. thought, Action
28. braided, Action
29. enter, Action
30. was, Linking; felt, Action

C. Application in Writing
Description

Answers will vary.

B. APPLICATION IN LITERATURE

Identifying Verbs Write the verbs in italics from the following passage. Label each verb *Action* or *Linking*. Notice how the writer mixes the use of action and linking verbs.

21Jody *was* glad when [the boys] had gone. **22**He *took* brush and currycomb from the wall, took down the barrier of the box stall and *stepped* cautiously in. **23**The pony's eyes *glittered,* and he edged around into kicking position. **24**But Jody *touched* him on the shoulder and *rubbed* his high arched neck. . . . **25**The pony gradually *relaxed* his tenseness. **26**Jody curried and *brushed* until a pile of dead hair lay in the stall and until the pony's coat had taken on a deep red shine. **27**Each time he finished he *thought* it might have been done better. **28**He *braided* the mane into a dozen little pigtails, and he braided the forelock, and then he undid them and brushed the hair out straight again.

29Jody did not hear his mother *enter* the barn. **30**She *was* angry when she came, but when she looked in at the pony and at Jody working over him, she *felt* a curious pride rise up in her.

John Steinbeck, "The Red Pony"

C. APPLICATION IN WRITING

Description In the sentence "The girl went down the beach," *went* is a dull action verb. Notice how the sentence becomes livelier with a specific action verb that tells you just how the girl moved:

The girl *raced* down the beach.

Write a description of someone doing an activity, such as a friend playing with a pet or a family member enjoying a nice day. Use as many specific action verbs as you can.

FOR MORE PRACTICE
See page 423.

PROFESSIONAL NOTEBOOK

As students revise for verb usage, share with them the advice of professional writing teacher William Zinsser:

"Verbs are the most important of all your tools. They push the sentence forward and give it momentum. . . . Most verbs also carry somewhere in their imagery or in their sound a suggestion of what they mean: *flail, poke, dazzle, squash, beguile, pamper, swagger, wheedle, vex. . . .* Don't choose one that is dull or merely serviceable. Make active verbs activate your sentences."

from On Writing Well

MAIN VERBS AND HELPING VERBS

A verb may be a single word or a group of words.

You know that many verbs are single words. Read these sentences.

Dawn *makes* lunch.
Dave *mixes* the salad.

Often, however, a verb is made up of two or more words.

Dawn *is making* lunch.
Dave *was mixing* the salad.
Dawn *has been making* lunch.
Dave *might have mixed* the salad.

When there are two or more words in the verb, the last word is the **main verb.** Other words are **helping verbs.**

Helping Verbs	Main Verbs	Verb
is	making	is making
has been	making	has been making
was	mixing	was mixing
might have	mixed	might have mixed

Forms of the verbs *be, have,* and *do* are the most commonly used helping verbs.

be—be, am, is, are, was, were
have—have, has, had
do—do, does, did

Forms of *be, have,* and *do* can also be used as main verbs.

Used as Helping Verb	Used as Main Verb
Eric *is* cooking.	Eric *is* the cook.
Laura *has* finished.	Laura *has* the cookbook.
Kevin *did* stumble.	Kevin *did* his homework.

MAIN VERBS AND HELPING VERBS

Objectives

- To distinguish between main verbs and helping verbs
- To recognize the separate parts of a verb

Writing

- To use main verbs and helping verbs in a paragraph

Teaching Strategies

KEY TO UNDERSTANDING Point out that when forms of *be* act as main verbs, they are linking verbs:

Akiko *is* a figure skater. (*Is* links Akiko and figure skater.)

When forms of *have* and *do* act as main verbs, they are action verbs:

Hal *does* the dishes every night.

HELPFUL HINT: HELPING VERBS Tell students that in English a main verb can have no more than three helping verbs, as in "might have been caught."

INDIVIDUALIZING INSTRUCTION: ESL STUDENTS Many foreign languages, including Spanish, French, and Italian, use a one-word verb (with an inflected ending) where English uses a helping verb (or verbs) and a main verb. For example, the French use one pronoun and one verb, "je *dormais,*" to say "I *was sleeping.*" Point out to these students that in English, helping words change to show the time of an action. In their native languages, on the other hand, the ending of the main verb continually changes to indicate when something happens.

SPEAKING AND LISTENING Have students choose partners and play this verb game: Partner A chooses a helping verb from the list at the top of page 400 and forms a sentence. Partner B must identify the helping verb and the main verb in the sentence. Partner B should then make up a new sentence, using the same helping verb but a different main verb. Continue until all the verbs on the list have been used.

HELPFUL HINT: INTERVENING WORDS Point out that, except in questions, intervening words between a helping verb and a main verb are often negative words, such as *not, n't, never, scarcely*, or words that tell *when* or *how.* Ask students to find the intervening words between the helping verb and the main verb in the following sentences:

We did*n't* study on Saturday night.

Instead we were *happily* watching a video.

Have you *ever* done that?

Additional Resource

Grammar and Usage Practice Book, p. 25

Writing Theme: Foods

Suggest that students use these exercises as a springboard to writing. Other related areas that they might explore include the following:

- ways to make pizza
- how to use a wok
- tasty vegetarian dishes
- learning to be a chef

Answers to Practice Your Skills

A. Concept Check

Main Verbs and Helping Verbs

1. <u>Can</u> imagine
2. <u>had</u> heard
3. <u>were</u> growing
4. <u>had been</u> cultivated
5. <u>were</u> adopted
6. <u>were</u> enjoying
7. <u>have</u> become
8. <u>was</u> considered
9. <u>did</u> like
10. <u>may</u> be

Several other helping verbs can be used with main verbs.

be	must	will	should
being	can	would	may
been	could	shall	might

Separated Parts of the Verb

The main verb and its helping verbs are not always together. They may be separated by other parts of the sentence.

The children *are* not *eating* their dinner.
Sherry *has* never *liked* snacks.
Did the kindergartners *make* popcorn today?
We *could*n't *find* the recipe.

Notice that *not* and the ending *n't* in the contraction are not verbs. Also notice that in questions, one or more words often come between the helping verb and the main verb.

Practice Your Skills

Writing Theme
Foods

A. CONCEPT CHECK

Main Verbs and Helping Verbs Write the main verbs and helping verbs from each sentence. Underline the helping verbs.

1. Can you imagine a world without French fries or corn on the cob?
2. Before Columbus's voyages, Europeans hadn't even heard of potatoes and corn.
3. People in the Americas, however, were growing potatoes and corn long before anyone else.
4. Crops had been cultivated for centuries.
5. These vegetables were quickly adopted by the Europeans.
6. What other American foods were the Europeans enjoying?
7. Tomatoes have become popular around the world.
8. At first, the tomato was considered an exotic food.
9. Only after many years did most Europeans like tomatoes.
10. Chocolate may be the most popular food native to the Americas.

B. DRAFTING SKILL

Using Helping Verbs Write the following sentences. Add one or two helping verbs to each sentence. Choose from the lists on pages 399–400.

EXAMPLE I ___ made pancakes for breakfast.
I have made pancakes for breakfast.

11. Somewhere in the world today, someone ___ eat a pancake.
12. Pancakes ___ have different shapes, sizes, and names.
13. In France, people ___ eating pancakes for ages.
14. French pancakes ___ called crêpes.
15. Crêpes ___ filled with meat, cheese, or even fruit.
16. ___ you ever eaten a crêpe with chocolate sauce?
17. You ___ probably love it!
18. Many Mexican families ___ not eat a meal without tortillas.
19. First made centuries ago, these corn pancakes ___ still enjoyed today.
20. In the United States, people ___ eating tortillas in tacos, enchiladas, and burritos.
21. Chinese people ___ made pancakes for centuries too.
22. Chinese pancakes ___ made of flour and water.
23. People ___ wrap them around meat, vegetables, and sauces.
24. Then they ___ fold them into long, thin tubes.
25. These tubes ___ eaten just like a sandwich.

C. APPLICATION IN WRITING

Paragraph People write about food to describe how to cook, to describe what types of food people in other cultures eat, and for many other reasons. Write a paragraph about food. Use helping verbs and main verbs, such as the following:

Main Verbs

cook	simmer	make
fry	chop	enjoy

Helping Verbs

any form of *be*	any form of *do*	any form of *have*
will	should	can

FOR MORE PRACTICE
See page 423.

B. Drafting Skill
Using Helping Verbs

Answers may vary. Typical answers are shown below.

11. Somewhere in the world today, someone will eat a pancake.
12. Pancakes can (*or* may) have different shapes, sizes, and names.
13. In France, people have been eating pancakes for ages.
14. French pancakes are called crêpes.
15. Crêpes can be (*or* may be, are) filled with meat, cheese, or even fruit.
16. Have (*or* Had) you ever eaten a crêpe with chocolate sauce?
17. You will (*or* would) probably love it!
18. Many Mexican families do (*or* will, would) not eat a meal without tortillas.
19. First made centuries ago, these corn pancakes are still enjoyed today.
20. In the United States, people are (*or* have been) eating tortillas in tacos, enchiladas, and burritos.
21. Chinese people have made pancakes for centuries too.
22. Chinese pancakes are made of flour and water.
23. People can (*or* may, might) wrap them around meat, vegetables, and sauces.
24. Then they may (*or* can, might) fold them into long, thin tubes.
25. These tubes are (*or* can be) eaten just like a sandwich.

C. Application in Writing
Paragraph

Paragraphs will vary.

CHECK POINT

Writing Theme: Lunar Energy

Other related areas students might wish to explore as writing topics include the following:

- lunar calendars
- the Apollo 11 moon landing in 1969
- the myth of the "man in the moon"
- the satellites of other planets in the solar system

MIXED REVIEW • PAGES 396–401

You may wish to use this activity to check students' mastery of the following concepts:

- kinds of verbs
- main verbs and helping verbs

1. Have heard; Action
2. Do know; Action
3. howl; Action
4. stroll; Action
5. will be using; Action
6. pulls; Action
7. is; Linking
8. becomes; Linking
9. weakens; Action
10. have explained; Action
11. are studying; Action
12. may become; Linking
13. have built; Action
14. floods; Action
15. convert; Action
16. takes; Action
17. is; Linking
18. is located; Action
19. run; Action
20. can produce; Action
21. follow; Action
22. has ruled; Action
23. must find; Action
24. must seem; Linking
25. looks; Linking

Writing Theme
Lunar Energy

CHECK POINT

MIXED REVIEW • PAGES 396–401

Write the verb from each sentence. Underline the main verb twice. Underline each helping verb once, if there is one. Then write whether the main verb is *Action* or *Linking*.

1. Have you ever heard of solar power?
2. Do you know about lunar power?
3. Wolves howl at the full moon.
4. Sweethearts stroll hand in hand in the moonlight.
5. Perhaps someday people will be using the moon's forces for energy.
6. During the moon's orbits of the earth, the moon's gravity pulls on the earth.
7. Twice each day the moon is at its nearest point to the earth.
8. The pull becomes stronger at those times.
9. At other times, the distance of the moon from the earth weakens the force of the pull.
10. Scientists have explained the relationship between the rise and fall of the tides and the force of the moon's pull on the earth.
11. Many countries are seriously studying this force.
12. Tides may become a safe source of energy.
13. Some nations have built power plants on the ocean shore.
14. At high tide, water floods into the plant.
15. Machines convert the water's movement into energy.
16. This energy takes the form of electricity.
17. Tidal power is the name for the creation of energy from tidal movements.
18. One successful tidal power plant is located near St.-Malo, France.
19. Its giant machines run during high and low tides.
20. This plant can produce twice the power of other plants.
21. The tides, of course, follow the moon's cycle.
22. However, the sun's cycle, not the moon's, has always ruled human activities.
23. So, scientists must find ways of storing the energy.
24. All the problems must not seem too difficult, though.
25. The moon's future as an energy source looks bright!

402 Grammar Handbook

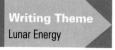

DIRECT OBJECTS OF VERBS

A **direct object** is the noun or pronoun that receives the action of the verb.

In some sentences, the subject and verb alone express a complete thought.

Subject	**Verb**
The scientist	shouted.
Jemma	waved.
We	applauded

Other sentences, however, are not complete until a word or words are added after the verb.

Paul found *the bone.*
Erika recorded *the discovery.*
The archaeologist appreciated *our work.*

The noun or pronoun that receives the action of the verb is the **direct object** of the verb. *Bone* tells what Paul found. *Discovery* tells what Erika recorded. *Bone* and *discovery* are direct objects. Only action verbs, such as *found* and *recorded,* can have direct objects. Linking verbs do not have direct objects.

To find the direct object in a sentence, first find the verb. Then ask *whom* or *what* after the verb. The word in the sentence that answers *whom* or *what* is the direct object. If no word answers these questions, there is no direct object.

Jeff collects fossils.
Jeff collects *what? fossils*
The direct object is *fossils.*

Lamarr studies in the laboratory.
Lamarr studies *whom?* Lamarr studies *what?*
This sentence has no direct object.

DIRECT OBJECTS OF VERBS

Objective

- To recognize direct objects in sentences

Teaching Strategies

KEY TO UNDERSTANDING: WORD ORDER Point out that the direct object almost always *follows* the verb in English (in some foreign languages, such as Japanese and German, it very often *precedes* the verb). You can reinforce this fact about word order in English sentences by giving students examples of declarative, interrogative, exclamatory, and imperative sentences, all with direct objects following the main verb. Cases of inverted word order, such as "Him I love deeply," are the only exceptions to this rule, and they are found more often in poetry than in prose.

CRITICAL THINKING: SYNTHESIZING Point out to students that quite a few verbs can be used either with or without a direct object, depending on the sentence. Write a pair of examples on the board, such as "Lamarr *studies* in the lab" and "Lamarr *studies biology* in the lab." Invite students to experiment by making up similar pairs of sentences with different verbs. You might start them off with the following list of verbs: *ride, leave, drive, eat,* and *cook.*

Additional Resource

Grammar and Usage Practice Book, p. 26

Writing Theme: Clues to the Past

Other related areas students might wish to explore as writing topics include the following:

- a prehistoric animal
- the La Brea tar pits in California
- fossils
- the discoveries of Louis and Mary Leakey in East Africa

Answers to Practice Your Skills

A. Concept Check
Direct Objects

Answers are shown on page.

B. Concept Check
Identifying Direct Objects

16. None
17. artifacts
18. screams
19. None
20. animals
21. None
22. discovery
23. paintings
24. drawings
25. None

Writing Theme
Clues to the Past

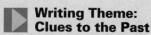

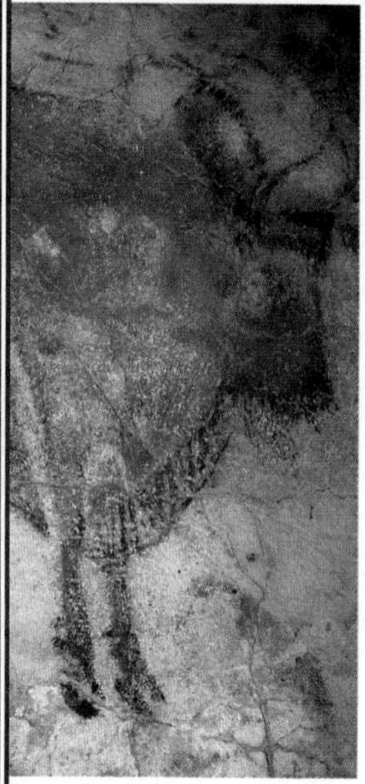

Cave painting of a bison, Altamira, Spain

FOR MORE PRACTICE
See page 424.

Practice Your Skills

A. CONCEPT CHECK

Direct Objects Write each sentence. Underline the verb once and the direct object twice.

1. Paleontologists study fossils for many reasons.
2. Like detectives, they hunt clues to the past.
3. Fossils often contain the images of ancient animals.
4. Close study reveals the fossils' shapes.
5. However, scientists must know their age, as well.
6. Long ago, paleontologists made educated guesses.
7. In the 1940s, Willard F. Libby invented a better method.
8. Libby developed the process of radiocarbon dating.
9. Every living thing contains a small amount of radiocarbon, a radioactive form of carbon.
10. Living plants and animals constantly absorb atoms of radiocarbon from the air or from their food.
11. Dead organisms, however, slowly lose their radiocarbon.
12. Libby understood an important fact about radiocarbon.
13. Dead organisms lose radiocarbon atoms at a constant rate.
14. Now scientists can measure the number of radiocarbon atoms in a fossil.
15. This number gives exact information about the fossil's age.

B. CONCEPT CHECK

Identifying Direct Objects Write the direct object from each sentence. If a sentence does not have a direct object, write *None.*

[16]Nine-year-old Maria de Sautuola wandered into a cave in northern Spain. [17]Nearby, her father was digging artifacts. [18]Suddenly, he heard screams. [19]He rushed to Maria. [20]Maria had seen animals on the cave ceiling! [21]The animals seemed very lifelike. [22]Maria had made an important discovery. [23]Experts soon were studying these fantastic paintings. [24]Ancient people created the drawings between 15,000 and 10,000 B.C. [25]The caves in Altamira are fine examples of prehistoric art.

LINKING VERBS

A **linking verb** connects, or links, the subject of a sentence with a word in the predicate that describes or renames the subject.

Linking verbs connect a word in the predicate with the subject. The word in the predicate says something about the subject.

The ocean *is* huge.   Many islands *are* small.

Linking verbs connect *ocean* with *huge* and *islands* with *small.* The words *huge* and *small* tell about the subjects. They are linked to the subjects by the linking verbs *is* and *are.*

The words *am, is, are, was, were, be, been,* and *become* are used as linking verbs. The words *seem, look, appear, smell, taste, feel,* and *sound* can also be linking verbs. (See pages 396–397 for a more complete list of linking verbs.)

The words that follow linking verbs and tell something about the subject can be adjectives, nouns, or pronouns. These words are called **predicate words** because they follow the verb and are part of the predicate.

The guests *feel* lucky. (*Lucky* is an adjective.)

The coconuts *taste* sweet. (*Sweet* is an adjective.)

Fish *became* their favorite food. (*Food* is a noun.)

The best cook *is* she. (*She* is a pronoun.)

Do not confuse predicate words with direct objects. Predicate words describe or rename the subject. In the above examples, *food* renames *fish* and *she* renames *cook.* To identify a linking verb, decide if the word following the verb either describes or renames the subject. If it does, the verb is a linking verb.

LINKING VERBS

Objectives

- To identify linking verbs and the words they link in sentences
- To identify predicate words as adjectives, nouns, or pronouns

Teaching Strategies

KEY TO UNDERSTANDING: LINKING VERBS Point out to students that one way to identify a linking verb is to substitute an equal sign (=) for the verb in the sentence. If the sentence still makes sense with the equal sign, the verb is a linking verb.

Linking Verb	Herb is the quarterback. Herb = the quarterback.
Action Verb	José eats bacon. José = bacon. (Sentence does not make sense)

CRITICAL THINKING: CATEGORIZING Remind students that linking verbs can never have a direct object since they do not express action. Action verbs, on the other hand, can never be followed by predicate words, because they do not link the subject to words that describe or rename it. Reinforce this distinction by giving students the following example.

He smells *smoke.* (*Smells* here is an action verb with a direct object, *smoke.*)

The room smells *smoky.* (*Smells* here links the subject, *room,* with the adjective *smoky,* which describes *room.*)

HELPFUL HINT Remind students that linking verbs—just like action verbs—can consist of more than one word. On the board, write some examples of linking verbs that include one or two helping verbs as well as the main verb: *had* ***been,*** *might have* ***been,*** *may* ***seem,*** *would have* ***become.*** Point out that the main verb is always the last one.

Additional Resource

Grammar and Usage Practice Book, p. 27

Writing Theme: Polynesia

Other related areas students might wish to explore as writing topics include the following:

- Hawaiian volcanoes
- Captain James Cook, explorer
- American Samoa
- marine birds of the Pacific
- Polynesian languages

Answers to Practice Your Skills

A. Concept Check
Linking Verbs

Answers are shown on page.

B. Concept Check
Identifying Linking Verbs and Predicate Words

	Subject	Linking Verb	Predicate Word
16.	Life	may seem	ideal
17.	Islanders	feel	grateful
18.	leaders	are	chiefs
19.	sons	become	chiefs
20.	solvers	are	they
21.	problems	appear	unsolvable
22.	Work	is	scarce
23.	Life	sounds	good
24.	Villagers	are becoming	dwellers
25.	cultures	may be	nonexistent

Writing Theme
Polynesia

Practice Your Skills

A. CONCEPT CHECK

Linking Verbs Write the linking verb in each sentence.

1. The origin of the Polynesian people remains a mystery.
2. They were not Asian or South American.
3. Historians feel certain about these facts.
4. Centuries ago, the Polynesians became masters of the ocean.
5. They were brave ocean travelers.
6. Their main form of transportation was travel by canoe.
7. Their slender dugout canoes with elaborate decorations look too fragile for dangerous ocean trips.
8. Nevertheless, these vessels were efficient.
9. Polynesian navigators seemed sure of their skills.
10. The navigators were familiar with the ocean currents, the stars, and the winds.
11. On the sea, Polynesian sailors felt free and independent.
12. The sea also became an important source of food.
13. Fishing remains an important industry in Polynesia today.
14. However, tourism appears a likely growth industry.
15. Thousands of tourists are visitors to Polynesia every year.

B. CONCEPT CHECK

Identifying Linking Verbs and Predicate Words Make three columns: *Subject, Linking Verb,* and *Predicate Word.* Find these parts in each sentence and write them in the proper columns. Include helping verbs in the *Linking Verb* column.

16. Life on a Pacific island may seem ideal.
17. Islanders feel grateful for their kinship with people on other islands.
18. Village leaders are often chiefs.
19. The chiefs' sons usually become chiefs too.
20. Skilled problem solvers are they.
21. However, some problems appear unsolvable.
22. Work in the villages is frequently scarce.
23. Life in the cities sounds good to the villagers.
24. Villagers are quickly becoming city dwellers.
25. Traditional cultures may one day be nonexistent.

FOR MORE PRACTICE
See page 424.

CHECK ✔ POINT

MIXED REVIEW · PAGES 403–406

Write the verb from each sentence. Then write the direct object or the predicate word. Write *DO* next to each direct object and *PW* next to each predicate word. If a sentence has no direct object or predicate word, write *None*.

1. Today, many women become doctors.
2. In the 1800s, people felt uneasy about women doctors.
3. The very idea of female physicians seemed outrageous.
4. Elizabeth Blackwell broke the barriers of prejudice with her leadership and determination.
5. As a young child, Blackwell lived in England.
6. In 1832, her family moved to the United States.
7. Even as a child, Blackwell wanted a career in medicine.
8. Later, she wrote applications to thirty medical schools.
9. Twenty-nine schools rejected her.
10. Finally, the thirtieth school, Geneva College, accepted her application.
11. Blackwell's training was difficult.
12. The future often looked bleak to her.
13. Nevertheless, she persevered in her studies.
14. In 1849, she finished her work at the college.
15. She became the first woman to receive a medical degree in the United States.
16. Her success, though, tasted bittersweet.
17. Hospitals closed their doors to her.
18. She couldn't even enter the wards of patients.
19. Fortunately, a persistent fighter was she.
20. For several years, she treated patients in Europe.
21. After a while, she returned to the United States.
22. However, prejudice appeared strong as ever.
23. In 1857, she opened a hospital with help from her sister.
24. The hospital served poor women in New York City.
25. It also included a medical school for women.

Writing Theme
Elizabeth Blackwell

Elizabeth Blackwell (1821–1910), first woman physician in the United States

Understanding Verbs **407**

CHECK ✔ POINT

◀ **Writing Theme: Elizabeth Blackwell**

Other related areas students might wish to explore as writing topics include the following:

- Barbara McClintock, Nobel Prize winner
- women doctors in Russia
- careers in medicine in the 21st century
- Gertrude B. Elion, Nobel Prize winner

MIXED REVIEW · PAGES 403–406

You may wish to use this activity to check students' mastery of the following concepts:

- direct objects of verbs
- linking verbs

1. become, doctors, PW
2. felt, uneasy, PW
3. seemed, outrageous, PW
4. broke, barriers, DO
5. lived, None
6. moved, None
7. wanted, career, DO
8. wrote, applications, DO
9. rejected, her, DO
10. accepted, application, DO
11. was, difficult, PW
12. looked, bleak, PW
13. persevered, None
14. finished, work, DO
15. became, woman, PW
16. tasted, bittersweet, PW
17. closed, doors, DO
18. could enter, wards, DO
19. was, she, PW
20. treated, patients, DO
21. returned, None
22. appeared, strong, PW
23. opened, hospital, DO
24. served, women, DO
25. included, school, DO

VERB TENSES

Objectives

- To recognize and form the present, past, and future tenses of verbs
- To use tenses accurately in sentences

Writing

- To correct verb tenses in a piece of writing

Teaching Strategies

HELPFUL HINT: FORM CHANGES

Across the top of the board, write three headings: *Change in Ending, Change in Spelling, Change in Helping Verb.* Then, write a vertical column of verbs down the left side of the board. Verbs might include *tell, paint,* and *live.* Have students fill in the chart with the correct verb form in each column as appropriate. For example, the verb *tell* can appear in the chart as *tells, told,* and *will tell.* Then ask students what effect, if any, these changes in form have on the tense of the verb. (*tells*—same tense; *told*—changed to past tense; *will tell*—changed to future tense) Continue the activity by calling on volunteers to suggest new verbs.

INDIVIDUALIZING INSTRUCTION: ESL STUDENTS Many foreign languages form tenses in ways different from English. They use various combinations of spelling changes, ending changes, and changes in helping verbs. Some languages, such as Turkish, have a large number of verb tenses. Japanese, on the other hand, has only two verb tenses: present and past.

To help students master English verb tenses, be sure all your ESL students understand the three basic concepts of time: *past*—happened before; *present*—happening now; *future*—will happen in the future.

VERB TENSES

> Different forms of a verb are used to show time. These forms are called **tenses.**

Verbs do more than tell of an action or a state of being They also tell about time. By changing their forms, verbs tell whether the action or state of being is past, present, or future.

The **present tense** tells about an action or a state of being that is happening now.

I *am* a jeweler. I *polish* gems. I *can work.*

The **past tense** tells about an action or a state of being that was completed in the past.

I *was* tired yesterday. I *polished* fifty gems.

The **future tense** tells about an action or a state of being that will happen in the future.

I *will receive* rubies tomorrow. I *will be* busy.

Notice that verb tense changes are made in three ways:

1. By a change in ending: *own, owned*
2. By a change in spelling: *see, saw*
3. By a change in helping verbs: *did work, will work*

A jeweler sorting diamonds

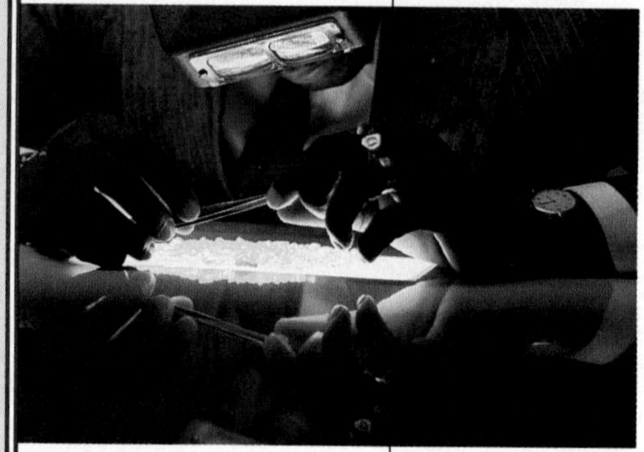

Forming the Present Tense

When the subject is plural, use the base form of the verb. The base form of the verb has no endings or changes. Use the base form of the verb with the pronouns *I* and *you.* Add *-s* or *-es* to the base form when the subject is singular.

We *look.* They *look.* I *look.*
You *look.* He *looks.*

Forming the Past Tense

Form the past tense of most verbs by adding *-d* or *-ed* to the base form of the verb. All verbs that form the past tense by adding *-d* or *-ed* to the base form of the verb are called **regular verbs.**

file	file*d*	wash	wash*ed*

Other verbs, called **irregular verbs,** undergo a change in their spelling to show the past tense. It's a good idea to memorize the past tense of irregular verbs.

go	*went*	wear	*wore*
choose	*chose*	do	*did*

There is another way that you can show a change in tense from the present form. You can use a helping verb along with the main verb.

rule	had ruled	cut	had cut

Forming the Future Tense

Form the future tense by using the helping verbs *will* or *shall* with the present tense.

shine	will shine	choose	will choose

Using Verb Tenses

Whenever you write, remember to keep your verbs in the same tense. Avoid switching from past to present or from present to past.

Incorrect The opal gleamed. It glows and glitters.
Correct The opal gleamed. It glowed and glittered.

Also, do not change the verb tense in the middle of a sentence.

Incorrect I *slip* on the ring and *wore* it proudly.
Correct I *slipped* on the ring and *wore* it proudly.

Writing TIP

You will need to change the ending of some regular verbs before adding *-ed* to form the past tense. For help with spelling past tense forms see Improving Your Spelling, pages 610–611.

Writing TIP

Notice how the use of verb tenses helps a reader understand the time order in these sentences.

Yesterday, I *fixed* the lock on the safe. Lady Markham *needs* a secure place to store her jewels. She *will bring* them tomorrow.

LINKING GRAMMAR AND WRITING Point out that writers sometimes use the present tense for special effect when they describe past events. Using the present tense can make a narrative or a description especially vivid and immediate for readers. Ask students if they can locate examples of newspaper or magazine articles in which the writer has used the present tense for events that occurred in the past. Remind students that if they use this technique in their writing, they must be sure to keep their verb tenses consistent.

Additional Resource

Grammar and Usage Practice Book, p. 28

Writing Theme: Precious Stones

Other related areas students might wish to explore as writing topics include the following:

- birthstones
- the use of rubies in lasers
- how diamonds are mined
- how pearls are formed

Answers to Practice Your Skills

A. Concept Check

Verb Tenses

1. Will come, Future
2. means, Present
3. surround, Present
4. will rule, Future
5. will wear, Future
6. sparkled, Past
7. belonged, Past
8. fell, Past
9. died, Past
10. glitters, Present

B. Drafting Skill

Using Tenses Accurately

11. fascinated
12. invented
13. give
14. brings
15. will fill
16. will predict
17. will increase
18. prevented
19. believe
20. will find

Writing Theme
Precious Stones

Practice Your Skills

A. CONCEPT CHECK

Verb Tenses Write the verb in each sentence. Then label the verb tense *Past, Present,* or *Future.*

1. Will the legends about the Kohinoor diamond come true?
2. *Kohinoor* means "the mountain of light" in Persian.
3. Two legends surround this fabulous gem.
4. First, its owner will someday rule the world.
5. Second, a man will never safely wear the stone.
6. The Kohinoor diamond sparkled through the destruction of two empires.
7. Long ago, it belonged to Emperor Mohammed Mogul.
8. His empire fell to the Shah of Persia.
9. The diamond's new owner, the Shah, soon died in a palace revolt.
10. At present, the diamond glitters in the collection of the Queen of England.

B. DRAFTING SKILL

Using Tenses Accurately Write the verb form given in parentheses.

11. Gems (past of *fascinate*) people of long ago in many unusual ways.
12. People even (past of *invent*) superstitions about gems and jewels.
13. Supposedly, diamonds (present of *give*) people strength in battle.
14. A sapphire (present of *bring*) wonderful happiness.
15. Rubies supposedly (future of *fill*) your life with love and joy.
16. An emerald under your tongue (future of *predict*) the future for you.
17. In other legends, amethysts (future of *increase*) your wisdom.
18. Turquoise supposedly (past of *prevent*) falls from horses and other accidents.
19. Of course, few (present of *believe*) these stories.
20. However, most people (future of *find*) the stories interesting.

410 Grammar Handbook

C. PROOFREADING SKILL

Correcting Verb Tenses Write the following paragraph, correcting errors in verb tenses. Also correct errors in spelling, capitalization, and punctuation. (10 errors)

Jade is a semiprecious stone, and it came in too kinds—jadeite and nephrite. Today, jadeite will be the more valuable of the two. Both kinds of jade are used for jewlery. In 1990, a huge boulder of nephrite jade was found in northeastern china. The boulder will weigh 291 tons. and it was 23 feet long by 20 feet high. can you imagine wearing that around you're neck.

FOR MORE PRACTICE
See page 425.

CHECK POINT

MIXED REVIEW • PAGES 408–411

Writing Theme
Horses

Write the following sentences using the verb form given in parentheses.

1. I (past of *attend*) a horse show last Friday.
2. My friend Amy (past of *show*) her horse Gypsy.
3. Gypsy (present of *perform*) many beautiful movements for the appreciative crowd.
4. Amy (past of *work*) with Gypsy for a month preparing for Friday's show.
5. He (present of *bow*) and (present of *prance*) gracefully in front of the reviewing stand.
6. Before every show, Amy (future of *braid*) his tail.
7. Gypsy (present of *seem*) like a member of her family.
8. Some riders (future of *decorate*) their horses' manes with colorful satin ribbons.
9. Amy (past of *shudder*) when she learned about prehistoric people.
10. They (past of *hunt*) wild horses and ate the meat.
11. No one ever (future of *turn*) Gypsy into a ponyburger!
12. Almost any horse (future of *learn*) to obey commands.
13. Amy (present of *train*) Gypsy every day.
14. Sometimes Gypsy (present of *disobey*) her commands.
15. Amy simply (present of *repeat*) the command patiently.

C. Proofreading Skill
Correcting Verb Tenses

Errors in proofreading exercises are counted as follows: (a) A misspelled word is one error; two initials and a last name not capitalized are counted as three errors. (b) Run-on sentences and sentence fragments are each counted as one error, even though the correction involves both punctuation and capitalization.

Errors are shown on page. The correctly rewritten paragraph appears below.

Jade is a semiprecious stone, and it comes in two kinds—jadeite and nephrite. Today, jadeite is the more valuable of the two. Both kinds of jade are used for jewelry. In 1990, a huge boulder of nephrite jade was found in northeastern China. The boulder weighed 291 tons, and it was 23 feet long by 20 feet high. Can you imagine wearing that around your neck?

CHECK POINT

Writing Theme: Horses

Other related areas students might wish to explore as writing topics include the following:

- a famous horse, real or fictitious
- the remaining wild horses of the American West
- how the horse and the zebra are related
- workhorses today

MIXED REVIEW • PAGES 408–411

You may wish to use this activity to check students' mastery of the following concept:

- verb tenses

1. attended
2. showed
3. performs
4. worked
5. bows, prances
6. will braid
7. seems
8. will decorate
9. shuddered
10. hunted
11. will turn
12. will learn
13. trains
14. disobeys
15. repeats

Understanding Verbs 411

THE PRINCIPAL PARTS OF VERBS

Objectives
- To identify the three principal parts of regular verbs

Writing
- To use the various verb forms in writing

Teaching Strategies

KEY TO UNDERSTANDING: PAST PARTICIPLES Stress to students that there is a distinction between the *principal parts* of a verb and a verb's *tenses*. The first and second principal parts correspond to the present and past tense forms of a verb, but the past participle form does not express any one tense. On the contrary, a participle in a verb phrase is always used with one or more helping verbs. It is these helping verbs that determine the tense.

ASSESSMENT: SPOT CHECK Give students a list of five additional regular verbs, such as *pull, wave, sip, marry,* and *pounce.* Have them write the principal parts of these verbs on index cards. Then have students exchange cards with a neighbor and check the accuracy of each other's verb forms and spelling.

THE PRINCIPAL PARTS OF VERBS

All verb tenses are made from the three **principal parts** of a verb: present, past, and past participle.

You have seen that every verb has many different forms. All of these different forms are made from just three **principal parts.** Look at the principal parts of the verbs below.

Present	Past	Past Participle
call	called	(have) called
halt	halted	(have) halted
print	printed	(have) printed
watch	watched	(have) watched
review	reviewed	(have) reviewed
carry	carried	(have) carried

The **present** part of the verb is its present tense. Add *-s* to form the singular. The present part used with *will* or *shall* forms the future tense.

The **past** part of the verb is its past tense. The spelling of the past tense of a verb may change if its present form ends in *y* or a consonant such as *-h, -d, -p,* or *-t.* For example, the past of *worry* is *worried;* the past of *snap* is *snapped.*

The **past participle** is always used with a helping verb such as *have.* Look at these other examples.

is called	has called	was being called
was called	have called	has been called
were called	had called	will have called
		will be called
		should have been called

Notice that with regular verbs, the past participle is the same as the past form. This is not always true of irregular verbs. You will learn more about the principal parts of irregular verbs later in this handbook.

Practice Your Skills

A. CONCEPT CHECK

Principal Parts of Verbs Make three columns: *Present, Past,* and *Past Participle.* Write each of the following words in the *Present* column. Then write the past and past participle forms in their columns. Choose helping verbs to include with the past participles.

1. try	**6.** record	**11.** flub
2. produce	**7.** plan	**12.** vary
3. hurry	**8.** play	**13.** pick
4. act	**9.** edit	**14.** rehearse
5. learn	**10.** accept	**15.** shop

B. DRAFTING SKILL

Using the Principal Parts of Verbs Write each sentence using the verb form given in parentheses.

16. Movies (past participle of *enjoy,* with *are*) by millions of people everywhere.
17. Movie making (present of *involve*) hundreds of people, from actors to costume designers to electricians.
18. Of course, no film ever (past of *start*) without a "property," or idea for a story.
19. The screenwriter's job never (present of *end*).
20. Scripts (past participle of *change,* with *must be*) often.
21. The director (present of *plan*) every detail.
22. His orders (past participle of *carry,* with *are*) out by the cast and crew.
23. For example, stunts (past participle of *practice,* with *should be*) many times for safety's sake.
24. In the past, stunt performers often (past of *injure*) themselves.
25. Today, safety equipment and procedures (present of *protect*) most stunt performers from harm during filming.

Writing Theme
Making Movies

FOR MORE PRACTICE
See page 425.

Additional Resource

Grammar and Usage Practice Book, p. 29

Writing Theme: Making Movies

Other related areas students might wish to explore as writing topics include the following:

- special effects in today's movies
- the role of the film editor
- changing black-and-white movies to color
- movies targeted for a young audience

Answers to Practice Your Skills

A. Concept Check
Principal Parts of Verbs

Helping verbs with the past participles may vary.

	Present	Past	Past Participle
1.	try	tried	(have) tried
2.	produce	produced	(was) produced
3.	hurry	hurried	(has) hurried
4.	act	acted	(have) acted
5.	learn	learned	(were) learned
6.	record	recorded	(has) recorded
7.	plan	planned	(are) planned
8.	play	played	(will be) played
9.	edit	edited	(had) edited
10.	accept	accepted	(is) accepted
11.	flub	flubbed	(have) flubbed
12.	vary	varied	(have been) varied
13.	pick	picked	(will have) picked
14.	rehearse	rehearsed	(was) rehearsed
15.	shop	shopped	(has) shopped

B. Drafting Skill
Using the Principal Parts of Verbs

Student answers should be in complete sentences.

16. are enjoyed
17. involves
18. started
19. ends
20. must be changed
21. plans
22. are carried
23. should be practiced
24. injured
25. protect

IRREGULAR VERBS

Objectives

- To identify the three principal parts of irregular verbs

Writing

- To use irregular verbs correctly in a piece of writing

Teaching Strategies

KEY TO UNDERSTANDING: IRREGULAR VERBS Tell students that verbs are irregular when they do not form the past tense by adding *-d* or *-ed.* To help students see the difference between regular and irregular verbs, write on the board the principal parts of the six regular verbs from the list on page 412 and six irregular verbs from the chart on page 415, and ask students to compare the forms.

MODELING Show students how to find the principal parts of irregular verbs. For example, have them look up the word *buy* in a dictionary. Point out and identify past tense and participle forms.

STUMBLING BLOCK Tell students that there are a few irregular verbs whose present tense, past tense, and past participle forms are the same. Write examples of these forms—such as *let, put, set, hit,* and *shut*—on the board. Tell students that the context in which a verb is used is the only clue as to whether the verb is in the past or the present tense. Give some examples of these verbs in sentences, such as "I always *let* (present) my hair grow in the winter" and "Yesterday I *let* (past) my dog run without his leash." Then have students offer some examples of their own in which the context indicates the present or past tense.

IRREGULAR VERBS

For some verbs, the past tense is formed by changing the spelling of the present form. These verbs are called **irregular verbs.**

You have already learned that the past form of all regular verbs is made by adding either *-d* or *-ed* to the present form of the verbs.

race   rac*ed*   jump   jump*ed*   dip   dipp*ed*

Some verbs, however, have past forms that are made by changing the spelling of the present form. These verbs are **irregular verbs.** Here are some examples.

run   *ran*   sing   *sang*   go   *went*

Sometimes, the past participle of an irregular verb is the same as the past form.

said   *(has) said*   taught   *(have) taught*

However, many irregular verbs have past participle forms that are different from the past forms.

threw   *(were) thrown*   swam   *(have) swum*

Remember these rules whenever you use regular or irregular verbs.

1. The past form of a verb is always used alone without a helping verb.

   The athlete *drank* the entire container of water.

2. The past participle must always be used with a helping verb.

   The athlete *had drunk* the entire container of water during the time out.

Here is a list of the principal parts of the most common irregular verbs. Refer to it whenever you are unsure about the proper form of an irregular verb. In addition, dictionaries list the principal parts of irregular verbs after the present form.

Principal Parts of Common Irregular Verbs

Present	Past	Past Participle
begin	began	(have) begun
break	broke	(have) broken
bring	brought	(have) brought
choose	chose	(have) chosen
come	came	(have) come
do	did	(have) done
drink	drank	(have) drunk
eat	ate	(have) eaten
fall	fell	(have) fallen
fly	flew	(have) flown
freeze	froze	(have) frozen
give	gave	(have) given
go	went	(have) gone
grow	grew	(have) grown
know	knew	(have) known
lay	laid	(have) laid
lie	lay	(have) lain
ride	rode	(have) ridden
rise	rose	(have) risen
run	ran	(have) run
say	said	(have) said
see	saw	(have) seen
sing	sang	(have) sung
sit	sat	(have) sat
speak	spoke	(have) spoken
steal	stole	(have) stolen
swim	swam	(have) swum
take	took	(have) taken
teach	taught	(have) taught
wear	wore	(have) worn
write	wrote	(have) written

CRITICAL THINKING: CLASSIFYING Point out to students that it may help them to master the chart of irregular verbs if they look for similar patterns of irregular forms. For example, *break, broke, broken* shows a pattern of changes similar to that of *speak, spoke, spoken.* Challenge students to identify other patterns, such as *teach, taught, taught* and *bring, brought, brought.* Have teams work on forming mini-lists of verbs with similar forms. Have students share their lists and quiz each other on the principal parts of verbs with similar forms.

INDIVIDUALIZING INSTRUCTION: ESL STUDENTS For many ESL students, it is frustrating to learn a language that always seems to "break the rules." Past tense irregular verb forms are especially difficult for these students because each form must be memorized separately. Pair ESL students with native English speakers to practice irregular verb forms orally. Below are some additional irregular verb forms that will be useful for ESL students to learn.

drive-drove	read-read
feel-felt	send-sent
forget-forgot	sleep-slept
lose-lost	tell-told
make-made	think-thought

INDIVIDUALIZING INSTRUCTION: BASIC STUDENTS Remind students to refer to the chart on page 415 when completing the exercises. You may want to do the first five sentences in Exercise A orally with these students to make sure they are able to select the proper verb forms from the chart.

Additional Resource

Grammar and Usage Practice Book, pp. 30–35

Writing Theme: Record-setting Feats

Other related areas students might wish to explore as writing topics include the following:

- Charles Lindbergh, aviator
- Olympic records
- the *Guinness Book of World Records*
- baseball statistics

Answers to Practice Your Skills

A. Concept Check

Irregular Verbs

1. done
2. said
3. chose
4. ran
5. went
6. broken
7. taught
8. began
9. came
10. worn
11. known
12. lay
13. fell
14. rose
15. drunk

B. Proofreading Skill

Using Irregular Verbs Correctly

Errors are shown on page. The correctly rewritten paragraph appears below.

In 1926, Gertrude Ederle stole the world's heart. She gave her best effort to a daunting task. At age nineteen, she swam the English Channel. Her time broke all previous records. The feat took fourteen hours and thirty-nine minutes. Other swimmers had nearly frozen in the cold water. Gertrude, however, wore a heavy coat of grease for warmth. Reporters had flown in from all over the world for the event. Some rode next to her in rowboats. In their articles, the reporters wrote about Gertrude's victory and sang her praises for the Olympic medals she had won earlier.

Writing Theme
Record-setting Feats

Practice Your Skills

A. CONCEPT CHECK

Irregular Verbs Write the correct form of the verb given in parentheses.

1. How many athletes have (past participle of *do*) what was thought to be impossible?
2. How many have (past participle of *say*), "I can do it"?
3. Sarah Covington-Fulcher (past of *choose*) a challenge that many believed impossible.
4. She (past of *run*) perhaps the longest distance ever.
5. She (past of *go*) 11,134 miles through 35 states.
6. Earlier records had now been (past participle of *break*).
7. This runner (past of *teach*) a lesson in endurance.
8. Her race (past of *begin*) on July 21, 1987.
9. It (past of *come*) to an end on October 2, 1988.
10. Twenty-six pairs of shoes were (past participle of *wear*) out during her run.
11. Could she have (past participle of *know*) the hazards?
12. Hazards, indeed, (past of *lie*) in wait along the route.
13. Once, the temperature (past of *fall*) way below zero!
14. In the desert, it (past of *rise*) to 124 degrees!
15. She must have (past participle of *drink*) lots of water!

B. PROOFREADING SKILL

Using Irregular Verbs Correctly Write the paragraph. Correct all errors, especially those in the use of irregular verbs. (18 errors)

In 1926, gertrude ederle stealed the worlds' heart. She gave her best effort to a daunting task. At age ninteen, she swum the English Channel. Her time breaked all previous records, The feat taked fourteen hours and thirty-nine minutes. Other Swimmers had nearly frozen in the cold water. Gertrude, however, weared a heavy coat of greese for warmth. Reporters had flew in from all over the world for the event. Some rided next to her in rowboats. In they're articles, the reporters wrote about Gertrude's victory. And singed her praises for the Olympic meddals she had won earlier.

FOR MORE PRACTICE
See page 426.

CHECK POINT

MIXED REVIEW • PAGES 412–416

Write the correct form of the regular or irregular verb given in parentheses.

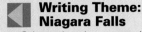

1. Have you ever (saw, seen) Niagara Falls?
2. Each year, millions (visit, visited) the falls.
3. The water (runs, ran) violently over a rocky cliff.
4. Over time, the falls actually have (grew, grown) smaller.
5. Water (worn, wears) away part of the cliff.
6. This erosion (stolen, steals) an average of three inches from the cliff each year.
7. Still, water has (rush, rushed) over the cliff since the end of the Ice Age.
8. Visitors have (tell, told) of many amazing sights at Niagara.
9. Several times, for example, the falls have (freeze, frozen) in extremely cold weather.
10. Daredevils have also (try, tried) spectacular stunts.
11. Some have (went, gone) over the falls in barrels.
12. Most of them (fell, fallen) to disastrous ends.
13. A few, however, have (swam, swum) to safety.
14. In the 1800s, a famous French tightrope artist (gave, given) his greatest performance at Niagara.
15. People (came, come) from all over to see Blondin's performance.
16. Blondin (crossed, cross) above the falls on a thin wire several times.
17. During one crossing, he (wore, worn) a blindfold.
18. Another time, he (carried, carry) a man on his back.
19. At one point, he (sat, sit) calmly on the wire and (eat, ate) an omelet!
20. Officials have since (pass, passed) laws against such stunts.

Writing Theme
Niagara Falls

CHECK POINT

Writing Theme: Niagara Falls

Other related areas students might wish to explore as writing topics include the following:

- Victoria Falls in Africa
- hydroelectric power
- how a waterfall is formed

MIXED REVIEW • PAGES 412–416

You may wish to use this activity to check students' mastery of the following concepts:

- the principal parts of verbs
- irregular verbs

Answers are shown on page.

CONFUSING PAIRS OF VERBS

Objectives

- To choose the correct form of these verbs: *can, may; let, leave; lie, lay*

Writing

- To use these verbs correctly in sentences

Teaching Strategies

KEY TO UNDERSTANDING: *CAN* AND *MAY* You may wish to share one or more of these notes with students: (a) *can* and *may* are almost always used as helping verbs; (b) while *can* has a past tense *(could), may* is used only in the present tense; (c) *can* is often substituted for *may* in informal speech and dialogue. Point out, however, that it is important to use *can* and *may* correctly in formal writing.

INDIVIDUALIZING INSTRUCTION: VISUAL LEARNERS Encourage each student to think of a sentence for one of the following verbs: *can, may, let, leave, lie,* and *lay.* The sentence should be one that can be illustrated on a poster; for example, "You can stop forest fires." Then invite the students to create posters illustrating their sentences. Displaying the posters in the classroom will provide visual reinforcement of correct usage.

CONFUSING PAIRS OF VERBS

Several pairs of verbs are often confused. These include **can** and **may, let** and **leave,** and **lie** and **lay.**

Look at the correct way to use these confusing verbs.

Can and *May*

1. *Can* means "to be able."
2. *May* means "to be allowed to," "to be permitted to," or "to have the possibility of."

Can you walk a tightrope?
You may go to the circus.

Let and *Leave*

1. *Let* means "to allow" or "to permit."
2. *Leave* means "to depart" or "to let stay or let be."

Principal Parts	let, let, let
	leave, left, left

Let me see your ticket.
What time do you *leave* for the show?
Do not *leave* your ticket behind.

Lie and *Lay*

1. *Lie* means "to rest" or "to recline."
2. *Lay* means "to put or place something."

Principal Parts	lie, lay, lain
	lay, laid, laid

The elephant *lies* down upon command.
The clown *lays* a red carpet in the ring.

Lay also means "to produce eggs": A hen *lays* eggs.

Practice Your Skills

A. CONCEPT CHECK

Confusing Verbs Write the correct verb from those given in parentheses.

1. I had just (laid, lain) down on the sofa for a nap.
2. Children's cries outside did not (let, leave) me sleep.
3. "(Can, May) I go to the circus?" cried a boy.
4. A girl cried, "(Leave, Let) me go too!"
5. I (can, may) imagine these same cries in ancient Rome.
6. The Romans (laid, lay) the foundations for the circus.
7. The circus's past also (lies, lays) in fairs and markets.
8. In the markets, vendors (lain, laid) out their goods.
9. I (can, may) picture the people shopping.
10. Vendors rarely (let, left) their stands.
11. Other people, though, would (lie, lay) down their purchases and watch jugglers, magicians, and minstrels.
12. Later, the idea of a market as a fair was (left, let) behind.
13. Fairs became separate celebrations that (left, let) people have fun.
14. People would (lie, lay) their troubles aside and laugh.
15. I (can, may) see why the children want to go to the circus!

B. REVISION SKILL

Using Verbs Correctly For each sentence, if a verb is incorrect, write the correct verb. If a verb is correct, write *Correct.*

16. Have you ever laid down with a ball on your nose?
17. Graduates of National Circus Project workshops claim they may juggle and perform other circus stunts.
18. Many schools let project members work with students.
19. The circus performers arrive and lie out the equipment.
20. They do not let students alone while learning.
21. Instead, they let students learn tricks and stunts.
22. Some find they may juggle balls easily after only one lesson.
23. For others, many balls still fall and lay on the floor.
24. By the time instructors leave, students feel confident.
25. Sometimes, schools may invite promising students back.

Writing Theme
The Circus

FOR MORE PRACTICE
See page 426.

Additional Resource

Grammar and Usage Practice Book, p. 36

Writing Theme: The Circus

Other related areas students might wish to explore as writing topics include the following:

- circus clowns
- big cats in circus acts
- circus buildings in ancient Rome
- the career of P.T. Barnum

Answers to Practice Your Skills

A. Concept Check
Confusing Verbs

Answers are shown on page.

B. Revision Skill
Using Verbs Correctly

16. lain
17. can juggle
18. Correct
19. lay
20. leave
21. Correct
22. can juggle
23. lie
24. Correct
25. Correct

Understanding Verbs 419

OTHER CONFUSING VERB PAIRS

Objectives

- To choose the correct forms of these often-confused verbs: *teach, learn; rise, raise; sit, set*

Writing

- To use these verbs correctly in sentences

Teaching Strategies

HELPFUL HINT Some dialects substitute *learn* for *teach.* To accustom students to the sound of standard English, provide them with the following oral drill:

The coach *taught* the team new plays.

The team *learned* quickly.

Some team members failed to *learn* the offsides rule.

The coach finally *taught* them by drawing a diagram.

KEY TO UNDERSTANDING It may help students to choose the correct form from these verb pairs if they know that *raise* and *set* almost always take direct objects, but *rise* and *sit* almost never do. Remind students that a direct object answers the question *whom* or *what* after a verb.

MANAGING THE PAPER LOAD To limit the number of exercises you have to correct, you may wish to have students do Exercise A orally. In Exercise B, students can write their answers and then exchange papers with partners to correct each other's work.

OTHER CONFUSING VERB PAIRS

Other verb pairs that are often confused are these: **teach** and **learn, rise** and **raise,** and **sit** and **set.**

Here are some other pairs of verbs that are often confused and used incorrectly.

Teach and *Learn*

1. *Teach* means to "to show how" or "to explain."
2. *Learn* means "to understand" or "to gain knowledge."

Principal Parts teach, taught, taught
learn, learned, learned

Can you *teach* an old dog new tricks?
My dog will not *learn* any tricks at all.

Rise and *Raise*

1. *Rise* means "to move upward" or "to get up."
2. *Raise* means "to move something upward" or "to lift."

Principal Parts rise, rose, risen
raise, raised, raised

The lazy dog *rises* from the cushion.
Raise your paw for a handshake.

Sit and *Set*

1. *Sit* means "to be in a seat" or "to rest."
2. *Set* means "to put or place something."

Principal Parts sit, sat, sat
set, set, set

The puppy *sits* on his blanket.
Set his bowl on the floor.

Practice Your Skills

A. CONCEPT CHECK

Confusing Verb Pairs Write the correct verb from those given in parentheses.

1. Almost any dog can be (learned, taught) new tricks.
2. Your skill level, too, will (rise, raise) with each trick.
3. (Set, Sit) reasonable goals for yourself and your pet.
4. A reward will (rise, raise) your dog's rate of success.
5. I (learned, taught) my dog several simple tricks.
6. Now she (rises, raises) her paw to shake hands.
7. At my command, she (sets, sits) and waits for me.
8. Also on command, she (raises, rises) up on her hind legs.
9. Eventually, she (learned, taught) to find toys and bring them to me.
10. Yesterday, she (set, sat) her favorite toy on my lap.
11. When she did that, my hopes (rose, raised).
12. I tried to (teach, learn) her to fetch my slippers.
13. However, she stubbornly (set, sat) on one slipper and chewed the other.
14. I guess I had (sat, set) my sights too high.
15. I (learned, taught) that some tricks might be too hard.

B. REVISION SKILL

Using Verbs Correctly Write the sentences and correct any errors in the verbs. If a sentence is correct, write *Correct.*

16. Special trainers rise guide dogs to help blind people.
17. These trainers learn the dogs valuable skills.
18. First, a family rises a dog for about a year.
19. The family sits typical goals for basic obedience.
20. Then, an intense training program learns the dog other skills.
21. A guide dog even learns when to disobey commands.
22. A dog is learned to stop at busy intersections.
23. When cars are approaching, the dog will set still and refuse to move rather than endanger its owner.
24. Time is also sat aside for dog and owner to work together.
25. A well-trained dog will raise to almost any occasion.

Writing Theme
Training Animals

FOR MORE PRACTICE
See page 426.

Additional Resource

Grammar and Usage Practice Book, p. 37

Writing Theme: Training Animals

Other related areas students might wish to explore as writing topics include the following:

- training racehorses
- performing dolphins
- seeing-eye or hearing-ear dogs

Answers to Practice Your Skills

A. Concept Check
Confusing Verb Pairs

Answers are shown on page.

B. Revision Skill
Using Verbs Correctly

Student answers should be in complete sentences.

16. raise
17. teach
18. raises
19. sets
20. teaches
21. Correct
22. taught
23. sit
24. set
25. rise

CHECK POINT

Writing Theme: Young Napoleon Bonaparte

Other related areas students might wish to explore as writing topics include the following:

- Napoleon's military campaigns
- the retreat of Napoleon's army from Moscow (1812)
- Napoleon's exile on the island of St. Helena
- Napoleon in art

MIXED REVIEW • PAGES 418–421

You may wish to use this activity to check students' mastery of the following concept:

- confusing pairs of verbs

Answers are shown on page.

Writing Theme
Young Napoleon Bonaparte

CHECK POINT

MIXED REVIEW • PAGES 418–421

Write the correct verb from those given in parentheses.

1. How many great world leaders (can, may) you name?
2. Their deeds have (raised, risen) above the ordinary.
3. Some leaders (rose, raised) themselves to fame.
4. The stories of others (lay, lie) hidden in history.
5. We all (can, may) benefit from studying great leaders.
6. You (can, may) choose to learn about their childhoods.
7. Did they (sit, set) in school and not pay attention?
8. Did they (let, leave) diaries behind for us to read?
9. (Let, Leave) us examine the young Napoleon Bonaparte.
10. The Bonapartes did not (raise, rise) their son for a career in the army.
11. Bonaparte children were (learned, taught) to be priests, lawyers, or public officials.
12. Napoleon, though, (sat, set) his mind on military glory.
13. He would (lay, lie) a trap for his six younger brothers and sisters and then give them orders.
14. You (may, can) want to consider him bossy.
15. His orders often (raised, rose) a family ruckus.
16. What (can, may) you expect from a boy nicknamed "the little wolf"?
17. Only his older brother Joseph would (set, sit) quietly.
18. Usually, Napoleon (raised, rose) to the occasion and restored the family peace.
19. Napoleon's parents would (leave, let) him discover his own strengths and weaknesses.
20. He easily (learned, taught) science and mathematics.
21. In boarding school, the other students would not (leave, let) young Napoleon alone.
22. However, the boy preferred to (lay, lie) in bed and dream of glory.
23. He would (sit, set) goals for himself.
24. In time, he would (rise, raise) to fame and power.
25. In fact, "the little wolf" later (sat, set) on a throne as the Emperor of France.

A. Finding Action Verbs and Linking Verbs Write the main verb from each sentence. Then write whether it is an *Action Verb* or a *Linking Verb.*

1. Does exploration interest you?
2. Unexplored areas fascinated President Thomas Jefferson.
3. In the eastern United States, people knew little about the land west of the Mississippi River.
4. Little information was available to mapmakers in 1800.
5. An exploration party seemed the best solution.
6. In 1804, Jefferson organized a grand expedition.
7. He chose Meriwether Lewis as the leader.
8. William Clark became the second in command.
9. Clark was an excellent mapmaker and leader.
10. Forty-five men joined the dangerous expedition.
11. Lewis described the trip in his journal.
12. Grizzly bears attacked the men on the journey west.
13. Lewis felt happy and excited near the Rocky Mountains.
14. The men traveled about 7,700 miles to the Pacific Ocean.
15. Lewis published his journal in 1814.

B. Identifying Main Verbs and Helping Verbs Write the verb from each sentence. Underline the helping verb(s) once and the main verb twice.

16. Can you name any women explorers?
17. Many women explorers have been ignored by history.
18. These valiant adventurers did not become famous.
19. By the time of her death, Louise Boyd had led seven expeditions to Greenland.
20. Delia J. Akeley is known for her African explorations and knowledge of Pygmy culture.
21. In 1929, Akeley was living in a Pygmy village.
22. Her greatest contribution may have been her open approach to different cultures.
23. Friendliness had always served her well with strangers.
24. Have other women undertaken dangerous expeditions?
25. Even in her fifties, Annie Smith Peck was scaling mountains in Peru!

GRAMMAR HANDBOOK 36

Writing Theme
Great Expeditions

GRAMMAR HANDBOOK 36

ADDITIONAL PRACTICE

Each of these exercises correlates to a section of Handbook 36, "Understanding Verbs." The exercises may be used for more practice, for reteaching, or for review of the concepts presented.

Additional Resource

Grammar and Usage Practice Book, p. 39

Writing Theme: Great Expeditions

Other related areas students might wish to explore as writing topics include the following:

- the Oregon Trail
- Sir Richard Francis Burton, English explorer
- Thor Heyerdahl's *Kon Tiki*
- Ruth Harkness's search for the giant panda in China (1936)

A. Finding Action Verbs and Linking Verbs

1. interest, Action Verb
2. fascinated, Action Verb
3. knew, Action Verb
4. was, Linking Verb
5. seemed, Linking Verb
6. organized, Action Verb
7. chose, Action Verb
8. became, Linking Verb
9. was, Linking Verb
10. joined, Action Verb
11. described, Action Verb
12. attacked, Action Verb
13. felt, Linking Verb
14. traveled, Action Verb
15. published, Action Verb

B. Identifying Main Verbs and Helping Verbs

Answers are shown on page.

C. Recognizing Direct Objects Write the verb in each sentence. Then write the direct object. If a sentence has no direct object, write *None.*

26. Antonio and Margarita Serra loved their son Miguel.
27. Their bright little boy received an excellent education.
28. Young Miguel became a priest of the Franciscan order.
29. The world knows Miguel as Father Junípero Serra.
30. He had chosen the name of Junípero, a friend of St. Francis of Assisi.
31. The Franciscan order sent the priest to the Americas.
32. In Mexico, during the 1700s, Father Junípero learned many skills for survival in the wilderness.
33. Father Junípero joined an expedition to California.
34. He worked hard in the region known as Upper California.
35. He earned the respect of the native peoples there.
36. Together, they built the California missions.
37. Father Junípero defended the rights of the native peoples.
38. The first mission was established in San Diego in 1769.
39. Some missions are still standing.
40. In time, the original settlements became cities.

D. Identifying Linking Verbs and Predicate Words Write the verb from each of the following sentences. If the verb is a linking verb, write the predicate word. If the verb is not a linking verb, write *NLV.*

41. In the 1900s, most expeditions were scientific.
42. Adventure remained an important part of them, though.
43. Roy Chapman Andrews's work seems an excellent example.
44. In time, he became director of the American Museum of Natural History.
45. The museum sponsored his expeditions.
46. At first, he was famous for adventures in faraway places.
47. Andrews's life sounded glamorous to many people.
48. One year, he traveled to Outer Mongolia.
49. There he found the first known dinosaur eggs.
50. Undoubtedly, he felt proud of this discovery.

424 Grammar Handbook

C. Recognizing Direct Objects

26. loved, son
27. received, education
28. became, None
29. knows, Miguel
30. had chosen, name
31. sent, priest
32. learned, skills
33. joined, expedition
34. worked, None
35. earned, respect
36. built, missions
37. defended, rights
38. was established, None
39. are standing, None
40. became, None

D. Identifying Linking Verbs and Predicate Words

41. were, scientific
42. remained, part
43. seems, example
44. became, director
45. sponsored, NLV
46. was, famous
47. sounded, glamorous
48. traveled, NLV
49. found, NLV
50. felt, proud

E. Recognizing Verb Tenses Write the tense of each verb in italics. Write *Present, Past,* or *Future.*

51. Millions of people *admire* Admiral Richard E. Byrd.
52. Few explorers ever *will rival* his daring or his vision.
53. Byrd *gained* fame as an aviator for the United States Navy.
54. In 1926, he *was* on the first flight over the North Pole.
55. We *remember* him mostly for his work at the South Pole.
56. Byrd *explored* the Antarctic for more than thirty years.
57. He *opened* the Antarctic to exploration by aircraft.
58. Byrd also *established* bases for scientific studies.
59. In a book, he *describes* one lonely winter at a base.
60. Because of his work, people someday *will understand* the mysterious and icy continent of Antarctica.

F. Identifying Principal Parts of Verbs Write the verb from each sentence. Then tell whether the main verb is in the *Present, Past,* or *Past Participle* form.

61. In 1937, Amelia Earhart started her last expedition.
62. She and her navigator had planned a flight around the world.
63. Earhart had first gained fame as a pilot in the 1920s.
64. Over the years, she recorded many aviation firsts.
65. She also established many long-distance flying records.
66. Some of her achievements still stand in the record books.
67. By 1937, she had prepared for the ultimate flight.
68. Many people can recall the excitement of the flight's early stages.
69. Then, over the Pacific Ocean, Earhart, her navigator, and the plane all disappeared.
70. Since then, many expeditions have combed the area in search of her.
71. In fact, people still search for traces of the flight.
72. Investigators have advanced many theories.
73. The mystery of her tragic flight has never been solved.
74. It remains one of the great mysteries of this century.
75. The legend of Amelia Earhart lives on long after her death.

E. Recognizing Verb Tenses
51. Present
52. Future
53. Past
54. Past
55. Present
56. Past
57. Past
58. Past
59. Present
60. Future

F. Identifying Principal Parts of Verbs
61. started, Past
62. had planned, Past Participle
63. had gained, Past Participle
64. recorded, Past
65. established, Past
66. stand, Present
67. had prepared, Past Participle
68. can recall, Present
69. disappeared, Past
70. have combed, Past Participle
71. search, Present
72. have advanced, Past Participle
73. has been solved, Past Participle
74. remains, Present
75. lives, Present

G. Using Irregular Verbs
76. brought
77. ate
78. took
79. seen
80. froze
81. went
82. told
83. rode
84. gone
85. chose
86. began
87. sat
88. come
89. done

H. Choosing the Right Verb
Answers are shown on page.

G. Using Irregular Verbs Write the verb form given in parentheses.

76. Expeditions to the South Pole have (past participle of *bring*) some people fame and glory.
77. Others (past of *eat*) humble pie after their failure.
78. In 1911, Englishman Robert Scott (past of *take*) an expedition to the Antarctic.
79. By the time Scott and his companions reached the pole, they had (past participle of *see*) only icy misery.
80. In the end, Scott (past of *freeze*) to death.
81. Norwegian explorer Roald Amundsen also (past of *go*) to Antarctica in 1911.
82. Many writers have (past participle of *tell*) of the race between Scott and Amundsen to the South Pole.
83. Amundsen's group (past of *ride*) dog sleds and walked.
84. Their journey to the South Pole and back had (past participle of *go*) fairly smoothly.
85. British adventurer Robert Swan (past of *choose*) two dangerous expeditions.
86. Swan (past of *begin*) a walk to the South Pole in 1986.
87. Seventy days later, he (past of *sit*) down at the pole.
88. By 1989, he had (past participle of *come*) back from a walk to the North Pole.
89. Why have people (past participle of *do*) such daring and dangerous feats?

H. Choosing the Right Verb Write the correct verb from those given in parentheses.

90. Armchair adventurers (sit, set) back and relax.
91. These people (lie, lay) around and dream.
92. Others have (risen, raised) flags in distant lands.
93. Real adventurers do not (lie, lay) aside their dreams.
94. They (can, may) put their dreams into practice.
95. Their exploits (learn, teach) them courage.
96. Their mistakes (let, leave) them grow and learn.
97. Has the spirit of adventure (raised, risen) in you?
98. Perhaps one day you (can, may) enter the record books.

426 Grammar Handbook

A. Kinds of Verbs Write the verb from each sentence. Then, tell whether it is an *Action Verb* or a *Linking Verb*. If the verb is an action verb, write the direct object. If the verb is a linking verb, write the predicate word.

1. A year without a summer seems impossible.
2. In 1816, people in New England experienced the coldest summer on record.
3. Snowstorms struck the Northeast in June.
4. Frost nipped noses in July and August.
5. The weather remained cool during that entire spring and summer.
6. This scientific oddity sounds unbelievable.
7. In 1815, the Mount Tambora volcano in Indonesia shot tiny particles of sulfur into the atmosphere.
8. These sulfur particles reflected much sunlight away from the earth.
9. In 1816, summer became winter in upstate New York and New England.
10. One single volcanic eruption cooled the globe!

B. Main Verbs and Helping Verbs Write each of the following sentences. Underline the helping verb or verbs once. Underline the main verb twice.

11. Volcanoes have not been the only causes of strange weather around the world.
12. Many parts of the world are affected by an area of unusually warm sea water in the Pacific Ocean.
13. This stream of water is called El Niño.
14. Scientists haven't discovered the causes of El Niño.
15. They are still studying this oddity of nature.
16. However, they do know its effects.
17. In the past, El Niño has set off jet streams of warm, moist air.
18. These jet streams have created heavy rainstorms and other severe weather patterns.
19. How can people prepare for the effects of El Niño?
20. They should listen to the most recent weather forecast!

Writing Theme
The Weather

GRAMMAR HANDBOOK 36

REVIEW

These exercises may be used as a mixed review or as an informal evaluation of the skills presented in Handbook 36, "Understanding Verbs."

Additional Resources

Grammar and Usage Practice Book, p. 40
Tests and Writing Assessment Prompts, Mastery Test, pp. 19–22
Elaboration, Revision, and Proofreading Practice, p. 25

Writing Theme: The Weather

Other related areas students might wish to explore as writing topics include the following:

- weather satellites
- how a hurricane or a tornado forms
- the greenhouse effect
- monsoons

A. Kinds of Verbs

1. seems, Linking Verb; impossible
2. experienced, Action Verb; summer
3. struck, Action Verb; Northeast
4. nipped, Action Verb; noses
5. remained, Linking Verb; cool
6. sounds, Linking Verb; unbelievable
7. shot, Action Verb; particles
8. reflected, Action Verb; sunlight
9. became, Linking Verb; winter
10. cooled, Action Verb; globe

B. Main Verbs and Helping Verbs

Answers are shown on page.

Understanding Verbs 427

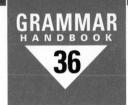

Writing Theme: Science at Work

Other related areas students might wish to explore as writing topics include the following:

- the Komodo dragon and other giant lizards
- Do fish feel pain?
- the language of whales and dolphins
- Are bats really blind?

C. Verb Tenses

Student answers should be in complete sentences.

21. snagged
22. traveled
23. will help
24. will improve
25. studied
26. reveals
27. fascinates
28. changed
29. will create
30. will owe

D. Principal Parts of Verbs

31. studied, Past Participle
32. rank, Present
33. spotted, Past Participle
34. investigated, Past
35. robbed, Past
36. love, Present
37. gathered, Past Participle
38. waits, Present
39. loaded, Past Participle
40. gobbles, Present

Writing Theme
Science at Work

C. Verb Tenses Write the following sentences. Use the tense of the verb given in parentheses.

21. A fishing net in the Mississippi River (past of *snag*) a foot-long mud puppy.
22. Then, the unhappy lizard (past of *travel*) to a laboratory in Colorado.
23. The mud puppy (future of *help*) scientists in their research on taste buds!
24. According to the scientists, mud puppies someday (future of *improve*) the taste of our foods.
25. For years, scientists (past of *study*) the lizard's large taste cells.
26. Research (present of *reveal*) new information about the sense of taste.
27. This complex sense (present of *fascinate*) scientists involved in taste research.
28. Their discoveries (past of *change*) some of their beliefs.
29. As a result, scientists (future of *create*) new taste sensations.
30. If so, we (future of *owe*) a lot to the large taste cells of the mud puppy!

D. Principal Parts of Verbs Write the main verb from each of the following sentences. Then write whether it is in the *Present, Past,* or *Past Participle* form.

31. Entomologists have studied thousands of the world's insects.
32. Robber flies rank among the most interesting.
33. These unusual insects have been spotted in many different parts of the world.
34. Scientists investigated the fly's behavior.
35. These insect pirates robbed other insects of food.
36. Many robber flies, for example, love pollen.
37. However, no robber fly has ever gathered its own pollen.
38. Instead, it waits near a beehive for the return of the worker bees.
39. Usually, the worker bees are loaded with pollen.
40. The fly simply gobbles up a bee!

E. Irregular Verbs For each sentence, write the form of the verb given in parentheses.

41. Between five and six P.M., the light (past of *grow*) dim.
42. Cecily (past of *fall*) over a skate on the sidewalk.
43. Cecily could never have (past participle of *see*) it.
44. Poor night vision has (past participle of *give*) doctors cause for concern.
45. Doctors (past of *know*) about the problem but not about its seriousness.
46. It has (past participle of *take*) years to recognize the extent of the problem.
47. Researchers have (past participle of *begin*) to study problems of contrast and lighting.
48. In fact, traffic accidents (past of *bring*) the problems to their attention.
49. Have you (past participle of *ride*) in a car at night?
50. One doctor (past of *say*) that dim light may cause about 80 percent of all accidents at night.

F. Confusing Pairs of Verbs Write the correct verb from those given in parentheses.

51. You (can, may) use weight equipment to strengthen your muscles.
52. Now, computer programs will (rise, raise) your level of brainpower!
53. You (can, may) think brain exercises are useless.
54. Have you (let, left) your mental powers weaken?
55. Better brainpower (lays, lies) within your grasp.
56. For starters, you (set, sit) at the computer.
57. A mental workout program (lays, lies) mind-expanding puzzles and brain teasers before you.
58. For example, a picture of a brick (raises, rises) onto the screen.
59. How many different uses for it (can, may) you think of?
60. The program (sits, sets) up dozens of problems for you to solve during each workout session.

E. Irregular Verbs
41. grew
42. fell
43. seen
44. given
45. knew
46. taken
47. begun
48. brought
49. ridden
50. said

F. Confusing Pairs of Verbs
Answers are shown on page.

WRITING CONNECTIONS

Elaboration, Revision, and Proofreading

This activity will allow students to see some of the concepts presented in this Handbook at work in a piece of informative writing. By revising and proofreading this passage, students will have the chance to use verbs to clarify ideas and combine sentences.

You might have students work in small groups to revise the passage. Then discuss the completed revision with the entire class. Revisions may vary slightly. A typical revision is shown below. Elements involving change are shown in boldface.

My grandfather told me this story about how his family came to the United States from Poland **one hundred years ago.** His father, Anton, was just a boy of twelve at the time. He **traveled** by ship with his father, sister, and mother. When their ship **arrived** at New York, **his mother** was ill. **The immigration officials examined her and put a cross on her jacket with chalk.** Anton **looked** around and **realized** that the people with crosses were being separated from the others. The immigration officials would not **let** these people come into the United States. **Immediately,** Anton **sat** next to his mother and put his arm around her. When no one **was** looking, he **wiped** away the cross. Thanks to his cleverness, his mother **was** not sent back like the others.

WRITING CONNECTIONS

Elaboration, Revision, and Proofreading

Informative Writing: Reports

Writing a family history allows you to explore your own past. (See Workshop 7.) When you revise a family history, make sure that your facts are correct and that you have presented them in the right order. Also check to see that you do not switch back and forth between the past and present tense.

Revise the following draft of a family history by using the directions at the bottom of the page. Then proofread your work, paying special attention to the use of verbs. Also look for other grammatical errors and mistakes in capitalization, punctuation, and spelling.

[1]My grandfather told me this story about how his family came to the United States from Poland. [2]His father, Anton, was just a boy of twelve at the time. [3]He came by ship with his father sister and mother. [4]When there ship arrives at New York, she was ill. [5]The immigration officials examine her. [6]The immigration officials put a cross on her jacket with chalk. [7]Anton looks around and realizes that the poeple with crosses were being separated from the others. [8]The immigation officials would not leave these people come into the United States. [9]Anton set next to his mother and put his arm around her. [10]When no one were looking, he wipes away the cross. [11]Thanks to his cleverness, his mother is not sent back like the others.

1. Make sentence 1 more complete by adding the information that the family came from Poland one hundred years ago.
2. In sentence 3, replace the weak verb "came" with the stronger "traveled."
3. In sentence 4, replace the unclear pronoun "she" with "his mother."
4. Combine sentences 5 and 6 to make one sentence with a compound verb.
5. Show Anton's quick thinking in sentence 9 by beginning the sentence with the adverb "Immediately."

Crazy English

Why do we say the alarm clock is going off when it goes on? How can a building burn up and burn down at the same time? Why is a boxing ring square? It's a crazy language, you say? You're right! As Richard Lederer explains, the English language is very strange indeed.

In the crazy English language, there is no butter in buttermilk, no egg in an eggplant, and no ham in a hamburger. . . .

To add to this insanity, blackboards can be green, hot dogs can be cold, darkrooms can be lit, nightmares can take place in broad daylight ("That test was a real nightmare"), tablecloths can be made of paper, and silverware (especially in fast-food eateries) can be made of plastic. . . .

A writer is someone who writes, and a stinger is something that stings. But fingers don't *fing,* grocers don't *groce,* hammers don't *ham,* and humdingers don't *humding.*

If you wrote a letter, why don't we also say that you *bote* your tongue? If the teacher taught, why isn't it also true that the preacher *praught?* If you conceive a conception and receive at a reception, why don't you grieve a *greption* and believe a *beleption?*

Yes, English is a crazy language.

Divide the class into small groups and have each group research the origins of some of the "crazy" words in the text. For example:

- *Buttermilk* is the sour liquid left after cream has been churned into butter.
- *Eggplant* is so named because the dark purple fruit is shaped like an egg.
- *Hamburger* is named for Hamburg, Germany, the city where Hamburg steak (a ground-beef patty) was popularized.
- *Hot dog* is thought to have been coined around 1900 by the cartoonist Tad Dorgan. He was probably alluding to the widely held belief that frankfurters (named for Frankfurt, Germany) were filled with dog meat.

Skills ASSESSMENT

Test 1

This test enables you to evaluate student mastery of the concepts taught in handbooks 34–36.

Additional Resources

Grammar and Usage Practice Book, pp. 41–42

Answer Key

Corrections for run-ons may vary.

1. B—Sundays
2. A—eaten
   C—That's
3. A—S.
   C—had ridden *or* rode
4. A—states from
5. B—birthday
   C—parties
6. A—sedimentary
   C—leaves
7. B—lie
   C—east
8. B—Ann Chovy. Can
   C—topping?
9. A—rises
10. D
11. A—Knives
    B—forks. Before
12. B—potatoes
    C—grew
13. A—written
    C—He
14. A—saw
    C—drank
15. B—Neither
    C—pianos

Skills

ASSESSMENT **TEST 1 Grammar Handbooks *34–36***

Directions One or more of the underlined sections in the following sentences may contain an error in grammar, punctuation, spelling, or capitalization. Write the letter of each incorrect section. Then rewrite the section correctly. If there is no error in an item, write *D.*

Example Some weasel's (A) coats turn white in the winter (B). These weasels (C) are called ermines. No error (D)

Answer A—weasels'

1. Blue laws forbid certain activities (A), such as dancing, on sundays (B). At one time, mothers could not kiss their children (C) on this day. No error (D)

2. Have you ever ate (A) 480 oysters in an hour? (B) Thats (C) the oyster-eating record. No error (D)

3. President Ulysses s. (A) Grant got a speeding ticket in Washington, D.C. (B) He ridden (C) his horse over the speed limit of twenty miles per hour. No error (D)

4. It is sometimes possible to see five states. From (A) the top of the Empire State Building (B) in New York (C). No error (D)

5. Do people who were born in a leap year have fewer (A) Birthday (B) partys (C) than other people do? No error (D)

6. Not all Sedimentary (A) rocks are made of particles of rock. Some (B) have been formed from fossils of animals and leafs (C). No error (D)

7. The Falkland Islands [A] lay [B] about three hundred miles to the East [C] of Argentina. No error [D]

8. A woman in Leeds, England, [A] is named Ann Chovy can [B] you imagine having the name of a pizza topping [C]. No error [D]

9. The tallest sea mountain raises [A] 28,500 feet above the ocean [B] floor. Yet its peak is still 1,200 feet below the water's [C] surface. No error [D]

10. Shakespeare wrote [A] *The Merry Wives of Windsor* [B] in fourteen [C] days. No error [D]

11. Knifes [A] have been around much longer than forks before [B] the invention of these tools, people ate with their [C] fingers. No error [D]

12. You probably don't think of tomatoes [A] and potatos [B] as foreign foods, but originally the natives of South America grown [C] them. No error [D]

13. Famous authors have wrote [A] many books on typewriters, but [B] Mark Twain was the first. he [C] typed *The Adventures of Tom Sawyer* himself. No error [D]

14. We seen [A] several camels in the zoo's [B] Asian exhibit. One drunk [C] a whole bucket of water while we watched. No error [D]

15. Don't raise [A] the curtain yet. Niether [B] of the pianoes [C] is working. No error [D]

List of Skills Tested

1. A—noun plural
B—capitalization—common/proper noun
C—noun plural

2. A—irregular verb form
B—punctuation—end mark
C—punctuation—contraction

3. A—capitalization—initials
B—punctuation—abbreviation
C—irregular verb form

4. A—sentence fragment/run-on
B—capitalization—common/proper noun
C—punctuation—end mark

5. A—comparative adjective form
B—capitalization—common/proper noun
C—noun plural

6. A—capitalization—common/proper noun
B—sentence fragment/run-on
C—noun plural

7. A—capitalization—common/proper noun
B—confusing pairs of verbs
C—capitalization—geographic name

8. A—capitalization—common/proper noun
B—sentence fragment/run-on
C—punctuation—end mark

9. A—confusing pairs of verbs
B—capitalization—common/proper noun
C—noun possessive

10. A—irregular verb form
B—capitalization—title
C—spelling

11. A—noun plural
B—sentence fragment/run-on
C—spelling

12. A—noun plural
B—noun plural
C—irregular verb form

13. A—irregular verb form
B—punctuation—comma
C—capitalization—first word

14. A—irregular verb form
B—punctuation—possessive
C—irregular verb form

15. A—confusing pairs of verbs
B—spelling
C—noun plural

Sketchbook

Objective

- To use a photograph and writing prompts as springboards to informal writing

WRITING WARM-UPS

Begin by reminding students that they will not be graded on these sketchbook activities. The writing prompts and the photograph are intended as springboards to get students thinking imaginatively about the concepts in the handbook. Unless students volunteer to explore more than one prompt, have them work on a single response.

Sketchbook

WRITING WARM-UPS

- You're in a baseball stadium when the home team scores the winning run. What happens? How does the crowd react?

- Tell about a time you were in a crowded place. It might have been a stadium, a theater, an elevator—anyplace where people are close together. Describe what you and the people around you were doing.

434

Understanding Pronouns

GRAMMAR HANDBOOK 37

- Pronouns and Antecedents
- Using Subject Pronouns
- Using Object Pronouns
- Possessive Pronouns
- Indefinite Pronouns

A good team needs more than just starting players. It also needs substitute players on the bench who can come in to give the starters a rest. Nouns and pronouns work like a team too. You can use pronouns in your sentences as substitutes for nouns.

This handbook explains how pronouns can take the place of nouns and make your writing smoother and less repetitious.

GRAMMAR HANDBOOK 37

Understanding Pronouns

Objectives

- To define pronouns and to identify pronouns and their antecedents in sentences
- To use pronouns correctly as subjects of sentences
- To use pronouns correctly after linking verbs
- To use pronouns correctly as objects in sentences
- To identify possessive pronouns and to use them correctly
- To distinguish between possessive pronouns and contractions
- To identify indefinite pronouns
- To use possessive pronouns that agree with indefinite pronoun antecedents

Writing

- To make writing smoother by using pronouns to avoid repetition of nouns and noun phrases
- To recognize errors and use pronouns correctly in writing

INTRODUCING THE HANDBOOK

You might ask students to discuss why teams need substitutes. (Regular players may get injured or overtired or may simply have a bad game.) Point out that just as a coach may want to replace an athlete, a writer may need to replace a word. If the same noun is used again and again in a short passage, the reader will find it monotonous.

Fortunately, there is a type of word that the writer can call upon to substitute for the overused noun. Introduce the term *pronoun;* tell students that they are about to study different kinds of pronouns and learn how to use them correctly.

PRONOUNS AND ANTECEDENTS

Objectives

- To identify pronouns and their antecedents
- To use pronouns that agree in number with their antecedents

Writing

- To substitute pronouns for overused nouns in writing

Teaching Strategies

HELPFUL HINT: GENDER Explain that sometimes the gender of a singular antecedent is not stated. In such cases, the pronoun phrases *he or she* or *his or her* should be used. For example:

An *artist* may choose to frame *his or her* work in a variety of ways.

PRONOUNS AND ANTECEDENTS

A **pronoun** is a word used in place of a noun. An **antecedent** is the word or words a pronoun stands for.

Read these sentences:

Leo made *Leo's* own flip book so *Leo* could play with the *book.*
Leo made *his* own flip book so *he* could play with *it.*

The second sentence is less awkward than the first because some nouns have been replaced with pronouns. *His, he,* and *it* are **pronouns.** Pronouns take their meaning from the words they replace. *His* and *he* refer to *Leo. It* refers to *book.*

The word a pronoun stands for is the **antecedent** of the pronoun. In the examples above, *Leo* is the antecedent of both the pronouns *his* and *he. Book* is the antecedent of *it.*

Two nouns may also serve as the antecedent of a pronoun.

Leo and *Iris* made many flip books for *their* friends.
(*Leo* and *Iris* are both antecedents of *their.*)

Note that when a pronoun refers to the person speaking, there may not be a stated antecedent.

I flip the pages to make the characters move.

In most sentences, a pronoun appears after its antecedent. However, sometimes a pronoun and its antecedent may appear in separate sentences.

The *artists* arrived. *They* displayed *their* work.
(*Artists* is the antecedent of *They* and *their.*)

Sometimes the antecedent of a pronoun is another pronoun.

Did *you* watch Leo's cartoon in *your* room?
(*You* is the antecedent of the pronoun *your.*)

Literature Connection

Stress that good writers use pronouns to make their writing less repetitious and wordy. Have students identify the pronouns (underlined here) in this passage from *My Friend Flicka* by Mary O'Hara.

"Nell McLaughlin saw the change in Kennie and <u>her</u> hopes rose. <u>He</u> went to <u>his</u> books in the morning with determination and really studied. . . . Examples in arithmetic were neatly written out and, as <u>she</u> passed <u>his</u> door before breakfast, <u>she</u> often heard the monotonous drone of <u>his</u> voice as <u>he</u> read <u>his</u> American history aloud."

Pronouns can be either singular or plural. Pronouns may be used to refer to yourself, to someone you are addressing, or to other persons, places, or things.

	Singular Pronouns		
Person speaking	I	my, mine	me
Person spoken to	you	your, yours	you
Persons, places, and things spoken about	he	his	him
	she	her, hers	her
	it	its	it
	Plural Pronouns		
Person speaking	we	our, ours	us
Person spoken to	you	your, yours	your
Persons, places, and things spoken about	they	their, theirs	them

Pronoun and Antecedent Agreement

Use a singular pronoun when the antecedent is singular. Use a plural pronoun when the antecedent is plural. This is called making the pronoun **agree** with its antecedent in number.

The *cartoon* (singular) began. *It* (singular) was funny.
People (plural) laughed. *They* (plural) were amused.

Practice Your Skills

A. CONCEPT CHECK

Pronouns Write each pronoun in the following sentences. After the pronoun, write its antecedent if one is given.

EXAMPLE Cartoons and their creation interest me.
their, Cartoons; me

1. I enjoy cartoons, but my friends think they are silly.
2. A cartoon may look simple, yet it is complicated to make.
3. At some time in your life, you have probably made your own flip book.

Writing Theme
Animated Cartoons

INDIVIDUALIZING INSTRUCTION: ESL STUDENTS Some languages use different pronouns to distinguish between polite and familiar direct address. In Spanish, for example, *tú* addresses someone with whom the speaker is on familiar terms; *usted (Vd.* or *Ud.)* addresses someone more formally. Explain that English makes no such distinction; *tú* and *usted* are both translated as "you."

Additional Resources

Tests and Writing Assessment Prompts, Pretest, pp. 23–24
Grammar and Usage Practice Book, p. 43
Grammar Test Generator

Writing Theme: Animated Cartoons

Suggest that students use these exercises as a springboard to writing. Other related areas that they might explore include the following:

- Walt Disney
- computer animation
- careers in art

Answers to Practice Your Skills

A. Concept Check
Pronouns

1. I; my, I; they, cartoons
2. it, cartoon
3. your, you; you; your, you

TEACHER'S LOUNGE

"Sure, I know what a pronoun is. It's a noun that plays for money."

4. We; our, We
5. their, Animators
6. He, Shamus Culhane
7. He, Shamus Culhane; us; his, He
8. they, Artists; them, sketches
9. his, artist; her, artist; its, sheet
10. they, pegs; it, drawing
11. it, table; he, artist; she, artist
12. their, animators
13. they, animators; them, cels
14. his, writer; her, writer; their, Artists
15. them, characters

B. Revision Skill
Substituting Pronouns for Nouns

Tom spends his free time in an animation studio. He is learning the skill of painting animation cels with opaque paint. This skill requires patience. It also requires careful attention to detail. The painter puts the opaque paint in the center of the area to be colored. Then he or she pushes it toward the outside of the area he or she is coloring. His or her hand must be very steady, and the strokes must be smooth. If they are not even, light can show through and ruin the cel. The work is sometimes very boring. To make it more fun, the artists often play practical jokes. They must be alert for upside-down paint jars on their desks or glue on their brushes.

As this work of the animator Arthur Babbitt illustrates, many drawings are necessary to create a simple walking sequence.

FOR MORE PRACTICE
See page 452.

438 Grammar Handbook

4. We flip the pages and see figures move before our eyes.
5. Animators make their cartoons in a similar way.
6. Shamus Culhane is an animator. He is also an author.
7. He explains animation to us in his book *Animation from Script to Screen.*
8. Artists make many sketches for a simple movement, and they draw them on special sheets.
9. An artist draws his or her ideas on a transparent sheet, called a cel, that has holes along its top.
10. The holes fit on pegs, and they hold each drawing in the same place as the one before it.
11. The drawing table has a light under it, so the artist can see what he or she has drawn before.
12. The animators only draw key movements on their cels.
13. Assistant animators get the cels next, and they draw other movements on them.
14. Artists work closely with a writer, since his or her opinion of their drawings is important.
15. The writer invents characters, and the artists bring them to life.

B. REVISION SKILL

Substituting Pronouns for Nouns Rewrite the following paragraph. Use pronouns in place of the words in italics to make the sentences flow smoothly.

Tom spends *Tom's* free time in an animation studio. *Tom* is learning the skill of painting animation cels with opaque paint. This skill requires patience. *This skill* also requires careful attention to detail. The painter puts the opaque paint in the center of the area to be colored. Then *the painter* pushes *the opaque paint* toward the outside of the area *the painter* is coloring. *The painter's* hand must be very steady, and the strokes must be smooth. If *the strokes* are not even, light can show through and ruin the cel. The work is sometimes very boring. To make *the work* more fun, the artists often play practical jokes. *Artists* must be alert for upside-down paint jars on *the artists'* desks or glue on *the artists'* brushes.

CHECKPOINT

MIXED REVIEW • PAGES 436–438

APPLICATION IN LITERATURE

Write each pronoun in the following sentences. Write the antecedent of each pronoun if there is one.

1. "First you tell a diary all your secrets, then you publish it!" **Richard Selzer**
2. "Writing is more fun than ever. The longer I write, the easier it gets." **Isaac Asimov**
3. "You must write every single day of your life." **Ray Bradbury**
4. "Keeping a journal helps you get in touch with your own feelings." **May Sarton**
5. "I think writers—especially young writers—should want to read all the books they can get their hands on." **Raymond Carver**
6. "When we write, we make a contract: *My words are addressed to the outside world . . .*" **Donald Hall**
7. "People want to know why I do this, why I write such gross stuff. I like to tell them I have the heart of a small boy—and I keep it in a jar on my desk." **Stephen King**
8. "A writer doesn't so much choose a story as a story chooses him." **Robert Penn Warren**
9. "You were provided with an imagination. Use it. . . . For every new writer, every new year remains unexplored until he or she explores it." **Irving Wallace**
10. "I shoot the moment, capture feelings with my poems." **Nikki Giovanni**
11. "I don't tell; I don't explain. I show; I let my characters talk for me." **Leo Tolstoy**
12. "Sometimes young poets make the mistake of writing about things they think they ought to care about—they write about 'friendship' and 'peace' and the 'avenues of life' instead of about a certain friend, a certain day, a certain street. . . . The simple and particular way you talk with your friends is most likely the way you can best say what you want to." **Kenneth Koch and Kate Farrell**

Writing Theme
Writers on Writing

CHECKPOINT

Writing Theme: Writers on Writing

Suggest that students use these exercises as a springboard to writing. Other related areas that they might explore include the following:

- Isaac Asimov
- a novel by Ray Bradbury
- a film adaptation of a Stephen King novel
- Nikki Giovanni's poetry

MIXED REVIEW • PAGES 436–438

You may wish to use this activity to check students' mastery of the following concept:

- pronouns and antecedents

Application in Literature

1. you; your, you; you; it, diary
2. I; it, writing
3. You; your, You
4. you; your, you
5. I; they, writers; their, writers
6. we; we; *My*
7. I; I; I; them, People; I; I; it, heart; my, I
8. him, writer
9. You; it, imagination; he, writer; she, writer; it, year
10. I; my, I
11. I; I; I; I; my, I; me, I
12. they, poets; they, poets; they, poets; you; your, you; you; you

USING SUBJECT PRONOUNS

Objectives

- To use subject pronouns correctly in single and compound constructions and after linking verbs

Writing

- To use subject pronouns correctly in writing

Teaching Strategies

INDIVIDUALIZING INSTRUCTION: ESL STUDENTS Subject pronouns are largely unnecessary in Spanish because the verb ending indicates person and number. Therefore, ESL students from Spanish-speaking backgrounds may tend to drop the subject pronoun, producing English sentences such as, "Is raining." Be alert for error patterns in ESL students' writing, and explain the difference between the ways in which the two languages use subject pronouns.

HELPFUL HINT: COMPOUND SUBJECTS Point out that while most compound subjects are linked by *and,* some are linked by *or* or its negative form, *nor.*

Shawn *or* I will drive.

Neither Shawn *nor* he argued in the car.

Point out, however, that students can still find the correct form of the pronoun by dropping the other part of a compound subject.

~~Neither Shawn nor~~ (I, me) will drive.

I will drive.

USING SUBJECT PRONOUNS

The **subject pronouns** are *I, you, he, she, it, we,* and *they.* Use these pronouns as subjects of sentences and after linking verbs.

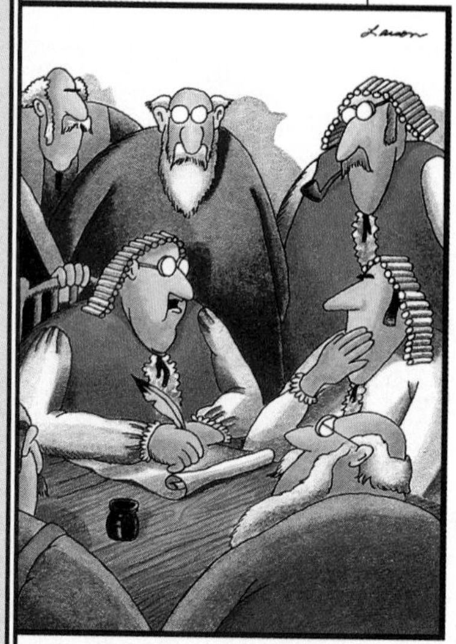

"So, then . . . Would that be 'us the people' or 'we the people'?"

Pronouns as Subjects

Use only subject pronouns as the subject of a verb.

While on vacation, Emma bought souvenirs.
She bought them for friends.

In the first sentence, *Emma* is the subject. In the second sentence, *She* is the subject. Only the pronouns *I, you, he, she, it, we,* or *they* can be used as the subject of a verb. For example, you would never say, "*Her* bought them for friends."

Pronouns in Compound Subjects

You probably have no trouble choosing the correct pronoun when it appears by itself as the subject. Sometimes, however, one or more pronouns appear in a compound subject.

Shawn and (he, him) argued in the car.

The pronoun is part of the compound subject in this sentence. Therefore, you would use the subject pronoun *he.* If you are unsure about what pronoun to use, try dividing the compound subject into two parts. Then try each part as the subject.

Shawn argued in the car. *He* argued in the car.

Put the parts together, using the same pronoun you used when it was alone in the sentence.

Shawn and *he* argued in the car.

Writing TIP

Subject pronouns can serve as a link between two sentences as shown in this example:

My friends are from Iowa. *They* lived in Des Moines.

Follow the same steps to choose pronouns for the following example sentence.

(She, Her) and (I, me) took snapshots.
She took snapshots. *I* took snapshots.
She and *I* took snapshots.

Sometimes a pronoun is followed by a noun in the subject of a sentence. To help you decide which pronoun to use in the sentence, try leaving out the noun.

(We, Us) girls hiked up Mount Victoria.
We hiked up Mount Victoria.
Us hiked up Mount Victoria.
We girls hiked up Mount Victoria.

Pronouns After Linking Verbs

Use subject pronouns after linking verbs. Look at these sentences:

He is a good driver. A good driver is *he.*

Both sentences make sense, even though the subject and the pronoun are reversed. The pronoun following the linking verb *is* renames, or identifies, the subject. Therefore, you would use the subject pronoun *he.*

Practice Your Skills

A. CONCEPT CHECK

Subject Pronouns Write the correct pronoun for each sentence.

Writing Theme
Family Travel

1. Why do (we, us) think family trips are fun?
2. My family and (I, me) have had many adventures.
3. (We, Us) travelers have been lost in ten states.
4. Dad never asks directions. (He, Him) relies on the road map.
5. Emil and my other brother always fight. Emil and (he, him) have a talent for getting on Mother's nerves.
6. An impatient traveler is (she, her).

HELPFUL HINT Tell students that one way to check whether a subject pronoun is necessary after a linking verb is to reverse the positions of the subject and predicate. If the two sentences mean substantially the same thing, students should use a subject pronoun:

The team captains are you and *I.*
You and *I* are the team captains.

STUMBLING BLOCK: CONTRACTIONS Remind students that forms of the linking verb *be* are sometimes contracted to *'m* (for *am,* as in *I'm*), *'s* (for *is,* as in *it's*), and *'re* (for *are,* as in *they're*). A pronoun that follows such a contraction should still be a subject pronoun: *I'm she. It's he.*

SPEAKING AND LISTENING Note that in the informal English of everyday speech, people often fail to use subject pronouns. For example, in informal conversation people say "It's him," although "It's he" is technically correct. Point out that the subject form should be used when a person is giving a presentation and in other formal speaking situations. Ask students to correct these common errors:

- It is me. (It is I.)
- The best students are us. (The best students are we.)
- It is her. (It is she.)

Additional Resource

Grammar and Usage Practice Book, p. 44

Writing Theme: Family Travel

Other related areas students might wish to explore as writing topics include the following:

- games for long car trips
- visiting a national park
- seeing the sights of your own state or community
- a "dream vacation"

Answers to Practice Your Skills

A. Concept Check
Subject Pronouns

Answers are shown on page.

B. Revision Skill
Using Subject Pronouns

13. We saw a strange sight near Scone.
14. It is a small town.
15. It never goes out.
16. They were wrong.
17. He *(or* She) found the coal to be five hundred feet below the surface of the mountain.
18. They thought a god lived there.
19. He (she, it) "speaks from smoke."
20. In the encyclopedia, she found the answer.
21. It is called "Burning Mountain" or Mt. Wingen.
22. It suggests that lightning started the fire.

C. Application in Writing
Speech

Speeches will vary. Check that students have correctly used subject pronouns to link sentences.

7. Dad and (she, her) always bring travel games.
8. (We, Us) kids have to play dumb games and be quiet.
9. Emil and (I, me) have counted a trillion license plates.
10. (We, Us) passengers have also named all the state capitals.
11. What more can (they, them) expect of us?
12. My brothers and (I, me) think family trips are dull!

B. REVISION SKILL

Using Subject Pronouns Write the second sentence of each pair. Replace the repeated words with a subject pronoun.

13. My family and I went to Australia. My family and I saw a strange sight near Scone.
14. Scone is north of Sydney. Scone is a small town.
15. Near Scone, a fire burns in a mountain. The fire never goes out.
16. Explorers first thought the fire was a volcano. The explorers were wrong.
17. A scientist learned that the fire is caused by a burning seam of coal. The scientist found the coal to be five hundred feet below the surface of the mountain.
18. The native people feared the place. These people thought a god lived there.
19. The people called the god Turramulan. The god "speaks from smoke."
20. My sister wondered how long the fire has burned. In the encyclopedia, my sister found the answer.
21. The mountain has been smoldering for centuries. The mountain is called "Burning Mountain" or Mt. Wingen.
22. One idea explains the fire. The idea suggests that lightning started the fire.

C. APPLICATION IN WRITING

Speech Have you ever been on a trip and had something exciting, funny, or very annoying happen? Write a short speech about your trip. Include details about who was on the trip with you. Then use subject pronouns to link sentences and make your speech concise.

FOR MORE PRACTICE
See page 452.

442 Grammar Handbook

CHECK POINT

MIXED REVIEW • PAGES 440–442

Write the following sentences, correcting errors in the use of subject pronouns. If a sentence has no errors, write *Correct.*

1. My friend and me found an old diary in a steamer trunk.
2. It was my great-grandmother's diary. C
3. In Oakland, California, her and others saw the test flight of an airship invented by George and Lizzie Heaton.
4. They made it around 1905. C
5. She and him worked as partners to make the engine.
6. An unusual pair were them.
7. I will tell you what my great-grandmother wrote. C
8. "Us spectators watched the airship rise with Mrs. Heaton aboard."
9. "It was held down by cables and was supposed to rise only to the treetops." C
10. "Mr. Heaton and us were horrified when the cables snapped and Mrs. Heaton was launched in the ship."
11. "She rose in the air with frightening speed." C
12. "Apparently, Mrs. Heaton was very brave and smart. She bit a hole in the airship's gas bag." C
13. "It released the gas and allowed the airship to go down." C
14. "At first, the airship and her dropped like a flash."
15. "My beau and me were much relieved to see it land safely."
16. "Him and I rushed to interview Mrs. Heaton."
17. Both the airship and she were safe. C
18. A courageous pilot was her.
19. Now, my friend and me want to make an airship.
20. Our classmates and us may have found a winning project for the science fair!

Writing Theme
Partners in Invention

At the conclusion of the 1903 Paris Exposition, line handlers move the *Lebaudy I*, the first practical airship.

CHECK POINT

Writing Theme: Partners in Invention

Other related areas students might wish to explore as writing topics include the following:

- Pierre and Marie Curie
- the Montgolfier brothers
- the Wright brothers

MIXED REVIEW • PAGES 440–442

You may wish to use this activity to check students' mastery of the following concept:

- using subject pronouns

Errors are shown on page. Correctly rewritten sentences appear below.

1. My friend and I found an old diary in a steamer trunk.
2. Correct
3. In Oakland, California, she and others saw the test flight of an airship invented by George and Lizzie Heaton.
4. Correct
5. She and he worked as partners to make the engine.
6. An unusual pair were they.
7. Correct
8. "We spectators watched the airship rise with Mrs. Heaton aboard."
9. Correct
10. "Mr. Heaton and we were horrified when the cables snapped and Mrs. Heaton was launched in the ship."
11. Correct
12. Correct
13. Correct
14. "At first, the airship and she dropped like a flash."
15. "My beau and I were much relieved to see it land safely."
16. "He and I rushed to interview Mrs. Heaton."
17. Correct
18. A courageous pilot was she.
19. Now, my friend and I want to make an airship.
20. Our classmates and we may have found a winning project for the science fair!

USING OBJECT PRONOUNS

Objectives

- To use object pronouns as objects of verbs and prepositions

Writing

- To use object pronouns correctly in writing

Teaching Strategies

HELPFUL HINT Note that pronouns used as objects of prepositions take the object form, even if the prepositional phrase is part of the complete subject of a sentence:

The girl *with her* is her sister.

The friendship *between him and me* grew stronger.

Additional Resource

Grammar and Usage Practice Book, p. 45

USING OBJECT PRONOUNS

The **object pronouns** are *me, you, him, her, it, us,* and *them.* Use these pronouns as the objects of verbs or prepositions.

Pronouns After Action Verbs

Nouns do not change their forms when they are used as the objects of verbs. Pronouns, however, have special object forms.

The object pronouns are *me, you, him, her, it, us,* and *them. You* and *it* can be used as both subject and object pronouns. Look at the object pronoun in this sentence:

The expert told *us* about the new computer.

Pronouns are sometimes part of a compound object.

Did the expert help (he, him) and (she, her)?

If you are unsure about what pronoun to use, try dividing the compound object into two parts. Then try each part as the object.

Did the expert help (he, him)?
Did the expert help (she, her)?
Did the expert help *him* and *her?*

Pronouns After Prepositions

A **preposition** usually has a noun or pronoun after it and shows a relationship between that noun or pronoun and the rest of the sentence. The noun or pronoun that follows a preposition is called the **object of the preposition.** Object pronouns are used as objects of prepositions.

He spoke to *Lee* and *Beth.* He spoke to *them.*

You will learn more about prepositions in Grammar Handbook 40. A list of common prepositions is on page 504.

Practice Your Skills

A. CONCEPT CHECK

Object Pronouns Write the correct pronoun given in parentheses for each sentence.

1. Computers can be programmed for people with special needs, such as my friends and (I, me).
2. Some help blind people by speaking to (they, them).
3. We can talk to the computer, and it "hears" (we, us) kids.
4. Jay and Ann can ask a computer a question and it answers (he, him) and (she, her).
5. The new programs are good. People like (them, they).
6. A program can tell the difference between Jay and (I, me).
7. The computer knows Jay's voice belongs to (he, him).
8. One program amazes Ann and (us, we). It understands thirty thousand words.
9. When Ann spoke to the computer, it answered (her, she).
10. The computer gave (she, her) a printed reply in Braille.

B. DRAFTING SKILL

Using Object Pronouns in Sentences Complete the following sentences using correct object pronouns.

11. My neighbors Bill and Maggie have inspired ___.
12. Bill's customers like ___ very much.
13. He is always cheerful and polite to ___.
14. His customers know they can rely on ___.
15. Bill contacts ___ through his computer.
16. Maggie's boss, Al, is very happy with ___.
17. She does his record keeping for ___.
18. He has praised ___ very highly.
19. Bill and Maggie are blind, but computers help ___ work.
20. Computers are the key to success for both ___ and ___.
21. A special computer helps my co-workers and ___ make phone calls.
22. We type a message on ___ and a voice talks to the listener.
23. It is very useful to ___ because we cannot talk.
24. One computer finishes our words for ___.
25. It predicts the word and shows ___ on the screen.

Writing Theme
Special Computer Programs

FOR MORE PRACTICE
See page 454.

Writing Theme: Special Computer Programs

Other related areas students might wish to explore as writing topics include the following:

- computer software for translating foreign languages
- computer software for writers
- how computer software is developed

Answers to Practice Your Skills

A. Concept Check
Object Pronouns

Answers are shown on page.

B. Drafting Skill
Using Object Pronouns in Sentences

11. me
12. him
13. them
14. him
15. them
16. her
17. him
18. her
19. them
20. him, her
21. me
22. it
23. us
24. us
25. it

POSSESSIVE PRONOUNS

Objectives

- To use pronouns to show possession
- To distinguish between possessive pronouns and contractions

Writing

- To use possessive pronouns correctly in writing

INDIVIDUALIZING INSTRUCTION: BASIC STUDENTS Explain that possessive pronouns, unlike nouns, never have apostrophes, since they are already possessive in form. Then write the following phrases on the board and ask students to substitute a possessive pronoun for each possessive noun.

Douglas's cat = his cat

the cat's meow = its meow

the dogs' bones = their bones

COOPERATIVE LEARNING Distinguish between possessive pronouns used by themselves and those that modify nouns (for example, *This book is mine; This is my book).* Then have volunteers prepare a chart that shows both kinds of pronouns in columns and each pronoun in a sentence.

KEY TO UNDERSTANDING Remind students that apostrophes in contractions stand for missing letters; they do not indicate possession.

Additional Resource

Grammar and Usage Practice Book, p. 46

Writing Theme: A Day in the Life

Other related areas students might wish to explore as writing topics include the following:

- the day of a physician (for example, an emergency-room doctor)
- the day of someone in public office (for example, a senator)
- the day of a journalist (for example, a TV reporter)

POSSESSIVE PRONOUNS

Possessive pronouns show ownership or relationship.

Possessive pronouns are used to show ownership or relationship. The possessive pronouns are *my, mine, his, her, hers, its, our, ours, their, theirs, your,* and *yours.*

My interview is with *your* cousin Amy.
His report about *her* job was interesting.

In the first sentence, the pronouns *my* and *your* tell whom the interview and the cousin belong to. In the second sentence, *his* and *her* point to the owners of the report and the job.

To make a noun show possession, you add an apostrophe and an *s.* Pronouns, however, have special possessive forms. Possessive pronouns never use apostrophes.

Possessive pronouns may be confused with contractions that are spelled similarly. Look at the difference in these pairs of italicized words.

Possessive Pronoun	The factory opened *its* doors.
Contraction	*It's* a computer business. (It is)
Possessive Pronoun	*Their* jobs sound interesting.
Contraction	*They're* programmers. (They are)
Possessive Pronoun	*Your* interview is in the paper.
Contraction	*You're* a celebrity! (You are)

Practice Your Skills

Writing Theme
A Day in the Life

A. CONCEPT CHECK

Possessive Pronouns and Contractions Write the correct possessive pronoun or contraction from the words given in parentheses. Then label the word *Pronoun* or *Contraction.*

1. Security officers spend (their, they're) time on guard.
2. In a hotel, (their, they're) workday may begin at 4 P.M.

446 Grammar Handbook

3. (Your, You're) probably wondering what these important employees do.
4. "Most of the time, (you're, your) helping guests."
5. "(Their, They're) always losing the room keys."
6. "You also have to stay on (your, you're) toes."
7. "(Its, It's) important to watch for troublemakers."
8. (Their, They're) job includes assisting hotel guests and having safety drills.
9. The hotel has a responsibility to protect (its, it's) guests in emergencies.
10. "I love to talk to kids. (Their, They're) fascinated by my walkie-talkie," says Sharona Lewis, an officer.

B. PROOFREADING SKILL

Correcting Pronoun Errors Rewrite the following paragraph, correcting all errors in grammar, punctuation, capitalization, and spelling. Pay special attention to errors in possessive pronouns. (15 errors)

Ivan is a speechwriter for sevral important people. Its not easy writing speeches for them. They're speeches may last only fifteen minites apiece, but Ivan spends about thirty-two hours writing each one. He follows standard writing steps. Your familiar with them. Their the ones you use in you're classes. He gathers information. Writes a draft, and then rerites it. Ivan doesnt rest until its perfect. He spends his day talking with clients, holding interviews, and doing research at librarys in boston. "Your probably not going to believe this," he says. "Research is the most important step, and its the one that takes the longest."

C. APPLICATION IN WRITING

Report Who is the most interesting person in the world to you? Write a report about a typical day in the life of this person. He or she may be an actual person or a character from fiction. Include some actual or imaginary quotations from the person. Use possessive pronouns to make your writing clear and concise.

FOR MORE PRACTICE
See page 453.

Answers to Practice Your Skills

A. Concept Check
Possessive Pronouns and Contractions

Correct words are shown on page.

1. their, Pronoun
2. their, Pronoun
3. You're, Contraction
4. you're, Contraction
5. They're, Contraction
6. your, Pronoun
7. It's, Contraction
8. Their, Pronoun
9. its, Pronoun
10. They're, Contraction

B. Proofreading Skill
Correcting Pronoun Errors

Errors in proofreading exercises are counted as follows: (a) Each word is counted as one error. For example, a misspelled word is one error; two initials and a last name not capitalized are counted as three errors. (b) Run-on sentences and sentence fragments are each counted as one error, even though the correction involves both punctuation and capitalization.

Errors are shown on page. The correctly rewritten paragraph appears below.

Ivan is a speechwriter for several important people. It's not easy writing speeches for them. Their speeches may last only fifteen minutes apiece, but Ivan spends about thirty-two hours writing each one. He follows standard writing steps. You're familiar with them. They're the ones you use in your classes. He gathers information, writes a draft, and then rewrites it. Ivan doesn't rest until it's perfect. He spends his day talking with clients, holding interviews, and doing research at libraries in Boston. "You're probably not going to believe this," he says. "Research is the most important step, and it's the one that takes the longest."

C. Application in Writing
Report

Answers will vary.

CHECK ✔ POINT

Writing Theme: Dinosaur Quiz

Other related areas students might wish to explore as writing topics include the following:

- dinosaur displays at museums
- fictional dinosaurs
- why dinosaurs became extinct
- dinosaurs that could fly
- Dinosaur National Monument in Colorado

MIXED REVIEW • PAGES 444–447

You may wish to use this activity to check students' mastery of the following concepts:

- using object pronouns
- possessive pronouns

1. my
2. me, my
3. You're, me
4. your, you're
   Answer: Torosaurus
5. my
6. them
7. they're
8. their
9. It's
   Answer: Maiasaura
10. You're, you're
11. me, them
12. me, them
13. her, her
    Answer: Deinosuchus
14. me
15. his, her
16. him, her
17. me
18. us, your
19. its
20. their, They're
    Answer: Tyrannosaurus

Writing Theme
Dinosaur Quiz

Maiasaura

Deinosuchus

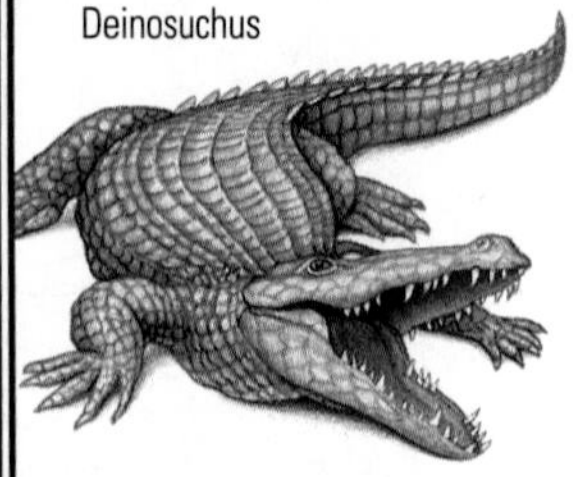

Tyrannosaurus

Torosaurus

CHECK ✔ POINT

MIXED REVIEW • PAGES 444–447

Fill in the blanks in the following sentences with the correct object pronoun, possessive pronoun, or contraction. You may wish to refer to lists on page 444 and page 446. Using each set of descriptions, see if you can identify each dinosaur in the margin.

1. My head is larger than that of any other dinosaur, and ___ body is very large too.
2. Three horns protect ___ from ___ predators.
3. You don't need to worry. ___ safe around ___ because I eat plants.
4. If ___ guess is Triceratops, ___ wrong! Who am I?

5. Everyone's name has meaning, and ___ name means "the good mother lizard."
6. I lay eggs in a nest to keep ___ warm.
7. The eggs are hidden; ___ covered with sand or plants.
8. After the babies hatch, I bring them ___ food.
9. ___ hard work being a mother. Who am I?

10. ___ probably thinking that I look like a crocodile, and ___ right.
11. Other dinosaurs are afraid of ___ because I eat ___.
12. My victims don't see ___ hiding in the swamps, but I see ___.
13. The good mother lizard better watch ___ step as she passes by because I might devour ___! Who am I?

14. Scientists call ___ "tyrant lizard."
15. Around me, every plant eater fears for ___ or ___ life.
16. My razor-sharp teeth can cut ___ or ___ to shreds.
17. Skeletons of other dinosaurs and ___ are in museums.
18. You have seen many of ___ awesome creatures on ___ field trips.
19. One museum in the Smithsonian Institution is especially famous for ___ dinosaur skeletons.
20. Scientists differ in ___ opinions about me. ___ not sure if I am a scavenger or a great hunter. Only I know. Who am I?

448 Grammar Handbook

INDEFINITE PRONOUNS

An **indefinite pronoun** is a pronoun that does not refer to a specific person or a specific thing.

Pronouns such as *anyone* or *everybody* do not refer to any definite person or thing. These pronouns are called **indefinite pronouns.** Indefinite pronouns often do not have clear antecedents because the persons or things they refer to are unknown. This chart lists singular and plural indefinite pronouns.

Indefinite Pronouns

Singular			Plural
another	either	nobody	both
anybody	everybody	no one	many
anyone	everyone	one	few
anything	everything	somebody	several
each	neither	someone	

Use the singular possessive pronouns *his, her,* and *its* with singular indefinite pronouns.

Someone left *her* purse on the boat.

Another of the tourists lost *his* hat.

When the person referred to could be either male or female, *his or her* may be used.

Everyone should bring *his or her* camera.

Use the plural possessive pronoun *their* with plural indefinite pronouns.

Both enjoyed *their* visit. Many bring *their* children.

Refer to page 536 for information on making indefinite pronouns agree with verbs.

INDEFINITE PRONOUNS

Objectives

- To identify indefinite pronouns
- To distinguish between singular and plural indefinite pronouns and to make other pronouns agree with them

Writing

- To correct errors in pronoun agreement in writing

Teaching Strategies

KEY TO UNDERSTANDING Point out that indefinite pronouns do not have special subject, object, and possessive forms; those that can show possession do so with an apostrophe and *-s,* as nouns do: *anyone's, everybody's.*

HELPFUL HINT Explain that many words used as indefinite pronouns can also be used as adjectives. When these words stand alone, they usually are pronouns. When they precede a noun, they are adjectives: in *Another tourist lost his hat, Another* is an adjective.

Additional Resource

Grammar and Usage Practice Book, p. 47

Writing Theme: Hannibal, Missouri

Other related areas students might wish to explore as writing topics include the following:

- events in *The Adventures of Tom Sawyer*
- the origin of Mark Twain's pen name
- Mark Twain's years in California
- steamboating on the Mississippi

Answers to Practice Your Skills

A. Concept Check
Indefinite Pronouns

Answers are shown on page.

B. Proofreading Skill
Making Indefinite and Possessive Pronouns Agree

Errors are shown on page. The correctly rewritten paragraph appears below.

One of Hannibal's yearly events is its summer festival called National Tom Sawyer Days. Anyone in the seventh grade can have his or her chance to play Tom Sawyer or Becky Thatcher. Many compete to spend their summer on a paddle wheeler named the *Mark Twain*. Judges choose three pairs of students to take turns greeting the passengers. Neither of the new greeters is nervous his or her first time. Both do their best to make riders feel welcome. Anybody would have the time of his or her life on the boat ride. One of the girls shows her tour group Inspiration Point, a high lookout over the Mississippi River.

Writing Theme
Hannibal, Missouri

Practice Your Skills

A. CONCEPT CHECK

Indefinite Pronouns Write the possessive pronoun that agrees in number with each indefinite pronoun.

1. Everyone has (his or her, their) reasons for visiting Hannibal, Missouri.
2. Many of the visitors carry (his or her, their) copies of *The Adventures of Tom Sawyer* by Mark Twain.
3. Everything looks like the 1800s because of (its, their) decor.
4. Someone tries (his or her, their) hand at the whitewash contest.
5. Everybody grabs (his or her, their) brush and bucket of paint.
6. Several of the contestants accidentally splatter paint on (his or her, their) clothes.
7. A few even get paint in (his or her, their) hair.
8. One of the girls is declared the winner and claims (her, their) prize.
9. Somebody still paints (his, their) part of the fence.
10. Nobody has it in (his or her, their) heart to stop him.

B. PROOFREADING SKILL

Making Indefinite and Possessive Pronouns Agree Rewrite the paragraph, correcting all errors in grammar, capitalization, punctuation, and spelling. Pay special attention to errors in pronoun agreement. (15 errors)

One of Hannibal's yearly events is it's summer festival called National Tom Sawyer Days. Anyone in the seventh grade can have their chance to play tom sawyer or becky thatcher. Many compeet to spend his or her summer on a paddle wheeler named the *Mark Twain.* Judges choose three pares of students to take turns greeting the passengers. Neither of the new greeters is nervous their first time. Both do his or her best to make riders feel welcome. Anybody would have the time of its life on the boat ride. One of the girls shows their tour group Inspiration Point, a high lookout over the mississippi river.

FOR MORE PRACTICE
See page 453.

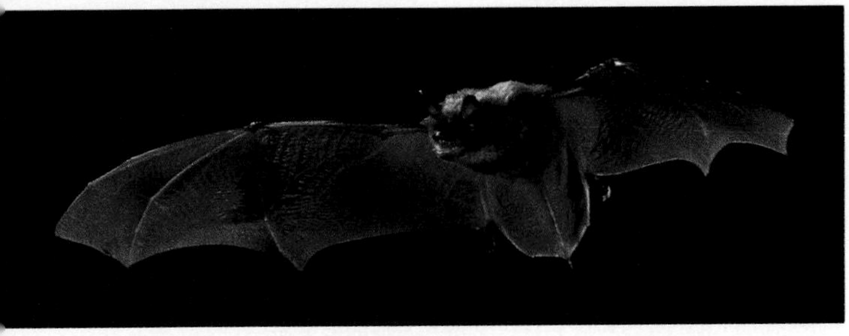

CHECKPOINT
MIXED REVIEW • PAGES 449–450

Write the possessive pronoun in parentheses that agrees with each indefinite pronoun.

1. Does anybody you know spend (his or her, their) time watching bats?
2. Many of the visitors come to see (his or her, their) favorite creatures living at Volo Bog near Chicago, Illinois.
3. Almost every one of the bats here makes (its, their) home in an old dairy barn.
4. Several of the visitors plan (his or her, their) evenings to see the bats fly from the dairy barn.
5. Everyone takes (his or her, their) place at sunset.
6. Many set up (his or her, their) cameras to take pictures.
7. Somebody raises (his or her, their) binoculars to get a closer look.
8. Several of the spectators clap (his or her, their) hands and cheer for the furry creatures.
9. Afterward, both of the tour guides give (his or her, their) daily speech about bats.
10. Neither misses (his or her, their) chance to praise bats.
11. Either explains bats' helpfulness in (his or her, their) talk.
12. Very few of the visitors discuss (his or her, their) fear of bats.
13. Nearly everybody shares (his or her, their) belief that bats are not creepy or dangerous.
14. Someone in the group enjoys (his or her, their) job taking care of bats at a nearby zoo.
15. Another has bats in (his or her, their) attic.

Writing Theme
Bats

CHECKPOINT

Writing Theme: Bats

Other related areas students might wish to explore as writing topics include the following:
- misconceptions about bats
- how bats navigate (echolocation)
- how bats benefit the environment
- vampire bats

MIXED REVIEW • PAGES 449–450

You may wish to use this activity to check students' mastery of the following concept:
- indefinite pronouns

Answers are shown on page.

GRAMMAR HANDBOOK 37

ADDITIONAL PRACTICE

Each of these exercises correlates to a section of Handbook 37, "Understanding Pronouns." The exercises may be used for more practice, for reteaching, or for review of the concepts presented.

Additional Resource

Grammar and Usage Practice Book, p. 49

Writing Theme: Water

Other related areas students might wish to explore as writing topics include the following:

- how animals survive in deserts
- glaciers
- how water filtration plants purify drinking water
- acid rain

A. Recognizing Pronouns

1. I; my, I
2. We, friends and I; our, We
3. her, Shinae
4. his, Tim
5. It, fire
6. our, friends and I; us, friends and I
7. them, wranglers
8. You; your, You
9. I; me, I; it, water
10. We; its, water

B. Using Subject Pronouns

Answers are shown on page.

C. Using Object Pronouns

Answers are shown on page.

GRAMMAR HANDBOOK 37

Writing Theme
Water

A. Recognizing Pronouns Write each pronoun—and its antecedent if there is one—in the following sentences.

1. I went hiking in the desert with my friends.
2. We lost our way in a large canyon.
3. By nightfall, only Shinae had water in her canteen.
4. Tim used his knife to cut scrub for a fire.
5. It was a wonderful fire.
6. Luckily, some wranglers saw our fire and found us.
7. The wranglers always carry extra water with them.
8. "You need a gallon of water for each day of your hike."
9. I only had two quarts of water with me, and it was gone.
10. We learned a lesson about water and its importance.

B. Using Subject Pronouns Write the correct pronoun given in parentheses.

11. You and (I, me) may never know the secret of an ancient mummy called Otze.
12. (He, him) was found by a German couple.
13. Hiking in the Alps, (they, them) spotted him in a glacier.
14. "(She, Her) and (I, me) saw a human form in the ice."
15. Scientists and (they, them) were puzzled.
16. A frozen mystery was (he, him).
17. (He, Him) died suddenly, but (we, us) don't know why.
18. His tools and (he, him) are being studied.
19. Otze and (they, them) were buried for five thousand years.
20. "(We, Us) scientists are amazed at this discovery."

C. Using Object Pronouns Write the correct pronoun given in parentheses.

21. Hard water affects (we, us) in many ways.
22. Water does not feel hard to you and (I, me).
23. It has mineral ions. Softeners remove (they, them).
24. Minerals make cloth feel stiff to you and (I, me).
25. These elements also stick to pipes and clog (they, them).
26. In the 1920s, an inventor gave a friend some zeolite and asked (he, him) to filter water through it.

452 Grammar Handbook

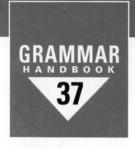

27. He did, and it impressed his wife and (he, him).
28. It occurred to (they, them) to wash diapers in it.
29. The diapers felt softer to (she, her) and (he, him).
30. Today, many of (we, us) have soft water in our homes.

D. Using Possessive Pronouns Write the sentences, correcting errors in possessive pronouns and contractions. If a sentence has no errors, write *Correct.*

31. Without water, its certain that you're going to die.
32. You're body needs water to turn food into energy.
33. Certain life forms do not have you're problem.
34. They're able to go long periods without water.
35. They're bodies shrivel up and look dead.
36. Add water and they regain their shape.
37. Their in a state of cryptobiosis.
38. Its a word that means "hidden life."
39. A life form's ability to "play dead" helps it's survival.
40. It's puzzling to scientists how cryptobiosis works.

E. Using Indefinite Pronouns Write the correct possessive pronoun from those in parentheses.

41. Everyone is concerned about (his or her, their) future.
42. Many want (his or her, their) environment free of pollution.
43. Nobody wants (his or her, their) planet destroyed.
44. Several of the factories still dump (its, their) garbage.
45. A few of the local farmers spray (his or her, their) crops with poisonous bug spray.
46. Both of these practices have (its, their) dangerous effects on animals and humans.
47. For example, no one wants (his or her, their) drinking water to cause diseases.
48. Anybody worried about (his or her, their) health should try to solve this problem.
49. Someone wrote (his or her, their) solutions in a letter to the editor.
50. Almost everybody has (his or her, their) opinions about how to prevent water pollution.

D. Using Possessive Pronouns

31. Without water, it's certain that you're going to die.
32. Your body needs water to turn food into energy.
33. Certain life forms do not have your problem.
34. Correct
35. Their bodies shrivel up and look dead.
36. Correct
37. They're in a state of cryptobiosis.
38. It's a word that means "hidden life."
39. A life form's ability to "play dead" helps its survival.
40. Correct

E. Using Indefinite Pronouns

Answers are shown on page.

GRAMMAR
HANDBOOK
37

REVIEW

These exercises may be used as a mixed review or as an informal evaluation of the skills presented in Handbook 37, "Understanding Pronouns."

Additional Resources

Grammar and Usage Practice Book, p. 50
Tests and Writing Assessment Prompts, Mastery Test, pp. 25–28
Elaboration, Revision, and Proofreading Practice, p. 26

Writing Theme: Mapmaking

Other related areas students might wish to explore as writing topics include the following:

- types of world maps
- computers in today's mapmaking
- weather maps
- how to read a road map

A. Finding Pronouns

1. you; your, you
2. his, Magellan
3. It, *Magellan*
4. it, *Magellan* (or satellite); their, Scientists
5. he, Francesco Bianchini
6. our
7. we; them, images
8. it, radar
9. their, scientists
10. We; it, crust

B. Using Subject and Object Pronouns

Answers are shown on page.

GRAMMAR
HANDBOOK
37

Writing Theme
Mapmaking

A. Finding Pronouns Write the pronouns from the sentences. Then write each pronoun's antecedent if there is one.

1. Do you remember Magellan from your history lessons?
2. Well, a new *Magellan* has taken his place.
3. Modern-day *Magellan* is not a man. It is a satellite.
4. Scientists use it to make their maps of Venus.
5. In 1726, Francesco Bianchini drew the first map of Venus, but he was unable to make an accurate drawing.
6. The planet is hidden by clouds that block our view.
7. However, *Magellan's* radar makes images of Venus, and we can study them.
8. In eight months, it recorded 84 percent of the surface.
9. Now scientists can't make up their minds.
10. We don't know if Venus's crust is thick or if it is thin.

B. Using Subject and Object Pronouns Write the correct pronoun from those given in parentheses.

11. The sea floor is hidden from you and (I, me).
12. (We, Us) creatures of the land need to make maps of it.
13. Sailors mapped the ocean floor. (They, Them) lowered lead weights over the side of the ship.
14. Then mapmakers and (they, them) recorded the depths.
15. Later, the echo sounder gave (we, us) more information.
16. It allowed scientists and (we, us) to measure depths.
17. A mapmaker uses data that are valuable to (he, him) or (she, her).
18. With computers, (he, him) or (she, her) draws maps.
19. You and (I, me) can study the three-dimensional maps.
20. The maps allow (we, us) to see trenches and volcanoes.
21. Better technology is available to mapmakers and (we, us).
22. For example, a sonar device named *Gloria* has helped scientists and (they, them.)
23. A technician lowers this sensitive machine, and it sends (he, him) acoustic, or sound, pictures.
24. *Gloria* and (he, him) receive accurate "snapshots."
25. *Gloria's* pulses of sound fan out to both sides. Each sound wave bounces back to (we, us) from the ocean floor.

26. With computers, a picture appears before you and (I, me).
27. Line by line, the ocean floor is visible to (we, us).
28. Besides you and (I, me), other people also thought the ocean floor was flat.
29. However, *Gloria's* pictures show (they, them) and (we, us) mountains, trenches, and volcanoes.
30. (We, Us) land beings can now see the ocean bottom.

C. Using Possessive Pronouns and Contractions Write the correct possessive pronoun or contraction for each sentence.

31. (Your, You're) not going to believe this.
32. Some people still cling to (their, they're) belief in a flat earth.
33. (Their, They're) known as the Flat Earth Society.
34. (Its, It's) leaders scorn all satellite pictures.
35. (Their, They're) sure the pictures are fakes.
36. They also scorn the moon landing and question (its, it's) truth.
37. According to them, (its, it's) a Hollywood trick.
38. Are you going to change (your, you're) mind?
39. Will you start (your, you're) subscription to the *Flat Earth News*?
40. (Your, You're) sure the earth is a sphere, right?

D. Using Indefinite Pronouns Write the following sentences and correct all errors in agreement. If a sentence has no errors, write *Correct*.

41. Almost everyone checks their maps before a trip.
42. Many will even plot his or her route carefully.
43. If no one had their maps, would anyone travel?
44. Somebody had to take his or her chances and explore the unknown.
45. Each of the early explorers made maps for their country.
46. Several made their observations with instruments.
47. Not everybody knew how to use his or her tools well.
48. A few relied only on his compass and surveyor's chain.
49. Either of these instruments proved their value on expeditions.
50. However, neither was known for their accuracy.

C. Using Possessive Pronouns and Contractions
Answers are shown on page.

D. Using Indefinite Pronouns
41. Almost everyone checks his or her maps before a trip.
42. Many will even plot their route carefully.
43. If no one had his or her maps, would anyone travel?
44. Correct
45. Each of the early explorers made maps for his or her country.
46. Correct
47. Correct
48. A few relied only on their compass and surveyor's chain.
49. Either of these instruments proved its value on expeditions.
50. However, neither was known for its accuracy.

51. Correct
52. Correct
53. Anything used as a tool is given its own name.
54. Many of these tools, such as Gunter's chain, get their names from their inventors.
55. Anyone can learn to use his or her tools for mapping.

E. Proofreading

Errors are shown on page. The correctly rewritten paragraphs appear below.

56 The chances of discovering buried treasure in your back yard are slim. **57** You and I find secret maps and treasure only in adventure stories. **58** Correct

59 All that we treasure hunters have to do is bury some valuable-looking objects. **60** Marcus, Jen, and I have done this for fun. **61** Correct **62** Marcus and she found an antique watch and rhinestone costume jewelry. **63** Everybody searched his or her neighborhood for an old object that we could use as a treasure chest. **64** Someone had thrown away his or her old silverware, bowls, and other kitchen things. **65** Correct

66 Jen and I were in charge of figuring out distances. **67** She and I used a yardstick to measure the length and width of our back yard. **68** It's not very big. **69** This part of our plan was easy for her and me to do. **70** Correct **71** Next, Jen and Marcus drew a grid on their graph paper. **72** Jen and he added symbols to represent things in the back yard, such as the elm tree, the rosebushes, and the toolshed. **73** Their grid and map symbols looked pretty good. **74** It was up to Jen and him to pick the burial spot. **75** No one will guess it in his or her whole lifetime. **76** They're really excited about our secret burial ceremony!

51. Another was the astrolabe. Its purpose was to help explorers navigate at sea.
52. One could calculate his or her position by measuring the angles of stars above the horizon.
53. Anything used as a tool is given their own name.
54. Many of these tools, such as Gunter's chain, get its names from its inventors.
55. Anyone can learn to use their tools for mapping.

E. Proofreading Rewrite the following sentences and correct all errors in the use of pronouns. If a sentence has no errors, write *Correct.*

56The chances of discovering buried treasure in you're back yard are slim. **57**You and me find secret maps and treasure only in adventure stories. **58**Yet treasure can really be ours.

59All that us treasure hunters have to do is bury some valuable-looking objects. **60**Marcus, Jen, and me have done this for fun. **61**They had the idea first. **62**Marcus and her found an antique watch and rhinestone costume jewelry. **63**Everybody searched their neighborhood for an old object that we could use as a treasure chest. **64**Someone had thrown away their old silverware, bowls, and other kitchen things. **65**Among them, we found an airtight container that was just the right size.

66Jen and me were in charge of figuring out distances. **67**Her and I used a yardstick to measure the length and width of our back yard. **68**Its not very big. **69**This part of our plan was easy for she and me to do. **70**Then we made a scale for our map: one inch equaled one foot. **71**Next, Jen and Marcus drew a grid on they're graph paper. **72**Jen and him added symbols to represent things in the back yard, such as the elm tree, the rosebushes, and the toolshed. **73**They're grid and map symbols looked pretty good. **74**It was up to Jen and he to pick the burial spot. **75**No one will guess it in their whole lifetime. **76**Their really excited about our secret burial ceremony!

456 Grammar Handbook

WRITING CONNECTIONS

Elaboration, Revision, and Proofreading

Revise the following draft of a friendly letter by using the directions below. Then proofread the letter for errors in the use of pronouns. Also correct any other errors in grammar, capitalization, punctuation, and spelling.

Dear Martin,

[1]We had a great time on our vacation in arizona. [2]My favrite place was Canyon de Chelly National Monument. [3]First we drove along the rim of the canyon and looked at the scenery. [4]Then Chuck and me went down a trail into the canyon. [5]It cut back and fourth for about a mile, finally, we reached a stream at the bottom. [6]Taking off our shoes and socks, we waded through the stream. [7]On the other side, we saw the ruins of a village. [8]Parts of the village were built into the cliff. [9]There are other cliff dwellings at Mesa Verde National Park in Colorado. [10]Some of the buildings still have all they're walls. [11]Even now the ruins look beatiful. [12]Chuck and me wish you could have been there with us to see it.

Your freind,
Rick

1. In sentence 4, replace the weak verb "went" with the more precise verb "hiked."
2. Replace the vague pronoun "it" in sentence 5 with the more precise noun "the trail."
3. Add details to sentence 6 by describing the stream as "cool and clear."
4. Add this information after sentence 7: "The Anasazi Indians built the village about one thousand years ago."
5. Delete the sentence that doesn't belong.

Personal and Expressive Writing

Writing a friendly letter is a good way to share your feelings and experiences with others. (See Workshop 1.) When you revise a letter you have written, make sure you present all of the details your reader will want to know. By using pronouns effectively, you can make your writing flow smoothly and present information clearly.

WRITING CONNECTIONS

Elaboration, Revision, and Proofreading

This activity will allow your students to see some of the concepts presented in this Handbook at work in a piece of personal and expressive writing. By revising and proofreading this friendly letter, students will have the opportunity to replace vague pronouns with precise nouns, to use elaboration, and to correct errors in pronoun use.

You may wish to have students revise the passage independently, then meet in small groups for peer review. Then briefly discuss the changes as a class. Revisions may vary slightly. A typical revision is shown below. Elements involving change are shown in boldface.

Dear Martin,

We had a great time on our vacation in Arizona. My favorite place was Canyon de Chelly National Monument. First we drove along the rim of the canyon and looked at the scenery. Then Chuck and I **hiked** down a trail into the canyon. **The trail** cut back and forth for about a mile. Finally, we reached a stream at the bottom. Taking off our shoes and socks, we waded through the **cool and clear** stream. On the other side, we saw the ruins of a village. **The Anasazi Indians built the village about one thousand years ago.** Parts of the village were built into the cliff. ~~**There are other cliff dwellings at Mesa Verde National Park in Colorado.**~~ Some of the buildings still have all their walls. Even now the ruins look beautiful. Chuck and I wish you could have been there with us to see them.

Your friend,
Rick

Sketch Book

Objective

- To use writing prompts and fine art as springboards to informal writing

WRITING WARM-UPS

Remind students that this assignment will not be graded. The art and writing prompts aim to help students begin thinking in a broad, imaginative way about the concepts in this Handbook. Unless students express an interest in more than one prompt, ask them to explore just one of these ideas.

For the first writing prompt, invite volunteers to suggest vivid words that describe Calder's creature. Have students close their eyes and imagine what it would look like in motion and how it would sound. Urge them to use such vivid words in writing their descriptions.

For the second writing prompt, remind students that a tall tale uses exaggeration to provide humor and entertainment. Point out that students' tall tales might make humorous exaggerations relating to size. Ask students to think about how the subject's size would affect movement, and how this person or thing might get along with people in an ordinary-sized world.

For the third writing prompt, tell students to focus on physical details. For example, ask students what they would do to avoid getting stepped on, if they were much smaller than everyone around them. How would they get enough to eat? Where would they go to get out of the rain? What other advantages or disadvantages would they have?

Sketch Book

WRITING WARM-UPS

- Imagine you see this creature walking down the street. Write a vivid description so your readers will be able to see it too.

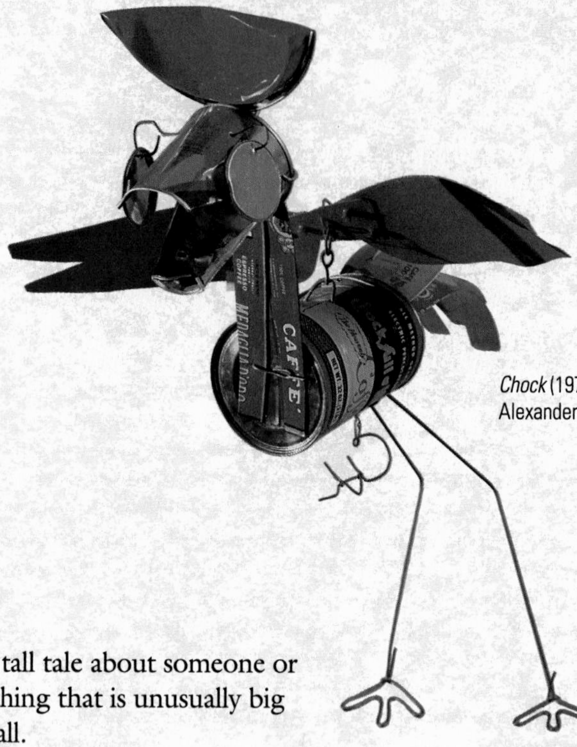

Chock (1972), Alexander Calder.

- Tell a tall tale about someone or something that is unusually big or small.
- Imagine that like Alice in Wonderland or Gulliver in the land of Lilliput, you have suddenly arrived in a place where you are much bigger or much smaller than all the things and people around you. Briefly describe your experience.

ART NOTE

Alexander Calder (1898–1976), the creator of the mobile, is famous for introducing motion into sculpture. Born near Philadelphia, Calder grew up in a family of artists and was making wire sculptures when he was only five. Later he studied engineering and attended art school in New York City and Paris. His first important works—such as an amusing wood carving called *The Flattest Cat*—often drew inspiration from the animal kingdom. In 1931 Calder devised his first mobile, or sculpture with moving parts. He created large and small mobiles, many of them for outdoor display.

Understanding Adjectives

GRAMMAR HANDBOOK 38

- What Are Adjectives?
- Kinds of Adjectives
- Articles and Demonstrative Adjectives
- Predicate Adjectives
- Making Comparisons with Adjectives

Click! A photographer captures an image on film. The color, the texture, the size, the detail—all make whatever the camera records seem very real. Yet a writer can do even more. A writer can capture and share the way something feels, sounds, tastes, and smells.

Adjectives help writers create clear, detailed, lively images. In this handbook you will learn how to recognize adjectives and use them to add color and precision to your writing and speaking.

GRAMMAR HANDBOOK 38

Understanding Adjectives

Objectives

- To identify and use adjectives
- To distinguish between common and proper adjectives
- To determine whether an adjective tells *which one, what kind* or *how many* about a noun or pronoun
- To identify and use articles and demonstrative adjectives correctly
- To recognize predicate adjectives
- To identify and use correctly the comparative and superlative forms of adjectives

Writing

- To use adjectives to make descriptions more vivid and more precise

INTRODUCING THE HANDBOOK

Ask students if they agree with the expression "A picture is worth a thousand words." Elicit that although pictures may vividly capture objects and scenes that we see, writing can also capture what we see, smell, taste, hear, and touch. To illustrate, ask students to describe the smell of a freshly repaired asphalt street, the taste of a pizza, the sound of the classroom as school ends for the day, and how an ice cube feels in their bare hands. Write on the board the adjectives students use in describing these situations. Explain that in this handbook, they will learn how to use adjectives to make their writing vivid and effective.

WHAT ARE ADJECTIVES?

Objectives

- To identify and use adjectives
- To distinguish between common and proper adjectives

Writing

- To use lively adjectives in writing

Teaching Strategies

STUMBLING BLOCK: PARTICIPLES
Students may have difficulty recognizing *aching* and *bruised* as adjectives. Point out that any word that describes a noun or pronoun is functioning as an adjective. Have students identify the noun or pronoun that *aching* and *bruised* modify. *(rider)* Then give students additional examples of similar forms:

I ate the *baked* potato.

The *bucking* broncos were angry.

Finally, ask students to generate their own examples of this type of adjective.

INDIVIDUALIZING INSTRUCTION: BASIC STUDENTS You may want to reinforce the use of proper nouns as adjectives by asking students to create sentences illustrating noun and adjective use of the sample words *African, Wyoming,* and *Independence Day*. (Samples: An *African* [noun] visited our school. Our *African* [adjective] visitor came from Senegal.)

Additional Resources

Tests and Writing Assessment Prompts, Pretest, pp. 29–30
Grammar and Usage Practice Book, p. 51
Grammar Test Generator

WHAT ARE ADJECTIVES?

An **adjective** is a word that modifies, or describes, a noun or a pronoun.

Look at these sentences:

A bull charged around the arena.
An angry bull charged around the hot, dusty arena.

What words in the second sentence tell you more about the bull and the arena? *Angry* describes *bull. Hot* and *dusty* tell about the *arena.* Each word adds more specific information to the sentence.

These words are **adjectives.** Adjectives describe, or modify, nouns and pronouns.

Adjectives may be placed before or after a noun or pronoun. Two or more adjectives modifying the same word sometimes need to be separated with commas. Use a comma after each adjective except the last one.

The *young, startled* cowpoke tumbled from the saddle.

Adjectives may also follow the word they modify.

This rider, *aching* and *bruised,* limped from the arena.

Writing TIP

If a noun is used as a describer, it becomes an adjective. In the sentence "I need *ham* for my *ham* sandwich," the word *ham* is used first as a noun and then as an adjective.

Proper Adjectives

Some adjectives, such as *Texan,* are made by adding endings to proper nouns. These are called **proper adjectives.**

Always begin a proper adjective with a capital letter. Common adjectives, those not formed from proper nouns, are not capitalized.

Africa + *-n* = African   China + *-ese* = Chinese

Other proper adjectives do not have special endings.

Wyoming rodeo   *Independence Day* celebration

Practice Your Skills

A. CONCEPT CHECK

Adjectives For the following sentences, write each adjective and the word it modifies. Label each adjective *Common* or *Proper.* You should find a total of twenty-one adjectives.

1. Cowhands in the brush country of the Southwestern hills are often called vaqueros.
2. Once, the term referred only to Spanish and Mexican cowpunchers.
3. Quickly, however, it came to mean any ranch hands.
4. South American historical records mention cowhands too.
5. For example, an Argentinian cowpoke was a gaucho.
6. Gauchos were good singers and storytellers.
7. Home was often a rough shack made of mud and twigs.
8. A gaucho wore loose white pants, a wool shawl at the waist, a shirt of bright color, and leather boots.
9. The gaucho, strong and brave, no longer exists.
10. Barbed wire ended the reign of this colorful figure.

B. REVISION SKILL

Using Lively Adjectives Careful choice of adjectives can make your writing more interesting. Write the following sentences. Replace each of the underlined overused or vague adjectives with one that is more lively or precise. If a (P) follows the sentence, use a proper adjective.

11. The rodeo, which originated among working cowboys, is a U.S. tradition and a nice contest of skills.
12. Year-round, big crowds file into arenas throughout the United States.
13. Competing can be dangerous, so rodeos attract good riders.
14. Bronc riding and steer wrestling are two good events.
15. Bulls, mean and mad, also provide a challenge for riders.
16. Riding a bucking bull can result in a bad fall.
17. Our rodeos are not the only ones; Canada also has them. (P)
18. Those riders, our neighbors to the north, are also skilled. (P)
19. Cowboys in Mexico have some rodeos, or *charreadas.* (P)
20. Australia has ranches too, and its rodeos are popular. (P)

Writing Theme
Cowpokes & Rodeos

FOR MORE PRACTICE
See page 475.

Writing Theme: Cowpokes & Rodeos

Suggest that students use these exercises as a springboard to writing. Other related areas that they might explore include the following:

- how horses came to the Americas
- Spanish settlement of the Southwest
- how horses are chosen and trained for rodeo performances
- the work of rodeo clowns

Answers to Practice Your Skills

A. Concept Check
Adjectives

1. brush, country, Common; Southwestern, hills, Proper
2. Spanish, cowpunchers, Proper; Mexican, cowpunchers, Proper
3. any, hands, Common; ranch, hands, Common
4. South American, records, Proper; historical, records, Common
5. Argentinian, cowpoke, Proper
6. good, singers, storytellers, Common
7. rough, shack, Common
8. loose, pants, Common; white, pants, Common; wool, shawl, Common; bright, color, Common; leather, boots, Common
9. strong, gaucho, Common; brave, gaucho, Common
10. Barbed, wire, Common; this, figure, Common; colorful, figure, Common

B. Revision Skill
Using Lively Adjectives

Answers will vary. Possible adjectives are shown below. Student answers should be in sentences.

11. remarkable
12. enormous
13. skillful
14. exciting
15. angry
16. nasty
17. United States
18. Canadian
19. Mexican
20. Australian

KINDS OF ADJECTIVES

Objectives

- To identify and understand the three functions of adjectives

Writing

- To use adjectives with different functions in writing

Teaching Strategies

LINKING GRAMMAR AND WRITING Stress the importance of choosing adjectives that add clarity and interest to writing. Avoid the use of tired, overused adjectives. Have students suggest replacements for the tired adjective *nice* in these phrases: *a nice view, a nice street, a nice day, a nice boy, a nice party.*

INDIVIDUALIZING INSTRUCTION: ESL STUDENTS In Spanish and many other languages, adjectives that tell *what kind* often immediately follow the nouns they modify; in English, they rarely do (except as a predicate adjective or in sentences like "The car, red and shiny, sped away."). Help students understand that constructions such as "the sky blue" and "the woman old" are not used in English.

Additional Resource

Grammar and Usage Practice Book, p. 52

KINDS OF ADJECTIVES

Writing TIP

Notice in "Yomarhi Purnima," pages 62–63, how the author Elizabeth Murphy-Melas uses adjectives to help the reader picture both Nepal and the thanksgiving festival she is describing.

An **adjective** modifies a word by telling *what kind, how many,* or *which one.*

Every adjective has one of three functions. It tells *what kind, how many,* or *which one.*

Some Adjectives Tell *What Kind*

Some adjectives describe by telling *what kind.*

The *gold medal* winners waved to the *cheering* crowd from a *twenty-foot-long* float.

Many adjectives that tell *what kind* are formed by adding an adjective ending to a noun.

rain*y*	adventur*ous*
fear*less*	color*ful*
comfort*able*	gold*en*

Some Adjectives Tell *How Many*

Some adjectives limit by telling *how many.*

There are *two* astronauts who orbited the moon *ten* times.

Some Adjectives Tell *Which One*

Some adjectives point out specific members of groups by telling *which one* or *which ones.* Remember that possessive pronouns can be used as adjectives. A complete list of possessive pronouns appears on page 446.

Adjectives that tell *which one* or *how many* almost always come before the words they modify.

That woman riding in the *third* car is *our* senator.

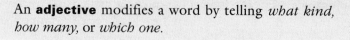

I designed *those three red robot* masks in the *second* row.

Practice Your Skills

A. APPLICATION IN LITERATURE

Recognizing Adjectives Read this passage about the two-time Olympic gold medal winner Jim Thorpe. Divide your paper into three columns. Label the columns *What Kind, How Many,* and *Which One.* Find all the adjectives in each sentence and write them in the correct columns. You should find a total of nineteen adjectives.

> **1** It was July 6, 1912. . . at the fifth Olympic games. **2** Around the cinder track marched hundreds of athletes. **3** They came from twenty-six different countries, from every part of the world. **4** They strode along to the cheers of 30,000 people who had come to watch. **5** The athletes went proudly past the royal box of King Gustav and Queen Victoria of Sweden. . . .
>
> **6** The American athletes were just coming past the box. **7** In the fourth row marched a tall, powerful-looking American Indian. **8** He had a shock of black hair. **9** His big square jaw was set firmly. **10** His half-closed eyes stared straight ahead.
>
> **Guernsey Van Riper, Jr.,**
> ***Jim Thorpe: Native American Athlete***

B. DRAFTING SKILL

Using Adjectives Act as screenwriter and add adjectives that complete the following stage directions for a historical film. Number your paper from 11 to 20 and write the kinds of adjective asked for in parentheses.

EXAMPLE ________ actors stand beside a flag. (how many)
Two actors stand beside a flag.

11. A(n) ______ spacecraft can be seen on the right. (what kind)
12. ________ craters dot the rocky landscape. (how many)
13. Some of ________ craters are several feet wide. (which ones)
14. The door on _______ spacecraft begins to open. (which one)
15. _________ figures dressed in spacesuits come slowly through the door. (how many)

Writing Theme
Celebrations and Accomplishments

Grammar TIP

Remember, when two or more adjectives modify the same noun, you will often add commas after all but the last adjective. However, adjectives that tell number, size, shape, color, and age often do not require commas.

Writing Theme: Celebrations and Accomplishments

Suggest that students use these exercises as a springboard to writing. Other related areas that they might explore include the following:

- Wilma Rudolph, Olympic star
- the origin of the Olympics
- a memorable personal accomplishment
- planning an awards celebration

Answers to Practice Your Skills

A. Application in Literature
Recognizing Adjectives

Student answers should be in columns.

1. fifth, Which One; Olympic, What Kind
2. cinder, What Kind
3. twenty-six, How Many; different, What Kind; every, How Many
4. 30,000, How Many
5. royal, What Kind (*King Gustav* and *Queen Victoria* are nouns. The titles *King* and *Queen* are part of the names and therefore are not adjectives.)
6. American, What Kind
7. fourth, Which One; tall, What Kind; powerful-looking, What Kind; American, What Kind
8. black, What Kind
9. His, Which One; big, What Kind; square, What Kind
10. His, Which One; half-closed, What Kind

B. Drafting Skill
Using Adjectives

Answers will vary. Sample adjectives are shown below.

11. (A) silvery
12. Several
13. those
14. that
15. Two

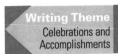

16. (an) American
17. his
18. dark
19. (a) busy
20. (An) excited

CHECK POINT

Writing Theme: Hiccups

Other related areas students might wish to explore as writing topics include the following:

- the scientific explanation of hiccups
- causes of and cures for snoring
- how germs are spread by coughing and sneezing

MIXED REVIEW • PAGES 460–464

You may wish to use this activity to check students' mastery of the following concepts:

- common and proper adjectives
- functions of adjectives

1. many, How Many; different, What Kind
2. numerous, How Many; unusual, What Kind
3. some, How Many; severe, What Kind
4. this, Which One; your, Which One
5. ancient, What Kind; his, Which One
6. Greek, What Kind, Proper Adjective
7. Many, How Many; this, Which One
8. Native American, What Kind, Proper Adjective; sugary, What Kind
9. small, What Kind; your, Which One
10. this, Which One
11. One, How Many; popular, What Kind
12. good, What Kind
13. many, How Many; folk, What Kind
14. opposite, Which One
15. brown, What Kind; paper, What Kind; few, How Many
16. your, Which One; several, How Many
17. one, How Many; tricky, What Kind
18. bad, What Kind
19. favorite, What Kind
20. your, Which One; worst, What Kind

16. One of the actors holds a(n) ________ flag. (what kind)
17. He raises ________ hand and plunges the flagpole into the soil. (which one)
18. The camera frames the image of the earth in the ________ sky behind the figures. (what kind)
19. The scene shifts to a(n) ________ TV studio. (what kind)
20. A(n) ________ commentator reports this historic event. (what kind)

FOR MORE PRACTICE
See page 475.

CHECK POINT

MIXED REVIEW • PAGES 460–464

Writing Theme
Hiccups

Write each adjective in the following sentences. Then write whether the adjective tells *What Kind, How Many,* or *Which One.* Identify each *Proper Adjective.* Ignore *a, an,* and *the.*

1. People have imagined many different causes for hiccups.
2. They have also invented numerous unusual cures.
3. According to some people, you get severe hiccups when someone talks about you.
4. If you guess who this person is, your hiccups will leave.
5. An ancient Greek tickled his nose so that he would sneeze.
6. Greek doctors believed that a sneeze chased away hiccups.
7. Many people still claim that this cure works.
8. The Aymara, a Native American people of Bolivia and Peru, say hiccups are caused by eating sugary sweets.
9. They say sweets make a small worm grow in your stomach.
10. Whenever this worm moves, you hiccup.
11. One popular cure today is to get someone to scare you.
12. A good fright almost always cures hiccups.
13. There are many folk remedies for hiccups.
14. Try drinking water from the opposite side of a glass.
15. Breathe into a brown paper bag for a few minutes.
16. Hold your breath and take several drinks of water.
17. Stand on one leg and say a tricky phrase quickly.
18. For bad hiccups, suck on a lemon.
19. Everyone seems to have a favorite cure for hiccups.
20. What is your secret for getting rid of the worst hiccups?

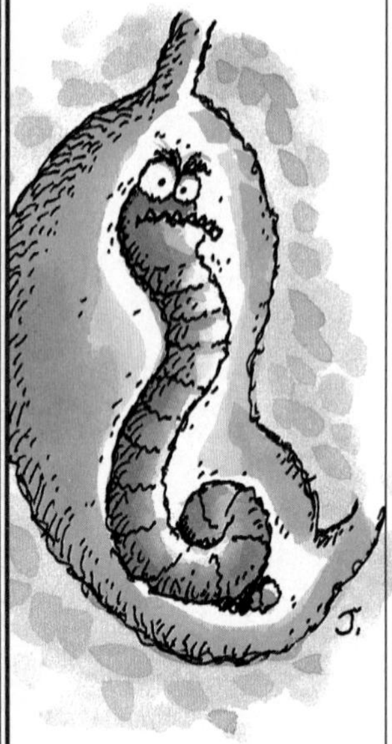

ARTICLES AND DEMONSTRATIVE ADJECTIVES

A, an, and *the* are special adjectives called **articles.** *This, that, these,* and *those* are **demonstrative adjectives.**

Articles

The words *a, an,* and *the* are **articles.** Because these words always modify nouns, they are also adjectives.

Use *a* before words beginning with consonant sounds.

a firefly a lamp a bulb a candle

Use *an* before words beginning with vowel sounds.

an afterglow an intense light an orange sunset

When you pronounce words that begin with a silent *h,* you do not say the *h* sound. Instead, you begin the word with the vowel sound after the *h*. Follow the rule for using *an.*

an hour an honor an heir

A and *an* are used with singular nouns. *The* may be used before either a singular or a plural noun. *The* is used when you want to refer to a specific person, place, thing, or idea. *A* and *an* are used when you want to be less specific.

The lantern shines brightly. (one specific lantern)
Brian turned on *a* light. (any light)

Demonstrative Adjectives

This, that, these, and *those* are **demonstrative adjectives.** They point out specific things. Use *this* and *that* with singular nouns. Use *these* and *those* with plural nouns.

This candle will burn longer than *that* one.
These candles are brighter than *those* candles.

ARTICLES AND DEMONSTRATIVE ADJECTIVES

Objectives

- To identify and use articles and demonstrative adjectives correctly
- To distinguish demonstrative adjectives from demonstrative pronouns

Writing

- To use articles and demonstrative adjectives in writing

Teaching Strategies

HELPFUL HINT: ARTICLES Point out that an article is a reliable signal that a noun is coming up. Sometimes the noun comes right after the article: *a firefly.* Sometimes adjectives or other words intervene: *a big firefly; a very big firefly; a yellow and brown firefly.*

Also point out that *a,* not *an,* should precede an *h* sound *(a horse; a hiccup; a hot platter; a happy infant).*

INDIVIDUALIZING INSTRUCTION: ESL STUDENTS Articles can cause ESL students particular difficulties. Some languages, such as Vietnamese and Russian, do not contain articles. Students who have been speaking these languages will need additional practice both in using articles and in identifying situations when articles should not be used. For these students, contrast and compare the following sentences:

A bus is coming. (nonspecific)

The bus is coming. (specific)

The buses are late today. (specific)

Buses come every ten minutes. (nonspecific)

INDIVIDUALIZING INSTRUCTION: ESL STUDENTS In many languages, adjectives change form to agree in gender or number with the nouns they modify. Remind ESL students that in English adjectives' forms do not change for gender and rarely change for number. Two exceptions are *this/these* and *that/those,* whose forms depend on whether the nouns they modify are singular or plural.

ADVANCED STUDENTS Have a group of students work together on a list of words that can be used as either pronouns or adjectives. Lists should expand beyond demonstrative words, to possessives such as *his;* relative pronouns that can be used as adjectives, such as *whose* and *which;* and indefinite pronouns that can be used as adjectives, such as *both, few, each, most,* and *many.* Ask students to create sample sentences illustrating the different uses of each listed word. Then have them share their work with classmates by preparing a wall chart or poster for permanent reference.

Additional Resource

Grammar and Usage Practice Book, p. 53

Demonstrative adjectives can show whether an object you are pointing out is nearer or farther away.

Near: this, these *Far:* that, those

Demonstrative adjectives are often paired with the nouns *kind* and *sort.* Both *kind* and *sort* are singular words. Therefore, say *this kind* and *that sort.* Use *these* and *those* only with the plurals: *these kinds* or *those sorts.*

This kind of flashlight is called a penlight.
Those sorts of light bulbs use the least electricity.

Adjectives or Pronouns?

Demonstrative words can be adjectives or pronouns. A demonstrative word is an adjective if it answers the question *which one?* about a noun. A demonstrative word is a pronoun if it takes the place of a noun. Look at these examples.

Adjective	*This* bulb is burnt out. (*This* tells which bulb.)
Pronoun	*This* doesn't work.
Adjective	*These* candles are new. (*These* tells which candles.)
Pronoun	*These* are new.
Adjective	*That* light is too bright. (*That* tells which light.)
Pronoun	*That* is too bright.
Adjective	Do you see *those* stars? (*Those* tells which stars.)
Pronoun	Do you see *those?*

Them is always a pronoun. It is never used as an adjective. The pronoun *them* is always used as an object, never as the subject of a sentence.

Incorrect	*Them* candles cannot be blown out.
Incorrect	*Them* are trick birthday candles.
Correct	*Those* candles are for Sarah's cake. I chose *them* myself. (*Them* is a pronoun functioning as a direct object. It replaces the noun *candles.*)

Practice Your Skills

A. CONCEPT CHECK

Articles and Demonstrative Adjectives Number your paper from 1 to 15. Write the correct word from the parentheses.

1. Do you see (those, them) floodlights on the playing field?
2. (A, The) development of the modern electric lamp made such lighting possible.
3. (These, Those) lights near us are incandescent.
4. Inside these (kind, kinds) of bulbs, wires are heated.
5. (Them, Those) heated wires produce light.
6. (A, An) fluorescent bulb, however, does not rely on wires.
7. Your school probably uses (this, these) kind of light.
8. (These, Them) tubes contain gases called argon and mercury vapor.
9. Currents run through (these, them) gases; light is produced.
10. (This, That) colorful tube over there contains neon gas.
11. (Those, Them) neon bulbs are used in signs for stores.
12. (A, An) advertisement in neon lights gets attention.
13. Look at (this, that) huge spotlight next to me.
14. (These, This) kind of bulb lights up when electricity leaps between two rods inside the bulb.
15. Spotlights produce (a, an) hot and very bright light.

Writing Theme
Sources of Light

The Ghost of Rock and Roll (1987), Lili Lakich.

B. DRAFTING SKILL

Using Adjectives Correctly You and a friend are in a park collecting fireflies, or lightning bugs, for a science project. The following situations describe what you see. Use these situations as starting points. Write five sentences using articles and demonstrative adjectives to describe what you see.

Two fireflies are close to you.
Your friend chases a firefly a long way.
There are two jars of fireflies—one nearby and one across the park.

FOR MORE PRACTICE
See page 475.

Writing Theme: Sources of Light

Other related areas students might wish to explore as writing topics include the following:
- moonlight and its source
- bioluminescence
- laser beams
- prisms

Answers to Practice Your Skills

A. Concept Check
Articles and Demonstrative Adjectives

Answers are shown on page.

B. Drafting Skill
Using Adjectives Correctly

Answers will vary. Check to see that students have used articles and demonstrative adjectives correctly. Look especially for correct use of *this, that, these,* and *those* to indicate distance. Sample sentences are shown below.

These fireflies flew right by my head.
Forget *that* firefly you are chasing.
Come get *the* firefly over here.
We can put *the* firefly in *this* jar right here or in *that* jar on the porch.
A firefly can look beautiful at night.

ART NOTE

Lila Lakish showed this neon sculpture in 1987 at the Museum of Neon Art in Los Angeles, a museum devoted to works of neon, electric, and kinetic (moving) art. Ask students what music they'd choose to go with this sculpture.

PREDICATE ADJECTIVES

Objectives
- To identify predicate adjectives

Writing
- To use predicate adjectives in writing

Teaching Strategies

KEY TO UNDERSTANDING: PREDICATE ADJECTIVES Stress that a predicate adjective must both follow a linking verb and modify the subject. If an adjective modifies another word in the predicate, it is not a predicate adjective. For example, in "The animal is a large cat," the adjective *large* modifies the predicate noun *cat.* However, in the sentence "The animal is large," *large* modifies the subject *animal* and is a predicate adjective.

KEY TO UNDERSTANDING: PRONOUNS WITH PREDICATE ADJECTIVES Explain that when the subject of a sentence is a pronoun, and the verb is a linking verb, the predicate adjective modifies the pronoun. Discuss the following example with students.

She is athletic.

Additional Resource

Grammar and Usage Practice Book, p. 54

Writing Theme: Comparison and Contrast

Other related areas students might wish to explore as writing topics include the following:
- crocodiles compared to alligators
- butterflies compared to moths
- turtles compared to tortoises
- wolves compared to dogs

Answers to Practice Your Skills

A. Concept Check
Predicate Adjectives

Predicate adjectives are underlined once and the words modified are underlined twice on the page.

PREDICATE ADJECTIVES

A **predicate adjective** is an adjective that follows a linking verb. It describes the subject of the sentence.

When an adjective follows a linking verb, it is part of the predicate. Therefore, it is called a **predicate adjective.** A predicate adjective modifies the subject. Notice that one predicate adjective may modify a compound subject and two predicate adjectives may be joined to describe the same subject.

The cat and dog seem gentle. (*Gentle* describes *cat* and *dog.*)
The lion looks fierce and dangerous. (*Fierce* and *dangerous* describe *lion.*)

A predicate adjective differs from other adjectives you have studied. Unlike most other adjectives, a predicate adjective comes after the word it modifies. Also, it is separated from the word it modifies by a linking verb.

Here are some linking verbs that often come before predicate adjectives. For more about linking verbs, see pages 405–406.

am	was	become	look	taste
are	were	feel	seem	sound
is	appear	grow	smell	remain

Writing TIP

To eliminate wordiness, try combining sentences to form a predicate adjective.

Practice Your Skills

A. CONCEPT CHECK

Writing Theme Comparison and Contrast

Predicate Adjectives Copy the following sentences. Draw one line under the predicate adjective in each sentence and two lines under the word or words it modifies. Remember that more than one predicate adjective can follow a verb.

1. To you, do frogs and toads look identical?
2. Both creatures are cold-blooded and amphibious.

Literature Connection

Have students identify predicate adjectives and other adjectives in these sentences from *Julie of the Wolves* by Jean Craighead George.

"Miyax was a classic Eskimo beauty, small of bone and delicately wired with strong muscles. Her face was pearl-round and her nose was flat. Her black eyes, which slanted gracefully, were moist and sparkling."

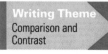

3. They are comfortable both on land and in water.
4. Yet the skin and shape of frogs and toads seem different.
5. Frogs feel smooth and slippery.
6. In contrast, toads appear dry and bumpy.
7. However, frogs and toads are similar as babies, or tadpoles.
8. Tadpoles of both animals appear fishlike.
9. Their tails are long and powerful.
10. Tadpoles can grow big in a short time.
11. After the tadpole stage, frogs become long and graceful.
12. Toads remain squat and pudgy.
13. People seem needlessly fearful about handling toads.
14. The rumor about toads and warts is untrue.
15. Somehow, toads look uglier to people than frogs do.

B. CONCEPT CHECK

Recognizing Predicate Adjectives Write the predicate adjectives in the following sentences. If a sentence does not contain a predicate adjective, write *None.*

[16]Some scientists feel comfortable about the classification of giant pandas as bears; others group pandas with raccoons. [17]In many ways, giant pandas and bears are similar. [18]Their body shape and size look alike. [19]Both grow quite large. [20]The movements of both appear slow and clumsy. [21]Bears and pandas can stand erect on their hind legs. [22]Differences are apparent too. [23]The panda's coloring is black and white. [24]To a panda, only bamboo shoots taste good. [25]To a bear, honey is perfect.

C. APPLICATION IN WRITING

Comparison and Contrast Write a brief paragraph comparing and contrasting two animals. Think about pets you've owned or animals you've seen at the zoo or in your back yard. Use at least five of the following linking verbs with predicate adjectives.

was	appear	seem	look	smell
are	become	grow	feel	

FOR MORE PRACTICE
See page 476.

B. Concept Check
Recognizing Predicate Adjectives

16. comfortable
17. similar
18. alike
19. large
20. slow, clumsy
21. None
22. apparent
23. black, white
24. good
25. perfect

C. Application in Writing
Comparison and Contrast

Answers will vary.

CHECK POINT

Writing Theme: Yo-Yos

Other related areas students might wish to explore as writing topics include the following:

- the origin of boomerangs
- the origin of kites
- how to play cat's cradle
- the art of origami

MIXED REVIEW • PAGES 465–469

You may wish to use this activity to check students' mastery of the following concepts:

- articles and demonstrative adjectives
- predicate adjectives

A.

Answers are shown on page.

B.

Answers are shown on page.

CHECK POINT

MIXED REVIEW • PAGES 465–469

Writing Theme
Yo-Yos

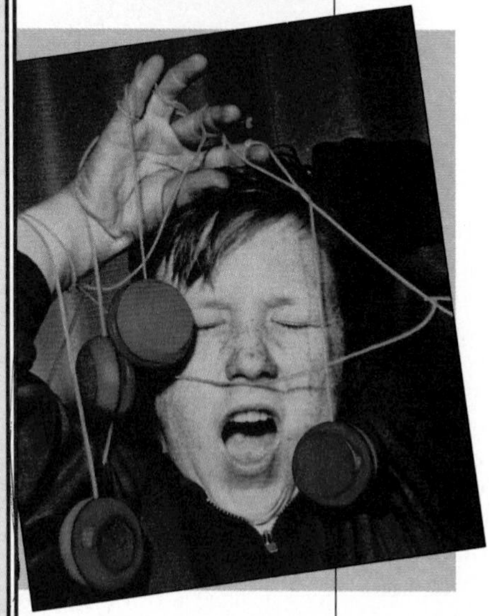

A. Write the correct word from those given in parentheses.

1. Have you ever played with (a, an) yo-yo?
2. You can get hooked playing with these (kind, kinds) of toys.
3. (A, The) yo-yo came to us from the Philippines.
4. (These, Them) yo-yos will do hundreds of tricks.
5. Grab one of (these, those) yo-yos over there.
6. Now throw (that, those) yo-yo to the end of its string.
7. When you can keep the yo-yo spinning down there at (this, that) end of the string, it is said to be "sleeping."
8. As you hold onto (this, that) end of the string, give a slight tug and the yo-yo will climb back up to your hand.
9. Once you master "sleeping," (this, these) yo-yo will do other tricks.
10. In (a, an) expert's hand, a yo-yo seems almost magical.

B. Write and label each Linking Verb and Predicate Adjective in the following sentences.

11. If yo-yos seem modern to you, you have a surprise coming.
12. Thousands of years ago, the Chinese were clever with yo-yos.
13. The ancient Greeks also became familiar with this toy.
14. In 1600, people in the Philippines grew serious about yo-yos.
15. To Filipinos, yo-yos appeared useful as hunting weapons.
16. Their yo-yos felt very heavy.
17. Made of rock, with twenty-foot-long strings, they looked awesome.
18. Filipino hunters became quite skillful with these yo-yos.
19. A repeat throw was easy after the return of the yo-yo on an unsuccessful attempt.
20. Today, after all these years, the yo-yo remains popular.

470 Grammar Handbook

MAKING COMPARISONS WITH ADJECTIVES

Use the **comparative form** of an adjective to compare two things. Use the **superlative form** of an adjective to compare three or more things.

A ruby is hard. A diamond is hard. An emerald is hard.

All of these gems are hard, but they do not all have the same degree of hardness. You can show the differences in hardness by using special forms of adjectives.

Use the **comparative form** to compare two things, two groups of things, or one thing with a group. *Harder* is the comparative form of *hard.*

A ruby is *harder* than an emerald. Rubies are *harder* than pearls. That gem is *harder* than the others.

Use the **superlative form** to compare three or more things. *Hardest* is the superlative form of *hard.*

The diamond is the *hardest* of all gems.

Follow these rules to make the comparative and superlative forms of adjectives.

1. **Use the comparative form to compare two things.** To make the comparative form of most short adjectives, add *-er.*
2. **Use the superlative form to compare three or more things.** To make the superlative form of most short adjectives, add *-est.*

Adjective	Comparative Form	Superlative Form
big	bigger	biggest
hard	harder	hardest
rare	rarer	rarest
lovely	lovelier	loveliest

MAKING COMPARISONS WITH ADJECTIVES

Objectives

- To make the comparative and superlative forms of adjectives correctly

Writing

- To use comparative and superlative forms of adjectives in writing

Teaching Strategies

HELPFUL HINT: COMPARATIVE AND SUPERLATIVE FORMS Explain that the comparative and superlative forms of one-syllable and most two-syllable adjectives are made by adding *-er* and *-est,* and that those of some two-syllable adjectives and all adjectives of three or more syllables are made by adding *more* and *most.*

One or Two Syllables

neat, neater, neatest

pretty, prettier, prettiest

Three or More Syllables

dangerous, more dangerous, most dangerous

Advise students to check their dictionaries if they are in doubt about correct forms. You may wish to demonstrate how to find forms of comparison by using the classroom dictionary.

SPEAKING AND LISTENING Hearing and saying the correct forms of adjectives used in comparisons will help reinforce learning. Have students take turns making up and saying sentences, using first a comparative form, then a superlative form. Encourage students to discuss any forms that "sound" incorrect.

CRITICAL THINKING: ANALYZING
Ask students what is illogical about this sentence: "Ms. Lopez is the most *perfect* pianist." Elicit that *perfect* already expresses an absolute condition; therefore, something cannot be "more perfect" or "most perfect." Remind students of other adjectives that express absolute conditions and have no comparative or superlative forms: *ideal, unique, transparent, lost,* and so on.

LINKING GRAMMAR AND WRITING Point out that students can use *less* and *least* to make negative comparisons: "This emerald is *less* colorful than that one. This emerald is the *least* colorful of all." In negative comparisons, *-er* and *-est* endings are not used.

Additional Resource

Grammar and Usage Practice Book, p. 55

Notice that when an adjective ends in a single consonan[t] following a single vowel, such as *big,* you must double the fina[l] consonant before adding the ending. When the adjective end[s] in silent *e,* such as *rare,* simply add an *r.* When the adjectiv[e] ends in a *y* following a consonant, such as *lovely,* change the *y* to *i* before adding *-er* or *-est.*

Using *More* and *Most*

The comparative and superlative forms of some adjective[s] are not made by adding *-er* or *-est.* For adjectives of more tha[n] two syllables, the word *more* is usually used before the adjectiv[e] to make the comparative form. Use the word *most* before th[e] adjective to make the superlative form.

Adjective	Comparative Form	Superlative Form
remarkable	more remarkable	most remarkable
colorful	more colorful	most colorful
brilliant	more brilliant	most brilliant

Never use the *-er* ending with the word *more.* Never use the *-est* ending with the word *most.*

Incorrect This emerald seems *more greener* than that one.
Correct This emerald seems *greener* than that one.

Grammar TIP

When you use the word *little* to mean small in size, you may use *-er* and *-est* to form the comparative and superlative forms: *littler, littlest.* Use less to indicate a small amount. You could say, "The *littler* boy drank less milk."

Irregular Adjectives

The comparative and superlative forms of some adjectives are completely different words. Here are some of those forms.

Adjective	Comparative Form	Superlative Form
good	better	best
bad	worse	worst
little	less	least
much	more	most
many	more	most
far	farther	farthest

Practice Your Skills

A. CONCEPT CHECK

Comparisons with Adjectives Choose the correct form of the adjective from the parentheses.

1. Diamonds are the (more, most) popular of all gems.
2. Those that are clear and that sparkle with light are (more, most) valuable than others.
3. The Cullinan diamond was the (larger, largest) ever found.
4. It weighed 1⅓ pounds before being cut into smaller but (more, most) valuable stones.
5. The (best, goodest) gem cutters split the Cullinan into 105 gems.
6. The (most big, biggest) of them weighs one-fourth of a pound.
7. The Hope diamond is (smaller, more small) than the Cullinan.
8. Nevertheless, it is the (more, most) famous of the two.
9. This is not because the Hope diamond is (more pretty, prettier) but because some people claim it is cursed.
10. Thomas Hope was a British banker, and he was one of the (wealthiest, most wealthiest) people in England.
11. After he bought the diamond, however, his luck became (worse, more worse) than before.
12. (More late, Later) owners of the gem also had misfortunes.

B. DRAFTING SKILL

Making Comparisons Write each sentence. Use the comparative or superlative form of the adjective in parentheses.

13. Without a doubt, diamonds are the (hard) of all gems.
14. They are also the (appreciated).
15. However, an emerald (large) than a diamond might cost more.
16. Sapphires are rare, but rubies are even (uncommon).
17. For that reason, rubies are (valuable).
18. How do experts judge which is the (good) of two sapphires?
19. They know that the (good) sapphires are a deep blue.
20. The (expensive) opals of all are the black ones.
21. In contrast, the (white) of two pearls would cost more.
22. It is often (important) for a gem to be flawless than large.

Writing Theme
Gems

The world's largest cut diamond is the 530-carat Star of Africa. Set in the British royal scepter, this jewel can be removed and worn as a brooch.

Writing Theme: Gems

Other related areas students might wish to explore as writing topics include the following:

- how diamonds form
- the Kohinoor diamond
- the crown jewels of England
- pearl diving in Japan
- turquoise jewelry of the Southwest

Answers to Practice Your Skills

A. Concept Check
Comparisons with Adjectives

Answers are shown on page.

B. Drafting Skill
Making Comparisons

Comparative and superlative forms are shown below. Student answers should be in sentences.

13. hardest
14. most appreciated
15. larger
16. more uncommon
17. more valuable
18. better
19. best
20. most expensive
21. whiter
22. more important

C. Proofreading Skill
Correcting Errors in Comparisons

Errors in proofreading exercises are counted as follows: (a) Each word is counted as one error. For example, a misspelled word is one error; two initials and a last name not capitalized are counted as three errors. (b) Run-on sentences and sentence fragments are each counted as one error, even though the correction involves both punctuation and capitalization.

Errors are shown on page. The correctly written paragraphs appear below.

Ancient peoples believed that precious jewels had great power and magic. The most precious gems of all had the greatest powers. Sometimes people didn't agree on whether a gem's magic was good or bad. Some thought opals were lucky. Others said opals brought the worst luck of all.

Gems were once used as medicine. They were crushed into powder and then swallowed. Red jewels, such as rubies, were thought to control or stop bleeding. Green ones, such as emeralds, were supposed to cure ailments of the eye. Of all the colors, people thought green was the best because it was more restful to the eye than a brighter color. In choosing between two gems, people claimed the costlier one produced stronger medicine than the cheaper one.

CHECK POINT

Writing Theme: Rivers

Other related areas students might wish to explore as writing topics include the following:

- John Powell and the exploration of the Colorado River
- steamboats on the Mississippi River
- the search for the source of the Nile
- tracing the course of a river (for example, the Amazon or the Danube)

MIXED REVIEW • PAGES 471–474

You may wish to use this activity to check students' mastery of the following concept:

- making comparisons with adjectives

Comparative and superlative forms are shown below. Student answers should be in sentences.

1. longer
2. more
3. lengthiest
4. greatest
5. smaller
6. most gigantic
7. more spectacular
8. most famous
9. deeper
10. least

C. PROOFREADING SKILL

Correcting Errors in Comparisons Proofread the following paragraphs. Rewrite them correctly. Pay special attention to the correct use of adjectives in comparisons. (15 errors)

Ancient peoples beleived that precious jewels had great power and magic. The most precious gems of all had the greater powers. Sometimes people didn't agree on weather a gems magic was good or bad. Some thought opals were lucky. Others said opals brought the worse luck of all.

Gems were once used as medicine they were crushed into powder and then swallowed. Red jewells, such as rubies, were thought to controll or stop bleeding. Green ones, such as emeralds, were supposed to cure ailmants of the eye. Of all the colors, people thought green was the better because it was most restful to the eye than a brighter color In chosing between two gems, people claimed the costlier one produced more stronger medicine than the cheapest one.

FOR MORE PRACTICE
See page 476.

Writing Theme
Rivers

CHECK POINT
MIXED REVIEW • PAGES 471–474

Write the following sentences, using the correct comparative or superlative form of each adjective given in parentheses.

1. Which river is (long), the Mississippi or the Missouri?
2. Many people think the Mississippi flows for (much) miles.
3. The Missouri is actually North America's (lengthy) river.
4. The Mississippi carries the (great) volume of water of any North American river because it is so wide.
5. By comparison, the Colorado is much (small) than the mighty Mississippi.
6. However, it has slowly carved the (gigantic) canyon in North America.
7. There is not a canyon (spectacular) than the Grand Canyon.
8. It is the (famous) canyon anywhere in the world.
9. The Snake River created Hell's Canyon, which is even (deep) than the Grand Canyon but not as wide.
10. Of these rivers, the Colorado carries the (little) water.

A. Identifying Adjectives Label three columns on your paper *What Kind, How Many,* and *Which One.* Write the adjectives in each sentence in the correct columns. Ignore articles.

1. Before 1600, people didn't have cloth or paper napkins.
2. In those days, even the king went without any napkin at all.
3. However, a wealthy family would own one fine tablecloth.
4. These tablecloths were imported from Damascus in Syria.
5. The famous weavers in Damascus made wonderful tablecloths with marvelous flower and animal patterns.
6. The white cloth had red borders and gold fringe.
7. These expensive tablecloths were part of the royal treasure.
8. Few households could afford them.
9. Picture a gorgeous tablecloth spread on a feast table.
10. In those days, people ate with their fingers.
11. They wiped their greasy hands on the tablecloth.
12. After a few feasts, the lovely tablecloth was a mess.
13. Finally, someone decided to protect these tablecloths.
14. A towel was given to each guest.
15. These towels were the first napkins.

B. Using Articles and Demonstrative Adjectives Write the correct word from the ones given in parentheses.

16. Have you heard (a, the) warning "Don't eat with your fingers"?
17. (This, These) kind of warning would have seemed foolish when people ate everything with their fingers.
18. The use of (a, an) fork for eating began in Asia.
19. (This, These) custom spread to Europe very slowly.
20. By 1500 (these, them) utensils were common in Italy.
21. The English thought the Italians were too dainty and made fun of (those, them).
22. The English had (a, an) humble view that fingers were made to eat with.
23. (This kind, These kinds) of utensil caught on slowly in England and America.
24. A fork was (a, an) unusual item in most homes before 1800.
25. Until then, (a, an) person who used a fork was laughed at.

GRAMMAR HANDBOOK 38

Writing Theme
Inventions

GRAMMAR HANDBOOK 38

ADDITIONAL PRACTICE

Each of these exercises correlates to a section of Handbook 38, "Understanding Adjectives." The exercises may be used for practice, for reteaching, or for review of the concepts presented.

Additional Resource
Grammar and Usage Practice Book, p. 57

Writing Theme: Inventions
Other related areas students might wish to explore as writing topics include the following:
- the history of a favorite invention
- a "new products" fair
- how to patent an invention
- a much-needed but not-yet-existing invention

A. Identifying Adjectives
Student answers will be in columns.
1. cloth, What Kind; paper, What Kind
2. those, Which One; any, How Many
3. wealthy, What Kind; one, How Many; fine, What Kind
4. These, Which One
5. famous, What Kind; wonderful, What Kind; marvelous, What Kind; flower, What Kind; animal, What Kind
6. white, What Kind; red, What Kind; gold, What Kind
7. These, Which One; expensive, What Kind; royal, What Kind
8. Few, How Many
9. gorgeous, What Kind; feast, What Kind
10. those, Which One; their, Which One
11. their, Which One; greasy, What Kind
12. few, How Many; lovely, What Kind
13. these, Which One
14. each, How Many or Which One
15. These, Which One; first, Which One

B. Using Articles and Demonstrative Words
Answers are shown on page.

C. Identifying Predicate Adjectives
Answers are shown on page. Predicate adjectives are underlined once; the words they modify are underlined twice.

D. Making Comparisons with Adjectives
Answers are shown on page.

C. Identifying Predicate Adjectives Write the following sentences. Draw one line under the predicate adjective or adjectives and two lines under the word that is modified.

26. Straight pins are very old.
27. Ice Age people were fond of fish-bone pins.
28. During the Bronze Age, people were happier with metal pins similar to today's safety pins.
29. Somehow through the years, the idea behind the efficient Bronze Age safety pin became unclear or lost.
30. Until 1849, straight pins remained popular.
31. That year, Walter Hunt became famous for his "invention," the safety pin.
32. Hunt's future looked bright.
33. However, his bank account remained small.
34. Furthermore, a friend of Hunt's was growing impatient about Hunt's unpaid fifteen-dollar loan.
35. The invention certainly appeared useful and practical.
36. The solution seemed obvious.
37. The friend would become rich from the ownership of the new invention.
38. Hunt would no longer be uncomfortable about his debt.
39. Furthermore, credit for the accomplishment would remain his.
40. Today, anyone with a missing button or a broken zipper is grateful to Walter Hunt.

D. Making Comparisons with Adjectives Write the correct form of the adjective shown in parentheses.

41. The (earliest, most early) houses did not have windows.
42. Even great castles of the (powerfullest, most powerful) kings had only a hole in the roof of the kitchen to let out smoke from the cooking fire.
43. A window is much (better, best) than a smoke hole.
44. The first windows let some rain in and were (worse, worst) about letting in cold.
45. In later times, they were stuffed with straw or covered with canvas so homes would be (comfortabler, more comfortable) in bad weather.

REVIEW

A. Identifying Adjectives Write the adjectives that modify each italicized noun in the sentences below. Include articles.

1. How would you like having a creepy *insect* living by your *bed?*
2. Strangely enough, many *people* enjoy having certain *kinds* of insects nearby.
3. These *bugs* that sing are often kept as pets.
4. Crickets and cicadas are two good *examples.*
5. They make wonderful *music.*
6. Chinese, Japanese, and Spanish *people* sometimes keep them.
7. These *owners* love their pets and give them special *care.*
8. Tiny *cages* are made for the *animals.*
9. An *owner* might keep several cricket *cages* near his or her *bed.*
10. The musical *crickets* then sing their *owner* to sleep.

B. Using Adjectives Correctly Write the correct adjective from those given in parentheses.

11. Imagine waking up to (a, an) alarming cry—"*To-kay!*"
12. Your eyes open and you see a monster straight out of your (worse, worst) nightmare.
13. It's a gray, golden-eyed lizard with red dots, and it stretches a foot long—although right now it looks much (longer, more long).
14. It's staring down at you from (a, the) ceiling over your bed!
15. (Faster, More fast) than lightning, you leap from your bed.
16. But wait—now you remember. (This, That) monster up there is your new pet!
17. It's a tokay gecko, one of the (more common, more commoner) pets in Asia.
18. Some people in the United States like (these, them) unusual animals too.
19. Geckos have the (beautifullest, most beautiful) eyes.
20. They are also (more, most) useful than many other pets.
21. They're (better, more good) hunters than most lizards.
22. Nighttime, when they busily seek insects, finds them (more, most) active than daytime.
23. Most geckos are gentle, but the tokay doesn't like being handled and has the (worse, worst) bite of all.

GRAMMAR HANDBOOK 38

Writing Theme
Unusual Pets

GRAMMAR HANDBOOK 38

REVIEW

These exercises may be used as a mixed review or as an informal evaluation of the skills presented in Handbook 38, "Understanding Adjectives."

Additional Resources

Grammar and Usage Practice Book, p. 58
Tests and Writing Assessment Prompts, Mastery Test, pp. 31–34
Elaboration, Revision, and Proofreading Practice, p. 27

Writing Theme: Unusual Pets

Other related areas students might wish to explore as writing topics include the following:
- how crickets chirp
- unusual lizards
- mongooses as pets
- unusual pet birds

A. Identifying Adjectives
Answers are shown on page.

B. Using Adjectives Correctly
Answers are shown on page.

C. Correcting Errors with Adjectives

31. What would be the best animal of all to have as a pet?
32. Of all pets, dogs and cats are the most typical.
33. Correct
34. If you're one of those people, you're in good company.
35. Correct
36. Perhaps the oddest was the alligator John Quincy Adams kept in the White House.
37. Those Adamses also kept silkworms.
38. Correct
39. Of all the presidents, Theodore Roosevelt may have had the largest assortment of creatures.
40. Parrots, snakes, lizards, pigeons, pigs, and rats—his children kept all those animals.
41. One of the best stories of all involves the snakes.
42. His son carried four of his newest snakes into a meeting.
43. Senators burst from the room, each trying to run faster than the others.
44. The Kennedy children also had a collection of pets. Theirs were less unusual than those in the Roosevelts' zoo.
45. The Kennedys' most remarkable pets were rabbits and hamsters.

24. The tokay is also the (largest, most large) gecko.
25. Because they have thousands of fine hairlike structures on the pads of their feet, (them, these) animals can walk up walls and across ceilings.
26. They can even walk across mirrors, as (this, that) one on the wall over there is doing.
27. Geckos are the (unusualest, most unusual) lizards because they are the only ones that talk.
28. The tokay, in its (loudest, most loud) voice, cries, *"To-kay!"*
29. (A, An) few geckos bark or quack, and some say *"Gecko!"*
30. Can you guess how (those, them) lizards got their name?

C. Correcting Errors with Adjectives Write each of the following sentences, correcting errors in the use of adjectives. If a sentence does not have an error, write *Correct.*

31. What would be the better animal of all to have as a pet?
32. Of all pets, dogs and cats are the more typical.
33. However, some people prefer more unusual animals.
34. If you're one of them people, you're in good company.
35. Some United States presidents chose stranger pets than you'd expect.
36. Perhaps the odder was the alligator John Quincy Adams kept in the White House.
37. Them Adamses also kept silkworms.
38. Silk was one of the costliest fabrics known, and Mrs. Adams's silkworms spun enough silk for her to make a dress.
39. Of all the presidents, Theodore Roosevelt may have had the larger assortment of creatures.
40. Parrots, snakes, lizards, pigeons, pigs, and rats—his children kept all them animals.
41. One of the better stories of all involves the snakes.
42. His son carried four of his most new snakes into a meeting.
43. Senators burst from the room, each trying to run more faster than the others.
44. The Kennedy children also had a collection of pets. Theirs were least unusual than those in the Roosevelts' zoo.
45. The Kennedys' more remarkable pets were rabbits and hamsters.

WRITING CONNECTIONS

Elaboration, Revision, and Proofreading

Revise the following draft of a description, using the directions at the bottom of the page. Then proofread the description, paying special attention to the use of adjectives. Also look for errors in grammar, capitalization, punctuation, and spelling.

1 Every year the recreation center is turned into a Haunted House for Halloween. 2 As we approached the building this year, we heard sounds coming from inside. 3 We walked to the door and timidly stepped into the dark and gloomy house. 4 Ahead of us was a zigzag path that led us passed all sorts of creepy things. 5 Arms reached out and grabed for us as we walked by. 6 A Monster jumped in our path and then vanished. 7 Compared to the monster, the swirling ghosts that swooped down from the rafters were definitately creepiest. 8 A witch zoomed by on a broomstick. 9 We reached the end. 10 We all agreed this years' haunted house was more better than last years'.

1. Add one or more adjectives to tell what kind of "sounds" in sentence 2.
2. In sentence 5, add two adjectives that tell how the arms looked and felt.
3. In sentence 6, use adjectives to describe what the monster looked like.
4. Make the order of events clearer by adding a transition word to sentences that signal the next event.
5. Add "finally" to the beginning of sentence 9 to indicate the end of the description.

Observation and Description

Descriptive writing provides a chance to create a picture with words. (See Workshop 2.) When you revise descriptive writing, look for ways to use a variety of words that appeal to the senses. Using precise adjectives is one way to make your descriptions come alive.

WRITING CONNECTIONS

Elaboration, Revision, and Proofreading

This activity will allow your students to see some of the concepts presented in this handbook at work in a piece of descriptive writing. By revising and proofreading this passage, students will have the opportunity to improve clarity and elaboration by using precise, vivid adjectives.

You may wish to allow students to work in pairs to revise the passage. After students have completed their revisions, discuss the changes with the class.

Revisions may vary slightly. Errors are underlined on the page. See a typical revision below. Elements involving change and transition words are shown in boldface.

Every year the recreation center is turned into a haunted house for Halloween. As we approached the building this year, we heard **strange, scary** sounds coming from inside. **Then** we walked to the door and timidly stepped into the dark and gloomy house. Ahead of us was a zigzag path that led us past all sorts of creepy things. **Cold and slimy** arms reached out and grabbed for us as we walked by. **Next** a **hairy** monster, **drooling and red-eyed,** jumped in our path and then vanished. Compared to the monster, the swirling ghosts that swooped down from the rafters were definitely creepier. **Then** a witch zoomed by on a broomstick. **Finally** we reached the end. We all agreed this year's haunted house was better than last year's.

Sketch Book

Objective

- To use writing prompts and a passage from literature as springboards to informal writing

WRITING WARM-UPS

Tell students that these activities will not be graded. They should have fun with writing while exploring, in an imaginative way, some of the concepts in this handbook. Urge students to choose at least one of the prompts to develop.

For the first writing prompt, explain that *A Connecticut Yankee in King Arthur's Court* is about a New Englander in Mark Twain's day (the late 1800s) who travels back in time to the days of King Arthur. Then have volunteers recall other books, films, or TV shows in which characters travel into the past. Tell students to keep these works in mind as they write.

Sketch Book

WRITING WARM-UPS

"Well, then," I said, "either I am a lunatic or something just as awful has happened. Now tell me, honest and true, where am I?"

"IN KING ARTHUR'S COURT."

I waited a minute, to let that idea shudder its way home, and then said:

"And according to your notions, what year is it now?"

"528—nineteenth of June."

Mark Twain
A CONNECTICUT YANKEE IN KING ARTHUR'S COURT

- What if you woke up one day and you were living in the past? It could be the time of King Arthur's court or the Roman Empire or any other time in history or legend. Write about how you would act, where you would go, and what you would do and see during your first day.
- Imagine you are a newspaper reporter witnessing an important event. Write a brief account for tomorrow's newspaper. Remember to include the five *w*'s—*who, what, when, where,* and *why*.
- How would you compare yourself to your best friend? What do you do better? What does your friend do better?

Literature Connection

Author Note Mark Twain (1835–1910) is the pen name of Samuel Langhorne Clemens, one of America's greatest writers. Twain grew up in the Mississippi River town of Hannibal, Missouri, and headed west after the Civil War. He first achieved fame with humorous tales about life on the rugged western frontier. *A Connecticut Yankee in King Arthur's Court* (1889) satirizes the romantic notions of King Arthur's day and the views of New Englanders in Twain's own time.

Understanding Adverbs

GRAMMAR HANDBOOK 39

- What Are Adverbs?
- Making Comparisons with Adverbs
- Adjective or Adverb?
- Double Negatives

Camelot. The wizard Merlin. Sir Lancelot. Queen Guinevere. You are probably familiar with the legends of King Arthur and the knights of the Round Table. To retell rich tales such as these, you need to use rich language. By using adverbs, you can include details about how, when, and where actions take place.

In this handbook you will study ways you can use adverbs to make your writing precise and lively.

GRAMMAR HANDBOOK 39

Understanding Adverbs

Objectives

- To recognize an adverb as a word that modifies a verb, an adjective, or another adverb
- To use the comparative and superlative forms of adverbs correctly
- To distinguish between adjectives and adverbs
- To avoid double negatives in speaking and writing

Writing

- To use adverbs to add clarity and precision to writing
- To recognize and correct errors in adverb usage

INTRODUCING THE HANDBOOK

If students are unfamiliar with the Arthurian legends, briefly explain that Arthur was a legendary King of Britain who invited the finest knights of his day to join him at his castle, Camelot. At his court, the knights were seated at a round table. Since no one knight sat at the head of the table, everyone felt equal. Merlin was Arthur's mentor and adviser; Guinevere was Arthur's wife; and Lancelot was one of the most famous knights of the Round Table. Ask students who have seen films or TV shows about King Arthur to describe the characters' actions. Point out that adverbs can help make such descriptions clearer and more vivid.

Objectives

- To identify adverbs and the information they provide

Writing

- To use adverbs to make writing more precise

Teaching Strategies

STUMBLING BLOCK Point out that some adjectives are often used incorrectly as adverbs. Write these sentences on the board; ask students what is wrong with each and how it should be corrected.

The stagecoach traveled the route regular. (regularly)

The impatient driver spoke loud to his horses. (loudly)

Two days late, the stagecoach rumbled safe into town. (safely)

HELPFUL HINT: *-LY* ENDINGS Point out that although the *-ly* ending is a clue that a word is an adverb, not all words ending in *-ly* are adverbs. Words such as *friendly, costly,* and *lovely* are adjectives: words such as *early* and *only* can be either.

LINKING GRAMMAR AND WRITING Note that when meaning isn't affected, adverbs can be placed in a variety of positions in sentences. For example, occasionally beginning a sentence with an adverb can make writing more interesting. Discuss the effect of the opening adverb in this sentence:

Instantly, they were pursued by squadrons of bomber-shaped dragons, who gobbled them up.

Jean Craighead George, *The Talking Earth*

Additional Resources

Test and Writing Assessment Prompts, Pretest, pp. 35–36
Grammar and Usage Practice Book, p. 59
Grammar Test Generator

WHAT ARE ADVERBS?

An **adverb** modifies a verb, an adjective, or another adverb.

Adjectives add excitement and clarity to your sentences. Adverbs can help you be more precise.

An **adjective** modifies a noun or pronoun.

An **adverb** modifies a verb, an adjective, or another adverb.

Mail moved *slowly.* (*Slowly* modifies the verb *moved.*)
Postage was *extremely* expensive. (*Extremely* modifies the adjective *expensive.*)
Settlers waited *very* impatiently for news. (*Very* modifies the adverb *impatiently.*)

An **adverb** tells *how, when, where,* or *to what extent* about the word it modifies.

Bill Cody rode *swiftly.* (*Swiftly* tells *how* Bill rode.)
He arrived *yesterday.* (*Yesterday* tells *when* he arrived.)
The coach went *west.* (*West* tells *where* the coach went.)
The rider was *completely* exhausted. (*Completely* tells *to what extent* the rider was exhausted.)

An adverb that modifies an adjective or another adverb often comes before the word it modifies.

extremely steep   *very* carefully

An adverb that modifies a verb may be found in one of several positions.

She wrote *often.*   She *often* wrote.   *Often,* she wrote.

Many common adverbs are formed by adding the ending *-ly* to adjectives. For example, the adjectives *quick* and *usual* become the adverbs *quickly* and *usually.*

Other adverbs include *there, now, never, almost,* and *too.*

Writing TIP

Adverbs can help make a story you're writing more specific. Use adverbs to tell more about the time, place, and extent of the action. See how adverbs add to this sentence.

Bob saddled his horse.
Bob *hurriedly* saddled his horse.

Literature Connection

Show students this passage from "The Circuit" by Francisco Jiménez and discuss how the adverbs (underlined) make characters' actions more vivid. Ask students to identify the word each adverb modifies. *(open, held; carefully, carried; out, carried; gently, placed; then, climbed; in, climbed; wearily, said)* "I held the front door open as Mamá carefully carried out her pot by both handles. . . . Papá gently placed it on the floor behind the front seat. All of us then climbed in. Papá sighed, wiped the sweat off his forehead with his sleeve, and said wearily: 'Es todo.'"

Practice Your Skills

A. CONCEPT CHECK

Adverbs Write each adverb and tell whether it answers *How, When, Where,* or *To what extent.* Then write the word it modifies.

EXAMPLE The stagecoach sped wildly downhill.
wildly, How, sped; downhill, Where, sped

1. In the Old West, mail service was unbelievably slow.
2. Until 1858, California had very irregular mail service.
3. It often took two to three months for a letter to arrive.
4. Finally, the Butterfield Overland Mail Service began.
5. Stagecoaches carried passengers and mail east and west.
6. Now, imagine a trip to California in 1858.
7. You eagerly board the train in St. Louis.
8. After nearly 150 miles, you transfer to a stagecoach.
9. Hold on tight, because the ride is really rough.
10. You and the mail travel almost constantly day and night.
11. Sleep is practically impossible.
12. The coach eventually jolts to a stop in San Francisco.
13. Shakily you climb down.
14. You're totally exhausted.
15. Just think, your trip took only twenty-four days!

B. REVISION SKILL

Using Precise Adverbs Sometimes you can make a sentence more precise or change the meaning by changing an adverb. Write each sentence. Replace each adverb in italics with another adverb that answers the same question of *how, when, where,* or *to what extent.*

EXAMPLE The rider galloped *fearlessly* into the night.
The rider galloped bravely into the night.

16. A Pony Express rider comes *quickly* into view.
17. A fresh rider and a horse stand *nearby.*
18. The first rider brings his horse *sharply* to a halt.
19. *Then* the new rider grabs the mail, leaps onto a waiting horse, and is off at top speed.

Writing Theme
The Old West and the U. S. Mail

Writing Theme: The Old West and the U.S. Mail

Suggest that students use these exercises as a springboard to writing. Other related areas that they might explore include the following:

- smoke signals for communication
- the invention of the telegraph
- the introduction of postage stamps
- the introduction of zip code

Answers to Practice Your Skills

A. Concept Check
Adverbs

Adverbs are shown on page.

1. unbelievably, To what extent, slow
2. very, To what extent, irregular
3. often, When, took
4. Finally, When, began
5. east, Where, carried; west, Where, carried
6. Now, When, imagine
7. eagerly, How, board
8. nearly, To what extent, 150
9. tightly, How, Hold; really, To what extent, rough
10. almost, To what extent, constantly; constantly, How, travel; day, when, travel; night, When, travel
11. practically, To what extent, impossible
12. eventually, When, jolts
13. shakily, How, climb; down, Where, climb
14. totally, To what extent, exhausted
15. Just, To what extent, think; only, To what extent, twenty-four

B. Revision Skill
Using Precise Adverbs

Answers will vary. Sample adverbs are given below. Student answers should be in sentences.

16. swiftly
17. here
18. promptly
19. Soon

20. east
21. usually
22. steadily
23. rarely
24. constantly
25. seldom

CHECK POINT

Writing Theme: Bullfighting

Suggest that students use these exercises as a springboard to writing. Other related areas that they might explore include the following:
- bullfighting in Spain or Mexico
- the history of bullfighting
- the running of the bulls in Pamplona, Spain
- famous bullfighters
- other workers in a bullring

MIXED REVIEW • PAGES 482-484

You may wish to use this activity to check students' mastery of the following concept:
- What are adverbs?

Application in Literature

Students need only list ten adverbs and the words they modify.
1. slowly, lifted; arrogantly, lifted
2. Back, came; again, controlled
3. back, looking
4. suddenly, charged; fast, charged; too, fast; fast, charged
5. None
6. up, tossed
7. None
8. automatically, acted
9. up, picked
10. backwards, ran; away, taking

FOR MORE PRACTICE
See page 495.

Writing Theme
Bullfighting

20. Riders carried mail 1,966 miles from St. Joseph, Missouri, to Sacramento, California, and then brought mail *back.*
21. Pony Express riders *always* rode as fast as possible.
22. They galloped *tirelessly* across the driest deserts.
23. They *scarcely* slowed down for steep mountain trails.
24. In deep snow, they *continually* urged their horses on.
25. Bad weather and rough trails *never* stopped them.

CHECK POINT
MIXED REVIEW • PAGES 482–484

Application in Literature Write ten adverbs from this paragraph and the word each modifies. If a sentence has no adverbs, write *None.* There are fourteen adverbs in all.

> [1]Juan . . . slowly, arrogantly, lifted the lure in both hands and let the animal charge under it. [2]Back came the bull, and again, with quiet assurance, the boy controlled the animal's speed and direction. [3]Without looking back, Juan walked towards Manolo. [4]The animal seemed to have been nailed to the sand by the last pass, but suddenly it charged fast, too fast for Manolo to warn Juan. [5]It happened in an instant. [6]The boy was tossed up in the air and landed with a thud on the ground. [7]The bull stomped the earth and moved his horns toward Juan, who had both arms thrown over his head. [8]But Manolo . . . acted automatically with no thought of what he was doing. [9]He picked up the muleta and waved it in front of the horns, and the horns charged the red cloth. [10]Manolo ran backwards, taking the bull away from Juan.
>
> **Maia Wojciechowska, *Shadow of a Bull***

Literature Connection

Author Note Poet, translator, and children's author Maia Wojciechowska (pronounced voi chə hov'skä) was born in Warsaw, Poland, in 1927. She escaped the Nazi occupation of her homeland and came to the United States when still a teenager. In her adventurous life, she has held dozens of jobs, including undercover agent, pro tennis player, and translator for Radio Free Europe; she has also raced motorcycles, parachuted from planes, and fought bulls. The last experience helped prompt *Shadow of a Bull* (1964), her Newbery Medal winner about the son of a bullfighter. Wojciechowska has also published works under the name Maia Rodman.

MAKING COMPARISONS WITH ADVERBS

Use the **comparative form** of an adverb when you compare two actions. Use the **superlative form** of an adverb when you compare three or more actions.

Since adverbs, like adjectives, are words that describe, they can be changed to the comparative or superlative form.

Use the **comparative form** when you compare one action with another.

Killer bees will attack *faster* than ordinary honeybees.

Use the **superlative form** when you compare three or more actions.

Of the three insects, yellow jackets, bumblebees, and wasps, yellow jackets will usually attack the *fastest.*

The comparative and superlative forms of adverbs are formed in three different ways.

1. Some short adverbs add *-er* to form the comparative. They add *-est* to form the superlative.

Adverb	Comparative	Superlative
high	higher	highest
loud	louder	loudest
early	earlier	earliest

2. Most adverbs that end in *-ly* form the comparative with the word *more.* They form the superlative with *most.*

Adverb	Comparative	Superlative
angrily	more angrily	most angrily
dangerously	more dangerously	most dangerously
painfully	more painfully	most painfully

Grammar TIP

Don't be confused by phrases such as "many other." Such phrases may signal that something is being compared to a group. Use the comparative form.

Jeff runs *faster* than many other players.

MAKING COMPARISIONS WITH ADVERBS

Objectives

- To identify the comparative and superlative forms of adverbs

Writing

- To use correct comparative and superlative forms of adverbs in writing

Teaching Strategies

HELPFUL HINT Point out that not all adverbs have comparative and superlative forms. Many adverbs that tell *when, where,* or *to what extent* have only one form (for example, *finally, up,* and *continually*).

CRITICAL THINKING: ANALYZING Ask students what is wrong with this comparison: *In 1988 track star Florence Griffith Joyner ran faster than any female runner.* Elicit that this wording says that Joyner is faster than any female; but she is a female and can't be faster than herself. Since she herself is a female, *other* must be used before *female* to make the comparison logical. Now ask students what word they need to add to make this comparison logical: *In 1991 Carl Lewis ran faster than anyone in the world.* (add *else* after *anyone*)

HELPFUL HINT Point out that the comparative form *more* and the superlative form *most* are combined with other adverbs to show comparisons: *more clearly, most clearly.* In addition, the forms *less* and *least* can be combined with adverbs to show negative comparisons: I work *less quickly* when I am tired than when I am rested. Jane works the *least quickly* of all of us.

Additional Resource

Grammar and Usage Practice Book, p. 60

Writing Theme: Dangerous Animals

Other related areas students might wish to explore as writing topics include the following:

- mosquitoes and tsetse flies
- poisonous spiders
- poisonous snakes
- poisonous fish

Answers to Practice Your Skills

A. Concept Check
Comparisons with Adverbs

Adverbs are shown on page.

1. more rapidly, Comparative
2. most viciously, Superlative
3. more accurately, Comparative
4. quickest, Superlative
5. best, Superlative
6. more agreeably, Comparative
7. most easily, Superlative
8. most, Superlative
9. more safely, Comparative
10. less productively, Comparative
11. better, Comparative
12. more profitably, Comparative
13. faster, Comparative
14. better, Comparative
15. more, Comparative

3. Some adverbs change completely to form the comparative and superlative.

Adverb	Comparative	Superlative
well	better	best
badly	worse	worst
much	more	most
little	less	least

Practice Your Skills

Writing Theme
Dangerous Animals

A. CONCEPT CHECK

Comparisons with Adverbs Write the adverb in each sentence that is used in comparison. Then write whether the adverb is used in the *Comparative* or *Superlative* form.

1. Killer bees are spreading more rapidly than we thought!
2. Of all honeybees, killer bees attack most viciously.
3. These bees are more accurately called Africanized bees.
4. They become angry the quickest and attack in swarms.
5. The common European honeybees behave best of all bees.
6. These bees don't behave more agreeably by chance.
7. Beekeepers sought wild bees they could manage most easily.
8. They worried most about finding bees that produced a great deal of honey.
9. They bred bees that could be handled more safely than those in the wild.
10. These bees produced honey successfully in Europe, Asia, and North America, but they performed less productively in tropical areas.
11. Then a scientist, who should have known better, imported African honeybees into Brazil.
12. He thought beekeepers could produce honey more profitably with this kind of bee.
13. The bees escaped and have been spreading through South America and into North America faster than anyone imagined.
14. Scientists predict that the bees will survive better in areas below 34 degrees north latitude than in northern regions.
15. That means that people in the southern United States should worry more about this threat than people to the north.

486 Grammar Handbook

B. DRAFTING SKILL

Using Adverbs in Comparisons Rewrite these sentences. Write the correct form of each adverb in parentheses.

16. Driven by a ceaseless hunger, army ants may hunt the (savagely) of all the inhabitants in a tropical forest.
17. You rarely find just a few army ants or even small swarms; they are (commonly) found in swarms of millions.
18. Nothing attacks (ferociously) than a swarm that has found some food.
19. These ants bite (viciously) than almost any other animal.
20. These ants tear the (efficiently) of all forest creatures.
21. An army ant can bite through a grasshopper's leg (easily) than you can bite through a stick of celery.
22. They don't run the (fast), but what they do catch, they eat.
23. Ants don't like to take on a big animal when it is alert, so they attack big animals (much) often when the animals are in pens or asleep.
24. The victims are eaten (rapidly) than you can imagine.
25. Of all insects, army ants scare me (bad).

C. PROOFREADING SKILL

Correcting the Use of Adverbs Rewrite the following paragraph, correcting all errors in grammar, capitalization, punctuation, and spelling. Pay special attention to the use of adverbs to make comparisons. (10 errors)

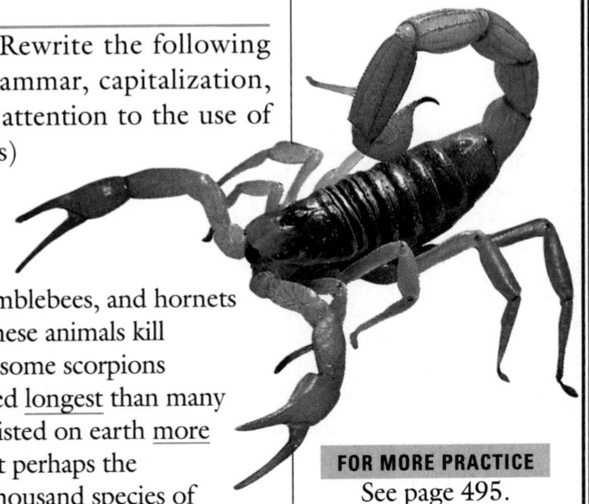

People fear scorpions worse than most other animals, and with good reason. Some scorpions inject a very harmful Poison. Even tarantulas, bumblebees, and hornets are not as great a threat poisons of these animals kill prey least effectivly than the poisons some scorpions inject. Have also adapted and survived longest than many other creatures. In fact, they have existed on earth more longer than all other creatures except perhaps the Cockroach. There are more than a thousand species of scorpions. They look like miniature lobsters. However, scorpions are most closely related to spiders than to lobster's.

FOR MORE PRACTICE
See page 495.

B. Drafting Skill
Using Adverbs in Comparisons

Adverbs are shown below. Students' answers should be in sentences.

16. most savagely
17. most commonly
18. more ferociously
19. more viciously
20. most efficiently
21. more easily
22. fastest
23. more
24. more rapidly
25. worst

C. Proofreading Skill
Correcting the Use of Adverbs

Errors in proofreading exercises are counted as follows: (a) Each word is counted as one error. For example, a misspelled word is one error; two initials and a last name not capitalized are counted as three errors. (b) Run-on sentences and sentence fragments are each counted as one error, even though the correction involves both punctuation and capitalization. Errors are shown on page. The correctly rewritten paragraph appears below.

People fear scorpions worse than most other animals, and with good reason. Some scorpions inject a very harmful poison. Even tarantulas, bumblebees, and hornets are not as great a threat. Poisons of these animals kill prey less effectively than the poisons some scorpions inject. Scorpions have also adapted and survived longer than many other creatures. In fact, they have existed on earth longer than all other creatures except perhaps the cockroach. There are more than a thousand species of scorpions. They look like miniature lobsters. However, scorpions are more closely related to spiders than to lobsters.

Objectives

- To distinguish between adverbs and adjectives
- To use *good, well, bad,* and *badly* correctly

Writing

- To correct errors in the use of adverbs and adjectives in writing

Teaching Strategies

LINKING GRAMMAR AND WRITING Point out that some words can be used as either adjectives or adverbs without changing form. To determine the part of speech of such a word, students must decide what word is being modified. Write these sentences on the board and have students state whether the italicized words are adjectives (Adj) that modify nouns or pronouns, or adverbs (Adv) that modify verbs, adjectives, and other adverbs.

Adj
This winter was *longer* than most and
Adj
hard on many plants.
Adv Adj
It snowed *hard* in *early* March.
Adv
Since the snow cover lasted *longer*
Adv
than usual, crocuses bloomed *late.*
Daffodils, which also flower
Adv Adj
early, were also *late* too.

INDIVIDUALIZING INSTRUCTION: VISUAL AND KINESTHETIC LEARNERS To distinguish adjectives from adverbs, both visual and kinesthetic learners may find it helpful to draw arrows to the words modified. For example:

The petals moved *gently.*

It was a *really good* play.

Fresh bread smells *wonderful.*

ADJECTIVE OR ADVERB?

An **adjective** describes a noun or pronoun. An **adverb** modifies a verb, an adjective, or another adverb.

Look at these lists of words.

Adjective	Adverb
cautious	cautiously
angry	angrily
slow	slowly
easy	easily
quick	quickly
beautiful	beautifully
sad	sadly

Grammar TIP

To decide whether an adjective or adverb should follow verbs such as *look* or *feel,* ask yourself whether the verb is functioning as an action verb or linking verb. Use an adverb only if the verb is an action verb.

Adjectives and adverbs are both modifiers. Because adverbs are often formed from adjectives, they look very much alike. For these reasons, it is sometimes difficult to know when to use each type of word.

To decide whether to use an adjective or an adverb in a sentence, ask yourself what word is being modified.

Read this example.

The petals moved (gentle, gently) in the breeze.

Which word is correct? In this case, the verb *moved* is being modified. Since adverbs modify verbs and *moved* is a verb, choose the adverb *gently.*

Now look at this sentence.

Little Shop of Horrors is a (real, really) good play.

Which word is correct? Here, the adjective *good* is being modified. Therefore, the adverb *really* is the correct choice.

Remember these rules:

Adjectives tell *which one, what kind,* or *how many* about nouns and pronouns.

Adverbs tell *how, when, where,* or *to what extent* about verbs, adjectives, and other adverbs.

Using *Good* and *Well,* or *Bad* and *Badly*

Choosing between *good* and *well* or *bad* and *badly* can be confusing. *Good* and *bad* are adjectives. They tell *what kind.*

> Those flowers smell *good.* (*Smell* is used as a linking verb here. Therefore, *good* is a predicate adjective that modifies *flowers.*)
>
> You shouldn't feel *bad* about picking them; picking them makes them grow. (*Feel* is a linking verb. *Bad* is a predicate adjective.)

The words *well* and *badly* are adverbs. Use them to modify verbs. *Well* and *badly* tell *how* something is done.

> Violets grow *well* in shade. (*Well* tells *how* they grow.)
>
> Seymour behaved *badly.* (*Badly* tells *how* he behaved.)

Note that *well* is an adjective when it describes a noun or pronoun and means "healthy," as in *Seymour does not feel well.*

Practice Your Skills

A. CONCEPT CHECK

Adjective or Adverb? Choose the correct modifier from those given in parentheses.

1. To Seymour, an assistant in a run-down florist shop, the plant seemed (pitiful, pitifully).
2. It looked small and (weak, weakly).
3. He knew (quick, quickly) that it was special.
4. Seymour nursed it (slow, slowly) to health.
5. It didn't do very (good, well), and he didn't know why.

Writing Theme
Unusual Plants

SPEAKING AND LISTENING Explain that in the informal English of everyday speech, adjectives sometimes are used where adverbs are grammatically correct. Especially common errors are the use of adjectives to modify other adjectives, as in "*real* good" and "*sure* terrific"; errors in brief commands, such as "Drive *slow*"; and the confusion of *good, well, bad,* and *badly.* You might ask students to compile a list of adverb errors that they hear spoken in a given week.

HELPFUL HINT Since *well* can be either an adjective or an adverb, students must find the word it modifies. Explain that if the verb shows action, *well* is an adverb: *I played well.* If the verb is a linking verb, *well* modifies the subject: *I feel well* (healthy) *today.*

Additional Resource

Grammar and Usage Practice Book, p. 61

Writing Theme: Unusual Plants

Other related areas students might wish to explore as writing topics include the following:

- sundew and pitcher plants
- air plants
- poison ivy and poison oak
- ferns and how they grow

Answers to Practice Your Skills

A. Concept Check

Adjective or Adverb?

Answers are shown on page.

B. Revision Skill
Using Adjectives and Adverbs Correctly

Errors are shown on page. The corrected paragraph is shown below.

Have you ever carefully observed a carnivorous plant such as the Venus's-flytrap? These plants grow especially well in damp and boggy areas. White blossoms rise brightly from the flower's leaves. The shape of the flytrap's hinged leaves appears strange. A fly buzzes unsuspectingly over the flower stalk. To the fly, the red centers of the leaves look attractive. Tiny hairs on the leaves are extremely sensitive. Buzzing closer, the fly lightly touches a hair. The leaves of the flytrap instantly clamp shut. The flytrap's digestive juices gradually set to work. Soon the fly does not feel too well.

6. Then one day, he (accidental, accidentally) cut his finger.
7. The plant moved (sudden, suddenly); it wanted blood!
8. The plant looked so (miserable, miserably) that Seymour fed it his blood.
9. Soon, the plant had grown (gigantic, gigantically).
10. Its appetite became (enormous, enormously).
11. To the plant, only human blood seemed (satisfactory, satisfactorily).
12. Because of the plant, Seymour behaved (bad, badly).
13. Who would guess he was capable of doing such (real, really) terrible things?
14. When you see the movie or play called *Little Shop of Horrors,* you can decide for yourself if it ends (good, well).
15. Remember, act (careful, carefully) around plants.

B. REVISION SKILL

FOR MORE PRACTICE
See page 495.

Using Adjectives and Adverbs Correctly Revise the following paragraph to correct errors in the use of adjectives and adverbs.

Have you ever careful observed a carnivorous plant such as the Venus's-flytrap? These plants grow especially good in damp and boggy areas. White blossoms rise bright from the flower's leaves. The shape of the flytrap's hinged leaves appears strangely. A fly buzzes unsuspecting over the flower stalk. To the fly, the red centers of the leaves look attractively. Tiny hairs on the leaves are extreme sensitive. Buzzing closer, the fly lightly touches a hair. The leaves of the flytrap instant clamp shut. The flytrap's digestive juices gradual set to work. Soon the fly does not feel too good.

490 Grammar Handbook

CHECK POINT
MIXED REVIEW • PAGES 485–490

Write the correct modifier from those given in parentheses.

1. Lacrosse has been played (longer, longest) than many other team sports.
2. It is (true, truly) an American game.
3. Native Americans, the inventors, were (real, really) skilled players.
4. Various groups played the game (different, differently).
5. All of them used a stick, or crosse, that was bent (sharp, sharply) at one end with a pouch for holding the ball.
6. Compared to a baseball, a lacrosse ball is (smaller, smallest).
7. Players catch the ball and pass it (quick, quickly).
8. Today's teams have ten players, but Native American teams had (more, most) players—usually about seventy.
9. At times, however, the number was (remarkable, remarkably), with as many as a thousand men on a team.
10. Native Americans played very (serious, seriously).
11. They would prepare (careful, carefully) for weeks.
12. When a team member played (bad, badly), he often suffered painful injuries.
13. Of all the players, the ones who ran the fastest were injured (less, least).
14. If a young brave played (good, well), he was considered ready for battle.
15. Often the team that was the (better, best) of the two was the one that severely hurt the largest number of the opposition's players.
16. Often winning players didn't feel too (good, well) either.
17. The Cherokee name for the game, little brother of war, is (sure, surely) appropriate.
18. French settlers in Canada learned the game (slow, slowly).
19. In 1867, Parliament declared it Canada's national game, and today Canadians point (more, most) proudly to their lacrosse players than to their football players.
20. Native Americans on reservations in both Canada and the United States still field excellent teams (regular, regularly).

Writing Theme
Lacrosse

CHECK POINT

Writing Theme: Lacrosse

Other related areas students might wish to explore as writing topics include the following:

- other games played by Native Americans
- polo
- curling
- jai alai
- ice hockey

MIXED REVIEW • PAGES 485–490

You may wish to use this activity to check students' mastery of the following concepts:

- making comparisons with adverbs
- Adjective or adverb?

Answers are shown on page.

DOUBLE NEGATIVES

Objectives

- To identify double negatives

Writing

- To correct double negatives in writing

Teaching Strategies

INDIVIDUALIZING INSTRUCTION: ESL STUDENTS In Spanish and in some other languages, double negatives are grammatically correct and can be used to emphasize a point. You may wish to call this fact to the attention of the class and have ESL students offer examples. As these students work through the Practice Your Skills exercise, you might have them check their work with students able to identify and explain examples of English double negatives.

STUMBLING BLOCK Most double negatives contain a form of the word *no* twice. Point out, however, that words such as *hardly, barely,* and *scarcely* are also negatives and should not be used with other negatives.

Incorrect: Peg couldn't hardly see.

Correct: Peg could hardly see.

Additional Resource

Grammar and Usage Practice Book, p. 63

Writing Theme: Lost Ships

Other related areas students might wish to explore as writing topics include the following:

- the *Mary Deare*
- the *Flying Dutchman*
- sunken treasure ships
- the Bermuda Triangle

Answers to Practice Your Skills

A. Concept Check
Double Negatives

Answers are shown on page.

DOUBLE NEGATIVES

Never use a **double negative** when you write or speak.

The word *not* is an adverb that often causes problems. It is a negative. A negative is a word that says "no."

You remember that many contractions end in *-n't.* The *-n't* ending is a shortened form of *not.* Therefore, contractions that use *-n't* are negatives. Look at this list of negatives.

was + not = wasn't	would + not = wouldn't
have + not = haven't	can + not = can't
will + not = won't	does + not = doesn't

Not all negatives are contractions. Look at these examples of negatives. They are easy to remember because most of them contain the word *no.*

no	no one	nothing	not
none	nobody	nowhere	never

When two negatives appear in one sentence, they result in a **double negative.** Avoid double negatives in both your writing and speaking.

Incorrect	The captain *couldn't* do *nothing* to save the ship.
Correct	The captain *couldn't* do anything to save the ship.
Correct	The captain could do *nothing* to save the ship.

Writing Theme
Lost Ships

Practice Your Skills

A. CONCEPT CHECK

Double Negatives Write the correct word from those given in parentheses.

1. Clearly, Christopher Columbus's last voyage (was, wasn't) no success story.
2. For a year, he searched for a route to the Indian Ocean but didn't find (anything, nothing).

3. Heat and humidity took their toll; there wasn't food without maggots (anywhere, nowhere).
4. At one point, his ships were anchored in a bay off Panama; Columbus didn't (never, ever) know he was one day's march away from the Pacific Ocean.
5. By then, his ships weren't very seaworthy (any, no) longer.
6. Worms didn't like (nothing, anything) better than ships.
7. Two ships were sinking and not fit for (no one, anyone) to sail.
8. There wasn't (anything, nothing) to do but set out across the Gulf of Mexico in the two remaining ships.
9. The ships never got (any, no) closer to home than Jamaica.
10. Marooned, Columbus didn't go (anywhere, nowhere) for a year.
11. Jamaica's governor hadn't (never, ever) liked Columbus.
12. The governor wouldn't use (any, none) of his ships or men to help Columbus.
13. On a chartered ship, Columbus made it back to Spain without (any, none) of the riches he had hoped for.

B. REVISION SKILL

Correcting Double Negatives Revise each of the following sentences to eliminate a double negative. Some sentences can be corrected in more than one way.

14. In 1912, no ships weren't better built than the *Titanic.*
15. Everyone said there wasn't nothing that could sink the ship.
16. However, the *Titanic* didn't never complete its only voyage.
17. On April 14, the crew sighted an iceberg that was so close that there wasn't nothing they could do to avoid hitting it.
18. The *Titanic* didn't take no more than three hours to sink.
19. Many passengers couldn't find no way to escape the ship.
20. The lifeboats couldn't hold no more than half of the people.
21. Today, ocean liners aren't never without strict safety rules and the help of the International Ice Patrol.
22. For years, people couldn't find the sunken *Titanic* nowhere.
23. In 1985, explorers found the sunken ship, but it is in such deep water it hasn't never been explored except with robots.

FOR MORE PRACTICE
See page 496.

B. Revision Skill
Correcting Double Negatives

Answers may vary slightly. Typical answers are shown below.

14. In 1912, no ships were better built than the *Titanic.*
15. Everyone said there wasn't anything that could sink the ship.
16. However, the *Titanic* didn't ever complete its only voyage.
17. On April 14, the crew sighted an iceberg that was so close that there wasn't anything they could do to avoid hitting it.
18. The *Titanic* took no more than three hours to sink.
19. Many passengers couldn't find any way to escape the ship.
20. The lifeboats could hold no more than half of the people.
21. Today, ocean liners are never without strict safety rules and the help of the International Ice Patrol.
22. For years, people couldn't find the sunken *Titanic* anywhere.
23. In 1985, explorers found the sunken ship, but it is in such deep water it has never been explored except with robots.

CHECK POINT

Writing Theme: New Madrid Earthquake

Other related areas students might wish to explore as writing topics include the following:

- causes of earthquakes
- how earthquakes are measured
- predicting earthquakes
- other famous earthquakes

MIXED REVIEW • PAGES 492–493

You may wish to use this activity to check students' mastery of the following concepts:

- Adjective or adverb?
- double negatives

Answers may vary slightly. Possible answers are shown below.

1. During the night of December 16, 1811, people in New Madrid, Missouri, had no idea what was happening.
2. They had never expected the earth to shake so violently.
3. It was late at night, but nobody could get any sleep.
4. People couldn't do anything but leave their houses.
5. Some probably thought this was the worst earthquake ever.
6. Correct
7. Today's scientists know that there haven't been many quakes anywhere that were stronger.
8. Log cabins, they know, don't ever fall down easily.
9. Most of New Madrid's cabins weren't anything but rubble.
10. Correct
11. In Tennessee, twenty-square-mile Reelfoot Lake formed rapidly when the land was no longer high enough for the water to drain off.
12. Huge cracks in the earth opened suddenly all over the region.
13. The Mississippi River became violent with massive waves.
14. Correct
15. The quake shook nothing less than a million square miles.
16. Correct
17. The earth shook so badly that it made a church bell in Charleston, South Carolina, ring.
18. It seemed as if the aftershocks would never end.
19. For a year, strong shocks occurred unexpectedly.
20. Two aftershocks weren't any weaker than the first tremors.

Writing Theme
New Madrid Earthquake

An engraving of inhabitants fleeing their homes in New Madrid, Missouri, during the great earthquake of 1811.

CHECK POINT

MIXED REVIEW • PAGES 492–493

Write each sentence and correct all errors in the use of adverbs. If a sentence has no errors, write *Correct.*

1. During the night of December 16, 1811, people in New Madrid, Missouri, didn't have no idea what was happening.
2. They hadn't never expected the earth to shake so violently.
3. It was late at night, but nobody could get no sleep.
4. People couldn't do nothing but leave their houses.
5. Some probably thought this was the worse earthquake ever.
6. Scientists back then didn't have any of the equipment we have today for measuring the intensity of earthquakes.
7. Today's scientists know that there haven't been many quakes nowhere that were stronger.
8. Log cabins, they know, don't never fall down easily.
9. Most of New Madrid's cabins weren't nothing but rubble.
10. Nothing less than thirty-thousand square miles of land sank abruptly by five to fifteen feet.
11. In Tennessee, twenty-square-mile Reelfoot Lake formed rapidly when the land wasn't no longer high enough for the water to drain off.
12. Huge cracks in the earth opened sudden all over the region.
13. The Mississippi River became violently with massive waves.
14. The Mississippi actually ran backwards for a short time.
15. The quake didn't shake nothing less than a million square miles.
16. No one in New Orleans could ignore the shocks.
17. The earth shook so bad that it made a church bell in Charleston, South Carolina, ring.
18. It seemed as if the aftershocks wouldn't never end.
19. For a year, strong shocks occurred unexpected.
20. Two aftershocks weren't no weaker than the first tremors.

ADDITIONAL PRACTICE

A. Finding Adverbs Find every adverb in these sentences. Write the adverb and the word it modifies.

1. In the 1700s, bicycles were pretty crude and slow.
2. There were bikes then, but you'd barely recognize them.
3. In 1791, a French count invented a two-wheeled device that people rather playfully called a *célérifère,* which means "swift-footed."
4. It more or less resembled a bicycle.
5. It was designed strangely; it had two wheels but no pedals.
6. The rider actually ran while he or she sat on the thing.
7. The count also somehow left off any steering mechanism.
8. For a change in direction, a rider picked the célérifère up to move it.
9. The machine's wood wheels produced an extremely rough ride.
10. Célérifères were somewhat clumsy, but they were much faster than walking.

B. Using Adverbs Correctly For each sentence, write the correct form of the adverb in parentheses.

11. Each year, engineering improvements create race cars that travel (more, most) rapidly than the previous year's models.
12. Certainly, early race cars traveled (more slowly, most slowly) than today's cars.
13. At the first automobile race, held in France in 1894, people were (more curious, most curious) about which cars would finish than about which car was fastest.
14. Of the twenty cars in the race, a car powered by a steam engine performed (more reliably, most reliably).
15. Not only was it reliable, but it ran the (faster, fastest).
16. Of the cars that finished, the winner puttered (more quickly, most quickly), averaging almost twelve miles per hour.
17. The other cars did (worse, worst), and most didn't finish.
18. The cars traveled (less, least) than seventy-five miles.
19. In 1895, the cars raced (farther, farthest) than they had the year before.
20. The car that ran (best, better) averaged fifteen miles per hour!

GRAMMAR HANDBOOK 39

Writing Theme
Speed

GRAMMAR HANDBOOK 39

ADDITIONAL PRACTICE

Each of these exercises correlates to a section of Handbook 39, "Understanding Adverbs." The exercises may be used for more practice, for reteaching, or for review of the concepts presented.

Additional Resource

Grammar and Usage Practice Book, p. 65

Writing Theme: Speed

Other related areas students might wish to explore as writing topics include the following:

- from sailing ships to steamships
- the invention of the airplane
- speed skating
- *Around the World in Eighty Days* by Jules Verne (book or film)

A. Finding Adverbs

Adverbs are shown on page.

1. pretty, crude, slow
2. then, were; barely, 'd (would) recognize
3. rather, playfully; playfully, called
4. more, resembled; less, resembled
5. strangely, was designed
6. actually, ran
7. also, left; somehow, left; off, left
8. up, picked
9. extremely, rough
10. somewhat, clumsy; much, faster

B. Using Adverbs Correctly

Answers are shown on page.

C. Choosing the Right Modifier

Correct modifiers are shown on page.

21. swiftly, travel, Adverb
22. good, horses, Adjective
23. really, fast, Adverb
24. frightening, trains, Adjective
25. real, blur, Adjective
26. rapidly, improved, Adverb
27. easily, broke, Adverb
28. unbelievable, It, Adjective
29. badly, do, Adverb
30. incredible, It, Adjective

D. Using Negatives Correctly

Answers may vary slightly. Typical answers are shown below.

31. No one had ever circled the world until Magellan did so in 1521.
32. His ships didn't make it in anything less than two years.
33. We have never quit trying to circle the globe faster.
34. The next noteworthy trip was made by nobody else but Nellie Bly, a reporter who in 1889 went around the world in about seventy-two days.
35. That record was nothing after people started flying.
36. In 1924, one plane had no trouble circling the earth in fifteen days.
37. Not even that record was safe, though.
38. Wiley Post and Harold Gatty took no time at all to break the record, taking less than eight days in 1931.
39. By 1957, the record was no more than two days.
40. None of these records means anything to space vehicles.

C. Choosing the Right Modifier Write the correct modifier the word it modifies, and whether it is an *Adjective* or *Adverb.*

EXAMPLE Trains can travel (safe, safely) at 120 mph.
safely, travel, Adverb

21. Until recently, people didn't travel very (swift, swiftly).
22. If someone was in a hurry, horses were pretty (well, good).
23. Then trains made it possible for people to travel (real, really) fast.
24. To some people, early trains appeared (frightening, frighteningly).
25. An 1825 train seemed like a (real, really) blur at 7 mph.
26. Trains improved (rapid, rapidly), however.
27. By 1850, trains broke 60 miles per hour (easy, easily).
28. It may sound (unbelievable, unbelievably), but in 1955 a French train set a record by traveling 205 miles per hour.
29. At 160 mph, a Japanese train doesn't do so (bad, badly).
30. It seems (incredible, incredibly), but a United States rocket train that tests spacecraft parts reaches a rate of 3,090 mph.

D. Using Negatives Correctly Write the following sentences, correcting all double negatives.

31. No one had never circled the world until Magellan did so in 1521.
32. His ships didn't make it in nothing less than two years.
33. We haven't never quit trying to circle the globe faster.
34. The next noteworthy trip wasn't made by nobody else but Nellie Bly, a reporter who in 1889 went around the world in about seventy-two days.
35. That record wasn't nothing after people started flying.
36. In 1924, one plane never had no trouble circling the earth in fifteen days.
37. Not even that record wasn't safe, though.
38. Wiley Post and Harold Gatty didn't take no time at all to break the record, taking less than eight days in 1931.
39. By 1957, the record wasn't no more than two days.
40. None of these records means nothing to space vehicles.

REVIEW

A. Identifying Adverbs Write each adverb below. Also write whether the adverb tells *How, When, Where,* or *To what extent.*

1. A newborn bear is usually only seven or eight inches long.
2. The tiny cub ordinarily weighs less than a pound.
3. It is completely blind and lacks both teeth and hair.
4. It grows quickly, though, and very soon it is not helpless.
5. In only a few years, it may weigh 300 to 1,500 pounds.
6. Alaskan brown bears are the tallest—sometimes nearly nine feet high when standing up on two legs.
7. They are powerful and dangerously unpredictable animals.
8. Some bears can run faster than a horse for short distances.
9. Bears once lived everywhere in the United States.
10. Now, many black bears and a few grizzlies still live here.

B. Making Comparisons Write the correct form of each adverb given in parentheses.

11. Of all Americans who have worked with animals, James Capen Adams may be the (well) known animal trainer.
12. People know him (well) as Grizzly Adams.
13. Adams had many jobs; the one he probably liked (little) was his first one as a shoemaker in Massachusetts.
14. In 1849, he joined the California Gold Rush, thinking he couldn't do (badly) as a prospector than he had done as a shoemaker.
15. He wanted (desperately) of all to work with animals.
16. He quit mining and traveled even (deep) into the mountains.
17. He caught and trained many animals; one, a bear he named Lady Washington, he trained the (carefully) of all.
18. Lady Washington fought back (hard) than a cub would have.
19. In time, Lady grew (much) gentle and they became friends.
20. Later, Grizzly captured a grizzly cub, which he named Benjamin Franklin; it was (easily) trained than Lady.
21. Ben had lived (briefly) as a wild animal than Lady.
22. Lady and Ben served Grizzly the (loyally) of all his animals.

GRAMMAR HANDBOOK 39

Writing Theme
Bears

GRAMMAR HANDBOOK 39

REVIEW

These exercises may be used as a mixed review or as an informal evaluation of skills presented in Handbook 39, "Understanding Adverbs."

Additional Resources

Grammar and Usage Practice Book, p. 66
Tests and Writing Assessment Prompts, Mastery Test, pp. 37–38
Elaboration, Revision, and Proofreading Practice, p. 28

Writing Theme: Bears

Other related areas students might wish to explore as writing topics include the following:
- famous fictional bears
- pandas or koalas—bearlike animals

A. Identifying Adverbs
Adverbs are shown on page.
1. usually, When; only, To what extent
2. ordinarily, When; less, To what extent
3. completely, To what extent
4. quickly, How; very, To what extent; soon, When; not, To what extent
5. only, To what extent
6. sometimes, When; nearly, To what extent; up, How
7. dangerously, How
8. faster, How
9. once, When; everywhere, Where
10. Now, When; still, To what extent; here, Where

B. Making Comparisons
11. best
12. better
13. least
14. worse
15. most desperately
16. deeper
17. most carefully
18. harder
19. more
20. more easily
21. more briefly
22. most loyally

C. Using the Correct Modifier

23. Correct
24. These creatures survived very well everywhere west of Ohio and Kentucky.
25. Native Americans lived uneasily with them from the beginning.
26. Some groups would hunt the grizzly only if they needed food badly.
27. They respected the animal and felt bad when they killed one.
28. Correct
29. They were really sure that their ancestors had become bears.
30. Bears appear frequently in their legends and stories.
31. Correct
32. When angry, it could overtake a rider on horseback easily.
33. It could knock down both the rider and the horse with one remarkably powerful swipe.
34. Early pioneers never felt too safe with grizzlies near.
35. The settlers killed bears rather regularly.
36. Correct

D. Using Negatives
Answers are shown on page.

C. Using the Correct Modifier Write the following sentences, correcting all errors in the use of adjectives and adverbs. If a sentence has no error, write *Correct.*

23. At one time, the sight of a grizzly bear was not unusual in North America.
24. These creatures survived very good everywhere west of Ohio and Kentucky.
25. Native Americans lived uneasy with them from the beginning.
26. Some groups would hunt the grizzly only if they needed food bad.
27. They respected the animal and felt badly when they killed one
28. Others worshipped the awesome grizzly and never hunted it.
29. They were real sure that their ancestors had become bears.
30. Bears appear frequent in their legends and stories.
31. No doubt, this extremely deadly bear deserved its reputation.
32. When angry, it could overtake a rider on horseback easy.
33. It could knock down both the rider and the horse with one remarkable powerful swipe.
34. Early pioneers never felt too safely with grizzlies near.
35. The settlers killed bears rather regular.
36. Most grizzlies south of Canada have been gradually destroyed.

D. Using Negatives For each sentence, write the correct word from those given in parentheses.

37. None of our presidents did (no, any) more to protect wilderness areas and wild animals than Theodore Roosevelt.
38. There wasn't (no one, anyone) who loved the outdoors more.
39. However, he wasn't in (any, no) way against hunting.
40. He didn't like (anything, nothing) much better than a bear hunt; but one time in Mississippi an old bear was caught.
41. Teddy didn't think (anybody, nobody) ought to shoot it.
42. He wouldn't (ever, never) shoot a helpless creature.
43. There wasn't (anybody, nobody) who ignored that story.
44. A toy maker (could, couldn't) not let the opportunity pass.
45. Nothing would sell (any, no) better than "Teddy" bears.
46. T.R. himself didn't have (any, no) objection to the toys.

498 Grammar Handbook

WRITING CONNECTIONS

Elaboration, Revision, and Proofreading

Revise the following draft of an opinion paper by using the directions at the bottom of the page. Then proofread your paper, paying special attention to the use of adverbs. Also look for other grammatical errors and errors in capitalization, punctuation, and spelling.

[1]Squirt guns don't seem like something for no one to get concerned about. [2]They are just a way for kids to have some good, clean (and wet) fun. [3]However, some people want to ban squirt guns. [4]My cousin has a squirt gun. [5]Why should all the kids who play safely with these toys be punished because a few kids act irresponsibly? [6]The gun that people are worried about is a new, high-powered squirt gun. [7]This gun holds more water. [8]It shoots it more forceful. [9]Critics say that if these guns are missused, they can be dangrous a few kids have been injurd. [10]Yet any toy is dangrous if it is missused. [11]Some toys are too expensive. [12]When these squirt guns are used properly, theyre a blast. And they are not unsafe.

1. Remove the two sentences that do not support the main idea.
2. Strengthen the argument by adding an example to sentence 10. "Even a tricycle can be dangerous if a child rides too fast or out into a street."
3. Improve the flow of sentences by combining 7 and 8 to make a sentence with a compound verb.
4. Replace the informal words *a blast* in sentence 12 with a more formal expression.
5. Make the conclusion of the paragraph stronger by placing sentence 5 after sentence 12.

Persuasive Writing

Stating your opinion allows you to share ideas on issues you feel strongly about. (See Workshop 5.) When you revise an opinion paper, look to see that you have stated your position clearly and supported it. Use adverbs to add details that tell *how, when, where,* and *to what extent.*

WRITING CONNECTIONS

Elaboration, Revision, and Proofreading

This activity will allow students to see some of the concepts presented in this Handbook at work in a piece of persuasive writing. By revising and proofreading this passage, students will have an opportunity to identify and correct errors in the use of adverbs. They will also become more aware of style.

You might have students work in small groups to revise the passage and then discuss the completed revision with the entire class. Revisions may vary slightly. See a typical revision below. Elements involving change are shown in boldface.

Squirt guns don't seem like something for anyone to get concerned about. They are just a way for kids to have some good, clean (and wet) fun. However, some people want to ban squirt guns. ~~**My cousin has a squirt gun.**~~ The gun that people are worried about is a new, high-powered squirt gun. **This gun holds more water and shoots it more forcefully.** Critics say that if these guns are misused, they can be dangerous. A few kids have been injured. Yet any toy is dangerous if it is misused. **Even a tricycle can be dangerous if a child rides too fast or out into a street.** ~~**Some toys are too expensive.**~~ When these squirt guns are used properly, they're **fun,** and they are not unsafe. **Why should all the kids who play safely with these toys be punished because a few kids act irresponsibly?**

Test 2

This test enables you to evaluate student mastery of the concepts taught in handbooks 37–39.

Additional Resource

Grammar and Usage Practice Book, pp. 67–68

Answer Key

Corrections for run-ons may vary.

1. A—aren't
   C—they're
2. A—really
3. B—well
4. C—her
5. A—its
6. B—most popular
7. B—his
8. B—most precious
9. A—Those
   B—anybody
10. A—August
    B—its name
11. B—he
12. A—This
13. D
14. B—poorly
    C—ever *or* don't need
15. D

Skills

ASSESSMENT TEST 2 Grammar Handbooks *37–39*

Directions One or more of the underlined sections in the following sentences may contain an error in grammar, punctuation, spelling, or capitalization. Write the letter of each incorrect section. Then rewrite the section correctly. If there is no error in an item, write *D.*

Example I watched the magician very close (A), but I don't understand. How did him (B) and his assistant make the rabbit disappear (C)? No error (D)

Answer A—closely; B—he

1. Big animals arent (A) always parents of big babies (B). Kangaroos are about an inch long when their (C) born. No error (D)

2. If a bus is going real (A) fast and stops suddenly (B), it is the force of inertia that pushes your (C) body forward. No error (D)

3. A bloodhound's (A) nose works really good (B). Some of these dogs can follow a trail that's (C) ten days old. No error (D)

4. The song "Happy Birthday" (A) was a gold mine for Mildred Hill. It was written (B) by she (C) and her sister Patty and has earned millions of dollars. No error (D)

5. If a salamander loses it's (A) tail, it (B) just grows (C) a new one. No error (D)

6. There (A) are a great many people named John and Jim. Muhammad, however, is the most popularest (B) name in the world (C). No error (D)

500 Skills Assessment

7. Neither John F. Kennedy (A) nor Warren G. Harding outlived their (B) father (C). No error (D)

8. Rubies (A), not diamonds, are currently the more precious (B) stones on this planet (C). No error (D)

9. Them (A) stingers on a queen bee won't hurt nobody (B). They (C) are only used as weapons against other queen bees. No error (D)

10. July and august (A) have something in common. Each got their name (B) from a Roman (C) emperor named Caesar—a Julius and an Augustus. No error (D)

11. My brother and I (A) are twins, but him (B) and my cousin look (C) more alike than he and I do. No error (D)

12. These (A) kind of penguin grows (B) four feet tall and can weigh nearly (C) one hundred pounds. No error (D)

13. Watch out! (A) Those (B) chili peppers are much hotter (C) than bell peppers. No error (D)

14. Two-thirds of all adult Americans (A) see poor (B) enough to need eyeglasses. That leaves one third that don't never (C) need to wear them. No error (D)

15. Has everyone in the string (A) section tuned his or her (B) instrument (C)? No error (D)

List of Skills Tested

1. A—punctuation—apostrophe
   B—noun plural
   C—confusion of possessive pronoun and contraction
2. A—adjective/adverb confusion
   B—adjective/adverb confusion
   C—confusion of possessive pronoun and contraction
3. A—noun possessive
   B—good/well
   C—punctuation—apostrophe; subject-verb agreement
4. A—capitalization—title
   B—irregular verb form
   C—pronoun case
5. A—confusion of possessive pronoun and contraction
   B—pronoun-antecedent agreement
   C—subject-verb agreement
6. A—spelling
   B—comparative adjective form—more/most
   C—capitalization—common/proper noun
7. A—capitalization—initials
   B—agreement of possessive pronoun and indefinite pronoun
   C—capitalization—common/proper noun
8. A—noun plural
   B—comparative adjective form—more/most
   C—capitalization—common/proper noun
9. A—demonstrative adjective
   B—double negative
   C—pronoun case
10. A—capitalization—name of month
    B—agreement of possessive pronoun and indefinite pronoun
    C—capitalization—nationality
11. A—pronoun case
    B—pronoun case
    C—subject-verb agreement
12. A—demonstrative adjective
    B—subject-verb agreement
    C—adjective/adverb confusion
13. A—punctuation—end mark
    B—demonstrative adjective
    C—comparative adjective form
14. A—capitalization—nationality
    B—adjective/adverb confusion
    C—double negative
15. A—capitalization
    B—pronoun-antecedent agreement
    C—spelling

Sketchbook

Objective

- To use visual writing prompts as springboards to informal writing

WRITING WARM-UPS

Encourage students to respond freely and informally to at least one of the Sketchbook prompts. Students may begin by discussing their reactions in small groups and then freewriting in their journals. Remind them that their responses will not be graded and will provide them with the opportunity to think creatively about the concepts presented in this handbook.

For the first writing prompt, elicit the response that information about color, shape, size, and location is especially useful in helping readers picture an unfamiliar object. Point out that phrases, or groups of words, often help clarify size (for example, *nearly three feet long*) and location (for example, *on the right* or *at the front*). Encourage students to use such phrases in their descriptions.

For the second writing prompt, suggest that students include in their written descriptions words and phrases that clarify the sequence of the episode's events: *at the start, next, after ten minutes,* and *near the end,* and so on.

For the third writing prompt, elicit the response that clear directions often include the following kinds of phrases about specific streets or roads *(on Main Street),* time *(in about fifteen minutes),* distance *(after ten miles),* and landmarks or sights along the way (*at the third light* or *by the middle school*). Tell students to include phrases like these in their directions.

Sketchbook

WRITING WARM-UPS

Extravaganza Televisione (1984), Kenny Scharf.

- This television gives new meaning to the question, What's on TV? Write a description of this television set. Use words that help you tell your readers exactly where things are located.
- Write about what happened in a recent episode of a television show you often watch.
- Imagine that you and a friend are going to meet at your home or some other specific place. Write directions to tell your friend how to get there.

502

ART NOTE

Do students agree that Kenny Scharf's TV sculpture is, in the words of one art critic, the "ultimate box"? Ask students how they would turn their headset, TV, or boom box into a work of art.

Prepositions and Conjunctions

GRAMMAR HANDBOOK 40

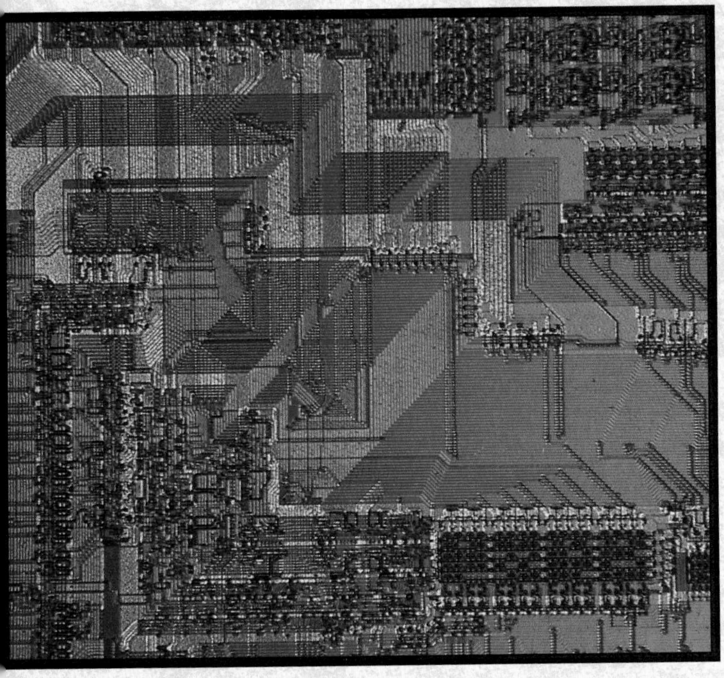

Circuits like this one provide the electrical connections that make a picture appear on your television set. When you write, you often need to provide connections between words and sentences.

In this handbook you will learn ways to use prepositions and conjunctions to show your readers how your ideas are connected and to add details to your writing.

- What Are Prepositions?
- Using Prepositional Phrases
- Pronouns After Prepositions
- More About Prepositions
- What Are Conjunctions?
- Using Words as Different Parts of Speech

GRAMMAR HANDBOOK 40

Prepositions and Conjunctions

Objectives

- To identify prepositions and their objects
- To identify prepositional phrases
- To use object forms of pronouns as objects of prepositions
- To distinguish between prepositions and adverbs
- To use *between* and *among* correctly
- To identify conjunctions and the sentence parts they combine
- To identify the part of speech of a word by its use in a sentence

Writing

- To use prepositions, prepositional phrases, and conjunctions correctly in sentences
- To use prepositional phrases as a means of adding details to writing
- To combine sentences by reducing one sentence to a prepositional phrase and inserting it in another sentence
- To use conjunctions to combine sentences
- To use proofreading skills to correct errors in preposition and conjunction usage

INTRODUCING THE HANDBOOK

Ask students to name some of their favorite electronic devices—such as compact disc players and computers—and to tell what they find entertaining about each. Ask what happens when the devices are unplugged or the batteries go dead. Point out that without connections to electrical power, the devices are useless. Then explain that sentences have special words that make important connections between words and ideas. Tell students they will learn more about these useful words, called *prepositions* and *conjunctions*, in this handbook.

WHAT ARE PREPOSITIONS?

Objectives

- To recognize prepositions and their objects

Writing

- To use appropriate prepositions to complete sentences

Teaching Strategies

KEY TO UNDERSTANDING: OBJECTS OF PREPOSITIONS Have a volunteer answer the question preceding the chart by identifying the object of the preposition in each sample sentence. (the noun *table*) Stress the change in the relationship brought about by the change in prepositions.

To show how pronouns can also be objects of prepositions, ask what pronoun can replace the noun *tunnel* and its modifier *the* in the statement "We walked through the tunnel." *(it)* With the pronoun, the sentence will read, "We walked through *it.*"

INDIVIDUALIZING INSTRUCTION: ESL STUDENTS Urdu, Hindi, and other South Asian languages utilize postpositions, not prepositions (postpositions *follow* their objects). Point out to students who speak these languages that prepositions have the same function as postpositions—to show relationships between words in a sentence—but that in relation to their objects, prepositions' position in a sentence is different from that of postpositions.

WHAT ARE PREPOSITIONS?

A **preposition** shows how a noun or a pronoun relates to another word in a sentence. The noun or pronoun that follows a preposition is the **object of the preposition.**

The girl is *on* the table.

The girl is *above* the table.

Prepositions help to show relationships. For example, *on* and *above* show the relationship between the girl and the table. The noun or pronoun following a preposition is called the **object of the preposition.** Which word is the object in the captions below the pictures?

Commonly Used Prepositions

about	before	down	of	to
above	behind	during	off	toward
across	below	for	on	under
after	beneath	from	onto	underneath
against	beside	in	out	until
along	between	inside	outside	up
among	beyond	into	over	upon
around	but (except)	like	past	with
at	by	near	through	without

Writing TIP

Choose prepositions carefully to make your meaning clear. Often, by changing prepositions, you can change the relationship between words in a sentence.

Practice Your Skills

A. CONCEPT CHECK

Prepositions Write the prepositions in the following sentences. Beside each preposition, write its object. Some sentences have more than one preposition and object.

1. Some magic tricks rely on appearances.
2. The laws of science are behind others.
3. Place a deck of cards on a table and cut the deck in half.
4. Look at the top card, show it to your audience, and then replace it.
5. Conceal a saltshaker in your pocket.
6. Reach inside that pocket.
7. Secretly coat the tip of your finger with salt and tap the top card with your finger.
8. Be sure you leave some salt on the surface of the top card.
9. Place one stack beneath the other.
10. The selected card seems lost in the middle of the deck.
11. Take a saltshaker from your pocket.
12. Sprinkle a little salt over the deck.
13. Also gently tap against the side of the deck with the shaker.
14. As if by magic, the deck will separate at the point where the selected card is.
15. Grains of salt on that card act like ball bearings, making the cards separate there.

B. DRAFTING SKILL

Using Prepositions Write prepositions that logically complete the following sentences.

16 Stick a piece ___ double-sided sticky tape ___ the front edge of a table. 17 Show a six-inch piece of thread ___ your audience, then attach one end ___ the tape. 18 Take a comb ___ your pocket. 19 Run the comb ___ your hair. 20 Say, "Rope, rise ___ the air." 21 Hold the comb ___ the free end of the thread. 22 Draw the comb up ___ the air, and the thread mysteriously rises. 23 This trick is done ___ static electricity caused by rubbing the comb ___ your hair.

Writing Theme
Science and Magic

FOR MORE PRACTICE
See page 521.

Additional Resources

Tests and Writing Assessment Prompts, Pretest, pp. 39–40
Grammar and Usage Practice Book, p. 69
Grammar Test Generator

Writing Theme: Science and Magic

Suggest that students use these exercises as a springboard to writing. Other related areas that they might explore include the following:

- other card tricks
- how to perform a magic trick
- famous magicians
- famous scientific hoaxes
- scientific advances that might seem magical to a person from an earlier time

Answers to Practice Your Skills

A. Concept Check
Prepositions

Answers are shown on page.

B. Drafting Skill
Using Prepositions

Answers may vary. See typical answers below.

16. of; on, against, *or* to
17. to; to
18. from
19. through
20. into
21. over, above, *or* near
22. into *or* through
23. with; on, through, *or* in

USING PREPOSITIONAL PHRASES

Objectives

- To identify prepositional phrases

Writing

- To use prepositional phrases in writing
- To combine sentences by reducing one sentence to a prepositional phrase and inserting that phrase in another sentence

Teaching Strategies

LINKING GRAMMAR AND WRITING Explain that some prepositional phrases can be positioned in more than one place in a sentence. For example:

Many trees were cut *in the forest.*

In the forest many trees were cut.

Point out that writers sometimes place the prepositional phrase at the beginning of a sentence, for variety. Emphasize, however, that wherever a prepositional phrase is placed, the meaning of the sentences should remain clear and there should be no possibility of confusion for the reader.

INDIVIDUALIZING INSTRUCTION: ADVANCED STUDENTS Explain that an entire prepositional phrase works as a modifier to describe words functioning as nouns or verbs in a sentence. In the first sample sentence, *in the Southwest* describes the verb *live* by telling *where.* In the third sample sentence, *of the Pueblos* describes the noun *ancestors* by telling *which ones.* Ask what words the prepositional phrases in the other sample sentences describe. *(for many centuries, have lived; in high cliffs, made; in New Mexico . . . , settled; of stone and adobe, built; of stone and adobe, homes)*

Additional Resource

Grammar and Usage Practice Book, p. 70

Writing TIP

Look at "The Circuit" on pages 142–145. Notice how the author Francisco Jiménez used prepositional phrases to add important details about events and places in the story.

USING PREPOSITIONAL PHRASES

A **prepositional phrase** is a group of words that begins with a preposition and ends with its object.

Look at the italicized prepositional phrases in the sentences below. Notice each preposition and its object.

Preposition — Object of Preposition

The Pueblo people live *in the Southwest.*

Preposition — Object of Preposition

They have lived there *for many centuries.*

In a prepositional phrase, one or more words that describe the object may come between the preposition and its object. The preposition, the object, and all the words that describe the object form the **prepositional phrase.**

Sentences often contain more than one prepositional phrase.

The ancestors *of the Pueblos,* the Anasazi, made their homes *in high cliffs.*

A preposition may have a **compound object** made up of two or more nouns or pronouns joined by *and* or *or.*

Object — Object — Object — Object

They settled *in New Mexico, Arizona, Utah, and Colorado.*

You can often make your writing smoother by reducing a sentence to a prepositional phrase and combining it with another sentence.

The Pueblos later built more elaborate homes. They built them *of stone and adobe.*

The Pueblos later built more elaborate homes *of stone and adobe.*

Always be sure to place the prepositional phrase close to the word or words it describes.

Literature Connection

Point out to students that prepositional phrases, like other modifiers, can make writing more precise and vivid. Write on the board the following lines from "Lob's Girl" by Joan Aiken. Ask students to identify the prepositional phrases (underlined). Discuss how the phrases add precision and vividness to the writing.

The whole family was playing cards by the fire in the front room after supper when there was a loud thump and a crash of china in the kitchen.

An adobe structure in a Pueblo community outside Taos, New Mexico.

Practice Your Skills

A. APPLICATION IN LITERATURE

Prepositional Phrases Notice how this writer uses prepositional phrases to add detail to her narrative. Write the prepositional phrases in these sentences. If a sentence contains no prepositional phrases, write *None.*

> **1**The house of Tassai was the last one in the little town, on the very edge of the mesa top. **2**She ran into the door and did not notice that the little white girl who had followed her had stopped suddenly just outside the doorway. **3**The child was watching, with wide, frightened eyes, a snake that lifted its head. . . . **4**It was a rattlesnake, and it moved its flat, ugly head closer and closer to the little girl. **5**She gave one sharp cry as Tassai came out . . . with the jar in her arms. **6**Tassai had thrown aside the blanket and held the jar unwrapped in her arms. . . .
>
> **7**Tassai did the only thing she could do. **8**With all her strength she threw the jar at the snake. **9**It broke into many pieces on the rock, and the snake lay flat and still.

Grace P. Moon, "The Jar of Tassai"

Writing Theme
Pueblo Communities

Writing Theme: Pueblo Communities

Suggest that students use these exercises as a springboard to writing. Other related areas that they might explore include the following:

- today's Pueblo peoples
- traditional Pueblo literature
- traditional Pueblo crafts
- Hopi or Zuñi history

Answers to Practice Your Skills

A. Application in Literature
Prepositional Phrases

1. of Tassai; in the little town; on the very edge; of the mesa top
2. into the door; outside the doorway
3. with wide, frightened eyes
4. to the little girl
5. with the jar; in her arms
6. in her arms
7. None
8. With all her strength; at the snake
9. into many pieces; on the rock

Literature Connection

Author Note Grace Purdie Moon (1877?–1947) is best known for her children's books about Native Americans. "When I was a little girl," she once explained, "I thought I really was an Indian because I was born in Indianapolis." She married artist-writer Carl Moon, who was also interested in Native American life, and the two lived for a time with Southwestern Native Americans, gathering material for books. Carl Moon coauthored some of her works and illustrated virtually all of them. They include *Lost Indian Magic, Chi-Wee: The Adventures of a Little Indian Girl, Daughter of Thunder,* and *One Little Indian.*

B. Drafting Skill
Using Prepositional Phrases

Answers may vary slightly. See typical answers below.

10. The kiva was a large underground space beneath the community's living quarters.
11. The kiva was carefully built in a circle or a rectangle.
12. The kiva had a deep pit in the middle.
13. For their most important ceremonies, the Anasazi built fires in this pit. *or* The Anasazi built fires in this pit for their most important ceremonies.
14. Over the pit there was often a roof of timbers. *or* There was often a roof of timbers over the pit.
15. A ladder led to the kiva from the buildings above.
16. Members entered easily through a hatchway.
17. The Anasazi created hundreds of communities in the area of Chaco Canyon.
18. Pueblo Bonito, in the famous Chaco Culture National Historical Park, is a remarkable example.
19. This city was four stories high, with almost 650 rooms and 32 kivas.
20. Nearly a thousand people lived there about nine hundred years ago. *or* About nine hundred years ago, nearly a thousand people lived there.
21. The largest of the kivas is two stories deep, with a diameter of over fifty feet.

C. Application in Writing
Using Prepositions in Directions

Answers will vary.

B. DRAFTING SKILL

Using Prepositional Phrases Rewrite each of the following pairs of sentences by reducing one sentence to a prepositional phrase and combining it with the other sentence.

EXAMPLE *Separate* At the heart of the community was a kiva. It was used *for meetings and ceremonies.*

Combined At the heart of the community was a kiva *for meetings and ceremonies.*

10. The kiva was a large underground space. It lay beneath the community's living quarters.
11. The kiva was carefully built. It was built in a circle or a rectangle.
12. The kiva had a deep pit. The pit was in the middle.
13. The Anasazi built fires in this pit. The fires were for their most important ceremonies.
14. There was often a roof over the pit. It was made of timbers.
15. A ladder led to the kiva. It came from the buildings above.
16. Members entered easily. They came through a hatchway.
17. The Anasazi created hundreds of communities. They were in the area of Chaco Canyon.
18. Pueblo Bonito is a remarkable example. It is in the famous Chaco Culture National Historical Park.
19. This city was four stories high. It was built with almost 650 rooms and 32 kivas.
20. Nearly a thousand people lived there. They lived there about nine hundred years ago.
21. The largest of the kivas is two stories deep. It was dug to a diameter of over fifty feet.

C. APPLICATION IN WRITING

Using Prepositions in Directions Prepositions and prepositional phrases are especially useful in giving directions. Write a set of directions. Tell a friend how to get somewhere—for example, how to get from the airport to your house—or how to do something, like fold a paper airplane.

FOR MORE PRACTICE
See page 521.

CHECK POINT
MIXED REVIEW • PAGES 504–508

Write the prepositional phrases in the following sentences. Draw a line under the object of each preposition.

1. A pinhole camera can easily be made from any box with a tight-fitting lid.
2. A pinhole will perform the job of a lens in the camera.
3. First, take a small square of aluminum foil about an inch on each side.
4. Lay the foil on a flat, hard surface.
5. Press the point of a needle through the foil.
6. The pinhole should be round and free of ragged edges.
7. Select a box and paint the inside with black paint.
8. Cut a hole in one side of the box.
9. Tape the aluminum foil over the hole in the box.
10. Be sure that the pinhole is in the center of the foil.
11. Take a piece of nontransparent tape and cover the pinhole.
12. Load the pinhole camera with a sheet of light-sensitive photographic paper.
13. Loading must be done in a darkroom with a safelight.
14. Center the photographic paper on the opposite side of the box from the pinhole.
15. Replace the lid of the box.
16. Take the pinhole camera outdoors and place it on a firm support.
17. Remove the tape from the pinhole for two minutes.
18. If the day is cloudy, open the pinhole for eight minutes.
19. Remove the exposed photographic paper and develop it in the darkroom.
20. A negative image will form on the paper.
21. If your negative is too dark, repeat the procedure and shorten the time of exposure.
22. Lengthen the time of exposure if your negative is too light.
23. You can make several pinhole cameras for multiple shots of various scenes.
24. Try making a pinhole camera from an oatmeal box.
25. Making a camera of this kind is fun and inexpensive.

Writing Theme
Cameras

CHECK POINT

Writing Theme: Cameras

Other related areas students might wish to explore as writing topics include the following:

- the early history of photography
- Ansel Adams or Margaret Bourke-White, famous photographers
- the invention of motion pictures
- how to use a video-recording camera

MIXED REVIEW • PAGES 504–508

You may wish to use this activity to check students' mastery of the following concepts:

- What are prepositions?
- prepositional phrases

Answers are shown on page.

PRONOUNS AFTER PREPOSITIONS

Objectives

- To use the object forms of pronouns as simple or compound objects of prepositions

Writing

- To use object forms of pronouns correctly in writing
- To use proofreading skills to correct errors in the use of object pronouns

Teaching Strategies

KEY TO UNDERSTANDING Point out that the pronouns listed here are personal pronouns. Other types of pronouns can also be used as objects of prepositions, but they do not have special object forms. An exception is *who,* which has a special object form, *whom.*

SPEAKING AND LISTENING One reason why students have trouble in selecting the correct form of a pronoun as the compound object of a preposition is that colloquial speech often misuses this construction, as in *Come with Anne and I.* Stress that students should develop an "ear" for correct object forms by doing oral drills such as the following:

- Come with Ann and *me.*
- Everyone but *him* volunteered to help.
- The secret is between *him* and *me.*
- The doctor gave a lecture on nutrition to *us* girls.

Additional Resource

Grammar and Usage Practice Book, p. 71

PRONOUNS AFTER PREPOSITIONS

When a pronoun is the object of a preposition, the object form of the pronoun must be used.

Object forms of pronouns must be used as objects of prepositions. Here are the object forms:

me you him her it us them

Notice the pronouns in these sentences.

The pioneers are an inspiration for *us* today.
They traveled west, taking all their possessions with *them.*

Sometimes a pronoun is part of a **compound object of a preposition.** When a pronoun is part of a compound object, you must use an object pronoun.

Simple Object	**Compound Object**
The girl rode with *me.*	The girl rode with *Hank and me.*
She held the reins for *me.*	She held the reins for *him and me.*

Pioneer families in canvas-covered wagons formed wagon trains and journeyed west.

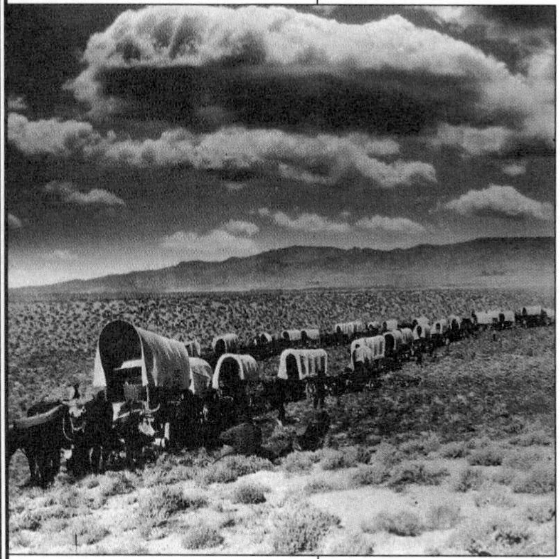

If you are unsure which form of pronoun to use in a compound object, say the sentence with just the pronoun following the preposition. Then write the sentence with the complete prepositional phrase.

Everyone was ready but the Cranes and (we, us).
Everyone was ready but *us.*
Everyone was ready but the Cranes and *us.*

For more information on using object pronouns, see Handbook 37, "Understanding Pronouns," pages 434–457.

510 Grammar Handbook

Practice Your Skills

A. CONCEPT CHECK

Pronouns After Prepositions Write the correct pronoun.

1. Your letter was a treat for Tina and (I, me).
2. It came to (we, us) just before our wagon train left St. Louis.
3. To Mom, Tina, and (I, me), that seems like years ago.
4. Imagine all these families taking everything they own with (they, them).
5. One of the drivers stands guard near (we, us) all night.
6. His rifle shots are an alarm clock for my family and (I, me).
7. To get ready for the day's journey, Pa gathers the oxen and puts harnesses on (they, them).
8. The oxen are always shoving against (he, him) because they don't like to be harnessed.
9. This morning Mom made pancakes and split the extra ones between Tina and (he, him).
10. Pa takes a lot of teasing from Tina and (she, her) about his healthy appetite.

B. PROOFREADING SKILL

Using the Correct Pronoun Forms Proofread the following paragraph. Then write the paragraph, correcting all errors in grammar, capitalization, punctuation, and spelling. Make sure that the correct pronoun forms are used. (10 errors)

Women preformed many important tasks in a pioneer community. A woman prepared meals. And washed clothes for she and her family. Women also drove wagons gathered fuel and food, and cared for the sick. Recording the births, deaths, and other events in a families life were part of a womans' role. Even when women's families were settled, life was just as hard for they and their husbands as it had been on the trail. Together they cleared the land, planted crops, and herded animals. Often, stores, mills, and even mines were started by they and their husbands. Sometimes because of death. or other misfortune, women had to run these busineses by themselves.

Writing Theme
Life as a Pioneer

FOR MORE PRACTICE
See page 521.

Writing Theme: Life as a Pioneer

Other related areas students might wish to explore as writing topics include the following:

- the Homestead Act
- the Oklahoma Land Rush
- types of pioneer wagons
- famous pioneer routes to the West
- *Little House on the Prairie* (book or former TV series)

Answers to Practice Your Skills

A. Concept Check
Pronouns After Prepositions

Answers are shown on page.

B. Proofreading Skill
Using the Correct Pronoun Forms

Errors in proofreading exercises are counted as follows: (a) Each word is counted as one error. For example, a misspelled word is one error; two initials and a last name not capitalized are counted as three errors. (b) Run-on sentences and sentence fragments are each counted as one error, even though the correction involves both punctuation and capitalization.

Errors are shown on page. The correctly rewritten paragraph appears below.

Women performed many important tasks in a pioneer community. A woman prepared meals and washed clothes for her and her family. Women also drove wagons, gathered fuel and food, and cared for the sick. Recording the births, deaths, and other events in a family's life was part of a woman's role. Even when women's families were settled, life was just as hard for them and their husbands as it had been on the trail. Together they cleared the land, planted crops, and herded animals. Often, stores, mills, and even mines were started by them and their husbands. Sometimes because of death or other misfortune, women had to run these businesses by themselves.

More About Prepositions

Objectives

- To distinguish between prepositions and adverbs
- To use *between* and *among* correctly

Writing

- To use prepositions and adverbs correctly in sentences

Teaching Strategies

STUMBLING BLOCK Remind students that prepositional phrases are sometimes split when they are used in questions. In such a case a preposition may appear at the end of the sentence and appear to be an adverb. Suggest that students turn the question into a statement, to determine whether such a word is a preposition. For example: *Did the dog go out?* becomes *The dog did go out.* (*Out* is an adverb.) The sentence *Which file does this belong in?* becomes *This does belong in which file.* (*In* is a preposition.)

LINKING GRAMMAR AND WRITING Point out that writers should use prepositions consistently in parallel constructions.

Inconsistent: The firm has offices *in* Miami, Atlanta, and *in* Tampa.

Consistent: The firm has offices *in* Miami, *in* Atlanta, and *in* Tampa. *Or* The firm has offices *in* Miami, Atlanta, and Tampa.

HELPFUL HINT: BETWEEN/AMONG Tell students the following everyday expressions will help them to remember how to use *between* and *among* correctly:

"Between the two of us, ..."

"To be among friends is great."

Additional Resource

Grammar and Usage Practice Book, p. 72

More About Prepositions

Some prepositions need special attention.

Several words that are used as prepositions are also used as adverbs. Some examples are *up, down, around, in,* and *out.*

Josh looked *up.* (adverb)
Josh looked *up* the street. (preposition)

The cat dashed *around.* (adverb)
The cat dashed *around* the room. (preposition)

To determine if a word is an adverb or a preposition, look at how it is used. If it is used alone, it is probably an adverb. If it begins a phrase, it is probably a preposition.

For more information on adverbs, see Handbook 39, "Understanding Adverbs," pages 480–499.

Using *Between* and *Among*

You may hear the prepositions *between* and *among* used as though there were no difference between them. However, there is a difference.

Usually, *among* is used to refer to three or more persons, objects, or groups.

Chris was *among* the many guests at Ann's party.
Joan's present was hidden *among* all the others.

Between is usually used to refer to two persons, objects, or groups.

Jenna sat between Ben and Chloe.

Between may also be used to refer to more than two items when you wish to show that each is related to the others.

A treaty *between* France, Germany, and Italy was drafted.

Writing TIP

Avoid using unnecessary prepositions.

Unnecessary
Where is the package *at?*
Improved
Where is the package?

Practice Your Skills

A. CONCEPT CHECK

Adverbs and Prepositions Write each italicized word. Label it *Adverb* or *Preposition.*

Writing Theme Celebrations Around the World

1. People *around* the world celebrate birthdays in many ways.
2. Have you ever seen birthday candles blown *out?*
3. Blowing out candles first became popular *in* Germany.
4. *Over* the years, the custom has spread to other countries.
5. *In* Korea a baby's first birthday may be used to tell the child's future.
6. The baby sits at a table covered *with* a variety of objects.
7. The baby reaches *among* the objects.
8. The first object the baby picks *up* foretells his or her future.
9. In China people associate long noodles *with* long life.
10. On birthdays, bowls *of* long noodles are exchanged between friends.
11. The noodles mean "Long life *to* you."
12. In England prizes are hidden in a tub of sawdust and guests dig *in* to find them.
13. In Mexico piñatas are hung *up* for birthdays and other celebrations.
14. A piñata is filled *with* candies, fruits, and gifts.
15. Blindfolded guests swing sticks *around,* hoping to hit the piñata.
16. When it breaks, the prizes spill *down* onto the guests.

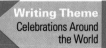

Writing Theme: Celebrations Around the World

Other related areas students might wish to explore as writing topics include the following:

- Chinese New Year celebrations
- totem-pole raising among Native Americans of the Northwest
- Independence Day celebrations in various countries

Answers to Practice Your Skills

A. Concept Check
Adverbs and Prepositions

1. around, Preposition
2. out, Adverb
3. in, Preposition
4. Over, Preposition
5. In, Preposition
6. with, Preposition
7. among, Preposition
8. up, Adverb
9. with, Preposition
10. of, Preposition
11. to, Preposition
12. in, Adverb
13. up, Adverb
14. with, Preposition
15. around, Adverb
16. down, Adverb

B. Revision Skill

Using Prepositions Correctly

17. The arrival of a new year has been a special day among people for ages.
18. Thousands of years ago, the Egyptians celebrated the new year between May and July, when the Nile overflowed.
19. From among their various gods, the ancient Romans chose Janus as the god of the new year.
20. Janus had two faces and so did not have to choose between looking forward and looking backward.
21. Correct
22. Correct
23. Celtic priests in what is now England gave out branches of mistletoe among their followers.
24. Among some Native Americans, the new year meant new possessions.
25. Correct

C. Application in Writing

Answers will vary.

Bahamian drummers welcome the New Year as they perform in the Junkanoo Parade. This event may be named after John Canoe, a local folk hero.

B. REVISION SKILL

Using Prepositions Correctly Revise the sentences in which *between* or *among* is used incorrectly. If a sentence contains no error, write *Correct.*

17. The arrival of a new year has been a special day between people for ages.
18. Thousands of years ago, the Egyptians celebrated the new year among May and July, when the Nile overflowed.
19. From between their various gods, the ancient Romans chose Janus as the god of the new year.
20. Janus had two faces and so did not have to choose among looking forward and looking backward.
21. January was named for Janus, and on the first day of January, good-luck gifts were exchanged between friends.
22. In contrast, ancient Persians shared new year's eggs among family members.
23. Celtic priests in what is now England gave out branches of mistletoe between their followers.
24. Between some Native Americans, the new year meant new possessions.
25. The Creeks, between July and September, threw out old things and got new clothes, furniture, and even new toys.

C. APPLICATION IN WRITING

Think of the funniest or most unusual party you ever attended. Did people wear costumes? Describe the party in a few sentences. Use at least two of these words as adverbs: *up, down, around, through,* and *in.* Use at least three of these words as prepositions: *for, from, with, out, behind,* and *of.*

FOR MORE PRACTICE
See page 522.

514 Grammar Handbook

CHECK ✔ POINT

MIXED REVIEW • PAGES 510–514

Choose and write the correct word from the two given in parentheses.

1. (<u>Between</u>, Among) barnstorming and air shows, many early pilots gained experience and skill.
2. Many of these pilots pleased large crowds by performing daring tricks for (they, <u>them</u>).
3. Many of their stunts would be thrilling even for (we, <u>us</u>) today.
4. The planes were flimsy, but the pilots did amazing stunts with (they, <u>them</u>).
5. One pilot, "Linc" Beachey, stood out; there was a difference between (he, <u>him</u>) and the other fliers.
6. For one trick this fearless daredevil would zoom (<u>between</u>, among) the doors of airplane hangars—in one side and out the other.
7. With six thousand feet between (he, <u>him</u>) and the crowd below, he would begin his "dive of death."
8. Gasps and cries could be heard (between, <u>among</u>) the amazed spectators as he turned off his engine and headed straight for them.
9. Just in time, he pulled out of the dive and landed safely (between, <u>among</u>) them.
10. Another important name (<u>among</u>, between) early pilots was Bessica Raiche.
11. For (she, <u>her</u>) and her husband, building a plane in their living room was no small accomplishment.
12. (Between, <u>Among</u>) the various materials available, they chose bamboo, silk, and piano wire.
13. (Between, <u>Among</u>) the aircraft builders of her day, Raiche became a pioneer.
14. After poor health forced her out of flying, she decided medicine was the career for (she, <u>her</u>), so she became a doctor.
15. Credit for the first solo flight by a U.S. woman is shared by (she, <u>her</u>) and Blanche Scott.

Writing Theme
Pioneers of Flight

Prepositions and
Conjunctions **515**

CHECK ✔ POINT

Writing Theme: Pioneers of Flight

Other related areas students might wish to explore as writing topics include the following:
- the Wright brothers
- Charles A. Lindbergh
- Beryl Markham
- "Wrong-Way" Corrigan

MIXED REVIEW • PAGES 510–514

You may wish to use this activity to check students' mastery of the following concepts:
- pronouns after prepositions
- differentiating between prepositions and adverbs
- *between* and *among*

 Answers are shown on page.

Objectives

- To recognize conjunctions and to identify the sentence parts they combine

Writing

- To use conjunctions to combine sentences

Teaching Strategies

CRITICAL THINKING: MAKING COMPARISON Have volunteers compare and contrast the functions of prepositions with those of conjunctions. (Both create links in sentences. Prepositions link a noun or pronoun to another word in a sentence, but conjunctions link complete sentences or parallel sentence parts, such as subjects, verbs, or direct objects.)

Additional Resource

Grammar and Usage Practice Book, p. 73

Writing Theme: Dog-Sled Racing

Other related areas students might wish to explore as writing topics include the following:

- types of sled dogs
- training teams of sled dogs
- tobogganing
- cross-country skiing
- other kinds of working dogs

Answers to Practice Your Skills

A. Concept Check

Compound Constructions

1. dogs and dog sleds; Subject
2. goods and people; Object

WHAT ARE CONJUNCTIONS?

A **conjunction** joins words or groups of words.

Writing TIP

Notice how in "The Monkey Garden" on pages 50–51, Sandra Cisneros uses conjunctions to link ideas and show the relationship between sentence parts.

A conjunction can be used to join sentence parts or whole sentences. The words *and, but,* and *or* are conjunctions. In the following sentences, the conjunctions join sentence parts.

Glenna *and* her dogs sped across the ice. (*And* joins subjects.)
The team was tired *but* raced on. (*But* joins predicates.)
By nightfall they might reach McGrath *or* Takotna. (*Or* joins direct objects.)

You have learned that *compound* means "having more than one part." In the examples above, conjunctions were used to join compound sentence parts. Conjunctions may also be used to join whole sentences that are closely related.

The team came to a stop. Glenna unhitched the dogs.
The team came to a stop, *and* Glenna unhitched the dogs.

Notice that a comma is used at the end of the first sentence, before the conjunction *and.* A comma is not used, however, when two sentence parts are joined. Also, you may omit the comma when the two sentences you join are very short.

Practice Your Skills

A. CONCEPT CHECK

Compound Constructions Write the compound part in each of the following sentences and label it *Subject, Verb, Object,* or *Sentence.*

Writing Theme
Dog-Sled Racing

1. For many years dogs and dog sleds provided the main form of winter transportation in Alaska.
2. Sleds carried goods and people across the countryside.

516 Grammar Handbook

3. In 1925, dog-sled teams proved their strength and value.
4. That year a diphtheria epidemic broke out in Nome, but the town was not prepared.
5. More serum was needed, or the town would face disaster.
6. Dog sleds and railroads combined their efforts.
7. Trains took the serum part of the way, and sleds carried it on to Nome.
8. Nineteen drivers and teams worked in a relay for a week.
9. Nome's residents cheered and celebrated the team's arrival.
10. Now every March the Iditarod Trail Sled Dog Race duplicates and honors that event.

B. DRAFTING SKILL

Sentence Combining Combine each of the following sentence pairs into a single sentence. Choose a conjunction and use a comma if necessary. Omit words in italics.

11. Susan Butcher is a dog-sled racer. *She is* a four-time winner of the Iditarod race.
12. This famous race covers over 1,100 miles. *It* lasts many days.
13. Sled dogs in the race must be strong. They could not survive.
14. Early in one race, Butcher's sled got stuck in an icy creek. *The sled* broke in four places.
15. Her sled no longer steered properly. She continued anyway.
16. Later, a brutal snowstorm came up. *There were* fierce winds.
17. Butcher could wait out the storm. She could go on.
18. Two opponents were close. They were forced to stop.
19. She trusted her dogs. They trusted her.
20. She drove all night through the storm. *She* beat the second-place dog-sled by fourteen hours.

The four-time Iditarod winner Susan Butcher poses with a hard-working friend.

FOR MORE PRACTICE
See page 522.

3. their strength and value; Object
4. That year a diphtheria epidemic broke out in Nome, but the town was not prepared; Sentence
5. More serum was needed, or the town would face disaster; Sentence
6. Dog sleds and railroads; Subject
7. Trains took the serum part of the way, and sleds carried it on to Nome; Sentence
8. drivers and teams; Subject
9. cheered and celebrated; Verb
10. duplicates and honors; Verb

B. Drafting Skill
Sentence Combining

Answers may vary slightly. See typical answers below.

11. Susan Butcher is a dog-sled racer and a four-time winner of the Iditarod race.
12. This famous race covers over 1,100 miles and lasts many days.
13. Sled dogs in the race must be strong, or they could not survive.
14. Early in one race, Butcher's sled got stuck in an icy creek and broke in four places.
15. Her sled no longer steered properly, but she continued anyway.
16. Later, a brutal snowstorm and fierce winds came up.
17. Butcher could wait out the storm, or she could go on.
18. Two opponents were close, but they were forced to stop.
19. She trusted her dogs (*or* dogs,) and they trusted her.
20. She drove all night through the storm and beat the second-place dog sled by fourteen hours.

USING WORDS AS DIFFERENT PARTS OF SPEECH

Objectives

- To identify the part of speech of given words

Writing

- To write sentences, using the same word as various parts of speech

Teaching Strategies

CRITICAL THINKING: ANALYZING Have volunteers explain why *farm* is a noun in the first sample sentence (it names a place and serves as the object of a preposition), a verb in the second (it expresses action and shows what the subject does), and an adjective in the third (it describes the noun *machinery*, telling *what kind*).

SPEAKING AND LISTENING Point out that some words that can be either nouns or verbs change pronunciation when used as a different part of speech. For example, the noun *object* has the stress on the first syllable, but the verb *object* has the stress on the second. Have volunteers offer more examples and use them in sentences. (Some examples are *conduct, contest, convict, present, produce, project, refuse,* and *use.*)

Additional Resource

Grammar and Usage Practice Book, p. 74

USING WORDS AS DIFFERENT PARTS OF SPEECH

Some words may be used as more than one part of speech. How a word is used in a sentence determines what part of speech it is.

On page 512 of this handbook, you learned that words lik *up, down, around, in,* and *out* can be used either as preposi tions or as adverbs. Many other words can function as mor than one part of speech. Before you can determine what part c speech a word is, you must decide how the word is used in sentence. Look at how the word *farm* is used in the followin sentences.

As a noun

Josh and Jenna live on a *farm.*

As a verb

Their family first *farmed* that land a hundred years ago.

As an adjective

Josh and his father take care of the family's *farm* machinery.

Remember the rules for each part c speech when using words in different way For example, when you use *farm* as noun, you add *-s* to form the plural *farm* When you use *farm* as a verb, you add *-e* to form the past tense *farmed.* To us *farm* in some tenses, you may need to ad a helping verb such as *did* or *will.*

There is only one sure way to tell wha part of speech a word is. Look at th sentence in which the word is used.

Practice Your Skills

A. CONCEPT CHECK

Parts of Speech Identify the part of speech of each word in italics. Write *Noun, Verb, Adjective, Adverb,* or *Preposition.*

1. Are you a good *weather* forecaster?
2. Certain signs have been used as *warning* signs of future weather for centuries.
3. Generally, *rain* is not likely if the wind is from the north.
4. In contrast, it will often *rain* or snow shortly after a south wind.
5. A *red* sky at sunrise can also be a warning of coming rain.
6. Red skies in the evening *promise* clear weather.
7. Trees with curling leaves are a *promise* of a coming storm.
8. If bees stay *inside* the hive, a storm is on the way.
9. Just before a storm, ordinary *daily* sounds are often louder.
10. With these tips you can predict the weather *daily.*

B. DRAFTING SKILL

Using Words as Different Parts of Speech For each sentence, write your own sentence, using the word in italics. Use the italicized word as the part of speech shown in parentheses.

11. Many people *turn* to an almanac for information about the weather and other topics. (Noun)
12. Almanacs have been *around* for ages. (Preposition)
13. *In* fact, almanacs are among the earliest published works. (Adverb)
14. An almanac from ancient Egypt has *lists* of religious festivals and lucky and unlucky days. (Verb)
15. Later almanacs even forecasted the *weather.* (Adjective)
16. These forecasts helped guide explorers like Christopher Columbus *across* the seas. (Adverb)
17. The oldest almanac published in this *country* first appeared in 1792. (Adjective)
18. It offered numerous tips *on* planting. (Adverb)
19. Most almanacs *forecast* the weather months in advance. (Noun)
20. These *forecasts* are right eight times out of ten. (Verb)

Writing Theme
Weather and Almanacs

FOR MORE PRACTICE
See page 522.

Writing Theme: Weather and Almanacs

Other related areas students might wish to explore as writing topics include the following:

- *The Old Farmer's Almanac*
- a meteorologist's training
- types of clouds
- how lightning forms
- the water cycle

Answers to Practice Your Skills

A. Concept Check
Parts of Speech

1. Adjective
2. Adjective
3. Noun
4. Verb
5. Adjective
6. Verb
7. Noun
8. Preposition
9. Adjective
10. Adverb

B. Drafting Skill
Using Words as Different Parts of Speech

Answers will vary. Sample answers are shown below.

11. It was not his *turn* to move his game piece.
12. She lives *around* the corner.
13. Bring the cat *in.*
14. The chart *lists* bestsellers.
15. Did you hear the *weather* report?
16. At this part of the stream, you need a boat to go *across.*
17. I like *country* music.
18. Turn the kettle *on.*
19. The weather *forecast* predicted snow.
20. A meteorologist *forecasts* the weather.

CHECK POINT

Writing Theme: Adventure Stories

Other related areas students might wish to explore as writing topics include the following:

- *Twenty Thousand Leagues Under the Sea,* the Disney film, compared to the novel
- lost pirate treasures
- the novels of H. G. Wells
- the first submarines

MIXED REVIEW • PAGES 516–519

You may wish to use this activity to check students' mastery of the following concepts:

- What are conjunctions?
- using words as different parts of speech

A.

1. was attacking and sinking; Verb
2. Ned Land and a French professor; Subject
3. An explosion sent them overboard, but they were rescued; Sentence
4. Captain Nemo and the *Nautilus;* Object P
5. oxygen, electricity, and fuel; Object
6. Food and clothing; Subject
7. walked and hunted; Verb
8. For months they sailed around the world, and they experienced many adventures; Sentence
9. Nemo or the ship; Object P
10. submarines or atomic power; Object P

B.

11. sail, Verb
12. pirate, Noun
13. pirate, Adjective
14. plan, Verb
15. plan, Noun
16. sail, Noun
17. inside, Adverb
18. treasure, Noun
19. gold, Noun
20. gold, Adjective

Writing Theme
Adventure Stories

CHECK POINT

MIXED REVIEW • PAGES 516–519

A. In each of the following sentences, write and label the compound part as *Subject, Verb, Object,* or *Sentence.* For a compound object of a preposition, use the label *Object P.*

1. Apparently a monster was attacking and sinking ships.
2. Ned Land and a French professor tried unsuccessfully to destroy the monster.
3. An explosion sent them overboard, but they were rescued.
4. They had come up against Captain Nemo and the *Nautilus.*
5. The underwater ship had oxygen, electricity, and fuel.
6. Food and clothing came from the sea.
7. With special equipment they walked and hunted on the ocean floor.
8. For months they sailed around the world, and they experienced many adventures.
9. They woke up one morning on an island, with no sign of Nemo or the ship.
10. Jules Verne published the story *Twenty Thousand Leagues Under the Sea* in 1870, before submarines or atomic power.

B. Write the italicized words in the following sentences and identify the part of speech of each.

11. Armed with a treasure map, Jim Hawkins, Squire Trelawney, and Dr. Livesey *sail* off to find gold.
12. Long John Silver, the ship's cook, is really a *pirate,* however.
13. Several of his *pirate* friends are part of the crew.
14. They *plan* to take over the ship.
15. Jim, however, overhears their *plan.*
16. Shortly after going ashore, Jim looks back to see a skull-and-crossbones flag flying above the *sail.*
17. On the island, the pirates find a chest, but nothing is *inside.*
18. Ben Gunn, a pirate marooned on the island for three years, has already found the *treasure.*
19. Eventually Jim and his friends get the *gold.*
20. Long John Silver escapes with a bag of *gold* coins.

ADDITIONAL PRACTICE

A. Recognizing Prepositions and Prepositional Phrases Write the prepositional phrases in the following sentences. Underline the object or objects of each preposition.

1. Imagine a huge forest growing in a hot, steamy environment.
2. In a tropical rain forest, the tallest trees rise nearly two hundred feet above the ground.
3. Direct sunlight reaches only the highest of their branches.
4. Only dim light filters through the leaves to the ground.
5. Thundershowers occur often throughout the year.
6. However, few raindrops fall directly to the ground.
7. Water drips down tree trunks or falls from leaves.
8. The place teems with wildlife.
9. Many animals spend their entire lives in the trees.
10. Frogs, toads, lizards, and snakes dwell among the branches.
11. Flying squirrels and flying lemurs glide from tree to tree.
12. Monkeys scamper along branches or swing from vines.
13. Bats, gibbons, monkeys, squirrels, and toucans eat nuts and fruits from the highest branches.
14. Few low-growing plants can live in the dim light of the forest floor.
15. You could easily walk through most parts of such a forest, among the fallen leaves.

B. Using Pronouns as Objects of Prepositions Write the correct form of the pronoun in parentheses.

16. One writer found an African rain forest quite useful to (he, him) as a setting for adventure stories.
17. Edgar Rice Burroughs wrote many books, but the most famous of (they, them) is *Tarzan of the Apes*.
18. The Tarzan stories are still familiar to (we, us) today.
19. The son of an English nobleman, Tarzan is lost as an infant in the jungle—where death waits for most people, but not for (he, him).
20. Instead, he is raised by a tribe of great apes, and an incredible series of exciting events unfold for Tarzan and (they, them).
21. It is easy for (he, him) to communicate with the animals.

GRAMMAR HANDBOOK 40

Writing Theme
Rain Forests

GRAMMAR HANDBOOK 40

ADDITIONAL PRACTICE

Each of these exercises correlates to a section of Handbook 40, "Prepositions and Conjunctions." The exercises may be used for more practice, for reteaching, or for review of the concepts presented.

Additional Resource

Grammar and Usage Practice Book, p. 76

Writing Theme: Rain Forests

Other related areas students might wish to explore as writing topics include the following:

- native peoples of the Amazon rain forest
- plant life of the rain forests
- rain forests of the northwestern United States
- efforts to save the rain forests

A. Recognizing Prepositions and Prepositional Phrases
Answers are shown on page.

B. Using Pronouns as Objects of Prepositions
Answers are shown on page.

22. Eventually Tarzan meets Jane and falls in love with (she, her).
23. The stories about (he, him) and (she, her) are widely read.
24. In the film version of the story, a chimpanzee named Cheeta lives in the jungle with Jane and (he, him).
25. Today, all this might seem unlikely to you and (I, me).

C. *Among* and *Between* Choose and write the correct preposition from the two given in parentheses.

26. (Among, Between) the world's tropical rain forests, the Amazon rain forest is the largest.
27. It lies (among, between) the Andes and the Atlantic.
28. It will be hard to keep a balance (between, among) protecting the environment and using the resources.
29. Scientists estimate that (between, among) 40 million and 60 million acres of rain forest are destroyed yearly.
30. Governments will have to choose (among, between) several different approaches to the problem.

D. Using Conjunctions Write each sentence pair as a single sentence, using *and, but,* or *or.* Add commas where needed.

31. The natives of the Amazon forest are highly inventive. They also value generosity.
32. Some are farmers. Most are hunters and gatherers.
33. They invented the hammock. They also created blowguns.
34. These forest dwellers have an interesting history. Their future is uncertain.
35. They could survive in many places. They could disappear.

E. Identifying Parts of Speech Write each italicized word and identify its part of speech.

36. The *outside* world knows little of life *inside* the forest.
37. The Amazon flows *past* the little villages as it did in the *past.*
38. However, times are changing *along* this river, and the forest people may have no choice but to go *along* with the changes.
39. The life they have lived *over* centuries may be almost *over.*
40. *On* the other hand, perhaps their traditions will live *on.*

C. *Among* and *Between*
Answers are shown on page.

D. Using Conjunctions
Answers may vary slightly. See typical answers below.

31. The natives of the Amazon forest are highly inventive, and they also value generosity.
32. Some are farmers, but most are hunters and gatherers.
33. They invented the hammock and also created blowguns.
34. These forest dwellers have an interesting history, but their future is uncertain.
35. They could survive in many places, or they could disappear.

E. Identifying Parts of Speech

36. outside, Adjective; inside, Preposition
37. past, Preposition; past, Noun
38. along, Preposition; along, Adverb
39. over, Preposition; over, Adjective
40. On, Preposition; on, Adverb

522 Grammar Handbook

REVIEW

A. Prepositional Phrases Write the prepositional phrases in the following sentences. Underline the object or objects of each preposition.

1. In 1991, two hikers made a strange discovery in the Alps.
2. They were walking along a snow-covered mountain ridge.
3. They spotted part of a skull in a melting glacier.
4. To their surprise, the skull was part of a mummified body.
5. Scientists were soon at work on this cold, lonely site.
6. In a short while, a startling discovery was made.
7. The body was that of a prehistoric man who had died, and whose body had lain there for over 5,000 years.
8. Around the body were many of his belongings.
9. Among them were leather clothes, a bow, arrows, and an ax.
10. Without a doubt, this was one of the most important discoveries of its kind in recent years.

B. Pronouns and Prepositions Write the correct pronoun or preposition given from the two in parentheses.

11. (Among, Between) the prehistoric man's belongings was a pair of shoes.
12. His shoes were different from those used by (we, us) today.
13. Scientists think that for (he, him) and others of his time, shoemaking may have been part of daily life.
14. Each shoe has a bottom sole and an upper flap, both of (them, they) made of leather.
15. (Among, Between) these parts is a socklike net sewn onto the sole.
16. Roswitha Goedecker-Ciolek is (among, between) the experts studying the shoes.
17. According to (she, her) and others on the team, the man stuffed grass into the nets so that the shoes would fit snugly.
18. It would have been easy for (he, him) to replace the grass when it became dirty or matted.
19. It seems clear to (she, her) that the man didn't remove his shoes often; they were too delicate.
20. These shoes may seem crude to you or (I, me), but they offered warmth and protection.

GRAMMAR HANDBOOK 40

Writing Theme
Stone-Age Man

GRAMMAR HANDBOOK 40

REVIEW

These exercises may be used as a mixed review or as an informal evaluation of the skills presented in Handbook 40, "Prepositions and Conjunctions."

Additional Resources

Grammar and Usage Practice Book, p. 77
Tests and Writing Assessment Prompts, Mastery Test, pp. 41–42
Elaboration, Revision, and Proofreading Practice, p. 29

Writing Theme: Stone-Age Man

Other related areas students might wish to explore as writing topics include the following:

- characteristics of Stone Age civilization
- Neanderthal or Cro-Magnon Man
- methods used by archaeologists

A. Prepositional Phrases
Answers are shown on page.

B. Pronouns and Prepositions
Answers are shown on page.

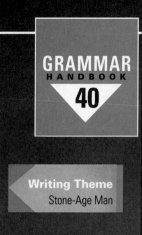

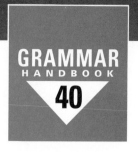

C. Conjunctions and Compound Constructions

Answers may vary slightly. See typical answers below.

21. Scientists do not know where this Stone Age man lived or why he was in the mountains.
22. A snowstorm or an avalanche probably killed him.
23. The man was 5 feet 4 inches tall and twenty-five to thirty-five years old.
24. Scientists may not be sure of the man's home, but they believe he was a herdsman or hunter from a nearby village.
25. There were many such villages, but scientists know little about them.
26. Most of the man's tools were made of copper or flint.
27. He carried a small box filled with leaves wrapped around pieces of charcoal, but we can only guess about their use.
28. The man probably carried glowing charcoal from his last fire and used it to start a fire at the next camp.

D. Words as Different Parts of Speech

29. about, Preposition
30. remain, Verb
31. about, Adverb
32. search, Adjective
33. search, Noun
34. use, Verb
35. use, Noun
36. around, Adverb
37. remains, Noun
38. Around, Preposition

C. Conjunctions and Compound Constructions Combine each of the following pairs of sentences to form a single sentence. Add conjunctions and commas where needed. Omit italicized words.

21. Scientists do not know where this Stone Age man lived. *They also do not know* why he was in the mountains.
22. A snowstorm probably killed him. *It might have been* an avalanche.
23. The man was 5 feet 4 inches tall. *He was* twenty-five to thirty-five years old.
24. Scientists may not be sure of the man's home. They believe he was a herdsman or hunter from a nearby village.
25. There were many such villages. Scientists know little about them.
26. Most of the man's tools were made of copper. *Some were of* flint.
27. He carried a small box filled with leaves wrapped around pieces of charcoal. We can only guess about their use.
28. The man probably carried glowing charcoal from his last fire. *He* used it to start a fire at the next camp.

D. Words as Different Parts of Speech. Write each word in italics. Identify its part of speech by writing *Noun, Verb, Adjective,* or *Preposition*.

29. Scientists believe the man died *about* 3000 B.C.
30. However, there *remain* many mysteries about this man.
31. For one thing, why was he walking *about* on this mountain?
32. Maybe he was part of a *search* party looking for copper.
33. Perhaps he was on a *search* for lost sheep or goats.
34. The man's bow is unfinished; clearly he did not *use* it.
35. An unfinished bow is of little *use* to anyone.
36. Possibly he was looking *around* for some materials to finish his bow.
37. As scientists study the man's *remains,* they may find the answers to their questions.
38. *Around* these mountains, they will also seek other clues to the ancient past.

WRITING CONNECTIONS

Elaboration, Revision, and Proofreading

On a separate sheet of paper, revise the following set of directions for assembling a pizza. Use the instructions given at the bottom of the page. Then proofread the directions for errors in grammar, capitalization, punctuation, and spelling. Notice the use of prepositions and conjunctions.

[1]Use a mix to prepare pizza dough and sauce or make them from scratch. [2]Then follow these directions to assemble the pizza. [3]Sprinkle flour on a cutting board. [4]Put the pizza dough on the cutting board. [5]Flatten the dough. [6]Use a rolling pin. [7]Push the rolling pin in all directions to make the pizza as round as possible. [8]Add more flour as necesary to prevent the dough from sticking. [9]Sprinkle the shreded Cheese on top of the sauce. [10]Spoon the pizza sauce on the dough and spread it evenly. [11]Finally, add your toppings. [12]Now your ready to put the pizza in the oven. [13]Bake it in an oven heeted to 425 degrees for ten to fifteen minutes. [14]You will know you're pizza is done when the crust turns golden brown.

1. Combine sentences 3 and 4, using the conjunction *and.*
2. Add the information in sentence 6 to sentence 5 as a prepositional phrase beginning with *with.*
3. Make sentence 8 clearer by adding the phrase "to the cutting board" at the end.
4. Add *next* to the beginning of sentence 10 to tell your readers you are moving on to a new step.
5. Switch the order of sentences 9 and 10 so that these steps are in the proper order.

Informative Writing: Explaining *How*

Writing directions involves giving step-by-step instructions. (See Workshop 4.) When you revise directions, look to see that you have included all the steps and have presented them in a clear order. Use prepositions and conjunctions to lead your readers clearly through the steps.

WRITING CONNECTIONS

Elaboration, Revision, and Proofreading

This activity will allow your students to see some of the concepts presented in this handbook at work in a piece of informative writing. By revising and proofreading the passage, students will have an opportunity to combine sentences using prepositions and conjunctions.

You may wish to make revision 1 with the class. Have students complete the remaining corrections and changes individually. Then read the passage line for line with the class, discussing the changes.

Rewritten paragraphs may vary slightly. See typical answer below. Proofreading errors are underscored on the page. Elements involving change are shown in boldface.

Use a mix to prepare pizza dough and sauce, or make them from scratch. Then follow these directions to assemble the pizza. **Sprinkle flour on a cutting board, and put the pizza dough on the board. Flatten the dough with a rolling pin.** Push the rolling pin in all directions to make the pizza as round as possible. Add more flour as necessary to prevent the dough from sticking **to the cutting board. Next, spoon the pizza sauce on the dough and spread it evenly. Sprinkle the shredded cheese on top of the sauce.** Finally, add your toppings. Now you're ready to put the pizza in the oven. Bake it in an oven heated to 425 degrees for ten to fifteen minutes. You will know your pizza is done when the crust turns golden brown.

Sketch Book

Objective

- To use newspaper headlines as springboards to informal writing

WRITING WARM-UPS

Begin by reminding students that they will not be graded for this assignment. The headlines and the activities are intended as springboards to get them to think imaginatively about the concepts of this Handbook. Unless students volunteer to explore more than one prompt, have them work on a single activity.

Students who have difficulty in thinking of topics will probably choose the first prompt, which supplies the beginnings of headlines. Encourage students who choose the second prompt to invent as many wacky headlines as they can within a time span you decide on.

Sketch Book

WRITING WARM-UPS

Dying planet
sends SOS to Earth

WOLF BITE TURNS TEEN GIRL INTO WEREWOLF!

Boy addicted to wood eats baseball bats!

- How would you complete these headlines? Be as outrageous as you please.

  Aliens from Outer Space ______________

  Escaped Gorilla ______________

  Dog with Two Heads ______________
- Try creating some weird and wacky headlines of your own.
- What is the strangest thing you ever saw? Describe what happened.

Subject-Verb Agreement

GRAMMAR HANDBOOK 41

WORLD TABLOID
Vol. 21, No. 4
Prehistoric crustacean terrorizes honeymoon cruise
EXCLUSIVE
Pet iguana rescues girl from burning building
Elvis spotted at Omaha drycleaner
Woman finds diamond bracelet in breakfast cereal
"What a crab!" Cleveland couple cries.

You may not agree with the outrageous claims of these headlines. Yet the headlines are in agreement—their subjects and verbs work together. When you match singular subjects with singular verbs and plural subjects with plural verbs, your sentences are in agreement.

This handbook shows you how to avoid confusion in your sentences by making sure your subjects and verbs agree.

GRAMMAR HANDBOOK 41

Subject-Verb Agreement

Objectives

- To identify and use verbs that agree with their subjects
- To avoid agreement errors with verbs that have special forms
- To avoid agreement errors in sentences beginning with *There, Here,* and *Where*
- To use verbs that agree in number with compound subjects
- To avoid agreement errors when subject and verb are separated by a prepositional phrase
- To avoid agreement errors when certain pronouns are used as subjects

Writing

- To identify and correct errors in subject-verb agreement

INTRODUCING THE HANDBOOK

You might use the *World Tabloid* headlines as springboards by asking questions that involve alternate subject-verb numbers. For example, what if more than one woman found a diamond bracelet? Point out that the verb in the headline would change: "Women *find* diamond bracelets in breakfast cereal." Then introduce the term *subject-verb agreement,* and tell students that they are going to learn about this topic in the upcoming Handbook.

SUBJECT AND VERB AGREEMENT

Objective

- To understand that subjects and verbs must agree in number

Writing

- To make subjects and verbs agree in sentences

Teaching Strategies

KEY TO UNDERSTANDING:
Remind students that the *subject* of a sentence is the word or words telling whom or what the sentence is about. The *verb* is the word or words telling what the subject does or is. Ask students to find the *subject* and *verb* in the following sentences:

The girls ride their bikes to school.

Lee's new mountain bike is black.

If students seem unsure about subject and verb, use pages 342–343 of Handbook 34, as a mini-lesson before beginning this Handbook.

INDIVIDUALIZING INSTRUCTION: ESL STUDENTS In Vietnamese, Chinese, Japanese, and many other languages, there is only one form for each verb; therefore, verbs do not have to agree in number with their subjects. Be aware that some students are unaccustomed to the concept of subject-verb agreement. Offer them many opportunities to hear and use English sentences containing present-tense verbs.

Additional Resources

Tests and Writing Assessment Prompts, Pretest, pp. 43-44

Grammar and Usage Practice Book, p. 78

Grammar Test Generator

SUBJECT AND VERB AGREEMENT

Subjects and verbs in sentences must agree in number.

A singular noun stands for one person, place, thing, or idea.

man county box invention

A plural noun stands for more than one person, place, thing, or idea.

men counties boxes inventions

Verbs can also be singular or plural. A verb must **agree in number** with its subject. A subject and verb agree in number when they are both singular or both plural.

Singular	**Plural**
One *dog barks* at the bike.	Two *dogs bark* at the bike.
The *rider falls* off.	The *riders fall* off.

Singular verbs in the present tense usually end in *s* or *es*. In the sentences above, the verbs *barks* and *falls* are singular. They are used with the singular nouns *dog* and *rider*.

When the subject is plural, the verb must be plural too. Plural verbs in the present tense do not usually end in *s*. The noun *dogs* is plural. Therefore, the plural verb *bark* does not have an *s*. The noun *riders* is plural, so *fall* does not end in *s*.

Not all singular verbs are formed by adding *-s*. Here are some examples.

Singular	Plural
match*es*	mat*ch*
scurr*ies*	scurry
miss*es*	mi*ss*
do*es*	d*o*

Practice Your Skills

A. CONCEPT CHECK

Subject and Verb Agreement Write the verb in parentheses that agrees with the subject.

1. Some problems (present, presents) unusual challenges.
2. Often an unusual solution (solve, solves) them.
3. Snoring (result, results) from a blocked air passage.
4. Experts (think, thinks) thirty million Americans snore.
5. Inventors (design, designs) anti-snoring aids.
6. Muzzles (hold, holds) snorers' mouths closed.
7. One invention (keep, keeps) sleepers from turning over.
8. Another device (strap, straps) the forearm to the chin.
9. One plan (remove, removes) salt from the snorer's diet.
10. Some people (try, tries) hypnotism to stop snoring.
11. Snorers (seek, seeks) surgery to enlarge nasal passages.
12. Earplugs (resolve, resolves) the problem for people sleeping near snorers.

B. DRAFTING SKILL

Making Subjects and Verbs Agree Write the following sentences, changing the verb in parentheses to the present tense. Make sure the verb agrees in number with the subject.

13. Inventions (helped) solve many practical problems.
14. A special book (presented) some fascinating inventions.
15. The book's title (attracted) readers: *Feminine Ingenuity: Women and Inventions in America.*
16. The book (showed) cyclists with a problem.
17. Some dogs (chased) bicycles recklessly.
18. A clever invention (repelled) the dogs.
19. Pepper boxes (attached) to the handlebars.
20. The rider (squeezed) a bulb on the box.
21. One squeeze (released) a cloud of pepper.
22. The sharp, spicy pepper (made) the dogs' eyes smart.
23. Also, the dogs (sneezed).
24. Just one dose (stopped) the dogs from chasing the bikes.
25. This unusual procedure (succeeded) in solving the problem.

Writing Theme
Unusual Solutions

FOR MORE PRACTICE
See page 539.

Writing Theme: Unusual Solutions

Suggest that students use these exercises as a springboard to writing. Other related areas that they might explore include the following:

- folk remedies
- the "inventions" of Rube Goldberg
- a personal experience with a problem and an unusual solution

Answers to Practice Your Skills

A. Concept Check
Subject and Verb Agreement

Answers are shown on page.

B. Drafting Skill
Making Subjects and Verbs Agree

13. Inventions help solve many practical problems.
14. A special book presents some fascinating inventions.
15. The book's title attracts readers: *Feminine Ingenuity: Women and Inventions in America.*
16. The book shows cyclists with a problem.
17. Some dogs chase bicycles recklessly.
18. A clever invention repels the dogs.
19. Pepper boxes attach to the handlebars.
20. The rider squeezes a bulb on the box.
21. One squeeze releases a cloud of pepper.
22. The sharp, spicy pepper makes the dogs' eyes smart.
23. Also, the dogs sneeze.
24. Just one dose stops the dogs from chasing the bikes.
25. This unusual procedure succeeds in solving the problem.

for FURTHER READING

Books to Read Students interested in problem solving may enjoy the following books:

- Vaune Ainsworth-Land and Norma Fletcher, *Making Waves with Creative Problem Solving*
- Patricia Elwell, *Creative Problem-Solving for Teens*
- Diane Draze, *Think Tank*
- Rob Nelson and Robin Smith, eds., *Mind Benders*
- Ruth B. Noller and Ernest Mauthe, *Scratching the Surface of Creative Problem Solving*

AGREEMENT WITH SPECIAL VERBS

Objectives

- To avoid agreement errors with verbs having special forms
- To avoid agreement errors in sentences that begin with *there, here,* or *where*

Writing

- To use verbs having special forms correctly in writing sentences

Teaching Strategies

CRITICAL THINKING: ANALYZING
After discussing the correct use of the forms of *be, have,* and *do* shown on the student page, have students help you list the negative contractions of these verb forms (*aren't, hasn't, doesn't,* and so on). Ask students which contractions would be correct with a singular subject and which with a plural one. Ask volunteers to use each contraction correctly in a sentence.

ASSESSMENT: SPOT CHECK
Before assigning the Practice Your Skills exercises, verify students' understanding by having them identify the subjects of the following sentences. (See single underlining below.)

Here (is/are) the pilot's gloves.

Where (is/are) the old biplanes?

There (is/are) one of them on the runway.

Then ask students to choose the correct verb form for each sentence. (See double underlining.) Have students share and explain their answers.

SPEAKING AND LISTENING In informal speech, some people use the singular verb *is* with the words *There* and *Here,* regardless of the subject. In these situations errors, such as "There's too many boys in the auditorium," are commonplace. Emphasize to students that in writing, they must be sure that a verb that accompanies an initial *There* or *Here* agrees with the subject. Encourage students to find the subject by looking at the nouns or pronouns that follow the verb.

AGREEMENT WITH SPECIAL VERBS

Some verbs have special forms. Follow the rules of agreement for these verbs.

Special Forms of Certain Verbs

A few verbs have special forms. Make sure you choose the verb form that agrees in number with your subject.

Is, Was, Are, Were The verb forms *is* and *was* are singular. The forms *are* and *were* are plural.

Singular Lily *is* a detective. Lily *was* a detective.
Plural The clues *are* here. The clues *were* here.

Has, Have The verb form *has* is singular. *Have* is plural.

Singular The investigator *has* no answer.
Plural The investigators *have* no answer.

Does, Do The verb form *does* is singular. *Do* is plural.

Singular Lewis *does*n't like mysteries.
Plural They *do*n't like mysteries.

Writing TIP

Remember to find the subject of the sentence when you use contractions.

Wrong
Here's the answers.
Correct
Here are the answers.

There Is, Where Is, Here Is

Many sentences begin with *There, Where,* or *Here.* These words are never subjects of sentences. To decide whether to use a singular or plural form of a verb in such a sentence, first find the subject by asking *who* or *what* before the verb.

There (is, are) the planes.

Who or *what* is *there?* The planes are.

The word *planes* is the subject, and the word *planes* is plural.

Use the plural verb *are.*

Additional Resource
Grammar and Usage Practice Book, p. 79

Practice Your Skills

A. CONCEPT CHECK

Agreement with Special Verbs Write the verb form in parentheses that agrees with the subject of each sentence.

1. The state of Vermont (has, have) many scenic mountains.
2. The Green Mountains (is, are) famous for their beauty.
3. However, the forests (has, have) a mysterious secret.
4. The mystery (is, are) more than forty years old.
5. There (was, were) six strange disappearances on a hiking trail called the Long Trail.
6. Authorities (does, do) not know what happened.
7. Two of the people (was, were) experienced hikers.
8. Here (is, are) another puzzling fact.
9. Only one person's body (was, were) ever found.
10. Mysteriously, the body (was, were) in an open spot in the woods.
11. Where (is, are) the other people?
12. Searchers (has, have) never found clues.
13. (Was, Were) the hikers victims of foul play?
14. (Doesn't, Don't) the mystery intrigue you?

B. DRAFTING SKILL

Making Subjects and Verbs Agree Write the present tense of each verb in parentheses in these sentences. Make sure the verb agrees in number with the subject.

15. There (be) strange tales about the Bermuda Triangle.
16. The Triangle (be) an area of the ocean near Florida.
17. Sometimes, vessels (have) difficulty there.
18. In fact, there (be) reports of vessels disappearing and strange radio signals.
19. Often, wreckage (do) not even appear.
20. Where (have) these vessels gone?
21. Here (be) one explanation.
22. The vessels (be) thrown off course by violent storms.
23. (Have) any investigator found definite evidence?
24. The many theories (do) not explain the mystery.

Writing Theme Unexplained Mysteries

FOR MORE PRACTICE
See page 539.

Writing Theme: Unexplained Mysteries

Suggest that students use these exercises as a springboard to writing. Other related areas that they might explore include the following:
- where the Anasazi came from and why they vanished
- the lost continent of Atlantis
- the Loch Ness monster
- the Yeti, or Abominable Snowman

Answers to Practice Your Skills

A. Concept Check
Agreement with Special Verbs

Answers are shown on page.

B. Drafting Skill
Making Subjects and Verbs Agree

15. are
16. is
17. have
18. are
19. does
20. have
21. is
22. are
23. Has
24. do

for FURTHER READING

Books to Read Students interested in unsolved mysteries might enjoy the following books:
- Daniel Cohen, *Mysteries of the World* and *Missing! The Stories of Strange Disappearances*
- Thomas G. Gunning, *Unexplained Mysteries*
- Stephen Tchudi, *Probing the Unknown: from Myth to Science*

CHECK ✓ POINT

Writing Theme: Help Yourself

Other related areas students might wish to explore as writing topics include the following:

- vending machines
- drive-through restaurants
- the ideal self-serve bagel bar

MIXED REVIEW • PAGES 528–531

You may wish to use this activity to check students' mastery of the following concepts:

- subject and verb agreement
- agreement with special verbs

1. Do most people like self-service in cafeterias?
2. Customers enjoy choosing their own food.
3. There are stories about the history of cafeterias.
4. The first cafeterias were for hungry factory workers.
5. Correct
6. There were many diners pleased with the low prices too.
7. Where were the first cafeterias located?
8. Correct
9. Today, almost every person has eaten in a cafeteria.
10. Correct
11. Before 1920, though, stores were not self-service.
12. Doesn't every shopper know about the first self-service market?
13. Correct
14. His store designs have a patent.
15. The diagram looks like a giant maze.
16. "Where are the canned soups?" asks a customer.
17. "Here are the soups, ma'am, in aisle two," answers a clerk.
18. Originally the stores were unusual to shoppers.
19. Now, however, most grocery stores use self-service.
20. Correct
21. Visitors have a unique chance to step back in time.
22. The museum's exhibit tries to recapture the era.
23. Old brands line the shelves.
24. There are old price stickers too.
25. Do shoppers believe a price of thirty-seven cents for pancake mix?

Writing Theme
Help Yourself

Clarence Saunders, inventor of the first self-service grocery store, developed a patented automated grocery machine for his store called the Keedoozle (adapted from the phrase "key does all").

CHECK ✓ POINT
MIXED REVIEW • PAGES 528–531

If a sentence has an error in agreement, write the sentence correctly. If a sentence is correct, write *Correct.*

1. Does most people like self-service in cafeterias?
2. Customers enjoys choosing their own food.
3. There's stories about the history of cafeterias.
4. The first cafeterias was for hungry factory workers.
5. In the 1890s, a quick meal was important to them.
6. There was many diners pleased with the low prices too.
7. Where was the first cafeterias located?
8. Kansas City was one of the first places.
9. Today, almost every person have eaten in a cafeteria.
10. The grocery store is another self-service business.
11. Before 1920, though, stores was not self-service.
12. Don't every shopper know about the first self-service market?
13. The inventor was Clarence Saunders.
14. His store designs has a patent.
15. The diagram look like a giant maze.
16. "Where are the canned soups?" ask a customer.
17. "Here's the soups, ma'am, in aisle two," answers a clerk.
18. Originally the stores was unusual to shoppers.
19. Now, however, most grocery stores uses self-service.
20. There's a model of Saunders's first store in Memphis.
21. Visitors has a unique chance to step back in time.
22. The museum's exhibit try to recapture the era.
23. Old brands lines the shelves.
24. There's old price stickers too.
25. Does shoppers believe a price of thirty-seven cents for pancake mix?

SPECIAL AGREEMENT PROBLEMS

Watch for compound subjects and prepositional phrases when making subjects and verbs agree.

Compound Subjects

When two or more parts of a compound subject are joined by the conjunction *and,* use the plural form of the verb.

The hiker and the guide *are* amazed.
Water and steam *shoot* into the air.
Geysers and hot springs *do* not *behave* in exactly the same way.

When the parts are joined by *or, either/or,* or *neither/nor,* use the form of the verb that agrees with the subject closest to the verb.

Clint or Ross *is* reading about geysers.
Either these books or that article *has* good pictures.
Neither a picture nor videotapes *show* the force of water.

Prepositional Phrases After the Subject

Be careful with prepositional phrases that come between the subject and the verb. Do not confuse the subject of the verb with the object of the preposition. Look at this example.

The explanation for geysers is simple.

What is the sentence about? *Explanation*
Explanation is the subject of the sentence.

Explanation is singular, so you use the singular verb *is.*
For geysers is a prepositional phrase. *Geysers* is the object of the preposition *for;* it is not the subject of the sentence.

For more information about prepositional phrases, see Grammar Handbook 40, pages 506–509.

Writing TIP

Casual conversation contains many errors. To make subjects and verbs agree, do not rely on what "sounds right." Follow the rules.

SPICE BOX

To reinforce students' awareness of subject-verb agreement and to encourage them to read newspapers and magazines, "hire" students as grammar sleuths. Give them one week to collect as many examples as possible of subject-verb agreement errors in the print media. Assign points as follows: error in daily newspaper—2 points, error in weekly magazine or newspaper—5 points, error in monthly magazine—10 points

At the end of the week, have students discuss and correct the errors. Consider providing prizes or rewards for first-, second-, and third-place winners.

SPECIAL AGREEMENT PROBLEMS

Objectives

- To use verbs that agree in number with compound subjects
- To avoid agreement errors when a prepositional phrase separates subject and verb

Writing

- To use proofreading skills to correct errors in subject-verb agreement

Teaching Strategies

HELPFUL HINT After discussing agreement with compound subjects, write the following sentences on the board. Ask students which verb is correct (underlined below) and why.

Hot springs and a geyser (warms, <u>warm</u>) the city of Reykjavik, Iceland.

Monkeys and other animals (enjoys, <u>enjoy</u>) the natural thermal pools of Northern Japan.

Spring or fall (<u>is</u>, are) best for visiting Yellowstone Park's geysers.

Neither Tony nor Anna (have, <u>has</u>) ever seen a geyser.

STUMBLING BLOCK As you discuss the use of prepositional phrases, emphasize that the subject of a sentence is never found in a prepositional phrase. (Students can also apply this rule as they learn about subject-verb agreement involving indefinite pronouns, discussed on page 536.)

LINKING GRAMMAR AND WRITING Point out that inserting a prepositional phrase between a subject and its verb is a way to add information to a sentence and a way to improve sentence variety. Remind students to double-check for subject-verb agreement when they insert prepositional phrases in this way.

Additional Resource

Grammar and Usage Practice Book, p. 80

Writing Theme: Geysers

Other related areas students might wish to explore as writing topics include the following:

- Iceland's geysers
- Yellowstone National Park
- hot springs
- geothermal power

Answers to Practice Your Skills

A. Concept Check

Special Agreement Problems

Answers are shown on page.

Writing Theme
Geysers

Practice Your Skills

A. CONCEPT CHECK

Special Agreement Problems Write the verb form in parentheses that agrees with the subject of each sentence.

1. Jubilee Grotto and Crystal Cone (erupts, erupt) regularly and spectacularly.
2. Neither lava nor rocks (comes, come) out, however.
3. Instead, plumes of steam (shoots, shoot) skyward.
4. The Valley of the Geysers (is, are) their home.
5. Geysers (is, are) the rarest wonders of the world.
6. Reports and studies about the region (mentions, mention) only twenty-three geysers.
7. However, shouts of delight (was, were) heard recently.
8. Visitors to the region (has, have) counted two hundred!
9. Few people on earth (has, have) seen them.
10. Only Russian scientists or officials (was, were) there.
11. Now these Russian frontiers on the Kamchatka Peninsula (is, are) open to outsiders.
12. Either earthquakes or temperature changes (causes, cause) less frequent eruptions.
13. Changes in geyser activity (happens, happen) often.
14. Heat or underground forces (affects, affect) eruption.
15. Drilling and other human activities (does, do) damage.
16. This valley of springs and steam (is, are) unspoiled.

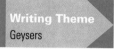

17. Steep trails and harsh terrain (hinders, hinder) visitors.
18. The possibility of tourism (is, are) being considered.
19. The valley and the geysers (needs, need) protection, however.
20. Neither tourists nor the weekend visitor (has, have) easy access to this incredible region—for now.

B. DRAFTING SKILL

Using Verbs That Agree with Subjects Write the sentences, using the present-tense form of the verb in parentheses.

21. Hot water or cold water (spout) from the earth.
22. Some spouts in Utah (be) called "soda-pop geysers."
23. Soda pop and other fizzy drinks (have) carbonation.
24. Dissolved carbon dioxide gas in underground pockets (make) these fake geysers erupt.
25. A well or other drilling operations (cause) them.
26. These wells of ice-cold water (erupt) like geysers.
27. Hot-water plumes or steam (be) necessary for true geysers.
28. Rest periods and activity periods (be) needed too.
29. Four phases of activity (occur) in true geysers.
30. Neither hot springs nor a "soda-pop geyser" (qualify).

C. PROOFREADING

Finding Errors in Agreement Rewrite the following paragraph, correcting any errors in subject-verb agreement. Also correct errors in grammar, spelling, capitalization, and punctuation. (15 errors)

Each year, millions of tourists flock to yellowstone national park. Here, minrals and the earth's inner heat creates unbeleivable effects. Lakes of colored mud bubbles furiously, springs and geysers burst from cracks in the ground. Hot water jets and vapor sprays high into the air. Tiny plants of brilliant color fills steaming pools. Hot water in the center of the pools stay blue. Because the water is so hot in the center, neither yellow algae nor brown algae grow there. Tiny red mushrooms or thick moss are found near the edges of the pools. A bordwalk for spectators go right to the water's edge.

FOR MORE PRACTICE
See page 540.

B. Drafting Skill
Using Verbs That Agree with Subjects

21. Hot water or cold water spouts from the earth.
22. Some spouts in Utah are called "soda-pop geysers."
23. Soda pop and other fizzy drinks have carbonation.
24. Dissolved carbon dioxide gas in underground pockets makes these fake geysers erupt.
25. A well or other drilling operations cause them.
26. These wells of ice-cold water erupt like geysers.
27. Hot-water plumes or steam is necessary for true geysers.
28. Rest periods and activity periods are needed too.
29. Four phases of activity occur in true geysers.
30. Neither hot springs nor a "soda-pop geyser" qualifies.

C. Proofreading
Finding Errors in Agreement

Errors in proofreading exercises are counted as follows: (a) Each word is counted as one error. For example, a misspelled word is one error; two initials and a last name not capitalized are counted as three errors. (b) Run-on sentences and sentence fragments are each counted as one error, even though the correction involves both punctuation and capitalization corrections.

Errors are shown on page. The correctly rewritten paragraph appears below.

Each year, millions of tourists flock to Yellowstone National Park. Here, minerals and the earth's inner heat create unbelievable effects. Lakes of colored mud bubble furiously. Springs and geysers burst from cracks in the ground. Hot water jets and vapor spray high into the air. Tiny plants of brilliant color fill steaming pools. Hot water in the center of the pools stays blue. Because the water is so hot in the center, neither yellow algae nor brown algae grows there. Tiny red mushrooms or thick moss is found near the edges of the pools. A boardwalk for spectators goes right to the water's edge.

AGREEMENT WITH PRONOUNS

Objectives

- To avoid errors in subject-verb agreement when the pronouns *I* and *you* and indefinite pronouns are used as subjects

Writing

- To use the pronouns *I* and *you* and indefinite pronouns correctly in sentences

Teaching Strategies

INDIVIDUALIZING INSTRUCTION: LEP STUDENTS Some students speak dialects in which singular verb forms are acceptable with *I* and *you.* Remind students that working "by ear" is not a sure test for correctness; the written forms used in standard English may differ from what people sometimes say or hear.

SPEAKING AND LISTENING Point out that some indefinite pronouns—such as *everyone* and *everybody*—can be tricky because they seem to refer to more than one person. To emphasize that these pronouns are singular, write the following sentences on the board. Have students read the sentences aloud, filling in different present-tense verbs for each sentence.

When the girls' track team goes out for pizza, everybody _______ for her favorite topping.

Nobody _______ her pizza plain.

Everyone ______ to choose her own extras.

Luckily, each of the girls ______ pepperoni.

Additional Resource

Grammar and Usage Practice Book, p. 81

AGREEMENT WITH PRONOUNS

Follow special rules of agreement with the pronouns *I* and *you* and with indefinite pronouns.

I and *You*

The pronoun *I* stands for a single person. However, th only singular verb forms used with it are *am* and *was* Otherwise, the plural form of the verb is always used.

I *am* a fussy eater. I *was* a young gourmet.
I *do* the cooking. I *have* an award. I *enjoy* winning.

Although *you* can be singular or plural, always use a plura verb with this pronoun.

"You *were* messy," the judge said to the contestant.
"You *were* messy," the judge said to the contestants.

Indefinite Pronouns

The indefinite pronouns below are singular. They use singular verbs.

either	each	everyone	anyone
neither	one	everybody	nobody

Either *likes* rice.
Neither *eats* with chopsticks.

In the sentences above, a singular verb follows a singular subject. When a prepositional phrase follows one of these pronouns, the verb must still agree with the pronoun subject.

Either of the boys *likes* rice.
Neither of the girls *eats* with chopsticks.

For more information about indefinite pronouns, see Grammar Handbook 37, pages 449–451.

Practice Your Skills

A. CONCEPT CHECK

Agreement with Pronouns Write the correct verb.

1. Everybody (has, have) a favorite food or snack.
2. Each of the world's nations (is, are) known for a particular kind of food.
3. If you (is, are) French, you (has, have) probably eaten escargots.
4. I (knows, know) that *escargots* is French for "snails."
5. Someday, I (am, is, are) going to try frog legs.
6. Each of these French dishes (is, are) cooked in butter.
7. Neither (is, are) prepared without garlic.
8. Anyone from Greek towns (talks, talk) about octopus.
9. One (cuts, cut) dried octopus into chunks and broils it.
10. (Has, Have) you ever tasted sushi?
11. Almost everyone in Japan (likes, like) this dish.
12. Nobody in the restaurants (turns, turn) down raw fish.

B. DRAFTING SKILL

Using Verbs with Pronouns Write each sentence, changing the verb in parentheses to its present-tense form.

13. Everyone in Asian countries (eat) rice daily.
14. You (do) not like rice as much as I (do).
15. (Have) you read that rice is a kind of grass?
16. Anyone (use) chopsticks or fingers to eat rice.
17. I (have) learned of other uses for rice, though.
18. Anybody with cows or pigs (feed) them rice bran.
19. Another of the uses (be) for oil.
20. Nobody (throw) away the rice hulls or stalks.
21. Almost everybody in industry (use) the byproducts.
22. Each of the uses (be) clever.
23. I (know) it's used for fuel, fertilizer, and clothes!
24. One of the varieties of rice (be) called miracle rice.
25. Someone (have) tried to solve world hunger.
26. Everyone (do) not have faith in miracle rice.
27. No one among the growers (be) discouraged, though.

Writing Theme
International Foods

Writing Theme: International Foods

Other related areas students might wish to explore as writing topics include the following:

- foods of other specific cultures
- a favorite family meal or recipe
- corn or beans, other dietary staples
- how plant hybrids are developed

Answers to Practice Your Skills

A. Concept Check

Agreement with Pronouns

Answers are shown on page.

B. Drafting Skill

Using Verbs with Pronouns

13. Everyone in Asian countries eats rice daily.
14. You do not like rice as much as I do.
15. Have you read that rice is a kind of grass?
16. Anyone uses chopsticks or fingers to eat rice.
17. I have learned of other uses for rice, though.
18. Anybody with cows or pigs feeds them rice bran.
19. Another of the uses is for oil.
20. Nobody throws away the rice hulls or stalks.
21. Almost everybody in industry uses the byproducts.
22. Each of the uses is clever.
23. I know it's used for fuel, fertilizer, and clothes!
24. One of the varieties of rice is called miracle rice.
25. Someone has tried to solve world hunger.
26. Everyone does not have faith in miracle rice.
27. No one among the growers is discouraged, though.

CHECK POINT

Writing Theme: Collaboration

Other related areas students might wish to explore as writing topics include the following:

- comedy teams, such as Burns and Allen or Laurel and Hardy
- Sir Edmund Hillary and Tenzing Norgay, conquerors of Mount Everest
- Seeing-Eye dogs, examples of human-animal collaboration
- the collaboration required for success in team sports

MIXED REVIEW • PAGES 533–537

You may wish to use this activity to check students' mastery of the following concepts:

- special agreement problems
- agreement with pronouns

1. Everyone has heard of famous collaborators.
2. Haven't you read stories by Ellery Queen?
3. Frederic Dannay and Manfred B. Lee were Ellery Queen.
4. Dannay and Lee were cousins and friends.
5. Neither of them was trained as a detective.
6. Each of them was famous only as a collaborator.
7. One team of inventors has not become famous.
8. Anybody with a knowledge of inventions remembers Samuel Morse, the inventor of the telegraph.
9. Neither you nor I know his partners' names today.
10. Neither of Morse's partners was able to get money for work on the telegraph.
11. Morse, without his partners, was given congressional help for an experiment.
12. Anyone from Baltimore or Washington remembers the location of the first experimental telegraph line.
13. The Morse code and the telegraph are what we remember Samuel Morse for.
14. Correct
15. William Hanna and Joseph Barbera are familiar to us.
16. Correct
17. Everyone loves the Tom and Jerry characters.
18. Each of the characters by this team is lovable and funny.
19. Correct
20. One of the hardest tasks is collaboration, I think.

Writing Theme
Collaboration

CHECK POINT

MIXED REVIEW • PAGES 533–537

Write the following sentences and correct all errors in subject and verb agreement. If a sentence is correct, write *Correct.*

1. Everyone have heard of famous collaborators.
2. Hasn't you read stories by Ellery Queen?
3. Frederic Dannay and Manfred B. Lee was Ellery Queen.
4. Dannay and Lee was cousins and friends.
5. Neither of them were trained as a detective.
6. Each of them were famous only as a collaborator.
7. One team of inventors have not become famous.
8. Anybody with a knowledge of inventions remember Samuel Morse, the inventor of the telegraph.
9. Neither you nor I knows his partners' names today.
10. Neither of Morse's partners were able to get money for work on the telegraph.
11. Morse, without his partners, were given congressional help for an experiment.
12. Anyone from Baltimore or Washington remember the location of the first experimental telegraph line.
13. The Morse code and the telegraph is what we remember Samuel Morse for.
14. Fortunately for us, teams or partners often succeed.
15. William Hanna and Joseph Barbera is familiar to us.
16. Nobody denies their success in the cartoon world.
17. Everyone love the Tom and Jerry characters.
18. Each of the characters by this team are lovable and funny.
19. Yogi Bear and Huckleberry Hound are my favorites.
20. One of the hardest tasks are collaboration, I think.

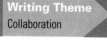

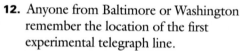

The animators William Hanna and Joseph Barbera with a few of their cartoon characters.

538 Grammar Handbook

GRAMMAR HANDBOOK 41

A. Using the Right Verb Form Write the form of the verb that agrees with the subject in each sentence.

1. People (takes, take) gears for granted.
2. Gears (makes, make) many things work.
3. Gears (connects, connect) in many different ways.
4. Usually, one gear (turns, turn) faster or slower than its partner.
5. Car ads (talks, talk) about rack-and-pinion steering.
6. A rack-and-pinion system (works, work) quite simply.
7. The driver (spins, spin) the steering wheel.
8. The pinion (rotates, rotate) like a wheel.
9. Its teeth (fits, fit) into the teeth of the rack.
10. The rack (slides, slide) back and forth.
11. Both elements (moves, move) in the same direction.
12. In this way, movement (becomes, become) easy.
13. Gears (comes, come) in a great variety of sizes and types.
14. Their names (reflects, reflect) their appearance.
15. A worm gear (looks, look) like a worm!
16. Cowboy spurs (inspires, inspire) the name "spur gear."
17. Planetary gears (resembles, resemble) planets moving around a sun.
18. Automatic transmissions (uses, use) planetary gears.
19. Books (tells, tell) about the different kinds of gears.
20. Remember, wheels (forms, form) part of most gears.

B. Writing the Correct Verb Form Write the form of the verb in parentheses that agrees with the subject.

21. (Was, Were) pens always ballpoints?
22. (Doesn't, Don't) people know how they work?
23. The process (is, are) called capillary action.
24. Capillaries (is, are) tubes, like veins in the body.
25. Where (does, do) the ink go?
26. (Here's, Here are) the answer!
27. Inside the ink tube, pressure (does, do) all the work.
28. There (is, are) pressure on the ballpoint.
29. Higher pressure (has, have) the job of releasing ink.
30. Low pressures (has, have) the job of holding in the ink.

Writing Theme
Processes

GRAMMAR HANDBOOK 41

ADDITIONAL PRACTICE

Each of these exercises correlates to a section of Handbook 41, "Subject-Verb Agreement." The exercises may be used for more practice, for reteaching, or for review of the concepts presented.

Additional Resource

Grammar and Usage Practice Book, p. 83

Writing Theme: Processes

Other related areas students might wish to explore as writing topics include the following:

- how zippers work
- the first computers
- Louis Daguerre and photography
- the invention of Braille
- why steel ships float

A. Using the Right Verb Form
Answers are shown on page.

B. Writing the Correct Verb Form
Answers are shown on page.

C. Choosing the Right Verb Form

31. Thelma, Ina, and Carl wash their hair every day.
32. Mostly, Ina or Carl fights over using the hair drier.
33. Neither the sisters nor the brother knows anything about driers.
34. Currents of electricity flow into the drier.
35. Wire coils inside the drier heat up.
36. The blades of a small fan blow the hot air out.
37. Heat and jets of air make water evaporate.
38. Soon the tangled locks of Ina's hair are dry.
39. At times, either the coil or other elements get too hot.
40. Burns and the hazards of fire are possible.
41. A thermostat inside the components senses the heat.
42. The power to the elements shuts off.
43. The heating units inside the drier cool down.
44. Before long, more wet heads require the hair drier again.
45. Aren't science and technology wonderful?

D. Making Verbs Agree with Pronouns

46. am
47. Have
48. Does
49. thanks
50. is
51. requires
52. learns
53. is
54. knows
55. remembers
56. saves
57. is
58. uses
59. Do
60. see

C. Choosing the Right Verb Form Write the sentences, correcting errors in subject-verb agreement.

31. Thelma, Ina, and Carl washes their hair every day.
32. Mostly, Ina or Carl fight over using the hair drier.
33. Neither the sisters nor the brother know anything about driers.
34. Currents of electricity flows into the drier.
35. Wire coils inside the drier heats up.
36. The blades of a small fan blows the hot air out.
37. Heat and jets of air makes water evaporate.
38. Soon the tangled locks of Ina's hair is dry.
39. At times, either the coil or other elements gets too hot.
40. Burns and the hazards of fire is possible.
41. A thermostat inside the components sense the heat.
42. The power to the elements shut off.
43. The heating units inside the drier cools down.
44. Before long more wet heads requires the hair drier again.
45. Isn't science and technology wonderful?

D. Making Verbs Agree with Pronouns Write the correct present-tense form of the verb for each sentence.

46. I (be) fascinated with photocopiers.
47. (Have) you ever made copies at the library?
48. (Do) either of us know about the inventor of copy machines?
49. Everyone who makes copies (thank) Chet Carlson.
50. One of the photocopying processes (be) completely dry.
51. Each of the other processes (require) liquid developers.
52. Everyone (learn) that Carlson invented the dry process.
53. One of his contributions (be) the process of xerography.
54. Anyone at his mother-in-law's beauty parlor (know) of him.
55. Everybody (remember) that is where he invented it.
56. Each of the uses of xerography (save) time and work.
57. Neither of these savings (be) trivial.
58. Everybody in offices (use) copy machines.
59. (Do) you recognize the corporation name that is based on the word *xerography?*
60. I (see) it: the Xerox Corporation!

540 Grammar Handbook

REVIEW

A. Making Subjects and Verbs Agree Write the verb that agrees with the subject in number.

1. Diaries (preserves, preserve) thoughts and feelings.
2. Many people (keeps, keep) diaries and journals.
3. Famous people (has, have) published theirs.
4. Where else (does, do) people share their hopes and dreams and disappointments?
5. Where else (has, have) a reader become acquainted with a queen?
6. There (is, are) important lessons to be learned from diaries.
7. Here (is, are) one example from Queen Victoria's diary.
8. Even English queens (likes, like) parties.
9. One entry (tells, tell) about her dancing until 3 A.M.!
10. Other entries (reveals, reveal) her crush on Prince Albert.
11. (Does, Do) a queen get nervous before her wedding?
12. Queen Victoria (was, were) nervous and happy.
13. "The ceremony (was, were) very imposing," she wrote.
14. Other diaries (has, have) fascinating insights too.
15. Readers (shares, share) Davy Crockett's last days.
16. There (is, are) an account of the battle at the Alamo.
17. Provisions (was, were) running out.
18. The diary (shows, show) Crockett's great courage and determination.
19. Many paragraphs (describes, describe) the battle.
20. "Shells (has, have) been falling into the fort. . . ."
21. Another paragraph (states, state) a wish for freedom.
22. His diary (recounts, recount) his last day.
23. Crockett's last entry (was, were) "Liberty and independence forever!"
24. Here (is, are) stirring pieces of eyewitness accounts.
25. Without a doubt, diaries (makes, make) fascinating reading.

B. Using the Correct Verb Write the correct present-tense form of the verb in parentheses.

26. Fame and money (be) only trifles to Thomas Edison.
27. Problems with dandruff (bother) him in July.
28. "Powerful itching of my head" (be) what he wrote.

GRAMMAR HANDBOOK 41

Writing Theme
Diaries

GRAMMAR HANDBOOK 41

REVIEW

These exercises may be used as a mixed review or as an informal evaluation of the skills presented in Handbook 41, "Subject-Verb Agreement."

Additional Resources

Grammar and Usage Practice Book, p. 83
Tests and Writing Assessment Prompts, Mastery Test, pp. 45–46
Elaboration, Revision, and Proofreading Practice, p. 30

Writing Theme: Diaries

Other related areas students might wish to explore as writing topics include the following:

- Robert F. Scott's South Pole diary
- the journals of Lewis and Clark
- notes from a naturalist's journal
- a personal memoir

A. Making Subjects and Verbs Agree
Answers are shown on page.

B. Using the Correct Verb
26. are
27. bother
28. is

29. tell
30. comes
31. are
32. are
33. does
34. haunts
35. are
36. fill
37. loves
38. has
39. do
40. has

C. Making Verbs and Pronouns Agree
Answers are shown on page.

29. Entries in Edison's diary (tell) us about the man.
30. The person behind the inventions (come) through in his plain, direct style.
31. Neither complaints nor embarrassing events (be) kept out of the diary.
32. Two keys on his piano (be) out of tune.
33. A clerk in a drugstore (do) not have peroxide.
34. A demon with eyes four hundred feet apart (haunt) his dreams.
35. Edison's comments and logic (be) keen.
36. Either nonfiction or novels (fill) part of every day for him.
37. This self-taught man of strong opinions (love) reading.
38. Lack of lessons or school (have) not discouraged or stopped him.
39. The walls of his office (do) not have diplomas.
40. He wonders if perhaps encyclopedia articles or the dictionary (have) facts about dandruff!

C. Making Verbs and Pronouns Agree Write the correct verb.

41. I (is, am, are) the famous fly on the wall—a diary!
42. (Does, Do) you know of me?
43. I (saves, save) the thoughts of John Quincy Adams, our sixth president.
44. Nobody in Congress (escapes, escape) his sharp comments.
45. Each of Thomas Jefferson's tales (is, are) retold and made fun of.
46. Everyone (knows, know) about Jefferson's tendency to exaggerate.
47. One of Adams's dislikes (is, are) newspaper editors and their stories.
48. Everybody in Congress (has, have) the same dislike, he believes.
49. Anyone from Washington also (understand, understands) Adams's notes about summer heat.
50. Neither of his two sons (wish, wishes) to swim in the Potomac River to cool off, however.

542 Grammar Handbook

WRITING CONNECTIONS

Elaboration, Revision, and Proofreading

Revise the following draft of a personal narrative by using the directions at the bottom of the page. Then proofread the narrative, making sure that all subjects and verbs agree in number. Also look for other errors in grammar, capitalization, punctuation, and spelling.

[1]When we started our band, we had a problem. [2]Bob's mom said we couldnt use there garage after just one session. [3]Because we was too loud. [4]None of the other parents even let us try. [5]Then one day Keith said, "I found a great studio for us." [6]He give us directions. [7]He told us to meat him there the next afternoon. [8]When Bob and I arrived, we was shocked. [9]Our "studio" was the parking lot of an old gas station. [10]"Don't worry," Keith said, "bands practices here all the time." [11]Then he pulled out his horn and blowed. [12]"That really sound great," Bob said. [13]"I like the way the sound echoes off the walls of the old building." [14]In addition, there were no one living nearby to complane. [15]We unpacked all of our gear. [16]We begun to play to our audience of passing cars.

1. After sentence 1, add information to explain the problem the band had: finding a place to practice without disturbing the neighbors.
2. Combine sentences 6 and 7 to make one sentence with a compound verb.
3. Make sentence 14 more complete by adding the phrase "about the noise" to the end.
4. Add "anxiously" to the beginning of sentence 15 to show how the band members prepared to play.
5. Divide the passage into paragraphs.

Narrative and Literary Writing

Writing a personal narrative is a chance to share your experiences with others. (See Workshop 3.) When you revise a narrative, make sure you have presented events in the order in which they occurred. Also make sure your subjects and verbs agree so that your readers can easily follow your story.

WRITING CONNECTIONS

Elaboration, Revision, and Proofreading

This activity will allow students to see some of the concepts presented in this Handbook at work in a personal narrative. By revising and proofreading this passage, students will have the chance to identify and correct errors in subject-verb agreement. They also will become more aware of paragraphing and style.

You might have students work in small groups to revise the passage. Then discuss the completed revision with the entire class.

Revisions may vary slightly. See a typical revision below. Elements involving changes are shown in boldface. Proofreading errors are shown on page.

When we started our band, we had a problem **finding a place to practice without disturbing the neighbors.** Bob's mom said we couldn't use their garage after just one session because we were too loud. None of the other parents even let us try.

Then one day Keith said, "I found a great studio for us." He gave us **directions and told us** to meet him there the next afternoon. When Bob and I arrived, we were shocked. Our "studio" was the parking lot of an old gas station. "Don't worry," Keith said. "Bands practice here all the time." Then he pulled out his horn and blew.

"That really sounds great," Bob said. "I like the way the sound echoes off the walls of the old building." In addition, there was no one living nearby to complain **about the noise. Anxiously,** we unpacked all of our gear. We began to play to our audience of passing cars.

Test 3

This test enables you to evaluate student mastery of the concepts taught in handbooks 40–41.

Additional Resource

Grammar and Usage Practice Book, pp. 85–86

Answer Key

Corrections for run-ons may vary.

1. D
2. B—more loosely
   C—this
3. D
4. D
5. A—makes
   B—yellow. It *or* yellow; it
6. B—aunt
7. A—are
8. A—principal
   B—Middle School
9. B—lies
10. C—has
11. C—form
12. C—Cleveland and
13. A—There are
    B—children's
14. B—calories. When
15. B—is

Skills

ASSESSMENT TEST 3 Grammar Handbooks *40–41*

Directions One or more of the underlined sections in the following sentences may contain an error in grammar, punctuation, spelling, or capitalization. Write the letter of each incorrect section. Then rewrite the section correctly. If there is no error in an item, write *D.*

Example Palindromes is (A) words or sentences that read the same forward and backward. "Madam, (B) I'm Adam" is one of the most famous (C). No error (D)

Answer A—are

1. Sometimes a flock of geese flies (A) as high as 26,000 (B) feet. That is almost five miles (C) above the earth! No error (D)

2. Which shoes fit (A) looser, (B) these (C) kind or that kind? No error (D)

3. There's (A) only one irregular verb in the Turkish (B) language. That verb is *imek,* and it means "to be." In English there are (C) sixty-eight irregular verbs. No error (D)

4. Where are (A) the science fiction (B) books shelved in this library? (C) No error (D)

5. Neither of these spices make (A) rice yellow, it (B) is saffron that turns rice golden (C). No error (D)

6. Either our neighbors (A) next door or my Aunt (B) feeds (C) our hamster when we are away. No error (D)

7. Bud Abbott and Lou Costello is (A) in the Baseball Hall of Fame (B), but neither of them ever played professional baseball. They (C) are honored for their "Who's on First?" comedy routine. No error (D)

8. The principle (A) said, "If it snows hard enough, everybody at John Wood middle school (B) goes (C) home early." No error (D)

9. A fjord is a long, narrow (A), deep inlet of the sea. A fjord lays (B) between steep cliffs (C). No error (D)

10. Neither (A) the brushes (B) nor the paint for our project have (C) arrived. No error (D)

11. Bubbles (A) in soda pop (B) forms (C) where carbon dioxide gas is present. No error (D)

12. Only two presidents of the United States have (A) entered the White House (B) as bachelors—Grover Cleveland, and (C) James Buchanan. No error (D)

13. There's (A) some childrens' (B) television shows that are really (C) educational. No error (D)

14. Cream is thicker (A) than milk and has more fat and calories when (B) you weigh each, however, milk is heavier (C) than cream. No error (D)

15. Each of these computer disks (A) are (B) full. You need (C) to get another disk. No error (D)

List of Skills Tested

1. **A**—subject-verb agreement
   B—punctuation—comma
   C—noun plural
2. **A**—subject-verb agreement
   B—comparative adjective form
   C—demonstrative adjective
3. **A**—subject-verb agreement
   B—capitalization—language
   C—subject-verb agreement
4. **A**—subject-verb agreement
   B—capitalization—common/proper noun
   C—punctuation—end marks
5. **A**—subject-verb agreement
   B—sentence fragment/run-on
   C—spelling
6. **A**—spelling
   B—capitalization—common/proper noun
   C—subject-verb agreement
7. **A**—subject-verb agreement
   B—capitalization—common/proper noun
   C—sentence fragment
8. **A**—spelling
   B—capitalization—common/proper noun
   C—subject-verb agreement
9. **A**—punctuation—comma
   B—confusing verb pairs
   C—noun plural
10. **A**—spelling
    B—noun plural
    C—subject-verb agreement
11. **A**—spelling
    B—capitalization—common/proper noun
    C—subject-verb agreement
12. **A**—subject-verb agreement
    B—capitalization—common/proper noun
    C—punctuation—comma
13. **A**—subject-verb agreement
    B—punctuation—possessive
    C—adjective/adverb confusion
14. **A**—comparative adjective form
    B—sentence fragment/run-on
    C—comparative adjective form
15. **A**—noun plural
    B—subject-verb agreement
    C—subject-verb agreement

Sketch Book

Objective

- To use writing prompts as springboards to informal writing

WRITING WARM-UPS

Tell students that this page is intended to prompt informal written responses that will not be graded. The illustration and the text provide an imaginative introduction to concepts that will be developed in the handbook. Allow students to work on one activity, unless they offer to respond to more than one prompt.

For the first writing prompt, have students brainstorm the names and some memorable attractions of theme parks they have visited or heard about. Ask one or two volunteers to name rides they particularly liked. Then have individuals begin writing about an ideal theme park.

Sketch Book

WRITING WARM-UPS

- Imagine you've been asked to develop a theme park like Safari Funland. Write a brief description of the park. What would it be called? What types of rides would the park have and what would you name them?
- Which movies or books do you like the best? Who do you think deserves to be called "great"? Make lists of movies, people, books, songs, products, or other items that are in your Top Ten.

Capitalization

GRAMMAR HANDBOOK 42

- Proper Nouns and Proper Adjectives
- More Proper Nouns
- First Words
- Outlines and Titles

Amusement park rides like the Zipper that spin 'round and 'round can make you really dizzy. Trying to remember all the rules for capitalization can make you really dizzy, too!

These rules, however, are important because capital letters are an important part of writing. Writers use them to name specific people, places, and things. This handbook will show you how to use capitalization in your writing.

GRAMMAR HANDBOOK 42

Capitalization

Objectives

- To recognize and capitalize proper nouns and proper adjectives
- To capitalize the names of months, days, holidays, and historical events
- To capitalize the names of races, religions, nationalities, and languages
- To capitalize words referring to God and to religious scriptures
- To capitalize the names of clubs, organizations, and business firms
- To capitalize the first words of sentences and of most lines of poetry
- To capitalize the first words of entries in outlines and of titles

Writing

- To identify and correct capitalization errors in writing
- To use capital letters correctly in a piece of writing

INTRODUCING THE HANDBOOK

Explain that capital letters play an important role in making written prose easier to read. Point out that they guide the reader to the beginning of a sentence and to the names of specific people, places, and things. Tell students that in this handbook, they will learn rules that will help them use capital letters correctly in their writing.

PROPER NOUNS AND PROPER ADJECTIVES

Objectives

- To recognize proper nouns and adjectives and capitalize them correctly
- To apply capitalization rules to personal and official titles
- To capitalize the pronoun *I*

Writing

- To proofread paragraphs, correcting errors in capitalization
- To capitalize words correctly in writing

Teaching Strategies

KEY TO UNDERSTANDING Before introducing the definitions of common and proper nouns and adjectives, invite students to discuss connotations of the words *common* and *proper*. For instance, which word suggests formality, uprightness, and distinctiveness? *(proper)* Then have students look at the examples of nouns on the pupil page and try to formulate their own definitions of common and proper nouns. Finally, discuss the definitions in the text with these student-generated definitions in mind.

INDIVIDUALIZING INSTRUCTION: ESL STUDENTS The writing systems of languages such as Arabic, Hindi, Chinese, Korean, and Japanese do not distinguish between lowercase and capital letters. For students who speak these languages, provide extra help with English capitalization rules. Suggest that they write each rule in a notebook, for handy reference.

ADVANCED STUDENTS Challenge students to work in groups of three to compile lists of birds, animals, or trees whose names are made up of a proper adjective and a noun, such as the Douglas fir. Students may use prior knowledge, a dictionary, an encyclopedia, or magazine articles to find examples. Invite volunteers to tell the class about a particular item on their lists, explaining the origin or significance of the proper adjective.

PROPER NOUNS AND PROPER ADJECTIVES

Capitalize proper nouns and proper adjectives.

A **common noun** is a general name for a person, a place, a thing, or an idea. A **proper noun** names a particular person, place, thing, or idea. A **proper adjective** is made from a proper noun. All proper nouns and proper adjectives are capitalized.

Common Noun	Proper Noun	Proper Adjective
peninsula	Arabia	Arabian
country	Ireland	Irish

A proper noun may be made up of one or more words. Capitalize all important words in a proper noun.

Rocky **M**ountains   **L**incoln **P**ark **Z**oo   **P**eter the **G**reat

Proper adjectives are often used with common nouns. Do not capitalize the common noun.

Irish wolfhound   **B**urmese cat   **A**merican saddle horse

There are many kinds of proper nouns. These rules will help you recognize words that need to be capitalized.

Capitalize the names of people and pets.

Begin every word in a name with a capital letter. An initial stands for a name. Write initials as capital letters. Put a period after each initial.

Ken **G**riffey, **J**r.   **E**. **B**. **W**hite   **L**assie

Often, a word for a family relation is used in place of the name of a particular person, or as part of the name. *Dad* and *Aunt Jane* are two examples. Capitalize a word used in this way.

MULTICULTURAL Connection

Some foreign languages include as part of a person's name a word (or words) that connects the first and last names. These short words are likely to begin with lowercase letters: Charles de Gaulle (French), Ludwig *van* Beethoven (German), Simon *van der* Meer (Dutch). Ask students to offer other examples of such names and to tell what the short words mean and whether or not they are capitalized.

Capitalize a personal title used with a person's name.

A **personal title** is a term of respect used in front of a name. Many titles have short forms called **abbreviations.** Capitalize abbreviations of personal titles. Follow an abbreviation with a period.

Mister—**M**r. **M**istress—**M**rs. **D**octor—**D**r.

The title *Miss* has no abbreviated form. Do not use a period after this title. *Ms.* has no long form.

Mrs. **C**asey saw **C**aptain **G**etz and **D**r. **Y**ung at the zoo.

Do not capitalize a title that is used alone or that follows a person's name.

The mayor met Joy Ortiz, the ambassador to China.

Capitalize the following titles when used before names, or when used alone to refer to the current holders of the positions.

the **P**resident (of the United States) **Q**ueen Elizabeth II
the **V**ice-**P**resident (of the United States) the **P**ope

Capitalize the word *I*.

Clarice and **I** took our dogs to obedience classes.

Practice Your Skills

A. CONCEPT CHECK

Proper Nouns and Adjectives Write the following sentences, using capital letters where necessary.

Writing Theme
Famous Animals

1. Yesterday i asked dad who he thought was the most popular fictional animal in the world.
2. He suggested garfield, the cartoon cat, but i think it is charlie brown's dog, snoopy.
3. The cartoonist charles m. schulz first drew this funny beagle over forty years ago, basing him on his own childhood dog, spike.

HELPFUL HINT: TITLE ABBREVIATIONS Students may note that the word *Mrs.* is not pronounced like the word *Mistress,* and that the word *Mistress* is not used as a title today. You might like to explain that two hundred years ago, every adult woman, married or single, was addressed as Mistress So-and-so, and that with time, the word became *Mrs.* (mis' əz), a title now used only for married women. You might also mention that *Ms.* (miz) is a title now used in front of a name of an adult woman, married or single.

INDIVIDUALIZING INSTRUCTION: BASIC STUDENTS Review with these students the capitalization rules on pages 548–549. Then do the first items in the Concept Check together, marking in colored chalk on the board the words that should be capitalized. Students can finish the rest of the exercise independently.

Additional Resources

Tests and Writing Assessment Prompts, Pretest, pp. 47–48
Grammar and Usage Practice Book, p. 87
Grammar Test Generator

Writing Theme: Famous Animals

Suggest that students use these exercises as a springboard to writing. Other related areas that they might explore include the following:

- the animals in *The Incredible Journey*
- an animal in an Aesop fable
- a favorite animal in a children's book, TV show, or film

Answers to Practice Your Skills

A. Concept Check

Proper Nouns and Adjectives

Answers are shown on page.

B. Proofreading Skill
Capitalizing for Clarity

Errors in proofreading exercises are counted as follows: (a) Each word is counted as one error. For example, a misspelled word is one error; two initials and a last name not capitalized are counted as three errors. (b) Run-on sentences and sentence fragments are each counted as one error, even though the correction involves both punctuation and capitalization errors.

Errors are shown on page. The correctly rewritten paragraphs appear below.

My mother claims that her Siamese cat, Albie, warned the family about a fire in the house. Such stories are not unusual, I have found. A British man, Ray Wakelin, fell on ice. His German shepherds, Rommel and Zeus, lay on Mr. Wakelin to keep him warm. A pig named Priscilla saved a Texan boy from drowning. Priscilla received the Stillman Award from the American Humane Association. The award is named for Dr. William O. Stillman, a past president of the association. The Quaker Oats Company also gives awards to brave animals. One went to a dog named Jet that alerted neighbors when its owner went into a diabetic coma. "I know I would have died without Jet's help," said Candy Sangster.

C. Application in Writing
Report

Answers will vary.

© 1970 United Feature Syndicate, Inc. From the feature film *Snoopy Come Home*, a Mendelson-Melendez Production.

4. Later mr. schulz named snoopy's brother spike.
5. Charlie brown once wrote about his pet, "He's kind of crazy."
6. This dog has been to france, the sahara, and the moon.
7. He fought the red baron, a german pilot, in a very popular series of cartoons that appeared in the late 1960s.
8. An american pop hit was "snoopy Versus the red baron."
9. In 1969, the apollo 10 astronauts named their command module charlie brown and their lunar module snoopy.
10. Snoopy sent personal get-well wishes to president reagan when the president was shot in 1981.
11. Fans from japan, finland, and chile follow the dog's story.
12. But snoopy is not always known by the same name—in swedish he is called snobben, and in norwegian he is sniff!

B. PROOFREADING SKILL

Capitalizing for Clarity Proofread the paragraph. Then write it, correcting mistakes in capitalization and other errors. (35 errors)

My Mother claims that her siamese cat, albie, warned the family about a fire in the house. Such stories are not unnusual, i have found. A british man, ray wakelin, fell on ice. His german Shepherds, rommel and zeus, lay on mr wakelin to keep him warm. A pig named priscilla saved a texas boy from drowning. Priscilla recieved the stillman Award from the american Humane Association. the award is Named for dr. william o. stillman, a past President of the association. The Quaker Oats company also gives awards to brave animals. One went to a dog named jet that alerted neighbors when its Owner went into a diabetic coma. "i know i would have died without jet's help," said candy sangster.

C. APPLICATION IN WRITING

Report Investigate a real or fictional animal and write a one- or two-paragraph report about it. Possibilities include Benji, Kermit the Frog, Flipper, Black Beauty, and Sounder. Make your writing more precise by using proper nouns and adjectives. Be sure to capitalize words correctly.

CHECKPOINT

MIXED REVIEW • PAGES 548–550

Write the sentences. Capitalize proper nouns and adjectives, and correct improperly capitalized common nouns.

1. In 1860, the irish immigrant michael moran came to new york city.
2. He became part Owner of a tugboat called the *ida miller.*
3. From his office on south street, facing the east river, he sold towing services to boats using new york harbor.
4. Here began the moran transportation and towing company.
5. Michael's son, eugene f. moran, worked on a tug too.
6. He said, "i was born practically on the Sea, and i have lived on and off it ever since."
7. Moran tugboats took part in major new york harbor events.
8. They were there when the brooklyn bridge opened in 1883.
9. With other american vessels, Moran's boats paraded with italian, french, and spanish Ships on the 400th anniversary of columbus's arrival in america.
10. Moran's tugs welcomed president theodore roosevelt home in 1910.
11. They have played an interesting role in american History.
12. They handled army transport in the spanish-american war.
13. In fact, the first commercial american boat to enter havana harbor after the war was the tugboat *m. moran.*
14. mr. moran advised assistant secretary of the navy franklin d. roosevelt on equipping Patrol Boats for world war I.
15. During world war II, moran boats worked on both the atlantic ocean and the pacific ocean.
16. The *edmond j. moran*, under capt. hugo kroll, had many adventures dodging german Submarines.
17. A moran tug hauled a german submarine to lake ontario.
18. The Sub is now at chicago's museum of science and industry.
19. In peacetime the tugboats have docked many famous ocean liners, including the queen mary and the queen elizabeth.
20. There is even a walt disney cartoon, named *Little toot*, about a moran tug.

Writing Theme

The Moran Tugboats

CHECKPOINT

Writing Theme: The Moran Tugboats

Suggest that students use these exercises as a springboard to writing. Other related areas that they might explore include the following:

- tugboat captains and their training
- the work of fireboats
- the small boats in the World War II evacuation of Dunkirk

MIXED REVIEW • PAGES 548–550

You may wish to use this activity to check students' mastery of the following concept:

- proper nouns and proper adjectives

Words to be capitalized and words incorrectly capitalized are shown on page.

1. In 1860, the Irish immigrant Michael Moran came to New York City.
2. He became part owner of a tugboat called the *Ida Miller.*
3. From his office on South Street, facing the East River, he sold towing services to boats using New York Harbor.
4. Here began the Moran Transportation and Towing Company.
5. Michael's son, Eugene F. Moran, worked on a tug too.
6. He said, "I was born practically on the sea, and I have lived on and off it ever since."
7. Moran tugboats took part in major New York Harbor events.
8. They were there when the Brooklyn Bridge opened in 1883.
9. With other American vessels, Moran's boats paraded with Italian, French, and Spanish ships on the 400th anniversary of Columbus's arrival in America.
10. Moran's tugs welcomed President Theodore Roosevelt home in 1910.
11. They have played an interesting role in American history.
12. They handled army transport in the Spanish-American War.
13. In fact, the first commercial American boat to enter Havana Harbor after the war was the tugboat *M. Moran.*
14. Mr. Moran advised Assistant Secretary of the Navy Franklin D. Roosevelt on equipping patrol boats for World War I.
15. During World War II, Moran boats worked on both the Atlantic Ocean and the Pacific Ocean.
16. The *Edmond J. Moran,* under Capt. Hugo Kroll, had many adventures dodging German submarines.
17. A Moran tug hauled a German submarine to Lake Ontario.
18. The sub is now at Chicago's Museum of Science and Industry.
19. In peacetime the tugboats have docked many famous ocean liners, including the *Queen Mary* and the *Queen Elizabeth.*
20. There is even a Walt Disney cartoon, named *Little Toot,* about a Moran tug.

MORE PROPER NOUNS

Objectives

- To capitalize the names of particular places and things
- To capitalize the names of months, days, holidays, and historical events
- To capitalize the names of races, religions, nationalities, and languages
- To capitalize words referring to God and to religious scriptures
- To capitalize the names of clubs, organizations, and business firms

Writing

- To use proofreading skills to correct capitalization errors in writing
- To use capital letters correctly in writing

Teaching Strategies

STUMBLING BLOCK Students may find it difficult to distinguish when a direction word is to be capitalized and when it is not. Provide additional examples of specific place names that contain direction words—such as Northern Ireland, South Carolina, North Beach, East Boston, and the Lower East Side—and then ask them to provide examples from their own area. Point out, as well, that when a word such as *south* or *east* stands by itself, with no other proper noun or no article, it is a direction word:

Direction: Head south one mile.

Region: We headed toward the [article] South Pacific [proper noun].

COOPERATIVE LEARNING Have students work together to create a class chart with categories of proper nouns (place names and historical events) and examples of words that illustrate the capitalization rule for each category.

MORE PROPER NOUNS

Capitalize the names of places, races, languages, religions, days, months, holidays, and historical events.

Capitalize the names of particular places and things.

1. Capitalize names of cities, states, and countries.

We stopped in **C**hicago, **I**llinois, on our way to **C**anada.

2. Capitalize names of streets, bridges, parks, and buildings.

We took **L**ake **S**hore **D**rive to **G**rant **P**ark and crossed the **M**ichigan **A**venue **B**ridge near the **W**rigley **B**uilding.

3. Capitalize geographical names. Do not capitalize *north, south, east,* and *west* when they refer to directions. Capitalize them only when they refer to particular areas or are parts of geographical names.

The highway runs east and west along **L**ake **O**ntario.
Many cities in the **E**ast lie along rivers and lakes.

Capitalize the names of months, days, holidays, and historical events.

Do not capitalize the names of the four seasons: *spring, summer, autumn,* and *winter.*

In **S**eptember, **L**abor **D**ay and the first day of autumn make me think of school and colorful leaves.
Last spring we studied the causes of **W**orld **W**ar II.

Capitalize the names of races, religions, nationalities, and languages.

Native **H**awaiians belong to the **P**olynesian race.
Both **H**induism and **B**uddhism began in **I**ndia.
Brazilian people speak **P**ortuguese.

SPICE BOX

The list of place names on this page is a natural springboard for a map-making activity. Encourage students to create a list of local landmarks and other points of interest: streets, stores, bridges, ponds, lakes, large buildings, and so on. To help students get started, you might show them some sample maps, as available. Then, after students draw a map, they can write the place names, showing correct capitalization on the map and in its location key.

Capitalize words referring to God and to religious scriptures.

the **D**eity	the **B**ible	the **G**ospels
the **L**ord	the **T**almud	the **B**ook of **P**salms
Allah	the **K**oran	the **O**ld **T**estament

Capitalize the names of clubs, organizations, and business firms.

The **S**ierra **C**lub has fought for one hundred years to protect the environment.
Clara **B**arton founded the **A**merican **R**ed **C**ross in 1881.
In 1972, **S**tandard **O**il of **N**ew **J**ersey became **E**xxon.

Practice Your Skills

A. CONCEPT CHECK

Capitalization of Proper Nouns Write the following sentences, using capital letters where necessary.

Writing Theme
Cultures Around the World

1. North America's first immigrants were asian nomads.
2. They came from siberia thousands of years ago.
3. The inuits and other native peoples of north, central, and south america are descended from these immigrants.
4. The first europeans to reach north america were the Vikings.
5. They landed on the eastern coast of what is now canada about a thousand years ago.
6. About five hundred years later, john cabot, an italian sailing for king henry VII of england, explored the area.
7. Later, french ships sailed west up the st. lawrence river.
8. During the winter of 1535 to 1536, french explorers camped at what is now cartier-brébeuf park in quebec city.
9. Members of the society of jesus and other french missionaries brought stories from the bible to the native people.
10. Both britain and france claimed canada as a colony, and for more than one hundred years, the french, the algonquins, and the hurons fought the british and the iroquois.
11. In 1763, after the seven years' war—called the french and indian war in the united states—the french surrendered.

INDIVIDUALIZING INSTRUCTION: ESL AND LEP STUDENTS Problems in deciding whether to capitalize unfamiliar English words such as *Inuits* and *nomads,* or a foreign compound such as *Cartier-Brébeuf* (kär' tyā brā bĕf'), as proper nouns will make this Concept Check difficult for many of these students. Offer your assistance when necessary, or pair these students with English-proficient peers to complete the exercise.

Additional Resource

Grammar and Usage Practice Book, p. 88

Writing Theme: Cultures Around the World

Other related areas students might wish to explore as writing topics include the following:
- Viking ships and sailors
- native peoples of North America
- the "old city" and "new city" in Quebec City
- cultures of the Amazon River basin

A. Concept Check

Capitalization of Proper Nouns

Words to be capitalized are shown on page.

B. Proofreading Skill
Focus on Capitalization

Errors are shown on page. The correctly rewritten paragraphs are shown below.

India, located on the continent of Asia, is the seventh largest country in the world. India stretches from the Indian Ocean to the Himalayas. Its largest cities are Bombay, Delhi, and Calcutta. Bombay lies on the west coast, between the Arabian Sea and the mountains called the Western Ghats. To the north, Delhi lies along the Jumna River. Calcutta lies in the east, near the border with Bangladesh. The most famous building in India is the Taj Mahal, at Agra in the north.

The majority of Indians believe in the Hindu religion. Many others are Muslims, who worship Allah and base their faith on the sacred book called the Koran. Fourteen major languages, including Hindi and Urdu, are recognized by the Indian government. Each winter, on January 26, Indians join to celebrate Republic Day. This holiday honors the birth of India as an independent, democratic country in 1950. In New Delhi, the capital, the celebrations are held on a wide avenue called the Rajpath.

C. Application in Writing
Report

Answers will vary.

12. From 1763 until 1870, much of canada was controlled by the hudson's bay company, a fur-trading organization.

13. On july 1, 1867, three canadian colonies formed the dominion of canada, which grew and became independent in 1931.

14. Every summer, on july 1, canadians celebrate canada day, the country's biggest national holiday.

15. Today canada has two official languages, french and english, and most canadians are either roman catholics or members of protestant denominations.

B. PROOFREADING SKILL

Focus on Capitalization Write these paragraphs, correcting the errors in capitalization, grammar, and punctuation. (35 errors)

India, located on the continent of asia, is the seventh largest country in the world. India stretches from the indian ocean to the himalayas. Its largest cities are bombay, delhi, and calcutta. Bombay lies on the west coast, between the arabian sea and the mountains called the western ghats. To the north, delhi lies along the jumna river. Calcutta lies in the east, near the border with bangladesh. The most famous building in india is the taj mahal, at agra in the north.

The majority of indians believe in the hindu religion. Many others are muslims, who worship allah and base their faith on the sacred book called the koran. Fourteen major languages, including hindi and urdu, are recognized by the indian government. Each winter, on january 26, indians join to celebrate republic day. This holiday honors the birth of india as an independent, democratic country in 1950. In new delhi, the capital, the celebrations are held on a wide avenue called the rajpath.

The Taj Mahal is one of the world's most beautiful tombs. It was built between 1630 and 1650 in memory of Mumtaz Mahal, the wife of the Indian ruler Shah Jahan.

C. APPLICATION IN WRITING

Report Imagine that a time machine has taken you to a strange place. In two or three paragraphs, describe the place. Tell about the land, the people, their language, religion, and any other interesting facts. Be sure to capitalize correctly.

CHECK POINT

MIXED REVIEW • PAGES 552–554

Write the following sentences, adding capital letters where necessary. If a sentence has no errors, write *Correct.*

1. Marian anderson believed that her voice was a gift from god and that god expected her to develop and share that gift.
2. She was born in philadelphia on february 17, 1902.
3. At age six, she joined the choir at the union baptist church.
4. In 1923, ms. anderson became the first african-american singer to win a vocal contest sponsored by the Philharmonic Society of Philadelphia.
5. She learned to sing in german, french, and italian.
6. In 1925, she won a competition to sing in new york city with the new york philharmonic orchestra at lewisohn stadium.
7. Then she went on several concert tours in Europe. C
8. She was cheered by the scandinavians, the french, and the swiss.
9. In december of 1935, she returned to the united states.
10. Marian anderson's 1935 concert at manhattan's town hall was a success, and she became a top concert singer.
11. However, some americans were not as accepting as the europeans.
12. Particularly in the south, some people rejected anderson on the basis of her color.
13. Because of her race, anderson was denied permission to perform at constitution hall in washington, d.c., in 1939.
14. This unjust act angered many people, including president Roosevelt's wife, eleanor.
15. Mrs. Roosevelt arranged for Anderson to sing at the Lincoln Memorial that year; over 75,000 people attended the concert. C
16. In 1955, marian anderson became the first african-american singer to perform at new york's metropolitan opera.
17. In 1958, president eisenhower made her a delegate to the united nations.
18. Her final concert was at carnegie hall on easter sunday, 1965.
19. Anderson retired to marianna farm near danbury, connecticut.
20. Yet she continued to work for charitable causes, including the american red cross and the eleanor roosevelt foundation.

Writing Theme
Marian Anderson, Singer

CHECK POINT

Writing Theme: Marian Anderson, Singer

Other related areas students might wish to explore as writing topics include the following:

- Marian Anderson's first Metropolitan Opera role
- Marian Anderson and the civil rights movement
- Leontyne Price or Kathleen Battle, African-American opera singers
- the training of opera singers

MIXED REVIEW • PAGES 552–553

You may wish to use this activity to check students' mastery of the following concept:

- more proper nouns

Words to be capitalized are shown on page. Sentences 7 and 15 are correct.

FIRST WORDS

Objectives

- To capitalize the first word of sentences and some lines of poetry

Writing

- To use proofreading skills to correct errors in capitalization

Teaching Strategies

KEY TO UNDERSTANDING: SENTENCES Point out that while sentences may end with different punctuation marks, as the example sentences on the pupil page do, they always begin with a capital letter. Be sure students understand, however, that this rule applies only to prose.

LINKING MECHANICS TO WRITING Point out that lines 2–4 of Langston Hughes's poem are part of a single sentence; the poem contains only two sentences, yet the first word in each of the four lines is capitalized. Emphasize that capitalization in regard to poetry allows the writer more creativity and "poetic license" than does prose.

CRITICAL THINKING: DRAWING CONCLUSIONS Ask students to describe the effect of the lack of capitalization in Phillip Booth's poem "Crossing." (Sample: There is no interruption in the flow or movement of words.) Invite the class to suggest a possible pattern. Then discuss the impact such a pattern might have.

Additional Resource

Grammar and Usage Practice Book, p. 89

FIRST WORDS

Capitalize the first words of sentences and lines of poetry.

Capitalize the first word of every sentence.

My brother likes to read Shel Silverstein's poems.
Have you read any of Eve Merriam's poems?
What an unusual title that poem has!

Sunset through the Golden Gate Bridge, San Francisco

Capitalize the first words in some lines of poetry.

In poetry, the first words of lines are often capitalized, even when they do not begin new sentences.

> **I** went to San Francisco.
> **I** saw the bridges high
> **Spun** across the water
> **Like** cobwebs in the sky.
> **Langston Hughes, "Trip: San Francisco"**

Sometimes, especially in modern poetry, the lines of a poem may not begin with capital letters.

> STOP LOOK LISTEN
> as gate stripes swing down,
> count the cars hauling distance
> upgrade through town:
> warning whistle, bellclang,
> engine eating steam,
> engineer waving,
> a fast-freight dream . . .
> **Phillip Booth, "Crossing"**

Practice Your Skills

A. CONCEPT CHECK

First Words Write each sentence, capitalizing letters where necessary. If a sentence is correct, write *Correct.*

1. listen, my children, and you shall hear
   of the midnight ride of paul revere
   on the eighteenth of april, in 'Seventy-five;
   hardly a man is now alive
   who remembers that famous day and year.
2. these are the opening lines of "Paul Revere's Ride."
3. The poem honors Revere's role in the American Revolution. C
4. it first appeared in a book called *Tales of a Wayside Inn.*
5. The book is a collection of tales in verse that are supposed to have been told by people at an inn in massachusetts.
6. did you know they were written by henry wadsworth longfellow, a famous american poet of the 1800s?
7. the tales are set in america, in spain, and elsewhere.
8. Longfellow is best known for his long narrative poems. C
9. a famous one is *Evangeline,* which is set in north america.
10. It tells about french immigrants to nova scotia who were forced to move south during the french and indian war.

B. PROOFREADING SKILL

Capitalizing Correctly Write this passage, correcting errors in capitalization, punctuation, and grammar. (15 errors)

The american Poet emily Dickinson was a very private Person. she did not write her Poetry for publication. Only a few of her poems was published during her Lifetime. After her death in 1886, her Sister found many of emily's poems and had them published. Dickinsons poems was usually short they often had unusual rhythms they explored everyday experiences of Life.

Writing Theme
Poets and Poetry

Writing Theme: Poets and Poetry

Other related areas students might wish to explore as writing topics include the following:

- Paul Revere's adventures on the night of his ride
- Craigie House, Longfellow's home near Harvard University
- other narrative poems about events in American history

A. Concept Check

First Words

Words to be capitalized are shown on page. Sentences 3 and 8 are correct.

B. Proofreading Skill

Capitalizing Correctly

Errors are shown on page. The correctly rewritten paragraph appears below.

The American poet Emily Dickinson was a very private person. She did not write her poetry for publication. Only a few of her poems were published during her lifetime. After her death in 1886, her sister found many of Emily's poems and had them published. Dickinson's poems were usually short. They often had unusual rhythms. They explored everyday experiences of life, as in this example:

A bird came down the walk:
He did not know I saw;
He bit an angle-worm in halves
And ate the fellow, raw.

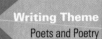

Objectives

- To capitalize the first words of entries in an outline
- To use capital letters correctly in titles

Teaching Strategies

KEY TO UNDERSTANDING You may want to begin the instruction by restating the second sentence in the opening paragraph, "In a title, capitalize the first and last words and all other words that are important." Explain that important words in titles are often nouns, verbs, and adjectives. Less important words are articles, prepositions (especially short ones of fewer than five letters), and conjunctions.

LINKING GRAMMAR AND WRITING Remind students that as they move into the higher grades, they will be planning and writing longer reports. Explain that a properly organized outline can help them structure their thoughts and notes and that sometimes they may be required to submit an outline before drafting a paper. If students have already written an outline for a report, have them check to see if they have capitalized their entries correctly.

Additional Resource

Grammar and Usage Practice Book, p. 90

OUTLINES AND TITLES

Capitalize the first words of entries in outlines. In a title, capitalize the first and last words and all other words except articles, coordinating conjunctions, and prepositions of four or fewer letters.

Capitalize the first word of each line of an outline.

Roman numerals (I, II) mark the major divisions of an outline. Capital letters (A, B) identify the next rank of items, and Arabic numerals mark the rank after that.

The **W**riting **P**rocess
I. **P**rewriting activities
  A. **C**hoosing a topic
    1. **B**rainstorming
    2. **R**eviewing journal notes and past writing
  B. **R**esearching the topic
II. **W**riting techniques

Capitalize the first and last words of a title and all other words except articles, coordinating conjunctions, and prepositions of four or fewer letters.

Do not capitalize articles (*the, a, an*), coordinating conjunctions (*and, but, or, nor*), or prepositions of four or fewer letters (*of, with, in*) except as the first or last word of a title.

Anne of Green Gables (book)
"Where Do These Words Come From?" (poem)
The Phantom of the Opera (movie, musical play)
"The Man Who Liked Dickens" (short story)
Los Angeles Times (newspaper)
National Geographic World (magazine)
"Surefire Steps to Strong Plots" (magazine article)
Bill of Rights (document)

Writing TIP

Some titles are underlined, and others are enclosed in quotation marks. Look on page 590 for rules on writing titles correctly.

Practice Your Skills

CONCEPT CHECK

Titles and Outlines Write each item, using capital letters where needed. If the item is correct, write *Correct.*

1. what is your favorite type of story or poem?
2. Is it short stories like O. Henry's "hearts and hands"?
3. Do you prefer novels such as Cleary's *the luckiest girl?*
4. Do you like poems like David McCord's "rollercoaster"?
5. These authors share something with the writer of the *Iliad* of ancient Greece and reporters for today's *New York Times.* C
6. Whether they write for a textbook or for *sesame street,* most writers use a similar writing process.
7. Imagine that you are a reviewer for the *Chicago tribune.*
8. you are to write an article titled "my favorite movie."
9. you want to explain why *the wizard of oz* is your favorite.
10. first, you might brainstorm about the movie, then write your ideas in a draft you could title "working draft."
11. you might organize your article this way:
12. I. elements of the movie *the wizard of oz*
  A. plot, action, and special effects
  b. performances
    1. main characters
    2. minor characters
 II. my reaction to the movie
13. reread your draft and revise it so that it expresses just what you want to say about *the wizard of oz.*
14. You could research facts in a book like *The Oscar Movies.* C
15. You might add a comparison with a film like *star wars.*
16. You could write about the contribution "somewhere over the rainbow" and other songs make to the film.
17. After revising and proofreading, you would prepare a final draft of "my favorite movie" for publication.
18. Authors use this process whether writing an article for *Newsweek,* a school report, or a legal document. C
19. for example, Thomas Jefferson revised the declaration of independence many times before it was finally approved.
20. Now you can write a report titled "the writing process."

Writing Theme
The Writing Process

Writing Theme: The Writing Process

Other related areas students might wish to explore as writing topics include the following:

- why writers write
- finding subjects to write about
- overcoming writer's block
- ways to share finished pieces of writing

Concept Check
Titles and Outlines

Words to be capitalized are shown on page. Sentences 5, 14, and 18 are correct.

Capitalization 559

CHECK POINT

Writing Theme: Poet, Biographer, Novelist

Other related areas students might wish to explore as writing topics include the following:

- writers and their cultural heritages
- a book I would like to write someday

MIXED REVIEW • PAGES 556–559

You may wish to use this activity to check students' mastery of the following concepts:

- first words
- outlines and titles

A.

Words to be capitalized are shown on page. Sentences 7 and 10 are correct.

B. Application in Literature

Words to be capitalized are shown on page.

Writing Theme
Poet, Biographer, Novelist

CHECK POINT

MIXED REVIEW • PAGES 556–559

A. Write the sentences, using capital letters where necessary. If a sentence is correct, write *Correct.*

1. should Eloise Greenfield be called a poet or a novelist or a biographer—or simply a writer?
2. If you had read the *hartford times* back in 1963, you would have enjoyed her first published poem, "to a violin."
3. since then, she has had many other poems published, including a book of poems entitled *honey, i love.*
4. Her poems use words and rhythms to put the reader in the middle of a scene, as in "*rope rhyme.*"
5. It begins this way:
   get set, ready now, jump right in
   bounce and kick and giggle and spin. . . .
6. But Greenfield has also written novels, such as *sister.*
7. She has written biographies of famous African Americans too. C
8. With her mother, Greenfield wrote the children's book *i can do it by myself.*
9. In addition to poems and books, she has written articles for magazines, including *ebony, Jr.*
10. Greenfield hopes her writing encourages young people to be proud of themselves, their heritage, and their abilities. C

The poet, novelist, and biographer Eloise Greenfield.

B. Application in Literature Write this paragraph, using capital letters where necessary.

i fell in love with langston terrace the very first time i saw it. our family had been living in two rooms of a three-story house when mama and daddy saw the newspaper article telling of the plans to build it. it was going to be a low-rent housing project in northeast washington, and it would be named in honor of john mercer langston, the famous black lawyer, educator, and congressman.

Eloise Greenfield and Lessie Jones Little, "Childtimes"

A. Capitalizing Proper Nouns and Adjectives Write the following sentences, using capital letters where necessary.

1. Steven spielberg once said, "Like peter pan, i never wanted to grow up."
2. Audiences from north america to asia are glad he didn't.
3. spielberg was born in december 1947 to a jewish family.
4. His family moved from cincinnati, Ohio, east to new jersey, then west to Phoenix, and eventually to california.
5. Mr. and mrs. spielberg encouraged Steven's interest in movies.
6. He made a short film to earn a merit badge in the boy scouts.
7. By 1969, spielberg was a director at universal studios.
8. His first big american film was *Jaws* in 1975.
9. spielberg then wrote and directed the 1977 science fiction blockbuster *Close Encounters of the Third Kind.*
10. *Raiders of the Lost Ark*, in the summer of 1981, was the first of three films about the archaeologist indiana jones.
11. It takes place in the middle east just before world war II.
12. The lost ark is a box that contained the ten commandments written in stone as handed down from god to moses.
13. Indiana hopes to find it in a temple called the well of souls in the sahara desert.
14. Another film, e.t.: *The Extra-Terrestrial,* from 1982, may be spielberg's best-known movie.
15. People from austria to zaire love the tale of e.t. and elliot.

B. Capitalizing First Words Write the following sentences, capitalizing where necessary.

16. can you name the first full-length animated film?
17. it was *Snow White and the Seven Dwarfs.*
18. producer walt Disney introduced this classic in 1937.
19. later, disney produced other animated films of children's stories, including *Pinocchio* and *alice in Wonderland.*
20. eventually Disney combined live action with animation.
21. the movie *Mary Poppins* used this technique.
22. usually disney's composers wrote new song lyrics and music.
23 in *Alice in Wonderland,* however, one song used these lines from the poem "Jabberwocky" in lewis carroll's book:

GRAMMAR HANDBOOK 42

Writing Theme
Moviemakers

GRAMMAR HANDBOOK 42

ADDITIONAL PRACTICE

Each of these exercises correlates to a section of Handbook 42, "Capitalization." The exercises may be used for more practice, for reteaching, or for review of the concepts presented.

Additional Resource

Grammar and Usage Practice Book, p. 92

Writing Theme: Moviemakers

Other related areas students might wish to explore as writing topics include the following:

- the adventures of Indiana Jones or another movie hero
- fantasy films
- special effects in filmmaking
- the role of the director in filmmaking

A. Capitalizing Proper Nouns and Adjectives

Words to be capitalized are shown on page.

B. Capitalizing First Words

Words to be capitalized are shown on page.

C. Capitalizing in Outlines and Titles
Words to be capitalized are shown on page.

24. 'twas brillig, and the slithy toves
did gyre and gimble in the wabe;
all mimsy were the borogoves,
and the mome raths outgrabe.

25. however, that lovable rodent mickey mouse was Disney's first great animated success!

C. Capitalizing in Outlines and Titles Write the following items, adding capital letters where needed.

26. the following outline shows some sources of popular movies:
27. I. existing literature
    A. books
        1. children's books like *the wonderful wizard of oz*
        2. novels like *gone with the wind*
    b. fairy tales, legends, and other traditional stories
    c. stage plays, musicals, and operas
   II. original screenplays
28. many children's books, such as *heidi, treasure island,* and *sounder,* have been turned into movies starring child actors.
29. Others—for example, *the wind in the willows* and *aladdin*—were put on screen with animated characters.
30. films based on novels, such as *around the World in 80 days* and *Dances with wolves,* have won Oscars for best picture.
31. The animated film *cinderella* was based on the fairy tale.
32. another fairy tale, "beauty and the beast," has been made into two feature films, one with actors and the other animated.
33. the movie *oliver!* was the film version of the musical stage play *oliver!,* which was based on the book *oliver twist.*
34. its stars sang such songs as "who will buy?" and "consider yourself."
35. The movie (and musical) *annie* was based on a comic strip!
36. Most of the classic comedies, such as Laurel and Hardy's short film *the music box*, were original movie scripts.
37. *citizen kane* was loosely based on William Randolph Hearst.
38. He published the *san francisco examiner* and *harper's bazaar.*
39. *gandhi* was a more factual account of its subject's life.
40. whatever their source, movies are great entertainment!

A. Using Capitalization Write the sentences, capitalizing where necessary. If a sentence is correct, write *Correct.*

1. Early flags of American colonies often showed a rattlesnake. C
2. The first flag for all the colonies joined thirteen red and white stripes with the british flag, called the Union Jack.
3. During the revolutionary war, patriots wanted a new flag.
4. Legend says Betsy Ross, a quaker seamstress, made the first u.s. flag in a house on arch street in philadelphia in 1776.
5. In her honor, the site is called the betsy ross house.
6. The new design replaced the union jack with thirteen white stars on a blue rectangle.
7. Records show that the continental congress adopted this flag on june 14, 1777, when it passed the Flag Resolution.
8. the new flag, the stars and stripes, was first used in a land battle on august 16, 1777, at the battle of bennington.
9. It was first flown at sea on november 1, 1777, on a ship commanded by captain john paul jones.
10. The Flag Act of 1818 set the number of stripes at thirteen, with the number of stars matching the number of states. C
11. From 1791 till 1959, when a star was added for hawaii, the flag of the united states changed twenty-six times!
12. The flag that flew over fort mcHenry during the war of 1812 had fifteen stripes and fifteen stars.
13. this flag inspired francis scott key to write a poem.
14. Key was an american lawyer held on a british ship in chesapeake bay on tuesday, september 13, 1814.
15. He watched into the night as british ships shelled baltimore.
16. The next morning, overjoyed that the U.S. flag still flew over the fort, Key wrote some words that would soon be set to music: C
17. "oh! say, can you see, by the dawn's early light, what so proudly we hailed at the twilight's last gleaming?"
18. The title "The star-Spangled banner" comes from a line in the song: "oh! say, does that star-spangled banner yet wave."
19. On march 3, 1931, president herbert hoover signed a bill adopting the song as the united states' national anthem.
20. the very flag that inspired the song can be seen at the smithsonian institution in washington, d.c.

GRAMMAR HANDBOOK 42

Writing Theme
Symbols of Patriotism

GRAMMAR HANDBOOK 42

REVIEW

These exercises may be used as a mixed review or as an informal evaluation of the skills presented in Handbook 42, "Capitalization."

Additional Resources

Grammar and Usage Practice Book, p. 93
Tests and Writing Assessment Prompts, Mastery Test, pp. 49–52
Elaboration, Revision, and Proofreading Practice, p. 31

Writing Theme: Symbols of Patriotism

Other related areas students might wish to explore as writing topics include the following:

- the rattlesnake on early American flags
- the meaning of each color in the United States flag
- war memorials
- national anthems of countries around the world

A. Using Capitalization

Words to be capitalized are shown on page. Sentences 1, 10, and 16 are correct.

B. Mastering Capitalization
Words to be capitalized are shown on page.

B. Mastering Capitalization For each sentence and outline item, write correctly only the words lacking correct capitalization.

[21]samuel francis smith was a student at andover theological seminary in massachusetts. [22]he studied the bible and other religious subjects. [23]in 1831, lowell mason gave smith some german song books. [24]mason wanted smith to write songs for children, using melodies from the song books. [25]On a dreary winter day in february 1832, smith chose a melody and wrote these words:

> [26]my country! 'tis of thee, sweet land of liberty,
> of thee i sing. . .

[27]His patriotic song was introduced to the public on independence day in 1832. [28]four years later, the song was published in a book called *the boston academy* under the title "america, national hymn." [29]dr. smith eventually became the pastor of the first baptist church in newton, west of boston. [30]His song, "america," was being sung throughout the united states. [31]during the civil war, it was very popular among citizens of the North. [32]they sang it at rallies, in army camps, and at meetings.

[33]this patriotic song is still popular. [34]Some are surprised to learn that it has the same melody as the british national anthem. [35]Smith himself did not know he had chosen the melody of "god save the king." [36]the song from which he took the tune had german lyrics. [37]The result is that the melody appeals to the patriotism of people in two nations—the united kingdom and the united states.

[38]In 1914, Smith's son donated the original manuscript of "America" to the library at harvard university. [39]This manuscript is considered one of the treasures of the united states.

[40]The song "america"—a history

I. Origin of the song "america"
   a. basic facts
      1. who, when, where
      2. what happened
   b. excerpt—first three lines
II. the song's growth in popularity

564 Grammar Handbook

WRITING CONNECTIONS

Elaboration, Revision, and Proofreading

Revise the following draft of a personal response to literature by using the directions at the bottom of the page. Then proofread your work, paying special attention to using capitalization correctly. Also look for errors in grammar, punctuation, and spelling.

[1]Reading The diary of a young girl by Anne frank made me think about my reactions to writing in my own journal. [2]Like anne, i sometimes wonders what the point is. [3]Why would anyone want to read the scribblings of someone like me. [4]On the one hand, her Dairy is a fascinating record of a terible time. [5]It tells about all the things she endured with her Parents and her Sister. [6]It also provide a chilling picture of what europe was like during world war II. [7]Anne's writing shows me the value of just getting my thoughs out. [8]Even if no one ever reads it, my thoughts have value for me. [9]Writing is a way to relese my emotions. [10]It is a way to figure out what I am thinking. [11]It is a way to figure out what I am feeling.

1. Add the following information after sentence 3 to introduce the sentences that follow. "Anne's diary gives two very powerful answers to that question."
2. Add emphasis to sentence 7 by beginning it with the phrase "more importantly, however."
3. Make sentence 8 clearer by replacing the vague pronoun "it" with the more precise "my journal."
4. Eliminate repetition by combining sentences 10 and 11 to make one sentence.
5. Divide the passage into three paragraphs.

Responding to Literature

Writing a personal response to literature allows you to share your thoughts and opinions about the things you read. (See Workshop 6.) When you revise this type of writing, make sure you present your reactions clearly and support them with specific details. Also check for errors in capitalization that could detract from your message.

WRITING CONNECTIONS

Elaboration, Revision, and Proofreading

This activity will allow students to see some of the concepts presented in this handbook at work in a personal response to literature. In revising and proofreading this passage, students will apply rules for capitalizing titles of books, the first words of sentences, and names of places. They will also be reminded of the ways in which using precise nouns and combining related sentences can strengthen a piece of writing.

Have students work in small groups to revise the passage. Finally, discuss the completed revisions with the entire class. Revisions may vary slightly. Typical changes are shown below. Elements involving change are shown in boldface.

Reading *The Diary of a Young Girl* by Anne Frank made me think about my reactions to writing in my own journal. Like Anne, I sometimes wonder what the point is. Why would anyone want to read the scribblings of someone like me? **Anne's diary gives two very powerful answers to that question.**

On the one hand, her diary is a fascinating record of a terrible time. It tells about all the things she endured with her parents and her sister. It also provides a chilling picture of what Europe was like during World War II.

More importantly, however, Anne's writing shows me the value of just getting my thoughts out. Even if no one ever reads **my journal,** my thoughts have value for me. Writing is a way to release my emotions. **It is a way to figure out what I am thinking and feeling.**

SKETCH BOOK

Objective

- To use writing prompts as springboards to informal writing

WRITING WARM-UPS

Begin by reminding students that they will not be graded for this assignment. The activities are intended as springboards to get them to think imaginatively about the concepts of this Handbook. Unless students volunteer to explore more than one prompt, have them work on a single activity.

For the first writing prompt, suggest that students imagine the alien. They might jot down a few descriptive words or phrases—or even draw this creature.

For the second writing prompt, have students recall some of the "other worlds" they remember from science fiction stories, movies, or TV shows. Then challenge students to imagine a science fiction setting that is completely different from these other alien worlds.

SKETCH BOOK

WRITING WARM-UPS

- Imagine you just arrived in another world. Write the conversation you have with the first alien you meet.

- What is the biggest difference between this new world and the earth? Write a letter to your best friend, telling him or her about the wonders you've seen.

566

Punctuation

GRAMMAR HANDBOOK 43

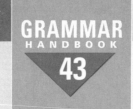

No matter how you get your message across—with your voice, with your hands, or with your writing—you need to use signals. Punctuation marks are the signals you use when you write. They point out stops and starts. They add emphasis, join together words, or show how ideas are related.

In this handbook, you will learn ways you can use punctuation to clearly signal your meaning to your readers.

Punctuation

Objectives

- To use periods correctly in sentences, initials, abbreviations, outlines, and lists
- To use question marks and exclamation points correctly
- To use commas in a series, in compound sentences, to avoid confusion, to set off special elements in sentences and letters, and to set off direct quotations
- To use apostrophes to form possessives and contractions
- To use hyphens in word division, compound numbers, and fractions
- To use colons in business letters, expressions of time, and Biblical references
- To use semicolons to combine related sentences
- To punctuate quotations and titles correctly

Writing

- To correct punctuation errors
- To combine sentences, using correct punctuation
- To change indirect quotations to direct quotations

INTRODUCING THE HANDBOOK

To get students thinking about the effects of punctuation, play a brief recording of a conversation. Then have two volunteers come to the board and transcribe the recorded material while listening to it a second time. Are both transcriptions punctuated in the same way? Which of the punctuation marks indicate pauses or stops? Which suggest the speaker's tone of voice? Tell students that they will learn more about the role of punctuation as they work through Handbook 43.

THE PERIOD

Objectives

- To use a period after declarative sentences and most imperative sentences, after some abbreviations and all initials, and after numbers and letters in outlines and lists

Writing

- To revise writing by adding missing periods

Teaching Strategies

HELPFUL HINT Explain that when an imperative sentence states a strong command, it ends in an exclamation point (see page 571).

HELPFUL HINT Point out that abbreviations for government agencies and political organizations are usually written without periods, particularly if they are acronyms, abbreviations pronounced as words: NASA, NATO, UNICEF, OPEC.

After pointing out the abbreviation for *meter (m)*, you might go over some additional metric abbreviations. Reinforce that (as noted in the Writing Tip) such metric measures also usually appear without periods:

cm (centimeter)	**g** (gram)
km (kilometer)	**mg** (milligram)
cc (cubic centimeter)	**ml** (milliliter)

HELPFUL HINT Point out that the two-letter postal abbreviations for states are generally used only for addresses that include the zip code (for example, on an envelope or in the inside address of a business letter). Tell students to spell out state names in formal writing.

THE PERIOD

Use a period after declarative sentences, after most imperative sentences, and after abbreviations, initials, and numbers and letters in lists.

Use a period at the end of declarative sentences and most imperative sentences.

A **declarative sentence** makes a statement.

Louis Pasteur developed the first rabies vaccine.

An **imperative sentence** states a command or a request.

Pour the solution into the beaker slowly.

Use a period after an abbreviation.

When taking notes or doing other kinds of informal writing, people often use shortened forms of words, or **abbreviations.** Notice how periods are used in these abbreviations:

P.O. (Post Office)	Co. (Company)
tsp. (teaspoon)	oz. (ounce)
Jan. (January)	Mon. (Monday)

Some abbreviations are written without periods.

FM (frequency modulation)	L (liter)
UPC (Universal Product Code)	m (meter)

The two-letter postal abbreviations of state names, such as *MA, AL,* and *CA,* are written with capital letters and no periods.

Dictionaries, newspapers, and magazines do not always punctuate abbreviations the same way. When deciding whether to use a period with an abbreviation, see what your teacher prefers or follow what your class dictionary says. Except for such abbreviations as *Mr., Mrs., Ms., Dr., A.M.,* and *P.M.,* avoid using abbreviations in formal writing.

MULTICULTURAL Connection

You might ask ESL students to share some common abbreviations from their first languages. For example, Spanish uses abbreviations for some terms not commonly abbreviated in English. In addition to all the words English typically abbreviated in English (months, weights and measures, honorary titles, addresses, etc.), Spanish shortens the phrases used as the greetings and closings of letters:

B.S.M. *(beso sus manos):* with great respect
S.S.S. *(su seguro servidor):* your faithful servant
E.S.M. *(estrecho su mano):* I press your hand

Use a period after an initial.

An **initial** is the first letter of a person's name. It is used alone to stand for the name.

R. L. Carson—Rachel Louise Carson
Albert B. Sabin—Albert Bruce Sabin

Use a period after each number or letter in an outline. Use a period after each number in a list.

Astronomy

I. Galaxies and stars
   A. Types of galaxies
      1. Spiral
      2. Elliptical
      3. Irregular
   B. Types of stars
      1. Dwarf
      2. Giant
II. Solar system

Scientific Measurements

1. Volume
2. Mass and weight
3. Density
4. Temperature
5. Length

For information about the use of capital letters in outlines, see page 608.

Practice Your Skills

A. CONCEPT CHECK

Periods Copy each word, abbreviation, letter, or number that should be followed by a period. Then add the period.

1. Everyone in Mr Ramos's class had to do a science project
2. This chart shows the growth of plants for one project

Date	With Fertilizer	Without Fertilizer
Mon, Sept 21	7 cm	8 cm
Fri, Nov 20	12 cm	9.5 cm

3. T L Fabbri, M L Gibbons, and J T Ortez recorded the data
4. Dr Sharon Adams of Biotech Ltd was their advisor
5. Tom, Mary Lou, and J T gave both their plants the same amount of water and light but gave only one plant fertilizer

Writing **TIP**

Do not use periods when abbreviating metric units of measurement. For example, use *g* for "gram" and *mm* for "millimeter."

Writing Theme
Science World

HELPFUL HINT Point out that if a person's name includes two or more initials, a space is left between the first period and the second letter: *C. S. Lewis* (not *C.S. Lewis*).

Additional Resources

Tests and Writing Assessment Prompts, Pretest, pp. 53-54
Grammar and Usage Practice Book, p. 94
Grammar Test Generator

Writing Theme: Science World

Suggest that students use these exercises as a springboard to writing. Other related areas that they might explore include the following:

- types of fertilizers
- a science project they have done
- growing plants indoors

Answers to Practice Your Skills

A. Concept Check
Periods

1. Mr., project.
2. project., Mon., Sept., Fri., Nov.
3. T. L., M. L., J. T., data.
4. Dr., Ltd., advisor.
5. J. T., fertilizer.

SPICE BOX

Students might enjoy playing this abbreviations game. Divide the class into two teams. Each team must list ten or so abbreviations and acronyms not included in the lesson; the other team must identify what each abbreviation stands for. For bonus points, you might provide additional abbreviations and acronyms for both teams to guess. Some suggestions: *CIA, FCC, FDA, HUD, VISTA, NAACP, EST, A.D., DOS, AWOL, ACLU, J.F.K., F.D.R., L.B.J., laser, radar, GIGO.* To simulate a TV game show, you might bring in two noisemakers—whistles, bells, buzzers, horns—to signal correct and incorrect answers.

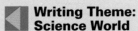

6. 1., 2., hr., min., 3., tsp.
7. growth.
8. I., II., A., B., III.
9. taller.
10. plants.

B. Revision Skill
Using Periods for Clarity

11. Tues., Sept., P.M.
12. E., St.
13. Co., Inc., St.
14. Dr., Mrs., B. J., eclipse.
15. Mt., difficult.
16. B. J., eclipse.
17. 1., sun., 2., projector.
18. IL.
19. Co., Inc., Mon., Tues., Oct., 4.
20. lb.
21. Ave.
22. P.M.

6. These are the measurements they used:
1 Water—50 ml per day
2 Sunlight—6 hr 30 min daily
3 Fertilizer—1 tsp per week
7. For two months they carefully observed the plants' growth
8. They wrote a project report based on this outline:
I What we thought would happen—our hypothesis
II Our procedures
A Daily watering and sunlight for both plants
B Organic fertilizer for only one plant
III Results and conclusions
9. Organic fertilizer caused one plant to grow taller
10. Use organic fertilizer if you want big, healthy plants

B. REVISION SKILL

Using Periods for Clarity All needed periods are missing from these notes. Copy each word, abbreviation, letter, or number that should be followed by a period, adding the period.

[11]The Science Club met Tues, Sept 6, at 7:00 PM [12]We were at 45 E Main St [13]I was asked to write to this address for a catalog:

Science Equipment Co, Inc
4652 Main St
Beloit, WI 53511

[14]Dr Robert Alvin and Mrs B J Craig showed slides of their trip to Hawaii to see a solar eclipse [15]Clouds and ashes from the Mt Pinatubo eruption the previous June made viewing difficult [16]Yet B J Craig took fascinating pictures of the eclipse [17]She described safe ways to view a solar eclipse:

1 Do not look directly at the sun
2 Look through a special filter or use a pinhole projector

[18]Our next trip is to the Adler Planetarium, Chicago, IL [19]Alicia made arrangements with Corren Bus Co, Inc, for Mon and Tues, Oct 3 and 4 [20]The baggage weight limit for each person is 40 lb [21]We'll stay at the Hillcrest Hotel on Michigan Ave

[22]The meeting ended at 9:30 PM

FOR MORE PRACTICE
See page 592.

570 Grammar Handbook

THE QUESTION MARK AND THE EXCLAMATION POINT

Use a question mark after an interrogative sentence. Use an exclamation point after an exclamatory sentence, after an imperative sentence that is exclamatory, and after an interjection.

Use a question mark after an interrogative sentence.

An **interrogative sentence** asks a question.

When does the game start**?** Who is the new pitcher**?**

Use an exclamation point at the end of an exclamatory sentence that expresses excitement or another strong feeling.

It's a home run**!** We're number one**!**

Use an exclamation point at the end of an imperative sentence that makes a strong command.

Run**!** Get that ball**!** Throw it**!**

Use an exclamation point after an interjection, a word or group of words used to express surprise or another strong feeling.

Wow**!** What a catch**!** Unbelievable**!**

Writing **TIP**

Exclamations express strong feelings, but too many exclamations in your writing can make the feelings seem less important.

Practice Your Skills

A. CONCEPT CHECK

Question Marks and Exclamation Points Copy this conversation. Add needed periods, question marks, and exclamation points. Try not to overuse exclamation points.

1. ED: We've won We've won
2. AL: What a fantastic game That's the way to play ball

Writing Theme
Sports Fans

PROFESSIONAL NOTEBOOK

Overuse of exclamation points dilutes their effectiveness. According to *The Elements of Style* by William Strunk, Jr., and E. B. White, "The exclamation mark is to be reserved for use after true exclamations or commands." It should not be used for simple statements like "It was a wonderful show." Note that several exercises in this Handbook ask students to make judgment calls about the use of exclamation points. Urge students to show restraint here and in their own writing.

THE QUESTION MARK AND THE EXCLAMATION POINT

Objectives

- To use a question mark after interrogative sentences
- To use an exclamation point after exclamatory sentences, some imperative sentences, and interjections

Writing

- To correct errors in the use of question marks and exclamation points

Teaching Strategies

INDIVIDUALIZING INSTRUCTION: ESL STUDENTS Punctuation rules vary from language to language. For example, Spanish questions and exclamations begin with an inverted question mark or exclamation point and end with a regular one. Spanish-speaking students may retain this practice with English. Watch for this and other consistent usage errors and work individually with students to help correct problem areas.

Additional Resource

Grammar and Usage Practice Book, p. 95

Writing Theme: Sports Fans

Suggest that students use these exercises as a springboard to writing. Other related areas that students might explore include the following:

- an exciting sports event
- a favorite sport or athlete
- reasons for liking or disliking a particular sport

Answers to Practice Your Skills

A. Concept Check

Question Marks and Exclamation Points

Some answers may vary, depending on whether a sentence is considered declarative or exclamatory. Possible answers are shown below.

1. ED: We've won! We've won!
2. AL: What a fantastic game! That's the way to play ball!

3. ED: Can you believe it? We beat the Cougars by nine runs.
4. MIA: Hurry! They're showing replays.
5. AL: Didn't.you think that ball was out of the park?
6. MIA: Yes, but Jackson's one-handed catch saved the day.
7. ED: Right! What an unbelievable catch!
8. MIA: I was so afraid the Cougars would score in the ninth.
9. AL: So was I, but we really held on.
10. ED: Weren't you impressed with Garcia today?
11. AL: That's for sure! He was incredible! *(or.)*
12. MIA: Can you imagine how it felt to hit three homers?
13. ED: Great! It had to feel just great!
14. AL: Do you think the Cougars regret trading him away?
15. ED: Who knows? I'm just glad he's on our team now! *(or.)*

B. Proofreading Skill

Using Question Marks and Exclamation Points

Errors in proofreading exercises are counted as follows: (a) Each word is counted as one error. For example, a misspelled word is one error; two initials and a last name not capitalized are counted as three errors. (b) Run-on sentences and sentence fragments are each counted as one error, even though the correction involves both punctuation and capitalization corrections.

Errors are shown on page. Some answers may vary. See a typical revision below.

ACTOR 1: Wow! What a stunning performance!

ACTOR 2: There's her score. It's a ten! A perfect ten!

ACTOR 1: Outstanding! T. A. Bukro is the new world champion. Listen to this crowd roar.

ACTOR 3: Are you a gymnastics fan? Do you enjoy watching track-and-field events? Or is soccer your favorite sport?

ACTOR 4: Do you know where you can see these and other exciting sports events?

ACTOR 3: You can see them on Super Sports Station. Super Sports offers you the best in sports all day long, every day.

ACTOR 4: You don't want to miss the most thrilling sports events shown on television, do you?

ACTOR 3: Of course not! Just call this number, and we'll add Super Sports to your cable package.

ACTOR 4: Hurry! Order today and get one month free. That's right! Absolutely free!

ACTOR 3: Call today! What sports fan could turn down this offer?

3. ED: Can you believe it We beat the Cougars by nine runs
4. MIA: Hurry They're showing replays
5. AL: Didn't you think that ball was out of the park
6. MIA: Yes, but Jackson's one-handed catch saved the day
7. ED: Right What an unbelievable catch
8. MIA: I was so afraid the Cougars would score in the ninth
9. AL: So was I, but we really held on
10. ED: Weren't you impressed with Garcia today
11. AL: That's for sure He was incredible
12. MIA: Can you imagine how it felt to hit three homers
13. ED: Great It had to feel just great
14. AL: Do you think the Cougars regret trading him away
15. ED: Who knows I'm just glad he's on our team now

B. PROOFREADING SKILL

Using Question Marks and Exclamation Points Write this script for a television advertisement. Correct the errors in punctuation and spelling. Use exclamation points in ways you think are correct for an advertisement. (24 errors)

ACTOR 1: Wow. What a stunning performance
ACTOR 2: There's her score. Its a ten A perfect ten
ACTOR 1: Outstanding T A Bukro is the new world champion. Listen to this crowd roar
ACTOR 3: Are you a gymnastics fan Do you enjoy watching track-and-feild events. Or is soccer your favorite sport
ACTOR 4: Do you know where you can see these and other exciteing sports events
ACTOR 3: You can see them on Super Sports Station. Super Sports offers you the best in sports all day long, every day?
ACTOR 4: You don't want to miss the most thrilling sports events shown on television, do you.
ACTOR 3: Of course not Just call this number, and we'll add Super Sports to your cable pakage.
ACTOR 4: Hurry! Order today and get one month free Thats' right Absolutely free
ACTOR 3: Call today What sports fan could turn down this offer.

FOR MORE PRACTICE
See page 592.

572 Grammar Handbook

CHECK POINT

MIXED REVIEW • PAGES 568–572

Write the following phrases and sentences, adding periods, question marks, and exclamation points where necessary.

1. Come one, come all See the Greatest Show on Earth
2. Under those huge words on the sign were several lines in smaller type
3. The other lines gave important information:
—Ringling Bros and Barnum & Bailey Combined Shows, Inc
—Opening in St Louis on Sun, Oct 15
4. Sara Hird, T J Hart, and I went to the circus that Sunday
5. Mr and Mrs Hart sat with us
6. The show was fantastic Truly fantastic
7. I couldn't believe my eyes
8. The show began at 7:00 PM with the grand entrance
9. Suddenly, things started happening in all three rings
10. Have you ever seen anyone let go of a trapeze and do four somersaults before being caught by a partner
11. Wow What a stunt
12. The high-wire performers were amazing
13. Can you imagine riding a bicycle on a thin wire high above ground with someone standing on your shoulders
14. What an awesome sight
15. Here's a list of my favorite acts:
1 The tightrope walkers
2 The trapeze artists
3 The clowns
16. I also liked the animals, especially the elephants and the seals
17. Now, those are really smart animals
18. I decided to write a report about the circus
19. This is part of my outline:
I Great circus owners
A James A Bailey and P T Barnum
B Ringling Brothers
II Outstanding circus performers
20. I can hardly wait until the circus comes back next year

Writing Theme
Circus

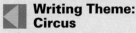

"Lorenzo and Lorenzo" of San Francisco's Pickle Family Circus.

CHECK POINT

Writing Theme: Circus

Other related areas students might wish to explore as writing topics include the following:

- a famous clown or trapeze artist
- a brief history of the circus
- how circus animals are trained
- a day at the circus

MIXED REVIEW • PAGE 568–572

You may wish to use this activity to check students' mastery of the following concepts:

- the period
- the question mark and the exclamation point

Some answers may vary. See typical answers below.

1. Come one, come all! See the Greatest Show on Earth!
2. Under those huge words on the sign were several lines in smaller type.
3. The other lines gave important information:
—Ringling Bros. and Barnum & Bailey Combined Shows, Inc.
—Opening in St. Louis on Sun., Oct. 15
4. Sara Hird, T. J. Hart, and I went to the circus that Sunday.
5. Mr. and Mrs. Hart sat with us.
6. The show was fantastic! Truly fantastic!
7. I couldn't believe my eyes!
8. The show began at 7:00 P.M. with the grand entrance.
9. Suddenly, things started happening in all three rings.
10. Have you ever seen anyone let go of a trapeze and do four somersaults before being caught by a partner?
11. Wow! What a stunt!
12. The high-wire performers were amazing!
13. Can you imagine riding a bicycle on a thin wire high above ground with someone standing on your shoulders?
14. What an awesome sight!
15. Here's a list of my favorite acts:
1. The tightrope walkers
2. The trapeze artists
3. The clowns
16. I also liked the animals, especially the elephants and the seals.
17. Now, those are really smart animals.
18. I decided to write a report about the circus.
19. This is part of my outline:
I. Great circus owners
A. James A. Bailey and P. T. Barnum
B. Ringling Brothers
II. Outstanding circus performers
20. I can hardly wait until the circus comes back next year!

COMMAS THAT SEPARATE IDEAS

Objectives

- To use commas to separate items in a series; to combine sentences joined by *and, but,* or *or;* and to avoid confusion in a sentence

Writing

- To combine groups of sentences into a series, adding commas where needed

Teaching Strategies

HELPFUL HINT If two items in a series are considered a single unit, they should not be separated by a comma:

We had bread and butter, salad, and spaghetti and meatballs for dinner.

HELPFUL HINT When combining sentences with the same subject, a writer might choose not to repeat the shared subject. In that case, the comma before *and, but,* or *or* is omitted:

Sara enjoyed the art fair but didn't buy anything.

Such a combination forms a sentence with a compound verb, rather than a compound sentence.

KEY TO UNDERSTANDING Point out that sometimes a comma is needed to prevent a humorous misreading, as in item 8 of the Concept Check on page 575. Caution students to be sure to insert a comma in introductory phrases and clauses that end in a verb or a preposition:

Confusing: When she woke up Mara was hungry.

Clear: When she woke up, Mara was hungry.

Additional Resource

Grammar and Usage Practice Book, p. 96

COMMAS THAT SEPARATE IDEAS

Use commas to separate items in a series. Use a comma when you use *and, but,* or *or* to join two sentences. Use a comma to avoid confusion.

Commas tell readers to pause. This pause keeps readers from running together words or ideas that should be kept separate.

Use commas to separate the items in a series. There are always three or more items in a series.

Roses, carnations, and other flowers were for sale.
Our class planned, advertised, and set up the art fair.
Sue, Cliff, Dave, and Shawna sold tickets on Friday, Saturday, and Sunday.

In a series, place a comma after each item except the last. Notice how the use of commas changes the meaning of this sentence.

At the food fest we tasted chicken, enchiladas, fruit, salad, cheese, ravioli, and bran muffins.
At the food fest we tasted chicken enchiladas, fruit salad, cheese ravioli, and bran muffins.

When you use *and, but,* and *or* to combine complete sentences, put commas before these words.

Sara enjoyed the art fair. She didn't buy anything.
Sara enjoyed the art fair, but she didn't buy anything.

Use a comma whenever the reader might be confused.

Some sentences can be very confusing without commas.

Confusing Soon after opening the farmers' market ran out of corn.

Clear Soon after opening, the farmers' market ran out of corn.

Writing TIP

Remember, do not overuse commas. Too many commas may make a sentence harder to read instead of easier.

Practice Your Skills

A. CONCEPT CHECK

Commas That Separate Ideas Write the following sentences, adding commas where necessary.

1. Growers sell food at markets or they sell it at roadside stands.
2. Farmers plant crops grow them and sell them in nearby towns.
3. Some supply fresh corn and others offer delicious tomatoes.
4. Yesterday, we went to a market and we looked for bargains.
5. We wanted to buy corn on the cob but it was sold out.
6. Instead, we bought tomatoes green beans and zucchini.
7. Dad said he would make bacon lettuce and tomato sandwiches.
8. As we ate Dad talked about the farm where he grew up.
9. Remembering the farm Dad always smiles.
10. His family grew apples and they shipped the apples out of state.

B. DRAFTING SKILL

Using Commas to Make Writing Concise Combine the sentences in each group, adding commas where necessary.

EXAMPLE The parking lot was crowded. The booths were crowded. The shops were crowded.
The parking lot, the booths, and the shops were crowded.

11. You may know them as flea markets. You may know them as swap meets. They are also known as outdoor marketplaces.
12. Today these events are popular throughout the United States. They are becoming even more widespread.
13. Flea markets are in parking lots. They are in stadiums.
14. Some attract just a few loyal fans. Others draw thousands.
15. Companies such as Sears may set up booths. J. C. Penney may set up booths. MCI Communications may set up booths.
16. People come to have fun. They are also looking for bargains.
17. Shoppers arrive early. They browse around. They make deals.
18. Browsers can find interesting items. They can find unusual items. They can find practical items.
19. They buy new cars. They buy antiques. They buy clothes.
20. Shoppers can enjoy just looking. They can buy treasures.

Writing Theme
Open-Air Markets

FOR MORE PRACTICE
See page 592.

Writing Theme: Open-Air Markets

Other related areas students might wish to explore as writing topics include the following:

- a visit to an outdoor market
- a meal your family might enjoy after shopping at a farmers' market
- the best bargain you ever found
- a flea market *versus* a mall

Answers to Practice Your Skills

A. Concept Check
Commas That Separate Ideas

1. Growers sell food at markets, or they sell it at roadside stands.
2. Farmers plant crops, grow them, and sell them in nearby towns.
3. Some supply fresh corn, and others offer delicious tomatoes.
4. Yesterday, we went to a market, and we looked for bargains.
5. We wanted to buy corn on the cob, but it was sold out.
6. Instead, we bought tomatoes, green beans, and zucchini.
7. Dad said he would make bacon, lettuce, and tomato sandwiches.
8. As we ate, Dad talked about the farm where he grew up.
9. Remembering the farm, Dad always smiles.
10. His family grew apples, and they shipped the apples out of state.

B. Drafting Skill
Using Commas to Make Writing Concise

Some answers may vary. Possible answers are shown below.

11. You may know them as flea markets, swap meets, or outdoor marketplaces.
12. Today these events are popular throughout the United States, and they are becoming even more widespread.
13. Flea markets are in parking lots and stadiums.
14. Some attract just a few loyal fans, but others draw thousands.
15. Companies such as Sears, J. C. Penney, and MCI Communications may set up booths.
16. People come to have fun, but they are also looking for bargains.
17. Shoppers arrive early, browse around, and make deals.
18. Browsers can find interesting, unusual, and practical items.
19. They buy new cars, antiques, and clothes.
20. Shoppers can enjoy just looking, or they can buy treasures.

COMMAS THAT SET OFF SPECIAL ELEMENTS

Objectives

- To use commas to set off introductory words or phrases, the names of people spoken to, and most appositives
- To use commas to separate parts of dates and addresses

Writing

- To revise paragraphs by adding missing commas

Teaching Strategies

HELPFUL HINT Explain that when an appositive is essential to the meaning of a sentence because it identifies a particular member of a group or category, it should not be set off by commas.

Here is a pair of sentences to help students see this distinction:

The English writer Charles Dickens is the author of *David Copperfield. (He is one of many English writers.)*

The author of *David Copperfield,* Charles Dickens, was born in 1812. *(Dickens is the book's only author.)*

STUMBLING BLOCK Writers frequently forget to use the *second* comma—the one that goes after an appositive, a year, or the name of a state or country. Discuss the difference between these sentences:

Abby, my best friend, plays the flute. *(Abby is the friend.)*

Abby, my best friend plays the flute. *(Abby is being told about the friend.*

HELPFUL HINT Point out that commas are not used when a date gives just the month and year: *I moved in May 1992.*

Additional Resource

Grammar and Usage Practice Book, p. 97

COMMAS THAT SET OFF SPECIAL ELEMENTS

Use commas to set off introductory phrases, the names of people spoken to, and appositives. Use commas to separate parts of dates and addresses.

Use a comma after *yes, no,* or *well* at the beginning of a sentence.

Yes, I'll take a bicycle tour. Well, have a great time.

Use commas to set off the name of a person spoken to.

One comma is needed when the name starts or ends the sentence. A comma is needed both before and after a name in the middle of a sentence.

Inez, don't forget your helmet. Do you have yours, Ted?
It's important, Lenore, to check the air in the tires.

Use commas to set off most appositives.

An **appositive** follows a noun and renames the noun. It is used to give more information.

Camille Morilla, a veteran cyclist, won the race.

Use commas to separate the parts of a date. Use a comma after the last part of a date in the middle of a sentence.

Our school will hold a bike rally on Monday, October 6.
On May 31, 1868, the first recorded bike race was held.

Use a comma to separate the name of a city from the name of a state or country. Use a comma after the name of the state or country in the middle of a sentence.

The Tour de France bicycle race ends in Paris, France.
The bike race in Bloomington, Indiana, drew a big crowd.

Grammar TIP

Remember to use a comma after a transition word such as *next, however,* or *therefore* at the beginning of a sentence.

Practice Your Skills

A. CONCEPT CHECK

Commas and Special Elements Write the following sentences. Add commas where needed.

1. TEACHER: Class our guest is Alex Doren a cycling fan.
2. SPEAKER: Thank you Ms. Farino.
3. Good morning students. Yes I do love to ride my bicycle.
4. I first rode a bicycle on June 7 1967 my fifth birthday.
5. I have toured all over Ohio my home state by bicycle.
6. Once I toured Toronto Canada with Barney my favorite bike.
7. Well my most recent tour began on Sunday April 18 1993.
8. Please dim the lights Ms. Farino so I can show my slides.
9. Friends and I started off from Hampton New Hampshire.
10. We cycled along the ocean to Newburyport Massachusetts.
11. Our scenic seaside tour ended on April 24 1993 at Hampton.
12. I also plan to cycle through Acadia a scenic national park in Maine.

B. REVISION SKILL

Using Commas for Clarity The paragraphs below are missing some commas. Copy the paragraphs, adding commas where needed.

13 Shelly did you know that the first bicycle was invented in the 1790s? **14** Well although it had two wheels, the *célérifère* wasn't much of a bike. **15** It could not be steered and a rider had to paddle his or her feet on the ground to make it move. **16** Baron Karl von Drais a German inventor added a steering bar to this kind of bike. **17** He displayed his improved bicycle in Paris France on April 6 1818.

18 In 1866, Pierre Lallement a French immigrant and James Carroll of Ansonia Connecticut received the first bicycle patent in the United States. **19** Their bicycle the bone-shaker had pedals on the front wheel. **20** The high-wheeler or penny-farthing was introduced in the 1860s. **21** Then the safety bicycle a bike more like bicycles of today came along in the 1870s. **22** Yes Shelly the bicycle has certainly come a long way since the *célérifère!*

Writing Theme
On the Bike

The English racer M.W. Wright stands beside his bicycle. Wright removed the brakes before each race and wore tightly fitted clothing in order to race as fast as possible.

FOR MORE PRACTICE
See page 592.

Writing Theme: On the Bike

Other related areas students might wish to explore as writing topics include the following:

- a memorable bicycle ride
- the Tour de France
- bicycles of today
- bicycle safety

Answers to Practice Your Skills

A. Concept Check
Commas and Special Elements

1. TEACHER: Class, our guest is Alex Doren, a cycling fan.
2. SPEAKER: Thank you, Ms. Farino.
3. Good morning, students. Yes, I do love to ride my bicycle.
4. I first rode a bicycle on June 7, 1967, my fifth birthday.
5. I have toured all over Ohio, my home state, by bicycle.
6. Once I toured Toronto, Canada, with Barney, my favorite bike.
7. Well, my most recent tour began on Sunday, April 18, 1993.
8. Please dim the lights, Ms. Farino, so I can show my slides.
9. Friends and I started off from Hampton, New Hampshire.
10. We cycled along the ocean to Newburyport, Massachusetts.
11. Our scenic seaside tour ended on April 24, 1993, at Hampton.
12. I also plan to cycle through Acadia, a scenic national park in Maine.

B. Revision Skill
Using Commas for Clarity

13 Shelly, did you know that the first bicycle was invented in the 1790s? **14** Well, although it had two wheels, the *célérifère* wasn't much of a bike. **15** It could not be steered, and a rider had to paddle his or her feet on the ground to make it move. **16** Baron Karl von Drais, a German inventor, added a steering bar to this kind of bike. **17** He displayed his improved bicycle in Paris, France, on April 6, 1818.

18 In 1866, Pierre Lallement, a French immigrant, and James Carroll of Ansonia, Connecticut, received the first bicycle patent in the United States. **19** Their bicycle, the bone-shaker, had pedals on the front wheel. **20** The high-wheeler, or penny-farthing, was introduced in the 1860s. **21** Then the safety bicycle, a bike more like bicycles of today, came along in the 1870s. **22** Yes, Shelly, the bicycle has certainly come a long way since the *célérifère!*

Objectives

- To use commas to set off direct quotations from explanatory words
- To use a comma after the greeting of a friendly letter and the closing of any letter

Writing

- To revise writing by adding missing commas

Teaching Strategies

KEY TO UNDERSTANDING Be sure students understand that when a quotation ends with a period, the period should be changed to a comma to separate the quote from the explanatory words, or speaker's tag, that follow. Also point out that if a quotation ends with a question mark or an exclamation point, no separating comma is needed:

"Did you watch the show?" asked Lee.

"Of course I did!" said Alex.

Additional Resource

Grammar and Usage Practice Book, p. 98

Writing Theme: Mysteries

Other related areas students might wish to explore as writing topics include the following:

- the Bermuda Triangle
- a famous unsolved mystery, such as the disappearance of Amelia Earhart
- a favorite mystery story, movie, or TV show

Answers to Practice Your Skills

A. Concept Check

Other Uses of Commas

1. "I just read a book about the *Mary Celeste,*" said Beth.
2. Curious, I asked, "What is the *Mary Celeste?*"

OTHER USES OF COMMAS

Use commas to set off direct quotations. Use commas after the greeting and closing of a friendly letter.

Use commas to set off explanatory words from direct quotations.

Compare the positions of the commas in these sentences:

Lee asked, "Did you see the mystery on TV last night?"
"I saw somebody sneaking away," insisted the witness.

In the first sentence, the explanatory words *Lee asked* come before the quotation. Therefore, a comma is placed after the last explanatory word. In the second sentence, the explanatory words come after the quotation. A comma is placed inside the quotation marks after the last word of the quotation.

Explanatory words can separate a quotation into two parts.

"No one knows," said the detective, "when it happened."

One comma is used inside the quotation marks that end the first part of the quote. Another comma is used after the last explanatory word. You will learn more about punctuating quotations on pages 586–587.

Use a comma after the greeting of a friendly letter and after the closing of any letter.

Dear Anita,   Your friend,

Writing Theme
Mysteries

Practice Your Skills

A. CONCEPT CHECK

Other Uses of Commas Write the following sentences, adding commas where needed.

1. "I just read a book about the *Mary Celeste*" said Beth.
2. Curious, I asked "What is the *Mary Celeste?*"

3. "It was a ship" replied Beth "that left New York with eleven crew members and passengers on November 7, 1872."
4. "A month later" Beth continued "the crew of another ship saw the *Mary Celeste* on course, but swinging left and right."
5. "A few sailors investigated the ship" Beth went on.
6. "Well" I asked "what did they find?"
7. Beth whispered "They found everything just as it should be, but no one, not one single person, was on the *Mary Celeste.*"
8. "They noticed that the lifeboat was missing" she added.
9. "The crew and passengers could have sailed away in it" I suggested.
10. "Could be" agreed Beth "but the lifeboat was never found."
11. "Also, no one from the ship was ever seen again" said Beth.
12. I concluded "Then their fate is a mystery of the sea."

B. REVISION SKILL

Using Commas in Friendly Letters Copy this letter, adding commas where needed.

[13]Dear Mr. Sherlock Holmes

[14]I must congratulate you on your solution to the last strange case. [15]Yes I know I should be used to your special abilities by now but I am still amazed. [16]After all Holmes who else would have suspected the timid servant? [17]As you questioned the witnesses the case became more puzzling to me. [18]I became confused but you grew more certain of the guilty person's identity.

[19]One of the family members wondered "Why does Holmes ask us so many questions?"

[20]"The solution" one brother suggested "must become clear soon if it is ever to be found."

[21]"I think Mr. Holmes is as stumped as the rest of us" said a family friend.

[22]Well Holmes you showed them once more that you are the smartest quickest and greatest detective who ever lived. [23]It is an honor to work with you and I am proud to call you my friend.

[24]Best regards
Dr. Watson

FOR MORE PRACTICE
See page 592.

3. "It was a ship," replied Beth, "that left New York with eleven crew members and passengers on November 7, 1872."
4. "A month later," Beth continued, "the crew of another ship saw the *Mary Celeste* on course, but swinging left and right."
5. "A few sailors investigated the ship," Beth went on.
6. "Well," I asked, "what did they find?"
7. Beth whispered, "They found everything just as it should be, but no one, not one single person, was on the *Mary Celeste.*"
8. "They noticed that the lifeboat was missing," she added.
9. "The crew and passengers could have sailed away in it," I suggested.
10. "Could be," agreed Beth, "but the lifeboat was never found."
11. "Also, no one from the ship was ever seen again," said Beth.
12. I concluded, "Then their fate is a mystery of the sea."

B. Revision Skill

Using Commas in Friendly Letters

13Dear Mr. Sherlock Holmes,

14 I must congratulate you on your solution to the last strange case. **15** Yes, I know I should be used to your special abilities by now, but I am still amazed. **16** After all, Holmes, who else would have suspected the timid servant? **17** As you questioned the witnesses, the case became more puzzling to me. **18** I became confused, but you grew more certain of the guilty person's identity.

19 One of the family members wondered, "Why does Holmes ask us so many questions?"

20 "The solution," one brother suggested, "must become clear soon if it is ever to be found."

21 "I think Mr. Holmes is as stumped as the rest of us," said a family friend.

22 Well, Holmes, you showed them once more that you are the smartest, quickest, and greatest detective who ever lived. **23** It is an honor to work with you, and I am proud to call you my friend.

24 Best regards,
Dr. Watson

CHECK POINT

Writing Theme: On the Road to Independence

Other related areas students might wish to explore as writing topics include the following:

- the Boston Massacre
- the Boston Tea Party
- *Common Sense* by Thomas Paine
- another nation's struggle for independence

MIXED REVIEW • PAGES 574–579

You may wish to use this activity to check students' mastery of the following concepts:

- commas that separate ideas
- commas that set off special elements
- other uses of commas

A.

1. The Second Continental Congress first met on May 10, 1775.
2. Delegates attended meetings in Philadelphia, Pennsylvania.
3. On June 7, 1776, Richard H. Lee gave a speech.
4. Lee proclaimed, "These United Colonies are, and of right ought to be, free and independent states."
5. Correct
6. Meanwhile, Thomas Jefferson, John Adams, Benjamin Franklin, and two others began working on the Declaration of Independence.
7. As Jefferson wrote, the others suggested changes.
8. Finally, on July 2, 1776, the congress voted for independence.
9. Members then discussed, debated, and passed the declaration.
10. Correct

B.

11 Dear Kristin,

12 Happy Fourth of July! 13 Today is July 4, 1993, and we had a huge family picnic. 14 My grandparents from Phoenix, Arizona, came, but my joke-loving grandmother from Green Bay, Wisconsin, couldn't come. 15 Without her, things were quieter than last year.

16 Yes, we all ate delicious food, played games, and watched a fireworks show.

17 My little brother asked, "Why do we celebrate on the fourth of July, Terry?"

18 "Well, that is the day," I answered, "that some American leaders decided to make a new country."

19 "David, we celebrate because this day marks the beginning of our nation, the United States of America," Mom explained.

20 Write and tell me what your family did, Kristin. 21 Did you go to a picnic like I did, or did you celebrate at home?

22 Your friend always,
Terry

Writing Theme
On the Road to Independence

CHECK POINT

MIXED REVIEW • PAGES 574–579

A. Write the sentences, adding commas where necessary. If a sentence is correct, write *Correct.*

1. The Second Continental Congress first met on May 10 1775.
2. Delegates attended meetings in Philadelphia Pennsylvania.
3. On June 7 1776 Richard H. Lee gave a speech.
4. Lee proclaimed "These United Colonies are, and of right ought to be, free and independent states."
5. Well, some delegates agreed with him, but others did not.
6. Meanwhile, Thomas Jefferson John Adams Benjamin Franklin and two others began working on the Declaration of Independence.
7. As Jefferson wrote the others suggested changes.
8. Finally, on July 2 1776 the congress voted for independence.
9. Members then discussed debated and passed the declaration.
10. John Hancock, president of the congress, signed it on July 4.

B. Write this friendly letter, adding commas where necessary.

11 Dear Kristin

12 Happy Fourth of July! 13 Today is July 4 1993 and we had a huge family picnic. 14 My grandparents from Phoenix Arizona came but my joke-loving grandmother from Green Bay Wisconsin couldn't come. 15 Without her things were quieter than last year.

16 Yes we all ate delicious food played games and watched a fireworks show.

17 My little brother asked "Why do we celebrate on the fourth of July Terry?"

18 "Well that is the day" I answered "that some American leaders decided to make a new country."

19 "David we celebrate because this day marks the beginning of our nation the United States of America" Mom explained.

20 Write and tell me what your family did Kristin. 21 Did you go to a picnic like I did or did you celebrate at home?

22 Your friend always
Terry

THE APOSTROPHE
AND THE HYPHEN

Use apostrophes to show possession and to form contractions. Use hyphens to divide words at the end of lines and to write compound numbers and fractions.

Use an apostrophe to show possession. To form the possessive of a singular noun, add an apostrophe and *s*.

musician + 's = musician's   Charles + 's = Charles's

To form the possessive of a plural noun that does not end in *s*, add an apostrophe and *s*.

children + 's = children's   women + 's = women's

To form the possessive of a plural noun that ends in *s*, add only an apostrophe.

composers + ' = composers'   violins + ' = violins'

Use an apostrophe in a contraction.

A **contraction** is two words written as one, with one or more letters left out. An apostrophe replaces the missing letter or letters.

can + not = can't   she + will = she'll
I + am = I'm   he + had = he'd

Use a hyphen after the first part of a word divided at the end of a line. Then write the second part on the next line.

Musicians in the orchestra watched closely as the conductor raised her baton.

Divide a word only between syllables. Never divide a word of one syllable, such as *count* or *score.* A dictionary shows how to divide a word into syllables.

THE APOSTROPHE AND THE HYPHEN

Objectives

- To use an apostrophe to show possession and to form contractions
- To use a hyphen to divide a word at the end of a line, in compound numbers, and in fractions

Writing

- To revise writing by adding necessary apostrophes and hyphens

Teaching Strategies

INDIVIDUALIZING INSTRUCTION: BASIC STUDENTS Explain that the first and third rules for forming possessives cover most English nouns. Provide the following additional examples:

glass + 's = glass's
doctors + 's = doctors'

ADVANCED STUDENTS Tell students that it is acceptable to add just an apostrophe to a singular noun if adding an additional *s* makes a word difficult to pronounce. Examples are words that contain more than one *s* or whose last syllable is pronounced *uz* or *eez.*

Jesus'	Achilles'
Moses'	Ulysses'

MODELING Write these contractions on the board and ask volunteers to provide the long form of each:

isn't	didn't	you're	we'd
aren't	wasn't	he'll	he's
don't	weren't	she'd	let's

Then have students state how each of the following words is shortened in a contraction: *not (n't), are ('re), will ('ll), had ('d), have ('ve), is ('s),* and *us ('s).* Usually, shortened forms are added to a verb or pronoun without any change in the first word's spelling. Ask students to think of exceptions. *(can't* and *won't)*

STUMBLING BLOCK Remind students that *it's* is the contraction of *it is,* but *its* is the possessive form of *it.* Add that *its* is a possessive pronoun and therefore does not need an apostrophe to show possession.

HELPFUL HINT Tell students that if a word is already hyphenated, as is *mother-in-law,* it should be divided at the end of a line only at an existing hyphen.

Additional Resource

Grammar and Usage Practice Book, p. 99

Writing Theme: Music

Other related areas students might wish to explore as writing topics include the following:

- great orchestras of the world
- a famous orchestra conductor, such as Arturo Toscanini, Leonard Bernstein, Herbert von Karajan, or Seiji Ozawa
- your school band or orchestra
- your response to a live concert or recording by an orchestra

Answers to Practice Your Skills

Concept Check
Apostrophes and Hyphens

1. ac-companied
2. audiences'
3. you've
4. conductor's, musicians'
5. conductor's
6. wouldn't
7. It's
8. orchestra's, player's
9. one-half, instru-ments
10. sixty-five
11. one-fourth
12. includ-ing
13. percussionist's
14. They're
15. Prokofiev's, children's

Do not write a single letter at the end or the beginning of a line. These divisions would be wrong: *a- dapt, regga- e.*

Use hyphens in compound numbers from twenty-one through ninety-nine and in fractions.

eighty-eight piano keys   two-thirds of the audience

Practice Your Skills

CONCEPT CHECK

Writing Theme
Music

Apostrophes and Hyphens Write the words that need apostrophes or hyphens in these sentences.

1. Originally, an orchestra was a group of musicians who ac companied opera performances.
2. Soon, audiences attention centered on the orchestras as much as on the opera singers.
3. If youve ever seen an orchestra play, then you know it has a leader, called a conductor.
4. A conductors baton and arm motions hold the musicians attention.
5. The conductors signals and gestures lead the orchestra.
6. Orchestra members wouldnt be able to play without direction
7. Its important that the musicians play together as a group.
8. The orchestras success depends on each players skill and sense of cooperation.
9. More than one half of the musicians play stringed instru ments, such as violins, violas, double basses, and cellos.
10. For example, in an orchestra of one hundred members, about sixty five usually play stringed instruments.
11. About one fourth play brass instruments, such as trumpets, French horns, trombones, and tubas.
12. The rest of the musicians play either woodwinds—includ ing clarinets, oboes, and flutes—or percussion instruments.
13. The timpani, or big kettledrums, are a percussionists most important instruments.
14. Theyre large, hollow copper kettles covered with drumheads
15. Listening to Sergey Prokofievs *Peter and the Wolf* often builds childrens interest in the orchestra.

FOR MORE PRACTICE
See page 592.

THE COLON AND THE SEMICOLON

Use a colon after the greeting of a business letter and between hours and minutes in an expression of time. Use a semicolon to join two related sentences.

Use a colon after the greeting of a business letter.

Dear Mrs. DeMille**:**   Dear Sir**:**

Use a colon between numerals representing hours and minutes. Also use a colon between chapter and verse in Biblical references.

10**:**14 A.M.   6**:**33 P.M.   Genesis 1**:**1–5

Remember to capitalize the letters and to use a period after each letter in the abbreviations A.M. and P.M.

Use a semicolon to combine two related sentences.

You can combine two related sentences into one by using a comma and a conjunction such as *and, but,* or *or* to connect the sentences.

We ran to the theater, but the show had already begun.

Another way to combine two related sentences is to use a semicolon (;). The semicolon takes the place of both the comma and the conjunction.

We ran to the theater**;** the show had already begun.
We ran to the theater**;** however, we were late.

You can use semicolons to avoid writing run-on sentences. For more about run-on sentences, see Handbook 34, pages 344–345.

Incorrect The lights dimmed the movie began.
Correct The lights dimmed**;** the movie began.

Bijou
THE ATTAC
OF THE KILLE
CONJUNCT
THOSE OF YOU WAITING TO BUY A TICKET, PLEASE FORM AN ORDERLY SENTENCE!
TALK TO THIS GUY, HE'LL MAKE SURE WE GET IT TOGETHER!

THE COLON AND THE SEMICOLON

Objectives

- To use a colon after the greeting of a business letter, in expressions of time, and in Biblical references
- To use a semicolon to join two related sentences

Writing

- To combine sentences by using either a semicolon or a comma along with a conjunction

Teaching Strategies

KEY TO UNDERSTANDING Tell students to think of the semicolon as a cross between a comma and a period (which is exactly what it looks like). It signals a pause stronger than that of the comma but weaker than that of the period.

HELPFUL HINT The semicolon can also be used to avoid another common writing problem: the comma splice. A comma splice occurs when two sentences are combined ("spliced" together) with a comma—but no conjunction. To correct this problem (and still combine the sentences), a conjunction can be added, or the comma can be changed to a semicolon. Discuss these sentences with the class:

Incorrect: The train was pulling into the station, I ran to catch it.

Correct: The train was pulling into the station, and I ran to catch it.

Correct: The train was pulling into the station; I ran to catch it.

Additional Resource

Grammar and Usage Practice Book, p. 101

Writing Theme: Entertainment

Other related areas students might wish to explore as writing topics include the following:

- how to use a video camera
- a proposal for a new video
- an outstandingly funny home video
- your favorite music video

Answers to Practice Your Skills

A. Concept Check

Colons and Semicolons

1 April 10, 19—

2 Dear Ms. Velez:

3 Please put this announcement in the school paper: 4 Mr. Wu's sixth-grade class has made a video; it's called *On a Sunny Day*. 5 It's about summer sports, hobbies, and activities. 6 The video will be shown on Tuesday, April 28, at 11:00 A.M. and 2:00 P.M. 7 The movie is free; however, a donation for the Food Bank is welcome. 8 Cans of fruit, vegetables, and soup are needed. 9 We hope people come; the class has worked hard.

10 Sincerely yours,
Andrea Giotti

B. Drafting Skill

Sentence Combining

11. Mr. Chandler's class made a video last fall; now they are making another one.
12. They discussed story ideas, and they chose one.
13. Anya wrote the script; Stacy helped her.
14. Class members are actors in the video, and (*or* or) they handle the technical jobs.
15. Jaina hopes to borrow her family's video camera, or Mr. Chandler may bring his camera.
16. Costumes are Sonya's job; she loves sewing.
17. Jason and Mike are collecting props, but they don't know where they will find a pair of stilts!
18. The actors must rehearse; they must learn lines.
19. The first rehearsals have been a little shaky, and everyone is nervous.
20. By the end of the month, everything must be ready; it will be time to start filming.

Writing Theme
Entertainment

Practice Your Skills

A. CONCEPT CHECK

Colons and Semicolons Write the following business letter, adding colons, semicolons, and commas where necessary.

[1]April 10 19—

[2]Dear Ms. Velez

[3]Please put this announcement in the school paper. [4]Mr. Wu's sixth-grade class has made a video it's called *On a Sunny Day*. [5]It's about summer sports hobbies and activities. [6]The video will be shown on Tuesday April 28 at 1100 A.M. and 200 P.M. [7]The movie is free however a donation for the Food Bank is welcome. [8]Cans of fruit vegetables and soup are needed. [9]We hope people come the class has worked hard.

[10]Sincerely yours
Andrea Giotti

B. DRAFTING SKILL

Sentence Combining Combine each pair of sentences, using either a comma and a conjunction or a semicolon, as indicated in the parentheses.

11. Mr. Chandler's class made a video last fall. Now they are making another one. (semicolon)
12. They discussed story ideas. They chose one. (conjunction)
13. Anya wrote the script. Stacy helped her. (semicolon)
14. Class members are actors in the video. They handle the technical jobs. (conjunction)
15. Jaina hopes to borrow her family's video camera. Mr. Chandler may bring his camera. (conjunction)
16. Costumes are Sonya's job. She loves sewing. (semicolon)
17. Jason and Mike are collecting props. They don't know where they will find a pair of stilts! (conjunction)
18. The actors must rehearse. They must learn lines. (semicolon)
19. The first rehearsals have been a little shaky. Everyone is nervous. (conjunction)
20. By the end of the month, everything must be ready. It will be time to start filming. (semicolon)

FOR MORE PRACTICE
See page 593.

CHECKPOINT

MIXED REVIEW • PAGES 581–584

A. Write the following business letter, adding apostrophes, hyphens, colons, semicolons, and commas where necessary.

[1]Dear Dr. Wasser

[2]Yesterday morning, about 600 A.M., I was walking on the beach near some cliffs when I saw the most incredible crea ture! [3]It had an eagles head and wings and a lions tail and body. [4]Ive heard youre an expert on unusual animals thats why I decided to write to you. [5]You must be used to peoples imaginations running wild. [6]However please dont tell me that I was dreaming. [7]I was only twenty five feet away from this animal and I saw it clearly. [8]I tried to get even closer but it flew away then. [9]Please answer soon nobody else believes me!

[10]Sincerely
Alice Stein

B. Write the following reply. Add apostrophes, hyphens, colons, semicolons, and commas where necessary.

[11]Dear Ms. Stein

[12]Thank you for writing to me I enjoy hearing about peoples unusual experiences. [13]The animal you saw was a griffin but I have to tell you that its thought to be an imagi nary creature. [14]Legend says that griffins lived in western Persia and guarded the gods gold mines from greedy humans. [15]A griffin was supposed to be stronger than ninety nine eagles one could carry off and devour oxen elephants and even people. [16]Griffins claws were thought to contain an antidote to poison and it is said that the claws were made into drinking cups.

[17]Please come to see me Id like to hear more about your ex perience on the beach. [18]My office hours are 100 P.M. to 500 P.M. on Tuesdays and Fridays. [19]Its not necessary to make an appointment.

[20]Yours truly
Dr. Alvin Wasser

Writing Theme
Mythical Animals

CHECKPOINT

Writing Theme: Mythical Animals

Other related areas students might wish to explore as writing topics include the following:

- the sphinx or the manticore, two other mythological creatures that are part lion
- a creature from Greek mythology, such as the centaur, the Minotaur, or Pegasus
- the legendary unicorn or phoenix

MIXED REVIEW • PAGES 581–584

You may wish to use this activity to check students' mastery of the following concepts:

- the apostrophe and the hyphen
- the colon and the semicolon

A.

1 Dear Dr. Wasser:

2 Yesterday morning, about 6:00 A.M., I was walking on the beach near some cliffs when I saw the most incredible crea-ture! 3 It had an eagle's head and wings and a lion's tail and body. 4 I've heard you're an expert on unusual animals; that's why I decided to write to you. 5 You must be used to people's imaginations running wild. 6 However, please don't tell me that I was dreaming. 7 I was only twenty-five feet away from this animal, and I saw it clearly. 8 I tried to get even closer, but it flew away then. 9 Please answer soon; nobody else believes me!

10 Sincerely,
Alice Stein

B.

11 Dear Ms. Stein:

12 Thank you for writing to me; I enjoy hearing about people's unusual experiences. 13 The animal you saw was a griffin, but I have to tell you that it's thought to be an imagi-nary creature. 14 Legend says that griffins lived in western Persia and guarded the gods' gold mines from greedy humans. 15 A griffin was supposed to be stronger than ninety-nine eagles; one could carry off and devour oxen, elephants, and even people. 16 Griffins' claws were thought to contain an antidote to poison, and it is said that the claws were made into drinking cups.

17 Please come to see me; I'd like to hear more about your ex-perience on the beach. 18 My office hours are 1:00 P.M. to 5:00 P.M. on Tuesdays and Fridays. 19 It's not necessary to make an appointment.

20 Yours truly,
Dr. Alvin Wasser

QUOTATION MARKS

Objectives

- To use quotation marks at the beginning and end of direct quotations

Writing

- To revise sentences by changing indirect quotations to direct quotations

Teaching Strategies

INDIVIDUALIZING INSTRUCTION: BASIC AND LEP STUDENTS You may want to provide some additional pairs of sentences illustrating the difference between direct and indirect quotations. Point out, as well, that an indirect quotation is often signaled by the word *that:*

I said *that* I would do the job.

HELPFUL HINT Point out that in writing dialogue, a new paragraph should begin every time a new speaker is quoted. (For examples, direct students to the letters on pages 579 and 580 and the Thurber excerpt on page 589.) Tell students that if you are quoting more than one paragraph spoken by the same person quotation marks should be placed at the beginning of each paragraph but at the end of only the last paragraph. Ask students to look in newspapers, magazines, and books for passages that illustrate these rules for punctuating dialogue.

QUOTATION MARKS

Use quotation marks at the beginning and the end of a direct quotation.

When you write what a person has said, you are writing a **quotation.** A **direct quotation** is a restatement of the person's exact words. If you do not write the exact words, you are writing an **indirect quotation.** Here are examples:

Direct Quotation	Jenny said, "I've met the mayor."
Indirect Quotation	Jenny said that she had met the mayor.

Put quotation marks before and after the words of a direct quotation.

In the first sentence above, Jenny's exact words are set apart by quotation marks. The second sentence tells what Jenny said without using her exact words.

Place a period inside the quotation marks if the quotation ends the sentence.

Jenny said, "He shook my hand."

Use a comma, exclamation point, or question mark to separate explanatory words from a direct quotation.

"I was surprised," said Jenny.
"I couldn't think of anything to say!" Jenny exclaimed.

Place question marks and exclamation points inside quotation marks if they belong to the quotation itself.

Rita asked, "What did the mayor say to you?"
"I can't remember!" answered Jenny.

In the first sentence, the question is quoted. Therefore, the question mark is placed inside the quotation marks. In the second sentence, the speaker is showing strong emotion. The exclamation point is also placed inside the quotation marks.

MULTICULTURAL Connection

Punctuation style for quotations varies from language to language. For example, French, Spanish, Italian, and Russian have small angle marks called *guillemets* (« ») that enclose quotations. Dialogue, however, is set off by dashes. In German, quotations begin with inverted lowered quotation marks and end with inverted raised marks („ "). Even British style is somewhat different from American: commas are generally placed outside the closing quotation marks. Ask students to share examples of quotation styles from languages they are familiar with.

Place question marks and exclamation points outside quotation marks if they do not belong to the quotation.

Did Christopher say, "Sometime I would like to talk to the mayor myself"?

How amazing that Jenny said, "Maybe you can"!

Divided Quotations

Sometimes a quotation is divided. Explanatory words, like *he said* or *she asked,* are in the middle of the quotation.

"The interview," said Jenny, "is scheduled for Friday."

Notice that two sets of quotation marks are used for this quotation. This sentence has a comma after the explanatory words because the second part of the quotation does not begin a new sentence. Use a period after the explanatory words if the second part of the quotation is a new sentence.

"Today is Tuesday," said Paul. "That gives me three days to get my questions ready."

In this sentence, the second part of the quotation begins with a capital letter because it is a new sentence.

Practice Your Skills

A. CONCEPT CHECK

Quotation Marks Write the sentences, adding quotation marks and other punctuation where necessary. Write *Correct* if no additional punctuation is needed.

1. Our guests today announced the talk show host are two famous world leaders.
2. Ladies and gentlemen, please welcome Genghis Khan and Abraham Lincoln she said.
3. Mr. Lincoln she asked you are our sixteenth president. How do you lead people?
4. First of all, you must earn their respect Lincoln answered That's vital.
5. I disagree shouted Genghis You must show strength.

Writing **TIP**

Use a variety of explanatory words when you write quotations. Some common explanatory words are *explained, shouted, asked, laughed,* and *replied.* Make sure the word you choose fits the situation.

Writing Theme
Interviews

KEY TO UNDERSTANDING Remind students that commas and periods always go inside closing quotation marks. You might also point out that semicolons and colons go outside (see page 590):

Terry whispered, "I'm afraid," and then he burst into tears.

Terry whispered, "I'm afraid"; then he burst into tears.

LINKING GRAMMAR AND WRITING Suggest that students might occasionally use verbs other than *said* in tag lines, for example, *whined, shrieked, whispered, muttered.* Also point out that good writers vary not only the kinds of explanatory words they use, but also the placement of those words to introduce, interrupt, or conclude a quotation. (See examples in the Literature Connection, below.)

Additional Resource

Grammar and Usage Practice Book, p. 102

Writing Theme: Interviews

Other related areas students might wish to explore as writing topics include the following:

- an interview with a grandparent or other older person about his or her life
- an interview with a student leader
- an interview with a local store owner
- the life of a famous world leader

Answers to Practice Your Skills

A. Concept Check
Quotation Marks

1. "Our guests today," announced the talk show host, "are two famous world leaders."
2. "Ladies and gentlemen, please welcome Genghis Khan and Abraham Lincoln," she said.
3. "Mr. Lincoln," she asked, "you are our sixteenth president. How do you lead people?"
4. "First of all, you must earn their respect," Lincoln answered. "That's vital."
5. "I disagree!" shouted Genghis. "You must show strength."

Literature Connection

Ask students to find the vivid explanatory words (underlined) in this passage from "Miss Awful" by Arthur Cavanaugh.

"Such was Roger's distress that his mother offered to stop at the Schrafft's on Thirteenth Street and treat him to a soda. "Who's got time for sodas?" he <u>bleated</u>. "I have homework to do. Punishment homework. Ten words, ten times each. On account of the . . . spelling test."

"Ten words, ten times each?" Mrs. Clark <u>repeated</u>. "How many words were on the test?"

"Ten," <u>moaned</u> Roger. "Every one wrong. Come on. I've got to hurry home. I don't have time to waste."

6. "I conquered Asia," Genghis boasted loudly, "by taking what I wanted."
7. Correct
8. "I agree," said Lincoln, "but a leader must also trust the people."
9. Correct
10. What was Lincoln's response when Genghis said, "My people trusted me to make the right choices"?

B. Revision Skill
Using Quotation Marks for Livelier Writing

Answers will vary. Explanatory words can appear in different positions. See typical answers below.

11. Andy asked, "How should I prepare to conduct an interview?"
12. Kris said, "First, I would try to learn about the person."
13. "Doing research is a good idea!" exclaimed Leon.
14. Janine said, "First, I would think of a list of questions."
15. "Would that be hard to do?" asked Kevin.
16. "The difficult part," replied Janine, "is thinking of open-ended questions."
17. "A reporter should ask questions that can't be answered just yes or no," said José.
18. "Thinking up good questions," declared Mai, "is the most important part of a reporter's job."
19. "Should I try writing some practice questions?" Andy asked.
20. Mai said, "It would probably help you if you did."

Abraham Lincoln (1809–1865) and Genghis Khan

6. I conquered Asia Genghis boasted loudly by taking what I wanted.
7. He said that a leader must be able to command loyalty.
8. I agree said Lincoln but a leader must also trust the people.
9. Lincoln said that the people could make the right choices.
10. What was Lincoln's response when Genghis said My people trusted me to make the right choices?

B. REVISION SKILL

Using Quotation Marks for Livelier Writing Change these indirect quotations to direct quotations. You may need to change some words in the sentences. Try to put the explanatory words in different positions in your sentences.

11. Andy asked how he should prepare to conduct an interview.
12. Kris said that she would try to learn about the person first.
13. Leon exclaimed that doing research was a good idea.
14. Janine said that she would think of a list of questions.
15. Kevin asked whether that would be hard to do.
16. Janine replied that the difficult part was thinking of open-ended questions.
17. José said that a reporter should ask questions that can't be answered just yes or no.
18. Mai declared that thinking up good questions is the most important part of a reporter's job.
19. Andy asked whether he should try writing some practice questions.
20. Mai said that it would probably help him if he did.

FOR MORE PRACTICE
See page 593.

CHECK POINT

MIXED REVIEW • PAGES 586–588

A. Write the sentences, adding quotation marks and other punctuation where necessary.

1. The planetarium guide said People around the world see different pictures when they look at the moon.
2. She asked Have you heard of the man in the moon
3. Marie nodded, and Thomas shouted Sure
4. To many Europeans explained the guide the markings on the moon look like a man carrying a bundle of twigs
5. Many Native American people she said see a frog
6. People in Tibet and Mexico see a hare she continued.
7. Samoans see a woman the guide added So do the Maori of New Zealand
8. What image do you see in the moon she asked the children.
9. Marie said I see a sleeping cat.
10. Did Thomas really say I see a monkey

B. APPLICATION IN LITERATURE

Punctuating Quotations Write the following passage, adding quotation marks and other punctuation as needed.

> [11]The Princess Lenore was awake, and she was glad to see the Court Jester but her face was very pale and her voice very weak.
>
> [12]Have you brought the moon to me she asked.
>
> [13]Not yet said the Court Jester but I will get it for you right away. [14]How big do you think it is
>
> [15]It is just a little smaller than my thumbnail she said for when I hold my thumbnail up at the moon, it just covers it
>
> [16]And how far away is it asked the Court Jester.
>
> [17]It is not as high as the big tree outside my window said the Princess for sometimes it gets caught in the top branches
>
> [18]It will be very easy to get the moon for you said the Court Jester [19]I will climb the tree tonight when it gets caught in the top branches and bring it to you

James Thurber, "Many Moons"

Writing Theme
Moonstruck

CHECK POINT

Writing Theme: Moonstruck

Other related areas students might wish to explore as writing topics include the following:

- Greek and Roman moon goddesses
- a Native American myth about the moon
- how the moon causes tides

MIXED REVIEW • PAGES 586–588

You may wish to use this activity to check students' mastery of the following concept:

- quotation marks

A.

1. The planetarium guide said, "People around the world see different pictures when they look at the moon."
2. She asked, "Have you heard of the man in the moon?"
3. Marie nodded, and Thomas shouted, "Sure!"
4. "To many Europeans," explained the guide, "the markings on the moon look like a man carrying a bundle of twigs."
5. "Many Native American people," she said, "see a frog."
6. "People in Tibet and Mexico see a hare," she continued.
7. "Samoans see a woman," the guide added. "So do the Maori of New Zealand."
8. "What image do you see in the moon?" she asked the children.
9. Marie said, "I see a sleeping cat."
10. Did Thomas really say, "I see a monkey"?

B. Application in Literature

Punctuating Quotations

11. The Princess Lenore was awake, and she was glad to see the Court Jester, but her face was very pale and her voice very weak.
12. "Have you brought the moon to me?" she asked.
13. "Not yet," said the Court Jester, "but I will get it for you right away.
14. How big do you think it is?"
15. "It is just a little smaller than my thumbnail," she said, "for when I hold my thumbnail up at the moon, it just covers it."
16. "And how far away is it?" asked the Court Jester.
17. "It is not as high as the big tree outside my window," said the Princess, "for sometimes it gets caught in the top branches."
18. "It will be very easy to get the moon for you," said the Court Jester.
19. "I will climb the tree tonight when it gets caught in the top branches and bring it to you."

PUNCTUATING TITLES

Objectives

- To punctuate titles correctly

Writing

- To revise a piece of writing by correcting errors in the punctuation of titles

Teaching Strategies

KEY TO UNDERSTANDING Point out that question marks and exclamation points are treated the same way in quoted titles as they are in quotations: They go outside the closing quotation marks if they are not part of the title, but inside if they are (see pages 586–587):

Have you read "The Circuit"?

Have you read the story "Fire!" by John MacDonald?

Additional Resource

Grammar and Usage Practice Book, p. 103

Writing Theme: Science Fiction

Other related areas students might wish to explore as writing topics include the following:

- one of the early science fiction writers mentioned in Exercise B: Mary Shelley, Edgar Allan Poe, Jules Verne, or H. G. Wells
- predictions about what life will be like in fifty years
- a plan to remake the movie *Frankenstein,* set in the 1990s
- taking a trip in a time machine

Answers to Practice Your Skills

A. Concept Check

Titles

1. "Time Travel"
2. <u>Amazing Stories</u>
3. "A Martian Odyssey"
4. <u>Star Trek</u>
5. <u>The Monsters Are Due on Maple Street</u>
6. <u>Star Wars</u>
7. "The Future Now"
8. <u>The Time Machine</u>
9. "The Raven"
10. <u>The Voyage</u>

PUNCTUATING TITLES

Use quotation marks to set off titles of short works. Underline the titles of longer works.

Put quotation marks around the titles of stories, poems, reports, articles, and chapters of a book.

In a sentence, a period or comma following the title is placed within the quotation marks. Place any other punctuation for the sentence outside the quotation marks.

In this issue, read the article "Window to the Future."
I enjoyed the story "Mars Morning"; it's imaginative.

Underline the titles of books, magazines, plays, movies, very long poems, and TV series. In print, these titles appear in italics.

<u>E.T.: The Extra-Terrestrial</u> *E.T.: The Extra-Terrestrial*

Underline the title of a painting or the name of a ship. These titles also appear in italics in printed materials.

<u>The Persistence of Memory</u> (painting)
<u>Flying Dutchman</u> (ship)

To review the guidelines for capitalizing words in titles, see Handbook 42, pages 546–565.

Writing Theme
Science Fiction

Practice Your Skills

A. CONCEPT CHECK

Titles Use quotation marks or underlining for these titles.

1. Time Travel (article)
2. Amazing Stories (magazine)
3. A Martian Odyssey (story)
4. Star Trek (TV series)
5. The Monsters Are Due on Maple Street (play)
6. Star Wars (movie)
7. The Future Now (chapter)
8. The Time Machine (book)
9. The Raven (poem)
10. The Voyage (painting)

B. PROOFREADING SKILL

Punctuating Titles Write the paragraph. Punctuate titles correctly and correct other errors in punctuation, capitalization, and spelling. (32 errors)

Mary Shelley's Frankenstein, written in 1818, may have been the first science fiction novel? Some of Edgar allan Poe's stories, such as The Balloon-Hoax, are close to science fiction. Poe is best known, of corse, for horrer stories, such as The Tell-Tale Heart. Jules verne's first book, Five Weeks in a Balloon, resembles Poe's The Balloon-Hoax. With the sucess of his book Journey to the Center of the Earth, Verne became the first author to earn a living writing science fiction. However; isaac asimov, in an artecle called The Science Fiction Breakthrough, claimed that h. g. wells was the first writer to put science fiction first. My favrite Wells novel is The War of the Worlds. His alien's are not frendly beings like those in the movie E.T. In another article, Beyond Our Brain, asimov said that The War of the Worlds opened a new chapter in science fiction! This novel, along with The Time Machine and The Invisible Man, set the tone for science fiction ever sence.

CHECK POINT

MIXED REVIEW • PAGES 590–591

Write the sentences. Add needed quotation marks and underlining.

1. At the age of nineteen, Isaac Asimov sold his first science fiction tale, Marooned Off Vesta, to Amazing Stories magazine.
2. At twenty-one, he wrote one of his best stories, Nightfall.
3. His story The Fun They Had appears in many collections.
4. Asimov said that his favorite story was The Last Question.
5. His first book was Pebble in the Sky, published in 1950.
6. He won a Hugo award for science fiction for his books Foundation, Foundation and Empire, and Second Foundation.
7. Asimov's Caves of Steel is a science fiction detective novel.
8. His other science fiction books include Nemesis and I, Robot.
9. He wrote a popular book based on the movie Fantastic Voyage.
10. Asimov also wrote dozens of nonfiction science books, including Our World in Space and Understanding Physics.

Writing Theme
Science Fiction Award Winner

Punctuation 591

B. Proofreading Skill

Punctuating Titles

Errors are shown on page. The correctly rewritten paragraphs appear below.

Mary Shelley's Frankenstein, written in 1818, may have been the first science fiction novel. Some of Edgar Allan Poe's stories, such as "The Balloon-Hoax," are close to science fiction. Poe is best known, of course, for horror stories, such as "The Tell-Tale Heart." Jules Verne's first book, Five Weeks in a Balloon, resembles Poe's "The Balloon-Hoax." With the success of his book A Journey to the Center of the Earth, Verne became the first author to earn a living writing science fiction. However, Isaac Asimov, in an article called "The Science Fiction Breakthrough," claimed that H. G. Wells was the first writer to put science fiction first. My favorite Wells novel is The War of the Worlds. His aliens are not friendly beings like those in the movie E.T. In another article, "Beyond Our Brain," Asimov said that The War of the Worlds opened a new chapter in science fiction. This novel, along with The Time Machine and The Invisible Man, set the tone for science fiction ever since.

CHECK POINT

Writing Theme: Science Fiction Award Winner

Other related areas students might wish to explore as writing topics include the following:

- your response to a story by Isaac Asimov
- a favorite science fiction or fantasy writer, such as Ray Bradbury, Robert Silverberg, or Ursula K. Le Guin
- your favorite science fiction movie or TV show
- starting a science fiction fan club

MIXED REVIEW • PAGES 590–591

You may wish to use this activity to check students' mastery of the following concept:

- punctuating titles

1. At the age of nineteen, Isaac Asimov sold his first science fiction tale, "Marooned Off Vesta," to Amazing Stories magazine.
2. At twenty-one, he wrote one of his best stories, "Nightfall."
3. His story "The Fun They Had" appears in many collections.
4. Asimov said that his favorite story was "The Last Question."
5. His first book was Pebble in the Sky, published in 1950.
6. He won a Hugo award for science fiction for his books Foundation, Foundation and Empire, and Second Foundation.
7. Asimov's Caves of Steel is a science fiction detective novel.
8. His other science fiction books include Nemesis and I, Robot.
9. He wrote a popular book based on the movie Fantastic Voyage.
10. Asimov also wrote dozens of nonfiction science books, including Our World in Space and Understanding Physics.

GRAMMAR HANDBOOK 43

ADDITIONAL PRACTICE

Each of these exercises correlates to a section of Handbook 43, "Punctuation." The exercises may be used for more practice, for reteaching, or for review of the concepts presented.

Additional Resource

Grammar and Usage Practice Book, p. 105

Writing Theme: Eyewitness to History

Other related areas students might wish to explore as writing topics include the following:

- another Apollo mission to the moon
- an event in nature you witnessed, such as an eclipse or a hurricane
- a famous event, such as the inauguration of the President, the Summer or Winter Olympics, or the World Series

A. Using Commas and End Marks
Some answers may vary.

1. John, my nephew, asked me if there was any day that I would always remember.
2. "Well, John, I will never forget Sunday, July 20, 1969," I replied.
3. Why is that date so memorable?
4. On that day, two American astronauts, Neil A. Armstrong and Edwin E. Aldrin, Jr., landed on the moon.
5. At 9:56 P.M. Central Time, Armstrong stepped down from the *Eagle,* the lunar landing module, onto the moon's surface.
6. "That's one small step for a man," he proclaimed, "one giant leap for mankind."
7. I stared at the TV and shouted, "Come quickly, Mom! Look!"
8. Wow! Incredible!
9. It was hard to believe, but a human was standing on the moon.
10. What did the astronauts do on the moon?
11. During their short stay on the moon, they did the following:
    1. Planted a U.S. flag
    2. Collected rock samples
    3. Set up scientific equipment
12. Have you ever seen the movies Armstrong and Aldrin took of each other bouncing across the lunar landscape?

ADDITIONAL PRACTICE

GRAMMAR HANDBOOK 43

Writing Theme Eyewitness to History

A. Using Commas and End Marks Write the sentences, adding commas and end marks where they are needed.

1. John my nephew asked me if there was any day that I would always remember
2. "Well John I will never forget Sunday July 20 1969" I replied.
3. Why is that date so memorable
4. On that day, two American astronauts Neil A Armstrong and Edwin E Aldrin, Jr landed on the moon
5. At 9:56 PM Central Time, Armstrong stepped down from the *Eagle* the lunar landing module onto the moon's surface
6. "That's one small step for a man" he proclaimed "one giant leap for mankind."
7. I stared at the TV and shouted "Come quickly Mom Look"
8. Wow Incredible
9. It was hard to believe but a human was standing on the moon
10. What did the astronauts do on the moon
11. During their short stay on the moon, they did the following:
    1 Planted a U.S. flag
    2 Collected rock samples
    3 Set up scientific equipment
12. Have you ever seen the movies Armstrong and Aldrin took of each other bouncing across the lunar landscape
13. Also I remember that on July 24 1969 the first men to visit the moon returned to earth
14. What an extraordinary mission
15. I can't imagine a more thrilling exciting or inspiring event

B. Using Apostrophes and Hyphens Write the following sentences. Make the words in italics contractions, make underlined words show possession, and add hyphens where needed.

16. On October 8, 1871, the watchman Mathias Schaffer *was not* sur prised when he spotted a fire across the river.
17. There had been twenty seven fires in Chicago that week.
18. This, however, was to be one of the worst fires in <u>America</u> history.
19. Supposedly, it began when <u>Mrs. O'Leary</u> cow kicked over a lantern.

20. *It is* certain that the fire did begin in the O'Learys barn.
21. In 1871, most of Chicago buildings were made of wood.
22. Most people *could not* afford to build with brick and stone.
23. A strong wind blew fiery sparks from building to building, de spite firefighters heroic efforts.
24. The fire even traveled across the river to the city downtown.
25. It burned for twenty six hours, destroying 17,450 buildings and taking 250 people lives, before rain finally put it out.

C. Using Colons, Semicolons, and Commas Write this letter. Add colons, semicolons, and commas where these punctuation marks are needed.

[26]June 18 1849

[27]Dear Mr. Hunt

[28]Please forgive my late reply your letter was one of many I have received recently. [29]I appreciate your writing to Smith & Hardwick about your invention however, I do not think we would be interested in your "safety pin." [30]There are many stylish pin designs already on the market another one is not needed. [31]Also, your pin is not good-looking enough to decorate hats coats or other clothing. [32]Not many people would use this pin and we could not expect to profit from making it. [33]We regret that we cannot use your pin however, you may have other clever inventions to show us. [34]If so, Mr. Smith and I can meet with you on Friday June 24 at 1030 A.M.

[35]Yours sincerely
Davidson Hardwick

D. Punctuating Quotations Write the sentences. Add quotation marks and other punctuation where necessary.

36. Can you imagine what it was like to see the Wright brothers' airplane fly at Kitty Hawk, North Carolina asked Jane.
37. It would have been so exciting she exclaimed.
38. David asked whether many people saw that famous flight.
39. I think so answered Jane Some local men were there.
40. She explained that they were from a nearby lifesaving station.

13. Also, I remember that on July 24, 1969, the first men to visit the moon returned to earth.
14. What an extraordinary mission!
15. I can't imagine a more thrilling, exciting, or inspiring event.

B. Using Apostrophes and Hyphens

16. On October 8, 1871, the watchman Mathias Schaffer wasn't sur-prised when he spotted a fire across the river.
17. There had been twenty-seven fires in Chicago that week.
18. This, however, was to be one of the worst fires in America's history.
19. Supposedly, it began when Mrs. O'Leary's cow kicked over a lantern.
20. It's certain that the fire did begin in the O'Leary's barn.
21. In 1871, most of Chicago's buildings were made of wood.
22. Most people couldn't afford to build with brick and stone.
23. A strong wind blew fiery sparks from building to building, de-spite firefighters' heroic efforts.
24. The fire even traveled across the river to the city's downtown.
25. It burned for twenty-six hours, destroying 17,450 buildings and taking 250 people's lives, before rain finally put it out.

C. Using Colons, Semicolons, and Commas

26 June 18, 1849

27 Dear Mr. Hunt:

28 Please forgive my late reply; your letter was one of many I have received recently. **29** I appreciate your writing to Smith & Hardwick about your invention; however, I do not think we would be interested in your "safety pin." **30** There are many stylish pin designs already on the market; another one is not needed. **31** Also, your pin is not good-looking enough to decorate hats, coats, or other clothing. **32** Not many people would use this pin, and we could not expect to profit from making it. **33** We regret that we cannot use your pin; however, you may have other clever inventions to show us. **34** If so, Mr. Smith and I can meet with you on Friday, June 24, at 10:30 A.M.

35 Yours sincerely,
Davidson Hardwick

D. Punctuating Quotations

36. "Can you imagine what it was like to see the Wright brothers' airplane fly at Kitty Hawk, North Carolina?" asked Jane.
37. "It would have been so exciting!" she exclaimed.
38. No change in punctuation
39. "I think so," answered Jane. "Some local men were there."
40. No change in punctuation

41. "The Wrights had been trying to fly their plane for some weeks," she continued, "before they finally succeeded."
42. Jane said that the Wrights took turns being the pilot.
43. "On December 17, 1903," she said, "they had more than one successful flight."
44. "Who was piloting the plane on the first flight?" asked David.
45. "Orville was," Jane replied. "Wilbur, however, piloted the longest flight."
46. "Just imagine!" she exclaimed. "They must have been so happy!"
47. "Did you know that they had worked on this project for seven years?" she asked.
48. Why did Jane smile when David said, "That's a long time"?
49. "Yes," she agreed, "but they were really determined to be the first to fly."
50. Was David surprised when Jane said, "I wish I had been at Kitty Hawk that day"?

E. Using Punctuation Marks

51. On August 19 [comma optional] a tornado destroyed Maystown, Ohio.
52. However, the townspeople weren't discouraged; they immedi-ately began rebuilding their houses, schools, and businesses.
53. Junior-high students wrote about their tornado experiences in a school magazine they called Twister!
54. Simone wrote a poem called "At Exactly 3:23 P.M."
55. Mr. Clybourn's class wrote a play called Where Were You?
56. David's eyewitness report, "It's Not a Freight Train," also appeared in the local newspaper.
57. Keisha wrote an article called "No Home in Maystown"; it told about people whose homes had been destroyed.
58. Theo focused on the speed, power, and random nature of the tornado in his short story, "Gone in Twenty-two Seconds."
59. Martin heard that his photographs of Maystown before and after the tornado might be used in a book, Forces of Nature.
60. Did you see Sarah's home video of the tornado when it was shown on the TV series Eyewitness Video?

41. The Wrights had been trying to fly their plane for some weeks she continued before they finally succeeded.
42. Jane said that the Wrights took turns being the pilot
43. On December 17, 1903 she said they had more than one successful flight.
44. Who was piloting the plane on the first flight asked David.
45. Orville was Jane replied Wilbur, however, piloted the longest flight.
46. Just imagine she exclaimed They must have been so happy!
47. Did you know that they had worked on this project for seven years she asked.
48. Why did Jane smile when David said That's a long time?
49. Yes she agreed but they were really determined to be the first to fly.
50. Was David surprised when Jane said I wish I had been at Kitty Hawk that day?

E. Using Punctuation Marks Copy the sentences. Add underlining, quotation marks, and other punctuation marks where necessary.

51. On August 19 a tornado destroyed Maystown Ohio
52. However the townspeople werent discouraged they immedi ately began rebuilding their houses schools and businesses
53. Junior-high students wrote about their tornado experiences in a school magazine they called Twister!
54. Simone wrote a poem called At Exactly 323 P.M.
55. Mr. Clybourns class wrote a play called Where Were You
56. Davids eyewitness report Its Not a Freight Train also appeared in the local newspaper
57. Keisha wrote an article called No Home in Maystown it told about people whose homes had been destroyed
58. Theo focused on the speed power and random nature of the tornado in his short story, Gone in Twenty two Seconds
59. Martin heard that his photographs of Maystown before and after the tornado might be used in a book, Forces of Nature
60. Did you see Sarahs home video of the tornado when it was shown on the TV series Eyewitness Video

A. End Marks and Commas Write this friendly letter, adding punctuation where necessary.

[1]Dear Alicia
[2]Wow What a surprise [3]After your letter arrived, I ran home and shouted "Mama look Look! [4]I have a letter from America" [5]As I read Mama listened carefully and urged me to write to you soon
[6]Well I am Celia A Katanga from Zambia an African nation and I am happy to be your pen pal [7]Zambia was once a British colony but it became independent on Saturday Oct 24 1964 [8]My family lives in a cement house in Livingstone Zambia [9]The city was named in honor of Dr David Livingstone the famous British explorer of Africa [10]Would you be surprised to learn that we usually cook eat study and visit outdoors rather than in the house
[11]Yes Alicia I like school very much [12]Our classes begin at 7:30 AM and they are not over until 3:50 PM [13]Is your school day longer or shorter [14]These classes are my favorites:
1 Social studies
2 English
3 Home economics
Write soon and tell me more about yourself.
[15]Sincerely
Celia your new pen pal

B. Commas Write the sentences, adding commas where necessary.

16. Ted asked "Raul have you heard of Ndoki a tropical region in northern Congo?"
17. "No I haven't Ted" I replied "but tell me about it."
18. "The Ndoki rain forest is a beautiful exotic and remote place, which very few people have seen" said Ted.
19. Ted said that Michael Fay a botanist with a wildlife conservation organization recently led an expedition there.
20. The expedition began in May of 1992 in Ouesso Congo.
21. The members of the expedition entered the forest several days later and they were often delighted by what they saw.

GRAMMAR HANDBOOK 43

Writing Theme
African Dream

GRAMMAR HANDBOOK 43

REVIEW

These exercises may be used as a mixed review or as an informal evaluation of the skills presented in Handbook 43, "Punctuation."

Additional Resources

Grammar and Usage Practice Book, p. 106
Tests and Writing Assessment Prompts, Mastery Test, pp. 55–58
Elaboration, Revision, and Proofreading Practice, p. 32

Writing Theme: African Dream

Other related areas students might wish to explore as writing topics include the following:
- an African writer, such as Chinua Achebe or Buchi Amecheta
- your response to an African folktale
- endangered species in Africa
- an African musician or group, such as Youssou N'Dour or Ladysmith Black Mambazo

A. End Marks and Commas

Some answers may vary. Possible answers are shown below.
1 Dear Alicia,
2 Wow! What a surprise! 3 After your letter arrived, I ran home and shouted, "Mama, look! look! 4 I have a letter from America!" 5 As I read, Mama listened carefully and urged me to write to you soon.
6 Well, I am Celia A. Katanga from Zambia, an African nation, and I am happy to be your pen pal. 7 Zambia was once a British colony, but it became independent on Saturday, Oct. 24, 1964. 8 My family lives in a cement house in Livingstone, Zambia. 9 The city was named in honor of Dr. David Livingstone, the famous British explorer of Africa. 10 Would you be surprised to learn that we usually cook, eat, study, and visit outdoors rather than in the house?
11 Yes, Alicia, I like school very much. 12 Our classes begin at 7:30 A.M., and they are not over until 3:50 P.M. 13 Is your school day longer or shorter? 14 These classes are my favorites:
1. Social studies
2. English
3. Home economics
Write soon and tell me more about yourself.
15 Sincerely,
Celia, your new pen pal

22. As they walked chimps would stare and screech at them.
23. A gorilla charged stopped and then walked away from them.
24. Conservationists hope that the forest will become a wildlife preserve but they fear it will soon be destroyed.
25. Ndoki must be saved or the world will lose a precious natural resource.

C. Apostrophes and Hyphens Write the sentences, adding apostrophes and hyphens where necessary.

26. Baobab trees grow only on Africas dry savannas.
27. Theyre unusual trees because their branches look like roots.
28. According to the Bushmen, thats a hyenas fault.
29. When the Great Spirit gave him the baobab to plant, he mistakenly planted it upside down!
30. A baobab may be thirty five feet across and fifty five feet tall.
31. But heres the most amazing fact—it can live 1,000 years!
32. Many animals food and shelter are provided by the baobab.
33. Birds nest in the hollows, baboons eat the fruit, bush babies drink the flowers nectar, and insects eat the wood.
34. What about the local peoples uses of the baobab?
35. They gather honey from the tree, use the bark to make baskets and rope, and use the roots and leaves to make medicines.

D. Colons, Semicolons, and Commas Write this business letter, adding colons, semicolons, and commas where necessary.

36 March 25 19—

37 Dear Ms. Khouri

38 Thank you for asking about Ruckomechi the enclosed brochure should answer your questions. **39** Ruckomechi may be remote but it is worth the trip. **40** Our safari camp has the best location in Africa it is perfect for wildlife watching. **41** We have game drives every day at 600 A.M. and 200 P.M. **42** You will see elephants lions and hyenas. **43** You can also canoe fish and bird watch. **44** Our busiest time is September to December however, the camp is open from April 1 to January 1.

45 Sincerely

Zena Gwelo, Manager

B. Commas

16. Ted asked, "Raul, have you heard of Ndoki, a tropical region in northern Congo?"
17. "No, I haven't, Ted," I replied, "but tell me about it."
18. "The Ndoki rain forest is a beautiful, exotic, and remote place, which very few people have seen," said Ted.
19. Ted said that Michael Fay, a botanist with a wildlife conservation organization, recently led an expedition there.
20. The expedition began in May of 1992 in Ouesso, Congo.
21. The members of the expedition entered the forest several days later, and they were often delighted by what they saw.
22. As they walked, chimps would stare and screech at them.
23. A gorilla charged, stopped, and then walked away from them.
24. Conservationists hope that the forest will become a wildlife preserve, but they fear it will soon be destroyed.
25. Ndoki must be saved, or the world will lose a precious natural resource.

C. Apostrophes and Hyphens

26. Baobab trees grow only on Africa's dry savannas.
27. They're unusual trees because their branches look like roots.
28. According to the Bushmen, that's a hyena's fault.
29. When the Great Spirit gave him the baobab to plant, he mis-takenly planted it upside down!
30. A baobab may be thirty-five feet across and fifty-five feet tall.
31. But here's the most amazing fact—it can live 1,000 years!
32. Many animals' food and shelter are provided by the baobab.
33. Birds nest in the hollows, baboons eat the fruit, bush ba-bies drink the flowers' nectar, and insects eat the wood.
34. What about the local people's uses of the baobab?
35. They gather honey from the tree, use the bark to make bas-kets and rope, and use the roots and leaves to make medicines.

D. Colons, Semicolons, and Commas

36 March 25, 19—

37 Dear Ms. Khouri:

38 Thank you for asking about Ruckomechi; the enclosed brochure should answer your questions. 39 Ruckomechi may be remote, but it is worth the trip. 40 Our safari camp has the best location in Africa; it is perfect for wildlife watching. 41 We have game drives every day at 6:00 A.M. and 2:00 P.M. 42 You will see elephants, lions, and hyenas. 43 You can also canoe, fish, and bird watch. 44 Our busiest time is September to December; however, the camp is open from April 1 to January 1.

45 Sincerely,

Zena Gwelo, Manager

596 Grammar Handbook

E. Quotation Marks Write the sentences, adding quotation marks where necessary. Write *Correct* if no quotation marks are needed.

46. The students said that they had enjoyed their safari in Zimbabwe, Africa.
47. I asked, What is your favorite memory of the safari?
48. I saw lions in the wild, said Hilton. That was very exciting!
49. We learned to track animals, said Doris, by studying the trails they left.
50. At night, Stuart said, we played games, sang songs, and put on plays.
51. I asked how they had felt on the last day of the safari.
52. I felt happy and sad at the same time, said Hilton.
53. Everyone nodded in agreement when Stuart exclaimed, It was wonderful!
54. Do you want to go on a safari again? I asked.
55. Would you be surprised to learn that everyone shouted, Yes?

F. Titles Write the sentences, adding either quotation marks or underlining for each title.

56. I need to find information for a report I'm writing, called The Influence of African Music on American Music: Blues, Jazz, and Rock.
57. First, I read the book The Music of Africa: An Introduction.
58. One chapter, The Music of Contemporary Africa, was helpful.
59. However, another book, African Music: A People's Art, dealt only with traditional African music.
60. More current was an article in Fortune magazine called Africa's Hot New Export: Music.
61. Another article, The Roots of the Blues, was also good.
62. It was one of a series of articles in Music magazine.
63. Now I'm looking for a book called A Celebration of African-American Music.
64. It is based on a program from a TV series, Music Travels.
65. I'm planning to begin my report with a quotation about African music from a poem called African Heaven.

E. Quotation Marks

46. Correct
47. I asked, "What is your favorite memory of the safari?"
48. "I saw lions in the wild," said Hilton. "That was very exciting!"
49. "We learned to track animals," said Doris, "by studying the trails they left."
50. "At night," Stuart said, "we played games, sang songs, and put on plays."
51. Correct
52. "I felt happy and sad at the same time," said Hilton.
53. Everyone nodded in agreement when Stuart exclaimed, "It was wonderful!"
54. "Do you want to go on a safari again?" I asked.
55. Would you be surprised to learn that everyone shouted, "Yes"?

F. Titles

56. I need to find information for a report I'm writing, called "The Influence of African Music on American Music: Blues, Jazz, and Rock."
57. First, I read the book <u>The Music of Africa: An Introduction</u>.
58. One chapter, "The Music of Contemporary Africa," was helpful.
59. However, another book, <u>African Music: A People's Art</u>, dealt only with traditional African music.
60. More current was an article in <u>Fortune</u> magazine called "Africa's Hot New Export: Music."
61. Another article, "The Roots of the Blues," was also good.
62. It was one of a series of articles in <u>Music</u> magazine.
63. Now, I'm looking for a book called <u>A Celebration of African-American Music</u>.
64. It is based on a program from a TV series, <u>Music Travels</u>.
65. I'm planning to begin my report with a quotation about African music from a poem called "African Heaven."

WRITING CONNECTIONS

Elaboration, Revision, and Proofreading

This activity will allow students to see some of the concepts presented in this Handbook at work in a piece of informative writing. By revising and proofreading this passage, they will gain practice in using correct punctuation, especially in quotations and titles. They will also begin to see how to organize information into compound sentences and paragraphs.

You might begin by having the class as a whole discuss which sentence does not belong. Then divide students into small groups or pairs to revise the passage; alternatively, have them work individually and then go over their revisions with a partner. Revisions may vary slightly. See a typical revision below. Elements involving change are shown in boldface.

An unusual military strategy of Hannibal's army in the Second Punic War involved its use of elephants. ~~Elephants come from Africa and Asia~~. When Hannibal invaded Italy in 218 B.C., his army included thirty-seven elephants. According to the book The Ancient Romans by Chester Starr, the elephants were used as "walking tanks" against enemy foot soldiers.

Even before the army entered Italy, the elephants played an important role. To reach Italy, Hannibal's troops had to **struggle** over the Alps. They were attacked along the way by mountain tribes, **but** the elephants scared away some of the attackers. The Greek historian Polybius said, "The enemy was so terrified of the animals' strange appearance that they dared not come anywhere near them."

WRITING CONNECTIONS

Elaboration, Revision, and Proofreading

Informative Writing: Reports

A report presents facts about a topic in a clear and organized way. (See Workshop 7.) When you revise a report, make sure your facts are presented accurately. Also make sure you have used punctuation correctly, especially in quotations and titles.

Revise this portion of a report, using the directions at the bottom of the page. Then proofread your writing, paying special attention to the use of punctuation. Also look for errors in grammar, capitalization, and spelling.

[1]An unusual military strategy of Hannibal's army in the Second Punic War involved it's use of elephants. [2]Elephants come from Africa and Asia. [3]When Hannibal invaded Italy in 218 bc, his army included thirty seven elephants. [4]According to the book "The ancient romans" by Chester Starr, the elephants were used as "walking tanks" against enamy foot soldiers. [5]To reach Italy, Hannibals troups had to go over the Alps. [6]They was attacked along the way by mountain tribes. [7]The elephant's scared away some of the attacker's. [8]The greek historian Polybius said "The enemy was so terrified of the animals' strange appearance that they dared not come anywhere near them".

1. Delete the sentence that does not belong.
2. Add this sentence after sentence 4 to introduce the information that follows: "Even before the army entered Italy, the elephants played an important role."
3. In sentence 5, replace the weak verb "go" with a more expressive verb.
4. Combine sentences 6 and 7 by using the conjunction "but."
5. Divide the passage into two paragraphs.

on the LIGHT side

Silly Signs

Signs are everywhere—on street corners and on diner counter tops, in store windows and in hotel lobbies. But do signs always mean what they say? Look at the examples below and judge for yourself. These signs appear in *English Well Speeched Here* by Nino Lo Bello.

WARNING: DOOR IS ALARMED

PLEASE DO NOT FEED THE ANIMALS. IF YOU HAVE ANY SUITABLE FOOD, GIVE IT TO THE GUARD ON DUTY.

We Take Your Bags and Send Them in All Directions.

If You Consider Our Help Impolite, You Should See the Manager.

Authentic Tie Cuisine

The Parade Will Take Place in the Morning If It Rains in the Afternoon.

Courteous and Efficient Self-Service

You might begin discussing this feature by making sure everyone in the class "gets" what makes these signs silly—and why they don't always say what they mean.

For example, what is the parade sign trying to say? ("The Parade Will Take Place in the Morning. If It Rains, It Will Take Place in the Afternoon.") What is the zoo sign apparently asking visitors to do? (Give suitable food to the guard so that he or she can feed it to the animals.) What's so nonsensical about the self-service sign?

Have students keep their eyes open for signs that could use some good editing or proofreading; then add them to your "bloopers" bulletin board (see page 263).

Test 4

This test enables you to evaluate student mastery of the concepts taught in handbooks 42–43.

Additional Resource

Grammar and Usage Practice Book, pp. 107–108

Answer Key

1. A—Captain Hook
2. A—ate, the
   B—*Nova*
3. A—Anchorage
   B—people, but
4. B—"Don't
5. B—It
6. B—P.M. The
   C—8:05
7. B—there
   C—stage.
8. B—Asian
9. D
10. A—Colorado River
11. B—liberty
12. C—God
13. C—"All Summer in a Day."
14. D
15. A—planets
    B—any room

Skills

ASSESSMENT

TEST 4 Grammar Handbooks *42–43*

Directions One or more of the underlined sections in the following sentences may contain an error in grammar, punctuation, spelling, or capitalization. Write the letter of each incorrect section. Then rewrite the section correctly. If there is no error in an item, write *D*.

Example Sonja's (A) grandmother (B) came to the United States from Norway in 1932 mine (C) came from Ireland the same year. No error (D)

Answer C—1932. Mine

1. Peter Pan fans all recognize the name captain Hook (A), but few know that Hook's (B) first name was James (C). No error (D)

2. After we ate the (A) electricity went off, so we couldn't watch *nova* (B) on public television (C). No error (D)

3. The biggest city in the United States is anchorage (A), Alaska. It doesn't have the most people but (B) it covers the largest (C) area. No error (D)

4. "The bus leaves in two hours," (A) the guide said. "don't (B) be late or you'll be left behind!" (C) No error (D)

5. The woolly mammoth (A) had tusks sixteen feet long. it (B) has been extinct since the Ice Age (C). No error (D)

6. The brochure says the museum (A) closes at 8:00 P.M. the (B) doors are locked at 8 05 (C). No error (D)

600 Skills Assessment

7. The usher at the concert told Eric and us (A) that "There (B) might be a few seats near the stage." (C) No error (D)

8. African elephants are larger and more dangerous (A) than asian (B) elephants. African elephants also have (C) larger ears. No error (D)

9. Charles Dickens named one of the worst (A) villains in his stories after his best friend, (B) Bob Fagin. Fortunately, (C) Fagin had a sense of humor. No error (D)

10. The colorado river (A) is important to millions of Americans. It (B) is the major source of water for all the states in the Southwest. (C) No error (D)

11. Who shouted, "Give (A) me Liberty (B) or give me death"? (C) No error (D)

12. On every U.S. coin there (A) is (B) the motto "In god (C) we trust." No error (D)

13. One of my favorite short stories by Ray Bradbury (A) is (B) "All summer in a Day." (C) No error (D)

14. Some bristlecone pine trees in California (A) are four thousand years old. They're (B) believed to be the oldest (C) living things in the world. No error (D)

15. The planet Jupiter is so large that all the other planet's (A) in our solar system could be placed inside it if it were hollow. However, there wouldn't be no room (B) for all of the planets' (C) moons. No error (D)

List of Skills Tested

1. A—capitalization—title with name
   B—punctuation—possession
   C—capitalization—common/proper noun
2. A—punctuation—comma
   B—capitalization—title
   C—capitalization—common/proper noun
3. A—capitalization—place name
   B—punctuation—comma
   C—comparative adjective form
4. A—punctuation—quotation
   B—capitalization—quotation
   C—punctuation—quotation
5. A—capitalization—common/proper noun
   B—capitalization—first word
   C—capitalization—time period
6. A—capitalization—common/proper noun
   B—capitalization—first word
   C—punctuation—colon
7. A—pronoun case
   B—punctuation—quotation/indirect quotation
   C—punctuation—quotation
8. A—comparative adjective form
   B—capitalization—nationality
   C—subject-verb agreement
9. A—comparative adjective form
   B—spelling
   C—punctuation—end mark
10. A—capitalization—river
    B—capitalization—first word
    C—capitalization—geographic region
11. A—punctuation—quotation
    B—capitalization—common/proper noun
    C—punctuation—quotation
12. A—spelling
    B—subject-verb agreement
    C—capitalization—deity
13. A—capitalization—common/proper noun
    B—subject-verb agreement
    C—capitalization—title
14. A—capitalization—common/proper noun
    B—punctuation—contraction
    C—comparative adjective form
15. A—noun plural
    B—double negative
    C—plural possessive

Post-Test

This test assesses your students' mastery of skills acquired in the Grammar and Usage Handbook.

Answer Key

Corrections for run-ons may vary.

1. C—he
2. B—Paris, France,
   C—Ontario?
3. A—are
   B—confusing. Can
4. B—telegraph, was
5. C—country"?
6. A—uncle
   B—likes
7. B—knows
   C—its *or* her
8. A—sits
9. B—indoors to
   C—mice
10. A—well
    C—poorly
11. A—lie
    B—north
12. C—me
13. C—bicycling
14. D
15. D

Skills

ASSESSMENT POST-TEST Grammar Handbooks

Directions One or more of the underlined sections in the following sentences may contain an error in grammar, punctuation, spelling, or capitalization. Write the letter of each incorrect section. Then rewrite the section correctly. If there is no error in an item, write *D.*

Example The statue of Crazy Horse in south dakota (A) will be the largest sculpture in the world when it is completed (B). It is being carved out of a mountain (C). No error (D)

Answer A—South Dakota

1. Christopher Columbus's (A) younger brother Bartholomew helped the famous navigator plan his voyages. Christopher (B) and him (C) were very close. No error (D)

2. Was the letter addressed (A) to Paris France (B) or Paris, Ontario. (C) No error (D)

3. The instructions for operating this VCR is (A) very confusing can (B) you help me please? (C) No error (D)

4. At first, Samuel B. Morse, the (A) inventor of the telegraph was (B) better (C) known as a painter than as an inventor. No error (D)

5. Was it Nathan Hale who said, " (A)I regret that I (B) have but one life to give for my country?" (C) No error (D)

6. My Uncle (A) has two pet ferrets. One of them like (B) to eat French fried potatoes. (C) No error (D)

7. Somehow each of the ewes in that large flock of <u>sheep</u> **A** <u>know</u> **B** how to find <u>their</u> **C** lambs. <u>No error</u> **D**

8. Mount Kenya <u>sets</u> **A** right along the Equator, but because of <u>its</u> **B** <u>height</u> **C**—over 17,000 feet—the top is covered with snow. <u>No error</u> **D**

9. Rural households in ancient <u>Greece</u> **A** often kept snakes <u>indoors. To</u> **B** control rats and <u>mouses</u> **C**. <u>No error</u> **D**

10. Most metals conduct electricity <u>good</u> **A**. On the other hand, <u>substances</u> **B** made of nonmetal conduct electricity <u>poor</u> **C**. <u>No error</u> **D**

11. Parts of Scotland <u>lay</u> **A** as far <u>North</u> **B** in latitude as southern Alaska, but warm air from the <u>Gulf Stream</u> **C** makes Scotland's climate quite mild. <u>No error</u> **D**

12. Stalactites <u>hung</u> **A** all around <u>us</u> **B**, and a bat flew at Tom and <u>I</u> **C**. <u>No error</u> **D**

13. The triathlon participants had <u>swum</u> **A** a <u>mile, but</u> **B** they still had the <u>bycycling</u> **C** and running events ahead of them. <u>No error</u> **D**

14. On <u>December 7, 1941,</u> **A** millions of Americans turned on <u>their</u> **B** <u>radios</u> **C** and heard about the Japanese attack on Pearl Harbor. <u>No error</u> **D**

15. Stevland Morris is a great musician. However, most people <u>wouldn't</u> **A** recognize that <u>name. They</u> **B** know <u>him</u> **C** as Stevie Wonder. <u>No error</u> **D**

List of Skills Tested

1. A—punctuation—possessive
   B—sentence fragment/run-on
   C—pronoun case
2. A—spelling
   B—punctuation—comma
   C—punctuation—end mark
3. A—subject-verb agreement
   B—run-on sentence
   C—punctuation—end mark
4. A—punctuation—comma
   B—punctuation—comma
   C—comparison form
5. A—punctuation—quotation marks
   B—pronoun case
   C—punctuation—quotation marks
6. A—capitalization—common/proper noun
   B—subject-verb agreement
   C—noun plural
7. A—noun plural
   B—subject-verb agreement
   C—agreement of possessive pronoun and indefinite pronoun
8. A—confusing verb pairs
   B—possessive pronoun
   C—spelling
9. A—capitalization—common/proper noun
   B—sentence fragment/run-on
   C—noun plural
10. A—adjective/adverb confusion
    B—noun plural
    C—adjective/adverb confusion
11. A—confusing verb pairs
    B—capitalization—common/proper noun
    C—capitalization—common/proper noun
12. A—irregular verb form
    B—pronoun case
    C—pronoun case
13. A—irregular verb form
    B—punctuation—comma
    C—spelling
14. A—punctuation—comma
    B—pronoun-antecedent agreement
    C—noun plural
15. A—punctuation—apostrophe
    B—sentence fragment/run-on
    C—pronoun case

Skills Assessment **603**

ART NOTE Help students unfamiliar with Asia to understand that Asia is the home of diverse cultures and religions. In some countries, such as Nepal, Buddhist and Hindu festivals and traditions intermingle.

The three papier-mâché masks shown here are used in various joyful religious festivals in Indonesia, Nepal, and Hong Kong. The upper mask and the one at the right portray a lion and a dragon.

Upper Mask. This ceremonial mask of a lion is from Bali. (Note the striped ears, fierce teeth, and leonine nose.) In Asia, lion-head masks are sometimes thought to bring good luck and wealth.

Lower Right Mask. On Chinese New Year, men snake through the streets, performing the dragon dance. The first dancer carries an elaborate dragon mask like the one shown here. According to Chinese mythology, four dragon kings rule the four seas surrounding the earth and also control rainfall. Lakes and rivers are ruled by local dragon kings, and people place a small dragon-king statue by each well. To the Chinese, the dragon is well-meaning and is a powerful symbol.

Lower Left Mask. This devil mask was photographed at a winter religious festival in Katmandu, the capital of Nepal (a country in the Himalayas between Tibet and India). This mask may have been used in either a Buddhist or a Hindu festival.

Encourage students to find and tell (or read aloud) a myth or folk tale from the Nepalese tradition.

Colorful ceremonial masks, such as the ones shown here from (counterclockwise from top) Indonesia, Nepal, and Hong Kong, are used in religious festivals to portray characters from mythology and legend.

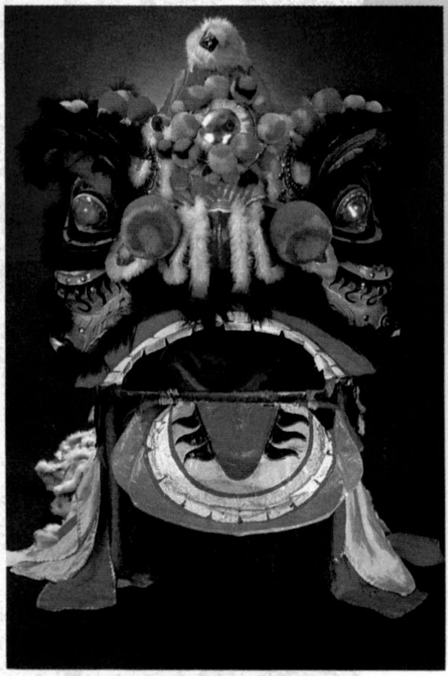

Appendix

Appendix

605

TECHNIQUES FOR PEER RESPONSE

Sharing your writing with others is a good way to ge encouragement and new ideas. It is also a way to find out wha things your readers like in your writing and what ideas may no be clear. Here are some techniques to help you get th responses you need to improve your writing.

Sharing

How to Use Share your writing with your peer readers by asking them to read or listen to it. Hearing how your words sound may help you and your peer readers discover new ideas or places where more details are needed.

At this stage your peer readers serve as your friendly audience. They should not evaluate your writing.

When to Use You may use this technique when you are exploring ideas. You may also use it to celebrate a finished piece of writing.

Pointing

How to Use Ask your readers to tell you about the things they like best in your writing. Ask them to be specific and to avoid simply saying, "I like it."

Have readers point out the words and phrases that create an image or express an idea clearly.

When to Use Use this technique when you want to find out what ideas are getting through to your readers. Also use it when you want encouragement and support for your writing.

606 Appendix

Summarizing

How to Use Ask readers to tell you the main idea in your writing. If readers stray from the main idea and start to talk about specific parts that they like or that confuse them, you might say, "For now, I want to know if I got my idea across to you."

Remind readers that at this stage you are not asking for an evaluation of your writing.

When to Use Use this technique when you want to know if your main idea or goals are getting through to readers.

Telling

How to Use Ask readers to tell you how they felt as they read your words. For example, did they feel sad or happy at any parts of your story? Did they get the characters mixed up? Did anything make them laugh?

As readers describe their feelings, ask them to point out the parts of the story that caused their reactions.

When to Use Use this technique when you want to find out which words and phrases are creating the effect you want and which ones are confusing your readers.

Identifying

How to Use Ask for feedback about things the readers don't understand, things they want to know more about, and questions that came to mind as they read.

Ask specific questions, such as these: What part was most interesting to you? Is there anything you'd like to know more about? Was anything confusing? How can I improve the organization? What are your views on this topic?

When to Use Use this technique to identify strengths and weaknesses in your writing.

Techniques for Peer Response 607

OUTLINING

An outline helps you plan your writing and take notes. In an outline main ideas are listed as headings. Details are shown as subpoints. A **sentence outline** uses complete sentences for the main ideas and details. A **topic outline** uses words or phrases, as in this model.

Sign Language

Thesis Statement: Sign language is a system of gestures and hand symbols developed to help hearing-impaired people communicate.

I. Types of sign language (Main idea)
- **A.** American Sign Language (Subpoint for I)
  - **1.** Based on ideas, not words (Detail for A)
  - **2.** Expresses ideas in gestures
- **B.** American Manual Alphabet
  - **1.** Based on the alphabet (Detail for B)
  - **2.** Uses finger symbols for letters
  - **3.** Combines finger symbols with gestures

II. Uses of sign language
- **A.** By deaf people (Subpoint for II)
- **B.** By hearing-impaired people
- **C.** By non-hearing-impaired people

Correct Outline Form

1. Write the title at the top of the outline.
2. Arrange main ideas and details as shown in the model.
3. Indent each division of the outline.
4. Break down each heading into at least two details. For example, if there is a 1 under A, there must be a 2.
5. In a topic outline, use the same form for items of the same rank. If A is a noun, then B and C should be nouns.
6. Begin each item with a capital letter. Do not use end punctuation in a topic outline.

608 Appendix

LETTER FORM

Business Letter

Heading 3148 Main Street
Downers Grove, IL 60516
September 22, 19—

American Assn. of Zoological Inside Address
Parks and Aquariums
4550 Montgomery Avenue
Suite 940N
Bethesda, MD 20814

Dear Sir or Madam: Salutation

Body I would like to learn about zoos that allow people to pay a small amount of money to "adopt" an animal. These zoos then use the money to buy food, improve habitats, and help support special programs for endangered animals. I understand that your association can send me information about adopt-an-animal programs.

Please send me information about programs in Illinois and Ohio. If you know of zoos that have unusual animals, such as cinnamon tarantulas, laughing thrushes, or pygmy hippos, please send me that information also.

Thank you for your help.

Sincerely, Closing

Laurie Douvris Signature

Laurie Douvris

Heading The heading contains your street address; your town or city, state, and ZIP code; and the date of the letter.

Inside Address Include the name of an individual if you know it and the name and address of the organization.

Salutation Begin the salutation two lines below the inside address and end with a colon. If you are writing to a specific person, include that person's name. If you do not know who will receive your letter, use a general greeting.

Body This section should be brief, courteous, and clear. State the purpose of your letter and indicate any items that you are requesting or have enclosed.

Closing This appears two lines below the body and is always formal. "Sincerely" and "Yours truly" are examples.

Signature Skip four spaces below the closing, print or type your name, and write your signature in the space.

Letter Form 609

IMPROVING YOUR SPELLING

Like hitting a fastball or mastering the backstroke, becoming a spelling whiz takes planning and practice. By following these tips and basic rules, you can become a better speller.

Spelling Tips

1. **Identify your own spelling demons.** Make a list of the words you have misspelled in your writing.
2. **Pronounce words carefully.** Sometimes people misspell words because they say them incorrectly. For example, if you say the word *schedule* correctly, you will not misspell it *s-c-h-e-d-u-e-l.*
3. **Make a habit of seeing the letters in a word.** Pay attention to every letter of a new or difficult word. For example, when you come upon a word like *library,* look at each letter to fix the spelling in your mind.
4. **Invent memory devices for problem words.** Here are some examples:

princi**pal** (pal)	The princi**pal** is my **pal**.
tr**age**dy (age)	Every **age** has its tr**age**dy.
emba**rra**ss (rr, ss)	I turned **r**eally **r**ed and felt **s**o **s**illy.

5. **Proofread what you write.** Reread your work word for word so that you don't miss incorrectly spelled words.

Steps for Mastering Difficult Words

1. Look at the word and say it one syllable at a time.
2. Look at the letters and say each one.
3. Picture the word in your mind as you write it.
4. Check to see that you have spelled the word correctly. If you misspelled the word, notice what the mistake was and repeat steps 1–3.

Words Ending in a Silent *e*

Before adding a suffix beginning with a vowel to a word ending in a silent *e*, drop the *e* (with some exceptions).

love + -able = lovable   improve + -ing = improving

Exceptions: dye + -ing = dyeing   mile + -age = mileage

When adding a suffix beginning with a consonant to a word ending in a silent *e*, keep the *e* (with some exceptions).

hate + -ful = hateful   excite + -ment = excitement

Exceptions: true + -ly = truly   argue + -ment = argument

Words Ending in *y*

When adding a suffix to a word that ends in a *y* preceded by a consonant, change the *y* to *i*.

noisy + -ly = noisily   nutty + -est = nuttiest

However, when adding *-ing,* do not change the *y.*

cry + -ing = crying   deny + -ing = denying

When a suffix is added to a word that ends in a *y* preceded by a vowel, the *y* usually does not change.

play + -ing = playing   enjoy + -ment = enjoyment

Words Ending in a Consonant

If a one-syllable word ends in one consonant preceded by one vowel, double the final consonant before adding a suffix beginning with a vowel, such as *-ing* or *-ed.* (Such a word is sometimes called a 1 + 1 + 1 word.)

sit + -ing = sitting   red + -est = reddest

The rule does not apply to words of one syllable that end in a consonant preceded by two vowels.

meet + -ing = meeting   dream + -er = dreamer

Improving Your Spelling 611

For a word of more than one syllable, double the final consonant (1) when the word ends in one consonant preceded by one vowel and (2) when the word is accented on the last syllable.

ad•mit′ be•gin′ pre•fer′

In these examples, note that after the suffix is added, the accent remains on the same syllable.

ad•mit′ + -ed = ad•mit′ ted
be•gin′ + -ing = be•gin′ ning

In this example, the accent does not remain on the same syllable; thus, the final consonant is not doubled.

pre•fer′ + -able = pref′ er•a•ble

Prefixes and Suffixes

When adding a prefix to a word, do not change the spelling of the base word.

un- + known = unknown mis + spell = misspell

When adding *-ly* to a word ending in *l,* keep both *l*'s. When adding *-ness* to a word ending in *n,* keep both *n*'s.

practical + -ly = practically mean + -ness = meanness

Special Spelling Problems

One English word ends in *-sede: supersede.* Three words end in *-ceed: exceed, proceed,* and *succeed.* All other words ending in the sound *seed* are spelled with *-cede.*

concede precede recede secede

When choosing between *ie* and *ei,* if the sound is long *e* (ē), you should usually spell the word with *ie* except after *c.*

i* before *e	belief	shield	yield	niece	field
except after *c*	conceit	receive	ceiling	deceive	receipt

Exceptions: either neither weird leisure seize

612 Appendix

USING THE RIGHT WORD

The following words are commonly misused or misspelled. Some of these words are **homonyms**, or words that have similar sounds but are spelled differently and have different meanings. Study this section to make sure you are using words correctly in your writing.

accept, except *Accept* means "to agree to" or "to receive willingly." *Except* usually means "not including."

My brother will *accept* the job at the grocery store.
Luis likes every flavor of yogurt *except* lemon.

a lot *A lot* is informal. Do not use it in formal writing. *Alot* is incorrect.

borrow, lend *Borrow* means "to receive on loan." *Lend* means "to give temporarily."

I *borrowed* my sister's watch.
Please *lend* me your eraser.

capital, capitol, the Capitol *Capital* means "very serious" or "very important." It also means "seat of government." A *capitol* is a building in which a state legislature meets. The *Capitol* is the building in Washington, D.C., in which the U.S. Congress meets.

The *capital* of Illinois is the city of Springfield.
The Illinois *capitol* is a stately building in Springfield.
The senator arrived at the *Capitol* in time to vote.

desert, dessert *Des′ ert* means "a dry, sandy, barren region." *De sert′* means "to abandon." *Des sert′* is a sweet food, such as pie.

Tall cactus plants grow in the *desert*.
The crane would not *desert* his injured mate.
Jake loves ice cream for *dessert*.

Using the Right Word 613

good, well *Good* is always an adjective. *Well* is usually an adverb that modifies an action verb. *Well* can also be an adjective meaning "in good health."

That dress looks *good* on you.
Anne performed her skating routine *well.*
Nikki didn't feel *well* today.

hear, here *Hear* means "to listen to." *Here* means "in this place."

Every time I *hear* this song, I feel happy.
The mayor's family has lived *here* for generations.

its, it's *Its* is a possessive pronoun. *It's* is a contraction of *it is* or *it has.*

The boat lost *its* sail during the storm.
It's nearly midnight.

lay, lie *Lay* is a verb that means "to place." It takes a direct object. *Lie* is a verb that means "to recline" or "to be in a certain place." *Lie* never takes a direct object.

Don't *lay* your coat on the couch.
The terrier likes to *lie* under the swing.
The island *lies* in the path of the hurricane.

lead, led *Lead* can be a noun that means "a heavy metal" or a verb that means "to show the way." *Led* is the past tense form of the verb.

These pellets contain *lead.*
The lieutenant *leads* her troops in the parade.
He *led* a group of explorers out of the jungle.

learn, teach *Learn* means "to gain knowledge." *Teach* means "to instruct."

In social studies we are *learning* about frontier life.
He is *teaching* us to use a computer.

614 Appendix

like, as, as if *Like* is a preposition. Use *as* or *as if* to introduce a clause.

He ran the pass pattern *as* he should.

loose, lose *Loose* means "free" or "not fastened." *Lose* means "to mislay or suffer the loss of."

The rider kept the horse's reins *loose.*
If you *lose* your book, tell the librarian right away.

of Use *have,* not *of,* in phrases such as *could have, should have,* and *must have.*

We should *have* invited her to our party.

peace, piece *Peace* means "calm" or "quiet." *Piece* means "a section or part."

After two years of war came *peace.*
The statue was carved from a *piece* of jade.

principal, principle *Principal* means "of chief or central importance" or "the head of a school." *Principle* means "basic truth," "standard," or "rule of behavior."

The *principal* export of Brazil is coffee.
The *principal* of our school organized a safety council.
One *principle* of science is that all matter occupies space.

quiet, quite *Quiet* means "free from noise or disturbance." *Quite* means "truly" or "almost completely."

The library is *quiet* in the afternoon.
The aquarium tank is *quite* full.

raise, rise *Raise* means "to lift" or "to cause to go up." It takes a direct object. *Rise* means "to go upward." It does not take a direct object.

Can you *raise* the sail by yourself?
The jury will *rise* when the judge enters the courtroom.

Using the Right Word 615

set, sit *Set* means "to place." It takes a direct object. *Sit* means "to occupy a seat or a place." It does not take a direct object.

I *set* the bag of groceries inside the door.
Sit still while we take your picture.

their, there, they're *Their* means "belonging to them." *There* means "in that place." *They're* is a contraction of *they are.*

Our neighbors sold *their* house and moved to a farm.
Please play with the squirt guns over *there.*
My sisters don't swim, but *they're* eager to learn.

to, too, two *To* means "toward" or "in the direction of." *Too* means "also" or "very." *Two* is the number 2.

The surgeon dashed *to* the emergency room.
It was *too* hot to run a race.
Only *two* of the six lifeboats reached shore.

weather, whether *Weather* refers to conditions such as temperature or cloudiness. *Whether* expresses a choice.

The *weather* is perfect for a picnic.
Whether we drive or take the train, we will arrive late.

whose, who's *Whose* is the possessive form of *who. Who's* is a contraction of *who is* or *who has.*

Whose wallet is lying under the chair?
Who's been chosen the student of the month?

your, you're *Your* is the possessive form of *you. You're* is a contraction of *you are.*

Please bring *your* cameras to the assembly.
You're doing much better this semester than last.

616 Appendix

Sentence Diagraming

A sentence diagram is a drawing that shows how the parts of a sentence are related. Use the following models as guides.

Subjects and Verbs

To diagram a subject and a verb, first draw a horizontal line. On this line write the subject and the verb. Then draw a vertical line between them. Capitalize words capitalized in the sentence. Do not use punctuation marks except in abbreviations.

Cars collided.

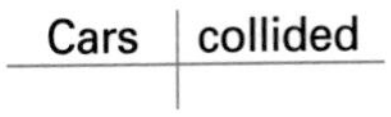

Questions, Exclamations, and Commands

In a sentence that asks a question, the subject often comes after the verb. When you diagram a question, put the subject before the verb.

Do dolphins communicate?

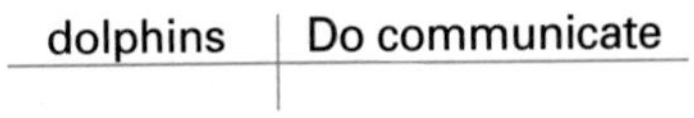

In a command or an exclamation, the subject is usually understood to be you. In diagraming, put the understood subject you before the verb and enclose it in parentheses.

Look.

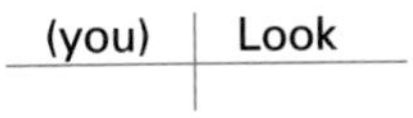

Go!

Sentence Diagraming 617

Compound Subjects and Verbs

To diagram a compound subject, split the subject line. Then write the conjunction on a dotted line between the subjects. Diagram compound verbs similarly.

Rose and Allan studied.
(Compound subject)

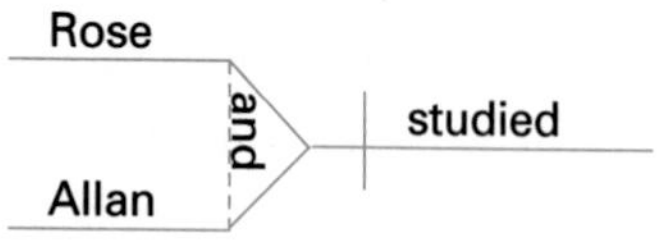

Raul fields and throws.
(Compound verb)

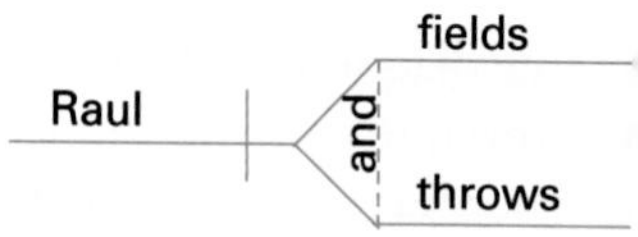

Direct Objects

Write a direct object after the verb. Then draw a short vertical line between the verb and the direct object.

Jody writes stories.

Predicate Words

Write a predicate word—noun, pronoun, or adjective—after the verb. Between the verb and the predicate word, draw a line slanting toward the subject.

Frogs feel slippery.

Caterpillars become butterflies.

618 Appendix

Adjectives

Write an adjective on a slanted line below the word it modifies. Treat possessive nouns and pronouns as adjectives.

The explorers searched a secret cave.

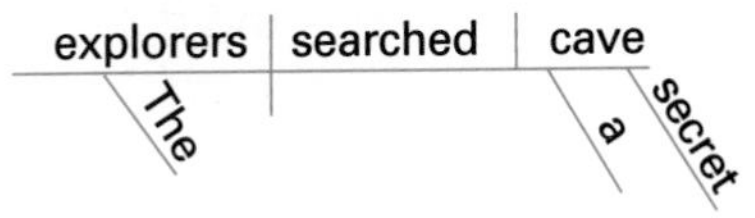

Adverbs

Write an adverb on a slanted line below the word it modifies.

Cats pounce silently.

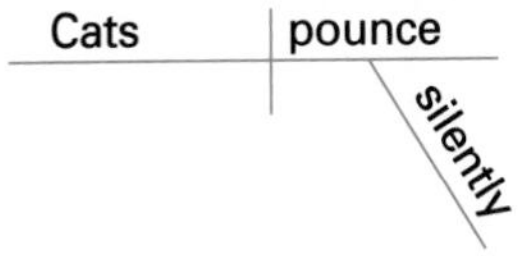

Prepositional Phrases

A prepositional phrase acts as an adjective or an adverb, so diagram it in a similar way. Draw an angled line below the word modified. Write the preposition on the slanted part and its object on the horizontal part. Put any modifiers on slanted lines below the object.

Fish darted through a coral tunnel.

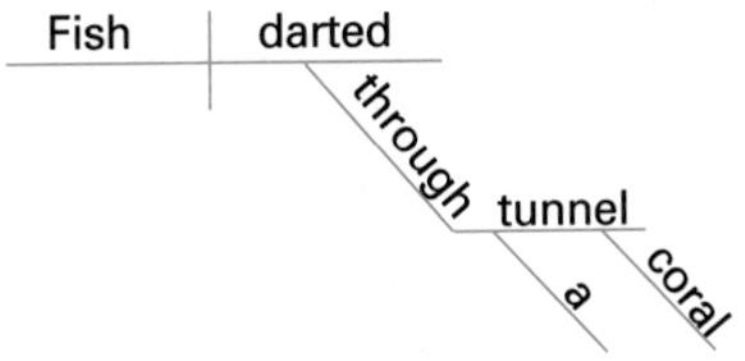

Sentence Diagraming 619

GLOSSARY FOR WRITERS

ADJECTIVE a word that modifies a noun or pronoun: *one* day.

ADVERB a word that modifies a verb, an adjective, or another adverb; in "She smiles often," *often* is an adverb modifying the verb *smiles.*

AUDIENCE your readers or listeners.

BRAINSTORMING a way of finding ideas that involves listing them without stopping to judge them.

CHRONOLOGICAL arranged in order of occurrence.

CLICHÉ an overused expression, such as "sly as a fox."

CLUSTER a kind of map made up of circled groupings of related details.

COHERENCE in paragraphs, logical flow from one sentence to the next; in compositions, logical ties between paragraphs.

CONJUNCTION a word or pair of words that connects other words or groups of words: Glenna *and* Gary won.

DIALECT a form of a language that has a distinctive pronunciation, vocabulary, and word order.

DIALOGUE spoken conversation; the conversation in novels, stories, plays, poems, and essays.

ELABORATION the support or development of a main idea with details, incidents, examples, or quotations.

FIGURATIVE LANGUAGE the imaginative and poetic use of words; writing that contains such figures of speech as similes, metaphors, and personification.

FREEWRITING a way of exploring ideas, thoughts, or feelings by writing down everything that comes to mind within a specific length of time.

GLEANING a way of finding ideas for writing by jotting down things you see, hear, read, do, think, and feel as they catch your attention.

GRAPHIC DEVICE a visual presentation of details; graphic devices include charts, graphs, outlines, clusters, and idea trees.

IDEA TREE a graphic device in which main ideas are written on "branches" and details related to them are noted on "twigs."

INTERJECTION a word or phrase used to express strong feeling.

JOURNAL a personal notebook in which you can freewrite, collect ideas, and record thoughts, feelings, and experiences.

LEARNING LOG a kind of journal in which you record and reflect on what you have learned and note problems and questions to which you want to find answers.

METAPHOR a figure of speech in which a comparison is made without the word *like* or *as;* "life is a journey" is a metaphor.

NONSEXIST LANGUAGE language that includes both men and women when referring to a role or group made up of people of both sexes; "A coach shares his or her skills and experience" and "Coaches share their skills and experience" are two nonsexist ways of expressing the same idea.

NOUN a word that names a person, a place, a thing, or an idea.

PARAGRAPH a group of related sentences that develop a single main idea or accomplish a single purpose.

PEER RESPONSE suggestions and comments on a piece of writing, provided by peers, or classmates.

PERSONIFICATION a figure of speech in which human qualities are given to nonhuman things.

PORTFOLIO a container (usually a folder) for notes on work in progress, drafts and revisions, finished pieces, and peer responses.

Glossary for Writers **621**

PREPOSITION a word that relates its object to some other word in the sentence; in "Alec waited near the fence," *near* is a preposition.

PRONOUN a word that is used to take the place of a noun or another pronoun; in "He will help us," *he* and *us* are pronouns.

RUN-ON SENTENCE two or more sentences incorrectly written as one.

SENSORY DETAILS words that show the way something looks, sounds, smells, tastes, or feels.

SENTENCE FRAGMENT a group of words that does not express a complete idea.

SIMILE a figure of speech in which the word *like* or *as* is used to make a comparison; "hands like ice" is a simile.

SPATIAL ORDER organization in which details are arranged in the order they appear in space, such as from left to right, front to back, top to bottom, or inside to outside.

TOPIC SENTENCE a sentence that states the main idea of a paragraph.

TRANSITION a connecting word or phrase that clarifies relationships between details, sentences, or paragraphs.

UNITY in a paragraph, the working together of all the sentences to support the same main idea; in a composition, the working together of all the paragraphs to support the overall goal.

VERB a word that expresses an action, a condition, or a state of being; in "The clown painted his face," *painted* is a verb.

WRITING VOICE the personality of the writer as it comes across through word choice and sentence structure.

622 Appendix

INDEX

Index 623

C

D

Index 625

Index 627

628 Index

Index 629

630 Index

Index 631

S

632 Index

Index 633

634 Index

ACKNOWLEDGMENTS

Sources of Quoted Materials

28: G. P. Putnam's Sons: For an excerpt from *Homesick: My Own Story* by Jean Fritz. Copyright © 1982 by Jean Fritz. Reprinted by permission of G. P. Putnam's Sons. **30:** Crown Publishers, Inc.: For excerpts from *The Diary of Latoya Hunter* by Latoya Hunter. Copyright © 1992 by Latoya Hunter. Reprinted by permission from Crown Publishers, Inc. **40:** Macmillan Publishing Company: For "letter of February 11, 1945," from *Letters to Children* by C. S. Lewis, edited by Lyle W. Dorsett and Marjorie Lamp Mead. Copyright © 1985 by C. S. Lewis PTE Limited. Reprinted with the permission of Macmillan Publishing Company. **50:** Susan Bergholz Literary Services: For an excerpt from "The Monkey Garden," from *The House on Mango Street* by Sandra Cisneros. Copyright © 1989 by Sandra Cisneros. Published in the United States by Vintage Books, a division of Random House, Inc., New York and distributed in Canada by Random House of Canada Limited, Toronto. Originally published in somewhat different form by Arte Publico Press in 1984 and revised in 1989. Reprinted by permission of Susan Bergholz Literary Services, New York. **62:** Elizabeth Murphy-Melas: For an edited version of "Yomarhi Purnima" by Elizabeth Murphy-Melas, from *Cricket*, November 1992 issue. Reprinted by permission of the author and thanks to Nepal Embassy, Washington. **72:** G. P. Putnam's Sons: For an excerpt from "A Child of the Movement," from *Freedom's Children* by Ellen Levine. Copyright © 1992 by Ellen Levine. Reprinted by permission of G. P. Putnam's Sons. **84:** Curtis Brown, Ltd.: For "Rain" by Adrien Stoutenburg, from *The Things That Are*. Copyright © 1964 by Adrien Stoutenburg. Reprinted by permission of Curtis Brown, Ltd. **85:** HarperCollins Publishers: "Reggie," from *Honey, I Love* by Eloise Greenfield. Text copyright © 1978 by Eloise Greenfield. By permission of HarperCollins Publishers. The Touchstone Center, Inc.: For "Scrapyard" by Michael Benson, from *Miracles: Poems by Children of the English-speaking World*, collected by Richard Lewis. Copyright © 1992 by Richard Lewis and The Touchstone Center, Inc. **94:** Ed Ricciuti: For "Take Tracks Home" by Ed Ricciuti, from *Field & Stream*, November 1992 issue. Reprinted by permission of the author. **116:** *Chicago Tribune:* For an adapted version of "Video Web Weaves an Inadequate Tale" by Barbara Brotman, from *Chicago Tribune*, March 22, 1992. Copyright © 1992 by Chicago Tribune Company. All rights reserved, used with permission of *Chicago Tribune*. **143:** Francisco Jiménez: For excerpts from "The Circuit" by Francisco Jiménez in *Arizona Quarterly*, Autumn 1973. Reprinted by permission of the author. **157:** GCT, Inc.: For "What Would We Do Without You?" by Jeff Hayden, from *Creative Kids*, March 1992 Vol. 10, No. 6. Reprinted with permission of *Creative Kids* magazine, Mobile, Alabama. **214:** Golden West Publishers: For excerpts from *Cowboy Slang* by Edgar R. "Frosty" Potter. Reprinted by permission from Golden West Publishers, Phoenix, Arizona. **264:** Marian Reiner, Literary Agent: For "The Sidewalk Racer," from *The Sidewalk Racer and Other Poems of Sports and Motion* by Lillian Morrison. Copyright © 1965, 1967, 1968, 1977 by Lillian Morrison. Reprinted by permission of Marian Reiner for the author. **393:** Macmillan Publishing Company: For six sniglets: "cinemuck," "glackett," "oatgap," "profanitype," "spork," and "wondracide," from *Sniglets* by Rich Hall and Friends. Copyright © 1984 by Not the Network Company, Inc. For one sniglet: "snacktivity," from *Angry Young Sniglets* by Rich Hall and Friends. Copyright © 1987 by Not the Network Company, Inc. For one sniglet: "pigslice," from *More Sniglets* by Rich Hall and Friends. Copyright © 1985 by Not the Network Company, Inc. Reprinted with the permission of Collier Books, an imprint of Macmillan Publishing Company. **394:** Gwendolyn Brooks: "Pete at the Zoo," from *Blacks* by Gwendolyn Brooks. Copyrighted by Gwendolyn Brooks, published by Third World Press, December 1991. By permission of the author. **431:** Weekly Reader Corporation: For excerpts from "English Is a Crazy Language" by Richard Lederer, from *Writing*, December 1986. Copyright © 1986 by Weekly Reader Corporation. Reprint permission granted by *Writing*, published by Weekly Reader Corporation.

The authors and editors have made every effort to trace the ownership of all copyrighted selections in this book and to make full acknowledgment for their use.

Illustration & Photography Credits

Commissioned Illustrations: Rondi Collette: **193, 295;** Pat Dypold: **106–107;** Joe Fournier: **278–279, 338;** Tyrone Geter: **84–85;** Mary Jones: **96–98, 100, 103, 105, 132, 215–216;** Linda Kelen: **247, 296, 321, 417, 504;** Keith Kraus: **87;** Jared D. Lee: **4, 6, 9, 305, 464, 513;** Rich Lo: **190;** Steven Mach: **94–95;** Eric Masi: **529;** Marlies Merk Najaka: **50–51;** Clinton Meyer: **526;** Richard Murdock: **307;** Kevin Pope: **222, 276;** Jesse Reisch: **142–145;** Douglas Schneider: **448;** Richard Shanks: *graphics* **166, 374;** Roni Shepard: **161, 214, 285, 393, 431;** Steve Skelton: **546, 583;** Kat Thacker: **28–29;** Russell Thurston: **180–181;** Meryl Treatner: **254;** Robert Voigts: **43, 109, 118, 194–196, 199, 202–203, 215–216, 235–236, 263, 299, 301, 309–312, 318, 527, 599;** Amy Wasserman: **120, 125, 127;** Don Wilson: **116–117;** Cheryl Winser *(hand-coloring)*: **167–168, 179, 207, 281, 325, 470, 532, 573.**

Assignment Photography: John Morrison: **14–15, 22–23, 26, 30–31, 41, 52–53, 67** *top,* **74–76, 78, 81, 83, 89, 96–97, 110** *top,* **118–119, 128, 140, 146–147, 166–169, 174, 201, 292;** Art Wise: **ii.**

Art and Photography: 2: Courtesy Michelle Ryan; **15:** Reprinted by permission of Sterling Publishing Co., Inc., NY, NY, from *John Hedgecoe's Complete Guide to Photography* by John Hedgecoe, © 1990 by Collins & Brown, Text © by Collins & Brown and John Hedgecoe, Photographs © 1990 by John Hedgecoe; **23:** © Tony Freeman/PhotoEdit; **24:** Slide MS 33-2-3, Leland C. Wyman Collection, Museum of Northern Arizona; **28–29:** Courtesy Jean Fritz; **30–31:** Copyright © 1992 by Latoya Hunter. Reproduced by permission of Crown Publishers, Inc., NY; **34:** © Mary Kate Denny/PhotoEdit; **39:** © Skjold; **40–41:** © Carr Clifton; **44:** *top,* Utah State Historical Society; *bottom,* Pablo Picasso, *Three Musicians,* Fontainebleau, summer 1921. Oil on canvas, 6'7" x 7'3 3/4" (200.7 x 222.9 cm). The Museum of Modern Art, New York. Mrs. Simon Guggenheim Fund; **52:** Courtesy Alisa Monnier; **53:** © Dave Bartruff/FPG; **54:** © J. Kugler/FPG; **61:** © J. Kugler/FPG; **62:** © Bill Wassman; **63:** *top,* © Eric Reynolds/Adventure Photo; *bottom left,* © Paula Bronstein/Black Star; *bottom right,* © Bill Wassman; **64:** © Andy Selters/Viesti Associates, Inc.; **67:** *bottom,* © Campbell Laird; **70:** The Granger Collection, New York; **72–73:** © James H. Karales/Peter Arnold, Inc.; **75:** © David Perry; **81:** Photograph of W. B. Johns courtesy of Corrine Johns; **89:** *top,* NASA; *bottom,* Reproduced by permission of HarperCollins Publishers. Cover photograph © Frans Lanting; **92:** Negative # DOM.APP. 022/Trustees of the Science Museum, London; **110:** *bottom,* Illustration and Character Designs © 1988 Danielle Jones; **114:** Marc Chagall. *I and the Village.* 1911. Oil on canvas, 6'3 5/8" x 59 5/8". The Museum of Modern Art, New York. Mrs. Simon Guggenheim Fund; **117:** Shooting Star; **118:** Courtesy Dave Smith; **118–119:** Reprinted by permission of the *Sarasota Herald-Tribune;* **128–129:** © Joe Viesti/Viesti Associates, Inc.; **135:** Reproduced by courtesy of the Trustees of the British Museum; **137:** *top,* Courtesy Robert B.

Acknowledgments 635

Mayer Family Collection, Chicago; *bottom,* © Laurie Rubin/Tony Stone Images; **146:** Courtesy Vanessa Ramirez; **147:** © Melanie Carr/Viesti Associates, Inc.; **149:** © Bill Aron/PhotoEdit; **152:** © Spencer Grant/Photo Researchers, Inc.; **155:** © Mary Kate Denny/PhotoEdit; **156–157:** © 1990 Kristin Finnegan/Allstock; **158:** from *What Would We Do Without You?* copyright © 1990 by Kathy Henderson. Used with permission of Betterway Books, a division of F&W Publications, Inc.; **160:** *top left,* © Weinberg/Clark/The Image Bank; *bottom right,* © Michael Grecco/ Sygma; **164:** © Jean-Francois Podevin/The Image Bank; **166:** *center,* Reprinted with permission of the Baltimore Sun Company; *bottom left,* UPI/Bettmann; *bottom right,* National Baseball Library, Cooperstown, NY; **167–168:** UPI/Bettmann; **170:** UPI/ Bettmann; **179:** UPI/ Bettmann; **180–181:** Zaremski Family photographs courtesy Merrill Wilk; Nieuw Amsterdam photograph from The Peabody & Essex Museum, Salem, Mass., Neg. #13704; **183:** Courtesy Holland America Line; **184:** The Granger Collection, New York; **185:** *top,* © Sterling FX/The Image Bank; *bottom,* India Office, London/The Bridgeman Art Library, London; **188:** Collection Chloe Sayer/Photography © David Lavender; **191:** © 1993 Cindy Lewis; **197:** Leonard McCombe, *LIFE* Magazine © Time Warner; **198:** Copyright © October 6, 1992, Chicago Tribune Company, all rights reserved, used with permission; **200:** Courtesy Beth & John Morrison; **203:** © Ken Merfeld; **205:** Shooting Star; **207:** UPI/Bettmann; **208:** © Tom McHugh/Allstock; **212:** © 1993 SIS/Jerry Werner; **218:** Baron Hugo Van Lawick, © National Geographic Society; **221:** Courtesy ACA Galleries, New York; **225:** © E. R. Degginger/Animals, Animals; **226:** © 1992 New World Computing. Spaceward Ho is a trademark of Delta Tao, Inc. under license to New World Computing. New World Computing is Registered trademark of New World Computing, Inc., Woodland Hills, CA; **229:** Chloe Sayer Collection/Photography © David Lavender; **230:** © The Detroit Institute of Arts, Museo Diego Rivera, Guanajuato (INBA); **234:** © Suzanne Murphy/FPG; **237:** Drawings copyright © 1989 by Chuck Jones Enterprises, Inc. Reproduced by permission. BUGS BUNNY, the character, name and all related indicia are property of Warner Bros. © 1993; **241:** © Chip Simons; **246:** © Steven E. Sutton/Duomo; **249:** © Fred Marcellino; **252:** © Norma Morrison/Hillstrom Stock Photo; **260:** Courtesy Pat Iversen; **264:** © 1993 The Estate of Keith Haring; **265:** © Walter Iooss Jr./ *Sports Illustrated;* **267:** © Francois Gohier/ Photo Researchers, Inc.; **269:** © Annie Griffiths Belt; **270:** *top,* © Bob Krist; *bottom,* © Doug Wechsler; **271:** *top left,* © Tom Ives; *top right,* © Eddie Adams/ courtesy 1989 H. J. Heinz Annual Report; **272:** *top,* © Will van Overbeek; *center,* © C. B. Harding; *bottom,* © Linda Gebhardt; **273:** © Gerald Farber; **281:** Photograph courtesy Harry Shunk; **283:** Reprinted by permission: Tribune Media Services; **286:** Sygma; **289:** © Edgar Moench/Allstock; **292:** *The Way Things Work,* © 1988 Dorling Kindersley Limited, London. Published in the United States by Houghton Mifflin Company, *Incredible Cross-Sections,* © 1992 Dorling Kindersley Limited, London. Published in the United States by Alfred A. Knopf, Inc. Distributed by Random House, Inc., Cover from *Knights in Armor* by John D. Clare, copyright © 1992, 1991 by Random House (UK) Limited, reproduced by permission of Harcourt Brace & Company; **293:** © James Marsh; **319:** Margaret Bourke-White, *LIFE* Magazine © Time Warner Inc.; **325:** public domain; **329:** The Granger Collection, NY; **333:** © Wendy Shattil & Bob, Rozinski/Tom Stack & Associates; **334:** Photograph courtesy of Thos. K. Woodard American Antiques and Quilts; **339:** © Robert E. Daemmrich/Tony Stone Images; **343:** Courtesy Louis K. Meisel Gallery, New York; **345:** © Martin Harvey/ The Wildlife Collection; **346:** © Peter Gridley/FPG; **351:** The Granger Collection, New York; **353:** © Travelpix/FPG; **357:** © Leon French; **358:** © Lee Balterman/FPG; **361:** © J. Carmichael, Jr./The Image Bank; **375:** © Mike Robins; **376:** © John Hanley; **379:** The Library of Congress; **386:** © Martha Cooper/Viesti Associates, Inc.; **395:** © Joe McDonald/Natural Selection; **398:** © Robert Frerck/Tony Stone Images; **404:** © Tom McHugh/Photo Researchers, Inc.; **407:** Courtesy New York Downtown Hospital; **408:** © Jon Love/The Image Bank; **413:** © 1993 Galen Rowell; **420:** © Ron Kimball; **434:** © Patrick Tehan; **435:** © Andy Levin; **438:** Sketches by the great Arthur Babbitt courtesy Mrs. Arthur Babbitt, reprinted from *Animation—From Script to Screen,* by Shamus Culhane; **443:** Mary Evans Picture Library; **451:** © Merlin D. Tuttle/Bat Conservation International; **458:** Alexander Calder, *Chock,* 1972. 11 x 28 x 22 inches. (27.9cm x 71.9cm x 55.9cm). Collection of Whitney Museum of American Art. Gift of the artist 72.55a-b; **459:** © Gerard P. Byrne. Reprinted from the Parade/Kodak We the People photo contest winners; **461:** The Library of Congress; **462:** © Jurgen Schmitt/The Image Bank; **467:** © 1987 Lili Lakich; **470:** UPI/Bettmann; **473:** © Her Majesty's Stationery Office; **480:** Illustration copyright © 1988 by Trina Schart Hyman from *A Connecticut Yankee in King Arthur's Court.* Reprinted by permission of Morrow Junior Books, a division of William Morrow and Co., Inc.; **481:** Illustration from *The Legend of King Arthur* by Alan Baker, published by Kingfisher Books. Copyright © Grisewood & Dempsey 1993; **484:** © Jeff Hunter/The Image Bank; **487:** © Joe DiStefano/ Photo Researchers, Inc.; **490:** © J.A.L. Cooke/Animals, Animals; **494:** State Historical Society of Missouri, Columbia; **502:** Courtesy Tony Shafrazi Gallery, New York, Photography by Tseng Kwong Chi; **503:** © Manfred Kage/Peter Arnold, Inc.; **507:** © Jack Parsons; **510:** Archive Photos/Wilgos; **514:** © Joe Viesti/ Viesti Associates, Inc.; **517:** © William R. Sallaz/ Duomo; **518:** © Peter Miller/ Photo Researchers, Inc.; **527:** © Joe Baraban; **532:** AP/Wide World Photos; **534:** © Mark Newman/Tom Stack & Associates; **538:** © and TM 1993 Hanna-Barbera Productions Inc. All Rights Reserved; **547:** © Eric Meola/The Image Bank; **554:** © Brian Vikander/ West Light; **556:** © 1990 Mark Downey; **559:** *THE WIZARD OF OZ,* © 1939 Turner Entertainment Co. All Rights Reserved. Photo courtesy of MGM/UA Home Video, Inc.; **560:** Courtesy Eloise Greenfield; **566:** The Everett Collection, Inc.; **567:** © Russ Kinne/Comstock; **570:** © Tobias Everke/Gamma-Liaison; **573:** © Terry Lorant; **577:** Smithsonian Institution Photo No. 33184; **580:** © Mark Green/ Tony Stone Images; **588:** The Granger Collection, New York; **604:** *top,* © E. C. Stangler/Leo de Wys, Inc.;*bottom left,* © Robert Holmes; *bottom right,* © Ken Haas/Leo de Wys, Inc.

Cover

Ryan Roessler

636 Acknowledgements